The Study of Second Language Acquisition

Published in this series

BACHMAN: Fundamental Considerations in Language Testing
BACHMAN and PALMER: Language Testing in Practice
BRUMFIT: Individual Freedom and Language Teaching
BRUMFIT and CARTER (eds.): Literature and Language Teaching
CANAGARAJAH: Resisting Linguistic Imperialism in Language Teaching
COOK: Discourse and Literature
COOK: Language Play, Language Learning
COOK and SEIDLHOFER (eds.): Principle and Practice in Applied Linguistics
COHEN and MACARO (eds.): Language Learner Strategies
DÖRNYEI: Research Methods in Applied Linguistics
ELLIS: SLA Research and Language Teaching
ELLIS: Task-based Language Learning and Teaching
ELLIS: The Study of Second Language Acquisition
ELLIS: Understanding Second Language Acquisition
ELLIS and BARKHUIZEN: Analysing Learner Language
FOTOS and NASSAJI (eds.): Form-focused Instruction and Teacher Education
HOLLIDAY: The Struggle to Teach English as an International Language
HOWATT: A History of English Language Teaching
JENKINS: The Phonology of English as an International Language
JENKINS: English as a Lingua Franca: Attitude and Identity
KERN: Literacy and Language Teaching
KRAMSCH: Context and Culture in Language Teaching
LANTOLF (ed.): Sociocultural Theory and Second Language Learning
LANTOLF and THORNE: Sociocultural Theory and the Genesis of Second Language Development
MACKEY (ed.): Conversational Interaction and Second Language Acquisition
MEINHOF: Language Learning in the Age of Satellite Television
NATTINGER and DECARRICO: Lexical Phrases and Language Teaching
PHILLIPSON: Linguistic Imperialism
SEIDLHOFER (ed.): Controversies in Applied Linguistics
SELIGER and SHOHAMY: Second Language Research Methods
SKEHAN: A Cognitive Approach to Language Learning
STERN: Fundamental Concepts of Language Teaching
STERN (eds. P. Allen and B. Harley): Issues and Options in Language Teaching
TARONE and YULE: Focus on the Language Learner
WIDDOWSON: Aspects of Language Teaching
WIDDOWSON: Defining Issues in English Language Teaching
WIDDOWSON: Practical Stylistics
WIDDOWSON: Teaching Language as Communication

The Study of Second Language Acquisition

Second Edition

ROD ELLIS

OXFORD
UNIVERSITY PRESS

OXFORD
UNIVERSITY PRESS

Great Clarendon Street, Oxford OX2 6DP

Oxford University Press is a department of the University of Oxford.
It furthers the University's objective of excellence in research, scholarship, and education by publishing worldwide in

Oxford New York

Auckland Cape Town Dar es Salaam Hong Kong Karachi
Kuala Lumpur Madrid Melbourne Mexico City Nairobi
New Delhi Shanghai Taipei Toronto

With offices in

Argentina Austria Brazil Chile Czech Republic France Greece
Guatemala Hungary Italy Japan Poland Portugal Singapore
South Korea Switzerland Thailand Turkey Ukraine Vietnam

First published 2008

2012 2011 2010

10 9 8 7 6 5 4 3

ISBN: 978 0 19 442257 4

Printed in China

Contents

Acknowledgements

I would like to thank the following for their helpful comments on individual chapters in this book: Kathleen Bardovi-Harlig, David Block, Zoltán Dörnyei, Willis Edmundson, Nick Ellis, Roger Hawkins, Scott Jarvis, Jim Lantolf, Alison Mackey, Lourdes Ortega, Dennis Preston, John Schumann, Merrill Swain. Also, the following doctoral students at the University of Auckland helped in proofreading and checking the bibliographical entries: Katherine Cao, Ute Knoch, Susan McKenna. I would also like to thank Cristina Whitecross of Oxford University Press, Simon Murison-Bowie and Ann Hunter for their editorial work. Finally, I would like to thank the University of Auckland for awarding me a research fellowship grant to complete the work on the book.

The author and publisher are grateful to those who have given permission to reproduce the following extracts and adaptations of copyright material:

p225 'Non-native/non-native conversations: a model for negotiation of meaning', E. Varonis and S. Gass. *Applied Linguistics* 6: 71-90, 1985. Reproduced by kind permission of *Applied Linguistics.*

p230-31 'Exploring the relationship between characteristics of recasts and learner uptake' by Y.Sheen. *Language Teaching Research* 10/4: 361-92, 2006. Reproduced by kind permission of Y. Sheen.

p243 'Negative feedback as regulation and second language learning in the zone of proximal development'. *Modern Language Journal* 78: 465-83, 1994. Reproduced by kind permission of Blackwell Publishers.

p368 'Some principles of second language phonology' by F. Eckman, A. Elreyes and G.Iverson. *Second Language Research* 19: 169-208, 2003. Reproduced by kind permission of F. Eckman.

p448 'Incidental vocabulary acquisition in a second language: a review' by T. Huckin and J. Coady. *Studies in Second Language Acquisition* 21: 181-94, 1999. Reproduced by kind permission of J. Coady.

p499 'The effects of pre-task and on-line planning on fluency, complexity, and accuracy in L2 monologic oral production', F. Yuan and R. Ellis. *Applied Linguistics* 24/1: 1-27, 2003. Reproduced by kind permission of *Applied Linguistics.*

p525 *Sociocultural Theory and the Genesis of Second Language Development* by J. Lantolf and S. Thorne. Oxford: OUP, 2006. Reproduced by kind permission of S Thorne and J Lantolf.

p793 'Progress in language classroom research: evidence from the *Modern Language Journal*, 1916-2000', C. Chaudron. *Modern Language Journal* 85:57-76, 2001. Reproduced by kind permission of Blackwell Publishers.

p806 'Corrective feedback and learner uptake: negotiation of form in communicative classrooms' by R. Lyster and L. Ranta. *Studies in Second Language Acquisition* 19: 37-66, 1997. Reproduced by kind permission of R. Lyster.

Preface

Second language acquisition research over the years

In the Introduction to the first edition of *The Study of Second Language Acquisition* I attempted a brief account of the developments that had taken place in SLA since its establishment as a field of enquiry in the 1960s.[1] One development concerned the scope of the field of enquiry. Whereas much of the earlier work had focused on the linguistic, and, in particular, the grammatical properties of learner language, and was psycholinguistic in orientation, later work attended to the pragmatic aspects of learner language and, increasingly, adopted a sociolinguistic perspective. A second development concerned the increasing attention paid by SLA researchers to linguistic theory, in particular the theory of language associated with Chomsky's model of grammar: Universal Grammar (UG). I noted that the relationship between SLA research and linguistics had become increasingly symbiotic and that SLA research, therefore, was no longer a consumer of linguistics, but also a contributor to it. A third development was the marked increase in theory-led research. Whereas much of the earlier research was of the 'research-then-theory' kind, typically consisting of the collection and analysis of samples of learner language, later research was increasingly theory-led and experimental in style. I also noted the evolution of two subfields of SLA, one addressing individual learner differences and the other, classroom L2 acquisition. Individual difference research, in fact, pre-dated the onset of mainstream SLA, as a rich tradition investigating such constructs as language aptitude and motivation was already in existence well before the 1960s. However, the study of the universal properties of L2 acquisition and of individual learner differences remained disconnected areas of enquiry in SLA in 1994 when the first edition of this book was published. Classroom studies of L2 learners dated back to the inception of SLA research but had grown to constitute a distinct subfield of SLA. These studies were directed at investigating issues important to language pedagogy but were also explicitly concerned with theoretical issues related to L2 acquisition.

I concluded my brief survey of the then current state of SLA by suggesting that it had become a rather amorphous field of study with elastic boundaries. I gave the opinion that SLA stood at the crossroads in the sense that it might continue as a coherent field of enquiry with its own recognized research community, or it might splinter into a series of subfields, and perhaps become submerged into the 'mother' disciplines that informed those subfields.

These comments were written in 1993. Some fifteen years have now passed and it seems apposite to again attempt to summarize the developments that have taken place over this intervening period. Where does SLA stand now as field of study? To what extent is there continuity with the earlier period, as described in the first edition? To what extent have the intervening years seen new avenues of research open up? Has SLA survived as a coherent field of enquiry?

Many of the developments evident at the time of the first edition have continued since. SLA is clearly no longer focused on the morphosyntactic aspects of L2 acquisition, although these have continued to attract interest. The study of the pragmatic aspects of learner language has expanded. In addition, there is an increasing body of research investigating the phonological and lexical aspects of L2 acquisition. There are specialist volumes devoted to all three of these aspects—for example, Kasper and Rose's (2002) survey of pragmatic development, Leather's (1999b) collection of articles on phonological issues in L2 learning, and Nation's (2001) comprehensive account of vocabulary learning. SLA has continued to figure mainly as a psycholinguistic area of study, but interest in the more social aspects, evident at the time of the first edition, has grown stronger, with some researchers (for example, Firth and Wagner 1997; Block 2003) now challenging the legitimacy of many of the key constructs that have informed psycholinguistic SLA—for example, the notions of 'native' versus 'non-native speaker' and 'target language'—on the grounds that such notions are inadequate to account for the complexity evident in the heteroglossic urban contexts where so much of the SLA research has taken place. This increased emphasis on the social aspects of L2 learning has been matched by the ongoing interest shown in linguistic theory. UG-based enquiry has continued unabated, despite the opposition that it has aroused in a number of quarters. The central tenets of a generative account of L2 acquisition have been defended stoutly by White (2003a, 2003b) and Gregg (2003) among others. There are now numerous collections of papers examining the grammatical properties of learners' interlanguages from the perspective of both 'old' Chomskyan models of grammar (i.e. the Government/Binding model) and more recent ones (for example, the Minimalist Program)—see Chomsky (1981b, 1995).

The two subfields of SLA noted in the introduction to the first edition are also still very much with us. Work on individual differences has figured strongly in the last fifteen years, with new instruments developed to measure established constructs such as language aptitude, motivation, and learning style and new theories advanced to account for the role that these factors play in L2 acquisition. It is pleasing to note that the separation between mainstream SLA and individual difference research, which I saw as a feature of SLA in 1994, is now beginning to disappear. Researchers are increasingly examining how key individual difference factors affect the actual mechanisms and processes through which knowledge of an L2 is acquired. Thus, there has been a coming together of the 'cognitive' and 'psychological' lines of enquiry in SLA. The second subfield—instructed SLA—has also flourished. This in part reflects the 'applied' nature of SLA as a sub-discipline of Applied Linguistics and in part the sheer convenience of using classroom learners as participants in studies designed to test theoretical claims about L2 acquisition. There has been a flurry of books addressing the effect that instruction has on acquisition—for example, Doughty and Williams (1998), R. Ellis (2001a), DeKeyser (2007a).

It would be wrong, however, to characterize the last fifteen years of SLA as simply 'more of the same'. There has been a number of new developments both in the methodological tools employed by SLA researchers and also in the theories that have informed enquiry. Indeed, it is these new lines of enquiry that most clearly demonstrate the dynamic nature of SLA today.

Two methodological advances are the use of concordancing tools for examining the properties of learner language, and of neuroimaging techniques for investigating the parts of the brain involved in L2 processing and learning. Computer-based analyses of learner corpora have made possible what Granger (1998b) has called a new research paradigm—'contrastive interlanguage analysis'. Researchers across the world have been busy collecting and analysing both written and oral corpora from L2 learners, deepening our understanding of the commonalities and differences evident across learners and across varieties of learner language. Neuroimaging, such as functional Magnetic Resonance Imaging (fMRI), has been made possible by the development of machines that reveal the blood flow to different parts of the brain as learners perform different tasks in the L2. It affords the intriguing possibility of testing some of the key claims in SLA, such as the existence of a critical period for language learning. These are exciting developments that have already impacted strongly on the field and will undoubtedly continue to do so in the years ahead.

Perhaps the major theoretical development in SLA since 1994 has been the emergence of 'sociocultural SLA'. It is of course not entirely accurate to claim that sociocultural accounts of SLA were not available pre-1994 (see, for example, Frawley and Lantolf 1985), but, they were marginal and they did not figure at all in the first edition of this book. Sociocultural SLA draws on the work of the Russian psychologists Vygotsky and Leontiev. It proposes that L2 learning, like any other form of higher learning, occurs intermentally as well as intramentally, as new forms and functions appear first in production mediated by social interaction and subsequently become internalized. It emphasizes the social and cultural nature of learning while also recognizing that language is a mental phenomenon. Sociocultural SLA provides an entirely different theoretical perspective on how an L2 is acquired to that available from the standard 'input-interaction-output model' (Block 2003)—the model that informed the bulk of the research reported in the first edition.

The second major theoretical development did receive a brief mention in the first edition. Connectionist (and other emergentist) accounts of L2 acquisition, driven in particular by a series of publications by N. Ellis (see, for example, N. Ellis 1996, 2002, 2006b), have now assumed central importance in SLA. Connectionist views about language learning exist in direct opposition to UG-based accounts. That is, they view language learning as like any other type of learning, drawing on a common set of neural mechanisms. Learning is viewed as largely implicit in nature, driven by exposure to sequences of language in the input and fine-tuned through feedback. Language is represented in the mind not as a set of abstract rules but rather as a complex network of weighted connections that are constantly adjusted over time in the light of experience. Learning is slow, gradual, and emergentist. Connectionism emphasizes the importance of formulaic chunks in the learning process. Connectionist modelling of language acquisition has taken the form of computer-based studies that make use of software designed to mirror the parallel-distributed processing that characterizes the operation of the human brain. Not surprisingly, connectionist accounts of language and language learning have aroused opposition from UG-based SLA theorists (for example, Gregg 2003).

Thus, in the fifteen years that have passed since the first edition of this book, there is evidence of both continuity with the earlier period of SLA and of new developments. The earlier period concluded (in 1993) with a special issue of *Applied Linguistics* that was given over to a metatheoretical discussion of SLA. Contributions from a variety of scholars evinced markedly different views about the state of the field and, in particular, what to do about the plethora of theories of L2 acquisition that were current at that time. The number of theories has not notably reduced since, despite the call for 'culling' by some of these scholars. Rather, the theoretical plenitude has continued and has even further expanded. Arguably, the boundaries of SLA are even more elastic than they were in 1993. Old theories have by and large continued to attract attention (albeit in modified form) while new theories have appeared. The field of SLA is characterized by marked controversy about both what the facts of L2 acquisition are and also how to explain the facts. As in 1993, there are those who wish to circumscribe the field of enquiry in an attempt to cope with what they see as unwanted tensions and fragmentation. Doughty and Long (2003), for example, concluded their *Handbook of Second Language Acquisition* with a call for a common focus by placing SLA firmly within the boundaries of cognitive science. To do so, however, is to ignore the work done by more socially oriented SLA researchers and by neuroscientists who seek to identify how the brain itself handles an L2. L2 acquisition is an enormously complex phenomenon and will benefit from a multiplicity of perspectives, theories, and research methodologies. Like other areas of the social sciences, it should and undoubtedly will remain open to a multiplicity of lines of enquiry and, as a result, will continue to be characterized by controversy and debate. Thus, whereas in the 1994 edition I expressed concern over whether SLA would survive as a coherent field of study, today I am more prepared to acknowledge that this may not be important and that diversity of approach and controversy constitute signs of the field's vigour and an inevitable consequence of the attempt to understand a complex phenomenon.

The aims of the book

As with the first edition, the main aim of this book is to develop a framework for describing the field as it currently exists and to use this framework to provide an extensive account of what is currently known about L2 acquisition and L2 learners. I will attempt both to summarize the main findings of SLA research and to account for the main theories that have been advanced to explain these findings. I will also seek to evaluate the research to date by pointing out both the strengths and weaknesses of the different approaches. My goal is to be as encyclopaedic as possible so that the book can serve as a source of reference for both those beginning the study of SLA and those already members of the SLA community of scholars. As previously, I will endeavour to avoid taking up any particular position regarding what constitutes the most legitimate approach to SLA research. Instead, I shall aim to provide a balanced and objective account, while recognizing that my personal views will inevitably colour the picture I provide. I will admit, for example, a personal dissatisfaction with purely generative accounts of L2 acquisition.

I found the task of surveying SLA in 1993 a challenging one. I have found the same task for this edition of the book almost overwhelming. The sheer breadth and weight of the research is quite frightening and, arguably, it is beyond the ability of a single scholar to do justice to all of it. Thus, I have sympathy with other scholars who have opted for a 'handbook' approach to surveying the field, editing chapters written by specialists in each area of enquiry. The advantage of such an approach is a rich and informed account of each area. The danger, however, is a lack of coherence—a failure to make the necessary connections between the different areas—and also the absence of a unifying style. Thus, the justification for my second (and undoubtedly last) attempt to survey SLA is that I can show the whole picture and how the parts that compose it fit together, and I can do so with a single voice. The extent to which I am able to achieve this will hopefully compensate for the gaps and inaccuracies that will undoubtedly accompany my account of specific areas, especially those that lie at the margins of my own areas of expertise.

The book's readership

This edition has been written for two main kinds of reader. One is students of SLA research—those beginning their study of L2 acquisition and who wish to obtain an understanding of the principal issues that have been addressed, the methods used to research them, the main findings, and the theories that have been developed to explain them. It is hoped that the book will provide an accessible introduction to the field.

The second kind of reader is the SLA researcher who feels the need for a reference book that provides an overview of the main work accomplished in the different areas of SLA research. Such readers are likely to be experts in one or more areas of SLA research and, therefore, may have little need for the chapters that deal with their own areas of specialization, but may wish to benefit from a survey of the work undertaken in other areas with which they have less familiarity.

The first edition of the book was also aimed at a third kind of reader—second/foreign language teachers, many of whom may be completing a post-service programme of teacher education (for example, an MA in TESOL or Applied Linguistics) or engaging in doctoral research.[2] It is still my hope that the book will be of assistance to teachers and that it can be used as a textbook for an SLA course, perhaps alongside a shorter, simpler text such as my *Second Language Acquisition* (Ellis 1997a). This is how I have used the first edition of the book in my own teaching of SLA courses.

Second language acquisition research and language pedagogy

Whether or not the book is used as a course book, I have no doubt that it will be read by teachers in some capacity or another. It is pertinent, therefore, to consider why teachers should make the effort to read about L2 acquisition. The position I advanced in the earlier edition of this book seems equally tenable today. I argued that the study of SLA provides a body of knowledge that teachers can use to evaluate their own pedagogic practices. It affords a learning- and learner-centred view of language pedagogy, enabling teachers to examine critically the principles upon which the selection and organization of teaching have been based and also the methodological procedures they have chosen to employ. Every time teachers make a pedagogic decision about content or methodology, they are, in fact, making assumptions about how learners learn. The study of SLA may help teachers in two ways. First, it will enable them to make their assumptions about learning explicit, so that they can examine them critically. In this way, it will help them to develop their own explicit ideas of how the learners they are teaching acquire an L2. Second, it will provide them with information that they can use when they make future pedagogic decisions. Of course, SLA research is not the only source of information of relevance to language teachers.

SLA research, as we have seen, is, like language pedagogy itself, a hybrid discipline, drawing on a range of other disciplines. However, it would be a mistake to treat SLA research as a mediating discipline that takes concepts from other disciplines and moulds them into a form applicable to language pedagogy. SLA research has its own agenda and is best treated as another source discipline. The information provided by SLA research, then, needs to be 'applied' in the same way as that from other sources. SLA research is not capable of providing teachers with recipes for successful practice. It should be treated as providing teachers with 'insights' which they can use to build their own explicit theory. It is on the basis of this theory—not on the basis of SLA research itself or any theory it has proposed—that teaching practice should proceed.

The structure and contents of the book

The contents of this book have been organized in accordance with a general conceptual framework that takes account of (1) a general distinction between the 'description' and 'explanation' of L2 acquisition, and (2) the various subfields that have developed over the years. The following are the main sections with a brief summary of their contents:

Part one: Background

This section contains one chapter that introduces some of the key issues in SLA and outlines the conceptual framework of the whole book.

Part two: The description of learner language

This section reports some of the main findings regarding the nature of learner language. It considers learner errors, developmental patterns, variability, and pragmatic features.

Part three: Explaining second language acquisition: external factors

This section begins the task of explaining L2 acquisition by considering external influences—the role of input/interaction and social factors.

Part four: Explaining second language acquisition: internal factors

This section continues the work of explaining L2 acquisition by examining various theories of the mental processing that learners engage in.

Four perspectives on these processes are offered—language transfer, cognitive accounts of L2 acquisition, cognitive accounts of L2 performance, and linguistic universals. In addition, this section includes a new chapter on sociocultural SLA.

Part five: Explaining individual differences in second language acquisition

In this section the focus of attention switches from 'learning' to 'the learner'. Individual differences are considered from the point of view of general psychological factors (for example, motivation) and learner strategies. In the previous edition there were separate chapters on Individual Differences and Learning Strategies but in this edition I have included both areas of enquiry in the same chapter. This has meant somewhat less space devoted to learning strategies, which, to my mind, constitute a somewhat amorphous and messy area of study.

Part six: The brain and L2 acquisition

This constitutes an entirely new section for the second edition. It provides an account of the recent research that has investigated the neurological correlates of the mental mechanisms and processes involved in L2 acquisition.

Part seven: Classroom second language acquisition

This examines classroom-based and classroom-orientated research, from the point of view of both interaction and formal instruction.

Part eight: Conclusion

The book concludes with a critical look at the a number of key epistemological issues in SLA—the nature of the data used to make claims about L2 acquisition, theory construction, and the applications of SLA (in particular to language pedagogy). This section affords a reflective, 'state of the art' account of what SLA has achieved and where it has reached.

There is no separate chapter on research methodology in SLA, mainly because the methods used vary considerably according to the particular aspect of SLA being studied. However, where appropriate, information about the methods used to investigate specific areas is provided in the individual chapters.

A note on terminology

The term 'second language acquisition research' (SLA research) is used to refer to the general field of enquiry. It labels the discipline that is the focus of this book. The term 'L2 acquisition' serves as an abbreviation for 'the acquisition of a second language'. This is what learners try to do and is the object of study in SLA research. For reasons explained later, no distinction is made between 'acquisition' and 'learning', the two terms being used interchangeably.

Throughout the book, words explained in the Glossary are in SMALL CAPITALS.

Notes

1 Thomas (1988) pointed out that it is ahistorical to insist that SLA began in the 1960s as this ignores the substantial amount of work undertaken before this. This is correct. However, the 1960s did constitute a start of a kind as it was in this decade that the impact of the recent work on L1 acquisition was first felt in SLA with regard to both the methodologies used and the kinds of questions asked.

2 I am aware that some teacher educators will feel that *The Study of Second Language Acquisition* is too detailed and too long to be used as a course book of SLA for teachers. Ortega (2001), for example, declined to include it in her review of survey books of SLA for teachers on these grounds.

However, I know of many teacher educators who have elected to use the first edition as a course book and, naturally, hope that this will also be the case with this edition.

PART ONE
Background

Introduction

The purpose of this chapter is to provide a general introduction to SLA as a field of enquiry. As noted in the Preface, second language (L2) acquisition has continued to arouse enormous interest since its beginnings in the 1960s and now constitutes a somewhat amorphous field of enquiry, drawing on and contributing to a number of distinct disciplines—linguistics, cognitive psychology, psycholinguistics, sociolinguistics, and education. There has been a rapid growth in the number of publications dealing with all the key areas of SLA making it difficult to keep abreast of the developments that have taken place in the field. This has raised questions as to whether SLA research constitutes a coherent field, with identifiable goals and methods of enquiry, and has posed a problem as to how to introduce the field to readers.

I begin this chapter with an explication of 'second language acquisition', acknowledging that it constitutes a multi-faceted phenomenon that defies simple definition. In contrast to the first edition of this book, I have elected not to outline the specific areas that will be addressed in the subsequent chapters but rather (following an idea once put to me by Leo van Lier) to offer the reader a number of case studies of L2 learners. These serve to show the complexity of the phenomenon under discussion, to introduce the kinds of problems SLA researchers have faced in investigating L2 acquisition and to pinpoint a number of issues—such as what should be the focus of enquiry and how to explain the enormous variation in the success of individual learners. These are issues that will figure throughout the book. I then discuss two issues in some detail—fossilization (the cessation of learning before target-language competence is achieved) and the Critical Period Hypothesis (the claim that target-like ability in an L2 can only be achieved if learners commence learning before a certain age). These two issues lie at the centre of much of the descriptive and explanatory research into L2 acquisition and also serve to illustrate the problems that SLA researchers have faced in reaching clear conclusions.

The chapter concludes with a brief description of the framework that informs the rest of the book. This framework distinguishes 'General SLA' and 'Instructed SLA'. The former covers research aimed at describing and explaining the universal properties of L2 acquisition and also the factors responsible for individual differences in learning. The latter focuses on research that has examined classroom L2 learners. These two broad types of SLA enquiry are then divided into a total of seven different areas which provide a structure for the contents of the book.

1

An introduction to second language acquisition research

This chapter maps out the territory that will be covered in the rest of the book. It begins by examining some of the problems in defining 'second language (L2) acquisition'. By way of concrete illustration of L2 acquisition, this chapter will then present the results of a number of case studies of L2 learners. These will serve to introduce many of the issues that will be considered in greater depth later in the book. Next, the chapter examines a key issue in the study of L2 acquisition in greater depth—the role that age plays in the acquisition of an L2 together with an examination of FOSSILIZATION. This issue is central to an understanding of L2 acquisition and has figured strongly in SLA. Finally, the chapter outlines the framework for studying L2 acquisition that informs the structure of the whole book.

In this book I shall make a distinction between the terms 'SLA' and 'second language acquisition' or 'L2 acquisition'. I shall use the term SLA to refer to the field of study that we will be exploring—the research and the theories that comprise the discipline. I shall use the term 'second language acquisition' to refer to the object of study. Thus, we will be learning what SLA has to say about L2 acquisition. Readers are asked to note, however, that not all researchers use the terms in this way. Some researchers use the term 'SLA' to refer to what I am calling 'second language acquisition'. It is, however, useful, to make a distinction between the two.

What is 'second language acquisition'?

Sometimes a distinction is made between a 'second' and a 'third' or even a 'fourth' language. However, the term 'second' is generally used to refer to any language other than the first language. In one respect this is unfortunate, as the term 'second' when applied to some learning settings, such as those in South Africa involving black learners of English, may be perceived as opprobrious. In such settings, the term ADDITIONAL LANGUAGE may be both more appropriate and more acceptable. However, given that 'second' has become the generally accepted epithet, I will use the term 'second language acquisition' to refer to the acquisition of any language after the acquisition of the mother tongue.

Another distinction that is often made is that between SECOND and FOREIGN LANGUAGE acquisition. In the case of second language acquisition, the language plays an institutional and social role in the community (i.e. it functions as a recognized means of communication among members who speak some other language as their mother tongue). For example, English as a second language is learnt in the United States, the United Kingdom, and countries in Africa such as Nigeria and Zambia. In contrast, foreign language learning takes place in settings where the language plays no major role in the community and is primarily learnt only in the classroom. Examples of foreign language learning are English learnt in France or Japan. The distinction between second and foreign language learning is best treated as a sociolinguistic one rather than a psycholinguistic one. That is, for the time being at least, we need to keep an open mind as to whether the learning processes found in each are the same or different. Somewhat confusingly, the term 'second language acquisition' is used as a superordinate term to cover both types of learning.

A related distinction is that between NATURALISTIC and instructed second language ACQUISITION, according to whether the language is learnt through communication that takes place in naturally occurring social situations or through study with the help of 'guidance' from reference books or classroom instruction.[1] These terms clearly imply psycholinguistic differences. Klein (1986) argued that the learner focuses on communication in naturalistic second language acquisition and thus learns incidentally, whereas in instructed second language acquisition the learner typically focuses on some aspect of the language system. However, again, there is a need to keep an open mind as to whether the processes of acquisition are the same or different in naturalistic and classroom settings.

The main goal of SLA research is to characterize learners' underlying knowledge of the L2, i.e. to describe and explain their COMPETENCE. Researchers differ, however, in how they view 'competence'. Those working in the generative tradition associated with Chomsky have defined it somewhat narrowly as LINGUISTIC COMPETENCE (i.e. knowledge of the grammar of the L2). Other researchers, however, have adopted a broader perspective, examining how learners acquire COMMUNICATIVE COMPETENCE (i.e. knowledge of both the L2 grammar and of how this system is put to use in actual communication). SLA has increasingly adopted the broader perspective and, thus, while this book will consider the grammatical properties of L2s in detail (see for example Chapters 2, 3, and 4), reflecting the large number of studies in this area, it will also pay attention to other aspects, especially the learner's PRAGMATIC COMPETENCE. (See, for example, Chapter 5.)

In order to study how learners acquire a second language, a clear, operational definition of what is meant by the term 'acquisition' is needed. Unfortunately, researchers have been unable to agree on such a definition. 'Acquisition' can mean several things.

A distinction is sometimes made between 'ACQUISITION' and 'LEARNING' (for example, Krashen 1981). The former refers to the subconscious process of 'picking up' a language through exposure and the latter to the conscious process of studying it. According to this view, it is possible for learners to 'acquire' or to 'learn' L2 features independently and at separate times. Although such a distinction can have strong face validity—particularly for teachers—it is problematic, not least because of the difficulty of demonstrating whether the processes involved are or are not conscious (McLaughlin 1987). In this book the terms 'acquisition' and 'learning' will be used interchangeably.

However, it is useful to make a distinction between IMPLICIT LEARNING and EXPLICIT LEARNING, terms that are widely accepted in cognitive psychology (see, for example, Eysenck 2001) and which have become increasingly common in current accounts of L2 acquisition. Implicit learning is typically defined as learning that takes place without either intentionality or awareness. It can be investigated by exposing learners to input data, which they are asked to process for meaning, and then investigating (without warning) whether they have acquired any L2 linguistic properties as a result of the exposure. For example, learners could be asked to read a book and then tested to see if they had acquired any new vocabulary in the process. (See, for example, Dupuy and Krashen 1993.) However, while such an approach can guard against intentional learning it cannot guarantee that the learning took place without awareness. In fact, researchers disagree as to whether any learning is possible without some degree of awareness. Explicit learning, however, is necessarily a conscious process and is likely to be intentional. It can be investigated by giving learners an explicit rule and asking them to apply it to data or by inviting them to try to discover an explicit rule from an array of data provided. These two types of learning clearly involve very different processes and are likely to result in different types of knowledge (i.e. implicit knowledge or explicit knowledge of the L2). Chapter 9 considers these distinctions in depth.

Finally, there are some important methodological issues to consider. First, what and how learners learn an L2 is not open to direct inspection; it can only be inferred by examining samples of their performance. SLA researchers have used different kinds of performance to try to investigate L2 acquisition. Many analyse the actual utterances that learners produce in speech or writing. Some try to tap learners' intuitions about what is correct or appropriate by means of GRAMMATICALITY JUDGEMENT tasks, while others rely on the introspective and retrospective reports that learners provide about their own learning. The question about what kind of data afford the most reliable and valid account of L2 acquisition is a matter of controversy—a matter that is taken up at various points in this book and discussed in some detail in Chapter 17. Here it should be noted that different kinds of data will be needed to investigate whether what learners know about the L2 is implicit or explicit.

Second, there is the question of how we can determine whether a particular feature has been acquired. Some researchers (for example, Bickerton 1981) consider a feature has been acquired when it appears for the first time, while others (for example, Dulay and Burt 1980) require the learner to use it to some predetermined criterion level of accuracy, usually 90 per cent. Thus, a distinction can be made between acquisition as 'emergence' or 'onset' and acquisition as 'accurate use'.

Clearly, second language acquisition is a complex, multifaceted phenomenon and it is not surprising that it has come to mean different things to different people. It does, however, make it very difficult to compare the results of one study with those of another. Conflicting results can be obtained depending on whether the data used consist of learners' productions, introspections, or intuitions, or whether emergence or accuracy serves as the criterion of acquisition. It is for this reason that it is important to examine carefully the nature of the data used and the way in which acquisition has been measured, when reading reports of actual studies.

Case studies of L2 learners

One of the approaches for investigating SLA has involved the detailed study of individual L2 learners. These case studies have typically been longitudinal (i.e. they covered an extended period of time, often a year or longer) and have been based largely on data collected naturalistically (for example, typically spontaneous communicative speech). They have involved both naturalistic and instructed language learners and child and adult learners. They have provided information about the general course of L2 acquisition as well as individual differences among learners.

Many of the case studies were conducted in the 1970s or 1980s and then, for a while at least, fell out of fashion, in part because they are time consuming and they do not readily permit generalization (although generalization is possible if based on a number of studies). In more recent years, however, case studies have again become popular. The European Science Foundation conducted a number of case studies of adult migrant learners of different European languages directed at investigating L2 acquisition cross-linguistically (Klein and Perdue 1992, 1997). More recently still, Han (1998), Long (2003), and Lardiere (2007) employed case studies of single learners in order to investigate fossilization.

The case studies help to identify some of the key issues in SLA and for this reason serve as a useful way of introducing SLA to the reader. I will briefly review five studies, four early ones and one very recent, and then discuss the issues that they raise.

Wong Fillmore's (1976, 1979) study of five Mexican children

This was one of the earliest case studies. Wong Fillmore studied five Mexican children aged from 5.7 to 7.3 years over a nine-month period. They were attending an English-speaking school in California. Each child was paired with a native-English-speaking child and their interactions in a school playroom were recorded for one hour a week. The main purpose of the study was to investigate how their ability to communicate in English (their 'COMMUNICATIVE COMPETENCE') developed. Contrary to her initial expectation, Wong Fillmore found that the children varied greatly in the PROFICIENCY they developed over the period of the study. In order to explain these differences, Wong Fillmore considered and then discounted LANGUAGE APTITUDE (i.e. the special ability learners have for learning an L2). Instead, she examined the cognitive and social LEARNING STRATEGIES the children employed in their interactions. These are summarized in Table 1.1. Each social strategy was linked to one or more cognitive strategy. For example, S-1 was linked to C-1. By joining a group, the children gained access to L2 input which they were able to comprehend despite their very limited knowledge of English as a result of the repetition inherent in the input and contextual clues. S-2 is linked to C-2. The children's ability to give the impression they could speak English rested on their use of formulaic expressions such as 'let's go', 'I don't care', 'knock it off', and 'shaddup your mouth'. These enabled the children to participate in interactions with their native-speaking partners and thus to gain exposure to English. The formulaic expressions also provided the learners with data that they could subsequently analyse and, thereby, discover the underlying patterns of English (i.e. C-3). Wong Fillmore showed how the children slowly broke down formulaic sequences into their constituent parts, which were then subsequently used to create new utterances. Successful communication was achieved both with the help of their native-speaking partner (strategy S-3) and by making the most of their linguistic resources (strategy C-4). The final cognitive strategy (C-5) involved the children working on the 'big things' (for example, word order and lexical expressions) and leaving the 'details' (for example, grammatical morphemes) until later. This study, then, suggests that L2 acquisition arises out of learners' ability to participate successfully in communication, and shows that children vary in their ability to do this and thus develop at different rates. It also suggests that the pattern of acquisition is from 'wholes' to 'parts' rather than the incremental mastery of specific grammatical features.

Social strategies	**Cognitive strategies**
S-1 Join a group and act as if you understand what's going on, even if you don't. S-2 Give the impression, with a few well-chosen words, that you speak the language. S-3 Count on your friends for help.	C-1 Assume what people are saying is relevant to the situation at hand. Meta-strategy—guess. C-2 Get some expressions you understand, and start talking. C-3 Look for recurring parts in the formulas you know. C-4 Make the most of what you've got. C-5 Work on the big things first: save the details for later.

Table 1.1 Social and cognitive strategies used by five child L2 learners

Schumann's (1978b) study of Alberto

Schumann (1978b) conducted a 10-month study of the untutored acquisition of a 33-year-old Costa Rican called Alberto, who was living and working in the USA during this period. The data collection involved both naturalistic and elicited speech. The main finding of the analyses that Schumann carried out on the data was that Alberto showed very little linguistic development over the period of study. Schumann then explored a number of factors that might explain this, concluding that the most likely was Alberto's social and psychological distance from native speakers, especially the former. Alberto failed to acculturate to US society, remaining locked into an immigrant worker community, and thus experienced a 'bad learning situation' that restricted him to the 'communicative function' served by language at the expense of the 'integrative' and 'expressive' functions. As a result, Alberto's English remained pidginized. Table 1.2 summarizes this case study.

Learner's background	Alberto was a 33-year-old lower-middle-class Costa Rican. He was working in a factory in the USA with other non-native speakers of English. He lived within a small Spanish-speaking minority in a Portuguese area. Thus he experienced high enclosure as a member of a highly cohesive group of Spanish speakers, which very likely aroused negative attitudes on the part of native speakers.
Purpose of the study	The study of Alberto was part of a larger study by Cancino, Rosansky, and Schumann (1978b) that investigated the acquisition of English by five Spanish-speaking L2 learners in the USA. The overall purpose was to document the pattern of acquisition of specific grammatical structures (for example, negatives and interrogatives). As such, it was informed by similar studies of the L1 acquisition of English.

Data collection	Three types of audio recorded data were collected: 1 Spontaneous speech recordings of conversations with the researcher. 2 Experimental elicitations (for example, transforming a positive into a negative utterance). 3 Pre-planned sociolinguistic interactions involving taking Alberto to parties, restaurants, and sports events in order to collect speech in varied natural situations.
Analysis	The analysis focused on specific grammatical structures (for example, negatives, interrogatives, and auxiliary verbs). It involved an approach currently referred to as 'frequency analysis' (Ellis and Barkhuizen 2005). This entails identifying utterances where the learner attempts to perform the structure in question, describing the various non-target and target devices the learner uses and calculating the frequency of each device at different times within the total period of study. This enables the researcher to identify the dominant device used at different times and thereby to plot the pattern of development for the structure.
Main findings	Alberto showed very little linguistic development during the period of study—for example, his negatives were predominantly of the 'no + verb' type ('I no use television'), a large proportion of his interrogatives were not inverted ('Where you get that?'), and only one auxiliary (copula 'is') was mastered. In short, Alberto's English was 'pidginized' (i.e. manifested the same features as pidgin languages). Schumann also reported his attempt to teach Alberto negatives, noting that although this had some effect on his production of elicited negatives it had no effect on his production of spontaneous negatives.
Discussion	Schumann considered a number of factors that could explain Alberto's lack of development. He dismissed ability and age as factors and instead turned to a consideration of the factors that could cause pidginization of languages. He examined a range of factors that promote or inhibit social solidarity between two groups (for example, social dominance, acculturation, enclosure, cohesiveness, size of the L2 group, and ethnic attitudes) and concluded that Alberto experienced a 'bad learning situation' as a result of social distance from native-speaking groups. Schumann also suggested that Alberto experienced substantial psychological distance (for example, displayed negative attitudes and little motivation to learn English).

Table 1.2 Schumann's (1978b) study of Alberto

Schmidt's (1983) study of Wes

Like Wong Fillmore and Schumann, Schmidt investigated a learner who was acquiring English naturalistically through interacting with other speakers of the language. Schmidt's study of Wes, however, differs from the previous two case studies in that it was not exclusively focused on how linguistic competence is acquired. Schmidt took as his starting point Canale's (1983) model of communicative competence. This distinguishes four components:

linguistic competence, sociolinguistic competence (i.e. the ability to use language in socially appropriate ways), discourse competence (i.e. the ability to participate in coherent and cohesive conversations) and strategic competence (i.e. the ability to deal with communication breakdown). Schmidt showed that development of these abilities proceeded separately in Wes. That is, although, like Alberto, he showed little linguistic development, he progressed considerably in the other aspects of communicative competence. Schmidt also questioned the importance Schumann attached to social distance in explaining Wes' failure to acquire the L2 grammar as Wes clearly enjoyed regular contact with native speakers of English but nevertheless manifested a pattern of pidginization similar to that of Alberto. Schmidt's case study is summarized in Table 1.3.

Learner's background	Wes is a 33-year-old Japanese learner of L2 English who left school at 15 years old and thus had had very little experience of formal instruction. He was a successful artist. He divided his time between living in Hawaii and Japan, spending increasing amounts of time in the former. He mixed predominantly with English speakers in Hawaii and thus experienced very little social distance from native speakers of English.
Purpose of the study	Schmidt sought to investigate to what extent Wes' acculturation to American society could explain his development of communicative competence over a three-year period. This case study also addresses the extent to which Wes was able to acquire English through natural interaction.
Data collection	Data were collected over a three-year period predominantly by asking Wes to make one-hour tape recordings concerning business and daily activities on his visits back to Japan. These monologues were supplemented with some recordings of informal conversations with native speakers. In addition, Wes completed Scarcella's (1979) test of knowledge of verbal routines such as those involving apologies.
Analysis	Schmidt transcribed the spoken data and then analysed the transcripts in terms of Canale's four aspects of communicative competence. Linguistic competence was investigated by examining the extent to which Wes used a number of grammatical morphemes. The other aspects of communicative competence were analysed qualitatively and illustrated by examples taken from the transcripts.

Main findings	1 Wes' pronunciation was good (especially his intonation) but his grammar hardly developed over the three-year period. Of nine grammatical morphemes (for example, V-ing and 3rd person -s), only three reached the 90 per cent criterion level of accuracy deemed to indicate 'acquisition'. 2 Initially, Wes' directives relied extensively on formulaic expressions (for example, 'Can I have a __?'). These were not available for productive use (i.e. were unanalysed). By the end of the three-year period, gross errors in his use of directives had been eliminated. Also, his English utterances were largely socially appropriate, although sometimes idiosyncratic. 3 Wes demonstrated a high level of discourse competence, which compensated for his linguistic weaknesses. This was the area that showed the greatest improvement. By the end of the period, Wes demonstrated improved comprehensibility in his narratives and had become a good conversationalist in many respects, able to nominate topics freely. 4 Wes was able to repair communication breakdowns despite his limited linguistic competence. He made effective use of communication strategies such as paraphrase (for example, his use of 'money-girl' for 'prostitute'). He used adverbials to compensate for his lack of a verb tense system. However, he rarely repaired his utterances as a result of interactional feedback. Schmidt suggests that Wes operated on the principle that it was the responsibility of native speakers to make an effort to understand him.
Conclusion	Wes could be considered a 'good' language learner in terms of his overall communication skills but as a 'poor' learner in terms of his linguistic ability. His failure to develop grammatically cannot be explained in terms of social distance. Schmidt suggests that it is better explained in terms of psychological factors (for example, Wes' personality) which were responsible for his failure to attend to linguistic form. This study also shows the partial independence of grammatical competence from other aspects of communicative competence.

Table 1.3 Summary of Schmidt's (1983) study of Wes

Ellis' (1984a, 1992) study of three classroom learners

The next case study we will consider is my own. I investigated three children aged 10 to 13 years, who were learning English in a Language Centre in an outer suburb of London. The 10-year-old was Portuguese while the other two (a brother and sister) came from Pakistan. Like Wong Fillmore's learners, they were all complete beginners at the start of the study. I collected data by sitting in their English classes and noting down all the utterances they produced together with contextual information relating to the function and audience of their utterances. My initial purpose in conducting these case studies was to examine whether the pattern of development evident in naturalistic learners was the same as or different from the pattern found in the classroom learners. In other words, I wanted to know whether the instructional setting influenced the way in which the children learned English.

Like Wong Fillmore's learners, the three children all made extensive use of formulaic sequences as a means of performing the communicative acts that were needed of them in a classroom where English was not only the target of instruction but also the medium of instruction. Table 1.4 gives examples of the different types of formulas the learners produced. Like Wong Fillmore, I noted a number of ways in which these formulas were subsequently developed by the three learners. For example, the learners were subsequently able to modify and extend the 'I don't know' formula by substituting other verbs (for example, 'I don't understand'), changing the subject (for example, 'You don't know') and adding a constituent (for example, 'I don't know this one'). I suggested that this indicated that the learners were slowly unpackaging the formulas, releasing their constituents for creative language use.

Type of formula (based on Yorio 1980)	Examples
1 Situation formulas (i.e. those associated with a specific situation)	Finished (spoken after completing a task). Very good (a self-congratulation). What's the time? (spoken as break-time was approaching).
2 Stylistic formulas (i.e. those associated with a specific style of speaking)	Can I have a __? (requesting goods from the teacher or another pupil).
3 Ceremonial formulas (i.e. those associated with ritualistic interactions)	How are you? (greeting) Good morning (greeting). Excuse me miss (attracting teacher's attention). Oh my God (exclamation).
4 Gambits (i.e. those used to organize interactions and activities)	This one or this one? (identifying nature of classroom task). What's this? (identifying an object). I don't know (referring to either lack of knowledge or inability to respond). That's all right (confirming a course of action).
5 Euphemisms	No examples observed.

Table 1.4 Formulas observed in the speech of three classroom learners (from Ellis 1984a: 69)

Another feature of the three children's language was what I called 'semantic simplification'. This was only evident in the learners' creative communicative speech (i.e. not in utterances that were modelled for them by the teacher or were formulaic). It entails omitting constituents that perform semantic roles that would normally be encoded by a native speaker. For example, one of the learners produced the utterance 'Sir, sir, pencil' after the teacher had taken his pencil, omitting the semantic roles of 'agent' ('you') and action ('take') and encoding only the object ('pencil'). Such utterances were readily understood because the missing constituents could easily be recovered with the help of contextual clues. Over time such simplification diminished in the children's speech.

The use of formulaic sequences and semantic simplification has also been noted in naturalistic learners, suggesting that in these respects these three classroom learners were acquiring English in very similar ways to learners like Wes and Alberto. Further evidence for the similarity between naturalistic and classroom acquisition was obtained by comparing the stages of acquisition evident in the acquisition of grammatical structures such as negatives and interrogatives. The developmental profiles of the three children were very similar to each other and showed a striking similarity to that reported for naturalistic learners. I concluded that the children were relying largely on natural processing mechanisms to acquire English.

The main focus of these analyses was the learners' linguistic competence. However, later (Ellis 1992), I returned to the data I had collected to examine the pragmatic features of the three learners' use of requests, documenting how their repertoire of strategies for performing this speech act gradually increased but was still quite limited after nearly two years. Further information about this later analysis can be found in Chapter 5.

Lardiere's (2007) study of Patty

Patty was born in Indonesia in 1953 but was of Chinese origin. She left Indonesia for China in 1969 and lived there for two years before moving to Hong Kong, where English became the primary language of instruction. When she finished high school she worked in an import-export company in Hong Kong, rarely speaking English. She arrived in the United States in 1976 at the age of 22. She lived with her Vietnamese fiancé's family and began college-level study and, a little later, took a waitressing job. In 1985 she separated from her husband and began to live by herself but married again in 1989 to a native English speaker. Lardiere collected naturalistic production data from Patty on three occasions. Recording 1 was made in 1986 when Patty had been living in the United States for about 10 years. Recordings 2 and 3 were made two months apart, in 1995. Written samples, mainly from email messages, were also collected. The data for this case study, therefore, spanned a much longer period than for any of the other case studies reported above.

Lardiere investigated a number of grammatical features in Patty's English speech and writing, including finiteness (for example, morphological markers of tense/aspect and agreement), the acquisition of past tense, clausal word order and movement (for example, WH–movement in English question formation), and nominal phrases (for example, possessive pronouns and plural marking). This constitutes perhaps the most exhaustive account of an L2 learner's acquisition of grammar currently available.

Patty had not achieved a native-like grammar by the end of the study. However, there was a clear difference in her ability to use morphophonological aspects of English grammar correctly and her ability to employ English syntactical constructions correctly, as shown in Table 1.5. Whereas the former continued to be problematic, as evidenced in the frequent omission or overuse of inflectional markers on verbs and nouns, the latter were 'surprisingly target-like' (p. 204). A further finding was that Patty's written English was more accurate than her spoken English. The results of this case study suggest the need for an explanation of three points. (1) Why did Patty fail to achieve accuracy in the use of morphological features despite the facts that she had been in the United States for 10 years and that she had experienced favourable acquisition circumstances (i.e. immersion, acculturation, a high level of educational attainment and professional and personal success in her target-language community)? (2) Why was there such a difference between the morphological and syntactical aspects of Patty's acquisition of English grammar? (3) Why was her written English more accurate than her spoken English?

Morphophonological aspects	**Syntactical aspects**
Many morphological features were non-target-like: • omission of regular past-tense marking • omission of copular and auxiliary 'be' forms • past participle not inflected • omission and overuse of the progressive -ing form • omission of plural marking • omission of possessive marking.	Most syntactic and some morphological features were now target-like: • perfect knowledge of pronominal case marking • near-perfect use of possessive pronouns and demonstratives • proficient use of definite and indefinite articles • accurate placement of adverbs • robust relative clause formation • accurate WH–movement • appropriate stranding of prepositions • inversion/'do' support in questions • perfect use of overt subjects (as opposed to null subjects).

Table 1.5 Morphophonological and syntactical aspects of Patty's grammar

Lardiere advances a number of answers to these questions. First, Lardiere suggests that, although Patty's L1 may have played a role in her acquisition of English grammar, it cannot fully account for the findings of the case study. Instead, Lardiere suggests that Patty's continued variability in the use of morphological features, despite highly favourable conditions for learning, might be explained by the age factor:

> Maturational changes in the learner may influence the ability to perceive or statistically calculate the criterial percentage of information needed for deriving categorical generalization, resulting in variability. (p. 235)

Thus Patty failed to fully acquire 'categorical generalization' (i.e. full accuracy in the use of features like plural –s) because she did not begin to learn English until her adolescent years. To account for Patty's differential acquisition of morphophonology and syntax, Lardiere appeals to the notion of modularity in grammatical systems, suggesting that some domains (i.e. morphophonology) are inherently more susceptible to failure than others, possibly because they are not governed by the 'language faculty' that some SLA researchers have claimed governs L2 acquisition as it does L1 acquisition. Lardiere does not address the difference in accuracy in Patty's spoken and written English. One possible explanation for this is that Patty possesses metalinguistic knowledge of English grammar and was able to make use of this more easily when writing than when speaking.

Issues raised by the case studies

These case studies raise a number of important issues that will be revisited in subsequent chapters. They will be briefly considered here.

1 Methods of data collection

All five studies were based largely on spontaneous speech. In three of the studies (Wong Fillmore, Schumann, and Ellis) this took the form of conversational data. In Schmidt's study, however, the data consisted of oral monologues. Two of the studies (Schumann and Ellis) also collected data reflecting more planned language use, but in both care was taken to keep the unplanned and planned data separate. One study (Lardiere) also collected samples of written language. SLA researchers have generally held that learners' spontaneous communicative speech constitutes the best data for investigating acquisition, but, as we will see in later chapters, they have frequently resorted to elicited data of various kinds.

2 Focus of enquiry

The main focus of the four studies was learners' acquired linguistic competence (in particular, grammar). This is a feature of many early SLA studies but continues to attract interest today, as Lardiere's study demonstrates. The early case studies also presaged the later interest that SLA researchers have shown in other aspects of language. Schmidt examined four aspects of communicative competence. Wong Fillmore and Ellis examined how formulaic speech enabled learners to communicate at a time when they had very limited linguistic resources and also served as a platform for the acquisition of grammatical knowledge.

3 The pattern of L2 development

All the studies showed that learners apparently follow a very similar pattern of development. For example, all the studies documented how learners' early speech is 'pidginized' or 'semantically simplified' and that subsequent acquisition of grammatical structures is very gradual, manifesting common stages of development. The existence of universal properties of L2 acquisition that these studies testify to constitutes a key finding of SLA, which has informed a number of theories of L2 acquisition.

4 The acquisition of the morphological and syntactical aspects of an L2

The studies also indicate that L2 learners experience greater difficulty in acquiring the morphological (inflectional) properties of an L2 than they do the syntactical properties. Failure in acquisition is more likely in the former than the latter.

5 The role of instruction

None of these studies systematically investigated the effects of instruction on L2 acquisition. However, Schumann reported that his attempt to teach Alberto negatives had no effect on his spontaneously produced negatives. Also, Ellis noted clear discrepancies between his learners' spontaneous communicative speech and their modelled speech; and Lardiere noticed differences in her learner's speech and writing. The extent to which formal instruction can influence the course of L2 acquisition is a major theme in SLA. (See Chapters 15 and 16.)

6 Variation in the rate of development

While learners appear to manifest a very similar pattern of development, they also clearly vary in both how rapidly they develop and also in what aspects of the L2 they show most development in. This variation is evident in both adults and children—Alberto was chosen for study because his development was so much slower than that of other adult learners in the Cancino *et al.* (1978) study, and both Wong Fillmore and Ellis reported variation in the rate of development of the children they studied. Furthermore, none of the learners investigated achieved target-language competence by the end of the period of study. In part, this might be because the studies were not long enough, although Schmidt's study of Wes covered three years and Lardiere's study of Patty, ten years. It is possible, then, that L2 learners 'fossilize' (i.e. stop developing before they achieve full mastery). Fossilization is a key issue in SLA and will be considered more fully in the following section of this chapter.

7 Explaining L2 acquisition

There are two aspects of L2 acquisition that require explanation; the universal aspects (i.e. the general pattern of development evident in all learners) and the variable aspects (i.e. differences in the rate of development and in ultimate achievement). The universal aspects might be explained in terms of a common set of social and cognitive strategies (Wong Fillmore), or in terms of the unpackaging of formulaic sequences, or, perhaps, as the working of an innate 'language faculty'. These explanations (together with others) will be explored in subsequent chapters. The variable aspects can be potentially explained by a host of factors. These are of a social nature (for example, Schumann's notion of 'social distance'), of a more personal, psychological nature (for example, Wes' orientation towards the functional aspect of language at the expense of the formal aspect) and of a linguistic nature (for example, Lardiere's proposal that some aspects of grammar are governed by the learner's 'language faculty' whereas others lie outside it). Age may also be a factor, as Lardiere has suggested. Age is potentially of considerable significance to theory building in SLA and has attracted considerable attention from researchers. For this reason it will be considered more fully below.

The case studies I have considered are all of learners of English. This reflects a bias that has continued in SLA; the majority of studies that will be considered in the following chapters have examined the acquisition of L2 English. However, interest in other languages has increased over the years and I will be reporting studies of both European languages (for example, German and French) and of Asian languages (for example, Chinese, Korean, and Japanese).

The role of age in L2 acquisition

In this section I will consider an issue that has figured consistently in discussions of L2 acquisition—the role that age plays in L2 acquisition and, in particular, whether there is a critical period during which the acquisition of full target-language competence is possible and after which it becomes impossible. Both the age issue and fossilization are topics of continued debate in SLA.

The role that age plays in L2 acquisition has attracted the attention of researchers since the inception of SLA as a field of study. Krashen, Long, and Scarcella (1979: 161) reviewed a number of the earlier studies, reaching three conclusions:

1 Adults proceed through the early stages of syntactic and morphological development faster than children (where time and exposure are held constant).

2 Older children acquire faster than younger children (again, in the early stages of syntactic and morphological development where time and exposure are held constant).
3 Acquirers who begin natural exposure to a second language during childhood achieve higher second-language proficiency than those beginning as adults.

It should be noted that these conclusions do not entirely accord with the lay belief that 'younger is better' where L2 learning is concerned. While it is true that learners who start learning in childhood often achieve higher levels of ultimate proficiency than learners who start later (i.e. in adolescence or as adults), the research indicates that in the earlier stages of L2 acquisition, older learners outperform younger learners, especially where knowledge of grammar is concerned. In discussing the role of age, then, it is important to distinguish the effects that the 'age of onset' has on the rate of acquisition and on ultimate achievement. Accordingly, I will first consider age in relation to rate of learning and then address ultimate achievement and the related issue of whether there is a critical period for acquiring language.

The effects of age on the rate of second language learning

The study most often cited in support of Krashen *et al.*'s conclusions regarding the effect of age on the rate of L2 acquisition is Snow and Hoefnagel-Höhle (1978). This study investigated the naturalistic acquisition of Dutch by 8- to 10-year-old English-speaking children, 12- to 15-year-old adolescents, and adults over a 10-month period. The learners' proficiency was measured on three separate occasions (after three months, after six months, and at the end of the study). With regard to morphology and syntax the adolescents did best, followed by the adults, with the children last. However, there were only small differences in pronunciation, and the grammar differences diminished over time as the children began to catch up.

The Barcelona Age Factor Project (Muñoz 2006) investigated the effects of age of onset in an instructed setting. This project examined the acquisition of English by classroom learners of English in Catalonia (Spain), comparing students who began their study at the age of 8, 11, and 14 and controlling for exposure to English outside the classroom. Data from a battery of tests providing measures of both implicit and explicit types of knowledge were collected on three occasions—after 200 hundred hours of instruction, 416 hours, and 726 hours. The main finding was that the older learners progressed faster than the younger learners. In contrast to Snow and Hoefnagel-Höhle's findings, the younger learners did not catch up over time, probably because the number of hours available for learning in this instructed setting was insufficient to enable them to do so. However, as in Snow and Hoefnagel-Höhle's study, there was evidence that age had a differential effect on the acquisition of different aspects of the L2. Thus, the advantage for the older learners was strong and durable on measures of grammar and least evident in the case of measures of speech perception, listening comprehension, and oral fluency. In the latter measures, no statistically significant differences between the young and older starters were evident on the final occasion. Similar results for instructed learners had been obtained by Burstall (1975) in a study that compared students who started learning L2 French at either the primary- or secondary-school level in England.

Experimental studies have also shown that adults outperform children in the short term. For example, Olsen and Samuels (1973) found that American English-speaking adolescents and adults performed significantly better than children after ten 15–25 minute German pronunciation sessions. Cochrane (1980) investigated the ability of 54 Japanese children and 24 adults to discriminate English /r/ and /l/. The average length of naturalistic exposure was calculated as 245 hours for the adults and 193 for the children (i.e. relatively little). Nevertheless, the children outperformed the adults. However, in a follow-up experiment in which the two groups were taught the phonemic distinction, the adults benefited while the children did not. Overall, the experimental research indicates that in formal learning situations adults seem to do better than children, even in this area of learning (pronunciation) that most favours children.

Overall, then, the research supports the earlier conclusion of Krashen *et al.*—learners who start learning an L2 in adolescence or as adults learn more rapidly than those who start in childhood. However, to fully understand the results of the research it is useful to distinguish the effects of age on the rate of acquisition in terms of the distinction between implicit and explicit learning. (See DeKeyser 2000.) The greater cognitive development of older learners is advantageous where explicit learning is concerned, as the results of the experimental studies show. Late-starting learners do better in tests that tap into explicit knowledge of the L2 language (for example, traditional grammar tests). In contrast, they do not necessarily outperform early-starters in the long-term where implicit learning is involved. Implicit learning is a slow and gradual process and thus the advantage that younger learners may have where this kind of learning is involved will not show up until after many hours of exposure to the L2—that is, typically only in a naturalistic setting. Thus, in the case of the naturalistic learners in Snow and Hoefnagel-Höhle's study, the exposure was sufficient to enable the younger learners to catch up with the older learners. But in the case of the Barcelona Age Factor Project, the exposure in the instructed setting was very limited, even after several years of schooling, with the result that the early-start learners failed to catch up. The difference between implicit and explicit learning can also explain why the advantage for older learners in some aspects of language (for example, listening ability and pronunciation) is not—or at least, is less—evident. These are aspects that cannot easily be mastered through explicit learning—they develop primarily through exposure and practice.

The effects of age on ultimate achievement

It would follow that if learners who start learning as children have an advantage in the long term, especially where the acquisition of implicit knowledge is concerned, then ultimately they can be expected to achieve higher levels of proficiency. A number of studies have investigated whether this is the case—allowing for a minimum of five years of exposure in the case of naturalistic learners.

As Singleton (1989) noted, school-based studies cannot address this issue, as formal learning environments typically do not provide learners with the amount of exposure needed for the age advantage of young learners to emerge. An exception can be found in the school-based studies involving immersion education. In immersion programmes students are taught a range of school subjects through the medium of the L2 and thus receive far greater exposure than is the case in traditional foreign language programmes. (See Chapter 7.) Harley (1986), for example, investigated the levels of attainment of children in French bilingual programmes in Canada. She focused on the learners' acquisition of the French verb system, obtaining data from interviews, a story-repetition task, and a translation task. She compared early and late immersion students after both had received 1,000 hours of instruction. Neither group had acquired full control of the verb system. The older students demonstrated greater overall control when hours of exposure were controlled for, but the early immersion group showed higher levels of attainment at the end of their schooling. However, this result may reflect the additional number of years' instruction they had received rather than starting age.

Naturalistic learners who start as children achieve a more native-like accent than those who start as adolescents or adults. Oyama (1976) investigated 60 male immigrants who had entered the United States at ages ranging from 6–20 years and had been resident there for between 5 and 18 years. She asked two adult native speakers to judge the nativeness of the learners' accents in two 45-second extracts taken from performance on a reading-aloud task and a free-speech task. Oyama reported a very strong effect for 'age of arrival' but almost no effect for 'number of years' in the United States. She found that the youngest arrivals performed in the same range as native-speaker controls. Other studies which have investigated the effects of age on pronunciation (see Flege 1999 for a review of these studies) support the younger-is-better position. There is substantial evidence to suggest that ultimate attainment in pronunciation declines linearly as a product of learners' starting age. However, there is also some evidence that learners who begin as adults are capable of achieving native-like accents. Bongaerts (1999), for example, reported three studies that showed that a number of advanced late learners of L2 English were judged as native-like by native speakers on a variety of measures of pronunciation.

Similar results have been obtained for the acquisition of grammar. Patkowski's (1980) study of 67 educated immigrants to the United States found that learners who had entered the United States before the age of 15 were rated as more syntactically proficient than learners who had entered after 15. Furthermore, there was a marked difference in the distribution of the scores (based on native speakers' ratings on a five-point scale) for the two groups. The adult group's scores were evenly distributed, with the majority at midpoints on the rating scale. The child group's scores clustered at the high end of the rating scale, with 29 out of 33 achieving a rating of 4+ or 5. Patkowski also investigated the effects of number of years spent in the United States, amount of informal exposure to English, and amount of formal instruction. Only the amount of informal exposure had any significant effect, and even this was negligible in comparison with the age factor. Patowski's findings are confirmed by Johnson and Newport's (1989) study of 46 native Koreans and Chinese who had arrived in the United States between the ages of 3 and 39, half before the age of 15 and half after 17. The subjects were asked to judge the grammaticality of 276 spoken sentences, about half of which were grammatical. Overall the correlation between age at arrival and judgement scores was –0.77 (i.e. the older the learners were on arrival, the lower their scores). Neither the number of years of exposure to English beyond five, nor the amount of classroom instruction was related to the grammaticality judgement scores and, although an effect for 'identification with American culture' was found, this was much weaker than that for age. However, as we will see below, when we turn to an examination of the CRITICAL PERIOD HYPOTHESIS, Johnson and Newport's study has been subject to considerable criticism.

In his summary of a wide range of research investigating the effects of age on L2 acquisition, Singleton (1989) wrote:

> Concerning the hypothesis that those who begin learning a second language in childhood in the long run generally achieve higher levels of proficiency than those who begin in later life, one can say that there is some good supportive evidence and that there is no actual counter evidence. (1989: 137)

This is one of the few definite conclusions that Singleton felt able to reach in his comprehensive survey of age-related research and it has withstood the test of time. It is worthwhile noting, however, that this conclusion may not hold true for the acquisition of L2 literacy skills. Cummins and Nakajima (1987) examined the acquisition of reading and writing skills by 273 Japanese children in Grades 2–8 in Toronto. They found that the older the students were on arrival in Canada, the more likely they were to have strong L2 reading skills and, to a lesser extent, better L2 writing skills. The explanation Cummins and Nakajima offer is that the older learners benefited from prior literacy experience in Japanese. (See the discussion of the INTERDEPENDENCY PRINCIPLE in Chapter 7.)

The Critical Period Hypothesis

The CRITICAL PERIOD HYPOTHESIS (CPH) claims that there is a fixed span of years during which language learning can take place naturally and effortlessly, and after which it is not possible to be completely successful. Penfield and Roberts (1959), for example, argued that the optimum period for language acquisition falls within the first ten years of life, when the brain retains its plasticity. Initially, this period was equated with the period taken for lateralization of the language function to the left side of the brain to be completed. Work on children and adults who had experienced brain injuries or operations indicated that damage to the left hemisphere was rapidly repaired in the case of children but not adults (Lenneberg 1967). There is, however, no clear consensus on when the 'window of opportunity' for language learning ends. Singleton (2005), in a survey of the literature that has addressed this issue, reported claims ranging from near birth to late adolescence. Also, it has become clear that, if there is a critical period, this varies depending on the aspect of language under examination (see, for example, Seliger 1978) with the end point coming earlier for pronunciation than for grammar.

There are different conceptualizations of the critical period. One is that the end of the critical period signals the point at which performance begins to decline. That is, up to that point, age has no or very little effect on L2 acquisition. Birdsong (2006a) refers to this as the 'unconventional notion of the critical period' (p. 19). The conventional view is that the end of the critical period constitutes the point at which the decline in performance as a result of age ceases. According to this version of the hypothesis, maturation signals the end rather than the beginning of age effects as, once past the critical age, acquisition is blocked for all learners irrespective of whether they are just past it or many years past it.

What both conceptualizations have in common is the notion of a discontinuity in learning; that is, after a certain age, the pattern of learning changes, as Patkowski found for grammar in the studies referred to above. Johnson and Newport (1989) interpreted the results of their study as evidence for the CPH (conventional version). They endeavoured to show that there was a sharp break in the effects evident for age at the critical period. In the case of the early starters (prior to age 15), there was a gradual decline in performance according to age. However, in the case of the late starters (after age 17), the relationship between age and performance was essentially random. However, as Bialystok and Hakuta (1994) showed, if the cut-off for the end of the critical period was moved to 20 years, then the age of the older group in Johnson and Newport's study was found to be related to performance. In other words, when the data were analysed in this way, there was no evidence of a clear discontinuity. Birdsong (2006a), in a review of a number of studies, including Johnson and Newport, concluded that there is no consistent evidence of a discontinuity effect. Bialystok and Hakuta's (1999) investigation of the English-language proficiency of 24,903 speakers of Chinese and 38,787 speakers of Spanish, all of whom had been resident in the US for a minimum of ten years, found a clear linear effect for age of arrival for both sets of speakers and 'nothing special about the age range before puberty' (p. 175).

A second way of assessing whether learners can achieve native-speaker levels in an L2 is to see whether they are able to recognize spoken or written 'accents' in the same way as native speakers. Scovel (1981) asked four groups of judges (adult native speakers, child native speakers, adult non-native speakers, and adult aphasics) to rate speech samples and written pieces produced by a mixture of native and non-native speakers. He found that even the most advanced non-native speakers achieved an accuracy rate of only 77 per cent, which was about the same as the child native speakers (73 per cent) but less than the adult native speakers (95 per cent) and even the aphasic native speakers (85 per cent). This study suggests that even very advanced learners lack some of the linguistic abilities of native speakers.

Another approach to investigating the CPH involves investigating learners who began learning as adults and are now very advanced to see if they can perform similarly to native speakers. Two frequently cited studies exemplify this approach. Coppetiers (1987) tested 21 highly proficient speakers of French, all of whom had begun learning as adults, and compared their performance on a grammaticality judgement task with that of 20 native speakers. Coppetiers noted that it was not possible to distinguish the two groups by the mistakes they made, their choice of lexis, or grammatical constructions, and six of the subjects were also described as having no traces of a foreign accent. The results of the grammaticality judgement test, however, showed clear differences between the two groups, suggesting that despite the native-like performance of the learners in language production, their grammatical competence differed from that of native speakers. However, Birdsong (1992) identified 'numerous procedural and methodological features of the Coppetiers study that compromise its conclusions' (1992: 711). His replication of Coppetiers' study produced very different results. Birdsong administered a grammaticality judgement test to 20 English-speaking learners of L2 French, who were near-native in their oral ability, and to 20 native speakers of French. The study was motivated by Long's challenge to researchers to investigate 'whether the very best learners actually have native-like competence' (1990a: 281). Contrary to Coppetiers, Birdsong found no evidence of any dramatic differences in the judgements of the non-native speakers and native speakers. A number of the non-native speakers performed in the same range as the native speakers on the grammaticality judgement test. Furthermore, Birdsong could find no evidence of marked differences between the two groups in the think-aloud data that he collected from the subjects as they performed their judgements. This study, then, suggests that at least some learners who start learning an L2 after puberty achieve a level of competence indistinguishable from that of native speakers.

Other later studies (for example, Ioup, Boustagui, El Tigi, and Moselle 1994; Bongaerts 1999) have also produced evidence to show that at least some learners who start as adults cannot be distinguished from native speakers, even when the comparison involves pronunciation. Again, though, much may depend on how performance is assessed. Hyltenstam and Abrahamsson (2003) produced evidence to suggest that when detailed analyses of learners' spontaneous speech are undertaken some differences between learners and native speakers always emerge. Birdsong (2006a), responding to this point, suggested that 'it is more reasonable to argue that minor quantitative departures from monolingual values are artefacts of the nature of bilingualism, wherein each language affects the other and neither is identical to that of the monolingual' (p. 22). In other words, absolute similarity in performance between an L2 learner and a native speaker is simply not possible because of the very nature of bilingualism.

A final approach that has figured strongly in recent research is to examine brain measures of highly proficient bilinguals. In this kind of research, the participants are given language tasks to perform and the activity in their brains is measured in a variety of different ways (for example, using MAGNETIC RESONANCE IMAGING (MRI).[2] The aim of such studies is to establish whether processing in the L2 is accomplished in the same way as processing in the L1. Summarizing the results of a number of such studies, Birdsong (2006a) concluded that, where tasks involving production are concerned, it is L2 proficiency level rather than age of arrival in an L2-speaking environment that is the strongest predictor of the degree of similarity between processing in the L1 and L2. Comprehension studies have produced similar results. However, Birdsong noted one difference. There is evidence that processing is more effortful in the L2 than in the L1 even with highly proficient bilinguals. In general, these studies support Green's (2005) 'convergence hypothesis', according to which L1 and L2 processing become increasingly similar as L2 proficiency increases. Research that has examined neurolinguistic aspects of L2 acquisition is considered in Chapter 14.

What conclusions can be drawn from this research? Birdsong (2005) conducted a meta-analysis of studies that have investigated the L2 end state. He reached three conclusions:

a In all analyses of pooled data from early and late arrivals, age effects persist indefinitely across the span of surveyed age of arrival (AoA) (i.e. they are not confined to a circumscribed period).
b In analyses of disaggregated samples (and in studies that look only at late AoA), most studies find significant AoA effects for the late learners, indicating postmaturational declines in attainment.
c In analyses of early-arrival data alone, AoA effects are inconsistent: some are flat, some are random, and some are monotonically declining (pp. 14–15).

Overall, then, the available evidence speaks against the CPH. There is no clear end point beyond which L2 learners will fail to achieve native-speaker proficiency. Rather there is a gradual decline in the ability to learn an L2 with age starting from early childhood.

The CPH is the subject of ongoing debate. Birdsong (1999a) summarized the positions adopted by the 'whys' and the 'why nots'. He also described the various mechanisms that different researchers have proposed to account for why late starters have difficulty in acquiring an L2. These are summarized in Table 1.6. He then reviewed the evidence for the other side of the fence (which he acknowledges is where he sits). He emphasized that although in general the research is not consonant with the CPH, there are nevertheless clear maturational effects evident in L2 acquisition. That is, the ability to learn a language (like most other things) declines gradually and steadily with age.

Hypothesis	**Description**
Loss of neural plasticity in the brain	After the closure of the critical period (CP), the neural substrate responsible for language learning is not fully available due to loss of organizational plasticity and lateralization (Penfield and Roberts 1959).
Loss of (access to) the language learning faculty	A strong version of this hypothesis is that Universal Grammar (UG) is no longer available on closure of the CP. A weak version is that UG is mentally represented but no longer accessible. See Bley-Vroman's (1989) Fundamental Difference Hypothesis.
Maladaptive gain of processing capacity with maturation	The greater processing capacity of adults enables them to extract more from the input and thus they are faced with the problem of analysing everything at once, whereas children's limited processing capacity means they extract less from the input but can handle it.
Use it and then lose it	The language learning faculty has served its purpose once a language has been learned; evolution has ensured that it is dismantled once it is no longer needed as keeping it would incur costs.
Use it or lose it	This draws on 'a mental muscle metaphor'; that is, if the language learning faculty is not used, it will atrophy but if it is used it is maintained. Bever (1981) suggests that acquisition requires that perception and production systems need to work together but once one stops learning a language this ceases.
Learning inhibits learning	Connectionist theories[3] see learning as a matter of the strengthening of neural connections but once the connections have been firmly established they are difficult to undo. Thus the ability to learn may change over time as a function of previous learning.
Other hypotheses	Other variables that may account for age-related difficulty in L2 learning are availability of input, social-psychological factors such as learner attitudes and motivation, and availability of instruction.

Table 1.6 Explanations of age-related difficulties in L2 learning (based on Birdsong 1999a: 2–9).

Fossilization

Irrespective of their age (but especially if they start in adolescence or later), many learners do not achieve full native-speaker competence—they stop short, continuing to manifest grammatical and lexical errors in their L2 production and, even if overcoming these, failing to achieve a native-like pronunciation or to behave in accordance with the pragmatic norms of the target language (TL). The term *fossilization* was introduced by Selinker (1972) to refer to this phenomenon. Selinker and Lamendella (1978) defined fossilization as:

> ... a permanent cessation in learning before the learner has attained target language norms at all levels of linguistic structure and in all discourse domains in spite of the learner's positive ability, opportunity, and motivation to learn and acculturate into target society. (p. 187)

Selinker (1972) suggested that only 5 per cent of learners succeed in achieving full competence. Other researchers have suggested that this figure may be too generous and it is more like 1 per cent or 2 per cent. None of the learners in the five case studies was successful in achieving target-language competence despite favourable learning conditions. Hyltenstam and Abrahamsson (2003) argued that no L2 learner can achieve full native-speaker proficiency.[4] In this respect, L2 acquisition differs from L1 acquisition, where, except for highly unusual cases of children who are deprived of opportunities to hear and speak—such as the case of Genie[5] (Curtiss 1977)—all learners succeed in becoming native-like in their home dialect.

Fossilization is not an all-or-nothing phenomenon. First, there is considerable variation in the extent to which individual learners fossilize. That is, learners vary at what point in their development of an L2 they fossilize, with some ceasing development at a very elementary level, manifesting continued pidginized forms in their production (as in the case of Alberto), and others at a much more advanced level. Second, as Han (2004) pointed out there is 'intra-learner differential success/failure'. That is, a learner may reach target-language norms in some aspects of the L2 but not in others. Readers may be familiar with learners like Henry Kissinger, whose English grammar is essentially native-like, but whose accent remains conspicuously foreign. Differential success/failure can also arise within the grammatical system of the L2 itself (as seen in Lardiere's study of Patty). Syntactical features (for example, basic subject-verb-object word order) are relatively easy to acquire while morphological features (for example, subject-verb agreement in English) are much more difficult. Thus, it is perfectly possible for a learner to be fossilized in some aspects of the L2 but to continue to develop in others.

Fossilization can refer to both a product (i.e. a state of fossilization) and a process (a cognitive view). Han (2004) offered these definitions:

> *Cognitive level*: Fossilization involves those cognitive processes, or underlying mechanisms that produce permanently stabilized IL forms.

> *Empirical level*: Fossilization involves those stabilized interlanguage forms that remain in learner speech or writing over time, no matter what the input or what the learner does. (p. 20)

However, there is a conspicuous lack of detail in the SLA literature addressing the nature of the cognitive processes that comprise fossilization. Instead, researchers have focused on demonstrating the existence of fossilized states and the putative causes of fossilization. Han (2004) identified a total of 49 different variables that have been invoked to account for fossilization. Some of these explanations refer to cognitive processes—lack of attention, inappropriate learning strategy, the inability to notice input-output discrepancies, false automatization, reluctance to restructure, processing constraints, a natural tendency to focus on content rather than form, reduction in the computational capacity of an innate language faculty, and neural ENTRENCHMENT. There is an equally long list of social-psychological variables (for example, the learner's will to maintain his or her own identity). Han opted for a primarily cognitive explanation:

> I have argued that fossilization is internally determined due to the constant functioning of maturational and native language constraints, yet it can be modulated (aggravated or alleviated) by environmental, social, and psychological forces. (p. 43)

However, she also acknowledged Selinker and Lakshmanan's (1992) Multiple Effects Principle, according to which fossilization is more likely when two or more factors work in tandem.

Fossilization is, however, a problematic construct. Learners can only be considered 'fossilized' in relation to some set of norms—usually those of some standard variety. Bialystok and Hakuta (1999) noted 'there is an assumption in all research into second language acquisition that the learner is striving toward some stateable goal, a standard and perfect version of the language that is embodied in the mind of every native speaker' (p. 165). However, such an assumption may not be warranted, as many L2 learners may not be committed to performing like native speakers. In particular, learners in the multilingual melting pots of large cities such as London and New York may be targeting MULTICOMPETENCE (Cook 2002), involving varying abilities in a number of different languages, rather than target-like use of a single L2. It is problematic to term such learners 'fossilized' even if they manifest non-native norms in some (or even all) of the codes at their disposal, as their overall ability in language may outweigh that of monolingual speakers. This view is compatible with Larsen-Freeman's (2005) claim that the very notion of a target 'end state' is theoretically untenable, for 'when we entertain a view of language as a dynamic complex adaptive system ... we recognize that every use of language changes its resources, and the changed resources are then available for use in the next speech event' (p. 408). In other words, all language systems, including that of the native speaker, are constantly changing and thus it does not make sense to measure a learner's competence against some static notion of a native-speaker target.

There are also methodological problems associated with research that has claimed to investigate fossilization. Long (2003) presented a detailed critique of the research, identifying only three studies (one of which was his own) that met the stringent methodological requirements he argued were needed to claim that fossilization has taken place—i.e. fossilization must be demonstrated not assumed, the learners under investigation must have had ample opportunity and motivation to learn the L2, the data collected should be longitudinal and include samples of spontaneous speech, and the analyses should involve stability/change measures of individual learners. Lardiere's study satisfies these requirements and thus it would seem reasonable to conclude that Patty is a fossilized learner, as indeed Lardiere claims.

Long proposed that SLA researchers would do better to investigate STABILIZATION phenomena, which are well attested in L2 acquisition, rather than fossilization, which he claimed is almost impossible to demonstrate. 'Stabilization' refers to a state of L2 development where fluctuation has *temporarily* ceased. Many L2 learners are familiar with a situation where they appear to plateau, failing to develop despite their continuing efforts to do so, but then make a 'breakthrough' some time later. Stabilization is easier to demonstrate empirically as it does not constitute a permanent condition—that is, a stabilized L2 system can subsequently become destabilized. All that is required to demonstrate that a learner has stabilized is evidence to show that over a given period of time some specific non-target feature of the learner's L2 system has persisted. In contrast, to demonstrate fossilization it is necessary to provide evidence that the learner's L2 system is permanently stabilized. This requires showing that even after many years of exposure to the language the learner continues to manifest the same non-target features.

There is also another reason for preferring 'stabilization' to 'fossilization'. Talk of fossilization positions L2 learners as failures but, in fact, many achieve very considerable success in acquiring an L2. A key factor in determining success is undoubtedly instruction (see Chapter 16); learners who have received some instruction generally outperform those who rely entirely on naturalistic learning. Bardovi-Harlig (2000), for example, reviewed the results of a number of longitudinal studies undertaken as part of the European Science Foundation Project which investigated the acquisition of a number of languages by migrant workers in Europe—see Dietrich *et al.* 1995—in order to examine whether the instructed learners differed from the uninstructed learners. The more successful instructed learners acquired a rich repertoire of tense/aspect features. In contrast, the uninstructed learners did not. Of course, instruction was not the only factor that distinguished the successful and unsuccessful learners—for example, the amount of contact with the target language was another factor—but instruction was clearly a major explanatory factor. Instructed learners, then, may be successful in acquiring the morphological features the absence of which has been taken as a defining characteristic of a fossilized learner (as in Lardiere's study of Patty). It would follow that a learner who displays 'stabilization' might be able to continue learning with the help of instruction.

It is clear that fossilization is a problematic construct—both conceptually and methodologically. As Fidler (2006) pointed out, there has been little progress made in achieving the twin goals of reaching consensus on what fossilization is and how it can be described empirically. However, fossilization/stabilization are important constructs in SLA because they raise what is a central question: is L2 acquisition largely the product of a learner-internal capacity for language learning, which atrophies once the first language has been acquired, or is it driven by exogenous and endogenous factors such as the availability of instruction and the learner's motivation to learn?

Age-related effects: some general conclusions

The following is a summary of the main findings of research into age-related effects and fossilization in L2 acquisition:

1 Adult learners have an initial advantage where rate of learning is concerned, particularly in grammar. They will eventually be overtaken by child learners who receive enough exposure to the L2. This is less likely to happen in instructional than in naturalistic settings because the critical amount of exposure is usually not available in the former.
2 Child learners are more likely to acquire a native accent and grammar than adult learners but there is now sufficient evidence to suggest that a native accent and grammar is possible for at least some adult learners.
3 Children are more likely to reach higher levels of attainment in both pronunciation and grammar than adults but only providing there is sufficient exposure to the L2. Where there is not sufficient exposure (as is the case in many instructed learning contexts) late-starting learners may continue to outperform child learners, especially in grammar.
4 There is no agreement as to whether there is a critical period for learning an L2. Researchers who argue for a critical period acknowledge that it may vary depending on the aspect of language involved (for example, the critical period may differ for pronunciation and for grammar). Disagreements among supporters of the critical period also exist with regard to the span involved for any particular aspect of language. Long (1990a), for example, puts the onset critical age for pronunciation at six years, but Scovel (1981) argues that there is no evidence to support this and argues for a pre-puberty start.
5 Overall, however, the research indicates no clear discontinuity in learning as a result of age. Rather, the ability to learn an L2 declines gradually with increasing age. Also, there is growing evidence that some learners who start learning as adults can achieve a native-like competence (i.e. fossilization is not inevitable).

6 As evidenced by measures of brain activity, there is no clear evidence that language processing in the L2 is substantially different from that in the L1 in balanced bilinguals. Neural activity is more influenced by the learner's general level of proficiency in the L2.
7 Many learners fail to achieve full native-speaker ability in an L2, which has led some researchers to posit that 'fossilization' is a characteristic of L2 acquisition. However, methodological problems exist in both defining fossilization and also determining whether it exists. While in many cases L2 learning may be slower than L1 acquisition, it has not yet been clearly established that L2 learners necessarily fail to reach the same end state as L1 learners, especially if they have access to instruction.

As Larsen-Freeman and Long (1991) point out, the age issue is an important one for theory-building in SLA research, for educational policy-making, and for language pedagogy. A key theoretical issue is whether there is an innate, biologically endowed capacity for language learning and whether this is available in L2 as well as L1 acquisition. Language educators are concerned with whether foreign-language learning is likely to be more successful if started in childhood (i.e. at primary school) than in adolescence (i.e. at secondary school). Language teachers want to know whether children learn in different ways from adults and thus whether they need different approaches and techniques to teaching an L2, depending on the age of the learner.

There are, however, no easy answers to these questions. Initially, it was believed that child language acquisition relies on an innate capacity for language learning (what Chomsky has termed 'Universal Grammar' (UG)) and that this was no longer available after a certain age. This is now in some doubt. But even if child and adult language acquisition are seen as drawing on the same learning mechanisms, this would not constitute evidence against UG, as it is possible that this is available in both. In other words, arguments about UG cannot be resolved with reference to the role of age in L2 acquisition.

It would appear that the research on the age factor does not support an early start for L2 learning in school settings, given that late starters appear to do as well and sometimes better than early starters. But it remains a possibility that those instructed learners who start early may outperform those who start late if they subsequently have opportunities to learn in a naturalistic setting which affords them the quantity of exposure they need to benefit from an early start. Also, there are strong educational reasons for an early start; there are intellectual and cultural benefits in studying a foreign language. Finally, the fact that there is no obvious discontinuity in the achievement of early and late starters does not obviate the need to take account of general cognitive differences between young and older learners in deciding what constitutes the most appropriate instructional approach. It is not clear, therefore, that the research on age in L2 acquisition affords clear guidance to SLA theory builders, educational language planners, or teachers.

What the research on both fossilization and age demonstrates is the enormous complexity of the issues involved in L2 acquisition and the methodological problems that exist in SLA. The controversies and mixed findings that characterize research in both areas are, in fact, evident in SLA as a whole. I hope that the above examination of these two issues will prepare readers of this book to expect controversy and the uncertainty that it accompanies. In my final chapter, Chapter 17, I will examine the epistemological problems that arise from this indeterminacy. Before that, however, I would like to lead readers through the main areas of enquiry in SLA so that they can see for themselves what has been discovered about L2 acquisition and where the divisions of opinion are to be found. To this end, I conclude by outlining the framework for exploring SLA that informs the whole book.

A framework for exploring SLA

The framework is shown in Table 1.7. A distinction is made between 'General SLA' and 'Instructed SLA'. The former investigates issues relative to all L2 learners, irrespective of whether they are in a naturalistic or an instructed setting. The latter is concerned with how learners acquire an L2 in a classroom setting. In the case of General SLA a distinction is made between 'Description', where the emphasis is on identifying the properties of learner language, and 'Explanation', where the attention shifts to theoretical accounts of L2 acquisition and of individual learner differences. Instructed SLA involves both the study of how the kinds of interaction found in classrooms influence L2 acquisition and whether learners actually learn what they are taught. This framework affords seven distinct areas of enquiry, which are outlined below.

Area 1 addresses the characteristics of learner language. The study of these provides the researcher with the main source of information about how acquisition takes place—the 'facts' that need to be explained. One of the major goals of SLA research is to describe learner language and to show how it works as a system. Four aspects of learner language will receive attention: (1) ERRORS, (2) ORDER OF ACQUISITION AND SEQUENCE OF DEVELOPMENT, (3) VARIABILITY, and (4) PRAGMATIC FEATURES relating to the way language is used in context for communicative purposes.

Area 2 examines learner-external factors that can account for how an L2 is acquired. We will adopt both a narrow and broader view of such factors. In the narrow view, we will focus on the linguistic environment by investigating the properties of the input and interaction learners experience and how these affect learning. Taking a broader view, we will study the macro and micro social contexts of acquisition, examining such issues as learner identity and its influence on learning.

Area 3 addresses the psycholinguistic processes involved in both L2 acquisition and L2 use. Three views of these processes are considered. In one view, these are seen as mental and largely hidden from view, although not necessarily completely unconscious. They involve (1) the transfer of knowledge

General SLA					Instructed SLA	
Description of learner language	Explanation of learning					
Area 1 Characteristics of learner language	**Area 2** Learner external factors	**Area 3** Psycholinguistic processes	**Area 4** Inter-learner variability	**Area 5** The brain and L2 acquisition	**Area 6** Inside the 'black box'	**Area 7** Intervening directly in interlanguage
Errors (Chapter 2)	Input and interaction (Chapter 6)	L1 transfer (Chapter 8)	Individual differences in L2 learners (Chapter 13)	Neurolinguistic accounts of L2 acquisition (Chapter 14)	Classroom interaction and L2 acquisition (Chapter 15)	Form-focused instruction and L2 acquisition (Chapter 16)
Acquisition order and developmental sequences (Chapter 3)	Social accounts of L2 learning (Chapter 7)	Cognitive accounts of L2 acquisition (Chapter 9)				
Variability (Chapter 4)		Cognitive accounts of L2 use (Chapter 10)				
Pragmatic features of interlanguage (Chapter 5)		Sociocultural accounts of L2 acquisition (Chapter 11)				
		Linguistic accounts of L2 acquisition (Chapter 12)				

Table 1.7 A framework for investigating L2 acquisition

from the learner's L1, (2) the universal processes involved in converting input into INTAKE and RESTRUCTURING existing L2 knowledge systems, and (3) the processes for using L2 knowledge in L2 production. All of these draw on cognitive theories of language, language use, and language acquisition. The second perspective can be found in (4): SOCIOCULTURAL SLA. This explains L2 acquisition in terms of the interplay between learner-external and learner-internal factors, treating acquisition as something that happens both outside and inside the learner's head. The third perspective, seen in (5), is linguistic in orientation; that is, an explanation of how learners learn language is based on the claim that learners have innate knowledge of LINGUISTIC UNIVERSALS.

Area 4 addresses individual learner differences and what causes them. Learners set about the task of acquiring an L2 in different ways. They differ with regard to such general factors as MOTIVATION and LANGUAGE APTITUDE, and also in the use of various strategies such as inferencing and self-monitoring for obtaining input and for learning from it.[6] The study of these general factors and LEARNING STRATEGIES helps to explain why some learners learn more rapidly than others and why they reach higher levels of proficiency.

An alternative approach to explaining L2 learning is offered in Area 5. This looks at attempts to understand how learners learn an L2 by examining what parts of the brain are involved in storing and accessing L2 knowledge. Key topics in this area are whether different parts of the brain are implicated in the storage of implicit and explicit L2 knowledge and whether L1 and L2 processing involve different neural activity.

Area 6 is the first of two areas to examine instructed SLA. This area attempts to go inside the 'black box' of the classroom to examine the ways in which language is used there and how this may influence the course and success of acquisition. It views instruction broadly as 'interaction' affording (or sometimes limiting) opportunities for language learning.

Area 7 investigates whether direct attempts to intervene in the course of interlanguage development through FORM-FOCUSED INSTRUCTION are effective and, given that there is growing evidence that they are, which types are more effective than others. The research in this area, while of obvious relevance to language pedagogy, also addresses issues of key theoretical importance in SLA.

It is not always clear where specific lines of enquiry fit best. For example, the study of the communication processes involved in using L2 knowledge is viewed by some researchers as an aspect of interaction (Area 2), by others as an aspect of psycholinguistic processing (Area 3) and by yet others as one type of learner strategy (Area 4). Also, the areas interrelate, so not surprisingly many investigations will figure in more than one area. For example, the errors that learners make (Area 1) reflect the operation of internal processing mechanisms (Area 3) and may also be influenced by the social context in which learning takes place (Area 2) and the learner's preferred LEARNING STYLE (Area 4). In other words there will always be more than one way of carving up the content of SLA. The way I have chosen reflects my own conceptualization of this content and how to make sense of it for my readers.

The book concludes with a chapter that examines a number of epistemological issues in SLA. These concern the nature of the data that can best inform about L2 acquisition, the scope and evaluation of theories of L2 acquisition, and to what extent and in what ways SLA can be applied to language pedagogy.

Summary and conclusion

This chapter began by defining the term 'second language acquisition', pointing out the diversity of phenomena which have been investigated under its banner. It then went on to present the results of a number of case studies of L2 learners before examining the role of age in L2 acquisition. A framework for reviewing SLA research was then proposed. This consisted of seven major areas: (1) learner language, (2) learner-external factors, (3) psycholinguistic processes, (4) inter-learner variability, (5) the brain and L2 acquisition, (6) inside the black box of the classroom, and (7) direct intervention in interlanguage development.

It is useful to distinguish two main goals of SLA research: description and explanation. In the case of description, the goal is to provide a clear and accurate account of the learner's competence and, in particular, to uncover the regularities and systematicities in the learner's development and control of L2 knowledge. In the case of explanation, one goal is to reveal how learners are able to develop knowledge of an L2 from the available input and how they use this knowledge in communication. A second goal is to specify the factors that cause variation in individual learners' accomplishment of this task.

It is also useful to distinguish two branches of enquiry within SLA research. One has as its focus learning, and the other, the language learner. In the case of the former, the emphasis is on identifying the universal characteristics of L2 acquisition. In the case of the latter, the aim is to account for differences in the ways in which individual learners learn an L2. The ultimate goal of SLA is to develop a theory that can interconnect the findings from both branches and thus account for both the universal aspects of L2 acquisition and the individual differences observed in L2 learners. However, we are still a long way from such a theory, although, arguably, some progress has been made in this direction.

SLA continues to be characterized by a plethora of theories and models, some of which overlap and some of which are complementary. There is little sign of this plethora thinning out. Nor is there agreement as to whether this is desirable and, if it is, how it could be achieved. At this point in the history of the development of SLA, the reader must be prepared for different perspectives, controversy, and uncertainty, as illustrated in the above accounts of fossilization and the role of age in L2 acquisition. In this respect, perhaps, SLA is no different from other social sciences. The compensation for the lack of a single, highly focused picture is the richness of forty odd years of enquiry into L2 acquisition and the excitement this engenders—in me and, I hope, in the readers of this book.

Notes

1 The terms 'naturalistic' and 'instructed' are not favoured by all SLA researchers. Alternative terms are 'untutored'/'tutored' or 'uninstructed'/'instructed'. The point has been made that there is really nothing 'unnatural' about classrooms. However, I have elected to keep the terms 'naturalistic'/'instructed' in part because they are commonly used but also because they offer distinct terms for the two kinds of setting in which acquisition can take place rather than labelling one as simply the negative of the other. It should be noted that learners often do not belong exclusively to the 'naturalistic' or 'instructed' categories but rather to a third category, often called 'mixed'.

2 Magnetic resonance imaging uses a radiology technique to produce images of body structures. It has been used in language research to investigate what parts of the brain are active in performing different language tasks and also whether there are differences in brain functioning in L1 and L2 language use.

3 Connectionist theories of L2 acquisition view acquisition as driven primarily by input which enables learners to strengthen the connections in a neural network. This network links together linguistic sequences of varying shapes and sizes.

4 Birdsong (2006a) rightly notes that estimates regarding the incidence of native-like achievement in L2 learning are more a matter of guesswork than empirical evidence. He also notes that the estimates may have included foreign language learners who may not have reached their end state due to lack of learning opportunities.

5 Genie was kept in virtual isolation for most of her life and did not receive substantial exposure to English before the age of 13. When discovered, she had no language. Genie was successful in learning English but did not achieve full grammatical competence, although it is not clear whether this was because she had passed the critical period for language acquisition or because of the emotional disturbance she continued to manifest.

6 A distinction is generally drawn between those cognitive processes responsible for the general pattern of L2 acquisition (i.e. its universal characteristics) and those strategies that are employed, often consciously, by learners to improve their learning. The terminological distinction between 'processes' and 'strategies' is not always adhered to, however. 'Strategies' are often invoked to account for developmental regularities. The problems of definition are dealt with in Chapter 13.

PART TWO
Description: the characteristics of learner language

Introduction

An obvious starting point in the study of second language (L2) acquisition is the study of the language that learners produce at different stages of their development. Learner language can provide the researcher with insights into the process of acquisition. For many researchers—although not all[1]—it constitutes the most important source of information about how learners learn an L2. This section, therefore, focuses on the description of learner language. Its purpose is to provide an overview of the principal ways in which it has been studied and to describe its main characteristics. An understanding of these characteristics is fundamental to the study of L2 acquisition. It provides a basis for examining and evaluating the various explanatory accounts of L2 acquisition that will be considered in Parts 3, 4, and 5 of the book.

A number of different approaches to the description of learner language can be identified:

1 learners' errors
2 developmental patterns
3 variability
4 pragmatic features.

It is possible to see a progression in the way enquiry has proceeded. Thus, initially (in the 1960s) the main approach was the study of learners' errors, but this was rapidly superseded by the study of developmental patterns (in the late 1960s and 1970s) and, a little later, variability. The study of L2 pragmatic features is a more recent phenomenon but has attracted considerable interest in the last two decades. This section follows this historical progression, beginning with (1) and concluding with (4). The opening chapters, therefore, focus on the early research in SLA. However, as all these approaches have continued to figure in SLA research, at least to some extent, each chapter will also examine relevant recent research. In the case of the chapter on interlanguage pragmatics much of the research is of recent origin.

As we noted in the Preface, prior to the late 1960s there was very little empirical study of L2 acquisition. Why, then, did researchers suddenly become interested in it? There appear to have been two principal reasons. One concerned the need to investigate the claims of competing theories. The other concerned the desire to improve L2 pedagogy.

According to the CONTRASTIVE ANALYSIS HYPOTHESIS, learners were strongly influenced by their L1. Where the L1 matched the L2, learning was facilitated; where it differed, learning was impeded. In the view of some (for example, Lado 1957), errors were mainly, if not entirely, the result of transfer of L1 'habits'. This theory of learning was challenged both by Chomsky's attack on behaviourism (see his famous review of B. Skinner's *Verbal Learning* in 1959) and also by research on L1 acquisition, which showed that children did not seem to learn their mother tongue as a set of 'habits' but rather seemed to construct mental 'rules', which often bore no resemblance to those manifest in their caretakers' speech. This challenge to the received opinion of the day created the necessary climate for the empirical study of L2 acquisition. Were learners' errors the result of L1 transfer? Did L2 learners, like L1 learners, construct unique mental 'rules'? These were questions that could only be answered by looking at learner language.

Second, many L2 researchers were directly concerned with language pedagogy. The prevailing methods of the day were the audiolingual method and the oral/situational approach. (See Richards and Rogers 1986.) Both of these emphasized tightly structuring the input to the learner and controlling output in order to minimize errors. It was noted, however, that children were successful in acquiring their mother tongue without such a structured learning environment. Also, many L2 learners, children and adults, seemed to be very successful in learning an L2 in natural settings. Newmark (1966), in a seminal paper, argued that L2 learning in the classroom would proceed more efficiently if teachers stopped 'interfering' in the learning process. But how did L2 learners learn in natural settings? What strategies did they use? What made some learners more successful than others? Again, these were questions that invited empirical enquiry. Many of the early studies in SLA research investigated L2 learners in naturalistic or mixed settings, motivated in part by the desire to find what experiences worked for them, so that suitable copies could be introduced into the language classroom.

This, then, constitutes the background to the study of learner language. It should be clear that, although the empirical studies were primarily descriptive in nature, they were not atheoretical. In the late 1960s and 1970s a growing consensus was reached that behaviourist theories of L2 learning were inadequate. L2 learners, like L1 learners, were credited with a 'built-in-syllabus' (Corder 1967), which guided their progress. Selinker (1969, 1972) coined the term 'interlanguage' to refer to the special mental grammars that learners constructed during the course of their development. Interlanguage theory credited learners with playing an active role in constructing these grammars. It treated their behaviour, including their errors, as rule-governed. The language they produced, therefore, reflected the strategies they used to construct provisional grammatical rules (i.e. rules which they subsequently revised). The research that we will now consider helped to shape interlanguage theory and, in many cases, was influenced by it. Thus, although the main concern of this section is the description of learner language, some attention to theory is inevitable. Interlanguage theory is considered more fully in Chapter 9.

The research reported in these chapters was often conducted by researchers whose primary concern was L2 acquisition and L2 pedagogy. Inevitably, however, these researchers drew on various fields to help them in their enquiry. The fields of most obvious importance were linguistics (which provided researchers with well-defined linguistic categories to investigate), first language acquisition research (which provided them with useful procedures for collecting and analysing learner language), sociolinguistics (which provided both theories and methodologies for examining variability), and pragmatics/discourse analysis (which facilitated the study of learner language in a wider social and textual context). The account of learner language that follows, therefore, reflects one of the prevailing characteristics of SLA research—the utilization of a wide range of concepts and methods that have been borrowed from different fields and adapted to the particular needs of L2 researchers.

Note

1 Some researchers prefer to work with intuitional data, obtained by asking learners to judge the grammaticality of sentences. However, as this introduction to Part Two makes clear, the primary data in SLA research—both historically speaking and in terms of importance—has been learner language.

2

Learner errors and error analysis

Introduction

The study of 'bad language' in the context of native-speaker usage has a long history, as reflected in such well-known publications as Fowler's *The King's English* (1906) and, more recently, Howard's *Good English Guide* (1994). In the context of foreign/second language pedagogy, there have been a number of books detailing 'common errors' (for example, Fitikides' *Common Mistakes in English* (1936) and Turton and Heaton's *Good English Guide* (1996)). There are also dictionaries of errors specific to particular groups of learners, as illustrated by Swan and Smith's *Learner English: A Teacher's Guide to Interference and Other Problems* (2001).

In this chapter, however, we are concerned with the use of ERROR ANALYSIS (EA) as a tool for investigating how learners acquire a second language (L2). This has a much shorter history, dating from the 1960s. In a series of articles published in the late 1960s and early 1970s, Corder spelt out the theoretical rationale and empirical procedures for carrying out an error analysis. Corder (1967) noted that ERRORS provided the researcher with evidence of how language was learnt, and also that they served as devices by which the learner discovered the rules of the target language (TL). George published his influential *Common Errors in Language Learning* in 1972, developing a model to account for why learners produced errors. In 1974, Richards published *Error Analysis*, a seminal collection of empirical studies of learner errors. Subsequently, interest in EA declined and today it is rare to find published articles devoted solely to descriptions and explanations of learner errors. Nevertheless, EA has continued to figure in the study of L2 acquisition. James' *Errors in Language Learning and Use: Exploring Error Analysis* (1998) constitutes a powerful defence of EA, rebutting many of the criticisms that have been levelled at it. EA also figures in current studies that address accuracy in L2 production. (See, for example, Foster and Skehan 1996.) In short, although EA no longer constitutes the preferred means for examining L2 acquisition, it is nevertheless far from extinct.

L2 learners are, of course, not alone in making errors. Children learning their first language (L1) also make 'errors'. (See, for example, Bloom 1970.) They regularly produce utterances[1] like the following:

*I goes see Auntie May. (= I went to see Auntie May.)

*Eating ice cream. (= I want to eat an ice cream.)

*No writing in book. (= Don't write in the book.)

But it is probably true to say that these 'errors' are not generally thought of as errors in the same sense as those produced by L2 learners. Whereas L2 learners' errors are generally viewed as 'unwanted forms' (George 1972), children's 'errors' are seen as 'TRANSITIONAL FORMS'. Similarly, adult native speakers' errors are treated as 'slips of the tongue'.[2]

This chapter will consider the procedures involved in each of the steps involved in conducting an EA identified by Corder (1974):

1 collection of a sample of learner language
2 identification of errors
3 description of errors
4 explanation of errors
5 evaluation of errors.

In so doing, this chapter will examine some of the research carried out in the 1970s and, where appropriate, the methodological problems faced. A general critique of EA follows. Finally, it will look at some more recent research which has made use of the techniques of error analysis.

Collection of a sample of learner language

The type of data collected can have a marked effect on the results of an EA, as a result of the different production processes which they typically involve. For example, LoCoco (1976) found differences in the number and type of errors in samples of learner language collected by means of free composition, translation, and picture composition. In particular, the nature and quantity of errors is likely to vary depending on whether the data consist of natural, spontaneous language use or careful, elicited language use. For this reason, natural samples are generally preferred. A drawback, however, is that learners often do not produce much spontaneous data, which led Corder (1973) to argue the case for elicited data. He distinguished two kinds of elicitation. Clinical elicitation involves getting the informant to produce data of any sort, for example, by means of a general interview or by asking learners to write a composition. Experimental elicitation involves the use of special instruments designed to elicit data containing the linguistic features which the researcher wishes to investigate. An example of such an elicitation instrument is the BILINGUAL SYNTAX MEASURE (Burt, Dulay, and Hernandez 1973). This consisted of a series of pictures which had been devised to elicit specific features and which the learners were asked to describe.

Table 2.1 lists some of the factors that need to be considered in collecting a sample of learner language. Unfortunately, many EA studies paid little attention to these factors, with the result that they are difficult to interpret and almost impossible to replicate. A further problem is that the majority of EAs have been cross-sectional rather than longitudinal, thus making it difficult to determine accurately the different errors that learners produce at different stages of their development. The limitations of EA, as practised in the late 1960s and 1970s, are evident in the samples of learner language collected. Svartvik, for instance, notes that 'most error analyses use regular examination papers (composition, translations, etc.) for material' (1973b: 12).

Factors	Variables	Description
Learner	Proficiency level	Elementary, intermediate, or advanced.
	Other languages	The learner's L1; other L2s.
	Language learning experience	This may be classroom or naturalistic or a mixture of the two.
Language sample	Medium	Learner production can be oral or written.
	Genre	Learner production may take the form of a conversation, a lecture, an essay, a letter, etc.
	Content	The topic the learner is communicating about.
Production	Unplanned	The discourse is produced spontaneously.
	Planned	The discourse is produced spontaneously or under conditions that allow for careful online planning.

Table 2.1 Factors to consider when collecting samples of learner language

Errors

Identification of errors

The definition of 'error' is problematic, as James (1998) admits. The difficulty centres around a number of issues. The first is whether *grammaticality* (i.e. well-formedness) or *acceptability* should serve as the criterion. An utterance may be grammatically correct but pragmatically unacceptable. For example,

'I want to read your newspaper' addressed to a complete stranger is grammatical but pragmatically unacceptable. In general, EA has attended to 'breaches of the code' and ignored 'misuse of the code' (Corder 1974: 124), but increasingly attention has been paid to the latter (for example, Thomas 1983; Kasper and Schmidt 1996). Errors of this pragmatic kind will be considered in Chapter 5. Nor is grammaticality itself always easy to determine. If this is defined as a 'breach in the rule of the code', the question arises as to what particular variety of the target language is chosen as the 'code'. In particular, phonological or semantic well-formedness can vary considerably depending on the variety of language.[3] As James (1990) points out 'nobody would seriously think of designating the differences between, say, British English and any of the "colonial" varieties of English as "error"' (p. 209). Also, what constitutes rules of well-formedness differ for spoken and written language. (See Carter and McCarthy 1995.)

The second issue concerns whether a distinction should be made between ERRORS and MISTAKES (Corder 1967). An error (in this technical sense) takes place when the deviation arises as a result of lack of knowledge (i.e. a lack of competence).[4] Mistakes are performance phenomena and are, of course, regular features of native-speaker speech, reflecting processing failures that arise as a result of competing plans, memory limitations, and lack of automaticity. Corder argues that the EA should be restricted to the study of errors (i.e. mistakes should be eliminated from the analysis). However, apart from the problems of identification that this distinction raises, it also assumes that competence is homogeneous rather than variable. Thus, if learners sometimes use a correct target form and sometimes an incorrect, non-target form, it cannot necessarily be concluded that the learner 'knows' the target form and that the use of the non-target form represents a mistake. For example, a learner may have no difficulty in using the target-language form in some linguistic contexts:

My sisters are older than me.

but produce an error in others:

*My three sister are older than me.

Traditional EA largely ignored the problem of variability in learner language.

A third issue concerns whether the error is overt or covert (Corder 1971a). An overt error is easy to identify because there is a clear deviation in form, as when a learner says:

*I runned all the way.

A covert error occurs in utterances that are superficially well formed but which do not mean what the learner intended them to mean. For example, the utterance (from Corder 1971a):

*It was stopped.

is apparently grammatical until it becomes clear that 'it' refers to 'the wind'. Furthermore, a superficially correct utterance may only be correct by chance. For example, the learner may manifest target-like control of negative constructions in ready-made chunks such as 'I don't know' but fail to do so in 'created' utterances (i.e. utterances that are constructed on the basis of rules the learner has internalized). The existence of covert errors led Corder to argue that 'every sentence is to be regarded as idiosyncratic until shown to be otherwise' (p. 21).

A final issue is whether infelicitous uses of the L2 should be considered erroneous. There are instances where a learner produces a form that is grammatical (i.e. conforms to the norms of the code) but this may not be the form *preferred* by native speakers of the code. Consider the use of 'was coming' in the following text:

> One day an Indian gentleman, a snake charmer, arrived in England. He was coming from Bombay.

The preferred form is probably 'had come'. However, 'was coming' can be considered possible if the speaker wishes to emphasize the duration of the action. The probabilistic nature of the use of forms can only be considered if the analyst has access to a corpus of native-speaker language which can serve as a baseline for comparing learners' choice of forms. Recent work in the computer-based analysis of language corpora (learner and native speaker) has made such comparisons possible—see, for example, Granger and Tyson 1996—with the result that infelicitous usage can now be more easily investigated.

Lennon's (1991) definition of an error constitutes an attempt to take into account these issues:

> A linguistic form or combination of forms which, in the same context and under similar conditions of production, would, in all likelihood, not be produced by the speaker's native speaker counterparts. (p. 182)

Applying such a definition to actual data, however, is not easy. Recognizing this, Corder (1971a, 1974) proposed an elaborate procedure for identifying errors. This acknowledged the importance of 'interpretation' and distinguished three types: normal, authoritative, and plausible. A normal interpretation occurs when the analyst is able to assign a meaning to an utterance on the basis of the rules of the target language. In such cases, the utterance is 'not apparently erroneous', although it may still only be right 'by chance'. An authoritative interpretation involves asking the learner (if available) to say what the utterance means and, by so doing, to make an 'authoritative reconstruction'. A plausible interpretation can be obtained by referring to the context in which the utterance was produced or by translating the sentence literally into the learner's L1. However, it is not at all clear whether Corder's procedure will work. For example, reliance on the learner as an informant has been criticized on the grounds that retrospective accounts of intended meaning are often not reliable (Van Els *et al.* 1984).

Perhaps, though, the problems of identification have been overstated. Duskova (1969) discusses them at some length and concludes that 'the number of cases in which it was hard to decide whether an error had been made ... did not exceed 4 per cent of all the errors examined'. The problems do point to the need for researchers to provide inter-rater reliability measures for the errors they have identified. Unfortunately, they have rarely done so.

Description of errors

The description of learner errors involves a comparison of the learner's idiosyncratic utterances with a reconstruction of those utterances in the target language or, more recently, with a baseline corpus of native-speaker language.

Perhaps the simplest type of descriptive taxonomy is one based on linguistic categories. A very general distinction can be drawn between lexical and grammatical errors. Politzer and Ramirez (1973) distinguished errors of morphology, syntax, and vocabulary. One general finding is that lexical errors generally exceed grammatical errors. Blaas (1982; cited in Meara 1984) for example found that there were three times as many lexical errors as grammatical in one corpus of errors. Grammatical errors are typically subdivided into categories. An example can be found in Burt and Kiparsky's *The Gooficon: A Repair Manual for English* (1972). This identifies a number of general grammatical categories (for example, the auxiliary system, passive sentences, temporal conjunctions, and sentential complements). Each of these general categories is then broken down further. For example, the auxiliary system is subdivided into 'do', 'have' and 'be', modals, and mismatching auxiliaries in tag questions. Such taxonomies allow for both a detailed description of specific errors and also for a quantification of errors.

The 1960s saw a number of studies which provided descriptions of the different kinds of linguistic errors produced by learners. Richards (1971b), in a paper designed to challenge the widely held belief that learner errors were the result of L1 interference, provided a taxonomy of different categories of linguistic error based on a number of previous studies. He examined errors made by learners from different language backgrounds and illustrated the different kinds of errors relating to the production and distribution of verb groups, prepositions, articles, and the use of questions. However, he made no attempt to quantify the errors. Nor do we know to what extent his linguistic categories accounted for all the errors he examined. Duskova (1969)—one of the studies Richards drew on—is better in this respect. She identified a total of 1,007 errors in the written work of 50 Czech learners of English, who were postgraduate students studying science. She found 756 'recurrent systemic errors' and 251 'nonce errors' (i.e. errors that occurred once only). Errors in articles were most common (260), followed by errors in lexis (233) and morphology (180). In comparison, there were only 54 errors in syntax and 31 in word order. Duskova noted, however, that the frequency of the errors did not necessarily reflect the level of difficulty the learners experienced with different linguistic features, as some features (such as articles) were attempted more often than others (for example, adverbs). Duskova also noted that although she had few difficulties in assigning errors to general linguistic categories such as 'word order', it often proved very difficult to classify them accurately into subcategories.

These studies were cross-sectional in design. Of greater interest for SLA research are longitudinal studies of learners' errors as these can show in what areas of language errors persist over time. Chamot's (1978, 1979) study of the acquisition of English by a bilingual French/Spanish boy is interesting in this respect. She found that the main linguistic problem areas were omission of constituents, verb forms, sentence formation, articles, and prepositions. In some of these (for example, omission of constituents) the number of errors reduced sharply over a 44-month period, while in others (for example, question formation) little improvement was evident. In all the areas, however, there was considerable fluctuation in error frequency throughout the period. Chamot's study suggests that it may be difficult to provide a satisfactory description of learners' L2 development by quantifying the types of errors they make.

An alternative to a linguistic classification of errors is a surface strategy taxonomy. This 'highlights the ways surface structures are altered' (Dulay, Burt, and Krashen 1982: 150) by means of such operations as omissions, additions, and regularizations. Table 2.2 provides a part of the total taxonomy together with examples of the categories. Dulay, Burt, and Krashen claim that such an approach is promising because it provides an indication of the cognitive processes that underlie the learner's reconstruction of the L2. This seems a doubtful claim, however, as it presupposes that learners operate on the surface structures of the target language rather than create their own, unique structures. There have, in fact, been few attempts to describe learner errors using such a taxonomy.

Although linguistic and surface strategy taxonomies of errors may have a pedagogic application (for example, by demonstrating which errors are the most frequent and, therefore, most in need of attention), in general they shed little light on how learners learn an L2. Corder's (1974) framework for describing errors is more promising in this respect. He distinguishes three types of error according to their systematicity:

1 Pre-systematic errors occur when the learner is unaware of the existence of a particular rule in the target language. These are random.
2 Systematic errors occur when the learner has discovered a rule but it is the wrong one.
3 Post-systematic errors occur when the learner knows the correct target-language rule but uses it inconsistently (i.e. makes a mistake).

Category	Description	Example
Omissions	The absence of an item that must appear in a well-formed utterance.	She sleeping.
Additions	The presence of an item that must not appear in well-formed utterances.	We didn't went there.
Misinformations	The use of the wrong form of the morpheme or structure.	The dog ated the chicken.
Misorderings	The incorrect placement of a morpheme or group of morphemes in an utterance.	What daddy is doing?

Table 2.2 A surface strategy taxonomy of errors (categories and examples taken from Dulay, Burt, and Krashen 1982)

Type 1 occurs when the learner cannot give any account of why a particular form is chosen, Type 2 occurs when the learner is unable to correct the errors but can explain the mistaken rule used, and Type 3 occurs when the learner can explain the target-language rule that is normally used. Such a taxonomy, therefore, requires that the researcher has access to the learners and that the learners are capable of providing explanations for their L2 behaviour. For this reason it may prove difficult to operate.

The description of errors, like their identification, is problematic. Even if the error itself can be easily identified, it is often problematic to determine what the error consists of. In many cases—even with sentences that are overtly idiosyncratic—the reconstruction of the target-language version—and, therefore, its description—is problematic. For example, if a learner produces the following sentence:

*I am worried in my mind.

it is not clear what constitutes the best reconstruction. One possibility is 'I am feeling worried'. Another is 'I have a problem on my mind'. Even if the learner is available for consultation, it may not be possible to choose between these two reconstructions. But the description of the error will obviously vary according to which reconstruction is finally chosen. The reconstruction of covertly idiosyncratic sentences will prove even more difficult.

Another problem concerns the failure to quantify the different types of errors that have been identified and described. In some studies error frequencies are not given at all (for example, Jain 1974; Richards 1971b), while in others only absolute frequencies are given (for example, Duskova 1969). But as Schachter and Celce-Murcia (1977) point out, to say anything worthwhile about error frequency we need to know the number of times it would be possible for learners to have committed different errors. In other words, relative rather than absolute frequencies are needed.

Explanation of errors

Explanation is concerned with establishing the source of the error, i.e. accounting for why it was made. This stage is the most important for SLA research as it involves an attempt to establish the processes responsible for L2 acquisition.

As Taylor (1986) points out, the error source may be psycholinguistic, sociolinguistic, epistemic, or may reside in the discourse structure. Psycholinguistic sources concern the nature of the L2 knowledge system and the difficulties learners have using it in production. Sociolinguistic sources involve such matters as the learners' ability to adjust their language in accordance with the social context. Epistemic sources concern the learners' lack of world knowledge, while discourse sources involve problems in the organization of information into a coherent 'text'. In general, however, SLA research has attended only to the first of these. As Abbott puts it: 'The aim of any EA is to provide a psychological explanation' (1980: 124).

A number of different sources or causes of psycholinguistic errors have been identified. Richards (1971b) distinguishes three:

1 INTERFERENCE ERRORS occur as a result of 'the use of elements from one language while speaking another'. An example might be when a German learner of L2 English says 'I go not' because the equivalent sentence in German is 'Ich gehe nicht'.
2 INTRALINGUAL ERRORS 'reflect the general characteristics of rule learning such as faulty generalization, incomplete application of rules and failure to learn conditions under which rules apply'.
3 DEVELOPMENTAL ERRORS occur when the learner attempts to build up hypotheses about the target language on the basis of limited experience.

However, Schachter and Celce-Murcia (1977) find the distinction between intralingual and developmental errors 'curious', and most researchers have operated with a general distinction between transfer errors (Richards' Category 1) and intralingual errors (an amalgam of Richards' Categories 2 and 3).

It is not easy to distinguish TRANSFER and intralingual errors, and even more difficult to identify different types of transfer and intralingual errors. In an attempt to deal with the problem of identifying sources, Dulay and Burt (1974b) classified the errors they collected into three broad categories:

1 Developmental (i.e. those errors that are similar to those in L1 acquisition)
2 Interference (i.e. those errors that reflect the structure of the L1)
3 Unique (i.e. those errors that are neither developmental nor interference).

However, Dulay and Burt's research has often been criticized on the grounds that reliable classification of errors in terms of these categories is still not possible.

A possible source of unique errors is the instruction that learners receive. Stenson (1974) provides a number of examples of such instructionally INDUCED ERRORS in the classroom speech of Tunisian learners of English. Faulty explanation of grammatical points can give rise to errors (for example, the use of 'any' to mean 'none' when the students were told that 'any' has a negative meaning). Drills performed without consideration for meaning can also result in error. Svartvik (1973b) suggests that overdrilling may be one of the reasons why Swedish learners of L2 English overused infinitival complements (for example, *'He proposed her to stay'). Stenson argues that such errors are not systematic and therefore do not reflect competence. However, there are probably cases when learners do internalize faulty rules derived from instruction and in such cases the resulting errors will reflect their competence. Instruction may constitute one source of what Dulay and Burt call 'unique errors', as Weinert (1987) has shown.

The bulk of the empirical work in SLA has focused on determining what proportion of the total errors in a corpus are transfer as opposed to intralingual. This research was motivated by the need to test the competing claims of a behaviourist, habit-formation account of L2 acquisition and a mentalist, creative-construction account. According to behaviourist accounts, errors were viewed as the result of the negative transfer of L1 habits. According to mentalist accounts, errors were predicted to be similar to those found in L1 acquisition because learners actively construct the grammar of an L2 as they progress (i.e. they are intralingual). This issue dominated early work in SLA. It should be noted, however, that subsequently researchers have come to recognize that the correlation between BEHAVIOURIST LEARNING THEORY and transfer errors on the one hand and MENTALIST LEARNING THEORIES and intralingual errors on the other is simplistic and misleading. Transfer is now treated as a mental process in its own right. (See Chapter 8.)

A good example of the kind of 'proportion study' that investigated this behaviourist/mentalist question is Dulay and Burt (1974b). In a corpus of speech collected by means of the Bilingual Syntax Measure, 513 unambiguous errors produced by Spanish children acquiring L2 English were extracted. These errors occurred in six syntactic structures which differed in English and Spanish. The errors were classified as 'developmental', 'interference', or 'unique', and detailed results for each structure were provided. In each case the developmental errors far outweighed the interference errors. For example, for the structure NP + V + Pronoun (for example, 'The dog ate it'), which is realized as NP + Pronoun + V in Spanish (for example, 'El perro se lo comio'), there were 93 developmental errors and no interference errors. Overall less than 5 per cent of the total errors were attributed to interference. This led Dulay and Burt to propose that L1 and L2 acquisition were very similar—the L2 = L1 HYPOTHESIS, discussed in Chapter 3. It should be noted, however, that other studies (for example, George 1972 and Flick 1980) found a much higher proportion of transfer errors. (See Chapter 8.)

One reason for the discrepancy in research findings has been the problem of error classification. As Flick notes:

> The assignment of a particular error to such categories as 'transfer', 'overgeneralization' or 'ambiguous' has been largely an arbitrary matter, subject to the individual biases and point of view of the researcher. (Flick 1979: 60)

Schachter and Celce-Murcia (1977) argue that a large number of learners' errors are ambiguous with regard to source and that 'one must be extremely cautious when claiming to have identified the cause of any given error type'. Such caution has not always been exercised, however. It is, therefore, difficult and perhaps dangerous to attempt to synthesize the results of studies that have sought to explain errors in learner language. The following is a tentative list of some of the main findings:

1 A large number—and in some cases perhaps most—of the errors that learners produce are intralingual in origin rather than transfer. However, the precise proportion of the kinds of error varies considerably from study to study.
2 According to Taylor (1975), learners at an elementary level produced more transfer errors than learners at an intermediate or advanced level. Conversely, he found that learners at an intermediate or advanced level produced more intralingual errors (for example, overgeneralization) than learners at an elementary level. However, as we will see in Chapter 8, other researchers (for example, Kellerman 1983) have challenged the view that transfer is more prevalent in beginners.
3 The proportion of transfer and intralingual errors varies in accordance with the task used to elicit samples of learner language. For example, translation tasks tend to result in more transfer errors than tasks that call for free composition (Lococo 1976).
4 Transfer errors are more common in the phonological and lexical levels of language than in the grammatical level. Also some areas of grammar acquisition are more likely to be influenced by the learners' L1 than others. Grauberg (1971) found that interference accounted for 25 per cent of the lexical errors produced by adult German learners of L2 English, 10 per cent of their syntactic errors, and none of their morphological errors.
5 Transfer errors are more common in adult learners than in child learners. For example, White (1977) found that 21 per cent of the errors made by adult Spanish learners of English were transfer. White used the same instrument to collect data as in the Dulay and Burt (1974b) study of Spanish children referred to above, so this study is directly comparable.
6 Errors can have more than one source. For example, the 'no' + verb error (as in 'No look my card') is universal, suggesting an intralingual explanation, but Spanish learners of L2 English have been noted to make this error

more frequently and for a longer period of time, suggesting that the L1 pattern for negatives ('no' + verb) is also having an influence.

Evaluating errors

Whereas all the preceding stages of EA have involved an examination of errors from the point of view of the learner who makes them, ERROR EVALUATION involves a consideration of the effect that errors have on the person(s) addressed. This effect can be gauged either in terms of the addressee's comprehension of the learner's meaning or in terms of the addressee's affective response to the errors. Error evaluation studies proliferated in the late 1970s and in the 1980s, motivated quite explicitly by a desire to improve language pedagogy.[5] The studies surveyed in Table 2.3 constitute only a part of the total. Ludwig (1982) provides a survey of twelve early studies.

The design of error evaluation studies involves decisions on who the addressees (i.e. the judges) will be, what errors they will be asked to judge, and how they will be asked to judge them. The judges can vary according to whether they are native speakers (NSs) or non-native speakers (NNSs), and also according to whether they are 'expert' (i.e. language teachers) or 'non-expert'. The errors they have been asked to judge cover semantic or lexical aspects of English, different grammatical features, and spelling. The instruments used to elicit judgements vary in a number of ways. In most cases they consist of decontextualized lists of sentences containing either one or several errors. These sentences are usually taken from actual samples of learner language (mainly written compositions) but they are sometimes contrived. In some studies the sentences are contextualized. The errors can be presented orally but are usually presented in writing. The judges may be asked to evaluate the 'comprehensibility' of the sentences containing the errors, the 'seriousness' or the 'naturalness' of errors, or the degree of 'irritation' they arouse. Sometimes they may be asked to correct the errors and to give reasons for why they judged some errors as especially problematic. In some studies the judges' comprehension of the erroneous sentences is also tested.

Error evaluation studies have addressed three main research questions: (1) Are some errors judged to be more problematic than others? (2) Are there differences in the evaluations made by NSs and NNSs? and (3) What criteria do judges use in evaluating learners' errors? We will briefly consider the main findings on each of these issues.

NS judges tend to judge lexical errors as more serious than grammatical errors (for example, Burt 1975; Tomiyana 1980; Khalil 1985). They also tend to judge global grammatical errors as more likely to interfere with comprehension than local errors, although, as Santos (1987) points out, there have been conflicting results on this point. Burt defines GLOBAL ERRORS as errors that affect overall sentence organization. Examples are wrong word order, missing or incorrectly placed sentence connectors, and syntactic overgeneralizations. LOCAL ERRORS are errors that affect single elements in a sentence (for example, errors in morphology or grammatical functors). NS judges may also be influenced by MARKEDNESS factors. Santos' study, for example, lends some credence to the idea that errors involving the substitution of marked for unmarked forms (for example, 'an book' for 'a book') are judged more severely than errors in which unmarked forms replace marked forms (for example, 'a apple' for 'an apple'). NS judges also find it easier to deal with insertion than with omission or wrong choice errors (Tomiyana 1980). It should be noted, though, that there can be considerable variation in the judgements of native speakers. Thus Vann, Meyer, and Lorenz (1984) found that some academic faculty members were inclined to view all errors as equally serious—'an error is an error'.

There are clear differences in the judgements made by NSs and NNSs. Overall, NNSs are much more severe (James 1977; Hughes and Lascaratou 1982; Davies 1983; Sheorey 1986). NNS judges seem to be especially hard on morphological and functor errors in comparison to NS judges. However, they tend to evaluate lexical and global errors less severely than NS judges.

Judges appear to use different criteria in assessing ERROR GRAVITY. Khalil (1985) identified three general criteria: intelligibility, acceptability, and irritation. Intelligibility concerns the extent to which sentences containing different kinds of error can be comprehended.' Acceptability is a rather vague criterion, involving judgements of the seriousness of an error. Irritation concerns the emotional response of an addressee but is also related to the frequency of errors. Albrechtsen, Henriksen, and Færch (1980), who had NS judges rate the errors made by Danish learners of English in oral interviews, found that 'all errors are equally irritating ... irritation is directly predictable from the number of errors regardless of the error type or other linguistic aspects'(1980: 394).

NS and NNS judges vary in the criteria they use. NS judges appear to be more concerned with the effect that an error has on their comprehension, whereas NNS judges are more influenced by their ideas of what constitute the 'basic' rules of the target language (Hughes and Lascaratou 1982). However, Davies (1983) points out that NNS judgements will be influenced by a number of factors relating to the particular context in which they operate. Thus NNS teachers in a foreign language context will be influenced by their background knowledge of the syllabus and text book the learners are following and by explicit knowledge of their L1. Transfer errors are viewed leniently, but errors in grammatical structures that have already been taught will be seen as more serious.

Study	Subjects	Measures	Procedure	Main Results
Burt 1975	Non-expert NS	Partially corrected versions of 300 sentences containing multiple errors.	Subjects were asked to judge comprehensibility of different corrected versions.	Subjects found versions in which 'global' errors had been corrected more comprehensible than versions in which 'local' errors had been corrected.
Albrechtsen, Henriksen, and Færch 1980	120 non-expert adult NSs (e.g. hotel workers in UK; 180 British sixth-formers)	Samples of oral language taken from Grade 10 Danish learners of L2 English; the samples varied with regard to error density.	Subjects listened to tapes and rated each sample using bipolar adjective scales (e.g. easy to understand–difficult to understand).	The oral texts containing few errors (syntactic as well as lexical) and few communication strategies (CSs) received positive evaluations. Frequent use of CSs had greater negative effect than number of errors.
Tomiyana 1980	NS graduates in education and language departments	2 constructed passages (200 words in length), designed to include 7 instances of 6 kinds of errors involving articles and sentence connectors.	Subjects were asked to read the passages and correct the errors and to rate likely academic achievement of the writer of the passage.	Subjects corrected insertion errors more accurately than omission or wrong choice errors, and article errors more accurately than connector errors. Errors in articles not perceived as so damaging to academic success as errors in connectors.
Chastain 1981	27 native Spanish speakers: undergraduates at university in Spain	10 paragraphs written by American university students of Spanish.	Subjects were asked to read the passages, underline each error, and then evaluate it as comprehensible and acceptable, comprehensible but not acceptable, or not comprehensible.	The overall seriousness of the different errors was (1) word errors in noun phrases (most serious); (2) form errors in verb phrases; (3) word errors in verb phrases; and (4) form errors in noun phrases (least serious).

Hughes and Lascaratou 1982	10 Greek-speaking teachers; 10 NS teachers; 10 non-expert NSs	32 sentences containing errors in 8 categories (vocabulary, grammar, and spelling) taken from learners' compositions; 10 error-free sentences.	Subjects were asked to underline errors, write correct versions, and judge their seriousness. Also asked to give reason if error judged 'very serious'.	NNSs judged errors overall as more serious than NSs. NNSs more lenient on spelling errors. NNSs judged according to whether error constituted infringement of 'basic' rule; NSs judged according to intelligibility. Evaluation of specific errors inconsistent.
Davies 1983	43 Moroccan teachers of English; 43 non-expert NSs	82 contrived sentences (some correct) containing typical errors of Moroccan secondary school students.	Subjects were asked to rate seriousness of the errors and to add comments.	NSs more lenient than NNSs. NNSs very hard on morphological and tense choice errors, but NNSs less hard on obvious transfer errors and 'global' errors.
Vann *et al.* 1984	319 faculty members of US university	24 sentences containing multiple errors and 12 containing single errors; errors in 12 error categories.	Subjects were asked to judge acceptability of sentences.	Subjects more prepared to accept errors of kind made by NS students (e.g. in spelling), but less likely to accept 'global' errors (e.g. word order).
Khalil 1985	240 American undergraduate NSs	20 grammatically deviant and 12 semantically deviant sentences taken from compositions by Arab first-year students, some contextualized and some not.	Subjects were asked to judge intelligibility and naturalness of sentences. They were also tested on the ability to understand the sentences' meaning.	Semantic errors were judged less intelligible and found less comprehensible than grammatical errors. Contextualization of sentences did not improve intelligibility.
Sheorey 1986	64 NS teachers and 34 NNS (Indian) teachers	20 sentences reflecting 8 categories of error taken from compositions written by foreign students at university in USA.	Subjects were asked to judge seriousness of errors.	NNSs judged errors overall more serious than NSs. NSs judged lexical errors more serious than NNSs. NNSs judged errors in tense, agreement, prepositions, question formation, and spelling more serious than NSs.

Santos 1987	40 university professors in physical sciences	4 written compositions; in 2 of them 5 errors of the marked-to-unmarked kind (e.g. 'a' instead of 'an') were inserted and in the other 2, 5 errors of the unmarked-to-marked kind (e.g. 'an' instead of 'a') were inserted.	Subjects were asked to rank each composition and to underline each error and to assess the degree of irritation it aroused.	No significant difference in rankings of the compositions. Overall, unmarked-to-marked errors were found to be more irritating than marked-to-unmarked errors. Syntactic errors were also found more irritating than morphological errors.

Table 2.3 A summary of selected evaluation studies

Error evaluation studies have often been pedagogically motivated. They have sought to identify criteria for establishing error gravity so that teachers can be guided in what errors to pay more attention to. The general conclusion is that teachers should attend most carefully to errors that interfere with communication (i.e. semantic and global grammatical errors). Johansson (1973) suggests that errors should be evaluated by first asking whether they are comprehensible, and second whether they cause irritation. Other, secondary factors—the frequency and generality of the feature involved—also need to be considered. In this way, Johansson constructs a hierarchy of errors. However, he acknowledges that 'it is not possible to illustrate the scale of errors at the present time since there is no available information concerning the degree of comprehensibility/irritation caused by different errors' (1973: 109).

Like other aspects of EA, the evaluation of learner error poses a number of problems. It is not at all clear what criteria judges use when asked to assess the 'seriousness', 'intelligibility', or 'acceptability' of an error. Error evaluation is influenced by the context in which the errors occurred. Thus, the same error may be evaluated very differently depending on who made it and where, when, and how it was made. The experimental studies which have been conducted to date, however, take no account of these contextual factors, often presenting errors for evaluation in isolated sentences. It is perhaps not surprising that these studies have produced conflicting results. (See Santos 1987.) The appearance of rigour given by the use of descriptive and qualitative statistics may therefore be spurious.

The limitations of error analysis

There have been a number of critiques of EA (Bell 1974; Schachter and Celce-Murcia 1977; Long and Sato 1984; Van Els *et al.* 1984). Bell goes so far as to call EA a 'pseudo procedure'. The criticisms levelled at EA fall into three main categories: (1) weaknesses in methodological procedures, (2) theoretical problems, and (3) limitations in scope. The first type have already been considered in the previous sections, so we focus on the second and third here.

According to some SLA researchers, EA is theoretically flawed in that it takes some target language variety as its reference point. We have seen that this is problematic because it is not always clear what the learners' reference group is and that, in some cases (for example, Hispanics living in an African American area of New York), they may be targeted on some non-standard variety. But there is a more major problem. Bley-Vroman (1983) pointed out that learner language needs to be considered as a variety in its own right and that EA is guilty of the COMPARATIVE FALLACY (i.e. it seeks to account for learner language solely in terms of target-language norms). In the next chapter we will examine research that avoids this by examining the forms that learners acquire and use irrespective of whether they do or do not confirm to target-language norms. James (1998), however, has responded to this criticism of EA by pointing out that learners are typically targeted on native-speaker norms and as such perform 'cognitive comparisons' in the process of learning an L2.

A frequently mentioned limitation is that EA fails to provide a complete picture of learner language. We need to know what learners do correctly as well as what they do incorrectly. This problem has been overstated, however. First, Corder (1971b) explicitly recognized the importance of examining the totality of the learner's production. Second, there is nothing to prevent the researcher doing this. At the very least, EA can be considered to have a place 'as a partial and preliminary source of information at an initial stage of investigation' (Hammarberg 1973: 34).

EA is limited in a second way. Most of the studies are cross-sectional in nature (i.e. data were collected at a single point in time) and thus afforded only a very static view of L2 acquisition. In many cases little care has been taken to separate out the errors made by learners at different stages of development. As a result, EA has not proved very effective in helping us understand how learners develop knowledge of an L2 over time. This weakness is, again, not a necessary one. EA can be used in longitudinal studies of L2 learners (i.e. by collecting data from the same learners at different points in time) as in the Chamot (1978, 1979) study referred to earlier. A study of how learners' errors change from one stage to another can shed light on the process of L2 acquisition.

The third problem is more substantive, however. Schachter (1974) conducted an analysis of the relative clause errors produced by two sets of learners (one Arabic and Iranian, and the other Chinese and Japanese). She found that the first group of learners made more errors than the second group, despite the fact that relative clause structures existed in their L1s and did not exist in Chinese and Japanese. However, she also discovered that the Arabic and Iranian learners made many more attempts to use relative clauses than did the Chinese and Japanese learners. She concluded that learners may resort to AVOIDANCE if they find a structure difficult. Subsequent studies by Kellerman (1977), Kleinmann (1978), Dagut and Laufer (1985), and Hulstijn and Marchena (1989) testify to the prevalence of avoidance in L2 acquisition.

EA, which focuses exclusively on what learners do, has no way of investigating avoidance and is, therefore, seriously limited. Avoidance is clearly an important issue for SLA research; it is examined more fully in Chapter 8.

Summary

Error analysis was one of the first methods used to investigate learner language. It achieved considerable popularity in the 1970s, replacing contrastive analysis. The first step in carrying out an EA was to collect a sample of learner language. The sample could consist of natural language use or be elicited either clinically or experimentally. It could also be collected cross-sectionally or longitudinally. The second stage involved identifying the errors in the sample. Corder distinguished errors of competence from mistakes in performance and argued that EA should investigate only errors. Corder also proposed a procedure for identifying errors by reference to normal, authoritative, and plausible interpretations. The third stage consisted of description. Two types of descriptive taxonomies have been used: linguistic and surface strategy. The former provides an indication of the number and proportion of errors in either different levels of language (i.e. lexis, morphology, and syntax) or in specific grammatical categories (for example, articles, prepositions, or word order). The latter classifies errors according to whether they involve omissions, additions, misinformations, or misorderings. The fourth stage involves an attempt to explain the errors psycholinguistically. Errors can result from transfer, intralingual, or unique processes. They can also be induced through instruction. EA studies produced widely differing results regarding the proportion of errors that are the result of L1 transfer, but most studies concur that the majority of errors are intralingual. The precise proportion varied as a product of such factors as the learners' level, the type of language sampled, the language level (for example, lexis versus grammar) and the learners' ages. Also, errors were shown to have more than one cause. Finally, evaluation studies entailed establishing the effect that different errors have on the person addressed—either in terms of comprehension or affective response. They produced evidence to show that global errors affect comprehension more than local errors, that non-native speakers are inclined to be harsher judges of errors than native speakers, and that different criteria involving intelligibility, acceptability, and irritation are used to make judgements.

EA has lost popularity as a result of its perceived weaknesses. These weaknesses include methodological problems involving all stages of analysis and, also, limitations in the scope of EA. Focusing solely on the errors which learners produce at a single point in time—as most of the studies have done—can only provide a partial picture. It takes no account of what learners do correctly, of development over time, and of avoidance phenomena.

However, it is important not to be over-dismissive of EA. It has made a substantial contribution to SLA research. It served as a tool for providing empirical evidence for the behaviourist/mentalist debates of the 1970s, showing that many of the errors that learners make cannot be put down to interference. Perhaps, above all, it helped to make errors respectable—to force recognition that errors were not something to be avoided but were an inevitable feature of the learning process. Indeed, the very concept of 'error' came to be challenged on the grounds that learners act systematically in accordance with the mental grammars they have constructed and that their utterances are well formed in terms of these grammars. As Corder put it, 'everything the learner utters is by definition a grammatical utterance in his dialect' (1971a: 32).

More recent EA research

The heyday of EA was in the 1960s and 1970s. It then went temporarily out of fashion, as a result of the perceived weaknesses in procedure and scope discussed above. However, some work in EA continued and, recently, it has had something of a rebirth with the advent of computer-based analyses of learner language.

As we have already noted, some of the weaknesses are not inherent in EA. Taylor (1986) outlined a number of principles that he believes should guide the practice of EA. These principles are based on the general claims that 'what constitutes significant error is not strictly quantifiable' and that we should 'conceive our analytical aims to lie rather more in the interpretative traditions of a humanistic discipline than has recently been customary' (1986: 162). Taylor demonstrated, through the detailed analysis of a piece of writing produced by a native speaker, how the study of errors should be located in the 'whole text' and how it can afford valuable insights into the process of language use.

In contrast, Lennon (1991) remained more committed to the quantification of errors, seeking to show how some of the problems of error identification could be overcome. He pointed out that most 'erroneous forms are, in fact, in themselves not erroneous at all, but become erroneous only in the context of the larger linguistic unit in which they occur' (1991: 189). To take account of this in error identification he proposed two new dimensions of error: domain and extent. Domain refers to the breadth of the context (word, phrase, clause, previous sentence, or discourse) which needs to be considered for determining whether an error has occurred. Extent refers to the size of the unit (morpheme, word, phrase, clause, sentence) that requires deleting, replacing, reordering, or supplying in order to repair an erroneous production. For example, in an error like *'a scissors', the domain is the phrase and the extent is the word, while in an error like *'well, it's a great hurry around', both domain and extent are the whole sentence.[7] Lennon illustrated how the concepts of domain and extent can help to distinguish different kinds of lexical error.

EA, in fact, continues to be practised, although now it is more likely to serve as a means for investigating a specific research question rather than for providing a comprehensive account of learners' idiosyncratic forms. For example, Felix (1981) and Pavesi (1986) used EA to compare the language produced by instructed and naturalistic learners. Bardovi-Harlig and Bofman (1989) wished to investigate the differences between a group of learners who successfully passed the Indiana University Placement exam and a group who failed to do so. They examined the nature of the errors which the two groups produced in one part of the examination—written compositions—and found, unremarkably, that the pass group made fewer overall errors than the non-pass group and, more interestingly, that the major differences were in the number of lexical and morphological rather than syntactical errors. Santos (1987), in the study already referred to, carried out an error evaluation in order to investigate linguistic claims regarding markedness.

EA is also used to provide a measure of ACCURACY in studies that have investigated the effects of task design and implementation on learner production. (See Chapter 10.) Foster and Skehan (1996), for example, calculated the percentage of error-free clauses as a general measure of accuracy in their study of tasks. This measure involved examining each clause to determine whether it contained an error. Mehnert (1998) computed the number of errors per 100 words. Other task-based studies have focused on specific areas of language to obtain measures of accuracy. Crookes (1989) calculated the percentage of target-like use of plurals while Skehan and Foster (1997) examined target-like use of vocabulary. Obviously all these measures involve a much more limited EA than that described in the preceding sections of this chapter as they only entailed the identification of errors (i.e. no attempt was made to describe or explain the errors). Interestingly, none of these studies included any report of the kinds of problems with error identification discussed above, casting some doubt on the reliability of the accuracy measures they employed.

EA has been reborn in computer-based analyses of learner language. Learner corpora such as that collected for the INTERNATIONAL CORPUS OF LEARNER ENGLISH (ICLE) project (Granger 1998) are tagged for errors.[8] The hierarchical error-tagging system developed for the ICLE project assigned a tag to each instance of error in a large corpus of written language. Errors were first classified in terms of whether they were grammatical (G), lexical (L), lexico-grammatical (X), formal (F), register (R), syntax (W), or style (S) and then according to subdivisions of these categories, for example, grammatical verb error (GV) and grammatical auxiliary verb error (GVAUX). The ICLE consisted of a written corpus collected from learners who were not clearly distinguished in terms of their level of proficiency. The Standard Speaking Test Corpus (SST) project (Izumi *et al.* 2004) collected samples of oral language use from Japanese learners of English, who were asked to complete the Standard Speaking Test, a 15-minute oral interview test, that served to provide not only samples of oral language use but also a means of determining the overall proficiency level of the learners—nine levels were distinguished. This project made use of mark-up software, called the *TagEditor*, to facilitate the tagging of errors (Tono *et al.* 2001). Both discourse tagging (for example, filled pauses, repetitions, self-corrections) and error tagging were undertaken. In the case of the latter, three broad types of errors (i.e. omissions, replacements, and insertions) and 42 error categories were distinguished. An error tag provided three pieces of information—the part of speech involved, the grammatical/lexical rule that has been transgressed, and the corrected form. The following is an example of an error-tagged sentence from Izumi *et al.* (2004: 35):

*I belong to two baseball **<n_num crr = "teams">** team **< n_num>**

Once a corpus has been electronically tagged it becomes possible to carry out a detailed computer-based analysis, identifying the frequency of different error types. Such an approach allows for both the analysis of very large corpora and also for the comparison of the errors produced by different learners according to such variables as proficiency, L1, or age. Clearly, computer-based analyses provide an opportunity to carry out large and sophisticated EAs. However, as Barlow (2005) points out, such analyses are subject to the same problems and limitations as traditional error analysis.

Finally, error analysis continues to have a role to play in remedial approaches to the teaching of writing. Ferris (2002), for example, has revived Hendrickson's (1978) earlier appeal for researchers to examine L2 learner errors as a basis for deciding what L2 features to teach.

Notes

1 These examples of sentences containing an error—and others in this chapter—are intended to reflect the kind of errors that are often made. In cases where attested sentences are used to illustrate a point their source will be indicated.

2 The study of production errors in native speakers has received explicit attention by Fromkin (1971), among others. As Crookes (1991) points out, speech errors serve as the primary data for the construction of models of language production. In retrospect, it is somewhat surprising that the L2 researchers who developed and made use of error analysis techniques made so little reference to work on L1 production.

3 Learners also have 'model preferences' (Beebe 1985), which are a reflection of their REFERENCE GROUP and the variety they are targeted on, a point discussed in Chapter 7.

4 The distinction between COMPETENCE and PERFORMANCE in an L2, which here is discussed in terms of 'errors' and 'mistakes', has more recently been considered in terms of the general distinction between 'knowledge' and 'control' (for example, Bialystok and Sharwood Smith 1985). This distinction is discussed in the Introduction to Part 4.

5 Svartvik (1973b) refers to error evaluation as 'therapy'.

6 The claim that greater attention should be paid to errors that affect comprehension does not mean that no attention should be paid to local errors in morphology or the use of grammatical functors. Indeed, the fact that

such structures do not have much communicative value may be one reason why they are often not acquired and why an instructional focus on them may be necessary.

7 Lennon (1991: 192) claims that 'for any given error, domain will be at higher rank than or equal rank to extent, but never at a lower rank'.

8 Not all computer-based analyses of learner corpora have utilized EA. Many studies examine the extent to which learners use specific target-language forms, tagging words and constructions in terms of target-language categories.

3
Developmental patterns in second language acquisition

Introduction

One of the most powerful ideas to have emerged from descriptive research of learner language is that L2 acquisition proceeds in a regular, systematic fashion. In this chapter we will examine the evidence that lends support to the existence of regular developmental patterns in L2 acquisition, reserving theoretical and pedagogical considerations until later.

A distinction will be made between the idea of an ORDER and a SEQUENCE OF DEVELOPMENT. One question we can ask is 'Do learners acquire some target-language (TL) features before others?' This is a question about the order of acquisition. We can answer it by showing that one feature, say plural –s in English, is acquired before another. A second and entirely different question is 'How do learners acquire a particular TL linguistic feature?' To answer this question we need to investigate some specific feature (such as negation) in detail and, preferably, over time. Showing that learners pass through stages *en route* to the TL construction provides evidence for a sequence of acquisition. DEVELOPMENTAL PATTERN will be used as a cover term for the general regularities evident in language acquisition. As such, it subsumes the ideas of order and sequence.

The starting point for this chapter will be an account of the main methods that have been used to study developmental patterns in language acquisition. A brief examination of developmental patterns in L1 acquisition follows, setting the scene for a more thorough account of L2 acquisition. The emphasis will be on description (explanation being handled in later chapters) and on research carried out primarily with naturalistic L2 learners.[1] The survey will begin with a description of three aspects of early L2 acquisition: (1) the SILENT PERIOD, (2) the use of FORMULAIC SEQUENCES, and (3) STRUCTURAL/SEMANTIC SIMPLIFICATION. It continues with an account of research that has investigated the order and sequence of acquisition of grammatical features (which have received the most attention), vocabulary, and phonology. A brief discussion of the L2 = L1 HYPOTHESIS follows. Finally, there will be a general evaluation of the claims regarding developmental patterns.

Methods for investigating developmental patterns

There are a number of different ways in which researchers can set about trying to identify developmental patterns. One way is to examine whether learners' ERRORS change over time. There is some evidence to show that this does happen, but as we saw in the last chapter, ERROR ANALYSIS has not succeeded in providing clear and conclusive evidence of developmental patterns. A second way is to examine samples of learner language collected over a period of time in order to identify when specific linguistic features emerge. According to this approach, 'acquisition' is defined as 'first occurrence'. It has been used extensively in first language acquisition research (for example, Wells 1985) and to a lesser extent in SLA research (for example, Pienemann 1984).

One common method for identifying and describing developmental patterns is OBLIGATORY OCCASION ANALYSIS. This has been widely used by L2 acquisition researchers and is clearly described in Brown (1973). The basic procedure is as follows. First, samples of naturally occurring learner language are collected. Second, obligatory occasions for the use of specific TL features are identified in the data. In the course of using the L2, learners produce utterances which create obligatory occasions for the use of specific target-language features, although they may not always supply the features in question. Thus, if a learner says: 'My sister visited us yesterday' or *'My father arrive yesterday', obligatory occasions for the use of past –ed have been created in both utterances. Third, the percentage of accurate use of the feature is then calculated by establishing whether the feature in question has been supplied in all the contexts in which it is required. A criterion level of accuracy can then be determined in order to provide an operational definition of whether a feature has been 'acquired'. Usually, the level is set at 80–90 per cent, below 100 per cent, to take account of the fact that even adult native speakers may not achieve complete accuracy. Brown (1973) considered a feature to be 'acquired' if it was performed at the 90 per cent level on three consecutive data collection points—a very rigorous definition.

One problem with obligatory occasion analysis is that it takes no account of when a learner uses a feature in a context for which it is not obligatory in the TL. For example, the learner who says *'I studied last night and now I *understood* better' has overgeneralized the past tense, using it where the TL requires the present tense. Clearly, acquisition of a feature such as past tense requires mastering not only when to use it but also when not to use it. To take account of over-uses as well as misuses a number of researchers (for example, Pica 1983) have suggested a procedure known as TARGET-LIKE USE ANALYSIS. Pica (1984) has shown that substantial differences in estimates of learners' abilities arise depending on whether obligatory occasion or target-like use analysis is employed.

Both obligatory occasion and target-like use analysis are target-language-based—that is, like error analysis, they seek to compare learner language and the TL—and thus reflect the COMPARATIVE FALLACY (Bley-Vroman 1983). That is, they ignore the fact that learners create their own unique rule systems in the process of learning an L2. One way of investigating these is to catalogue the various linguistic devices that learners use to express a particular grammatical structure (such as negatives) and then to calculate the frequency with which each device is used at different points in the learners' development. (See, for example, Cazden *et al.* 1975.) This method is called FREQUENCY ANALYSIS or INTERLANGUAGE ANALYSIS. It is able to show the 'vertical variation' in learners' development (i.e. how different devices become prominent at different stages) and serves as one of the best ways of examining developmental sequences.

Many of the studies considered in this chapter are longitudinal, involving data collection over a period of many months and, in some cases (for example, Schmidt 1983) several years. Such studies provided the strongest evidence of developmental patterns. In addition, there have been a number of cross-sectional studies (i.e. data were collected only at a single point in time). In order to make claims about the order of acquisition on the basis of cross-sectional data, researchers resorted to a number of statistical procedures. Some researchers argued that the accuracy order with which different features were performed corresponded to their acquisition order (for example, Dulay and Burt 1973, 1974c). Thus, for example, if the data showed that short plural –s (as in 'boys') was performed more accurately than long plural –es (as in 'churches'), then this indicated that the short plural form was acquired before the long plural form. An alternative procedure for establishing order of acquisition from cross-sectional data involves IMPLICATIONAL SCALING. This technique was first used in Creole studies (Decamp 1971). It seeks to exploit the inter-learner variability that exists in a corpus of learner language in order to establish which features different learners have acquired and whether the features can be arranged into a hierarchy according to whether the acquisition of one feature implies the acquisition of one or more other features for each learner. For interested readers, Hatch and Farhady (1982: Chapter 14) provide a clear explanation of how implicational scaling is carried out. An example can be found in Figure 4.1. The extent to which cross-sectional data, so processed, can provide valid information about developmental sequences is a matter of some dispute.

The existence of developmental patterns can be investigated in different areas of language: linguistic (phonological, lexical, and grammatical), semantic, and functional. This chapter will deal more or less exclusively with linguistic systems. Chapter 5 will examine the acquisition of pragmatic features.

Developmental patterns in L1 acquisition

Early work on L1 acquisition in the 1960s and 1970s consisted of detailed case studies of individual learners based on the speech they produced (for example, McNeill 1970; Slobin 1970; Brown 1973), of cross-sectional studies of larger numbers of learners (for example, de Villiers and de Villiers 1973), and of some experimental studies of children's production and comprehension of specific linguistic features (for example, Berko 1958; C. Chomsky 1969). These early studies attempted to identify the general pattern of children's language development. This empirical tradition continued into the 1980s and 1990s, spawning an enormous amount of research in a great range of languages. Notable projects include the Bristol Study, 'Language at Home and at School' (Wells 1985), which involved the longitudinal study of more than 60 children and the enormous cross-linguistic project initiated by Slobin. (See Slobin 1985a.) Inevitably during this time-span there have been shifts in emphasis, but in this tradition researchers largely continue to follow a research-then-theory approach, emphasizing the description of children's language as a basis for theory-building. An alternative tradition grew up in the 1980s. This eschews empirical enquiry and instead seeks to examine L1 acquisition from the point of view of learnability theory and UNIVERSAL GRAMMAR. In this chapter we will be concerned exclusively with the empirical, descriptive tradition, although we will also briefly consider some of the theoretical issues with which this tradition is concerned. The theory-driven tradition is considered in Chapter 12.[2]

One of the pervasive findings in first language acquisition research is that children appear to follow a fairly well-defined pattern of development. This pattern is evident in the way in which all linguistic systems are acquired. Children typically begin with one-word utterances which function as holophrases (i.e. they express whole propositions). They gradually extend the length of their utterances, passing through stages when the bulk of their speech consists of first two-word, then three- and four-word utterances. At the same time, they systematically acquire the various syntactical and morphological rules of the language. The result is that remarkable regularities are evident in both the overall pattern of development and in the acquisition of specific linguistic systems (for example, tense markings or negatives). These regularities are often described with reference to mean length of utterance as a general measure of development. Crystal (1976), for example, describes the specific grammatical features that are evident in children's language when the mean length of their utterances is one word, two words, three words, etc.

In one of the most influential studies of L1 acquisition—the Harvard Study—Brown (1973) found evidence for the fixed order of acquisition of various English morphological features in three children. The same order was obtained in de Villiers and de Villiers' (1973) cross-sectional study of twenty children. The acquisition of individual morphemes also involves stages. For example, the acquisition of English past tense forms involves an initial stage in which there is little or no use followed by sporadic use of some irregular forms, then use of the regular –ed form including overgeneralization to irregular verbs, and finally target-like use of regular and irregular forms. Thus, the acquisition of forms such as 'went' follows a U-shaped pattern of development, with children first using it correctly (for example, 'went') and then incorrectly (for example, 'goed') before they finally once again produce the correct form ('went').

Clear examples of developmental sequences in L1 acquisition are those found in the acquisition of English negatives and interrogatives. Klima and Bellugi (1966), for example, identified three stages in the acquisition of negatives. (See Table 3.1.) Bloom (1970) found evidence of the systematic acquisition of the semantic functions which negatives can realize in English. The children she studied first used 'no' and 'not' to refer to non-presence (for example, 'No cookie'), then to refer to rejection of an offer or suggestion (for example, 'No car' = 'I don't want the car'), and finally to denial. Similar regularities are evident in the acquisition of the formal and semantic aspects of English interrogatives. (See Klima and Bellugi 1966; Cazden 1972.)

Stage	**Description**	**Examples**
1	Negative utterances consist of a 'nucleus' (i.e. the positive proposition) either preceded or followed by a negator.	Wear mitten no. Not a teddy bear.
2	Negators are now incorporated into the affirmative clauses. Negators at this stage include 'don't' and 'can't', used as unitary items. Negative commands appear.	There no squirrels. You can't dance. Don't bite me yet.
3	Negators are now always incorporated into affirmative clauses. The 'auxiliary + not' rule has been acquired, as 'don't', 'can't', etc. are now analysed. But some mistakes still occur (e.g. copula 'be' is omitted from negative utterances and double negatives occur).	I don't have a book. Paul can't have one. I not crying. No one didn't come.

Table 3.1 The L1 acquisition of English negatives (examples from Klima and Bellugi 1966)

These regularities in grammatical development are the product of the acquisition task which the child faces. Clark and Clark (1977) described this task as follows:

> From the outset children are faced with two general problems. First of all, they have to figure out how to map their ideas and general knowledge onto propositions ... Second, they have to find out how to communicate speech acts and thematic information along with the propositional content of their utterances.
> (Clark and Clark 1977: 296)

They emphasized that the two tasks of mapping and communicating go hand in hand. This claim is supported by the fact that regularities are also evident in the way in which the different pragmatic and textual functions of the TL are mastered. Thus, for example, Clark and Clark illustrate how initially children learn to perform assertions and requests and only later develop the ability to express directives (for example, asking, ordering, forbidding, and permitting) and commissives (such as promising). Expressives (for example, thanking) and declarations follow even later. A full account of the developmental path, therefore, must describe how children master the formal, functional, and semantic properties of a language. It is important to recognize, however, that although certain stages of acquisition can be identified, development is, in fact, continuous. Children do not usually jump from one stage to the next but rather progress gradually with the result that 'new' and 'old' patterns of language use exist side by side at any one point in time.

It is also important to acknowledge the inter-learner variability that exists in L1 acquisition. This is most evident in the rate of acquisition. Some children learn their L1 with great rapidity while others do so much more slowly (Wells 1986b). The individual differences go further than rate, however. They concern the overall strategy that children appear to follow. For example, although many children use an ANALYTICAL STRATEGY and show evidence of the developmental progression described above, other children use a GESTALT STRATEGY, typically remaining silent for a longer period before producing full sentences when they first start talking (Peters 1977). All children make use of unanalysed units (formulaic speech) but some seem to rely on them much more extensively than others (Nelson 1973). There is a considerable body of research into L1 acquisition that has sought to identify the factors responsible for inter-learner variation. The variables studied include sex, intelligence, personality and learning style, social background, and experience of linguistic interaction (Wells 1986b).

Developmental patterns in second language acquisition

Most of the research that we shall be reviewing has investigated learners in naturalistic settings and has been based on what might roughly be called UNPLANNED language use (i.e. the learner language that results from attempts by learners to express their meaning intentions more or less spontaneously). L2 learners, particularly adults, have the capacity to engage in PLANNED language use, by paying deliberate attention to the language forms they choose (for example, by using EXPLICIT L2 KNOWLEDGE of grammatical rules or by translating). Unplanned and planned language use display markedly different features, as we shall see in the next chapter. The idea of 'developmental patterns' is based on unplanned language use.

The distinction between the descriptive/empirical and linguistic/theoretical traditions, made in the context of L1 acquisition research, is also relevant to the study of developmental patterns in L2 acquisition. Sharwood Smith and Truscott (2005) distinguished these two perspectives; the developmental perspective sees acquisition as a gradual process with overlapping stages while the linguistic perspective views acquisition as a stepwise movement from one rule system to another. In this chapter only the developmental perspective will be considered; consideration of the linguistic perspective can be found in Chapter 12.

The early stages (The silent period/Formulaic sequences/ Structural and semantic simplification)

The early stages of L2 acquisition in naturalistic settings are often characterized by a SILENT PERIOD, by the use of FORMULAIC SEQUENCES, and by STRUCTURAL AND SEMANTIC SIMPLIFICATION.

The silent period

In the case of L1 acquisition, children go through a lengthy period of listening to people talk to them before they produce their first words. This silent period is necessary, for the young child needs to discover what language is and what it does. In the case of L2 acquisition, the silent period is not obligatory, as the learner already knows about language, having already acquired one. Yet many learners—especially children—opt for a silent period. Itoh and Hatch (1978), for instance, describe how their subject, Takahiro—a two-and-a-half-year-old Japanese boy—refused to speak English at an American nursery school and also to the researcher in his own home for the first three months. Hakuta (1976) reports the difficulty he had in obtaining any data from his subject, Uguisu—a 5-year-old Japanese girl—for the first three months, but then comments that her English suddenly 'blossomed'. Saville-Troike (1988) reports that six out of the nine children learning L2 English that she studied opted for a silent period. Hanania and Gradman's (1977) study of the acquisition of English in the USA by Fatmah, a 19-year-old Saudi woman, also indicates that some adults go through a silent period. Krashen (1985) cites Rodriguez (1982) as another example of an adult learner who began with an extensive silent period. Rodriguez describes his own case history of learning L2 English, noting that he said nothing in class in the American school he attended for the first six months.

Of course, not all learners go through a silent period, as Saville-Troike's study shows. Many learners—particularly classroom learners—are obliged to speak from the beginning. But even when production is not required, some learners opt for it. Paul, a 5-year-old Taiwanese boy studied by Huang and Hatch (1978), appears to have begun talking in English almost immediately, although most of his early utterances involved imitation. Studies of GOOD LANGUAGE LEARNERS report that many adult learners (82 per cent in a study carried out by Naiman *et al.* 1978) claim they begin to speak right from the start. Gibbons (1985) reviewed the evidence in favour of a silent period in both children and adults and found it inconclusive. His own survey of 47 children learning English as an L2 in Sydney primary schools revealed considerable individual variation, with a mean length of just two weeks' silence. It is also interesting to note that in many of the studies which Krashen cites as providing evidence of a silent period, the learners were not, in fact, completely silent, but often produced some formulaic expressions right from the beginning.[3]

The question arises as to why some learners opt for a silent period while others do not. Saville-Troike (1988) suggested that the reason may lie in differences in the learners' social and cognitive orientation. She distinguished OTHER-DIRECTED and INNER-DIRECTED LEARNERS. The former 'approach language as an interpersonal, social task, with a predominant focus on the message they wish to convey', while the latter 'approach language learning as an intrapersonal task, with a predominant focus on the language code' (p. 568). She suggested that while other-directed learners do not typically go through a silent period, inner-directed learners do.

There is some disagreement regarding the contribution that the silent period makes to language learning. Krashen (1982) argued that it provides an opportunity for the learner to build up competence via listening. According to this view, speaking ability emerges naturally after enough competence has been developed through listening. Itoh and Hatch (1978), however, took a different view, referring to Takahiro's silent period as a 'rejection stage', during which he tried to avoid learning English. Rodriguez (1982) claimed that he only began to learn English when he started to speak it at home with his parents. Gibbons (1985) concluded that the initial silent period is in many cases a period of incomprehension that does little or nothing to promote acquisition and that if the silent period is a prolonged one it may reflect psychological withdrawal.

One possibility is that the silent period provides learners with opportunities to prepare themselves for social use of the L2 by means of PRIVATE SPEECH, which they engage in while they are 'silent'. Saville-Troike, in the study of child L2 learners referred to above, defines silent speech as speech that is produced at a very low volume so as to be inaudible to anyone present and with no apparent expectation of a response. She used a radio-microphone hung round the neck of the children to record it. Five of the children who went through a silent period manifested private speech, using a variety of intrapersonal strategies. These included repeating other speakers' utterances, recalling and practising English words and phrases, creating new linguistic forms, substituting items in utterances, and expanding them and rehearsing utterances for overt social performance. All five learners eventually began to speak, using at first single words, memorized chunks, and repetitions of other children's L2 utterances. A sixth child who manifested a silent period, however, did not engage in private speech and, unlike the others, remained silent throughout the study (approximately 18 weeks), apparently not learning any English. Saville-Troike's study suggests that while some child learners may use silence as a strategy for avoiding learning, many make active use of it to prepare for the time when they begin speaking the L2. However, as Saville-Troike acknowledged, her study does not show whether the learning strategies some learners employ during their silent period are related to long-range L2 development.

Formulaic sequences

Formulaic sequences consist of 'expressions which are learnt as unanalysable wholes and employed on particular occasions' (Lyons 1968: 177). Formulaic speech differs from creative speech, which is speech that has been constructed by stringing together individual lexical items, often by drawing on underlying abstract patterns or rules. Everyday native-speaker speech is composed of a mixture of formulaic sequences and creative elements.

Hakuta (1976) and Krashen and Scarcella (1978) distinguished two types of formulaic sequences—ROUTINES and PATTERNS—to refer respectively to whole utterances learnt as memorized chunks (for example, 'I don't know') and to utterances that are only partially unanalysed and have one or more open slots (for example, 'Can I have a ___?'). In Ellis 1984b, I too suggested that formulaic speech can consist of entire scripts, such as greeting sequences, which the learner can memorize because they are fixed and predictable. Wray (2000: 465) uses the term 'formulaic sequence' as a cover term, defining it as follows:

> A sequence, continuous or discontinuous, of words or other meaning elements, which is, or appears to be, prefabricated; that is stored and retrieved whole from memory at the time of use, rather than being subject to generation or analysis by the language grammar.

The identification of formulaic sequences is problematic, however, not least because any attested learner utterance may constitute a ready-made unit or may have been generated by the learner's grammar or may be partially formulaic and partially rule-based. For example, when a learner produces 'I don't know' the utterance may be formulaic or may be the product of the application of an internalized rule for English negation.

Researchers have suggested a number of criteria for determining whether an utterance is formulaic. The following are the criteria proposed by Myles, Hooper, and Mitchell (1998):

1 at least two morphemes in length
2 phonologically coherent (i.e. fluently articulated, non-hesitant)
3 unrelated to productive patterns in the learner's speech
4 greater complexity in comparison with the learner's other output
5 used repeatedly in the same form
6 may be inappropriate (syntactically, semantically, or pragmatically or otherwise idiosyncratic)
7 situationally dependent
8 community-wide in use.

However, these criteria are not always easy to apply, even with the advent of concordancing software for analysing learner corpora. Read and Nation

(2004) pointed out that no single criterion is adequate in itself and endorsed Wray's (2002) emphasis on the need to consider multiple criteria. However, the key criteria applied in the studies of early learner language referred to below appear to be (3) and (4).

Formulaic speech can also be observed in the speech of native speakers. Nattinger and DeCarrico (1992: 1) suggested that what they call 'lexical phrases' (defined as 'multi-word lexical phenomena that exist somewhere between the traditional poles of lexicon and syntax') are commonly used by native speakers, reflecting the ritualization of language behaviour. Pawley and Syder (1983) argued that achieving native-like control involves not only learning a rule system that will generate an infinite number of sentences, but also 'memorized sequences' and 'lexicalized sentence stems'. They stated that 'the number of memorized complete clauses and sentences known to the mature English speaker is probably many thousands' (1983: 205). Erman and Warren (2000) estimated that formulaic sequences made up 58.6 per cent of the spoken English discourse they analysed. Examples given by Pawley and Syder included 'Can I come in?', 'What's for dinner?', and 'Speak for yourself', as well as sequences longer than simple, single clauses. They also pointed out that native speakers internalize sentence stems in which the structure is fully specified together with a nucleus of lexical and grammatical morphemes. An example is:

NP be-*tense* sorry to keep-*tense* you waiting

which can be realized in a number of forms:

I'm sorry to keep you waiting.
I'm so sorry to have kept you waiting.
Mr X was sorry to keep you waiting the other day.

Pawley and Syder characterized the task facing the language learner as to precisely what permutations of a sentence stem are possible—a view of learning which bears a strong resemblance to that which underlies some current models of language use and acquisition, such as emergentist models of the kind promulgated by N. Ellis (1996, 1998, 2005), which are considered fully in Chapter 9. Formulaic expressions frequently embody the societal knowledge which a given speech community shares and, according to Coulmas, 'are essential in the handling of day-to-day situations' (1981: 4). They enable the speaker to say the right thing at the right time in the right place. They also perform a psycholinguistic function in speech production. Dechert (1983) suggested that fixed expressions serve as 'islands of reliability' that help speakers to construct and execute production plans.

Formulaic sequences have been observed to be very common in L2 acquisition, particularly in the early stages. They figure frequently in the speech of all learners, irrespective of their age. Itoh and Hatch noted two very common patterns in the speech of Takahiro, once he began talking—'I get ...' and 'I wanna ...'. Ervin-Tripp (1974) noted that one of the first utterances produced by young English-speaking learners of L2 French was 'Peut-je jouer avec Corinne?' and noted that 'the size of the unit stored is impressive'. Hakuta (1976) discussed three patterns in the speech of his subject, Uguisu—those using copula, 'do you' in questions, and 'how to' in embedded questions. Rescorla and Okuda (1987) reported similar patterns in their subject, Atsuko, a 6-year-old Japanese child. Hanania and Gradman (1977) observed that at the start of their study, Fatmah relied almost entirely on 'memorized items'. They noted that 'the use of these expressions does not imply that she recognized the individual words within them, or that she was able to use the words in new combinations' (p. 78). Initially, Fatmah seemed to resist segmentation of expressions such as 'Thank you, I can't ...' and 'Do you like ... ?' There are, in fact, few case studies based on naturally occurring learner language that do not make some mention of the prevalence of formulaic sequences. Formulaic sequences are not restricted to naturalistic learners either. They have been observed in adolescent classroom learners, even when the instruction is grammar-oriented. Indeed, studies by Weinert (1987), Myles, Hooper, and Mitchell (1998), and Myles, Mitchell, and Hooper (1999) suggest that classroom learners extract and internalize ready-made chunks out of the grammar practice activities they engage in. However, most of the studies to date have examined child or adolescent L2 learners. As Wray (2000) pointed out, with the exception of Hanania and Gradman, there have been few studies of formulaic speech in adult L2 learners.

The particular formulaic sequences learnt by individual learners are likely to vary, but some seem to figure in just about every learner (for example, 'I don't know' and 'What's this?'). Each formula is closely tied to the performance of a particular language function which is communicatively important to the learner. Hakuta (1976) noted that Uguisu's formulas enabled her to express functions which would have been beyond her if she had relied on her rule-governed knowledge. In Ellis (1984b), I observed that the three classroom learners I studied learnt formulas to enable them to meet their basic communicative needs in an ESL classroom, where English functioned as the medium of instruction. Krashen (1982) claimed that formulaic speech occurs when learners are forced to speak before they are ready and that, left to their own devices, they will remain silent. But Krashen's view seems to ignore the fact that it is perfectly natural for any language user to seek to simplify the burden of processing language—by using formulaic sequences to establish 'islands of reliability', for example. Learners, like native speakers, learn formulaic sequences because it reduces the learning burden while maximizing communicative ability.

It is not surprising, therefore, to find that learners sometimes use the formulaic sequences they have acquired in unique ways. For example, they do not always use them to perform the same functions as native speakers. Huebner (1980) provides a detailed account of how an adult Vietnamese learner of L2 English used two formulas 'waduyu' (= 'what d'you') and 'isa' (= 'is a'). 'Waduyu' served initially as a general question marker. It was used ubiquitously where native speakers would employ a variety of WH–question words ('what', 'how', 'why', and 'when'). Over time the learner gradually and systematically replaced 'waduyu' with these target forms. 'Isa' functions initially as a topic marker, but it was only used when the topic was not an agent or object and was not identical to the topic of the immediately preceding sentence. The general point that Huebner makes is that the acquisition of the functions performed by formulaic sequences may be an evolutionary process.

A key question is that posed by Hakuta (1976): 'To what extent do these routines and patterns facilitate or hinder the acquisition of TL grammar?' A number of researchers have suggested that formulaic speech serves as the basis for subsequent creative speech when the learner comes to realize that utterances initially understood and used as wholes consist of discrete constituents which can be combined with other constituents in a variety of rule-bound ways. Clark (1974) illustrated how in L1 acquisition new structures can result from the juxtaposition of two routines or from the embedding of one within another. Wong Fillmore (1976), in a study of five Spanish-speaking learners of English, suggested that in L2 acquisition, formulaic sequences are slowly analysed, releasing constituent elements for use in 'slots' other than those they initially occupied. For example, to begin with, Nora (the fastest of Wong Fillmore's learners) used two formulas:

I wanna play wi' dese.
I don' wanna do dese.

and then discovered that the constituents following 'wanna' were interchangeable:

I don' wanna play dese.
I wanna do dese.

Wong Fillmore commented that this 'formula-based analytical process ... was repeated in case after case' (1976: 645). In Ellis 1984b, I too found evidence to support the view that formulaic sequences are worked on systematically by learners. I demonstrated how the 'I don't know' formula was built on by combining it with other formulas:

That one I don't know.
I don't know what's this.

It was also broken down, so that 'don't' came to be used in similar but different expressions:

I don't understand.
I don't like.

'Know' was eventually used without 'don't':

I know this.

and with subjects other than 'I':

You don't know where it is.

Further evidence of the role played by formulaic sequences in L2 acquisition comes from Myles (2004). As in my 1984 study, Myles drew on longitudinal data from classroom learners but, in this case, of L2 French. She characterized the first stage of development as that of associating semantic content with words/formulaic sequences. At this stage syntactic categories are underspecified or absent. It is only in the second phase, that true grammatical categories emerge. Myles suggested that this occurs when learners are able to unpack the verbs from their earlier acquired sequences. The pattern of development that Myles outlines, then, is:

Formulaic sequences → verb extraction → morphosyntactic elaboration.

Further, Myles suggested that learners who failed to acquire a set of formulaic sequences showed very little development over a year whereas those that did manifested clear development.

A rather different view is taken by Krashen and Scarcella (1978). They argued that formulaic speech and rule-created speech are unrelated. According to this view, learners do not unpackage the linguistic information contained in formulaic sequences, but internalize L2 rules independently through attending to input. Their conclusion is that 'the use of routines and patterns is certainly part of language, but it is probably not a very large part'. This view is supported by Bohn (1986), who analysed data that Wode (1981) collected from four German children learning English in the United States. This study found that these child learners relied on formulaic speech very little in most situations, although Bohn admits that they may not have been subject to the same communicative pressures as other L2 learners. Formulaic-like speech was evident when the children were involved in playing games, leading Bohn to suggest that the prevalence of formulas in Wong Fillmore's subjects' speech was an artifact of the fact that she collected most of her spontaneous data during games. Bohn concluded that formulaic sequences serve only 'short-term production tactics' and play no role in acquisition. A similar view was taken by Granger (1998a), on the basis of computer-analysed corpora of adult L2 learner language. She commented:

> There does not seem to be a direct line from prefabs to creative language ... It would thus be a foolhardy gamble to believe that it is enough to expose learners to prefabs and the grammar will take care of itself. (pp. 157–8)

It is not easy to choose between these two interpretations of the role played by formulaic sequences. McLaughlin (1985), in a lengthy discussion of formulaic sequences, came down on the side of Wong Fillmore, at least where children are concerned. Wray (2000) commented that 'there is very little evidence that adult learners naturally extrapolate grammatical or lexical information from larger strings' (p. 472), as illustrated in Schmidt's (1983) longitudinal study of Wes, who demonstrated considerable gains in fluency by acquiring and using formulaic sequences but no concurrent gain in accuracy. In considering this controversy, we should remember that it is not easy to make a clear distinction between formulaic and creative speech. In many instances, learners seem to make use of patterns which are varied to a greater or lesser extent through lexical substitutions. Such speech has both formulaic and creative elements, suggesting that 'we should move beyond misleading dichotomies such as prefabricated formulas versus creative constructions' (Rescorla and Okuda 1987: 293). Even if Krashen and Scarcella are right and formulaic frames do not evolve into productive rules, they almost certainly underestimated the importance of formulaic sequences for L2 learners. As Pawley and Syder have shown, the task facing the learner is not just that of acquiring a rule system but also of mastering a set of lexicalized sentence stems that will enable them to process language efficiently. The development of target-like L2 ability, then, requires the memorization of a large set of formulaic chunks and patterns.

Interest in formulaic sequences has increased considerably over the years, as evidenced by two full-length books (Schmitt 2004; Wray 2002). In part, this has been made possible by the availability of concordancing packages for analysing large corpora of learner language (as in Granger 1998b and 1999). Much of the recent research, however, has been cross-sectional, often experimental, and does not directly address the focus of this section—the use of formulaic sequences in early L2 acquisition. For this reason, it will be considered in later chapters. (See in particular Chapters 6 and 9.)

Structural and semantic simplification

In comparison with formulaic speech, the learner's early creative utterances are typically truncated, consisting of just one or two words, with both grammatical functors and content words missing. Hanania and Gradman (1977) give the following examples produced by their adult subject, Fatmah:

> library (= He is in the library.)
> clean floor (= Give me something for cleaning floors.)

Pienemann (1980) gives similar examples from the speech of children learning L2 German:

> ein junge ball weg (= Ein Junge wirft den Ball weg.)
> ein mädchen bier (= Ein Mädchen kauft Bier.)

In Ellis 1984a, I found further evidence of simplified speech in the speech of three children learning English in a classroom setting:

> me no blue (= I don't have a blue crayon.)
> eating at school (= She eats meat at school.)

Such speech, therefore, is very common in the unplanned speech of both child and adult learners.

These utterances, which bear a strong resemblance to those found in pidgin languages, indicate that both structural and semantic simplification are taking place. Structural simplification is evident in the omission of grammatical functors such as auxiliary verbs, articles and bound morphemes like plural –s and past tense –ed. Semantic simplification involves the omission of content words—nouns, verbs, adjectives and adverbs—which would normally occur in native-speaker speech. (See Ellis 1982.) Both structural and semantic simplification may occur either because learners have not yet acquired the necessary linguistic forms or because they are unable to access them in the production of specific utterances. In other words, they may reflect processes of language acquisition or of language production.[4]

Structural simplification can be described by means of the traditional categories of a descriptive grammar. Semantic simplification is best accounted for in terms of the descriptive categories provided by a case grammar (Fillmore 1968; Greenfield and Dent 1980). For example, if a learner wishes to encode the proposition:

He is hitting me.

which involves these semantic categories:

(agent) (action process) (patient)

the message can be conveyed by producing any one of these abridged versions:

Hitting (= action process)
He hitting (= agent + action process)
Hitting me (= action process + patient)
He me (= agent + patient).

Which version the learner chooses will reflect: (1) the linguistic resources available or readily accessible, and (2) which constituents will be maximally informative in context.

There is some evidence to suggest that learners, particularly children, tend to begin speaking first in single-word utterances and then in increasingly longer utterances, many of which are novel. (See Saville-Troike 1988.) However, the nature of this progression is not as well defined as in L1 acquisition, perhaps because L2 learners have more developed processing capacities. Often, utterances that manifest structural and semantic simplification are used along with others that display little or even none.

The prevalence of structural and semantic simplification in the speech of beginner learners is acknowledged in the work of Klein and Perdue (1997) and Perdue (2000). They characterized L2 acquisition in terms of a series of evolving varieties, each with its own distinguishing characteristics. The starting point is the 'pre-basic variety', which is characterized by nominal utterance organization. At this stage, utterances are scaffolded (i.e. constructed over more than one turn) and context-dependent. In time, this gives way to the

BASIC VARIETY, characterized by non-finite verbal organization. Utterances are now constructed in accordance with the general pragmatic principle that the 'controller' is mentioned first and the 'focus' last. The semantic and structural simplification illustrated in the sentences above suggest that they are characteristics of both these varieties. It is not until the 'post-basic variety', where finite verbal organization finally appears, that simplification of utterance structure begins to disappear. However, when learners are under pressure to communicate, it can always resurface.

The acquisition of grammatical morphemes: order and sequence

As we have already noted, it is possible to consider acquisition in terms of both the order in which different features are acquired and also the sequence of stages evident in the acquisition of a single feature. Much of the early research focused on the order of acquisition. Subsequent research has increasingly paid attention to sequence as well as order.

The morpheme studies

In the 1970s a number of studies, commonly referred to as the MORPHEME STUDIES, were carried out to investigate the order of acquisition of grammatical functors such as articles and inflectional features such as plural –s. These studies were motivated by similar studies in L1 acquisition. (See the previous section on L1 acquisition.) In particular, they sought to establish whether, as in L1 acquisition, there was an invariant order of acquisition. The studies were both cross-sectional and longitudinal, although the former predominated.

The studies employed obligatory occasion analysis in order to establish the accuracy with which learners of L2 English performed a range of morphemes. In the case of cross-sectional studies, an accuracy order was calculated and this was equated with acquisition order by some researchers, on the grounds that the more accurately a morpheme was used, the earlier it must have been acquired.

In two early studies, Dulay and Burt (1973, 1974c) investigated Spanish and Chinese children, eliciting 'natural' spoken data by means of the BILINGUAL SYNTAX MEASURE (BSM). They found that the 'acquisition order' for a group of English morphemes remained the same irrespective of the learners' L1 or of the methods they used to score the accuracy of the morphemes. Bailey, Madden, and Krashen (1974) replicated these studies with adult subjects, again using the BSM. They found an 'acquisition order' that correlated significantly with those obtained by Dulay and Burt. Larsen-Freeman (1976b) extended these studies in two ways. First, she used learners with a wider range of L1s (Arabic, Spanish, Japanese, and Farsi) and secondly she used five tasks to collect data: the BSM, a picture-cued sentence repetition test, a listening comprehension task, a multiple-choice reading cloze test, and a writing test involving filling in blanks. She found that the learners' L1s made little difference to the accuracy orders she obtained. However, there were some differences in the orders for the different tasks. The most notable was that between the speaking/imitation tasks and the reading/writing tasks. Some morphemes (for example, plural -s and third person -s) rose in the rank order in the reading and writing tasks. One possibility, then, is that different orders exist for oral and written learner language. This finding is not problematic where production is concerned, as speaking and writing are influenced by different sociological and psycholinguistic conditions. It becomes problematic if the goal is to determine a single, invariant order of acquisition that is distinct from actual use. However, Krashen, Butler, Birnbaum, and Robertson (1978) found that the accuracy orders obtained from written data did correlate significantly with those reported by Dulay and Burt for oral data. In this study, two kinds of writing task were used—one requiring 'fast' writing and the other 'careful' writing—but neither encouraged attention to discrete items as was the case with Larsen-Freeman's writing task. The distinction between 'free' and 'careful' writing did not affect the morpheme orders. These studies are summarized in Table 3.2. They constitute only a small selection of the total morpheme studies that were undertaken. Goldschneider and DeKeyser (2001) identified 25 morpheme studies carried out between 1973 and 1996.

One of the problems of rank orders is that they disguise the difference in accuracy between various morphemes. Thus a morpheme that is just 1 per cent lower than another morpheme is given a different ranking in just the same way as a morpheme that is 30 per cent lower. To overcome this problem, Dulay and Burt (1975) and later Krashen (1977) proposed a grouping of morphemes. They argued that each group constituted a clear developmental stage in that the morphemes within it were 'acquired' at more or less the same time. Figure 3.1 presents Krashen's 'natural order' of morpheme acquisition.

Study	**Subjects**	**Data collection**	**Results**	**Conclusions**
Dulay and Burt 1973	3 separate groups of 6–8-year-old Spanish-speaking children; total 151	Oral data from Bilingual Syntax Measure.	1 85 per cent of errors were developmental.	1 There may be a universal or natural order in which L2 children acquire certain morphemes.
			2 The 'acquisition orders' for the three groups were strikingly similar, but different from L1 orders; 8 morphemes investigated.	2 Exposing a child to a natural communication situation is sufficient for L2 acquisition to take place.

Dulay and Burt 1974b	60 Spanish-speaking children	Oral data from Bilingual Syntax Measure.	1 The 'acquisition orders' for both groups of children were basically the same; 11 morphemes investigated.	1 The learner's L1 does not affect the order of development in child L2 acquisition.
	55 Chinese-speaking children; both groups 6–8 years		2 The orders obtained by different scoring methods were the same.	2 'Universal cognitive mechanisms' are the basis for the child's organization of the target language.
Bailey, Madden, and Krashen 1974	73 adults aged 17–55 years; classified as Spanish- and non-Spanish-speaking; members of 8 ESL classes	Oral data from Bilingual Syntax Measure.	1 The 'acquisition orders' for both Spanish and non-Spanish groups were very similar.	1 Adults use common strategies independent of L1 or L2 acquisition.
			2 The adult orders of this study were very similar to those reported for all but one of Dulay and Burt's (1973) groups.	2 Adults process linguistic data in similar ways to children.
			3 The adult orders were different from L1 order.	3 The most effective instruction is that which follows observed order of difficulty.
Larsen-Freeman 1976b	24 adults (L1s = Arabic, Japanese, Persian, Spanish); learning English at University of Michigan	Battery of 5 different tests of reading, writing, listening, speaking, and imitating.	1 L1 did not have a significant effect on way adults learn English morphemes.	1 There is a standard morpheme order for production tasks.
			2 Differences in morpheme orders occurred on different tasks but orders on production	2 The frequency counts for morphemes on speaking task reflect the actual occurrence

			tasks (speech and imitation) agreed with Dulay and Burt's order.	in real communication. Frequency in native-speaker speech is main determinant of accuracy orders.
			3 Accuracy orders correlate with frequency orders for production of morphemes.	
Krashen, Butler, Birnbaum, and Robertson 1978	70 adult students from 4 language backgrounds; at University of Southern California	Free compositions, with (1) time limit; (2) no time limit and chance for self-correction.	1 The 'acquisition' order for the 'fast' writing was the same as that for the 'careful'.	1 The students were focused on communication in both tasks, hence a 'natural order' was obtained.
			2 The orders obtained in both written tasks were very similar to those reported for adults in the Bailey, Madden, and Krashen study.	2 The processes involved in L2 acquisition underlay both the oral and the written mode.

Table 3.2 A summary of key morpheme studies (from Ellis 1985a)

The picture that emerges from these studies is of a standard 'acquisition order' that is not rigidly invariant but is remarkably similar irrespective of the learners' language backgrounds, of their age, and of whether the medium is speech or writing. A different order occurs only when the learners are able to focus on the form rather than the meaning of their utterances. As Krashen (1977: 148) put it, whenever the data reflect a focus on meaning there is 'an amazing amount of uniformity across all studies'.

A number of later cross-sectional morpheme studies have been carried out, including some of languages other than English (for example, Van Naerssen's (1980) study of L2 Spanish). One of the best is Pica's (1983) study of the morpheme orders of three separate groups of L2 learners—a 'naturalistic' group, an instructed group, and a mixed group. Pica—who was careful to claim only an 'accuracy order'—found the same 'natural order' even when she took account of learners' over-use of morphemes in her scoring procedure (i.e. used target-like use analysis rather than obligatory occasion analysis). This is important because it helps counter one of the main criticisms levelled at the morpheme studies, namely that they have failed to consider inappropriate morpheme use in non-obligatory contexts.

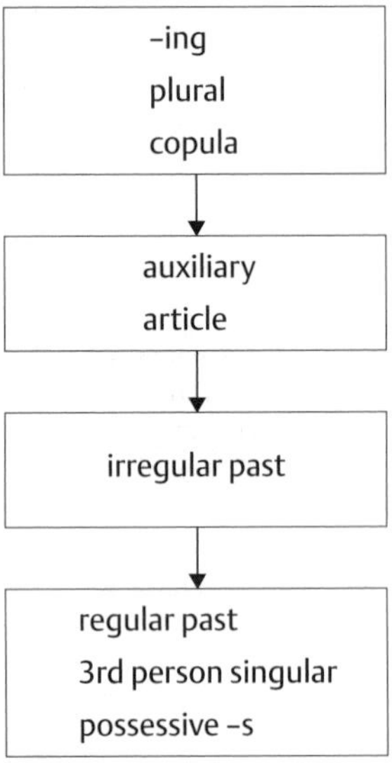

Figure 3.1 Proposed 'natural order' for L2 acquisition (Krashen 1977)

There have been fewer longitudinal morpheme studies. Rosansky (1976) examined the order of acquisition of the same morphemes investigated by Dulay and Burt in the speech of Jorge, a Spanish learner of English, over a period of ten months. She concluded that the order of acquisition of this individual learner did not conform to the 'natural order' reported for groups of learners. Also, when she carried out cross-sectional analyses with data collected at different points in time she found varying orders. Hakuta (1974) collected spoken data from a 5-year-old Japanese girl, Uguisu, over several months. The acquisition order he obtained did not match that of Dulay and Burt. Articles, for instance, which have a high ranking in the cross-sectional accuracy orders, had a low ranking in the acquisition order for Uguisu. Schmidt's (1983) study of Wes (see Chapter 1), also found some discrepancies with the cross-sectional order (plural, article, and past regular having lower ranks). One possible explanation for the difference in results between the cross-sectional and longitudinal studies is that the results of the latter were misleading because accuracy levels were sometimes calculated using fewer than ten obligatory occasions, a point that Krashen (1977) emphasized. Nevertheless, the differences do cast some doubt on the validity of equating cross-sectional accuracy with acquisition orders.

There have been few recent morpheme studies. However, Shin and Milroy (1999) reported an interesting study of young Korean-American children's acquisition of English grammatical morphemes, focusing on whether the L1 and L2 acquisition order were the same or different and also whether the learner's L1 background affects the order. They examined 10 grammatical morphemes, including all of those that figure in the earlier studies. The morphemes performed least accurately by the L2 learners were plural –s and third person –s. The rank orders for L1 and L2 acquisition were clearly different, leading Shin and Milroy to conclude that 'L1 and L2 learners of English do not acquire English grammatical features in the same sequence' (p. 164). They also reported clear differences in the orders for Chinese and Spanish learners of English and the Korean learners in their study but a similar order with that reported for Japanese learners. They concluded that there are 'language specific influences on second language acquisition'. Thus the study contradicts the finding of the earlier studies, namely that there is a more or less universal order of acquisition for English morphemes.

The morpheme studies have been subject to some stringent criticisms in addition to the doubts about using accuracy order as a basis for discussing acquisition. (See Hatch 1978d, 1983a; Long and Sato 1984.) One criticism is that the method of scoring morphemes does not take account of misuse in inappropriate contexts. But, as we have seen, Pica's (1983) study suggests that even when overuse is taken into account it does not affect the order. Another criticism is that the use of rank order statistics hides meaningful differences, but Krashen's grouping of features into a 'natural order' (see Figure 3.1) goes some way to overcoming that objection. Other objections are that the research has been restricted to a small set of morphemes, that the morphemes studied constitute a rag-bag of disparate features (the acquisition of articles and third person –s, for instance, pose the learner very different tasks, as one involves semantic considerations and the other is a purely formal feature), and that the research has lacked theoretical motivation. However, Larsen-Freeman and Long (1991) concluded their own survey of these studies with the claim that they provide strong evidence of a developmental order:

> Contrary to what some critics have alleged, there are in our view too many studies conducted with sufficient methodological rigor and showing sufficiently consistent general findings for the commonalities to be ignored. (1991: 92)

Although with one or two exceptions the morpheme studies ceased in the early 1980s, interest in the 'natural order' did not. Researchers switched attention from description to explanation by focusing on the factors that accounted for the accuracy order. Two key studies in this respect were Zobl and Liceras (1994) and Goldschneider and DeKeyser (2001), which will be considered later. The descriptive research that followed the morpheme studies seized on the most serious criticism—their conceptualization of acquisition in terms of what Rutherford (1988) calls 'accumulated entities', i.e. the mastery of grammatical items one at a time. In the next section we examine more recent research that focused on a single grammatical sub-system and attended to how learners acquire individual morphemes by examining meaning as well as form.

The acquisition of tense and aspect

Whereas the morpheme studies belong to an early period in SLA (the 1970s and 1980s), tense and aspect, both of which involve the acquisition of morphological features, have been studied intensively in SLA in more recent years. This research has been reviewed comprehensively in Bardovi-Harlig (1999a and 2000) and Zielonka (2005). It is of particular interest because it has investigated both how learners acquire the meanings ultimately realized by tense and aspectual systems and the emergence of verbal morphology. As Bardovi-Harlig noted 'the meaning-oriented approach and the form-oriented approach together afford a better opportunity for understanding the acquisition of tense-aspect than either approach alone' (p. 93). Also, parallel studies of a number of different languages have been conducted, thus allowing for cross-linguistic generalizations about the order of acquisition.

Meaning-based analyses have focused on how learners express temporality at different stages of acquisition. The cross-linguistic study of adult L2 acquisition conducted under the auspices of the European Science Foundation (Klein and Perdue 1992, 1997; Perdue 1993) investigated the acquisition of Dutch, English, French, German, and Swedish by adult migrants. In this longitudinal study covering 2½ years, samples of learner language were collected by means of conversational interviews and oral film retell tasks. The corpus for the analysis of temporality was drawn from the narrative data. Dietrich *et al.* (1995) reported on 23 learners of Dutch, French, German, Swedish, and English. They distinguished three broad stages in learners' expression of past time:

1 Initially, the learners did not possess any L2 linguistic means for expressing past time, relying instead on pragmatic means. A number of different ways were identified. The learners relied on what they called scaffolded discourse (for example, they produced utterances that contained no explicit marker of past time but could be interpreted as such in the context of a previously produced utterance). They also relied on implicit reference by drawing on context to make their meaning clear. A third strategy made use of contrasting events and a fourth chronological order. Frequently, they employed more than one of these pragmatic means at a time. What all these strategies have in common is that there is no explicit reference to pastness, thus requiring the learner's interlocutor to infer it from the pragmatic clues provided.
2 In the lexical stage, reference to past time is now made explicit by means of various lexical expressions (for example, locative adverbials such as 'in the morning' and 'yesterday' and connectives such as 'and' and 'then'). At this

stage verbs are not marked morphologically for pastness and are invariant. Any verbs used are either in the base form (for example, 'go' in English) or some idiosyncratic form (for example, 'going').

3 It is in the third stage that morphological markers of pastness appear. To begin with, they are used non-systematically; that is, learners sometimes supply a morphological feature but on other occasions continue to rely on pragmatic and lexical means to convey pastness. (See Schumann 1987.) Bardovi-Harlig (2000) commented that instructed learners are more likely to make appropriate use of morphological markers than naturalistic learners. Past-tense morphology only stabilizes over time and is accompanied by a decrease in the use of adverbials.

This sequence of development also seems to hold for other temporal meanings. For example, when learners begin to make reference to past events that occurred before other past events (expressed by means of the past perfect in English) they rely initially on pragmatic and lexical means before using morphological devices.

Form-oriented studies of the acquisition of verbal morphology differed from the earlier morpheme studies in a number of respects. First, they examined a self-enclosed grammatical system, thus avoiding the criticism of the morpheme studies that very disparate morphological features were being compared. Second, they were longitudinal rather than cross-sectional in design, thus allowing for acquisition as opposed to accuracy of use to be examined. Third, as a result, they were able to address the sequence as well as order of acquisition. Finally, they defined acquisition in terms of emergence (i.e. when specific forms established themselves in the learner's verb-morphology repertoire) rather than approximation to target-language accuracy. This is important for, as Bardovi-Harlig (2000) noted 'learners revise their form-meaning associations for any given tense-aspect morpheme as new morphemes are added to the system' (p. 95).

Studies that have investigated the emergence of verbal morphology provide evidence of a consistent order of acquisition. Interestingly, despite the differences between the target-language systems of Romance languages (such as French and Italian) and Germanic languages (such as English), there are clear parallels in the acquisitional order of these L2s. All learners initially employ some basal form of the L2 and then systematically accrue the various tense-aspect morphological forms. Klein (1995) reported the acquisition of English tense-aspect morphology in a longitudinal study of one Italian learner (Lavinia). He identified the following order of emergence:

1 Third person –s and present tense copula
2 Irregular past tense forms and Verb–ing
3 Present perfect forms
4 Regular past tense forms
5 Future with 'shall' or 'will'
6 Past perfect forms.

Bardovi-Harlig (2000) reported a similar order in her longitudinal study of 16 learners of L2 English from 4 different language backgrounds:

Past > past progressive > present perfect > past perfect

She also noted that there was no obvious influence of the learners' L1. For L2 French, Schlyter (1990) posited the following order, based on her own longitudinal study of two untutored learners and a cross-sectional study of seven adult learners:

1 Passé composé
2 '*veux*'/'*va*' + infinitive to refer to the future
3 Imparfait
4 Past perfect

Harley and Swain (1978) in a study of immersion learners of French in Canada also reported that passé composé emerged before imparfait, which remained underused even after many years of exposure. Perfect forms emerge late and occur only infrequently in naturalistic learners. Noyau *et al.* (1995), for example, reported that in their Swedish data the perfect was used with only a limited number of high frequency verbs and that there were only two instances of the use of the past perfect.

In addition to documenting the order of emergence of different tense-aspect morphemes, researchers have also described the acquisitional stages involved in the development of individual morphemes. Bardovi-Harlig (1992, 2000) reports on the sequence of acquisition of past progressive, present perfect and past perfect. For example, the present perfect only appeared after learners had achieved stability in the use of the past tense. Once it had emerged, learners manifested OVERGENERALIZATION into contexts requiring past tense forms, only gradually sorting out the appropriate uses of the two forms. Later when learners began to attempt to express anteriority in pastness (a function calling for past perfect in the target language) they also overgeneralized the present perfect. The detailed study of how learners acquire tense-aspect morphemes demonstrates the gradual nature of acquisition, reflecting the learners' need to constantly restructure form–meaning mappings as new morphemes are added to their repertoire.

The study of tense-aspect in the ESF project and in Bardovi-Harlig's research has been descriptive in nature and focused on naturalistic or mixed learners. Lantolf and Thorne (2006) report a longitudinal study of tense-aspect acquisition by of a group of university-level instructed learners of L2 Spanish (Negueruela 2003). Focusing on these learners' acquisition of the preterite and imperfect tenses, Negueruela found that although the learners had largely acquired the linguistic forms of these tenses they were not always able to use them appropriately in their communicative speech or writing. In particular, they experienced difficulty with the use of the imperfect tense. However, after explicit instruction on the form–function mappings of the two tenses and as a result of encouraging the learners to think consciously about their choice of forms and to verbalize the rules, the learners demonstrated increased control over both forms, including more appropriate use of the imperfect. This study then suggests that instructed learners follow a similar developmental route of tense-aspect to that of naturalistic learners and also that improved conceptual understanding of explicit rules appears to assist development. The role of instruction in L2 acquisition is considered further in Chapter 16 while the role of explicit knowledge in acquisition is examined in Chapter 9.

To summarize, Zielonka (2005) provided the following account of the initial stages of tense-aspect acquisition:

> At the initial stage of L2 acquisition, naturalistic learners produce simple utterances using some content words, mainly nouns, and omitting grammatical morphemes. When verbs begin to emerge, they appear mainly in uninflected forms. Past temporal reference is initially made through pragmatic devices such as situational context, or chronological order of events ... At a later stage, temporal reference is established by means of temporal adverbs of different types, among others, calendrical expressions.
> (p. 76)

Bardovi-Harlig (2000) identified four general principles. First, acquisition is slow and gradual. Second, form often precedes function, as Negueruela found. That is, when a given morpheme first appears it is overgeneralized and thus lacks a clear contrast with existing forms. Base forms tend to be used alongside other forms even at later stages of acquisition. The third principle is that irregular morphology precedes regular morphology, as illustrated by the prior acquisition of irregular past tense forms in English. This is likely to reflect the fact that irregular forms are acquired as distinct lexical items. The fourth principle is that when learners are acquiring compound verb tenses such as the present/past progressive and the present/past perfect they begin by using a verb with verbal suffix (for example, 'eating') and only subsequently produce verbs with auxiliaries (for example, 'is eating'). It should be noted, however, that it is not always easy to test this principle in the case of the perfect tenses in Germanic languages, as the past participle and past tense forms are not always distinguishable (for example, 'said' in English). Still, studies of languages such as French or Italian (for example, Giacalone Ramat 1997), where there is a clear distinction between past and perfect forms, lend support to the fourth principle. Many learners do not succeed in acquiring the full L2 tense-aspect system.

The acquisition of syntactic structures

We will look at three sets of syntactic structures to see to what extent they provide support for the existence of developmental patterns in second language acquisition. First, we will review a number of early studies which examined the acquisition of negatives in English and German and which provide evidence of a clear sequence of development. Second, we will consider relative clauses, which also provide evidence of an order of acquisition. Third, we will look at the acquisition of word-order rules in L2 German. This provides evidence of both an acquisition order (as different TL rules are acquired one after another) and also of a developmental sequence (as learners also manifest TRANSITIONAL CONSTRUCTIONS which differ from the TL norms). Finally, we will look at an attempt to characterize general grammatical development in an L2.

The acquisition of negatives in English and German

The development of negatives in English outlined below is based on several early studies (Ravem 1968; Milon 1974; Cazden *et al.* 1975; Wode 1976, 1981; Adams 1978; Butterworth and Hatch 1978). These studies cover learners of English with Japanese, Spanish, German, and Norwegian as their L1, and also children, adolescents, and adults. Schumann (1979) provides an excellent overview of a number of studies involving Spanish learners of English.

The acquisition of negation shows clear transitional structures (see Dulay, Burt, and Krashen 1982). That is, it involves a series of forms or structures which learners use *en route* to mastering the TL form. These interim forms are indicative of the developmental stages that learners pass through on the way to TL competence. Initially, negative utterances are characterized by external negation. That is, the negative particle (usually 'no' but sometimes 'not') is attached to a declarative nucleus:

No very good.
No you playing here.

A little later, internal negation develops; that is, the negative particle is moved inside the utterance. This often coincides with the use of 'not' and/or 'don't', which is used variably with 'no' as the negative particle. 'Don't' at this stage is formulaic as it has not been analysed into its separate components 'do' and 'not'.

Mariana not coming today.
I no can swim.
I don't see nothing mop.

A third step involves negative attachment to modal verbs, although this may again occur in unanalysed units initially:

I can't play this one.
I won't go.

In the final stage, the TL rule is acquired. The learner has developed an auxiliary system and uses 'not' regularly as the negative particle (i.e. the use of 'no' with verb is eliminated). Negative utterances are now marked for tense and number, although not always correctly:

He doesn't know anything.
He didn't said it.
She didn't believe me.

This sequence is summarized in Table 3.3.

Stage	Description	Example
1	External negation (i.e. 'no' or 'not' is placed at the beginning of the utterance).	No you are playing here.
2	Internal negation (i.e. the negator—'no', 'not' or 'don't' is placed between the subject and the main verb).	Mariana not coming today.
3	Negative attachment to modal verbs.	I can't play that one.
4	Negative attachment to auxiliary verb as in target language rule.	She didn't believe me. He didn't said it.

Table 3.3 Summary of general stages in the sequence of acquisition in L2 English negation

The way along this route is a gradual one. Some learners can take longer than two years and some never travel the whole distance. The stages are not clearly defined but overlap considerably. Development does not consist of sudden jumps, but of the gradual reordering of early rules in favour of later ones. There are also some differences among learners, reflecting their L1. These are discussed in Chapter 8. Individual learners display different preferences in the choice of negative particle—'no' is the most common, but 'not' and unanalysed 'don't' have also been attested.

German negation differs from English in a number of respects. Like English, German places the negative particle after the finite verb:

Ich kann nicht kochen. (= I can not cook.)

but unlike English, German does not have a dummy auxiliary, so 'nicht' follows the main verb in sentences like:

Ich koche nicht (= I cook not.)

Also, when there is a direct object and a 'free' adverb, 'nicht' follows them as in:

Ich habe den Wagen gestern nicht gefahren.
(= I have the car yesterday not driven.)

Studies of the naturalistic acquisition of sentential negation in L2 German include those by Felix (1978), Lange (1979), Pienemann (1981), and Clahsen (1982). Weinert (1987) and Eubank (1990) provide summaries of the general pattern of development. The first stage involves sentence external negation, using 'nein' usually in sentence-initial position:

nein spielen Katze (= no play cat)

Learners then move on to internal negation, placing the negator in both preverbal or postverbal position. Main verbs tend to be negated preverbally and other verb types postverbally:

ich das nicht mach (= I that not do)
ich kann das nicht (= I can that not)

As learners master internal negation, they eliminate preverbal negation, positioning the negative particle after the verb even with main verbs:

ich fallst nicht runter (= I fall not down)

In the final stage, learners master the position of negator after direct objects and free adverbials (i.e. they are able to separate 'nicht' from the verb). Thus, despite the differences in the 'final states' towards which learners of English and German are targeted, marked similarities in the sequence of acquisition of negatives in the two languages can be seen.

The acquisition of relative clauses in English and Swedish

The acquisition of relative clauses presents learners with two tasks. In the case of English, they must first learn that relative clauses can modify noun phrases that occur both before the verb (i.e. as subject of the main clause) and after the verb (i.e. as object or in a prepositional phrase):

The man who lives next door is getting married.
We met the man who lives next door.

Second, they must learn the various functions that the relative pronoun can serve. English permits a range of functions, as shown in Table 3.4. These two tasks amount to a substantial learning burden. How do learners tackle it?

Function	**Example**
Subject	The man who lives next door ...
Direct object	The man whom I saw ...
Indirect object	The man to whom I gave a present ...
Oblique (object of preposition)	The man about whom we spoke ...
Genitive	The man whose wife had an accident ...
Object of comparative	The man that I am richer than ...

Table 3.4 Relative pronoun functions in English

Studies which have investigated the acquisition of relative clauses in L2 English include those by Cook (1973), Schachter (1974), Ioup (1977), Gass (1979), Schumann (1980), Chiang (1980), Gass and Ard (1980), Hyltenstam (1984), Pavesi (1986), and Hansen-Strain and Strain (1989). See also the collection of articles in *Studies in Second Language Acquisition* 29.2. The learners in these studies again come from a variety of language backgrounds.

With regard to the first task, Schumann found that the five Spanish-speaking learners he investigated began by attaching a relative clause to a noun phrase that follows the verb. Often learners include a pronominal copy:[5]

I know the man who he coming.

in which case the relative pronoun may be functioning in a similar way to the co-coordinator 'and', joining two main clauses. Only when learners omit the pronominal copy can they be said to have acquired the use of relative clauses:

Joshua's a boy who is silly.

Relative clauses modifying the subject of the main clause appear later:

The boys who doesn't have anybody to live they take care of the dogs.

With regard to the second task, learners may begin by omitting the relative pronoun (see Schumann 1980):

I got a friend speaks Spanish.

Next, they may use an ordinary personal pronoun:

I got a friend he speaks Spanish.

and finally the relative pronoun proper is used:

I got a friend who speaks Spanish.

The first function to be mastered is that of subject. The order of acquisition then proceeds as shown in Table 3.4. Two studies, one of L2 Swedish (Hyltenstam 1984) and the other of L2 English (Pavesi 1986), both of which used implicational scaling, could find no clear evidence for differentiating the order of acquisition of indirect object/oblique and genitive/object of comparison, however.

The retention of pronominal copies is also linked to the acquisition of the functions of the relative pronouns. Hyltenstam's study indicated that the extent to which learners retain copies is influenced by their L1. Thus, Persian learners, whose L1 permits copies, are much more likely to retain them than Finnish learners, whose L1 does not. However, all learners use at least some copies and, interestingly, are more likely to use them with the relative pronoun functions that are difficult to acquire. Hyltenstam and Pavesi provided evidence to suggest that copies disappear from learners' language in the same order as the relative pronoun functions are acquired.

The study of the acquisition of relative clauses is an important area of work in SLA research because it has been used to test predictions based on MARKEDNESS. We will return to it later in the book. (See Chapter 12.)

A general pattern of L2 grammatical development

We will conclude this section on the order and sequence in L2 acquisition by examining research that has found evidence of a general pattern of L2 grammatical development. This research originated in the Zweitspracherwerb Italienischer und Spanischer Arbeiter (ZISA) project, which focused on the naturalistic acquisition of German by learners with a Romance language background. This was reported in a series of articles by Meisel, Clahsen, and Pienemann (for example, Meisel, Clahsen, and Pienemann 1981; Clahsen 1980; Clahsen 1984; Clahsen, Meisel, and Pienemann 1983; Pienemann 1980). Subsequent work has also examined Turkish learners (for example, Clahsen and Muysken 1986). Jordens (1988) provides a helpful survey of the relevant research. It continued in the research into the acquisition of L2 learners of English in Australia undertaken by Johnston and Pienemann (1986). Subsequently the theoretical basis of this approach was further developed by Pienemann (1998) and applied to other L2s such as Swedish (Pienemann and Hakansson 1999) and Japanese and Italian (Biase and Kawaguchi 2002).

A clear developmental pattern of the acquisition of German word order rules emerged from the ZISA project. This is summarized in Table 3.5. Pienemann, Johnston, and Brindley (1988: 222) claim that this pattern 'is now probably one of the most robust empirical findings in SLA research, because the same sequence has been found with a considerable number of further informants in studies carried out independently of each other'. The pattern does allow for some variation, however. Thus, stage 1 (canonical order) may not necessarily consist of subject-verb-object (SVO) for all learners. Whereas learners with Romance language backgrounds begin with SVO, other learners (for example, Turkish) begin with different basic word orders that reflect their L1. Also, learners vary in how they progress along the sequence. Some learners appear to move slowly, consolidating each new stage before they move on to the next, whereas others move on to a new stage very rapidly, not bothering if they have not achieved a high level of accuracy in the structure belonging to the prior stage. For example, in stage 4 (inversion) some learners acquire the rule in one linguistic context (for example, with sentence initial adverbials) and then move on to stage 5 (verb-end) before acquiring inversion in other linguistic contexts (such as interrogatives). Other learners take time to acquire the rule in all its contexts before they progress to verb-end. Differences among learners also exist with regard to their ultimate level of achievement. Many of the learners in the ZISA project failed to reach stages 4 and 5.

Stage	Name	Description	Examples
1	Canonical order	Romance learners begin with SVO as their initial hypothesis about German word order. Adverbials appear in sentence-final position.	die kinder spielen mit ball (= the children play with the ball).
2	Adverb preposing	Learners are now able to move an adverbial into sentence-initial position. However, they do not yet invert the subject and verb as is required when a sentence begins with an adverbial. This is not acquired until stage 4.	da kinder spielen (= there children play).
3	Verb separation	Learners move non-finite verbal elements into clause-final position, as required in the target language.	alle kinder muss die pause machen (= all the children must the pause make).
4	Inversion	Learners learn that in certain contexts such as sentence-initial adverbials and interrogatives, the verb must precede the subject.	dann hat sie wieder die knocht gebringt (= then has she again the bone bringed).
5	verb-end	Learners learn that the finite verb in subordinate clauses goes in clause-final position.	er sagte dass er nach hause kommt (= he said that he to home comes).

Table 3.5 Sequence of acquisition of German word order rules (based on Pienemann, Johnston, and Brindley 1988)

This developmental pattern in the acquisition of German word order rules was explained in terms of a set of cognitive processing operations that were claimed to underlie the production of sentences in German. These operations formed the basis of the MULTIDIMENSIONAL MODEL (Meisel, Clahsen, and Pienemann 1981) and were later incorporated into Pienemann's (1998) PROCESSABILITY THEORY. Both theories propose processing operations which can serve as a basis for predicting the development of the L2 grammar of any language. Johnston and Pienemann (1986), for instance, tested the predictions afforded by the Multidimensional Model on the acquisition of English by migrant workers in Australia and found evidence to support it. Similarly, Pienemann and Hakansson (1999) found evidence to support the operations that Pienemann claims underlie the acquisition of an L2 grammar in a study of L2 Swedish. Doi and Yoshioka (1990) also used Pienemann's Processability Theory to make predictions about the order of acquisition of '*wa*' (a topic marker), '*ga*' (subject marker) and '*o*' (object marker) and confirmed that '*wa*' was acquired before the other two markers in accordance with the theory. Biase and Kawaguchi (2002) tested the claims of Processability Theory on two typologically different languages, Italian and Japanese, reporting that the structures they investigated in these languages emerged in the implicational order predicted by the theory.

Table 3.6 shows the general hierarchy of stages of acquisition proposed by Pienemann's Processability Theory as applied to English. It is important to recognize that each stage is linked to acquisition of not just one but potentially a number of different features. However, as previously noted, individual learners do not necessarily learn all the features associated with a particular stage before moving on to another stage.

Stage	**L2 process**	**Morphology/syntax**
6	Main and subordinate clauses	Embedded questions: 'I wonder why he sold the car.'
5	Subject-verb agreement involving non-salient morphology	3rd person -s: 'This man owns a dog.'
4	Inversion	Yes/no inversion: 'Has he seen you?'
3	Noun phrase agreement	Plural: 'He own many dogs.'. Adverb: 'He sleep always.' Do fronting: 'Do he like you?'
2	Plural/possessive pronoun	Canonical order (Subject-verb-object: 'He buy car.')
1	Invariant forms	Single constituent (including formulaic chunks: 'eating'/'I don't know.')

Table 3.6 A hierarchy of acquisition in L2 English (based on Pienemann 1998: 171)

Finally, the work on L2 German and English suggests that not all features are developmental in the sense that their acquisition occurs at a particular stage of learners' overall development. Some are variational, i.e. they may or may not be acquired by individual learners and can be acquired at any stage of development. Meisel, Clahsen, and Pienemann (1981) gave copula as an example of a VARIATIONAL FEATURE, pointing out that learners vary enormously regarding both whether and when they acquire it.[6]

The acquisition of vocabulary

There has been a notable growth of interest in the acquisition of L2 vocabulary in the last ten years, as evidenced by the publication of a number of single-authored books (for example, Nation 2001; Singleton 1999) and collections of articles (Bogaards and Laufer 2004a; Schmitt and McCarthy 1997; Wesche and Paribakht 1999). Bogaards and Laufer (2004b) listed the various themes that this research has addressed. These include the distinction between receptive and productive knowledge, the relationship between vocabulary knowledge and language PROFICIENCY, the role of word frequency in vocabulary learning, the implicit and explicit learning of vocabulary and the learning strategies learners employ to learn new words. Here, however, our concern is solely with the patterns of development over time. Somewhat surprisingly, there are still very few descriptive studies of these patterns, so it is pertinent to ask why. The probable reason is that it is not entirely clear what it means to 'know' a word. In the case of the study of the acquisition of L2 grammar, there is a clearly defined terminal stage—the target-language grammar—making it possible to plot the transitional stages of acquisition learners pass through *en route* to the terminal stage. However, this is less easily done with vocabulary. There is no agreed terminal stage for knowledge of a word. In fact, there is no such thing as a target-language lexicon because vocabulary, in contrast to grammar, constitutes an open system and individual native speakers vary enormously in both the size of their lexicon and in their DEPTH OF KNOWLEDGE of specific words. It is not surprising, then, that there is no agreement as to how to characterize lexical development.

Nor is lexical development just a matter of learning 'words'. As N. Ellis (1997) pointed out, vocabulary is not necessarily learnt word by word but often enough, especially in the early stages of development, in lexical phrases. If a learner produces a formula such as 'I don't know' it cannot be said that this learner knows the words 'I', 'don't', and 'know'. Ellis argued that lexical acquisition takes place through the process of segmentation when learners come to see that formulaic sequences are made up of separate words as they acquire additional formulas (for example, 'I don't understand'), identify recurring elements and establish open slots in them (i.e. 'I don't' + word). In this respect the process by which a word is acquired may not be so different from the process by which grammar is developed.

The study of a learner's vocabulary development involves a consideration of both quantitative changes in vocabulary size over time and qualitative changes in the learner's knowledge of individual words. Given that it is not possible to determine absolutely how many words a learner knows at any point in time, it is necessary to obtain estimates, usually by means of some form of test, such as Laufer and Nation's (1995) Productive Vocabulary Level Test. The investigation of qualitative changes in the learner's lexicon requires information about a number of dimensions of word knowledge. Haastrup and Henriksen (1998) distinguished three dimensions:

1 the partial to precise understanding continuum (i.e. the extent to which a given word is only vaguely or clearly understood)
2 depth of knowledge (i.e. the extent to which the learner has acquired various properties of the word such as its syntactical function and its collocations)
3 the receptive-productive continuum (i.e. whether the learner understands and is able to produce the word).

These dimensions are viewed as continua but Meara (1997) queried whether this is appropriate. He argued the need to formally model vocabulary acquisition in terms of how connections between a newly acquired word and a word already in the learner's lexicon are built. Irrespective of how vocabulary acquisition is to be characterized qualitatively, there is general agreement that it constitutes a cumulative activity not just an all-or-nothing affair.

How, then, have researchers set about investigating vocabulary development? Two broad approaches to the study of developmental patterns can be identified: (1) longitudinal studies of L2 learners' productive vocabulary, and (2) experimental studies of learners' acquisition of individual words. We will briefly consider some of the research based on these approaches.

There has been a conspicuous absence of longitudinal studies of vocabulary development in learners. Two exceptions to this generalization are Yoshida (1978) and Wode *et al.* (1992), both of which report children's incidental acquisition of vocabulary in naturalistic settings and thus are analogous to the studies of the acquisition of grammar reported in the previous sections. Yoshida investigated the acquisition of English by a young Japanese child. One finding was that this child showed a marked propensity for nouns over verbs in the early stages of development, a finding supported in later research (for example, Myles 2004). In this respect, L2 acquisition (at least by a young child) mirrors L1 vocabulary acquisition (Singleton 1999). Wode *et al.* reported the results of their study of the English vocabulary acquired by four German children in a natural setting. They pointed to a number of differences between L1 and L2 vocabulary acquisition. Whereas vocabulary growth is slow in L1 acquisition up to the first fifty words and then rapidly accelerates, it is initially much more rapid but soon decelerates in L2 acquisition. The kind of overgeneralizations evident in L1 acquisition (for example, 'cat' is used to refer to a variety of four-legged animals) is not apparent in L2 acquisition. Closed-class items like prepositions, articles and pronouns are acquired late in L1 children, while L2 learners manifest a high percentage of such items early on. Wode *et al.* explained these differences in terms of the cognitive abilities and background knowledge of the two types of learner.

There have also been studies of classroom learners. Palmberg (1987) reported a longitudinal study of vocabulary growth in Swedish learners of English in a classroom setting. He elicited productive vocabulary by giving the 11-year-old learners one minute to list as many English words as they could think of beginning with the letters M and R. He noted a steady increase in words over time. In the case of M words, for example, the number increased from a mean of 3.8 in session 1 to 7.2 in session 5. Two thirds of the words produced were traceable to the textbook vocabulary. This study demonstrates the obvious: the size of learners' lexicons increases over time and reflects the nature of the input to which they have been exposed. Laufer and Nation (1999) reported a pseudo-longitudinal study of quantitative growth in classroom learners' lexicons. Using the Productive Vocabulary Levels Test, they examined the relationship between general proficiency (operationalized in terms of the number of years the learners had been studying English) and passive vocabulary size. They found clear evidence that the learners' test scores increased in line with general proficiency. Laufer (1998) examined the development of passive and active vocabulary in foreign language learners over one year. She found that whereas passive knowledge progressed considerably and controlled active knowledge to a lesser extent, free active vocabulary did not progress at all.

To summarize, few generalizations about how learners' lexicons develop quantitatively are possible. Over time, given input, learners will learn more words. However, productive vocabulary may only develop very slowly. Meara (1997) makes the obvious point that the uptake rate of new vocabulary is a function of proficiency. Initially, acquisition is slow, but then speeds up, until at advanced stages, a threshold is reached, slowing acquisition down, dependent on whether new domains of use become important to individual learners.

Experimental studies of qualitative changes in learners' knowledge of individual words have adopted two different approaches, labelled the 'developmental approach' and the 'dimensional approach' by Read (1997). Paribakht and Wesche's (1993) Vocabulary Knowledge Scale is a good example of a developmental scale. This proposes five levels based on whether learners are able to recognize a word, give a definition, and produce the word appropriately and accurately:

Stage 1: The word is not familiar at all.
Stage 2: The word is familiar but the meaning is not known.
Stage 3: A correct synonym or translation is given.
Stage 4: The word is used with semantic appropriateness in a sentence.
Stage 5: The word is used with semantic appropriateness and grammatical accuracy in a sentence.

Schmitt (1998) pointed to a number of disadvantages of such a scale. It is not clear how the stage boundaries can be clearly defined. There is no principled basis for determining the number of stages required to characterize the acquisitional process. The relationship between receptive and productive knowledge of a word remains unclear; an assumption is made that the early stages involve only receptive knowledge.

Schmitt's preferred approach is the dimensional one. This seeks to describe the level of mastery of various aspects of word knowledge, drawing on work by Richards (1976), among others, that specified the various components of word knowledge. Such an approach makes no assumption that the relationship among these components is hierarchical (i.e. that one aspect of word meaning is necessarily acquired before another) but allows for such a possibility. Indeed, Schmitt and Meara (1997), in a study involving Japanese learners of English with limited proficiency, reported a correlation between word association knowledge and suffix knowledge. Schmitt (1998) reports a longitudinal study of four advanced learners of L2 English that investigated in what ways their knowledge of 11 polysemous target words changed over time. He focused on four components of word knowledge: form (i.e. spelling), association (i.e. the extent to which the learners' word associations corresponded to those of native speakers), grammatical characteristics (i.e. word class and word derivations), and meaning. The learners were interviewed in three sessions at approximately half-yearly intervals. The learners experienced few problems in spelling the words from the beginning. Their associations became increasingly native-like in line with gains in meaning knowledge. Progress in grammatical knowledge was erratic with the learners demonstrating obvious gaps in their knowledge of the morphological properties of the target words. Few new meanings of the words were acquired but meaning knowledge moved from unknown to receptive and from receptive to productive. Schmitt also investigated to what extent progress in the different components was interrelated but found no evidence of a developmental hierarchy. In other words, the learners demonstrated increased knowledge of the words but it was not possible to identify a sequence of acquisition.

Jiang (2000) presented a psycholinguistic model of L2 vocabulary acquisition directed at describing 'how a specific word evolves in the learning processes' (p. 51). He distinguished three stages. In the first stage, the learners' initial entry for a word contains only formal information with semantic, syntactic, and morphological information stored separately. At this stage, there are likely to be strong links between the L2 word and L1 translation equivalents. The second stage is the 'L1 lemma mediation stage'; access to the conceptual meaning of an L2 word is mediated by the L1 translation equivalent. At this stage the direct connections between the L2 items and their conceptual meaning are weak. The third stage only occurs when the L2 lexical entry incorporates its own semantic, syntactic, and morphological information. At this stage the structure of L2 entries is essentially the same as that for L1 lexical entries. This stage requires plentiful contextualized input and, according to Jiang, is rarely reached.

To summarize the research on qualitative aspects of vocabulary development, it is clear that acquisition of individual words proceeds cumulatively, with learners gradually accruing additional information relating to form and meaning, as suggested by Schmitt and Jiang. However, whether it is possible to identify a clearly defined sequence of acquisition either in terms of developmental stages or a hierarchy of word components remains uncertain. As Meara (1997) has pointed out 'maybe acquisition events involve the establishment of random connections between words' (pp. 120–1).

The acquisition of phonology

As with vocabulary, there has been a conspicuous growth of interest in L2 phonology in recent years, as reflected both in a number of books devoted to this topic (for example, Leather 1999b) and a series of review articles (for example, Leather 1999a; Eckman 2004a). Phonology, like grammar and unlike vocabulary, constitutes a closed system, and thus it is not surprising to find researchers searching for evidence of developmental sequences. Invariably, learners experience difficulty in producing L2 phonological forms in the early stages, becoming more target-like only very gradually. Often, however, they fail to achieve target-like accuracy, continuing to manifest a non-native accent even after many years of exposure or study.

Much of the research into L2 phonology has been theory driven. That is, theoretically derived hypotheses have been developed and research, often experimental, designed to test the hypotheses. The literature is replete with such hypotheses, for example the MARKEDNESS DIFFERENTIAL HYPOTHESIS (Eckman 1977), the Structural Conformity Hypothesis (Eckman 1991), the Similarity Differential Hypothesis (Major and Kim 1996) and the Ontogeny Phylogeny Model (Major 2001). These hypotheses seek to account for three general characteristics of L2 phonology:

1 the presence of L1 phonological features in the learners' speech
2 the tendency for learners to substitute unmarked forms where the target language requires marked forms (where markedness refers to the inherent linguistic characteristics of phonological forms that determine their naturalness.)
3 the occurrence of unique phonological forms in the learner's L2 production, including those found in L1 acquisition. Wode (1977), for instance, found that the German children he studied followed the same developmental sequence for /r/ as that observed in native, English-speaking children.

However, these need not concern us here as they relate to how observed patterns of development can be *explained* and so will be considered in later chapters. As in previous sections, we will focus on *description*, considering the evidence for developmental sequences by drawing primarily on longitudinal studies.

For reasons of space we will focus on one area of L2 phonology—SYLLABLE STRUCTURE. Eckman (2004b) gives a number of reasons for the syllable being a particularly viable domain for L2 research: the construct of the syllable and its structure is not a matter of controversy among phonologists; there are clear and well-defined ways in which languages differ in their syllable structure (compare, for example, Chinese with English); and the strategies that learners utilize in modifying target language syllables have been shown to be developmentally ordered in a series of longitudinal studies.

Syllables can be open or closed. An open syllable consists of an onset (one or more consonants) and a rhyme (a vowel). Closed syllables contain a coda (i.e.

one or more final consonants). Closed syllables are generally considered to be more difficult to acquire than open syllables. Learners learning a language such as English or Swedish resort to simplification strategies when attempting to produce closed syllables. These strategies consist of deletion, EPENTHESIS, and substitution. Thus when faced with articulating a closed syllable such as 'sad' they are likely to either omit the final consonant (i.e. say 'sa'), add a vowel (i.e. say 'sadi'), or devoice the /d/ (i.e. say 'sat'). The question arises as to whether these simplification strategies are employed randomly until the learner finally masters the production of closed syllables or whether they are developmentally ordered.

First, there is clear evidence that learners do substitute open syllables for closed syllables and also reduce final consonant clusters. Two early studies testify to this. Tarone (1978) investigated learners from three L1 backgrounds—Cantonese, Korean and Portuguese—finding a general preference for open syllables. She argues that this reflected a universal tendency rather than L1 transfer because the L1s differed in the extent to which they allowed closed syllables. Sato (1984) found clear evidence of consonant reduction in a longitudinal study of two Vietnamese children's spontaneous speech. High error frequencies in final consonants were evident at the beginning of the study (85 per cent and 94 per cent) which first increased before finally decreasing after 18 weeks.[7] This study pointed to an important characteristic of development, namely that it is not entirely linear but more U-shaped. Other later studies have confirmed the general preference for open syllables and consonant reduction. Osburne (1996) observed that a Vietnamese learner of English improved his coda cluster production over a six-year period (from a 95 per cent to an 81 per cent error rate). Carlisle (1998) reported a low–high–low pattern of development in two of the four Spanish learners of L2 English he investigated, although the other two exhibited different patterns of development (one improving linearly and the other regressing linearly).

The study we will focus on is that of Abrahamsson (2003) as this provides one of the most detailed analyses of learners' acquisition of syllable structure to date. It examines not just the overall developmental profile but also explores how contextual factors influence learners' choice of syllable structure, thus pointing to the existence of systematic variability in learner language. Abrahamsson studied three Chinese learners of L2 Swedish, collecting data by means of conversations conducted over just short of a two-year period. An important feature of his study was that the learners were complete beginners at the onset of the study. His analysis addressed both developmental aspects and grammatical/functional aspects in the word final codas of the participants' speech. Error frequencies were characterized by four phases: (1) an initial phase of relatively high error rates followed by a rapid decrease in error frequency, (2) a linear increase in error frequency, (3) a stable plateau of relatively high error frequencies, and (4) a final decrease in error rates. In other words, the learners manifested a U-SHAPED PATTERN OF DEVELOPMENT. Errors involved both consonant deletion and epenthesis. The epenthesis–deletion ratio increased over time during the first year, showing that the learners gradually replaced deletion with epenthesis as a simplification strategy. In the second year, epenthesis also reduced. Drawing on the results of his own study and Hammarberg's (1988) study of five German learners of L2 Swedish, which examined substitutions of word final codas, Abrahamsson proposed the following developmental sequence:

deletion > epenthesis > feature change (for example, devoicing) > target form

He explained the U-shaped pattern of development in terms of the learners' developing fluency. Initially, the learners focused on accurate production but, as they focused more on fluency, their errors increased until they had sufficient control of Swedish to once again pay attention to accuracy. Regarding grammar/functional aspects, Abrahamsson showed that error frequencies were higher for inflected words (for example, noun or verb + inflection) than for non-inflected ones (i.e. content words). To explain this, he drew on Weinberger's (1987) Recoverability Principle, according to which learners are less likely to simplify syllable structure when they estimate that their interlocutors will have difficulty in understanding what they mean. Whereas content words contribute substantially to the meaning of an utterance, form words are often meaning redundant.

This study, then, attests to some of the key features in L2 development—the fact that development is not always linear, the existence of relatively well-defined sequences of acquisition, the role of context in determining the learners' choice of forms and the trade-off between fluency and accuracy. These are themes that will be revisited throughout this book. The study also points to another important aspect of L2 development—there is individual variation. For example, whereas one learner in Abrahamsson's study continuously increased her use of epenthesis during the first year, another of the learners consistently produced more deletions than epenthesis right up to the end of the first year. This points to the importance of individual differences in L2 learning, a topic addressed in Chapter 13.

The L2 = L1 hypothesis

The L2 = L1 HYPOTHESIS (also referred to as the 'identity hypothesis') has received considerable attention in SLA research as it raises a number of important theoretical issues. (See Clahsen 1990.) These concern whether the language acquisition device which mentalists claim is responsible for L1 acquisition is available to L2 learners. In another line of research, comparisons of the language produced by L1 and L2 learners have been conducted with a view to establishing to what extent developmental patterns are the same or different. (See for example, McNamara 1973; Dulay and Burt 1974c; Ervin-Tripp 1974; Cook 1977; McLaughlin 1978a, 1985; Felix 1978; Ellis 1985b.) Foster-Cohen (2001) rightly argued that these two approaches need to be clearly distinguished, suggesting that the former concerns 'acquisition' (a theoretical construct) and the latter 'development' (an empirical phenomenon). Our concern here is with 'development' in Foster-Cohen's sense of this term.

The similarities in learner language in L1 and L2 acquisition are perhaps most pronounced in the early stages of development. There is evidence of a silent period, of the use of formulas, and of structural and semantic simplification in both types of acquisition. However, there are also obvious differences. Whereas all L1 learners necessarily pass through a silent period, many L2 learners—especially adults—do not. Many L2 learners appear to make greater use of formulaic sequences than L1 learners in the early stages of acquisition. Also, L2 learners are able to produce some longer and less propositionally reduced utterances from the beginning. A correct characterization of early L1 and L2 acquisition might be to say that L2 learner language displays many of the features of L1 learner language plus some additional ones. Felix (1978) pointed to a number of differences in a comparison of sentence types in the acquisition of German. He found that the L2 children he studied produced only three different multi-word utterance types, and argued that this contrasts with L1 acquisition, where learners have been shown to produce a multitude of different structures from the two-word stage.

The morpheme order acquisition is not the same in the two types of acquisition. Dulay and Burt (1974c) compared the 'acquisition order' they obtained for nine English morphemes with the acquisition order for the same morphemes obtained in both longitudinal studies (for example, Brown 1973) and cross-sectional studies (for example, de Villiers and de Villiers 1973) of L1 English. They found that the orders were different. Articles, copula, and auxiliary 'be' were acquired earlier by L2 learners, while irregular past tense was acquired later. However, the L2 order they obtained did correlate with the L1 order obtained by Porter (1977), who used the same data collection instrument—the Bilingual Syntax Measure (BSM). This has led some researchers (for example, Rosansky 1976; Hakuta and Cancino 1977) to suggest that Dulay and Burt's acquisition order is an artifact of the Bilingual Syntax Measure.

The process by which individual morphemes are acquired displays both similarities and differences. For example, both L1 and L2 learners omit pronouns and they both overgeneralize individual pronouns. The substitution of nouns for pronouns also occurs in both types of acquisition. However, L1 learners commonly substitute their own name in place of the first person singular pronoun for example, 'Lwindi eating' (= I am eating), which has not been attested in L2 acquisition, except by very young children.

The similarities between L1 and L2 acquisition are, perhaps, strongest in syntactical structures. The evidence from studies of negation (and also interrogatives) suggests that learners pass through a remarkably similar sequence of acquisition for these structures. Readers are invited to compare the order of L1 acquisition for English negatives shown in Tables 3.1 and 3.3. The similarities are striking. However, once again, the sequences in the two types of acquisition are not identical. For example, children acquiring German as an L1 begin with the verb in final position (Clahsen 1988):

wurst hier schnitt (= sausages here cut)

whereas, as we have seen, L2 learners begin with a canonical order derived from their L1, which in the case of Romance language learners results in an SVO word order.

Differences between the L1 and L2 acquisition of vocabulary can be expected given that L2 learners are equipped with a developed conceptual system to anchor the acquisition of word forms, whereas L1 learners are faced with the dual task of developing a conceptual system and acquiring lexical forms. Also, L2 learners do not go through an extensive period of pre-verbal development. However, as Singleton (1999) points out, there are also similarities. Both sets of learners face difficulties in extracting lexical units from the speech stream. Also, L2 learners are faced with acquiring at least some new meanings as there is no one-to-one correspondence between the lexical meanings of their L1 and L2.

Similarities are also evident in the acquisition of phonology, despite the fact that L2 learners are known to transfer features from their L1. Abrahamsson (2003), for example, claims that sequence of development for the acquisition of closed syllable structure is essentially the same for L1 and L2 learners. He notes that although many L1 children do not seem to pass through an epenthesis stage, moving directly from consonant deletion to the target form, some precocious children do manifest epenthesis, possibly because, like adult L2 learners, they are more aware of their listener's needs and seek to make their meaning clear by avoiding consonant deletion.

Given the mixed results available from comparative studies of L1 and L2 acquisition, it is perhaps not surprising to find widely diverging conclusions regarding the L2 = L1 hypothesis. Bley-Vroman (1988) emphasized the differences between L1 and adult foreign language learning (see Table 3.7) and ended up with the following claim:

> These general characteristics of foreign language learning tend to the conclusions that the domain-specific language acquisition of children ceases to operate in adults, and in addition, that foreign language acquisition resembles general adult learning in fields for which no domain-specific learning system is believed to exist. (1988: 25)

Ervin-Tripp (1974), however, emphasized the similarities she found in naturalistic child learners of L2 French and L1 learners:

> We found that the functions of early sentences, and their form, their semantic redundancy, their reliance on ease of short-term memory, their overgeneralization of lexical forms, their use of simple order strategies were similar to processes we have seen in first language acquisition. In

> broad outlines, then, the conclusion is tenable that first and second language learning is similar in natural situations.
> (cited in Hatch 1978a: 205)

These two quotations reveal why researchers have reached such different conclusions. Whereas Bley-Vroman concentrates on acquisitional outcomes, Ervin-Tripp focuses on the process. Whereas Bley-Vroman talks about foreign language learners, Ervin-Tripp refers to naturalistic learners.

Feature	**L1 acquisition**	**L2 (foreign language) acquisition**
Overall success	Children normally achieve perfect mastery of their L1.	Adult L2 learners are very unlikely to achieve perfect mastery.
General failure	Success is guaranteed.	Complete success is very rare.
Variation	There is little variation among L1 learners with regard to overall success or the path they follow.	L2 learners vary in both their degree of success and the path they follow.
Goals	The goal is target-language competence.	L2 learners may be content with less than target-language competence and may also be more concerned with fluency than accuracy.
Fossilization	Fossilization is unknown in child language development.	L2 learners often cease to develop and also backslide (i.e. return to earlier stages of development).
Intuitions	Children develop clear intuitions regarding what is a correct and an incorrect sentence.	L2 learners are often unable to form clear grammaticality judgements.
Instruction	Children do not need formal lessons to learn their L1.	There is a wide belief that instruction helps L2 learners.
Negative evidence	Children's 'errors' are not typically corrected; correction not necessary for acquisition.	Correction generally viewed as helpful and, by some, as necessary.
Affective factors	Success is not influenced by personality, motivation, attitudes, etc.	Affective factors play a major role in determining proficiency.

Table 3.7 Differences between L1 and L2 acquisition (based on Bley-Vroman 1988)

L2 learners appear to tackle the problem of learning a language in similar ways to L1 learners. These similarities are most clearly evident in informal learning situations when learners are attempting to engage in unplanned language use. But there are also differences in the ways in which L2 learners go about 'cracking the code', and these become most evident in formal learning situations. The differences between the kinds of learning involved in these two settings are described by McNamara (1973) and d'Anglejan (1978). For example, informal learning typically takes place in contexts where the input is not consciously structured and the primary focus is on message conveyance, while formal learning occurs in contexts where the input is usually carefully organized and the primary focus is on form. Informal learning involves implicit knowledge, while formal learning is likely to involve at least some explicit knowledge of L2 rules.

Formal and informal learning can also be differentiated in the kind of memory learners rely on. Adult L2 learners have access to a more developed memory capacity than L1 learners and when they can use it (or are required to use it, as in many pedagogic learning activities), differences between the language they produce and that produced by L1 learners occur. However, when they are not able to use it, they will produce language that resembles young children's. Cook (1977) found that when adults were unable to utilize their memory capacity to process relative clauses they behaved in the same way as L1 learners. In another experiment, designed to establish the number of digits adult learners could remember in the L2, Cook found that they behaved like native-speaking adults. This led Cook to conclude that when the memory process depends on features of syntax, the same restrictions apply to the L1 and adult L2 learner, but where the memory process is minimally dependent on language, the adult L2 learner exploits his or her general memory capacity. In other words, when L2 learners make use of their special language-learning faculties, the identity hypothesis receives support, but when they rely on learning procedures of a general kind it does not.

Another obvious source of difference between L1 and L2 acquisition lies in the fact that L2 learners have access to a previously acquired language, in some cases to several. There is clear evidence to show that this results in differences between L2 and L1 acquisition—for example, in the case of the acquisition of German word order rules. Chapter 8 considers the various ways in which the learner's L1 influences L2 acquisition.

The L2 = L1 acquisition hypothesis is important because it raises so many key issues. The evidence that we have considered here suggests that the hypothesis is partially supported. Given the immense cognitive and affective differences between very young children and adults, the similarities in the language they produce are striking. However, there are also significant differences which have been shown to exist and, as we will see in Chapter 12, when we consider whether L2 learners have continued access to Universal Grammar.

Summary

The investigation of developmental patterns in learner language was motivated by the desire to describe learner language in its own right, as a system of rules that learners constructed and repeatedly revised. It has proceeded by means of cross-sectional and longitudinal research. It has employed a number of methodological procedures, including obligatory occasion analysis, target-like use analysis, frequency analysis, emergence and implicational scaling.

First language acquisition researchers sought evidence with which to test the rival behaviourist and mentalist accounts of language learning. They provided evidence of (1) an order of acquisition for morphemes, (2) sequences of development in the acquisition of specific structures such as negatives, and (3) cross-linguistic similarities.

In L2 acquisition, early learner language is characterized by (1) a silent period (although not in all learners), (2) extensive use of formulaic sequences and (3) structural and semantic simplification, particularly in unplanned language use. Early studies of the order of acquisition of grammatical morphemes such as plural –s and articles produced mixed results. The cross-sectional studies reported a consistent accuracy order when the learner was focused on communicating meaning, which some researchers equated with acquisition order. Krashen (1977) proposed a 'natural order' of acquisition based on these studies. However, longitudinal studies did not always confirm this order. A major criticism of the morpheme studies is that acquisition is viewed as one of 'accumulated entities', and insufficient attention is paid to the ways in which learners achieve gradual mastery over specific linguistic features. However, studies of the acquisition of tense and aspect and syntactical structures, such as negation, lend strong support to the existence of developmental sequences. Learners of different L2s manifest similar patterns of development when acquiring tense and aspect. This is evident in both meaning-based and form-based analyses. In the case of syntactic structures, regularities are also evident. The acquisition of English and German negation involves a series of transitional stages in which learners gradually switch from external to internal negation and from preverbal to post-verbal negation. Relative clauses constitute a complex learning task. There is evidence to suggest that learners solve it piecemeal by learning first to modify noun phrases before the verb, and then noun phrases that follow the verb. Also, learners acquire the functions that relative pronouns can perform in a fairly well-defined order. Finally, the ZISA project and research based on Pienemann's Processability Theory have provided some impressive evidence to show that learners acquire a range of features in a predictable order. ZISA researchers have also distinguished developmental and variational features.

L2 lexical acquisition, like the acquisition of grammar, is a slow and gradual process. Learners gradually extend their lexicons while simultaneously accumulating knowledge of lexical forms and meanings (i.e. they extend both the breadth and depth of their lexicons). However, there is little evidence of any order or sequence. There is some evidence that early acquisition is characterized by nouns and adjectives, with verbs only appearing later. But there does not appear to be any clear hierarchy in learners' acquisition of the properties of individual words. It is to be noted that vocabulary constitutes an open system that is not subject to 'rules' in the same way as grammar or phonology. The acquisition of vocabulary is best seen as involving item rather than system learning and for this reason is inherently 'variational'.

The study of L2 phonology has provided evidence of developmental sequences. Various influences (the learner's L1, the universal properties of language, and uniquely developmental processes) conspire to shape the path of acquisition. Thus, learners' acquisition of closed syllable structure shows a staged progression from consonant deletion to epenthesis to feature substitution to target form. As in the case of grammar acquisition, these phases are not clearly separated; rather learners shift gradually from one simplification strategy to another.

A comparison of the developmental patterns found in L1 and L2 acquisition lends partial support to the identity hypothesis. Some striking similarities have been found in syntactic structures such as negatives, but there are also differences. It has been suggested that adult L2 learners are more likely to manifest similar patterns of acquisition to children acquiring their native language when they engage in informal learning, but that they also have access to formal learning strategies, which results in differences.

Conclusion

In the Introduction to an influential collection of papers, Hatch (1978a) wrote:

> Nothing can be certain until second language acquisition has been studied in tangible case histories or until empirical evidence has been obtained (p. 10).[8]

A considerable amount of empirical evidence is now available. This chapter has reviewed a selection of it in order to examine the extent to which there are testifiable developmental patterns (orders and sequences) in L2 acquisition of the kind that have been observed in L1 acquisition.

What constitutes evidence for a developmental pattern? This question has rarely been addressed in an explicit manner, but the following would seem to be the criteria that researchers have applied:

1 Developmental patterns can be established by looking at either the order in which different target structures emerge or are mastered, or the sequence of stages through which a learner passes *en route* to mastery of a single TL structure.

2 In the case of transitional structures, a 'stage' consists of a period during which learners use a particular form or structure in a systematic manner, although not necessarily to the exclusion of other forms and structures.
3 The forms and structures that a learner produces at different points during the process of L2 acquisition can be ordered implicationally in such a way that one form or structure implies the emergence/mastery of one or more other features.
4 Learners progress step-by-step in an order or sequence, mastering or using one particular structure—target-language or transitional—before another. However, progress is not necessarily linear (i.e. it can be U-shaped).
5 Strong evidence for developmental patterns occurs when it can be shown that an order or a sequence is universal (i.e. applies to different L2s and to all learners). Weaker evidence is found if it is shown that an order or a sequence applies only to specific L2s and/or to specific groups of learners.

These criteria raise many questions to do with the definition of such key terms as 'form', 'structure', 'systematic use', and 'master'. Different researchers have worked with rather different operational definitions, with the result that it is not easy to compare results across studies. Inevitably, then, the picture is often a fuzzy one, suggesting that it may be better in many cases to talk of 'regularities' than of 'definite patterns'.

The strongest evidence for developmental patterns comes from studies of syntactic structures and phonology. We have seen that the morpheme studies, once highly regarded, are of doubtful validity, because their view of acquisition as one of 'accumulated entities' is seriously flawed. But in the case of grammatical sub-systems such as tense and aspect, negatives, relative clauses, word order rules (as well as other areas of syntax such as interrogatives),and aspects of phonology such as syllable structure, there is evidence to support at least the 'weak' definition of developmental patterns referred to in (5) above. The acquisition of these features in a particular L2 shows surprising uniformity, and in some cases the regularities hold across different L2s. For example, learners of all L2s so far investigated appear to go through an initial stage of preverbal negation and to master closed syllable structure in a similar manner.

There is plenty of evidence that acquisitional sequences are not completely rigid. A sequence can also be influenced by the learner's L1. Thus, the starting point for the acquisition of German word order rules seems to vary according to the basic word order of the learner's L1. Also, the L1 may result in an additional stage, as when German and Norwegian learners of L2 English add a negator after the main verb at a certain developmental point.

In addition, there is individual learner variation, with some learners missing out stages of development. If the variability between learners becomes too great, it makes little sense to continue to talk of a standard developmental route, a point raised by Lightbown (1984). She claimed that for every study that reports an order or a sequence, there is another study which has produced counter-evidence and argued that the learners' L1, the input they experience, and their social-psychological attitudes can all result in variant patterns. But Lightbown's conclusion is not that clear patterns do not exist, merely that we need to examine how these variables interact with universal tendencies. Again, this raises the whole question as to what constitutes a 'definite pattern' of L2 acquisition, a question partly but not completely answered by the criteria listed above.

It is easy to find methodological flaws with many of the studies. Lightbown (1984) listed a number of them. Some studies have been carried out in a manner that makes replication of them difficult and yet, clearly, replication is essential if claims about the universality of sequences are to be substantiated. Another problem is that researchers have tended to base their claims on data collected by means of a single instrument and, thus, have ignored the variability in learner language produced in different contexts. Increasingly, however, researchers have recognized the importance of collecting evidence of acquisition by means of a range of instruments. (See, for example, Norris and Ortega 2003.) Lightbown also suggested that some researchers have used inappropriate data collection procedures for their subjects, while others have presented the results anecdotally rather than quantitatively. The need for quantification is not something that all researchers would acknowledge, however.[9]

Despite all these problems, the work on developmental patterns has been substantial and in many cases convincing. The discovery that learners do follow identifiable routes owes much to early research into L2 acquisition, research that was based largely on longitudinal studies of learners in naturalistic environments. This work was essentially descriptive and in more recent years has given way to theory-driven research involving experimental studies designed to test specific hypotheses. With some notable exceptions such as the ESF project, Bardovi-Harlig's work on tense and aspect, and studies of L2 phonology such as Abrahamsson's, the focus of attention in SLA has shifted to identifying the cognitive and social processes involved in L2 acquisition. This research has often been cross-sectional and laboratory-based rather than longitudinal and naturalistic. Later sections of this book will consider this research.

Arguably, any theory of L2 acquisition will need to account for developmental patterns. The general theory that has been dominant in SLA—INTERLANGUAGE theory (Selinker 1972)—was initially formulated to provide such an account. It claimed that learners construct a series of interlanguages (i.e. mental grammars that are drawn upon in producing and comprehending sentences in the L2) and that they revise these grammars in systematic and predictable ways as they move along an interlanguage continuum. It has also proposed that this continuum involves both recreation and restructuring (Corder 1978a). Learners create unique rules not to be found in either the L1 or the TL and then gradually complexify these rules in the direction of those in the TL, particularly in the case of syntax learnt in informal environments.

They also make use of their L1, gradually restructuring it as they discover how it differs from the TL. Interlanguage theory is considered in more detail in Chapter 9.

Notes

1 In fact, though, many of the subjects of the studies reported in this chapter were of the 'mixed' kind. That is, although they had opportunities for exposure in non-instructional settings, they were also receiving some classroom instruction. This is particularly true of children learning the L2 in a country where it functions as an official language. (See, for example, Dulay and Burt 1973; Pienemann 1980.)

2 Atkinson (1986) has labelled these two traditions in language acquisition research the FLAT and SHARP traditions. The label SHARP is not an acronym, in fact. Atkinson chose it as an antonym to FLAT. This is an acronym, referring to 'First Language Acquisition Theories'.

3 There is also the general problem of determining exactly what a learner's 'silence' signifies. Silence can be used as a conversational strategy—a means of indicating disagreement, disapproval of someone's behaviour, or plain uncooperativeness, for example.

4 The fact that structural/semantic simplification can reflect the processes either of acquisition or production raises an epistemological and methodological problem in SLA research. What actually counts as 'acquisition'? To what extent is it possible to distinguish between what learners 'know' and what they 'do', given that the primary evidence for what they know rests in what they do? This issue raises its head at various points throughout this book and is discussed in some detail in Chapter 17.

5 The retention of pronominal copies may be a manifestation of the same psycholinguistic mechanism underlying the choice of nouns over pronouns—the learner's attempt to be transparent by ensuring that all meanings map on to overt forms.

6 The claim that variational features like copula are not acquired in a fixed order does not preclude their acquisition involving a sequence of stages. Indeed, there is some evidence to suggest that the acquisition of copula 'be' does involve transitional stages. (See Ellis 1988a and Chapter 4.) Thus, copula may first appear in learner language at any time; its mastery, however, takes time and involves stages of development.

7 However, Sato (1987), found negligible use of epenthesis in her Vietnamese learners of English, which she saw as 'evidence against the hypothesized universal preference for the CV (i.e. open) syllable' (1987: 260). Riney (1990) provides evidence to suggest that the crucial factor may be the age at which the learner began learning the L2.

8 It is assumed that Hatch's use of 'or' is not meant to suggest that 'case studies' do not constitute 'empirical research'. They clearly do.

9 There is a rich ethnographic and descriptive tradition in SLA research which eschews quantification in favour of rich, illustrative accounts of L2 learners. (See Johnson 1992, in particular Chapters 4 and 6, for an account of these.)

4
Variability in learner language

Introduction

In Chapters 2 and 3, evidence was provided to suggest that learner language displays significant systematicity. However, we also noted that a pervasive feature of learner language is its variability. Learners sometimes make an error and sometimes do not. Within a single stage of acquisition, learners do not consistently make use of a single form or pattern, but rather show a preference for the use of one form among others that they use during the same period.

The types of variability found in learner language are not unique. All natural languages will manifest VARIABLE FORMS that have two or more VARIANTS. A variable form is a feature (phonological, lexical, or grammatical) that is realized linguistically in more than one way. Variants are the linguistic devices that realize a variable form. A good example of a variable form is negation in native speaker English. There are two standard variants of the negator: full 'not' and the contracted 'n't'. Of course, the variants found in learner language will not necessarily be the same as those found in the target language. Thus, learners' interlanguages have been found to manifest three rather than two variants of the negator: 'no', 'not', and 'n't'. Negation also varies structurally in both native-speaker speech (where the double negative exists alongside the standard verbal negative) and in learner speech (where preverbal and post-verbal negation occur). It should be noted that the types of variability and their sources are the same in natural languages, including learner language.

How then can the apparent contradiction between variation and systematicity in learner language be accounted for? There are four possible approaches. The first approach is that practised by linguists in the Chomskyan tradition (for example, White 1989a and Gregg 1989), who adopt what Tarone (1983) has called 'a homogeneous competence model'. In this approach variation is seen as a feature of performance rather than of the learner's underlying knowledge system. The type of data often preferred by researchers who operate within the homogeneous competence paradigm consist of speakers' intuitions regarding what they think is correct in the L2 rather than actual instances of language use.[1] In effect, then, variability is either discounted in this paradigm as simply 'slips' or 'performance errors' or, in some cases, explained in terms of multiple competencies.

The second approach is sociolinguistic in orientation. Sociolinguists such as Labov (1970) view a speaker's competence as itself inherently variable. They identify two major sources of variability. INTERNAL VARIATION arises as a result of linguistic factors that condition which specific variant of a linguistic form a speaker selects. For example, whether syllable simplification takes place (see Chapter 3), depends in part on whether the consonant cluster is integral to a content word (for example, 'mist') or arises as a result of a grammatical inflection (for example, 'missed'), with final consonant deletion more likely in the latter than the former. EXTERNAL VARIATION arises as a result of social factors that lead a speaker to select one form rather than another. The influence of social factors such as age, gender, and social class is evident in both different varieties of a language preferred by groups of speakers (i.e. in inter-speaker variation) and also in stylistic variation within the performance of a single speaker in different SOCIAL CONTEXTS (i.e. in intra-speaker variation). SLA researchers who adopt a sociolinguistic orientation prefer to work with data (often multiple sets of data) that reflect actual instances of language use. In this approach, the problem of variability is addressed by demonstrating that it is systematic.

The third approach is psycholinguistic. Psycholinguistic processing models seek to account for the variation that results from factors that influence the learner's ability to process L2 knowledge under different conditions of use. For example, systematic differences in performance have been found to exist in learner language depending on whether it is planned or unplanned (Ellis 1987b; Crookes 1989). Researchers in this tradition collect samples of language use elicited under experimental conditions. They seek to show that planning variability is systematic and to explain it in terms of mental processing. However, the distinction between the psycholinguistic and sociolinguistic approaches is not clear-cut, as sociolinguists such as Labov have evoked the notion of ATTENTION to account for the variability evident when speakers switch styles depending on the addressee. (See the following section.) Thus, attention can be viewed as both a psycholinguistic and sociolinguistic construct.

L2 variability has attracted increasing attention in SLA research, drawing on a range of different theoretical perspectives. Wolfram (1991: 104), in a review of a number of books on L2 variability, found the 'range of models and perspectives almost overwhelming in its inclusiveness' and considered the 'search for a unitary model of SLA variation very elusive'. Similarly, Zuengler argued that 'it is misguided to search for one comprehensive theory since one theory will most likely be insufficient in explaining the complexity of performance variation ...'(1989: 66). However, Preston (1989, 2002) has gone some way to developing a model of learner variability that incorporates both sociolinguistic and psycholinguistic perspectives.

The starting point for this chapter is a brief discussion of the sociolinguistic and psycholinguistic theories that have informed variability research in SLA. There follows a typology of variability in learner language, which serves as a framework for the rest of the chapter. The typology distinguishes free and systematic variation. The latter is accounted for in terms of sociolinguistic and psycholinguistic factors. Theories of L2 acquisition that have sought to explain attested patterns of variability in learner language are considered in Chapter 9.

Some theoretical perspectives

Sociolinguistic models

The Labovian paradigm

The Labovian paradigm has exerted considerable influence on the study of variability in SLA research, particularly in much of the earlier work. Two constructs are of particular importance: speech styles and variable rules.

Labov (1970) listed five axioms relating to the study of speech styles:

1. '... there are no single style speakers.' All speakers vary their language to some degree when the social context or topic changes.
2. 'Styles can be ranged along a single dimension, measured by the amount of attention paid to speech.' Language users vary in the degree to which they monitor their speech in different situations.
3. The VERNACULAR STYLE is the style in which minimum attention is given to monitoring speech. It is the style associated with informal, everyday speech and it provides 'the most systematic data' for linguistic study.
4. It is not possible to tap the vernacular style of users by systematic observation of how they perform in a formal context (such as an experiment).
5. The only way to obtain good data on the speech of language users is through systematic observation.

The conflict between the fourth and the fifth axioms leads to what Labov called the OBSERVER'S PARADOX. Good data require systematic observation, but this prevents access to the user's vernacular style.

As an example of how Labov set about examining speech styles, let us consider one of his studies. Labov (1970) examined the speech patterns of New Yorkers. He collected data using a variety of tasks in order to sample a range of speech styles, which he classified as (1) casual speech (i.e. the relaxed speech found in the street and in bars), (2) careful speech (for example, the speech found in interviews), (3) reading, (4) word lists, and (5) minimal pairs. These styles were spread along a continuum according to the amount of attention paid by the speakers to their own speech, the least attention being paid in (1) and the most in (5). Thus, attention is seen as the mechanism through which other factors can affect style. Labov's model, therefore, although primarily sociolinguistic, also incorporates a psycholinguistic factor—attention. Attention serves as the mechanism through which causative social factors such as verbal task (in particular), topic, interlocutor, setting, or the roles of the participants influence actual performance. However, Labov appeared to view 'attention' as a global sort of activity rather than as involving a conscious focus on the variable in question. He investigated a number of pronunciation features and was able to show that the use of sounds like /θ/ (i.e. the first sound in 'thing') and their variants (for example, /t/) signalled sociolinguistic meaning. Speakers used the prestige /θ/ more frequently in styles where they were able to pay attention and the less prestigious sounds such as /t/ in styles where little or no attention to speech was paid. Labov referred to these changes in speech as STYLE SHIFTING. He distinguished INDICATORS (i.e. features that showed no style shifting but which differed according to social stratification), MARKERS (i.e. features that signalled both style shifting and social stratification), and STEREOTYPES (i.e. features that are socially stigmatized and therefore actively avoided).

Labov's work indicated that style shifting was systematic either categorically or probabilistically. Categorical style shifting is evident when it can be shown that speakers always use one particular feature (such as /θ/) in one style and another (such as /t/) in a different style. In such cases it is possible to write a categorical rule to describe the speech behaviour. Such a rule has this form:

X→Y/__A

where X refers to the variable itself, Y to its actual realization, and A the particular context (for example, the first sound of 'thing' is realized as /t/ in a context calling for a casual style). The actual behaviour of Labov's subjects, however, was not usually categorical in this way. They tended to use one variant in one style and another variant in another style to a greater or lesser extent. In other words, their behaviour was probabilistic. To account for this, Labov proposed the use of variable rules. These state that a given variable feature, X, is manifest as either Y or Z with differing levels of probability depending on the context/style. Such a rule can account for the patterns of variability in the choice of /θ/ and /t/ which Labov found in the speech of New Yorkers. It can show that speakers are much more likely to use the prestige feature /θ/ in a careful style than in a more casual style and, conversely, that they are more likely to use a less socially prestigious feature /t/ in casual than in a careful style.

Variable rules have been used to describe the extent of the systematic variation that occurs in relation to situational factors (i.e. in style shifting) and also that which arises as a result of linguistic context. For example, Labov (1969) was also able to show that the use of variants of copula 'be' (full, contracted, and zero copula) in Black English Vernacular (BEV) was influenced by the preceding and following elements in the sentence. Thus, zero copula was most likely to occur when the preceding word ended in a vowel and 'gonna' followed:

He gon' try to get up. (+ vowel/+ verb)

and least likely to occur when the preceding word ended in a consonant and a noun phrase followed:

Bud is my friend. (+ consonant/+ noun phrase)

A variable rule can express the probability of a particular form being used in a particular linguistic context.

Powerful statistical procedures such as logistic regression (as used in VARBRUL) have been developed to account for the effects that various factors relating to both situational and linguistic context can have on speakers' choice of language forms. These provide a means of determining the differential effect of a number of factors and how they interact.

The Labovian paradigm has come in for considerable criticism (for example, Wolfson 1976; Beebe 1982; Bell 1984; Rampton 1987). One of the main problems consists of Labov's use of 'attention to speech' as a causative factor in style shifting. As Wolfson pointed out, very little is known about the relationship between audio-monitoring and speech style and it is difficult to obtain independent measures of attention. Thus we cannot be sure that a speaker really does attend to speech more in a 'careful' than in a 'casual' style. Sometimes speakers may pay attention to their choice of language in an informal setting, if a particular feature is important for communicating in this kind of language use. A further serious criticism, advanced by Bell (1984), is that the attention-to-speech model ignores the effect that the addressee has on the interaction. It cannot account for the role played by such factors as feelings of ethnic identity and solidarity with one's in-group. Beebe argued that 'attention to speech is inadequate as an explanation for style' (1982: 13) and pointed to a number of studies (for example, Bourhis and Giles 1977) where style shifting does not appear to involve attention on the part of speakers. Variable rules have also been attacked. In particular, doubts have been expressed as to whether the probabilities expressed in a variable rule can be seen as part of the native speaker's competence, as Labov claims. As we will see in the next section, Bickerton (1975) has shown how variability can be accounted for entirely through categorical rules. However, other sociolinguists such as Preston (1989) continue to see value in the inherent variability expressed in variable rules.[2]

The dynamic paradigm

Whereas Labov sought to account for variability in groups of speakers by means of variable rules, Bailey (1973) and, in particular, Bickerton (1975), developed alternative means, based on a view of how language change takes place.

Bailey sought to show how a theory of language change can account for synchronic variability in language use. According to his WAVE THEORY, linguistic innovation is first introduced by one group of speakers. By the time it is taken up by a second group, the first group has introduced a second innovation. And so as old rules spread, new rules arise. The spread, or diffusion, of new rules also takes place in another way. Initially, a rule may be restricted to a specific linguistic environment and then gradually come to be used in an increasing range of environments. Linguistic environments can be distinguished according to their weight. Change originates in 'heavy environments' (i.e. those environments that favour the use of a particular variant) and then spreads through intermediate to 'light environments' (i.e. those environments that do not favour the use of the variant). Thus, like Labov's variable rule, the wave theory accounts for the systematic effects of both social and linguistic factors.

The relationship between language change and synchronic variation (i.e. the variation evident in speakers at a single point in time) is clearly evident in CREOLES—languages that began as pidgins but then developed rapidly when they came to be used and learnt as first languages. A creole generally has several varieties, or 'lects' as they are called: (1) the basilect manifests the 'deepest' creole features, (2) the mesolect contains middle-level features, and (3) the acrolect is the variety closest to the standard language. Together the lects constitute a creole continuum, going from the simplest, most basic variety to the most complex. In a study of Guyanese Creole, Bickerton (1975) was able to show how different speakers could be located at different points on the continuum by using implicational scaling. Table 4.1 provides an example. Six speakers are listed on the vertical axis while four Guyanese Creole features are listed on the horizontal axis. The matrix shows whether each of the six learners uses a particular feature (signalled by X) or not (signalled by o). The table indicates that speakers 1 and 2 (whose speech provided evidence of only one of the four grammatical features Bickerton examined) were basilectal speakers, while speakers 3 and 4 (who provided evidence of two or three of the features) were mesolectal, and speakers 5 and 6 (who used all four features) were acrolectal. Table 4.1 constitutes an implicational scale because it can be shown that the presence of a feature to the left in the horizontal list of features entails the presence of all features to the right. Bickerton claims that it is possible to write separate grammars consisting only of categorical rules to account for each lect. The resulting description is called a polylectal grammar.

Different types of variability can be accounted for using Bickerton's model. First, there is INTER-SPEAKER VARIATION. Some speakers may have access to one variety and others to other varieties, although the full continuum of varieties will only be evident in the 'langue' of the speech community as a whole. Second, there is INTRA-SPEAKER VARIATION. This occurs when speakers who have access to more than one lect engage in CODE-SWITCHING. In accordance

Speaker	Linguistic features			
	Ving	**Ning**	**doz**	**a**
1	0	0	0	X
2	0	0	0	X
3	0	0	X	X
4	0	X	X	X
5	X	X	X	X
6	X	X	X	X

X = occurs; 0 = does not occur

Table 4.1 Varieties of Guyanese Creole in the speech of six speakers (simplified table from Bickerton 1975: 79)

with situational factors such as the topic of the discourse, its purpose, and the addressee, a speaker may choose to use one lect sometimes and another at other times. Code-switching works in much the same way as style shifting, the difference being that in the dynamic paradigm it can be accounted for in terms of a polylectal grammar rather than variable rules. Third, there is FREE VARIATION. When a speaker first acquires a new feature, this is likely to exist alongside an existing feature and to be used to realize the same meanings. Bickerton claimed that this occurs only in those speakers whose language systems are still unstable—a relatively small set of the total population. He also claimed that free variation is short-lived.

The dynamic paradigm offers the SLA researcher some powerful theoretical constructs—for example, the notion of environmental weight (also offered by the Labovian paradigm), of distinct lects, and of code-switching—together with some useful tools for investigating L2 variability, such as implicational scaling and form–function analysis. However, it is not without its problems. It is not clear, for instance, to what extent it is possible to identify distinct varieties in learner language as Bickerton was able to do for Guyanese Creole. L2 acquisition involves even more rapid change than creolization, with the result that the stages of development are not sharply defined. The idea of a polylectal grammar, while attractive, may not be applicable to L2 acquisition. Also, as Preston (1989) notes, Bickerton's dismissal of variable rules may not be warranted, given that at least some creole speakers manifest a variable grammar—a point that may be even more relevant in the case of L2 learners.

Social-psychological models

Social-psychological models attempt to explain variation in language use by reference to the speakers' views about the social, institutional, and ethnic status of their own in-group, and also that of out-groups with whom they come into contact. A good example of a social-psychological model is Giles' SPEECH ACCOMMODATION THEORY.

Speech accommodation theory identifies three principal types of variation, according to the nature of the adjustments which speakers make to their speech during interaction. Convergence occurs when speakers adjust their normal speech to make it more similar to their interlocutor's speech or to a stereotype of it (i.e. the speaker converges towards some prestige norm that they believe their interlocutor values). Divergence occurs when the opposite takes place—speakers seek to make their speech dissimilar from that of their addressee. Speech maintenance occurs when speakers do not make any changes. However, Giles views this as a failure to converge (the expected type of behaviour) and therefore considers it a subtype of divergence. Both convergence and divergence can take place upwards or downwards. Upward convergence takes place when speakers adjust their speech in the direction of the speech norms of persons of higher social status. It is the most common type because it is based on the universal human desire for approval. Downward convergence involves adjustments in the direction of the speech norms of persons of lower social status. Downward divergence involves speakers emphasizing the non-standard features in their repertoire, while upward divergence involves emphasizing the standard features.

An example (based on Giles 1971) will make this clear. Let us imagine that a shop assistant who normally speaks standard English is communicating with a customer who speaks a non-standard variety. If the shop assistant adopts some of the non-prestige forms used by the customer, downward convergence takes place. If the customer adopts some of the prestige forms of the shop assistant, upward convergence takes place. This is what we might normally expect to happen. But let us now imagine that the customer is trying to return some article she bought yesterday and the shop assistant is refusing to refund her the money it cost. The shop assistant may gradually diverge upwards by emphasizing the standardness of her language, while the customer may diverge downwards by resorting to the 'vernacular' forms of her dialect.

Accommodation can take place at any level of language use—in the choice of language used in a bilingual situation, or in terms of volume, speed, pronunciation, choice of vocabulary, and grammatical structures, and also in discourse features such as length of turn and choice of topic in monolingual situations.

One of the strengths of speech accommodation theory is that it recognizes the central importance of the addressee in accounting for variation. It also makes the shifting patterns of variation which occur within a single interaction a focus of study. Speakers can switch from convergence to divergence as they reassess their addressee during the course of an interaction. One disadvantage of the model, claimed by Bell (1984), is that it rests on the concept of 'response matching', and therefore provides only a responsive dimension. Bell argues that stylistic variation also needs to take into consideration an initiative dimension (i.e. where stylistic choice is used dynamically to redefine an existing situation). Finally, speech accommodation theory cannot account for all patterned variability. Beebe (1982: 22) recognized that there is also 'extravergence' (i.e. 'variation which cannot or should not be described as converging towards or diverging from an interlocutor') and listed several kinds including the interlanguage variation that results from learning, communication, or performance strategies, and systematic variation according to the linguistic environment.

Speech accommodation theory has been used in SLA research by Beebe (1981), Beebe and Zuengler (1983), and Zuengler (1989) among others. It also underlies Tarone and Liu's (1995) study of the effect addressees have on the rate and route of L2 acquisition.

Psycholinguistic models

These concern the way in which speech is planned and monitored by speakers.

The concept of planning has been widely used in models of both first and second language production. If, as de Bot argued, 'many aspects of speaking are the same for monolingual and bilingual speakers' (1992: 2), it should be possible to make use of a general model of speech production, such as that proposed by Levelt (1989)—the model de Bot favours. LEVELT'S MODEL OF SPEECH PRODUCTION suggests a number of possible psycholinguistic sources of variability, in accordance with different stages of speech production:

1 in the 'conceptualizer', where decisions are taken regarding which variety of language to use in accordance with situational factors, and also which specific communicative intentions are to be realized in the spoken message
2 in the 'formulator', where the 'preverbal message' provided by the conceptualizer is converted into a speech plan by selecting the appropriate words from the lexicon and by applying grammatical and phonological rules
3 in the 'articulator', which converts the speech plan into actual speech
4 in the 'speech comprehension system', which provides the speaker with feedback regarding the presence of possible mistakes in the phonetic plan or in overt speech and which also enables the speaker to make adjustments in the 'conceptualizer'.

De Bot emphasized that in the Levelt model 'the different components are at work simultaneously' and 'that various parts of the same sentence will be at different processing stages' (1992: 6).

L2 variability research has focused somewhat narrowly on the effect of 'planning time' on this production process, influenced no doubt by the fact that, whereas L1 production is largely automatic, L2 production is often not, so that the amount of time a learner has to plan the different processing stages is likely to affect output. Ochs (1979), again discussing production in the L1, distinguished PLANNED and UNPLANNED DISCOURSE. The former is 'discourse that lacks forethought and organizational preparation', while the latter is 'discourse that has been thought out and organized prior to its expression' (1979: 55). The distinction constitutes a continuum. There are linguistic differences in the two types of discourse. In unplanned discourse, Ochs found that speakers rely more on the immediate context to help them convey their message, make use of syntactic structures that tend to emerge early during acquisition (for example, demonstrative modifiers, active voice, and present rather than past tenses) and make extensive use of repetition and word replacement. In Ellis (2005b), I reviewed a wide body of L2 research into the effects of planning time, distinguishing two types of planning—PRE-TASK (or STRATEGIC) PLANNING and ONLINE PLANNING. The former consists of actions a speaker/writer takes to plan the propositional content and the linguistic formulations of a message prior to actual production. The latter involves the within-task planning that takes place during production; this can be unpressured if the speaker/writer has ample time to conceptualize and formulate messages or pressured if the speaker/writer is required to plan and produce rapidly. As we will see later in this chapter, these two types of planning can have different effects on the nature of the language produced.

Speakers may MONITOR their output (i.e. pay conscious attention to specific elements of the utterance in order to correct or improve them). Morrison and Low (1983) made use of a similar production model to that of Levelt to distinguish post-articulatory monitoring, which operates on overt speech, and pre-articulatory monitoring, which occurs prior to the implementation of the phonetic plan. Levelt (1983), cited in Crookes (1991: 116), similarly distinguished a 'production theory of monitoring', according to which learners respond to 'alarm signals' during the course of implementing a plan and make appropriate adjustments, and a 'perceptual theory of monitoring', according to which users compare the final result of the production process with their original intention. Macro- and micro-monitoring can also be distinguished. The former involves adjustments to the communicative goal of discourse and sentence plans. The latter takes place as the speaker/writer begins the process of filling out constituent plans with linguistic forms and involves the substitution of one selected form with another, preferred form. Micro-monitoring can be carried out on lexis, syntax, morphology, and the phonetic realization of the utterance. Speakers are better able to carry out such monitoring when the communication event allows them plenty of time for planning online than when it requires rapid, fluent production. Kormos (1999) provides a detailed taxonomy of learner self-corrections.

The effects of planning time on L2 use have been extensively investigated in both early studies (for example, Ellis 1987b and Crookes 1989) and more recently in studies that have examined both pre-task planning (for example, Foster and Skehan 1996; Mehnert 1998) and online planning (for example, Yuan and Ellis 2003). Monitoring plays a key role in Krashen's Monitor Model (see Krashen 1981) and in a study by Hulstijn and Hulstijn (1984).

Summary and final comment

The sociolinguistic and psycholinguistic models outlined in the previous sections are summarized in Table 4.2. These models offer the L2 acquisition researcher a number of tools for investigating learner language.

The Labovian paradigm has provided an excellent means for examining stylistic variation in learner language. The dynamic paradigm has served as a basis for exploring how the learner's interlanguage develops in terms of shifting form–function relationships. Speech accommodation theory has contributed to the study of how learners vary in the way they use their L2 repertoire according to addressee factors operating in a particular interactional context. There is, however, one important caveat regarding the use of sociolinguistic models in the study of L2 acquisition, in particular the Labovian and dynamic paradigms. Sociolinguists like Labov, Bailey, and Bickerton are concerned with variability in the speech of social groups. As Preston (1989) has pointed out, such a view of language does not fit easily with the goal of SLA research, which is to describe and explain the acquisition of L2s by *individual* learners. Nor is it clear whether the notion of 'social group' is applicable to many language learners. For example, it does not seem appropriate to suggest that the L2 learners in a classroom in Spain or Japan make up a social group in the same way as street gangs in New York City do. Thus, while it may be possible to transfer the techniques used by sociolinguists such as Labov and Bickerton to the study of individual learners, there are obvious problems regarding the applicability of the 'social' explanations that sociolinguists have provided. However, current work in sociolinguistics focuses on the 'linguistic individual', in reaction to the group approach of much earlier research, and this is more clearly relevant to SLA.

Psycholinguistic models of speech production such as Levelt's enable us to recognize that whereas some variability is socially motivated some is not. In part, variability reflects the tension between the amount of effort needed to access words from the lexicon, execute a grammatical encoding, and then assign a phonological coding, and the availability of planning time. Production involves a constant trade-off of the competing demands on memory and control mechanisms. The result will be systematic differences in language use in accordance with opportunities available for pre-task and online planning and monitoring.

Romaine (2003) points out that 'variation is usually conditioned by multiple causes' (p. 431). These causes are both sociolinguistic and psycholinguistic in origin. It follows that what is needed is an approach that accounts for 'the psycholinguistic problem of variation' (Preston 2002: 141)—one that acknowledges that the distribution and selection of forms is socially motivated and also addresses the psycholinguistic mechanisms involved.

Type of model	Main constructs	Methods	Key SLA studies
Sociolinguistic: Labovian paradigm	Inter- and intra-learner variation; multiple sources of variability (e.g. linguistic and sociolinguistic); style shifting occurs as a result of varying attention to speech.	Tasks designed to elicit varying attention to speech; variable rules; logistic regression (e.g. VARBRUL) statistical models.	Dickerson 1975; Tarone 1985; Young 1996
Dynamic paradigm	Language change as a source of variability; environmental weight; lectal variation; code-switching; grammar-internal variation; free variation.	Implicational scaling; form–function analysis.	Huebner 1983, 1985; Ellis 1985c
Social-psychological paradigm	Speech shifts involving convergence and divergence; importance of addressee and of speaker's attitudes to addressee's social group.	Experimental investigation of factors that induce convergence and divergence.	Beebe 1981; Tarone and Liu (1995)
Psycholinguistic models	Levelt's (1989) model of speech production; conceptualizing, formulating, and articulating.	Experimental manipulation of pre-task and online planning conditions.	Crookes 1989; Foster and Skehan 1996; Yuan and Ellis 2003
	Macro- and micro-monitoring; pre- and post-articulation monitoring; production-based and perception-based monitoring	Experimental manipulation of conditions that affect monitoring.	Kormos (1999)

Table 4.2 Summary of different types of models used to explain variability in language production

A typology of variability in learner language

This section draws on many of the constructs that have already been introduced (and which are summarized in Table 4.2) to present a typology of the different kinds of formal variation that can be found in the use of natural languages—including learner language. The outline of the typology is shown in Figure 4.1. The typology addresses variation in choice of linguistic form. It excludes functional variation (i.e. variation in the choice of language function), which is considered in the next chapter.

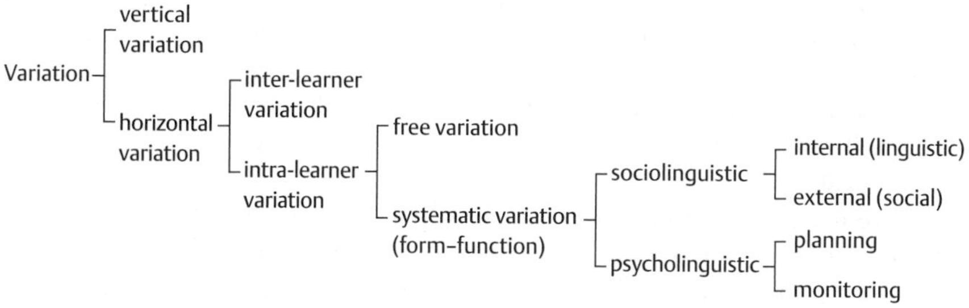

Figure 4.1 A typology of variation in the choice of linguistic form found in learner language

A basic distinction is made between HORIZONTAL and VERTICAL VARIATION. Horizontal variation refers to the variation evident in learner language at any single time, while vertical variation refers to variation over time and is, therefore, coterminous with 'order/sequence of development'. There is some evidence to suggest that horizontal variation mirrors vertical variation for, as Widdowson puts it, 'change is only the temporal consequence of current variation' (1979b: 195), a view that accords with the role of change in the dynamic paradigm.

Horizontal variation is subdivided into inter-and intra-learner variation. Inter-learner variability reflects individual learner factors such as motivation and personality, but it also arises as a result of social factors such as social class and ethnic grouping, as the Labovian paradigm has demonstrated, and also as a result of psycholinguistic factors, such as working memory. As these same social and psycholinguistic factors are also involved in intra-learner variation, there is clearly an interaction between individual learner factors such as sex, social class, and working memory and the situational factors involved in style shifting; as we noted earlier, the markers involved in stylistic variation also function as social indicators. In this chapter the focus is on intra-learner variation; Chapters 7 and 10 examine the social and psychological sources of inter-learner variation.

Intra-learner variation can take the form of either free variation or systematic variation. Free variation arises when linguistic choices occur randomly, making it impossible to predict when a learner will use one form as opposed to another. The existence of free variation in learner language is, however, controversial. Many sociolinguists consider that free variation does not exist or that it occurs for only a very short period of time and is of minor interest.[3] Gatbonton (1978) and I (Ellis 1985c, 1989c, 1999c) have, however, argued that free variation constitutes an important mechanism of development. Systematic variation occurs when it is possible to identify some factor that predisposes a learner to select one specific linguistic form over another. Systematic variation is evident in form–function analyses that demonstrate that, at any one time of development, learners' grammars reflect particular configurations of form–function mapping. That is, learners organize their linguistic systems in such a way that specific forms are used to realize specific language functions. Thus, the choice of one linguistic form in preference to another is determined by the language function the learner wishes to perform. The bulk of the research discussed in this chapter has examined systematic variability.

Systematic variation is conditioned by both sociolinguistic and psycholinguistic factors. Sociolinguistic accounts of variation (see, for example, Romaine 2003) distinguish internal and external sources. Internal variation is determined by linguistic context (i.e. the elements that precede and follow the variable structure in question) and other linguistic factors such as markedness. External variation is accounted for in terms of the social factors that are configured in different situational contexts of language use that conspire to categorically or probabilistically influence the learner's choice of linguistic forms. The situational context covers a whole host of factors. Preston (1989) offers a detailed breakdown (for example, time, topic, purpose, and tone). It is probably true to say that to date SLA research has examined only a few of these situational factors. We will consider two bodies of research that have explored sociolinguistic sources of variability—studies that have investigated style shifting and those that have investigated social-psychological aspects of variability. Psycholinguistic sources of variability include the means learners use to control their linguistic resources (i.e. planning and monitoring) under different conditions of language use. They have been investigated in terms of task-induced variability.

The goal of variationist research is to describe and account for learners' choice of linguistic forms. The assumption is made that variability in learner language is systematic (i.e. that it is possible to identify the factors that will account for why one form is preferred to another in different SOCIOLINGUISTIC and PSYCHOLINGUISTIC CONTEXTS). There remains the possibility, however, that at least some of this variability is non-systematic (i.e. learners select randomly from their linguistic repertoires). The review of the research that now follows begins by looking at free variation. A detailed examination of systematic variation in relation to first sociolinguistic and then psycholinguistic contexts follows.

Free variation in learner language

Variationists differ in their views about free variation. Labov (1971) in a discussion of the notion of 'system' in pidgins and creoles, argued that 'important and significant linguistic behaviour can be non-systematic' (p. 449) and further asserted that 'it would be meaningless to say that linguistic relations are systematic if there were not also forms of communication that were unsystematic' (p. 451). However, other variationists have been reluctant to accept the existence of free variation. Preston (1996), for example, commented 'I am suspicious that language variation which is influenced by nothing at all is a chimera' (p. 25).

Matthews (1997) defined free variation as the relation between sounds or forms which have similar or partly similar distributions but are not described as being in contrast. How then does one determine that sounds/forms are not in contrast? In Ellis (1999c), I suggested that free variation can be held to exist when two or more sounds/forms are seen to be used randomly by individuals with regard to *all* of the following:

1 the same situational context(s)
2 the same illocutionary meaning(s)
3 the same linguistic context(s)
4 the same discourse context(s)
5 the same planning conditions.

This operational definition of free variation constitutes a modified version of my earlier definition (see Ellis 1985c, 1994a), in response to criticisms by Preston (1989, 1996). This revised definition seeks to establish that the locus of the study of free variation in SLA must be the individual learner rather than a social group (in accordance with the goal of variationist research in SLA) and also that, in order to claim that free variation exists, it must be demonstrated that neither the sociolinguistic nor psycholinguistic context impacts on selection. It is of course possible that there are other significant variables not included in the above definition that influence selection but, I would argue, the default position should always be that free variation does exist unless systematicity can be demonstrated.[4]

In my earlier discussion of free-variation I gave the following example. 'J'—a 10-year-old Portuguese boy—produced the following two utterances in close proximity to each other during a game of word bingo:

No look my card.
Don't look my card.

I noted that the 'don't' negative was the single instance out of 18 spontaneous negative utterances produced during the first month of the study and was used in an identical way to the predominant 'no' + V form of this period. Subsequently, however, this learner did employ these two negative forms in a systematic way. Citing this example, Romaine (2003) comments 'it is still an open question, however, whether cases of seemingly free variation are instead the result of inadequate research methods and lack of sufficient data for analysis' (p. 411), a comment that unfortunately views systematicity as the default position.

There is, in fact, substantial evidence to support the claim that free variation in learner language is not uncommon. Cancino, Rosansky, and Schumann (1978) found that their subjects made use of a variety of forms to express negation at each stage of their development. Jorge (one of the five learners they investigated), for instance, used two forms initially ('no' + V and 'don't' + V). From the second month of the study, Jorge began to use four forms (the previous two plus an auxiliary negative and analysed 'don't'), and continued to do so for the remaining eight months of the study. Cancino *et al.* were unable to write 'rules' to account for the use of the different forms, suggesting that they were in free variation. Wagner-Gough (1975), in a longitudinal study of Homer, a Persian boy, reported that he used English simple and progressive verb forms for an identical range of functions over an extended period of time. Eisenstein, Bailey, and Madden (1982) also found that their beginner learners used these two verb forms indiscriminately, while their more advanced learners used them more systematically. Vogel and Bahns (1989) reported on the general pattern of acquisition of the two verb forms, based on data collected by Wode in his longitudinal study of the naturalistic acquisition of English by five German children. (See Wode 1981.) They also found evidence of free variation. One verb after another appeared in its inflected (–ing) form and its simple form before the learners distinguished the use of the two forms functionally. Nicholas (1986) found that his subject, Cindy—a 3-year-old learner of L2 German—rapidly acquired three first person pronoun forms ('ich', 'mich', and 'mir') but used them variably to perform the same functions. Nicholas claimed that Cindy set about diversifying her L2 system by incorporating as many features into it as possible. Huebner (1985) found that at one stage of the development of an adult Hmong learner of English, there were no functional constraints on this learner's use of 'da' (an article form)—'da' was used randomly and randomly omitted. All of these studies investigated learners' vernacular styles.

Further evidence of free variation comes from a number of later studies. Towell *et al.* (1993), for example, investigated the use of the French prepositions 'à' and 'de' in such sentences as 'Quelque chose est difficile à faire' and 'C'est difficile de faire quelque chose' by means of a grammaticality judgement test administered three times over an 18-month period. They found evidence for a variety of strategies on the part of the learners, including a free-variation strategy, where they accepted both forms in all the sentences. The researchers commented 'where a subject is seen to use different forms in a single set of sentences, it is difficult to see how this can be anything but unsystematic variation' (p. 445). This study is important because it suggests that free variation is also evident in a superordinate style (assuming that this is what a grammaticality judgement test measures, as Tarone (1983) proposed).

However, the claim that these studies provide evidence of free variation can be disputed on the grounds the researchers failed to investigate all the possible sources of systematicity listed in the above definition of free variation. In this respect, Young's (1996) study of low- and high-proficiency Czech and Slovak learners of English provides more convincing evidence. Using a VARBRUL analysis of these learners' use of 'the', Young investigated the effects of a large number of internal and external factors. He found no evidence of any form–function relation in the use of 'the' and concluded that free-variation can occur in interlanguage. However, he suggested that it arises only under specific conditions:

- the L2 form does not have a corresponding form in the L1
- the L2 form is perceptually salient
- there is no clear form–function relation between the L2 form and meaning
- free variation in the L2 form consists of initial overuse of the form
- systematic use of the form begins when the form disappears from some environments.

(Young 1996: 170)

A general finding of these studies is that free variation occurs when a new form first emerges and then disappears as learners develop better organized L2 systems. Given this, two positions are possible. The first is that this constitutes a theoretically uninteresting phenomenon because what is important is how learners build 'systems'. This is the view adopted by Schachter (1986). She considers free variation of little interest on the grounds that it occurs before the onset of the productive use of a new feature. She comments: 'Those isolated occurrences of a structure prior to onset remind me of the puts-puts of a motor just before it catches on with a roar.' For her, acquisition begins 'where the structure/form occurs across different lexical items with some (unquantified) regularity' (1986a: 127).

The alternative position is that free variation is an inherent feature of interlanguage and constitutes a significant stage in the development of linguistic competence. Gatbonton's (1978) GRADUAL DIFFUSION MODEL proposes two broad stages of L2 development: an 'acquisition phase' and a 'replacement phase'. In the former, the learner first uses one form in a variety of situations and contexts, and then introduces another form which is used in free variation with the first in all contexts. In the replacement phase, each form is restricted to its own contexts through the gradual elimination of the other in first one context and then another. Gatbonton developed this model to account for the patterns of variation which she found in the production of three phonological features (/θ/, /ð/, and /h/) in the speech of 27 French-Canadian learners of English, elicited by means of reading-aloud and spontaneous-speaking tasks. In Ellis (1999b), I extended Gatbonton's model, drawing also on Towell *et al.* (1993) to account for the elimination of free variation as learners come to use each form to perform specific functions. This extended model is discussed in Chapter 9.

Systematic variation

In accordance with the typology of variability outlined in Figure 4.1, we will now examine the factors that account for systematic variability in learner language. We will begin by looking at the research that has examined variability in terms of form–function systems. These systems can be viewed as the joint product of both sociolinguistic and psycholinguistic factors. In subsequent sections we will examine the specific sociolinguistic and psycholinguistic factors that account for variability.

Variability in form–function systems

Tarone (1988) noted that the term 'function' includes 'pragmatic function' (for example, requests and denials), 'discourse function' (for example, topic and cohesion), 'semantic function' (for example, specific and non-specific information), and even 'grammatical function' (for example, subject and object). She suggested that the study of the way learners use particular forms to express particular functions is relevant to the study of interlanguage variation because 'it provides a method of analysis which can reveal the linguistic system hidden in a learner's apparently unsystematic use' (1988: 54). We saw this in Chapter 3 when we considered FORM–FUNCTION ANALYSES of the temporal-aspect system.

A good example of the value of form–function analyses in explaining variability can be found in Schachter (1986), a study already briefly referred to. Schachter set out to re-examine the data for one of Cancino, Rosansky, and Schumann's learners (Jorge) in order to establish whether his use of negative forms was as random as the original authors suggested. She argued that the variability was not explicable in terms of different situation requirements, as the data collection took place on a regular basis with the same situational constraints throughout. However, Schachter was able to find evidence of 'a rich system, complex from the very beginning, which became even more so as time progressed' (1986: 123–4). The main basis for this claim was a form–functional analysis. Schachter identified seven functions performed by Jorge's productive negative utterances and found surprising regularity in his pairing of forms and functions. For example, the formula 'I don't know' was always used to perform the same function of 'no information' (i.e. to indicate that the speaker was not in a position to confirm or deny whether something is the case), while 'no' + V with one exception carried the 'denial' function (i.e. to assert that an actual, supposed, or proposed state of affairs did not hold for the speaker). Only 'no' by itself was functionally ubiquitous.

Even more powerful evidence of the systematic way a learner uses language to realize different functions can be found in a series of studies that investigated learners' use of English articles. Huebner's (1979, 1983) longitudinal study of Ge, also referred to earlier, showed that although Ge did not use forms to perform the same set of functions that they perform in the target language, he did nevertheless establish systematic form–function relationships. Huebner began by identifying a number of linguistic forms for analysis, one of which was Ge's use of articles ('da' and zero article). He analysed these in terms of two binary categories of semantic function:

+/– information assumed to be known by the hearer (HK)
+/– specific referent (SR)

which, when combined, yield four categories of noun phrases, as shown in Table 4.3.

Type	Standard English forms	Examples
1 - SR/+ HK	'the', 'a', or zero	Lions are beautiful.
2 + SR/+ HK	'the'	Ask the man over there.
3 + SR/- HK	'a' or zero	She gave me a present.
4 - SR/- HK	'a' or zero	He's a nice man.

Table 4.3 Noun phrase types

Initially, Ge used 'da' mainly for (2), unless the noun phrase in question functioned as a topic of the sentence, in which case he used zero article. Later he used 'da' for all four types of noun phrase. Later still, he dropped 'da' for type (4) and finally for type (3). In a subsequent paper, Huebner (1985) also showed how Ge introduced 'a' with type (3) noun phrases. Huebner's main point is that what appears to be random use of articles in an obligatory occasion analysis, turns out to be largely systematic in a form–function analysis.

The same functional analysis of the use of articles was also employed in another study (Tarone and Parrish 1988). They re-analysed data which Tarone (1985) had collected using three different tasks: (1) a grammaticality judgement test, (2) an oral interview, and (3) an oral narration task. Tarone and Parrish re-examined the data from the two oral tasks. The accuracy level of the ten Japanese and ten Arabic-speaking learners' use of articles varied according to task. Tarone and Parrish were able to show that the different tasks elicited different types of noun phrases to a different extent, and that this went a long way to explaining the overall pattern of task variation. For example, both accuracy and use of Type 2 articles was greater on the narrative than on the interview task. It was this combination that accounted for the overall difference in performance on the two tasks. The point here, however, is that the different tasks favoured the use of different noun phrase types because they required the performance of different functions involving articles. Again, this study demonstrates that the communicative function of particular forms must be taken into account if we are to understand the underlying systematicity of learner language.

Yet further evidence of systematic variation in the use of articles according to function comes from Young's (1996) study of English articles by low- and high-proficiency Czech and Slovak learners of L2 English. Young, it will be recalled, did find that the low-proficiency learners used definite articles in free variation. He also found evidence of systematic form–function mapping in the use of indefinite articles by both low- and high-proficiency learners and also in definite articles by the high-proficiency learners. His learners used indefinite articles to mark information not assumed to be known by the learner (i.e. –HK). The tendency to use indefinite articles with this function increased with proficiency. The high-proficiency learners used definite articles predominantly to mark specific and unique reference. Young's study shows not only that variability is systematic when learners' use of specific linguistic forms is subjected to a careful form–function analysis but also that the pattern of variability differs according to the proficiency level.

Other studies have investigated what is known as the DISCOURSE HYPOTHESIS. This states that speakers will systematically distinguish between foregrounded and backgrounded information when performing narratives. Hopper (1979) suggested that this distinction is a universal in narrative discourse. He claims that speakers 'mark out the main route through a narrative and divert in some way those parts of the narrative which are not strictly relevant to this route' (p. 239). Several L2 studies (for example, Godfrey 1980; Véronique 1987) showed that learners vary their use of syntactic devices according to whether information is foregrounded or backgrounded. Bardovi-Harlig (1998) analysed learners' use of verbal morphology in a cross-sectional sample of narratives. She found that, irrespective of their overall correct use of past tense, the learners used a higher proportion of past tense forms to convey foregrounded information than backgrounded information in both oral and written narratives. In contrast, progressive verb forms were preferred for backgrounded information. However, learners' choice was not entirely dependent on narrative structure. Systematicity was also evident in accordance with the lexical aspect of the verbs used (i.e. whether the verb referred to an achievement, an accomplishment, or a state). Lexical aspect is considered below as it relates to the role of linguistic context in determining variability.

What these studies show is that learners construct form–function systems in which specific linguistic forms are linked probabilistically to specific functions. Over time they revise these form–function systems with the result that the patterns of variability shift dynamically. Form–function analyses of learner language are very promising because they afford a window through which to view how learners construct their L2 systems. The following are the main conclusions that can be drawn from the research:

1 A form–function analysis can identify systematic patterns of variability where a target-based analysis has failed.

2 Learners construct form–function systems in the process of learning and using an L2. These systems are likely to differ from the form–function systems found in the target language.
3 The learner's form–function systems evolve over time. Thus at any stage of development different form–function systems are likely to be observed.
4 Learners will seek to use their linguistic resources to perform those functions that are communicatively important for accomplishing specific tasks.

Sociolinguistic accounts of L2 variability

As noted earlier, sociolinguistic accounts of variability distinguish internal variation due to linguistic factors and external variation that reflect social factors. We will consider internal and external variation in learner language separately.

Internal variation

1 Linguistic environment

The effects of the linguistic environment are evident at the phonological, morphological, and syntactic levels of language.

One of the earliest studies to investigate the effects of linguistic context on learners' production was Dickerson's (1975) study of ten Japanese learners' production of English /z/. Dickerson examined four different phonological environments and found that in a dialogue-reading task, the learners used the correct target-language form whenever /z/ was followed by a vowel, but were progressively less accurate in the other environments (+ consonants such as /m/ and /b/, + silence, and + consonants such as /θ/ and /t/). Dickerson collected data at three different points in time and found that the same pattern occurred at each. Although the learners improved in their ability to use target-language /z/ in the more difficult contexts over time, the environmental effects observed at time 1 were also evident at time 3.

The form of a word can affect the learners' use of specific grammatical features. Thus, Wolfram (1989) reported that Vietnamese learners of L2 English in the United States were more likely to manifest past tense marking on suppletive forms (for example, 'go'/'went') than on replacive forms (for example, 'make'/'made'). Wolfram suggested that this may reflect a 'principle of perceptual saliency', according to which the more distant the past tense form is phonetically from the present tense form, the more likely it is to be marked for past tense. Whereas Wolfram's study demonstrates an effect for the phonetic form of a word, Saunders' (1987) study indicates that the grammatical form is also influential. He studied Japanese learners' production of the –s morpheme in consonant clusters (–ps, –ts, and –ks) in nouns and verbs. He found that they were more likely to omit or shorten the –s in verbs than in nouns. Saunders suggests that this may be due to the 'amount of information contained in the morpheme; the third person singular is almost always redundant while the plural usually gives some information not available in the rest of the sentence' (1987: 261).

Bardovi-Harlig's (1998) study of narratives, mentioned above, shows how the inherent meaning of a word can influence learners' choice of morphological form. In addition to the Discourse Hypothesis, she investigated the ASPECT HYPOTHESIS. This claims that the distribution of interlanguage verbal morphology is determined by lexical aspectual class and draws on Vendler's (1967) classification of verb phrases into those that refer to states (for example, 'seem' and 'know'), achievements (for example, 'arrive' and 'fall asleep'), activities (for example, 'sleep' and 'study') and accomplishments (for example, 'build a house' or 'paint a picture'). Earlier research has demonstrated how lexical aspect can influence interlanguage development. For example Andersen (1991) provided evidence to show that Spanish perfective past first emerged in verb phrases expressing achievements, followed, in order, by accomplishments, activities, and states. Bardovi-Harlig set out to examine whether lexical aspect can also be shown to explain learners' variable use of verbal morphology. She found similar patterns in both oral and written narratives; past tense was used most consistently in achievements, followed by accomplishments, and then activities. Past was not used at all with states although there were very few lexical statives used by the learners. Bardovi-Harlig concluded that 'lexical aspect and narrative structure conspire to shape the distribution of tense-aspect morphology in interlanguage' (p. 501).

Bayley's (1996) study of Chinese learners of English also found evidence of a complex, additive effect of two distinct factors—a variable phonological process (–t/d deletion) and a variable grammatical process (past tense marking). In this case, both factors related to linguistic environment. The learners were less likely to delete –t/d following a liquid than an obstruent or nasal, as were native speakers in this study. However, unlike native speakers, the preceding phonological environment had no effect. The learners also differed from native speakers with regard to the effects of grammatical category: –t/d deletion was more likely in monomorphemes such as 'mist' than in past tense verbs such as 'missed'. Interestingly, however, the grammatical effect was a variable one. Whereas semi-weak verbs (for example, 'left') were subject to both the grammatical and phonological process, past tense marking of strong verbs ('talked') was affected only by the grammatical process. Bayley concluded that 'Chinese-English interlanguage diverges from native-speaker English when competing rules are involved' and that, in such cases, 'even highly proficient learners, who mark most underlying inflectional forms, are unlikely to perform like native speakers' (p. 116).

The above studies examined phonological and morphological features. Linguistic context also affects the choice of syntactic features. Hyltenstam (1977) showed that two environmental factors had an effect on where learners of L2 Swedish placed the negator; whether the negative clause was a main or subordinate clause and whether the finite verb was an auxiliary or a lexical verb. Using implicational scaling he showed that the learners went through several stages of development, mastering the placement of the negative in first one environment and then another. This study, then, also indicates that the acquisition of syntactic forms proceeds from one context to another.

The relationship between linguistic context and acquisition over time is of considerable importance for SLA. One possibility is that learners begin with a single feature which they use in all environments (i.e. initially learners display categorical use of a language form), then manifest free variation as they acquire new variants for the form before progressing to a stage when they distribute the variants systematically according to context. Dickerson's study, however, found no support for this. Systematic variation was evident at time 1 in her study, although it should be noted that her subjects were not complete beginners. However, Gatbonton's (1978) study of English /θ/, /ð/, and /h/ in the speech of 27 French-Canadians does support a diffusion model. (See the discussion on page 137.) Gatbonton obtained independent measures of the subjects' proficiency and found that in the least proficient (those in the 'acquisition stage') a single variant or free variation was evident, whereas in the more proficient (those in the 'replacement phase') systematic variation in accordance with linguistic context occurred. However, as Tarone (1988) points out, Gatbonton's study is cross-sectional in design and thus does not constitute totally convincing evidence for acquisition as a process of gradual diffusion.

There have been some longitudinal studies. In Ellis 1988a, I investigated the effects of linguistic context on two morphological features (third person –s and copula –s) in the English speech of three classroom learners (one Portuguese and two Punjabi-speaking) over a two-year period. For purposes of space, only results for copula –s (which is a variable form in native speaker use) will be considered here. The main findings were:

1 Three variants of copula –s were identified (zero, full, and contracted).
2 These variants emerged in the same order for all three learners. The learners first used the zero form, then the full form, and finally the contracted copula.
3 The target-language variants (full and contracted copula) were used more consistently when the preceding subject was a pronoun than when the preceding subject was a noun. Conversely, the non-target-language variant (zero copula) occurred more frequently when the subject was a noun.
4 Some pronoun environments also favoured the use of the target-language variants more than others.
5 The acquisition of the target-language variants took place initially in 'easy' environments (i.e. those involving a closed class of items), and then appeared to spread to more 'difficult' environments. (i.e. those involving an open class).

6 None of the learners achieved the pattern of variability for copula use which has been reported for native-speaker speech (i.e. they did not acquire the target-language variable rule).

This study, therefore, suggests that the acquisition of target-language forms may be closely linked to their use in specific linguistic environments.

There have been several other studies that have investigated linguistic context (for example, Carlisle 1991; Bailey 1989; Véronique 1987; Regan 1996; Hansen 2001; Zielonka 2005), providing conclusive evidence that it plays a major role in determining the process by which phonological, morphological, and syntactic features are acquired. A number of issues remain unclear, however. First, it is still not certain what the learner's starting point is. Is it categorical use of a single form followed by free variation, as Gatbonton and I propose? Or do learners begin with the systematic use of two or more variants in accordance with linguistic context, a view Dickerson and Tarone favour? Secondly, it is not clear to what extent the idea of systematic 'diffusion' is applicable to all learners. Meisel, Clahsen, and Pienemann argue that 'learners differ greatly with respect to which context is most suitable for the application of a new rule' (1981: 126). But several studies (such as Carlisle's study of EPENTHESIS in initial consonant clusters) have shown that at least some of the effects of linguistic context hold across learners.

2 *Other sources of internal variability*

Romaine (2003), in her review of variation in L2 acquisition, considered two other sources of internal variability—MARKEDNESS and L1 TRANSFER. As both of these are considered in detail in later chapters (see Chapter 8 for language transfer and Chapter 12 for markedness), these sources will be treated only briefly here.

A feature can be considered 'unmarked' if it is, in some sense, natural, easy, and universal. Conversely, a feature is 'marked' if it is unnatural (or less natural), difficult, and its occurrence in the world's language is more restricted. Thus, closed syllables are marked in relation to open syllables because they are more difficult to pronounce and learn (see Chapter 3) and because they figure less frequently in the world's languages. It is important to note that markedness effects, such as consonant simplification in closed syllables, are evident in both L1 and L2 language use.

Markedness can help to explain why some linguistic contexts favour the target form and others do not. Major's (1996b) study of four adult speakers of Brazilian Portuguese learning English in an instructional setting provides clear evidence of markedness effects in initial and final consonant cluster simplification. One example will have to suffice. Major noted that there is a universal tendency for final stops in consonant clusters to be devoiced more consistently than final fricatives—that is, it is easier to maintain voicing for fricatives than for stops. Thus, for example, the final cluster in 'rigged' can be considered marked in comparison to the final cluster in 'rigs'. Major found that the learners were indeed more likely to devoice final stops than fricatives in such contexts. He concluded that 'interlanguage phonology behaves in a similar fashion to adult natural language phonology in terms of universal hierarchical relationships involving markedness' (p. 92).

However, markedness cannot provide a complete explanation of the patterns of variability in learner language. In some cases a more marked feature will be performed more accurately than a less marked one if the marked feature is present in the L1. In Major's study, the learners performed initial consonant clusters with a fricative and a stop (for example, 'spy') more accurately than initial consonant clusters consisting of a fricative and a liquid (for example, 'slap') even though the latter is unmarked. This can be explained by transfer. In Portuguese fricative + stop clusters occur in running speech whereas fricative + liquid clusters do not. Major concluded that 'the specifics of Portuguese phonology in some cases mediate a markedness relationship' (p. 92).

Summary and final comment

It is clear that systematic internal variation is a common phenomenon in learner language. Linguistic context, discourse context, markedness and L1 transfer also influence the extent to which one form is preferred over another. Which of these sources of internal variation is primary is not clear. For example, Kumpf (1984) suggested that the variable use of past tense forms is influenced primarily by whether the information is foregrounded or backgrounded, whereas Wolfram (1985) claimed that the main factor is linguistic context. It may not be useful to look for single causes; internal variability can have more than one source.

Many of the studies reported above did not exclusively examine the effects of linguistic factors but rather investigated sociocultural factors as well, using VARBRUL. The results of these multi-factor studies will be considered later. First we will consider external variation.

External variation

External variation arises as a result of the constraints exerted by situational and social factors on learners' choice of linguistic forms. The basis for many of the studies considered in this section, is Labov's notion of style shifting. Other studies have examined variability from a social-psychological perspective and in relation to social networks.

1 Style shifting

Tarone (1982) suggested that L2 learners possess a continuum of styles, ranging from the SUPERORDINATE (or CAREFUL) to the VERNACULAR. The former reflects the kind of language found in formal situations that require careful language use, while the latter is evident in informal situations that permit more spontaneous language use. Each style has its own linguistic norms. Learners style shift between the two styles in accordance with the demands of the situation. Tarone argued that both the superordinate and vernacular norms constitute part of the learners' overall language competence or, as she later called it, their CAPABILITY (Tarone 1983).

To study STYLE SHIFTING, Tarone adapted Labov's methodology. She accepted that the psycholinguistic mechanism responsible for style shifting is attention to speech and suggested that different styles can be elicited using tasks that require different degrees of attention to speech. Figure 4.2 demonstrates the relationships between task, attention, and style that Tarone recognized. Thus, to examine learners' vernacular style it is necessary to collect 'unattended speech data', while to investigate their careful style, data from grammaticality judgement tasks can be used. Various other kinds of task elicit intermediate styles.

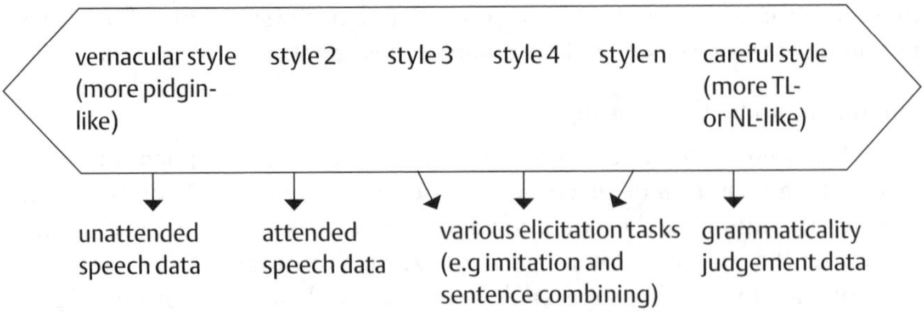

Figure 4.2 Style shifting in learner language (from Tarone 1983)

A number of studies have used this methodological framework for investigating variability. For example, Dickerson (1975), in the study already referred to, used three different tasks to elicit data and found that the use of the target-language variant of /z/ was used least frequently in free speech, and most consistently when her subjects were reading word lists aloud; performance on a task that required learners to read dialogues aloud was intermediate. The learners increased their use of the target-language variant over time, but manifested the same order of accuracy in the three tasks on each occasion. Dickerson also found that her subjects were more likely to use those non-target-language variants that were closest to the target-language variant in tasks that allowed them to attend more closely to their speech.

However, learners do not always manifest the target-language variant more in careful language use. Sometimes they transfer forms from their L1, particularly if these forms have prestige value in their speech community. Beebe (1980) found that her subjects (adult Thai learners of English) produced fewer instances of the target sound, /r/, in formal language use than in informal language use. This was because they used a prestige Thai variant of /r/, which they associated with formal language use in their own language. Beebe's study and similar studies by Schmidt (1977) and Major (1987) provided evidence of the complex nature of style shifting in learner language. They showed that the careful style may not always be the most target-like. To accommodate this,

Tarone (1983) revised her view of the careful style to allow for use of either a target-language or L1 variant. It is this view that is reflected in Figure 4.2.

A later study by Tarone (1985) also testifies to the complexity of style shifting. She investigated three grammatical morphemes (third person –s, the article, plural –s) and one grammatical structure (direct object pronouns) using data collected from three tasks. In the case of third person –s, the results demonstrated the expected pattern of style shifting. That is, the learners were most accurate in the test and least accurate in the oral narrative. However, the pattern was reversed for the article and direct object pronouns—the learners were most accurate in the task that had been designed to require the least attention to form. Tarone attempted to explain these results by suggesting that the narrative task led the learners to attend to discourse cohesiveness to a greater extent than the other two tasks, the article and object pronouns serving as important markers of discourse cohesiveness. In other words, the functional demands of the task imposed unexpected demands on the learner's attention. It was this that led Tarone and Parrish (1988) to investigate form–function relations in the use of the article. (See the discussion earlier in this chapter.)

Style shifting does not always arise, as shown by Sato's (1985) study of a 12-year-old Vietnamese boy's acquisition of English. Sato collected data over a ten-month period using three different tasks (free conversation, oral reading of a continuous text, and elicited imitation of words and short phrases). She looked at target final consonants and consonant clusters. The accuracy rankings of the first of these on the three tasks changed from one time to the next. Greater consistency was evident for the second feature. Sato concluded that not all variables yield the same pattern of variation.

Sato's findings should not be considered inconsistent with those of Tarone or, indeed, Labov. Both Tarone and Labov have made it clear that not all linguistic features function as markers and, therefore, not all will style shift. (See definitions of INDICATORS, MARKERS, and STEREOTYPES in the Glossary.) In the case of Labov's work, it is possible to predict which features are likely to style shift on the basis of whether they display sensitivity to social factors (i.e. also function as indicators). However, social factors may not affect many L2 learners (for example, foreign language learners in a classroom setting). This raises the important question as to why some L2 features style shift and others do not. Sato suggested that one factor might be linguistic difficulty. Features that are particularly difficult may not be subject to much variation for the simple reason that learners cannot alter their performance whatever the task.

More recent studies have included 'style' as one of the factors investigated in multi-factorial studies. Bayley (1996) found that the –t/d variable in consonant clusters was sensitive to speech style in the language produced by 20 native Mandarin learners of English who had lived in the United States for varying lengths of time. The learners were less likely to delete final –t/d in their careful style (i.e. when reading aloud) than in their casual style (i.e. in informal conversation). This effect was found for both the low- and high-proficiency learners. Regan investigated the effects of style in 'ne' deletion in the negative constructions of seven advanced learners of L2 French. This study is of special interest as, unlike most variability studies, it was longitudinal, involving data collected before the learners spent time in France and after. At time 1 the learners deleted 'ne' more in their casual style than in their careful style. This reflected their explicit knowledge of the rule for 'ne' deletion (i.e. 'when you are being formal in French you retain "ne"; in casual speech you delete it'). Interestingly, however, style made less of a difference at time 2 (one year later). This was because the learners now deleted it more regularly in their careful style. Regan suggested that this may have occurred because the learners realized 'it is good and native-like to delete "ne"' and extended this to monitored speech. By time 2, in fact, the learners' deletion rates were very close to those of native speakers. Berdan (1996) also investigated the effects of style alongside a number of other factors on one of Cancino *et al.*'s learners (Alberto). Berdan's aim was to challenge Schumann's claim that Alberto showed no development in his use of 'don't' as a negative marker over the period of study (40 weeks) by using sociolinguistic methods of analysis. He found no main effect for style but there was a significant interaction between style and time. Initially, Alberto did not differentiate in his use of 'don't' in conversation and elicited speech but by the end of the data collection he did, manifesting much more frequent use in elicited speech than in conversation.

All of these studies point to an effect for style on learners' choice of forms. They provide evidence of both CHANGE FROM ABOVE (i.e. change associated with a socially prestigious feature that speakers are aware of) and CHANGE FROM BELOW (i.e. change associated with a non-prestigious feature that occurs below the level of conscious awareness). (See Preston 1989: 243.) In the case of formal target-language features (for example, –t/d suppliance in consonant clusters and 'don't' in negative constructions), suppliance is greater in the careful than casual style. But in the case of an informal target-language feature ('ne' deletion) suppliance is greater in the casual style and spreads later to the careful style. Berdan's study also suggests that learners need to have achieved some level of proficiency in the L2 before style shifting kicks in—a finding that echoes Sato's claim that 'difficult' features are immune to style shifting.

These studies—and others—indicate that style shifting is influenced by a number of different factors (for example, the learner's L1, the learner's stage of development, and the difficulty of the target-language feature). Although the studies were informed by a sociolinguistic model designed to account for how situational factors affect language use, they have not shed much light on the relationship between the situational context and learners' use of the L2. This is because the nature of the link between attention and social factors—the primary causative variables—is particularly unclear in the case of L2 learners. SLA researchers have ignored what is central to the Labovian model, namely social organization. As a result, in SLA, the STYLISTIC CONTINUUM is perhaps more of a psycholinguistic construct than a sociolinguistic one. Tarone (1988), in fact, treats L2 models based on Labov as exemplars of 'psychological processing theories'. This is understandable given the problematicity of applying the concept of 'social group' to many L2 learners.

2 *Social-psychological influences*

Other studies of external variation have taken place within a social-psychological framework, and these have proven more illuminative of the relationship between social/situational factors and L2 use in so far as they have examined what social factors activate psycholinguistic factors such as attention. Studies by Beebe (1977) and Beebe and Zuengler (1983) demonstrate that learners are sensitive to their interlocutor. The subjects (adults in the first study and children in the second) were Chinese-Thai bilinguals who were interviewed twice on the same topics, once by a Chinese interviewer and once by a Thai. Both interviewers, however, were fluent in Thai. The bilinguals adapted their speech to their interlocutor by using more Thai phonological variants with the Thai interviewer and more Chinese variants with the Chinese interviewer. Beebe and Zuengler (1983) also reported a similar study involving Puerto Rican learners of English in New York, who were interviewed in English by a monolingual native English speaker, an English-dominant Hispanic, and a Spanish-dominant Hispanic. They found that the learners used more dependent clauses with the monolingual English speaker than with the English-dominant Hispanic. They suggested that learners have difficulty in identifying with members of their own ethnic group when speaking in the L2 and, therefore, do not converge. This idea receives some support from Takahashi's (1989) study of the effects of Japanese and non-Japanese listeners on the speech patterns of Japanese speakers of L2 English. She found that the learners became more hesitant and briefer when addressing a listener with the same native language background, and also were less prepared to negotiate any communication problem. They also reported feeling more uncomfortable.[5] Dowd, Zuengler, and Berkowitz (1990) reviewed the L2 research that has investigated 'social marking' by learners and concluded that it can occur even during the early stages of learning, despite the learners' obvious limitations in repertoire, and that learners seem to be aware of specific linguistic features that 'stereotype' native speakers of a language.

All these studies point to the influence the learners' addressees have on their selection of forms. A study by Tarone and Liu (1995) provides further evidence of addressee-induced variation. They reported a 26-month case study of a 5-year-old Chinese boy named 'Bob' learning English in Australia in four interactional contexts involving three different interlocutors—teachers, peers, and a researcher (who was a familiar adult). Clear differences according to addressee were found. For example, Bob produced more complex structures when interacting with the researcher than with peers. Also, he initiated far fewer utterances with the teacher than with his peers or the researcher. This study is of particular interest because it suggests that the different interactions

Bob engaged in influenced not only his choice of linguistic forms but also the rate and route of his development. The general pattern for the emergence of new structures was researcher → peers → teacher. Tarone and Liu also reported that Bob did not follow the universal route of development for interrogatives. They explained this by suggesting that the intensive interactions with the researcher provided a context in which Bob was able to acquire later stage forms before some of the earlier stage forms. They comment 'social demands can be so strong that they can cause alteration in internal psychologically motivated sequences of acquisition' (p. 122).

Learners also seem to be aware of their own identity as learners and, at times, to exploit it. Rampton (1987) noted that intermediate learners of L2 English sometimes resorted to 'me no' constructions (for example, 'me too clever' and 'me no do it'), even though they clearly possessed the competence to produce target-like utterances. He suggested that the learners used this primitive negative construction as a means of IMPRESSION MANAGEMENT—to tone down the force of their speech acts by drawing attention to their insignificant status as learners. Once again, then, we see the importance of a form–function analysis. Selinker and Douglas (1985) found that a Polish learner of L2 English varied markedly on a number of linguistic features according to whether the 'discourse domain' concerned an everyday topic (telling your life-story) or a specialized, technical topic (critical path schedules). Zuengler (1989) also referred to evidence that shows that the attitude learners have towards a topic—whether they see themselves as experts or non-experts on it relative to their native-speaker interlocutors—will affect their language behaviour, making them more or less likely to interrupt, for example.

Social-psychological factors are also evident in the relationship between gender and variability in language use. Female speakers have been shown to make more frequent use of prestigious or standard forms than male speakers. Trudgill (1983: 208) described this as 'the single most consistent finding to emerge from sociolinguistic studies'. Broeders (1982) found that female learners were more favourably disposed towards 'Received Pronunciation' (the prestigious British accent) than males. Adamson and Regan (1991) reported that their learners, Cambodian immigrants in the United States, used the prestigious form of the –ing suffix more frequently than male speakers. Lin (2003) investigated the use of two consonant simplification strategies, epenthesis, and deletion (see Chapter 3) by female and male L2 learners of English. Overall, the females used simplification strategies less than the males, although the difference was not statistically significant. However, when the comparison was made in terms of an epenthesis/deletion ratio, the difference was significant: females were more likely to prefer epenthesis over deletion than males. Interestingly, this study also found a gender effect for interlocutor differences. The males did not differ in their epenthesis/deletion ratio when talking to a non-native-speaking peer or a native speaker. In contrast, the females accommodated more fully to the speech of their addressees.

3 Social networks

Another approach to investigating external variability is in terms of the influence exerted by a speaker's SOCIAL NETWORK. Milroy (1980) developed an approach to investigating linguistic variability that involved examining the social networks that individuals were members of. She distinguished social networks in terms of whether they were 'dense' (i.e. where all the individual members know each other), 'diffuse' (i.e. where the individuals are not known to each other), 'multiplex' (i.e. where the relationships among individuals are complex, involving a number of different social institutions such as family and workplace) and 'simplex' (i.e. where relationships are governed by a single role). Milroy developed a way of measuring the strength of a network and then examined the relationship between network scores and linguistic variables as these were used in the speech of individuals. Her study of Belfast working-class communities showed that change came about because of unstable conditions which led to disruptions in an individual's social network.

Work in SLA based on Milroy's theory has focused on macro-linguistic choices involving bilingual communities rather than the micro-linguistic choices of individual learners. In this respect, it differs from the research based on the style shifting and social-psychological models. A good example of the application of Milroy's theory can be found in a study by Raschka, Wei, and Lee (2002). They examined L1 maintenance in a Chinese community in Tyneside in the United Kingdom. They used participant observation, semi-structured interviews, and questionnaires to collect social and linguistic data. On this basis the primary networks of the children in the Chinese families were established. The main finding was the social networks of the children had changed as they grew older. Not surprisingly, in their early years their social network comprised their immediate family, and this resulted in a high level of exposure to Chinese. Later, peer networks became more influential and 'social-group pressure from within these peer-oriented networks encourages accommodation and conformity to the group norms to the extent that the dominant peer language (English or mixed code) increasingly becomes the preferred medium' (p. 23). The result was a 'struggle' between the family's desire to maintain Chinese and the children's increasing desire to conform to their peer networks.

Summary and final comment

It is clear that learners, like native speakers, are influenced by situational factors and, in particular, by their addressee and their social networks. Learners exploit their linguistic resources in order to behave in sociolinguistically appropriate ways. Sometimes this results in more target-like behaviour and sometimes in less, depending on who their addressee is, the particular language functions they wish to perform, the topic of the discourse, their perceptions of their own expertise on a subject', and their gender. The extent to which their social networks support the use of the L2 or of their mother tongue will exert a powerful influence on both the learning of the L2 and L2 maintenance. In general, however, the research to date has relied on the concept of 'style' and has been disappointing in its failure to tease out the contributions that different situational factors make to overall variation in learner language.

The question arises as to what the relative effects of internal and external constraints are on patterns of variability. Preston (1996) is adamant that it is linguistic factors that play the major role. Reviewing a number of variability studies he concluded 'the most important influencing factors on the variability of interlanguage performance are linguistic ones' (p. 38), while in a later article (Preston 2002: 146) he commented 'linguistic influences are nearly always probabilistically heavier than sociocultural influences'.

Psycholinguistic accounts of L2 variability

Psycholinguistic sources of variability have been investigated in a number of ways. As we saw in the discussion of style shifting, a number of studies have found differences in learners' production according to the nature of the task they were asked to perform and have inferred from this that 'attention' is a key factor. Other studies have investigated the role of pre-task and online planning on the FLUENCY, COMPLEXITY, and ACCURACY of learners' productions. These will only be considered briefly here as they are examined in greater depth in Chapter 10. Finally, a few studies have examined the role of monitoring.

Task-based variation

Learners' performance varies according to task. Larsen-Freeman (1976b) used five different tasks—speaking, listening, reading, writing, and elicited imitation—in her study of grammatical morphemes. She found different accuracy orders, in particular between those tasks involving speaking of some kind and the reading/writing tasks. (See Chapter 3.) LoCoco's (1976) error analysis study also found that the number of errors made by adult elementary learners of L2 Spanish varied according to task. For example, preposition errors were more common and adjective and determiner errors less common in the translation task than in the free composition and picture description tasks. LoCoco suggested that the learners' perception of the task might be one factor influencing the results. Thus, the learners might have focused on accuracy in the translation task and on expressing ideas clearly in the picture description task.

One of the key factors, then, is whether learners are focused on meaning or form. Bahns and Wode (1980) reported differences in two German children's use of English negative constructions in naturally occurring speech and structured interviews (which involved translation). They found evidence of clear form–function distributions for 'don't' and 'didn't' in the spontaneous data but not in the elicited data. Hulstijn and Hulstijn (1984) investigated the effects of time pressure, focus of attention (i.e. whether on information or on linguistic form), and METALINGUAL KNOWLEDGE on the accuracy with which two Dutch word order rules (inversion and verb-end) were performed in a story-retelling task in L2 Dutch. These rules operate in very similar ways to the same rules in L2 German. (See Chapter 3 for a description.) The results indicated that neither time pressure nor metalingual knowledge by themselves had any effect, but that focusing attention on form increased accuracy in both structures. It should be noted, however, that the time factor did influence two other aspects of the learners' performance: response duration and speech rate.

The effects of planning

The effects of planning on L2 production have been investigated within the framework of information processing models according to which learners' limited processing capacity (especially in the case of low L2 proficiency) makes it difficult for them to attend to form and meaning at the same time and thus obliges them to make decisions about how to allocate their attentional resources by prioritizing one aspect of language over others. Skehan (1996) has distinguished three aspects of linguistic performance: fluency 'concerns the learner's capacity to produce language in real time without undue pausing or hesitation'; complexity 'concerns the elaboration or ambition of the language that is produced' and reflects learners' preparedness to take risks; accuracy 'concerns the extent to which the language produced conforms to target language norms' (p. 22). Skehan argued that there are two types of knowledge—lexicalized and rule-based—and that learners draw differentially on these two types of knowledge depending on the conditions of production. If the task conditions call for fluency, then learners will draw on their lexicalized knowledge. Other conditions (in particular planning) will enable learners to draw on their rule-based knowledge with the result that complexity/accuracy is enhanced. A series of studies that have investigated the effects of pre-task planning (i.e. the planning that learners do before they start the task) and online planning (i.e. the planning they do while they are performing the task) demonstrate that both kinds of planning can have an effect on all three aspects. Pre-task planning typically facilitates fluency and complexity (and sometimes accuracy) whereas online planning facilitates accuracy. Skehan's DUAL-MODE SYSTEM is considered in Chapter 9 while a detailed account of studies that have investigated planning in task-based performance is available in Chapter 10.

Monitoring

Kormos (1999, 2000) points out that the role of attention in monitoring is a neglected area of investigation even though there has been a substantial body of research that has studied learner self-corrections. We will consider two studies here.

Schmidt (1980) investigated second-verb ellipsis in sentences like 'Mary is eating an apple and Sue a pear'. He found that learners from a variety of language backgrounds always included the second verb in free oral production where the focus was predominantly on meaning; however, they increasingly omitted it in proportion to the degree of monitoring that different tasks (imitation, written sentence-combining, and grammaticality judgements) were hypothesized to permit.

Kormos (2000) reported a study of 30 Hungarian learners of English, made up of 10 intermediate learners, 10 upper-intermediate and 10 advanced. There was also a group of 10 native speakers of Hungarian. The participants completed a role-playing task followed by a retrospective interview. The analysis was based on a psycholinguistic system of classification of self-repairs, which distinguished four major groups: (1) different-information repairs (i.e. the speaker decides to encode different information than he/she is currently formulating; (2) appropriacy repairs (i.e. the speaker decides to encode the original information but in a modified way; (3) error repairs (i.e. the speaker repairs an accidental lapse); and (4) rephrasing repairs (i.e. the form of the speaker's original message is revised without changing the content). Kormos reported that error repairs were the most frequent with the learners attending equally to lexical and grammatical errors. High-proficiency learners attended more to appropriacy than low-proficiency learners. There were differences between the L2 learners and native speakers. The L2 learners monitored more (not surprisingly as they made more errors) and focused on correcting linguistic errors, whereas the native speakers focused more on correcting the informational content. The native speakers also corrected a higher proportion of their lexical errors than the learners. In explaining these results, Kormos argued that high-proficiency learners were able to focus more on appropriacy because they had extra attention available to address this aspect of message formulation. He also suggested that the correction rate of errors reflected not just the learners' capacity to monitor but also their conscious decisions about the worthwhileness of monitoring in specific linguistic contexts.

Summary and final comment

It is clear that both the nature of the task that learners are asked to perform and the conditions under which they perform it have systematic effects on the language produced. Some tasks predispose learners to focus their attention on meaning whereas other tasks lead to a focus on form. When learners are focused on form they are likely to produce more target-language variants. Pre-task planning leads to more fluent and more complex but not necessarily more accurate language. Online planning is what appears to be important for accuracy. Monitoring also induces variability, with the learners' proficiency determining the specific aspect of their production they choose to repair.

A full account of variability in learner language must consider psycholinguistic sources. The key mechanism is 'attention'. This underlies the variability resulting from performing different tasks, planning, and monitoring. Attention is a key construct in cognitive theories of L2 acquisition and is considered further in Chapter 9.

A multi-factor approach

Young and Bayley (1996) identified two key principles in the study of learner variation: (1) the principle of quantitative modelling, which states that interlanguage variation can be modelled quantitatively by examining the forms that linguistic variables take and the contextual features that influence their selection, and (2) the principle of multiple causes, which states that to explain a given pattern of variability it is necessary to examine a number of different sources. In the preceding sections we followed the principle of quantitative modelling in considering a number of sociolinguistic factors—form–function relationships, linguistic context, markedness, the learner's L1, audience design, learner identity—and psycholinguistic factors—attention, planning, and monitoring—that contribute to systematic internal and external variability in learner language. However, we considered each of these factors in isolation and therefore could not consider the differential contribution of particular factors or how they interact. Clearly, though, to account for the complexity and multidimensionality of learner language, such a multi-factor approach is needed. The tool that has been increasingly used in such approach is a statistical procedure known as VARBRUL.

VARBRUL is a form of logistic regression. It identifies which out of a set of independent variables predict a dependent variable. The independent variables are possible constraints on the choice of the form of the dependent variable—in others words, function, linguistic context, style, planning, etc. The dependent variable is a variable linguistic form with two or more values—typically a phonological or morphological feature where it is possible to identify values that are unambiguous (for example, either zero or –s for the English plural morpheme). In order to run a VARBRUL analysis a large number of tokens of the variable linguistic form are needed. Young and Bayley (1996) provide a detailed account of the use of VARBRUL.

A good example of a multi-factor approach using VARBRUL is Young's (1988a, 1991) study of one linguistic variable—plural –s on English nouns—in the speech of twelve Chinese learners. The learners were interviewed in English twice, once by a native English speaker and the second time by a fellow Chinese speaker. Data relating to four general factors were obtained: (1) the context of the situation (in particular the extent to which each learner converged with the interviewers in terms of general social factors such as ethnicity, sex, education, and occupation), (2) the subjects' proficiency in English (whether 'high' or 'low'), (3) the linguistic context (whether the plural nouns were definite or animate, the syntactic function of the noun phrase, and the phonological environment), and (4) redundancy in plural marking (whether plural –s was omitted because plurality was indicated by some other linguistic device such as a numeral or verb-subject agreement).

Young reports that the learners marked 65 per cent of nouns correctly for plural –s. Using VARBRUL, Young was able to calculate the effect that each factor had on the learners' use of plural –s. Table 4.3 summarizes the main results. As predicted, Young found that all four general factors accounted for the variability present in the data. One of the most interesting findings was that different factors influenced the performance of low- and high-proficiency learners. Thus, for instance, the phonological environment of –s had a significant impact on variation only during the early stages of acquisition, while social convergence with an interlocutor had a significant effect only during the later stages. Another interesting discovery was that the presence of some other marker of plurality (for example, a numeral) seemed to trigger –s. One reason for this was that the learners, particularly those of low proficiency, made frequent use of a closed set of 'measure expressions' (for example, numeral + years, days, hours, dollars). These expressions were formula-like; the nouns in them were more or less invariably marked with –s.

Adamson and Regan (1991) investigated the acquisition of variable –ing, which occurs in a number of English grammatical structures including tenses, participles, and nouns and has two phonetic forms, [ɪn] and [ɪŋ], the latter constituting the prestige target-language variant. Hypothesizing that the learners would begin with [ɪŋ] as a result of transfer from their L1, Adamson and Regan investigated the factors that contributed to the appearance of the non-prestige [ɪn], arguing that this would signal the learners' integration into the local speech community. Data were collected using interviews designed to control for shifts of formality. The results showed that the learners' sex, the opportunity to monitor production by attending to speech, and the grammatical category of –ing all had a significant effect on the variant used. Thus, males favoured the non-standard [ɪn] to a greater extent than females and, when monitoring, were more likely to use it. The authors suggest that this reflected the males' desire to match male native-speaker norms.

Other multi-factor studies are Bayley (1996), Young (1996), Regan (1996), Berdan (1996), and Lin (2003). They produce conclusive evidence that variation is conditioned by multiple causes. They also support Preston's claim that the primary source of variation is linguistic rather than social. However, these studies have generally examined only sociolinguistic variation and have not also examined psycholinguistic sources of variation (for example, the effect of pre-task and online planning). Ideally, multi-factor studies need to consider both types of variation.

Summary

The research reported in the previous sections has focused on variability in linguistic form (i.e. the starting point has been a specific linguistic form or forms) in the output of individual learners. In accordance with the overall goal of this section of the book, the main aim has been to describe rather than to explain the variability. For this reason, there has been no in-depth discussion of theories of L2 acquisition based on variability. These are considered

Factor	Low proficiency	High proficiency	Combined proficiency
1 Social convergence with an interlocutor	–	+	+
2 Definiteness	–	–	–
3 Animacy	+	+	–
4 Position of noun within noun phrase	+	+	+
5 Syntactic function of noun phrase	+	+	+
6 Phonological context (preceding segment)	+	–	+
7 Phonological context (following segment)	–	–	+
8 –s marked irrespective of existence of other + markers of plurality in noun phrase	+	+	+
9 Noun-verb concord	–	–	–

+ = factor accounts significantly for observed variability

– = factor does not account significantly for observed variability

Table 4.3 The contribution of different factors to the variable production of plural –s (simplified from Young 1988a: 293)

in Chapter 9. The main characteristics of learner language variability are summarized below.

First, somewhat controversially, a number of researchers have claimed to have observed instances of free variation (i.e. the unsystematic use of two or more forms). In most cases evidence for this kind of variability is only found in the rich data available in longitudinal case studies of individual learners. It appears to be most common in the early stages of development and may rapidly disappear. It has been suggested that learners go through an 'acquisition phase', involving free variation as new features are acquired, and then a 'replacement' phase, during which variability becomes systematic as the learner sorts out when to use the new features. This is reflected in the commonly observed S-curve of development (slow–quick–slow) noted in studies based on the dynamic paradigm.

Researchers do agree that much of the variability found in learner language is systematic. Systematic variation can arise as a result of both sociolinguistic and psycholinguistic sources. Sociolinguistic variation arises as a result of internal and external constraints on the selection of linguistic forms. Form–function analyses have shown that what appears to be unsystematic may in fact be systematic. A number of studies—again mainly longitudinal—indicate that learners construct form–function networks in which individual forms are used to perform specific functions. These networks may not be target-like, and they evolve over time. Linguistic context has been shown to have an effect on phonological, morphological, and syntactic features. Some environments favour target-language variants, while others favour interlanguage variants, suggesting that learners find it easier to use the target-language form in particular environments to begin with. As they progress, so they master the use of the form in the more difficult environments. Other internal factors are linguistic markedness and the learner's L1. External variation arises as a result of social factors. A number of studies have demonstrated that style shifting occurs in learner performance, but, as has now become clear, learners do not always use the target-language variant in tasks requiring formal language use and interlanguage variants in tasks requiring informal language use. The learners' stage of development, their L1, and the linguistic feature under study all influence whether and in what direction style shifting occurs. More promising is the research that indicates that learners are sensitive to both their audience and the discourse topic, but to date the research in these areas has been limited. Other studies have examined psycholinguistic sources of variation, such as the focus of learners' attention (on form or meaning), planning, and monitoring. These show that accuracy is enhanced when learners are attending to form and when they have an opportunity for online planning. Pre-task planning facilitates fluency and complexity of language use but not necessarily accuracy. Whether learners attend primarily to form or meaning when monitoring depends on their proficiency.

A multi-factor approach to identifying sources of variability has been described. This suggests that the patterns of variability in the use of a single linguistic variable (such as plural –s) can only be fully identified and accounted for if a range of possible factors that affect learner language are taken into account. This approach also suggests that different factors may be important at different stages of the learner's development and linguistic influences are paramount.

The research to date suggests that horizontal and vertical variability are inextricably intertwined. This is most clearly evident in the studies that have investigated linguistic context, form–function relationships, and planning variability. Initially learners begin with 'simple' systems, characterized by the use of a given form in 'heavy' environments only (often in closed classes) and in planned discourse, and also by unique form–function mappings. Over time they learn to use the form in a target-like way by extending its use to increasingly 'lighter' contexts and to unplanned discourse and by reorganizing form–function networks so that they correspond more closely to those of native speakers. Studies of style shifting suggest that change from above and change from below can occur. Preston (1996) has argued that marked linguistic forms develop more quickly in monitored interlanguage performances while unmarked forms are acquired earlier in the vernacular style.

Conclusion

In this chapter we have explored the nature of variability in learner language and have seen that there is ample evidence to show that variability is systematic, traceable to particular causes. It remains for us to consider whether variability is a significant phenomenon—whether it constitutes, as Tarone has argued, 'a phenomenon that must be accounted for by any theory of second language acquisition' (1988: 142). Here we find conflicting opinions, depending on whether the approach is a linguistic one following the Chomskyan tradition or a sociolinguistic/psycholinguistic one.

Researchers in the Chomskyan tradition argue that the primary goal of SLA research is to build a theory of L2 COMPETENCE, and that in this respect variability is of no interest. As Gregg (1990) put it:

> The variationist is committed to the unprincipled collection of an uncontrolled mass of data, running the real risk that the object of study will become as Roger Brown once put it, 'cognitively ... repellent'.

Although Gregg acknowledged that variability is 'a fascinating and puzzling phenomenon', he believes that variable features are the exception rather than the rule in learner language. In this he is surely mistaken, as the studies reported in this chapter provide indisputable evidence of extensive variability in learner language. Gregg argued that, although the study of variability might contribute to a theory of performance, it will tell us nothing about competence. Variability studies, he argued, describe, but Gregg seeks to explain. For Gregg, knowledge is categorical—we either know a rule or we do not. He is unable to accept the notion of a fuzzy, probabilistic knowledge and is particularly dismissive of variable rules.

On the other hand, researchers in the functionalist tradition see the study of language in its social context as necessary for theory-building. In responding to Gregg's arguments, Tarone (1990) quoted Romaine (1984: 78–9), who took a very different view of what knowledge of a language involves:

> Rule acquisition is not an all or nothing affair ... There may be a number of aspects of the internal workings of a rule, some of which may be acquired before others. There are also social dimensions of a rule relating to its use.

Similarly, Preston (2002: 144) argued:

> Speakers have two (or more) forms available in their linguistic competence or competences, and another device (some sort of sociocultural one) tells them which to choose.

In other words, competence itself may be seen as variable, although there is still no clear way of distinguishing between the inherent variability in a single competence and the code-switching between two or more competences.

Other researchers have emphasized that knowledge cannot be considered in isolation from learners' ability to use their knowledge. Tarone (1990) argued that a theory of L2 acquisition must account for the learner's 'capability'—the actual ability to use particular rules that a learner has—and not just knowledge about what is grammatically correct. For Tarone it is this capability rather than competence that underlies actual performance. In Ellis 1990c I made a similar point in arguing that even if competence (narrowly defined) is itself not variable, the learner's proficiency is. I used this term with the meaning assigned to it by Taylor (1988)—the ability to use knowledge in specific contexts.[6] I argued that for many researchers—especially those interested in educational issues—it is not the learners' competence that is important but their proficiency.

We can therefore identify three distinct positions: the homogeneous competence position of Gregg, the variable competence position of Romaine and Preston, and the capability position of Tarone and myself. The first position views variability as of no theoretical interest. The second and third treat it as of both theoretical (and practical) significance. This debate is an old one and is likely to continue into the future. As Widdowson has pointed out, 'as soon as you talk about competence as *ability*, or what people can actually *do* with language, you get into all kinds of difficulty' (1989: 134). This is because it necessarily involves consideration of a multitude of interacting factors, as indeed the discussion of variability in this chapter has demonstrated. Whereas 'universalists' see this as a reason for viewing competence as homogeneous and so avoiding the 'difficulty' that Widdowson talks about, variationists are prepared to accept it in order to undertake what they see as an essential task—to account for learners distribution and selection of linguistic forms.

Notes

1 While many linguists—including those who work with L2 data—continue to make use of data based on speakers' intuitions regarding what is gram-

matical, many now recognize the need to work with other kinds of data, including those derived from natural language use.

2 Preston (1989: 20) commented: 'the psycholinguistic possibility for a variable rule does not seem to be arcane'.

3 Fisher (1958) stated the position adopted by many sociolinguists on free variation as follows:

> 'Free variation' is of course a label, not an explanation. It does not tell us where the variants come from nor why the speakers use them in differing proportions, but is rather a way of excluding such questions from the scope of immediate inquiry.

4 The *de facto* position adopted by most variationists is that variability should be assumed to be systematic unless it can be shown to be non-systematic. However, I have argued (Ellis 1999b) that it is more appropriate to assume that variability is free until it can be shown to be systematic as this constitutes the null hypothesis. This is, in fact, the stance adopted by Young (1996).

5 It may be that the difficulty the learners experienced in communicating with members of their own ethnic group reflected the fact they found using the L2 with them bizarre.

6 Widdowson (1983: 8) uses the term 'capacity' to refer to 'the ability to produce and understand utterances by using the resources of the grammar in association with features of context to make meaning'. It is clear that 'capability', 'capacity', and 'proficiency' have much in common.

5
Pragmatic aspects of learner language

Introduction

The focus of enquiry in the preceding chapters has been the formal linguistic properties of learners' INTERLANGUAGES. Increasingly, however, SLA researchers have paid attention to pragmatic aspects of learner language. This has been motivated in part by the belief that a full understanding of how formal properties are learnt will not be achieved without examining the way in which these properties are used in actual communication (hence the form–function analyses discussed in Chapters 3 and 4). It has also been motivated by the belief that the study of learner language requires a consideration of pragmatic aspects in their own right. According to this view the goal of SLA research is to describe and explain not only learners' LINGUISTIC COMPETENCE, but also their PRAGMATIC COMPETENCE.

Pragmatics is not any easy term to define. It refers to the field of study where linguistic features are considered in relation to users of the language (Morris 1938; Levinson 1983) but, as Shriffrin (1994) pointed out, despite devoting a whole chapter to defining pragmatics, Levinson found it difficult to effectively delimit its scope. In the case of interlanguage pragmatics, however, the scope is relatively well defined. Researchers have investigated what speakers accomplish when they perform utterances in terms of: (1) INTERACTIONAL ACTS and (2) SPEECH ACTS. The former give structure to the discourse by ensuring that one utterance leads smoothly to another; they concern how speakers manage the process of exchanging turns, how they open and close conversations, and how they sequence acts to ensure a coherent conversation. Speech acts, on the other hand, constitute attempts by language users to perform specific actions, in particular interpersonal functions such as compliments, apologies, requests, or complaints. Of course speech acts are also interactional acts given that they cannot be performed outside interaction. Nevertheless, the distinction between how interaction is organized and the specific actions performed by speaker utterances is a useful one.

This chapter will not attempt to provide a comprehensive overview of the work undertaken in interlanguage pragmatics to date. Instead, we will adopt what Kasper and Dahl (1991) referred to as the 'narrow sense' of interlanguage pragmatics—the performance and acquisition of speech acts by L2 learners. The justification for this decision lies in the fact that it is this aspect of pragmatics which has received the greatest attention in SLA research. However, as a reflection of the increasing interest in how L2 learners perform interactional acts, some consideration will also be given to this aspect of interlanguage pragmatics. We will also concentrate on the pragmatic aspects of learners' spoken rather than written language. The main concern of this chapter is the same as that of the previous ones—description rather than explanation. Theoretical issues are addressed in later chapters.

There are a number of problems in the study of interlanguage pragmatics. One concerns the same problem we noted with error analysis (see Chapter 2), that is, the extent to which it is appropriate to assume that learners' are targeted on native-speaker norms. This is arguably even more of an issue where pragmatics is concerned, as many learners may wish to adhere to their L1 pragmatic norms when speaking in an L2. A second problem concerns the relationship between linguistic and pragmatic competence. Clearly, learners will need at least some linguistic competence in order to perform even a primitive version of a speech act. The possibility arises, then, that the development of pragmatic competence cannot be considered in isolation from the development of linguistic competence. However, I will put discussion of these (and other problems) on hold until the Conclusion section of this chapter in order to first consider what has been found out about interlanguage pragmatics.

Speech acts and illocutionary meaning

According to speech act theory (Austin 1962; Searle 1969), the performance of a speech act involves the performance of three types of act: a locutionary act (the act of saying), an ILLOCUTIONARY ACT (the performance of a particular language function by what is said), and a perlocutionary act (the achieving of some kind of effect on the addressee). Levinson (1983) pointed out that the term 'speech act' is generally used to refer exclusively to 'illocutionary act'.

Searle (1975) identified five general classes of speech acts:

- Representatives: e.g. asserting, concluding
- Directives: e.g. requesting, ordering
- Commissives: e.g. promising, threatening
- Expressives: e.g. thanking, congratulating
- Declarations: e.g. excommunicating, declaring war, marrying, firing.

In this chapter, we will examine research that has investigated directives and expressives. Searle also distinguished 'direct' and 'indirect' speech acts. In a direct speech act, there is a transparent relationship between form and function, as when an imperative is used to perform a request (for example, 'Pass me the salt.'). In an indirect speech act, the illocutionary force of the act is not derivable from the surface structure. For example, an interrogative form can serve as a request as in 'Can you pass me the salt?'.

The successful performance of an illocutionary act is achieved when the speaker meets a number of conditions associated with that particular act. Searle (1969) distinguished three types of conditions: preparatory conditions, sincerity conditions, and essential conditions. For example, the illocutionary act of 'ordering' is successfully performed when both the speaker and hearer recognize that the speaker is in a position of authority over the hearer (preparatory condition), that the speaker wants the ordered act to be done (sincerity condition), and that the speaker intends the utterance as an attempt to get the hearer to do the act (essential condition). If any one of these conditions is not met or is challenged by the hearer, the act may not be successfully performed. For this reason, they are seen as of primary importance in a theory of speech acts.

Other considerations of a secondary nature also enter into speech act performance—in particular, politeness. (See Leech 1983; Kasper 1990; Scollon and Scollon 2001.) Speakers have to take account of their relationship with the addressee and the degree of imposition imposed by the illocution and its propositional content in order to ensure that harmonious social relations between the speakers are not endangered. In so doing they give recognition to the need to signal solidarity with and/or power over their hearers, both of which determine the nature of their relations with them. Brown and Levinson (1978) have developed a model of politeness, in which they distinguished a number of options or 'strategies' available to the speaker. (See Figure 5.1.) First, the speaker can choose to perform the act or not to perform it. If the act is performed it can be 'off-record' (i.e. performed in such a way that it can be ignored by the addressee) or 'on-record'. On-record acts can be 'baldly on record' (i.e. performed by means of a direct speech act) or can involve a 'face-saving activity'. The latter can take the form of a 'positive strategy' or a 'negative strategy'. The former involves some kind of attempt to establish solidarity with the addressee by emphasizing commonality. It is likely to occur when there is minimal social distance and little power difference between the participants. A 'negative strategy' involves performing the act in such a way that deference is shown to the hearer—the aim is to give the hearer a way out of compliance with the act. It is used when the power difference between the participants is considerable. Building on Brown and Levinson's model, Scollon and Scollon (2001) distinguished three politeness systems. A solidarity system, characterized by [– power/– distance], employs positive politeness strategies. In a deference system, characterized by [– power/+ distance], negative politeness strategies figure. In a hierarchical system, where one participant is in a [+ power] position and the other in a [– power] position and where the relationship may be either close or distant, the participant with power uses positive politeness strategies while the participant without power uses negative politeness strategies. Brown and Levinson, and Scollon and Scollon argued that these strategies are universal. However, research (see Kasper 1990 for a review) suggests that this may not be the case. As we will see, how L2 learners handle politeness has attracted the attention of a number of researchers.

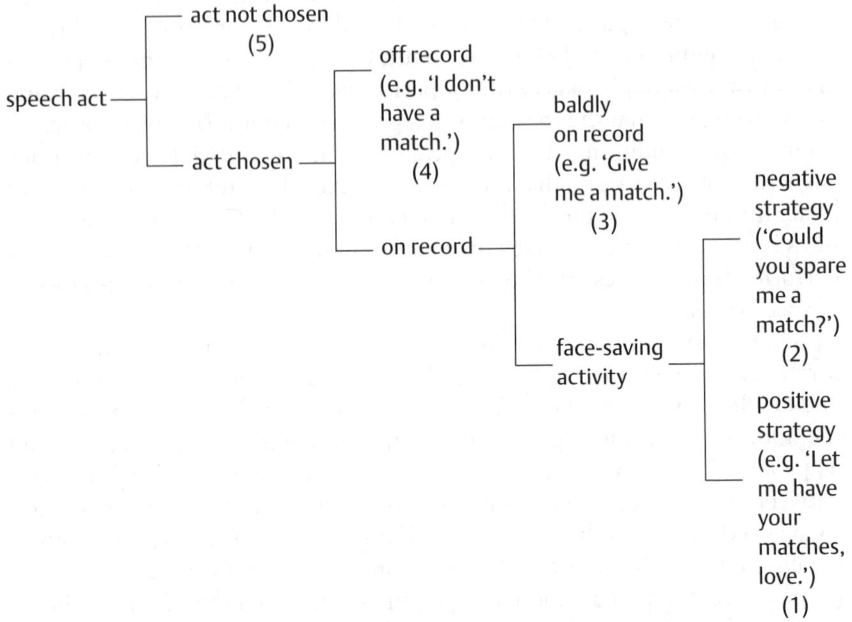

Figure 5.1 A schematic representation of Brown and Levinson's (1978) politeness model

The study of speech acts in interlanguage has concentrated on illocutionary meanings or language functions as they are commonly known. The questions that have been addressed are: (1) To what extent and in what ways do learners perform illocutionary acts in the L2 differently from native speakers of the target language? Are there differences in the form of the illocutionary act and/or the appropriateness of its use on a particular occasion? and (2) How do learners learn to perform different illocutionary acts? The bulk of the research has been cross-sectional, so little is currently known about the second question. However, a few longitudinal and pseudo-longitudinal studies cast some light on the process by which learners gradually master the performance of specific illocutionary acts.

We will begin by considering the research methods that have been used to investigate illocutionary acts in learner language. A survey of the research that has studied a number of L2 illocutionary acts follows, with a focus on three particular acts: requests, apologies, and refusals. Several general features of learners' attempts to perform and to acquire illocutionary acts are then discussed. Finally, although the focus of this chapter is on description, a number of explanatory factors will be considered.

Research methods for studying pragmatic aspects of learner language

The growth of interest in interlanguage pragmatics has been accompanied by an ongoing debate about the research methods to be used. See Kasper and Dahl 1991; Rose 1994; Rose and Ono 1995; Gass and Houck 1999; Kasper 2001; Yuan 2001; Kasper and Rose 2002; Golato 2003; Bardovi-Harlig and Hartford 2005b. These researchers address a number of methodological issues: (1) research design (cross-sectional versus longitudinal), (2) the modality of the data (perception/comprehension versus production, (3) data collection methods, (4) the discourse type (genre) to be investigated and (5) methods of data analysis.

Many of the early studies of interlanguage pragmatics (for example, Scarcella 1979; Olshtain and Blum-Kulka 1985; House and Kasper 1987; Rintell and Mitchell 1989) were cross-sectional in design. Two early longitudinal studies were Schmidt (1983) and Ellis (1992). There have also been a number of more recent longitudinal studies (for example, Ohta 2001a; Kanagy 1999; Achiba 2003). However, cross-sectional studies still dominate (for example, Hill 1997; Rose 2000). Kasper and Rose (2002) considered the strengths and weaknesses of cross-sectional and longitudinal studies. Cross-sectional studies can be conducted quickly and allow for large samples that enable inferential statistics to be used but they do not permit the analysis of causal relationships and cannot chart individual differences in development over time. However, it should be noted that cross-sectional studies that compare groups of learners with different levels of general PROFICIENCY do allow researchers to describe putative growth and development. Still, longitudinal studies are clearly desirable for plotting DEVELOPMENTAL PATTERNS, as they enable change to be analysed in a single learner at the micro level. They are also helpful in identifying causal relationships. But they are very time-consuming and there is the danger that repeated observation or interviewing will influence the learner's behaviour. Kasper and Rose advocate 'a sequential or parallel research program' (p. 78) that incorporates both types of design.

Kasper and Dahl (1991) distinguished data collection methods according to the modality of the data elicited (perception/comprehension/intuition versus production) and the degree of control over learners' speech (elicited versus observational). They also pointed out that some of the most successful studies have employed combined methods of data collection. Table 5.1 summarizes the main methods that have been used and identifies their main advantages and disadvantages.

Many studies have used questionnaires and DISCOURSE COMPLETION TASKS (DCTs) to elicit learners' intuitions about how to perform specific acts appropriately in different situations. Olshtain and Blum-Kulka (1985), for example, investigated learners' perceptions about politeness in Hebrew by means of a questionnaire consisting of descriptions of situations calling for apologies and requests followed by lists of possible strategies for performing these acts in each situation. The learners were asked to rate each strategy for politeness on a three-point scale. Here is an example:

> A friend of yours at the university comes up to you after class and tells you that she has finally found an apartment to rent. The only problem is that she has to pay $200 immediately and at present she only has $100. She turns to you and says:
>
> a Say, could you lend me $100 until next week?
> b You can lend me $100 until next week right?
> c Lend me the money, please.
> d Could you lend me $100 until next week?
> e Do you think you could lend me $100 until next week?
> f Maybe you have a little money to give me so that I could take the apartment?
>
> (Olshtain and Blum-Kulka 1985: 324)

Observational performance data have also been used to investigate the comprehension of illocutionary acts. Carrell (1981), for example, had learners listen and react to requests, while Kasper (1984a) gauged learners' comprehension on the basis of the kinds of responses that they provided to their interlocutor's previous turn.

The study of the pragmatic aspects of learners' production has made use of discourse completion tasks, clinical elicitation activities (i.e. communication tasks and sociolinguistic interviews), role plays, and spontaneous conversation. In addition, a number of studies have elicited participants' own interpretations of their pragmatic behaviour by means of stimulated recall and retrospective oral and written self-reports.

DCTs have been extensively used. In the CROSS-CULTURAL SPEECH ACT REALIZATION PROJECT (Blum-Kulka, House, and Kasper 1989a) a series of studies involving participants from a variety of language backgrounds (for example, American, British, and Australian English, Canadian French, Hebrew, German, and Danish) made use of a questionnaire consisting of eight request and eight apology contexts. Each context was briefly described and was then followed by a short dialogue with an empty slot which the learners were asked to fill in by writing down the request or apology they would make. Here is an example, designed to elicit an apology:

> A student has borrowed a book from her teacher, which she promises to return today. When meeting her teacher, however, she realizes that she forgot to bring it along.
>
> TEACHER: Miriam, I hope you brought the book I lent you.

MIRIAM: ___
TEACHER: OK, but please remember it next week.
(Blum-Kulka, House, and Kasper 1989b: 14)

Similar tasks were used by Beebe and her colleagues (for example, Beebe, Takahashi, and Uliss-Weltz 1990), and, subsequently, by a number of other researchers.

Role plays also provide the learners with a description of a context which has been designed with the performance of a particular illocutionary act in mind. But in this case the learners are asked to respond orally. The role plays may be performed with the help of puppets (for example, Walters 1980), or by the learners interacting with other learners (for example, Kasper 1981), or with the researcher. Participants can be asked to play themselves or take on imaginary roles. The data collected from role plays provide information about learners' ability to construct a discourse context for the specific act under investigation.

The use of naturally occurring speech as a basis for studying interlanguage pragmatics has been less common, partly because of the difficulty of assembling a sufficient corpus of data. Wolfson (1989b), however, used this approach to investigate learners' complimenting behaviour (compliments together with compliment responses). It has also been used in studies of institutional talk. For example, Bardovi-Harlig and Hartford (1990) used data collected from academic advising sessions while Jessica Williams's (2005b) corpus came from writing centre sessions in a university setting. Various methods have been used to collect natural samples of speech—field observation, audio and video recordings and recall protocols.

As Table 5.1 shows, each of these methods has its advantages and disadvantages. A number of studies (for example, Beebe and Cummins 1985; Rintell and Mitchell 1989; Wolfson, Marmor, and Jones 1989; Yuan 2001; Golato 2003) have compared data obtained from discourse completion tasks with those from observational studies. They have found both similarities and differences. With regard to the similarities, both methods result in the use of the same strategies. For example, Golato (2003) found that data collected by means of a DCT and audio-recordings of naturally occurring language behaviour revealed that compliment responses in both data sets were realized by means of 'compliment assessments' (i.e. a positive assessment of a compliment). However, Golato also reported a number of differences. Notably, in the DCT data there were numerous instances of 'appreciation tokens' (for example, 'thank you') whereas in the observational data there were none. Other differences reported by researchers who have compared the two types of data include the semantic formulas employed, the length of learners' responses, and the size of the discourse context created. These differences raise questions about the extent to which the elicited data can serve as evidence of learners' pragmatic competence, as they may not accurately reflect actual language use. Wolfson (1989a) argued strongly that learners' intuitions about what they would say in a particular situation are not reliable, as the sociolinguistic knowledge they draw on in performing illocutionary acts lies beneath the threshold of consciousness. Golato (2003) similarly argued that a DCT is metapragmatic and suggested that it is 'a valid instrument not for measuring pragmatic action, but symbolic action' (p. 92). Bonikowska (1988) pointed out a further problem with DCTs; in naturally occurring contexts speakers always have the option of 'opting out', whereas discourse completion questionnaires oblige learners to perform linguistically even when they would normally keep quiet.[1] Nevertheless, there are advantages to using questionnaires and DCTs. Ideally, as Kasper and Rose (2002) pointed out, researchers need to combine methods. However, there have been few studies to date that have done this.

In general, the study of interlanguage pragmatics has focused on conversational discourse. However, there is growing interest in institutional discourse (i.e. talk that takes place in a specific institutional context such as a workplace or an educational institution). Bardovi-Harlig and Hartford (2005b) claimed that institutional discourse differs from ordinary conversations in three main ways. It is goal-oriented in a relatively restricted way, it involves special and particular constraints on what constitutes appropriate pragmatic behaviour and it involves the specific procedures associated with a particular institutional context. Bardovi-Harlig and Hartford suggested that ideally data need to satisfy three criteria; (1) comparability (i.e. there is adequate control of the variables influencing behaviour to enable comparison of different samples), (2) interactivity (i.e. the data display the interactional facets associated with turn-taking) and (3) consequentiality (i.e. the talk is directed at achieving a real-world outcome). They compared conversational and institutional talk in terms of these three criteria, demonstrating that whereas the former satisfies (2) and (3), it does not satisfy (1), as it is not usually possible to control the variables involved in naturally occurring conversational behaviour. In contrast, institutional talk satisfies all three criteria. They noted that the 'goal oriented nature of institutional talk allows for comparison across speakers in the same way that experimental interactions allow researchers to compare speakers' (p. 13).

Methods of data analysis reflect the disciplinary orientation of the research. Kasper and Rose (2002) distinguished the methods associated with contrastive pragmatics, sociology, linguistic anthropology, developmental pragmatics, cognitive psychology, and social psychology. Broadly speaking, however, two different approaches to data analysis can be identified. A quantitative approach is based on the definition and classification of pragmatic phenomena, which allows for the tallying of frequencies and, potentially, the use of inferential statistics to compare different groups of participants. A qualitative approach, such as conversational analysis, is directed at describing and understanding the complex interactional facets evident in online talk. Whereas quantitative methods have been used to examine illocutionary acts,

Method	Description	Advantages	Disadvantages
1 Discourse completion tasks	These consist of a description of a situation and an instruction to learners to either select from a range of choices about how to respond or to say/write how they would respond. They can be presented orally or in writing and the response can also be oral or written.	• They allow the researcher to control for variables related to the situation (e.g. status of interlocutors). • Responses from native speakers and learners (and also different groups of learners) can be statistically compared.	• They do not show the interactional facets of a speech event (e.g. multi-turn sequences). • They do not reflect actual language behaviour only learners' beliefs about how they would behave. • They are not suitable for lower-proficiency learners unless the task is presented in the L1. • They cannot reliably show 'opting out' behaviour.
2 Clinical elicitation activities	There are two types: (1) conversation tasks: participants are either asked to converse about a topic or to jointly reach some predetermined goal. (2) sociolinguistic interviews: an interviewer asks informants about their life history, experiences, and attitudes. They afford both a sample of language that can be analysed and information about the learner's background. In both types the learners perform as themselves.	• Conversational tasks allow for both symmetrical and asymmetrical role configurations to be studied. • Both types can shed light on a range of interactional facets (e.g. conversational organization and management).	• They allow for only a limited range of communicative acts to be investigated. • They do not necessarily reflect actual language behaviour as there may not be any meaningful consequence of interacting on the learner's part.
3 Role plays	These involve simulations of communicative encounters. Learners are given an imaginary situation and can be asked to perform as themselves or in imaginary roles.	• They allow for a range of communicative acts to be investigated in online language use. • They allow for both symmetrical and asymmetrical role configurations to be studied. • They can shed light on a range of interactional facets.	• The participants are only imagining how they would behave. • The participants' real roles may interfere with their imaginary roles. • The verbal actions performed have no real consequences for the participants.

4 Recall protocols	Participants are asked to remember the last exemplar of a specific pragmatic feature (e.g. a request) they received or gave and the situation in which it occurred.	• They provide data relating to natural target behaviour.	• Participants typically have to be selected on the basis of convenience. • Participants may not be able to recall accurately what was said or the situational context. • Recall protocols do not yield rich information about a range of interactional facets.
5 Self-report	Participants are asked to comment on their own pragmatic behaviour either concurrently (i.e. through think-aloud protocols) or retrospectively through interviews or diaries.	• Self-report provides the researcher with the participants' interpretations of their behaviour, which can be triangulated with interpretations from other sources.	• Self-report does not provide data relating to the actual performance of a pragmatic feature. • Concurrent self-reports may interfere with normal pragmatic behaviour.
6 Methods for collecting spontaneous conversation			
a Field observation	The researcher (or field worker) writes down exemplars of a specific pragmatic feature (e.g. an illocutionary act) as they come across them in everyday life. They also record contextual information.	• It allows for the collection of a large data base from a wide range of speakers in different settings. • The data collected reflect actual language use (i.e. consequential behaviour). • It affords rich contextual information.	• The researcher may not be able to record data at the time it is produced and so may have to rely on memory with the result that the data may not be accurate. • The researcher may not be able to record crucial indexical information (e.g. pausing and non-verbal actions).
b Audio/video recordings	The researcher audio- or video-tapes naturally occurring interactions which are then transcribed for detailed analysis.	• The data collected reflect consequential behaviour. • Rich contextual information is available (especially from video recordings). • This method allows for detailed analysis of a full range of interactional facets of utterances in relation to their sequential context.	• Large amounts of data may be needed to afford sufficient exemplars of the specific phenomenon under investigation. • Recording may interfere with participants' normal language behaviour. • It is difficult to control for variables such as power, status, gender and age.

Table 5.1 Different data collection methods in interlanguage pragmatics research

qualitative methods have explored the sequential nature of interactional acts (for instance turn-taking mechanisms) and the socialization processes involved in acquiring L2 pragmatic norms. Quantitative studies of interlanguage pragmatics have been dominant but there is an increasing interest in more qualitative methods.

It remains to consider two additional methodological issues: the participants to be investigated and the problem of target-language norms. Ideally, the study of illocutionary acts in learner language should involve the collection of three sets of data: (1) samples of the illocutionary act performed in the target language by L2 learners, (2) samples performed by native speakers of the target language, and (3) samples of the same illocutionary act performed by the learners in their L1. Only in this way is it possible to determine to what extent learner performance differs from native-speaker performance and whether the differences are traceable to transfer from the L1. Increasingly, L2 studies are collecting all three sets of data.

The study of pragmatics in learner language faces the problem of target-language norms. In order to decide in what way the learner's performance differs from the native speaker's, it is necessary to determine what is normative in the latter. We need to know, for example, how native speakers handle compliments. The difficulty is that native speakers are likely to vary considerably in this respect. For example, middle-class Americans have different norms for complimenting from those of middle-class white South Africans (Herbert 1989). Similarly, females do not compliment in exactly the same way as males. (See Holmes 1988.) As Kasper (1992) pointed out, the obvious solution to this problem is to choose those norms found in whatever variety the learner is typically exposed to as the 'target'. However, as Kasper also pointed out, many learners are exposed to more than one variety. Kasper's conclusion is that 'investigators might want to give more attention to "choosing the right stuff" as an L2 norm in interlanguage pragmatics' and that this is 'largely a matter of logistics' (1992: 225). In many learning situations, however, the 'logistics' may be very complicated.

Illocutionary acts in learner language

We can distinguish two ways of examining illocutionary acts in SLA. The first and earlier way belongs to error analysis and thus focuses on learners' failure to perform acts in native-like ways. The second way reconceptualizes illocutionary acts as part of communicative competence.

Thomas (1983) distinguished SOCIOPRAGMATIC FAILURE, which takes place when a learner fails to perform the illocutionary act required by the situation (i.e. deviates with regard to appropriateness of meaning), and PRAGMALINGUISTIC FAILURE, which occurs when a learner tries to perform the right speech act but uses the wrong linguistic means (i.e. deviates with regard to appropriateness of form). A good example of sociopragmatic error can be found in Wolfson's (1989a) account of how L2 learners typically respond to compliments. Wolfson argues that compliments are used by native speakers of American English as a means of establishing and maintaining solidarity. It is for this reason that they are most common among status-equal acquaintances and co-workers rather than among intimates; the former involve more uncertain relationships which have to be negotiated. Compliments serve as one of the ways in which Americans (particularly women) undertake this negotiation. Wolfson pointed out that many negotiating sequences involving native speakers are long and elaborate. In comparison, those involving non-native speakers are typically short, because learners often fail to take up a compliment, preferring instead to give no response at all:

NS: You have such a lovely accent.
NNS: (No response)

Wolfson argues that by failing to conform to native-speaker complimenting norms, learners deprive themselves of the opportunities to establish relationships with native speakers and, thereby, of the input that they need to develop both their linguistic and sociolinguistic competence.

Not all of Wolfson's learners manifested sociopragmatic failure through failing to respond to a compliment. Many displayed pragmalinguistic failure—that is, they responded to a native-speaker compliment but in linguistically inappropriate ways. Middle-class, white Americans are likely to respond by giving unfavourable comments about the object that is the target of a compliment:

NS: I like your sweater.
NS: It's so old. My sister bought it for me from Italy a long time ago.

In this way, American native speakers often refused the compliment or tried to downgrade themselves. In contrast, learners tended to respond with a simple 'thank you'. Such a response served to act as a dampener on the conversation.

Pragmalinguistic failure by learners is widely reported in the literature. Another good example comes from Eisenstein and Bodman's (1986) study of expressions of gratitude. This made use of a discourse completion questionnaire administered to 67 learners with different L1 backgrounds. Baseline data were collected from native speakers of English. Eisenstein and Bodman reported that the learners performed very differently from the native speakers—in fact, their responses were similar only 30 per cent of the time. They experienced difficulty with both syntax and vocabulary, and also in identifying the formulas and conventionalized routines that characterized native-speaker thanking. In a subsequent study (Bodman and Eisenstein 1988), learners were asked to role play situations calling for expressions of gratitude. Lower-proficiency learners often translated expressions from their L1. For example, in thanking someone for a loan they might say 'May God increase your bounty'. More advanced learners avoided this kind of pragmalinguistic error, but instead displayed considerable hesitation and awkwardness. Pragmalinguistic difficulty, therefore, can also be manifested in the failure to conform to the temporal norms of native-speaker speech.[2]

The distinction between sociopragmatic and pragmalinguistic errors, however, is not as clear-cut as these examples may have suggested. Kasper pointed out that 'the distinction becomes fuzzy in the case of indirectness' (1992: 210). For example, the decision regarding whether to provide an explanation for having committed some offence can be seen as a sociopragmatic one, but if providing an explanation is seen as one of several possible strategies for performing the act of apologizing (as in Olshtain and Cohen's 1983 framework discussed later), its inclusion or omission constitutes more of a pragmalinguistic decision. Nevertheless, Kasper acknowledged that the distinction is 'analytically useful'.

The alternative view of illocutionary acts involves viewing them in terms of knowledge rather than failure. Kasper (2001), for example, offered the following reformulation of Thomas' distinction:

> Pragmalinguistic knowledge requires mappings of form, meaning, force, and context ... Sociopragmatics refers to the link between action-relevant context factors and communicative action (e.g. deciding whether to request an extension, complain about the neighbour's barking dog) and does not necessarily require any links to specific forms at all.
> (2001: 51)

Seen in this way the ability to perform illocutionary acts constitutes part of COMMUNICATIVE COMPETENCE. Canale included this ability in sociolinguistic competence, which he defined as 'the extent to which utterances are produced and understood appropriately in different sociolinguistic contexts' (1983: 7). He went on to point out that appropriateness involves both appropriateness of meaning (i.e. when it is proper to perform a particular illocutionary act) and appropriateness of form (i.e. the extent to which a given act is realized in a verbal or non-verbal form proper for a given situation). The former constitutes sociopragmatic competence and the latter pragmalinguistic competence.

Research has begun to cover the use and acquisition of a number of illocutionary acts, but remains somewhat limited in its depth of coverage. It has tended to make use of rough-and-ready categories of sociocultural reality—the problem of norms referred to earlier. It has also tended to concentrate on a fairly small set of speech acts. Much of the research has focused on requests, apologies, and refusals (the three acts to be considered in detail in the following sections of this chapter). In addition, complaints have been investigated by Olshtain and Weinbach (1985) and Bonikowska (1988), thanking by Eisenstein and Bodman (1986), invitations by Scarcella (1979), suggestions by Bardovi-Harlig and Hartford (1990, 1993) and Rintell (1981), compliments by Wolfson (1989b) and Billmyer (1990), greetings by DuFon (2000), arguing by Adger (1987), complaints/criticisms by Murphy and Neu (1996), and disagreements Bardovi-Harlig and Salsbury (2004). Many of these acts have two points in common. First, they constitute 'relatively well-defined' acts (De Beaugrande and Dressler 1981: 117) in the sense that they are realized by means of a small set of easily recognizable linguistic elements (many formulaic). For example, Wolfson (1983) has shown that nine syntactic patterns account for 95 per cent of the compliments in her native-speaker corpus. Second, many of these acts are face-threatening in nature and, therefore, provide a means of studying to what extent L2 learners with different L1 backgrounds are able to use native-like politeness strategies. In this chapter we will consider only descriptive studies, reserving discussion of research that has investigated the effects of instruction on the development of pragmatic competence to Chapter 16.

Requests

Requests are attempts on the part of a speaker to get the hearer to perform or to stop performing some kind of action in the interests of the speaker. A number of general illocutionary and sociolinguistic features of requests can be identified:

1 The speaker wishes the hearer to perform the request, believes the hearer is able to perform the act, and does not believe the act will be performed in the absence of the request (Fraser 1983).
2 A request can be more or less direct (Searle 1976). Blum-Kulka, House, and Kasper (1989b) identified eight 'strategy types', which they ordered according to directness. These strategies are realized by means of identifiable 'semantic formulas', as shown in Table 5.2. Following Fraser (1981), a 'semantic formula' is defined as 'a word, phrase or sentence which meets a particular semantic criterion or strategy' (cited in Olshtain and Cohen 1983: 20).
3 Requests are also subject to internal and external modification. Internal modification takes the form of downgraders, which are intended to mitigate the force of the act, and upgraders, which are intended to increase the degree of coerciveness of the act. External modification consists of moves that occur either before or after the head act (i.e. the act that actually performs the request); these moves can also be classified according to whether the purpose is to downgrade or upgrade the force of the act.
4 Requests can be encoded from the speaker's perspective (for example, 'Give me the book'), from the hearer's perspective (for example, 'Could you give me the book?'), from a joint perspective ('Let's read a book') or from an impersonal perspective ('It would be nice to read a book').
5 Requests are 'inherently imposing' (Blum-Kulka, House, and Kasper 1989b). For this reason they call for considerable 'face-work'. The choice of linguistic realization depends on a variety of social factors to do with the relationships between the speaker and the addressee, the perceived degree of imposition which a particular request makes on the hearer (i.e. it involves a choice of politeness strategy), and the goal of the act (for example, requesting goods or initiating joint activity).

6 Although the main sociopragmatic categories of requests can be found in different languages, there are pragmalinguistic differences relating to the preferred form of a request that is used in a particular situation. Also, cross-linguistic differences exist in the choice of other linguistic features such as internal and external modification devices.

Level of directness	Strategy	Semantic formulas
Direct	1 Mood-derivable	You shut up.
	2 Performative	I am telling you to shut up.
	3 Hedged performative	I would like to ask you to shut up.
	4 Locution-derivable	I want you to shut up.
Conventionally indirect	5 Suggestory formula	Let's play a game.
	6 Query-preparatory	Can you draw a horse for me?
Non-conventionally indirect	7 Strong hint	This game is boring.
	8 Mild hint	We've been playing this game for over an hour now.

Table 5.2 Request strategies (summarized from Blum-Kulka, House, and Kasper 1989b)

Requests have received considerable attention in SLA research for a number of reasons. They are clearly important in social life, they are face-threatening and, therefore, call for considerable linguistic expertise on the part of the learner, they differ cross-linguistically in interesting ways and they are often realized by means of clearly identifiable formulas.

A number of studies (see Table 5.3) have investigated learners' intuitions about what constitutes an appropriate request. A focus of enquiry is whether L2 learners are able to recognize the distinctions between polite and less polite forms. Advanced learners appear to have few problems. Olshtain and Blum-Kulka (1985) found that learners of L2 Hebrew, who had been resident in Israel for over 10 years, showed the same high level of tolerance for direct and positive politeness strategies as native speakers of Hebrew. Walters (1979) and Carrell and Konneker (1981) also reported that the advanced learners they studied perceived the politeness level of different requests in accordance with native-speaker norms. However, there is also evidence of some differences. In particular, advanced learners appear to develop a greater sensitivity to the use of politeness strategies in requesting than is evident in native speakers. Walters noted that there was greater unanimity between his learners and native-speaker females, who tended to distinguish polite and impolite forms more sharply than native-speaker males. Carrell and Konneker found that their advanced learners tended to perceive more distinct levels of politeness than native speakers. A tentative conclusion, therefore, is that with sufficient exposure to the L2, learners are able to perceive the sociolinguistic distinctions encoded by native speakers in requests but that they may become oversensitive to them.

There is less information available about how low-level (as distinct from advanced or intermediate) learners understand different kinds of requests. One possibility is that such learners rely more on situational than linguistic clues as a means of comprehending requests, as Ervin-Tripp *et al.*'s (1987) study of child learners of L2 French suggests. Low-level learners are likely to have problems selecting request strategies that are appropriate to different situations. Thus, Tanaka and Kawade (1982) found that Japanese ESL learners (who had probably had little exposure to the sociolinguistic norms of native speakers) tended to opt for less polite strategies overall. Further evidence of the problems that learners face in their choice of request strategy is to be found in Olshtain and Blum-Kulka (1985). They noted that learners of L2 Hebrew who had spent less than two years in Israel were reluctant to accept the informal, positive-orientated request strategy or the direct request strategy found in native-speaker speech. For example, learners were inclined to reject the Hebrew equivalent of 'I hope you can take me back to town' when asking for a ride, whereas native speakers were more likely to accept it. The learners may have responded in accordance with the politeness norms of their L1.

However, not all studies have found an effect for the learners' proficiency level. Takahashi (1996) did not find any difference according to proficiency in learners' perceptions of transferability of L1 request strategies, although this may have been because the higher-level learners in this study (Japanese university students) were not sufficiently advanced for a proficiency effect to become evident.

Study	**Participants**	**Data collection instruments**	**Main results**
Walters 1979	75 advanced ESL learners (mixed L1s); 60 NSs of English	Judgement tasks involving paired comparisons.	Learners performed like NS females in making clearer distinctions between polite and impolite forms than NS males.
Fraser, Rintell, and Walters 1980	Adult ESL learners (L1 Spanish); NS controls	Ratings of speech produced in role-playing situations on a deference scale of 1–5.	Learners perceived deference to older and female addressees in a similar way to NSs (i.e. they did not transfer L1 pragmatic rules).
Carrell and Konneker 1981	73 advanced and intermediate ESL learners (mixed L1s); 42 NSs	Sorting task requiring subjects to rank strategies according to politeness.	Learners performed like NSs but tended to perceive more distinctive levels of politeness, i.e. they were oversensitive to syntactic/form distinctions.

Tanaka and Kawade 1982	ESL learners (L1 Japanese); NS controls	M/C questionnaire; subjects select strategy most appropriate to situation.	Both learners and NSs chose more polite strategies with increased social distance but learners chose less polite strategies overall.
Olshtain and Blum-Kulka 1985	172 NSs of English; 160 NSs of Hebrew; 124 learners of Hebrew	M/C questionnaire in English and Hebrew; subjects asked to rate each of 6 strategies for politeness on a 3-point scale.	Learners showed increased preference for direct request strategies and positive politeness (i.e. NS norms) according to length of stay in target community; learners capable of achieving NS acceptability patterns.
Ervin-Tripp *et al.* 1987	Learners of French (3 age groups 3–9); NSs of English and French	Participants asked to explain implicit requests based on narratives; also to carry out implicit requests.	The child learners relied on situational rather than linguistic clues to interpret requests; accuracy of interpretation increased with age.
Takahashi 1996	142 low- and high-proficiency male Japanese university students	Transferability judgement questionnaire to measure perceptions of the contextual appropriateness of five Japanese indirect request strategies and also equivalence between Japanese request strategies and English equivalents.	The Japanese strategies were perceived as differentially transferable. However, only minimal proficiency effects were evident on learners' transferability perceptions.
Matsuura 1998	77 Japanese university English majors; 48 American university students	Likert-scale questionnaire measuring perceptions of politeness and appropriateness for addressee.	The Japanese learners under-estimated the politeness level of 'May I ...?' They indicated a preference for casual, direct requests in situations involving close friends whereas NSs preferred conventionally indirect forms.

Table 5.3 Cross-sectional studies of learners' perception/comprehension of requests

Most of the research on requests that has investigated production has been cross-sectional. (See Table 5.4.) These studies have elicited requests in the form of written responses to a discourse completion task or oral responses in role play tasks. These studies do provide evidence of differences in requesting behaviour between low- and high-proficiency learners. Lower-level learners display only a limited range of politeness features. Scarcella (1979), for instance, reported that 'low level L2 speakers showed much less variety in the politeness strategies they used and lacked any apparent distribution of politeness features' (p. 287). For example, they used imperative requests to all addressees irrespective of social distance and power differences, and deployed hedges in totally inappropriate ways. Tanaka (1988) found that Japanese students at an Australian university differed markedly from native English speakers in their requesting behaviour. They failed to give concrete reasons for their requests and also showed less uncertainty regarding whether the conditions for a request were met. In general, they were less indirect and tentative. Thus, whereas Australians were likely to say 'Do you think I could have ...?' when requesting a book from a lecturer, the Japanese used 'Can I...?' They also differed in their choice of strategies, using negative politeness strategies (for example, 'If you don't mind ...') where the native speakers did not, and failing to use them in other situations where the native speakers employed them. They avoided positive politeness strategies (for example, mention of first name). These lower-level learners had no difficulty in performing the illocutionary meaning of requesting, but they were unable to do so in socially appropriate ways. They made an attempt to vary their request in accordance with social factors such as addressee—as Cathcart (1986) also found in a study of the communicative behaviour of children in a bilingual kindergarten—but could not do so very effectively. In contrast, higher-level learners produce longer requests than lower-level learners (Blum-Kulka and Olshtain 1986), more conventionally indirect requests and fewer direct requests (Hill 1997), and opt out less (Rose 2000). Higher-proficiency learners approximate closer to native-speaker norms in terms of both their choice of strategies and their use of mitigation devices (Trosberg 1995).

However, one of the strongest findings of these studies is that even advanced learners do not acquire fully native-like ways of requesting. In particular, they tend to produce longer requests than native speakers—the 'waffle phenomenon'. (See Blum-Kulka and Olshtain 1986; House and Kasper 1987; Færch and Kasper 1989; Rintell and Mitchell 1989: Edmondson and House 1991.) This is the result of the over-suppliance of politeness markers, of syntactic downgraders, and, in particular, of supportive moves. This verbosity is more evident in high-intermediate than in advanced learners (Blum-Kulka and Olshtain 1986). A number of explanations have been suggested for this phenomenon. It may reflect a desire to 'play it safe' by making propositional and pragmatic meanings as transparent as possible. The need to 'play it safe' may in turn derive from the fact that although advanced learners have access to the standardized routines needed to perform requests, they make less use of them than native speakers because they are not sure about the range and

Study	Participants	Data collection instruments	Main results
Scarcella 1979	10 beginners & 10 advanced learners (L1 Arabic); 6 NSs	Role play involving different addressees	Some politeness forms (e.g. 'please') acquired early; others (e.g. inclusive 'we') acquired late. Learners acquire forms before their social meanings. L1 learners use a limited range of politeness features.
Cathcart 1986	8 ESL learners (children; L1 Spanish) in bilingual classroom	Audio-recording of classroom speech	Children used longer and more complex requests addressed to adults than to other children. Requests also longer and more complex with other children in tasks with joint goals.
Blum-Kulka and Olshtain 1986	Learners of L1 Hebrew (mixed proficiency); NS controls	Discourse completion questionnaire	High-intermediate learners used longer requests than low-intermediate or advanced learners.
House and Kasper 1987	Advanced learners of L1 English (L1 = Danish and German)	Discourse completion questionnaire	Learners showed similar choice of directness levels but used less varied syntactic and lexical down-graders less frequently. Also, learners produced longer requests.
Tanaka 1988	8 Japanese ESL learners in Australia; NS controls	Role play involving two hearers (friend and lecturer)	The learners were more direct than native speakers and used politeness inappropriately.
Færch and Kasper 1989	200 learners of English & 200 learners of German (L1 = Danish); NS of Danish, British English, and German	Discourse completion questionnaire	Learners tend to be more verbose e.g. tend to use double markings (e.g. 'Could you 'possibly' ...?). 'Please' is over-used, but 'possibly' is underused.
Rintell and Mitchell 1989	34 ESL learners (low-advanced level mixed L1); 37 NSs	Discourse completion questionnaire; role play	Learners' requests longer than NSs'; no major differences in choice of forms/strategies.
Trosberg 1995	Three groups of Danish learners of English—Grade 9 secondary school, high school and commercial school, university	Discourse role-play task	Learners approximated more closely to native-like request strategies with increased proficiency and also manifested more native-like patterns of mitigation.

Hill 1997	60 university-level Japanese learners of English at three levels of proficiency	Discourse completion questionnaire	Low-proficiency group showed heavy reliance on direct requests with few indirect requests; the advanced group showed the opposite. But the advanced students also showed more evidence of transfer for some conventionally indirect strategies (i.e. expressions of willingness).
Rose 2000	Cantonese-speaking primary school learners of English at three levels	A cartoon oral production task; single frame cartoons developed to represent 10 request scenarios	Conventionally indirect requests used more by the more proficient learners; less proficient used more opting out. Almost no situational variation evident in any of the groups. The most advanced group used more supportive moves but still not as many as they used in their L1.

Table 5.4 Cross-sectional studies of learners' production of requests

appropriateness of their application in particular situations (Edmondson and House 1991: 285). Verbosity may also reflect a desire on the part of such learners to display their linguistic competence or, conversely, it may be indicative of the learners' awareness of their own status as second language users—an acknowledgement of the diminished identity they feel in certain situations. Again, though, conclusions about learners' pragmatic competence on the basis of their elicited performance can only be tentative.

Other differences between high-level learners and native speakers have been noted. For example, they tend to overuse the politeness marker 'please', to employ more double-markings (for example, '*Could you possibly* present your paper this week?') and to make more extensive use of external (as opposed to internal) modification (Færch and Kasper 1989). These high-level learners, however, show control over a wide range of forms and strategies for performing requests.

Ideally, detailed information is needed about how individual learners with different L1 backgrounds gradually develop the ability to perform requests over time. Unfortunately, there have been few longitudinal studies on requests so far. Table 5.5 summarizes three studies. Schmidt's (1983) study of Wes (L1 Japanese) examined his acquisition of directives (a general class of speech acts that includes requests) over a three-year period. Initially, Wes relied on a small set of formulas (for example, 'Can I have a ...?'). On occasions he used V + –ing in place of the imperative form, and he tended to rely heavily on lexical clues such as 'please' (a phenomenon that Scarcella also noted in beginner learners). Wes also made substantial use of hints, which Schmidt says native speakers often had difficulty in interpreting. Over three years, considerable development took place so that 'by the end of the period gross errors in the performance of directives had largely been eliminated' (1983:154). Wes could use request formulas productively, he had abandoned V + –ing in commands, he had increased the range of request patterns at his disposal (for example, 'Let's ...' and 'Shall we ...?' had appeared), and in general gave evidence of much greater elaboration in his requesting behaviour. However, Schmidt noted that Wes was still limited in his ability to vary the use of directive type in accordance with situational factors, and also sometimes used a particular pattern in inappropriate ways. In general, Wes's strategic competence in performing requests developed considerably, but without much corresponding linguistic development.

The second longitudinal study indicates a similar PATTERN OF DEVELOPMENT to that of Wes, although in this case the two learners (L1 = Portuguese/Punjabi) were children acquiring L2 English in a classroom context in London. In Ellis 1992, I claimed that there was clear evidence of a developmental progression. For example, requests for goods were first performed by means of verbless utterances (such as 'Pencil please?'), reflecting the PRE-BASIC VARIETY discussed in Chapter 3. Next, mood derivable requests with an imperative verb appeared (such as 'Give me a paper') and only a short time afterwards query preparatory requests using 'Can I have ...?' This formula was frequently used and alternative ways of requesting goods did not appear until much later. It also took time for 'Can I ...?' to appear in a range of syntactic frames (for example, 'Can I take a book with me?' and 'Can you pass me the pencil?'). I also identified a number of general areas of development. For example, the overall range of request types expanded, the range of exponents of a specific request type increased, and requests that encoded the hearer's perspective (as opposed to the speaker's) emerged. However, the learners' requests were still limited in a number of ways by the end of the two-year period. The majority of their requests were still of the direct kind. There were few examples of non-conventional requests. Certain types of requests (performatives and hedged performatives) did not occur at all. The range of formal devices was still very limited. There was little attempt to employ either internal or external modification. The learners failed to modify their choice of request strategy systematically according to addressee (teacher or another pupil). I suggested two possible explanations for these developmental limitations. One was that the learners were still in the process of acquiring the linguistic and pragmatic knowledge needed to perform requests. According to this explanation, many features of requests are acquired late. The other explanation was that the classroom setting did not afford the appropriate communicative conditions for full acquisition of request forms and strategies.

The third longitudinal study (Achiba 2003) investigated the acquisition of English requests by one 7-year-old Japanese girl called Yao living in Australia. Achiba identified four phases of development. In the first phase all strategy types were used but with limited linguistic realization devices (i.e. they were mainly formulaic). In this phase, modification of the head request act (i.e. the act that performs the actual request) was also very restricted with the learner relying on attention-getters and repetition. 'Please' was used during this phase but more as a marker of requesting than of politeness. The second phase was characterized by a dramatic reduction in the use of FORMULAIC SEQUENCES and the development of metalinguistic awareness. Greater variety of modification devices was also evident (for example, toners such as 'just', and explanations). 'Please' was now used as a marker of politeness. The third phase was a period of pragmatic expansion. Many new linguistic forms were added to Yao's repertoire (for example, 'Shall we ...?', 'Could you (I/we) ...?' and different types of obligation statements). Yao was now able to mitigate the impositive force of her requests by modifying her requests with explanations. In the final phase, the linguistic devices for performing indirect strategies increased (for example, 'Would you like to ...?', 'Is there ...?' and 'Do you have a ...?'). Yao was also now able to mask both the object requested and the action required when hinting. Concurrent with Yao's pragmalinguistic development was her growing sociocultural awareness of Australian requestive behaviour. Achiba was also able to show that Yao varied in her choice of request strategy depending on the goal of her requests. For example, in phase one Yao used mood derivable requests for requesting goods, initiation of action, and cessation of action but suggestory formulas for requests for joint activity. The choice of strategy according to goal changed over time. Thus by phase four, growing differentiation was evident (for example, PREPARATORY ACTS that preceded the head request act were used primarily to initiate joint activity). In contrast, the addressee had only a limited effect on strategy choice. Overall, Achiba considers that Yao's pragmatic competence increased significantly but she also noted that her development was not complete, as even in the final phase instances of unmotivated rudeness in her requests occurred.

These three longitudinal studies are suggestive of a developmental profile for requesting in an L2. Kasper and Rose (2002: 140), drawing on the same three studies, suggested that development involves five stages:

1 the pre-basic stage (i.e. context-dependent requests lacking in verbs)
2 the formulaic stage (i.e. reliance on unanalysed formulaic sequences and imperatives)
3 the unpacking stage (i.e. formulaic sequences are analysed allowing for more productive use and a general shift to conventional indirectness)
4 the pragmatic expansion stage (i.e. the pragmalinguistic repertoire is extended, greater mitigation, more complex syntax)
5 the fine-tuning stage (i.e. fine-tuning of the requestive force to participants, goals and contexts).

Wes was at stage 2 at the beginning of Schmidt's study and advanced only as far as stage 3. Ellis' learners were complete beginners and thus were at stage 1 to begin with progressing as far as stage 3. Yao started off at stage 2 and progressed all the way to stage 5. However, Kasper and Rose noted that there are dangers in characterizing development in terms of macro-strategies without also considering how learners' use of specific sub-strategies develops.

Study	**Participants**	**Data collection instruments**	**Main results**
Schmidt 1983	One adult ESL learner (L1 Japanese); naturalistic setting	Audio recordings in different natural settings	Learner showed initial reliance on small set of formulas and lexical clues ('please'); by end he had control of wide range of request formulas but could not always use them appropriately.
Ellis 1992	2 ESL learners (10–11 yrs old; L1s Portuguese and Punjabi) classroom setting	Pencil and paper records and audio recordings	Clear evidence of developmental progression, but learners did not make elaborated requests and were limited in their ability to use requests in a number of ways (e.g. used few hints and little modification).
Achiba (2003)	One 7-year-old child Japanese learner of English in Australia; naturalistic setting	Audio and video recordings of the learner's interactions with three interlocutors (classmates, teenager, and adult)	Clear evidence of development in the repertoire of strategies and linguistic forms used and the types of modification observed. The learner's choice of strategy also depended on the goal of her request.

Table 5.5 Longitudinal studies of learners' acquisition of requests

What general conclusions can we come to regarding L2 learners' use and acquisition of requests? Learners—even relative beginners—appear to have few problems in understanding the illocutionary force of a request, probably because they are able to make use of situational cues. Advanced learners are able to perceive the sociolinguistic meanings encoded by different request types, although they may be oversensitive to these. With regard to production, learners begin with very simple requests and then slowly build up their repertoire, learning not only an increasing number of formal devices for performing them, but also how to mitigate their requests in accordance with the impositive load. In other words, there is clear evidence of pragmalinguistic development, although even very advanced learners do not conform fully to target-language norms, showing a tendency to verbosity, perhaps because they are aware of the dangers inherent in making requests. There is less clear evidence of sociopragmatic development, especially in the case of adults in foreign language contexts. In particular, the studies to date do not provide clear evidence that learners are sensitive to their addressees (i.e. able to select strategies in accordance with power and status differences). As Kasper and Rose (2002: 145) commented in conclusion to their survey of studies of L2 requests:

> ... despite already possessing considerable universal pragmatic knowledge, adult L2 learners appear to require a great deal of time to develop the ability to appropriately map L2 forms to social categories.

Apologies

An apology requires the speaker to admit responsibility for some behaviour (or failure to carry out some behaviour) that has proved costly to the hearer. Thus, it can be viewed as a face-saving act. Apologies differ from requests in an important respect—speaker/hearer orientation. That is, they impose on the speaker rather than the hearer. Apologies also differ from requests in that they refer to past rather than future events.

Apologies may also differ from requests in another important way. Whereas there are substantial cross-cultural differences in the way requests are realized in different situations, this does not appear to be the case with apologies. Olshtain (1989), in a study that was part of the Cross-cultural Speech Act Realization Project, investigated the strategies used to realize apologies by speakers of four different languages: Hebrew, Australian English, Canadian French, and German. As in most of the other studies in this project, data were collected by means of a discourse completion task. Olshtain reached the following conclusion:

> ... we have good reason to expect that, given the same social factors, the same contextual factors, and the same level of offence, different languages will realize apologies in very similar ways.
> (1989: 171)

However, although apologizing constitutes a universal illocutionary act, it would seem likely that different cultures will realize apologies in different ways.[3] For example differences have been observed between English and Japanese. Nonaka (2000), for instance, suggested that Japanese say 'I'm sorry' to show consideration towards their interlocutor's feelings even if the speaker is not at fault, whereas Americans only apologize if they consider themselves in the wrong. Kumagai (1993) made a similar distinction, describing Japanese apologies as 'penitent' and American as 'rational'. Thus whereas some learners may be able to make effective use of their L1 strategies to apologize, other learners may not. As we will see, all learners experience some degree of difficulty in apologizing in an L2.

The principal strategies for apologizing have been described by Olshtain and Cohen (1983). They pointed out that when a speaker is confronted with a situation in which the interests or rights of a hearer have been violated, one of two things can happen: the speaker can reject the need for an apology, or can accept responsibility for the violation and apologize. In the case of the former, the speaker may deny that there is a need to apologize or deny responsibility for the violation. In the case of the latter, there are a number of strategies which the speaker can choose from and perform with different levels of intensity.

The basic strategies (based on Olshtain and Cohen 1983), together with examples of the semantic formulas that realize them, are shown in Table 5.6. The apology strategies and formulas shown in Table 5.6 have been confirmed in subsequent studies. Blum-Kulka, House, and Kasper (1989b), for instance, provided a similar list. The first ('an expression of an apology'), which is realized by an explicit illocutionary force indicating device of a formulaic nature, constitutes a direct strategy, and is clearly necessary for the performance of the speech act, whereas the other strategies are more indirect and serve as ways of elaborating the speech act. An apology can be performed with different levels of intensity. For example, the speaker can say 'I'm sorry' or 'I'm very sorry', or can use multiple strategies to increase the intensity. There are also strategies for downgrading apologies, such as when the speaker says 'Sorry, but you shouldn't be so sensitive' (Blum-Kulka, House, and Kasper 1989b: 21). It should also be noted that paralinguistic features such as tone of voice are likely to be important in apologizing. However, these have not been systematically investigated.

Strategy	**Semantic formulas**
1 An expression of an apology	
a expression of regret	I'm sorry.
b an offer of apology	I apologize.
c a request for forgiveness	Excuse me.
2 An explanation or account of the situation	The bus was late.
3 An acknowledgement of responsibility	
a accepting the blame	It's my fault.
b expressing self-deficiency	I wasn't thinking.
c recognizing the other person as deserving apology	You are right.
d expressing lack of intent	I didn't mean to.
4 An offer of repair	I'll pay for the broken vase.
5 A promise of forbearance	It won't happen again.

Table 5.6 The speech act set for apologies (information and examples taken from Olshtain and Cohen 1983)

Apologies in an L2 have been studied by Cohen and Olshtain (1981), Olshtain and Cohen (1983), Fraser (1981), Olshtain (1983), Blum-Kulka and Olshtain (1984), House (1989), Olshtain and Cohen (1989), and Rintell and Mitchell (1989). Later studies include Linnell *et al.* (1992), Maeshiba *et al.* (1996), Kondo (1997) and Rose (2000). All these studies made use of data elicited by means of either a written discourse completion or an oral role-play task. The subjects of these studies came from a variety of language backgrounds. In most of them baseline data from the learners' L1 and from native speakers of the target languages were also collected. The studies suggest that L2 learners' performance of apologies is influenced by a number of factors: (1) the learners' level of linguistic proficiency, (2) their L1, (3) their perception of the universality or language specificity of how to apologize, (4) the nature of the specific apology situation, and (5) the learning context.

Evidence that the learners' level of linguistic proficiency influences how they apologize is forthcoming when it can be shown that learners' L1 apologies and those of native speakers of the target language are very similar, but differ from the learners' L2 apologies. In such cases L1 TRANSFER is possible but does not actually occur, presumably because the learners lack the necessary L2 proficiency to do so. Cohen and Olshtain (1981), in a study of Hebrew learners of L2 English, found situations where the learners did not seem to be familiar with the semantic formulas needed for the apology. For example, they were less likely to offer repair when they had backed into someone's car, and less likely to acknowledge responsibility when they had bumped into and shaken up an old lady than when they performed the same apologies in their L1. In a later paper, Olshtain and Cohen (1989) distinguished three types of deviation resulting from gaps in linguistic competence. OVERT ERRORS occur when the learner is evidently trying to apologize but produces a linguistic error as in this example:

> Situation: bumping into a woman in the way. 'I'm very sorry but what can I do? It can't be stopped.'

where the speaker uses 'stopped' instead of 'avoided'. COVERT ERRORS occur when the learner's apology is linguistically correct but is inappropriate. For example, a Hebrew learner of L2 English apologized for failing to keep an appointment with a friend with 'I really very sorry. I just forgot. I fell asleep. Understand'. Faulty realization of a semantic formula occurs when the learner has chosen an appropriate formula but phrases it incorrectly, as when one learner wanted to offer repair for forgetting a meeting with someone by using this formula: 'I think I can make another meeting with you'. In other words, lack of linguistic proficiency may be reflected in the use of general formulas and saying too little.

However, not all studies provide clear evidence of the effect of L2 proficiency. Linnell *et al.* (1992) found no relationship between their learners' performance of apologies and TOEFL scores. Also, Rose (2000) found relatively few differences in the three groups of primary school learners he investigated, although, as proved the case for requests, the more advanced learners did use more modification devices. It is possible that the learners in these studies were not sufficiently advanced for the differences in their general proficiency to impact on how they performed apologies.

L1 transfer has been noted in a number of studies. Maeshiba *et al.* (1996) reported that the effects of positive transfer were much more pervasive than negative transfer in the intermediate and advanced Japanese learners they investigated. Some negative transfer was also evident, more so in the intermediate than the advanced learners. Thus, the advanced learners showed more positive and less negative transfer than the intermediate learners. L1 transfer may influence the intensity with which apologies are performed. Cohen and Olshtain (1981) found that Hebrew speakers of English were less likely to accept responsibility for an offence or to make offers of repair than native English speakers. Also, they did not intensify their expressions of regret as much. Olshtain and Cohen (1983) refer to an unpublished study by Wu (1981) which found that Chinese learners of English intensified regret much more than native English speakers. Olshtain and Cohen commented 'while Hebrew L2 speakers may appear somewhat rude to native English speakers when expressing regret, Chinese L2 speakers may appear overly polite, even obsequious' (1983: 30). The Chinese learners also tended to offer explanations, where native English speakers did not. This resulted in the same phenomenon observed in studies of L2 requests—a tendency to say too much.

However, it may not be the actual differences between languages, but rather the learners' attitudes about how apologies should be performed cross-linguistically, that matter. Olshtain (1983) found that the overall frequency of semantic formulas was higher in native English speakers than in native Hebrew speakers, with native Russian speakers somewhere in the middle:

English > Russian > Hebrew

She hypothesized that 'transfer from Russian or English into Hebrew as the target L2 might therefore be expected as an increase in the overall frequency of use of semantic formulas' (1983: 245). However, this was not quite what she found. Whereas the English learners decreased the frequency of their use of semantic formulas to a level approximating to that of native Hebrew speakers, the Russian learners maintained the same level as in their native Russian. Olshtain suggested that this reflects the different perceptions of the English and Russian learners. Whereas the former perceived Hebrew speakers as apologizing less than native English speakers, the latter viewed apologizing as a universal phenomenon, 'claiming that people needed to apologize according to their feelings of responsibility, regardless of the language which they happen to be speaking ...' (op. cit.: 246). Thus, transfer was governed by whether the learners saw apologies as language-specific or universal in nature. However, as Kasper (1992) noted, the Russian learners in fact supplied apology strategies in three out of five situations more frequently in L2

Hebrew than in their native Russian, despite their perceptions of universality. This suggests that learners' attitudes can be overridden by other factors.

The extent to which learners acquire the sociocultural rules of the L2 has been shown to be situation-dependent. Olshtain (1983) suggested that transfer might be more likely in situations where the learners' culturally determined perceptions of the importance of status and distance and of the severity of the offence are different from those of native speakers of the target language. For example, in the case of a situation involving backing into someone's car and causing damage, English speakers of L2 Hebrew apologized in much the same way as they did in their L1, whereas in the situation where they had insulted someone at a meeting, they did not transfer their L1 strategies but rather behaved in a similar way to native Hebrew speakers. Linnell *et al.* (1992) only found significant differences between learners and native speakers in two out of eight of the situations they investigated. The learners were less explicit and used less modification than the native speakers in an unintentional insult situation and when acknowledging responsibility for forgetting a meeting with their boss.

The learning context has also been shown to have some influence on learners' performance of apologies. Kondo (1997) investigated 45 Japanese learners of English before and after one year abroad in the United States. While these learners continued to display more concern for the hearer than native speakers (for example, by humbling themselves), they did modify their apologies in the direction of native-speaker behaviour by increasing their use of the repair strategy.

To sum up, the study of L2 apologies bears out many of the findings of the research on L2 requests. Lower-level learners may be too direct and concise while higher-level learners may be verbose. In general, however, advanced learners are more native-like. The sociocultural norms of learners' L1 influence how they apologize in an L2. The extent to which transfer takes place can be influenced by the learners' perceptions of the universality of how to apologize, transfer being *less* likely if learners recognize the language-specificity of apologies. Transfer is also more likely in situations where learners feel the need to act in accordance with the sociocultural norms of the native culture. The opportunity to interact in an L2-speaking environment enables learners to become more native-like. Somewhat disappointingly, there have been no longitudinal studies of apologies and thus it is not possible to comment on the developmental profile.

Refusals

Refusals do not fit easily into Searle's (1975) classification of speech acts. They occur in the form of responses to a variety of illocutionary acts (for example, invitations, offers, requests, and suggestions). It might be better to treat refusals as an informal 'interactional' turn rather than a 'speech act' proper. Clearly, though, they constitute another face-threatening act and require a high level of pragmatic competence.

L2 learners' refusals were studied in a series of early investigations involving Beebe and her co-researchers (Beebe and Takahashi 1989a, 1989b; Takahashi and Beebe 1987; Beebe, Takahashi, and Uliss-Weltz 1990) and also by Bardovi-Harlig and Hartford (1991). They have continued to attract attention from researchers (for example, Gass and Houck 1999; Felix-Brasdefer 2004). These studies relied primarily on data elicited by means of written discourse completion tasks or role plays but some specific examples of naturally occurring refusals are also discussed.

On the basis of an analysis of native-speaker refusals, Beebe and Takahashi were able to show that they are performed by means of a fairly limited set of direct and indirect strategies, which are shown in Table 5.7. Individual refusals are made up of different selections from these strategies in accordance with the status and power relationships holding between speaker and hearer. The analysis of learners' refusals considered (1) the order of the strategies, (2) the frequency of the strategies, and (3) the choice of semantic formulas for realizing the individual strategies in relation to native-speaker use.

Type	**Strategies**[4]	**Semantic formulas**
Direct	1 Performative	I refuse.
	2 Non-performative statement	I can't.
Indirect[5]	3 Statement of regret	I'm sorry.
	4 Wish	I wish I could help you.
	5 Excuse, reason, explanation	I have a headache.
	6 Statement of alternative	I'd prefer to...
	7 Set condition for past or future acceptance	If you'd asked me earlier I'd have ...
	8 Promise of future acceptance	I'll do it next time.
	9 Statement of principle	I never do business with friends.
	10 Statement of philosophy	One can't be too careful.
	11 Attempt to dissuade interlocutor	I won't be any fun tonight.
	12 Acceptance that functions as refusal	Well, maybe.
	13 Avoidance (e.g. silence or hedging)	I'm not sure.

Table 5.7 Semantic formulas used in refusals (based on information provided in Beebe, Takahashi, and Uliss-Weltz 1990)

The subjects of most of the studies were Japanese learners of English. Beebe and Takahashi are at pains to point out that there are certain stereotypes regarding Japanese people. Japanese people are supposed to apologize a lot, to be less direct and less explicit than Americans, to avoid making critical remarks to someone's face, to avoid disagreement, and to avoid telling people things that they do not want to hear. The results of their research indicate that these stereotypes are not warranted. Frequently, for instance, the learners were more direct than the native speakers and in certain situations they showed no reluctance to impart unpleasant information. There were, however, a number of differences between the way Japanese learners and Americans performed refusals.

One type of pragmalinguistic error concerned the order of the strategies. Beebe, Takahashi, and Uliss-Weltz (1990) found that although even proficient Japanese speakers of English in the United States employed the same range of strategies as Americans, they differed in the order in which they were typically used. For example, the Japanese speakers omitted expressions of apology or regret in refusing invitations made by people lower in status than themselves. They reacted differently according to whether the invitation originated from a higher- or lower-status person, whereas the native speakers responded according to how familiar they were with their interlocutors. The same difference was evident in the frequency with which different strategies were used. The Japanese English speakers increased the number of strategies they used when refusing a higher-status interlocutor, while the American English speakers did so when addressing familiar equals. In other words, where Americans adopted strategies consonant with solidarity, the Japanese preferred power-orientated strategies. A similar difference is evident in the content of strategies, the Japanese excuses tending to be less specific than American excuses (except when refusing food) and sounding more formal in tone. This was particularly evident in the frequent use of lofty-sounding appeals to principle and philosophy. For example, refusing the offer of a new diet, one Japanese learner responded 'I make it a rule to be temperate in eating'.

The main focus of Beebe and Takahashi's research was pragmatic transfer—the extent to which learners transfer the 'rules of speaking' of their native language into the L2. The key question was the extent to which transfer is influenced by the learners' level of L2 proficiency. Takahashi and Beebe (1987) hypothesized that Japanese learners (EFL and ESL) with higher proficiency would display more Japanese communicative characteristics in their English than less proficient learners. They based this hypothesis on the argument that lower-level learners lack the linguistic resources to encode socioculturally appropriate Japanese patterns and so resort to a simplification strategy, whereas the higher-level learners have acquired the linguistic means to make sociocultural transfer possible. The results of an analysis of the refusals produced by Japanese ESL learners gave support to this hypothesis. The more proficient learners (defined in this study as those who had been resident longer in the United States) made more frequent use of native-language patterns—in particular, the high level of formality in the tone and content of refusals (for example, 'I am very delighted and honoured to be asked to attend the party, but ...'). However, the results for the EFL learners (i.e. those studying English at college level in Japan) failed to support the hypothesis, there being no difference in the refusals of undergraduates and graduates. Takahashi and Beebe suggested that this was because 'pragmatic competence is not affected by just a few years' difference in school in the EFL context' (p. 149). Again, this study suggests that the development of pragmatic competence depends on whether the learners experience any sociolinguistic need to vary their performance of specific acts.

Gass and Houck (1999) also investigated Japanese learners. The focus of their study was the sequencing of strategies in refusals to suggestions, offers, invitations and requests. They emphasized that 'refusals are played out events, rather than instances characterized by a brief exchange or single utterance' (p. 35). For this reason, they used video-recorded open role plays, in which the participants played themselves rather than a DCT to collect data. They provided qualitative accounts of lengthy refusal sequences when the interlocutor did not accept an initial refusal. These sequences involved multiple episodes containing the same strategies identified by Beebe, Takahashi, and Uliss-Weltz but used to negotiate an outcome. The learners experimented with different responses. They did not just transfer strategies from Japanese but rather actively searched for linguistic and attitudinal resources to achieve their refusals.

Felix-Brasdefer's (2004) study extended Gass and Houck's work in two respects. First, it examined the sequential organization of politeness strategies in advanced native-speaking English learners of L2 Spanish. Second, it also examined what effect the learners' length of residence in a Spanish-speaking environment had on their use of politeness strategies. Data were collected by means of role plays. Felix-Brasdefer found clear evidence of L1 transfer. For example, the learners, like native speakers of English but unlike native speakers of Spanish, frequently made use of pre-refusal strategies to initiate a refusal. The pre-refusals involved various positive politeness strategies such as expressing a positive opinion or willingness. The learners' length of residence in a Spanish-speaking environment was found to influence the extent to which they employed internal modification of the refusals by means of lexical and syntactical devices. Learners who had spent nine months or more approximated the levels of mitigation found in native speakers of Spanish.

The study of L2 refusals is more limited than the study of requests or apologies. There have been fewer studies, none of them longitudinal, and a narrow range of participants. However, the work done raises a number of interesting points. First, L2 learners' pragmatic behaviour is not always in accordance with stereotypical views. Second, although advanced L2 learners have no difficulty in performing refusals, they do not always do so in the same way as native speakers. One possible reason for this is pragmatic transfer. Thus, highly proficient Japanese learners respond to the status of their interlocutors with negative politeness strategies, rather than to how familiar with them they are, by means of positive politeness strategies. Third, learners may need to reach a threshold level of linguistic proficiency before pragmatic transfer can take place. Fourth, some learners are able to engage in lengthy negotiations using a variety of semantic formulas to achieve a refusal. Fifth, learners who have lived in an environment where the L2 is the medium of communication for some time are more likely to perform refusals in a native-like way.

Final comments

There have now been a substantial number of studies of L2 learners' perceptions and performance of a range of illocutionary acts. However, most of these studies have been cross-sectional, making it difficult to reach reliable conclusions about developmental sequences. Below are some general conclusions that are supported by the research to date.

1 Just as learners make linguistic errors, so too they make pragmatic errors. These are of two kinds: sociopragmatic and pragmalinguistic (Thomas 1983). Learners appear better able to overcome their pragmalinguistic than their sociopragmatic errors. Learners progress steadily in developing a full range of strategies for performing illocutionary acts and in learning how to perform them using varied linguistic means. However, it takes learners a long time to learn the sociocultural rules underlying the performance of specific illocutionary acts. Many learners may never do so.
2 There does not appear to be a linear relationship between how learners perform specific illocutionary acts and their general proficiency. In addition to the studies already mentioned, Matsumara's (2003) study of Japanese university-level students' advice-giving in English reported that proficiency, as measured by the TOEFL had only a weak and non-significant effect. However, some proficiency-related effects have been observed. Learners with little lexical or grammatical knowledge of the L2 are restricted not only in what illocutionary acts they can perform, but also in how they perform them. Advanced learners are more native-like but have a tendency to verbosity. Proficiency can also have an indirect effect on pragmatic development. Matsumara found that the higher-proficiency learners in his study benefited more from exposure to English in Canada.
3 Transfer is the other major factor identified. According to the positive correlation hypothesis, the more proficient the learner the more likely transfer is to take place. In other words, transfer only becomes possible when learners have achieved sufficient L2 resources to make it possible, as Takahashi and Beebe (1987) proposed. A second hypothesis is that the more proficient the learner the greater the positive transfer but the less the negative transfer will be, as Maeshiba *et al.* (1996) proposed. It is possible that the relationship between proficiency and transfer will depend on the specific illocu-

tionary act being investigated. It is also possible that the extent to which transfer takes place may be governed by the learners' perceptions about transferability, in particular by the extent to which learners view their L1 and the L2 strategies as equivalent in terms of contextual appropriateness (Takahashi 1996).

4 Factors other than L2 proficiency and L1 transfer may impact on how learners perceive and perform illocutionary acts in the L2. Beebe and Takahashi (1989a) invoke SPEECH ACCOMMODATION THEORY (see Chapter 4) to suggest that Japanese learners' directness may reflect 'psychological convergence'. That is, they may attempt to converge towards a stereotypical norm of native-speaker behaviour, but overshoot the mark, thus diverging. Such convergence can be teacher-induced, as when Japanese teachers advise their students to be direct when in the United States, resulting in learners producing such refusals as 'Hell no!'. Another possibility is found in Preston's (1989) observation that learners may sometimes wish to appear 'learner-like' as this brings communicative advantages in certain situations, a point taken up later in the discussion of impression management. Preston suggests that this may account for the greater verbosity of advanced learners' speech acts. It is possible that learners vary their style of speaking, sometimes opting to perform in accordance with their stereotypes of native speakers and sometimes emphasizing their status as learners.

5 The extent to which length of stay in an environment where the L2 is a medium of communication assists learners to approximate more closely to native-speaker pragmalinguistic and sociopragmatic norms is a matter of controversy. Some studies (for example, Blum-Kulka and Olshtain 1986; Matsumara 2003) have shown that length of stay or amount of exposure to the L2 has a greater effect than linguistic proficiency. However, Kasper and Rose (2002) did not find length of residence a reliable predictor of L2 pragmatic ability.

6 Finally, the extent to which learners are able to encode illocutionary acts in socially appropriate ways may also depend on psycholinguistic factors (i.e. whether their attention is focused on simply getting the propositional content of their utterance across or also on its modality). Kasper (1984a) found that when learners were under communicative pressure they tended to engage in MODALITY REDUCTION.[6] That is, they omitted grammatical features such as modal verbs and adverbials associated with the expression of modal meanings like possibility and tentativeness.

This account of pragmatic development tends to assume that learners are targeted on some set of native-speaker norms. As Blum-Kulka (1991) noted, such an assumption is questionable, however. Learners may prefer to maintain their own ethnic identity or they may wish to establish a separate identity as an L2 learner/user. In such cases, behaving in accordance with native-speaker norms will be perceived as inappropriate. The distinctive pragmatic features evident in the language of even very advanced L2 learners may reflect not so much a failure to achieve target-language norms as the attainment of a mode of behaviour compatible with the learners' chosen sense of identity. (See Chapter 7 for further discussion of this aspect of L2 acquisition.) This observation may apply more to sociopragmatic than pragmalinguistic choices, for, as Thomas points out, 'sociopragmatic decisions are *social* before they are linguistic, and while foreign learners are fairly amenable to corrections they regard as linguistic, they are justifiably sensitive about having their social ... judgement called into question' (1983: 104).

Interactional acts in learner language

The development of pragmatic competence involves more than learning how to perform illocutionary acts in pragmalinguistically and sociopragmatically appropriate ways. It also involves learning how to take part in interactions in the L2. Broadly speaking this entails the acquisition of 'discourse ability', including topic initiation and development, conversational organization and management (for example, openings and closings), repair of miscommunication, conversational strategies, narrative structure, and small talk. As these aspects are dealt with elsewhere (see Chapter 6), we will focus here on one aspect of discourse ability that underlies the other aspects–impression management. This concerns how a speaker's pragmatic behaviour impacts on the attitudes of their interlocutors and is thus closely connected with the idea of 'face', so central in speech act theory. However, the study of impression management has been informed by INTERACTIONAL SOCIOLINGUISTICS (Erickson and Schultz 1982; Gumperz 1982; Scollon and Scollon 1983) rather than speech act theory and thus warrants separate consideration. Interactional sociolinguistics examines how speakers achieve communicative effects by manipulating their linguistic and non-linguistic resources.

The choices that individual speakers make from the repertoire of signs available to them serve as one of the ways in which they seek to form and change the attitudes that other speakers have towards them. Speakers exploit CONTEXTUALIZATION CUES (i.e. the signals that trigger how speakers view the context they are attempting to build through interaction) to channel the listeners' interpretations of what is being said. In particular, cues that are in some way unexpected serve as devices for managing the listener's impressions of a speaker. The study of these cues has involved the qualitative analysis of social encounters in which potential problems of communication arise because the speakers do not share the same cues or because they attribute different values to those cues they do share. (See Gumperz 1982.)

Learners often experience problems in impression management. Chick (1985, cited in Wolfson 1989a) found that black students in South Africa were unable to overcome the negative cultural stereotypes held by their white professors in discussions of their examination results despite the fact that they were fluent L2 speakers. Chick argued that this failure arose from 'a mismatch of contextualization cues'. Roberts and Simonot (1987) reported a study of minority ethnic workers in encounters with an estate agent and in more informal conversations with a researcher. They describe the interactional style of one worker who was content to play a subservient role in the estate agent encounter. He never offered information, he developed only those themes which the estate agent had explicitly sanctioned, and he omitted affective responses that might have conveyed to the estate agent that his wishes were not satisfied. Roberts and Simonot suggested that this learner's repeated failure to negotiate a context in which he could participate as an equal resulted in his failure to acquire the interactional knowledge needed to escape from his disadvantaged social position. They noted that this learner was typical of their learners. Kerekes (2005) reported that one reason why non-native-speaking light industrial candidates in the United States were unsuccessful in job interviews was because they did not share a common discourse style with their interviewers. She suggested that the interviewers represented a higher prestige discourse style than the candidates and that discourse style served as an indicator of social and educational background.

Learners are likely to experience difficulties in identifying the right contextualization cues to deal with problems that arise in interaction. Fiksdal (1989) used the techniques developed by Erickson and Schultz (1982) to investigate how Chinese speakers of English handled uncomfortable moments during academic advisory sessions with native-speaker advisers. In this kind of situation, problems arise when the learners need to reject the advice offered by the native speaker. Fiksdal found that, unlike native-speaker students, the Chinese students either delayed or omitted offering verbal repair of uncomfortable moments and, in the case of delayed repair, showed a preference for an implicit rather than an explicit statement. She suggested that this may reflect their wish to avoid forcing the advisers to lose face by indicating that their advice is not acceptable.

Sometimes learners may be able to substitute alternative contextualization cues, by drawing creatively on their interlanguage resources. Rampton's (1987) study of ESL learners in a London language unit indicates one way in which this might take place. He observed these learners using primitive interlanguage forms such as 'me no like' and 'me too clever', even though they clearly possessed the competence to produce more target-like forms. A form–function analysis revealed that the 'broken English' forms were used to perform potentially face-threatening acts such as rejection/refusal and boasting. Rampton suggested that the learners made deliberate use of 'me' constructions to symbolize their cultural and social incompetence as a way of mitigating the force of these face-threatening speech acts. By emphasizing their learner status, they were able to challenge the teacher or play down their attempt to claim superiority over their peers.

Learners also need to acquire the devices that signal an affective common ground. In Japanese this involves learning to use acknowledgement expression such as 'hai' (yes) and 'aa soo desu ka' (I see) and alignment markers such as 'ii desu ne' (nice, great). In a longitudinal study of two American learners of L2 Japanese enrolled in a first year JFL course, Ohta (2001a) showed that they developed from an early reliance on repetitions and formulaic expressions to more productive use of expressions. By the end of the year the faster of the two learners was able to use a range of expressions spontaneously and appropriately.

To sum up, when learners participate in conversations with native speakers and other learners—particularly if the encounters are of the unequal kind—they need to negotiate the impression they wish to create. Frequently, they lack knowledge of the relevant contextualization cues. One solution is to accept the social role allocated to them—a kind of avoidance strategy. Another is to substitute cues from their native language—a form of transfer. A third solution is to make creative use of their interlanguage resources to exploit their status as language learners. Over time, however, learners develop more native-like ways of managing impression.

The relationship between linguistic and pragmatic development

What is not clear in the foregoing account of research into interlanguage pragmatics is the extent to which the acquisition of pragmatic knowledge is distinct from or related to the acquisition of linguistic knowledge. It can be assumed that L2 learners already possess knowledge of the illocutionary acts that can be performed in the L2 as these are essentially universal. Similarly, many of the strategies for realizing specific illocutionary acts are universal and so do not need to be acquired. It can also be assumed that learners have sociopragmatic knowledge although, of course, they will still need to discover how the sociopragmatic norms of the L2 differ from those of their L1. Arguably, then, the main learning task facing the learner is acquiring the pragmalinguistic tools (i.e. the semantic formulas) for performing illocutionary strategies and achieving sociopragmatic appropriateness. This raises the key question of the relationship between pragmalinguistic development and grammatical development. Do learners acquire grammar and then put this to use to convey pragmatic meanings? Or do they acquire pragmalinguistic devices and derive grammar from these? Or does pragmalinguistic and grammatical development take place concurrently with each feeding off the other? As Bardovi-Harlig (1999b) pointed out, such questions are not easy to answer because the bulk of the research has been comparative rather than acquisitional in nature (i.e. it has compared L2 and native-speaker pragmatic behaviour rather than investigated how learners develop pragmatic competence over time).

There is evidence to support the separateness of pragmatic and grammatical development in a second (as opposed to foreign) language context. Schmidt's (1983) longitudinal study of Wes documented considerable development in pragmatic competence without any commensurate development in linguistic competence. Schmidt commented that Wes 'developed considerable control of the formulaic language that acts as social grease in interaction' (p. 154) and that this enabled him to show pragmatic development while not advancing much linguistically. Similarly, the classroom learners I investigated in Ellis (1992) relied extensively on formulaic expressions especially in the early stages of their development of L2 requests. Achiba (2003) likewise noted that Yao's early requests were largely formulaic. Dittmar and Terborg's (1991) longitudinal study of 16 Polish learners of German found that learners first used 'bitte' (please) to signal the requestive force of an utterance and did not acquire its use as a politeness marker until later. These studies and other studies of naturalistic learners (see Chapter 3) suggest that the early stage of acquisition is essentially pragmatic rather than grammatical. That is, learners grab at the slender linguistic resources at their disposal (formulaic sequences, simple lexis, and intonation) to perform the illocutionary acts that are communicatively important to them. At this stage they are simply not in a position to attend to sociolinguistic niceties. If, as has been strongly argued in Chapter 3, lexis and formulaic sequences serve as the foundation for the development of grammar, then, at least in the case of learners in a second language context, the development of some minimal pragmatic competence can be seen as the basis for the subsequent development of grammar.

However, it does not follow that the pragmatics-precedes-grammar sequence continues throughout the course of a learner's development. We have already seen that learners whose overall proficiency is very advanced (and therefore can be assumed to have a high level of grammatical competence) may still be lacking in pragmatic skills. There is also considerable evidence that the acquisition of grammar constitutes the condition for the performance of more subtle pragmatic meanings. Bardovi-Harlig (1999a), for example, presented evidence to suggest that 'acquisitionally, we cannot expect pragmatic extension of tense-mood aspect forms until the core deictic meanings have been acquired' (p. 695). Similarly, Takahashi (1996) reported that where native speakers preferred biclausal request formulas (for example, 'I was wondering if you could ...') Japanese university students opted for monoclausal formulas, a finding most easily explained by the fact that they had not yet acquired the biclausal constructions involved. Grammar serves as a resource for encoding different kinds of meaning—semantic meaning (for example, indicating the duration of an action or expressing a reason) as well as pragmatic meaning. As Kasper (2001) put it, 'linguistic expressions have a double life as symbols and indexicals'. For example, the modal *can* serves to convey ability (semantic meaning) as in:

I can swim one hundred metres.

and to perform a request (pragmatic meaning) as in the formulaic sequence:

Can I have a ...?

When learners acquire new grammatical forms they may do so either in conjunction with their symbolic/semantic or indexical/pragmatic meaning. In later stages of development, grammatical forms may be first acquired in relation to their core semantic meanings and only take on a pragmalinguistic function later. If this line of argument is accepted, then, it can be argued that grammatical development precedes pragmatic development.

Clearly, though, much may depend on the context of acquisition. In a second language context, where learners are exposed to the communicative uses of the L2, the pattern of development may be as described above. However, in a foreign language context, learners may have both limited opportunity and limited need to perform a range of illocutionary acts while the type of instruction they are exposed to may prioritize grammar. In such a context, grammatical development is likely to precede pragmatic development even in the early stages. Such learners acquire grammar and only later learn how to put this to use pragmatically. Thus, we might expect differences in the kind of competence evinced by second and foreign language learners. A study by Bardovi-Harlig and Dörnyei (1998) set out to investigate if this is the case. They elicited judgements of English utterances (presented in scenarios) from high- and low-proficiency ESL and EFL learners. The judgements required the participants to indicate whether each utterance was appropriate or correct and in the case of negative judgements to assess the severity of the deviation. Clear differences were found in the judgements of the ESL and EFL learners. The ESL learners identified more pragmatic errors and rated them as more severe than the grammatical errors, whereas the EFL learners found more grammatical errors which they rated as more serious than the pragmatic errors. Niezgoda and Rover (2001) also found differences between EFL and ESL learners in a replication of Bardovi-Harlig and Dörnyei's study. However, the differences were not quite the same. Whereas the ESL learners again rated pragmatic errors as more serious than grammatical errors, the EFL learners judged both pragmatic and grammatical errors as more serious than the ESL learners, possibly because they were very exam-oriented learners. Kasper (2001) concluded her own review of these studies by stating that they 'strongly suggest that pragmatic and grammatical awareness are largely independent' (p. 505).

Bardovi-Harlig (1999b) feels that it is probably premature to reach any definite conclusion about the relationship between grammatical and pragmatic competence. She suggests that clear answers will only be forthcoming when there are more studies of beginning-level learners, when elicitation procedures appropriate to such learners are available, when there are more longitudinal studies, and when researchers specifically set out to integrate the study of emergent grammar and pragmatic ability. I would concur. Tentatively, I have suggested that in naturalistic learners, pragmatic development precedes grammatical development in the early stages but subsequently grammatical development is required to perform in pragmatically sophisticated ways. In foreign language learners, however, grammatical development may precede pragmatic development from the beginning.

Conclusion

Studies of interlanguage pragmatics have concentrated on describing the differences between the way in which L2 learners and native speakers perform the same illocutionary acts. They have also focused on the pragmatic problems that learners experience. Less attention has been given to how learners' pragmatic competence develops over time. As a result, although quite a lot is now known about how learners *use* an L2, much less is known about how rules of speaking are acquired. For this, longitudinal studies are needed.

The studies to date suggest that three factors are of major importance in the acquisition of pragmatic competence. The first is the level of the learners' linguistic competence. Learners cannot construct native-speaker-type discourse unless they possess the linguistic means to do so. Learners with limited L2 proficiency find few problems in performing the speech acts that are communicatively important to them but considerable difficulty in performing them in native-like ways. However, the relationship between pragmatic and linguistic development is still poorly understood. It may differ depending on the learner's stage of development and the acquisitional context.

The second factor of obvious importance is transfer. There is ample evidence that learners transfer 'rules of speaking' from their L1 to their L2. As Riley (1989: 247) emphasized, cultural transfer is evident in the types of communicative events that learners expect to occur in a given situation, the manner of their participation in them, the specific types of acts they perform and the way they realize them, the way topics are nominated and developed, and the way discourse is regulated. Yet it is important not to overstate the role of the non-native speaker's L1 and culture. First, as we saw in the case of requests, learners have to develop a satisfactory level of linguistic competence before transfer of complicated L1 strategies and routines becomes possible. While acknowledging the importance of transfer, we also need to recognize that other factors are involved. Second, as Kasper and Dahl (1991) pointed out, researchers of interlanguage pragmatics have tended to take a very product-orientated view of transfer, which has been rejected in current process-orientated accounts. Transfer needs to be viewed as a complex process, constrained by other factors such as the learner's stage of development. (See Chapter 8.) Takahashi's (1996) transferability scale constitutes a step in this direction.

The third factor is the status of the learner. Learners do not usually participate in communicative events as equals—at least when their interlocutors are native speakers. One reason for the lack of equality may be the learner's overall social status in the native-speaker community. This is reflected in the discourse which has been observed to take place in 'gate-keeping encounters'.

But learners also have a reduced status simply because they are learners. As Harder (1980: 268) put it, 'the learner is a coarse and primitive character from an interactional point of view'. Learners are, in a sense, 'clients', and this status determines the kind of discourse they typically take part in and the role they play in it. For example, adult learners in conversations with native speakers are likely to have few opportunities to nominate topics and tend not to compete for turns. This restricts the range of speech acts they will need to perform. It is not yet clear what the repercussions of this are for the acquisition of both linguistic and pragmatic competence, but there is sufficient evidence to suggest that learners may benefit from opportunities for a more equal discourse role, such as occurs in communication with other learners.

Finally, I would like to draw attention to two limitations in the interlanguage pragmatics research to date. First, more attention needs to be given to the role that the acquisitional CONTEXT plays in learners' pragmatic development. Summing up what is currently known about the effect of the learning environment Kasper and Rose (2002) commented:

> For developing pragmatic ability, spending time in the target community is no panacea, length of residence is not a reliable predictor, and L2 classrooms can be a productive social context.
> (p. 230)

This might suggest that little is to be gained by comparing pragmatic development in different environments, but this is surely mistaken. For one thing, differences in pragmatic ability, depending on whether the context is a second or a foreign one, have been found, and length of residence has been shown to be a factor. But, more importantly, the effects of the acquisitional context need to be explored at the micro- rather than macro-level (i.e. in terms of the specific types of input and interactions learners are exposed to). In this respect, the study of pragmatic development lags behind that of linguistic development, which has for some time recognized the importance of examining specific features of the learner's linguistic environment. (See Chapter 6.) Interlanguage pragmatics research has focused more or less exclusively on learners' perceptions and productions. Even the longitudinal studies of myself (Ellis 1992) and Achiba (2003) have made no attempt to examine input and interaction.[7]

Second, it should be pointed out that the study of interlanguage pragmatics has focused on the spoken medium and has paid little attention to writing. This is particularly the case with illocutionary acts. In effect, therefore, although we know something about how 'contextualized' acts such as requests, apologies, and refusals are acquired, we know little about how learners acquire the ability to perform acts found in decontextualized, written language. Snow's (1987) study of the acquisition of definitions by French/English bilingual children indicates that 'formal definitional knowledge' constitutes an area of learning that is independent of 'communicative adequacy'. This suggests that the ability to perform speech acts like requests, apologies, and refusals in face-to-face interaction may be distinct from the ability needed to perform speech acts like definitions in writing.[8] Perhaps, though, researchers investigating interlanguage pragmatics would do well to keep clear of written language, as, it might be argued that the ability to perform discourse acts such as definitions in formal writing lies beyond the boundaries of SLA.

Notes

1 Some questionnaires do allow for opting out in the list of choices given to the participants. However, participants may be too biased by the nature of the instrument to commit to 'saying something'.

2 It should also be noted that learners may prefer to retain the patterns of pragmatic behaviour of their L1 (i.e. refuse to conform to native-speaker norms). This may be because they wish to maintain their own identity or it may be done for strategic reasons. (See the section on 'impression management' in this chapter.)

3 Olshtain (1989) added a caveat to her claim that apology strategies are universal. She noted that it may be 'an artefact of our data collection instrument—the seven apology-inducing situations were selected intentionally to create contexts that were cross-culturally very similar' (1989: 171). It remains a possibility, therefore, that there are cross-cultural differences regarding *when* speakers apologize.

4 Beebe *et al.* (1990) labelled what I have called 'strategies' in Table 5.7 'semantic formulas'. However, to achieve consistency with the earlier tables, I have used the term 'strategies' to refer to the different ways in which the act is performed and have kept the term 'semantic formulas' to refer to the linguistic devices used to realize the strategies. It should be noted, however, that interlanguage pragmatic researchers are not consistent in their use of these terms.

5 The strategies that Beebe classified as 'indirect' appear to be of two kinds, which perhaps should be distinguished. Some of the formulas, for example, (4) 'Wish', are likely to be used alongside direct refusals (for example, by preparing for them), while others, for example, (5) 'Excuse, reason, or explanation' can be used in place of a direct refusal.

6 Learners are not alone in ignoring modality under certain conditions. Native speakers are also likely to forsake politeness markers if the context does not favour the explicit indication of social positions.

7 Gass and Houck's (1999) study of refusals is an exception in that consideration is given to the role played by input and interaction in pragmatic development.

8 There is, of course, a substantial amount of work on the performance of decontextualized speech acts by native speakers. (See, for example, Flowerdew's (1992) study of definitions in science lectures.)

PART THREE
Explaining second language acquisition: external factors

Introduction

The chapters in the previous section concentrated on the description of learner language. The chapters in the next three sections will attempt to explain learner language by addressing three major questions:

1 *How do learners learn a second language?*

   To answer this question it is necessary to explain how learners obtain L2 data and how they process this information in order to develop their interlanguages.

2 *Why do learners vary in how fast they learn a second language?*

   Learners vary in the speed with which they acquire an L2. What factors account for this inter-learner variation?

3 *Why do many learners fail to achieve full target-language competence?*

   As we have already seen in Chapters 1 and 3, learners vary in the ultimate level of proficiency they achieve, with most of them failing to reach target-language competence. A full explanation of L2 acquisition must account for this phenomenon.

To answer these questions we will need to consider three aspects of L2 acquisition: (1) the linguistic and social environment, (2) the 'black box' (i.e. the learner's existing knowledge and the internal mechanisms that guide L2 acquisition), and (3) individual learner factors, such as language aptitude and motivation. The focus of the chapters in Part 3 is the first of these—the linguistic and social environment. Part 4 will consider the language processing mechanisms of the 'black box', while Part 5 will examine individual learner factors. This way of categorizing explanations of L2 acquisition reflects identifiable orientations in SLA research and provides a means of organizing the information produced by research. However, it should be emphasized that there is no single nor simple explanation of L2 acquisition. A complete explanation will need to consider all three aspects and how they interact. Social factors/settings and input/interaction cannot be considered in total isolation from individual learner factors or language processing. In the two chapters in this section, therefore, while focusing attention on external factors, we will also need to give some consideration to the other two aspects.

The linguistic and social environment of L2 acquisition will be examined from two perspectives. In Chapter 6, I will examine research that has investigated the nature of the input and interactions that L2 learners experience. The theoretical perspective that informs this chapter is that of interactionist SLA. Norris and Ortega (2003) characterize this as 'based on functionalist views of language as a symbolic system that develops from communicative needs' (p. 727). In other words, interactionist SLA views L2 acquisition as a cognitive process that occurs inside the 'black box' of the mind but which is facilitated (or impeded) by the nature of the 'data' that learners obtain from the input to which they are exposed and the opportunities they have for producing the L2. It seeks to explain L2 acquisition in terms of how learners operate on the input they receive. Interactionist SLA originated in the work of Evelyn Hatch in the 1970s. It was developed through Krashen's Input Hypothesis and Long's Interaction Hypothesis and has continued as a major strand of enquiry in SLA to this day. Chapter 6 will also introduce recent work undertaken from a different theoretical perspective—sociocultural theory. This views input and interaction not simply as a source of 'data' but as a context in which acquisition itself takes place. In this chapter we will examine what sociocultural theory has to say about the kinds of interaction that are important for L2 acquisition, reserving a fuller account of this theory until Chapter 11. Chapter 6 offers an answer to the first of the questions above—how learners learn a second language.

Chapter 7 addresses the role of social factors. It draws on a broad sweep of research that is sociolinguistic in nature. It is self-evident that the social contexts in which learners find themselves influence the rate of learning and their ultimate success. Learners who have plenty of opportunities to hear and speak the L2 will generally learn more rapidly than those that have few such opportunities. It is obvious, too, that factors such as gender, ethnicity, and social identity will affect the extent to which learners are able to obtain the requisite opportunities. Nevertheless, the role of social factors in SLA is a matter of controversy. Whereas some researchers view them as central, others see them as relatively peripheral and uninteresting. For Atkinson (2002), for example, 'just as surely as language is social, so is its acquisition' (p. 527), whereas for Long and Doughty (2003) it is only the learner's mental states that constitute 'the proper domain of inquiry' (p. 866). This constitutes one of the major controversies in SLA today. In Chapter 7, I will discuss the main differences between psycholinguistic and sociolinguistic SLA before examining how social settings have been found to affect learning outcomes, how social factors such as age, gender, and ethnicity impact on learning, and how situational factors can influence the actual course of L2 acquisition. I will also outline a number of social theories of L2 acquisition. I will also, in line with Long and Doughty's objections, acknowledge that sociolinguistic SLA has shed little light on the first of the three questions above, while arguing that its is an important source of answers to the second and third questions.

6

Input, interaction, and second language acquisition

Introduction

Input can be non-interactive in the form of texts that learners listen to or read. Alternatively, it can arise out of interaction, as when learners participate in conversations. Interaction affords learners opportunities to receive input in the form of 'models' (i.e. exchange-initial utterances in the form of statements, questions and instructions that provide exemplars of specific linguistic features). It also affords learners opportunities to produce 'output' and to receive feedback on their attempts at production, in particular feedback that points out and corrects their errors (i.e. CORRECTIVE FEEDBACK). This chapter is primarily concerned with the input, output, and corrective feedback that arise through interaction but it will also consider non-interactive input.

Although all theories of L2 acquisition acknowledge a role for input, they differ greatly in the importance that is attached to it (VanPatten and Williams 2006). BEHAVIOURIST THEORIES of L2 acquisition propose a direct relationship between input and output. They emphasize the possibility of shaping L2 acquisition by manipulating the input to provide appropriate stimuli and by ensuring that adequate feedback is always available. Acquisition is thus controlled by external factors, and the learner is viewed as a passive medium. MENTALIST THEORIES view input as only a 'trigger' that sets off internal language processing (Cook 1989). Learners are equipped with innate knowledge of the possible forms that any single language can take, and use the information supplied by the input to arrive at the forms that apply to the L2 they are trying to learn. A common assertion of mentalist theories is that the input is 'indeterminate' i.e. the information that it supplies is, by itself, insufficient to enable learners to arrive at the rules of the target language. INTERACTIONIST THEORIES on input view verbal interaction as being of crucial importance for language learning in a number of ways. Interaction provides learners with input containing the data they need for acquisition. It also affords opportunities to experiment through production and to receive feedback on these attempts, thereby making the 'facts' of the L2 salient.

However, as Gass (2004) pointed out, an interactionist model is agnostic as to whether input determines acquisition or feeds the learner's innate LANGUAGE ACQUISITION DEVICE. The final type of theory offers a very different view of the relationship between input and learning. SOCIOCULTURAL SLA does not distinguish between 'input' and 'output' but rather views language acquisition as an inherently social practice that takes place within interaction as learners are assisted to produce linguistic forms and functions that they are unable to perform by themselves. Subsequently, 'internalization' takes place as learners subsequently move from assisted to independent control over a feature.

This chapter begins with a brief discussion of the main methods used to investigate input and interaction. The following two sections describe the L2 input received by learners and the interactions that learners participate in. This provides a basis for considering how input and interaction are involved in L2 acquisition through an examination of the research undertaken within the compass of interactionist and sociocultural theories.

Methods for investigating input and interaction

Descriptive methods

Many of the early input and interaction studies (for example, Hatch and Wagner-Gough 1976; Hatch 1978b; Peck 1978; Schmidt 1983) used data that had been collected to study learner production. In many cases, these data consisted of naturally occurring samples of learner language although they were sometimes supplemented by means of clinical elicitation, defined by Corder (1976) as devices for 'getting the informant to produce data of any sort'. Increasingly, researchers have used TASKS (i.e. activities that involve the exchange of information or opinions in a communicative manner) to elicit such data. Long (1981), for instance, asked sixteen pairs of subjects (consisting of American native speakers of English, and Japanese non-native speakers) to perform six different tasks, three of them involving one-way information exchange (giving instructions, vicarious narrative, and discussing the supposed purpose of the research) and three involving two-way information exchange (conversation and playing two communication games). There has been a gradual but steady move away from studying input/interaction in natural settings to studying them in laboratory settings. This raises the important question as to whether the data collected in these settings are the same or different. Gass, Mackey, and Ross-Feldman (2005), however, found very few differences in the interactional patterns resulting from the completion of three different tasks in a classroom setting (which constitutes one kind of natural setting) and a laboratory setting. However, they did find differences according to task. (See Chapter 15 for further discussion of tasks in SLA research.)

Both naturally occurring samples and clinically elicited samples need to be transcribed and then submitted to analysis. Transcription can be broad (for example, a straightforward orthographic record of the words said) or narrow (for example, include pauses, dysfluencies and suprasegmental information), depending on the goals of a study. The two main methods of analysis are (1) discourse analysis and (2) conversational analysis.[1] The former is 'the study of how sentences in spoken and written language form larger meaningful units such as paragraphs, conversations, interviews, etc.' (Richards, Platt, and Platt 1992). Good examples of a 'larger meaningful unit' in input/interaction studies are the 'negotiation of meaning' sequence (see p. 229 of this chapter) and 'language-related episodes' (see p. 271). Discourse analysis has been used to develop coding systems for quantifying the occurrence of specific speech acts arising in interactions involving learners (for example, Lyster and Ranta's (1997) typology of corrective feedback). Conversational analysis seeks to account for the 'preferential practices' that are evident in 'the sequential structure of talk-in-interaction' (Markee 2000: 25). It has focused in particular on the conversational behaviours of turn taking and repair (for example, Schwartz 1980) and figures increasingly in the study of classroom interaction (Seedhouse 2004; Markee and Kasper 2004).

Experimental methods

Increasingly, and in line with the move towards studying input/interaction in laboratory settings, experimental and quasi-experimental methods have been used to investigate the effect of specific variables on input and interaction. Experimental studies make it possible to collect baseline data consisting of conversations between native speakers performing the same tasks. Such data enable the researcher to identify what is special about the input addressed to the learners. Another advantage of such methods is that they enable the researcher to manipulate individual variables deemed likely to influence the quantity or quality of the input and thereby affect learners' comprehension of the input and acquisition. For example, Leeman (2003) designed an experimental study to investigate the effect of four different interactive conditions on learners' acquisition of gender and number marking of nouns in Spanish. In this study, different groups of learners completed the same communicative tasks in the different interactive conditions. The disadvantage of experimental studies is that it is difficult to determine to what extent the data collected are representative of the kind of communication the learners would take part in naturally. In many cases, the interlocutors have no prior knowledge of each other, as was the case in Leeman's study. As we saw in the discussion of addressee effects in Chapter 4, this may influence the language used. Interactionist SLA has generally preferred authentic data or as close a replica of this as possible given the need to manipulate the conditions under which the interaction takes place in experimental studies.

Self-report methods

SELF-REPORT methods have not been widely used in input research, as neither learners nor native speakers are likely to recall detailed features of the input and thus will not be able to provide retrospective comments that are accurate or reliable. However, Ferguson (1975) collected data on FOREIGNER TALK by asking students at Stanford University to rewrite standard English sentences in the way they thought they would say them to illiterate non-Europeans with no English. This method suffers from the same drawbacks that we noted with respect to DISCOURSE COMPLETION TASKS in Chapter 5. We cannot be sure that what people think they would say is what they would actually say. Another source of introspective information is diary studies. Brown (1985) used diaries to investigate the kinds of requests for input expressed by L2 learners. She analysed the comments the diarists made in 'any reference to input desired, to amount of input given, to type, complexity or meaningfulness of input' (p. 275). Schmidt and Frota (1986) also made use of a diary study as a means of investigating what one learner *noticed* in the input. This study demonstrated that self-report is an important tool for the input/interaction researcher, as it provides one of the best ways of discovering what it is in the input that learners attend to.

Introspective methods

Researchers have increasingly turned to introspective methods to investigate what learners attend to in the input they are exposed to. A number of studies (for example, Alanen 1995; Leow 1998; Rosa and O'Neill 1999) have used THINK-ALOUD TASKS. These require learners to say aloud what they are thinking as they concurrently process a written text. (It must necessarily be a written text as thinking at the same time as listening is well-nigh impossible.) Jourdenais (2001) reviewed the use of protocol analyses in SLA. Mackey and Gass (2005) summarized the procedures recommended for conducting think-aloud in SLA research. A potential problem of this method is reactivity. Thinking aloud potentially involves learners in 'dual processing—performing some learning task and commenting on their thinking processes' (Ellis 2001b: 37) and, as such, is likely to influence how they perform the task. However, Leow and Morgan-Short (2004) specifically set out to investigate whether this was the case and found that thinking aloud had no effect on the learners' comprehension and intake.

Another introspective method that has proved popular in recent studies is STIMULATED RECALL. In input/interaction research, this involves asking learners to retrospectively consider what they were thinking at the time when they were previously exposed to some input. To facilitate this, learners are provided with a prompt consisting of the actual snippet of oral or written text the learners were earlier exposed to. As Gass and Mackey (2000) pointed out, 'the theoretical foundation for stimulated recall relies on [an] information processing approach whereby the use of and access to memory structures is enhanced, if not guaranteed, by a prompt that aids in recall of the information' (p. 17). A good example of the use of this technique is Mackey, Gass, and McDonough's (2000) study of how learners perceived the corrective feedback they were exposed to when performing a task. The danger of this method is that learners' comments will not actually reflect what they were attending to earlier but what they notice in the prompts during the stimulated recall session. For this reason it is important that the session occurs as soon after the event as possible and that the learners are correctly prompted.

A third introspective method is IMMEDIATE RECALL. Philp (2003) cued L2 learners to repeat the last utterance they had heard by interrupting the interaction by means of two loud knocks on the table. In this way, she was able to ascertain whether the learners had noticed the native-speaker's recasts of their erroneous utterances. The danger of this method is that the interruption primes the learners to start paying attention when they would not normally have done so.

Comment

These methods have their advantages and disadvantages. For example, think-aloud favours veridicality but suffers potentially from reactivity whereas stimulated recall is likely to avoid the problem of reactivity, but veridicality becomes an issue. Immediate recall may result in untypical learner behaviour. These different methods should not be seen as mutually exclusive. Many input/interaction studies have employed multiple methods. For example, Rosa and O'Neill (1999) used an experimental design to examine the effect of different conditions of exposure to L2 input and assessed the level of the learners' awareness in the different conditions by means of think-aloud protocols.

The characteristics of input to language learners

A number of researchers have warned of the dangers of making assumptions about the nature of the input that is addressed to language learners on the basis of descriptions of the abstract system of the target language.[2] Lightbown and d'Anglejan (1985) argued the case for detailed empirical studies of actual usage, pointing out that such studies are particularly important before any claims can be made about universals of language acquisition. They found discrepancies between the declared norms for three French structures (interrogatives, negatives, and word order) and the use of these structures in everyday spoken French. They found that non-inverted interrogative forms and questions with 'est-ce-que' (which also adhere to declarative word order) are predominant in native-speaker input, contrary to the claims of the formal descriptions of linguists and grammarians and also to native-speaker intuitions. In the case of negation, 'ne' is often deleted in rapid informal speech (for example, 'Elle vient pas avec vous.'), making French a post-negation rather than double-negation language. They also note that although French is considered to be a subject-verb-object (SVO) language typologically, spoken French provides copious examples of alternative orders (VOS, VS and even OSV).

An additional problem facing the researcher is determining which kind of target language norms to consider when evaluating the learner's interlanguage. Learners vary in their choice of REFERENCE GROUP. (See Chapter 7.) Valdman (1992) talks of the 'illusive ideal native speaker', pointing out that even in cases where there is a single norm (for example, Metropolitan Standard French), 'the norm allows considerable leeway' (p. 84). Valdman goes on to argue that 'an invariant target language norm, based on the planned discourse of educated and cultivated speakers, is an illusory target for learners' (p. 94). Even assuming that accurate information regarding target-language norms is available, the problem is not overcome, as in many cases native speakers do not adhere to these norms when communicating with non-native speakers. For example, when caretakers speak to young children who are in the process of acquiring their L1, they typically adjust their speech in a number of ways. The register that results has been referred to variously as 'baby-talk', 'motherese', CARETAKER TALK (the term used in this chapter), and 'child-directed language'. Similarly, when native speakers talk to L2 learners they also modify their speech; the resulting register is known as FOREIGNER TALK. Krashen (1981: 121) also referred to INTERLANGUAGE TALK (i.e. the language that learners address to each other) but this term is rarely used today. We will now examine the formal and interactional characteristics of these registers.

Caretaker talk

Partly as a response to mentalist claims that the input that children receive from their caretakers is 'degenerate' (see Miller and Chomsky 1963), in the 1970s L1 acquisition researchers set out to examine the nature of caretaker talk empirically. Pine (1994) provides a survey of the motherese studies. More recent accounts of caretaker talk can be found in Shore (1997) and Kuhl (2000).

Caretakers adjust their speech formally so that the input that children receive is both clearer and linguistically simpler than the speech they address to other adults. Broen (1972) found that speech addressed to two-year-olds has only half the speed used with adults. Garnica (1977) showed that adults use a higher pitch when talking to children. Sachs (1977) found that mothers tune the pitch, intonation, and rhythm of their speech to the perceptive sensitivity of their children. Such modifications are often linked with additional clues provided by gesture and gaze. Caretakers also make adjustments in lexis and syntax (Snow 1976). They use a higher ratio of content words to functors and also restrict the range of vocabulary items employed (i.e. they manifest a low type-token ratio). Kuhl (2000) noted that parents often introduce new words in stereotyped phrases such as 'Where's the ___?' which help children to attend to them. Modifications in syntax are evident in a lower mean length of utterance (MLU), a measure that reflects both the length and the overall linguistic complexity of utterances. Caretakers use fewer subordinate and coordinate constructions, and correspondingly more simple sentences. They avoid sentence embeddings and they produce sentences which express a limited range of syntactical and semantic relations. Furthermore, adults' speech to children has been shown to be remarkably well formed, thus refuting the mentalist claim that the input children receive is degenerate. For example, Newport, Gleitman, and Gleitman (1977) reported that only one out of 1,500 utterances was dysfluent.

It has been suggested, however, that these characteristics are not necessarily found in the talk of caretakers in non-Western cultures (see Lieven 1994) and, thus, may reflect the particular child-rearing practices of middle-class, English-speaking parents. Harkness (1977) and Ochs (1982) respectively provided evidence to suggest that formal simplifications are not the norm in caretaker talk in Kenya and Western Samoa. Ochs and Schieffelin (1984) argued that many of the characteristics of talk observed in white, middle-class American caretakers are a reflection of a cultural predisposition for experts to assist novices and that this may not be evident in other cultures. However, they argued that 'all cultures change something about the structure with the resulting effect of aiding the child through the maze of language' (p. 55).[3]

One way in which this might be achieved is in terms of adjustments to the kinds of topics that get talked about. Parents of all cultures tend to follow the here-and-now principle by talking about topics which can be understood in terms of objects physically present and actions that are taking place at the time. Ferrier (1978) pointed out that much of the communication with young children centres on routine activities such as eating, having a bath, getting dressed, looking at picture books, playing games, etc. These activities involve caretaker and child in joint attention on a common set of objects and actions.

Caretaker speech is also characterized by INTERACTIONAL MODIFICATIONS. Both child and adult caretakers make plentiful use of attention-getters (for example, 'Look!' or 'Hey!'). Adult caretakers make special efforts to ensure that what they say is understood by their children by frequently checking comprehension and repeating all or parts of their utterances, as in this example from Snow (1972):

> Pick up the red one. Find the red one. Not the green one. I want the red one. Can you find the red one?

They are also ready to allow the child to initiate and control the development of topics. Some caretakers appear to be particularly skilful in the strategies they use to sustain and extend a conversation which their children have started. Frequently, however, their attempts to communicate are not successful, either because they fail to understand what the child has said or because the child cannot understand the caretaker. In the case of the former the caretaker is likely to probe further by means of requests for clarification (such as 'Mm?') or requests for confirmation which often take the form of a reformulation or an expansion of what the caretaker thinks the child has tried to say. When the child does not understand, the caretaker uses repetitions and paraphrases to sort out the problem. These features, of course, are not unique to caretaker talk but they have been shown to be especially frequent in comparison to discourse involving adult–adult interaction. The availability of semantically contingent input (i.e. input that is closely linked in meaning to something that the child has already said) has been found to be an excellent predictor of the child's rate of progress (Wells 1985).

It is important to recognize that caretaker talk is a dynamic register and for this reason cannot be considered restricted in scope, as claimed by some mentalists (for example, White 1987a). That is, the nature of the modifications adults make to their speech varies in accordance with their assessment of their child's linguistic competence and, in particular, their ability to comprehend (Cross 1977). Thus, the nature and extent of the modifications they make change as the child develops. Interestingly, while the relationship between the input complexity of the adult's speech and the child's linguistic competence at any one developmental point has been found to be only a weak one (Newport, Gleitman, and Gleitman 1977),[4] adults seem to step up the frequency of specific linguistic features in their input shortly *before* their children first use them in their own speech (Wells 1985). In other words, adults seem to pitch their input at a level slightly beyond the child's existing competence. In this respect, the input can be considered to be fine-tuned (Cross 1977).[5]

Researchers also considered the purposes served by caretaker talk. Ferguson (1977) suggested three possible functions: (1) to aid communication, (2) to teach language, and (3) to socialize the child. It is the first of these that seems to be the most important. As Brown (1977: 26) put it, the primary motivation is to communicate, to understand and to be understood, and to keep two minds focused on the same topic. Brown and Hanlon (1970) showed that mothers do correct children to ensure that what they say is true. Thus, if a child mislabels an object (for example, refers to a horse as 'doggie'), the mother is likely to respond with either an explicit correction (such as 'No, it's a horsie') or an implicit correction (for example, 'Yes, the horsie is jumping'). Mothers also pay attention to their children's pronunciation of words and draw their attention to politeness formulae (for example, when to say 'thank you'). However, they pay little attention to the grammatical correctness of their children's speech, allowing even blatant errors to go uncorrected. The claim that children receive no corrective feedback directed at their grammatical errors is based on only one study—Brown and Hanlon (1970)—and, as Snow (1986) noted, this study used a very narrow definition of corrective feedback (i.e. explicit corrections). Children may be able to use other clues in the caretaker's speech, such as requests for clarification and reformulations of incompletely understood utterances, as suggested in studies by Farrar (1992) and Saxton (1997). These studies support Kuhl's (2000) general claim that caretaker talk is important because it helps children to 'map native-language input' (p. 11855). There is also evidence that caretaker speech aids children's mental development as well as their linguistic development (Shore 1997).

In summary, there is now plentiful evidence to show that the speech that caretakers use in addressing children is well adapted to their linguistic abilities, particularly comprehension. Three main features of caretaker talk stand out: (1) it is more grammatical than speech addressed to adults, (2) it is simpler, and (3) it is more redundant. However, as Snow (1986) pointed out, it cannot be concluded on the basis of these findings that there is no innate component in L1 acquisition, as the studies do not enable us to determine the relative importance of innate and input factors. The studies show only that the claim that children receive degenerate or restricted input is unwarranted.

Foreigner talk

The FOREIGNER TALK (FT)[6] used by native speakers when communicating with non-native speakers displays many of the characteristics of caretaker talk. There are also some differences, however, particularly when the non-native speakers are adults. Freed (1980; 1981) compared the speech of 15 mothers studied by Newport (1976) with that of native speakers of American English to 11 adult non-native speakers. She found no differences in the degree of well-formedness and syntactic complexity (although instances of ungrammatical FT are not uncommon—see below) but she did find some in the distribution of sentence types and the interpersonal functions they encoded. In particular, declaratives were much more common in the foreigner talk, and yes/no questions and imperatives less common. Freed suggested that this reflects a general difference in purpose. Whereas the main functional intent of caretaker talk is that of directing the child's behaviour, that of foreigner talk is the exchange of information. It should be noted, however, that when FT is addressed to young children, it appears to resemble caretaker talk fairly closely. Hatch, Peck, and Wagner-Gough (1979) analysed the input in Huang's (1970) study of a 5-year-old learner and found that imperatives and questions far outweighed declaratives. The crucial factor, therefore, may be age.

A detailed study of foreigner talk necessitates a consideration of a number of issues: (1) the extent to which it occurs in native speaker–non-native speaker interactions, (2) ungrammatical input modifications, (3) grammatical input modifications, (4) interactional modifications, (5) the discourse structure of FT, and (6) the functions served by FT. As we will see later in this chapter, foreigner talk is important because it constitutes a source of input that can facilitate acquisition.

1 The universality of modifications

The majority of studies have shown that native speakers modify their speech when addressing non-native speakers. However, such modifications do not always occur and when they are found they are not always consistent. Gass (1997a) cited a number of studies that reported little or no modification. For example, Smith, Scholnick, Crutcher, Simeone, and Smith (1991) used a matched guise format to compare how 18 native speakers addressed a non-native speaker and a native speaker (actually the same person—a professional actress). They found evidence of some modifications—for example, shorter utterances—but there were also instances of what the authors called 'counter-accommodating behavior'. That is, on occasions the native speakers increased their speech rate, used complex and confusing syntax and vocabulary, and inappropriate repair strategies. Some of the native speakers expressed acute frustration, one concluding that it was 'fruitless' to try to communicate with such a linguistically incompetent non-native speaker. Gass also illustrated (in an extract from Gass and Varonis 1985) how native speakers can vary the extent of their modifications within a single conversation, reflecting their changing perception of what the non-native speaker is capable of comprehending. Finally, fairly obviously, native speakers will vary in their ability to engage in foreigner talk depending on their communicative style or skills and their prior experience of communicating with non-native speakers.

2 Ungrammatical input modifications

In one of the earliest discussions of FT, Ferguson (1971) noted that in languages where native speakers employ a copula in equational clauses in normal communication (for example, 'Mary is a doctor') they often omit it in talk directed at foreigners. Ferguson suggested that this is because the absence of the copula is considered simpler than its presence. The omission of copula is a clear example of ungrammatical FT. In subsequent publications (Ferguson 1975; Ferguson and DeBose 1977), Ferguson suggested that ungrammaticality is evident in three ways: (1) omission of grammatical functors such as copula, articles, conjunctions, subject pronouns, and inflectional morphology, (2) expansion, as when 'you' is inserted before an imperative verb (for example, 'You give me money.'), (3) replacement/rearrangement, as when post-verbal negation is replaced by preverbal negation in English FT (for example, 'No want play'). Frequently utterances will manifest all three types of ungrammaticality. As Ferguson (1971) noted, many of the features found in FT are also evident in pidgins.

A number of studies provide evidence of ungrammatical FT. (See Long 1981 and Larsen-Freeman and Long 1991 for reviews.) It is particularly likely in what Ferguson and DeBose (1977) referred to as 'talking down' situations. Thus, Clyne (1978) reported finding examples in the speech that Australian factory foremen used to address foreign workers. Germans have been found to address guest workers in the same way (Heidelberger Forschungs Projekt

1978). However, it has also been found in situations of a more neutral kind, as when passers-by give directions to tourists (Larsen-Freeman and Long 1991) and even in conversations between friends (Hatch, Shapira, and Wagner-Gough 1978).

There are striking similarities between ungrammatical FT and learner language. Table 6.1 compares the speech of an adult learner (Zoila) with that of a native-speaker friend (Rina) in the same conversation. It shows that Rina's input matched Zoila's output in a number of ways. Hatch, Shapira, and Wagner-Gough (1978) observed that Rina felt unable to stop herself producing ungrammatical utterances, but they also pointed out that her speech was not an exact copy of Zoila's. The similarity between FT and learner language should not be taken as evidence in favour of the matching hypothesis (i.e. that the source of learners' 'errors' is ungrammatical FT), for, as both Long (1983a) and Meisel (1983) noted, it may reflect a common set of cognitive processes. However, native speakers may well introduce ungrammatical forms of the kind they observe in learner language into their speech as part of the process of accommodating to their addressee. (See Chapters 4 and 7 for a discussion of accommodation theory.)

Grammatical structure	**Learner language**	**Foreigner talk**
Copula	Regularly deleted, but does occur in some contexts.	Only deleted in 5 out of 43 instances.
Pronoun 'it'	Pervasive deletion.	Also pervasively deleted.
Verb tense	Uninflected verb form used for all time reference; also V -ing used in apparent free distribution. No aux-'do'.	V -ing used grammatically Aux-'do' regularly deleted.
Negatives	'no' + V and 'I don't know' used.	Mixed 'no' + V and grammatical negatives used; 'no' + V -ing negatives most common.
Possessives	No possessive -s.	Nouns consistently marked with possessive -s.
'For'	'For' used in expressions like 'Is upset for you?'.	Similar use of 'for' found in 3 out of 15 instances.

Table 6.1 A comparison of learner language and foreigner talk (based on data from Hatch, Shapira, and Wagner-Gough 1978)

Non-standard forms are also evident in other levels of language: pronunciation and lexis, for instance. Epenthesis (the insertion of an additional vowel), the replacement of reduced vowels by full vowels, and exaggerated intonation similar to the kind observed in caretaker talk have all been noted in FT pronunciation. Interestingly, though, native speakers practising FT do not seem to follow caretakers in using a higher pitch. In lexis, 'ungrammatical' adaptations include the use of names in place of pronouns, a special lexicon of quantifiers, intensifiers and modal particles and, in highly marked forms of FT, the use of foreign or foreign-sounding words such as 'amigo', 'capito', and 'compris', which Meisel (1980) reported observing in German FT.

A number of factors appear to induce ungrammatical FT. Long (1983a) suggested that four factors may be involved:

1 The learner's level of proficiency in L2—ungrammatical FT is more likely when the learner's proficiency is low.
2 The status of the native speaker—ungrammatical FT is more likely when the native speaker is or thinks he or she is of higher status.
3 The native speaker has prior experience of using FT but only of the limited kind used to address non-native speakers of low proficiency.
4 The extent to which the conversation is spontaneous—ungrammatical FT is less likely in planned, formal discourse or in experimental situations.

However, ungrammatical FT can occur both with interlocutors who are familiars (as in the conversations between Rina and Zoila) and with strangers, suggesting that factors other than those listed by Long are at work. It is, in fact, not yet possible to identify the exact conditions that will result in ungrammatical FT, perhaps because native speakers vary both culturally and individually in the kind of FT they prefer to use.

As Meisel (1980) pointed out, ungrammatical FT is generally felt to imply a lack of respect. Meisel reported that Italian and Spanish workers in Germany reacted negatively when played recordings of speech samples containing ungrammatical FT, claiming that it showed contempt on the part of the native speakers. However, it may not be the presence of ungrammatical modifications *per se* that arouses negative responses in learners, but their awareness of being addressed in a special manner. Lynch (1988) found that some learners objected to the speech of a teacher because they perceived it as 'talking down', even though it did not contain obvious ungrammatical modifications. Also, in cases of very close relationships (as that between Rina and Zoila) ungrammatical adjustments do not appear to be objected to.

3 Grammatical input modifications

Ungrammatical FT is highly marked. In many situations it does not occur, suggesting that it constitutes a particular discourse type. Arthur *et al.* (1980) recorded 60 telephone conversations between adult non-native speakers of English and airline ticket agents and reported no instance of ungrammatical input modifications. Studies of teacher talk (for example, Henzl 1973, 1979;

Gaies 1977; Hakansson 1986) also, not surprisingly, report an absence of ungrammatical modifications, although other studies (for example, Hatch, Shapira, and Wagner-Gough 1978) did find instances in the language that teachers use to organize and manage classroom activities. Grammatical modifications are the norm in most classrooms and, not surprisingly, in the modified texts of the kind found in graded readers.

Grammatical FT is characterized by modifications reflecting both simplification and elaboration. Table 6.2 illustrates both types in examples of written text modifications from Long and Ross (1993). In the case of oral language a third type of modification—regularization—can occur. It should be noted that whereas simplification involves an attempt on the part of native speakers to simplify the language forms they use, regularization and elaboration are directed at simplifying the learners' task of processing the input and can, in fact, result in the use of language that is not always simple in itself. This is important because it means that FT provides not only simple input, corresponding perhaps to what learners already know, but also input containing linguistic features that they have not yet learnt.

Type of speech	**Example**
Baseline (i.e. speech addressed to native speakers)	Catfish have gills for use under water and lungs for use on land, where they can breathe for twelve hours or more. The hot daytime sun would dry them out, but they can slip out of their ponds at night and still stay cool while they hunt for food.
Simplified FT	Catfish have both gills and lungs. The gills are used for breathing under water. The lungs are for use on land. The fish can breathe on land for twelve hours or more. At night these fish can slip out of ponds. They move at night so they can stay cool. The hot sun would dry them out. They hunt at night too.
Elaborated FT	Catfish have two systems for breathing: gills, like other fish, for use under water, and lungs, like people, for use on land, where they can breathe for twelve hours or more. Catfish would dry out and die from the heat of the sun, so they stay in water during the daytime. At night, on the other hand, they can slip out of their ponds and stay cool while they hunt for food.

Table 6.2 Simplification and elaboration of a written text (Long and Ross 1993)

One way of simplifying is by adjusting temporal variables such as speech rate (measured usually in syllables per second), articulation rate (measured by calculating the ratio of the total number of syllables to the total articulation time) and silent pause phenomena (pause duration, pause distribution, and pause frequency). Griffiths (1991a) summarized the research in this area of FT. His survey showed that although temporal variables have frequently been commented on in the literature (for example, Freed 1981; Hatch 1983a), these comments are not accompanied by reports of detailed empirical results. Henzl's (1973, 1979) study of the teacher talk in three different languages (Czech, English, and German) addressed to advanced and beginner L2 learners and native speakers, did give results, however. The study showed that the teachers adjusted their speech rate in accordance with the listeners' proficiency, as does Hakansson's (1986) study of Swedish teachers' classroom talk. Griffiths pointed out a number of methodological flaws in both studies (for example, failure to control for the sequence of audiences and to account for classroom activity silences) and also drew attention to the fact that in Henzl's study there was enormous variability from one language to another and, in both studies, from one teacher to another within the same language. In the case of lexical modification, simplification is achieved both by avoiding difficult items in the target language and also by reducing use of them, resulting in a lower type-token ratio. One common means of achieving syntactic simplification is through avoiding the use of subordinate constructions, as illustrated in the simplified text in Table 6.2.

Regularization entails the selection of forms that are in some way 'basic' or 'explicit'. Examples include: fewer false starts; a preference for full forms over contracted forms; a preference for canonical word order noted by Long, Gambhir, Gambhir, and Nishimura (1982) in English, Hindi, and Japanese; the use of explicit markers of grammatical relations (for example, 'He asked if he could go' rather than 'He asked to go'); movement of topics to the front of sentences (for example, 'John, I like him'); avoidance of forms associated with a formal style (for example, 'tu' is preferred to 'vous' in French FT); and avoidance of idiomatic expressions and use of lexical items with a wide coverage (for example, 'flower' rather than 'rose'). Hatch (1983b: 66–7) suggested a number of ways learners might benefit from regularizations of these kinds. For example, they help to make the meanings of utterances more transparent. This may be achieved by increasing the processing time available to learners or by making key structural elements more salient, thereby helping them to identify constituent boundaries in utterances.

Elaboration is the opposite of simplification, but to claim that FT evidences both is not contradictory, as both processes can occur at different times. Elaboration often involves lengthening sentences in an attempt to make the meaning clear. Native speakers often use analytic paraphrases of lexical items they consider difficult. For example, in the elaborated text in Table 6.2, the semantic link between 'gills' and 'lungs' is made explicit in the opening phrase 'systems for breathing'. Chaudron (1983) provided a number of examples in the speech used by a university lecturer to a class of ESL learners ('hold on tightly' is used in place of 'cling'; 'there's still this feeling ...' instead of 'we have this myth'). Native speakers also sometimes offer synonyms ('funds or money') and they define items. Chaudron suggested that such elaborations are designed to make the message more 'cognitively simple', but he also made the point that they can result in too much redundant and confusing information. The lecturer he studied sometimes over-elaborated, making the interconnections between ideas difficult to comprehend. Ehrlich, Avery, and Yorio (1989) distinguished native speakers who adopted a 'skeletonizing' strategy (i.e. provided only the basic information needed to perform a task) from those who adopted an 'embroidering' strategy (i.e. providing information that expanded and embellished beyond what is required to perform the task). Derwing (1996) distinguished three types of elaboration; (1) marked paraphrase where a paraphrase is preceded with a discourse marker such as 'in other words', (2) an unmarked paraphrase, and (3) elaborative detail which included irrelevant information.

As in caretaker talk, these different kinds of adjustments are continuous in nature; speakers make more or less use of them depending on their perception of the learner's ability to understand. Hakansson (1986), for instance, found that the input provided by a teacher to learners of L2 Swedish increased in length over time as a result of an increased use of subordinations and an expansion of nominal phrases through increased modification. Kleifgen (1985) found that a kindergarten teacher's input became more complex over time with children who showed improvement, but remained static with those who did not. Age might also be a factor; children are more likely to receive simplified input than adults. (See Scarcella and Higa 1981).

4 The functions of foreigner talk

Overall, three functions of foreigner talk can be identified: (1) it promotes communication, (2) it signals, implicitly or explicitly, speakers' attitudes towards their interlocutors, and (3) it teaches the target language implicitly. Hatch (1983b) argued correctly that (1) is primary in that most adjustments are geared to simplifying utterances to make them easier to process or to clarify what has been said by either the native speaker or the non-native speaker. Hatch characterized (2) in terms of the special kind of affective bond that FT can create between the native speaker and non-native speaker, but it is also manifest in FT whose purpose is 'talking down'. (See Ferguson and DeBose 1977). In fact, it can reflect either downward divergence (such as when a native speaker deliberately employs ungrammatical forms with a competent non-native speaker to signal lack of respect), or downward convergence (such as when a native speaker approximates the interlanguage forms used by the non-native speaker as a way of signalling solidarity). This double function of (2) may help to explain why ungrammatical FT can occur between non-familiar interlocutors in service or workplace encounters and between familiar interlocutors in ordinary conversation. (3) is only 'implicit' because native speakers do not usually have any pedagogic intent, although Naro (1983) in a response to Hatch argued that FT can occur with an explicit teaching function (i.e. with the intention of helping a learner learn).

Many of the formal characteristics of FT are very similar to those found in other simplified registers such as learner language, caretaker talk, and pidgins. This suggests that it reflects universal processes of simplification, knowledge of which constitutes part of a speaker's linguistic competence. However, as Meisel (1980) pointed out, there are differences between the simplification found in FT and that observed in learner language. Whereas both manifest RESTRICTIVE SIMPLIFICATION (for example, the use of an infinitive in place of inflected verb forms), only learner language manifests ELABORATIVE SIMPLIFICATION (for example, the use of novel verb forms through processes such as overgeneralization). Meisel suggested that restrictive simplification in both registers serves 'the purpose of achieving an optimal result in communication' (1980: 36), but elaborative simplification occurs when learners are trying to complexify their interlanguage system.

An interesting question is how native speakers come to be able to adjust the level of their FT to suit the level of individual learners. Hatch (1983a) considered three ways: (1) regression (native speakers move back through the stages of development that characterized their own acquisition of language until they find an appropriate level), (2) matching (native speakers assess a learner's current interlanguage state and then imitate the forms they observe in it), and (3) negotiation (native speakers simplify and clarify in accordance with the feedback they obtain from learners in communication with them). The second was the explanation offered by Bloomfield (1933), but it seems unlikely, as it is probably asking too much of learners' interlocutors to measure simultaneously the learners' phonology, lexicon, syntax, and discourse with sufficient accuracy to adjust their own language output. The most likely explanation is (3), although (1) is also possible.

Interlanguage talk

INTERLANGUAGE TALK (ILT) consists of the language that learners receive as input when addressed by other learners. ILT constitutes the primary source of input for many learners. (See Chapter 7.) A key issue is the extent to which ILT provides learners with adequate access to the grammatical properties of the target language. Not surprisingly, ILT has been found to be less grammatical overall than FT or teacher talk (Pica and Doughty 1985a and 1985b). Porter (1986) in a detailed study of the ILT produced by intermediate and advanced L2 learners in pairwork and comparable FT found that whereas only 6 per cent of FT was 'faulty', 20 per cent of ILT proved to be so. Porter also found ILT to be sociolinguistically deficient. She looked at a number of speech acts such as expressing opinions, agreement, and disagreement and found that the learners failed to use politeness strategies to the same extent as native speakers. In general they did not generate the kind of sociocultural input needed for language learning. On the plus side, however, both Pica and Doughty and Porter found that the learners in their studies repeated only a very small amount of the faulty input they heard.

In another respect, however, interlanguage talk can be considered superior to foreigner talk. When learners talk amongst themselves in the L2 they are more likely to experience communication problems and more likely to negotiate solutions to these problems. Porter (1986), for example, found that learners prompted each other five times more than the native speakers prompted non-native speakers, while repair frequencies were similar. Mackey, Oliver, and Leeman (2003) compared NS–NNS speech with NNS–NNS speech in terms of the feedback provided and the learners' response to this feedback. They found that feedback from NNSs was more likely to result in the child learners modifying their output than feedback from the NSs although there was no difference in the case of the adult learners. Overall, these studies suggest that the input that learners obtain from others learners may be beneficial.

Summary

This section has examined three simple registers of language addressed to learners. First, in studies of caretaker talk, it has been shown that the input children receive when learning their L1 is well formed and dynamically adjusted to their level of development. Also, some caretakers seem adept at helping children to establish and develop topics that they want to talk about. Foreigner talk resembles caretaker talk in some respects, but also differs from it in others (for example, there are fewer yes/no questions). Both ungrammatical and grammatical FT occur, although it is not possible to identify the precise social conditions that favour one over the other. In the case of grammatical FT, three processes are evident: simplification, regularization, and elaboration. The modifications are continuous, influenced by the learner's stage of development, and age. Finally, we looked at interlanguage talk. This, not surprisingly, tends to be less grammatical than FT, but it is characterized by more interactional modifications associated with the negotiation of meaning. I will now consider these interactional modifications.

The characteristics of interactions involving language learners

As noted above, L2 learners do not always obtain access to the kinds of input modifications found in FT. More ubiquitous are INTERACTIONAL MODIFICATIONS. In a study that examined both interactional and input modifications, Long (1981) found few input differences between the speech native speakers addressed to other native speakers and the speech they addressed to non-native speakers. He did, however, find substantial interactional differences.

A useful distinction can be made between those interactional modifications that involve DISCOURSE MANAGEMENT and those that involve DISCOURSE REPAIR. The former are motivated by the attempt to simplify the discourse so as to avoid communication problems, while the latter occur when some form of communication breakdown has taken place or in response to a learner utterance that contains an error of some kind (factual, linguistic, or discourse).[7] A somewhat different perspective is provided by sociocultural

SLA; learners are seen as experiencing SCAFFOLDING (i.e. a dialogic process by which a speaker—a native speaker or another learner—assists the learner in performing a function that he or she cannot perform alone).

Discourse management

One of the most effective ways of managing discourse with native speakers is to ensure that the topic of the conversation is understood. Long (1983a), in his early work, identified a number of strategies which native speakers use to achieve this end: selecting salient topics, treating topics simply and briefly, making new topics salient, and, when necessary, relinquishing topic control.

One method used by native speakers to control topic concerns the amount and type of information that is communicated. Arthur *et al.* (1980) compared the number of 'information bits' that native-speaker airline agents included in their answers to a specific telephone enquiry from native speakers and non-native speakers ('What kind of plane is a __?'). A distinction was made between 'simple' information (such as 'size' and 'jet') and 'complex' information (for example, 'seating capacity', 'name of manufacturer', and 'seating arrangement'). There was no difference in the amount of simple information given to native speaker and non-native speaker callers, but significant differences were found in the amount of complex information, non-native speakers receiving far less. Derwing (1989) found that native speakers adjusted the information they provided about a film they had seen when speaking to low-proficiency L2 learners. The information was classified as belonging to one of three categories: (1) crucial information, (2) non-essential major information, and (3) minor information, consisting of background or irrelevant information. There was no difference in the amount of crucial information which the native speaker and non-native speaker addressees received, but differences were evident in the relative proportions of major and minor information. Overall the narrators included less major information and more minor information in speech to the learners. Ehrlich, Avery, and Yorio (1989) also found evidence of variation in the amount of information supplied by individual native speakers in a problem-solving task. They distinguished 'skeletonizing', where the barest details are provided, from 'embroidering', where the information is expanded and embellished. Interestingly, they found both strategies present in interactions with both native speakers and non-native speakers, suggesting that individual native speakers may have preferred interactional styles which they use irrespective of their interlocutors. It is clear, though, that native speakers often do seek to manage discourse with non-native speakers by regulating the amount and type of information they provide.

Native speakers also make use of questions to establish and control topics. We have already noted that questions appear to be more frequent in FT than in caretaker talk. Long (1981) found that in conversations between native English speakers and elementary level Japanese learners, the native speakers initiated most of the topics, typically making use of questions to do so. Questions constituted 96 per cent of all topic initiations, whereas in NS–NS conversations only 62 per cent were questions. Long suggested a number of reasons why questions were favoured: they compel answers, they signal to the non-native speaker that a turn is approaching, and they lighten the learner's conversation burden because they encode part (and sometimes all) of the propositional content required to respond. Long also found differences in the types of questions used. In conversations with the learners, the native speakers made greater use of 'yes/no' and 'or' type questions. Gaies (1982) obtained similar results in a study in which, unlike in Long's study, the native speakers and non-native speakers were already acquainted with each other. It should be noted, though, that in all these studies the native speakers were adults; child native speakers seem less inclined to establish and develop topics through questioning. (See Hatch 1978b; Peck 1978.)

A third strategy in discourse management is to select topics that have a here-and-now orientation. (See the discussion of this feature in caretaker talk.) Long (1981) and Gaies (1982) both reported significantly more present-tense verbs in native-speaker speech addressed to non-native speakers than in speech addressed to other native speakers, suggesting such an orientation. The here-and-now orientation allows learners to make use of the immediate context to interpret the meaning of utterances.

Finally, native speakers have been noted to try to manage discourse by frequently checking whether the learner has understood. Comprehension checks (for example, 'You understand?', 'Okay?') have been found to occur more frequently in NS–NNS discourse than in NS–NS discourse (Long 1981; Scarcella and Higa 1981). Teacher talk, in particular, seems to be rich in comprehension checks. Pica and Long (1986) found that ESL teachers were much more likely than native speakers in informal conversations to check comprehension.

Discourse repair

1 Negotiation of meaning and of form

The need for discourse repair arises when some kind of problem occurs. Two different kinds of problems can be identified: (1) communication problems and (2) linguistic problems. Frequently, the two coincide, especially when the source of the problem lies in something the non-native speaker has said, as in the example below. Here the non-native speaker's incorrect pronunciation of 'closed' leads to a communication breakdown. In solving the communication problem, however, the linguistic problem is addressed.

NNS The windows are crozed.
NS The windows have what?
NNS Closed?

NS Crossed? I'm not sure what you are saying here.
NNS Windows are closed.
NS Oh, the windows are closed, OK, sorry.
(From Pica 1994b)

Gass and Varonis (1991) developed a taxonomy of communication problems. An initial distinction is made between 'non-engagement' and 'miscommunication'. The former occurs either when there is 'non-communication' (for example, when a non-native speaker avoids talking to a native speaker) or when there is 'communication break off' (for example, when native speakers stop communicating as soon as they discover they are talking to a non-native speaker). 'Miscommunication' occurs when some message other than that intended by the speaker is understood. It can take the form of a 'misunderstanding' or an 'incomplete understanding' (either 'non-understanding' or 'partial understanding'), depending on whether or not the participants overtly recognize a problem and undertake repair. In the case of an 'incomplete understanding' (as in the sequence above) remediation occurs, but in the case of a 'misunderstanding' no repair occurs and the speakers are likely to lapse into silence. Gass and Varonis also noted that miscommunication can occur both as a result of cross-cultural differences in the way language is interpreted and because of purely linguistic difficulties.

Repair also occurs even when there is no communication difficulty. In such cases, the problem is purely linguistic in nature. Such repairs are uncommon in conversational interaction (although sometimes learners do request them) but very common in classroom contexts. The following example illustrates this kind of repair. Here the student mispronounces 'patriot'. The teacher, who clearly understands what the learner meant, immediately corrects him. In this case, then, there is no miscommunication but negotiation still occurs.

S yeah, I'm a patriost.
T a patriot
S yeah
(From Ellis, Basturkmen, and Loewen 2001)

Such sequences are very common in language lessons whose objective is production accuracy but they can also occur in lessons based on communicative tasks, as shown in Lyster's studies of immersion classrooms in Canada (Lyster and Ranta 1997; Lyster 1998a; Lyster 1998b) and in Ellis, Basturkmen, and Loewen's (2001) study of adult ESL classrooms in New Zealand.

Both of the above examples illustrate negotiation. NEGOTIATION OF MEANING takes place through the collaborative work which speakers undertake to achieve mutual understanding when there is some kind of communication problem. NEGOTIATION OF FORM[8] takes place when one speaker (a native speaker or teacher) elects to address a linguistic problem in the speech of a learner. Gass and Varonis (1985) and Varonis and Gass (1985) developed a model to describe the structure of 'non-understanding routines' where negotiation takes place. (See Figure 6.1.) It consists of a 'trigger', i.e. the utterance or part of an utterance that creates a problem of understanding, an 'indicator' which indicates that something in a previous utterance was not understood, a 'response' to the indicator, and finally a 'reaction to the response', which is optional. The 'indicator–response–reaction to the response' portion of a non-understanding sequence is called a 'pushdown', because it has the effect of pushing the conversation down rather than allowing it to proceed in a forward manner. The model is recursive in that it allows for the 'response' element itself to act as a 'trigger' for a further non-understanding routine.

Trigger	Resolution
T	I R RR

T = trigger (i.e. the utterance which causes misunderstanding)
I = indicator (i.e. of misunderstanding)
R = response
RR = reaction to response

Example:

S1	And what is your mmm father's job?	
S2	My father now is retire.	T
S1	Retire?	I
S2	Yes	R
S1	Oh, yes.	RR

Figure 6.1 The structure of meaning of negotiation sequences (Varonis and Gass 1985)

Modifications to the structure of negotiation sequences have been observed in computer-mediated interaction. Smith (2003a) reports that the model shown in Figure 6.1 failed to account for the pattern of interaction he observed in 14 NNS–NNS dyads completing four communicative tasks using a browser-based chat programme. One of the key differences lay in the delay that often occurred between the initial trigger (T) and the indicator (I). This delay arose because the chat-room interaction did not adhere to strict turn adjacency, causing some triggers to go unanswered. Smith identified what he called 'split negotiation routines,' where the response (R) only occurred after one or more repeat indicator moves. Smith's study suggests that the medium through which negotiation takes place can influence how it is realized.

A considerable amount of research has been undertaken to establish the conditions that promote negotiation, motivated by the claim that the COMPREHENSIBLE INPUT that can result from it is of particular benefit to L2 acquisition. (See the section Input Hypothesis in this chapter.) Pica (1987) argued that the most important factors concern the social relationships between the interactants. Interaction involving participants of equal status ensures that 'learners and their interlocutors share a need and desire to understand each other.' This can explain why negotiation occurs more frequently when NNSs interact with NNSs. Conversely, unequal status makes it difficult and even unnecessary for participants to restructure interaction. This claim mirrors that made by Wells and Montgomery (1981) for caretaker interaction. When mothers act as conversational partners, plentiful negotiation takes place, but when they adopt a tutorial role it is inhibited. It also explains why interactional modifications are more frequent outside than inside the classroom, as roles are unequally distributed in the classroom, with the teacher assigned many more discourse rights than the learners. (See Pica and Long 1986.)

A number of other factors have been found to influence negotiation: for example, the nature of the task, the characteristics of the participants, and participatory structure. Oliver (2002), for example, found that the nativeness of the child dyads (i.e. whether a learner was paired with another learner or a native speaker) and the level of proficiency influenced the amount of negotiation. Negotiation occurred most frequently in low-proficiency NNS–NNS pairings. Two-way information gap tasks that require information exchange and are performed in small groups or pairs can lead to plentiful negotiation (Pica, Kanagy, and Falodun 1993). Much of the research that has investigated the factors influencing negotiation has involved classroom learners or has been conducted for a clear pedagogic purpose, for example, to identify which tasks are likely to result in high levels of negotiation. (See Ellis 2003.) For this reason it will be considered in Chapter 15.

2 Negotiation strategies

Negotiation exchanges are accomplished by means of a variety of strategies. These are described and illustrated in Table 6.3. Three of these strategies figure prominently in the negotiation of meaning—requests for clarifications, confirmation checks, and recasts—as these lead to different learner responses and afford different kinds of opportunities for learning. Long (1996) distinguished between 'negotiation of meaning' and RECASTS. This is problematic, however, as a CONFIRMATION CHECK (a negotiation move) often cannot be distinguished formally from a recast unless intonation (rising versus falling) is used as the distinguishing feature. Oliver (1997) recognized this problem, admitting that she double coded such utterances as both confirmation checks and as 'other repetitions' (i.e. as recasts). All the strategies in Table 6.3 can figure in the negotiation of form. Metalinguistic feedback, elicitation, and explicit correction are all clearly didactic. The other strategies are less obviously so but Lyster (2002) noted that, in the IMMERSION classrooms he investigated, the teachers frequently feigned incomprehension in order to intentionally draw attention to form. In many cases, however, it is not easy to determine whether it is meaning or form that is being negotiated.

Negotiation strategies can be implicit or explicit. (See Ellis, Loewen, and Erlam 2006.) Implicit strategies such as requests for clarification or confirmation checks are only covertly corrective (i.e. they do not directly signal that a correction of a learner form is being undertaken). In contrast, explicit strategies such as METALINGUISTIC FEEDBACK or explicit correction make it clear to learners that they are being corrected. The distinction between implicit and explicit strategies, however, is best seen as reflecting a continuum rather than a dichotomy as many of the strategies can be more or less implicit/explicit. This point will become clearer when recasts are examined in the section that follows.

Negotiation strategies can also be distinguished in terms of whether they are input-providing or output-prompting (Ellis 2006a). Recasts and confirmation checks provide learners with input demonstrating target language norms. In contrast, all the other strategies, labelled 'prompts' by Lyster (2004), indicate that an error has been made but do not supply the correct forms. Instead, they constitute an encouragement for learners to try to self-correct. The distinction between input-providing strategies and output-prompting strategies is of theoretical importance because it is related to the nature of the data that learners obtain, i.e. whether the data afford both POSITIVE and NEGATIVE EVIDENCE or just negative evidence.

Negotiation strategy	**Description**	**Example**	**Type**
Request for clarification	An utterance that elicits clarification of the preceding utterance.	NNS When I get to Paris, I'm going to sleep for one whole day. NNS What? (Varonis and Gass 1985)	Implicit; output-prompting
Confirmation check	An utterance immediately following the previous speaker's utterance intended to confirm that the utterance was understood.	NNS Mexican food have a lot of ulcers. NS Mexicans have a lot of ulcers? (Young and Doughty 1987)	Implicit; input-providing
Recast	An utterance that rephrases the learner's utterance by changing one or more components (subject, verb, object) while still referring to its central meaning. (Long 1996)	NNS En las mesa hay una taza rojo. NS Um, hmm, una taza roja. (Leeman 2003)	Implicit; input-providing
Repetition	An utterance that repeats the learner's erroneous utterance highlighting the error.	S le .... le giraffe? T Le giraffe? (Lyster and Ranta 1997)	Implicit; output-prompting

Metalinguistic feedback	An utterance that provides comments, information, or questions related to the well-formedness of the learner's utterance.	S Euhm, le, le elephant, le elephant gronde. T Est-ce-qu'on dit le elephant?	Explicit; output-prompting
Elicitation	A question aimed at eliciting the correct form after a learner has produced an erroneous utterance.	S The chien peut court. T The chien peut court? Le chien peut ... (Lyster and Ranta 1997)	Explicit; output-prompting
Explicit correction	An utterance that provides the learner with the correct form while at the same time indicating an error was committed.	S La note pour le shot. T Oh, pour la, oh, pour ça. Tu veux dire pour la piqure. Oui? (Lyster and Ranta 1997)	Explicit; output-prompting

Table 6.3 Strategies used in the negotiation of meaning and form

3 Recasts

Of the strategies listed in Table 6.3, recasts have received the most attention. They have attracted a number of review articles (Nicholas, Lightbown, and Spada 2001; Long 2006b; Ellis and Sheen 2006; Mackey 2007a) and numerous empirical studies, including cross-sectional studies documenting the use of recasts in different settings and under different participatory structures such as NS–NNS as opposed to NNS–NNS interaction, (for example, Braidi 2002; Iwashita 2003; Leeman 2003; Mackey, Oliver, and Leeman 2003; Mackey and Philp 1998; Panova and Lyster 2002; Philp 2003; Sheen 2004), longitudinal studies (for example, Han 2002; Ishida 2004; Nabei and Swain 2002) and experimental studies designed to investigate the relative effectiveness of recasts as opposed to other strategies in acquisition (for example, Ayoun 2004; Long *et al.* 1998; Lyster 2004). There are theoretical reasons for this level of interest but another reason is undoubtedly convenience. Sheen (2004), in a study that compared the frequency of recasts in immersion, communicative ESL and EFL contexts found that, on average, 60 per cent of all the feedback moves involved recasts. Braidi (2002), in a laboratory study of NS–NNS dyads performing communicative tasks, reported that up to 45 per cent of the NS's responses to erroneous utterances were recasts, a lower proportion, but still substantial, especially so, given that Braidi excluded confirmation checks from her count.

Recasts are not monolithic. Rather they come in a number of different forms. Sheen (2006) offers a description of the key characteristics. (See Table 6.4.) To use this scheme, a recast is first judged to be a multi-move or single-move recast. If it is a multi-move recast then it is classified as either a corrective recast, a repeated recast or a combination recast. A single-move recast is coded in terms of each of the seven characteristics shown in Table 6.4. For example, the recast in this sequence:

S I think she'll travel together her boyfriend after the course.
T I think she'll travel together with her boyfriend.

would be coded as mode (= declarative), scope (= isolated), reduction (= non-reduced), length (= clause), number of changes (= one change), type of change (= addition), and linguistic focus (= grammar). Such a description is useful because it enables researchers to examine the relationship between different types/characteristics of recasts and learner uptake (i.e. whether the learner's response successfully incorporates the correction) and acquisition (i.e. whether as a result of exposure to a recast the learner is subsequently able to use the corrected form accurately). The results of such research are discussed later in the chapter.

The prevailing view in the recast literature is that recasts constitute an implicit form of negative feedback. Lyster (1998a) referred to their 'function of *implicitly* providing a reformulation' (p. 59) while Long (2006b) asserts unequivocally that 'a recast is a discourse move that is by definition *implicit*' (italics added). But what exactly does 'implicit' mean here? Arguably, recasts should not be viewed as necessarily implicit but rather, depending on the linguistic signals that encode them and the discoursal context, as *more or less* implicit/explicit. Corrective recasts are clearly explicit, as is evident in this example from Doughty and Varela (1998):

L I think that the worm will go under the soil.
T I *think* that the worm *will* go under the soil?
L (no response)
T I *thought* that the worm *would* go under the soil.
L I *thought* that the worm *would* go under the soil.

In other words, recasts can lie at various points on a continuum of linguistic implicitness/explicitness depending on their linguistic and discoursal features. An alternative way of determining if recasts are implicit might be to ask the learners. Mackey, Gass, and McDonough (2000) used stimulated recall to investigate L2 learners' perceptions of feedback moves, including recasts. They found that feedback on morpho-syntax was seldom perceived as being about morpho-syntax whereas feedback on phonology and lexis was perceived more accurately. Feedback on morpho-syntax typically took the form of recasts whereas feedback on phonology and lexis involved other strategies (for example, requests for clarification). This study then indicates that learners were not aware of the corrective force of the recasts and did not attend to the reformulated morphological features, suggesting that the recasts were functioning implicitly. It should be noted, however, that the recasts were not focused on any specific grammatical target in this study and, judging from the examples provided, the recasts were predominantly communicative rather than didactic in nature. Didactic recasts used to negotiate form are more likely to be explicit. In short, recasts cannot be viewed as a purely implicit form of negative feedback. In many cases their illocutionary force as corrections is quite transparent and, therefore, they should be seen as an explicit form of negative feedback. What is important is to resist theorizing about recasts as if they are a homogeneous entity and instead to acknowledge the diversity of their form and function, and of learners' responses to them.

Characteristic	**Description**	**Example**
1 Multi-move recasts		
a Corrective recasts (Doughty and Varela 1998)	An other-repetition precedes the recast.	S I pay the cost. T I pay? I'll pay the cost.
b Repeated recasts	A recast that is repeated either partially or fully.	S They probably like ... horse or ride horse. T Okay, a race horse? A race horse.
c Combination recasts	A recast that occurs with some other corrective strategy.	S In San Francisco, I didn't need a car. I used transportations. T Transportation. Uncountable.
2 Single-move recasts		
a Mode	Whether the recast is declarative in form or interrogative.	S Yes, I stand in the first row. T You stood in the first row?
b Scope (Lyster 1998a)	The extent to which the recast differs from the learner's ill-formed utterance. The recast can be 'isolated' (i.e. an erroneous part of the learner's utterances is reformulated with no new information added) or 'incorporated' (i.e. the reformulation involves additional semantic content).	S I think she'll travel her boyfriend after course. T I think she will travel together with her boyfriend. S I think he's not pride. T He's not proud because he cheated.
c Reduction (Lyster 1998a)	The reformulation of the learner's utterance may result in reduction (i.e. the recast is shorter than the learner's utterance) or non-reduction (i.e. the recast repeats the learner's entire utterance).	S Yeah, Kal told me your height is rather shorter. T Rather short. Rather short. S I'm a freshman. T I was a freshman. S What's feed up? T Fed.

d Length	A recast can consist of a single word or short phrase (only one content word), a long phrase (more than two words), or a clause (including a finite verb).	S Eighteenth of January T Yeah, the eighteenth of January. S I think Haynes is uh murder. T Haynes is the murderer.
e Number of changes	A recast can involve a single change to the learner's utterance or more than one change.	S The leader said, taste the alcohol, and then he said change, change the glass. T Exchange the glasses. S I worry about side effect. T Side-effects (i.e. 's' added)
f Type of change (based on Dulay *et al.*'s (1982) taxonomy of errors)	The recast can involve (i) an addition to the learner's utterance, (ii) a substitution, (iii) a reordering, or (iv) a combination of the above types.	S Whitman comes to my mind. T Comes to mind. (i.e. 'my' deleted) T How did you meet your partner? S On a, on a party T At a, at a party (i.e. substitution) S The voice tone is different. T Tone of voice (i.e. reordering)
g Linguistic focus	The recast can correct (i) pronunciation, (ii) vocabulary, or (iii) grammar.	S I think world people will don't need any food. T Will NOT need any food. (i.e. grammar)

Table 6.4 Characteristics of recasts (based on Sheen 2006a)

4 Learner uptake

The term UPTAKE refers to the response move in the negotiation sequence shown in Figure 6.1 (i.e. when S2 responds to S1's confirmation check—'Retired?'—with 'Yes'). Lyster and Ranta (1997) distinguished two broad types of uptake; 'repair' (i.e. the student's utterance successfully repairs the initial problem) and 'needs repair' (i.e. the student's response fails to successfully repair the initial utterance). They identified a number of ways students perform these two types of uptake. For example, repair can involve 'repetition', where the learner repeats the teacher's feedback or 'incorporation', where the learner incorporates repetition of the correct form in a longer utterance. Needs repair can take the form of an acknowledgement (for example, the student responds 'yes' or 'no' to a confirmation check) or of production of the same error again.

A number of studies that have investigated recasts have also examined the extent to which learners respond to recasts and, more interestingly, the extent to which they repair the errors in their initial utterances by incorporating the correct forms from the recasts (for example, Braidi 2002; Ellis, Basturkmen, and Loewen 2001; Loewen 2005; Loewen and Philp 2006; Lyster 1998a;

Panova and Lyster 2002; Lyster and Ranta 1997; Oliver 2000; Sheen 2004). Sheen (2004) showed that both uptake and repair vary according to setting. They occur more frequently in contexts where learners are oriented to language as an object (such as adult EFL classes) than in contexts where the interlocutors are predominantly concerned with content (such as immersion classrooms). One reason for this appears to be that in classrooms where there is a strong focus on message content, teachers often do not allow time for students to uptake their recasts, preferring instead to continue with topic development. Oliver (2000) found that learner uptake of feedback is also more likely in a teacher-fronted lesson than in a pairwork situation. She suggests that this was because many of the recasts in the pairwork situation consisted of confirmation requests where the appropriate response was simply 'yes' or 'no'. Thus, the extent to which uptake with repair occurs depends to a large extent on the instructional or social context of the interaction.

There is general acknowledgement that uptake does not demonstrate that acquisition has taken place. Long (2006b) argued that it is necessary to demonstrate that learners are capable of using a target feature on their own, without assistance, before any claim about acquisition can be made. Clearly, repaired uptake does not meet this criterion. It can be more convincingly argued that repaired uptake signals that noticing has taken place. If learners correct their original errors by incorporating the target forms from the recasts, then they must have noticed these forms at some level or other. However, failure to repair the original errors cannot be taken as evidence of a failure to notice the target forms. Indeed, as Ohta's (2000) study of Japanese foreign language classrooms showed, learners' responses to corrective feedback often take the form of private rather than social speech. The role which noticing plays in acquisition will be considered later.

5 Limitations of the research on interactional modifications

The study of interactional modifications related to negotiation has blossomed and there is now a rich literature to draw on. There are, however, a number of limitations that need to be recognized:

1 The research has focused on a rather narrow set of interactional phenomena associated with the negotiation of meaning. The categories themselves are less watertight than researchers sometimes admit (for example, the original distinction made between confirmation checks and recasts).
2 Much of the work has involved the quantification of negotiation strategies on the grounds that higher frequencies constitute evidence that higher levels of negotiation of meaning are occurring. This is, however, questionable. Aston (1986) pointed out that these strategies do not unambiguously indicate repair is taking place, as the same procedures can be used in non-problematic conversation. He argued that they are often used 'to achieve a formal display of convergence of the participants' worlds' by allowing them to perform 'a ritual of understanding or agreement'.
3 In the case of linguistic modifications, there is substantial evidence that their extent in native-speaker speech varies according to the learners' level

> of development. Somewhat surprisingly, there have been few studies that have investigated whether this is also true for interactional modifications. Ellis (1985d) found that a teacher used significantly fewer self-repetitions, but more expansions, in interactions with two learners when they had progressed beyond the stage of absolute beginners. However, no change was observed in other interactional features such as requests for clarification and confirmation checks.

However, the methodology for examining interactional modifications has improved considerably since the early days. For example, researchers have increasingly developed more operationally-convincing and fine-grained coding systems. As Mackey and Gass (2006) noted, the research methods employed by interactionist researchers have broadened considerably, for example, by focusing on the cognitive processes that learners engage in during negotiation through the use of stimulated recall.

The work currently undertaken by conversational analysts and sociocultural theorists offers alternative approaches that afford rich descriptions of repair work involving learners, and thus helps to overcome some of the limitations of the research completed to date. It is to these that we now turn.

Repair in conversational analysis

CONVERSATIONAL ANALYSIS seeks to demonstrate how conversation constitutes an accomplishment that is achieved through the collaborative efforts of the participants. Repair, like other types of conversational activity, is viewed as a joint production. Early studies focused on repair in naturally occurring conversations. Schwartz (1980) reported a general preference for self-correction over other-correction in NNS–NNS discourse. The same seems to be the case in NS–NNS discourse. Gaskill (1980) examined the types of repair which an Iranian learner of English experienced in both elicited and naturally-occurring conversations with native speakers. He found only 17 examples of other-correction in 50 pages of transcript. It would appear, then, that native speakers typically ignore learners' errors, a conclusion supported by Chun, Day, Chenoweth, and Luppescu's (1982) study of 28 ESL learners of mixed proficiency in Hawaii. In this case, fewer than 9 per cent of the total errors were corrected. Also, it was 'factual' errors and 'discourse errors' (for example, inappropriate openings, closings, and refusals) rather than lexical or syntactic errors that were more likely to attract repair from native speakers. Chun *et al.* suggested that the low level of repair reflects the native speakers' desire not to impair the cohesion of the discourse. When other-correction does take place, it is typically on-record rather than off-record, i.e. the native speaker responds to the source of a learner's language problems directly and unambiguously, by means of a statement with declarative intonation (Day, Chenoweth, Chun, and Luppescu 1984) but this may only be possible when the native speaker is a personal friend of the learner.

Later research (for example, Kasper 1985; Markee and Kasper 2004; Seedhouse 1997b, 2004) has addressed repair in classroom interaction. Markee and Kasper noted that conversational analysts treat classroom talk as 'a type of institutional talk that is empirically distinct from the default speech exchange system of ordinary conversation' because 'teacher-fronted classroom talk is an unequal power speech exchange system' (p. 492). Seedhouse (2004) distinguished what he calls 'didactic repair' in form-and-accuracy contexts and 'conversational repair' in meaning-and-fluency contexts, a distinction that mirrors the negotiation of meaning/form distinction. He notes that in his data from meaning-and-fluency contexts, errors were frequently ignored unless they led to communication breakdown. However, other studies (for example, Ellis, Basturkmen, and Loewen 2001) have shown that didactic repair is quite common in communicative activities. Seedhouse (1997b, 2004) offers a detailed account of the preference organization of repair in form-and-accuracy contexts. The strategies he describes are considered in detail in Chapter 15. It can be noted here that many of the strategies are very similar to those described in Table 6.3. For example, the strategy 'supply a correct version of the linguistic forms' is the same as a 'recast'. This raises the question as to whether the repair strategies associated with the negotiation of meaning/form in meaning-and-fluency contexts are necessarily very different from those found in form-and-accuracy contexts.

Conversational analysts have often been critical of mainstream SLA researchers' reliance on coding schemes of the kind shown in Table 6.3. Hauser (2005), for example, argued that 'the practice of coding results is a transformation of the data that obscures what is happening in the interaction' (p. 295). He was especially critical of mainstream SLA researchers' assumption that the propositional content of an error turn and the subsequent recast are clearly identifiable and identical—an assumption that is implicit in the definition of a recast as referring to the 'central meaning' of the learner's error turn. Using conversational analysis techniques, he demonstrated that recasts do not simply refer back to the meaning of the error turn but rather meaning is something that emerges continuously through the interaction.

Scaffolding

The term SCAFFOLDING comes from SOCIOCULTURAL THEORY (SCT), the central claim of which is that cognition needs to be investigated without isolating it from social context. SCT sees learning, including language learning, as dialogically based. Artigal (1992) even proposes that the 'language acquisition device' is located in the interaction that takes place between speakers rather than inside learners' heads. That is, acquisition occurs *in* rather than *as a result of* interaction. From this perspective, then, L2 acquisition is not a purely individual-based process but shared between the individual and other persons. One of the principal ways in which this sharing takes place is scaffolding. Other terms used to refer to much the same idea are 'collaborative dialogue'

(Swain 2000) and 'instructional conversation' (Donato 2000). Scaffolding (a social construct) is closely linked to another key construct, the ZONE OF PROXIMAL DEVELOPMENT (ZPD). This refers to 'the distance between the actual developmental level as determined by independent problem-solving and the level of potential development as determined through adult guidance or in collaboration with more capable peers' (Vygotsky 1978: 86). SCT is described in more detail later in this chapter and also in Chapter 11.

Scaffolding is an inter-psychological process through which learners internalize knowledge dialogically. That is, it is the process by which one speaker (an expert or a novice) assists another speaker (a novice) to perform a skill that they are unable to perform independently. Wood, Bruner, and Ross (1976) identified the following features of scaffolding:

1 recruiting interest in the task
2 simplifying the task
3 maintaining pursuit of the goal
4 marking critical features and discrepancies between what has been produced and the ideal solution
5 controlling frustration during problem solving
6 demonstrating an idealized version of the act to be performed.

In Ellis (2003) I used the extract below (taken from Ellis 1985d) to illustrate a number of these features of scaffolding.

1 T I want you to tell me what you can see in the picture or what's wrong with the picture.
2 L A /paik/ (= bike)
3 T A cycle, yes. But what's wrong?
4 L /ret/ (= red)
5 T It's red yes. What's wrong with it?
6 L Black.
7 T Black. Good. Black what?
8 L Black /taes/ (= tyres)

A teacher is showing a beginner learner a picture of a bicycle with no pedals. The teacher wants the learner to explain what is wrong with the bicycle, but clearly the learner is unable to perform this function. This interaction shows the teacher eventually simplifying the original task and controlling frustration by accepting the learner's contributions. It also shows the teacher providing idealized versions of the learner's one-word utterances (for example, 'Red' – 'It's red.'). Finally, the extract shows how the learner's final utterance ('black /taes/'), which constituted this learner's first attested two-word utterance, is constructed with assistance from the teacher. The teacher's question, 'Black what?' provides the learner with a frame that he uses to form his own utterance. In this way, the learner's final utterance can be said to be 'co-constructed'.

Like the research based on the negotiation of meaning/form constructs, SCT research investigating scaffolding has focused on corrective feedback. However, as Lantolf and Thorne (2006) pointed out 'research based on SCT addresses feedback from a different and more holistic vantage point' in that feedback and negotiation are viewed as 'a collaborative process where the dynamics of the interaction itself shape the nature of the feedback and inform its usefulness to the learner' (p. 276).

The key study is Aljaafreh and Lantolf (1994). This examined the one-to-one interactions arising between three L2 learners and a tutor who provided corrective feedback on essays they had written. Aljaafreh and Lantolf developed a 'regulatory scale' to reflect the extent to which the help provided by the tutor was implicit or explicit. For example, asking learners to find and correct their own errors is considered an implicit strategy while providing examples of the correct pattern is highly explicit. An intermediate level occurs when the tutor indicates the nature of an error without identifying it for the learner. The complete scale is shown in Table 6.5. In detailed analyses of selected protocols, Aljaafreh and Lantolf show how the degree of scaffolding provided by the tutor for a particular learner diminished (i.e. the help provided became more implicit over time). This was possible because the learners assumed increased control over the L2 and, therefore, needed less assistance. Aljaafreh and Lantolf identified a number of general principles governing the effectiveness of feedback: (1) it must be graduated (i.e. no more help than necessary is provided at any one time), (2) it must be contingent (i.e. it must reflect actual need and cease when the learner demonstrates an ability to function independently, and (3) it is dialogic (i.e. it involves dynamic assessment of a learner's ZPD).

Whereas the scaffolding examined in Aljaafreh and Lantolf's study was provided by a native speaker (in expert–novice interaction), learners can also scaffold each other in novice–novice interaction. Donato (1994) described the collective scaffolding employed by groups of university students of French performing an oral activity. In a detailed analysis of an exchange involving the negotiation of the form 'tu t'es souvenu', Donato showed how they jointly manage components of the problem, distinguish between what they have produced and what they perceive as the ideal solution, and use their collective resources to minimize frustration and risk. The scaffolding enables the learners to construct the correct form of the verb even though no single learner knew this prior to the task. Ohta (2000) also showed how students were able to produce utterances collaboratively that were beyond them individually and described the various techniques that learners used to scaffold each other's L2 speech. These included the use of prompts, co-constructions, and recasts. Ohta also reported that although the students did not always produce error-free utterances they only infrequently incorporated incorrect utterances. Both of these studies show that scaffolding is not dependent on there being a breakdown in communication.

0	Tutor asks the learner to read, find the errors, and correct them independently, prior to the tutorial.
1	Construction of a 'collaborative frame' prompted by the presence of the tutor as a potential dialogic partner.
2	Prompted or focused reading of the sentence that contains the error by the learner or the tutor.
3	Tutor indicates that something may be wrong in a segment (for example, sentence, clause, line)—'Is there anything wrong in this sentence?'
4	Tutor rejects unsuccessful attempts at recognizing the error.
5	Tutor narrows down the location of the error (for example, tutor repeats or points to the specific segment which contains the error).
6	Tutor indicates the nature of the error, but does not identify the error (for example, 'There is something wrong with the tense marking here').
7	Tutor identifies the error ('You can't use an auxiliary here').
8	Tutor rejects learner's unsuccessful attempts at correcting the error.
9	Tutor provides clues to help the learner arrive at the correct form (for example, 'It is not really past but something that is still going on').
10	Tutor provides the correct form.
11	Tutor provides some explanation for use of the correct form.
12	Tutor provides examples of the correct pattern when other forms of help fail to produce an appropriate responsive action.

Table 6.5 Regulatory scale—implicit to explicit (Aljaafreh and Lantolf 1994: 471)

A number of other researchers have examined the scaffolding that occurs in L2 group work. In a series of studies, Swain and her co-researchers examined the contribution of 'collaborative dialoguing' to language learning. Kowal and Swain (1997), for example, examined learners' ability to reconstruct a text jointly from notes after listening to the teacher read it twice to them. They identified a number of 'language-related episodes', in which the learners talked about language form and were often able to decide collectively what forms to use to reconstruct a text. However, Kowal and Swain also reported that heterogeneous dyads worked less effectively together, possibly because 'neither student's needs were within the zone of proximal development of the other' (p. 86) and because they failed to respect each other's perspective. Swain's work is considered further in Chapter 11. Storch (2001) identified four patterns of interaction in learner dyads depending on the degree of collaboration she observed. Some learners were successful in creating a joint action space where they mutually supported each other. Other learners (in a dominant-dominant configuration) demonstrated considerable disagreement and failed to reach agreement. In the third pattern, where one of the learners adopted an authoritative stance, there was little negotiation. In the fourth pattern, one of the learners took on the role of expert, assisting the other to participate in the task. These studies, then, support Donato's and Ohta's finding that learners are able to scaffold each other but also suggest that how effectively they do this depends on the interactional configuration.

Summary

In this section we have explored a number of perspectives on interactions involving L2 learners. These can be broadly divided into two groups:

1 Taxonomic accounts of L2 interactions. Included in this group are the descriptions of strategies involved in discourse management and the negotiation of meaning/form. The former seek to make the discourse easier for learners to process (i.e. they are pre-emptive). The latter seek to deal with problems of understanding and/or problems of form that arise in communication (i.e. they are reactive). One specific strategy in this group that has attracted the attention of researchers is recasts. Such taxonomies enable researchers to examine the frequency with which different strategies occur in the input and thus cater to quantitative and experimental research methodologies.
2 Holistic and qualitative accounts of L2 interactions. Conversational analysts treat conversations as 'accomplishments', seeking to explain how they are achieved. They have focused on the turn-taking mechanisms and repair work. Other researchers have drawn on sociocultural theory to examine how scaffolding enables learners collaboratively to perform skills which are beyond them individually.

These two approaches reflect very different theoretical orientations. The taxonomic approach has drawn on a message model of communication, which views communicative language use as involving the 'successful sending and receiving of linguistic tokens' (Donato 1994: 34) and a computational model of acquisition (Lantolf 1996), which views interaction as a source of data which are processed by the internal mechanisms responsible for acquisition. In contrast, the holistic/qualitative approach views interaction as a site where learners can appropriate linguistic knowledge at the same time as learning new cultural meanings. In the next section, we explore these theoretical positions more closely, beginning with a brief examination of research in L1 acquisition that has investigated the roles of input and interaction.

Input and interaction in first language acquisition

It is helpful to first examine research that investigated the roles of input/interaction in L1 acquisition as this was the origin of many of the methods and theoretical issues that SLA researchers have taken up.

A number of early studies investigated the relationship between the language that caretakers address to children (i.e. input features) and acquisition, with somewhat mixed results. Newport, Gleitman, and Gleitman (1977) found little evidence of a close relationship between the frequency of specific linguistic features in mothers' speech and the growth of the same features in their children. In contrast, Furrow, Nelson, and Benedict (1979) found much greater evidence of an effect for input. In this study, four aspects of L1 development (mean length of utterance, verbs per utterance, noun phrases per utterance, and auxiliaries per verb phrase) were related to a number of input measures. Barnes, Gutfreund, Satterly, and Wells (1983) reported significant correlations between the frequency of polar interrogatives and subject-verb inversion in the input, and general semantic and syntactic development in the children. Wells (1985) found that caretakers increased the frequency of specific auxiliary verbs in their input just before the same verbs appeared for the first time in their children's speech. All these studies found some relationships involving input and acquisition. FRAGILE FEATURES[9] such as auxiliary verbs, in particular, seem to be sensitive to input. One of the problems with such correlational studies is that they typically did not take account of the children's age and stage of development, both of which have been shown to influence caretaker input. Snow (1986: 76) pointed out that 'the task of learning a language is quite different in different stages of acquisition' and that, consequently, it is reasonable to presume that different aspects of caretaker talk may be important at different stages.

The age-dependent effects of input are clearly evident in more recent observational and experimental studies reviewed by Tomasello (2000a, 2000b). In accordance with the VERB-ISLAND HYPOTHESIS 'a 2-year-old child's syntactic competence is comprised totally of verb-specific constructions with open nominal slots' (2000a: 314). In other words, there is no evidence of abstract syntactic categories until the child reaches around 3 years. Even nominals are lexically specific, i.e. represented, for example, as 'seer' and 'thing seen' rather than as 'subject' and 'object'. Tomasello reviews a number of experimental studies that investigated children's use of the English transitive construction with different verbs. For example, Tomasello, Akhtar, Dodson, and Rekau (1997) exposed children aged 1:6 to 1:11 years to sentences containing novel nouns and verbs (for example, ' Look! The wug!, 'Look! Meeking!'). They found that whereas the children combined the nouns quite freely with their existing linguistic resources (for example, 'I pushing wug'), they almost entirely failed to combine the new verbs with existing words. Tomasello concluded that children of this age are only able to use verbs in the construction in which they have heard it. Thus, if they have encountered a specific verb in a transitive construction, they can use it in that construction but, if they have not (as was the case with 'meeking' in the example above), they are not able to do so. Input, then, plays an important role at this stage. Tomasello suggests that it is evident in two key acquisitional processes. The first is 'entrenchment'; the more frequently children hear a verb used in a specific construction, the less likely they are to extend the use of this verb to other constructions. The second is 'pre-emption'; if the child experiences a particular verb in a specific construction (for example, 'He made the rabbit disappear'), the child infers that the verb cannot be used in a simple transitive construction (for example, *'He disappeared the rabbit'). Tomasello argued for a usage-based account of L1 acquisition, according to which linguistic knowledge is item-based and input-dependent in the first instance, with abstract categories only emerging later.

A different position has been taken by Pinker (1999). He argued for a dual-mechanism model, according to which computation of regular morphological features such as past tense –ed in English involves rule-based or symbolic processing, whereas irregular features such as irregular past tense forms like 'swam' are sensitive to input frequency. He cited a number of studies that provide support for the dual mechanism model. Thus, the extent to which some grammatical features (as claimed by Pinker) as opposed to all (as claimed by Tomasello) are sensitive to input frequency in L1 acquisition remains a matter of controversy.

Tomasello (2000b) also theorized that grammar evolved historically out of socio-interactive processes and that the same processes account for children's acquisition of language. A number of studies have documented how interaction fosters acquisition. One way in which interaction may help children learn language is by providing them with opportunities to form vertical constructions. A vertical construction is built up gradually over several turns. Scollon (1976) provided a number of examples of mother–child discourse, where the child produces a meaningful statement over two or more turns:

BRENDA Hiding
ADULT What's hiding?
BRENDA Balloon

He suggested that vertical constructions prepare the child for the subsequent production of horizontal constructions (the production of a meaningful statement within a single turn).

Other researchers point to the contribution that specific discourse acts make to acquisition. Interaction rich in directives appears to foster rapid language acquisition, at least in the early stages (Ellis and Wells 1980), perhaps because children are equipped with an 'action strategy' (Shatz 1978) that makes them particularly receptive to directives, perhaps because directives are frequently related to the here-and-now and perhaps because they are often linguistically very simple. Expansions also appear to promote development. These are full, correct versions of telegraphic child utterances, which often occur in the form of acknowledgements or requests for confirmation:

CHILD Pancakes away
Duh Duh stomach
MOTHER Pancakes away in the stomach, yes, that's right.

Snow (1986) cited a number of studies that provide evidence of the positive effect of expansions (for example, Malouf and Dodd 1972; Nelson 1977; Cross

1978; Wells 1980), perhaps because they provide crucial bits of information about syntax and morphology, although, as Snow noted, the same information may also be made available to children in other kinds of input. Farrar (1990) found that different types of feedback moves were related to different grammatical features; recasts were strongly related to the development of two bound morphemes (plural –s and progressive –ing) while expansions were related to past tense and copulas. In another study, Farrar (1992) showed that children were more likely to imitate corrective recasts than other types of reformulations. This suggests that recasts may be of special importance in helping learners 'crack the code'.

Children also seem to benefit from assistance in building conversations about topics in which they are interested. Wells (1986a) and Snow (1986) both emphasized the importance of 'collaborative meaning making' and discussed some of the ways in which this is achieved. Successful conversations are achieved when caretakers regularly check their understanding of what their children have said, when they work hard to negotiate misunderstanding, when they help to sustain and extend topics that their children have initiated, when they give children opportunities to contribute to the conversation, no matter how minimally, and when they are responsive to feedback cues. The result is what Snow calls 'semantically contingent speech'.

Input and interaction in second language acquisition

We will distinguish two broad approaches to studying the role that input/interaction plays in L2 acquisition depending on whether the basis is the computational model of L2 acquisition or sociocultural theory. The first approach has given rise to a number of theories (labelled 'hypotheses' by their originators): (1) the Frequency Hypothesis (Hatch and Wagner-Gough 1976; N. Ellis 1996, 2002), (2) the Input Hypothesis (Krashen 1985), (3) the Comprehensible Output Hypothesis (Swain 1985, 1995), (4) the Interaction Hypothesis (Long 1983b, 1996), and (5) the Noticing Hypothesis (Schmidt 1990, 1994, 2001). Gass (1988, 1997a) offered a model of L2 acquisition that incorporates these different hypotheses. Mackey and Goo (2007) provided a meta-analysis of 28 studies undertaken within the compass of these theories. The second approach draws on Vygotsky's theory of mediated learning and, in particular, the role attributed to interaction in assisting learners to acquire (or rather 'appropriate') linguistic skills in goal-directed activity (Lantolf 2000c).

Research based on the computational model of L2 acquisition

1 The Frequency Hypothesis

As initially formulated by Hatch and Wagner Gough (1976), the FREQUENCY HYPOTHESIS stated that the order of L2 acquisition is determined by the frequency with which different linguistic items occur in the input and was investigated by examining the relationship between input frequency and the order of acquisition. (See Chapter 3.) Hatch and Wagner-Gough (1976) suggested that the limited range of topics about which learners (particularly children) typically talk results in certain grammatical features occurring with great frequency in the input. The hypothesis was subsequently investigated in a series of correlational studies (summarized in Table 6.6), which produced very mixed results. Whereas Larsen-Freeman (1976a, 1976b), Lightbown (1983), Hamayan and Tucker (1980), and Long (1981) all found significant positive correlations between input frequency and accuracy, Snow and Hoefnagel-Höhle (1982), Long and Sato (1984), and Lightbown (1983) did not find any direct relationship. These studies do not permit a clear conclusion to be reached and suffer from a number of limitations. For example, some of the studies did not obtain measures of input frequency from the same data sets used to examine learner accuracy (for example, Larsen-Freeman 1976a; Long 1981b), thus making the correlations they report additionally difficult to interpret. More importantly, it can be argued that it makes little sense to investigate input-output relationships in data collected at the same time, as any effect for frequency will not be immediately apparent. Only Lightbown's (1983) study of Grade 6 ESL learners in Canada provides some indication of how input available at one time can affect acquisition that becomes apparent at a later time. In this study, the learners manifested overuse of V + –ing after having received massive classroom exposure to this feature previously at the end of Grade 5.

Study	**Design**	**Main results**
Larsen-Freeman 1976a	L2 accuracy orders of grammatical morphemes correlated with input frequency orders of same morphemes in the classroom speech of 2 ESL teachers.	Spearman rank order correlations generally positive and significant.
Larsen-Freeman 1976b	L2 accuracy orders of grammatical morphemes correlated with frequency order of same morphemes in parental speech to children (based on Brown 1973).	Spearman rank order correlations were positive and significant except for imitation task.
Hamayan and Tucker 1980	The accuracy order of 9 French syntactic structures in speech elicited from L1 and L2 learners correlated with frequency order of same structures in teacher classroom input.	Significant rank order correlations reported for both L1 and L2. The frequency order reported for two classrooms differed but was significantly related to accuracy orders in both cases.

Lightbown 1983	Order of appearance of L2 French question words in speech of 2 children correlated with frequency order of same question words in speech addressed to the children by a French research assistant.	Frequency with which question words appeared in NS's speech matched closely the sequence of question word development in L2 learners' speech.
Long 1981	Krashen's average order of acquisition of grammatical morphemes correlated with the frequency order of same morphemes in the speech that NSs addressed to 36 elementary Japanese ESL students.	Spearman rank order correlation positive and significant.
Snow and Hoefnagel-Höhle1982	Achievement and gain scores of American children acquiring L2 Dutch in Holland correlated with (1) quantity of Dutch heard in the classroom, (2) percentage of speech directed specifically at learners, and (3) amount of speech directed at individual learners.	No significant relationships found.
Long and Sato 1984	Krashen's average order of acquisition of grammatical morphemes correlated with the frequency order of the same morphemes in ESL teachers' speech.	No significant relationship found. However, teachers' frequency order did correlate significantly with NSs' frequency order, which in turn correlated significantly with Krashen's average order.
Lightbown 1983	Grade 6 ESL students' accuracy order of -s morphemes in oral communication activity correlated with frequency order of same features in samples of one teacher's speech and in textbook used by students.	No direct relationship between accuracy and input frequencies found, but some evidence that high level of frequency of V + -ing in input at earlier period (Grade 5) led to overuse by the students.

Table 6.6 Input frequency–output accuracy studies in early SLA research

Later studies have produced more convincing evidence that input frequency influences acquisition. Palmberg (1987) found that the vocabulary remembered by beginner learners of English in a classroom context in Sweden reflected the frequency of the items in the textbook. Elley (1989) found that frequency produced the highest correlation with vocabulary gains made by

7- and 8-year-old children from stories read to them. Gass and Lakshmanan (1991) reanalysed data from two of the learners investigated by Cazden *et al.* (1975)—Alberto and Cheo—and found a striking correlation between the presence of subjectless utterances in the input and in the production of the two learners over time. They were also able to demonstrate that in the case of Alberto, deviant input in a grammaticality judgement test was followed by a jump in this learner's production of subjectless sentences shortly afterwards. It should be noted, however, that the learners' L1 (Spanish) permits subjectless sentences. It is possible, therefore, that input and transfer work jointly to shape interlanguage development. As Gass and Lakshmanan put it, 'the learner initially searches for correspondences or matches in form between the native and the second language'.[10] Goldschneider and DeKeyser (2001) carried out a meta-analysis of the determinants of the natural order of acquisition. One of the factors they investigated was input frequency, operationalized in terms of Brown's (1973) parental frequency data. They reported a statistically significant correlation of .44 between this frequency measure and the accuracy scores for the six morphemes they investigated. However, notably higher correlations were reported for phonological salience (.63) and syntactic category (.68).[11] Goldschneider and DeKeyser found that a combination of all the determinants they studied accounted for a very large proportion of the variance in the accuracy scores for the functors in the natural order and suggested that all the determinants constituted aspects of a single general factor—salience. From this perspective, then, input frequency works together with other characteristics of the input to determine acquisition.

The Frequency Hypothesis has received its strongest support from N. Ellis' (2002) review of a range of research that investigated frequency effects in phonology, reading and spelling, lexis, morphosyntax, and formulaic language production. Ellis draws on a connectionist theory of language acquisition (considered in Chapter 9). This disputes the view that linguistic competence is comprised of rules derived from some form of innate language acquisition device and instead views linguistic knowledge in terms of a network of interconnected nodes. The strengths of the connections in this network are highly sensitive to input frequency. Like Tomasello (see previous section), Ellis argued that acquisition proceeds initially by the memorization of exemplars which are subsequently analysed to extract underlying categories and rules. He characterized language learning as 'the associative learning of representations that reflect the probabilities of occurrence of form–function mappings' (p. 144). From this perspective it follows that 'frequency is thus the key determinant of acquisition because "rules" of language … are structural regularities that emerge from learners' lifetime analysis of the distributional properties of the language input'. For N. Ellis, frequency learning constitutes a basic human capacity; language learners count and they do so unconsciously. However, N. Ellis recognized that the effects of frequency are modulated in various ways. First, the power law of practice operates; the amount of improvement decreases as a function of increasing practice or frequency. Second, the need to simultaneously attend to the constraints of all the other constructions that are represented in the learner's system influence what is attended to in the input. Third, learners respond differently to token and type frequency. Token frequency concerns how often specific linguistic forms appear in the input; it promotes the entrenchment and conservation of irregular forms (for example, irregular past tense forms like 'swam'). Type frequency refers to the items that can occur in a given slot in a construction; it facilitates the development of a general category governing the items that occur in a particular slot (for example, regular past tense –ed).

Evidence for N. Ellis' claims about input frequency comes from computer-based simulations that manipulate linguistic input in order to examine its effect on output. For example, N. Ellis and Schmidt (1997) demonstrated that there were frequency effects for both regular and irregular morphological forms. Research based on the COMPETITION MODEL (MacWhinney 2001), which also draws on connectionist theory, provides further evidence of frequency effects. The model claims that the probabilities of occurrence of specific form–function mappings in the input (termed 'cue availability') predict learning outcomes. MacWhinney (2001: 74) stated that 'the most basic determinant of cue strength is the raw frequency of the basic task'. Many of the studies (for example, Sasaki 1997a; Harrington 1987) have looked at the cues that signal agency. In the case of English, learners rapidly tune in to the fact that agency is signalled by word order because the input provides copious examples of utterances where the noun phrase preceding the verb is the agent. However, cue availability is not the only factor influencing cue strength. Cue reliability (i.e. the extent to which a cue always maps the same form onto the same function) is also involved. For example, Kempe and MacWhinney (1998) showed that Russian case marking is acquired more easily than that of German because the Russian inflections provide more reliable information about the functions they encode. The Competition Model, which is considered in greater detail in Chapter 9, also recognizes that the learner's L1 influences how input is processed. In this model, then, input frequency operates in conjunction with other determinants of learning.

However, there is mixed evidence from L2 studies regarding the dual-mechanism model. (See section above on input and interaction in L1 acquisition.) Beck (1997) investigated native speakers' and learners' response times in a task that required them to produce simple past tense forms verbally when presented with a mixture of high- and low-frequency regular and irregular verb stems on a computer screen. Both the native speakers and the learners showed no significant effects on regular verbs. The native speakers but not the learners manifested frequency effects on irregular verbs. Thus in the case of the native speakers there is evidence of a DUAL MECHANISM operating (as claimed by Pinker) but not in the case of the learners. Beck explained this finding by suggesting that the instruction in irregular verb forms that the learners most probably received may well have overridden the effects of input frequency. Birdsong and Flege (2001), however, did find clear evidence of a dual mechanism in the learners they investigated (educated Spanish and Korean native speakers who were at or near to asymptote in their acquisition of English). They measured these learners' acquisition of regular and irregular morphological forms (past tense and plural nouns) by means of a multiple choice test. They reported frequency effects in both groups of learners. That is, input frequency (established by reference to Francis and Kucera's (1982) frequency dictionary of English) predicted performance on the irregular items but not on the regular items.

There is now sufficient theory and empirical evidence to make the case that input frequency plays a major role in L2 acquisition. However, it is also clear that input frequency alone cannot explain L2 acquisition. This is, in fact, obvious. For example, the English definite and indefinite articles are both among the most frequent forms in both oral and written input but they pose considerable learning problems for all learners and are acquired later than other forms that occur much less frequently. Other factors that interact with input frequency in determining acquisition include syntactic category (in particular, whether the feature is regular or irregular), phonological salience, the learner's L1, communicative value (for example, third person –s is acquired late because it is redundant) and innate constraints on learning. In their response to N. Ellis' claims about frequency effects, Gass and Mackey (2002) noted 'an issue of central importance that remains to be addressed relates to exactly how frequency effects interact with other aspects of the L2 acquisition process' (p. 257). Goldschneider and DeKeyser's meta-analysis is a start in this direction. Crucially, also, frequency effects need to be investigated separately in relation to the acquisition of linguistic forms (i.e. the appearance of new forms in learners' production) and of form–function mappings (i.e. the way these forms are used to realize meanings).

2 The Input Hypothesis

Krashen (1981, 1982) distinguished between ACQUISITION and LEARNING. The former is an implicit, subconscious process and is reflected in the natural order of acquisition. The latter is an explicit, conscious process and results in metalinguistic knowledge. (See Chapter 9 for further discussion of implicit/explicit learning and knowledge.) The INPUT HYPOTHESIS (Krashen 1985, 1994) relates only to acquisition. It makes the following claims:

1 Learners progress along the natural order by understanding input that contains structures a little bit beyond their current level of competence (i + 1).
2 Although comprehensible input is necessary for acquisition to take place, it is not sufficient, as learners also need to be affectively disposed to 'let in' the input they comprehend.
3 Input becomes comprehensible as a result of simplification and with the help of contextual and extralinguistic clues; 'fine-tuning' (i.e. ensuring that learners receive input rich in the specific linguistic property they are due to acquire next) is not necessary.

4 Speaking is the result of acquisition, not its cause; learner production does not contribute directly to acquisition. (However, Krashen (1989) did allow for speaking to have an indirect effect by assisting the learner's conversational partner to make input comprehensible.)

Krashen subsequently continued to reject any direct role for output in L2 learning. In Krashen (1998) he outlined a number of reasons why output is not effective: (1) learners have very limited opportunities to speak, especially in classrooms, (2) there is plenty of evidence to show that high levels of linguistic competence can be achieved without output, (3) 'pushing' learners to speak is anxiety-provoking, and (4) there is no direct evidence that output leads to acquisition. The case for output, which is in fact substantial, is considered in a later section in this chapter.

The test of the Input Hypothesis is whether (1) simplified input aids comprehension and (2) comprehension results in acquisition. We will examine both issues.

One type of simplification concerns speech rate. A number of studies (for example, Long 1985a; Kelch 1985; Mannon 1986) provided evidence to suggest that a slower rate aids comprehension, but in many cases speech rate was investigated alongside other variables and these early studies also suffered from methodological problems, making it difficult to assess the effect of speech rate *per se*. However, two other, better-designed studies indicated that rate of speech was a significant factor. Conrad (1989) asked 29 native speakers, 17 high-level non-native speakers, and 11 medium-level non-native speakers to recall five time-compressed recordings of 16 English sentences. Each sentence was presented five times at different speeds: 450, 320, 253, 216, and 196 words per minute. The native speakers managed nearly complete recall of all the sentences by the second trial (320 words per minute), but the non-native speakers of both proficiency levels experienced considerable difficulty even with the slowest rate after the fifth hearing. Griffiths (1990) investigated the effects of varying the speech rate in three 350–400 word passages on the comprehension of 15 lower-intermediate level adult non-native speakers. The speeds varied from 94–107 wpm (slow) to 143–54 (medium) and 191–206 (fast). The subjects manifested significantly reduced comprehension, measured by means of true/false questions, at fast rates, but there was no difference between the 'medium' and 'slow' rates. These studies suggest that there may be a threshold level—around 200 wpm—below which intermediate and advanced level learners experience little difficulty in comprehending.

Other studies have explored the effect of different kinds of input modifications on comprehension. Parker and Chaudron (1987) reviewed 12 experimental studies (including Johnson 1981; Blau 1982; R. Brown 1987; Chaudron and Richards 1986) of the effects of input modifications on comprehension and concluded that although linguistic modifications (for example, simpler syntax and vocabulary) helped comprehension they did not do so consistently. In contrast, what they called 'elaborative modifications' had a consistent effect on comprehension. They distinguished two types of elaborative modifications: those that contribute to redundancy (such as repetition of constituents, paraphrase, use of synonyms, use of left dislocation, and slower speech), and those that help to make the thematic structure explicit (such as extraposition and cleft constructions). Long and Ross (1993) compared the effects of three text conditions (unsimplified, simplified, and elaborated) on Japanese college students' reading comprehension. They found that the simplified text (but not the elaborated text) resulted in significantly higher comprehension scores. They suggest that the reason why the elaborated text was less successful than expected was because the elaboration process made it one grade level harder in readability. Oh's (2001) study found in favour of elaborated input. She reported that whether a text was elaborated or simplified did not affect Korean high school students' comprehension, but argued that elaborated texts were preferable because they retained more native-like qualities and thus better prepared learners to read unmodified materials.

Some studies have failed to demonstrate that input modifications assist comprehension. Parker and Chaudron's (1987) own study of 43 undergraduate and graduate ESL learners, who read one of two reading passages which differed according to whether they had been modified by incorporating linguistic or elaborative modifications, failed to find any significant differences in comprehension. They explained this result, which they considered unexpected, by suggesting that the overall lexical and syntactic difficulty of both passages may have been so great as to negate the effects of the elaborative modifications. If this is right, it suggests that elaborative modifications will only benefit comprehension if the level of linguistic difficulty of the input does not exceed a certain threshold. Issidorides and Hulstijn (1992) examined the effects of simplifying Dutch AdvVSO sentences by replacing them with the ungrammatical AdvSVO and AdvSOV sentences. These 'simplifications' were motivated by the fact that learners of L2 Dutch and L2 German have been found to experience production difficulties with verb-subject inversion after initial adverbs. (See Chapter 3.) In an experimental study that required three groups of subjects (Dutch native speakers, English and Turkish learners of L2 Dutch) to state what the subject or agent of a series of sentences was, AdvVSO sentences were found to be no more difficult to understand than modified, ungrammatical sentences (providing that the messages conveyed by the sentences were semantically plausible). Issidorides and Hulstijn concluded that 'the fact that non-native speakers have difficulties in producing a certain grammatical structure ... does not imply that such a structure is also more difficult to understand in the speech of others' (1992: 167). Loschky (1994) and Ellis, Tanaka, and Yamazaki (1994) also failed to find consistent evidence that premodified (simplified) input worked better for comprehension than baseline (unsimplified) input.

The research evidence relating to the relationship between comprehension and acquisition is also quite mixed. Much of the early research was correlational in nature and therefore cannot be said to demonstrate that comprehensible input *causes* acquisition. This evidence is summarized in Table 6.7. Long (1983b) considered the fact that deprivation of comprehensible input results in delayed acquisition the strongest evidence, but Larsen-Freeman (1983) argued quite convincingly that learners can assimilate useful information about an L2 without understanding input (for example, information relating to the phonology of an L2). She also made the point that learners can work by themselves on unmodified input—such as that found in TV programmes—and so gain input that helps them learn. Thus, at least some L2 learning may take place without comprehensible input and, more importantly, comprehending input may not result in acquisition.

Source of evidence	**Brief explanation**
Caretaker speech	Caretaker speech to young children is roughly tuned to the children's receptive abilities and is motivated by the need to aid comprehension.
Foreigner talk	Foreigner talk to NNSs is also roughly tuned and functions as an aid to comprehension.
Silent period	Some young children go through a silent period in L2 acquisition. During this period they do not produce but nevertheless learn the L2.
Age difference	Krashen (1985: 12) argued that 'older learners obtain more comprehensible input' and that this may explain why they learn more quickly initially than younger learners.
Comparative method studies	The studies show that methods that supply plenty of comprehensible input (e.g. Total Physical Response) are more successful than methods that supply little (e.g. audiolingualism).
Immersion programmes	Immersion programmes have generally been found superior to foreign/second language programmes—again because they supply plenty of comprehensible input.
Bilingual programmes	The success of different kinds of bilingual programmes is related to the extent to which they supply comprehensible input.
Delayed L1 and L2 acquisition	Studies of children in both L1 and L2 acquisition who are deprived of comprehensible input (e.g. because their parents are deaf) show that acquisition is delayed or non-existent.
Reading and vocabulary acquisition	Studies indicate that children are able to increase their L1 vocabulary and also develop a 'deep' understanding of new words through pleasure reading.
Reading and spelling acquisition	Studies indicate that spelling can be most effectively acquired through exposure to the written word in extensive reading undertaken for pleasure.

Table 6.7 Indirect evidence in support of the Input Hypothesis

More direct evidence has come from experimental studies involving a comparison between instructional methods that supply plentiful comprehensible input and more traditional methods. These studies drew for inspiration on earlier research by Elley (1989) which demonstrated the effectiveness of book-flood programmes in promoting incidental language learning in Fiji. These programmes, involving graded readers, were aimed at providing learners with extensive comprehensible input. Krashen (1989, 1993b) himself also promoted extensive reading as a source of comprehensible input for acquisition. In a series of small-scale studies he and his co-researchers (for example, Dupuy and Krashen 1993; Mason and Krashen 1997; Rodrigo, Krashen, and Gribbons 2004) sought to demonstrate that learners who experience comprehensible input through extensive reading outperform those taught by traditional, grammar-centred methods. In Rodrigo, Krashen, and Gribbons, for example, three methods were compared: (1) a reading method consisting of an extensive reading programme of graded books, (2) a reading-discussion method, where students read books and then participated in debates and discussions about them, and (3) a traditional grammar and composition method. The reading and reading-discussion groups outperformed the traditional group on a vocabulary test while just the reading-discussion group outperformed the traditional group on a grammar test. No statistically significant differences were found on a cloze test. Interestingly, it was the reading-discussion group that proved the best, suggesting that the speaking that this group engaged in might have contributed. However, Rodrigo *et al.* rejected this, suggesting instead that it was the high level of affective engagement in this group that explained their superiority. However, given the small sample sizes and design problems (for example, the groups had different teachers) this study does not constitute strong evidence in favour of the Input Hypothesis. It should also be noted that learners' ability to learn incidentally through reading will depend on their level of reading ability; Swanborn and de Glopper (2002) found that the low-ability readers in their study learnt hardly any words incidentally.

Other experimental studies have failed to find that simplified input aids acquisition. Leow (1993) exposed university learners of Spanish to simplified and unsimplified reading passages that contained exemplars of two verb structures (present perfect and present subjunctive). The learners were tested by means of a multiple-choice assessment task. Leow concluded from this study that simplification did not have a significant effect on the learners' intake of either structure. In a later study, Leow (1997a) examined the effects of text length and text enhancement (by means of underlining and bolding) on a similar group of learners' comprehension and intake of the Spanish impersonal imperative structure. He found that text length but not text enhancement resulted in higher comprehension scores while neither type of input modification assisted acquisition.

These mixed results regarding the effects of modified input on acquisition may reflect the different designs of the studies considered above. Krashen investigated the global effects of comprehensible input by means of extended COMPARATIVE METHOD STUDIES whereas Leow investigated the effects of specific types of input modification on the acquisition of particular grammatical structures. However, it is perhaps not surprising that the results have been inconsistent as what probably matters is not so much the input itself as what learners do with the input they are exposed to.

There have been a number of critiques of the Input Hypothesis (Gregg 1984; Færch and Kasper 1986a; Sharwood Smith 1986; McLaughlin 1987; White 1987a; Gass 1988; Ellis 1990a, 1991a). Perhaps the major problem is that Krashen paid little attention to what 'comprehension' entails. Rost defined listening comprehension as 'essentially an inferential process based on the perception of cues rather than straightforward matching of sound to meaning' (1990: 33). This suggests that understanding does not necessitate close attention to linguistic form. Færch and Kasper (1986a) also recognized the importance of 'top-down processes', in which learners utilize contextual information and existing knowledge to understand what is said, but they also point out that they may sometimes make use of 'bottom-up processes', where they pay closer attention to the linguistic forms in the message. The question that remains unanswered, then, is what type of comprehension processes are needed for acquisition to take place. If learners can rely extensively on top-down processing they may pay little attention to the form of the input and may therefore not acquire anything new. Færch and Kasper argued that only when there is a 'gap' between the input and the learner's current interlanguage and, crucially, when the learner perceives the gap as a gap in knowledge, will acquisition take place. Sharwood Smith (1986) argued similarly that the processes of comprehension and acquisition are not the same, and suggested that input has a 'dual relevance'—there is input that helps learners to interpret meaning, and there is input that learners use to advance their interlanguages. Thus, as Gass (1988) pointed out, it is not comprehensible input but rather *comprehended* input that is important. Krashen (1983) appeared to have recognized this when he proposed that learners learn through comprehension by linking form to meaning and by noticing the gap between the i + 1 form and their current interlanguage rule. Unfortunately, however, he did not consistently emphasize this in presentations of the Input Hypothesis. As Carroll (1999) pointed out, what is required of any account of the role of input in acquisition is 'explicit statements of how what is detected in the acoustic and visual stimuli is mentally represented and how detection and encoding are guided by internal mechanisms' (p. 39).

A second major criticism focuses on the claim that comprehensible input is *necessary* for acquisition. L. White (1987a) argued that a considerable part of acquisition is 'input-free'. She claimed that certain types of overgeneralizations which learners make cannot be unlearnt simply by understanding input. They require negative evidence (for example, in the form of corrective feedback) which in naturalistic acquisition may not be available to the learner. She also claimed that learners are able to go beyond the evidence available in the input, and develop knowledge of target-language rules by projecting from their existing knowledge (a point discussed more fully in Chapter 12). Finally, she argued that in the case of some structures (for example, English passive constructions), it may be the failure to understand input that leads to learning. As she puts it 'the driving force for grammar change is that input is *incomprehensible*, rather than comprehensible ...' (1987a: 95). White's idea was that failure to understand a sentence may force the learner to pay closer attention to its syntactical properties in order to obtain clues about its meaning and, as such, reflected the views of Færch and Kasper (1986a) and Sharwood Smith (1986) about comprehension and learning discussed above.

3 The Interaction Hypothesis

The origins of Long's INTERACTION HYPOTHESIS (IH) lie partly in Hatch's work on discourse analysis and L2 acquisition and partly in Krashen's Input Hypothesis. Hatch (1978b: 404) claimed:

> One learns how to do conversations, one learns how to interact verbally, and out of this interaction syntactic structures are developed.

A number of researchers (for example, Wagner-Gough 1975; Peck 1978; Hatch 1978a, 1978b) sought to show how this might happen. One way is through the use of an INCORPORATION STRATEGY, as shown in this example from Wagner-Gough:

MARK Come here.
HOMER No come here.

Such a strategy may explain why 'no + verb' constructions are so common in early L2 acquisition (see Chapter 3), although other explanations also exist. Another way is vertical constructions of the kind reported by Scollon (1976) in L1 acquisition. Hatch (1978b: 407) provided this example in an interaction involving Paul, Huang's (1970) subject:

PAUL Oh-oh!
J What?
PAUL This (points at an ant)
J It's an ant.
PAUL Ant.

The construction that Paul builds over three utterances is 'Oh-oh, this, ant'.

In his initial formulation of the IH, however, Long (1983a) emphasized the role played by interaction in making input comprehensible. In the later version, Long (1996) was more faithful to the earlier work of Hatch in that he acknowledged that interaction can facilitate acquisition by assisting learners' L2 production. The later version of the hypothesis has also been closely associated with another construct—FOCUS ON FORM. We will examine both versions of the hypothesis and focus on form in turn.

The general claim of both early and late versions of the IH is that engaging in interpersonal oral interaction in which communication problems arise and are negotiated *facilitates* incidental language acquisition. Long and other IH researchers have been careful to emphasize that interaction involving meaning negotiation only facilitates acquisition; it does not *cause* acquisition to take place. Modified interaction can only 'set the scene for potential learning' (Gass, Mackey, and Pica 1998: 304). Furthermore, as Pica (1996) pointed out, the IH does not claim that meaning negotiation is the only type of interaction in which the conditions that foster learning arise; 'uninterrupted communication' (i.e. communication where there is no problem of understanding) can also contribute to acquisition.

In his early version of the IH, Long (1983a), acknowledged that simplified input and context can play a role in making input comprehensible, as Krashen claimed. However, he stressed the importance of the interactional modifications that occur in negotiating meaning when a communication problem arises. In other words, he argued that interactive input is more important than non-interactive input because it supplied learners with information relating to linguistic forms that were problematic to them.

To facilitate empirical research based on the IH, Long (1985a) suggested that researchers follow three steps: (1) they need to show that conversational adjustments that arise when meaning is negotiated promote the comprehension of input, (2) they need to show that comprehensible input promotes acquisition, and (3) they can then deduce that conversational adjustments assist acquisition. However, the early version of the IH received somewhat mixed support from research relating to (1) and (3). Pica, Young, and Doughty (1987) compared learners' comprehension of directions under three conditions: a baseline condition (which involved listening to directions of the kind native speakers address to other native speakers), a PREMODIFIED INPUT condition (where baseline directions were simplified in accordance with the kinds of modifications native speakers make when they address non-native speakers), and an INTERACTIONALLY MODIFIED INPUT condition (where the learners were given the opportunity to negotiate the directions if they did not understand them). They found that learners comprehended the directions best in the interactionally modified condition (as claimed by the IH) and worst in the baseline condition, with comprehension in the premodified condition somewhere in between. Other studies (for example, Gass and Varonis 1994; Loschky 1994; and Ellis, Tanaka, and Yamazaki 1994) also reported that interactionally modified input was more effective in promoting comprehension than premodified input. However, a problem with all these studies was that the interactionally modified input treatment took considerably longer than the premodified treatment. Thus, its superiority may have been simply due to more time-on-task. To address the role of time, Pica (1991) carried out a study where the length of time taken up by the premodified input and interactionally modified input was controlled. In this study, the comprehension scores of the two groups were not statistically different. Other studies (for example, Loschky 1994) failed to show that interactionally modified input is privileged in promoting acquisition while some (for example, Derwing 1994; Ehrlich, Avery, and Yorio 1989) showed that native speakers sometimes have a tendency to over-elaborate when negotiating meaning and that this has a detrimental effect on comprehension. Also, even with studies that have shown interactionally modified input to be superior to premodified input where acquisition is concerned (for example, Gass and Varonis 1994; Ellis, Tanaka, and Yamazaki 1994) the same problem with time-on-task arises. Thus, Ellis (1995d), in a further analysis of the data used in Ellis, Tanaka, and Yamazaki, showed that if words-per-minute was used to compare the effects of the two types of input then the premodified input was the more effective. Finally, interactional modifications may remove the need for learners to develop their linguistic competence and thus have a negative effect on acquisition. Sato (1986) found that the two Vietnamese children she investigated failed to show any progress in acquiring past tense markers over a 10-month period and suggested that one reason for this was that the interactional support they were given obviated the need for them to attend to these features.

The early version of the IH was subjected to a number of criticisms. (See Ellis 1991a.) First, as Hawkins (1985) showed, learners often fake comprehension. That is, they frequently pretend they have understood as a result of negotiating a comprehension problem when, in fact, they have not. Clearly, there are social constraints that influence the extent to which learners are prepared to negotiate to achieve understanding. Second, Aston (1986) pointed out that the forms used to realize the topic management functions associated with meaning negotiation can also be used to realize entirely different functions. For example, modified repetitions of learner utterances need not be confirmation checks; they might simply function as conversational continuants. The identification of negotiation sequences, therefore, is problematic, although this is rarely acknowledged by IH researchers. A third problem is that the early version of the IH, like the Input Hypothesis, failed to explain how the comprehensible input resulted in acquisition.

Long's (1996) updated IH, which emphasized that the role of negotiation is to facilitate ATTENTION to form, addressed this last criticism. Long wrote:

> ... negotiation for meaning, and especially negotiation work that triggers interactional adjustments by the NS or more competent interlocutor, facilitates acquisition because it connects input, internal learner capacities, particularly selective attention, and output in productive ways. (pp. 451–2)

In contrast to the early version of the IH, which simply postulated an effect for comprehensible input, this later version sought to account for *how* interactionally modified input contributes to acquisition by specifying the learner internal mechanisms involved. Interactionally modified input works for acquisition when (1) it assists learners to notice linguistic forms in the input and (2) the forms that are noticed lie within the learner's 'processing capacity'.

The updated version of the IH also afforded a much richer view of how negotiation can assist language learning. As in the early version, negotiation was seen as providing learners with comprehensible input, thereby supplying them with POSITIVE EVIDENCE (i.e. 'models of what is grammatical and acceptable'—Long 1996: 413). Pica (1992) illustrated how the negotiation of meaning provides learners with information about the semantic and structural properties of the target language (English). Native speakers respond to non-native speakers' triggers by modifying their utterances semantically and/or formally through the segmentation and movement of input constituents, as in this example:

NS with a small pat of butter on it and above the plate
NNS hm hmm what is buvdaplate?
NS above
NNS above the plate
NS yeah
(Pica 1992: 225)

However, as Pica admitted, it is not clear from such data whether learners use the information supplied by such exchanges to adjust their interlanguage systems.

The later version of the IH also posits two other ways in which interaction can contribute to acquisition: through the provision of NEGATIVE EVIDENCE and through opportunities for MODIFIED OUTPUT. Long (1996: 413) defined negative evidence as input that provides 'direct or indirect evidence of what is ungrammatical'. It arises when learners receive feedback on their own attempts to use the L2. Gass (1997a) suggested that the negative evidence learners obtain through negotiation serves to *initiate* interlanguage change but that permanent restructuring may only take place after an 'incubation period' during which the learner has access to input that provides further evidence of the need for the change. In other words, the effects of negative evidence may be delayed. Modified output occurs in cases where there is learner uptake-with-repair. In positing a role for this, Long was incorporating Swain's (1985, 1995) Comprehensible Output Hypothesis, which is considered in detail below.

The updated version of the IH is also implicated in Long's views about 'focus on form' (Long 1991; Long and Robinson 1998). FOCUS ON FORM constitutes a type of form-focused instruction that contrasts with FOCUS ON FORMS. In focus on form instruction, attention to form arises out of meaning-centred activity derived from the performance of a communicative task. Focus-on-forms instruction involves the pre-selection of specific features based on a linguistic syllabus and the intensive and systematic treatment of those features. These two types of instruction are considered in greater detail in Chapters 15 and 16. Here we are concerned with the role that negotiation of meaning and form plays in drawing learners' attention to linguistic forms they are experiencing problems with. Doughty (2001) noted 'the factor that distinguishes focus on form from other pedagogical approaches is the requirement that focus on form involves learners briefly and perhaps simultaneously attending to form, meaning and use during one cognitive event' (p. 211). One of the chief ways in which this takes place is through recasts.

Whereas research based on the early version of the IH focused on demonstrating that interactionally modified input assisted comprehension (rather than acquisition), research based on the later version has attempted to investigate whether it facilitates acquisition. This research has consisted primarily of studies of corrective feedback. As we noted earlier in this chapter, corrective feedback can be input-providing (through recasts) or output-prompting. Both of these are relevant to testing the claims of the updated IH but we will only consider studies of recasts here, reserving studies of corrective prompts to the next section of this chapter. Also, we will limit the review to laboratory-based studies, reserving consideration of classroom-based studies to Chapters 15 and 16. In this respect, note is taken of Long's (1996) claim that 'nonclassroom studies are more revealing because spontaneous conversation with no metalinguistic focus before negative evidence is provided is the norm for most L2 learners and the only experience available to many' (p. 438).

Long (1996) argued that recasts constitute an implicit correction strategy that assist acquisition by providing opportunities for 'cognitive comparison' (i.e. for learners to compare their own deviant productions with grammatically correct input). In Long (2006), he listed other advantages: they convey information about language in context; they involve joint attentional focus; the learner has prior comprehension of at least part of the message; the learner is likely to be motivated to attend and is thus primed to notice the correction; and the learner has freed up attentional resources which can be allocated to form–function mapping. Table 6.8 summarizes a number of laboratory studies that have investigated the effects of recasts on L2 acquisition. A number of these studies (see, for example, Han 2002) indicate that recasts can facilitate acquisition. However, recasts are not always effective. They had no effect on three out of the four structures investigated by Long, Inagaki, and Ortega (1998), for example. Also, Iwashita (2003) found that the number of recasts her learners experienced only predicted scores on one of the two structures she investigated. One reason why recasts do not always work can be deduced from Mackey and Philp's (1998) study; they found that recasts assisted the developmentally ready learners but not those who were unready. In other words, recasts may only prove effective if they are tuned to the learner's stage of development. Another factor is the nature of the recasts provided. As we noted earlier, recasts vary in their degree of implicitness/explicitness. For recasts to work as negative evidence, learners have to recognize their corrective force, which is more likely if the recasts are of the more explicit kind. Egi (2007), in a study that made use of stimulated recall, found that learners failed to perceive recasts as corrective when they were long and expanded on the initial erroneous utterance but did do so with shorter, simpler recasts. Han (2002) suggested that the recasts in her study resulted in acquisition because they satisfied four key conditions: (1) they afforded the learner individualized attention, (2) they had a consistent focus (tense consistency), (3) the learners were developmentally ready to acquire the targeted feature, and (4) they were intense (i.e. were repeated over an 8-week period). It is unlikely, however, that the recasts that most learners receive in the context of everyday interaction can satisfy such conditions. Thus, while the research does lend support to the efficacy of recasts, care should be taken not to overestimate their value. As we will see in Chapters 15 and 16, classroom studies (for example, Ellis, Loewen, and Erlam 2006; Loewen and Philp 2006) that have investigated corrective feedback (including recasts) suggest that other forms of corrective feedback, such as metalinguistic feedback and prompts, produce better results than recasts and, also that recasts themselves vary in the extent to which they impact on acquisition. A variety of factors, such as the learners' developmental level, the specific context, the kinds of tasks the learners are asked to do, and the interlocutor's skill in performing recasts, will influence whether and to what extent recasts are effective.

The updated version of the IH, with its emphasis on the contributions of negative feedback and modified output as well as comprehensible input and its recognition that interaction works by connecting input, internal learner capacities, and output via selective attention is obviously a major advance on the early version. There are, however, a number of caveats.

The main one is that a theory of language acquisition based on a single type of interaction (negotiation sequences) or a single interactional strategy (for example, recasts), which constitutes only a small part of the total interaction a learner experiences, would seem to be quite limited. For example, Cook (2000) and Broner and Tarone (2001) made a strong case for the interactions that arise in language play constituting an ideal interactive context for acquisition. Nakahama, Tyler, and Van Lier (2001) contrasted the meaning negotiation resulting from an information exchange task with the negotiation of global problems (for example, relating to anaphoric reference and interpretation of an entire utterance) in a conversation task. The former was mechanical in nature and centred on lexical items. The latter involved significantly longer and more complex turns and wider use of discourse strategies (for example, paraphrase). Nakahama *et al.*'s main point was that there are types of interaction other than the negotiation of meaning that may prove to be more facilitative of acquisition. IH researchers, however, have acknowledged this limitation (for example, Pica 1996).

The IH is limited in another respect, also acknowledged by Pica (1996). Negotiation may work best with intermediate learners; beginner learners lack the resources to negotiate effectively while advanced learners tend to focus on opinion and interpretation rather than comprehension or linguistic clarity. Also negotiation has been shown to centre on lexical problems and larger syntactic units and rarely involves inflectional morphology except in

Study	Participants	Target structure	Design	Tests	Results
Long, Inagaki, and Ortega (1998)	24 young adult 2nd semester learners of Japanese; 30 young adult 3rd semester learners of Spanish	Adjective ordering and locative construction in Japanese; direct object placement and adverb placement in Spanish	For each language group, 3 groups were formed: (1) a models group, which listened to sentences containing the target structures, repeated them, and then demonstrated understanding; (2) a recasts group, which received recasts of any utterances containing errors in the target structures; and (3) a control group. Groups (1) and (2) performed communicative tasks.	Picture description tasks for Japanese; a picture description and grammaticality judgement test for Spanish.	No statistically significant group differences evident for either of the Japanese structures; the recasts group outperformed both the models and control groups on Spanish adverb placement but no group differences for direct object placement were observed.
Mackey and Philp (1998)	35 adult beginner/ lower-intermediate ESL learners from two private language schools in Sydney	WH– and SVO questions	Five groups completed the same communicative tasks. The groups differed in terms of whether (1) they participated in negotiated interaction or just received recasts and (2) their developmental readiness.	The participants completed tasks similar to those used in the treatment immediately after the final treatment, 2 weeks later, and again 5 weeks later. Acquisition was measured in terms of ability to produce developmentally more advanced questions.	The only group to show significant improvement in terms of stage development was the developmentally ready recasts group. Only low levels of repetition or modification of the recasts were recorded (22 per cent and 5 per cent respectively).
Mackey (1999)	34 adult ESL learners in a private school in Sydney.	WH– and SVO questions	Five groups completed the same communicative tasks with NS. The groups varied in terms of (1) whether they received interactionally modified or premodified input, (2) whether they participated in meaning negotiation or not, (3) their developmental readiness to acquire question forms. The interactionally modified input consisted of feedback made up of a mixture of recasts and clarification requests.	As in Mackey and Philp (1998)	Only the learners who received interactionally modified input demonstrated clear-cut evidence of development—they advanced along the developmental sequence and produced more developmentally advanced questions.
Han (2002)	8 adult female upper intermediate ESL learners in a university intensive English language programme	Tense consistency	The participants completed oral and written narratives based on cartoon scripts. One group received recasts when performing the oral narratives while the other just completed the tasks. All participants completed 11 sessions over a period of 2 months.	The degree of present tense and past tense consistency in the oral and written narratives was calculated on three occasions (pre-test, post-test, and delayed post-test).	The recast group improved significantly more in tense consistency in both oral and written narratives than the non-recast group. Thus, there was evidence of cross-modal transfer.

Leeman (2003)	74 first-year university learners of Spanish	Spanish noun-adjective agreement	Four groups performing communicative task one-to-one with researcher; (A) recast group, (B) negative evidence group (source of problem indicated but not corrected), (C) enhanced salience with no feedback, (D) control group.	Post and delayed post picture descriptions tasks.	Only groups (A) and (C) outperformed the control group on any post-test measure. No difference between (A) and (C).
Iwashita (2003)	55 learners of L2 Japanese enrolled in a beginning level course.	Japanese locative construction s and verb (te–) form	Experimental group interacted with NS in performing two communicative tasks. Control group completed a discussion task. Different categories of interactional moves identified.	Pre-test, immediate post-test, and delayed post-test consisted of an oral picture description task.	Recasts less frequent in the input than models. Recasts did not predict accurate performance of locative constructions but did predict accurate performance of the verb (te–) form.
Ishida (2004)	4 adult learners of L2 Japanese (4th and 5th semester language course)	Japanese te i (ru) structure and other items	A time series design: 2 weeks for pre-test, 4 weeks for treatment, and 2 weeks for post-test; 30 minutes conversation sessions about daily activities, weekly schedules, and photographs. Recasts supplied along with other types of feedback.	Obligatory occasional analysis of use of target structure in conversations.	Accuracy in use increased between pre-test and treatment sessions but not between treatment and post-test sessions. However, number of recasts directed at target structure was strongly correlated with gains. Learners had difficulty in developing progressive use of target structure despite the large number of recasts directed at it.
McDonough and Mackey (2006)	58 Thai university EFL learners at stage 4 of Pienemann's development-al sequence for questions (See Chapter 3.)	English question forms	A pre-test, treatment, immediate post-test, delayed post-test design. The experimental group received recasts of incorrectly formulated questions. The control group received no feedback.	The highest stage a learner had reached in Pienemann's developmental sequence as evidenced by at least 2 questions produced in different tasks.	Recasts were a significant predictor of development in question formation. Immediate uptake was not related to development but 'primed production' (i.e. production of the question form provided by the recast within 6 turns of the recast) was related.

Table 6.8 Laboratory studies investigating the effects of recasts on L2 acquisition

experimental studies, such as Ellis, Loewen, and Erlam (2006), which have specifically targeted a morphological feature. The IH, therefore, may not be able to explain how all learners acquire all aspects of linguistic competence. Gass (2003) concluded her own review of the negotiation research by stating 'it is likely that there are limitations to what can and cannot be learnt through the provision of negative evidence provided through conversation' (p. 248).

This suggests the need to attend to individual learner differences. The IH, like other theories in SLA, is universalistic in its frame of reference: it seeks to identify the environmental conditions that pertain to L2 acquisition in general. It would seem obvious, however, that learners vary enormously in their ability or their preparedness to negotiate. The bulk of the research has studied adolescent or adult learners. Do children negotiate in similar ways? Oliver (1997) found that children aged between 8 and 13 years negotiated in similar ways to adults but differed in their proportional use of individual strategies (for example, they made less use of comprehension checks). Van den Branden (1997) also found that 11- to 12-year-old children negotiated each other's output, although he noted that this negotiation was directed principally at meaning and content rather than form. However, younger children (under 7 years) appear to differ more radically in their ability to negotiate (Ellis and Heimbach 1997). Another area of difference concerns interactants' negotiation styles. Polio and Gass (1998) found marked differences in the way native speakers engaged learners in communicative tasks, some adopting a 'leading' role by asking questions to elicit the information they needed while others allowed the learners, who had control of the information to be communicated, to lead. They provided evidence to suggest that learners comprehend better when they have control over the content and form of the discourse. Gass, Mackey, and Pica (1998) asked for INDIVIDUAL DIFFERENCES to be looked at carefully in IH research but their plea has been responded to only to a limited extent. In Chapter 13 we examine a number of studies that have investigated how individual differences affect interaction and mediate acquisition.

However, these limitations do not warrant a dismissal of the IH. The hypothesis has generated considerable interest in the field, has spawned numerous studies and, despite the caveats, has demonstrated ample explanatory power. No theory of L2 acquisition is complete without an account of the role played by interaction and the IH continues to be one of the most convincing statements of this role to date.

4 The Comprehensible Output Hypothesis

Swain (1985, 1995) advanced the COMPREHENSIBLE OUTPUT HYPOTHESIS as a complement to Krashen's Input Hypothesis. She argued that immersion programs in Canada had demonstrated that comprehensible input alone was insufficient to ensure that learners achieved high levels of grammatical and sociolinguistic competence. A number of studies (for example, Harley and Swain 1978) had shown that although immersion learners achieve considerable confidence in using the L2 and considerable discourse skills, they fail to develop more marked grammatical distinctions, such as that between French passé composé and imparfait, and full sociolinguistic competence. Swain argued that this cannot be explained by a lack of comprehensible input, as immersion classrooms are rich in this. She speculated that it might be because the learners had limited opportunity to talk in the classroom and were not 'pushed' in the output they did produce. This was later demonstrated to be the case when Allen, Swain, Harley, and Cummins (1990) showed that immersion students' responses were typically 'minimal' (i.e. less than 15 per cent of students' utterances in French were more than a clause in length).

On these grounds, Swain proposed that production (especially PUSHED OUTPUT[12]) may encourage learners to move from semantic (top-down) to syntactic (bottom-up) processing. Whereas comprehension of a message can take place with little syntactic analysis of the input, production forces learners to pay attention to the means of expression especially if they are 'pushed' to produce messages that are concise and socially appropriate. As Swain (1995) puts it, 'learners ... can fake it, so to speak, in comprehension, but they cannot do so in the same way in production' (p. 127). Production requires learners to process syntactically; they have to pay some attention to form.

Skehan (1998a), drawing on and extending Swain (1995), suggested that production has six roles: (1) it serves to generate better input through the feedback that learners' efforts at production elicit, (2) it forces syntactic processing (i.e. it obliges learners to pay attention to grammar), (3) it allows learners to test out hypotheses about the target-language grammar, (4) it helps to automatize existing L2 knowledge, (5) it provides opportunities for learners to develop discourse skills, for example by producing 'long turns', and (6) it is important for helping learners to develop a 'personal voice' by steering conversations onto topics they are interested in contributing to. To these, another role might be added; (7) production provides the learner with 'auto-input' (Schmidt and Frota 1986) in the sense that learners can attend to the 'input' provided by their own productions. (1), (3), (6), and (7) constitute indirect ways that output can contribute to acquisition, through the input that learners secure for themselves by their efforts to speak. The other roles Skehan mentioned, however, suggest that production can contribute more directly and centrally to acquisition. In effect, there would seem to be two basic arguments relating to the contribution of production. The first is that production enables learners to practise what they already know, thus helping them to automatize their discourse and linguistic knowledge. Roles (4) and (5) belong here. The second argument relates to (2)—the central idea that production engages syntactic processing in a way that comprehension does not.

Evidence in support of a role for output in L2 acquisition is both indirect and direct. Indirect evidence is forthcoming from studies that have investigated the extent to which learners produce modified output. This evidence is reliant on the claim that modified output constitutes evidence of learning or, at least, serves as a mechanism of learning. This is controversial, with some researchers (for example, Long 2006b) arguing that it plays no role in acquisition and others (for example, Lyster 2002) arguing that it probably does. Two kinds of modified output can be identified—other-initiated (i.e. uptake) and self-initiated (i.e. monitoring). Direct evidence involves demonstrating that pushed output results in the internalization of new linguistic forms or increased control over partially acquired forms. The bulk of the research has been of the indirect kind. As Shehadeh (2002: 601) noted:

> After well over a decade of research into Swain's (1985) comprehensible output hypothesis, few definitive conclusions can be made, because the question of whether and how learners' output, or output modification, helps with L2 learning is still largely unanswered.

We will first consider the indirect evidence and then the direct.

A series of studies by Pica have addressed other-initiated output modification. Pica (1988) examined the interactions between a native speaker and 10 non-native speakers of English in order to discover whether corrective feedback led to improved output. She found that the learners did produce more grammatical output when the native speakers requested confirmation or clarification, but in less than half of their total responses. In a subsequent study, however, Pica, Holliday, Lewis, and Morgenthaler (1989) found that the crucial factor was the nature of the indicator the native speaker provided. The learners (10 Japanese adults) were much more likely to produce output modifications in response to clarification requests than to recasts. This was because clarification requests constitute an 'open signal', leaving it up to the learners how to resolve the comprehension problems, whereas recasts, where the native speaker models what the learner intended to mean, remove the need for improved output. Interestingly, this study also showed that many of the modifications that learners made were grammatical and not just semantic in nature. Pica's learners were adults but Van den Branden (1997) showed that 11- to 12-year-old learners were also able to produce modified output following corrective feedback. As we noted, Krashen dismissed such output modification on the grounds that it rarely occurred. This is the case in some studies but in other studies (for example, Shehadeh 1999; Mackey, Oliver, and Leeman 2003) it has been shown to occur frequently.

Two studies that have examined learner-initiated modified output are Swain and Lapkin (1995) and Shehadeh (2002). Using think-aloud protocols, Swain and Lapkin examined the ability of Grade 8 immersion students to reprocess their output when they experienced a problem during a report-writing task. The students experienced a problem on 190 occasions and on each occasion succeeded in modifying their output by making it either more comprehensible or more accurate. They argued that 'on each occasion, the students engaged in mental processing that may have generated linguistic knowledge that is new for the learner or consolidated existing knowledge' (p. 284). Shehadeh examined learners' 'hypothesis-testing episodes' when performing a picture-description task with a native-speaker partner. These episodes involved learners in monitoring and modifying their initial output as in this example:

> You have two chairs (0.8) one near of the bed (0.8) near of the bed (0.9) near to the bed (1.0).

Shehadeh reports that in 87 per cent of such episodes the NS did not provide any feedback on the learners' output and speculates that in such cases the learners would be likely to assume that the hypotheses represented by their self-corrections were confirmed. However, neither of these studies demonstrated conclusively that self-initiated modified input resulted in acquisition.

Let us now consider studies that sought direct evidence that pushed output leads to acquisition. These have produced somewhat mixed results. In an exploratory study involving just six learners (three experimental and three control), Nobuyoshi and Ellis (1993) sought to establish whether pushed output resulted in improved performance over time. In two-way information gap tasks, which each learner performed with the researcher, the experimental subjects experienced 'focused meaning negotiation', where they received a clarification request every time they produced an utterance containing a past tense error. The control subjects experienced 'unfocused meaning negotiation' (i.e. negotiation only took place when there was a genuine communication problem). Both sets of learners believed they were communicating rather than practising language. Nobuyoshi repeated the information-gap task with both groups one week later, this time without a special focus on past tense. Two out of three experimental learners improved the accuracy of their use of the past tense as a result of the requests for clarification and maintained this improvement one week later. The control subjects showed no improvement on either occasion. This study intriguingly suggests that pushing learners to produce more comprehensible output may have a long-term effect, but not necessarily for all learners.[13] Loewen (2005) found that learners' successful uptake in classroom-based communicative lessons was a strong predictor of their ability to subsequently correct their errors in tailor-made tests administered to individual students. However, Smith (2005) found no relationship between degree of uptake (with or without repair) and the acquisition of L2 vocabulary items by intermediate-level ESL learners, who participated in computer-mediated communication based on jigsaw tasks. Clearly, more research on this issue is needed. McDonough and Mackey (2006) also found no evidence that the learners' repetitions of recasts assisted acquisition although they did find that what they called 'primed production' (i.e. the learner correctly produced the corrected form within six turns of the recast that provided it) predicted acquisition.

Two other studies compared the relative effect on acquisition of premodified input, interactionally modified input (where learners have no opportunity to uptake) and modified output (where learners were pushed to use the target items). Ellis and He (1999) used a listen-and-do task performed under four different conditions: (1) baseline (unmodified) input, (2) premodified input, (3) interactionally modified input, and (4) modified output. In (1) learners listened to a set of instructions about where to position items of furniture in a plan of an apartment, in (2) they listened to the same set of directions but in a simplified form, in (3) they were given the opportunity to request clarification if they did not understand a direction, and in (4) they had to make up their own directions and then negotiate them so their partner could understand them. In each case, the directions were seeded with lexical items which the learners did not know. The results were clear-cut. (4) proved superior to all the other conditions with regard to comprehension of the instructions, recognition of the target items, and production of these items. In other words, the learners who produced the comprehensible output outperformed those who received input (comprehensible or otherwise). De la Fuente (2002), in a study of L2 Spanish vocabulary acquisition, also found that negotiated interaction that included pushed output promoted productive acquisition (but not receptive acquisition) of new words to a greater extent than either premodified input or negotiated interaction without pushed output.

One way in which output may promote acquisition is by priming learners to attend to linguistic features in the input. Izumi, in a series of studies (for example, Izumi and Bigelow 1999; Izumi *et al.* 1999) investigated this possibility. The aim of these studies was to compare the relative effects of enhanced input and output on both comprehension and acquisition. In Izumi *et al.* (1999) this was achieved by comparing five groups; (1) + output/+ enhanced input, (2) + output/– enhanced input, (3) – output/+ enhanced input, (4) – output/– enhanced input (i.e. baseline input), (5) a control group that just completed the pre- and post-tests. Output was elicited by means of a text reconstruction task. Enhanced input consisted of a reading text with the target structure (relative clauses) highlighted. The output groups outperformed the non-output groups. There was no difference between groups (1) and (2). In other words, the visual INPUT ENHANCEMENT had no measurable effect on learning. Izumi *et al.* interpreted these results as suggesting that output caused the learners to undertake a cognitive comparison between the target language form and their interlanguage (IL) form leading them to eradicate the IL form.

Finally, Swain and her co-researchers have conducted a series of studies designed to investigate the effects of collaborative talk on metalinguistic awareness and acquisition. These studies were initially informed by the Comprehensible Output Hypothesis but later Swain drew on sociocultural theory to explain her findings. (See Swain 2000 for an explanation of this switch.) Of particular interest here are studies (for example, Kowal and Swain 1994, 1997; LaPierre 1994) which sought to demonstrate that the awareness of form generated by output tasks resulted in learning. In the LaPierre study, Grade 8 French immersion students completed a dictogloss task (Wajnryb 1990). This required them to take notes while listening to a text and then to reproduce it in groups. LaPierre identified 250 LANGUAGE-RELATED

EPISODES that occurred during the reconstruction stage. Swain (1998: 70) defined a language-related episode as 'any part of a dialogue in which students talk about the language they are producing, question their language use, or other- or self-correct'. To establish what effect these episodes had on acquisition, LaPierre designed tailor-made tests which were administered to individual learners one week later. The learners' responses in these tests showed a 70–80 per cent correspondence with the solutions (right or wrong) they had reached in their text reconstructions. Swain (1998) argued that these results show that collaborative talk can mediate language acquisition.

The Comprehensible Output Hypothesis constitutes an important addition to work on the role of interaction in L2 acquisition. It is becoming clear that output contributes to language acquisition. What is not yet clear, however, is whether output assists learners to acquire new linguistic forms or only to automatize use of partially acquired forms (i.e. to eliminate IL variants when the TL variant is already part of a learner's interlanguage). Further work is also needed to establish whether (and under what conditions) the modified output in repaired uptake constitutes acquisition.

5 The Noticing Hypothesis

The theories we have examined up to this point vary in the role they allocate to consciousness in L2 acquisition. The Frequency Hypothesis neither claims nor does not claim that learners need to pay conscious attention to linguistic form in the input. Krashen's Input Hypothesis explicitly rejects a role for consciousness, claiming that 'acquisition' is a subconscious process. Long's Interaction Hypothesis, especially the updated version, claims that learners do need to pay conscious attention to form in order to benefit from negotiated interaction. Swain's Comprehensible Output Hypothesis emphasizes the importance of consciousness, both in terms of learners' noticing gaps in their interlanguage and developing metalinguistic awareness. We will now briefly consider Schmidt's NOTICING HYPOTHESIS, noting that Schmidt's work has been drawn on extensively by theorists such as Long and Swain. A fuller treatment of Schmidt's work can be found in Chapter 9 when information processing theories of L2 acquisition are considered.

Schmidt (1990, 1994, 2001) claimed that attention to input is a conscious process. He viewed NOTICING (i.e. registering formal features in the input) and NOTICING-THE-GAP (i.e. identifying how the input to which the learner is exposed differs from the output the learner is able to generate) as essential processes in L2 acquisition:

> The allocation of attention is the pivotal point at which learner-internal factors (including aptitude, motivation, current L2 knowledge, and processing ability) and learner-external factors (including the complexity and the distributional characteristics of input, discoursal and interactional context, instructional treatment, and task characteristics) come together. What then happens within attentional space largely

> determines the course of language development, including the growth of knowledge (the establishment of new representations), fluency (access to that knowledge), and variation.
> (Schmidt 2001)

In Schmidt and Frota (1986), he referred to his own experience as a learner of Portuguese in Brazil to demonstrate the importance of attention, showing that in nearly every case new forms that appeared in his spontaneous speech were consciously attended to previously in the input. He also drew on a wide body of research in SLA and cognitive psychology to support his central contention that little (possibly no) learning of new linguistic material from input is possible without attended processing.

But what exactly does 'attended processing' consist of and is any learning possible without it? Schmidt (2001) drew on the work of Tomlin and Villa (1994) in distinguishing three subsystems of attention. Attention as 'alertness' refers to motivation and readiness to learn. Here he made the point that noticing and acquisition are not dependent on learner intention (i.e. involuntary noticing can occur). 'Orientation' concerns the general focus of attention (for example, whether on meaning or on form), which can also be influenced by the design of the task. (See Chapter 5.) Schmidt suggested that orientation plays a role in both facilitating and inhibiting processing. In the case of the former it causes certain stimuli to be attended to at the expense of others. In the case of the latter, it helps learners to avoid interference by attention-capturing information that is not relevant to their orientation. 'Detection' refers to the cognitive registration of stimuli that allows for the further processing of information. It is here that controversy exists both regarding whether detection involves awareness and whether it requires only global attention (for example, general attention to form) or more specific attention (for example, attention to a specific aspect of language). With regard to the first of these controversies, Schmidt (2001) distinguished a strong and weak form of the Noticing Hypothesis. The strong form, which reflects his earlier position, states that 'there is no learning whatsoever from input that is not noticed', while the weak form, indicative of his later position, allows for representation and storage of unattended stimuli in memory but claims that 'people learn about the things they attend to and do not learn much about the things they do not attend to'. On the second issue, Schmidt argued that attention needs to be specifically directed. As he put it, 'nothing is free'.

6 Gass' model of second language acquisition

While to some extent the hypotheses we have considered are in conflict (for example, regarding the relative roles of input and output), it is also possible to see them as affording complementary insights into how input and interaction affect L2 acquisition that can be integrated into an overarching framework. We conclude this section with Gass' (1988, 1997) model of second language acquisition, which constitutes an attempt to develop such a framework. A slightly simplified version of the model is shown in Figure 6.2.

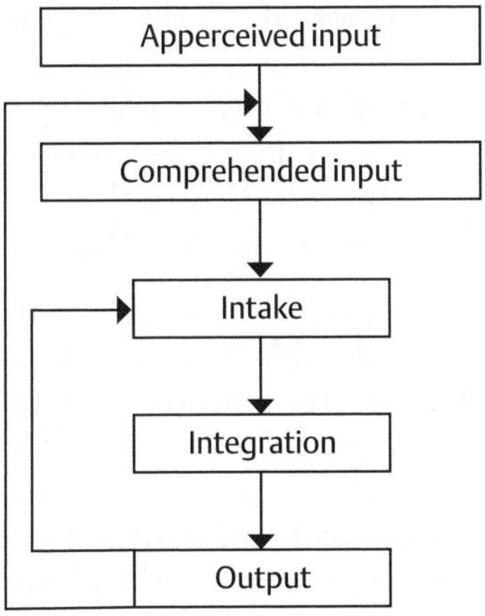

Figure 6.2 An integrated model of second language acquisition (based on Gass 1997: 3)

The model identifies five stages to account for the conversion of input to output. It also incorporates a role for output in the acquisitional process.

1 Apperceived input: this occurs when the learner realizes that there is a gap in his/her L2 knowledge. 'Apperception is an internal cognitive act in which a linguistic form is related to some bit of existing knowledge (or gap in knowledge)' (Gass 1997: 4). Thus, the stage of the model draws on Schmidt's Noticing Hypothesis. Gass also acknowledged the role played by input frequency.
2 Comprehended input: Gass stressed the difference between 'comprehensible' and 'comprehended input'. Whereas comprehensible input positions the speaker as controlling comprehensibility, comprehended input focuses on the learner. She also noted that comprehension is not an all-or-nothing affair; there are different levels, reflecting the difference between processing input for meaning and for learning. This stage draws on criticisms of Krashen's Input Hypothesis.
3 INTAKE: this referred to 'the process of assimilating linguistic material; it refers to the mental activity that mediates input and grammars' (1997: 5). It is where noticing-the-gap or cognitive comparisons occur. Gass viewed interaction, in conjunction with the learner's innate knowledge of linguistic universals and his/her L1 knowledge, as instrumental in causing intake.
4 INTEGRATION: Gass identified four possibilities. The first involves the acceptance or rejection of an existing IL hypothesis. The second involves the use of the intaken feature to strengthen an existing IL hypothesis. The third involves 'storage'. That is the intaken feature is not immediately incorporated into the IL system but is rather treated as an item and placed in the learner's lexicon. Later, however, when the learner has gathered more evidence, the learner may be able to utilize this item to confirm or disconfirm

an IL hypothesis. The final possibility is that the learner makes no use of the intaken feature.

5 Output: Gass viewed output both as an overt manifestation that acquisition has taken place and also as a source of acquisition when it serves as a means for testing hypotheses. She drew explicitly on Swain's Comprehensible Output Hypothesis, envisaging a loop back to input.

It is clear that Gass' model incorporates aspects of all the five hypotheses we have considered, although only obliquely so in the case of Krashen's Input Hypothesis. The model, therefore, constitutes the fullest and clearest statement of the roles played by input and interaction in L2 acquisition currently available.

Gass' model is a computational-type model and, as such, has been criticized. In the following section we turn to the objections that sociocultural theorists have raised with computational models of this type and examine their alternative approach to theorizing the role played by interaction. First, though, to conclude this section, we will consider Mackey and Goo's (2007) meta-analysis of studies that have examined the effect of interaction on L2 acquisition.

7 A meta-analysis of interaction studies

A meta-analysis involves a sampling of primary studies, which are then coded according to the features the reviewer sees as important (for example, type of feedback) and then subjected to statistical analysis in order to identify the magnitude of the effect of the coded features. Norris and Ortega (2006a) offered a compelling argument for pursuing this approach, while also acknowledging its limitations. A number of meta-analyses are considered in Chapter 16 when the results of form-focused instruction are considered. Mackey and Goo (2007) identified 28 interaction studies that met the conditions for a statistical meta-analysis. The main results of their analysis are summarized in Table 6.9.

Overall, then, this meta-analysis produces convincing evidence that interaction is highly effective in facilitating L2 acquisition and, moreover, that the effect is not just short term but durable. It should be noted, however, that Mackey and Goo are very tentative about a number of the findings summarized in Table 6.9 due to various methodological problems, in particular the confounding of variables; for example, there have been more studies of vocabulary in foreign than in second language settings, making it difficult to carry out an effective comparison of the overall effects of interaction in these different contexts. Further, the fact that only a very small number of studies could be included in some of the analyses has the result that the 'analysis suffered at times from an insufficient amount of data available on the stated constructs of interest' (p. 445). Mackey and Goo concluded, as so many researchers do, that more (and better) research is needed.

Research question	Main findings
1 How effective is interaction at promoting the acquisition of linguistic forms?	The interactional treatments produced a strong effect on acquisition in both immediate and delayed tests. The effect was stronger in the delayed than in the immediate tests.
2a How does the type of target structure mediate the relationship between interaction and L2 developmental outcomes?	Learners gained more from interaction on lexical than grammatical items in the immediate post-tests but learners showed greater gains on grammatical than on lexical items in both short-term and long-term delayed post-tests.
2b How does the presence or absence of interactional feedback mediate the relationship between interaction and L2 developmental outcomes?	No significant difference between feedback and no feedback conditions was found on the immediate post-tests. A large difference was evident on the short-term delayed tests but this disappeared on the long-term delayed tests.
2c How does the type of feedback which is provided mediate the relationship between interaction and L2 developmental outcomes?	Recasts showed large effects on all post-tests.
2d How does the focus of the feedback provided mediate the relationship between interaction and L2 developmental outcomes?	No difference on the immediate post-tests was found between the feedback that was broadly focused and feedback that focused on specific linguistic targets. However focused feedback was more effective on the short-term delayed tests.
2e How does the presence or absence of opportunities for modified output mediate the relationship between interaction and L2 developmental outcomes?	Feedback without the opportunity to produce modified output proved more effective than feedback with this opportunity on the immediate post-tests and longer-term delayed tests. There was no difference on the short-term delayed tests.
2f What are the relationships between context and the L2 developmental outcomes that have been found in interaction research?	Interactional treatments were more effective in foreign than in second language contexts with this difference significant on the immediate post-tests.
2g What are the relationships between research setting and L2 developmental outcomes that have been found in interaction research?	Laboratory studies showed strong effects across all tests; classroom studies only showed significant effects on the delayed tests. Overall, the laboratory studies showed the stronger effect.
2h What is the relationship between the type of dependent measure that is employed and the L2 developmental outcomes that have been found in interactional research?	The largest effect was found for 'closed-ended prompted production'. However, a significant effect was also found for 'open-ended prompted production'.

Table 6.9 Summary of the results of a meta-analysis of interaction studies (based on Mackey and Goo 2007)

Sociocultural accounts of interaction and L2 acquisition

Sociocultural theory is now very prominent in SLA due in particular to the advocacy of Lantolf and his fellow researchers (Lantolf and Appel 1994a; Lantolf and Pavlenko 1995; Lantolf 2000a, 2000b; Lantolf and Thorne 2006). Our focus here is not on the complete theory but on the place of social interaction in the theory and the research that has investigated this. I will briefly outline the relevant parts of the theory and then consider the theoretical critique that sociocultural theorists have levelled against the input-output model. Finally, a number of studies of interaction based on sociocultural theory will be considered.

1 The role of interaction in sociocultural theory

As Lantolf (2000a) pointed out 'the central and distinguishing concept of sociocultural theory is that higher forms of mental activity are *mediated*'. External MEDIATION serves as the means by which internal mediation is achieved. Lantolf suggested that mediation in second language learning involves (1) mediation by others in social interaction, (2) mediation by self through private speech, and (3) mediation by artefacts (for example, tasks and technology). Our concern here is only with (1). It should be noted, however, that Lantolf also viewed private speech as a form of interaction (i.e. the learner interacting with him/herself). Swain (2000) noted that language learning involves learning how to use language to mediate language learning. This is primarily achieved by means of verbal interaction, which can be monologic or dialogic. Whereas both can serve to mediate learning, dialogic interaction is seen as central. Dialogic interaction enables an expert (such as a teacher) to create a context in which novices can participate actively in their own learning and in which the expert can fine-tune the support that the novices are given (Anton 1999). In particular, dialogic discourse is better equipped to identify what a learner can and cannot do without assistance.

In sociocultural theory, then, there is a close relationship between interpersonal activity and intramental activity, the former serving as the precursor of the latter. As Vygotsky (1981) put it, new, more elaborate psychological processes become available as a result of the initial production of these processes in social interaction. Vygotsky provided this explanation of how children develop mental skills:

> Any function in the child's development appears twice or on two planes, first it appears on the social plane, and then on the psychological plane; first it appears between people as an interpsychological category, and then within the child as an intrapsychological category.
> (p. 163)

Children progress from object-regulation, where their actions are determined by the objects they encounter in the environment, to other-regulation, where they exhibit control over an object but only with the assistance of another, usually more expert person, and finally to self-regulation, where they become capable of independent strategic functioning. Verbal interaction, especially dialogic, serves as the principal means by which children progress from other- to self-regulation. Similarly, sociocultural SLA researchers consider that L2 learning proceeds in the same way. Foley (1991) suggested, for example, that the strategies involved in the negotiation of meaning constitute devices for achieving self-regulation.

The theory also has a psychological dimension. This entails the extent to which an individual is ready to perform the new skill. Vygotsky (1978) evoked the metaphor of the zone of proximal development (ZPD) to explain the difference between an individual's actual and potential levels of development.[14] The skills that the individual has already mastered constitute his or her actual level. The skills that the individual can perform when assisted by another person constitute the potential level. Thus, learnt skills provide a basis for the performance of new skills. For interaction to work for acquisition it needs to assist the learner in constructing zones of proximal development. As we saw earlier in the chapter, this is achieved with the help of scaffolding.

Sociocultural theorists prefer to talk of 'participation' rather than 'acquisition' (Sfard 1998) to emphasize the point that development is not so much a matter of the taking in and the possession of knowledge but rather of the taking part in social activity. In this view of learning, then, the distinction between 'use' of the L2 and 'knowledge' of the L2 becomes blurred because knowledge is use and use creates knowledge. For this reason, research based on SCT has typically eschewed the use of pre- and post-tests in favour of detailed 'micro-genetic' analyses of interactional sequences. However, research by Swain and her co-researchers (for example, Swain and Lapkin 2001) employed pre- and post-tests to examine the changes that result from performing collaborative tasks.

2 A critique of the input-output model of L2 acquisition

Two major criticisms have been levelled at the input-output model by sociocultural theorists. The first targets the assumption that acquisition is something that happens inside the head of learners. The second is directed at the view that interaction is simply a 'provider of input' (Gass 1997).

In all versions of the computational model acquisition is construed as taking place inside the head of the individual learner. In Chomskyan accounts of language acquisition, this process is dependent on a pre-wired capacity for language learning (a language acquisition device) which is activated by the triggering effect of the input. In accounts based on information-processing models, the learner is credited with a more general capacity to respond to the frequencies of sequences in the input, but, again, acquisition is entirely an inside-the-head phenomenon. Sociocultural theory views such a position as fundamentally mistaken because it perpetuates the view of the learner as 'a disengaged self ... metaphysically independent of society' (Claude and Weaver 1949). In contrast, the theory claims 'that specifically human psychological processes do not pre-exist inside the head waiting to emerge at just the right maturational moment' (Lantolf 2000a: 14). That is, learning is viewed as an interpsychological as well as an intrapsychological phenomenon with the latter only understood with reference to the former.

Sociocultural theorists also reject the view that interaction serves as a provider of input or of opportunities for output. Indeed, they object to the terms 'input' and 'output', viewing them as indicative of a mechanistic view of communication and learning.[15] Platt and Brooks (1994) argued that input and interaction models fail to characterize the rich nature of the interactions in which learners participate. They also rejected the key assumption of the Interaction Hypothesis, namely that the type of interaction that works best for language acquisition is information-providing and meaning centred. They noted that the learners they had observed frequently talked to themselves about conceptual content, task procedures, linguistic form, or their own language production and implied that such talk was of potential importance for language acquisition (as indeed Swain's studies of 'language-related episodes' have demonstrated). Van Lier (2000) made a similar point. He argued that interaction cannot be properly investigated by breaking it down into its component elements (as the input-output model seeks to do); rather it is necessary 'to look at the active learner in her environment' and study interaction in its totality in order to show the emergence of learning. In short, sociocultural theorists argue for a much richer view of interaction and for treating it as a cognitive activity in its own right.

3 Studies of interaction and L2 acquisition based on sociocultural theory

What have studies based on sociocultural theory discovered about interaction and L2 acquisition? We will consider representative studies that have examined both expert–novice interactions (i.e. interactions between a native speaker and learners) and novice–novice interactions (i.e. interactions between learners). Many of these studies adopted the MICROGENETIC METHOD. This involves detailed analysis of sequences of interaction with a view to documenting the shift towards self-regulation that occurs within them. (See Ellis and Barkhuizen (2005) for a description of this method.) However, a number of studies have also employed an experimental design involving pre-tests and post-tests.

Nassaji and Swain's (2000) examination of a native-speaking tutor's oral feedback on the written compositions of two Korean learners of English is an example of a study of expert–novice interactions. A particular strength of this study is that it incorporated mircrogenetic analyses within an experimental design. The study sought to compare the effectiveness of feedback on the two learners' acquisition of articles. The assistance to one learner was provided within her ZPD. That is, the tutor systematically worked through Aljaafreh and Lantolf's scale (see Table 6.5) to negotiate the feedback she supplied) while the assistance to the other learner was random (i.e. the tutor was supplied with a random list of correcting strategies drawn from the scale). The results showed that providing feedback within the learner's ZPD was effective in (1) helping the learner to arrive at the correct form during the feedback session, (2) enabling the learner to arrive at the correct form with much less explicit assistance in subsequent sessions, and (3) enabling the learner to use the correct form unassisted in a post-test consisting of a cloze version of the compositions she had written previously. In contrast, random feedback did not always succeed in enabling the learner to identify the correct article form in the feedback sessions and was much less effective in promoting unassisted use of the correct forms in the post-test. Also, interestingly, the tutor who provided the random feedback reported that he found it very difficult and unnatural. This study supports the claim that, when scaffolding works to construct a ZPD for a learner, learning results.

Swain, Brooks, and Tocalli-Beller (2003) reviewed research that has investigated peer–peer dialogue. They suggest that in such dialogue, learners can act concurrently as experts and novices and support learning 'through, for example, questioning, proposing possible solutions, disagreeing, repeating, and managing activities and behaviours (social and cognitive)' (p. 173). They reviewed studies where learners interacted collaboratively in completing writing tasks (for example, Swain and Lapkin 2001b), speaking (for example, Ohta 2001b), listening (for example, Ellis and He 1999) and reading (for example, Klingner and Vaughn 2000), concluding that the 'collaborative dialogue in which peers engage as they work together on writing, speaking, listening and reading activities mediates second language learning' (p. 181). In accordance with the view that learning occurs in interaction rather than as a result of interaction, most of the studies they reviewed studied learners' *use* of language rather than demonstrating that collaborative dialogue led to internalization of linguistic forms.

A study that did investigate transfer to new contexts is Donato (1994). I considered this study earlier in the section that addressed scaffolding. The learners were able to collaboratively construct the correct form of the verb construction 't'es souvenu' even though no single learner knew this prior to the task. Donato went on to provide evidence to suggest that internalization was taking place. The joint performance of new structures on one occasion was frequently followed by independent use of them by individual learners on a later occasion. Thus, this study goes further than most in demonstrating the essential claim of a sociocultural theory of mind, namely that 'higher mental functioning is situated in the dialectal processes embedded in the social context' (p. 46).

In their review of peer–peer dialogue, Swain *et al.* (2003) found 'few adverse effects of working collaboratively' (p. 181). However, as LaPierre (1994) and Swain and Lapkin (1998) showed, peer mediation is not always effective; occasions can arise when 'expert' mediation is required. Lantolf (2000a), for example, refers to a study by Platt and Troudi (1997), which showed how a teacher's belief that peer rather than expert mediation was more effective in promoting learning had a negative effect when it came to certain content areas (for example, maths). Lantolf went on to comment 'while peer assistance is effective for learning everyday functional language, it may not be as effective for development of academic language'. There will obviously be situations in which the mediation provided by an 'expert' language user is required to negotiate a learner's ZPD. Thus, Swain and Lapkin (1998) argued that teacher feedback on the recorded oral dialogue generated by a task or the written product of the task was needed to resolve learner uncertainty and to point out incorrect solutions to linguistic problems.

Research based on sociocultural theory offers important insights into the role interaction plays in L2 acquisition. It offers a refreshing alternative to the rather narrow, atomistic view of interaction projected by the input-output theories. Its strength lies in the demonstration of interpsychological learning through the analysis of a wide variety of interactional behaviours. However, the research to date has been less successful in demonstrating how the interpsychological becomes the intrapsychological (i.e. how full self-regulation is achieved). In part, this is because sociocultural researchers have been trapped by their axiomatic acceptance that use *is* acquisition. Sociocultural SLA will come of age when there are more studies like Nassaji and Swain's that document 'the transfer of knowledge to new contexts' (Swain *et al.* 2003).

Conclusion

In this chapter we have examined theory and research that has addressed the role of input and interaction in L2 acquisition. Much of the research has been descriptive, directed at identifying the key features of the input that L2 learners receive and the interactions (especially those occurring in naturalistic contexts) that they participate in. This led Young (1988b: 128) to conclude his survey of input and interaction research with the comment that 'there is still a great deal of beating about the bush', by which he meant that relatively few studies had tried to investigate to what extent and in what ways input and interaction influence acquisition. The position has changed somewhat in the years since Young's review and we now have a clearer idea of what kinds of input and interaction facilitate acquisition. It is now acknowledged, for example, that input frequency plays a significant role in item learning (but possibly less in system learning), that learners can learn from exposure to comprehensible input providing they pay attention to form, that negative evidence in the form of recasts and other forms of corrective feedback helps learners to carry out the cognitive comparisons necessary for acquisition, and that acquisition is not driven by input alone but that output also contributes. Studies have also shown that the scaffolding that arises in both expert–novice and novice–novice interactions enables learners to produce and subsequently internalize linguistic constructions that they could not perform independently.

These studies have drawn on two very different theoretical approaches—the computational model of L2 acquisition, as reflected in Gass' model, and socio-cultural theory. The computational model is concerned with documenting how input feeds into the universal mechanisms responsible for acquisition. It assumes that acquisition is something that happens inside the mind of the learner. Implicit in such a view is the Cartesian internal/external dualism. That is, the job of the researcher is characterized as identifying how input, viewed as external phenomena, interacts with mental knowledge and capacities, viewed as internal phenomena. The perspective is inherently cognitive. Sociocultural theory, in contrast, seeks to overcome this dualism by integrating social and biological factors. The linguistic environment is viewed not as a resource but as the source of learning; acquisition takes place in interaction that is shaped by social and cultural factors. The job of the researcher in this paradigm is to show how interaction mediates acquisition. The perspective is socio-cognitive. These approaches have been presented as oppositional—and, indeed, they are, as reflected in the publications of proponents of each approach. However, I prefer to see them as complementary, two strands of what Norris and Ortega (2003) called the 'interactionist paradigm' in SLA, incommensurable rather than incompatible (Sfard 1998). Arguably, to explain the complex relationship between input/interaction and L2 acquisition we need both perspectives.

Notes

1 The term 'discourse analysis' is often taken to include 'conversational analysis'. Hatch and Long (1980), for example, identified a wide variety of work that has been referred to as discourse analysis, including speech act analysis, the analysis of discourse structure and conversational analysis.

2 In Ellis 1988a, I also made the point that much of native-speaker usage is variable (for example, English copula has a full and contracted form) and the learner's target, therefore, is to achieve the same pattern of variability as that found in native-speaker usage. However, much of SLA research has been based on the assumption that the learner's target consists solely of categorical rules (such as the 3rd person –s rule in English) that specify the conditions requiring the obligatory use of a single linguistic form.

3 It should be noted that in some cultures adult caretakers do seem to give something resembling 'language lessons'. Ochs and Schieffelin (1984) give examples of how Kaluli mothers in Papua New Guinea require their children to engage in imitation exercises without any attention to the meaning of utterances being imitated.

4 Gleitman, Newport, and Gleitman (1984) noted that several studies have reported a strong correlation between adult and child speech involving subject-aux inversion in yes/no questions. Gass (1997a) suggested this

may reflect the greater 'engagement' that such questions elicit from children that makes this feature salient to them.

5 Snow (1986) made the point that in order to consider to what extent there is 'fine-tuning' it is essential to examine correlations between child variables and complexity of caretaker talk at the right stage of development. She also discussed a number of other factors that may attenuate the relationship; for example, fine-tuning may be situation-specific.

6 The term 'foreigner talk' was initially used by Ferguson (1971) to refer solely to the kind of ungrammatical talk that native speakers sometimes address to non-native speakers. Arthur *et al.* (1980) used the term 'foreigner register' to refer to grammatical FT while the term 'foreigner talk discourse' has been used to refer to interactionally modified FT. Increasingly, though, 'foreigner talk' was used as a general cover term for the modified language native speakers use with non-native speakers, and this is how the term is used in this chapter.

7 The distinction between discourse management and discourse repair of communication breakdowns mirrors Long's (1983a) distinction between 'strategies' for avoiding trouble and 'tactics' for dealing with trouble when it occurs.

8 The terms 'negotiation of meaning' and 'negotiation of form' are used variably in the literature. Lyster (2002), for example, used the former term to refer to strategies that dealt with communication breakdown (as in my definition) but the latter to refer to utterances that served as 'prompts' (i.e. elicited a correction from the learner). It should also be noted that some researchers (for example, Mackey) dispute whether there is such a thing as negotiation of form, preferring instead to view exchanges such as the one from Ellis, Basturkmen, and Loewen (2001) as 'form oriented discussions'.

9 Goldin-Meadow (1982) distinguished RESILIENT and FRAGILE PROPERTIES in the sign language of deaf children. The former are those properties such as recursion and word order that appear to develop irrespective of environmental conditions, whereas the latter (for example, plural and verb tense) need special care.

10 Another purpose of Gass and Lakshmanan's (1991) study was to show the dangers of conducting studies based on descriptions of language which assume that the input to the learner is target-like. They comment: 'considering principles of UG, or any other principles, devoid of context is insufficient and often misleading in accounting for how L2 grammars develop'.

11 Syntactic category was determined with reference to functional category theory. That is, a distinction was drawn between lexical and functional categories and between free and bound morphemes.

12 Plentiful opportunities to speak, such as those that Wes undoubtedly had in Hawaii (see Schmidt 1983), will not in themselves guarantee acquisition. Learners like Wes who develop high levels of strategic competence

may be able to communicate efficiently without much grammatical competence, and so may never experience the need to improve their output in order to make themselves understood. Lardiere's (2007) case study documents a similar finding. (See Chapter 1 for more information on these studies.)

13 Nobuyoshi and I noted that the one experimental learner who failed to improve past tense accuracy was adept at making himself understood in other ways. He manifested what Meisel, Clahsen, and Pienemann (1981) referred to as a 'communicative orientation'.

14 On the face of it the ZPD is analogous to Krashen's i + 1 (i.e. the notion that what learners can acquire is governed by their current interlanguage and what structure comes next in the 'natural order' of development). Such is the position adopted by some SCT researchers (for example, Schinke-Llano 1993). However, Dunn and Lantolf (1998) disputed such a comparison, arguing that whereas Krashen's i + 1 relates to features of language, the ZPD applies to individuals involved in the learning. Lantolf, in fact, disputes the existence of a universal 'natural order of acquisition'.

15 Swain (2000), in an article in which she documented the development of her own thinking from its earlier reliance on the input-output model to sociocultural theory, expressed a dislike of the term 'output' but admitted she could not think of a suitable alternative. Later, however, she hit on LANGUAGING.

7
Social aspects of second language acquisition

Introduction

In Chapter 4 we considered research that examined the variability found in learner language and the factors that account for this variability. We noted that there are both psycholinguistic and sociolinguistic sources of variability. In this chapter we explore further the sociolinguistic sources but adopt a broader perspective by asking how social factors influence learning and also how learners participate in the construction of social contexts of acquisition.

The perspective adopted in this chapter is, therefore, sociolinguistic rather than psycholinguistic in nature. Tarone and Swain (1995) characterized the difference in these two approaches as follows:

> Where psycholinguists tend to treat individuals as isolated for the purposes of research, sociolinguists prefer to treat individuals as representative members of the speech communities in which they function.
> (p. 167)

With the partial exception of variability studies, early SLA research was predominantly psycholinguistic in nature. Later research, however, has increasingly adopted a sociolinguistic outlook, often stridently so by insisting on the narrowness and illegitimacy of what Block (2003) has termed the 'Input-Interaction-Output Model' (i.e. the model of L2 acquisition that informed the work of Gass and Long considered in Chapter 6). Firth and Wagner (1997), for example, criticized this model on the grounds that it is 'individualistic and mechanistic' and 'fails to account for the interactional and sociolinguistic dimensions of language' (p. 285). They considered such an approach 'flawed' and sought to reconceptualize SLA in order to afford an integrated account of the social and cognitive dimensions of L2 use and acquisition. Tarone (2000) began her review of sociolinguistic SLA by claiming 'too much SLA research focuses on psycholinguistic processes in the abstract and does not consider the social context of L2 learning' (p. 182).

Atkinson (2002) offered a similar criticism: '... our obsession with the decontextualized, autonomous learner has prevented us from conceptualizing SLA as a situated, integrated, *sociocognitive* process' (p. 526). Roberts (2001) noted that even sociocultural accounts of L2 acquisition and interlanguage pragmatics have failed to view language as 'a discourse—a social process—into which members of a community are socialised' (p. 109). These (and other) commentaries point to a concerted attempt on behalf of a growing number of researchers to expand the boundaries of SLA by recognizing that 'just as surely as language is social, so is its acquisition' (Atkinson 2002: 527) and advancing the case for a SOCIOCOGNITIVE SLA.

Sociolinguistic SLA, however, does not constitute a single, homogeneous line of enquiry. Rather like sociolinguistics itself, it adopts a number of different approaches. Coupland (2001) distinguished three types of sociolinguistic theory, each with its own approaches to investigating the relationship between social factors and language. These are summarized in Table 7.1. These approaches are, in part, historically aligned. Thus, the Type 1 approach figured in the early decades of sociolinguistics in the study of variation and language change (which we considered in Chapter 4) with Type 2 following later. As Coupland noted, these two approaches are radically different and have often been the subject of antagonistic debate. Type 3 represents an attempt to develop a unifying theory of sociolinguistics. All three types are evident in the research that will be considered in this chapter.

Type	**Description**	**Methodological approaches**
Type 1 Socio-structural realism	Social life is viewed as 'a structured set of social categories which, to some extent, control our social characteristics and opportunities' (p. 2). It prioritizes the macro-level of social organization.	Labov's variationist sociolinguistics; quantification of linguistic features in relation to pre-determined social factors such as social class and age.
Type 2 Social action perspectives	This assumes that 'social life and our entire experience of society is best seen as structured through local actions and practices' (p. 2). This approach prefers to examine 'discourse' and 'interaction' rather than formal linguistic features. Social meaning is negotiated continuously through interaction.	Two distinct versions: (1) Sociolinguistic discourse analysis—actors are aware of the social norms for language, which influences how they interact (e.g. Accommodation theory) and (2) social meanings are contingent and co-constructed by the actors (e.g. Conversational Analysis).

Type 3 Integrationism	This attempts to transcend the dualisms of Type 1 and Type 2 sociolinguistics by acknowledging that social structures do impact directly on linguistic behaviour but also that actors function as agents who reproduce and also modify these structures.	Hymes' ethnography of speaking constitutes an early form of integrationism. Critical discourse analysis examines how socio-political contexts shape discourse and are also disputed through discourse.

Table 7.1 Three types of sociolinguistics (based on Coupland 2001)

Reflecting these different approaches, sociolinguistic SLA is replete with a bewildering set of terms referring to the social aspects of L2 acquisition. Barkhuizen (2004) lists the following: 'social influences', 'social factors', 'social context', 'social setting', 'situational environments', 'situational variables', 'environmental factors/influences' and 'social milieu'. Sociolinguistic SLA also displays a number of theoretical strands. Mitchell and Myles (2004) considered five in their overview: (1) variability in second language use, (2) second language socialization, (3) communities of practice and situated L2 learning, (4) L2 learning and the (re)construction of identity, and (5) affect and emotion in L2 learning.

This heterogeneity poses problems for anyone wishing to offer a survey of sociolinguistic SLA. I will not follow Mitchell and Myles in attempting to deal discretely with the different theoretical strands. It does not seem to me that these can be clearly distinguished as shown by the fact that Mitchell and Myles sometimes draw on the same range of studies in their accounts of the different strands. Instead, I will adopt an approach based on different levels of social structure, starting with 'sociolinguistic settings', and then moving on to examine the role first of specific 'social factors' and then 'situational factors'. In so doing I will draw on research that belongs to all three types of sociolinguistics. First, though, I will delve further into the differences between psycholinguistic and sociolinguistic SLA.

Psycholinguistic versus sociolinguistic SLA

A summary of the main differences between psycholinguistic and sociolinguistic SLA is provided in Table 7.2.

As should be clear from the chapters in Part 2 of the book, the focus of enquiry in psycholinguistic SLA has been the acquisition of L2 linguistic and pragmatic competence. The study of learner ERRORS, of ORDERS and SEQUENCES OF ACQUISITION, of variability in learner language and even of INTERLANGUAGE PRAGMATICS has been mainly concerned with documenting how learners develop specific L2 linguistic resources. In contrast, as Mitchell and Myles (2004) point out, sociolinguistic SLA has had a broader focus, addressing learners' pragmatic and discourse competence. This approach has also examined the relationship between SOCIALIZATION and language (i.e. how specific sociocultural forms influence the language that is learnt and how language serves as the means by which these forms are internalized). With the exception of work on variability, sociolinguistic SLA has also preferred to consider the rate and success of acquisition rather than the acquisition of specific features of the L2 code.

The two approaches also differ in the way they view SOCIAL CONTEXT. Siegel (2003) distinguished a structural view of social context corresponding to Coupland's Type 1 sociolinguistics (where social factors such as power and prestige are seen as determining social context) and an interactional view corresponding to Coupland's Type 2 (where social context is seen as created in each situation through an interplay of social factors). Psycholinguistic SLA adopts a structural view—social context is seen as determining the types of input and interaction a learner is exposed to and also the attitudes the learner has towards the target language, the target language community, and language learning. It also tends to view social context very broadly, for example in terms of the distinction between 'second' and 'foreign' language contexts, which, as Block (2003) pointed out, denies the enormous variation that exists within each of these contexts. Sociolinguistic SLA reflects both a structural and an interactional view. The former is evident in research that seeks to document how social constructs such as class, gender, and age impact on L2 learners as shown through their use of the L2 and their rate/success of learning. The latter is evident in research that treats the social context as a complex and constantly changing arena for learning that is constructed and reconstructed by all participants, including the learner. Coupland's Type 3 sociolinguistics (where the macro role of social factors is acknowledged but individuals can shape their own social reality through local action) is evident in Watson-Gegeo's (1992: 51) view of sociolinguistic SLA which she describes as involving 'the whole set of relationships in which a phenomenon is situated', including both macro-dimensions such as the institutional, social, political, and cultural aspects of context and the micro-dimensions of the immediate context of situation.

Differences in psycholinguistic and sociolinguistic SLA are also evident in how researchers conceptualize the learner's SOCIAL IDENTITY and its role in acquisition. As Firth and Wagner (1997) noted, psycholinguistic SLA characterizes the learner as a 'non-native speaker'; it views learners as 'inherently defective communicators' and, as we saw in the previous chapter, typically characterizes interaction as occurring between 'native speakers' and 'non-native speakers'. The 'native speaker' of psycholinguistic studies is also often idealized as a standard language speaker. In contrast, sociolinguistic SLA acknowledges that learners possess many different identities other than that of 'learner' and that these identities are dynamic. It also acknowledges that many of the interactions that learners take part in are with other learners rather than native speakers. It emphasizes that in many cases the so-called 'native speakers' that learners come into contact with are not speakers of the standard variety but rather of some regional or community variety. Not surprisingly, then, sociolinguistic SLA challenges the terms typically used in psycholinguistic SLA. Leung, Harris, and Rampton (1997), for example, suggested that terms such as 'native speaker' and 'non-native speaker' are replaced with 'language expertise' (how proficient people are in a language), 'language inheritance' (i.e. the ways in which individuals can be born into a language tradition whether or not they claim affiliation to that language) and 'language affiliation' (i.e. the attachment or identification they feel for a language). Rampton (1997) proposed replacing the term 'second language learner' with 'additional language learner'.

As Block (2003) pointed out, psycholinguistic research typically fails to provide rich descriptive accounts of the learners under study. He noted that there is 'a certain monolinguistic bias'(p. 33) in the descriptions of learners. That is, there is an assumption that the learners have a single L1 and that this remains intact despite contact with the L2. In contrast, sociolinguistic SLA typically provides rich descriptions of learners, acknowledging that in many cases they are multilingual and engage in heteroglossic practices. Block, following Cook (2002), emphasized the MULTICOMPETENCE of many learners. Leung, Harris, and Rampton (1997) pointed out that in psycholinguistic SLA, so-called 'bilingual learners' are 'frequently attributed a kind of romantic bilingualism and turned into reified speakers of a community language, and in the process their ethnicities are also reified' (p. 553). Sociolinguistic SLA, as this quotation indicates, has typically focused on learners in urban majority-language settings (for example, Bangladeshi learners of English in the United Kingdom) rather than on learners in classrooms in foreign language settings (for example, Japanese learners of English in Japan) and it is perhaps obvious that in such settings simplistic distinctions, such as that between 'L1' and 'L2 speakers', are not tenable.

Input and interaction are also viewed very differently in the two approaches. As we saw in the previous chapter, psycholinguistic SLA views input as the linguistic 'data' that learners can process internally in order to advance their interlanguages. Interaction serves as the means by which learners obtain input, especially the kinds of input hypothesized to promote acquisition. In contrast, in sociolinguistic SLA, there are few references to input. This is because no clear distinction is made between input and interaction. Rampton (1995), exemplifying Type 2 sociolinguistics, saw interaction as 'a sociohistorically sensitive area in which language learner identity is socially negotiated' (p. 293). It is seen as context-sensitive and is constructed dynamically by the participants on a moment-by-moment basis. Atkinson (2002) pointed out that input and interaction are integral aspects of a 'sociocognitive whole' that includes non-linguistic features (for example, facial expressions) as well as linguistic ones.

Not surprisingly, given the nature of these conceptual differences, the two approaches have typically employed very different research methodologies.

Whereas psycholinguistic SLA has been typically atomistic, quantitative, and confirmatory, sociolinguistic SLA (especially Type 2) has been holistic, qualitative, and interpretative. It is true that much of the early work in SLA was descriptive in nature, based on case studies of individual learners (for example, Schmidt 1983; Wode 1981) but this work also attempted to quantify the accuracy with which learners performed specific linguistic features in order to establish orders and sequences of acquisition. Much recent research in psycholinguistic SLA has been correlational or experimental in nature, seeking, for example, to identify relationships between measures of input/interaction and L2 acquisition (as in the studies reviewed in Mackey and Goo's (2007) meta-analysis considered in Chapter 6). Type 2 sociolinguistic research in the interactional tradition has been conducted by means of ethnographic studies of individual learners that aim to provide rich descriptions of the learners' backgrounds and the social contexts in which they participate. It has eschewed quantification in favour of looking at speech events in a holistic way. Thus, whereas psycholinguistic SLA has attempted to describe input and interaction in terms of taxonomic coding schemes (see Chapter 6), sociolinguistic SLA has preferred CONVERSATIONAL ANALYSIS (Markee 2000) or MICROGENETIC ANALYSIS (Aljaafreh and Lantolf 1994) as the methodological tools for examining how acquisition-in-interaction takes place.

Underlying the differences in the two approaches is a fundamental distinction in the way in which the object of enquiry (L2 learning) is conceptualized. In psycholinguistic SLA, learning is viewed as something that takes place inside the mind of the learner. It can only be demonstrated by showing that a change in learners' ability to comprehend or produce some specific linguistic feature has taken place. In sociolinguistic SLA, in contrast, no clear distinction between learning and language use is made. Rather it is assumed that because learning necessarily entails language use, it is sufficient to simply examine how learners use language and how social factors shape and are shaped by this use. In SOCIOCULTURAL SLA (see Chapter 11), for example, there is a preference for talking about 'participation' rather than 'acquisition' (Sfard 1998) on the grounds that development is not so much the taking in and possession of linguistic knowledge as the taking part in social activity. This blurring of the difference between language use and learning has led to the criticism that sociolinguistic SLA has failed to show that social factors impact on the process of acquisition itself. Long (1998), responding to Firth and Wagner's (1997) injunction to redress what they saw as an imbalance in perspectives and approaches in SLA by evolving a 'bio-social SLA', presented the following challenge:

> Instead of dismissing all work as 'narrow' and 'flawed', and simply asserting that SLA researchers should therefore change their data base and analyses to take new elements into account, [critics] should offer at least some evidence that, for example, a richer understanding of

> alternative social identities or people currently treated as 'learners', or a broader view of social context makes a difference, and a difference not just to the way this or that tiny stretch of discourse is interpretable, but to our understanding of acquisition.
> (p. 92)

Long went on to assert that changes in the social setting have not been shown to have any effect on the way in which the learner acquires an L2 (for example, no differences in error types or developmental sequences are evident).

This clash of perspectives is not easy to resolve because of the radically different conceptualizations of the object of enquiry. However, clearly, the case for a sociolinguistic SLA will be stronger if Long's challenge is taken up. What is important, perhaps, is to make a sharper distinction between research that has demonstrated the impact of social factors on language use and on acquisition. In this respect, sociolinguistic SLA has been lacking. However, as Collentine and Freed pointed out, 'at the very least, the study of SLA within and across various contexts of learning forces a broadening of our perspective of the most important variables that affect and impede acquisition in general' (2004: 158).

Dimensions	**Psycholinguistic SLA**	**Sociolinguistic SLA**
Focus of enquiry	Narrow focus on the universal aspects of how learners acquire an L2. Priority is given to linguistic competence.	Rate and success of L2 acquisition with a focus on differential outcomes. Priority is given to pragmatic and discourse competence. In addition, researchers have examined the relationship between socialization and the L2.
Social context	The structural view is dominant—the social context determines the L2 data made available to the learner and the learner's attitudes to learning.	Both the structural and the interactional view figure. The social context is seen as both determining L2 use and developmental outcomes (as in variationist studies) and as something that is jointly constructed by the participants.
Learner identity	The learner is viewed as a 'non-native speaker'. Learner identity is static.	The learner is viewed as having multiple identities that afford different opportunities for language learning. Learner identity is dynamic.

Learner's linguistic background	The learner has full linguistic competence in his/her L1.	Learners may be multilingual and may display varying degrees of proficiency in their ethnic language.
Input	Input is viewed as linguistic 'data' that serves as a trigger for acquisition.	Input is viewed as contextually constructed; it is both linguistic and non-linguistic.
Interaction	Interaction is viewed as a source of input.	Interaction is viewed as a socially negotiated event and a means by which learners are socialized into the L2 culture.
Research methodology	Quantitative and confirmatory	Qualitative and interpretative

Table 7.2 Psycholinguistic and sociolinguistic SLA compared

The social settings of L2 learning

As Tollefson (1991) noted, most theories of L2 acquisition are based on a neoclassical view of language learning, according to which individual learners make choices by weighing up the personal benefits and costs of learning the language. There is a need, however, to also consider how structural factors, such as the social setting, shape these choices.

I will use the term 'social setting' to refer to the milieu in which learning takes place. Any one setting is realized through a variety of social contexts. A good example of what I mean by this can be found in Caldas and Caron-Caldas (2002). This study investigated three bilingual children's choice of language in two *settings*—Louisiana, where the majority language was English, and Quebec where the majority language was French. The particular social context they studied was dinner-time talk. They found that when the children reached pre-adolescence the setting exerted a strong effect on their choice of language in this social context. Thus, when the children were living in Louisiana they displayed a strong preference for English when talking to their parents at the dinner table but when they moved to Quebec, French became the language of choice. Interestingly, the parents' own use of language (French in both settings in this social context) did not appear to influence the children's choice.

'Social setting' is clearly a somewhat crude construct. Block (2003) rightly pointed out that settings vary enormously within themselves. For example, the foreign language classroom setting varies in terms of teacher/student ratios, teacher preparation, the intensity of instruction, technological backup, the availability of teaching materials, and the relative importance of learning the foreign language. This might suggest that there is little point in considering acquisition in relation to such macro settings. However, there is plenty of evidence to suggest that both language use and acquisition do vary according to setting. Caldas and Caron-Caldas' study is a good example.

We can begin by asking in what ways the setting might influence L2 acquisition. There are three obvious possibilities. First, the setting can have an effect on learners' attitudes. Learners manifest different attitudes towards (1) the target language, (2) target-language speakers, (3) the target-language culture, (4) the social value of learning the L2, (5) particular uses of the target language, and (6) themselves as members of their own culture. Learner attitudes have an impact on the level of L2 proficiency achieved by individual learners and are themselves influenced by this success. In general, positive attitudes towards the L2, its speakers, and its culture can be expected to enhance learning and negative attitudes to impede learning but, as we will see, this need not necessarily be so.

Second, the setting may influence learners' choice of REFERENCE GROUP. Much of SLA research has been predicated on the assumption that learners are targeted on the standard dialect of the L2. Such an assumption, however, is not warranted in the case of many learners. As Beebe (1985: 404) observes, learners may be 'active participants in choosing the target-language models they prefer'. They do not just learn 'a language' but rather 'adopt a variety or varieties of that language'. Some deviations from Standard English, therefore, may not be 'errors', but may simply reflect the dialect which the learner has targeted. For example, learners who display copula deletion may do so because they are targeted on Black English Vernacular, in which this feature occurs.

In recent years, the term ENGLISH AS AN INTERNATIONAL LANGUAGE (EIL) (Jenkins 2000) has been coined to refer to the use of English across the range of contexts throughout the world and ENGLISH AS A LINGUA FRANCA (ELF) (Seidlhofer 2005) to refer to the communication in English that takes place between speakers with different first languages. English is increasingly functioning as a contact language with the result that 'English is being shaped at least as much by its non-native speakers as by its native speakers' (Seidlhofer 2005: 339). This has led to a call for the systematic description of ELF and the collection of corpora such as the Vienna-Oxford International Corpus of English (VOICE) to investigate its linguistic properties. This research serves to challenge stereotypes of correctness based on native-speaker usage.

Third, different settings might afford very different opportunities for language learning (for example, in terms of the typical types of input and interactions they give rise to). For example, Norton (1997, 2000) demonstrated the difficulty that learners in majority language settings experience in exercising their 'right to be heard' and suggested that this has a negative impact on their learning of the majority language. Also, it has been frequently noted that classroom settings do not afford much opportunity for learners to produce extended output (Swain 1985; Allen *et al.* 1990), which as we saw in the previous chapter is claimed to be important for acquisition.

We will now consider a number of macro social settings in terms of how they influence learners' attitudes, their choice of reference group, and their learning opportunities.

Natural versus educational settings

A general distinction can be made between NATURAL and EDUCATIONAL SETTINGS. The former arise in the course of the learners' contact with other speakers of the L2 in a variety of situations—in the workplace, at home, through the media, at international conferences, in business meetings, etc. The latter are traditionally found in institutions such as schools and universities but, increasingly, in computer-mediated environments. There will be some learners who experience the L2 entirely in natural settings and others whose only contact with it is in educational settings. However, many learners will experience the L2 in both natural and educational settings.

A general assumption is that the learning that takes place in natural and educational settings is very different in nature. In natural settings informal learning occurs. That is, learning is considered to result from direct participation and observation without any articulation of the underlying principles or rules. (See Scribner and Cole 1973.) Also, there is an emphasis on the social significance of what is being learnt rather than on the mastery of subject matter. In contrast, formal learning is held to take place through conscious attention to rules and principles, and greater emphasis is placed on mastery of 'subject matter' treated as a decontextualized body of knowledge. However, the correlation between informal learning and natural settings on the one hand, and formal learning and educational settings on the other, is at best only a crude one. (See Krashen 1976.)

Much depends on how individual learners orientate to the setting. Batstone (2002) distinguished two different dimensions of 'context'. There is the 'external context', which consists of the context of situation. This can be described in terms of such features as the participants, channel, topic, discourse type, and location. There is also the 'internal context', which concerns how the learner orientates to the external context. This distinction intersects with two types of context—communicative and learning contexts. A communicative context is one where the learner is primarily focused on the message; a learning context is one where the learner is primarily engaged in the effort to learn the L2. Batstone's framework helps us to see why there is no *necessary* connection between setting and type of learning. Externally a context may be viewed as a communicative context, but internally it may function as a learning context for a particular learner. Thus, learners in natural settings, where communicative contexts are dominant, sometimes resort to conscious learning and may deliberately seek out opportunities to practise specific linguistic items they have studied, as Lennon's (1989) study of advanced German learners of English in Britain demonstrated. Conversely, a context that externally constitutes a learning context may be treated by the learner as a communicative context.

Another common assumption is that natural settings lead to higher levels of L2 PROFICIENCY than educational settings. Schinke-Llano (1990: 216), for instance, claimed that 'second' language acquisition results in native-like use of the target language, while FOREIGN LANGUAGE ACQUISITION does not. This assumption is also evident in the 'year-abroad' built into university-level foreign language education in many European countries or the periods of 'study-abroad' offered to students of foreign languages in North American universities, and the growing popularity of 'home-stay' programmes among Japanese learners. The aim of these is to provide foreign-language learners with opportunities for informal learning, so that they can reach higher levels of oral proficiency. There is some support for this position. D'Anglejan (1978) reported that Canadian civil servants freed from their jobs for as long as a year to improve their L2 proficiency in intensive language classes did not generally become fluent in the L2, despite a strong motivation to learn. D'Anglejan suggested that one reason for this was the absence of any opportunities for contact with native speakers. In contrast, Vietnamese immigrants in California who were placed in occupational settings after a short training programme proved highly successful. Fathman (1978) found that 12- to 14-year-old ESL learners in the United States achieved a higher level of oral proficiency than EFL learners of similar ages in Germany, and also displayed greater strategic competence. The ESL learners' speech was rated higher in fluency than in grammaticality, while the opposite was true of the EFL learners. Interestingly, however, the ESL learners were much less certain about their ability to speak English than the EFL learners, perhaps because they were using a different yardstick to measure themselves against. Gass (1987) conducted a comparative study of ESL/EFL learners and also of Italian as a second language (ISL) and as a foreign language (IFL). Focusing on sentence interpretation strategies, she found no difference between the EFL/ESL groups, but a significant difference in the case of the IFL/ISL. Gass noted that sentence interpretation in English is unproblematic because it rests primarily on one type of cue (word order), whereas in Italian it is more problematic because several cue types (word order, inflectional, and pragmatic) are utilized. Thus, 'foreign' and 'second' language learners will manifest no differences when relatively simple learning targets are involved, but will differ when the targets are more complex. Complex rules cannot easily be taught, and classrooms do not offer sufficient input for them to be learnt naturally.

It is by no means certain, however, that naturalistic settings lead to high levels of proficiency—even oral proficiency. Fathman (1978) observed that there was considerable variation in the levels achieved by the ESL learners in her study, suggesting that some at least were not so successful. Schinke-Llano's claim that 'second' language learning is characterized by native-speaker levels of ability is very doubtful. Gass observed that 'most learners, be it classroom or non-classroom learners, do not attain complete mastery of an L2' (1990:

37), and queried whether native-language proficiency is ever possible for adults—a point considered in Chapter 1 when the role of age in L2 acquisition was examined. Longitudinal studies, such as those reported by Schumann (1978b), Schmidt (1983), Klein and Dittmar (1979), and Meisel (1983), also show that learners in natural settings often fall far short of native-language proficiency. The longitudinal studies conducted as part of the EUROPEAN SCIENCE FOUNDATION PROJECT (see Chapter 3) showed that it was the learners who had received instruction who reached the higher levels of L2 development.

These studies suggest that it may be inappropriate to examine the relative effects of natural and educational settings on overall proficiency and that a better approach might be to investigate their effects on different aspects of proficiency. The available evidence suggests that, whereas natural settings are likely to enhance oral fluency and pragmatic ability, educational settings will lead to higher levels of grammatical knowledge. Bardovi-Harlig and Dörnyei (1998) found that whereas ESL learners demonstrated greater sensitivity to pragmatic errors, EFL learners were more responsive to grammatical errors. (See Chapter 5 for further information about this study.) Comparisons of learners in a foreign language educational setting and a study abroad setting also point to differentiated benefits. Summarizing the results obtained from the studies in the special issue of *Studies in Second Language Acquisition* on 'Learning context and its effects on second language acquisition', Collentine and Freed (2004) reported that whereas the foreign language educational setting results in greater gains in morphosyntactic control, the study abroad setting leads to greater oral fluency, lexical breadth, and narrative ability. Interestingly, no difference in native-like phonological control was observed.

The notions of 'natural' and 'educational' settings are inevitably somewhat crude. The differences within each setting regarding both quality and quantity of learning opportunities are likely to exceed the differences between them. As a result, comparisons of the learning outcomes associated with each setting are, perhaps, of doubtful value. A more useful approach is to examine what factors within each setting are important for successful L2 learning. We will now do this by identifying and discussing more specific learning settings.

Natural settings

Following Judd (1978), three broad types of natural L2 learning settings can be identified. The type that has been most thoroughly researched (majority language settings) is found in situations where the target language serves as the native language (or one of the native languages) of the country—as is the case for L2 learners of English in the United States or the United Kingdom or L2 learners of French in France or Belgium. The second type (official language settings) is found in the decolonized countries of Africa and Asia, where the L2 functions as an official language. In such settings it is not learnt as a mother tongue by more than a few people. The third type (international settings) occurs when the L2 is used for interpersonal communications (usually of fairly specific kinds) in countries where it is neither learnt as a mother tongue nor used as an official language (for example, the use of L2 English for business communication in Japan). Following Siegel (2003), a fourth type (minority language settings) can be added, where speakers of the dominant language are learning the language of the minority group (for example, English speakers learning Punjabi in London). In all four types of setting, contexts may arise where the L2 learner communicates with either native speakers of the language or with other L2 users, but clearly the former is more likely in the first and last types of setting and the latter in the other two types. Table 7.3 summarizes these different types.

Type	**Definition**	**Example**
Majority language settings		
• monolingual	Learners have taken up residence in a country where the L2 constitutes the language of both informal and institutional communication and their L1 has no or very limited functional value.	Immigrant learners of L2 English in the USA, UK, and Australasia
• bilingual	Learners are members of an indigenous group that speaks a different language from that of majority (the L2).	Speakers of L1 French learning L2 English in Canada
Official language settings	Learners are indigenous members of a country where the L2 functions as an official language, and often as the medium of instruction in education.	The 'New Englishes' of countries like Nigeria and India
International settings	The L2 serves as a means of international communication, often with other L2 speakers (rather than with native speakers).	The use of English in 'Airspeak'
Minority L2 settings	Learners whose L1 is the majority language learn an L2 that is a minority language.	English-speaking learners of Welsh in the United Kingdom

Table 7.3 Types of natural settings

Second language learning in majority language settings

Second language learners in majority language contexts are typically members of ethnic minorities: immigrants (as in the case of Vietnamese immigrants to the United States), migrant workers (as in the case of Turkish workers in Germany or Mexican migrants in the United States), or the children of such groups. These learners and the specific social contexts they experience are inevitably very varied and as a result the learners vary in both the variety of the target language they acquire and the level of proficiency they achieve.

First, it should be noted that learners vary in their choice of REFERENCE GROUP. Goldstein (1987) investigated the preferred variety of 28 advanced Hispanic ESL learners from urban high schools in the New York metropolitan area, and what factors could account for this preference. Two linguistic variables associated with Black English were examined: negative concord and distributive 'be'. Samples of the learners' speech were collected by means of an interview and a role play. Goldstein found significant correlations between the amount of reported contact with black Americans and presence of both variables in the learners' speech. However, reported identification with black Americans did not prove to be significantly related to the two variables, although Goldstein queries whether the measures of identification she obtained were valid. Goldstein concluded by suggesting a number of other variables that may affect learners' choice of reference group: covert prestige of the target-language group, the status of the target-language group vis-à-vis one's own or one's desired status, the difficulty or ease of establishing and maintaining relationships with members of the target-language group, the attitudes of one's own ethnic group to the target-language group and vice versa, and the instrumental value of using the target language.

Some groups of learners in majority language settings do develop varieties close to the target language (for example, Norwegian and Swedish groups in the United States). How can this be explained? Taylor (1980) identified three stages in the social mobility of immigrant groups. Initially there are rewards for maintaining the L1, as individuals compete for position from within the minority group. Next, rapid learning of the L2 takes place as individuals identify with the majority group and seek to improve their social status. This may lead to what Lambert (1974) called SUBTRACTIVE BILINGUALISM. Finally, conscious attempts to maintain the L1 (the minority language) may be made as individuals react to discrimination by members of the majority group, whom they perceive as responsible for their lack of social advancement. Learners who reach this final stage are likely to achieve ADDITIVE BILINGUALISM. The extent to which different groups of learners progress is influenced by specific social factors. For example, the Heidelberger Forschungsprojekt 'Pidgin-Deutsch' (1978) found that the length of residence in Germany functioned as a major explanatory factor in the workers' acquisition of L2 German for the first two years of their stay but was subsequently overridden by other social factors, such as contact with Germans during leisure time, contact with Germans at work, professional training in the country of origin, and number of years of formal education.

In other groups a stable 'immigrant interlanguage' (Richards 1972) develops as in this example from the Puerto Rican community in New Jersey where the speaker is talking about shopping:

> No make any difference, but I like when I go because I don't have too many time for buy and the little time we buy have to go some place and I find everything there.

Such varieties are the product of the social conditions in which the learners live. The Heidelberger Forschungsprojekt 'Pidgin-Deutsch' referred to the 'miserable social situation' of the foreign migrant worker population in West Germany which is due 'not only to economic factors, such as insecurity of employment, low-prestige work, and so on, but also in large measure to a rather thorough exclusion from the local social and political life' (p. 2).

Later research has documented how social relations in majority language settings affect the quality of the interactions between migrant workers and native speakers. Bremer *et al.* (1996), as part of the European Science Foundation Project, showed how power relations affect these interactions and thereby constrain the opportunities for learning. They focused on gate-keeping speech events such as job interviews and service encounters where there was a clear mismatch of power and status. A good example of the kinds of communicative problems the learners experienced is found in the case of Abdelmalek, a Moroccan learner of French in France. Abdelmalek misheard a travel agent's request about *how* he wanted to travel as *why* he wanted to travel:

A je partir à Casablanca, Maroc
I am leaving for Casablanca, Morocco.
B par quoi vous voulez partir
How do you wish to go?
A [C'est] beaucoup problèmes là-bas papa malade
A lot of problems, there father is ill.

Bremer *et al.* suggested that this misunderstanding arose because Abdelmalek was used to being interrogated about his reasons in previous gate-keeping encounters and assumed that the travel agent was doing likewise. Such cases of misunderstanding, Bremer *et al.* argued, deny learners sustained opportunities for language learning. Further evidence of the difficulties that immigrant learners experience in their encounters with native speakers can be found in Norton (1997: 2000). Her research will be examined later in this chapter.

In a number of documented cases, very little L2 learning takes place, especially if the learner has limited opportunity for contact with speakers of the majority language. A frequently cited example is Schumann's (1978b) Alberto. (See Chapter 1.) Goldstein (1995) reported a study of Portuguese female immigrant workers in a Canadian factory. These women learnt very little English partly because of a lack of opportunity but also because it was Portuguese rather than English that was associated with social and economic benefits. The women relied on their Portuguese networks to find jobs and once working in the factory developed close social ties with the other Portuguese workers through speaking Portuguese. They developed a 'sisterhood' by working together to ensure they met their workloads and kept their jobs. In this context, English took on a negative value as it alienated them from their sisters.

The children of immigrants who are born into or grow up in the majority language setting constitute a somewhat special group. They have been the object of enquiry in the context of urban centres in the United Kingdom in a number of studies (for example, Harris 1995; Harris, Leung, and Rampton 2001) and, indeed, throughout the world (for example, Bayley and Schecter 2003). The central finding of these studies is that these children develop hybrid cultures involving a mixing and fusing of disparate elements, which is reflected in their repertoire and use of languages. Leung, Harris, and Rampton (1997) offered a series of vignettes of 13- and 14-year-old pupils that exemplify the richness and variety of their linguistic repertoires. One of these (NK, a female) is reproduced here:

> My first language is English. I read, write, speak and think in English. I also speak Gujarati because my mum and dad are Gujarati first language speakers. At home we speak mostly English, but my mum speaks to me in Gujarati and I answer back in English which is common ... My own language style is using a lot of slang and not enough Standard English. I have tried speaking Standard English ... but I can't ... In Gujarati I can only speak a few sentences and words ... My parents say my English is not good because I speak too much slang.

Drawing on the work of Hall (1992), Leung, Harris, and Rampton suggested that such adolescents are illustrative of a general phenomenon—transitional cultural identities, pluralistic repertoires, and CODE-SWITCHING and code-mixing in relation to social context. This is borne out in Schechter and Bayley's (1997) case studies of four Mexican-descent families. This study focused on the patterns of communication in the home and on the relationships between language choice and dimensions of language use such as topic, register, mode, and the speaker's age. They asked the children in these families this question: 'We'd be interested to know how you see yourself. Let's say someone asked you about your cultural identity. What would you call yourself?' They found evidence of substantial differences in the language socialization practices of the four families, reflecting divergence in the ways in which the families chose to pursue their goal of maintaining Spanish while their children were learning English. This study (and research by Heller 1999) testifies to the variety of ways in which the cultural and linguistic hybridist that Hall talks about becomes manifest. As Bayley and Schechter (2003) noted, in the fluid societal and situational contexts that arise in majority language settings, identity is not fixed and 'the bilingual persona ... may indeed have an ephemeral quality' (p. 6). Such learners have been studied within the framework provided by socialization theory, which will be considered later in this chapter.

A somewhat different majority setting arises in countries like Canada and Belgium, where there are two official languages. In Canada, native French speakers learn English as an L2, while in Belgium, Flemish speakers learn L2 French—and vice versa. These settings are of considerable interest because they enable us to compare the differential levels of proficiency achieved by minority community members learning the language of the majority and, vice-versa, majority members learning the language of the minority. In both Canada and Belgium, minority learners of the majority language tend to reach higher levels of proficiency than majority learners of the minority language. Edwards (1977) found that French-speaking learners of English in Ottawa maintained their English language skills, whereas English-speaking learners of French tended to lose their French. Edwards suggested that long-term retention of linguistic and communicative competence is a function of successful prior learning, opportunity to use the skills acquired, and interest in using them. The French-speaking learners reported both more opportunities for using their L2 and greater interest in doing so than the English-speaking ones. Lambert (1974) claimed that subtractive bilingualism characterizes many French Canadians learning L2 English, whereas additive bilingualism is more characteristic of English Canadians learning L2 French.

In another case of learners of a minority language learning the majority language, negative rather than positive attitudes towards the L2 culture promoted learning. Lanoue (1991) provided a fascinating account of the Sekani's linguistic development in British Columbia, Canada. This remote Indian tribe rejected its own mother tongue in favour of L2 English for even inter-ethnic communication not because they felt positively disposed towards Anglo-Canadian culture (in fact, they held negative attitudes) and not because of the socioeconomic advantages of English, but because English had become a symbol of pan-Indianism, which was seen as the only way of ensuring the tribe's identity in the future. What this study suggests is that if learners have a strong enough reason to learn the L2 they will do so even if social conditions are not favourable.

L2 learning in official language settings

Under colonial rule the languages of Europe (predominantly English, French, Portuguese, Spanish, and Dutch) were introduced to a substantial number of African, American, and Asian countries. At independence, some countries chose an indigenous language as the official language but many countries adopted the language of the ex-colonial power and maintained it in most of its previous social and official functions (for example, Nigeria chose English and Zaire chose French, while India also felt the need to maintain English alongside Hindi). Whether an indigenous or foreign language was chosen as the official language, it constituted an L2 for the vast majority of the population. Social and economic advancement depended to a large extent on its successful mastery—a fact that constituted a powerful motivation for acquiring it.

Official language settings are characterized by the emergence of new, indigenized varieties of the ex-colonial languages. Bolton (2004), in a survey of approaches to the study of these new varieties, shows that there has been a general shift from an early pre-occupation with purely linguistic description to approaches that share both a linguistic and socio-political concern (as evident in the World Englishes approach of Kachru 1986) and finally to approaches that are primarily socio-political and political (as in the critical linguistic work of Phillipson (1992) and Pennycook (2001). The latter will not be discussed here as they do not address the acquisition of second languages. Instead we will focus on work that has addressed linguistic matters from a socio-political perspective.

Kachru's work has been especially influential in socio-political discussions of the new varieties. Kachru (1986) divided 'world Englishes' into three groups: (1) the Inner Circle, where English is spoken as a first (native) language, (2) the Outer Circle, where English is learnt as a second or additional language, and (3) the Expanding Circle, where it is learnt as a foreign language. This section is concerned with (2). However, as Yano (2001) noted, the distinction between (1) and (2) is becoming blurred given the influx of immigrants to Inner Circle countries and the accompanying hybridity and permeability in language evident in these, as discussed in the preceding section. Increasingly, the processes of change and language use that have been evident in the Outer Circle for some time are becoming evident in the Inner Circle. However, there is one major difference. Whereas the language situation in Inner Circle settings is characterized by subtractive bilingualism (i.e. immigrants or indigenous populations frequently manifest L1 attrition), the situation in Outer Circle settings is typically one of additive bilingualism (i.e. the L1 is maintained).

The non-indigenous languages that assumed the role of official language in Outer Circle settings rapidly took on a life of their own, developing a set of norms that differed from those found in the Inner Circle, a process referred to as 'nativization'. Bamgbose (1998) suggested that these originate in the different 'behavioural norms' (i.e. the set of conventions that go with speaking) found in the cultures of the Outer Circle. For example, West-African speakers of English say 'sorry' when they observe someone experiencing the misfortune of falling down. A key issue concerns the status of these norms. Are they to be viewed as non-standard in comparison to the norms of the Inner Circle varieties or standard in terms of the local varieties that have developed in the Outer Circle? Bamgbose suggested that to determine the status of an observed linguistic feature in such settings it is necessary to establish whether it constitutes an innovation or an error. He suggested a number of criteria for achieving this—demographic (i.e. the number of educated users of the feature), geographic (i.e. how widespread the innovation is), authoritative (i.e. the extent to which the feature is used or approved by teachers, media practitioners, examination bodies, etc.), codification (i.e. whether the feature has a written form in a reference manual) and acceptability (i.e. the extent to which the feature is positively evaluated). However, Bamgbose acknowledged that the indeterminacy of many features is a result of the 'dearth of codification'.[1] For this reason, it is not always easy to decide whether a particular usage in these new varieties of colonial languages constitutes an error or an innovation. Thus, the problems of identifying errors (see Chapter 2) are accentuated in the new varieties of colonial languages found in the Outer Circle.

The existence of these new varieties raises further questions about what constitutes a 'native speaker'. Kachru and Nelson (1996) argued that the traditional definition of a native speaker as someone who learnt language in a natural setting from childhood as a first or sole language needs to be challenged. Kachru (1999) distinguished 'genetic nativeness' and 'functional nativeness', suggesting that educated speakers of the new varieties of English achieve the same degree of functionality as educated speakers of varieties in the Inner Circle even though they learnt English as a second or additional language. The view widely espoused in these sociolinguistic circles is that there is a need to recognize pluralistic norms for languages such as English around the world. Concerns that the development of local standards will result in their unintelligibility to speakers of other varieties (see, for example, Prator's (1968) critique of 'the British heresy') are dismissed on the grounds that such worries have probably been overstated and, in any case, little can be done to change the situation as in most cases learners have no access to Inner Circle models. The acceptance of pluralistic norms acknowledges the sociolinguistic realities and bilingual creativity of Outer Circle societies.

It should be clear from all this that sociolinguists such as Kachru and Bamgbose reject the view that these new varieties constitute INTERLANGUAGES. While it is true that such varieties are likely to reflect structural features of the speakers' mother tongue(s) and also overgeneralization of rules, processes evident in L2 acquisition, 'nativization' and L2 acquisition cannot be viewed as the same, as Sridhar and Sridhar (1986) and Lowenberg (1986) pointed out. There are differences both with regard to the linguistic contexts in which apparently similar strategies are employed, and also in the motivations underlying their use. For example, Lowenberg (1986: 6) claimed that the use of prefixes to coin new lexical items as in 'outstation' (meaning 'out of town' in Singaporean English) resembles the kind of productive process found in established varieties of English rather than a transitional L2 rule.[2] Also, whereas L2 learners view their interlanguage grammars as transitional and imperfect, users of the new Englishes treat their grammars as fully developed and display positive attitudes towards them. Further, as Kachru and Nelson (1996) pointed out, learners in the Outer Circle are not targeted on any Inner Circle model nor do they have such a model available to them in the broader social context. However, there has been very little research on L2 acquisition itself in official settings and clearly there is a need for such studies (Brown 2000).

In fact, though, the attitudes of learner communities to the non-indigenous official language are often ambivalent. Kachru and Nelson (1996) referred to 'attitudinal schizophrenia'. Bamgbose (1998) characterized this schizophrenia as follows: 'On the one-hand non-native norms are seen as an expression of identity and solidarity, while, on the other, there continues to be admiration for native norms' (p. 5). Michieka (2005) illustrated the mixed attitudes that exist in Kenya. Whereas some politicians and literary figures (for example, Ngugi) reject the continued use of the colonial language on the grounds that it serves to introduce new, insidious forms of colonialism, English has continued to survive because of the impracticality of replacing it with local languages. Michieka referred to a study by Sure (1991), which showed that primary and secondary students held favourable attitudes towards the use of English but she also noted that economically and socially marginalized Kenyans are likely to have less favourable attitudes.

L2 learning in international settings

A number of languages—in particular English—are now widely used as international languages. That is, they serve as a means of communication between speakers of different languages. These speakers may or may not be native speakers of the language and the speech events may or may not take place inside a country where the language is spoken as a mother tongue. Graddol (1997) predicted that the number of people who speak English as a second language would soon exceed those who speak it as a native language, while Yano (2001) claimed that the numerical majority of 'non-natives' has already been reached.

The use of an L2 in an international setting, then, is characterized by both NNS–NS interaction and NNS–NNS interaction, but, as Kachru (1986: 16) pointed out, the latter is more common. This has implications for acquisition, as discussed in Chapter 6. For example, Kachru argued that in NNS–NNS interactions 'the *British* English or *American* English conventions of language use are not only not relevant, but may even be considered inappropriate by interlocutors'. The culture-bound localized strategies of, for example, politeness, persuasion, and phatic communion 'transcreated' in English are more effective and culturally significant.

In such situations, then, the learners' reference group is not speakers of standard British or American English but, instead, a prestige local group. Also, in these situations, we can expect to see creative use made of interlanguage resources for impression management. (See Chapter 5.)

Garcia (2002) described the conditions that have led to the increased use of English as an international language:

> As globalization takes hold, new communicative functions are created that respond to the movement of capital and people around the globe and a proliferation of new products and services. Speakers who wish to participate in this new world order are then increasingly aware and

> favourably inclined to learn and adopt the language or language variety that will enable them to partake of this new economic order. The increased use of English on the Internet is the most obvious example. (p. 359)

However, Garcia went on to point out that views differ regarding whether the spread of English as an international language has taken place naturally as a result of the processes outlined above or as a result of an implicit or explicit 'language spread policy' on the part of economically powerful English-speaking nations, as claimed by Phillipson (1994). He cited Ammon (1997) who identified five goals of such a policy: (1) to increase communication, (2) to spread one's ideology, (3) to develop economic ties, (4) to gain revenue from language study and products, and (5) to preserve national identity and pride.

Much of the work on English as an international language (for example, Strevens 1980; Quirk 1982a, 1985; Kachru 1982; Smith 1983; Crystal 1997; Jenkins 2000) has focused on either describing the varieties of language associated with particular contexts of use (for example, the use of English for air-traffic control) or on arguing the merits of some form of 'basic' language which will facilitate communication, teaching, and learning (for example, Quirk's (1982a) Nuclear English and Wong's (1934) Utilitarian English). There has been little work on how target-language varieties associated with international use are mastered by L2 learners, or to what extent international use promotes or restricts interlanguage development. Davies (1989) made the point that although both international varieties and interlanguages can be described as 'simplified', they are in fact different, as the former involve functional simplification and the latter formal simplification. Thus, whereas an interlanguage manifests formal reduction—as when functors are omitted or overgeneralized—and then gradually gets more complex, international varieties employ standard language forms and are 'simplified' only in the sense that they are used to perform a restricted set of functions. We can speculate that where international varieties are of the very restricted kind (for example, 'Seaspeak' or 'Airspeak'), they can be mastered by learning to understand and use a small set of formulas and a limited lexicon, which, as we saw in Chapter 3, are well within the compass of a beginner learner. In a sense, then, these varieties are both sociolinguistically and psycholinguistically 'simple'. We can also speculate that learners who define their learning task as the mastery of these restricted varieties will achieve only a limited proficiency. In contrast, learners who engage in international communication that involves the full resources of the standard language (for example, the preparation of academic papers for publication) are more likely to develop a higher level of proficiency.

An alternative approach is that adopted by Seidlhofer (2002). She advocated establishing an 'index of communicative redundancy' (i.e. the identification of a commonly used set of constructions, lexical items, and sound patterns which are ungrammatical in terms of a standard variety but cause no communicative difficulty), which could serve as 'the kind of language that is most effective in language education' (p. 296). However, from the perspective of L2 acquisition, it is difficult to see how ENGLISH AS A LINGUA FRANCA (ELF) could constitute a target for individual learners, even though the interlanguages that they develop might well manifest the generalized properties that characterize ELF. L2 learners are unlikely to consciously adopt ELF as their target variety.

L2 learning in minority L2 contexts

L2 learning in minority contexts arises when learners whose L1 constitutes the majority language learn the language of some minority group in their setting as an L2. Such a situation arises when English speakers learn Welsh or Punjabi in the United Kingdom or Spanish in the United States. Highly relevant to work in this setting is Rampton's discussion of LANGUAGE CROSSING, 'the use of speech varieties which are not normally thought to belong to the speaker' (Rampton 1999: 335), in multi-ethnic urban settings. One way in which this manifests itself is in terms of the use of an ethnic language by members of ethnic out-groups. Rampton (1995) gave the example of the use of West Indian Creole by White and Asian adolescents. He noted that majority language speakers often demonstrate a strong interest in minority languages but also that 'adolescents do not necessarily require *all* members of their peer group to speak *all* its languages (Rampton 1995: 328). Access to minority languages provides a means by which members can play with different identities in their interactions with members of their peer group. Again, though, there has been little work on how such learners acquire minority languages as opposed to the use they make of them.

Educational settings

Skuttnab-Kangas (2000) distinguished a number of different types of 'bilingual education' settings, which she divides into 'non-forms' (i.e. types that do not use two languages as the media of teaching and learning), 'weak forms' (i.e. types that have monolingualism, strong dominance of one language, or limited bilingualism as their aim) and 'strong forms' (i.e. types that aim to promote high levels of bi- or multilingualism and multiliteracy for all participants). Table 7.4 summarizes the different types that Skuttnab-Kangas lists under these headings. However, for reasons of space, only the more commonly found will be considered in any detail.

Category	Type	Description	Example
Non-forms	Language teaching	The language of the school curriculum is the learners' L1; the L2 is taught as a subject only.	Teaching of English as a foreign language in Japan.
	Submersion	Linguistic minority students with a low-status L1 are taught the school curriculum through the medium of a high status L2.	Ethnic minority children in the UK or USA taught in English-medium mainstream classrooms.
	Segregation	Linguistic minority children with a low status L1 are taught the school curriculum through the medium of their L1. The L2 may be taught as a subject.	Mother tongue medium schools for the children of Turkish migrant workers in Germany.
Weak forms	Transitional	Linguistic minority children with a low status L1 are instructed through the medium of the L1 until they have acquired sufficient competence in the L2 for that to become the medium. Skuttnab-Kangas (2000) sees this as a more sophisticated version of submersion (p. 592).	Ethnic minority children in the UK or USA taught initially in their L1 but subsequently placed in English-medium mainstream classrooms.
Strong forms	Mother tongue maintenance	Linguistic minority children with a lower status L1 receive instruction in their L1 with a view to maintaining and developing skills in this language.	The programme in Italian for children of Italian-speaking parents in Bedford, UK (Tosi 1984).
	Immersion	Linguistic minority children with a high status language are instructed through the medium of a foreign/minority language in classes consisting entirely of L2 learners.	French immersion programmes in Canada.
	Dual language	A mixed group of linguistic minority and majority students are taught through the medium of the learners' L1 and L2, with the dominant language taught as a subject.	Two-way Spanish-English programmes in the USA.
	Alternate days	A mixed group of linguistic minority and majority students are taught using their L1 and L2 on alternate days.	The alternate day programme in English and Spanish in Castiloga, California.
	Plural multilingual	Students with different L1s are taught the school curriculum through the medium of their L1 with an L2 taught as a foreign language in Grade 1. This then increasingly becomes the medium of instruction in later years when other L2s are also offered as foreign languages.	The 10 European Union Schools in six countries.

Table 7.4 Educational settings

The language classroom setting

'The language classroom' is defined here as a setting where the target language is taught as a subject only and is not commonly used as a medium of communication outside the classroom. In this sense it includes both 'foreign' language classrooms (for example, Japanese classes in the United States or English classes in China) and 'second' language classrooms where the learners have minimal or no contact with the target language outside the language classroom (for example, 'ESL' classes in a francophone area of Canada).

Whereas the second language classroom has been the subject of a number of sociolinguistic studies (see, for example, Miller 2004 and Poole 1992), the foreign language classroom has been largely neglected by sociolinguists. Rampton (2006) offered a number of reasons for this neglect. First, in accordance with Type 1 sociolinguistics, the social significance of the target language has been deemed minimal because its speakers are remote from the learners. Second, sociolinguistic enquiry has focused on the interface between the home language and the language of the nation-state (i.e. with language use in majority language settings) and such an interface does not arise in foreign language classrooms. Third, the overarching concern with 'competence' and with the tacit acquisition of language has led sociolinguists to view the 'specialized languages' of the foreign language classroom as of no real interest.

The distinction between Type 1 and Type 2 sociolinguistics affords a way of examining the language classroom setting from a social perspective. I will first adopt a Type 1 perspective by considering the differences between the foreign-language and second-language classroom in terms of choice of target, the different roles that teachers and students adopt, parental support for language learning, and the impact these factors have on what and how well a learner learns. I will then draw on Rampton's (2006) interesting study of how learners of German as a foreign language in an urban school in London appropriated 'Deutsch' for their own purposes as a way of exploring a Type 2 approach to the language classroom.

Foreign-language classroom contexts can be distinguished from second-language classroom contexts in that native-like cultural and pragmatic competence is not a high priority in the former (Nayar 1997). To make it so would constitute a threat to the learners' own ethnic identities and also might not be favourably received by native speakers. Janicki (1985) commented:

> It has been noticed that non-natives are likely to face social consequences when their linguistic behaviour complies with sociolinguistic rules saved (by some norm) for the natives. Examples are the usage of obscenities, slang expressions, or very formal pronunciation. It seems that there exists a set of as yet unidentified norms which proscribe the use of some forms on the part of the non-native speaker.

Preston (1981) suggested that an appropriate model for the L2 learner is that of 'competent bilingual' rather than a native-speaker model. This may well be the implicit model of many learners in foreign-language settings.

The role relationships between teacher and student influence learning in a classroom. In the case of traditional approaches to language teaching, where the target language is perceived primarily as an 'object' to be mastered by learning about its formal properties, the teacher typically acts as a 'knower/informer' and the learner as an 'information seeker' (Corder 1977a). In the case of innovative approaches (for example, communicative language teaching) where the emphasis is on the use of the target language in 'social behaviour' a number of different role relationships are possible, depending on whether the participants are 'playing at talk', as in role-play activities, or have a real-life purpose for communicating, as in information gap activities; the teacher can be 'producer' or 'referee' and the learner 'actor' or 'player'. However, Corder noted that even 'informal learning' inside the classroom may differ from that found in natural settings. As noted earlier, classroom learners often fail to develop much functional language ability, which may reflect the predominance of the knower/information seeker role set in classrooms.[3]

Parents may play an active role by monitoring their children's curricular activities. They may also play a more indirect role by modelling attitudes conducive to successful language learning. A number of studies have found a positive relationship between parental encouragement and achievement in L2 classroom learning (for example, Burstall 1975; Gardner and Smythe 1975). Gardner (1985) argued that parents' influence on proficiency is mediated through the students' motivation.

I will turn now to examine a Type 2 approach to examining language classroom settings. Rampton (2006), drawing on the techniques of INTERACTIONAL SOCIOLINGUISTICS, documented how foreign language learners of German in a London school used 'Deutsch' (i.e. their spontaneous improvisations of German) outside their German classes—in break-time, in corridors, and in other subject lessons. Rampton found that the boys he studied made much greater use of Deutsch than the girls but put this down to differences in their interactional dispositions rather than their sex (i.e. the boys used it to show off). Rampton suggested that the use of German words and phrases served as a resource for the 'voluntary "performance" of exuberant students intent on embellishing the curriculum discourse in whatever ways they could' (p. 163), for making 'music' out of their linguistic resources, and for ritual purposes (for example, thanking and apologizing). Rampton also noted that German did not belong to anyone and therefore served as a racially-neutral language that was 'safe' for linguistically heterogeneous students. Rampton noted however, that the use of Deutsch was a 'passing fad'. In an interview some 18 months after the last classroom recording, the students who had been shown to use Deutsch said they no longer used it and expressed a dislike of their German classes. Thus, whereas Rampton's study sheds light on how students can appropriate elements of a foreign language to enact their social lives in and out of the classroom, it also suggests that such use may not contribute much to their actual proficiency in the foreign language.

In fact, as Skuttnab-Kangas (2000) noted, foreign language classroom settings are characterized by very varying degrees of success. In countries where the learners' L1 does not function as a lingua franca the teachers are well qualified and the language curricula are well designed (for example, in the Nordic countries and the Netherlands), high levels of proficiency are often achieved. In such countries, learners may also have some exposure to the target language outside the classroom (for example, through TV). In other countries (for example, the UK, France, Japan, and the USA) the results are less impressive. Ultimately, success in learning a language in a foreign language classroom may depend on the extent to which the learners see the language playing a role in whatever identity they wish to construct for themselves.

L2 learning in classroom settings is discussed in detail in Chapters 15 and 16.

Submersion

Skuttnab-Kangas (1988) defined a SUBMERSION programme as:

> a programme where linguistic minority children with a low-status mother tongue are forced to accept instruction through the medium of a foreign majority language with high status, in classes where some children are native speakers of the language of the instruction, where the teacher does not understand the mother tongue of the minority children, and where the majority language constitutes a threat to their mother tongue—a subtractive language learning situation.
> (p. 40)

Submersion is common in Britain and the United States, where ethnic minority children are educated in mainstream classrooms. Skuttnab-Kangas (2000) also noted that deaf children also experience submersion education as there are very few schools in the world teaching deaf children through the medium of sign languages.

The characteristics of submersion settings are discussed by Cohen and Swain (1979) and Baker (2006). Right from the beginning, L2 learners are taught with native speakers. This can create communication problems and insecurity in the learners. If L1 support is provided, it is of the 'pull-out' kind, which stigmatizes the L2 child and also deprives learners of the opportunity to progress in content subjects. The language teachers are typically monolingual and thus unable to communicate with the learners in their L1. In some cases, the learners are actively discouraged from speaking in their L1. The students' low academic performance may reflect the low expectations that teachers often have of the students, particularly those from certain ethnic groups (for example, Mexican American students in the United States). Reading material and subject-matter instruction in the L1 are not available, resulting in increased insecurity in the learners. Parental involvement in the school programme is usually limited. There are often problems with the learners' social and emotional adjustment to school.

For many learners, the disjunction between L1 use in the home and L2 use at school constitutes a painful experience, as Rodriguez' (1982) autobiography illustrates. Rodriguez was the son of a Mexican immigrant who settled in a mainly white locality of California. At school he was required to use English exclusively. At home Spanish was spoken, until his parents accepted the advice of the Catholic nun teachers at his school to speak English. Gradually, Rodriguez lost the ability to communicate in Spanish, signalling his rejection of his Spanish-Mexican identity. Although Rodriguez was ultimately successful in developing a high level of L2 proficiency, this was achieved at considerable personal and social cost. Rodriguez himself, however, while acknowledging the discomfort he experienced at both school and home, did not question the subtractive model of bilingualism to which he was exposed. In contrast, other learners do question it and refuse to assimilate (for example, Skuttnab-Kangas (2000) mentioned two case studies of members of the Sami group in Nordic countries in Europe who made strenuous efforts to maintain their L1 and develop literacy skills in it).

Although submersion settings do not invariably result in lack of success in learning an L2 (as the Rodriguez example demonstrates), in general they do not facilitate it and they can lead to L1 attrition. Cummins (1988) identified three characteristics that are important for L2 acquisition; (1) a bilingual teacher who can understand students when they speak in their L1, (2) input that has been modified to make it comprehensible (see Chapter 6 for a discussion of comprehensible input), and (3) effective promotion of L1 literacy skills. Submersion contexts have none of these. Baker (2000) argued that the basic assumption of submersion is assimilation, commenting that 'the school has become a melting pot to help create common social, political and economic ideals' (p. 196).

Segregation

SEGREGATION occurs where the L2 learner is educated separately from the majority or a politically powerful minority, who speak the target language as their mother tongue. As Baker (2006) put it, it 'forces a monolingual policy on the relatively powerless' (p. 198). Immigrants or migrant workers who are educated in special schools, centres, or units designed to cater for their language needs constitute an example of segregation in a majority setting. 'Bantu education' in Namibia prior to independence is an example of segregation in a setting where a powerful minority spoke the official language (Afrikaans) as a mother tongue.

Skuttnab-Kangas (1988) claimed that segregation settings produce poor results. She argued that the overall aim of education in these settings is the development of a limited L2 proficiency—sufficient to meet the needs of the majority or powerful minority and to ensure their continued political and economic control. Although some support for L1 development is provided, this is also usually limited. Negative L2-related factors identified by Skuttnab-Kangas include the poor quality of L2 instruction and the lack of opportunity to practise the L2 in peer-group contexts.

However, the case against segregation is not as clear-cut as Skuttnab-Kangas makes out. In certain situations, the provision of separate educational facilities may have beneficial effects. For example, short-term programmes for refugee populations newly arrived in the United States or European countries can help them adjust socially, affectively, and linguistically to the demands of their new country. It can also be argued that the maintenance of minority languages requires at least some segregation. Magnet (1990), for example, drew on the Canadian experience to argue that a minority language will only be viable if its speakers enjoy a 'degree of autonomy and segregation in order to develop in their own way' (1990: 295). The advantages of segregation are also recognized by minority communities themselves, as illustrated by their attempts to set up separate schools for their children. In a later discussion of segregation, Skuttnab-Kangas (2000) acknowledged that it has 'a somewhat better record than submersion' (p. 592).

Segregation also has some advantages where L2 learning is concerned. In particular, because the learners are likely to be at the same level of development, it is possible to tailor input to their level. Where the learners have different L1s, the L2 is likely to serve as a language of classroom communication and not just as a learning target. This is likely to broaden the functions that it typically serves. For these reasons, segregation may facilitate the development of 'survival skills' in the L2. However, as Skuttnab-Kangas (2000) pointed out, it has a number of disadvantages, such as the failure to develop high levels of bilingualism and, in some contexts, negative societal consequences. She argued that, in contrast to mother tongue maintenance settings it is distinctly inferior.

Mother tongue maintenance

Skuttnab-Kangas pointed out that MOTHER TONGUE MAINTENANCE can take two forms. In the weaker form, pupils are given classes in their mother tongue, directed at developing formal language skills, including full literacy. In the stronger form, pupils are educated through the medium of their mother tongue. Examples of the former are the programmes for Punjabi established in Bradford, UK (Fitzpatrick 1987), and the Heritage Language Program established in Ontario, Canada (Cummins 1992). These programmes were all funded by government or regional agencies. However, there is often reluctance on the part of such agencies to pay for community language programmes. Saravanan (1995), for example, reported that it took several years of lobbying to persuade the Singaporean government to support community run classrooms in Hindi, Punjabi, Bengali, and Urdu. In the USA, Chinese heritage community language schools are funded through tuition and private fund-raising (Wang 1996). Examples of programmes where learners are educated through the medium of their mother tongue can be found in the Finnish-medium classes for Finnish migrant workers in Sweden (Skuttnab-Kangas 1988). Summing up national policies and practices regarding minority language maintenance in Western countries, Skuttnab-Kangas (2000) commented: 'Despite the small recent improvements, it seems clear that Western countries have so far not respected what should be basic linguistic human rights, especially in education, and that the world so far does little to prevent linguistic and cultural genocide' (p. 563).

Mother tongue maintenance programmes are based on enrichment theory, according to which high levels of bilingualism are seen as a cognitive and social advantage. This contrasts with deficit theory, which views bilingualism as a burden and as likely to result in cognitive disadvantage. The results of research strongly suggest that additive bilingualism (the goal of mother tongue maintenance) confers linguistic, perceptual, and intellectual advantages. (See Swain and Cummins 1979 for a review.)

There is also evidence that mother tongue maintenance settings, particularly those of the strong kind, result in considerable educational success (Skuttnab-Kangas 1988). They are characterized by positive organizational factors (for example, appropriate cultural content in teaching materials), positive affective factors (for example, low anxiety, high internal motivation, and self-confidence in the learners), success in developing full control of the L1, metacultural awareness, and a high level of proficiency in the L2.

Mother tongue maintenance provides support for L2 learning in two main ways. First, it ensures that the L2 is an additional rather than a replacement language and thus results in learners developing a positive self-identity. As Spolsky noted, learning an L2 is intimately tied up with one's personality and being forced to learn an L2 as a replacement for the L1 is a 'direct assault on identity' (1986a: 188). Mother tongue maintenance, then, is more likely to result in the positive attitudes needed for successful L2 development.

The second way involves a consideration of Cummins' INTERDEPENDENCY PRINCIPLE (Cummins 1981). This claims that whereas basic interpersonal communication skills (BICS) develop separately in the L1 and L2, cognitive academic language proficiency (CALP) is common across languages.[4] Cummins noted that whereas L2 communicative skills are typically mastered by immigrant learners in about two years, it can take from five to seven years for the same learners to approach grade norms for L2 academic skills. The interdependency principle has been demonstrated in a number of studies (for example, Verhoeven 1991). Studies of the Portuguese-Canadian community in Toronto (Cummins *et al.* 1990), of Japanese immigrant children in Canada (Cummins and Nakajima 1987), and of Turkish immigrant children in Holland (Verhoeven 1991) support the importance of L1 academic skills as a basis for successful development of L2 CALP. Swain and Lapkin (1991) also showed that literacy in a community language benefits the learning of a second L2 (in this case, French) as a result of the transfer of knowledge and learning processes. The notion of interdependency is an important one because it suggests that the development of full L1 proficiency confers not only cognitive and social advantages attendant on mother tongue use but also benefits the acquisition of L2 proficiency.

Immersion

IMMERSION PROGRAMMES began with the St. Lambert Experiment (Lambert and Tucker 1972), a French immersion programme for English-speaking children living in Quebec, Canada. Similar programmes were then started in other parts of Canada. Subsequently, immersion programmes sprang up in many different parts of the world, for example in Hungary (Duff 1997), Finland (Bjorklund 1997), and Catalonia (Artigal 1997).

The term 'immersion' has come to refer to a number of different contexts, which need to be clearly distinguished. Initially, in the context of the Canadian French immersion programmes, it referred to programmes where members of a majority group (native speakers of English) were educated through the medium of French, the language of a minority group. There are a number of variants of these programmes, depending on whether the programme begins early (for example, in kindergarten) or late (for example, in Grades 4 or 7), and whether it is full (more or less all instruction is conducted in the L2) or partial (only part of the curriculum is taught through the L2). However, as Cummins (1988) pointed out, the term 'immersion' is used to refer to a variety of programmes for minority students. He distinguishes 'L2 monolingual immersion programs for minority students', which provide English-only instruction directed at classes consisting entirely of L2 learners; 'L1 bilingual immersion programs for minority students', which begin with L1-medium instruction, introducing L2-medium instruction some time later; and 'L2 bilingual immersion programs for minority students', which emphasize instruction in and on the L2 but which also promote L1 skills. He noted in addition that, misleadingly, even submersion programmes have been referred to as 'immersion'. Skuttnab-Kangas (2000) took the view that the term 'immersion' should be reserved for programmes where learners with a high-status L1 are taught through the medium of a low-status L2.

In an attempt to resolve definitional problems, Johnson and Swain (1997) identify a number of core features of immersion programmes. These are:

1 The L2 is the medium of instruction.
2 The immersion curriculum parallels the local L2 curriculum.
3 Overt support for the L1 exists.
4 The programme aims for additive bilingualism (a feature that Skuttnab-Kangas considers pivotal).
5 Exposure to the L2 is largely confined to the classroom.
6 Students enter with similar (and limited) levels of proficiency.
7 The teachers are bilingual.
8 The classroom culture is that of the local L1 community.

Swain and Lapkin (2005) reviewed these features in the light of the dramatic increase in ethnic diversity in Canada's urban centres which make feature (8) problematic. They also revised their views about restricting the learners' use of the L1, acknowledging that 'judicious use' may be warranted.

The Canadian French immersion programmes have met with considerable success. Genesee (1984, 1987) and Swain and Lapkin (1982) reviewed the various programmes, reaching similar conclusions. Immersion students acquire normal English language proficiency and show the same or a better level of general academic development. Furthermore, immersion students tend to have less rigid ethnolinguistic stereotypes of the target-language community, and place greater value on the importance of inter-ethnic contact. These advantages are evident in 'disadvantaged' as well as 'advantaged' children. Evaluation of the different kinds of programmes shows that in general, total immersion produces better results than partial immersion, and also that early immersion does better than late.

The Canadian French immersion settings also lead to a high level of L2 French proficiency, particularly with regard to discourse and strategic competence, where learners achieve near-native-speaker levels (Swain 1985). However, such levels are not usually reached in grammatical proficiency and, as Hammerley (1987, 1989) pointed out, in some cases a kind of 'classroom pidgin' can develop.[5] Also, in comparison to younger immersion students (i.e. second graders), older immersion learners (i.e. fifth and sixth graders) have been observed to rely more on their L1 when interacting with each other. Tarone and Swain (1995) suggested that this is because, whereas change from above occurs in early immersion (i.e. learners are predominantly influenced by the superordinate style, represented in this case by L2 French), older learners experience increasing pressure for change from below to perform important interpersonal functions such as play, competition, and positioning within their peer group and resort to L1 English because they do not have access to vernacular-style French. Swain and Tarone's argument is supported by Caldas and Caron-Caldas' (2002) study, which reported that two adolescent children in a French immersion programme in Louisiana resisted using French when speaking outside class with their peers.

Overall, however, immersion programmes are very successful in promoting L2 acquisition. There are many reasons for this. One undoubtedly has to do with the fact that immersion settings ensure a plentiful supply of input that has been tailored to the learners' level and is therefore comprehensible. There are also social reasons. The learners' L1 and their ethnic identity is not threatened, so it is easy for the learners to adjust to the immersion setting. Furthermore, the immersion programmes are optional and, therefore, are well supported by those parents who elect to send their children to them.

Dual language

DUAL LANGUAGE PROGRAMMES are often referred to as 'bilingual minority immersion programmes'. They are common in the United States, where they have been controversial. (See, for example, Epstein 1977 and Danoff *et al.* 1978, cited in Cummins 1988.) There has been considerable opposition to bilingual programmes for linguistic minorities, as reflected in the Official English Movement—the attempt to have English designated as the official language of the United States and to ensure that educational resources are directed towards teaching English rather than some other language. (See Bingaman 1990.) Cummins (1988) pointed out that the debate has centred on two arguments, both of which are mistaken. Supporters of minority bilingual programmes have advanced the 'linguistic mismatch' argument, according to which minority children will be retarded academically if they are required to learn exclusively through the L2. This is mistaken because the French Canadian immersion programmes have shown conclusively that early instruction through the medium of the L2 has no negative effects. Critics of bilingual immersion programmes have also advanced the 'maximum exposure' argument, according to which bilingual education is detrimental because it deprives learners of the exposure to the L2 necessary for successful acquisition. This is refuted by programmes which show that minority children who spend less time on English while they are developing L1 literacy skills ultimately do just as well in L2 academic skills as those who are educated exclusively through the L2. Cummins argued that minority programmes that are designed in such a way that they reflect the interdependency principle and the comprehensible input hypothesis have been shown to be successful. Genesee, however, suggested that the success of minority immersion programmes also depends on 'changing the sociocultural fabric of the school' (1987: 168–9). He noted that ways are needed to upgrade the status and power attached to the minority language and to teachers and support personnel who speak it as an L1. Genesee's comment points to the need to consider social as well as organizational factors in immersion education.

Summary

We have considered the relationship between different social settings and L2 learning. The aim has been to identify the potential learning outcomes associated with different types of settings, broadly defined. A basic distinction (and rather crude) between 'natural' and 'educational' settings has been proposed. There is some evidence to suggest that learners in natural settings achieve greater functional proficiency than those who are limited to educational settings but this will depend on a variety of social factors that determine the amount and quality of the contact with the L2. In contrast, learners with access to instructional settings may achieve greater linguistic accuracy. However, there will be considerable variance in learning outcomes within settings as well as between settings. Research to date has focused on identifying the actual or potential 'learning opportunities' that arise in the different settings rather than investigating 'learning outcomes'. Only in immersion programmes have learning outcomes been systematically studied.

It is possible to identify a set of general principles that underlie likely language learning success in natural and educational settings. The following is a list of such principles, based on the literature referred to in the previous sections:

1 L1 maintenance—ensuring that learners achieve a high level of both oracy and literacy in their L1 will promote learning of the L2.
2 Perceptions of L1—learning is enhanced when the setting confers status on both their L1 and the L2.
3 Social need—learners learn best when they have a clear social need for the L2. This social need is highly varied, however. For example, it can derive from the desire for power and status, from the use of the L2 as a medium of instruction, from the importance learners attach to achieving social cohesion, or from the 'gaming' that takes place in peer groups.
4 Target norms—success in L2 learning cannot always be measured in terms of a set of norms based on a standard form of the language. Learners may be targeted on a nativized variety of the language or on a local dialect.
5 Initial learning—initial L2 learning is more successful if learners have the opportunity to learn within an L1 speaking group (as opposed to a context where they are immersed in a group of native speakers).

Arguably the key finding from this discussion of different learning settings is the enormous complexity of L2 acquisition, when viewed from a social perspective. The distinction between 'native speaker' and 'non-native speaker/learner' becomes blurred. It is no longer always clear what can be considered an 'error' in L2 use, making definition of what it means to talk of someone having 'acquired' an L2 difficult. What is clear, however, is that this social dimension is essential for understanding how opportunities for learning are created and how learners are likely to respond to these opportunities.

Social factors and second language acquisition

We will now consider a number of specific social factors which operate in the settings discussed in the previous section, influence the attitudes held by different groups of learners, and lead to different levels of L2 proficiency. These factors can be viewed as facets of the learner's identity (McKay 2005). Discussion will be restricted to the four variables which have received the most attention in SLA research: (1) age, (2) sex and gender, (3) social class, and (4) ethnic identity.

Age

One way of viewing age from a social perspective is to downplay the importance of biological age and to emphasize social factors as determinants of learning. This was the approach adopted by Moyer (2004) in her study of the accents of 25 immigrants to Germany. Moyer argued that, although biological age was important, it needed to be considered in relation to social-psychological factors which determined the quality of contact the learners experienced.

This position is further supported by Piller's (2002) study of L2 learners in cross-cultural marriages. Piller found that age of first exposure was not a crucial factor and that the learners themselves distinguished between age of first exposure and when they 'really' started. What proved more significant in Piller's study was whether the learners created an 'L2 environment' or an 'L1 environment' in their adopted countries.

Another approach is to treat age as sociolinguistic variable. Chambers and Trudgill (1980), for instance, documented variants of /ŋ/ in the speech of different generations of speakers in Norwich (England). The younger generation (10–19 years) used non-standard variants, while middle-aged speakers (30–60 years) preferred the standard variant. Older speakers (70+ years) demonstrated use of non-standard variants, although not to the same extent as the younger generation. Chambers and Trudgill explained this pattern by suggesting that younger speakers are subject to social pressures from their peer group, while middle-aged speakers are more influenced by mainstream societal values. In older, retired people, social pressures lessen and social networks again become narrow. However, it would be wise to heed Eckert's (1997) warning regarding such generalizations: 'Age groups are not necessarily uniform across or between communities as different cultural and material conditions make different life trajectories' (p. 167). This, plus the fact that age interacts with other variables such as gender and social class, make comparisons between different age groups far from straightforward.

The general pattern of social influence that Chambers and Trudgill documented may help to explain age-related factors in L2 acquisition. (See Chapter 1.) Learners who commence learning an L2 after the onset of puberty (and possibly earlier) are unlikely to acquire a native-speaker accent, while those who begin after the age of about 15 years are less likely to develop as much grammatical ability as those who begin before. Preston (1989) suggested that children may be more prepared to share external norms because they are not subject to peer pressure and have not formed stereotypes of their own identities. He argued that the threat to identity in older learners occurs even in 'short-term, restricted' L2 acquisition, which may account for why many adolescents are resistant to L2 learning in foreign language settings. However, this does not explain why adolescent learners have been shown to progress more rapidly than younger learners initially. Nor does it explain why adolescents tend to do better than middle-aged learners, who ought to outperform the younger generation given their greater openness to prestige social norms.

Age has been shown to be a factor related to generational differences in bilingual communities. Dubois and Horvath (1999) considered language change in Cajun English. For the older generation English functioned entirely as a second language because English became the compulsory language of education when they were children. The middle-aged generation spoke a more native-like English because they were subject to the imposition of an external norm for speaking English as a result of urbanization and industrialization.

The English of the younger generation, in contrast, was more influenced by Cajun and the desire to adopt a Cajun identity. Dubois and Horvath also found clear effects for gender. They concluded 'The effects of gender are strongly conditioned by generation, and the generations are strongly conditioned by sociohistorical contexts' (p. 311).

Sex and gender

A distinction is often made between 'sex' and 'gender'. The former constitutes a biological distinction, while the latter is a social one. Many sociolinguists prefer the term 'gender' because it places the emphasis on the social construction of 'male' and 'female'. (See Kramarae 1990.) Whereas early research in SLA typically investigated 'sex' as a static, bipolar opposite in relation to language use and learning, later research increasingly focused on 'gender', viewing it as 'a complex system of social relations and discursive practices differentially constructed in local contexts' (Norton and Pavlenko 2004a).

Sociolinguists researching sex differences in language use have traditionally sought to account for general and stable patterns of language variation. Labov (1991: 206–7) identified two apparently contradictory principles:

1 In stable sociolinguistic stratification, men use a higher frequency of non-standard forms than women.
2 In the majority of linguistic changes, women use a higher frequency of the incoming forms than men.

Women, therefore, nearly always outstrip males in the standardness of their speech and use of prestige forms, and yet they also tend to be in the forefront of linguistic change. Both principles suggest that women might be better at L2 learning than men; they are likely to be more open to new linguistic forms in the L2 input and they will be more likely to rid themselves of interlanguage forms that deviate from target-language norms.

These predictions are borne out by several studies. Female learners generally do better than male, as illustrated in Burstall's (1975) longitudinal study of some 6,000 children beginning L2 French at 8 years old in English primary schools. Boyle (1987) reported on a study of 490 (257 male and 233 female) Chinese university students in Hong Kong. The female students achieved higher overall means on ten tests of general L2 English proficiency and in many cases the differences were significant. Nyikos (1990) reported that women outperformed men in a German vocabulary memorization task. Eisenstein (1982) found that females consistently and significantly outperformed males in discriminating among different American English accents. A possible explanation for the superiority of females is that they have more positive attitudes to learning an L2 than males. Burstall found that the girls in her study displayed consistently more favourable attitudes towards learning French than did the boys. Gardner and Lambert (1972) also reported that female learners of L2 French in Canada were more motivated than male learners and also had more positive attitudes towards speakers of the target language. Spolsky (1989) found that girls learning L2 Hebrew in Israel (a majority language setting) demonstrated more favourable attitudes to Hebrew than boys. Bacon and Finnemann (1992) reported that female learners of L2 Spanish at university level had a stronger instrumental motivation.

Other studies, however, have produced results suggesting males are the better learners or that there is no difference. Boyle (1987) reported that the male students in his study performed better on two tests of listening vocabulary. Bacon (1992) found no difference between the sexes in two authentic listening tasks. Nor are male learners always more negative than females in their attitudes. Ludwig (1983) found that male learners were more instrumentally motivated (i.e. more motivated to learn the L2 for purely functional reasons). Different results have also been found regarding sex differences in interactions involving learners. Gass and Varonis (1986) concluded that men use the opportunities to interact to produce more output, whereas women use it to obtain more input. However, Pica *et al.* (1991) failed to find much evidence to support sex differences in interactions involving adult male and female Japanese learners of L2.

The explanation for these mixed results almost certainly lies in the fact that it is gender rather than sex that is important for language learning. It will not always be the case that females outperform males. Asian men in Britain generally attain higher levels of proficiency in L2 English than do Asian women for the simple reason that their jobs bring them into contact with the majority English-speaking group, while women are often 'enclosed' in the home. Ehrlich (1997, 2004) convincingly argued against an essentialist account of male/female differences in language use and learning, presenting in its place a social constructionist account of the relationship. This emphasizes the importance of communicative settings and the specific tasks in which learners are engaged in explaining why men and women behave linguistically in the way that they do. Drawing on the work of Eckert and McConnell-Ginet (1999), Ehrlich suggested that gender is not an attribute of the individual but rather something that emerges out of the social practices that men and women engage in (i.e. she adopted a Type 2 approach to gender). Because these social practices vary from one social setting to another there are likely to be differences in whether it is men or women who prove the better learners.

To demonstrate this key point Ehrlich discusses a number of studies that have produced apparently conflicting results. Hill (1987) found that rural Mexican women's L2 Spanish was generally poorer than the men's because they lacked access to wage labour and the market place. However, in some respects (for example, Spanish stress patterns on borrowed Spanish nouns) it was more Spanish-like than the men's. This was because they were excluded from the social practices that led men to maintain Mexicano features in their Spanish as a means of displaying solidarity within their social group. Harvey (1994) found gender differentiated the use of Quechua and Spanish in men and women in Peru. Women were less likely than men to become fully bilingual or fluent in Spanish. However, this asymmetry was not simply due to differential exposure to the target language but also to the reluctance of the women to learn Spanish because of the severe social costs—men saw Spanish as threatening women's traditional role in society. In contrast, Gal (1978) reported that young peasant women in Austria were leading the shift from Hungarian to German in their community. This was because learning German was seen as the means by which they could escape from the drudgery of their life as peasants. The men, in contrast, viewed their work as affording self-employment and independence and thus clung to Hungarian. Ehrlich argued that these studies indicate that gender is something that people 'do' rather than something that they are. For this reason the relationship between gender and language learning is highly variable, reflecting the fact that 'gendering' in language learning varies from context to context.

All these studies examined learners in naturalistic settings. However, it has become clear that 'essentialized gender dichotomies' (Pavlenko 2004) also fail to account for how gender interacts with language learning or opportunities for language learning in educational settings. Pavlenko dismissed the traditional view that females are disadvantaged in classroom interaction and are thus less successful learners than males. This view fails to take account of the diversity of classrooms or the different values assigned to discursive practices within them and also simplistically assumes that sheer quantity of interaction is what is important for learning. Drawing on studies by Willett (1995) and Heller (2001), Pavlenko demonstrated that both boys and girls can be interactionally disenfranchised in different classroom contexts. Pavlenko argued that while learners enter classrooms as individuals whose options and motivations will have been shaped by their gender, they also gain access to the 'imaginary worlds of other languages where gender and sexuality may be constructed and performed differently than in their own culture' (p. 55). In other words, classroom learners, like naturalistic learners, can reconstruct their gender through the learning of an L2.

However, while emphasizing that gender is socially constructed and reconstructed, both Ehrlich and Pavlenko accepted that it is also socially determined by the 'regulatory norms' that arise out of institutionalized language practices and define what linguistic behaviour is socially appropriate. That is, their position corresponds to Coupland's Type 3 sociolinguistics. A good example of this can be found in Polyani's (1995, cited in Ehrlich 2004) study of American university students in a Russian study-abroad programme. Polyani described how the women and the men acquired different types of proficiency as a result of their interpersonal experiences with Russians. Whereas the women acquired the linguistic skills to cope with the harassment they received from Russian men, the men experienced the opportunity to develop greater fluency in Russian as a result of the pleasant, flirtatious encounters they enjoyed with Russian females. Not surprisingly the women made fewer gains than the men in listening and speaking skills, as measured on standardized tests of these skills. Ehrlich (2004) commented on this study 'the linguistic identities performed by these young men and women were saturated by the gendered ideologies and power relations that characterized the foreign language learning situation' (p. 322).

Social class

An individual's social class is typically determined by means of a composite measure that takes account of income, level of education, and occupation. It is customary to distinguish four groups: lower class, working class, lower middle class, and upper middle class. Finer distinctions (e.g. 'upper working class') are also sometimes made. Much of the work on social class has adopted a Type 1 approach.

As Preston (1989: 117) pointed out, there is a clear parallel between sociolinguistic phenomena associated with social class and interlanguage development. *Hypercorrection* (for example, the overextension of a feature like /h/ to words such as 'hour'), which occurs when lower-middle-class speakers seek to incorporate a prestige feature into their careful speech, parallels OVERGENERALIZATION in learner language. Hypocorrection (the retention of an old norm which has covert prestige in the speech of the working class) is like NEGATIVE TRANSFER. An INDICATOR (defined as 'a form not involved in change') is similar to FOSSILIZATION (the persistence of a non-standard form in interlanguage). CHANGE FROM ABOVE can be compared to monitoring (Krashen 1981), in so far as both involve conscious attention to linguistic form. However, as Preston recognized, while these processes seem very similar, it does not follow that they are motivated by the same social factors. The similarity may rest more in the psychological processes which underlie both linguistic change and L2 learning. Interestingly, however, Rehner, Mougeon, and Nadasdi (2003) provided evidence to show that middle-class French immersion students displayed a stronger preference for formal standard variants of French such as 'nous' as opposed to 'on' (i.e. of change from above) than upper-working-class students, a finding they explained in terms of a carry over of the same tendency the middle-class students were assumed to have in their L1.

There is clearer evidence of a relationship between social class and overall L2 achievement, especially for learners in a language classroom setting. Burstall (1975) found that children from middle-class homes regularly outperformed those from lower- and working-class homes in learning French. Also, working-class children tended to drop French after their second year in secondary school, while middle-class children were likely to continue. Olshtain, Shohamy, Kemp, and Chatow (1990) investigated the levels of proficiency in L2 English reached by 196 Grade 7 learners in Israel. The learners were divided into an 'advantaged' and a 'disadvantaged' group on the basis of socioeconomic status. Olshtain *et al.* found that the two groups differed significantly in L1 (Hebrew) cognitive academic level proficiency (CALP) and that a number of measures of this correlated significantly with L2 English achievement. One interpretation of this result was that the 'advantaged' children were better at learning English in a classroom setting because they had a more developed L1 CALP. Interestingly, variance in the 'advantaged' group was not attributable to differences in self-reported attitudes and motivation, whereas in the 'disadvantaged' group it was. Overall, though, L1 CALP explained much more of the variance in L2 achievement than did motivation and attitudes. Finally, Skehan (1990) also reported moderate correlations between the family background of 23 secondary school children in Bristol and both language learning aptitude and foreign language achievement in French and German, with middle-class children again outperforming lower-class ones. Skehan suggested that these relationships may reflect the learners' underlying ability to deal with context-disembedded language, thus bearing out Olshtain and her colleagues' main conclusion.

The results of these studies mirror the general finding that children from lower socioeconomic groups are less successful educationally than those from higher groups. Another study, however, suggests that the disadvantage in language learning shown by lower-status groups is not inevitable. Holobrow, Genesee, and Lambert (1991) reported on a study of partial immersion involving kindergarten and Grade 1 pupils in Cincinnati (USA). They found no difference in either French listening comprehension or oral production in children from different socioeconomic and ethnic groups:

> ... the working-class and black students were able to benefit from the second language experience as much as middle-class and white students. In other words, the disadvantaged students were not disadvantaged when it came to second language learning.
> (1991: 194)

One possible reason for this is that the early immersion programme placed greater emphasis on BASIC INTERPERSONAL COMMUNICATION SKILLS (BICS) The researchers suggest that 'the development of oral/aural interpersonal communication skills in a second language does not appear to be dependent on individual differences of a cognitive, linguistic and ... social nature'. In other words, where BICS are concerned, social differences in learners have no effect.

It is important to heed Milroy and Milroy's (1997) warning regarding the correlation that might be found between social class (or, indeed, any other social factor) and L2 achievement. They point out 'there may be many aspects of social behavior that are not accounted for in a single social variable, and also underlying social factors that are subsumed under a label such as 'social class' (such as educational level) may sometimes yield more precise correlations than the main composite variable' (pp. 53–4). In other words, it is the particular experiences of the world which members of the different social classes are likely to have that are important for acquisition. This is illustrated in two studies that have examined the role that literacy plays in L2 acquisition—literacy being closely associated with social class. Bigelow, Delmas,

Hansen, and Tarone (2005) found that the more educated and literate learners in a group of Somali learners of English were better at recalling recasts of their erroneous utterances than the less educated and literate learners. In another study involving the same group of learners, Tarone and Swierzbin (2005) reported that the more literate learners supplied more verbal morphology, more plural –s forms, more target-like articles, and more dependent clauses in oral narratives than the less literate learners.

Social class is, however, no longer a straightforward construct, at least in the complex urbanized societies of cities like London. Rampton (2006) pointed out that economic, social, and cultural changes have made it less easy to provide water-tight definitions of what constitutes working class and middle class. He noted that 'some linguists have also suggested that class may be losing its clarity in everyday speech' (p. 216) and that this may be especially true in the case of young people. It is possible, then, that class is less important for success in language learning than it has been in the past.

Ethnic identity

ETHNIC IDENTITY can be viewed from both a Type 1 and a Type 2 perspective. From a structural perspective, ethnic identity is seen as determined by the social contexts in which learners find themselves. From an interactional perspective, ethnic identity is seen as something that is constantly negotiated by learners and as a result is ambivalent, contested, and dynamic. May (2001) adopted a middle position (reflecting Coupland's Type 3 integrationist sociolinguistics):

> Negotiation is a key element ... to the ongoing construction of ethnicity. Individual and collective choices are circumscribed by the ethnic categories available at any given time and place. These categories are, in turn, socially and politically defined and have varying degrees of advantage or stigma attached to them ... Moreover, the range of choices available to particular individuals and groups varies widely.

In a similar vein, Tabouret-Keller (1997) wrote that 'identity is endlessly created anew, according to the various social constraints (historical, institutional, economic, etc.), social interactions, encounters, and wishes that may happen to be very subjective and unique' (p. 316). These quotations, then, highlight a number of important points about the relationship between ethnic identity and L2 acquisition:

- Ethnic identity is both a social and an individual construct and for that reason alone it is of special importance for SLA.
- Acquiring an L2 is likely to involve some change or addition to the learner's sense of identity.

- A change or addition to the learner's identity may involve the learner overcoming a number of social obstacles and the extent to which this is achieved will affect how successfully the L2 is acquired.

Research into L2 learners' ethnicity has been informed by normative, social-psychological, socio-structural, and post-structural views of the relationship between ethnic identity and L2 acquisition. As these perspectives (and the theories that derive from them) are considered in depth later in this chapter, we will focus here on representative samples of the kinds of research to which each has given rise.

Research based on a normative view of the relationship between ethnic identity and L2 learning seeks to establish to what extent membership of a particular ethnic group affects L2 achievement. Svanes (1988) investigated the acquisition of L2 Norwegian by three ethnic groups in Norway. One group (the 'near' group) consisted of learners from Europe and America who shared a common 'western' culture. The second group (the 'intermediate' group) consisted of learners from the Middle East and Africa, all of whom had contact with western culture. The third group (the 'distant' group) contained students from Asian countries (for example, India and Vietnam). Svanes found a clear relationship between cultural distance and L2 achievement, measured by an examination that tested a wide variety of knowledge and skills. The Western students had the best grades, the Middle Eastern and African students the next best, and the Asians the poorest results. It should be noted, however, that there is no way of knowing whether the difference in the grades obtained by the three groups was a reflection of cultural distance or linguistic difference.

A social-psychological view of the relationship between ethnic identity and L2 proficiency emphasizes the role of attitudes. The attitudes that learners hold towards the learning of a particular L2 reflect the intersection of their views about their own ethnic identity and those about the target-language culture. These views will influence (although not determine) both L1 maintenance and L2 learning, as shown in Table 7.5. Lambert (1974) distinguished *additive* and *subtractive bilingualism*. In the former, learners maintain their L1, adding the L2 to their linguistic repertoire. In such cases, learners may become *balanced bilinguals*. This is likely to occur when learners have a positive view of their own ethnic identity and of the target-language culture. In the case of subtractive bilingualism learners replace their L1 with the L2, failing to develop full competence in their mother tongue or, in some cases, actually losing competence that has already been acquired. This arises when learners have a low estimation of their own ethnic identity and wish to assimilate into the target-language culture. When learners have negative attitudes towards both their own culture and that of the target language, SEMILINGUALISM may result. That is, the learners may fail to develop full proficiency in either language. It should be noted, however, that semilingualism (so defined) is a controversial notion, as it runs the risk of depicting as deficit what is in fact only difference, and that the heteroglossic competencies of minority language children may be fully functional in the out-of-school contexts in which they are used, as Rampton's (1995) research has demonstrated. MONOLINGUALISM (i.e. failure to acquire the L2) is associated with a strong ethnic identity and negative attitudes towards the target-language culture.

The role of attitudes in L2 learning has been extensively researched by Lambert and Gardner and their associates (for example, Gardner and Lambert 1972; Gardner 1985), primarily in Canada but also in other settings (for example, the United States and the Philippines). The theoretical framework which has informed these studies is described in the final section of this chapter, so here we will focus on some of the research it has led to. A number of studies have supported Gardner and Lambert's original claim that a socially based motivation involving a 'willingness to be valued members

	Attitudes towards native culture	**target culture**
Additive bilingualism	+	+
Subtractive bilingualism	–	+
Semilingualism	–	–
Monolingualism	+	–

Key: + = positive attitudes – = negative attitudes

Table 7.5 Attitudes and L2 learning

of the (second) language community' (Gardner and Lambert 1959: 271) results in high levels of L2 proficiency. (See Gardner and Clement 1990.) Learners' attitudes also affect language attrition. Gardner, Lalonde, and McPherson (1985) found that learners of L2 French with favourable attitudes showed little decline, while those with less favourable ones showed significant loss in self-rated proficiency six months after an intensive course. However, other studies suggest that the relationship between positive attitudes and L2 proficiency is less clear-cut. In some cases no significant relationship has been found and in others there have been negative correlations. For example, Oller (1977) found that Chinese students with high levels of L2 English rated Americans lower on traits such as cleverness and happiness than did those with lower levels. Svanes, in the study referred to earlier, found that the Asian group, which had the lowest level of achievement, displayed the most positive attitudes towards Norwegians. In this study, too, there was a negative correlation between attitudes and language proficiency. Svanes suggested that 'for groups of adult students living in a foreign country, it is more important to have a balanced and critical attitude to the host people than to admire it uncritically' (1988: 365–6). It is also possible, of course, that learners of a non-international language like Norwegian may respond positively to Norwegian *people* and their culture while showing little interest in their *language*.

A more recent social-psychological study is Gatbonton, Trofimovich, and Magid (2005). This investigated the relationship between ethnic group affiliation (defined as 'one's sense of belonging to a primary ethnic group'—p. 489) and L2 pronunciation accuracy in a matched guise study. They compared two groups of L2 learners—Francophone learners and Chinese learners of L2 English in Quebec. In the case of the former the setting was deemed to be conflictual given the Francophone learners' perceptions of the threat English posed to their own ethnic group identity while in the latter it was considered non-conflictual, as the Chinese learners of English held no obvious animosity towards English or its speakers. Learners in both groups, regardless of their own degree of ethnic affiliation, treated their peers' L2 accent as an indicator of these peers' ethnic affiliation. However, there were differences when it came to the two groups' choice of leaders in mono- and bi-ethnic situations. Whereas the Chinese learners invariably preferred non-accented speakers in both situations (suggesting they were motivated primarily by the desire for efficient communication), the more nationalistic Francophone learners opted for the moderately and heavily accented learners as their leaders (suggesting a more ethno-centric attitude). In an interesting discussion of these results, Gatbonton *et al.* identified a number of possible learning outcomes as a result of differences in ethnic affiliation:

1 Recognizing the rewards of L2 learning, L2 learners may strive towards the highest possible level of L2 pronunciation.
2 Recognizing the need to maintain in-group identification, learners may be satisfied with a lower level of L2 pronunciation.
3 Recognizing that the rewards and costs of L2 learning can balance out, learners aim for high levels of L2 pronunciation while also finding ways to manipulate their pronunciation in order to demonstrate in-group membership.

This study indicates that attitudes towards in- and out-group ethnicity are socially determined. However, it is important to recognize that learners can also have very personal views. Okamura-Bichard (1985), in a study of Japanese children temporarily residing in the United States, argued that the 'personal translation of social factors is ... critical in motivating individual learners to make efforts in their learning attempts' (1985: 85). She suggested that what she called the 'happiness' factor may be more important than interest in or attitudes towards the target language/culture when the learner is a young child.

A socio-structural view of the relationship between attitudes and L2 learning is evident in work which has examined the effect that ethnic identity has on the interactions between members of different ethnic groups. This view has been explored within the general theoretical framework of interpersonal accommodation discussed in Chapter 4. According to ETHNOLINGUISTIC

IDENTITY THEORY (Giles and Johnson 1981), the members of an in-group may or may not adopt positive linguistic distinctiveness strategies when communicating with members of an out-group. Giles and Ryan (1982) suggested that speakers evaluate a situation and then decide whether to adopt status or solidarity and person-centred or group-centred strategies. In situations where people emphasize solidarity with their own in-group, linguistic divergence from the out-group is likely, whereas in situations where they are more concerned with status and are person-centred, convergence is likely. Successful L2 learning is held to occur when learners engage in frequent and long-term convergence. A number of studies have found statistically significant relationships between measures of subjective ethnolinguistic vitality and educational achievement. Ellinger (2000), for example, found that measures of subjective ethnolinguistic vitality were significant predictors of reading comprehension scores and final examination results in a group of Russian learners of English as a foreign language at a university in Israel. However, perceptions of vitality regarding Hebrew were inversely related to examination scores. Interestingly, the measures of ethnolinguistic identity proved much stronger predictors than other less social measures (for example, self-confidence and emotional distance).

More recent research has adopted a post-structural approach to the relationship between identity and L2 learning. Post-structuralism 'views language as an array of discourses imbued with meaning' which 'serve to reproduce, maintain or challenge existing power and knowledge structures' (Pavlenko 2002: 283). Pavlenko dismissed the assumption that the way people behave is determined by their membership of certain groups as a 'correlational fallacy'. Instead, language is seen as both constituted by and constituting social context, including ethnic membership—it serves as a 'site of identity construction' (p. 285). A good example of how this operates in the case of ethnic identity can be found in Caldas and Caron-Caldas' (2002) study referred to earlier. Their bilingual children had access to both an English and a French ethnic identity; which identity they drew on depended on the social context in which they found themselves. Thus, in Louisiana, they prioritized their English identity when communicating with their peers, even if these could speak French and were members of their French immersion class, while in Quebec they prioritized their French identity. They constructed and revealed their sense of identity through their choice of language in these different contexts. In both contexts, however, it was their identity as pre-adolescents that led them to opt for one or the other ethnic identity. This study suggests, therefore, that ethnic identity cannot be easily separated from other types of identity. It is for this reason that post-structuralist accounts present identity not as something unitary and stable but rather as multiple and dynamic. This view of identity is further developed later in this chapter.

Summary

In this section we have examined in what ways specific social factors affect L2 learning. With regard to age, it has been found that younger learners are generally more successful than older learners, possibly because their identity is less threatened by target-language norms. In the case of gender, mixed results have been obtained. Whereas some studies have shown that female learners generally outperform male learners in language classroom settings and also display more positive attitudes, other studies have found males superior in some aspects of learning. Current views emphasize 'gendering' rather than 'gender', viewing the relationship between gender and L2 learning as highly context-sensitive. The effects of social class may also depend crucially on the setting; in language classrooms that emphasize formal language learning, working-class children are often less successful than middle-class children, whereas there is some evidence to suggest that in immersion settings they do just as well. The central factor, and the one that has attracted the most attention, is ethnic identity. A normative view emphasizes the effect of 'cultural distance' on L2 learning; learners who are close to the target-language culture are likely to outperform those who are more distant. A social-psychological model emphasizes the role of attitudes. In general, learners with positive attitudes towards their own ethnic identity and towards the target culture can be expected to develop a strong motivation and high levels of L2 proficiency, while also maintaining their own L1. Successful L2 learning is also possible, however, in learners with non-integrative attitudes towards the target culture. In a socio-structural model, attitudes based on learners' sense of ethnic identity influence learning through the interactions in which learners participate. Learners who are status- and person-centred are more likely to converge on L2 norms and therefore more likely to be successful learners than those whose solidarity with their own in-group encourages divergence. A post-structural model does not clearly distinguish between ethnic identity and other forms of identity. It views identity as multiple and dynamic; identity and language learning are interrelated, each influencing the other.

There are obvious dangers in seeking to isolate the effects of individual social factors such as age, gender, social class, and ethnic identity. Pavlenko (2002) is dismissive of this 'laundry list' approach. Rampton (1997) rightly pointed out that 'people don't sit contentedly in the social categories society tries to fix them in' (p. 9). Learners have agency and are likely to try to shape the social context in which they learn rather than passively let it position them. This is one reason why post-structural (i.e. Type 2 and Type 3) accounts of the role of social factors in learning, which are increasingly in favour, have eschewed an etic, quantitative approach to the study of social factors in learning in favour of an emic, qualitative approach.

Situational factors and L2 acquisition

Situational factors refer to the specific characteristics of a social context that impact on L2 learning. The situational factor that we will focus on here is that of addressee. We have already seen in Chapter 4 that the addressee exerts an influence on learners' choice of linguistic forms. Here we will consider what effect it has on the actual process of learning, as manifest in learners' development over time. The research we will consider here, then, challenges Long's (1998) assertion that changing the social context of learning has no effect on how a learner acquires an L2.

First, there is clear evidence that native speakers vary in the extent to which they engage in FOREIGNER TALK with different addressees. In some cases, they engage in what Gass (1997a) referred to as 'counter-accommodating behavior'. She presented as evidence of this a telephone conversation between a native speaker in a TV repair shop and an L2 learner who thinks he is calling a TV sales outlet. Gass commented 'despite the obvious fact of non-understanding, the NS did little linguistically to help her partner' (p. 66). Tarone (2000) referred to a study by Bondevik (1996) that produced a similar finding: native speaker salesmen in an electronic store failed to make linguistic and conversational adjustments when misunderstandings with non-native speakers arose. The results from these studies contrast with the results from other studies which show that native speaker addressees do make such adjustments when talking to learners. (See Chapter 6.) Tarone (2000) cited other studies (for example, Bardovi-Harlig and Hartford 1996) which demonstrate how the situational context influences the nature of the input learners receive. She concluded 'because the TL input provided in different social situations is different, the IL grammars which can be acquired in these contexts must also be different' (p. 190). Such a claim, however, rests on the assumption that it is input/interaction that determines the nature of acquisition rather than the learner's internal mechanisms and, as we will see in later chapters, this assumption has been challenged. What is needed is actual evidence that interlocutor factors influence the actual course of acquisition.

Such evidence is available from Tarone and Liu's (1995) account of Liu's longitudinal study of a 6-year-old Chinese boy (called Bob) learning English in Australia. Liu collected data from Bob's interactions with three different addressees: (1) classroom teachers, (2) classroom peers, and (3) a familiar adult (Liu himself). Different patterns of language use were evidenced with these interlocutors. For example, Bob did not initiate interactions when talking to his teachers and was disinclined to take risks, whereas he adopted a more assertive stance with his peers, initiating interactions, speaking more fluently, and using a much wider range of speech acts. Bob also initiated interactions with the familiar adult and produced more complex structures. The adult was more likely to give Bob negative feedback than the teachers. Tarone and Liu summed up as follows:

> Bob's use of his interlanguage varies in its general shape as he moves from one situation to another: his use of his interlanguage knowledge is affected by the different interactional contexts, as defined by the different role relationships which pertain.
> (pp. 117–8)

They then acknowledged that this only demonstrates that the situational differences affect performance not development. In a further analysis, however, they provided evidence to suggest that they also affected Bob's interlanguage development.

First, they showed that the different interactions Bob participated in affected his rate of acquisition. Following Pienemann and Johnston's framework for the acquisition of English (see Chapter 3), the onset of features relating to each stage in the different data sets was established. Tarone and Liu reported that with very few exceptions every new stage was first evidenced in interaction with the familiar adult and only much later with the other interlocutors. The general pattern was for new structures to appear first in interactions with the familiar adult, some time later in interactions with the peers, and last of all in interactions with the teacher. Stage 5 interrogative forms, for example, appeared in session 23 with the familiar adult but only in session 36 with the peers, and still later with the teacher. In other words, if Bob had not had the opportunity to interact with the familiar adult, his overall rate of development would have been much slower. Tarone and Liu suggested that one reason why interactions with the familiar adult were so facilitative might have been because of the support this interlocutor provided when Bob attempted to produce pushed output.

Second, Tarone and Liu also showed that the interactional context affects the SEQUENCE OF ACQUISITION. They noted that stage 4 and stage 5 interrogative forms emerged in interactions with the familiar adult long before stage 3 forms appeared, thus contradicting the claims of Pienemann and Johnston's theory that the sequence of acquisition is universal. The explanation offered for this is that the familiar adult's input was especially rich in stage 4 and 5 interrogative forms. This provided Bob with the data he needed to acquire these features, while the nature of the interactions with the familiar adult constituted a context that gave him the incentive to acquire them. Further evidence that the situational context can influence the sequence of acquisition can be found in Gupta's (1994) study of two children's acquisition of Singapore Colloquial English. Gupta also found a different developmental pattern from that reported in both the first and second language acquisition literature. As Tarone and Liu pointed out, 'the social demands can be so strong that they can cause an alteration in internal psychologically motivated sequences of acquisition' (p. 122).

This is a very strong claim and one that runs counter to the findings of the numerous studies that have investigated the order and sequence of acquisition. (See Chapter 3.) It must be treated with circumspection given that it is based on very limited evidence. However, Tarone and Liu's study is important because it challenges an established finding in SLA and also because it shows the need to conduct longitudinal studies that carefully distinguish data sets collected in different situational contexts.

Social theories of L2 acquisition

We will now examine a number of theories which seek to account for the role of social factors in L2 acquisition. The theories are (1) Schumann's Acculturation Model, (2) Gardner's Socio-Educational Model, (3) Gile's Inter-group Model, (4) Language Socialization, and (5) Norton's Theory of Social Identity.

The Acculturation Model

Schumann's ACCULTURATION MODEL was established to account for the acquisition of an L2 by immigrants in majority language settings. It specifically excludes learners who receive formal instruction. The model recognizes the developmental nature of L2 acquisition (as discussed in Chapter 3) and seeks to explain differences in learners' rate of development and also in their ultimate level of achievement in terms of the extent to which they adapt to the target-language culture.

Acculturation, which can be defined generally as 'the process of becoming adapted to a new culture' (Brown 1980: 129), is seen by Schumann as governing the extent to which learners achieve target-language norms. As Schumann put it:

> ... second language acquisition is just one aspect of acculturation and the degree to which a learner acculturates to the target-language group will control the degree to which he acquires the second language.
> (1978a: 34)

In fact, Schumann (1986) distinguished two kinds of acculturation, depending on whether the learner views the second language group as a reference group or not. Both types involve social integration and therefore contact with the second language group but in the first type, learners wish to assimilate fully into its way of life, whereas in the second they do not. Schumann argued that both types of acculturation are equally effective in promoting L2 acquisition.

Schumann proposed the Acculturation Model as a means of accounting for the apparent fossilization of one of the six learners studied by Cazden, Cancino, Rosansky, and Schumann (1975). (See Chapter 1.) Whereas the other five manifested considerable development over the 10-month period of the study, Schumann (1978b) claimed that Alberto did not advance in most of the structural areas investigated, although as we saw in Chapter 4 when we considered Berdan's (1996) re-examination of Alberto's negative utterances this claim may not be entirely justified. Alberto's lack of development could not be satisfactorily explained by either his cognitive abilities, as he demonstrated normal intelligence, or age, as many older learners achieve satisfactory levels of L2 proficiency. The problem appeared to be that he had a very limited need to communicate in the L2.

The extent to which learners acculturate depends on two sets of factors which determine their levels of SOCIAL DISTANCE and PSYCHOLOGICAL DISTANCE (Schumann 1978a, 1978b, 1978c). Social distance concerns the extent to which individual learners become members of the target-language group and, therefore, achieve contact with them. Psychological distance concerns the extent to which individual learners are comfortable with the learning task and constitutes, therefore, a *personal* rather than a *group* dimension. The various social and psychological factors which Schumann identified as important are described in Table 7.6. The social factors are primary. The psychological factors mainly come into play where social distance is indeterminate (i.e. where social factors constitute neither a clearly positive nor a negative influence on acculturation).

Factor		**Description**
Social distance		
1	Social dominance	The L2 group can be politically, culturally, technically, or economically superior (dominant), inferior (subordinate), or equal.
2	Integration pattern	The L2 group may assimilate (i.e. give up its own lifestyle and values in favour of those of TL group), seek to preserve its lifestyle and values, or acculturate (i.e. adopt lifestyle and values of TL group, while maintaining its own for intra-group use).
3	Enclosure	The L2 group may share the same social facilities (low enclosure) or may have different social facilities (high enclosure).
4	Cohesiveness	The L2 group is characterized by intra-group contacts (cohesive) or inter-group contacts (non-cohesive).
5	Size	The L2 group may constitute a numerically large or small group.
6	Cultural congruence	The culture of the L2 group may be similar or different from that of the TL group.
7	Attitude	The L2 group and TL group may hold positive or negative attitudes towards each other.
8	Intended length of residence	The L2 group may intend to stay for a long time or a short time.

Psychological distance		
1	Language shock	The extent to which L2 learners fear they will look comic in speaking the L2.
2	Culture shock	The extent to which L2 learners feel anxious and disorientated upon entering a new culture.
3	Motivation	The extent to which L2 learners are integratively (most important) or instrumentally motivated to learn the L2.
4	Ego-permeability	The extent to which L2 learners perceive their L1 to have fixed and rigid or permeable and flexible boundaries and therefore the extent to which they are inhibited.

Table 7.6 Factors affecting social and psychological distance (based on Schumann 1978b)

A learning situation can be 'bad' or 'good' (Schumann 1978c). An example of a 'good' learning situation is when (1) the L2 and TL groups view each other as socially equal, (2) both groups are desirous that the L2 group assimilate, (3) there is low enclosure, (4) the L2 group lacks cohesion, (5) the group is small, (6) both groups display positive attitudes towards each other, and (7) the L2 group envisages staying in the TL area for an extended period. Several 'bad' learning situations are possible, as many of the social variables permit three-way alternatives. Also, different learning situations manifest degrees of 'badness' in accordance with the extent of the overall social distance.

In his early writings, Schumann suggested that acculturation affects L2 acquisition by its effect on the amount of contact learners have with TL speakers: the greater the contact, the more acquisition takes place. Subsequently, Schumann (1986) proposed that acculturation may also affect the nature of the verbal interactions that learners take part in and thus the quality as well as the quantity of L2 input. The Acculturation Model, however, does not specify the internal processes that are involved in acquisition.

The test of any model is whether it is supported by the results of empirical research. The Acculturation Model has received only limited support, as Schumann (1986) acknowledged. Maple's (1982) study of 190 Spanish-speaking students enrolled in an ESL programme at the University of Texas found a strong relationship between social distance and measures of L2 English proficiency. Seven out of the eight social factors shown in Table 7.6 were negatively correlated with proficiency. Other studies have failed to support the model either because they found that psychological distance correlated with advanced proficiency in situations where social distance was high (for example, Kelly 1982), or simply because no relationship between social distance and development was found when one might have been expected it (for example, Stauble 1984; Schmidt 1983).

There have been relatively few studies since the 1980s testing the Acculturation Model. Hansen (1995) examined the relationship between the degree of acculturation of 20 German-born immigrants to the US and their English pronunciation. An overall social factor, based on the social distance variables, correlated significantly with the degree of accent ($r = -.55$), with enclosure and cohesiveness being the most influential factors. Graham and Brown (1996) reported a study involving native Spanish speakers in a small town in northern Mexico with an English-speaking minority population. They investigated a number of variables, including those relating to social distance. They noted that 'in Schumann's terms, the conditions in the community are very favourable toward the acquisition of English by the Spanish speaking community' (p. 247). However, a regression analysis showed that none of the social distance variables predicted proficiency as measured by an oral proficiency test. Only attendance at local bilingual schools and the age of the learners emerged as significant predictors. Thus, the mixed results of the earlier studies are also reflected in the results of the later studies. One of the reasons for these mixed results is the difficulty of measuring acculturation. Apart from the problem of obtaining reliable measures of each social factor, there is no principled way of weighting the different variables.

A number of theoretical objections have also been lodged against the model. (See Larsen-Freeman and Long 1991.) A major concern is Schumann's assumption that it is contact that mediates the relationship between social distance and acquisition. It is not clear to what extent more contact correlates with higher levels of acquisition. The Heidelberger Forschungsprojekt 'Pidgin-Deutsch' (1978) reported a strong relationship between the initial contact that migrant workers in West Germany had with native Germans and their syntactic development in the L2. Similarly, the ZISA Project, also based in West Germany (see Chapter 3) found clear evidence of a relationship between contact and *restrictive simplification* (the continued use of simplified structures, such as deletion of function words, by learners who had developed the ability to use the corresponding non-simplified structures). However, Day (1985) failed to find a significant relationship between contact with native speakers and L2 proficiency in studies they carried out in Canada and Hawaii respectively.

However, perhaps the greatest failing of the Acculturation Model is that it has nothing to say about how social factors influence the *quality* of contact that learners experience. The model represents a Type 1 theory. (See Table 7.1.) That is, it assumes that social factors determine the rate and success of L2 acquisition. As such, it allows no room for the possibility that learners have agency and can challenge the social factors that impede their learning. To account for the quality of contact, a Type 2 approach is needed.

The Socio-educational Model

Gardner's SOCIO-EDUCATIONAL MODEL reflects the results of work begun at McGill University in Montreal in the 1950s and still carried on today. Unlike the other theories considered in this section, which were designed to account for the role that social factors play in natural settings, in particular majority language contexts, Gardner's model was developed to explain L2 learning in classroom settings, in particular the foreign language classroom. It exists in several versions (Gardner 1979, 1983, 1985). The following account is derived from the 1985 version. This was subsequently extended in Tremblay and Gardner (1995) to include additional factors (for example, goal salience—the extent to which the learners' goals are clearly specified) but as these were not found to appreciably improve the prediction of measures of achievement they will not be referred to here.

The model, which is shown schematically in Figure 7.1, seeks to interrelate four aspects of L2 learning: (1) the social and cultural milieu, (2) individual learner differences, (3) the setting, and (4) learning outcomes. The basis of the model is that L2 learning—even in a classroom setting—is not just a matter of learning new information but of 'acquiring symbolic elements of a different ethnolinguistic community' (Gardner 1979: 193).

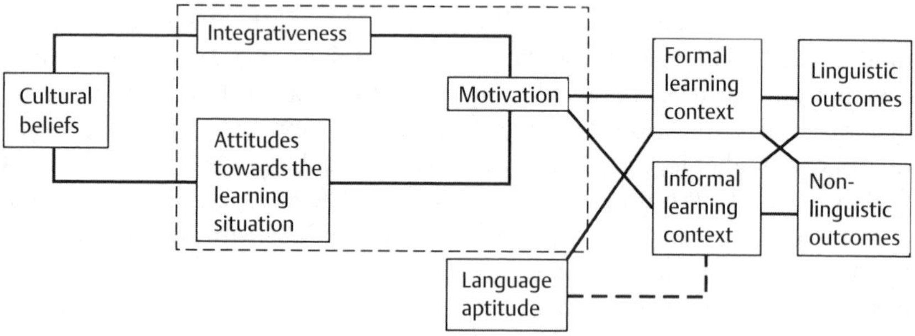

Figure 7.1 Gardner's (1985) Socio-educational Model

The social and cultural milieu in which learners grow up determines their beliefs about language and culture. Gardner identified a number of variables that result in individual differences. The two shown in Figure 7.1 are MOTIVATION and LANGUAGE-LEARNING APTITUDE. As both of these are discussed in detail in Chapter 13, we will say little about them here. The learners' social and cultural milieu determines the extent to which they wish to identify with the target-language culture (their integrative orientation) and also the extent to which they hold positive attitudes towards the learning situation (for example, the teacher and the instructional programme). Both contribute to the learners' motivation. Whereas motivation has a major impact on learning in both formal and informal learning contexts, aptitude is considered to be important only in the former, although it can play a secondary role in the latter. These two variables (together with intelligence and situational anxiety) determine the learning behaviours seen in different learners in the two contexts and, thereby, learning outcomes. These can be linguistic (L2 proficiency) and non-linguistic (attitudes, self-concept, cultural values, and beliefs). Learners who are motivated to integrate develop both a high level of L2 proficiency and better attitudes. The model is dynamic and cyclical.

One of the predictions of the Socio-educational Model is that the relationship between the social/cultural milieu and L2 proficiency and also between learners' attitudes and their proficiency is an indirect one, whereas that between integrative motivation and proficiency is more direct and, therefore, stronger. Gardner, Lalonde, and Pierson (1983) and Lalonde and Gardner (1985) investigated this using a statistical technique known as Linear Structural Analysis, which claims to be able to identify causal paths and not merely correlations among variables. These studies provide support for the view that factors in the social and cultural milieu are causally related to attitudes (integrativeness) which in turn are causally related to motivation and via this to achievement. Other studies suggest that there may be further intervening variables between setting and L2 achievement. Clement (1980), for instance, proposed that there is a 'secondary motivational process' connected with self-confidence. The results of studies that have investigated the relationship between measures of integrativeness and L2 proficiency have been somewhat mixed. These will be considered in Chapter 13.

Gardner's model constitutes another example of a Type 1 sociolinguistic theory. Its strength lies in its explanation of how setting is related to proficiency—one of the primary goals of any social theory of L2 acquisition—by positing a series of intervening variables (attitudes, motivation, self-confidence) and by trying to plot how these are interrelated and how they affect learning. Missing from the model, however, is any account of how particular settings highlight different factors that influence attitudes, motivation, and achievement. Not surprisingly, it has been criticized by proponents of Type 2 and Type 3 sociolinguistics. As Pavlenko (2002) noted, social-psychological approaches of the kind represented by Gardner's model lack explanatory validity because they do not consider the local social contexts of learners' motivations. Norton (2000) also attacked Gardner for failing to recognize that inequitable relations of power can limit learners' access to the L2. Also missing from the model is any reference to the concept of 'interlanguage development' and how this takes place through the process of social interaction.

The Inter-group Model

We have already seen that Giles and his associates were concerned with exploring how inter-group uses of language reflect the social and psychological attitudes of their speakers. Giles and Byrne (1982), Beebe and Giles

(1984), Ball, Giles, and Hewstone (1984), and Hall and Gudykunst (1986) have extended this approach in their INTER-GROUP MODEL to account for L2 acquisition. The following account is based primarily on Giles and Byrne's original formulation.

Drawing on the work of Tajfel (1974), Giles and Byrne identified a number of factors that contribute to a group's 'ethnolinguistic vitality'—the key construct in the theory. (See Table 7.7.) They then discussed the conditions under which subordinate group members (for example, immigrants or members of an ethnic minority) are most likely to acquire native-like proficiency in the dominant group's language. These are (1) when in-group identification is weak or the L1 does not function as a salient dimension of ethnic group membership, (2) when inter-ethnic comparisons are quiescent, (3) when perceived in-group vitality is low, (4) when perceived in-group boundaries are soft and open, and (5) when the learners identify strongly with other groups and so develop adequate group identity and intra-group status. When these conditions prevail, learners experience low ethnolinguistic vitality but without insecurity, as they are not aware of the options open to them regarding their status *vis-à-vis* native-speaker groups. These five conditions are associated with a desire to integrate into the dominant out-group (an integrative orientation), additive bilingualism, low situational anxiety, and the effective use of informal contexts of acquisition. The end result is that learners will achieve high levels of social and communicative proficiency in the L2.

Variable	**Description**
1 Identification with own ethnic group	This concerns the extent to which learners see themselves as members of a specific group that is separate from the out-group, and also consider their L1 an important dimension of their identity.
2 Inter-ethnic comparison	This concerns the extent to which learners make favourable or unfavourable comparisons with the out-group. Learners may or may not be aware of 'cognitive alternatives'.
3 Perception of ethno-linguistic vitality	This concerns the extent to which learners see their in-group as having low or high status and as sharing or being excluded from institutional power.
4 Perception of in-group boundaries	This concerns the extent to which learners see their group as culturally and linguistically separate from the out-group (hard boundaries), or as culturally and linguistically related (soft boundaries).
5 Identification with other social groups	This concerns the extent to which learners identify with other social groups (occupational, religious, gender) and, as a consequence, whether they hold an adequate or inadequate status within their in-group.

Table 7.7 Variables affecting L2 acquisition according to the Inter-group Model

Learners from minority groups will be unlikely to achieve native-speaker proficiency when their ethnolinguistic vitality is high. This occurs if (1) they identify strongly with their own in-group, (2) they see their in-group as inferior to the dominant out-group, (3) their perception of their ethnolinguistic vitality is high, (4) they perceive in-group boundaries as hard and closed, and (5) they do not identify with other social groups and so have an inadequate group status. In such cases, learners are likely to be aware of 'cognitive alternatives' and, as a result, emphasize the importance of their own culture and language and, possibly, engage in competition with the out-group. They will achieve low levels of communicative proficiency in the L2 because this would be seen to detract from their ethnic identity, although they may achieve knowledge of the formal aspects of the L2 through classroom study.

Whereas Schumann's model emphasizes 'contact' as the variable that mediates between social factors and L2 acquisition, Giles and Byrne see 'interaction' as crucial. The factors they identified determine the extent to which learners engage in upward convergence, and they defined L2 learning as 'long-term convergence'. As we saw in Chapter 4, much of the work in SLA research based on Giles' accommodation framework has been directed at discovering which linguistic features are subject to convergence or divergence and under which interactional conditions they operate. As such, the Inter-group Model integrates a macro- and micro-linguistic approach to the study of L2 acquisition and serves as a good example of a Type 2 sociolinguistic approach—one that utilizes 'sociolinguistic discourse analysis'.

However, the model represents a big leap from Giles' work on variation to acquisition seen as variation over time. The published work has focused only on the description and explanation of local phenomena in learner language (for example, Beebe and Zuengler's (1983) study of Puerto Rican and Chinese-Thai learners' use of specific linguistic phenomena in one-to-one interviews).[6] As such, there has not been any real test of the Inter-group Model. McNamara (1997) considered that the theory has proved somewhat 'disappointing' and suggested that this might be because SLA researchers were not primarily engaged in its formulation.

Tollefson (1991) offered a lengthy critique of the Inter-group Model. His main point was that it failed to consider the various historical and structural variables that explain why learners from minority language backgrounds make the choices they do. According to Tollefson, the concepts of ethnolinguistic vitality and ethnolinguistic group can only be properly understood by considering issues of power and domination in the majority and minority groups involved. He also argued that by emphasizing the role of convergence in language learning, the Inter-group Model suggests that 'learners who identify with their mother tongue cannot also be fully bilingual' and thus, inadvertently, 'provides a theoretical justification for language education programmes that seek to weaken learners' ties to their mother tongue and their community' (1991: 76). Tollefson's critique, then, draws on the theoretical perspective of Type 3 sociolinguistics by insisting on the need for a critical stance.

Language socialization

LANGUAGE SOCIALIZATION theory has attracted increasing attention in the last decade. Key publications include the collections of papers in Kramsch (2002) and Bayley and Schechter (2003) and various articles by Duff (for example, Duff, Wong, and Early 2002). However, relatively few of these publications have addressed how socialization impacts on language learning.

Language socialization research in SLA constitutes more of an approach than a distinctive theory. Schieffelin and Ochs (1986) defined language socialization as the practice by which novices in a community are socialized both to the language forms and, through language, to the values, behaviours, and practices of the community in which they live. Thus, it entails 'socialization through the use of language and socialization to use language' (p. 163). As such, it affords a promising way of examining the complex relationship between social behaviour and language learning. The theory proposes that in the process of learning to become a member of a community, learners learn the L2, and, conversely, that part of learning an L2 is becoming a member of the community that speaks it. One clear implication of such a theory is that language learning will be facilitated if socialization takes place and impeded if it does not.

A socialization paradigm challenges many of the assumptions of more traditional SLA research. Watson-Gegeo (2004), for example, advanced the sweeping claim that 'new research has made older cognitivist theoretical assumptions about development and learning obsolete' (p. 337) and went on to reject the view that there are universal stages of development in L2 acquisition or that there is a CRITICAL PERIOD for learning an L2. In particular, she challenged the view that knowledge (including linguistic knowledge) can be considered to exist independently of the specific contexts in which it was acquired, arguing instead that cognition was invariably 'situated'. However, she offered very little evidence to support such claims, relying instead on argument at a very high level of generality.

In contrast, Zuengler and Cole (2005) did review a number of SLA studies that have adopted a language socialization approach. However, most of these studies were macro-analytic in nature focusing on how learners acquired (or did not acquire) specific classroom socialization practices. Only one or two of these studies addressed the other side of the language socialization coin–'socialization to use language'. As it is these studies that seem more relevant to SLA we will focus on them here. Yoshimi (1999) investigated English learners' acquisition of Japanese 'ne', a pragmatic feature that conveys empathy and sharedness of knowledge. Whereas the majority of the learners' uses of 'ne' were pragmatically appropriate, some were not, reflecting L1 socialization. Matsumura (2001) compared a group of Japanese learners of English in Canada with a group in Japan in terms of their perceptions of status and their ability to give advice appropriately. Whereas the group in Japan only made modifications to the way they gave advice for higher-status addressees, the group in Canada showed a finer-grained awareness of status and were able to give advice accordingly. This study suggests that these learners' perception of status and advice-giving went hand in hand and that when they had the opportunity to interact with and become socialized into a target-language community their L2 use was more pragmatically target-like. Li (2000) reported an 18-month case study of a Chinese-speaking woman (Ming) working in a filing department in a US medical equipment company. Li focused on Ming's socialization with regard to her development of more target-like requests. Ming demonstrated agency in rejecting the way she was treated by some of her American co-workers, using polite request forms to demand what she considered appropriate behaviour from them. These three micro-analytic studies all addressed pragmatic features of the L2 in relation to socialization, reflecting Kasper's (2001) observation that language socialization is eminently suitable for investigating interlanguage pragmatics. However, Zuengler and Cole argued that Schieffelin and Ochs would disagree with Kasper, because in their view language socialization is concerned with 'a different (i.e. broader) scope of explanation' (p. 312). Yet, it is precisely this narrower, more linguistic focus that will make language socialization theory relevant to SLA.

Ideally, language socialization theory needs to marry a broad scope of explanation with a narrow, linguistic focus. A good example of how this can be achieved can be found in Bongartz and Schneider's (2003) study of two English-speaking brothers learning German in Germany. Bongartz and Schneider investigated two aspects of these boys' socialization through the interactions they took part in with their German-speaking playmates—language play (for example, sound play, narratives, insults and 'tough' talk) and negotiation (for example, about what, when, and how to play). They examined the boys' linguistic inventories by analysing their syntactic development (for example, sentence types and negation) and phrasal structure (for example, prepositions and determiners). They found that there were marked differences in the frequencies of the different tokens used by the two boys. For example, whereas the older brother used dependent clauses more frequently, the younger boy used imperative verbs more often. Bongartz and Schneider suggested that these differences were linked to the different patterns of socialization experienced by the two boys. That is, whereas the older boy interacted with his playmates through narratives, the younger interacted by attempting to initiate and control interactions. Thus, the 'lexical and syntactic choices for both boys are directly related to their interactional practices' (p. 32).

Zuengler and Cole concluded their review of language socialization in L2 learning by noting that there is a need to adopt a more critical stance that recognizes that 'practices come with ideologies' (p. 313). They suggested that the process of language socialization needs 'problematizing' by acknowledging the role that power and ideology play in the 'discourses' experienced by learners in majority language settings. In effect, then, Zuengler and Cole were arguing that socialization theory needs to move beyond a Type 2 approach (where the emphasis is on learners' social actions) to a Type 3 approach (where greater consideration is given to the socio-political forces that shape learners' learning opportunities.

Social identity theory

Norton's theory of SOCIAL IDENTITY and language learning, formulated in a series of publications (Peirce 1995; Norton 1997, 2000), addresses Tollefson's critique of the Inter-group Model and takes up Pennycook's (1990: 26) challenge to 'rethink language acquisition in its social, cultural, and political contexts, taking into account gender, race, and other relations of power as well as the notion of the subject as multiple and formed within different discourses'. In this respect, it is radically different from the preceding theories and constitutes a clear example of Coupland's Type 3 sociolinguistics.

Norton defined 'social identity' as 'the relationship between the individual and the larger social world, as mediated through institutions such as families, schools, workplaces, social services, and law courts (Norton 1997: 420). It contrasts with both 'cultural identity' ('the relationship between individuals and members of a group who share a common history, a common language, and similar ways of understanding the world') and 'ethnic identity' ('the relationship between the individual and members of the race to which the learner belongs'). Norton expressed a preference for the term 'social identity' because she believed that this term best captures the heterogeneous and dynamic nature of identity in the learners she investigated.

Norton's theory is concerned with the relationship between power, identity, and language learning. It draws on a number of sources. West (1992) saw identity as related to desire (for example, the desire for recognition, affiliation, security, and safety). These desires are closely related to material sources and to how people perceive themselves in relation to the world. According to West, 'Who am I?' has to be understood in terms of 'What can I do?'. Bordieu (1977) focused on the relationship between identity and symbolic power. A person's identity has to be understood in terms of the wider, often unequal relationships, in which they participate. These determine whether the individual has 'the right to speak' or the 'power to impose reception'. Weedon (1997), working from a feminist post-structuralist tradition, emphasized the agency of the individual. She proposed a 'theory of subjectivity'. The individual is seen as both the subject of and subject to the relations of power within different social sites. In other words, the individual is the product of social forces but is also able to shape his/her own identity. Underlying all of these perspectives is the view that language learning is inextricably connected with social conditions, in particular power relations, and that it can only be promoted if these are addressed.

The theory seeks to address three general questions: (1) under what conditions do language learners speak? (2) how can we encourage learners to become more communicatively competent? and (3) how can we facilitate interaction between language learners and target-language speakers? Answers to these questions are provided by three central propositions:

1 Social identity is multiple, contradictory, and dynamic. That is, each person possesses a number of different identities, some of which may be in opposition. Identities are modified, abandoned, or added to at any time depending on circumstances.
2 L2 learners need to 'invest' in a social identity that will create appropriate opportunities for them to learn the L2. They need to be prepared to struggle to establish such an identity.
3 L2 learners need to develop an awareness of the right to speak. This requires that they understand how the rules of speaking are socially and historically constructed to support the interests of a dominant group within society. In other words, identity construction has to be understood in relation to larger social processes.

Implicit in this view of social identity, L2 use, and L2 learning is the idea of 'ownership' of the language being learnt. Like Tollefeson and Pennycook, Norton challenged the view that native speakers own the language and asserted that learners need to see themselves as legitimate speakers of it. Thus, like others, Norton challenged the traditional notions of 'native speaker' and 'non-native speaker'.

The theory is made concrete through reports of case studies of a number of adult female immigrants to Canada. Norton documented how these women had social identities attributed to them which denied them the opportunity to speak and be heard and which they were uncomfortable with. In such a situation, they had a choice. They could either withdraw from contact with native speakers or they could fight to establish a preferred social identity that would afford them opportunities to learn. Martina, a Czech woman who came to Canada with her husband and children at the age of 37, was able to make use of her identity as the primary caregiver in her family, which involved finding accommodation, organizing telephones, buying appliances, choosing schools for the children, to create numerous opportunities for speaking English. She refused to be silenced despite experiencing frequent feelings of shame. Instead, she used her investment in her role as caregiver to challenge the 'rules' that govern interactions between immigrants and Anglophones—for example, by arguing with her landlord that she had not broken the terms of their lease. Another woman, Mai, was not so successful. Mai was subject to her brother's patriarchal authority at home and became the subject of derision at work because of the preferential treatment she received from the management on account of her single status. As a result, she was not able to establish an identity that created the conditions where she could learn English.

Further evidence for the relationship between identity and language learning can be found in McKay and Wong's (1996) study of adolescent Chinese immigrant students in junior high schools in California. They document how these students 'constantly conduct delicate social negotiations to fashion viable identities' (p. 603). One of the points that emerged from this study is that investment can be highly selective and will result in different kinds of language proficiency. Different learners were observed to prioritize different language skills or combinations of skills depending on how they defined their social identity.

Norton's theory was developed to account for under-privileged learners in a majority language setting. However, it can also help to account for a different kind of learner—privileged, short-stay learners in a majority setting. Two studies of Japanese women, although not undertaken explicitly within Norton's theoretical framework, clearly speak to it. Block (2006), for example, reported a number of case studies of learners with multilingual identities in London. Included in these is an account of five Japanese female graduate students. In contrast to the kinds of learners that Norton investigated, these learners were all middle class, highly educated, and economically secure. That is, they all possessed 'the requisite social and cultural capital to make the move from Japan to London' (p. 104). While there were some marked differences in the identities these learners assumed, they could all be characterized as 'internationalist women' (Kelsky 2001)—that is, women who elect to live their lives, to some degree at least, outside the confines of traditional Japanese society. This involved a partial rejection of Japanese culture through treating English as 'a language of liberation in which they can develop new femininities' (p. 97). Piller and Takahashi (2006) also investigated Japanese women's identities in an English-speaking environment, in this case in Sydney, Australia. Like Block's learners, these women manifested 'akogore' (i.e. desire) for the emancipated lifestyle of the West but unlike Block's graduates, they had come to Australia not to study but to find Western sexual and romantic partners, as a way of both liberating their lives and also improving their English. Both Block and Piller and Takahashi discussed the contradictions in the women's stories as they struggled to reconcile their conflicting identities as 'internationalist' and 'Japanese women'.

The importance of Norton's theory is that it provides a non-deterministic account of how social factors influence L2 acquisition by attributing 'agency' to the learner. It is capable of explaining why some learners are successful and others less so in a more convincing way than any of the preceding theories. However, it is also limited in scope in a number of ways. It deals exclusively with learners learning an L2 in a majority setting and it is therefore not clear to what extent it can explain L2 learning in foreign language settings. It addresses how 'learning opportunities' are created but has nothing to say about how these opportunities actually result in acquisition. Indeed, at times, Norton is guilty of uncritically equating 'learning opportunities' with 'learning'. Neither Norton, Block nor Piller and Takahashi provide any evidence to show what the learners they investigated actually learnt as a product of the identities they assumed. Nor do they show that learners who achieved the right to speak learnt more rapidly than those who do not.

There has been a plethora of recent publications reporting studies of learner identity. (See, for example, Block 2006; Pavlenko and Blackledge 2004; Pavlenko 2006a; Ricento 2005.) Clearly the learner's social identity constitutes a major factor determining success in L2 learning. However, it would be a mistake to overemphasize the role of identity. Purely contextual factors are as important, and perhaps in some contexts, more important than identity. Piller (2002), for example, reported that 'the passing of expert L2 users (as native speakers) is contextual rather than identity-related' (p. 198). That is, whether these learners made the effort to appear native-like depended on their interlocutors not on who they thought they were.

Conclusion

In this chapter we have explored a number of social aspects of SLA. It is probably true to say that by and large these aspects have been explored primarily with reference to learners in majority language settings. The social aspects of learning in classroom settings have received much less attention. Indeed, several of the theories considered in the previous section explicitly exclude instructed learning.

I have chosen to eclectically examine a number of different approaches, including (1) the more traditional ones that have sought to establish correlations between particular social settings or factors and language use/learning in accordance with Type 1 sociolinguistics and (2) the more current ones that, drawing on language socialization, post-structuralist, and critical views of society, emphasize the complex, heterogeneous nature of the social world that learners inhabit and the power asymmetries that may inhibit their opportunities for learning, as in Types 2 and 3 sociolinguistics. My position is that all three types afford valuable insights about how social context and learning are related and that their respective methodologies—quantitative and ethnographic, micro-analytic and macro-analytic—are needed. While accepting that both social settings and social factors such as age and gender cannot be assumed to be stable and causal of learning in any simple unidirectional way, I wish to argue that there is virtue in seeking to isolate specific social variables for study, for, otherwise, there is the danger of losing sight of the trees for the sake of the wood. Pavlenko (2002) claimed correctly that post-structuralist approaches 'allow SLA researchers to avoid monolingual and monocultural biases, to examine the multilingual reality of the contemporary world, and to see all individuals as users of multiple linguistic resources and as members of multiple communities of practice' (p. 295). But such approaches also run the risk of being perceived as ideologically motivated and, more seriously for the purposes of this book, of consistently failing to address actual 'learning' by focusing instead on 'learning opportunities'. This latter failing is evident in the traditional, correlational approaches, but to a lesser extent. Post-structuralist accounts have elected to examine language in terms of 'discourses', but in so doing have failed to recognize that these discourses must still involve the utilization of linguistic resources. Ultimately, the study of L2 acquisition cannot escape addressing how learners develop their linguistic resources and, until post-structuralist researchers demonstrate how such constructs as 'gendering' and 'social identity' relate to interlanguage development, their contribution to SLA will remain limited and their work be perceived as marginal by many SLA researchers. While it is self-evident that 'just as surely as language is social, so is its acquisition' (Atkinson 2002: 527), it is also clear that sociolinguistic SLA needs to demonstrate how social context influences acquisition of the linguistic systems of an L2.

The key issue remains whether the social context has a direct impact on L2 acquisition (i.e. affects the processes of interlanguage development as reflected in the route of development) or whether its influence is felt only on the rate of acquisition and the ultimate level of proficiency achieved. We have seen that there is only limited evidence of a direct effect. There is more evidence to show that the social context affects the rate of acquisition and ultimate achievement. It is in this respect that the study of social context has the most to offer SLA, for as Breen (2001a) has pointed out there is a need to account for differential outcomes as well as universals in L2 acquisition.

Notes

1 Bamgbose's (1998) comments about the dearth of codification of local norms describe the situation in Nigeria. As Bolton (2004) pointed out, codification is more evident in some Outer Circle countries such as India and the West Indies.

2 This claim, however, can be challenged. L2 learners make use of a similar set of COMMUNICATION STRATEGIES to native speakers, including word-coinage. (See Chapter 13.) A new coinage such as 'outstation' might figure in learner language in the same way it figures in native-speaker speech. Perhaps the difference lies not so much in the 'process' involved, as Lowenberg suggested, as in the permanence of the item. In learner language, 'outstation' constitutes a temporary solution to a communication problem, with little chance of it becoming a fixed element in the learner's lexicon, whereas new coinages in native-speaker varieties often become fixtures.

3 This discussion of roles focuses on the interactional roles adopted by teachers and learners in the classroom. Such roles reflect the status of the participants as teachers and students. They reflect the positions which educational institutions expect them to adopt. These are socially and culturally determined. This may be why teachers in some African and Asian countries seem to find it especially difficult to abandon the traditional role of 'knower'.

4 Contrary to Cummins' claim, there is also some evidence that BICS is interdependent. Both Snow (1987) and Verhoeven (1991) show that children's ability to produce context-embedded language in an L2 matches their ability to do so in their L1.

5 Hammerley's attack on the Canadian French immersion programmes has come in for considerable criticism. Collier (1992: 87), for example, characterized his 1989 book as an 'emotional, polemical, one-sided account of his personal views ... with scant research evidence cited to undergird his opinions'.

6 In fact, the research reported by Beebe and Zuengler (1983) was completed before Giles and Byrne (1982) proposed the Inter-group Model. It constituted an attempt to reinterpret earlier work by Beebe (see Beebe 1974) in terms of SPEECH ACCOMMODATION THEORY.

PART FOUR

Explaining second language acquisition: internal factors

Introduction

The chapters in the last section considered the role that external factors play in L2 acquisition. In this section we will consider the learner-internal mechanisms that enable learners to construct knowledge of the L2 from or though the input/interaction they experience. Thus, the chapters in this section build on Chapter 6 where we examined the role of input and interaction by focusing on the mental processes that enable learners to convert input to intake and thereby build their interlanguages.

The perspective of this section is psycholinguistic. Field (2003) provided this definition of psycholinguistics:

> Psycholinguistics explores the relationship between the human mind and language. It treats the language user as an individual rather than a representative of society—but an individual whose linguistic performance is determined by the strengths and limitations of the mental apparatus which we all share.
> (p. 2)

Field went on to suggest that psycholinguistics has two major goals; the first is to understand the processes which underlie the system of language and the second is to use the study of the mental processes involved in language in order to examine how these structure the way we think and see the world. The theories and research we will examine in this section are directed primarily at the first of these two goals but are also of relevance to the second goal, specially Chapter 11 which examines sociocultural theory.[1]

The first chapter in this section examines the role of the learner's first language in L2 acquisition. The study of *L1 transfer* is a good starting point because of its historical place in SLA. Much of the earlier research was directed at testing the rival claims of behaviourist and mentalist theories of L2 acquisition. Indeed, the case for viewing L2 acquisition as primarily a cognitive process was initially made through the study of transfer. L1 transfer is a good starting point for another reason. It is such a pervasive factor in L2 acquisition that it figures in all theories and thus in all the other chapters in this section. No account of L2 acquisition is complete without an explanation of the role played by the L1.

A key distinction that emerges in the chapter on language transfer and can be traced through all the subsequent chapters in this section, is that between 'knowledge' and 'control'. Bialystok and Sharwood Smith (1985) defined knowledge as 'the way in which the language system is represented in the mind of the learner' and control as 'the processing system for controlling knowledge during actual performance' (1985: 104). They also distinguished two types of knowledge—linguistic and pragmatic. The relationship between these two aspects of acquisition is shown in the figure below. However, while a number of psycholinguistic accounts of L2 acquisition are based on a clear-cut distinction between 'knowledge' and 'control' (for example, the Universal Grammar (UG)-based theories considered in Chapter 12), others are not. In the cognitive accounts we will consider in Chapter 9, knowledge is not seen as distinct from control. There is no clear dividing line between what learners know and what they can do with their knowledge, as the way linguistic knowledge is represented in the mind of the learner is influenced by the uses to which this knowledge is put.

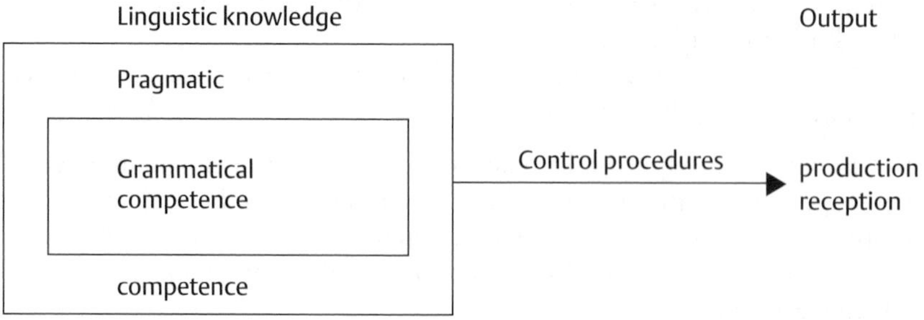

The relationship between control procedures and two aspects of linguistic knowledge (Bialystok and Sharwood Smith 1985: 106)

Irrespective of whether one takes the view that 'knowledge' and 'control' are distinct aspects of learners' interlanguages or part and parcel of the same phenomenon, there is a need to consider not just what a learner knows of the L2 but also to what extent this knowledge is usable under different conditions of language use. It does not follow, for example, that because learners can display knowledge of a linguistic feature in a controlled test that they can also access it in communicative language use. Thus, there is a need to examine the extent to which learners are able to exercise control over their knowledge. This has led to the study of learner production and, in particular, of how learners develop fluency in an L2. Chapter 10 examines a number of aspects of L2 production from a psycholinguistic perspective.

Another important distinction is between the 'acquisition of language' and 'language use'. It is self-evident that these are related, as the opportunities that learners have to use the L2 in comprehension and production will undoubtedly influence what and how fast they learn. However, differences arise as to whether acquisition is to be seen as something arising out of use but distinct from it, or as something that actually takes place in the course of attempts to use the L2. This difference is important because it implies the need for a different methodology for investigating L2 acquisition. If acquisition is seen as distinct from use, it follows that there is a need to show that learners are able to demonstrate knowledge of a particular feature independently of their initial experience of it in language use. This requires some sort of post-experience evidence as in experimental studies that have a pre-test → treatment → post-test design. But if acquisition is seen as occurring within language use, it follows that it can be demonstrated by showing that learners are simply able to use a feature that they could not use before. This can be achieved through the detailed analysis of the interactions in which learners participate. These conceptual and methodological differences distinguish mainstream cognitive theories of L2 acquisition (considered in Chapter 9) and sociocultural SLA (considered in Chapter 11).

The theories we will consider in this section are not compatible. Cognitive theories adopt a radically different view of L2 acquisition to linguistic theories based on UG. Sociocultural theory is again distinct. The differences are evident in the model of language they adopt. Cognitive theories favour some form of functional grammar (for example, Klein 1986) or cognitive grammar (for example, Bolinger 1975). Sociocultural SLA has paid little attention to the model of language but recently Lantolf and Thorne (2006) have suggested that both conceptual metaphor theory (Lakoff and Johnson 1999) and emergent grammar (Hopper 1998) constitute suitable linguistic paradigms. Linguistic theories of L2 acquisition have drawn on both typological linguistics and Chomsky's theory of Universal Grammar. The differences between these theories are also evident in how they view the role of input and interaction. In cognitive theories, interaction is seen as supplying learners with 'data' in various forms; acquisition is seen as largely driven by the input data. In sociocultural theory, interaction is seen as the matrix in which acquisition takes place. In linguistic theories, input is typically treated simply as a 'trigger', with the primary responsibility for learning placed on the language faculty. Further differences are evident in how these theories view sequences of acquisition, how they characterize the initial and final states of acquisition, and in the methodologies they employ to investigate L2 acquisition. The incompatibility of these theories raises a question: are there evaluative criteria that would make it possible to identify which of these theories provides the most adequate account of L2 acquisition? The answer to this is probably 'no', but I will reserve consideration of theory-evaluation until the final chapter of this book.

Note

1 Field's textbook, however, does not include SLA as one of the six areas that he considered psycholinguistic research falls into. He argued that SLA is 'best regarded as a different discipline' as it draws on a range of disciplines (i.e. sociolinguistics and educational psychology) whereas psycholinguistics is anchored in cognitive psychology. I would agree that SLA is broad-

based (as is reflected in the contents of this book) but I would also argue that a substantial body of research in SLA is psycholinguistic as it clearly draws on cognitive psychology. A better way to view SLA is as having both psycholinguistic and sociolinguistic strands. Field noted that 'some commentators include second language acquisition in the study of psycholinguistics' (p. 3). So they should!

8
Language transfer

Introduction

This chapter begins the study of the cognitive structures involved in second language acquisition by considering how the learner's existing linguistic knowledge influences the course of L2 development. This constitutes a suitable starting point, as this was the first factor to receive serious attention in SLA.

Odlin (2003) traced interest in the role of the first language (L1) in SLA to Weinreich's (1953) seminal publication *Language in Contact*. This sought to identify the influence that one language had on another in situations where two or more languages came into contact (for example, Afrikaans, English, and Bantu languages in South Africa) and emphasized negative transfer (i.e. how one language 'interfered' with the acquisition of another). However, whereas Odlin emphasized Weinreich's influence on early studies of L1 transfer, other researchers (for example, James 1980) pointed to the influence of behaviourist psychology and, indeed, the debates that took place in the 1960s and 1970s concerning the role of L1 transfer centred on the competing claims of BEHAVIOURIST and MENTALIST THEORIES of acquisition.

According to behaviourist theories of language learning, the main impediment to learning was INTERFERENCE from prior knowledge. PROACTIVE INHIBITION occurred when old habits got in the way of attempts to learn new ones. In such cases, the old habits had to be 'unlearnt' so that they could be replaced by new ones. In the case of L2 learning however the notion of 'unlearning' made little sense, as learners clearly did not need to forget their L1 in order to acquire an L2, although in some cases loss of the native language might take place eventually. For this reason, behaviourist theories of L2 learning emphasized the idea of 'difficulty', defined as the amount of effort required to learn an L2 pattern. The degree of difficulty was believed to depend primarily on the extent to which the target-language pattern was similar to or different from a native-language pattern. Where the two were identical, learning could take place easily through POSITIVE TRANSFER of the native-language pattern, but where they were different, learning difficulty arose and errors resulting from NEGATIVE TRANSFER were likely to occur. Such errors or 'bad habits' were considered damaging to successful language learning because they prevented the formation of the correct target-language habits. The commonly held view was that 'like sin, error is to be avoided and its influence overcome, but its presence to be expected' (Brooks 1960).

This chapter is primarily concerned with the cognitive accounts of language transfer that have now superseded behaviourist views. It begins with a discussion of terminological issues, the term 'transfer' itself being somewhat controversial. It then considers the methodology of transfer studies. A discussion of the CONTRASTIVE ANALYSIS HYPOTHESIS and Dulay, Burt, and Krashen's (1982) minimalist position follows. This leads into an examination of the evidence and arguments that led to a reappraisal of the role of transfer in the 1980s. The next section deals with transfer effects evident in production in the different levels of language (pronunciation, vocabulary, grammar, and discourse) and then in reception (reading). This section also includes consideration of conceptual transfer. Next, various constraints on transfer that account for the fact that transfer is sometimes apparent and sometimes not—the 'now you see it, now you don't' nature of language transfer (Kellerman 1983)—are examined. The chapter concludes with a summary of the various factors that a theory of language transfer will need to consider.

In subsequent chapters we will need to return to the issue of L1 transfer, as no theory of L2 acquisition that ignores the learner's prior linguistic knowledge can be considered complete. In particular, the section dealing with the Competition Model in Chapter 9 and that dealing with UG-based empirical studies of L2 acquisition in Chapter 12 will further address the role of the L1.

Terminological issues

The terms 'interference' and 'transfer' are closely associated with behaviourist theories of L2 learning. However, it is now widely accepted that the influence of the learner's native language cannot be adequately accounted for in terms of habit formation. Transfer is not simply a matter of interference or of falling back on the native language. Nor is it just a question of the influence of the learner's native language, as other, previously acquired 'second' languages can also have an effect. This suggests that the term 'L1 transfer' itself is inadequate. Sharwood Smith and Kellerman (1986) argued that a superordinate term that is theory-neutral is needed and suggest CROSSLINGUISTIC INFLUENCE. They commented:

> ... the term 'crosslinguistic influence' ... is theory-neutral, allowing one to subsume under one heading such phenomena as 'transfer', 'interference', 'avoidance', 'borrowing' and L2-related aspects of language loss and thus

> permitting discussion of the similarities and differences between these phenomena.
> (1986: 1)

There is much to be said for this proposal, not least the precise definition of 'transfer' that it permits. However, as is often the case in terminological disputes, usage does not always conform to reason, and the term 'transfer' has persisted, although its definition has now been considerably broadened to include most of the crosslinguistic phenomena that Kellerman and Sharwood Smith considered to be in need of attention. Following Odlin (2003), I will alternate freely between the use of the terms 'transfer' and 'crosslinguistic influence'.

I would like to propose the following definition of transfer, as an amalgam of Odlin's (1989) often cited 'working definition', which allows for BIDIRECTIONAL TRANSFER and the influence of previously acquired 'second' languages, and Jarvis' (2000) critique of this on the grounds that it fails to acknowledge that crosslinguistic influences are likely to manifest themselves as 'general tendencies and probabilities':

> Language transfer refers to any instance of learner data where a statistically significant correlation (or probability-based relation) is shown to exist between some feature of the target language and any other language that has been previously acquired.

It should be noted, however, that not all studies referred to in this chapter have been based on such a definition of transfer. Indeed, one of the reasons for the mixed and often contradictory findings of transfer studies is this lack of a common definition.

The methodology of transfer studies

The study of language transfer, like other areas of enquiry in SLA, faces a number of methodological problems. These include (1) whether transfer is best seen as a facet of communication, or learning, or both, (2) the nature of the data that are required to provide valid evidence of transfer, (3) the identification of incidences of transfer, and (4) the different ways in which the effects of transfer can be measured. I will consider each of these in turn.

Transfer as a communication and learning process

The study of language transfer entails the collection of evidence demonstrating that a learner's L1 influences the learner's *use* and *acquisition* of the L2. This distinction is theoretically and methodologically important because the presence of transfer effects in communication (production or reception) does not necessarily demonstrate that L1 forms have penetrated the learner's interlanguage (IL) system. Corder's (1983) view of transfer, for example, was that it is primarily a COMMUNICATION STRATEGY, which he termed 'borrowing'. He emphasized that borrowing is 'a *performance* phenomenon, not a *learning* process, a feature, therefore, of language use and not of language structure' (1983: 92). It is invoked in order to compensate for deficiencies in the interlanguage system. Such a view, however, contrasts with that of mainstream transfer researchers such as Kellerman (1983, 1995) and Odlin (1989, 2003), who clearly consider L1 transfer as a phenomenon of acquisition as well as use. It is difficult to see how the effects of the L1 on use and acquisition can be clearly distinguished given that the prima facie evidence of its role in acquisition comes from identifying transfer effects in language use (usually production). One possibility might be to examine temporal phenomena (for example, pausing and intonation) in learners' speech for signs that they are either attempting to cope with a communication difficulty by borrowing from their L1 or are accessing an automated IL form. Poulisse and Bongaerts (1994), for example, distinguished intentional and unintentional L1 switches by examining whether items were preceded by hesitation. In general, however, transfer studies have made no attempt to distinguish transfer as a COMMUNICATION or LEARNING STRATEGY.

Choice of data for the study of transfer

Transfer effects can be examined in terms of either reception (listening and reading) or production (speaking and writing). Most studies have investigated production but there are a number of studies (for example, Paribakht 2005; Akamatsu 2003) that have explored crosslinguistic influences in learners' listening and reading in an L2. Production data can be naturalistic, clinically elicited by means of tasks, or experimentally elicited by means of tests. Samples of spontaneous speech are likely to provide the best evidence of L1 forms that have become part of a learner's IL system but Odlin (2003) argued that they are likely to seriously underestimate the influence of the L1, as some structures may simply not be needed in this type of language use. Kellerman (2001) proposed that narratives may serve as a particularly fruitful type of data because they constitute a context for examining both linguistic and conceptual aspects of transfer. Odlin claimed that 'the most convincing evidence will come from multiple sources; spoken and written performances as well as responses to measures of perception, comprehension, or intuition' (p. 452).

Identifying instances of transfer

The third problem in transfer studies involves the actual identification of transfer in the data collected. Jarvis (2000) identified three criteria for identifying transfer: (1) intra-group homogeneity, (2) inter-group heterogeneity, and (3) similarities between the native language and interlanguage performance. Jarvis argued that at least two and preferably all three of these types of evidence are needed to make a reliable claim about transfer. (1) ideally requires a relatively large sample size, while (2) recognizes the need to investigate groups of learners with different native languages. (3) is the crucial criterion, as crosslinguistic influences can only be identified by means of some kind of comparison involving the learner's L1.

Various types of comparison are possible. Table 8.1 identifies five different types and the limitations of each. These comparisons involve the linguistic variables identified many years ago by Selinker (1969): (1) the learner's IL, (2) the learner's L1, and (3) the target language (TL). It is worth noting that whereas (1) is established empirically by inspecting some kind of language performance, (2) and (3) are often determined by reference to some published description, such as a reference grammar or dictionary, which may or may not reflect actual usage. (See Chapter 6.) These comparisons also involve important learner variables: whether the learners are from a single L1 background or from two (or more) L1 backgrounds and, in the case of the latter, whether the learners are bilingual or different monolingual learners. Finally, the comparisons can be one-way as in Types 1, 2, 3, or 4 or two-way as in Type 5. There is general agreement that the most valid comparison is one involving the IL, two (or more) L1s in bilingual learners and the TL, as in Ringbom's (1978) seminal study of Swedish/Finnish bilingual learners of English. However, Odlin (2003) rightly pointed out that it would be unwise to reject studies that do not meet this rigorous standard and that even Type 1 comparisons can provide reliable evidence of transfer effects. Nevertheless, an overall weakness of transfer studies has been their reliance on Type 1 and Type 2 comparisons.

Method	**Description**	**Example**	**Limitations**
Type 1 Comparison of the use of a particular feature in the IL and L1.	IL errors are identified; the learner's L1 is then inspected to determine if the error type corresponds to an L1 feature.	The 'after' perfect found in Irish and Scottish dialects of English (e.g. 'I'm after forgetting that'). A similar construction exists in Gaelic—see Odlin (2003).	1 Overestimation of transfer effects (i.e. the IL error might also reflect natural principles of acquisition). 2 Only serves to identify incidences of negative transfer.
Type 2 Comparisons of the use of a particular feature in the IL, the L1, and the TL.	IL features (deviant and otherwise) are identified. These features are then compared with the learner's L1 and the TL. Transfer (negative or positive) is held to occur if the IL feature is evident in the L1 but not in the TL.	Japanese learners' of English failure to use articles (i.e. English has both a definite and indefinite article but Japanese has neither).	Overestimation of negative transfer effects (i.e. the IL error might also reflect natural principles of acquisition).

Type 3 Comparisons of the use of a particular feature in the IL of learners from two or more different L1 backgrounds.	Differences are identified in the IL features of learners with different L1s. Transfer (negative or positive) is held to exist if the differences in the IL features can be shown to correspond to differences in the L1s.	Mesthrie and Dunne (1990, cited in Odlin 2003) compared learners with a Dravidian and an Indic L1 and found that structurally different patterns in relativization in their IL English corresponded closely to the L1 patterns.	Differences other than the differences in the learners' L1s (e.g. cultural differences) may account for the differences in their IL features.
Type 4 Comparisons of the use of a particular feature in the IL of learners who have two L1s (i.e. are bilingual).	As above except that only a single group of learners (who are bilingual) are investigated.	Ringbom (1978) investigated learners who were bilingual in Swedish and Finnish and showed that they were more likely to transfer word morphology from Swedish than from Finnish when learning English.	No obvious limitation; provides clear evidence of L1 transfer.
Type 5 Two-way comparisons involving learners with different L1s each learning the other's language as an L2.	Differences in the transfer of specific forms are investigated in two groups of learners; one group has language A as an L1 and is learning language B as the L2 while the other group has B as an L1 and is learning A as the L2.	Eckman (1977) investigated transfer in English learners of L2 German and in German learners of L2 English, focusing on voice contrast in pairs of phonemes such as /t/ and /d/.	Unless this design incorporates a Type 3 comparison, it will face the same limitations as Type 1 and 2 comparisons. However, incorporating a Type 3 comparison will necessitate a very complicated design.

Table 8.1 Methods for investigating L1 transfer

Measuring crosslinguistic effects

A further methodological issue is how to measure crosslinguistic effects. A number of different measures are possible: (1) errors (negative transfer), (2) facilitation (positive transfer), (3) avoidance (or underproduction), and (4) over-use. Somewhat different problems arise with each of these measures.

1 Errors

Learners' ERRORS were considered in detail in Chapter 2, where the procedure for conducting an error analysis was described. We noted that a substantial amount of empirical work in SLA research has been devoted to establishing to what extent errors are the result of transfer (i.e. interference) or are INTRALINGUAL in nature (i.e. the result of general processes of language development similar to those observed in L1 acquisition). Table 8.2, from Ellis 1985a, illustrates the considerable variance in the proportion of transfer errors reported by different investigators. Whereas Dulay and Burt (1973) reported that transfer accounted for only 3 per cent of the errors in their corpus of Spanish-speaking learners' L2 English, Tran-Chi-Chau (1975) reported 51 per cent in adult, Chinese-speaking learners' English. As we saw in Chapter 2, one of the main reasons for this variation is the difficulty in determining whether an error is the result of transfer or intralingual processes.

Study	Percentage of interference errors	Type of learner
Grauberg 1971	36	First language German—adult, advanced
George 1972	33 (approx)	Mixed first languages—adult, graduate
Dulay and Burt 1973	3	First language Spanish—children, mixed level
Tran-Chi-Chau 1975	51	First language Chinese—adult, mixed level
Mukkatesh 1977	23	First language Arabic—adult
Flick 1980	31	First language Spanish—adult, mixed level
Lott 1983	50 (approx)	First language Italian—adult, university

Table 8.2 Percentage of interference errors reported by various studies of L2 English grammar (from Ellis 1985a: 29)

2 Facilitation (positive transfer)

The learner's L1 can also facilitate L2 learning. This occurs when there are similarities between the L1 and L2. Ringbom (2007: 1) emphasized that 'learners, consciously or not, do not look for differences, they look for similarities wherever they can find them'. Ringbom made a convincing case for viewing similarity as 'basic' and difference as 'secondary'.

Odlin (1989) pointed out that the facilitative effects can only be observed when learners with different native languages are studied and Type 3 or 4 comparisons (see Table 8.1) are carried out. Facilitation is evident not so much in the total absence of certain errors—as would be expected on the basis of behaviourist notions of positive transfer—but rather in a reduced number of errors and, also, in the rate of learning. Ringbom (2007) provided a detailed description of the different types of crosslinguistic similarity, including the difference between 'objective' and 'perceived similarity', which is considered later in this chapter. (See Chapter 2 of his book.)

Two studies of relative clauses illustrate how transfer can have a facilitative effect. Gass (1979, 1983) investigated 17 adult learners of L2 English with diverse language backgrounds. Data relating to a number of structural aspects of relative clauses were collected but only one—pronoun retention—provided clear evidence of transfer effects. Gass divided her subjects into two groups according to whether their L1 allowed pronoun retention (for example, Persian and Arabic) or did not allow it (for example, French and Italian). She found that learners in the first group were much more likely to accept sentences like:

*The woman that I gave a book to *her* is my sister.

as grammatical than learners in the second group. Those learners in the second group, whose languages resembled English in not permitting pronoun retention, also made fewer errors in a sentence-joining task. Interestingly, though, facilitative transfer effects were not evident in all relative clause types, there being no difference between the two groups in the case of clauses where the pronoun functioned as subject, genitive, or object of comparison in the sentence-joining task. This led Gass to claim that transfer interacts with linguistic universals that determine the difficulty of different structures—an important point which we will take up later.

The second study (Hyltenstam 1984) investigated relative clauses in L2 Swedish, a language that does not permit pronoun retention. The subjects were 45 adult learners from five language groups. These languages differed in the extent to which they manifested pronominal copies in relative clauses. Hyltenstam used pictures to elicit oral sentences for each relativizable function. The results showed that pronominal copies occurred in the speech produced by all the language groups irrespective of whether their L1 permitted retention or not, but that the frequency of the copies varied according to language group. The Persian learners produced the most copies, followed by the Greek, with the Spanish and Finnish learners producing the fewest. This order corresponded exactly to that predicted on the basis of the structural properties of the learners' native languages.

The facilitative effect of the L1 is evident in other aspects of L2 acquisition. In many cases this is obvious, as when two languages share a large number of cognates (for example, English and French), thus giving the learners a head start in vocabulary. Chinese learners of L2 Japanese have an enormous advantage over English learners because of the similarity of the Chinese and Japanese writing systems. They are able to make use of written as well as spoken input straight away. The positive contribution of the L1 has been ignored by some researchers who, in staking out a minimalist transfer position, have chosen to attend only to learner errors.

It is clear that in order to establish the extent of crosslinguistic influences it is important to look for evidence of both positive and negative transfer.

It is also important, however, to establish whether learners' use of a target-language feature is due to positive transfer or some intralingual process.

3 Avoidance

Learners also avoid using linguistic structures which they find difficult because of differences between their native language and the target language. In such cases, the effects of the L1 are evident not in what learners do (errors) but in what they do not do (omissions). The classic study of avoidance, which we considered briefly in Chapter 2, is Schachter (1974). Schachter found that Chinese and Japanese learners of L2 English made fewer errors in the use of relative clauses than Persian or Arabic learners because they produced far fewer clauses overall. (See Table 8.3.) In Levenston's (1971) terms, 'under-representation' occurs. However, as Levenston (1979) pointed out, this is best characterized as an aspect of 'use' rather than 'acquisition'.

	Correct	Error	Total	Percentage of errors
Persian	131	43	174	25
Arab	123	31	154	20
Chinese	67	9	76	12
Japanese	58	5	63	8
American	173	0	173	0

Table 8.3 Relative clause production in five languages (Schachter 1974: 209)

The difficulty for the Chinese and Japanese learners may lie in the fact that while their mother tongues are left-branching (i.e. nouns are pre-modified):

Aki ga kinoo honya de kat-ta hon...
(Aki NOM yesterday bookstore LOC buy-PAST) book ...[1]

English is primarily right-branching (i.e. nouns are post-modified):

The book which Aki bought yesterday at the bookstore....

Persian and Arabic are also right-branching. Schachter hypothesized that it is this factor which leads Chinese and Japanese learners of L2 English to avoid using relative clauses.

The identification of avoidance is not an easy task. Seliger (1989) pointed out that it is only possible to claim that avoidance has taken place if the learner has demonstrated knowledge of the form in question, and if there is evidence available that native speakers of the L2 would use the form in the context under consideration. In other words, it only makes sense to talk of avoidance if the learners know what they are avoiding. Kamimoto, Shimura, and Kellerman (1992) argued that even demonstrating knowledge of a structure is not sufficient. Hebrew speakers of English may know how to use the passive, but their infrequent use of it in the L2 may simply reflect the general preference for active over passive in L1 Hebrew rather than avoidance (i.e. negative transfer). Thus, it is also necessary to demonstrate that the structure is not under-used simply because the equivalent structure is rare in the L1.

Avoidance is a complex phenomenon. Kellerman (1992) attempted to sort out the complexity by distinguishing three types. Avoidance (1) occurs when learners know or anticipate that there is a problem and have at least some sketchy idea of what the target form is like. This is the minimum condition for avoidance. Avoidance (2) arises when learners know what the target is but find it too difficult to use in the particular circumstances (for example, in the context of free-flowing conversation). Avoidance (3) is evident when learners know what to say and how to say it but are unwilling to actually say it because it will result in them flouting their own norms of behaviour.

4 Over-use

The over-use or 'over-indulgence' (Levenston 1971) of certain forms in L2 acquisition can occur as a result of intralingual processes such as OVERGENERALIZATION. (See Chapter 2.) For example, L2 learners have often been observed to overgeneralize the regular past tense inflection to irregular verbs in L2 English (for example, 'costed'). Similarly, learners may demonstrate a preference for words which can be generalized to a large number of contexts (Levenston 1979). OVER-USE can also result from transfer—often as a consequence of the avoidance or underproduction of some 'difficult' structure. Japanese learners of English for example, may overproduce simple sentences and may even be encouraged to do so, as this professional advice from a Japanese translator shows:

> Translate a main clause with a relative clause in English into two main clauses and connect them with conjunctions.
> (Kamimoto, Shimura, and Kellerman 1992: 268)

Over-use as a result of transfer is also evident at the discourse level. Olshtain (1983) examined the apologies offered by 63 American college students learning L2 Hebrew in Israel. She was able to show that the native speakers of English used more direct expressions of apology than native speakers of Hebrew and that they tended to transfer this into L2 Hebrew. This tendency was evident across situations. (See Chapter 5 for a fuller discussion of the research on apologies.)

Over-use of linguistic and discourse features as a result of L1 influence is probably more common than generally acknowledged. As in the case of avoidance, it can only be detected by comparing groups of learners with different L1s (i.e. by means of a Type 3 or 4 comparison).

Each of these ways of measuring transfer effects is problematic in its own way. The problems are exacerbated by the failure of many studies to provide reliability estimates of the effects identified, although one should not to be too hard on transfer studies as this continues to be a general failing in many areas of SLA research. Current discussions of transfer emphasize the necessity of considering the multiple ways in which L1 influence can exert itself. It is clearly insufficient to focus exclusively on production errors, as many of the subtle manifestations of transfer will be missed. Transfer scholars, therefore, also look for evidence of facilitation (positive transfer), avoidance, and over-use. However, again, there are relatively few studies that have examined all four types of evidence of transfer. Most have relied on the identification of errors. This runs the risk of seriously underestimating the extent of crosslinguistic influences. One approach might be to investigate the effects of transfer by rolling the various types of transfer into a single variable with two levels (use versus non-use).

Early days

We will begin this section with a consideration of early formulations of the CONTRASTIVE ANALYSIS HYPOTHESIS, consider some of the problems it gave rise to and then offer a reconsideration of the 'difference = difficulty' equation and of the role of CONTRASTIVE ANALYSIS. We will then go on to consider challenges to this hypothesis in the form of the minimalist position advanced by Dulay, Burt, and Krashen (1982).

The Contrastive Analysis Hypothesis

The Contrastive Analysis Hypothesis (CAH) as formulated by Lado (1957) was based on this assumption:

> ... the student who comes into contact with a foreign language will find some features of it quite easy and others extremely difficult. Those elements that are similar to his native language will be simple for him, and those elements that are different will be difficult.
> (1957: 2)

Lado's book *Linguistics Across Cultures* described the technical procedures needed to carry out detailed contrastive analyses. This spawned a series of contrastive analyses involving the major European languages (for example, Stockwell and Bowen 1965; Stockwell, Bowen, and Martin 1965). They were designed to provide course developers with information regarding where the differences and hence the difficulties lay for learners of different language backgrounds. The analyses were based on surface 'structuralist' descriptions of the two languages concerned. The procedure they followed involved (1) description (i.e. a formal description of the two languages was made), (2) selection (i.e. certain areas or items were chosen for detailed comparison), (3) comparison (i.e. the identification of areas of difference and similarity), and (4) prediction (i.e. determining which areas were likely to cause errors).

The scholars of the 1960s recognized different kinds of 'difference' and also attributed to them different degrees of 'difficulty'. Table 8.4 below provides a simplified version of the hierarchy of difficulty produced by Stockwell, Bowen, and Martin (1965). It shows that 'difficulty' will be greatest when there is a split and least in the case of coalesced forms. No difficulty arises when there is a complete correspondence of items in the two languages.

Type of difficulty	L1: English	L2: Spanish	Example
1 Split	x	x/y	'for' is either 'por' or 'para'
2 New	o	x	grammatical gender
3 Absent	x	o	'do' as a tense carrier
4 Coalesced	x/y	x	'his/her' is realized as a single form su
5 Correspondence	x	x	-ing, -ndo as complement with verbs of perception, e.g. 'I saw the men running'; 'vi a los hombres corriendo'.

Table 8.4 Simplified version of the hierarchy of difficulty (based on information given in Stockwell, Bowen, and Martin 1965)

In its strongest form, the CAH claimed that all L2 errors could be predicted by identifying the differences between the learners' native language and the target language. Lee (1968: 180), for instance, stated that 'the prime cause, or even the sole cause, of difficulty and error in foreign language learning is interference coming from the learner's native language'. However, given the empirical evidence that soon became available suggesting that many errors were not the result of transfer (see Table 8.2), a weaker form of the hypothesis was proposed (Wardhaugh 1970). According to this, only some errors were traceable to transfer, and contrastive analysis could be used only *a posteriori* to explain rather than predict. In other words, contrastive analysis needed to be used hand in hand with error analysis.

The CAH had its heyday in the 1960s, but gradually fell out of favour in the 1970s. There were several reasons for this. The strong form became untenable when it was shown that many errors were apparently not caused by transfer—see Dulay and Burt 1974a—and that many errors predicted by contrastive analysis did not actually occur. (See Jackson and Whitman 1971.) However, the weak form is also problematic. First, an *a posteriori* contrastive analysis is something of a 'pseudo procedure' (James 1980) in the sense that it makes little sense to undertake a lengthy comparison of two languages simply to confirm that errors suspected of being caused by transfer are indeed so. James argued that a contrastive analysis was only worthwhile if it was predictive. Schachter (1974) also argued that an *a priori* contrastive analysis was needed in order to identify those areas of the L2 system which learners might try to avoid. Neither version of the CAH was convincing, therefore; the strong version was theoretically untenable and the weak version was impractical and inadequate. It was not surprising to see contrastive analysis lose ground to error analysis in the 1970s.

The minimalist position

The minimalist position arose in the 1970s as dissatisfaction with the CAH grew. It sought to play down the importance of the L1 and to emphasize the contribution of universal processes of language learning, such as hypothesis-testing. It found expression in two major ways: the conduct of empirical studies designed to test the CAH, and the development of alternative theoretical arguments.

Empirical research and the CAH

A number of studies of learner language carried out in the late 1960s and early 1970s indicated that the influence of the L1 was much less than that claimed by the CAH. These studies were based on attempts to quantify the number of transfer errors. For example, in the most frequently cited study, Dulay and Burt (1974b) examined six structures in the L2 speech of Spanish learners of English. They selected only those structures that could provide unambiguous evidence of transfer. For example, negative constructions such as the following:

*I not have a bike.

were not included in the study, because although similar constructions are present in Spanish:

Yo no tengo bicicleta.

they are also found in the L1 acquisition of English, thus making it impossible to decide whether they constitute examples of interference or developmental errors. In contrast, the presence of a preclitic in sentences like:

*The dog it ate.

constitutes clear evidence of interference because, while the same construction is found in Spanish:

El perro se lo comió.

it is not evident in the L1 acquisition of English. The study showed that fewer than 5 per cent of the total errors in the corpus were of the 'interference' type, the rest being either 'developmental' or 'unique'. (See Chapter 2 for a definition of these categories.) Other studies have also claimed to show that the learner's L1 plays only an insignificant role. For example, Felix (1980b) examined three syntactic structures in English-speaking children's acquisition of L2 German and concluded that 'interference does not constitute a major strategy' (1980b: 107).

Studies of word order acquisition have also attempted to play down the role of transfer. Languages vary in (1) their basic word order (the majority of languages being VSO, SVO, or SOV) and (2) the extent to which their basic word order is rigid or flexible (for example, English has a rigid word order, while Russian is flexible). Thus, there is the potential for transfer to take place. For example, given that Japanese is rigidly SOV and English SVO, transfer might have been expected. However, Rutherford (1983) claimed that 'Japanese learners of English do not at any time produce writing in which the verb is wrongly placed sentence finally' (1983: 367). Zobl (1986) similarly argued that L2 learners do not have recourse to L1 knowledge where basic word order is concerned, except where the target language has more than one basic word order, as in the case of Dutch and German, which have SVO (and other patterns) in main clauses and SOV in subordinate clauses. Rutherford and Zobl's universalist position is in direct opposition to a transfer position.

Minimalist accounts of transfer seek to explain away apparent instances of L1 effects on word order. For example, Turkish learners of German have been observed to sometimes manifest constructions where the verb appears at the end of a sentence, suggesting that L1 transfer is taking place. However, Clahsen and Muysken (1986) argued that what appears to be transfer is in fact a discourse strategy. Odlin (1989: 89), too, accepted that there is 'detailed evidence for the heavy reliance of some learners on topic-comment patterning in the early stages of acquisition'. He cited these examples from Huebner's (1983) study of a Hmong refugee in Hawaii:

mii wok (As for me, I walked.)
hos, ai reis (As for horses, I raced.)

Learners of German, irrespective of their L1, have been found to produce similar utterances. (See Klein 1986; Clahsen and Muysken 1986.) These studies, then, suggested that the learner's L1 has little influence on basic word order and that, even when transfer is apparent, it can be better explained in terms of a discourse strategy. Thus, they lent support to the minimalist position.

Minimalist theoretical positions on transfer

Minimalist theoretical positions on transfer have tended to emphasize the similarity between L2 and L1 acquisition. Newmark (1966), for instance, drew extensively on research in L1 acquisition in dismissing behaviourist accounts of L2 learning. He was primarily concerned with rejecting the view of language as an incremental process, according to which learners were supposed to acquire a language structure by structure, proceeding from the simplest to the most complex. He acknowledged 'interference' but saw it as of little importance, arguing that it simply reflected ignorance. Newmark and

Reibel (1968) produced the following description of what has become known as the IGNORANCE HYPOTHESIS:

> ... a person knows how to speak one language, say his native one; but in the early stages of learning his new one, there are many things that he has not yet learnt to do ... What can he do other than use what he already knows to make up for what he does not know? To an observer who knows the target language, the learner will be seen to be stubbornly substituting the native habits for target habits. But from the learner's point of view, all he is doing is the best he can: to fill in his gaps of training he refers for help to what he already knows.
> (1968: 159)

Krashen (1983) adopted a similar position, drawing directly on Newmark's ideas. He viewed transfer as 'padding', the result of falling back on old knowledge when new knowledge is lacking. The cure is 'comprehensible input'. (See Chapter 6.) In effect, Newmark and Reibel and Krashen treated L1 transfer as a kind of COMMUNICATION STRATEGY (i.e. a means of overcoming a communication problem) rather than as a LEARNING STRATEGY (i.e. a device for developing interlanguage). This distinction between communication and learning transfer, which has already been touched on, is considered further in the conclusion to this chapter.

In place of the behaviourist notions of 'habit formation' and 'interference', researchers such as Dulay and Burt (1972) posited the existence of 'general processing strategies', which were seen as universal in the sense that they were used by all language learners, first and second. They identified a number of general production strategies to account for the various types of errors they observed. For example, the absence of grammatical functors was explained in terms of 'the pervasiveness of a syntactic generalization' while the use of intonation to signal questions in the early stages of learning was the result of 'using a minimal number of cues to signal the speaker's intentions'. Occasional instances of transfer errors were explained away as the result of the pressure to perform in the L2 (Newmark's idea), of the nature of the learning environment (for example, Ervin-Tripp (1974) claimed that interference was more likely in contexts where the L2 was not part of the learner's larger social milieu[2]), and of the use of tasks, such as translation, that predisposed learners to refer to their L1.

In retrospect, there can be little doubt that some scholars were too ready to reject transfer as a major factor in L2 acquisition. This over-reaction was caused by the close connection between the ideas of transfer and behaviourism, which, as we have seen, had become discredited. In clambering onto the mentalist bandwagon, however, researchers like Dulay and Burt mistakenly dismissed transfer, often on the basis of flimsy evidence. We will now consider the reappraisal of transfer which took place in the 1980s and has stayed with us today.

Reappraisal

Reappraisal of the role of transfer in L2 learning began in the late 1960s and was well established by the time of the seminal conference entitled 'Language Transfer in Language Learning' which took place at the University of Michigan, USA, in 1981. The reappraisal involved both theoretical challenges to the CAH (in particular the claim that 'difference = difficulty') and a rejection of Dulay, Burt, and Krashen's minimalist position.

It was soon clear that learning difficulty could not be defined solely in terms of L1–target-language differences. Thus, researchers continued to make use of contrastive analysis, but only as a tool for identifying *potential* areas of difficulty (Fisiak 1981a). It became generally recognized that the claims of a contrastive analysis needed to be subjected to careful empirical inquiry. As Selinker (1969) pointed out, 'experimentation in language research' is needed 'whenever it becomes clear that extrapolation from pure linguistic research is improper'. Similarly, Nemser (1971) saw the 'direct and systematic examination of learner speech' as a 'prerequisite for the validation of both the strong and weak claims of the contrastive approach'.

Researchers recognized that L1 transfer was just one of many possible explanations of L2 acquisition. Selinker (1972), for example, saw 'language transfer' as one of the five processes responsible for FOSSILIZATION, placing it, in fact, at the top of his list. Nemser (1971) claimed that learner speech was 'structurally organized' in the sense that it constituted a system in its own right. However, like Selinker, he saw the learner's native language as one of the major determinants of these 'approximative systems'.

Researchers came to recognize that it was similarity with some underlying developmental process that induced learners to transfer an L1 feature. For example, Wode (1983), following an analysis of phonological development in both instructed and naturalistic contexts, claimed that 'only certain L2 elements are substituted by L1 elements, namely, those meeting specifiable similarity requirements' (p. 185). Andersen (1983) offered his Transfer to Somewhere Principle (see p. 395 in this chapter), which also emphasized the importance of some degree of congruity between the L1 and the target language. Both Wode and Andersen claimed that L1 transfer would only take place if the features transferred accorded with universal developmental principles. As Wode put it 'those elements which do not meet the similarity requirements are acquired via developmental sequences similar to (identical with?) L1 acquisition'. In emphasizing similarity with L2 processes, however, Wode and Andersen may have overstated their case. Kellerman (1995) argued out that 'there can be transfer which is not licensed by similarity to the L2, and where the way the L2 works may very largely go unheeded' (p. 137). He proposed the Transfer to Nowhere Principle as a complement to the Transfer to Somewhere Principle. A balanced position, then, is one that acknowledges that the CAH was partly correct (difference can equal difficulty) but also acknowledges that L1 transfer works in tandem with other factors. Thus, while the claim that L1/L2 differences *will* lead to difficulty was shown to be incorrect, it also became clear that they *might* do so. The trick was to show when they did and when they did not. As Kellerman (1987) put it, there was a need to establish the 'potential for transfer' of a given structure and to identify the nature of the constraints that govern its transferability. We will take up this challenge in a later section in this chapter.

Reappraisal was also fostered by evidence that studies like those of Dulay and Burt and Felix seriously underestimated the role of the L1. James (1971) in pointing out that contrastive analysts had never claimed that L1 interference was the *sole* source of error, noted, prophetically, that 'it will probably turn out that many of the errors which are now not traceable to the L1, and are therefore attributed to L2 overgeneralization, will ... be recognized as errors of interference' (1971: 56). Researchers recognized that it was not always easy to decide whether an error is interference or developmental, and that this could result in estimations of transfer errors that were too conservative. As we have seen, it can be argued that 'no' + verb constructions produced by Spanish learners of English do not constitute a transfer error because the same error is evident in the L1 acquisition of English. It is possible, however, that 'no' + verb constructions reflect transfer and developmental processes working in conjunction. The point is that by eliminating structures with a potential for transfer (for example, negative constructions) and by investigating constructions, such as preclitics, where transfer is theoretically possible but unlikely—for reasons to be considered later—Dulay and Burt contrived to ensure that they found few interference errors. In other words, the assumption that errors were either the result of interference or intralingual was unwarranted. Also, before transfer can be dismissed, it is necessary to demonstrate through Type 2 and 3 comparisons (see Table 8.1) that the L1 is indeed having no effect.

Further evidence against the minimalist position was provided by Odlin's (1990) account of crosslinguistic influences in the acquisition of basic word order—a structure that was considered to be highly amenable to a universalist explanation—see previous section. Odlin collected evidence from 11 studies of SUBSTRATUM TRANSFER (i.e. from the L1 to the L2) and BORROWING TRANSFER (i.e. from the L2 to the L1) of word order rules. For example, Nagara (1972) reported that Japanese speakers of Hawaiian pidgin produce sentences like:

Mi: cu: stoa gecc (me two store get = I got two stores.)
hawai kam (Hawaii came = I came to Hawaii.)

It is possible that such utterances reflect a topic-comment patterning. However, Bickerton and Givón (1976) demonstrated that Japanese and Filipino speakers of Hawaiian Pidgin English manifest a word order that differs in accordance with their L1. Givón (1984) provided further evidence against a discourse explanation. He showed that Filipino and Korean speakers of Hawaiian pidgin displayed a preference for different word order patterns which directly reflected their L1s. Odlin also argued convincingly that Lujan, Minaya, and Sankoff's (1984) study of Spanish spoken in Peru and Ecuador provided evidence of influence from the L1 word order of local Indian languages, again dismissing Muysken's (1984) claim that the observed OV patterns are the result of 'stylistic considerations'. Further examples of substratum transfer cited by Odlin were in Korean Bamboo English, a pidgin used in contacts between American soldiers and Japanese and Korean civilians in the 1940s and 1950s, and Pidgin Fijian. Odlin concluded that 'there is no universal constraint on the transfer of basic word order' (1990: 107), contradicting the claim of Rutherford and Zobl.

However, Odlin (1990) did admit that there are relatively few instances of basic word order transfer in the literature and suggested two principal reasons why this might be so. First, he pointed out the relative lack of research on beginner learners, in whom word order transfer is most likely. Second, learners are likely to be highly conscious of word order as it involves the arrangement of semantically important elements. He noted that learners are very successful in identifying word order errors and, also, adept at imitating the word order patterns of other languages. He reported that Korean–English and Spanish–English bilinguals were much more consistent in judging word order errors than article errors. Teachers are also likely to pay attention to word order violations. The high level of awareness that word order seems to arouse may help learners to monitor their production in order to eliminate the effects of transfer. This might explain why Rutherford's Japanese learners displayed no evidence of the L1 order in their written compositions.

To sum up, the reappraisal of the role of transfer that took place in the 1970s and 1980s was based on the recognition that contrastive analyses could only identify potential errors and that there was a need to test out predictions based on differences between the TL and the L1 by examining learners' use of their IL. It was also recognized that L1 transfer was only one of several factors that could be invoked to explain L2 acquisition. Finally, the minimalist claims of Dulay, Burt, and Krashen were challenged by studies that showed that they had seriously underestimated the instances of transfer, even in structures like word order, where transfer might be considered unlikely to occur.

Evidence of transfer effects

In this section we will examine some of the research that has investigated crosslinguistic effects. We will consider studies that have found evidence of such effects in all aspects of production—pronunciation, vocabulary, grammar, and discourse (including PRAGMATICS)—and in reception. In addition, we will consider research that has explored what Odlin (2003, 2005) terms CONCEPTUAL TRANSFER (i.e. the influence of concepts associated with the cultural viewpoint of one language on the linguistic choices made in another language).

It may be possible to assess the overall level of transfer in a learner's IL. As Ringbom (2002) noted this will be determined by 'how much crosslinguistic similarity the learner can generally perceive, beginning from a common alphabet and phonemes in common over the division into grammatical categories (case, gender, word classes) to the number of cognates and other lexical similarities' (p. 1). However, as Odlin (2003) pointed out, it is very difficult to quantify the extent of transfer in the different language levels, not least because there is no reliable way of measuring the relative contributions of the L1 to the ease and difficulty of learning the different subsystems. Odlin noted that the frequency of occurrences of different features varies from one subsystem to another. For example, he pointed out the absurdity of comparing the transfer related to a phoneme such as /r/ with grammatical clefting (as in 'It's tomorrow she arrives'); transfer is more likely to be evident in the former than the latter as a reflection of occasions for the use of these two features. A further problem of quantifying crosslinguistic effects in the different subsystems resides in the difficulty of comparing transfer in reception and production. In this section, therefore, no attempt will be made to quantify the extent of transfer in the different language levels or in reception/production.[3] Instead, the aim will be to examine a number of studies relative to each aspect of language. Given the abundance of research in each area, the choice of studies to be examined is necessarily highly selective.

Production

1 Pronunciation

According to the difference = difficulty hypothesis, L2 sounds that are conspicuously different from the target language will be difficult to acquire and thus be acquired later than sounds that are similar. There is some evidence to support such a position. For example, Purcell and Suter (1980) asked native speakers to judge the pronunciation accuracy of L2 learners of English with different L1s (Thai, Japanese, Arabic, and Persian). They found that the greater the difference between the L1 and the L2, the lower the rating. Thus, Thai and Japanese learners were rated as less accurate than Arabic and Persian.

However, the difference = difficulty hypothesis does not account adequately for the L1 transfer effects that have been observed in L2 pronunciation. As we saw in Chapter 3, three general characteristics of L2 phonology have been identified:

1 the presence of L1 phonological features in the learners' speech,
2 the tendency for learners to substitute unmarked forms where the target language requires marked forms (where MARKEDNESS refers to inherent characteristics of phonological forms that determine learning difficulty)
3 the occurrence of unique phonological forms in the learner's L2 production, including those found in L1 acquisition.

In other words, learners do not invariably transfer the phonological features of their L1. Phonological transfer (like syntactical transfer) is governed in part by universal developmental tendencies, which reflect general principles that apply to the phonology of any natural language.

As an example of the selective nature of L1 phonological transfer we will consider a study by Eckman, Elreyes, and Iverson (2003). They identified three different ways in which the target language can differ from the L1 regarding phonemic contrasts. These are shown in Table 8.5. The strict application of the difference = difficulty hypothesis would lead to the following hierarchy of difficulty 1 > 2 > 3. In fact, 3 has been shown to be more difficult than 1 or 2, reflecting the general principle that learners find it more difficult to acquire similar sounds than dissimilar sounds (Flege 1995; Major and Kim 1996). Eckman, Elreyes, and Iverson then went on to show how what they call the Derived Environment Constraint that governs the phonology of any language also governs interlanguage phonology. This principle states that learners should never acquire a type (3) contrast, such as between [d] and [th] for Spanish speakers of English, in derived contexts (for example, in a word such as 'bathing') before they acquire it in basic contexts (for example, in contexts such as 'bathe'). Using a picture description task designed to elicit words with the English target sounds in basic and derived contexts from Spanish learners of English, Eckman *et al.* were able to show that this hypothesis was supported. Further, when a group of learners were given instruction in the production of these sounds in one or the other context, no case that contradicted the hypothesis was observed. The key point of this study is that 'target language contrasts between native language allophones are incorporated into interlanguages progressively, not at once' (p. 194) and that this progression is governed by general phonological principles such as the Derived Environment Constraint.

Target language	**Native language**	**Examples**
1 Sounds A and B contrast.	Contains neither A nor B.	English contrasts /f/ and /v/ but Korean has neither phoneme.
2 Sounds A and B contrast.	Contains A but lacks B.	English contrasts /p/ and /f/ whereas Japanese only has /p/.
3 Sounds A and B contrast.	Contains both A and B allophones of the same phoneme.	English contrasts /d/ and /t/ whereas in Spanish these are in complementary distribution (i.e. are allophones).

Table 8.5 Possible native language distribution for target language contrast (from Eckman et al. *2003: 171, with examples added)*

2 Vocabulary

Kellerman (1987: 42) commented 'there are enormous quantities of evidence for the influence of the L1 on IL (interlanguage) when it comes to lexis'. For example, Ringbom (1978) found that the majority of lexical errors made by Swedish and Finnish learners of L2 English living in Finland could be attributed to the transfer of partial translation equivalents. Also, the acquisition of lexis appears to be facilitated if the L1 and L2 are related languages. Thus, Sjöholm (1976) reports that Swedish learners of L2 English did better in vocabulary learning than Finnish learners, Swedish being closer than Finnish to English.

The L1 effects evident in Finland Swedish and Finnish learners' of L2 English lexis were further explored in Jarvis' (2000) study. This study is of particular importance because it constituted an attempt to achieve methodological rigour by obtaining all three types of evidence that Jarvis argued are needed to claim transfer (see the earlier section on the methodology of transfer studies in this chapter) and also by controlling for a number of other variables that potentially interact with transfer (for example, age, type and amount of language exposure, target language proficiency, and task). Jarvis investigated lexical reference, collecting L2 data from carefully selected samples of Swedish and Finnish speakers and L1 data from native speakers of Swedish, Finnish, and English, using tasks that tapped both production and reception. The statistical analyses produced only weak evidence of any transfer effects (i.e. there was no clear evidence of inter-L1 group differences and the levels of L1–IL correlation accounted for less than 50 per cent of the variance in the data). However, Jarvis argued that there were subtle and clearly detectable examples of transfer. For example, the Finnish-speaking learners preferred the words 'hit' (as in 'She hit a man') and 'crash' (as in 'She crashed with a man') to refer to a collision scene in a film, whereas the Swedish-speaking learners used 'run on' (as in 'She ran on a man'), differences that could be traced to differences in the underlying Finnish and Swedish concepts relating to collisions. Also, the L1 effects were notably stronger than the effects of any of the other variables.

A key issue relating to lexical transfer is whether learners form a new semantic specification for an L2 word or map it onto an existing semantic representation of their L1. Jiang (2002) investigated this question. He administered two semantic judgements tasks to Chinese learners of English. One task required the learners to determine the degree of semantic relatedness of two English words. The other experiment asked them to state whether two English words were related in meaning. The L2 word pairs varied according to whether they shared the same L1 translations or not. Jiang found that the learners provided higher rating scores and responded faster to L2 word pairs with the same translations. A control group of native speakers, however, responded in the same way to all the word pairs. This study provided clear evidence of L1 lemma mediation. The positive lexical transfer reported for learners of L2s with cognate L1s (as in the case of Swedish learners of English) may derive not just from the similarity of lexical forms but also from the availability of translation equivalents that allow for easy mapping of L2 forms onto L1 lemmas.

Vocabulary is also a source of BIDIRECTIONAL TRANSFER (i.e. transfer both from L1 to L2 and from L2 to L1), a point recognized by Weinreich (1953) in his initial formulation of interference between languages. Pavlenko and Jarvis (2002) investigated instances of bidirectional transfer in the oral narratives produced by advanced Russian learners of English who had learnt English post-puberty and had been living in the USA for a number of years. Examples of the lexical transfer they found are provided in Table 8.6. Interestingly, whereas L1 → L2 transfer occurred in grammar as well as vocabulary, the influence of the L2 on the L1 was predominantly lexical in nature. In the case of 'lexical borrowing' (defined in Table 8.6), only L1 → L2 transfer was evident. Pavlenko and Jarvis suggested that this was because such borrowing only occurs rarely in learners in majority language situations. In the case of 'semantic extension' and 'loan translation' the transfer was bidirectional. Pavlenko and Jarvis investigated a number of factors (for example, length of exposure and age at arrival) but found none that could explain individual learner variation in either the amount or directionality of the transfer. They concluded that bidirectionality reflects 'the flexible nature of MULTICOMPETENCE' (cf. Cook 1999). Further evidence of crosslinguistic effects of the L2 on the L1 can be found in Cook (2003).

Type	**Definition**	**L1–L2 transfer**	**L2–L1 transfer**
Semantic extension	Extension of a word in one language to include the meaning of a perceived translation of the word in another language.	'Neighbour' → 'roommate' (by extension from Russian *sosed* which refers to both next-door neighbours and apartment mates).	'Sozhitel'nitsa' → 'mistress' for 'roommate'.
Lexical borrowing	The use of a phonologically or orthographically adapted word from one language into another.	None	'boyfriend' (adapted phonologically).
Loan translation	The use of the literal translation of compound words, lexical collocations, or idioms from one language into another.	'deep inside herself' (from the Russian 'uiti v sebia'—'to go inside oneself').	'On vtorhaetsia v ee odinochestvo' (from the English 'he invades her privacy').

Table 8.6 Bi-directional lexical transfer (based on Pavlenko and Jarvis 2002)

3 Grammar

One of the prevailing findings of studies that have investigated crosslinguistic influences in the acquisition of grammar is that transfer works alongside other universal and developmental factors. Collins' (2002) study bears testimony to this. She investigated the roles of lexical aspect and L1 influence in adult French learners' acquisition of English temporal morphology by examining the choice of verb form in obligatory contexts for the use of the past tense. Drawing on the ASPECT HYPOTHESIS (see Chapter 4 and Glossary), she showed that the Francophone learners applied tense/aspect forms in ways that were consistent with the hypothesis. Thus, for example, they showed a greater preference for progressive forms (in place of the correct past tense forms) with activities than with other aspectual classes and used an uninflected verb form as an alternative to past tense with statives. In this respect, therefore, her study replicated previous studies by Bardovi-Harlig (for example, Bardovi-Harlig 2000) and provided further evidence of the universality of the Aspect Hypothesis. However, Collins also found evidence of L1 transfer in the Francophone learners' preference for the use of the perfect as an alternative for past tense with verbs expressing telic aspect (i.e. achievements and accomplishments). In this respect her findings differed from those reported by Bardovi-Harlig for other groups of learners. The Francophones' use of the perfect reflects the fact that French employs the passé composé to refer to indefinite past, as in this example:

> Oui, je l'ai commandée [passé composé] il y a une demi-heure. Tout à l'heure, j'ai entendu [passé composé] un bruit dehors. Peut-être qu'elle est arrivée [passé composé].

where English requires the simple past:

> Yes, I ordered it [simple past] half an hour ago. I heard [simple past] a noise outside a minute ago. Maybe it has arrived [present perfect].

Collins concluded that 'the L1 influence does not appear to override the effect of lexical aspect; rather it occurs within it' (p. 85). She also noted that the learners were more likely to use the perfect in place of the past tense when they had reached a stage of proficiency characterized by some productive use of the English past tense, pointing to an interaction between developmental stage and L1 transfer.

One type of crosslinguistic effect that may be especially evident in grammar is avoidance, possibly because learners find it relatively easy to monitor their production at the level of grammar. Table 8.7 summarizes four studies that have investigated the avoidance of phrasal verbs in English. These studies provide clear evidence that the learners' L1 affects avoidance behaviour. If the L1 contains phrasal verbs (as in Dutch), avoidance is limited but if the L1 does not contain any clear equivalent to phrasal verbs (as in Hebrew and Chinese) avoidance is much more prevalent. Two other findings emerge from these studies. One is that there is also an intralingual influence on avoidance behaviour, with learners from all language backgrounds more likely to avoid the use of phrasal verbs that have figurative meaning (for example, 'turn up' = 'appear') rather than literal meaning (for example, 'come in'). The other finding is that avoidance reduces as learners gain in proficiency and this is evident in all learners, irrespective of their L1. These studies also illustrate an important methodological point; there is much to be gained by researchers investigating a single grammatical feature, such as phrasal verbs, in a series of studies that employ the same basic design.

Study	**Participants**	**Tests**	**Results**
Dagut and Laufer (1985)	Advanced adult learners in an Israeli university; L1 = Hebrew	Three tests: 1 a multiple choice test; 2 a verb translation test; 3 a verb memorizing test.	Learners only selected phrasal verb option in fewer than 50% of m/c items. They were more likely to select phrasal verbs that were literal and least likely with figurative phrasal verbs.
Hulstijn and Marchena (1989)	Intermediate and advanced learners in Holland; L1 = Dutch	Same types of tests as in Dagut and Laufer.	The learners did not avoid phrasal verbs categorically but did avoid those they perceived as too Dutch-like and preferred one-word verbs over phrasal verbs with idiomatic meanings.
Laufer and Eliasson (1993)	Advanced learners of English in Sweden; L1 = Swedish	Two types of tests: 1 a multiple choice test, 2 a translation test. Also a comprehension test to test passive knowledge of phrasal verbs.	The learners did not avoid phrasal verbs. Neither did the inherent complexity nor the idiomaticity of the phrasal verbs induce avoidance.
Sjöholm (1995)	Mixed proficiency Finnish and Swedish learners of L2 English	A multiple choice test of phrasal verbs,	Both language groups tended to avoid or under-use English phrasal verbs, but Finns significantly more than Swedes in the early stages of learning. U-SHAPED BEHAVIOUR was evident in the Swedish group. Choice reflected both the L1 and the semantic properties of the verbs.

Liao and Fukuya (2004)	Advanced and intermediate learners in the US; L1 = Chinese Native speakers of American English	Same types of tests as in Dagut and Laufer. Two types of phrasal verbs: literal and figurative.	The intermediate learners used phrasal verbs less than the advanced learners or native speakers. All learners were more likely to use literal than figurative phrasal verb, but only in the translation test.

Table 8.7 Studies of the effects of L1 on learners' use of English phrasal verbs

Another key finding is that crosslinguistic influences in grammar can involve another non-native language as well as the L1. That is, in cases where a learner is learning an L3, transfer from the L2 as well as the L1 can take place. De Angelis (2005) investigated two groups of learners' written use of L3 (or L4) Italian. One group had English as their L1 and either Spanish or French as their L2. Another group had Spanish as their L1 and prior knowledge of English or English and French. She investigated their use of Italian function words. One finding was that both groups of learners relied extensively on their non-native languages for function words but only if they perceived the target and source languages as close to each other. A second major finding was that the learners were selective about which non-native function words they chose to transfer. Thus, those learners from both groups who had prior knowledge of French transferred the French subject pronoun 'il' extensively and also were less likely to omit the grammatical subject, as required in Italian. De Angelis' study together with earlier work by Ringbom (1987) and Williams and Hammarberg (1998) indicates that multilingual learners may draw on all their linguistic resources, not just their L1, but that the extent to which they do is determined by their perceptions of the typological similarities between the source and target languages. The importance of learners' perceptions about what is and is not transferable is considered later in this chapter.

4 Discourse

There is also general acceptance that transfer is a major factor at the level of discourse. Empirical evidence can be found in studies of L2 pragmatic development and in a series of studies that have investigated what are called 'pseudo-passives' in Chinese learners of L2 English.

In Chapter 5 we examined instances of language transfer in learners' performance of the illocutionary act of apologizing. There we presented evidence to show that both positive and negative transfer did take place in learners' choice of apology strategies (Maeshiba *et al.* 1996; Olshtain and Cohen 1983) and made the point that it might not be so much the actual linguistic differences between languages as learners' attitudes about how they should be performed crosslinguistically that influenced how they realized apologies in the L2.

According to the 'positive correlation hypothesis', lower-proficiency learners are less likely to manifest pragmatic transfer than higher-proficiency learners because they lack the necessary linguistic resources. A number of studies have supported this hypothesis (for example, Cohen 1997 and Hill 1997). However, other studies (for example, Maeshiba *et al.*) have not. Kasper and Rose (2002) considered that these conflicting results are unlikely to be reconciled until studies are carried out that investigate how the grammatical complexity of speech act strategies in the L1 and target language and pragmalinguistic transfer interrelate developmentally. Kasper and Rose emphasized the need to also examine learners' perceptions of transferability, as in Takahashi's (1996) study, which was considered in Chapter 5.

In a frequently cited paper, Schachter and Rutherford (1979) argued that what might at first sight appear to be transfer-induced syntactic errors are, in fact, transfer-induced discourse errors. They examined errors in the pseudo-passives produced by Chinese and Japanese learners of L2 English as in these examples:

> Most of food which is served in such restaurant have cooked already.
> Irrational emotions are bad but rational emotions must use for judging.

These errors were judged by native speakers to reflect a confusion between active and passive. Schachter and Rutherford, however, claimed that these sentences reflect the transfer of the topic-comment structure found in Chinese and Japanese. They suggested that learners learn a particular target-language form and then hypothesize that the form is used to express a particular discourse function. The topic-comment structure is, in fact, a universal feature of early interlanguage (see Chapter 4), but where the L1 supports its use—as in the case of the Japanese and Chinese learners—it is more prevalent. In a subsequent paper, Rutherford (1983) argued that whereas there is clear evidence of transfer involving topic prominence and pragmatic word order in Japanese learners of English, there is no evidence of transfer involving grammatical word order. He commented: 'I take these observations as evidence that it is therefore discourse and not syntax that gives gross overall shape to interlanguage' (1983: 368). However, as we have seen earlier in this chapter, Rutherford's rejection of word order transfer is open to criticism. Thus, while there can be few objections to his claim that discourse and pragmatic transfer is common, his assertion that it is more prevalent than syntactical transfer needs to be treated with circumspection. As we have already noted, it is not clear how the relative occurrences of transfer in different levels of language should be measured.

Building on the earlier research by Rutherford, Han (2000) reported a longitudinal study of two Chinese advanced learners of English (TOEFL 600 plus), focusing again on pseudo-passives. This study produced two major findings. First, it showed that in these learners the pseudo-passive was a hybrid 'in the sense that it functions as the topic at the same time as bearing some syntactic features of the subject, for example, controlling verb agreement' (p. 91). For example, one of the learners produced the following sentence:

The letter about graphics file has not received.

which Han analysed as a topic ('the letter about the graphics') and comment ('has not received') but also noted that the first noun phrase also functions as subject because it shows morphological agreement with the verb. Han suggested this constitutes an example of function–form transfer. Second, the study provided evidence that the L1 topic-comment influence was persistent in these learners because it occurred not just in non-target sentences but also in sentences that were superficially target-like (i.e. reflected covert errors). For example, the sentence:

The list will be sent to you later.

seems target-like but is inappropriate when viewed in its discourse context and, in fact, is best seen as another topic ('the list')/comment ('will be sent to you later') construction. Han argued that pseudo-passives persist in the interlanguages of even advanced Chinese learners of English and may, in fact, reflect fossilization.

Reception

Ringbom (1992) pointed out that 'transfer is at least as important in comprehension as it is in production' (p. 88). He provided evidence from Swedish-speaking Finns and Finnish-speaking Finns to show that the advantage which the former derive from the closer proximity of their L1 to English enables them to outperform the latter in both reading and listening comprehension. He suggested that the L1 constitutes 'potential knowledge' that can be drawn on more easily in decoding, which involves form-to-function mapping, than in encoding, which involves function-to-form mapping.

We will focus on reading studies that have examined the crosslinguistic differences in writing systems by comparing learners with L1s that have alphabetic and non-alphabetic writing systems (for example, Akamatsu 2003; Koda 1999; Wang, Koda, and Perfetti 2003; Wang and Koda 2005). By way of illustration we will consider two studies here. Akamatsu (2003) compared two groups of learners' reading rate and comprehension of L2 English texts. The groups differed in terms of whether their L1 orthographic background was logographic (Chinese and Japanese) or alphabetical (Persian). The texts were presented in two conditions; in one normal English orthography was used while in the other individual letters alternated between lower and upper case. The following are examples of these two conditions:

> There is no absolute limit to the existence of any tree. (normal case)
> ThErE iS nO aBsOlUtE lImIt To ThE eXiStEnCe Of AnY TReE. (alternated case)

Not surprisingly, perhaps, Akamatsu found that all the learners, irrespective of their L1 orthographic background, spent significantly longer on and comprehended less of the alternated case text than the normal case text. However, the Chinese and Japanese learners were more adversely affected by case alternation than the Persian learners. Akamatsu concluded that the learners' L1 orthography affected their ability to process constituent letters in words. In other words 'word processing skills or strategies developed in an L1 are transferred to L2 reading' (p. 221).

Wang and Koda (2005) investigated the word identification skills of Chinese and Korean college students in an intensive English language programme in the USA. They used a naming task that required students to say aloud words that appeared on a computer screen. The words had been carefully selected to reflect high and low word frequency and regular and irregular letter–sound patterns. The task also included a number of non-words. In addition, the learners completed an auditory semantic judgement task that required them to listen to a word and map it onto a meaning category. As in studies of L1 reading, they found a clear effect for both word frequency and word regularity (i.e. both groups of learners recognized high-frequency and regular words more accurately and faster than low-frequency and exception words). This testifies to a universal effect of input on acquisition. However, they also found a number of L1 effects. The Korean learners were better at recognizing high- and low-frequency regular and exception words than the Chinese. They were also more accurate in naming non-words and better at retrieving the correct meaning of spoken English words in the auditory semantic judgement task. These results reflect the fact that the Korean learners were able to make use of the fact that Hangul (the Korean writing system) is alphabetic like English whereas the Chinese learners were disadvantaged by the fact that their writing system is logographic. Wang and Koda concluded by stating that 'although the interplay of the nature and properties of the L1 and L2 is evident ... it appears that L2 factors may exert a greater degree of influence in English L2 word recognition than L1 experience' (p. 93).

Another way in which the L1 can exert an influence on L2 reading is through inferencing. Paribakht (2005) conducted a study to test the LEXICALIZATION HYPOTHESIS, according to which learners will find it easier to infer the meanings of lexicalized than non-lexicalized words because the former correspond to overlapping lemmas in their mental lexicon. The study investigated 20 Farsi-speaking university students' ability to infer the meanings of unknown words from English texts. The learners were all of an advanced level of English proficiency. The unknown words were selected to represent lemmas with equivalent L1 Farsi forms (i.e. lexicalized items such as 'proactive') and lemmas for which no ready-made L1 equivalent existed (i.e. non-lexicalized items such as 'clone'). The main finding was that the learners were about three times more successful in inferring the meanings of the lexicalized than the unlexicalized items. Paribakht pointed out that L1 lexicalization facilitated the process of successful inferencing but it was not essential, as the learners were also successful in inferencing the meanings of some of the non-lexicalized words. She also noted that there was no difference in the learners' retention of the two word sets; in other words, L1 lexicalization did not have any significant effect on acquisition in this study.

Conceptual transfer

CONCEPTUAL TRANSFER is closely linked to the notion of linguistic relativity. This concerns how the way people view the world is determined wholly or partly by the structure of their native language. Linguistic relativity is closely associated with Benjamin Whorf and the eponymous Whorfian Hypothesis. However, as Odlin (2005) pointed out, a more or less identical view of the relationship between mind and language was propagated much earlier by Von Humboldt. While the Whorfian Hypothesis has been controversial, receiving criticisms from universalists such as Pinker (1994), it has continued to attract the attention of a number of transfer researchers. These have sought evidence to show that an L1-specific world view affects the acquisition of another language. Odlin (2005) provided a survey of this research. Here we will consider just two examples.

Von Stutterheim (2003, 2005) examined conceptual transfer in very advanced learners with a view to determining if they differed from native speakers. She compared the principles for organizing information in different languages, claiming that 'preferences in construing content for expression developed in the course of L1 acquisition are maintained in solving verbal tasks in a second language'. For example, she claimed that German, French, and English differ conceptually in terms of whether they are 'bounded' (i.e. view events in terms of the end points of the events—as an accomplishment) or 'unbounded' (i.e. view events as a series of continuous actions—as a process). Whereas German and French are bounded, English is unbounded. She used a film narration to examine whether this conceptual difference is reflected in linguistic differences in the speech of native speakers of German, French, and English and in the speech of the same French and German participants speaking L2 English. She looked for linguistic realizations of the different perspectives in the choice of aspect (non-progressive versus progressive), reference to endpoints of actions (for example, in terms of locative expressions) and the use of 'dann'/'then' to punctuate the action-sequence. The results, which are shown in Table 8.8, show a clear effect for the speakers' conceptual orientation in both their L1 and L2 speech. Thus, while both the German and French learners produced more unbounded events in their English L2 narratives than in their L1 narratives, the percentage did not match that of the native speakers of English. The key point that von Stutterheim sought to make was that transfer effects were not just linguistic but reflected underlying ways in which learners perceived and conceptualized the world. One problem with her research, however, is that the distinction between bounded and unbounded ways of conceptualized events is not made independently of the linguistic devices that realize this distinction. Thus, it is not entirely clear whether her research provides evidence of linguistic or conceptual transfer (or, perhaps, both). Also, although the language examples she examines clearly reflect learners' conceptualizations, it is not clear whether the crosslinguistic influence in question originated at the level of conceptualization or at the level of 'thinking for speaking', where conceptualizations are fitted into the categories of language.

	L1 English	**L1 French**	**L1 German**	**L1 German/ L2 English**	**L1 French/ L2 English**
Bounded	27.4%	48.6%	51.4%	34.4%	43.2%
Unbounded	44.7%	29.2%	20.2%	33.9%	30.1%

Table 8.8 Bounded versus unbounded events (von Stutterheim 2005)

It seems reasonable to expect that if transfer is conceptual it will be reflected in non-linguistic systems of expression as well as linguistic. Yoshioka (2005) provided evidence to support this prediction. She compared the gestures used by L1 speakers of Dutch and Japanese in a story-retelling task and then examined the gestures of Dutch learners of L2 Japanese. She noted two differences in the gestures of the Dutch and Japanese L1 speakers. The Japanese used gestures more frequently to mark the introduction of main characters in the story and to track animate referents. Yoshioka suggested that this was linked to linguistic differences in the two languages. Whereas Dutch has a variety of linguistic devices (for example, articles and pronouns) for marking the informational status of referents, Japanese has fewer such devices with the result that Japanese speakers need to rely more on gestures to establish the identities of referents. The second difference involved the use of gesture to indicate inanimate referents (mainly locations) referred to in the story; the Japanese speakers frequently employed gesture whereas the Dutch speakers did not. Yoshioka found that the gestures used by Dutch learners of L2 Japanese were both unique in the case of referent marking and tracking (i.e. did not reflect those observed in the native or source languages) and reflected L1 usage in the case of inanimate referents where the learners attempted to map L1-packaged information onto L2 production (i.e. gesture was rarely used).

Evidence of the existence of a 'gesture interlanguage' can be found in Stam (2006). Her research demonstrated that the speech and gesture of Spanish learners of L2 English manifested aspects of both the L1 and L2 thinking in their expression of motional direction (i.e. path). Taking gesture as evidence of thinking, Stam found that some learners' manifested L1 thinking even when their speech was grammatically correct and fluent, whereas other learners appeared on the point of learning the L2 thinking pattern. Stam argued that investigating learners' gesture in relation to speech provides a window into their mental representations.

The study of conceptual transfer is still in its infancy. Odlin (2005) characterized it as 'exploratory'. One problem is distinguishing 'meaning transfer' (as reflected in the linguistic devices of a language) and 'conceptual transfer'. The study of GESTURAL ACCENT would seem an ideal way of achieving this.

Constraints on transfer

We have seen that a minimalist position on the role of transfer is not justified; transfer constitutes an important factor in L2 acquisition. However, we have also seen that behaviourist accounts of transfer, as reflected in the CAH in particular, overpredict both the transferability of specific items (that is, they fail to explain when they are transferred and when they are not), and transfer load (how much is transferred). Increasingly, as reflected in the evidence for transfer reviewed in the previous section, researchers have sought to identify the conditions that promote and inhibit transfer (i.e. constraints on transfer).

Odlin (2003) provided this useful definition of a 'constraint':

> ... a constraint could be anything that prevents a learner from either noticing a similarity in the first place or from deciding that the similarity is a real and helpful one.
> (p. 454)

He further noted that constraints can involve 'general cognitive capacities including perception and memory' and 'principles of language either totally or partially independent of other human capacities', i.e. they can be 'cognitive' or 'linguistic'. In this section we will consider a number of differing constraints on transfer: (1) social factors (the effect of the addressee and of different learning contexts on transfer), (2) MARKEDNESS (the extent to which specific linguistic features are 'special' in some way), (3) PROTOTYPICALITY (the extent to which a specific meaning of a word is considered 'core' or 'basic' in relation to other meanings of the same word), (4) language distance and PSYCHOTYPOLOGY (the perceptions that speakers have regarding the similarity and difference between languages), and (5) developmental factors (constraints relating to the natural processes of interlanguage development). It should be noted that these are not the only constraining factors. Non-structural factors such as the nature of the tasks a learner is performing and individual learner differences (for example, personality and age) also constrain L1 transfer. However, as these are considered in some detail elsewhere (see Chapters 4 and 13) they are not dealt with here.

Sociolinguistic factors

Sociolinguistic factors have been shown to influence when and to what extent transfer takes place. We will consider the effects of (1) the social context and (2) the relationship between the speaker and the addressee on transfer.

The social context can influence the extent to which transfer occurs. Odlin (1989, 1990) suggested that negative transfer is less likely in focused contexts, where there is concern to maintain the standardness of languages, than in unfocused contexts. This distinction between focused and unfocused contexts is taken from Le Page and Tabouret-Keller (1985), who claimed that whereas some communities have a very clear idea of what constitutes a language, others do not, mixing languages without much concern for what is 'grammatical' or 'ungrammatical'. Odlin suggested that negative transfer is less common in classroom settings than in natural settings because in the former, learners constitute a 'focused' community and as a consequence treat L1 forms as intrusive and even stigmatized. In natural settings learners may comprise either a 'focused' or an 'unfocused' community; where they are unfocused, language mixing will be freely permitted, thus encouraging negative transfer to take place. In addition, classroom learners are often explicitly warned when interference might occur through the contrastive presentation of items. Odlin (2003) noted that these differences in setting can explain the conflicting results regarding the transferability of idioms. Kellerman (1977) and Abdullah and Jackson (1998), on the basis of research in foreign language settings (Holland and Syria respectively), argued that learners are reluctant to transfer L1 idiomatic expressions, but Sridhar and Sridhar (1986) claimed that learners in official language settings such as India and Nigeria often create English idioms based on their L1.

However, it may be misleading to talk of 'communities'. It is likely that when learners are in a classroom setting, they will adhere to target-language norms and thus try to avoid negative transfer. However, when the same learners are outside the classroom, they may show much less regard for target-language forms and transfer quite freely.[4] Thus, where L2 learners are concerned, rather than talk of 'communities', it may be better to consider the effect of social context in relation to the kind of norm—external or internal—that learners have in mind. If the context requires attention to external norms (as manifested in textbooks, reference books, and the teacher), negative transfer is inhibited; if, however, the context encourages attention to internal norms (as in free conversation involving speakers with shared languages), learners may resort more freely to the L1 if this helps comprehensibility and promotes positive affective responses. Such variable transfer behaviour is most likely in official language settings (see Chapter 7), where the L2 is used both inside and outside of the classroom, but it may also be found in other settings as well. Of course, learners with access to only one type of setting (such as the classroom) may behave more like a 'community' where transfer is concerned.

Generalizations regarding the effect of macro contexts or settings on L1 transfer in general are dangerous, however. For a start, such generalizations overlook the possibility that the influence of the setting may vary according to the *type* of transfer that takes place. Pavlenko and Jarvis (2002), for example, found that advanced L2 learners in a majority language setting manifested instances of semantic extension and loan translation but not of lexical borrowing. Such generalizations also overlook the influence that specific social factors can have on learners' use of their L1. Studies by Beebe (1977) and Beebe and Zuengler (1983) examined the effect of addressee factors on transfer. Bilingual Thai/Chinese learners of English drew variably on their two L1s depending on whether their interlocutor was Thai or Chinese. Beebe (1980) found that Thai learners of English made use of a native variant of /r/ to a greater extent in a formal than in an informal context. Drawing on these and other studies of variability, Tarone (1982) argued that L1 transfer is likely to be more evident in learners' CAREFUL STYLE than in their VERNACULAR STYLE, on the grounds that when learners are paying greater attention to how they speak, they are more likely to make use of all their potential resources, including L1 knowledge. This variable use of the L1 was considered in more detail in Chapter 4.

It is interesting to note that the conclusion reached by Odlin on the basis of a macro-sociolinguistic perspective is very different from that reached by Tarone on the basis of a micro-sociolinguistic perspective. Given that 'focused' classroom learners are likely to make extensive use of a 'careful style', it seems contradictory to claim that transfer is inhibited in such learners and yet also prevalent in the careful style. This contradiction may be more apparent than real, however. Classroom learners may indeed seek to avoid transfer in general recognition of the importance of external norms, but in cases where the use of an L1 norm appears socially appropriate (because, for example, it gives prestige) they may still resort to transfer. Clearly, though, much work needs to be done to sort out such apparent contradictions.

Markedness

One of the strongest claims in research on transfer is that the transferability of different features depends on their degree of MARKEDNESS. The term 'marked' has been defined in different ways, but underlying all of the definitions is the notion that some linguistic features are 'special' in relation to others, which are more 'basic'. Thus, for example, the adjectives 'old' and 'young' can be considered unmarked and marked respectively, because whereas 'old' can be used to ask about a person's age:

How old is she? (= what is her age?)

'young' cannot, except in some very special sense:

How young is she? (= is she as young as she makes out?)

More technical definitions of markedness can be found in different linguistic traditions. These are discussed in some detail in Chapter 12, so here we will provide only a brief account to enable us to examine the hypothesized relationship between markedness and transfer. One definition of 'markedness' derives from Chomsky's theory of UNIVERSAL GRAMMAR (UG). This distinguishes the rules of a language that are core and periphery. Core rules are those that can be arrived at through the application of general, abstract principles of language structure, which Chomsky and other generative linguists have held to be innate. Basic word order, for example is considered part of the core. Peripheral rules are rules that are not governed by universal PRINCIPLES; they are idiosyncratic, reflecting their unique historical origins. The structure 'the more ... the more' is an example of a peripheral rule in English. Peripheral rules are marked. Core rules, as we will see in Chapter 12, can be both unmarked and marked.

UG theories of L2 acquisition differ in the role they attribute to the L1. The differences relate to what is referred to as 'access' (i.e. whether L2 learners are able to access universal grammar either fully or partially). A number of different possibilities have been identified. (See White 2000.) One possibility is that learners have complete access to universal grammar and thus do not need to rely on their L1—a zero transfer position. As should be clear from the preceding review of the evidence of transfer effects, this is not tenable. Another position is the 'full access/full transfer' according to which learners use their L1 grammar as the initial hypothesis which is then modified when the input data is found to be incompatible with this hypothesis. Schwartz and Sprouse (1996) claimed support for this position from a study of a Turkish learner of L2 German. However, Hakansson (2001) correctly pointed out that any claim about L1 transfer requires a comparison of learners with L1s that vary with regard to the features being investigated (i.e. a Type 3 comparison in Table 8.1). Hakansson's own study of Swedish learners of L2 German failed to support the full access/full transfer position; instead, the results of this study together with those from Schwartz and Sprouse pointed to the universality of developmental stages, as predicted by Pienemann's Processability Theory. (See Chapter 3.)

There are several other possibilities involving combinations of full/partial transfer and full/partial access to UG. Reviewing research that examined these possibilities, Odlin (2003) commented 'research for some two decades has led to many conflicting results' (p. 459). Odlin also noted that research on L1 transfer based on UG has tended to ignore research that lies outside the UG framework. He cited Vainikka and Young-Scholten's (1998) sweeping claim that functional projections are not available for transfer. Functional projections relate to function-word categories like articles but there is plenty of evidence to show that the presence of articles in the L1 results in positive transfer. Evidence of the transfer of functional projections can be found in Fuller's (1999) study of a German-Spanish bilingual's acquisition of English as an L3. Although not common, examples of the functional transfer of verb inflections in this learners' English speech did occur, as in this example, where the German –en affix is attached to an English verb:

I can every, every time sit-en und watch TV.

A further problem of much of the UG-inspired research is that it has relied on grammaticality judgements to measure transfer. Controversy exists as to whether these constitute a valid measure of L2 acquisition (Ellis 1991c). As pointed out earlier in this chapter, the most convincing evidence of the presence or absence of transfer can be found in studies that employ multiple measures. All in all, UG-based transfer research has been less than convincing.

Another approach to markedness can be found in language typology (the study of different types of language carried out in order to identify those properties that are universal). The identification of TYPOLOGICAL UNIVERSALS has been used to make claims about which features are marked and which ones are unmarked. The broad claim is that those features that are universal or present in most languages are unmarked, while those that are specific to a particular language or found in only a few languages are marked. Drawing on language typology, Zobl (1984) offered three senses in which rules can be marked. The first is typological specialization. For example, whereas English adheres to the universal tendency of languages to avoid non-extractable 'how' in 'how' + adjective phrases:

I didn't realize how comfortable I was.
*I didn't realize how I was comfortable.

French permits extraction of 'combien' in equivalent sentences. The structural properties of a language may also be marked as a result of typological inconsistency. Zobl cited the example of German and Dutch, which permit two different word orders, one in main clauses (SVO) and the other in subordinate clauses (SOV). Thus, German and Dutch word order can be considered marked in relation to English word order, which displays a high level of consistency. Finally, typological indeterminacy occurs when a structure predicted on the basis of a language's overall typology is not found. For example, English, as an SVO language, might be expected to manifest a noun + adjective ordering, but does not do so. Also, some linguistic properties—such as adverbial position—are not stringently controlled by overall typology and so can be considered 'fuzzy'. Typologically indeterminate features are seen as marked.

There is somewhat mixed evidence regarding the effects of typological markedness on the transferability of L1 features. Two general hypotheses have been investigated: (1) learners will transfer unmarked forms when the corresponding TL form is marked, and (2) learners will resist transferring marked forms, especially when the corresponding TL form is unmarked. As Hyltenstam (1984) put it:

> Unmarked categories from the native language are substituted for corresponding marked categories in the target language ... Marked structures are seldom transferred, and if they are transferred, they are much more easily eradicated from the target language.
> (1984: 43)

Zobl provided several examples of how learners tend to fall back on their L1 if the corresponding L2 rule is obscure because it is typologically inconsistent or indeterminate. For example, Zobl (1983a) noted that the following errors are common in French learners of L2 English:

*They have policeman for stop the bus.
*He do that for to help the Indians.

The 'for' + infinitive error corresponds closely to the L1 structure ('pour' + infinitive). Zobl pointed out that there are dialects of English where 'for to' occurs, that generative grammar posits 'for to' as the deep structure, and that it appears in Old and Middle English. He suggested that this creates a 'structural predisposition' for transfer. In other words, 'for to' can be considered unmarked in relation to the modern English structure. Zobl's basic point—reiterated in a number of papers (Zobl 1980a, 1980b, 1982, 1983a, 1984)—was that an L1 rule must meet certain conditions before it will be transferred; it must be productive in the L1 (not some kind of exception), it must be used frequently, and it must not be 'on the way out' historically speaking.

Evidence for the second hypothesis comes from Zobl (1984). On the grounds that extraction is typologically specified (i.e. marked), Zobl predicted that French learners of English will not accept ungrammatical English sentences such as the following:

*How many do you want oranges?
(1984: 86)

even though such extraction is permitted in L1 French. The results of a study in which a grammaticality judgement task was administered to mixed proficiency learners lent broad support to this hypothesis. Interestingly, though, the low-intermediate learners were more inclined to accept extraction than either the beginner or advanced level learners (i.e. there was evidence of U-shaped development involving transfer[5]). Zobl suggested that this may reflect the intermediate learners having noticed that English is tolerant of extraction in other grammatical areas (for example, *preposition stranding*, as in 'Who did he give it to?'). This study suggests that (1) learners do resist transferring marked forms when the corresponding TL structure is unmarked, but that (2) this resistance can be overcome if learners obtain evidence that transfer is possible. There is counter-evidence relating to (1), however. A study by Liceras (1985) suggested that learners may be prepared to accept transfer of a marked structure manifesting extraction. Liceras investigated preposition stranding by English-speaking learners of L2 Spanish. English permits extraction of the preposition in sentences like:

Who did John give the book to?

whereas Spanish does not. In this study, 43 per cent of the beginners accepted stranding in Spanish. Liceras' results, therefore, contradict Zobl's.

Indeed, not all researchers take the view that learners will resist transferring marked L1 forms. White (1987b: 266–7) argued forcefully 'that transfer is not confined to unmarked forms, that L2 learners may transfer marked forms from the L1 to the interlanguage, and that such transfer is compatible with the theory of markedness currently invoked in generative grammar'. She pointed out that the crucial test of the markedness hypothesis occurs only in situations where the L1 has a marked structure but the L2 does not. Such a situation arises for English learners of L2 French in the case of double object constructions, as in:

John gave Fred the book.

and preposition stranding, as in:

Who(m) did John give the book to?

neither of which occur in French. White found that whereas the English learners she investigated provided evidence of resisting the transfer of the marked preposition stranding construction in their grammaticality judgements, they showed a readiness to transfer the marked double object construction. Interestingly, another group of learners with different L1 backgrounds but with knowledge of English as their first L2, were prepared to transfer both structures. The learners with L1 English, therefore, behaved anomalously, in that they alone resisted transferring one of the marked structures. White suggested that one possible explanation for this exceptional behaviour could be the influence of prescriptive English mother-tongue teaching, where stranding is often presented as stylistically undesirable. White concluded that overall her study supported the view that marked forms are transferred and referred to other studies that show the same (for example, Selinker, Swain, and Dumas 1975 and Tarallo and Myhill 1983).

Some of the most convincing evidence of markedness effects on transfer can be found in studies that have examined asymmetrical patterns. A straight contrastive analysis is unable to cope with evidence that shows that a given feature (Z) is transferred in one direction (i.e. transfer of Z occurs from language X to language Y) but not in the other (i.e. transfer of Z does not occur from language Y to language X). A theory of transfer that incorporates markedness, however, can provide an explanation for such phenomena.

The study that is most commonly cited to illustrate asymmetrical patterns is Eckman (1977). Eckman investigated transfer in English learners of L2 German and German learners of L2 English, focusing on voice contrast in pairs of phonemes such as /t/ and /d/. In English this contrast exists word initially (for example, 'tin' versus 'din'), medially (for example, 'betting' versus 'bedding'), and finally (for example, 'wed' versus 'wet'). In German, however, the distinction only exists word initially and word medially; in word-final position, only voiceless stops occur. Both the German and the English L2 learners, therefore, are faced with learning to make a known distinction (i.e. voiced/voiceless stops) in a new position. Eckman argued that typologically, voice contrast in word-final position is more marked than in the other two positions. He provided evidence to show that English learners have no difficulty in learning that German has no voicing in word-final stops, but that German learners experience considerable problems in learning that English does. In other words, no transfer effects are evident when the L1 position is marked and the L2 position unmarked, but they appear when the L1 position is unmarked and the L2 marked.

In a subsequent study, Eckman (1981) provided evidence to show that devoicing of English stops in the most marked position (i.e. word finally) occurs in learners whose L1s, like English, include voicing. Cantonese learners, for instance, sometimes say 'pick' for 'pig'. This suggests, as Eckman acknowledged, that the devoicing of final stops is a 'natural' phenomenon. In the case of the German learners, therefore, the transfer may be reinforcing what is a universal tendency—a point we take up later when we consider developmental constraints on transfer.

In order to explain how markedness affects transfer, Eckman advanced the MARKEDNESS DIFFERENTIAL HYPOTHESIS (MDH):

> Those areas of difficulty that a second language learner will have can be predicted on the basis of a comparison of the native language (NL) and the target language (TL) such that:
> a those areas of the TL that are different from the NL and are relatively more marked than in the NL will be difficult;
> b the degree of difficulty associated with those aspects of the TL that are different and more marked than in the NL corresponds to the relative degree of markedness associated with those aspects;
> c those areas of the TL that are different from the NL but are not relatively more marked than the NL will not be difficult.
> (Eckman 1977: 321)

The notion of 'markedness' is defined typologically; that is, an area (X) is to be considered relatively more marked than some other area (Y), if crosslinguistically X implies the presence of Y, but Y does not imply the presence of X. An example is found in the comparison of voiced and voiceless stops in English and German discussed above. The Markedness Differential Hypothesis constituted an attempt to reformulate the CAH to take account of markedness factors. As Eckman (1985) pointed out, it differs from the CAH in a number of important ways: it seeks to explain (1) not only where learning difficulty will occur, but also the relative degree of difficulty, (2) where differences between the native and target languages will not result in difficulty, and (3) why certain structures are typically acquired before other structures. As such it constitutes a much more powerful theory. However, Eckman (2004a) also discussed the Structural Conformity Hypothesis (SCH) which addresses the role of markedness in general. This hypothesis simply claims that learners will perform better on less marked structures relative to more marked structures irrespective of any L1–L2 differences.

One problem with work involving markedness is the vagueness of the concept. Eckman (1985: 306) acknowledged this by admitting that 'one area in which more research is needed is in defining markedness relations'. The situation has not changed much since. The concept is characterized by a fuzziness that sometimes makes it difficult to determine which features are marked in relation to others. One way in which greater precision can be given to the concept is by defining it with reference to 'native speakers' own perceptions of the structure of their language' (Kellerman 1977). Thus, instead of determining markedness through reference to some linguistic description or theory, as was the case in the studies discussed in this section, it can be determined by asking native speakers whether they perceive specific features as 'infrequent, irregular, semantically or structurally opaque, or in any other way exceptional' (Kellerman 1983: 117). We now turn to Kellerman's work on markedness, or, as he calls it, PROTOTYPICALITY.

Prototypicality

In a series of papers, Kellerman (1977, 1978, 1979, 1986, 1989) sought to demonstrate that learners have perceptions of the structure of their own language, treating some structures as potentially non-transferable and others as potentially transferable, and that these perceptions influence what they actually transfer. The majority of the studies that Kellerman carried out to test this hypothesis have examined lexico-semantics. They made use of native speakers' intuitions regarding their L1.

The best known of Kellerman's studies is the 'breken' study (Kellerman 1978). This study had two stages. In the first stage, native speakers of Dutch were asked to sort seventeen sentences containing the verb 'breken' (see Table 8.8) into groups so that the sentences in each group were similar in meaning. Kellerman then examined the number of times a given pair of sentences was placed in the same group. A multidimensional scaling analysis was carried out to investigate the 'dimensions' of the 'semantic space' occupied by 'breken'. Kellerman (1979) reported two major dimensions, which he labelled 'core'/'non-core' and 'concrete'/'abstract'. In the second stage of the study, Kellerman asked 81 Dutch students of English in their first and third years at university to say which of the 17 sentences containing 'breken' they would translate using the English verb 'break'. There were clear differences in the percentage of students prepared to translate each sentence. For example, whereas 81 per cent considered 'hij brak zijn been' (= he broke his leg) translatable only 9 per cent identified 'sommige arbeiders hebben de staking gebroken' (= some workers have broken the strike) as translatable. Kellerman found that the rank order for the 'transferability' of the 17 sentences correlated poorly with the 'concrete'/'abstract' rank order derived from native-speaker intuitions. However, it correlated strongly and significantly with the 'core'/'non-core' order. This led Kellerman (1979: 51) to conclude that native speakers' intuitions about semantic space can be used to predict transferability, at least for the meanings of 'breken' and also that 'the most important factor is "coreness"'. It should be noted that Kellerman's results could not have been predicted on the basis of a contrastive analysis, as the learners clearly resisted transferring 'brekens' that had exact equivalents in English.

	Dutch	**English**
1	Hij brak zijn been.	He broke his leg.
2	'T Kopje brak.	The cup broke.
3	Na't ongeluk is hij 'n gebroken man geworden.	After the accident, he became a broken man.
4	Zij brak zijn hart.	She broke his heart.
5	De golven braken op de rot sen.	The waves broke on the rocks.
6	De lichtstralen breken in het water.	The light rays refract in the water.
7	Dankzij 'n paar grapjes, was't ijs eindelijk gebroken.	Thanks to a couple of jokes, the ice was finally broken.
8	Hij brak zijn woord.	He broke his word.
9	De man brak zijn eed.	The man broke his oath.
10	'Nood breekt wet.'	'Necessity breaks law' (a saying).
11	Zij brak't wereldrecord.	She broke the world record.
12	Zijn val werd door 'n boom gebroken.	His fall was broken by a tree.
13	Zijn stem brak toen hij 13 was.	His voice broke when he was 13.
14	Sommige arbeiders hebben de staking gebroken.	Some workers have broken the strike.
15	Welk land heeft de wapenstilstand gebroken?	Which country has broken the ceasefire?
16	Het ondergrondse verzet werd gebroken.	The underground resistance was broken.
17	N' spelletje zou de middag enigszins breken.	A game would break up the afternoon a bit.

Table 8.9 Sentences with 'breken' ranked according to coreness (prototypicality) (adapted from Kellerman 1979: 49)

In an extension of the 'breken' study, Kellerman (1979) asked 291 learners of English (including the 81 subjects in the study described above), who ranged from 12-year-olds in their second year of English to third-year university students, to assess the translatability of 9 of the 17 'breken' sentences. He found that the rank orders for the different groups of learners were 'remarkably consistent' and concluded that 'the effects of teaching, learning, and growing older do not significantly alter learners' beliefs about the *relative* transferability of the "brekens"' (1979: 52). Kellerman's study, therefore, suggests that learners' perceptions of what is transferable are not influenced by their L2 proficiency.

The concepts of 'coreness' and 'markedness' are obviously related, which Kellerman (1983) acknowledged. In this later paper, he referred to 'psycholinguistic markedness' in recognition of the importance he attached to native speakers' *perceptions* of the structure of their own language. In a further terminological switch, Kellerman (1986) referred to prototypicality to label the same basic idea. Kellerman suggested that the prototypical meaning of a lexical item, such as 'breken', is that which a dictionary gives as the primary meaning of the item.

As noted above, the bulk of Kellerman's empirical work concerned lexico-semantics—the early 'breken' study and the later 'eye' study (Kellerman 1986), for example. However, one study has also examined a syntactical structure, conditionals. Kellerman (1989) provided evidence to show that advanced Dutch learners of L2 English are likely to produce errors of this kind:

*If it would rain, they would cancel the concert in Damrosch Park
(= If it rained they would cancel the concert in Damrosch Park).

despite the fact that Dutch makes use of verb forms that are equivalent to English in main and subordinate clauses. Kellerman suggested that the failure to transfer the Dutch verb forms is the result of two tendencies. One is the learners' resistance to transferring a marked form. In this case, markedness is associated with the idea of a 'semantically transparent grammar'. It is more transparent to say 'would rain' than 'rained' because the verb is explicitly marked for future time. The second tendency is that of symmetry—the attempt to match the verb forms in the main and subordinate clauses. Kellerman pointed out that the same tendencies are also evident in both standard and non-standard varieties of the target language (English), suggesting that there is 'an interaction between natural tendencies and the native language' (1989: 111). This, he speculated, may explain why fossilization occurs.

A number of points emerge from Kellerman's work on prototypicality. The first is that it is possible to provide a clear operational definition of 'markedness' or 'prototypicality' by making use of native speakers' judgements of 'similarity'. The second is that learners have perceptions about what is transferable from their L1 and act in accordance with these perceptions. The third is that these perceptions reflect learners' ideas about what is prototypical or semantically transparent in their L1. Kellerman (1983) suggested that learners prize 'reasonableness in language' and 'attempt to keep their L2s transparent' (1983: 129). L1 structures that they perceive to be working against this principle—such as idioms that are highly metaphorical or grammatical structures where meanings are not overtly encoded—are not transferred. Finally, Kellerman showed that learners' perceptions regarding the translatability of L1 items are not influenced by their experience with the L2.

While Kellerman's work has gone a long way to teasing out the nature of the constraints on positive transfer, a few words of caution are in order. With the exception of the study on conditionals, Kellerman's research has been based on the elicitation of native speakers' intuitions regarding the similarity and translatability of decontextualized sentences. Kellerman (1986) justified this by pointing out that corpora of spontaneous speech are unlikely to supply the crucial data needed to test hypotheses. The weakness of such an approach, which Kellerman acknowledged, is that we do not know to what extent learners' judgements about what can be done accurately reflect what they actually do when using the L2. It is perhaps also wise to exercise caution about equating 'translatability' with 'transferability'. In Chapter 4 we examined a number of studies which show that differences in L1 transfer occur depending on whether the task requires translation or some other kind of performance. It does not follow that learners are prepared to make the same use of their L1 in natural speech as they are in translation.

Language distance and psychotypology

We now turn to consider another constraint on L1 transfer—the 'distance' between the native and the target languages. Distance can be viewed as both a linguistic phenomenon (i.e. by establishing the degree of actual linguistic difference between two languages) or a psycholinguistic phenomenon (i.e. by determining what learners *think* is the degree of difference between their native language and the target language). Kellerman (1977) used the term PSYCHOTYPOLOGY to refer to learners' perceptions about language distance.

Language distance is a factor in both positive and negative transfer. Evidence for this claim comes from the research conducted in Finland on the acquisition of English by Swedish-speaking and Finnish-speaking Finns. (See Sjöholm 1979; Ringbom 1976, 1978, 1987, 2007.) Finland constitutes an ideal setting for testing the effects of language distance. Whereas 93 per cent of the population speak Finnish as their mother tongue, a language distant from English, 6 to 7 per cent speak Swedish, a language much closer to English. Both groups consider themselves to belong to the same culture, however. Sjöholm, Ringbom, and their co-researchers have been able to show that Swedish-speaking Finns enjoy a substantial learning advantage over Finnish-speaking Finns. Interestingly, however, there is evidence to suggest that, contrary to the predictions of the CAH, the Finnish-speaking Finns often make fewer errors, i.e. they manifest less negative transfer. Sjöholm (1976), for instance, found fewer L1-based errors in Finnish-speaking university students than in the Swedish speakers. Ringbom (1978) was able to show that both the Swedish- and Finnish-speaking groups (both of whom are bilingual in the two languages) were much more likely to transfer word morphology from Swedish than from Finnish. Language switch was entirely from Swedish and word blends were almost always Swedish-English. In other words, whereas the Finnish speakers avoided transferring elements from their L1, preferring instead to fall back on their first L2 (Swedish), the Swedish speakers did transfer elements from their L1 but avoided doing so from their first L2 (Finnish).

Ringbom (2007) surveyed studies that have investigated the effects of language distance on transfer. He noted that similarity is a factor in L2 learning for both comprehension and for production but that there can be some differences. Thus, whereas similarity in grammar is important for both comprehension and production, lexical similarity is more important for production than for comprehension, because comprehension is often approximate and does not leave a permanent mark in the mental lexicon.

Studies of transfer in L3 acquisition where the previously learnt languages vary in their typological distance from the target language constitute an exemplary means of investigating the effects of language distance. Cenoz (2001), for example, studied lexical transfer in school students who were learning English and who spoke both Spanish and Basque, languages that differ widely in their proximity to the target language, English. She found, as predicted, that transfer from Spanish was much more common than transfer from Basque and, interestingly, that whereas the number of borrowed Spanish content and function words was the same, the number of borrowed content Basque words greatly exceeded the number of borrowed Basque function words. Cenoz suggested that this was because Basque-Spanish bilinguals often borrowed content words but not function words from Spanish and were simply using the same strategy for English.[6] Typological proximity between French and English can also explain Dewaele's (1998) finding that the lexical inventions of French L3 speakers with Dutch as their L1 and English as their L2 were more likely to draw on L2 than L1 lemmas. However, Dewaele also found that learners of L2 French with L1 Dutch and L3 English transferred more from Dutch than English. Clearly, other factors can override the effect of typological distance—for example, the learners' proficiency in the other non-native language.

Kellerman (1977) claimed that learners possess a psychotypology (a set of perceptions about language distance), and that it is this—rather than actual distance—that triggers or constrains transfer. Learners form 'projections' about what can be transferred on the basis of their beliefs as to whether the native and target languages are the 'same'—either in terms of 'linguistic detail' or 'in very general terms'. On the basis of these projections, learning decisions, or 'conversions', are made.

Kellerman's (1979) 'breken' study provides support for the idea of a psychotypology. Kellerman compared Dutch learners' judgements regarding the translatability of the 'brekens' into L2 German (a language close to Dutch) with their judgements regarding their translatability into L2 English (a language more distant from Dutch). The results showed that, in general, whereas they accepted the sentences in German, they sometimes rejected them in English. These results demonstrated a clear effect for perceived language distance.

Further evidence for the role of pyschotypology comes from Singleton's (1987) case study of Philip, an English-speaking learner of French. Philip displayed a high level of communicative efficiency in French, despite the fact that he had minimal opportunities to learn it. Singleton provided evidence to show that he borrowed extensively from his known languages (Latin, Spanish, and Irish, as well as English). Philip utilized Romance sources (i.e. those that were close to French) and, furthermore, was often able to attribute the forms he borrowed to a particular language. He demonstrated well-informed notions about which languages would assist him most in learning French. It would seem, then, that learners do have clearly defined perceptions regarding the similarities and differences between languages.

Kellerman (1979) argued that learners' psychotypology is not fixed. Rather, it is revised as they obtain more information about the target language. Thus, Dutch learners of German may start out with the assumption that the target language is very similar to their mother tongue, but later on come to adjust this perception as they recognize the many differences. Kellerman commented:

> Thus experience affects the provisional typology the learner is building up. This means that at any given moment certain NL (native language) features will be available for transfer to the given TL (target language), and others will not be.
> (1979: 40)

It follows that L1 items are not perceived as inherently 'neutral' (and so available for transfer) or 'specific' (and so not available for transfer).

According to Kellerman, learners' psychotypologies interact with their intuitive feel for prototypicality, which, it should be remembered, does not appear to change with developing proficiency. Prototypicality determines what learners are prepared to risk transferring. Their psychotypology determines what is actually transferred in performance. On the basis of the perceived distance between the native and target languages, learners decide whether to go ahead and transfer those items that they perceive to be prototypical and, therefore, potentially transferable.

Developmental factors

The constraints that developmental factors impose on L1 transfer will be considered with reference to (1) the extent to which transfer is evident at different levels of development, and (2) the complex interplay between natural principles of L2 acquisition and transfer.

The learner's general level of development

In an important survey of transfer research, Jarvis (2000: 246–7) noted a number of possible ways in which transfer might relate to PROFICIENCY:

1 LI influence decreases with increasing L2 proficiency.
2 L1 influence increases with increasing L2 proficiency.
3 L1 influence remains constant with increasing L2 proficiency.
4 L1 influence decreases, but nonlinearly.

5 L1 influence ultimately increases, but nonlinearly.
6 L1 influence ultimately never decreases nor increases but its presence continually fluctuates as L2 proficiency increases.

A strong version of the first possibility views interlanguage as a RESTRUCTURING CONTINUUM (Corder 1978a). That is, the starting point of L2 acquisition is the learner's L1, which is gradually replaced by the target language as acquisition proceeds. Such a view suggests that transfer will be more evident in the early than the later stages of development. However, although there is evidence to suggest that learners do gradually restructure their interlanguage by replacing L1 features with L2 features (see, for example, Wenk's (1986) study of French learners' acquisition of English rhythm), caution is needed. As we noted in Chapter 2, not all errors in early interlanguage are traceable to transfer; many are intralingual and resemble those found in L1 acquisition. Also, as Hakansson (2001) showed, L2 features that at first sight may appear to be the result of transfer may turn out, following careful analysis, to reflect universal developmental stages.

There is also evidence for the second possibility. Kellerman (1983), for example, pointed out that transfer errors involving pronominal copies in relative clauses can only occur when the learner is at a sufficiently advanced stage of development to produce relative clauses. Klein (1986: 27) also argued that 'the possibilities of transfer increase as knowledge of the second language increases'. Bhardwaj, Dietrich and Noyan (1988) illustrated this in a detailed study of an adult learner of L2 English. This learner was unable to express his Punjabi conception of location until he had acquired some idea of the meaning of words like 'up', 'down', and 'on', and had also developed the linguistic means to make these elements the head of definite noun phrases. Only then did the influence of L1 Punjabi appear in phrases like 'the up', 'the down', etc. Finally, as we noted earlier, it has been proposed that pragmalinguistic transfer only manifests itself when learners have developed sufficient L2 proficiency.

Nor can it be assumed that transfer errors which appear at an early stage of development are subsequently eliminated (the third possibility). Some transfer errors that appear at an initial stage continue to manifest themselves in advanced learners. Bohn and Flege (1992), for instance, found that German learners of L2 English failed to develop target-like categories for vowels that were similar but not identical to vowels in their L1, perhaps because 'category formation is blocked by equivalence classification' (1992: 156). Jarvis (2000) also cited studies that support the other three positions he mentions.

Interlanguage is clearly not a restructuring continuum. Although some aspects of L2 development, such as rhythm, may reflect the gradual replacement of L1 by target-language features, other aspects do not. In some cases, transfer is only evident in the later stages of development, while in others early transfer is never eliminated. In other words, studies have produced very mixed results, reflecting differences in the way transfer was defined and investigated. Jarvis (2000) suggested that no clear conclusion can be reached regarding the relationship between the learner's general level of proficiency and transfer. Proficiency clearly interacts with transfer but the interaction is too complex to capture with a simple generalization.

Natural principles of language acquisition

There is clear evidence to suggest that the L1 and developmental factors work together in determining the course of interlanguage—or, to put it another way, 'transfer is selective along the developmental axis' (Zobl 1980a). This selectivity is evident in a number of ways: (1) the effects of the L1 only become evident when the learner has reached a stage of development that makes transfer possible, (2) development may be retarded when a universal transitional structure arising naturally in early interlanguage corresponds to an L1 structure, and (3) development may be accelerated when an early transitional structure is not reinforced by the corresponding L1 structure.

A number of studies show that the influence of the L1 is developmentally constrained in the sense that it only occurs when the learner has reached a stage of development that provides a 'crucial similarity measure' (Wode 1976). Wode (1976, 1978, 1980) illustrated how this works. In the case of negation, for instance, the children that he studied initially manifested the universal pattern of development (see Chapter 3), but when they learnt that the negative particle could follow the verb 'be' or an auxiliary/modal verb in English, as in German, they assumed that it could also follow a main verb, as it does in German but not in English. In other words, when confronted with evidence that L2 negation worked in the same way as L1 negation, they assumed that the two languages were completely identical in this structure.[7] A similar pattern of development has been observed in the acquisition of L2 English by other learners whose L1 possesses post-verbal negation (for example, Norwegian—see Ravem 1968), but has not been observed in learners whose L1s have other ways of conveying negation—for example, Japanese (Milon 1974), Chinese (Huang 1970), or Spanish (Cazden *et al.* 1975). Wode (1978) found further evidence for developmentally constrained L1 transfer in interrogatives. He concluded that L2 learners make use of L1 syntactical knowledge in systematic ways, depending on the formal properties of the structures involved. He admitted, though, that the exact nature of the 'crucial similarity measure' is not clear.

The notion of 'developmental transfer' is also applicable to L2 phonology. Wode (1980) found that L2 phonological systems are acquired 'through the grid of the learner's L1 system' (1980: 129). Thus, elements of the L2 that are sufficiently similar to elements in the learner's L1 repertoire will be substituted by L1 elements to begin with. However, L2 elements that fall outside these 'crucial similarity measures' are not replaced with L1 elements, but instead undergo autonomous development, similar to that observed in L1 acquisition. Wode also noted that some elements appear to pose no learning difficulty even when there is no equivalent L1 element.

There is also the possibility that errors can be doubly determined—that is, reflect both 'naturalness' factors and L1 influence. Hatch (1983a) identified a number of 'naturalness' factors that are independent of the L1, such as how salient a feature is to the L2 learner and how transparent the relationship between a particular form and meaning is. In a similar vein, Andersen (1983a) also advanced the view that 'transfer can only function in conjunction with operating principles that guide language learners and users in their choice of linguistic forms to express the intended meaning' (p. 180). Examples of the kinds of universal operating principles that govern how learners acquire from the input are 'pay attention to the end of words' and 'avoid exceptions'. Andersen advanced the TRANSFER TO SOMEWHERE PRINCIPLE, which states:

> A grammatical form or structure will occur consistently and to a significant extent in interlanguage as a result of transfer *if and only if* there already exists in the L2 input the potential for (mis-)generalization from the input to produce the same form or structure.
> (p. 178)

In line with this principle, Andersen argued that transfer works in conjunction with general strategies such as simplification. (See Chapter 3.) That is, when an L1 structure matches a simplified structure in interlanguage transfer takes place. For example, learners may delete subject pronouns as a simplification strategy but if their L1 also allows for subject deletion (as is the case in Romance languages) this strategy will be reinforced. Similarly, if the 'no' + verb negative pattern found in early L2 acquisition corresponds to the L1 negative pattern, as in the case of Spanish learners of English, then the 'no' + verb pattern is likely to persist longer than is the case with other learners whose L1s do not have a matching pattern (Cazden *et al.* 1975).

Finally, the L1 has also been shown to have a facilitative effect when there is a lack of correspondence between the L1 pattern and a natural developmental pattern. Hammarberg (1979) re-analysed the data from Hyltenstam (1977) to show that, although the original conclusion (i.e. learners with different language backgrounds go through the same stages of development in acquiring Swedish negation) holds true, some learners progressed through these stages more rapidly than others and that this could be explained by their language background. Thus, English-speaking learners, whose L1 has post-verb negation, appeared to miss out the first stage (pre-verb negation). As Kellerman (1987) put it, the L1 can provide 'a leg-up along the developmental ladder'.

It is clear that an acceptable theory of transfer must take account of how learners' previous L1 knowledge interacts with the linguistic and cognitive principles responsible for the universal properties of interlanguage development. The relative strength of contributions from these two sources also needs to be determined. It is probably true to say that current work in transfer treats the linguistic and cognitive principles as primary and L1 knowledge as secondary. Gass, for instance, concluded her study of pronoun retention (see page 356) by stating that 'in considering the relationship between NL facts and language universals, the latter were found to play the leading role' (1983: 79). However, such a conclusion may not be valid for all levels of language, nor even for all aspects of syntax. Certainly, where phonology is concerned, there are grounds for considering L1 knowledge as primary, as suggested by Wode's study.

What is missing is precise information about the conditions under which L1 transfer is activated. Thus, Andersen (1983a) acknowledged that, although it is clear that transfer interacts with natural acquisitional principles, there is still 'leakage' (i.e. it is not possible to fully predict when, how, and to what extent transfer will take place). Leather and James (1991) reached a similar conclusion following their detailed survey of studies of L2 speech acquisition. This position has not changed greatly since.

Summary

We have now examined a number of constraints on L1 transfer. These are summarized below. Some of these factors are clearly external in nature, for example social factors, whereas others are equally clearly internal, for example developmental factors. Other constraints, however, have both an external and internal dimension—for example, markedness and language distance/psychotypology.

1 Sociolinguistic factors

It has been suggested that when learners attend to external norms, as they are likely to do in classroom settings, transfer will be impeded. However, learners may also make use of L1 forms in their careful style if they have a strong social motivation to do so.

2 Markedness

There is some evidence to suggest that learners are ready to transfer unmarked L1 forms, but resist transferring L1 marked forms; however, not all the research points clearly in this direction. Eckman's Markedness Differential Hypothesis constituted an improvement on the Contrastive Analysis Hypothesis by indicating how markedness interacts with linguistic difference to determine when transfer will and will not take place. Markedness, however, remains a somewhat ill-defined concept.

3 Prototypicality

Kellerman tapped native speakers' intuitions to determine which meanings of a lexical item are unmarked or 'prototypical'. Learners resist transferring non-prototypical meanings.

4 Language distance/psychotypology

The actual distance between languages affects positive transfer; learners find it easier to learn an L2 that is similar to their own language. However, perceived distance may be more important than actual distance. Kellerman suggested that whereas prototypicality influences what learners are prepared to risk transferring, their psychotypology (which changes as their proficiency develops) governs what they actually transfer.

5 Developmental factors

Whereas some researchers have claimed that negative transfer is more evident in beginners, other researchers have argued that learners may need to reach a certain stage of development before transfer of some L1 properties becomes possible. In general, except possibly where phonology is concerned, the evidence does not support the claim that interlanguage constitutes a restructuring continuum. Transfer interacts with natural principles of L2 acquisition, sometimes occurring early on and sometimes later. It can both retard and accelerate natural development.

Towards a theory of language transfer

It should be clear from the preceding section that a theory of transfer is likely to also be a general theory of L2 acquisition, in that the role of the L1 cannot easily be separated from other factors that influence development. Thus, just as there is no single general theory of L2 acquisition that receives broad acceptance within the SLA community so there is no single, widely accepted theory of L1 transfer. As Odlin (2003), in concluding his own survey of L1 transfer research, commented, 'the problems relating to crosslinguistic influence are so varied and so complex that there does not exist any really detailed theory of language transfer' (p. 475). It is clear that such a theory will have to be cognitive in nature—a behaviourist account of transfer such as that informing the Contrastive Analysis Hypothesis cannot account for the crosslinguistic effects that have been observed. The approach that I will take here is to identify some of the key elements that a cognitive theory of transfer will need to incorporate.

1 Transfer occurs in both communication and in learning

A theory of language transfer needs to account for transfer in both L2 communication and transfer in L2 learning and the relationship between them. This distinction mirrors the distinction we made in Chapter 6 between the role that input plays in comprehension and the role it plays in acquisition.

Researchers like Corder (1983) seek to explain transfer entirely in terms of communication; it is either a performance phenomenon or it is learnt as a product of repeated performance. Corder rejected the idea that learners transfer directly from their L1 into their interlanguages. Such a position is difficult to maintain, however. For one thing, there is evidence that particular transfer errors occur in whole populations with the same L1. It is far-fetched to suggest that all these learners engaged persistently in borrowing and as a result learnt the L1 structure. It is also not clear how communication transfer can account for the fossilization of certain L1-influenced structures in learners' interlanguages of the kind that Kellerman (1989) identified in advanced Dutch learners of English and Han (2000) found in Chinese learners of English.[8] Thus, whereas some instances of transfer can be put down to the use of a communication strategy, it is also necessary to recognize a more direct role for the L1 in L2 acquisition (i.e. transfer in learning).

Communication and learning transfer are related, as Corder recognized:

> ... persistent communicatively successful borrowing works backwards, as it were, and the successfully borrowed forms are eventually incorporated into the interlanguage grammar, both the correct and the incorrect.
> (1983: 94)

Ringbom (1992) also claimed a relationship between transfer in communication and learning:

> Transfer in communication is motivated by the learner's desire to comprehend or produce messages, but it may also have an effect on the process of hypothesis construction and testing, which many scholars see as central to interlanguage development. In other words, transfer in communication may lead to transfer in learning.
> (p. 106)

Ringbom suggested that it is transfer in comprehension that is most likely to induce a change in the learner's mental grammar. Such a view accords with theories that give centrality to comprehensible input in L2 acquisition. However, while acknowledging the legitimacy of Ringbom's claim, we should also recognize, as claimed by the Comprehensible Output Hypothesis (see Chapter 6), that L2 output and, therefore, transfer in production can also contribute significantly to interlanguage development.

2 Transfer arises as a result of both differences and similarities between the target language and the L1

The central claim of the Contrastive Analysis Hypothesis was that differences between the target language and the L1 resulted in learning difficulty and similarities in learning ease. However, as we have seen, this was not substantiated by research. In fact, as Kleinmann (1978) showed, when a target language feature is notably different from an L1 feature a 'novelty effect' is evident and acquisition may actually be facilitated. Conversely, a close correspondence between two features can result in learning difficulty. Major and Kim (1996), for example, showed that Korean learners of English found it easier to learn dissimilar sounds like /z/ than similar sounds like /dʒ/ (as in 'Joan') when acquisition was measured in terms of rate of acquisition. As a result of such studies, it is now generally accepted that transfer can take place as a result of both difference between and similarity with the target language and that it is similarity that is the more important (Ringbom 2007). But what is not clear is *when* differences or similarities will lead to transfer and also on what aspect of acquisition the transfer will impact (for example, production errors as in Kleinmann's study or rate of acquisition as in Major and Kim's study). In order to resolve these problems it is necessary to consider how similarity/difference interacts with other factors.

3 Transfer works in conjunction with other factors

The constraints on transfer were considered in detail in the previous section. It is because transfer is influenced by other factors of both an external and internal nature that it will not be possible to develop a theory that addresses transfer in isolation. Transfer needs to be incorporated into a general theory of L2 acquisition.

The research that has investigated the various constraints on transfer has helped us to understand what is transferred and what is not and also when transfer takes place and when it does not. However, as Odlin (2003) pointed out 'there remains much uncertainty about how many kinds of constraints there are or what their exact nature is' (p. 454). It is, therefore, unlikely that any theory that accounts satisfactorily for these constraints will emerge in the near future. What is more likely is that researchers will continue to focus on specific hypotheses that address the role of particular constraints.

4 Transfer is both a conscious and subconscious process

In the case of communication transfer, learners are likely to be fully aware that they are drawing on their L1. In the case of learning transfer, different positions have been advanced. Krashen (1983) argued that transfer played very little role in 'acquisition' (a subconscious process) but could contribute to 'learning' (a conscious process). Other researchers (for example, Möhle and Raupach 1989), however, have argued that L2 development can involve both subconscious and conscious transfer. Schachter's (1983) cognitive account of transfer is also compatible with such a view. Schachter proposed that transfer be viewed as a source of information that learners can use to construct and reconstruct hypotheses by means of inductive inferencing (scanning data, observing regularities, and generalizing) and deductive inferencing (testing hypotheses by looking in the first instance for confirming evidence and subsequently for disconfirming evidence). Hypothesis testing, whether of the inductive or deductive kind, can take place consciously or subconsciously.

A related issue is whether transfer contributes to learners' L2 IMPLICIT KNOWLEDGE or to their EXPLICIT KNOWLEDGE or to both. This distinction between explicit and implicit knowledge is considered in depth in Chapter 9.

5 Transfer is both conceptual and linguistic

If the Whorfian Hypothesis is accepted in either its weak form (i.e. language predisposes people to view the world in certain ways) or its strong forms (i.e. language 'binds' people to a particular way of viewing the world), then it follows that conceptual transfer is likely. Two issues arise for a theory of L2 acquisition that incorporates transfer. The first is when, how, and to what extent conceptual differences between the L1 and the target language result in the transfer. As we have seen in Yoshioka's (2005) study of gesture, conceptual differences do not necessarily lead to transfer. The second issue is whether there is L2–L1 transfer (i.e. whether the acquisition of an L2 results in learners acquiring new ways of viewing the world). Before these issues can be addressed, however, it will be necessary to identify valid and reliable ways of distinguishing conceptual and linguistic transfer.

6 Transfer is ultimately a subjective phenomenon

Many years ago, Lado (1957) acknowledged that individual learners respond differently to the problems that arise as a result of differences between the target language and their L1. He commented: 'Not all the speakers of a language will have exactly the same amount of difficulty with each problem' (p. 72). Odlin (2003) also recognized the inevitability of individual differences as a result of the subjective nature of L1 transfer:

> Much of what is called crosslinguistic influence depends on the individual judgments of language learners and bilinguals that there exist certain crosslinguistic similarities.
> (p. 443)

The nature of learners' judgements will depend in part on inherent linguistic factors such as those that determine the distance between languages but even then subjectivity is evident. Kellerman found individual differences in his Dutch learners' judgements regarding the translatability of sentences involving 'breken'. Over and above linguistic factors, a variety of individual learner factors have been found to influence transfer—age, motivation, literacy, and social class. As Odlin pointed out these 'combine in myriad ways that make the learning situations of virtually all individuals unique'. Odlin's comment points to the necessity of incorporating individual difference factors into an account of transfer. However, this constitutes an enormous challenge to theory development, not least because any theory must necessarily identify and explain general patterns of behaviour.

Conclusion: problems in the study of transfer

There have been considerable advances made in the study of L1 transfer, not least in the methods used to investigate it. (See Jarvis 2000.) In early studies, there was a tendency to claim that any L2 error that showed a similarity to an L1 feature was the result of transfer. Jackson (1981), for instance, argued that non-inverted WH– questions (such as 'How I do this?') were indicative of the L1 influence in Punjabi-speaking learners of English. As we have seen, such conclusions are not warranted unless it can be shown that these errors are not 'developmental' (i.e. do not occur in the interlanguages of all learners). There is plenty of evidence that non-inverted WH– questions are universal features of L2 acquisition. More recent studies have avoided such misjudgements by carrying out learner comparisons (comparing the output of learners with L1s that differ with regard to the presence or absence of particular linguistic features). Another promising approach, illustrated in a number of studies referred to in this chapter (for example, Pavlenko and Jarvis 2002) involves the bidirectional study of transfer. Yet another is the study of crosslinguistic influences in third language acquisition, as in the collection of papers in Cenoz, Hufheisen, and Jessner (2001). Both the crosslinguistic, bidirectional and third language acquisition studies not only result in more reliable research but also provide insights not readily available from the more traditional contrastive approach.

There are still a number of problems faced by transfer researchers, however. We will consider two: (1) the problem of how to distinguish communication and learning transfer, and (2) the problem of how to compare two languages. Neither problem is specific to the study of transfer, of course. All L2 acquisition researchers face the general problem of distinguishing what is strategic—the product of some compensatory strategy—and what is evidence of the learner's L2 knowledge system. Also, comparative linguists and writers of pedagogical grammars have to cope with the theoretical and practical difficulties involved in comparing two languages. Both problems, however, seem quite central to the work of transfer researchers.

We have seen that it is possible to make a clear theoretical distinction between communication and learning transfer. It is less clear, however, whether these two types of transfer can be distinguished empirically, given that the main data for the study of transfer come from language performance. The problem is acute because, as Kasper pointed out, 'learners sometimes transfer in want of a better solution even though they consider a given concept non-transferable' (1984b: 20). Not surprisingly, most researchers ignore this problem and assume that evidence of transfer in performance (usually production) is also evidence of transfer in learning. One solution lies in collecting introspective data from the learner, as in Poulisse's (1990) study of communication strategies. In this study, the learners were invited to comment retrospectively on the strategies they used to describe referents for which they had no available L2 word. They frequently commented on their L1-based strategies without being prompted. Introspective data may also be helpful in identifying instances of avoidance.

Comparisons of the target language and the learners' previously acquired languages are still essential to the study of transfer. Many of the problems that arise in comparing two languages were evident in the early days of contrastive analysis. One was that contrastive analysts generally failed to meet the criteria of descriptive and explanatory adequacy that any description of language must meet. They faced the same challenges found in the study of single languages—how to develop comprehensive descriptions, to what extent the linguistic data should be idealized, and how to cater for the interaction of linguistic subsystems (the influence that one system, say discourse, has on other systems). There was the problem of equivalence—whether it was possible to find a theoretically sound basis for comparing two languages. Sajavaara (1981a) listed the procedures that could be followed: (1) identify linguistic categories common to the two languages and compare how they are realized in each language, (2) search for equivalents of a given category in one language in the other, (3) compare rules or hierarchies of rules in the two languages, (4) examine how a given semantic category is realized in the two languages, and (5) investigate how a given language function is performed in both languages. All of these procedures were used, but there was little agreement about which constituted the optimal method. However, these problems are perhaps less acute now than earlier, given that less emphasis is placed on preparing comprehensive contrastive analyses and more on the detailed examination of specific linguistic elements.

Crosslinguistic effects are extensive, varied, and persistent. They are also illuminative of the cognitive processes involved in L2 use and acquisition. No theory of L2 use or acquisition can be complete without an account of L1 transfer. This will become apparent in the next two chapters when we consider a variety of cognitive theories, such as the Competition Model in which the L1 constitutes a major factor, and also theories based on *linguistic universals*. In both, the learner's L1 is a central factor.

Notes

1 This example of left-branching in Japanese is taken from Kamimoto *et al.* (1992: 268).
2 Ervin-Tripp's claim amounts to the assertion that transfer will be more common in classroom than in naturalistic language learning. This claim is not supported by research, which in fact suggests the opposite, as is clear in the discussion of transfer in relation to social setting on page 380–1.
3 I am grateful to Kellerman for pointing out to me the problems of measuring the frequency of transfer effects at different language levels.
4 I am grateful to Kellerman for helping to clarify the role of social context in language transfer and, in particular, for pointing out that learners can behave very differently, where transfer is concerned, inside and outside the classroom.

5 U-shaped behaviour involving transfer in an early stage can also be investigated by means of pseudo-longitudinal studies. These involve the cross-sectional examination of groups of learners with the same L1 but different stages of L2 development. The developmental pattern is evident in the differences between the groups. One difficulty with this approach, however, concerns how to determine what stage of development each learner in the sample has reached. Given that learners can produce the same correct feature at both an early and a late stage of development, this is obviously not an easy task.

6 Jarvis has pointed out to me that Cenoz' interpretation of her results is suspect. In his comments as a reviewer of this chapter, he argues that there are only two clear findings from her study: (1) learners transfer more from Spanish than from Basque, and (2) whereas transfer of both content and function words seems to occur relatively freely from Spanish, transfer of function words from Basque is very rare.

7 Jarvis has pointed out to me that the German children's transfer of the German negation pattern once they had found some evidence for it in the L2 contradicts the claim made earlier that learners' perceptions are not influenced by their experience with the L2. The children in Wode's study may have been influenced by the L2 in this case because they preferred a simple solution to the problem of negation in English. That is, they were looking for a single negative pattern that applied to all verbs (copula and main verbs) as in German. This solution was triggered by their discovery that English permits post-verbal negation with the copula.

8 Again, I am grateful to Kellerman for pointing out these problems with a communication-based account of transfer.

9
Cognitive accounts of second language acquisition

Introduction

In the last chapter we noted that language transfer has been increasingly understood as a cognitive process; that is, L2 learners make strategic use of their L1 in the process of understanding and producing messages in the L2 and in the acquisition of an L2. In this chapter, we will examine a number of other accounts of L2 acquisition which adopt a broadly 'cognitivist' stance in the sense that they see language acquisition as involving mental processes that explain how L2 knowledge is represented and acquired. In the following chapter we will examine cognitive accounts of L2 communication.

All of these accounts draw heavily on cognitive psychology, so it is useful to begin with a definition of this area of study:

> ... the subject matter of cognitive psychology consists of the main internal psychological processes that are involved in making sense of the environment and deciding what action might be appropriate. These processes include attention, perception, learning and memory, language, problem solving, reasoning and thinking.
> (Eysenck 2001: 1)

For reasons of space, I will focus on the SLA research that has examined these processes as they occur in L2 acquisition and use and make only passing reference to the theories and research in cognitive psychology that have informed SLA enquiry. Readers wishing to learn more about cognitive psychology are referred to Eysenck's (2001) excellent textbook and to Robinson's applications of the psychological research to SLA (for example, Robinson 1995a and 2003).

In the context of SLA, two somewhat different cognitive paradigms can be identified. One of these draws on a COMPUTATIONAL MODEL of L2 acquisition (Lantolf 1996), which characterizes acquisition in terms of input, the internal computation of data from the input, and output. This is the mainstream model informing SLA. The second account is perhaps better characterized as sociocognitive rather than cognitive. It affords a sociocultural explanation of L2 use and acquisition by viewing acquisition as originating in use and involving subsequent processes of internalization (Lantolf and Thorne 2006). Both the computational and the sociocultural paradigms share a point in common: they treat L2 acquisition as essentially similar in nature to other kinds of learning in drawing on a common set of processes. In this respect both paradigms contrast with the linguistic paradigm, which treats linguistic knowledge as unique and separate from other knowledge systems, and sees acquisition as guided by mechanisms that are (in part at least) specifically linguistic in nature. This chapter addresses theory and research in the computational paradigm. Chapter 11 examines sociocultural SLA and Chapter 12 deals with linguistic accounts of L2 acquisition.

This chapter is divided into three main subsections. The first deals with the representation of L2 knowledge (for example, the distinction between IMPLICIT and EXPLICIT KNOWLEDGE), the second with the cognitive processes involved in the acquisition of L2 knowledge (for example, the role of ATTENTION), and the third with cognitive theories of L2 acquisition (for example, CONNECTIONISM). While distinguishing representation and acquisition in this way is somewhat artificial (and, to an extent, controversial) it reflects the frequently made distinction between 'the representational problem' and the 'developmental problem' in psycholinguistic studies of language acquisition (for example, Bialystok and Sharwood Smith 1985; White 2003b). First, though, the chapter offers a brief outline of the computational model.

The computational model

In Chapter 6, we examined Gass' (1997a) model of second language acquisition. Gass distinguished (1) apperceived (or noticed) input, (2) comprehended input, (3) INTAKE, (4) INTEGRATION, and (5) output. Gass' model is a standard computational model, reflecting the information-processing approach common in cognitive psychology. Eysenck (2001) identified four key assumptions of this approach. First, input (information) derived from the environment is handled through cognitive processing systems such as attention, perception, and SHORT-TERM MEMORY. Second, as a result of such processing, information (i.e. input in SLA terms) is modified in systematic ways. Third, this processing draws on processes and structures such as WORKING MEMORY and LONG-TERM MEMORY, which, as McLaughlin and Heredia (1996) noted, can be isolated and studied separately. Fourth, the information processing that occurs in people is similar to that in computers—hence, the choice of main heading for this section. Over the years, various information processing models have been promulgated. The simplest is a serial-processing model, according to which processing takes place 'bottom-up', instigated by the input and with one only one process occurring at a time. More complex models recognize that cognition involves a mixture of bottom-up and top-down processing (involving schemata stored in long-term memory) and also that processes can occur in parallel. Gass' model is essentially a simple, serial-processing one.

Information-processing models typically propose three types of memory stores: (1) sensory stores (sometimes referred to as 'sensory buffers' in theories of attention), which are capable of holding information only very briefly, (2) a short-term store that includes working memory, where information is held for a short but sufficient period of time to enable processing to take place, and (3) a long-term store. It is the sensory stores that enable features of the input to be apperceived. They are modality specific. An iconic store is responsible for visual information while the echoic store handles auditory information. Most of the work in SLA discussed in this chapter has addressed the auditory modality. Working memory is where the key processes of perception, attention, and rehearsal take place and is of central importance in cognitive SLA. A key distinction is between a capacity-limited view of working memory and a multiple-resources view. As Robinson (2003) pointed out, much of the cognitively oriented research in SLA (for example, Skehan 1998b; VanPatten 1996) has assumed that working memory is limited in capacity. An implication of such a model is that L2 learners, especially beginners, will experience difficulty in attending to more than one aspect of language (for example, form or meaning) simultaneously and thus will have to prioritize one at the expense of the other(s). Capacity-limited models also assume a single working-memory resource. In contrast, a multiple resource model of working memory proposes that there are separate resource pools (for example, for auditory and visual processing) with competition for resources taking place within but not between pools. Such a model predicts, for example, that while learners will struggle to attend simultaneously to meaning and form in the auditory medium they would experience no difficulty in attending to one aspect of language in the auditory medium and another in the visual medium. A multiple-resource model of working memory has proved less popular with SLA researchers but, as we will see, Robinson himself favours such a model, while increasingly SLA is influenced by Baddeley's (1986) theory of working memory which distinguishes three separate components (a phonological loop and a visual/spatial sketchpad coordinated by means of a central executive) and which is a clear example of a multiple-resource model.

The final component of an information-processing model is long-term memory—where the products of processing in working memory are stored and where restructuring of existing knowledge as a result of processing takes place. This corresponds to the 'integration' component of Gass' model. In contrast to working memory, long-term memory is seen as unlimited in capacity and capable of holding information for long periods of time. Cognitive psychologists distinguish various types of long-term memory—episodic versus semantic memory, declarative versus procedural memory and explicit versus implicit memory. However, as Eysenck (2001) pointed out, it is not easy to distinguish these dichotomies. He commented:

> ... there have been clear changes over the years in the definitions of key concepts such as declarative memory, procedural memory, explicit memory, implicit memory, episodic memory, and semantic memory ... As a result, it is increasingly difficult to decide the extent to which different theories actually make significantly different predictions. (p. 213)

SLA researchers have drawn extensively on the distinction between declarative/procedural memory and EXPLICIT/IMPLICIT MEMORY and the types of L2 knowledge associated with each. In particular, these distinctions have been invoked in discussions of the role of 'awareness' in L2 acquisition.

The cognitive processes involved in L2 acquisition cannot be observed directly. Wigglesworth (2005) discussed three principal methods for investigating them: (1) introspection and verbal protocols, (2) learners' talk about language, and (3) measures derived from learner discourse. The first of these includes both concurrent and retrospective reports by learners, with Wigglesworth advocating the former (for example, THINK-ALOUD) because the latter are unlikely to reveal much about processes that are unconscious or involve only low levels of awareness. Learners' talk about language has been used extensively by Swain (see Chapters 6 and 11) to investigate noticing, hypothesis testing, and attention to feedback. Measures derived from learner discourse have been used to investigate the effects of planning on the FLUENCY, COMPLEXITY, and ACCURACY of L2 production, as in a series of studies conducted by Skehan and Foster (for example, Foster and Skehan 1996; Skehan and Foster 1997). (See Chapters 4 and 10.) All three methods are based on learners' performance of tasks in the L2 and thus are essentially descriptive in nature. N. Ellis (1999) also recommended the use of laboratory-type experimentation and simulation to investigate cognitive processes. As we will see, SLA researchers have followed in the steps of cognitive psychologists in making use of artificial languages to investigate specific processes. (See, for example, DeKeyser 1997.) Computerized connectionist simulation systems have also been devised to investigate the mechanisms involved in extracting regularities from sets of input data. (See, for example, N. Ellis and Schmidt 1997.) In the sections that follow we will find examples of studies that have used all of these methods.

This quick sketch of the structure and processes contained in the computational model provides a basis for examining how SLA researchers have set out to explain the nature of L2 representation and L2 acquisition. We will now examine each of these in turn.

The representation of L2 knowledge

Any theory of L2 acquisition must specify the nature of L2 knowledge—that is, address how L2 knowledge is represented in the minds of learners. We will begin with a brief account of (1) how early interlanguage theory represented L2 knowledge, and then move on to consider a number of more recent accounts of a broadly cognitive nature, (2) the extension of early interlanguage theory to incorporate variable L2 knowledge, (3) functionalist views of L2 knowledge, (4) implicit versus explicit L2 knowledge, (5) declarative versus procedural L2 knowledge, and (6) dual-mode representation.

Early interlanguage theory

INTERLANGUAGE, the term coined by Selinker (1972)[1] refers to both the internal linguistic system that a learner constructs at a single point in time ('an interlanguage') and to the series of interconnected systems that characterize the learner's progress over time ('interlanguage' or 'the interlanguage continuum'). This construct has been subject to both cognitive and linguistic interpretations, but we will be concerned with only the former here.

Cognitive theories of interlanguage postulated that learners build mental grammars of the L2. These grammars account for performance in the same way as a native-speaker grammar; that is, learners draw on the 'rules' they have constructed to interpret and produce utterances. Interlanguage is said to be systematic because learners behave 'grammatically' in the sense that they draw on the rules they have internalized—a view that casts doubt on the use of the term ERROR itself (Jakobovits 1970; Cook 1971), as learners' utterances are only erroneous with reference to target-language norms, not to the norms of their own grammars.

These mental grammars are perceived as dynamic and subject to rapid change. Thus, the interlanguage continuum consists of a series of overlapping 'grammars'. Each grammar shares some rules with the previously constructed grammar, but also contains some new or revised rules. A rule has the status of a 'hypothesis'. Each grammar or interlanguage is likely to be characterized by competing rules, or, as Corder (1976) put it, there will be 'several concurrent hypotheses, leading to a set of coexistent approximative systems'. It is this that accounts for systematic variability in learner performance.

One of the outcomes of this view of the interlanguage continuum is that L2 acquisition is characterized not by 'simplification' but by 'complexification'. Each grammar the learner builds is more complex than the one that preceded it. Corder (1977b) suggested that the learner's starting point is the same as in L1 acquisition: a 'basic' system consisting of lexical items and a few simple rules for sequencing them. This system constitutes the 'initial hypothesis' and may be universal (i.e. all languages, when stripped down, result in the same basic system). It follows that L2 knowledge entails a RECREATION CONTINUUM rather than a RESTRUCTURING one; that is, the starting point is not the full L1 which is gradually replaced by L2 rules and items, but a simple, reduced system of the L1, which is gradually complexified. Corder suggested that this explains why interlanguage systems manifest universal properties, particularly in the early stages of development. (See Chapter 3.)

As we will see later, the nature of the learner's 'initial hypothesis' is controversial. If, as Corder suggested, the starting point is the same as in L1 acquisition—a claim that is in itself controversial—then the question arises as to whether this starting point is some remembered early version of the L1, which is complexified through the general process of hypothesis-testing (Corder's position and one that is essentially cognitive), or whether it is the same innate knowledge of language which all children bring to the task of learning their L1, as proposed by Chomsky (1965). In essence, this is an argument between a cognitivist and a linguistic explanation of L2 acquisition. In addition, as we saw in Chapter 8, there are grounds for believing that in some aspects of language (for example, phonology) the starting point may be the L1 and that interlanguage may be, in part at least, a restructuring continuum.

Variable L2 knowledge

Theories that view L2 knowledge as inherently variable have drawn extensively on concepts from variationist sociolinguistics (see Chapter 4), but they are essentially cognitive in nature as they have sought to account for the way in which learners organize their L2 knowledge. These theories can all be seen as extensions of early interlanguage theory.

Tarone's 'Capability Continuum'

Tarone (1983) considered three paradigms for studying interlanguage. According to the 'Homogeneous Competence Paradigm', as reflected in Adjemian (1976):

> learners have grammatical intuitions which the linguist may use as data in modelling that competence. Variation is a phenomenon which occurs in speech performance and not in the grammatical intuitions on the basis of which the 'grammar itself' is written.
> (1976: 150)

This paradigm, which is the one that informs the linguistic theories to be considered in Chapter 12, is inadequate according to Tarone, because it does not satisfactorily account for the results of variability research, which show that the CAREFUL STYLE is more permeable to invasion from the target language than the VERNACULAR STYLE. The Homogeneous Competence Paradigm predicts the opposite.

Tarone's own model, the Capability Continuum, is based on the Labovian paradigm. CAPABILITY is preferred to 'competence' because she needed a term that refers broadly to the linguistic knowledge that underlies '*all* regular language behaviour' (1983: 151). The learner's capability, therefore, is evident in the regularities observed in production and perception, writing and reading, and making judgements on grammaticality. Tarone suggested that it is composed of 'regularities' (defined as 'patterns which underlie phenomena in observed behaviour') rather than 'rules' (defined as 'normative standards of behaviour'), but still constitutes 'an abstract linguistic system' which exists apart from its use (1983: 151–2). Capability consists of a continuum of styles, ranged from the 'careful' to the 'vernacular', and is, therefore, heterogeneous. (See Figure 9.1.) The vernacular style is considered to be 'primary' in the sense that it is the most stable and consistent.

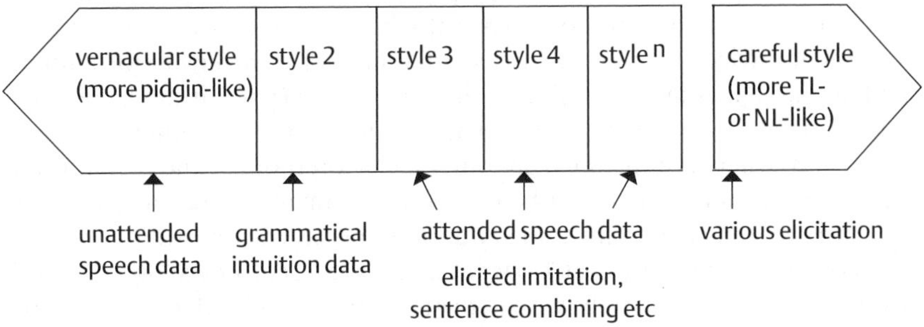

Figure 9.1 Tarone's interlanguage continuum

Tarone's theory is more than just an attempt to model L2 representation. It also provides an explanation of how knowledge is acquired. In fact, like other models to be considered later in this chapter, it blurs the distinction between representation and development. The model posits that new forms enter interlanguage in two ways: (1) directly into the learner's vernacular style, in which case they may subsequently 'spread' to more formal styles over time, and (2) initially into the learner's most formal style, manifest only when the learner is paying close attention to speech production, and subsequently by 'spreading' into the less formal styles where they replace those forms that entered these styles earlier. In the case of (1), there may be a tendency for the new forms to appear in a 'universal order'.

Whereas Tarone's 1983 paper did not offer much detail about the key notion of 'spreading', her 1988 book did, drawing on the work of Dickerson (1975) and Gatbonton (1978). Dickerson proposed that learners initiate change in one linguistic environment, which then spreads to other linguistic environments in a clear order. Thus, learners move systematically towards target-language norms over time. Gatbonton saw acquisition as proceeding in two phases: in the acquisition phase and the replacement phase. (See Chapter 4.)

Ellis' Variable Competence Model

In my account of L2 variability, I assumed that the way language is stored is a reflection of the way it is used. There are two strands to this position. One draws on the idea of a relationship between a differentiated knowledge store and different types of language use, and the other on the idea of L2 representation as form–function networks.

Like Bialystok (1982; see discussion later in this chapter), I saw L2 knowledge as represented differently in the mind of the learner according to how analysed and how automatic it is (Ellis 1984a). The unanalysed/analysed and the non-automatic/automatic distinctions constitute intersecting continua in which any L2 item or rule is located. In the case of native-speaker competence, the most usual form of representation is unanalysed/automatic, although many native speakers, especially literate ones, also have access to analysed knowledge. Language use is differentiated according to the amount of planning that takes place. Thus, following Ochs (1979), it can be planned or unplanned. PLANNED DISCOURSE is discourse that is thought out prior to expression, whereas unplanned discourse lacks forethought and preparation. UNPLANNED DISCOURSE can be considered primary in that it is the type found in everyday communication and spontaneous conversation.

According to this VARIABLE COMPETENCE MODEL, L2 development takes two forms. Learners learn how to activate items and rules that are available initially only in planned discourse for use in unplanned discourse. In this respect, my position is similar to that of Tarone. Also, learners acquire new L2 rules through participating in different types of discourse. In other words, as Widdowson (1979b: 62) suggested, 'we create discourse and commonly bring new rules into existence by so doing'. It is this latter type of development that I explored in my subsequent work on variability by drawing on the idea of form–function networks.

The starting point for my ideas on how learners construct variable form–function networks as a result of participating in discourse is free variation. (See Chapter 4 for an account of this.) I suggested (see Ellis 1985c) that the learner's interlanguage is composed of competing rules at any stage of its development. In some cases, these competing rules are systematic, as they relate to situational and contextual factors. In other cases, the competing forms are used arbitrarily, in free variation. I argued that new linguistic forms emerge in all natural languages 'quite spontaneously', and that interlanguage is no different. However, it is inefficient to operate a system in which two forms have total identity of function, so learners seek to remove free variation by (1) eliminating forms that are deemed non-standard or unnecessary, and (2) building form–function networks in which different forms are used to perform different functions. An implication of this position is that interlanguages do not invariably constitute 'systems' and, also, that, at any one stage of development, there may be parts of a learner's interlanguage that are organized as a system and parts that are not. In Ellis (1999b) I further developed this theory (drawing on Towell, Hawkins, and Bazergui 1993) by proposing a series of stages involved in the development of each grammatical subsystem. (See Table 9.1.) I also argued that underlying this pattern of development is the distinction between linguistic knowledge as 'items' (i.e. discrete features, words, and formulaic sequences) and as 'system' (i.e. as rules) and that L2 knowledge typically commences as the former and then gradually transmogrifies into the latter. As we will see, this distinction also underlies theorizing based on the implicit/explicit knowledge distinction and reflects the view expressed in Chapter 3 that rule-based knowledge originates in the FORMULAIC SEQUENCES that learners have internalized.

Stage	**Description**
1 Non-linguistic	Learners operate in accordance with an 'accept what I am offered' strategy. During this stage they have no awareness of the form–meaning mapping.
2 Acquisition	Learners operate an overgeneralization-phase strategy, selecting one form and using it in contexts that in target-language use would require two forms.
3 Replacement	Learners allow an alternate form into their interlanguage but are unable to determine the functional differences between the two forms. This phase is characterized by free variation.
4 Interlanguage	Learners now begin to use the two-forms phase systematically but in accordance with interlanguage norms rather than target-language norms. This stage may be characterized by categorical use or systematic variation.
5 Completion	Learners now use the two-forms phase in accordance with target-language norms, which may be categorical or variable.

Table 9.1 Stages in the development of a grammatical subsystem (based on Towell, Hawkins, and Bazergui 1993)

Preston's Socio-psycholinguistic Model

Preston's model, which is shown in Figure 9.2, rests on the idea of the learner's knowledge of the L2 as 'a complex variation space' (Preston 1989: 265), which can be accounted for in terms of (1) planning, (2) depth, and (3) stability. The concept of planning is envisaged as a continuum, as in Ellis' Variable Competence Model. Preston, however, saw 'planning' not just as something that learners do when using their knowledge, but as actually reflected in the knowledge system itself. He talked of the 'planned and unplanned sides of learner systems'. Learners will vary as to which side—or type of knowledge—is most fully represented in their interlanguage systems.

The 'depth' dimension of the model is an attempt to take account of the social uses that learners make of their variable systems. Thus, there are likely to be different frequencies of use that reflect gender, class, age, genres, relationships, etc. These differences reflect the attempts of learners to use their knowledge functionally for social purposes. Learners, like native speakers, will use forms symbolically for these purposes.

'Stability' is a characteristic of both the surface structure of the learner's interlanguage system and also of the way this system is used to convey social meanings. In the case of the former, a stable system is one where there is an absence of variation because no new forms are entering the system and

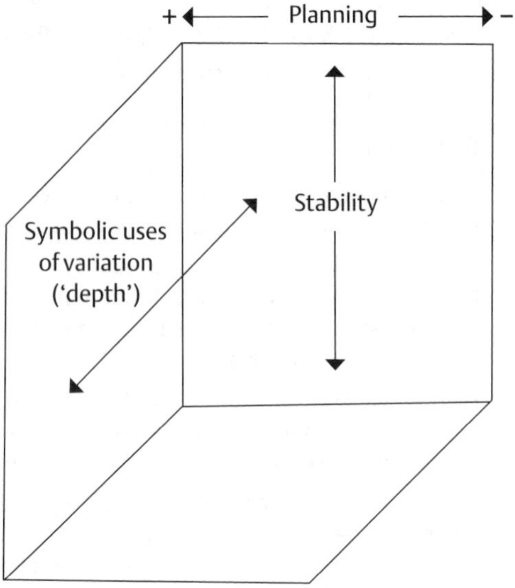

Figure 9.2 An integrated model of language variation (from Preston 1989)

existing forms have become categorical. In the case of the latter, 'stability' is evident when continued association of a given feature with a given social meaning halts or slows the development of that feature. When this kind of stability is found, fossilization may occur.

Preston raised the interesting possibility that learners will differ in the extent to which the variability of their systems is a product of the planning or the depth dimensions. He noted that 'where there is no real community of learners and no previous accretion of symbolic depth, ... change will be more linguistically determined along the shallow, surface plane of the model proposed here'. Thus classroom learners are more likely to manifest planning than social variability, although, as Preston was careful to point out, even these learners are likely to assign some symbolic value to developing forms.

Preston (2002) further addressed the nature of the L2 'grammar' that learners develop from a sociolinguistic perspective. He proposed that learners develop grammars consisting of variable rules that account for their choice of linguistic forms in accordance with social factors (responsible for external variation) and linguistic context (responsible for internal variation). A key feature of this later modelling of linguistic competence is that some features may be 'weaker' than others. Whereas Gregg (1990) and Chomsky (1988) claimed that elements of LINGUISTIC COMPETENCE are either there or not there, Preston argued that they may be 'less there'. He proposed that those features that are learnt as part of the 'vernacular' are more deeply entrenched than those features that are learnt 'post-vernacular'. In other words he conceived of 'grammars that have post-vernacular areas in which the constructions are 'there' in competence but 'weaker' (Preston 2002: 150).

Finally, Preston acknowledged that an elaborated psycholinguistic model of learner variability would also need to incorporate a memory and processing component.

Final comment on variability theories

While there can be no argument that learner-language is variable (see Chapter 4), there is considerable disagreement as to whether this variability is to be viewed as an aspect of linguistic competence (i.e. a matter of representation) or simply of performance. Whereas Tarone, myself, and Preston have advanced the case for viewing the learner's linguistic competence as variable, Gregg (1990) has viewed it as homogeneous, consisting entirely of categorical rules, and has relegated variability to the lesser status of a purely performance phenomenon. This constitutes a fundamental disagreement about the nature of the learner's interlanguage. Needless to say the cognitive accounts of L2 acquisition examined in this chapter very clearly favour the variationists, whereas the linguistic accounts considered in Chapter 12 promote the idealized view favoured by Gregg.

Functionalist views of L2 knowledge

Functionalist theories of L2 acquisition share a number of concerns with variability theories. For instance, both are concerned not just with how linguistic knowledge is represented in the mind of the learner, but also with how this knowledge is used in discourse. Also, both types assume that syntax cannot be considered separately from semantics and pragmatics and, as such, are opposed to accounts of L2 acquisition based on a clear distinction between LINGUISTIC and PRAGMATIC COMPETENCE (for example, Gregg 1989).

In a FUNCTIONALIST MODEL, learning a language is seen as a process of mastering a number of fundamental functions of language—spatial and temporal reference, for example—and the linguistic means for conveying them. Thus, from this perspective, L2 knowledge is comprised of a network of form–function mappings. Initially the network is a relatively simple one but it gradually complexifies as the learner acquires new L2 forms, matches these to existing functions and uses them to realize new functions.

This functional view of interlanguage development is closely associated with the work of Klein and Perdue. According to Klein (1991) language acquisition is functionally driven:

> It is ... functions ... which drive the learner to break down parts of the input and to organize them into small subsystems, which are reorganized whenever a new piece from the flood of input is added, until eventually the target system is reached (or more or less approximated).
> (p. 220)

Perdue (1991) reported a study demonstrating how this takes place. As part of the EUROPEAN SCIENCE FOUNDATION PROJECT ON ADULT SECOND

LANGUAGE ACQUISITION, the study examined how two learners handled spatial and temporal reference. Initially, the learners acquired a few simple words to express 'essential' reference and relations (for example, 'up'/'above' and 'left'/'right'), they used transparent form–meaning relationships, they decomposed complex relations into simpler ones (for example, instead of 'between two chairs' they used circumlocutions like 'side of chair, side of other chair, middle'), and they relied on the inferencing capacities of their interlocutors. This was characteristic of a 'pre-basic variety'. (See Chapter 3.) Some learners progress beyond this by GRAMMATICALIZING their interlanguage but other learners do not. Perdue and Klein (1992) reported on a study of two adult Italian learners of L2 English in London, who differed in the extent to which their interlanguages became 'grammaticalized' over time. Both learners began by producing very simple utterances, but whereas one of the learners, Andrea, proceeded to 'grammaticalize' his speech over a period of about 20 months (for example, by developing systematic verb morphology and case markings), the other, Santo, maintained the 'basic variety' throughout.

Functionalist researchers such as Perdue and Klein also emphasize the importance of discourse-contextual constraints on linguistic representation and interlanguage development. As Perdue (2000) put it 'the learner has to learn how to reconcile the informational structure with the linguistic means available, and if this is not possible to acquire further means' (pp. 301–2). Learner varieties are not just structured linguistically. They reflect the interaction of a limited set of organizational principles that operate at different levels—syntactic, semantic, and discoursal—with the specific interaction determining the nature of the learner variety from one time to the next. Development arises because the organizing principles clash, pushing the learner to reorganize and extend the existing variety. An example of such a clash can be found in the principles that govern the macrostructure of a text or conversation and those relating to the structure of individual utterances. For example, Bernini (2000) showed how 'development of negation (in L2 Italian) appears to be directly related to the articulation of the utterances in terms of information structure rather than to its syntactic structure' (p. 431). Bernini described two negative constructions used at stage 2 in learners' development: 'No(n) + X' and 'X + no'. He then showed how, although both constructions were used to realize the same pragmatic function, they could be distinguished in terms of information structure, with 'No(n) + X' used to negate the topic of the discourse and 'X + no' having a focus status (i.e. negating an element mentioned in the preceding discourse).

Like Klein and Perdue, Givón (1979) also saw syntax as inextricably linked to discourse—it is 'a dependent, functionally motivated entity' in the sense that its formal properties reflect its communicative uses. He distinguished two types of language, reflecting two different types of interlanguage system. There are the loose, paratactic structures found in informal/unplanned discourse, which constitute the 'pragmatic mode' (later referred to as the 'pre-grammatical mode' in Givón 1995). There are also the tight, 'grammaticalized' structures found in formal/planned discourse, which constitute the 'syntactic mode' (later called the 'grammatical mode'). An example of the former is the topic-comment structure of an utterance like:

Ice cream, I like it.

while an example of the latter is the subject-predicate structure of an utterance like:

I like ice cream.

Givón argued that learners progressively syntacticize their interlanguages as they move from a pre-grammatical to a grammatical mode. However, they retain access to the pre-grammatical mode which they employ when the conditions are appropriate. Givón also argued that other aspects of language—such as the historical evolution of languages and creolization—are also characterized by the same process of SYNTACTIZATION.

A number of studies have tested Givón's claims regarding syntactization (for example, Schumann 1987; Givón 1984; Sato 1988; Pfaff 1992; Ramat 1992). They have produced mixed results. For example, Sato's 10-month study of two children, Vietnamese learners of English, found little evidence of paratactic speech (non-propositional utterances, vertical constructions, and scaffolded utterances). In fact, both learners, contrary to the theory, encoded plenty of simple complete propositions from the start and were able to do so without the help of interlocutor scaffolding. Pfaff (1992), however, showed that grammatical markers developed out of independent lexical items in the acquisition of L2 German by pre-school and early school-age Turkish children in Berlin-Kreuzberg. She found, for instance, that main verb use of 'sein' and 'haben' preceded the auxiliary use of the same verbs.

Implicit and explicit L2 knowledge

Whereas the variationist view of L2 representation draws on the work of sociolinguists and the functional view on the work of cognitive linguists, the view we will now discuss is firmly rooted in cognitive psychology. The distinction between implicit and explicit knowledge and their correlates implicit and explicit memory have attracted the attention of a number of cognitive psychologists (for example, Reber 1989; Berry 1994) and, not surprisingly, a number of SLA researchers (for example, Krashen 1981; R. Ellis 1994c; N. Ellis 2005). The latter have been particularly concerned with the nature of the interface between the two types of knowledge/memory. We will begin by offering a definition of implicit and explicit knowledge and then move on to examine the different positions adopted by SLA researchers.

Defining implicit and explicit knowledge

I have identified seven ways in which implicit and explicit knowledge of language can be distinguished. (See Ellis 2004a.) These are summarized in Table

9.2. In line with these distinguishing characteristics the following definitions can be formulated:

IMPLICIT KNOWLEDGE is intuitive, procedural, systematically variable, automatic, and thus available for use in fluent, unplanned language use. It is not verbalizable. According to some theorists it is only learnable before learners reach a critical age (for example, puberty).

EXPLICIT KNOWLEDGE is conscious, declarative, anomalous, and inconsistent (i.e. it takes the form of 'fuzzy' rules inconsistently applied) and generally only accessible through controlled processing in planned language use. It is verbalizable, in which case it entails semi-technical or technical metalanguage. Like any type of factual knowledge, it is potentially learnable at any age.

Characteristics	**Implicit knowledge**	**Explicit knowledge**
Awareness	Learner is intuitively aware of linguistic norms.	Learner is consciously aware of linguistic norms.
Type of knowledge	Learner has procedural knowledge of rules and fragments.	Learner has declarative knowledge of grammatical rules and fragments.
Systematicity	Knowledge is variable but systematic.	Knowledge is often anomalous and inconsistent.
Accessibility	Knowledge is accessible by means of automatic processing.	Knowledge is accessible only through controlled processing.
Use of L2 knowledge	Knowledge is typically accessed when learner is performing fluently.	Knowledge is typically accessed when learner experiences a planning difficulty.
Self-report	Non-verbalizable.	Verbalizable.
Learnability	Potentially only learnable within the 'critical period'.	Learnable at any age.

Table 9.2 Key characteristics of implicit and explicit knowledge

Eysenck (2001) defined IMPLICIT MEMORY as 'memory that does not depend on conscious recollection' (p. 334) and EXPLICIT MEMORY as memory that does. This distinction, which Eysenck considered of 'major importance', corresponds closely to the definitions of implicit/explicit knowledge above. However, studies such as that of Tulving and Schachter (1990) suggested that implicit memory consists of multiple systems rather than a single system. It is possible, therefore, that implicit linguistic knowledge is better conceptualized in terms of separate stores for a perceptual and a conceptual system.

The implicit/explicit distinction, however, is not without controversy. One issue of debate is whether it constitutes a continuum or a dichotomy. Dienes and Perner (1999) claimed that the distinction represents a continuum rather than a dichotomy, a position they see supported by Karmiloff-Smith's (1992) account of how implicit linguistic knowledge becomes progressively more explicit in children. However, others (for example, Krashen 1981 and Schwartz 1993) argued strongly that it constitutes a dichotomy. This view is supported by Paradis (1994), who presented evidence to suggest that the two types of knowledge are neurolinguistically distinct. (See Chapter 14.)

A further problem concerns the extent to which the distinction can be operationalized and thus investigated empirically. This is a matter of special importance in studies of form-focused instruction (see Chapter 16), where it is obviously necessary to determine whether such instruction can only assist the development of explicit knowledge, as claimed by the likes of Krashen (1982), or whether it is able to contribute to implicit knowledge. (See Doughty 2003 for a discussion of this issue.) DeKeyser (2003) suggested that it might not be possible to distinguish the two types of knowledge empirically given that explicit knowledge may be proceduralized to a degree that makes it functionally indistinguishable from implicit knowledge (i.e. both types of knowledge may be available for use in unplanned language use). However, there is some evidence that DeKeyser may be wrong. Han and Ellis (1998) analysed scores derived from a battery of tests, some of which had been designed as measures of implicit knowledge—an oral production test and a timed grammaticality judgement test (GJT)—and others as measures of explicit knowledge—an untimed GJT and a measure of metalinguistic ability based on learners' verbalizations of a grammatical rule. In a Principal Component Factor Analysis, scores from the oral production test and the timed GJT loaded on one factor, demonstrating that they were strongly related to each other, while the untimed GJT and the metalinguistic comments scores loaded on a second factor. Han and Ellis labelled these two factors 'implicit L2 knowledge' and 'explicit L2 knowledge' respectively in accordance with the principles that informed the design of the tests. This study was limited, however, in that it focused on a single grammatical structure (verb complementation). In Ellis (2005a) I reported a follow-up study that investigated the extent to which tests of 17 different grammatical structures provided relatively separate measures of the two types of knowledge. These tests were based on the distinguishing characteristics shown in Table 9.2. They were administered to 92 L2 learners of mixed L2 proficiency. The results of a factor analysis indicated that the three tests designed to measure implicit knowledge (an oral elicited imitation test, an oral narrative, and a timed GJT) and the two tests designed to measure explicit knowledge (an untimed GJT[2] and a test of METALINGUAL KNOWLEDGE) accounted for different patterns of variation, suggesting that they were measuring distinct constructs. This study, then, lends support to the distinctiveness of the two types of knowledge while suggesting that it may be possible to measure them independently. It supports Hulstijn's (2002) claim that although it may be possible to 'speed up the execution of algorithmic rules to some extent' (p. 211), it is still possible to distinguish implicit and explicit knowledge.

Further debates centre around the processes responsible for the development of the two types of knowledge—in particular, whether implicit learning requires conscious attention or whether it can take place without making demands on central attentional resources. This key issue is addressed later. Suffice it to say here that a distinction needs to be drawn between implicit/explicit knowledge and implicit/explicit learning (Schmidt 1994). Thus, it is perfectly possible to claim that conscious attention is involved in implicit learning while maintaining that the products of such learning are not themselves available to consciousness.

Krashen's Monitor Theory

The distinction between implicit and explicit knowledge underlies Krashen's MONITOR THEORY. It was the basis of the first and, in many ways, the most central of the five hypotheses that comprised this model.[3] Krashen (1981, 1982, 1994) claimed that learners possess an 'acquired system' and a 'learnt system' which are totally separate. The former is developed by means of ACQUISITION, a subconscious process which arises when learners are using language for communication. The latter is the result of LEARNING, the process of paying conscious attention to language in an effort to understand and memorize rules. It is clear that the acquisition/learning distinction mirrors the implicit/explicit distinction, a point that Krashen himself acknowledged (1982: 10).

Whereas the claim that there are two types of knowledge is not controversial, Krashen's insistence that 'learnt' knowledge is completely separate and cannot be converted into 'acquired' knowledge is. This position has become known as the NON-INTERFACE POSITION. Krashen argued that 'acquired knowledge' can *only* be developed when the learner's attention is focused on message conveyance, and that neither practice nor error correction enables 'learnt knowledge' to become 'acquired'. Furthermore, he claimed that utterances are initiated by the 'acquired' system, and that the 'learnt' system only comes into play when learners monitor the output from it. Monitoring is possible when learners are focused on form rather than meaning and have sufficient time to access their 'learnt' knowledge. However, learners can also modify their output by means of 'feel', using 'acquired' knowledge. Krashen (1985) argued that an INTERFACE POSITION (i.e. explicit knowledge converts into implicit knowledge through practice) does not account for cases such as 'P', an advanced L2 learner who displayed conscious knowledge of rules like third person –s and yet could not use them in free speech, nor for other cases of learners who have 'acquired' rules without ever having learnt them. He has continued to maintain a non-interface position over the years (for example, Krashen 1994, 2003).

The Monitor Theory has been subjected to considerable criticism from McLaughlin (1978b, 1987), Sharwood Smith (1981), and Gregg (1984), among others. McLaughlin (1987: 21), for example, argued that Krashen's acquired/learnt distinction is not tenable because it cannot be falsified; Krashen failed to provide adequate definitions of what he means by 'subconscious' and 'conscious', and 'he has provided no way of independently determining whether a given process involves acquisition or learning'. McLaughlin's criticisms, however, appear to be levelled primarily at Krashen's attempt to distinguish 'acquired' and 'learnt' knowledge at the level of process, but as Bialystok (1981a) noted, the existence of two types of knowledge is widely recognized in cognitive psychology. Perhaps the main problem with Krashen's theory is his insistence that learnt knowledge cannot contribute to the acquisition of acquired knowledge.

Bialystok's Theory of L2 learning

Bialystok's (1978) Theory of L2 Learning was also based on the distinction between implicit and explicit knowledge but allows for an interface between explicit and implicit knowledge. Bialystok proposed that implicit knowledge is developed through exposure to communicative language use and is facilitated by the strategy of 'functional practising' (attempts by the learner to maximize exposure to language through communication). In contrast, explicit knowledge arises when learners focus on the language code, and is facilitated by 'formal practising', which involves either conscious study of the L2 or attempts to automatize already learnt explicit knowledge. There is an interaction between the two types of knowledge. Formal practising enables explicit knowledge to become implicit, while inferencing allows explicit knowledge to be derived from implicit. The model also distinguishes two types of output. Type I output is 'spontaneous and immediate', while Type II is 'deliberate and occurs after a delay' (Bialystok 1978: 74). As might be expected, Type I relies entirely on implicit knowledge, whereas Type II involves both implicit and explicit. A feedback loop from both types allows for continual modification of a response. Thus, Bialystok's theory is premised on an interface between the two types of knowledge.

Whereas Krashen's position has remained more or less immutable over the years, Bialystok's has undergone considerable revision (see Bialystok 1981a, 1982, 1990, 1991, and also Hulstijn 1990). The development that concerns us most here is her reconceptualization of L2 knowledge. In the early model this was represented as a dichotomy—knowledge was either implicit or explicit—but in subsequent formulations it is represented in terms of two intersecting continua reflecting the extent to which rules and items are 'controlled' or 'analysed'. Again, Bialystok's definition of 'control' has shifted somewhat. Whereas initially (for example, in Bialystok 1982), it concerned the ease and rapidity with which knowledge can be accessed in differing types of language use, in later formulations (for example, Bialystok and Ryan 1985) it refers to three different functions: the selection of items of knowledge, their coordination, and the extent to which selection and coordination can be carried out automatically.

By 'analysis', Bialystok refers to the extent to which the learner has abstracted an account of some linguistic phenomenon:

> Analysis of knowledge is the process by which mental representations of this knowledge are built up, structured, and made explicit for the learner. (Bialystok 1991: 65)

One way in which this can take place is by analysing formulas (i.e. discovering the parts that make them up). It is tempting to see this 'analysis' dimension as equivalent to the explicit/implicit distinction, with analysed knowledge corresponding to explicit knowledge and unanalysed to implicit. Bialystok, in fact, did equate analysis with the development of an explicit representation of knowledge, but she emphasized that analysed knowledge need not involve consciousness. As she put it 'a criterion of consciousness seriously underestimates the level of analysis with which linguistic knowledge is represented' (1991: 68).

In explaining how analysed knowledge is developed, Bialystok (1991) drew on the work of Karmiloff-Smith's (1986) three phases of skill development. The first phase is called 'Implicit'. Here, knowledge of a linguistic item is closely associated with procedures for using it in communication and is not represented independently. For example, the learner may supply linguistic determiners with a variety of nouns and yet not have organized them into a system of determiners. The second phase is called 'Explicit 1', during which learners examine, analyse, and organize their performances in order to construct explicit and independent representations of linguistic knowledge. In the final phase—Explicit 2—linguistic knowledge is available for conscious consideration. This model was intended to account for language development in children, and thus progress is reflected in movement from Implicit to Explicit 1 and finally to Explicit 2. It is not clear how—or whether—this model can be applied to L2 acquisition, nor did Bialystok consider this in her later work.

The goal of much of Bialystok's later work was to show the relationship between different types of knowledge and different types of language use (conversations, tests, reading, studying, etc.). Hulstijn (1990: 38), in fact, characterized it as 'a functional model, aimed at explaining language use in terms of task demands' rather than a theory of acquisition. The primary effect of analysing knowledge is to increase the potential for use in cognitively demanding tasks. Unanalysed knowledge also has its use—in conversation, for example.

There are a number of problems with Bialystok's views of language acquisition. (See Hulstijn 1990.) In particular, the claim that language must begin with unanalysed knowledge seems unwarranted in the case of L2 acquisition. Many instructed L2 learners begin with explicit knowledge. Hulstijn came out strongly in favour of the kind of skill-learning theory of L2 acquisition that we will consider later.

R. Ellis' Weak Interface Model

My own theory of instructed language acquisition (see Ellis 1994c) is also based on the implicit/explicit distinction. I presented a weak-interface position, as shown in Figure 9.3. This claims that explicit knowledge can be converted into implicit knowledge in the case of VARIATIONAL FEATURES (for example, copula 'be') but not DEVELOPMENTAL FEATURES (for example, negation or third person –s) unless the learner has reached the stage of development that allows for the integration of the feature into the interlanguage system. This distinction draws on Meisel, Clahsen, and Pienemann's MULTIDIMENSIONAL MODEL (discussed later in the chapter), which was based on studies of the L2 acquisition of German that had shown that whereas somewhat grammatical features appear to be constrained so that they can only be acquired in a fixed sequence, others are acquirable at any time. My theory also posited a role for explicit knowledge as a facilitator of implicit knowledge. That is, it contributed indirectly to the development of implicit knowledge by helping learners to notice linguistic forms in the input and to carry out a comparison between what they have noticed and their own current interlanguage. A corollary of this model is that not all L2 knowledge originates in an explicit form—more often than not knowledge commences as implicit knowledge. Thus, the model claims that there is both a direct interface between explicit and implicit knowledge (albeit one circumscribed by developmental constraints) and an indirect interface. In my later publications (for example, Ellis 2006c), however, I have tended to emphasize the indirect nature of this interface.

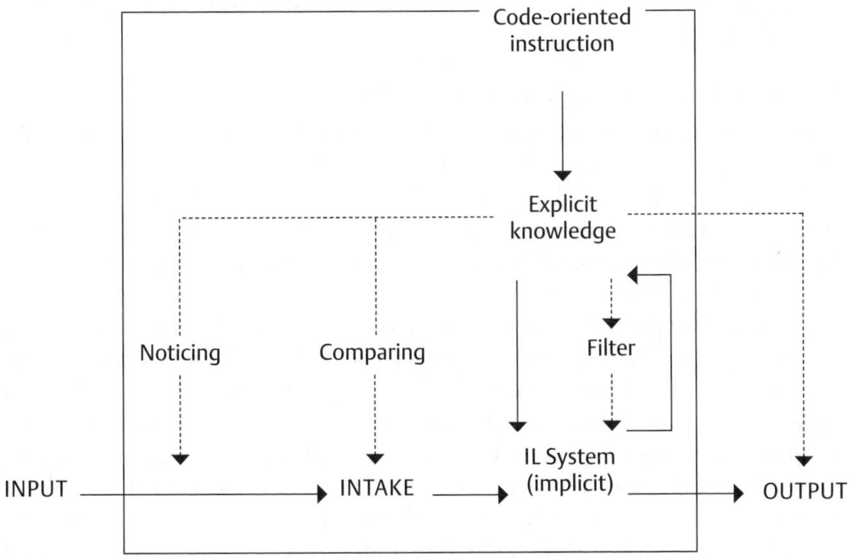

Figure 9.3 The role of explicit knowledge in L2 acquisition (Ellis 1994c: 97)

N. Ellis' account of the explicit/implicit interface

N. Ellis (1994a) has also posited a connection between explicit and implicit knowledge. He described the two types of knowledge as 'dissociable but cooperative' (N. Ellis 2005). He saw implicit knowledge as primary; 'most knowledge is tacit knowledge; most learning is implicit; the vast majority of our cognitive processing is unconscious' (p. 306). He supported Krashen's claim that implicit and explicit knowledge are distinct and disassociated—'they involve different types of representation and are substantiated in different parts of the brain' (p. 307). Unlike me, however, he argued that explicit cannot be converted into implicit knowledge, but like me he also acknowledged an indirect role for explicit knowledge as a facilitator of implicit knowledge. In particular, he considered explicit knowledge (and the consciousness it presupposes) to support and enhance the unconscious processes involved in acquiring implicit knowledge. For example, he saw explicit knowledge playing a role in the initial registration of the sequences that make up CONSTRUCTIONS, which are then tuned and integrated into the implicit system through subsequent implicit processing of L2 input. He proposed the following learning sequence:

> external scaffolded attention → internally motivated attention → explicit learning → explicit memory → implicit learning → implicit memory, automatization, and abstraction

and went on to suggest that 'conscious and unconscious processes are dynamically involved together in every cognitive task and in every learning episode' (p. 340). N. Ellis' account of the two knowledge sources and their interaction, then, can also be viewed as a weak interface model, in fact, even weaker than my own model.

Empirical studies of implicit/explicit knowledge

A number of early studies examined the relationship between learners' implicit and explicit knowledge (for example, Seliger 1979; Hulstijn and Hulstijn 1984; Sorace 1985). In all of these studies explicit knowledge was operationalized as learners' explanation of specific linguistic features, while implicit knowledge was determined by examining the learners' use of these features in oral or written language.

A good example of this early research is Green and Hecht's (1992) study of the L2 knowledge of 300 German learners of English with between three and twelve years' exposure to formal teaching, and, also, of 50 native English speakers. The participants were shown sentences containing different kinds of grammatical errors and asked to correct each sentence and in each case to state the rule that had been violated. The native speakers were able to correct 96 per cent of the errors, while the German learners corrected 78 per cent overall. The most advanced group of learners, however, corrected 97 per cent. Green and Hecht found that the German learners could only state the correct explicit rule in less than half the cases (46 per cent). Again, the more experienced learners showed higher levels of explicit knowledge, the university students with the most experience formulating correct rules in 85 per cent of the cases. Although the learners nearly always produced an accurate correction when they had produced a correct rule (97 per cent of such cases), they were able to make successful corrections without recourse to explicit knowledge in 43 per cent of the cases. This study suggests that the learners relied primarily on implicit knowledge, but that the availability of accurate explicit rules facilitated performance of the correction task. Explicit rules obviously constitute only a subset—and a fairly small one at that—of available implicit knowledge, a point which Krashen (1982) emphasized.

Later studies have continued to explore the relationship between the two types of knowledge. Macrory and Stone (2000), for example, investigated British comprehensive school students' 'perceptions' of what they knew about the formation of the French perfect tense (measured by means of self-report), their 'actual knowledge' of the tense (measured by means of gap-filling exercises), and their ability to use the tense in an informal interview and in free written production. They found that the students had a fairly good explicit understanding of the perfect tense (for example, they understood its function, they knew that some verbs used 'avoir' and some 'être', they were familiar with the forms required by different pronouns, and they were aware of the need for a final accent on the past participle). In general, this study found only weak relationships between students' perceptions, their performance in the gap-filling exercise, and their use of the tense in free oral and written production. For example, whereas they typically supplied an auxiliary (not always the correct one) in the gap-filling exercise, they typically omitted it in free production except in formulaic expressions involving 'j'ai'. Macrory and Stone concluded that what they term language-as-knowledge and language-for-use may have derived from different sources—instruction about the rule system and routines practised in class.

Hu (2002) conducted a study of 64 Chinese learners of English. His main purpose was to investigate to what extent explicit knowledge was available for use in spontaneous writing. He asked the learners to complete two spontaneous writing tasks and then to carry out an untimed error-correction task and a rule-verbalization task before again completing two similar spontaneous writing tasks and a timed error-correction task. The idea was that the correction and rule verbalization tasks would serve a consciousness-raising function, making the learners aware of the structures that were the focus of the study. Hu focused on six structures, selecting a prototypical and peripheral rule for each structure (for example, for articles 'specific reference' constituted the prototypical rule and 'generic reference' the peripheral rule). Overall, when correct metalinguistic knowledge was available, the participants were more accurate in their prototypical use of the six structures. Also, accuracy in the use of the six structures increased in the second spontaneous writing task, suggesting that, when made aware of the need to attend to specific forms, the learners made fuller use of their metalinguistic knowledge. However, Hu admitted that it is not possible to claim that the participants actually used their metalinguistic knowledge in the writing tasks although he did argue that the results are compatible with such an interpretation.

These studies were correlational in design. That is, they either sought to establish whether there was any relationship between learners' explicit and implicit knowledge (Green and Hecht and Macrory and Stone) or whether explicit knowledge was available for use in tasks that were hypothesized to require implicit knowledge (i.e. Hu). Such studies do not constitute tests of the interface position (nor were they intended to do so), as demonstrating a relationship does not show that knowledge that originated as explicit was subsequently transformed into implicit knowledge. However, they do provide support for the existence of the two types of knowledge and also for their relative separateness.

One study that has directly tested the interface position is DeKeyser (1995). DeKeyser's study examined the effects of two kinds of form-focused instruction (explicit-deductive and implicit-inductive) on two kinds of rules in an artificial grammar ('simple categorical rules' and 'fuzzy prototypical rules'). Learning outcomes were measured by means of a computerized judgement test, which required the learners to say whether a sentence matched a picture and a computerized production test, which required them to type in a sentence to describe a picture. DeKeyser claimed that the production test was to some extent 'speeded' (i.e. the learners had 30 seconds to respond). The learners were also asked to complete fill-in-the-blank tests to demonstrate their understanding of the grammatical rules. The learners in the explicit-deductive condition provided clear evidence of being able to produce the simple categorical rules in new contexts and did better than the learners in the implicit-inductive condition. Thus, on the face of it, this study suggests that, at least in the case of simple grammatical forms, learners who are taught explicit knowledge about the forms and then practise them are able to use them. But, as DeKeyser admitted, it was not clear to what extent the production task allowed for monitoring using explicit knowledge.

There have also been a number of other studies that have investigated the extent and nature of learners' explicit knowledge. (See Ellis 2004a, Table 1 on pp. 246–8, for a review.) This research has focused almost exclusively on explicit knowledge of L2 grammar (but see Newman and White's (1999) study of pronunciation). It has investigated explicit knowledge both in terms of conscious awareness (typically by means of eliciting judgements of grammaticality) and in terms of knowledge of metalinguistic terms. These studies demonstrate that, contrary to Krashen's (1982) claim that most L2 learners are capable of learning only very limited explicit knowledge (for example, of 'simple' and 'portable' rules like third person –s), learners often develop quite extensive explicit knowledge of a range of grammatical features.

Final comment on the implicit/explicit distinction

There is now widespread acceptance that learners' representation of their L2 knowledge is both implicit and explicit and that the distinguishing characteristic is 'consciousness'. There is also general agreement that these two types of knowledge require different processing conditions and therefore will be accessed in relation to the type of language use (planned versus unplanned) that learners engage in. However, there is disagreement about the relationship between these two knowledge sources. Whereas some researchers support a non-interface position, others project a strong interface position, and yet others a weak interface position. However, it has not yet proved possible to investigate these different claims as, to date, distinctive measures of the two types of knowledge have not been available. It should also be noted that SLA researchers do not always take note of the distinction between implicit and explicit knowledge, opting instead to simply investigate undifferentiated L2 knowledge and to talk about what learners 'have learnt' or 'know' without bothering about the nature of knowledge they are investigating. As Douglas (2001) noted, this constitutes a failure to consider the construct validity of the instruments used to measure learning. In lamenting this, Douglas pointed to what is needed:

> ... construct validity may be demonstrated by the construction of theoretical arguments linking hypothesized aspects of language ability to features of the test tasks, demonstrating the appropriacy of the tasks for making interpretations regarding the construct, and then providing empirical evidence that the links are in fact present.
> (p. 447)

One of the soundest ways of achieving this is by developing tasks that provide separate and valid measures of implicit and explicit knowledge.

Declarative and procedural L2 knowledge

A somewhat similar distinction to the explicit/implicit distinction is the declarative/procedural distinction. However, whereas the former distinction has been variably viewed as a dichotomy and a continuum, the latter is seen very definitely as a continuum, with declarative knowledge evolving into procedural knowledge through practice. We will begin by examining Anderson's account of declarative/procedural knowledge and then McLaughlin's information-processing model, which provides a basis for combining the implicit/explicit distinction with the declarative/procedural one.

Anderson's Adaptive Control of Thought (ACT) Model

Anderson's model (see Anderson 1976, 1980, 1983, 1993) rests on the distinction between DECLARATIVE and PROCEDURAL KNOWLEDGE.[4] While admitting that the distinction between the two types of knowledge is not watertight, Anderson (1976) characterized the essential differences in the form of three assumptions:

> 1 Declarative knowledge seems to be possessed in an all-or-none manner, whereas procedural knowledge seems to be something that can be partially possessed.
> 2 One acquires declarative knowledge suddenly, by being told, whereas one acquires procedural knowledge gradually, by performing the skill.
> 3 One can communicate one's declarative knowledge verbally, but not one's procedural knowledge.
> (1976: 117)

The transition of declarative to procedural knowledge takes place in three stages. In the declarative, stage information is stored as facts for which there are no ready-made activation procedures. For example, we may be aware that 'drowned' consists of 'drown' and '–ed', and yet be unable to produce 'drowned' correctly in conversation. The second stage is the associative stage. Because it is difficult to use declarative knowledge, the learner tries to sort the information into more efficient production sets by means of 'composition' (collapsing several discrete productions into one), and 'proceduralization', (applying a general rule to a particular instance). For example, the learner may have learnt 'drowned' and 'saved' as two distinct items, but may come to realize that they can be represented more economically in a production set: 'If the goal is to generate a past tense verb, then add –ed to the verb'. This may then serve as a general procedure for generating past tense forms, including incorrect ones (such as 'goed'). Anderson (1983) noted that errors are particularly likely during the associative stage. In the autonomous stage, in which procedures become increasingly automated, the mind continues both to generalize productions and also to discriminate more narrowly the occasions when specific productions can be used. For example, the learner may modify the past tense production set so that it applies to only a subset of verbs. At this stage the ability to verbalize knowledge of the skill can disappear entirely.

Anderson (1980 and 1983) discussed classroom L2 learning in the light of the ACT Model. He saw the kind of knowledge taught to the classroom learner as different from adult L1 knowledge:

> We speak the learnt language (i.e. the second language) by using general rule-following procedures applied to the rules we have learnt, rather than speaking directly, as we do in our native language. Not surprisingly, applying this knowledge is a much slower and more painful process than applying the procedurally encoded knowledge of our own language.
> (1980: 224)

However, Anderson saw the differences between L1 and foreign language learning as merely a question of the stage reached. Whereas L1 learners almost invariably reach the autonomous stage, foreign language learners typically only reach the associative stage. Thus, although foreign language learners achieve a fair degree of proceduralization through practice, and can use L2 rules without awareness, they do not reach full autonomy.

The ACT model is enormously complex. A single communicative act, for instance, is likely to involve an elaborate sequence of interrelated 'production systems'. It is not possible to do justice to this complexity here. The central points to grasp are the theoretical claims that learning begins with declarative knowledge which slowly becomes proceduralized, and that the mechanism by which this takes place is *practice*.

McLaughlin's Information-Processing Model

McLaughlin developed his Information-Processing Model of L2 acquisition over a series of publications. (See McLaughlin 1978b, 1980, 1987, 1990; McLaughlin, Rossman, and McLeod 1983; McLaughlin and Heredia 1996.) For McLaughlin, how knowledge is represented is closely linked to how it is processed. Drawing heavily on research in cognitive psychology into information processing (for example, Shiffrin and Schneider 1977), he proposed that learners are limited in how much information they are able to process by both the nature of the task and their own information-processing capacity. They are not capable of attending to all the information available in the input or their long-term memory. Some of it becomes the object of focused or selective attention, while other parts are attended to only peripherally. In order to maximize their information processing ability, learners routinize skills. Initially a skill may be available only through controlled processing, which McLaughlin, Rossman, and McLeod (1983) described as follows:

> ... not a learnt response, but a temporary activation of nodes in a sequence. This activation is under attentional control of the subject and, since attention is required, only one such sequence can normally be controlled at a time without interference
> (1983: 139).

In contrast, automatic processing 'involves the activation of certain nodes in memory every time the appropriate inputs are present'. Routinization, therefore, helps learners to reduce the burden on their information-processing capacity. It occurs when they have the opportunity to practise controlled processes. Routinization through practice results in quantitative changes in interlanguage by making an increasing number of information chunks available for automatic processing.

Representing L2 knowledge as two intersecting continua

The question now arises as to whether the explicit/implicit distinction is to be viewed as co-terminous with the declarative/procedural distinction or distinct from it. Bialystok (1982), in her reformulation of the implicit/explicit distinction proposed two distinct continua; (1) analysed/unanalysed knowledge (corresponding to the implicit/explicit distinction in her earlier model) and

(2) automatic/controlled knowledge. The intersection of these two continua affords four prototypical types of knowledge which manifest themselves in different kinds of language use. In Ellis (1993) I also suggested that the two distinctions are not isomorphic. I proposed that the terms 'explicit/implicit' label the type of knowledge learners possess according to whether it is conscious or intuitive, whereas the terms declarative/procedural concern the degree of control the learner has over both types of knowledge. Thus, it becomes possible to talk about both explicit and implicit knowledge existing in declarative and procedural form. (See Table 9.3.) Such modelling of L2 knowledge clearly makes the notion of 'interface' much more complex. While it is uncontroversial to envisage an interface between declarative and procedural knowledge (i.e. both explicit and implicit knowledge can be proceduralized), it is much more controversial to claim that either declarative or procedural explicit knowledge convert into implicit knowledge. The key interface issue is whether Type A knowledge (explicit/declarative) can convert into Type D knowledge (implicit/procedural). I argued that the results of research into the effects of grammar instruction on L2 learning indicate that such a conversion is not possible (i.e. grammar instruction directed at features learners are not ready to acquire as implicit knowledge is not successful. (See Chapter 16).

	Controlled	**Automatic**
Explicit	Type A Conscious knowledge of L2 items that can only be accessed slowly (e.g. rules and items that have been learnt formally and that require controlled processing in performance).	Type B Conscious knowledge of L2 items that can be accessed relatively rapidly (e.g. rules and items that have been learnt formally and practised so they have become automatic).
Implicit	Type C Intuitive knowledge of L2 items that has not yet been fully internalized (e.g. rules and items that have been learnt implicitly but which require controlled processing in performance).	Type D Intuitive knowledge of L2 items that is fully internalized (e.g. rules and items that have been learnt implicitly and are fully restructured so that they are available for automatic processing).

Table 9.3 L2 knowledge as intersecting continua

Final comment on the declarative/controlled distinction

SLA researchers have differed in their preference for a model of acquisition based on the implicit/explicit distinction or the declarative/procedural distinction, reflecting their stance on the interface issue. Those favouring an interface position (for example, DeKeyser 1998) have opted for the declarative/procedural distinction as it is relatively uncontroversial to claim that factual knowledge can be automatized through practice. Those favouring a non-interface or a weak-interface position have preferred the explicit/implicit distinction as this can more clearly be viewed as a dichotomy rather than a continuum. The notion of L2 knowledge as intersecting continua is an attractive one but it is difficult to see how it can be investigated empirically as it is likely to prove very difficult to design separate measures of the different types of knowledge shown in Table 9.3. It may be preferable to view the implicit/explicit distinction and the declarative/procedural distinction as essentially the same, for as Eysenck (2001) pointed out:

> It remains the case that declarative memory resembles explicit memory, in that it involves the integration or linkage of information. In contrast, procedural memory still resembles implicit memory, in that it involves specific forms of processing.
> (p. 213)

Indeed, the connectionist view of L2 learning we will consider later draws on the theoretical perspectives underlying both conceptualizations of L2 knowledge.

The dual-mode system

In Chapter 6, we saw that Pinker (1999) argued for a DUAL-MECHANISM MODEL, according to which computation of regular morphological features such as past tense –ed in English involves rule-based or symbolic processing, whereas features that are not constrained by readily identifiable rules, such as irregular past tense forms like 'swam', are stored as items. A not dissimilar position has been advanced by Skehan.

Skehan (1998b) proposed that speakers (native speakers and learners) possess a DUAL-MODE SYSTEM. Drawing on linguists such as Bolinger (1975), who claimed that language is more memory-based than has been commonly assumed and generally involves repetition rather than creation, and also on the work of linguists such as Biber (1988) and Carter and McCarthy (1995), who have shown that linguistic corpora manifest regular fixed combinations of lexical items, Skehan argued that much of language is exemplar rather than rule-based, reflecting the claims of Construction Grammar.[5] An implication of this position is that linguistic memory is not compact and efficiently organized but rather large and highly redundant, with multiple representations of the same item in what Skehan called 'item bundles'. Memory is organized in this way for convenience of use. That is, speaking (and, one might add, probably also rapid writing) is possible because of the way language is represented. Learners are able to draw on their exemplar-based system to obtain quick and easy access to the linguistic means needed to construct a phonetic plan. It is for this reason that speakers need to acquire a solid repertoire of formulaic chunks. Skehan's position echoes instance-based theories of fluency (for example, Logan 1988), which claim that fluent speech is not based on the rapid computation of rules but on the retrieval of ready-made exemplars that require minimal processing capacity because they are accessed as wholes. According to this view, then, language must be represented as an exemplar-based system because, if it was not, normal fluent speech would be impossible.

However, a memory-based system is limited and not all language use involves real-time processing. There are times when language users need to formulate precise and novel propositions. This requires a rule-based system and, when users are not under pressure to perform rapidly online, they have the time to access such a system. A rule-based system makes creativity and flexibility in what is said possible. Another advantage of such a system is its parsimony. It consists of a finite set of representations that can fit into a small memory space.

Thus, Skehan claimed 'two systems co-exist, the rule-based analytic, on the one hand, and the formulaic, exemplar-based on the other' (p. 54). The rule-based system consists of powerful 'generative' rules and is required to compute well-formed sentences. The exemplar-based system is capacious, with the contents organized in accordance with the 'idiom principle' (Sinclair 1991), and is required for fast, fluent language use. Skehan argued that 'language users can move between these systems, and do so quite naturally' (p. 54).

Skehan's theory of L2 representation is intuitively appealing. However, there is only limited empirical evidence to support it. First, while the theory may account for how our native language is represented, it does not follow that the L2 is represented in a similar fashion. Foster (2001), for example, found clear differences between native speakers and non-native speakers with regard to the frequency that they employed formulaic sequences (a measure of their memory-based systems). For example, when performing the same tasks requiring unplanned speech, the native speakers produced 621 formulaic sequences while the non-native speakers produced only 261. It appears, therefore, that non-native speakers have far fewer such sequences to draw on and thus must rely more extensively on their rule-based system. Foster's study, however, can only be taken as evidence of quantitative rather than qualitative differences between native and non-native speakers. L2 learners, especially those who have had little exposure to the L2, may be over reliant on their rule-based system.

One of the best tests of the dual-mode system was Prasada and Pinker (1993). This study showed that when native speakers were asked to produce the past tense forms of nonce verbs (for example, 'greem', 'plip') which varied in their similarity to actual verb forms, the degree of similarity had no effect with the regular nonce verbs but did with the irregular nonce verbs. This led Prasada and Pinker to claim that regular and irregular verb forms are disassociated in L1 representation and to view the study as support for the dual-mechanism model. Murphy (2004) replicated Prasada and Pinker's study on three groups; child native speakers, adult native speakers, and adult non-native speakers. All three groups produced the –ed suffix more consistently overall with the regular than the irregular nonce forms, thus confirming Prasada and Pinker's findings, and suggesting that they are applicable to L2 acquisition. However, Murphy suggested that disassociations can arise without having to invoke two separate representational systems, as she found a similarity effect for the regular as well as the irregular nonce forms in all three groups, which is contrary to the predictions of the dual-mechanism model. Murphy concluded by suggesting that the results of her study could be accounted for by a single-route associative model. Clearly, then, the whole question of whether L2 learners (or native speakers) operate a dual-mode system remains an open question. (See also discussion of this issue in Chapter 6 and Chapter 14.)

Concluding comments

It may appear from the multitude of models of L2 knowledge discussed in this section that there is no consensus in cognitive SLA. In attempting to construct a composite picture, there are obviously dangers of ignoring very real differences among the models, but it does seem to me that a number of generalizations are possible:

1 Learners construct mental systems (interlanguages) in long-term memory to represent what they have extracted from the input.
2 There is also widespread acceptance in cognitive SLA that an interlanguage consists of a network of form–function mappings rather than formal linguistic rules.
3 SLA researchers of a cognitive bent also acknowledge that interlanguage grammars are variable; that is, they store more than one form for realizing a particular function and alternate between these forms in accordance with both external (social) and internal (linguistic) factors.
4 Interlanguages vary in terms of how grammaticalized they are; changes in representation arise as grammaticalization takes place.
5 Changes in interlanguage are not just quantitative in nature. There are also qualitative changes as learners restructure their representations of the L2.
6 Learners possess unconscious procedural knowledge of L2 rules (implicit knowledge) as well as conscious, declarative knowledge (explicit knowledge). However, the relationship between these two types of knowledge remains a matter of controversy.
7 Any model of L2 representation must account for how knowledge is accessed in different types of language use (for example, planned versus unplanned).

An underlying assumption of cognitive approaches to L2 representation is that linguistic knowledge is differentiated. The main controversies surround how best to characterize this differentiated knowledge and the relationship between the different types of knowledge. Thus disagreement exists regarding the question of an interface between explicit and implicit knowledge (both whether there is one and, if there is, the nature of it) and also on whether in the implicit system it is necessary to posit a dual-mode representation or a single-mode, connectionist system.

It will have been apparent in the foregoing discussion of the different models of L2 representation that how L2 knowledge is represented is tightly linked to how input and output are processed. In the next section we will consider the cognitive processes involved in L2 acquisition.

The processes of L2 acquisition

This section considers a number of key cognitive processes involved in L2 acquisition. I have divided these (somewhat arbitrarily) into micro-processes and macro-processes. The term micro-processes is used to refer to the specific mental operations involved in different stages of acquisition. These processes figure to a greater or lesser extent in the macro-processes (i.e. the general approach to learning adopted by learners). This section serves as a basis for a consideration of cognitive theories of L2 acquisition, which draw on these various processes. These are considered later in this chapter.

Micro-processes

The micro-processes I will consider are (1) attention, (2) integration and re-structuring, and (3) monitoring.

Attention

Initially, the role played by ATTENTION in L2 acquisition was conceptualized in terms of 'consciousness'. As we have already seen, Krashen (1981) characterized the process responsible for the 'acquisition' of implicit knowledge as an unconscious one and that responsible for the 'learning' of explicit knowledge as a conscious one. McLaughlin (1990), however, viewed such a distinction as untenable on the grounds that the extent to which processes are conscious is not amenable to empirical study. Other SLA researchers, however, have been happy to grapple with the construct. In particular, Schmidt's contributions (1990, 1994, 1995a, 2001) have done much to give clarity to the role of consciousness. Schmidt (1994) distinguished four senses of 'consciousness'. First, there is consciousness as intentionality. That is, learners can set out to learn some element of the L2 deliberately, or they can learn something incidentally while focused on some other goal (for example, while processing input for meaning). This sense of 'conscious' then juxtaposes 'intentional' and 'incidental' learning. Second, there is consciousness as attention. Irrespective of whether acquisition takes place intentionally or incidentally, learners need to pay conscious attention to form. This sense of consciousness encompasses the

Noticing Hypothesis, which we considered briefly in Chapter 6. Third, there is consciousness as awareness. That is, learners may become aware of what they are learning. Schmidt acknowledged that this is a contentious issue. He noted that whereas some cognitive psychologists such as Reber (1993) have argued that learning is essentially implicit (i.e. takes place without awareness), others (such as Carr and Curran 1994) have argued that learners consciously form and test hypotheses. Thus, while it is not controversial to claim that awareness is involved in learning explicit knowledge, it is less clear whether consciousness is involved in the development of implicit knowledge. Fourth, there is consciousness as control. That is, the actual use of knowledge in performance involves conscious processes of selection and assembly. Schmidt proposed that whereas fluent performance is essentially unconscious, it may have originated in earlier guided performance, as proposed by Anderson (1993). Schmidt's seminal work has established a clear role for consciousness in L2 acquisition and helped to show what this consists of. The general position that Schmidt adopted is that the role of unconscious learning has been exaggerated.

Increasingly, SLA researchers have moved away from debating the role of consciousness to examining how attention functions in L2 acquisition. In making sense of the different positions that have been advanced, it is helpful to distinguish a number of different senses of 'attention'. Eysenck (2001), for example, pointed out that its primary use in cognitive psychology is to refer to selectivity in processing. He then distinguished 'focused attention', which is studied by asking participants to attend to only one of two or more input stimuli, and 'divided attention', which is studied by requiring participants to attend simultaneously to two or more input stimuli. With this important distinction in mind, we will examine how different SLA researchers have theorized the role of attention, starting with Schmidt.

1 Schmidt's Noticing Hypothesis

Schmidt's NOTICING HYPOTHESIS originated in the record of his experiences of learning L2 Portuguese in Brazil (Schmidt and Frota 1986). Schmidt kept a diary to establish which features in the input he had consciously attended to. His output was then examined to see to what extent the noticed forms turned up in communicative speech. In nearly every case the forms that Schmidt produced were those that he noticed people saying to him. Conversely, forms that were present in comprehensible input did not show up until they had been noticed.

Whereas Schmidt's earlier publications discussed noticing in terms of 'consciousness', in his 2001 article he directly addressed the nature and role of 'attention'. In this article, he made the following claim:

> ... the concept of attention is necessary in order to understand virtually every aspect of second language acquisition, including the development of interlanguages (ILs) over time, variation within IL at particular points in

> time, the development of L2 fluency, the role of individual differences, such as motivation, aptitude, and learning strategies in L2 learning, and the ways in which negotiation for meaning, and all forms of instruction contribute to language learning.
> (p. 3)

In other words, for Schmidt, learning an L2 entails attended learning. He identified the key attentional process as that of 'noticing' and the bulk of his article addressed this aspect of attention.

Schmidt acknowledged that it is not possible to separate attention and awareness completely, but argued that noticing is equivalent to Gass' 'apperception' (see Chapter 6) in that it involves only a very low level of awareness.[6] This is because noticing involves attention to only the surface structure of utterances not to abstract rules or principles and thus can be clearly distinguished from 'metalinguistic awareness'. Drawing on work in cognitive psychology, he identified a number of basic assumptions: attention is limited, it is elective, it is partially subject to voluntary control, it controls access to consciousness and it is essential for action control and learning. With respect to the last of these assumptions, which is perhaps the most crucial, Schmidt commented:

> It is argued that unattended stimuli persist in immediate short-term memory for only a few seconds at best, and attention is the necessary and sufficient condition for long-term storage to occur.
> (p. 16)

Schmidt went on to consider in some detail the key issue of whether there can be learning without attention. He noted, in line with Gass (1997a), that not all learning is dependent on input (i.e. learners are able to infer new knowledge by generalizing from their existing knowledge, as has been shown to occur in the case of relative clauses in English).[7] He also accepted that learners do not need to attend to input intentionally, while recognizing that intentional learning may sometimes help. He expressed less certainty regarding the degree of awareness that is needed for attention to result in learning. While he argued that 'global attention' (for example, attention directed at the meaning of the input) was not sufficient to ensure learning, he also accepted that different aspects of language (for example, syntax, morphology, and lexis) may differ in their attentional requirements. This claim is supported by Gass, Svetics, and Lemelin's (2003) study of L2 Italian, where focused attention was shown to have a significantly greater effect on the learning of syntax than of vocabulary. Schmidt rejected the view that many features of language are too abstract to be attended to on the grounds that learners only attend to surface structure exemplars of the features. Schmidt then offered his strong version of the Noticing Hypothesis—'while there is subliminal perception, there is no subliminal learning' (p. 26). That is, while learners may be able to notice elements in the input without conscious attention, they will not be able to process this information for storage in long-term memory. However, Schmidt later hedged somewhat on this strong position, by advancing a weaker version of the hypothesis—'people learn about the things they attend to and do not learn *much* about the things they do not attend to' (p. 30; italics added). In other words, while attention through noticing certainly aids learning, some learning (but not much) may be possible without it. Schmidt concluded his article by acknowledging that noticing is just the first step in language-building.

2 *Tomlin and Villa's Theory of Attention*

In an article that has had considerable impact on SLA, Tomlin and Villa (1994), drawing on the work of Posner and Petersen (1990), presented a very different view of the role of attention in L2 acquisition. They distinguished three kinds of attentional processes: (1) alertness, which involves a general readiness to deal with incoming stimuli and is closely related to the learner's affective/motivational state, (2) orientation, which entails the aligning of attention on some specific type or class of sensory information at the expense of others, and (3) detection, when the cognitive registration of a sensory stimulus takes place. It is during the last of these processes that specific exemplars of language are registered in memory. Tomlin and Villa then went on to make two claims, both of which have subsequently attracted opposition. The first claim is that detection can take place without alertness and orientation. In other words, learners can register an input feature even when they are not in an ideal state to attend and their attention is not focused on the feature in question. The second claim is that all three attentional processes can occur without awareness. They commented 'awareness requires attention, but attention does not require awareness'.

In order to test Tomlin and Villa's first claim, it is necessary to design ways of empirically distinguishing attention as alertness, orientation, and detection. Leow (1998) set out to do this in a study involving learners of L2 Spanish performing a crossword that required attention to the irregular third-person singular and plural preterite forms of stem-changing –ir verbs. There were four groups in this study. While all four groups were designated as + alertness, they differed in terms of whether they were – orientation/– detection (Group 1: the control group), + orientation/– detection (Group 2), + orientation/+ detection (Group 3), and – orientation/+ detection (Group 4). Orientation was operationalized through the instruction 'Please note that some of the forms of the verbs are irregular'. The opportunity for detection was provided by ensuring that the irregular forms needed to complete some of the crossword clues were available in a number of the other clues. The results showed that Groups 3 and 4 outperformed both the control group and Group 2 on all the post-tests but did not themselves differ significantly. In other words, the groups that had the opportunity to detect the target forms in the input outperformed those that did not, and simply orientating the learners to the existence of the form without the opportunity for detection had no effect.

Thus, detection proved to be the crucial attentional process. On the face of it, this seems to support Tomlin and Villa's first claim.

However, Simard and Wong (2001) presented a carefully argued challenge to Tomlin and Villa's claim and a convincing critique of Leow's study. They argued that Tomlin and Villa had misinterpreted Posner and Petersen's research about the neural locations of the three attentional processes. They pointed out that even though Posner and colleagues had identified separate neural locations, these were anatomically tied to each other and worked together in carrying out attentional processing. This is especially the case in higher-order tasks involving the processing of language data. Thus, they argued, there is no basis for claiming the separability of the three processes in Posner's research. With regard to Leow's study, Simard and Wong pointed out that no attempt was made to distinguish +/– alertness (as all conditions involved + alertness) and that this is not surprising as 'it is virtually impossible to design a task, particularly a language processing task, to do so' (p. 112). They also suggested that the study did not effectively distinguish the +/– orientation conditions, as the method of operationalization of this construct only resulted in different degrees of orientation. In other words, Leow's study failed to produce the fine-grained analysis of attention that it was intended to.

Simard and Wong as well as Schmidt (2001) challenged Tomlin and Villa's second claim, namely that attention to input stimuli (including detection) can take place without awareness. They criticized the studies in cognitive psychology (for example, Marcel 1983) that have been cited as support for such a claim on methodological grounds—in particular the difficulty of demonstrating that attention without awareness has taken place. Schmidt noted that while psychological studies may have been successful in distinguishing levels of awareness, they have not succeeded in establishing that no awareness had occurred. The method usually taken to demonstrate lack of awareness is concurrent verbal report (i.e. participants are considered to be unaware if they do not explicitly indicate attention to a feature in their online reporting). But, as Schmidt (2001) pointed out, this lacks validity; learners may have noticed something even though they did not report it. The issue of learning without awareness is an important one and we will return to it later when we consider implicit language learning.

3 VanPatten's Input Processing Theory

VanPatten's (1996) INPUT PROCESSING THEORY is based on the standard information processing viewpoint. Namely, working memory is limited in capacity (at least in terms of each modality), making it difficult for learners to attend concurrently to different stimuli in the input. He identified 'detection' as the key attentional process, noting that detecting one bit of information can interfere with the detection of others by consuming available resources in working memory. Thus, for VanPatten, the main issue is how learners allocate attentional resources during online processing and in particular what causes them to detect certain stimuli in the input and not others. He formulated a number of input-processing principles to explain learners' attentional priorities, for example:

P1 Learners process input for meaning before they process it for form.
P1 (a) Learners process content words in the input before anything else.
P1 (b) Learners prefer processing lexical items to grammatical items (for example, morphological markings) for semantic information.
P1 (c) Learners prefer processing 'more meaningful' morphology before 'less or nonmeaningful morphology'.
P2 For learners to process form that is not meaningful, they must be able to process informational or communicative content at no (or little) cost to attention.
(pp. 14–15)

VanPatten has continued to work on these principles over time, modifying them slightly and adding to them in subsequent publications. (See, for example, VanPatten 2004a.) The principles serve as the basis for VanPatten's ideas about input-processing instruction, which are considered in detail in Chapter 16.

VanPatten's input processing principles owe much to his 1990a study. This addressed the key question: 'What happens when learners are asked to attend to meaning and form together or just to meaning or form?' The study asked learners to listen to a text in Spanish under four conditions. In one task, the learners were instructed to listen for content only. In a second task they listened for content and the word 'inflación', making a check mark each time it occurred. In the third task, they listened for content and checked each time they heard the definite article 'la'. In the fourth task they listened for content and checked each time they heard the verb morpheme '–n'. VanPatten reported a significant difference on the comprehension scores (derived from asking students to recall the text) for tasks one and two on the one hand and tasks three and four on the other. There was no difference between the scores for tasks one and two or for tasks three and four. In other words, when the learners attended to form, their comprehension suffered. VanPatten concluded that meaning and form compete for learners' attention and that only when learners can understand input easily are they able to attend to form. VanPatten's results were replicated in a study based on a reading text by Wong (2001).

4 *Robinson's Multiple-Resource Model*

Perhaps the fullest treatment of the part played by attention in L2 learning is that of Robinson (1995a, 2003). In his 2003 survey of work on attention in SLA, he distinguished three senses of attention: (1) attention as selection (corresponding to the first stage in an information-processing model where input is perceived), (2) attention as capacity (corresponding to the central control and decision-making stage), and (3) attention as effort (referring to the sustained attention involved in response execution and monitoring).

Attention as selection addresses how 'input' becomes 'intake' (Corder 1967). It is equated with Schmidt's 'noticing', which Robinson defined as 'detection plus rehearsal in short-term memory, prior to encoding in long-term memory' (Robinson 1995a: 296). Robinson (2003) juxtaposed two accounts of how selection takes place; early on in processing when input is initially attended to or later when information has already entered working memory. In accordance with his preference for a multiple-resources view of working memory, he favoured the latter account; learners are able to process stimuli in parallel and selection takes place after the stimuli have been fully analysed. Accordingly, he proposed that selection arises not because of limits in memory capacity but in response to the goals learners form to satisfy task demands. Selection need not but is likely to involve awareness.

Attention as capacity is discussed in terms of the differential attentional demands placed on working memory by L2 tasks. Robinson considered three theoretical positions. According to single-capacity models, more complex and less automatized tasks consume more attentional capacity. According to multiple-resources models, attention can be allocated to different tasks as long as these do not belong to the same domain (for example, making a mobile call will not interfere with driving a car if it does not involve manual activity). According to interference models, limits on task performance are not the result of limited memory capacity but are caused by involuntary attention shifts induced by changing or conflicting intentions. Robinson noted that current theories of attention are moving away from the notion of a limited capacity.

Attention as effort is 'a "state" concept referring to energy or activity in the processing system' (p. 651). It addresses the extent to which a learner is able to maintain performance on a task over time. Failure to sustain attentional effort can occur as a result of prolonged time on a task and complexity of the task. It is reflected in a decline in the frequency of self-repair and monitoring of output. Robinson suggested that Swain's notion of 'pushed output' (see Chapter 6) implies attention as effort, as pushed L2 output is more effortful than normal production.

Robinson clearly favoured a revised version of a multiple-resources model—one that does not assume a single, limited processing capacity. He presented such a model in Robinson (2001a and 2001b) in accounting for how task characteristics affect attentional allocation. This model is potentially relevant to L2 acquisition but, as presented, it addresses L2 production rather than acquisition and, as such it will be discussed in Chapter 10.

Concluding comment on the role of attention

These accounts of the role of attention share much in common but they also differ in a number of crucial respects. The following is a list of relatively uncontroversial points:

1 A distinction can be drawn between focused and divided attention. Learning is more likely to occur when attention is focused.
2 As Schmidt (2001) put it, 'attention is not a unitary phenomenon, but refers to a variety of mechanisms' (p. 3). Robinson, for example, distinguished attention as selection, attention as capacity, and attention as effort.
3 'Detection' is directed at specific items present in the input not at the abstract rules that underlie the items. It is exemplar-oriented.
4 Learners are likely to experience interference when attempting to attend to more than one aspect of the L2. In particular, conflict may arise when they try to attend to meaning and form simultaneously, leading them to prioritize one or the other.
5 Attended input (i.e. 'intake') is not the same as 'acquisition'. Not all attended input enters long-term memory.

The role of attention is, however, controversial. With regard to the last of these points, for example, there is evidence from vocabulary studies that have investigated the effect of providing word primes (i.e. words that cue selection of a target word by their phonological, orthographic, or semantic similarity to the target) on learning. As N. Ellis (2005) noted, these show some measurable effect for just about every attended percept, even in cases where the level of attention is insufficient for awareness.

The major controversies centre around two issues. First, does attention necessarily involve awareness? Whereas Schmidt assumed that noticing involves at least a low level of awareness, Tomlin and Villa claimed that attention can take place without awareness. Secondly, to what extent is working memory limited or unlimited in capacity? Whereas most SLA researchers presume a single, limited capacity, Robinson argued for a multiple-resourced and unlimited capacity working memory. These controversies will resurface in subsequent sections when we consider implicit learning and models of L2 production.

Integration and restructuring

These are the processes that remain least understood in cognitive SLA. INTEGRATION is a general term that refers to the processes involved in storing items noticed and processed into long-term memory. That is, it involves modification of learners' interlanguage systems. Modification is both quantitative and qualitative. Quantitative changes take place when new forms are added. They entail item learning and assume an exemplar-based representation. Qualitative changes to a learner's implicit knowledge system involve the assigning of new functions to old forms (i.e. the existing form–function network is reorganized). This entails 'mapping', which, following Slobin (1985b), involves forming a link between an existing notion and a phonological form. Context plays an important part in enabling learners to achieve these links. As Doughty (2001) pointed out, mapping assumes that learners are predisposed to construct systems, as reflected in the well-documented sequences of acquisition described in Chapter 3. One of the best accounts of the processes involved in mapping is that provided by Andersen (1984b). Drawing on the work of Slobin in L1 acquisition, Andersen posited a number of OPERATING PRINCIPLES, such as the One-to-One Principle. These are considered in a later section of this chapter. It should be noted that not all features processed in working memory can be incorporated immediately into the learner's implicit knowledge system so, as Gass (1988, 1997a) proposed, learners may place new features/items in a separate storage until they are ready to modify their interlanguage.

The term RESTRUCTURING refers to the qualitative changes that take place in learners' interlanguages. These changes relate to both the way knowledge is represented in the minds of learners and also the strategies they employ. One way of characterizing restructuring is in terms of Anderson's ACT Theory, whereby declarative knowledge is reorganized into procedural knowledge (see earlier section on procedural/declarative knowledge). Another way is in terms of the shift from exemplar-based to rule-based representation. McLaughlin (1990: 118) gave the 'classic' example of the U-shaped learning of the past tense in English and also the process by which formulaic sequences become analysed (Chapter 3).[8] The primary mechanism of restructuring is automatization. McLaughlin (1987) claimed that 'once procedures at any phase become automatized ... learners step up to a "metaprocedural" level which generates representational change and restructuring' (p. 138). In other words, restructuring involves the replacement of existing procedures with more efficient ones. This process is facilitated by the flexible use of learning strategies. In a series of experiments, McLaughlin and his associates were able to show that 'expert' language learners display greater flexibility in restructuring rules, and are therefore able to avoid making certain types of error.

McLaughlin emphasized the importance of practice for both the quantitative and qualitative aspects of learning. Practice is seen as serving two purposes. First, it helps learners to automate sub-skills thus freeing up processing capacity for more complex tasks. This takes place through the accretion of an increasing number of chunks which are then compiled into automated procedures. Second, it enables learners to shift strategies and thereby restructure their L2 representations. This may be accompanied by temporary decrements in performance. Thus, practice may not lead immediately to more target-like representations.

One of the key issues surrounding discussions of integration and restructuring is whether these processes involve awareness. As we will see when we consider implicit learning, a number of psychologists (in particular, Reber) have argued that learners are able to store the underlying rules of a language without awareness. That is, learning does not involve conscious hypothesis formation and testing. Doughty (2001) similarly argued that the processes of mapping and restructuring take place unconsciously, although she noted that the insights that arise from these processes may be available for metalinguistic comment. However, Schmidt (1994) concluded that overall there is very little evidence for induction of knowledge without awareness. Research in general has shown an advantage for learning accompanied by awareness at the level of understanding (as opposed to just noticing) but, as Schmidt pointed out, it is not clear to what extent such learning is robust and long-lasting, or peripheral and fragile.

Monitoring

The final process we will consider is MONITORING. This was considered briefly in Chapter 4 when the psycholinguistic dimension of variability in learner language was discussed. Here we will examine three key questions: (1) how extensive is monitoring? (2) what errors do learners monitor? and (3) in what ways does monitoring assist L2 acquisition? The reader is referred to Kormos (1999 and 2006) for excellent reviews of the research on monitoring.

Views differ as to learners' capacity to monitor. Krashen (1982) claimed that monitoring can only take place when the learner is focused on form, knows the explicit rule to be applied, and has sufficient time. As these conditions were difficult to meet, he believed that monitoring had only a limited role in L2 acquisition. Green and Hecht's (1992) study (discussed earlier in this chapter) suggested that Krashen may have overestimated one of these limitations, as the learners in their study demonstrated explicit knowledge of a wide range of L2 features. This study also showed that the more advanced learners were capable of successfully correcting a large percentage of their errors. Lennon (1994), however, reported that the bulk of the errors corrected in his study were phonological and morphological (43 per cent) and also proforms (20 per cent), which can be explained by the fact that the correction of such errors does not involve any major restructuring of the utterance. Other researchers (for example, Poulisse and Bongaerts 1994) have suggested that attentional limitations can explain why the learners they studied tended to focus on correcting content words rather than function words. Kormos (1999) speculated that the same constraints that govern what learners can notice in the input determine what errors they are able to correct.

Studies have shown that the number and nature of the errors that learners monitor is related to their overall proficiency. Kormos (2000) reported her own study of the correction rate of 30 Hungarian learners of English at three levels of proficiency. She reported that the amount of attention paid to linguistic form at different levels of development did not differ but that there were marked differences in the error correction behaviour of L1 and L2 speakers and also in the types of errors addressed by L2 learners at different proficiency levels. For example, whereas L1 speakers corrected almost twice as many lexical as grammatical errors, the L2 learners corrected a similar proportion of both. Advanced L2 learners repaired discourse-level errors more frequently than pre-intermediate students did. This supports the findings of other studies (for example, Van Hest 1996) which have shown that whereas beginners attend to simple errors, more advanced learners address more complex errors. Kormos (1999) explained such findings in terms of the growth of metalinguistic awareness and automatization of knowledge. Conscious, controlled knowledge is prone to error. As knowledge is proceduralized, the number of errors is reduced. Automatization also releases processing capacity that enables learners to gain more advanced access to their metalinguistic knowledge and to attend to more complex problems.

Kormos (1999) proposed that monitoring assists language acquisition in a number of ways. First, it serves as a means for converting receptive into productive knowledge. This claim is based on Levelt's (1989) perceptual loop theory of monitoring, which sees monitoring as one of the functions of the speech comprehension system. Second, uncertainty regarding whether an error has or has not been committed can motivate the learner to notice-the-gap. Third, correcting errors helps the learner to rehearse an error-free solution to a problem in short-term memory and thereby assists the process by which this is then stored in long-term memory. Fourth, Kormos suggested that the self-repair that results from monitoring may function in much the same way as uptake following CORRECTIVE FEEDBACK. In other words, it constitutes a mechanism that promotes PUSHED OUTPUT, which has been hypothesized to expand the learners' linguistic repertoire. (See Chapter 6 for a discussion of corrective feedback, uptake, and pushed output.)

Macro-processes

Learners differ in the approach they adopt to learning as a result of how they orientate to learning. Drawing on cognitive psychology, SLA researchers have distinguished four general approaches, presented as two dichotomies: (1) incidental versus intentional learning and (2) implicit versus explicit learning. However, it is not easy to distinguish these pairs of constructs. Table 9.4 is my attempt to show the similarities and points of difference in these constructs. The key distinguishing characteristics are intentionality and awareness.

The essence of INTENTIONAL LEARNING is that it involves a deliberate attempt to learn; this may or may not involve awareness. For example, a learner may set out to read a book with the express purpose of increasing his/her vocabulary and is therefore likely to consciously attend to new words in the text. In contrast, INCIDENTAL LEARNING is characterized by an absence of intentionality to learn, but may involve *ad hoc* conscious attention to some features of the L2.

IMPLICIT LEARNING takes place without either intentionality or awareness. However, as we have seen, there is controversy as to whether any learning is possible without some degree of awareness. Schmidt, for example, has disputed whether there is any such thing as implicit learning. EXPLICIT LEARNING is necessarily a conscious process and is likely to be intentional as well, in which case it cannot be distinguished from intentional learning. However, it is possible to envisage explicit learning taking place without intention if intention is defined as a general orientation to learn; that is, explicit attention to language may arise incidentally as a means of coping with some *ad hoc* linguistic problem. But in this case it cannot be easily distinguished from incidental learning.

By now readers may feel that it is splitting hairs to attempt to distinguish these two pairs of terms, as they really reflect a single distinction (what in layman's parlance is called 'picking up' versus 'studying' the L2). Nevertheless, as we will see there are distinct research traditions related to the two distinctions and also it may be possible to identify prototypical tasks for investigating the four types of learning, as shown in Table 9.4.

Approach	**Intentionality**	**Awareness**	**Typical task**
1 Incidental learning	No	Possibly	Learners are given a task that focuses their attention on one aspect of the L2 and, without being pre-warned, tested on some other aspect of the task (e.g. they are asked to read a passage for general understanding and then tested on whether they have learnt a set of words in the text).
2 Intentional learning	Yes	Yes	Learners are given a task (e.g. to memorize a set of words), told they will be tested afterwards and then tested on the task as set.
3 Implicit learning	No	No	Learners are simply exposed to input data, asked to process it for meaning and then tested (without warning) to see what they have learnt (e.g. input-flooding).
4 Explicit learning	Usually	Yes	Learners are either given an explicit rule which they then apply to data in practice activities (deductive explicit learning) or they are asked to discover an explicit rule from an array of data provided (i.e. inductive explicit learning).

Table 9.4 Distinguishing four approaches to learning

Intentional versus incidental learning

As Hulstijn (2003) pointed out, intentional and incidental learning were first investigated within the context of behaviourist psychology. Incidental learning was operationalized in what Hulstijn calls Type 1 studies by asking learners to learn a set of stimuli (for example, a list of words) with orienting instructions that did or did not inform them that they would be tested on completion of a task. In other studies (Type 2), additional stimuli (for example, specific morphological features in the list of words) that the participants were not told about were included in the task and subsequently tested. Cognitive psychologists later took over the Type 2 design. One of the important findings of the psychological research was that in order to measure the effects of the two types of learning it was important to ensure an appropriate match between the method of training and testing (for example, with regard to whether receptive or productive knowledge of the learning target is tested).

There have been only a few studies that have investigated the intentional and incidental learning of L2 grammar. Hulstijn (2003) could identify only three studies (Hulstijn 1989; Robinson 1996b, 1997a) that have explicitly used the term 'incidental'. There is also a later study by Robinson (2005b). However, none of these investigated intentional learning as well. We will consider two of these studies here.

Hulstijn (1989) conducted two studies involving a natural language (L2 Dutch) and an artificial language. Learners were presented with word order structures implicitly (i.e. the structures were not explained to them) and incidentally (i.e. they did not know they would be tested for recall of the structures). They were assigned to one of three treatments involving exposure to sentences containing the target structures. One group (the form-focused group) had to perform an anagram task that directed their attention to the structure without any need to consider its meaning. The second group (the meaning-focused group) were shown the same sentences on a screen and asked to respond meaningfully to them by saying 'yes', 'perhaps', or 'I don't know'. The third group (the form- and meaning-focused group) were simply told to pay attention to both form and meaning but were given no special task to perform. The results showed that the form-focused group outperformed the other two groups in terms of gains in scores on a sentence-copying task and a task requiring cued recall of the sentences used in the learning tasks. Hulstijn interpreted the results as showing that attention to form when encoding input is a 'sufficient condition' for implicit and incidental learning. However, as the meaning-focused group also produced significant gains, the hypothesis that exclusive attention to meaning will inhibit acquisition was not supported. It is possible, though, that the learners in this group engaged in some degree of 'noticing' of the target structures. As Hulstijn pointed out, meaning may be the learner's first priority, but attention to form occurs as a 'backup procedure' in case meaning fails to provide an adequate interpretation.

Robinson's (2005b) study[9] was a replication of Knowlton and Squire (1996). The latter study involved an artificial language but Robinson investigated a natural language—Samoan. Another interesting feature of Robinson's study was that it involved complete beginners. The learners (Japanese university students) were first asked to memorize the meanings of a number of Samoan words. They were then exposed to 150 tokens each of three Samoan grammatical rules, two of which involved the use of particles and the other incorporation of the direct object into verbs. The participants were asked to try as hard as possible to understand the meaning of each sentence. They were asked to respond to yes/no comprehension questions and received feedback on the correctness of their responses. Results showed clear evidence of learning of all three target structures on old items in a GRAMMATICALITY JUDGEMENT test (i.e. the same sentences as in the training materials) but only for one of the structures (the locative particle) on new items. Robinson also reported a negative relationship between chunk strength (measured in terms of whether the test items contained bigrams or trigrams that also occurred in the training items) and accuracy of judgements on both the grammatical and ungrammatical test items. Robinson suggested that this somewhat surprising finding can be explained by the fact that semantic salience as well as chunk strength influenced what the learners attended to in the training items.

In contrast to the paucity of studies of incidental learning of L2 grammar there have been a plethora of studies investigating L2 vocabulary. This is, in part, motivated by the claim that the acquisition of vocabulary, whether in the L1 or L2, must be largely an incidental affair. The sheer size of the vocabulary-learning task (for example, Goulden, Nation, and Read (1990) estimated that the average educated native speaker knows about 17,000 base words) would seem to preclude the possibility that it can be handled successfully by means of intentional learning and points to the need for continual exposure to L2 input through, for example, extensive reading. Even if intentional learning has a role to play in adding 'breadth' (i.e. more words) to a learner's vocabulary, it would seem unlikely that it does much for 'depth' (for example, in learning how words collocate), which requires multiple encounters with a word in different linguistic contexts. However, although the primacy of incidental vocabulary learning is widely acknowledged, there are constraints and limits and there is wide acceptance that intentional vocabulary learning may not only be helpful but possibly necessary to ensure a well-developed L2 lexicon. Huckin and Coady (1999) provided an excellent summary of the main issues surrounding the incidental and intentional learning of vocabulary. These are summarized in Table 9.5.

A number of studies have shown that incidental learning of vocabulary does take place. (See the section on Krashen's Input Hypothesis in Chapter 6.) It should be noted, however, that the power of incidental learning is a matter of some dispute (cf. Dupuy and Krashen 1993 and Horst *et al.* 1998). Other studies have examined the conditions which promote or inhibit incidental learning from exposure to oral or written input. In Ellis (1994c), for example, I identified four sets of factors that have been shown to influence incidental acquisition from oral input: (1) the intrinsic properties of L2 words (for example, the length of a word and its imageability), (2) input factors (for example, frequency and availability of contextual clues), (3) interactional factors (for example, opportunity to request clarification), and (4) learner factors (for example, the learner's immediate phonological memory or encyclopaedic knowledge). Another set of studies have compared the learning rates of incidental and intentional conditions. A clear finding of these studies is that learning rates are much higher for intentional than for incidental learning. For example, Hulstijn (1992) had native speakers of Dutch read an expository text containing 12 pseudo-English words under

1 Incidental learning is not entirely 'incidental', as the learner must pay at least some attention to individual words.
2 Incidental learning requires a basic sight-recognition vocabulary of at least 3,000 word families. For university level texts, a knowledge of 5,000–10,000 word families may be needed.
3 Although incidental acquisition takes place incrementally over a period of time, there is no agreement as to how many of what kinds of exposures are needed for successful acquisition.
4 Effective word guessing requires the flexible application of a variety of processing strategies, ranging from local ones such as graphemic identification to global ones such as the use of broader contextual meanings.
5 Some strategies arise naturally but others need to be taught.
6 Students generally benefit from explicit vocabulary instruction in conjunction with extensive reading.
7 Some kinds of texts are more conducive to incidental learning than others—in particular, texts that are personally interesting to learners.
8 Input modification, including glossing of specific words, is generally effective, especially if it involves the learner interactively.
9 Incidental learning depends on educated guesswork and thus can lead to imprecision, misrecognition, and interference with the reading process. To overcome these problems, learners have to have a well-developed core vocabulary, a stock of good reading strategies, and some prior familiarity with the subject matter.

Table 9.5 Key points in the incidental and intentional learning of vocabulary (Huckin and Coady 1999: 190–1)

an incidental condition (i.e. they were asked to read the passage carefully in order to answer some comprehension questions) and an intentional condition (i.e. they were informed there would be a test of vocabulary contained in the passage). On the immediate post-test, which tested the target words in isolation, the incidental group retained only 4 per cent of the target words and the intentional group 53 per cent. On the delayed post-test, where the words were tested in their original contexts, the retention rates were 43 per cent and 73 per cent. However, as Hulstijn (2003) pointed out, it is necessary to take into account two points in interpreting such studies. The first is that studies such as Hulstijn (1992) did not control for 'time on task' (i.e. nothing is known about how the learners in the two conditions actually spent their time when reading the passage). The second point is that the studies have only investigated the effects of the two learning conditions on 'first encounters' with words and thus do not address the crucial issue of the role played by multiple encounters in developing 'depth' of knowledge.

In concluding his review of research into intentional and incidental learning, Hulstijn (2003) emphasized the wide diversity of issues and approaches.

He argued that the distinction is still of value, but primarily methodologically, given that L2 experimental studies will always need to consider how learners are required to orientate to a learning task. But 'it is not likely that either term will soon receive (or regain) a strong theoretical meaning' (p. 373).

Explicit versus implicit learning

It is important to distinguish explicit/implicit instruction and explicit/implicit learning (Schmidt 1994). The terms explicit and implicit instruction need to be defined from a perspective external to the learner. That is, it is the teacher, materials writer, or course designer who determines whether the instruction is explicit or implicit. In contrast, the terms implicit and explicit learning can only be considered in relation to the learner's perspective. Thus, implicit learning takes place when the learner has internalized a linguistic feature without awareness while explicit learning involves awareness. But what exactly is meant by 'awareness'? As we have seen, Schmidt (1994, 2001) distinguished two types of awareness: awareness as noticing and metalinguistic awareness. The former involves conscious attention to 'surface elements' while the latter involves awareness of the processes involved in incorporating intake into long-term memory. Schmidt argued that noticing typically involves at least some degree of awareness. Thus, from this perspective, there is no such thing as complete implicit learning and so a better definition of implicit learning might be 'learning without any metalinguistic awareness'. That is, the processes responsible for integration and restructuring (see earlier section) take place autonomously and without conscious control. Other researchers (for example, John Williams 2005), however, have argued that learning without awareness at the level of noticing is possible. N. Ellis (2005: 306) claimed that 'the vast majority of our cognitive processing is unconscious'. Thus there is no consensual definition of implicit learning. Explicit learning is less problematic; it is conscious learning 'where the individual makes and tests hypotheses in a search for structure' (N. Ellis (1994a: 1). As Hulstijn (2002) put it, 'it is a conscious, deliberative process of concept formation and concept linking' (p. 206).

Schmidt (1994) also claimed that it is necessary to distinguish implicit/explicit learning and implicit/explicit knowledge. It is possible, for example, that learners will reflect on knowledge that they have acquired implicitly (i.e. without metalinguistic awareness) and thus develop an explicit representation of it subsequently. Also, it is possible that explicit learning directed at one linguistic feature may result in the implicit learning of some other feature. However, Hulstijn (2002) argued there is a necessary correlation between the type of learning and the type of knowledge.

The study of implicit and explicit learning in SLA draws heavily on cognitive psychology. The work of Reber (Reber 1993; Reber, Walkenfeld, and Hernstadt 1991) has been seminal in this respect. Reber, Allen, and Reber (1999) characterized implicit learning as follows:

> Implicit learning (a) operates largely independent of awareness, (b) is subsumed by neuroanatomical structures distinct from those that serve explicit, declarative processes, (c) yields memorial representations that can be either abstract or concrete, (d) is a relatively robust system that survives psychological, psychiatric, and neuroanatomical injury, (e) shows relatively little inter-individual variation, and (f) is relatively unaffected by ontogenetic factors.
> (p. 504)

Reber and colleagues investigated the two types of learning by means of studies involving artificial languages, where groups of participants were instructed to memorize a set of letter strings generated by the artificial language without the help of any feedback (the implicit learning condition) or try to figure out the underlying rules of the same letter strings (the explicit learning condition). Following training, both groups completed a judgement test that required them to decide if the strings of letters followed the same rules as the strings they saw during training. They were not forewarned that they would be tested in this way. The main findings of such studies were: (1) there was clear evidence of implicit learning, (2) there was no difference between the test scores of the implicit and explicit learning groups in the case of simple rules but implicit learning proved more efficient for complex rules, and (3) the test scores of the explicit group demonstrated much greater individual variation than those of the implicit group, reflecting the fact that whereas analytical skills played a role in the former they did not in the latter.

A key issue is whether implicit learning of an L2 (i.e. learning without conscious awareness) is possible. A number of studies have addressed this, including several that have examined the effects of enhanced input on language learning. (See Chapters 6 and 16.) In a series of studies (for example, John Williams 1999, 2005; Williams and Lovatt 2003), John Williams examined whether learners are able to induce grammatical rules from exposure to input when their attention is focused on meaning. The studies showed that learning does take place, that the inductive learning of form (i.e. segmentation) is dissociable from the learning of the functions realized by the forms (i.e. distribution), that learner differences in phonological short-term memory influence the extent to which learners are successful in inductive learning, and that language background (i.e. whether learners have prior experience of learning languages) impacts even more strongly on learning. However, Williams' tests of learning (translation or grammaticality judgement tests) may have favoured those learners who attempted to construct explicit rules during the training and thus cannot convincingly demonstrate that *implicit* learning took place. Indeed, John Williams (1999) noted that the learners in this study 'had high levels of awareness of the product of learning' (p. 38), although, as he pointed out, awareness of the product of learning does not necessarily imply that conscious analysis occurred while learning. What is needed to resolve this issue are studies that obtain information about the micro-processes involved in the training (learning) phase of such studies.

One study that has attempted this is Leow (1997b). Leow asked beginner learners of L2 Spanish to think aloud as they completed a crossword that exposed them to a number of morphological forms. Learning was measured by means of a multiple choice recognition task and a fill-in-the blank written production task. The think-aloud protocols were analysed qualitatively to establish to what extent the learners demonstrated meta-awareness in the form of hypothesis-testing and conscious rule-formation. Leow reported that the level of awareness learners demonstrated correlated with both their ability to recognize and produce correct target forms. This study, together with Leow's (2000) follow-up study, demonstrated that online measures of meta-awareness are related to offline measures of learning, strongly suggesting that the learning which took place in these studies was explicit rather than implicit. DeKeyser (2003), summarizing the results of a number of studies that have investigated implicit learning, concluded 'there is very little hard evidence of learning without awareness' (p. 317).[10]

This conclusion raises doubts about studies that have purported to compare implicit and explicit learning. It can be argued that such studies are really comparing two types of explicit learning—that is, covert as opposed to overt explicit learning. Table 9.6 summarizes a number of representative SLA studies of the two types of learning. I have only included those studies that were based on natural languages in line with Robinson's (2005b) arguments that the learning of artificial languages (on which many studies have been based) differs from the learning of natural languages in that the former only involve segmentation of form whereas the latter also involve form–function mapping. I have also focused on laboratory studies that purported to investigate implicit/explicit learning, leaving consideration of classroom studies of the effects of implicit/explicit instruction to Chapter 16.

Care must be taken in attempting to generalize on the basis of these studies as implicit and explicit learning were operationalized and their effects measured in very different ways. Several of the studies indicate that implicit learning is successful (Doughty 1991; Shook 1994; Gass *et al.* 2003), although, as noted above, whether or not the learners actually engaged in implicit learning is not demonstrated. All the studies show that explicit learning is effective. Several of the studies found explicit learning to be more effective than implicit learning (N. Ellis 1993; Rosa and O'Neill 1999; Gass *et al.* 2003) while, in contrast, no study showed that implicit learning worked better than explicit learning. However, two of the studies (Doughty 1991; Shook 1994) found no difference between implicit and explicit learning. There is also some evidence to suggest that explicit learning is more effective with some linguistic features than others. Robinson (1996b) reported that his explicit learners outperformed the implicit learners on the simple structure (subject-verb inversion) but not on the complex structure (pseudo-clefts). Gass *et al.* (2003) found that their focused condition (which involved explicit attention to form and meaning) proved more effective than the unfocused condition for lexis than for morphology or syntax. It would seem then that there may be linguistic constraints determining when explicit learning is effective. (See Hulstijn and de Graaf 1994 for an in-depth discussion of this issue.) Three of the studies investigated learners' awareness of the structures they were learning. Rosa and O'Neill (1999) replicated Leow's (1997b) finding; learners who demonstrated high awareness during the learning outperformed those with low awareness. N. Ellis and Robinson both tested the learners' ability to verbalize the rule they had been learning but with different results. N. Ellis found the most explicit group in his study were able to verbalize the rule whereas Robinson reported that very few learners in any of his conditions could although, where the simple rule was concerned, the most explicit group (the one receiving an explanation of the rule) outperformed the rest. Finally, Gass *et al.*'s study raises the possibility that learners' level of proficiency may mediate the effects of explicit instruction; in this study the focused condition proved most effective with the low-proficiency learners.

On balance, it would appear that the advantage lies with explicit learning. However, there are two reasons to reserve judgement. First, the treatments in these studies were all of short duration, which arguably creates a bias against implicit learning. Second, the effects of the training were measured by the kinds of tests (for example, grammaticality judgement tests) likely to favour explicit learning. DeKeyser (2003), summing up the research, commented: 'the amount of L2 research narrowly focused on the implicit-explicit distinction is quite limited, not only in the number of studies, but also in duration and in scope of the learning target' (p. 336).

Study	**Participants**	**Linguistic target**	**Design**	**Results**
Doughty (1991)	20 intermediate level ESL students	English relative clauses with direct object relativized.	Two experimental groups. Both of which read computerized passages: (1) Meaning-focused group—support provided by means of lexical and semantic rephrasings and sentence clarification strategies. (2) Rule-oriented group—support provided by means of explicit rule statements and on-screen manipulation.	Both experimental groups outperformed the control group. (1) outperformed (2) in a test of the comprehension of the passage.

N. Ellis (1993)	English-speaking university students	Soft mutation of linguistic consonants in Welsh.	Three groups: (1) Exposure to numerous examples of consonant modifications in a random order; (2) Explicit explanation of the rules plus same random exposure as (1); (3) Explicit explanation of the rules, plus two examples, plus random exposure. Tests of explicit knowledge of the rule and grammaticality judgements.	Group (1) was the fastest in judging old sentences but the slowest in generalizing to new sentences. (2) learnt the explicit rules but was limited in applying them when judging well-formedness. Group (3)—the rules + instances group—outperformed the other two groups.
Shook (1994)	Adult learners of L2 Spanish	(1) Present perfect; (2) relative pronouns	Three groups: (1) Reading passage with target items highlighted. (2) As in (1) but learners instructed to focus on target structures. (3) Same reading passage with no highlighted items and no instruction to focus on target structures.	Groups (1) and (2) outperformed (3). All participants did better on present perfect than relative pronouns.
Robinson (1996b)	104 predominantly intermediate-level Japanese ESL learners	(1) Pseudo-clefts of location (hard rule); (2) subject-verb inversion following adverbial fronting (easy rule).	Four instructional conditions: (1) Implicit condition (remembering sentences); (2) Incidental condition (exposure in meaning-centred task); (3) Rule-search condition (identifying rules); (4) Instructed condition (written explanations of rules). Grammaticality judgement test—measuring correctness of judgements and response times. Debriefing questionnaire to measure awareness.	The explicit learners did not outperform the implicit learners on the complex rule. The instructed learners outperformed all the others in learning the simple rule. Very few of the learners were able to verbalize either of the rules.

Rosa and O'Neill (1999)	64 fourth semester university-level learners of L2 Spanish	Spanish contrary-to-fact conditional in the past (a complex structure).	A multiple choice jigsaw puzzle presented under four conditions: (1) Rule explanation + rule search; (2) rule explanation + no rule search; (3) no rule explanation + rule search; (4) no rule explanation + no rule search. Time-pressured multiple choice recognition task; think-aloud protocols to measure awareness.	Groups (1) and (2), but not group (3), outperformed group (4) (i.e. the more explicit conditions were more beneficial than the implicit condition). Learners who demonstrated high awareness demonstrated more learning than learners with low awareness.
Gass, Svetics, and Lemelin (2003)	Adult learners of L2 Italian—three proficiency levels	(1) Lexis; (2) morphosyntax; (3) syntax	A + focused and a – focused condition was created for each of the linguistic targets (e.g. for lexis the + focused condition required students to read a story focusing on the target words underlined followed by further activities focusing on the words' meanings; the – focused condition required students to read a passage with no underlined words and answer some comprehension questions followed by activities that did not focus on target words.	+ focused condition resulted in greater gains than – focused. Some learning took place even in the – focused condition; + focused condition had a greater effect on lexis than on morphology and syntax; the + focused condition had the greatest effect with low-proficiency learners.

Table 9.6 Selected studies of the implicit and explicit learning of natural languages

Final comment on the study of processes of L2 acquisition

The study of the mental processes involved in L2 acquisition lies at the heart of cognitive approaches in SLA. These processes cannot be directly observed. They have to be either assumed to take place on the grounds that an instructional set will predispose learners to act in predictable ways, or examined through think-aloud or retrospective learner reports, or inferred from tests of learning. There are limitations in all of these methods. Learners may not act in the way they were intended to. Think-aloud is likely to encourage certain processes at the expense of others and may interfere with natural processing.

Tests provide knowledge of learning products and there can be no simple correlation between processes and products. A further limitation is that many of the studies have taken place in a laboratory setting raising doubts as to the ecological validity of their findings. Nevertheless, the study of these processes has hugely enriched SLA and illuminated our understanding of how acquisition takes place. We now have a much fuller understanding of the role played by attention and working memory, a somewhat more limited picture of how integration/restructuring takes place (more on this in the section on connectionist models below), and quite detailed information about monitoring. The research on macro-processes is perhaps less satisfying, in part because of the problems of distinguishing incidental/intentional learning from implicit/explicit learning, but perhaps more so because of the difficulty of determining exactly what kind of learning is taking place when learners perform a task. In general, theorizing (and speculation too) has tended to outrun empirical enquiry. But this may simply reflect a stage in the development of cognitive SLA. In the next section, we will examine a number of general theories of L2 acquisition which, in one way or another, are cognitive in nature. These theories all draw on the micro- and macro-processes described in this section.

Cognitive theories of L2 acquisition

A complete cognitive theory of L2 acquisition would need to account for the following:

1 how learners extract information about the L2 from the input
2 how they 'operate' on this information internally in order to construct an interlanguage
3 the role played by explicit knowledge of the L2 in the development of implicit (procedural) knowledge
4 the role played by learner output in (1) and (2)
5 the role played by the learner's L1 in (1) and (2).

There is no complete cognitive theory that addresses all of these. The theories considered below typically focus on one or two facets.

The Nativization Model and Operating Principles

The NATIVIZATION MODEL (Andersen 1979a, 1980) proposes that L2 acquisition consists of two general processes, nativization and denativization. In the former, learners make the input conform to their own internalized view of what constitutes the L2 system. That is, they simplify the learning task by forming hypotheses based on knowledge that they already possess (L1 knowledge and knowledge of the world). In Andersen's terms, they attend to an 'internal norm'. The result is the kind of pidginization evident in early language acquisition and documented in Schumann's work. (See Chapters 1 and 7.) In denativization, learners accommodate to an 'external norm';

that is, they adjust their interlanguage systems to make them fit with the input, making use of inferencing strategies. Denativization is apparent in depidginization (the elaboration of a pidgin language which occurs through the gradual incorporation of forms from an external source). Andersen's later work is an attempt to develop the nativization model by further specifying the 'processes, cognitive operating principles, and communicative strategies' (Andersen 1990: 48) that fit within it.

Andersen has been strongly influenced by Slobin's idea of Operating Principles. In a series of publications culminating in his two-volume *The Crosslinguistic Study of Language Acquisition* (1985a), Slobin described the universal principles that guide children in the process of L1 acquisition. These principles are conceived as the operating principles by which children extract and segment linguistic information in order to build a grammar of the language they are learning (for example, 'Pay attention to stressed syllables in extracted speech units' and 'Keep track of the frequency of occurrence of every unit and pattern that you store'). The identification of such principles requires the painstaking analysis of production data from many unrelated languages in order to separate out language-specific tendencies from universal principles.

OPERATING PRINCIPLES can explain the pattern of acquisition accounted for by the ASPECT HYPOTHESIS, discussed briefly in Chapter 4. Andersen and Shirai (1994, 1996) invoked four operating principles to show why L2 learners, like L1 learners, have been found to restrict their use of L2 verb morphology in such a way that each inflection is used with a separate and distinct semantic class of verbs. (For example, past and perfective inflections are restricted primarily to verbs expressing accomplishment and achievement whereas progressive inflections are used initially with verbs expressing activity.) Table 9.7 describes and illustrates the relevant operating principles. These principles, however, do not relate only to language acquisition. Native speakers also follow the Aspect Hypothesis, albeit in terms of distributional bias rather than absolutely. Thus, the principles reflect 'speakers' (both learners and non-learners) communicative need to distinguish reference to the main point/goal of talk from supporting information' (Andersen and Shirai 1994: 152). There are differences between L2 learners and native-speakers, however. The latter achieve the freedom to use verb markers in non-prototypical ways to serve their communicative purposes.

Operating Principles clearly afford only a limited account of how learners acquire an L2. They account for only one of the five requirements of a complete theory of L2 acquisition listed above, i.e. (2): how learners 'operate' internally on the information they obtain from the input in order to construct an interlanguage. Operating Principles have been criticized in both L1 and L2 acquisition research on a number of grounds. Dulay and Burt (1974d) and Larsen-Freeman (1975) argued that they are difficult to test and are not mutually exclusive. Also, it is not clear how many principles are needed to explain

Principle	Definition	Example
The Relevance Principle	A grammatical morpheme is first used by learners according to how relevant it is to the meaning of the verb.	Aspect is more relevant to the meaning of a verb than tense, mood, or agreement, so the first uses of verb morphemes are as aspect markers.
The Congruency Principle	Learners will choose, from the various aspectual morphemes they have noticed in the input, the morpheme whose aspectual meaning is most congruent with the aspectual meaning of the verb.	Past or perfective markers are initially used primarily with event verbs; progressive markers are used primarily with activity verbs.
The One-to-One Principle	'An interlanguage system should be constructed in such a way that an intended underlying meaning is expressed with one clear invariant surface form (or construction)' (Andersen 1984b: 79).	The past morpheme is used to signal completion or end point, the progressive morpheme ongoing activity, etc.
The Prototype Principle	Learners will infer from the input the most prototypical meaning of each inflection and associate the inflection with the most prototypical members of each semantic class of verbs. Gradually they extend its use to less prototypical members.	The past morpheme is first used with such verbs as 'fall' ('fell') and only later with verbs such as 'run' ('ran').

Table 9.7 Operating Principles in L2 acquisition (summarized from Andersen and Shirai 1994)

acquisition. These criticisms, which were levelled at Slobin's (1973) earlier list, still apply to the later list. Bowerman (1985) pointed out that Slobin only *lists* operating principles, but this is inadequate because we need to know how the various principles are related to each other and, importantly, what weight is to be attached to principles when they conflict. Andersen acknowledged these criticisms, but argued that they do not warrant rejecting the whole idea of operating principles. The solution is to work on them and refine them. His work with Shirai on the Aspect Hypothesis goes some way to achieving this. It also addresses Pleh's (1990) criticism of Slobin (1985a), namely, that there is no explanation of the principles themselves; the principles reflect natural processes of communication. Clearly, though, to be thoroughly convincing, it will be necessary to show how Operating Principles explain a wider range of phenomena than those examined to date.

The Multidimensional Model and Processability Theory

The two related theories (in fact one grew out of the other) that we will consider here—the MULTIDIMENSIONAL MODEL (Clahsen, Meisel, and Pienemann 1983) and PROCESSABILITY THEORY (Pienemann 1998 and 2005b)—were developed to account for the acquisitional sequences in L2 German and L2 English (described in Chapter 3) and subsequently for other L2s. They view the regularities in learner language as the product of cognitive procedures that govern the linguistic operations learners are able to handle. These theories constitute a considerable advance on the idea of operating principles in that they relate underlying cognitive processes to stages in the learner's development, explaining how one stage supersedes another.

The Multidimensional Model makes the following general claims:

1 Learners manifest developmental sequences in the acquisition of a number of grammatical structures, such as word order and some grammatical morphemes.
2 Learners also display individual variation with regard to the extent to which they apply developmental rules and also the extent to which they acquire and use grammatical structures that are not developmentally constrained.
3 Developmental sequences reflect the systematic way in which learners overcome processing constraints. These constraints are of a general cognitive nature and govern production.
4 Individual learner variation reflects the overall orientation to the learning task, which in turn is the product of social-psychological factors.
5 Formal instruction directed at developmental features will only be successful if learners have mastered the prerequisite processing operations associated with the previous stage of acquisition. However, formal instruction directed at grammatical features subject to individual variation faces no such constraints.

The account of the Multidimensional Model that follows will consider points (2) to (4). The evidence for (1) was considered in Chapter 3. Point (5) is considered in Chapter 16, where we will consider Pienemann's views on 'teachability'. Regarding (2), Meisel, Clahsen, and Pienemann (1981) noted that within the defined stages of development, there was considerable variation among learners. This variation is of two kinds. First, learners differ in the extent to which they apply a particular word order rule to different linguistic contexts. For example, the inversion rule in German applies in a number of contexts—after an interrogative pronoun, after a preposing adverbial, after the topicalization of a direct object, and after a sentence-initial adverbial clause—but when learners acquire this rule they do not invariably apply it to all these contexts. Meisel, Clahsen, and Pienemann (1981: 126) commented: 'whereas some learners seem to acquire a rule perfectly before they move on to the next learning task, others are less perfect in terms of the target language'. Second, learners vary in the extent to which they use RESTRICTIVE SIMPLIFICATION and ELABORATIVE SIMPLIFICATION. This distinction works in much the same way in learner language as it does in foreigner talk. (See the discussion in Chapter 6.) Thus, restrictive simplification is designed to achieve 'optimal results in communication' by 'reducing the grammar in a way that makes it easy to handle' (Meisel 1980: 36). It is always evident in the early stages of acquisition. Elaborative simplification is 'a strategy that helps to complexify the grammatical system' by formulating hypotheses that are 'approximations to the actual rule' and often involve overextensions of a rule (op. cit.: 37). Not all learners engage in elaborative simplification.

The model therefore has two principal axes, the developmental and the variational, as shown in Figure 9.4. This allows for learners to be grouped both in terms of their stage of development and in terms of the kind of simplification they engage in. For example, Figure 9.4 shows two learners (A and B) at stage 5, two at stage 4 (C and D), and two others at stage 3 (E and F), reflecting their progress along the developmental axis. It also shows differences between the learners at each level. For example, learner B produces more standard-like language than learner A. Meisel, Clahsen, and Pienemann (1981) emphasized that progress along one axis or dimension is independent of progress along the other. It is theoretically possible, therefore, for a learner who practises elaborative simplification to use more target-like language overall than a learner who is 'developmentally' far more advanced. Learner F, for instance, is only at stage 3, but uses more standard-like constructions than Learner A, who is at stage 5.

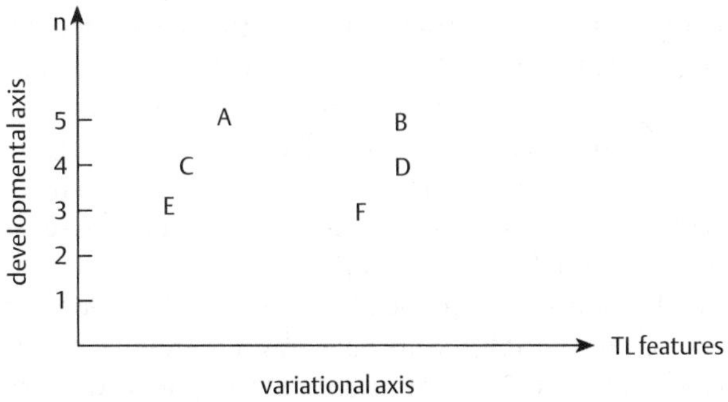

Figure 9.4 The two axes of the Multidimensional Model

The Multidimensional Model seeks to explain why learners pass through the stages of development they do (point (3)), and also, on the basis of this, affords predictions regarding when other grammatical structures (those that have not yet been investigated) will be acquired. In other words, the model has both explanatory and predictive power. This is achieved by specifying the processing constraints that learners need to overcome. Clahsen (1984) identified three language processing strategies, each one corresponding to the degree of psychological complexity involved in the production of a particular word order rule:

1 *Canonical Order Strategy (COS)*

No permutation or reordering of constituents in a structure occurs; utterances manifest a 'basic' order that reflects a direct mapping of meaning onto syntactic form. This strategy blocks the interruption of the underlying structure.

2 *Initialization/Finalization Strategy (IFS)*

No permutation involving the movement of an element from within a structure occurs, but movement of an initial element in a structure to final position and vice versa is possible.

3 *Subordinate Clause Strategy (SCS)*

No permutation of any element in a subordinate clause is possible, but movement of an element from within a main clause to another position in the clause is possible.

Progress entails the removal of the processing 'blocks'. For example, learners who have acquired the verb separation rule and thus can produce utterances like:

alle kinder muss die pause machen
(all the children must the pause make)

but have not yet acquired either inversion or verb-end (see Table 3.8 for examples) have overcome the constraint relating to the Canonical Order Strategy but not the constraints governing the other two strategies. The three strategies are hierarchical in that SCS is not manifest until IFS is evident, which in turn cannot be employed until COS has been accessed. The acquisition of grammatical structures occurs as learners systematically overcome the constraints identified in these processing strategies. The strategies are themselves developmental, not in the sense that learners do not already 'know' them—they clearly do, as they are involved in L1 production—but in the sense that they can only be accessed in the L2 incrementally.

The Multidimensional Model also has a social-psychological dimension that accounts for the simplification strategies employed by individual learners (point (4)). This is described in terms of a continuum reflecting learners' orientations towards learning the L2 (Meisel, Clahsen, and Pienemann 1981). At one end is segregative orientation, which arises when there is a lack of interest in contact with native speakers, discrimination on the part of native speakers, and a general lack of motivation. At the other end is integrative orientation, which is evident in learners with either a strong desire to assimilate into the L2 culture or in those with no desire to acculturate but with a strong instrumental need to learn the L2. The social-psychological dimension of the model echoes the social theories of L2 acquisition considered in Chapter 7. It explains the extent to which individual learners conform to target-language norms. The learner's orientation, however, has no effect on the general sequence of progression along the developmental axis.

Pienemann's Processability Theory is best seen as a development of the Multidimensional Model, as it also seeks to explain what is known about acquisitional sequences in terms of a set of processing procedures. As Pienemann (2005a: 2) put it 'once we can spell out the sequence in which language processing routines develop we can delineate those grammars that are processable at different points of development'. Drawing on LEVELT'S MODEL OF SPEECH PRODUCTION (see Chapter 4), he proposed that language production, whether in the L1 or the L2, could only be explained with reference to a set of basic premises: (1) speakers possess relatively specialized processing components that operate autonomously and in parallel, (2) processing is incremental (i.e. a processor can start working on the incomplete output of another processor), (3) in order to cope with non-linearity (i.e. the fact that a linguistic sequence does not match the natural order of events as in 'Before the man rode off, he mounted his horse'), speakers need to store grammatical information in memory, and thus it follows that (4) grammatical processing must have access to a grammatical memory store, which is 'procedural' rather than 'declarative'. It should be clear from this account that Processability Theory is in actuality a theory of language production. However, it can lay claim to being a theory of language acquisition in that it proposes that the processing procedures are hierarchical and are mastered one at a time. As Pienemann (2005: 13) put it 'it is hypothesised that processing devices will be acquired in their sequence of activation in the production process'. Thus, the failure to master a low-level procedure blocks access to higher-level procedures and makes it impossible for the learner to acquire those grammatical features that depend on them.

Pienemann (1998, 2005a) identified the following language generation processes:

1 word/lemma
2 category procedure (lexical category)
3 phrasal procedures (head)
4 S-procedure and word order rule
5 matrix/subordinate clause.

What distinguishes these processes is the nature of the grammatical information that the learner needs to deposit and exchange in what Pienemann called 'feature unification'.[11] Initially, learners are unable to control any of the processes involved. At this stage, learners can access L2 words but these are invariant in form and are used in single constituent utterances. The learners' lexicon is not annotated, while transfer of L1 annotation is blocked because the learner has not yet developed the specialized procedures to hold L2 grammatical information in memory. Thus, the beginning learner 'is unable to produce any structures which rely on the exchange of specific grammatical information using syntactic procedures' (Pienemann 2005a: 11). The first procedure to be mastered is the 'category procedure'. Lexical entries are now annotated with a number of diacritic features (for example, 'possessive' and 'number'). These can be accessed but only within a single constituent and are matched directly with the underlying conceptual content of a message, so still no exchange of grammatical information is required. At this stage, the learner is still not able to handle structures where diacritic features need to be matched across elements within a constituent or between constituents. The ability to handle this begins at the next stage—the level of phrasal constituents. Now it is possible for learners to handle such structures as articles, plural agreement, and do-fronting (for example, 'Do he like it?'). Exchange of information in the phrasal procedure is required to check the value of a diacritic feature of one lexical entry (for example, 'child') with that of another (for example, the indefinite article 'a') to ascertain that they match and thus enable the production of a structural phrase (for example, 'a child'). At this stage, however, exchange of information *between* structural phrases is still not possible. This is activated at the next stage—the S-procedure. This involves exchange of information between heads of different phrases, as in subject-verb agreement which entails the unification of features such as person and number *across* constituent boundaries. The features of one constituent (the subject noun phrase) are deposited in the S-procedure and subsequently placed in another constituent (the verb phrase). When this becomes possible learners are able to mark the third person of the present simple tense with the –s morpheme. The final procedure to be acquired enables learners to process the word order of subordinate structures such as that found in embedded questions in English (for example, 'He asked where I lived') and verb-end in German (for example, 'Er fragt warum ich traurig war'). Pienemann argued there is a basic difference between the first three procedures and the last two in the hierarchy in that structures appearing in levels 1–3 cannot be represented by constituent structure rules because the S-procedure has not been developed. Thus, in the early stages 'sentences are formed using simplified procedures based on a direct mapping of argument structure onto functional structure' (p. 14).

One of the strengths of Processability Theory is that it affords an explanation of how both syntactic features such as word order and morphological features are acquired. Thus, for example, the phrase procedure makes possible such syntactic structures as do-fronting and such morphological features as noun phrase agreement (as with plurals) while the S-procedure makes possible both yes/no inverted questions and tense agreement. The theory posits that different morphemes will be acquired at different times. Morphemes such as past tense –ed can be produced without the phrasal procedure and therefore emerge when lexical categories begin to be marked with diacritics. Morphemes such as indefinite article ('a') require a phrasal procedure so will only emerge when this procedure has been mastered. Inter-phrasal morphemes such as third person –s appear when the S-procedure becomes available.

Pienemann (1998, 2005a) also addressed a number of other key issues within the compass of Processability Theory: (1) the similarity/difference between L1 and L2 acquisition, (2) variability in learner language, (3) variability in rate of development and ultimate level of attainment, and (4) the role of the L1. He noted that although the sequence of acquisition in L1 and L2 may be different (as is the case in L1/L2 acquisition of German) this does not mean that both types of acquisition are not subject to the same processing constraints. He argued that the differences are the result of the fact that L1 and L2 learners' initial hypothesis may differ. For example in the case of German L1, learners' canonical word order is subject-object-verb (SOV) whereas in L2 learners it is typically SVO. This has implications for which procedures are now required for development. Whereas L2 learners need to instantiate the category and phrasal procedures, L1 learners do not because these are implicated in the verb-end order.

To account for variability, Pienemann suggested that if learners are unable to carry out a particular processing operation (such as S-procedure required for aux-second in WH– questions), they may resort to one of several solutions to the problem this poses them. They may leave out a constituent (for example, 'Where he going?') or utilize canonical word order (for example, 'Where he is going?'). Thus variability arises because 'processability leaves a certain amount of leeway which allows the learner a range of solutions' (2005: 49).

Variability in rate of development and ultimate level of attainment is explained with reference to VARIATIONAL FEATURES. If learners make 'inferior choices' with regard to these features then this may impede access to processing procedures. For example, if learners select the zero copula option in equational sentences (for example, 'me good') this has repercussions for the acquisition of question formation as they lose out on a prototypical form of inversion (i.e. 'Am I good?'). Thus the selections that learners make with regard to variational features determine rate and level of progress along the developmental axis. In this respect, Processability Theory appears to differ from the Multidimensional Model which claims that the developmental and variational axes of L2 acquisition are completely independent of each other.

Pienemann, Di Biase, Kawaguchi, and Hakansson (2005) addressed the role of the L1 in Processability Theory. The key points they made are that an L1 feature is not transferred even if it corresponds to an L2 feature unless it is processable (i.e. constitutes a feature that is located within the learner's current processing capacity), and following on from this, that the initial state of the L2 does not correspond to the final state of the L1.

It should be clear that both the Multidimensional Model and Processability Theory have predictive as well as explanatory power. The cognitive dimension afforded by the identification of underlying processing strategies and operations allows researchers to form hypotheses regarding which grammatical structures will be acquired at which general stage of development. The predictive framework has been applied to Japanese to test the validity of hypotheses relating to the acquisition of the particles 'wa', 'ga', and 'o' in a cross-sectional study by Yoshioka and Doi (1988) and a longitudinal study by Kawaguchi (2005), both of which supported predictions based on the theory. The predictive power of the model is possibly greater than that of any other model of L2 acquisition, with the possible exception of the Competition Model (considered below).

There are, however, several problems with the model. One concerns the reliance on emergence as the measure of acquisition, especially as this entails excluding formulaic sequences, which, as we have noted in Chapter 3, cannot be easily and reliably identified. If a learner, supposedly at stage 2, produces an utterance like 'Where does he live?', which belongs to stage 5, to what extent does this falsify the theory? It is very easy to immunize the theory by claiming that such an utterance is a 'formula' and thus not subject to processing constraints. But unless there is a clear method for identifying such formulas before the analysis proceeds, the theory runs the danger of becoming unfalsifiable. Another problem is the difficulty of establishing *a priori* which features are variational and, therefore, not subject to the constraints that govern developmental features. Unless we are able to stipulate beforehand which features are variational and which developmental, it is easy to dismiss any feature that fails to conform to the predictive framework of the model on the grounds that it is variational. These are serious problems.

Another problem concerns the operational definition of 'acquisition'. Whereas the original research on which the Multidimensional Model was based quantified all the features examined by indicating their overall proportion of suppliance in obligatory contexts (as in Meisel, Clahsen, and Pienemann 1981: 112), Pienemann and his co-workers subsequently redefined acquisition in terms of 'onset' (i.e. the first appearance of a grammatical feature). Hulstijn (1987), while accepting that the study of 'onset' is legitimate in a model that emphasizes the importance of processing operations, nevertheless felt that much of the work lacks rigour because Pienemann 'does not set quantitative or qualitative criteria to be met by the learner's production, in order to be considered as evidence for the operation of a predicted processing strategy' (1987: 14). The problem of defining 'onset', of course, derives in part from the difficulty of identifying formulas and variational features.

Yet another problem concerns the somewhat limited range of grammatical phenomena that the theories have addressed. Hudson (1993) noted that L2 development does not stop when learners have mastered the matrix/subordinate clause procedure and that there are many aspects of grammatical competence that the Multidimensional Model fails to address. However, Pienemann (2005a) went some way to address this failing by extending Processability Theory to include additional hypotheses: the Topic Hypothesis, for example, accounts for the procedures learners need to produce attention-getting linguistic devices involved in topicalization; and the Lexical Mapping

Hypothesis can account for such structures as the passive and causative, not originally included in the original processability hierarchy.

Finally, we should note that both the Multidimensional Model and Processability Theory only provide an explanation of acquisition in terms of learner production. They tell us nothing about how learners come to comprehend grammatical structures, nor do they inform us about how comprehension and production interact. In particular, neither theory addresses how learners obtain intake from input and how this is then used to reconstruct internal grammars. It is in this respect that the theories are most limited.

Emergentist models of L2 language acquisition

In EMERGENTIST accounts of language acquisition (first and second), knowledge is not seen as 'rules', nor is there any distinction drawn between 'declarative' and 'procedural' knowledge. A good example of an emergentist account can be found in Larsen-Freeman's (1997) application of chaos theory to L2 acquisition. Drawing on work in the physical sciences that has shown that complex systems are random, non-linear, unpredictable, self-organizing, and subject to 'strange attractors' (i.e. they home in on a pattern that determines the boundaries of the phenomenon), Larsen-Freeman proposed that language and L2 acquisition are best viewed as complex systems. She identified a number of features of L2 acquisition that justify this analogy: it constitutes a dynamic process characterized by variability, this process is self-evidently complex (i.e. it involves a number of interacting factors), it is non-linear (i.e. learners do not master one item and then move on to another), the learner's interlanguage system is self-organizing (i.e. it manifests 'restructuring'), and the learner's L1 functions as a 'strange attractor'. Larsen-Freeman's application of chaos theory is fundamentally emergentist in that it conflates how L2 knowledge is represented with how it is used and develops over time.

Probably the most influential emergentist model in SLA is CONNECTIONISM. This views learners' knowledge of language as a labyrinth of interconnections between 'units' that do not correspond to any holistic concepts of the kind we normally recognize (for example, a real-life person or object or, where language is concerned, a word or grammatical feature). Performance (i.e. information processing) involves the activation of the requisite interconnections; learning arises when, as a result of experience, the strength of the connections (i.e. 'weights') between units is modified. Connectionism affords 'a unified model of cognition, straddling the traditional competence/performance distinction' (Plunkett 1988: 307).

Connectionism originated in the relatively well-established notion in psychology of 'parallel processing'. This was advanced by the work of the PARALLEL DISTRIBUTED PROCESSING (PDP) group headed by Rumelhart and McClelland. (See Rumelhart, McClelland, and the PDP Research Group 1986a and 1986b.) This work entailed the development of both a theory to explain information processing and learning, and various computer models that simulated actual learning tasks. These simulations functioned as tests of the theory. An example of one of Rumelhart and McClelland's simulations is provided later in this section.

What exactly does a connectionist model of language learning claim? In a series of articles, N. Ellis (1994a, 1996, 1998, 1999, 2001, 2002, 2005, 2006a, 2006b) outlined an emergentist, constructivist, and empiricist view of language learning that incorporates the key precepts of connectionism. These are:

1 Learning is based on simple learning mechanisms.

Emergentism assumes a relatively simple learning mechanism and a massively complex environment. N. Ellis (1998) disputed the view held by generative linguistics that such a complex phenomenon as language can only be learnt if it is assumed that humans are endowed genetically with a language specific learning device:

> Simple learning mechanisms, operating in and across (cognitive) systems as they are exposed to language data as part of a communicatively-rich human social environment by an organism eager to exploit the functionality of language, suffice to drive the emergence of complex language representations
> (p. 644).

Connectionist models of language learning constitute one kind of emergentist account; the COMPETITION MODEL, considered next, is another.

2 Language is exemplar- rather than rule-based.

Learning consists of 'sequences' of sounds (letters), words and phrases. N. Ellis (2002) rejected the symbolist account of language and language learning, arguing that language is governed by an 'idiom principle' and that the data that learners obtain from the input are 'chunks' (such as 'lexical phrases') that are stored as 'memories':

> ... the knowledge underlying fluent language is not grammar in the sense of abstract rules or structure but a huge collection of memories of previous experienced utterances
> (p. 166).

In other words, learning entails item- rather than rule-learning. It involves the building of associations between phonological (or orthographic) elements. In other words, connectionists adopt a constructivist view of learning:

> Constructivists hold that grammatical development is a process of gradually assembling knowledge about distributional and semantic-distributional relationships between words.
> (N. Ellis 1996: 98)

The attested universal orders and sequences of acquisition (see Chapter 3) are not to be taken as evidence of an innate acquisition device but rather a reflection of how complex structures emerge out of simpler, basic forms.

3 Learning a language involves learning 'constructions'.

CONSTRUCTIONS are 'recurrent patterns of linguistic elements that serve some well-defined linguistic function' (N. Ellis 2003: 66). They can be at sentence level or below. Many constructions are based on particular lexical items which can be single words or whole sentences (i.e. they are formulaic in nature). Constructions can also be abstract such as the ditransitive pattern with verbs like 'fax' (for example, Pat faxed Bill the letter') or the caused motion pattern with verbs like 'push' (for example, Pat pushed the napkin off the table'). These abstract patterns cater to the creativity of language, allowing speakers to construct unique utterances such as 'Pat sneezed the napkin off the table'. N. Ellis (2003) proposed that the acquisition of constructions involves a developmental sequence from formula, through low-scope pattern (involving the partial analysis of formulaic chunks that enables learners to discover how particular lexical items work syntactically) to construction.

4 Learning is a process of gradually strengthening associations between elements.

That is, the association strengths among units are spontaneously modified. Learning consists of discovering the right connection strengths (i.e. those that reflect native-speaker competence) from the input. Interconnection strengths are derived through experience. It is this that the computer models of parallel distributed processing sought to capture. These models, like the cognitive architecture of the human mind, are 'dynamic, interactive and self-organizing systems' (McClelland, Rumelhart, and Hinton 1986: 42). It is for this reason that the distinction between representation (product) and learning (process) becomes blurred in connectionist accounts of learning. As N. Ellis (2001: 42) put it 'the same systems that perceive language represent language'.

5 Rule-like representations may arise out of the network of associations that learners build.

McClelland and Rumelhart claimed that PDP models can go beyond the input by means of 'spontaneous generalization'. They can extract 'regularities' in the patterns of interconnections; these resemble higher-order rules. However, PDP networks do not learn 'rules'; rather they learn to act as though they knew them. N. Ellis (2002) drew on Construction Grammar (Langacker 1987) to propose that learners gradually form constructions, some of which are schematic (for example, Det Noun) as well as purely lexical. These schematic constructions develop out into countless concrete instantiations of the construction. Learners analyse the sequences they have learnt, abstracting structural regularities from them, and in this way, bootstrap themselves to 'grammar'. N. Ellis also acknowledged that such constructions are symbolic in that their formal composition is linked to semantic, pragmatic, and discoursal meaning.

6 Processing is carried out in parallel rather than serially.

McClelland, Rumelhart, and Hinton (1986) pointed out that multiple constraints govern language processing, with semantic and syntactic factors constantly interacting without it being possible to say that one set is primary. They argue that if 'each word can help constrain the syntactic role, and even the identity, of every other word' (1986: 7), processing must take place not serially but simultaneously on different levels. A corollary of such a view of language learning is that it involves form–function mapping. Thus, connectionist models are very compatible with the functionalist views of linguistic representation discussed earlier in this chapter.

7 Language learning is frequency-driven.

In PDP models, processing is activated by 'input' which stimulates one or more units and, of course, their connections with other units in the system. Thus, in computer simulations selected input in the form of 'training sets' is fed into the computer, often in successive runs (as in Rumelhart and McClelland's study described below). The selection of 'training sets' in PDP models is usually based on information regarding the typical frequency with which the specific features or configurations of features that constitute the learning target occur in natural language use. In real-life learning, large amounts of input are needed to fine-tune the developing system. Learners are sensitive to the frequencies of sequences in the input. N. Ellis viewed input frequency as 'an all-pervasive causal factor'. As he put it 'in the final analysis of successful language acquisition and language processing, it is the language learner who counts' (2002: 179). N. Ellis (2002) argued that it is type rather than token frequency that learners respond to. (See Chapter 6.) In N. Ellis (2007), however, he proposed that frequency of token and type do rather different things; token frequency leads to entrenchment of a particular form, while type frequency drives the productivity of a pattern.

8 Learning is governed by the POWER LAW OF PRACTICE.

This law states that the logarithm of the reaction time and/or the error rate for a particular task decrease linearly with the logarithm of the number of practice trials taken. Put less technically, practice improves performance but with a gradually diminishing effect. The effects of practice are linked to 'chunking', which N. Ellis defined as 'the development of permanent sets of associative sections in long-term storage ... that underlie the attainment of automaticity and fluency in language' (1996: 107). Practice enables learners to develop higher-order chunks out of lower-order ones. For example, practice in processing input enables the learner to construct the higher-order chunk 'their' out of the lower-order sublexical chunks 'the' and 'ir' or 'their house' out of 'their' and 'house'. Chunking explains exponential learning. In this respect, connectionist models do not differ greatly from skill-building models (considered below) which are based on the proceduralization of declarative knowledge through practice.

9 Role of memory.

Working memory plays a major role in the processes outlined above. The more frequently items are rehearsed in phonological short-term memory, the more likely they are to be stored in long-term memory in a form that will make them more easily accessed later. The limitations of working memory drive learners to construct higher-order chunks out of lower-order chunks. Thus the learner who knows the chunks 'head' and 'ache' will find it less taxing on working memory to process 'headache' than the learner who has to process this item in terms of a series of lower-order chunks, such as non-meaningful sequences of letters. It follows from this that individual differences in short-term memory will impact on acquisition. N. Ellis (2001) claimed:

> The ability to repeat verbal sequences (for example, new phone numbers or non-words like 'sloppendish') immediately after hearing them is a good predictor of a learner's facility to acquire vocabulary and syntax in first, second, and foreign language learning. (p. 48)

Working memory then is where pattern detection takes place. Working memory is where commonalities between different modalities (for example, auditory and visual) are identified and the continuities and discontinuities between identified patterns in the input and existing schema are established.

10 Implicit learning.

The learning that results from the induction and subsequent analysis of sequences found in the input occurs without awareness. It is implicit learning. Indeed, as Hulstijn (2002) pointed out, it could not be anything else as it is an autonomous and unstoppable process, and learners cannot be aware of any change in the weights of the connections that comprise their neural system. As N. Ellis (1994a) put it, there are some things that we learn to do without conscious operations in the same way as swallows learn to fly. In N. Ellis' (2005) view 'the bulk of language acquisition is implicit learning from usage: the vast majority of our cognitive processing is unconscious' (p. 306). Learners count but they do not do so consciously.

11 Explicit learning and knowledge.

It does not follow, however, that *all* language learning is implicit. N. Ellis acknowledged that, as claimed by Schmidt, learners need to attend to sequences in the input and that this noticing is a conscious process. Thus, in part, language learning is also an explicit process. In N. Ellis (2005) he explained the inter-relationship of the two types of learning as follows:

> ... the primary mechanisms of explicit language learning is the initial registration of pattern recognizers for constructions that are then tuned and integrated into the system by implicit learning during subsequent input processing.
> (p. 308)

He also proposed that explicit knowledge plays a role in L2 production. For example, explicit rules of the kind provided by pedagogy are drawn on to construct novel utterances. These constructions are then subjected to the processes of implicit learning. Thus, N. Ellis, like me, adopts what might be called a weak-interface position. (See earlier discussion of interface positions.w

12 Role for L1.

The effects of the L1 are very evident in L2 acquisition (See Chapter 8.) How does a connectionist model of L2 acquisition account for this? In the case of L2 phonology, it assumes that learners initially project L1 phonetic categories onto the sounds of the L2. Similarly, crosslinguistic influence in the acquisition of grammar is acknowledged, especially in the initial stages of acquisition. Gradually, however, as learners are increasingly exposed to L2 data, an L2 network takes shape that is increasingly independent of the L1 network. This developing L2 network manifests very similar properties to those observed in L1 acquisition. According to this view, then, the effects of the L1 are most evident in the early stages of learning, gradually giving way to the 'recreation' continuum that Corder (1977) believed was the true characterization of interlanguage development.

N. Ellis (2006a, 2006c), however, argued that the L1 is the major reason why input fails to become intake due to 'learnt inattention'. This explains why most learners fail to achieve full target-language competence. This is true even in the case of features that occur with high frequency in the input (for example, tense and aspectual inflections). Drawing on theories of associative learning, he identified a number of factors, all linked to the L1 that could explain this. Two of these factors are OVERSHADOWING and BLOCKING. Overshadowing refers to a situation where two cues are associated with an outcome. Research has shown that in such cases the more subjectively salient of the two cues overshadows the weaker. As overshadowing continues over time, blocking results (i.e. learners learn to selectively attend to only the more salient of the two cues). As N. Ellis (2006b) put it, 'blocking is the result of an automatically learnt inattention' (p. 178). An example of blocking can be found in learners who acquire adverbials to express temporal reference but fail to acquire tense

> and aspectual markers (i.e. do not progress beyond the Basic Variety. (See Chapter 3.) The L1 contributes to overshadowing and blocking by making those L2 forms that are similar to L1 forms more salient. Learners know from their L1 that adverbials can express temporal meanings and how effective such devices are in communicating temporality. Thus, the high salience of these features prevents them from attending to tense and aspect markings.

There have been an increasing number of connectionist simulations of language learning. These have addressed the acquisition of phonological rules, lexis, morphology, and syntax. N. Ellis (1999) summarized their main finding as follows:

> These simple 'test-tube' demonstrations repeatedly show that connectionist models can extract the regularities in each of these domains of language and then operate in a rule-like (but not a rule-governed) way. (p. 29)

He then went on to claim that to the extent to which L1 and L2 learning are the same, these simulations are relevant to L2 acquisition.

One of the most frequently cited simulations is Rumelhart and McClelland's (1986a) study of past tense learning. Irregular past tense is of considerable interest to language researchers because, as we have seen, its natural acquisition typically involves U-shaped learning behaviour (for example, 'went'–'goed'–'wented'–'went'). Overgeneralization errors, such as 'goed', have been held to provide strong evidence that learners must organize their linguistic knowledge into 'rules'. Given that PDP systems are constructed in such a way that no rules of this nature are represented, past tense learning provides a rigorous test of the ability of such systems to account for language learning. The PDP system that Rumelhart and McClelland used was equipped with (1) an encoding device that operates on the root form of verbs (for example, 'hope') and converts them into a set of context-sensitive phonological features (called Wickel features); (2) a 'pattern associator' network that takes the output from (1) and computes the past tense form of the verbs, again in terms of Wickel features; and (3) a decoding device that converts the output of (2) into a normal set of phonological features. Large numbers of exemplars of both root and past tense verb forms were fed systematically into the model in a series of sets; they comprised the input. One of the most interesting results obtained by the simulation was that the pattern observed in the L1 acquisition of past tense forms occurred. For example, the model generated the familiar U-shaped learning curve, and errors involving double past tense marking. Thus, for 'eat', 'ated' occurred later than errors involving over-generalization ('eated'), a phenomenon also reported in L1 acquisition (Kuczaj 1977). Rumelhart and McClelland concluded that the simulation demonstrated that a 'reasonable account of the acquisition of past tense can be provided without recourse to the notion of "rule" as anything more than a *description* of the language' (1986: 267).

An example of a more recent simulation based on a connectionist model of language learning is N. Ellis and Schmidt (1997). This was a study of plural nouns in two parts, the first involving human participants and the second a connectionist simulation. The first required seven monolingual English university students to learn an artificial language. First they learnt the names for 20 picture stimuli. They were then trained first in the stem forms and then in the plural forms of the words they had learnt. The plural forms included high- and low-frequency regular and irregular forms. The dependent variables were the number of trials needed to achieve 100 per cent accuracy and response time. Both the regularity and frequency of the plural words in the input were shown to have an effect and there was also a regularity-by-frequency interaction (i.e. for the irregular items the frequency effect was more evident in the mid-order than in the early or late trials). The results supported the power law of practice in that the amount of improvement decreased as a function of increasing practice or frequency. In the second part of this study, a connectionist simulation was similarly directed at the learning of plural forms. At the outset, the connection weights of the PDP model were randomized. Initially the model was trained in singular nouns followed by intensive training in plural forms, with the design of this training resembling that provided to the human participants. The model produced a very good simulation of the pattern of acquisition demonstrated by the human subjects. Also, the model resulted in the same kind of overgeneralization of the regular plural form noted in natural language acquisition. Overall, this study supports a simple associative theory of learning involving a single distributed system.

Connectionist models of language learning constitute an enormous challenge to nativist theories of language and acquisition. Not surprisingly, therefore, they have been criticized by researchers working in the Chomskyan paradigm. Pinker and Prince (1989) observed that 'the fact that a computer model behaves intelligently without rules does not show that humans lack rules, any more than a wind-up mouse shows that real mice lack motor programs' (1989: 184). They pointed out that Rumelhart and McClelland's simulation met with only limited success, as even after extensive training it achieved only 67 per cent accuracy in a test of the model's ability to generalize its knowledge to new verbs. In many cases, it resulted in errors not attested in natural language acquisition (for example, 'typeded' for 'typed' and 'membled' for 'mailed'). For Pinker and Prince, then, connectionist theories are 'revisionist' in a way that is 'not scientifically defensible' (1989: 198).

Connectionists have responded to these criticisms. They reject the claim that the theory underlying their work is 'revisionist' (i.e. behaviourist) in nature, pointing out that they are concerned with internal states and mental processes. PDP models do have an 'initial state', which is, in a sense, 'innate' and, as Gasser (1990) noted, connectionists are increasingly concerned with what it consists of. Gasser (and subsequently N. Ellis) also pointed out that there are linguistic theories (for example, Langacker 1987) that are compatible with PDP models in that they emphasize the continuous nature of the differences between rules and exceptions. Similarly, Schmidt (1988) observed that PDP is good at dealing with variability and '*fuzzy* concepts'. MacWhinney (1989) also argued that connectionism offers 'a powerful formal framework that correctly expresses the processing and learning claims of the Competition Model' (1989: 457). This is not surprising, perhaps, given that both PDP and the Competition Model (considered below) share a number of features, such as the notions of 'network' and the 'weight' of cues or connections.

The debate has continued, however. In particular, N. Ellis' emergentist position has been challenged. Major (1996a), for example, argued that while a connectionist-type model is able to explain a number of aspects of language (for example, lexis), other aspects (for example, the universal phenomenon of epenthesis) are better accounted for by universal innate linguistic capacities. Ioup (1996) challenged N. Ellis' claim that rule-like behaviour is achieved when learners unpack the grammatical baggage in the formulaic sequences they have acquired. However, both Major and Ioup differed from N. Ellis in degree rather than fundamentally (i.e. they acknowledged the legitimacy of a connectionist account for some aspects of L2 learning). In contrast, Gregg (2003) offered a complete rejection of N. Ellis' claims. In particular, he was dismissive of connectionism because, in his view, it fails to provide an adequate PROPERTY THEORY of language (i.e. it does not specify what it is that learners have to learn). He argued that no connectionist model has demonstrated or is capable of demonstrating how learners acquire the concept of grammatical 'subject' and concluded that 'giving up a moderately successful theory merely in the hope that something better will come along is simply not an option that any rational scientist would choose' (p. 123). It is likely that the debate between emergentists like N. Ellis and nativists like Gregg will carry on for some time—until, perhaps, increasingly sophisticated connectionist models succeed in generating the kind of linguistic concepts that nativists view as indicative of concepts they claim are innate. Meanwhile, Gasser's (1990) conclusion strikes a neat balance between connectionism and symbolism:

> It is now clear that some form of connectionism will figure in a general model of human linguistic behavior. The only question is whether the role will be a minor one, relegated to low-level pattern matching tasks and the learning of exceptional behavior, or whether the connectionist account will supersede symbolic accounts, rendering them nothing more than approximations of the actual messy process.
> (1990: 186)

The growing significance of emergentist models for SLA is highlighted in the special issue of *Applied Linguistics* (27/4), which is given over to the examination and application of these models. In their introduction to this issue, Ellis and Larsen-Freeman (2007) viewed language as 'a complex adaptive system' and argued that an emergentist perspective can best account for the self-organizing property of L2 systems. Similarly, MacWhinney (2007a) saw emergentism as 'the most promising new trend in language studies' (p. 731), arguing that it offered 'new methods of prediction, new understandings of complex dialogic interactions, and new views of the learning process'. However, both Larsen-Freeman and Ellis and MacWhinney express caveats. MacWhinney noted that 'it is easy to come up with emergentist accounts that are appealing, but wrong' (p. 718). Ellis and Larsen-Freeman recognized the need for an eclectic, broad-based approach to the study of L2 acquisition, on the grounds that common dichotomies in SLA (for example, property theory–TRANSITION THEORY; competence–performance) are 'complementary, more mutually dependent than mutually exclusive' (p. 580) and reflect the emergent nature of the field itself—a point examined in greater detail in Chapter 17.

The Competition Model

The COMPETITION MODEL is another emergentist theory of L2 acquisition and is entirely compatible with connectionist theory, as MacWhinney (2001) explicitly recognized. It can also be seen as a functionalist model and like other such models seeks to account for the kind of knowledge that underlies real-time processing in real-world language behaviour, although, as we will see, it has been investigated by means of experimental studies which elicited rather artificial language responses. It also resembles other functionalist models in that it is interactionist; that is, the learner's grammar is viewed as resulting from the interaction between input and cognitive mechanisms relating to perceptual abilities, channel capacity, and memory.

Central to the model is the idea of form–function mappings. As MacWhinney, Bates, and Kligell (1984) put it: 'The forms of natural languages are created, governed, constrained, acquired and used in the service of communicative functions'. Any one form may realize a number of functions and, conversely, any one function can be realized through a number of forms. The learner's task is to discover the particular form–function mappings that characterize the target language. Form–function mappings are characterized as being of varying 'strengths' in different languages. This is usually illustrated with reference to the function of 'agency', which has a number of possible formal exponents:

1. Word order: in the case of transitive constructions, the first noun mentioned in a clause is likely to function as the agent. For example, in the English sentence 'Mary kissed John', 'Mary' is the agent.
2. Agreement: the noun phrase which functions as agent may agree in number with the verb. Thus, in English, a singular noun phrase functioning as agent takes a singular verb form (for example, 'She likes ice-cream'), while a plural noun phrase takes a plural verb form (for example, 'They like ice-cream'). The object of the sentence has no effect on the verb form.

3 Case: the noun phrase functioning as agent may be morphologically marked in some way. For example, the agent is signalled in German by nominative case marking on the article, while the object is signalled by means of accusative case marking (for example, 'Der Mann isst den Apfel' = 'The man is eating the apple').
4 Animacy: agents are normally animate, patients are normally inanimate.

Any one language is likely to utilize several devices for signalling the 'agent' of a sentence. English, for instance, uses all four, as illustrated in these sentences:

Mary kissed John. (word order).
Money they like. (agreement)
She kissed him. (case)
This book Mary likes a lot. (animacy)

However, a language is likely to assign different weights to these devices in terms of the probability of their use in signalling a given function. English, as the above examples show, relies primarily on word order to encode agency, while Russian uses case marking, and Japanese, animacy. Like variability models, the Competition Model is probabilistic in nature.

The model takes its name from the 'competition' that arises from the different devices or cues that signal a particular function. For example, in a sentence like 'that lecturer we like a lot' there is competition between 'lecturer' 'we' and 'lot' for the role of agent of the verb. 'Lot' rapidly loses out because, unlike 'lecturer' and 'we', it is inanimate, and because it follows rather than precedes the verb. The candidacy of 'lecturer' is promoted by its position in the sentence–it is the first noun–but, ultimately, this cue is not strong enough to overcome two other cues. 'We' is the strongest candidate for agent because it is nominative in case and because it agrees in number with the verb.

The task facing the L2 learner is to discover (1) which forms are used to realize which functions in the L2, and (2) what weights to attach to the use of individual forms in the performance of specific functions. This is what is meant by 'form–function mapping'. The input supplies the learner with cues of four broad types: word order, vocabulary, morphology, and intonation. The usefulness of a cue is determined by several factors: (1) 'cue reliability' (the extent to which a cue always maps the same form onto the same function), (2) 'cue availability' (how often the cue is available in the input), and (3) 'conflict validity' (whether a cue 'wins' or 'loses' when it appears in competitive environments). For example, if we consider the information available to the L2 learner regarding the role of word order in realizing agency in English, we can characterize this 'cue' as relatively reliable (the noun phrase preceding the verb is typically the agent) and readily available (the input is likely to supply plentiful examples of this mapping). Also, in English, word order tends to override other cues (except agreement). Thus, in a sentence like 'Mary bit the dog', 'Mary' is the agent, even though experience of the world might lead one to suspect that 'the dog' is the more likely agent. As MacWhinney (2001) put it, the Competition Model 'provides a minimalist, empiricist prediction for the ways in which cues are acquired' (p. 76).

There has also been some attempt to specify how learners use the information available from 'cues' to construct their language systems. MacWhinney (2001: 74) stated that 'the most basic determinant of cue strength is the raw frequency of the basic task'. Feedback also plays a role. McDonald (1986) proposed a learning-on-error model, according to which the weights attached to specific form–function mappings are changed when the learner interprets an input cue incorrectly and is subsequently provided with feedback. McDonald suggested that this may account for the developmental shift noted in L1 acquisition from an initial dependence on cue reliability/availability to dependence on conflict validity. To begin with, children respond to those cues which are salient and easily detectable (such as word order), but once these have been established they turn their attention to sentences containing conflicting cues (for example 'That person we all love', where there is conflict between the word order and agreement cues). Ultimately it is these sentences that help them to establish the dominance patterns of the cues. McDonald and Heilenman (1991) provided evidence from an experimental study of French/English bilinguals that supports such a view.

The Competition Model has informed a number of studies of L2 acquisition (for example, Harrington 1987; Gass 1987; Kilborn and Cooreman 1987; Kilborn and Ito 1989; McDonald and Heilenman 1991; Sasaki 1991, 1997a; Kempe and MacWhinney 1998). These studies take the form of sentence-interpretation experiments using bilingual subjects in a within-subjects, cross-language design. That is, speakers of different languages are asked to identify the function of different cues in L1 and L2 sentences that have been designed to reflect both the coordination and competition of cues. For example, they may be asked to say which noun is the agent of an action in acceptable sentences like 'The boy is chopping the log' and in semantically unlikely sentences such as 'The logs are chopping the boy', where the animacy cue is in competition with the word order cue, but the agreement cue is in coordination. The studies then compare the responses of learners with different language backgrounds.

We will consider two studies based on the Competition Model. Harrington (1987) investigated the effects of three factors—word order, animacy, and stress—on the processing strategies used by native speakers of English (the NL English group), native speakers of Japanese (the NL Japanese group), and Japanese speakers of English (the interlanguage (IL) group). There were twelve adult subjects in each group. They were asked to interpret 81 test sentences by stating which of two nouns in each sentence was the logical subject (i.e. agent). The sentences had been designed to incorporate the three factors systematically, either in competition or in coordination. The subjects, however, were not informed of this. Inevitably, some of the sentences were ungrammatical or unnatural, but Harrington argued that this was appropriate and that, in any case, information regarding the effects of converging and competing cues was 'extraordinarily difficult to obtain from natural speech' (1987: 360). The analysis of the results was based on 'choice' (which noun each subject chose in each sentence) and 'latency' (the time it took each subject to make each choice). The results are extremely complex, reflecting a number of interactions between the learner and language variables. We will focus here on the results obtained for word order cue effects, which are summarized in Table 9.8. As expected, the NL English group interpreted the first noun in canonical NVN sentences and the second noun in the unnatural NNV and VNN sentences[12] as the agent. Also, as expected, the NL Japanese group demonstrated little sensitivity to word order as a signal of agency, exhibiting no more than a slight tendency to choose the first noun as the agent and no use at all of a 'second noun strategy'. In contrast to these results for the word order cue, the NL English showed less sensitivity to the animacy cue than the NL Japanese, although to complicate matters, a subgroup of the NL English did appear to be influenced strongly by this cue. The IL group were midway between the NL English and NL Japanese groups in their choice of agent in canonical NVN sentences, but, as predicted, behaved like the NL Japanese group in their interpretation of the unnatural NNV and VNN sentences. Harrington also showed that even in the case of the NVN sentences, the IL group were responding more to the animacy than to the word order cue. He concluded that a word order strategy was evident but was 'only of limited strength' in the IL group. In contrast, there was clear evidence that animacy cues were of primary importance in the IL group's responses.

Group	**Canonical sentences**	**Unnatural sentences**	
	NVN	**NNV**	**VNN**
NL English	81%	35%	33%
NL Japanese	59%	56%	54%
IL subjects	68%	59%	56%

Table 9.8 Choice of first noun as agent in a sentence interpretation task (based on results reported in Harrington 1987)

The results of this study are encouraging for the Competition Model. They demonstrate that L2 learners are influenced by their L1 processing strategies, which they transfer when interpreting L2 sentences. Furthermore, the results suggest that the processing strategies utilized by L2 learners can be located somewhere on the continuum between the strategies used by native speakers of the two languages concerned. This suggests that the idea of a restructuring continuum may after all make some sense in the case of syntax, at least where sentence processing is concerned. Further evidence for this is available in

Kilborn's (1987) study of German learners of L2 English, which shows that a group of advanced learners were much closer to a NL English group than were a group of novice learners where word order cues were concerned. It should be noted, however, that restructuring involves strategies rather than forms; it is not L2 forms that replace L1 forms, but rather L2 processing strategies.

In the second study we will consider, Kempe and MacWhinney (1998) investigated the acquisition of case marking by adult learners of Russian and German. The key difference between these languages lies in 'cue reliability'. Case marking constitutes a much more reliable cue in Russian than in German. Beginner learners of Russian and German were presented with a sentence on a computer and asked to select which of two pictures showed what the agent of the sentence was. Altogether they judged 128 sentences. These had a simple noun-verb-noun pattern and were designed to permutate five factors; animacy of the first noun, animacy of the second noun, case marking of the first noun, case marking of the second noun, and noun configuration (SVO versus OVS). The learners' decisions and also latencies were recorded. The results supported the hypothesis that informed this study, namely that the learners of Russian would be able to rely correctly on case marking at an earlier stage in learning than the learners of German. In other words, the learners of Russian were much quicker in learning to process the case cues than the learners of German. This was especially true in non-canonical sentences, where the learners of German demonstrated a bias towards selecting the pre-verbal subject as agent. Kempe and MacWhinney followed up this study based on the Competition Model with a second study involving a connectionist network simulation. This study confirmed the results of the first study, indicating that 'an associative learning mechanism provides a good account for the learning of L2 sentence cues such as case marking' (p. 577).

Other studies have shown that some interpretation strategies are more universal than others. Gass (1987) found that while English-speaking learners of L2 Italian made little use of their L1 syntax-based strategy, Italian-speaking learners of L2 English did transfer their lexical-semantic strategy (i.e. animacy cues). Sasaki's (1991) bi-directional study of the acquisition of English and Japanese also testified to the primacy of a semantics/pragmatics strategy, confirming the findings of other functionally-orientated models of L2 acquisition. These studies suggest that the more universal a strategy is, the more likely it is to be transferred. Once again, then, we see evidence of constraints on transfer. (See Chapter 8.)

MacWhinney (2007b) outlined a development of the Competition Model, which he called the Unified Model because it sought to provide an account of both L1 and L2 learning. According to this model, forms are stored in associative maps for syllables, lexical items, constructions, and mental models. For example, in lexical maps, words are viewed as associations between forms and functions. Construction maps consist of patterns that show how a predicate (verb, adjective, preposition) can combine with its arguments. The idea of self-organizing associative maps is derived from computer modelling of language learning. These show learning involving three phases. In the first, all units in the model are activated by the input with each unit computing its current activation. In the second phase, units compete with the best matching unit emerging as the winner. In the third phase, the weights of the responding unit are adjusted to increase the precision of future activation. Within these associative maps, learning is self-organized, modulated by a number of processes—buffering, chunking, and resonance. Buffering serves as a mechanism for preserving competing information in short-term storage to enable selection of the final form/interpretation. Chunking (the process of storing formulaic sequences) provides a data base from which grammar can emerge through analogic processing (as discussed in Chapter 3). Resonance is the process by which robust connections within neural structure of the brain are formed. It is achieved through careful timing of practice to stimulate 'resonant activation' of the relevant neurons.

The strength of the Competition Model is that it provides a convincing account of a number of aspects of L2 acquisition which any theory must consider: the role of the L1, the effect of input, and the gradual way in which native-like ability is acquired. There are, of course, other aspects which it does not address, at least not at the moment. It is not clear, for instance, what kind of knowledge (implicit or explicit) learners use in sentence interpretation. The early version of the model did not have much to say about the cognitive mechanisms responsible for obtaining intake from input or for using L2 knowledge in production. However, the later Unified Model with its account of buffering, chunking, and resonance has largely filled this gap.

Probably the main weakness of the model is over-reliance on rather artificial interpretation tasks, a problem that is aggravated by the unnatural sentences that figure in such tasks. The justification for such a methodology is the Ecological Validity Hypothesis, according to which 'the processing of both grammatical and ungrammatical sentences proceed by reference to the same set of cues and processing patterns' (MacWhinney, Pleh, and Bates 1985: 199). But this has been queried by McLaughlin and Harrington (1989):

> ... it may be wise to question the 'ecological validity' of an experimental procedure in which subjects have to make decisions about sentences that are as deviant in English as: 'The apple is eating the man'. Perhaps subjects are not processing such sentences as they would in actual communicative situations, but are settling on a particular problem-solving strategy to get them through the many judgements of this nature they have to make.
> (1989: 125)

Nevertheless, the Competition Model is a powerful theory in that, like Processability Theory, it affords very precise predictions about L2 acquisition, which, as MacWhinney (2001) pointed out, have received uniform support in the studies that have investigated the model.

Skill-acquisition theories

SKILL-ACQUISITION THEORIES of language acquisition draw on the distinction between declarative and procedural knowledge (Anderson 1983) or between controlled and automatic processes (McLaughlin 1987) discussed earlier in this chapter. That is, they are based on the view that language learning, like other kinds of skill, is characterized by a progression from an initial declarative knowledge stage involving controlled processing, to a final procedural stage where knowledge is automatic. Skills are learnt as a result of 'practice'. Practice, however, needs to be skill-related. So the development of skill in listening requires practice in processing input while the development of speaking requires practice in oral production (DeKeyser and Sokalski 1996). According to this view, procedural knowledge is uni-directional; that is, automatization of one skill, such as listening, does not directly assist automatization of a different skill, such as speaking. However, automatization of one skill may have an indirect effect on a different skill by improving and strengthening declarative knowledge which is bi-directional (i.e. can be utilized in the development of different skills).

According to skill-acquisition theorists, L2 learners achieve proceduralization through extensive practice in using the L2. However, 'practice' is a relatively crude concept, especially when applied to language learning. What exactly does it entail? The traditional view is that practice involves the process of repeatedly and deliberately attempting to produce some specific target feature. It was this view that led to the use of the mechanical drills found in the audiolingual and oral-situational methods of language teaching. (See Richards and Rodgers 2001.) What was missing from this view, according to DeKeyser (1998), was recognition of the importance of practice directed at 'behaviour' rather than at 'structures'. Ellis (1988b) showed that practice is often not effective in enabling learners to use new structures autonomously—'practice does not make perfect' as Lightbown (1985) put it. This is because practising a structure in a mechanical way reifies the structure by decontextualizing it and thus does not affect long-term memory or lead to any change in behaviour. To change behaviour (i.e. develop automatic processes) it is necessary to provide practice of the actual behaviour itself. In the case of language learning, 'behaviour' must entail attempts to communicate. Thus, for practice to work for the development of the speaking skill it must involve learners producing the target structure in the context of communicative activity.

According to this view, then, communicative practice serves as a device for proceduralizing knowledge of linguistic structures that have been first presented declaratively. Instruction that incorporates such practice can be seen as an attempt to intervene directly in the process by which declarative knowledge is proceduralized. DeKeyser (1998: 49) drew on Anderson's skill-learning theory to argue for such an intervention:

> ... proceduralization is achieved by engaging in the target behavior—or procedure—while temporarily leaning on declarative crutches ... Repeated behaviors of this kind allow the restructuring of declarative knowledge in ways that make it easier to proceduralize and allow the combination of co-occurring elements into larger chunks that reduce the working memory load.

Johnson (1988, 1996) also drew on skill-learning theory to justify practice. He emphasized the importance of feedback in the learning process, suggesting that the instructional sequence is best seen as one of 'learn → perform → learn' rather than the traditional sequence of 'learn → perform'. During (or perhaps after) the 'perform' stage learners must have the opportunity to receive feedback. This feedback, Johnson suggested, should consist of 'mistake correction' (i.e. negative evidence about the misuse of features that the learners already have knowledge of but cannot yet use automatically). Johnson emphasized that for feedback to be effective learners 'need to see for themselves what has gone wrong in the operating conditions under which they went wrong' (1988: 93). He suggested that this can probably be best achieved by means of extrinsic feedback (i.e. feedback from an outside source) that shows the learner what is wrong by modelling the correct form while they are attempting to communicate.

Skill acquisition theories of the kind promoted by DeKeyser and Johnson underlie mainstream accounts of how to teach grammar. Ur (1996), for example, proposed a sequence of practice activities designed to lead a learner from 'accuracy' (i.e. performance based on declarative knowledge) to 'fluency' (i.e. performance based on procedural knowledge). This sequence involves 'controlled drills', 'meaningful drills', 'guided meaningful practice', 'structure-based free sentence composition', 'structure-based discourse composition' and 'free discourse'. It should be noted, however, that such a sequence finds a place for mechanical as well as communicative practice, seeing the former as a way of preparing for the latter, and, as such, does not conform with DeKeyser's and Johnson's views about the need to ensure that the practice involves 'behaviour' in 'real operating conditions'.

There can be little doubt that language learning, in part at least, does involve skill-learning in the sense that practice aids the process by which L2 knowledge is automatized—as also claimed by the emergentist theories discussed above. However, skill-acquisition theories are problematic in two related respects. First, they provide no explanation for the orders and sequences of acquisition that were described in Chapter 3. As Mitchell and Myles (1998) commented 'the route followed by L2 learners is not convincingly explained by such approaches' (p. 99). Second, it is difficult to accept that the acquisition of all L2 features begins with declarative knowledge. This implies a role for metalinguistic awareness in L2 acquisition that far exceeds that sketched out in this chapter.

Summary

At the beginning of this section, when examining the various cognitive theories of L2 acquisition, I suggested that a complete theory would need to account for five key aspects of learning. Table 9.9 indicates which of these aspects have been covered by each theory we have considered. This analysis shows that whereas some theories focus on the role of input and input-processing mechanisms (for example, Operating Principles and the Competition Model), other theories focus on production (for example, Processability Theory), and yet others on the role of explicit knowledge (for example, skill-acquisition theories). It also suggests that the most comprehensive theory is the connectionist model of the kind described by N. Ellis. The theories also differ with regard to the precision of hypotheses about L2 acquisition that they afford and the extent to which they are capable of predicting as well as explaining acquisition. In these respects, the Multidimensional Model/Processability Theory and the Competition Model score highly.

Key aspects of L2 acquisition	**Cognitive theories**				
	1	**2**	**3**	**4**	**5**
1 How learners extract information about the L2 from the input.	Yes	No	Yes	Yes	No
2 How learners 'operate' on this information internally in order to construct an interlanguage.	No	No	Yes	Yes	No
3 The role played by explicit knowledge of the L2 in the development of implicit (procedural) knowledge.	No	No	Yes	No	Yes
4 The role played by learner production.	Yes	Yes	Yes	No	Yes
5 The role played by the learner's L1.	No	Yes	Yes	Yes	No

Key: 1 Operating Principles
2 Multidimensional Model/Processability Theory
3 Connectionist models
4 The Competition Model
5 Skill-acquisition theories

Table 9.9 The aspects of L2 acquisition addressed by different cognitive theories

Conclusion

In their introduction to the *Handbook of Second Language Acquisition*, Long and Doughty (2003) advance the following claim:

> ... language learning, like any other kind of learning, is ultimately a matter of change in an individual's internal mental state. As such, research on SLA is increasingly viewed as a branch of cognitive science. (p. 4)

The claim that the appropriate object of study in SLA is the learner's 'internal mental state' is one that many researchers might challenge (see Chapter 7), but Long and Doughty were right to emphasize the centrality of cognitive aspects of L2 acquisition in SLA. This chapter has demonstrated the range and richness of theorizing and research in this branch of SLA.

Readers may wonder, in fact, if the theorizing and research has not become too rich, spawning a whole range of terms—'strategies', 'operations', 'mappings', 'principles', 'procedures', 'item/rule learning', 'incidental/intentional learning', 'implicit/explicit learning'—that defy precise definition and overlap in uncomfortable ways. It is, perhaps, in the field of cognitive SLA, that the dangers of theory proliferation are most evident. It is not easy to see to what extent theories resemble or differ from each other. To what extent, for example, can a clear distinction be drawn between explicit/implicit knowledge and declarative/procedural knowledge or between incidental/intentional learning and implicit/explicit learning? What exactly is the difference between a connectionist model of language learning and a skill-building model? I have attempted to answer such questions in this chapter but perhaps not entirely satisfactorily because clear answers are not really possible. An easier way of making sense of this field of enquiry lies in identifying the 'owners' of each approach. For connectionism read N. Ellis, for processability read Pienemann, for the role of competition between input cues read MacWhinney, etc. This is, in essence, what I have tried to do.

There is no comprehensive cognitive theory of L2 acquisition. What we have is a set of perspectives and theories that differ with regard to (1) provenance, (2) scope, (3) the type of data they aim to account for, and (4) the precision of the hypotheses they advance. Theories like Processability Theory and functionalist accounts of L2 representation have originated in work undertaken by L2 researchers, others were devised to account for L1 acquisition and were subsequently used in SLA research (for example, Slobin's operating principles), while still others are general cognitive theories applied to L2 acquisition (such as the skill-learning theories of McLaughlin and Johnson). We have seen that some theories focus on the way input is processed (for example, the Competition Model), some on the way L2 knowledge is represented (the Dual Mechanism Model), while others seek to account for L2 knowledge in relation to output (Processability Theory). Some theories have been constructed to account for naturalistic L2 data (Processability Theory) while others are based on data elicited through experiments or computer simulations (emergentist models). Finally, there are theories that afford very precise hypotheses that can be systematically tested (The Competition Model and the Processability Theory) while others offer more general statements that provide only a broad-brush picture of how acquisition takes place (skill-building theories).

However, in emphasizing the theoretical and methodological diversity of enquiry in cognitive SLA and the overlapping and sometimes conflicting constructs that inform it, I do not wish to be dismissive of the contribution it has made. It has hugely enriched our understanding of how the mind tackles the task of learning an L2. Apart from this, cognitive SLA has also afforded a number of practical applications, especially to language teaching, as will become apparent in Chapter 16.

In this chapter, I have distinguished two domains of enquiry in cognitive SLA: (1) the representation of L2 knowledge, and (2) the processes involved in acquiring this. In the next chapter I will consider a third domain—the processes involved in L2 use. It is heuristically useful to distinguish these three domains, but also artificial as the interweaving of them is an essential characteristic of cognitive SLA.

Notes

1 Various alternative terms to 'interlanguage' have been used. Corder (1971a) referred to 'idiosyncratic dialects' and 'transitional competence', whereas Nemser (1971) used 'approximative systems'. Although these terms have different shades of meaning, they all refer to the same general phenomenon. The term 'interlanguage' has stuck and will be the one used here.

2 The untimed grammaticality judgement scores loaded on both the implicit and explicit factors in my study. However, when just the scores for the ungrammatical sentences were entered into the analysis these were found to load strongly on just the explicit factor. Other research on grammaticality judgement tests (for example, Hedgcock 1993) has shown that the grammatical and ungrammatical sentences in a judgement test are measuring different constructs and this is reflected in the fact that they load differently in the factor analysis.

3 Krashen's five hypotheses are: (1) the Acquisition-learning Hypothesis, (2) the Natural Order Hypothesis, (3) the Input Hypothesis, (4) the Monitor Hypothesis, and (5) the Affective Filter Hypothesis. In this chapter we focus on (1) and (4). Hypotheses (2), (3), and (5) are considered in Chapters 3, 6, and 12 respectively.

4 Anderson's model has changed somewhat over the years. The 1983 version became known as ACT* (to be read 'ACT-star'). The distinction between declarative and procedural knowledge, however, is basic to all the ACT models.

5 The idea that language can be accounted for in terms of item-specific knowledge underlies what has become known as 'Construction Grammar'. This claims that grammar is represented in the mind as a set of items and, possibly also, ready-made patterns that are acquired from the input on the basis of their frequency. Generalizations are derived through the process of

identifying similarities and differences in the items and patterns. See Goldberg (2006: Chapter 10) for a useful survey of constructionist approaches to describing grammar. N. Ellis (2003, 2006a) draws on construction grammar in his connectionist account of L2 learning.

6 While Schmidt's 'noticing' and Gass' 'apperception' have much in common, there is a difference. Schmidt argued that whatever is noticed becomes intake; Gass (1997a) argued that not all apperceived input becomes intake as other factors (such as developmental stage) might intervene.

7 Gass' claim about some learning being independent of input is based on studies of relative clauses that have shown that when learners receive instruction in a marked type of clause (for example, preposition + relative pronoun) they manifest acquisition of unmarked types (for example, where the relative pronoun functions as subject of the clause) as well. This research draws on the Accessibility Hierarchy, which is considered in detail in Chapter 12. (See also Chapter 3.)

8 McLaughlin's (1990) account of 'restructuring' is not dissimilar to Bialystok's idea of 'analysis'. Exemplar-based representation corresponds to 'unanalysed knowledge' while rule-based representation corresponds to 'analysed knowledge'.

9 Robinson's (2005b) was a very complicated study that also included a replication of Reber *et al.*'s (1991) artificial grammar (AG) study. One of his aims was to establish to what extent learning AGs is the same as learning natural languages. He concluded that it is not the same.

10 N. Ellis, in his review of this chapter, noted that DeKeyser is wrong to claim that there is very little hard evidence of learning without awareness; he cited his own review of research in N. Ellis (2005), which investigated frequency effects in L2 acquisition and showed that these effects can only be explained if it assumed that learning without awareness is possible.

11 Pienemann drew on Lexical Functional Grammar (LFG) to provide a linguistic description of the feature unification that takes place at each processing stage. I have not included an account of this here as my focus is on the cognitive processes involved in Processability Theory. Readers are referred to Pienemann (1998 and 2005a) for a full account of the relationship between processing stages and LFG.

12 The choice of second noun in unnatural NNV and VNN sentences by native speakers of English has been noted in a number of previous studies and is considered to reflect the subjects' knowledge of the transformation which allows a direct object to take up an initial noun position (as in 'Mary John likes a lot') and which, as a consequence, moves the agent noun into the second noun position.

10

Cognitive accounts of second language production

Introduction

In this chapter, we turn to theoretical accounts of the procedures that learners employ when using their L2 knowledge in production. The focus shifts from how learners construct their L2 systems to how they use them in communication. Of course, as we have already noted, the distinction between 'acquisition of L2 knowledge' and 'use of L2 knowledge' is not clear-cut in cognitive theories—the general assumption is that the way in which knowledge is stored reflects the way in which it is used. This is most evident in the skill-learning models of Anderson and McLaughlin, where the ideas of 'proceduralization' and 'automatization' relate very obviously to the idea of how knowledge is controlled in language use. However, as Schmidt (1992: 359) pointed out, a distinction can be drawn between PROCEDURAL KNOWLEDGE (Anderson's concern) and PROCEDURAL SKILL ('the performance aspect of actually doing something in real time'). The focus of this section is on procedural skill rather than procedural knowledge. However, we will also consider ways in which the development of procedural skill interacts with and contributes to L2 acquisition. To account for procedural skill it is necessary to explain how learners make use of their existing L2 knowledge and also how they overcome the problems that result from insufficient L2 knowledge or inability to access L2 knowledge.

There has been a substantial body of research that has investigated production in a second language, especially the use that bilinguals make of their L1 and L2. (See, in particular, Kroll and De Groot's *Handbook of Bilingualism: Psycholinguistic Approaches*.) I will make no attempt to provide a comprehensive review of this research. Instead, I will focus on two aspects of L2 production that have figured strongly in the SLA literature and that address procedural skill: (1) L2 speech planning and (2) communication strategies.

Second language speech planning

L2 speech planning was considered briefly in Chapter 4 in relation to variability in learner language. Here we will focus on three areas of research and theory-building that are specifically cognitive in orientation: (1) aspects of L2 production (especially fluency), (2) the effects of planning on L2 production, and (3) the development of procedural skill in an L2.

Aspects of L2 production

Early research undertaken by researchers at the University of Kassel in Germany (see Dechert, Möhle, and Raupach 1984) focused on two key aspects of oral production: temporal variables and hesitation phenomena. Table 10.1 summarizes the main variables, as described in Wiese (1984). Both temporal variables and hesitation phenomena are online measures of speech related to the idea of fluency.

Speech planning phenomena		**Description**
A	Temporal variables	Variables related to the rate of speaking
	1 Speech rate	The number of syllables per second. This measure includes pause time.
	2 Articulation rate	The number of syllables per second of time of articulation. This measure excludes pause time.
	3 Pause length	The mean length of pauses above a stated threshold level (e.g. 0.20 seconds).
	4 Length of run	The mean number of syllables between pauses.
B	Hesitation phenomena	Variables relating to linguistic features that disturb the smooth flow of speech
	1 Filled pauses	The use of phonetic devices such as 'uh' or 'mhm' to fill pauses.
	2 Repetitions	The unchanged re-occurrence of a substring of an utterance that has no syntactic/semantic function.
	3 Corrections	A change made to some part of the preceding utterance—from a single phoneme to a long sequence of text.

Table 10.1 Speech planning phenomena (derived from Wiese 1984)

The basic methodology employed by the Kassel researchers involved recording L2 learners performing an oral task such as telling a story in their L2 and their L1 and, (in many cases) obtaining a native-speaker performance of the same L2 task. The recorded speech was then carefully transcribed indicating such features as pause length, intonation contours, vowel lengthening, fillers, drawls, and false starts. These were then analysed using both qualitative methods (the detailed discussion of sections of a text) and quantitative ones (measuring speech rate, etc.). The overall aim of this work was to describe the processes learners employ in the production of L2 speech.

As an example of this work, we will consider Raupach's (1983) analysis of FORMULAIC SEQUENCES. Through an analysis of the spontaneous productions of German students of French from the Kassel corpus, Raupach showed that formulas function both as 'fillers' and 'organizers'. For example, in the case of the former, the learners resort to such expressions as 'je ne sais pas' and single words such as 'mais' and 'vraiment' to fill pauses and, in so doing, give themselves time for further planning activities. Organizers (for example, 'je crois que ...' and 'on peut ...') contribute to the development of ongoing speech by helping learners to establish a structure for phrases and sentences. These formulaic chunks provide learners with 'islands of reliability' that they can fall back on when they experience planning problems.

More recent work on speech-planning phenomena has focused on fluency and automaticity. Segalowitz (2003, 2007) examined a number of cognitive issues that underlie fluency in an L2 and proposed a number of laboratory-type measures. He defined fluency as 'those aspects of productive and receptive language ability characterized by fluidity (smoothness) of performance' (2007: 181). Two key aspects are 'access fluidity' and 'attention control'. Access fluidity concerns the learner's ability to connect words and expressions to their meanings. This can be measured by means of reaction time (for example, the amount of time it takes a person to decide whether a word names an object in a particular category), but this is not very satisfactory as simple processing speed is entirely relative (i.e. it depends on the situation and the choice of comparison group). Thus Segalowitz proposed that what is needed is a measure of 'automatic processing' (i.e. the 'unstoppable or ballistic linking of symbol to meaning' (2007: 182)). Automatic processing involves considering how efficient or noise-free it is as, clearly, learners will be able to process their L2 more rapidly in noise-free situations. Segalowitz and Segalowitz (1993) proposed the coefficient of variation as a way to measure fluidity of mental flow apart from simple speed of processing. This is calculated by dividing the standard deviation of an individual's response time in a task by his or her mean response time. It provides a measure of whether there has been an increase over and above simple speed-up effects and assumes that changes in fluency are not just quantitative in nature but also qualitative (i.e. represent an improvement in efficiency).[1]

The second aspect of fluency that Segolowitz (2007) considered was 'attention control'. Function words (for example, 'the', 'under', 'above') are used by speakers to show how they construe a given situation. For example, the sentences '*A* balloon rose *above the* people' and '*Some* people stood *under the* rising balloon' involve different construals of the same situation. Speakers need to constantly focus and refocus attention on the relationships among meanings by means of the appropriate attention-directing devices. They have been shown to be less adept at using these relation words to achieve this when speaking in their L2 than in their L1. One way of measuring this aspect of fluency is to compare the response times when the task set involves performing the same operation repeatedly and when it involves switching from one operation to another.

Fluency is of course just one aspect of L2 performance. Other researchers have examined L2 performance more broadly by investigating COMPLEXITY and ACCURACY in addition to fluency. Table 10.2 provides a sample of the kinds of measures they have employed. Skehan (1998a) proposed that the three different aspects of production draw on different systems of language. (See Chapter 9 where Skehan's DUAL-MODE SYSTEM was described.) Fluency requires learners to draw on their memory-based system, accessing and deploying ready-made chunks of language and, when problems arise, using communication strategies to get by. In contrast, accuracy and, in particular, complexity are achieved by learners drawing on their rule-based system and thus require syntactic processing. Complexity is distinguished from accuracy in that it is related to the 'restructuring' that arises as a result of the need to take risks whereas accuracy reflects the learner's attempt to control existing resources and to avoid errors.

Skehan's research has been motivated by the hypothesis that, as a result of their limited processing capacity, learners will be hard pressed to focus simultaneously on all three aspects of production and thus will prioritize one, as demonstrated by VanPatten's (1990) study considered in Chapter 9. As a result, trade-offs are likely to become evident, for example, if learners elect to focus on accuracy, then either complexity or fluency or both will suffer. In contrast, Robinson's (2003) research is premised on a multiple-resources view of processing. (See Chapter 9.) According to this view, structural accuracy and functional complexity are not in competition, as Skehan claims, but are closely connected, so that increasing the cognitive complexity of a task is hypothesized to lead to greater linguistic complexity *and* accuracy. However, as Robinson (2001b) admitted, the majority of studies have not supported his claim, while there is some evidence of the kind of trade-off that Skehan's theory predicts. Skehan and Foster (1997), for example, factor analysed a number

Measure	Definition	Sample studies
A Fluency		
1 Pause length	This can be measured as either total length of pauses beyond some threshold (e.g. 1 second) or as the mean length of all pauses beyond the threshold. Pause length provides a measure of silence during a task.	Foster and Skehan (1999)
2 Reformulations	Phrases or clauses that are repeated with some modification.	Foster and Skehan (1999)

B Complexity		
Grammatical		
1 Amount of subordination	The total number of separate clauses divided by the total number of 'sentential' units (e.g. T- or c-units).	Foster and Skehan (1996)
2 Use of some specific linguistic feature (e.g. different verb forms)	The number of different verb forms used.	Yuan and Ellis (2003)
3 Mean number of verb arguments	The total number of verb arguments (subjects, direct objects, indirect objects, adjectival complements, prepositional phrases) divided by the total number of finite verbs.	Bygate (1999)
Lexical		
1 Type–token ratio	The total number of different words used (types) divided by the total number of words in the text (tokens).	Robinson (1995b)
C Accuracy		
1 Percentage of error free clauses	The number of error-free clauses divided by the total number of independent clauses, sub-clausal units, and subordinate clauses multiplied by 100.	Foster and Skehan (1996)
2 Target-like use of plurals	The number of correctly used plurals divided by the number of obligatory occasions for plurals multiplied by 100.	Crookes (1989)

Table 10.2 A selection of measures of fluency, complexity, and accuracy

of measures of fluency, complexity, and accuracy as applied to production from three different tasks. They argued that if the learners' L2 proficiency was the key factor, there would be a single factor with all the measures loading on this factor. If 'task' was the key factor, then a three-factor solution could be expected with measures for each task loading on a different factor. If, however, there was a trade-off involving fluency, complexity, and accuracy, then a three-factor solution corresponding to these constructs should occur (i.e. the measures of each construct would load on the same factor). The results of the factor analysis clearly supported the third of these possibilities, supporting the claim that 'the three aspects of performance are distinct, and even enter into competition with each other' (pp. 203–4).

In his later publications, however, Skehan (2003) recognized that a construct such as fluency is itself multi-faceted. Skehan distinguished 'breakdown fluency', as evidenced by the length and number of unfilled pauses, filled pauses and silence, 'speed', as evidenced by the number of syllables produced in a given time, and 'repair fluency', as evidenced in the frequency of reformulations, replacements, repetitions, and false starts. The first and third of these correspond to the 'hesitation phenomena' in the Kassel research project while the second corresponds to 'temporal features'. Tavakoli and Skehan (2005) factor analysed measures of these aspects of fluency, together with measures of complexity and accuracy. Although the solution did not entirely support the separateness of the various constructs, it did demonstrate a difference between two aspects of fluency (repair fluency and breakdown fluency) and between these and the measures of linguistic form of both complexity and accuracy. Shepherd (2006) also reported a factor-analytic study of various measures of fluency, complexity, and accuracy. In this case, six distinct factors were identified. By and large, Skehan's model was confirmed. That is, there were separate factors for 'break-down fluency', 'speed', and 'repair fluency' (as predicted by Skehan's model) and also for complexity and accuracy. Repair fluency, however, was reflected in two separate factors, thus explaining why six rather than five factors were found. That is, there was a separate factor for repetitions/fillers and for reformulations, suggesting that this aspect of fluency might need to be further differentiated.

These psycholinguistic studies have focused on the formal aspects of learner production although Segalowitz suggested that the measures of fluency he proposed were also applicable to pragmatic aspects. They address learners' control of their linguistic resources as shown in both clinically elicited production based on communicative tasks (in the case of the Kassell researchers and Skehan) and on experimental tasks (as in the case of Segalowitz). They show that fluency is a complex construct and also that learners' ability to speak fluently is, to some extent at least, distinct from their ability to use complex linguistic forms accurately. The attention given to fluency is particularly welcome given that the cognitive accounts of L2 acquisition discussed in Chapter 9 have been primarily concerned with how linguistic knowledge is represented and acquired.

The effects of speech planning on L2 production

In Ellis (2005b), I distinguished two principal types of task-based planning—PRE-TASK PLANNING and WITHIN-TASK PLANNING—in terms of when the planning takes place, either before the task is performed or during its performance. As shown in Figure 10.1, pre-task planning can be further divided into REHEARSAL and STRATEGIC PLANNING. Rehearsal entails providing learners with an opportunity to perform the task before the 'main performance'. In other words, it involves task repetition with the first performance of the task viewed as a preparation for a subsequent performance. Strategic planning entails learners preparing to perform the task by considering the content they will need to encode and how to express this content. Within-task planning can be differentiated according to the extent to which the task performance is pressured or unpressured. In an unpressured performance learners can engage in careful online planning resulting in what Ochs (1979) has called PLANNED LANGUAGE USE. In pressured performance learners will need to engage in rapid planning resulting in what Ochs calls UNPLANNED LANGUAGE USE (although, of course, all language use involves some level of planning). Different combinations of these two planning conditions are possible. The most demanding combination is when there is no pre-task planning and pressured within-task planning, while the least demanding is pre-task-planning together with unpressured online planning. Both pre-task and within-task planning can be further differentiated. For example, learners can be left to their own devices when planning a task strategically (unguided planning) or they can be given specific advice about what and how to plan (guided planning). In Sangarun's (2005) study, for example, different groups of learners were directed to attend to linguistic form, to meaning, or to both form and meaning.

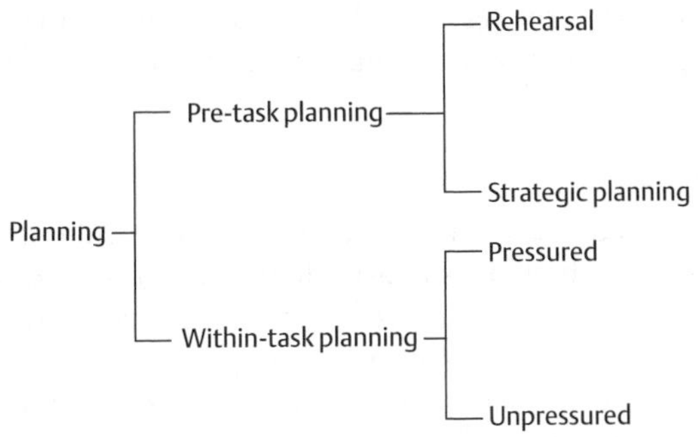

Figure 10.1 Types of task-based planning (from Ellis 2005b: 4)

The main theoretical basis for research into the effects of planning on speech production is LEVELT'S (1989) MODEL OF SPEECH PRODUCTION.[2] This was outlined in Chapter 4. The model distinguishes three overlapping processes: conceptualization, formulation, and articulation. It also allows for speakers to 'monitor' both prior to and after an utterance has been produced. Levelt also identified two characteristics of speech production which are relevant to task planning: (1) controlled and automatic processing and (2) incremental production. According to Levelt, some of the components of the speech production process (specifically, the conceptualizer and the monitor) operate under controlled processing, while other components (specifically, the formulator and the articulator) operate automatically in the main. Levelt's model provides a basis for considering what components of language production learners focus on while planning and also for examining what effects planning strategies have on actual production. Rehearsal, for example, may provide an opportunity for learners to attend to all three components in Levelt's model—conceptualization, formulation, and articulation—so it would seem reasonable to assume that this type of pre-task planning will lead to all-round improvements when the task is repeated, as found by Bygate (2001). Strategic planning can be considered likely to assist conceptualization in particular and thus contribute to greater message complexity and also to enhanced fluency, as found in a number of studies. Unpressured within-task planning may prove beneficial to formulation and also afford time for the controlled processing required for MONITORING. As a result, accuracy might increase. In other words different types of planning can be predicted to ease the pressure on the learner's limited working memory in different ways, variably affecting the competition and trade-offs evident in different aspects of language production. However, a full explanation of the results obtained to date requires a consideration of the role of context, or, more precisely 'psychological context'. Batstone (2005) has convincingly argued that the way in which learners orientate to a task will influence how they perform it. This may explain why a testing context seems to produce different kinds of performance from a laboratory context.

The following review of the research that has investigated the effects of the different kinds of planning shown in Figure 10.1 will consider the three types of planning separately.

Planning as rehearsal

Bygate (1996) compared one learner's retelling of a Tom and Jerry cartoon on two separate occasions, three days apart. He found that rehearsal enhanced complexity, with the learner using more lexical verbs (as opposed to copula), more regular past tense forms (as opposed to irregular), a wider range of vocabulary and cohesive devices (for example, words like 'then', 'so', and 'because'), and fewer inappropriate lexical collocations on the second occasion. There were also more self-correcting repetitions on the second telling of the story. Bygate (2001) reported a larger study that sought to investigate the effects of practising specific types of task (involving narrative and interview) on both a second performance of the same task and on performance of a new task of the same type. The study showed that the second performance manifested greater fluency and complexity and also that the opportunity to practise that particular type of task helped. However, the practice did not appear to assist performance of a new task of the same type. In other words, disappointingly, there was no transfer of practice effect. Gass *et al.* (1999) reported very similar findings in a study that compared learners' use of L2 Spanish in tasks with the same and different contents. In this study an effect for task repetition on ratings of overall proficiency, accuracy in the use of 'estar' (to a lesser extent), and lexical complexity (type–token ratio) was found. However, again there was no transfer of these effects to a new task. Lynch and McLean (2000, 2001) made use of a unique rehearsal task that required students to read an academic article and prepare a poster presentation based on it. Students then stood by their posters while other members of the group visited and asked questions. Given that the visitors tended to ask the same questions, there was substantial opportunity for retrial. A main finding of this study was that different learners appeared to benefit in different ways according to their proficiency. Thus, whereas one learner with low proficiency appeared to benefit most in terms of accuracy and pronunciation, a learner with higher proficiency used the opportunity for retrial to improve the clarity and economy of her explanations of a complex idea. Bygate and Samuda (2005) suggested that repeating a task serves as a kind of 'integrative planning' which can lead to qualitative improvements. They illustrated these in case studies of three learners' repetitions of a narrative, showing how these enabled them to progress from initial disjointed reports to coherent stories.

Overall, then, the research on rehearsal suggests that it has a beneficial effect on learners' subsequent performance of the same task but that there is no transference of the rehearsal effect to a different task, even when this is the same type as the original task.

Pre-task planning

A whole host of studies have investigated pre-task planning (for example, Ellis 1987b; Foster 1996; Foster and Skehan 1996; Skehan and Foster 1997, 2005; Mehnert 1998; Ortega 1999, 2005; Yuan and Ellis 2003). In an early study (Ellis 1987b), I asked 17 adult learners of English to perform three narrative tasks. Task 1 consisted of a written composition for which one hour was allowed; Task 2 was an oral reproduction of the same composition (without recourse to the written version); Task 3 consisted of a different composition which the subjects were asked to relate orally without any advance planning. I compared the accuracy with which the learners used three past tense morphemes (regular –ed, irregular, and copula). In the case of the regular past tense, a clear pattern emerged. The learners were most accurate in Task 1 and least accurate in Task 3, with Task 2 intermediate. This study suggests that, contrary to Hulstijn and Hulstijn's study, the availability of planning time systematically affects the accuracy with which at least some target variants are performed.[3]

Further evidence of substantial effects on L2 production resulting from planning time comes from Crookes' (1989) seminal study. Forty intermediate and advanced Japanese learners of L2 English were asked to complete tasks involving a description of how to construct a Lego model and an explanation for the siting of a set of buildings on a map. Some of the tasks were performed under a 'minimal planning condition' (no planning time allowed) and others under a 'planning condition' (ten minutes was provided to plan words, phrases, and ideas). The tasks performed under the planning condition resulted in more complex language as measured, for instance, by the number of subordinate clauses per utterance. However there were no statistically significant differences in general measures of accuracy.

More recent planning studies (summarized in Table 10.3) have drawn on Skehan's three aspects of production. A number of conclusions can be drawn from these studies. The first is that pre-task planning has a stronger effect on fluency and complexity than on accuracy. This suggests that when learn-

Study	Participants	Design	Task	Measures	Main results
Foster and Skehan (1996)	32 pre-intermediate ESL learners in the United Kingdom	Four groups: 2 planning groups each subdivided (10 minutes either detailed or undetailed pre-task planning); 2 control groups	Three tasks: narrative; personal; decision.	1 reformulations 2 replacements 3 false starts 4 repetitions 5 hesitations 6 pauses 7 total silence 8 average number of clauses per c-unit 9 syntactic variety 10 error-free clauses	Planning aids fluency as measured by (6) and (7). Planning led to greater complexity: detailed planning > undetailed planning > no planning. Detailed planning also resulted in greater variety of past tense usage. Undetailed planning led to greater accuracy but this was only statistically significant in the decision task.
Wendel (1997)	40 Japanese junior college females	Two groups: planning group (10 minutes pre-task planning); no-planning group	Two narrative tasks: retelling a film.	1 syllables per minute 2 mean length of pause 3 average number of clauses per T-unit 4 lexical richness (numbers of word families) 5 percentage of correctly used verbs	Planning resulted in increased fluency as measured by (1) and (2). It also led to greater syntactical complexity but not greater lexical richness. No effect on accuracy was evident.
Mehnert (1998)	31 adult learners of German as a foreign language at a university in London	Four groups: one-minute planning group; five-minute planning group; ten-minute planning group; no-planning group	Two tasks: instruction; exposition.	1 number of pauses 2 total pausing time 3 mean length of run 4 speech rate 5 average number of clauses per T-unit 6 average number of clauses per c-unit 7 length of c-units 8 percentage of error-free clauses 9 number of errors per 100 words 10 accuracy of word order 11 lexical errors	Planners produced more fluent speech than non-planners; the effect of planning on fluency increased with more planning time. Only the 10-minute planners produced more complex language as measured by (5). The planners produced more accurate language than the non-planners but most of the differences were not statistically significant. Accuracy did not increase with longer planning time.

Yuan and Ellis (2003)	42 undergraduate Chinese learners of English in a university in China	Three groups: no-planning group (NP); pre-task planning group (PTP); online planning group (OLP)	Oral narrative task based on pictures.	1 number of syllables per minute 2 number of pruned syllables per minute 3 average number of clauses per T-unit 4 number of different grammatical verb forms 5 mean segmental type–token ratio 6 error-free clauses 7 correct verb forms	The order of the groups for fluency was: PTP > NP > OLP. The only significant difference was between the PTP and the OLP for (2). Both planning groups produced more syntactically complex language; there was no difference between PTP and OLP. But the PTP produced more lexically varied language than the OLP. The order of the groups for accuracy was: OLP> PTP > NP. Only the difference between the OLP and the NP was statistically significant.
Tavakoli and Skehan (2005)	80 EFL adult elementary/ intermediate female learners in Tehran	Four groups: 10-minute planning (low proficiency); 10-minute planning (low proficiency); no planning (low proficiency); no planning (high proficiency)	Four narrative tasks with varying degrees of structure. These tasks were administered as 'tests'.	1 mean length of pause 2 number of pauses 3 time spent speaking 4 total silence 5 speech rate 6 reformulations 7 false starts 8 replacements 9 repetitions 10 length of run 11 average number of clauses per AS-unit 12 error-free clauses	Planning resulted in more fluent language as measured by (1), (3), (4), (5), and (10) for both low- and high-proficiency learners. Planners produced more complex and accurate language than non-planners but proficiency had a greater effect on both complexity and accuracy than planning.
Skehan and Foster (2005)	61 adult intermediate ESL learners in a college in London	Three planning groups: guided planning (10 minutes); unguided planning (10 minutes); no planning	Decision-making task; performance on first 5 minutes was compared with performance on the second 5 minutes.	1 end of clause pauses 2 mid-clause pauses 3 filled pauses 4 length of run 5 reformulations 6 false starts 7 average number of clauses per AS unit 8 error-free clauses	In the first five minutes, planning resulted in significantly increased fluency (but only as measured by (1)), increased complexity and increased accuracy. However, in the second five minutes, planning benefited only fluency.

Table 10.3 Selected planning studies

ers plan strategically they give more attention to drawing up a conceptual plan of what they want to say rather than to formulating detailed linguistic plans. Even when asked to engage in form-focused planning they may not do so, preferring to use the time given them to sequence ideas and to work out the semantic linkages among propositions. Alternatively, it is possible that even when learners do attend to form when planning, they find it difficult to carry over the forms they have planned into the performance of the task. Such an explanation is supported by Skehan and Foster's (2005) finding that the effects of pre-task planning are more evident in the first five minutes of performing a task than the second five minutes. The second conclusion is that trade-off effects are evident. When learners plan they have to choose what aspect of production to focus on; focusing on fluency and complexity is at the expense of accuracy and vice-versa. Finally, there is some evidence to suggest that strategic planning has a greater effect on production in general when the task is cognitively demanding. If a task is easy learners are able to perform it fluently using accurate and complex language without the need for planning.

Within-task planning

In contrast to pre-task planning, within-task planning does appear to have an effect on the accuracy of learners' production, as Ellis' (1987b) study described above shows. Yuan and Ellis (2003) set out to investigate the relative effects of pre-task and online planning on a group of Chinese learners' performance of an oral and written narrative task. The design of the oral narrative study in Yuan and Ellis is shown in Table 10.4. The pre-task planners performed more fluently and used more complex language than the no-planning group and the online planning group. Both planning groups produced more complex grammar than the no-planning group. Interestingly, only the online planning group performed more accurately than the no-planning group—pre-task planning did not result in greater accuracy. Ellis and Yuan (2004) obtained very similar results for written narratives. These studies suggest that the key factor where accuracy is concerned is the opportunity to plan carefully online. When this is available, learners are better able to search through their linguistic repertoires during the formulation stage of language production and also to engage in either pre- or post-production monitoring. However, this effect may only be evident when learners are drawing on their rule-based system. In both Hulstijn and Hulstijn (1984) and Ellis (1987b) the effects of reduced time pressure were only evident on grammatical structures that are clearly rule-based (i.e. Dutch word-order rules and English regular past tense); they were not evident in structures that are more lexical in nature (i.e. irregular and copula past tense forms). One explanation for these findings is that the greater accuracy in unpressured language use was the result of monitoring utilizing explicit knowledge of well-learnt rules.

Task condition	Pre-task planning	Online planning
No-planning group	0.5 minute	Limited time
Pre-task planning group	10 minutes	Limited time
Online-planning group	0.5 minute	Unlimited time

Table 10.4 Task conditions in Yuan and Ellis (2003)

Final comment on planning studies

Most of these studies were conducted in laboratory-like contexts. That is, L2 learners were invited by the researcher to perform a task either by themselves or in a small group outside their normal learning environment. Other studies (for example, Iwashita, Elder, and McNamara 2001; Elder and Iwashita 2005; Wigglesworth 1997, 2001) have examined the effects of planning on learners' production in a testing context. In these studies, learners' production was measured using the same kinds of discourse analytic measures as in the laboratory studies and also by means of ratings (a more standard method of measurement in a testing context). The studies failed to find a consistent effect for strategic planning. It is possible, then, that the testing context constrains the beneficial effects of strategic planning, perhaps because learners tend to be naturally focused on accuracy in such a context irrespective of whether they have the opportunity to plan before they do a task.

The development of procedural skill in an L2

The study of L2 production phenomena can shed light on the nature of the development that learners undergo in acquiring procedural skill. As well as acquiring L2 knowledge, learners need to increase their control over knowledge already acquired (i.e. learn how to process this knowledge in unplanned as well as planned language use). Studies that have researched this have investigated L2 learners in study-abroad contexts.

In a series of studies, Towell (1987, 2002; Towell, Hawkins, and Bazergui 1996) reported on the development of fluency in a number of British university students of L2 French over a period of four years, during which they spent a study-abroad year in France. Towell made audio-recordings of the students' performance of a personal adventure task and a story continuation task on three different occasions and used the kinds of temporal measures shown in Table 10.1 to analyse the learners' productions. Towell (1987) reported results for a single learner in this sample, showing that this learner increased her speaking rate by 65 per cent, her pause/time ratio by 37 percent, her articulation rate by 20 per cent, and the length of runs between pauses by 95 per cent. Towell (2002) reported the results for 11 of the learners. He demonstrated a clear pattern. There was an increase in speech rate, mean length of run, and phonation/time ratio. The learners reduced the amount of time they spent pausing between the first and third administration of the tasks and also between the second and third, but not between the first and the second. Towell argued that these results reflected changes in how the learners stored, accessed, and produced speech. A second general finding was that there was a marked difference between the low and high performers in this sample. The increase in fluency, which was largely due to the reduction in pausing time, was much greater in those learners with low fluency in the first task, although these learners did not quite catch up with the high performers. Towell then undertook a qualitative analysis of one low and one high performer. This showed that the low-performer increased her phonation/time ratio and length-of-run by pausing less, especially at syntactic boundaries rather than within them. The high-performer, however, still outperformed the low-performer on length-of-run as a result of her greater ability to produce subordinating structures. Thus, whereas the two learners grew closer in terms of fluency, they remained distinct in terms of complexity. Towell speculated that the differences in complexity may reflect differences in short-term memory or access to the processing abilities that Pienemann claims are required for subordination. (See Chapter 9.) An alternative explanation, however, might be that learners concerned with developing their communicative skills (as these advanced learners were) need first to establish a threshold of fluency before turning their attention to complexity. In other words, Skehan's idea of a trade-off may apply over time as well as synchronically.

Evidence for such a developmental trade-off between fluency and complexity can be found in Ellis (1990b). I examined the relationship between the development of fluency (measured in terms of speech rate) and the development of complexity (measured in terms of production of word-order rules) in 39 adult classroom learners of L2 German. I found that word-order acquisition was significantly and negatively correlated with gains in speech rate. One interpretation of this result is that learners who opted to increase their store of L2 knowledge paid a price in terms of procedural skill and vice versa. Schmidt (1992) also considered that the acquisition of knowledge and procedural skill may proceed separately. He gave as an extreme example a speaker of a pidginized interlanguage who can speak it very fluently.

Segalowitz and Freed (2004) compared groups of learners of L2 Spanish in two different contexts—a formal classroom in their home university and a study-abroad setting. They obtained three sets of measures: (1) measures of oral fluency based on hesitation and temporal phenomena, (2) a general measure of oral proficiency based on the Oral Proficiency Interview (OPI), and (3) cognitive measures of speed of lexical access, efficiency of lexical access, and speed and efficiency of attention control. (See above for a description of these.) The study-abroad learners showed greater gains in (1) and (2) than the at-home learners. However, no statistically significant gain differences were evident in the case of (3)—i.e. the cognitive measures. Segalowitz and Freed also examined the relationships between the three sets of scores. They reported positive correlations between (1) and (2). Also, there were a number of significant correlations between (1) and (3). In one case, the correlation was negative; the efficiency of attention control was negatively related to speech rate in the post-test, suggesting that as learners developed the ability to shift attention, they did so with a concomitant loss of temporal fluency. Finally, the study also found statistically significant relationships between gains in oral performance as measured by the OPI and pre-test levels of cognitive ability. This study indicates that the learning context makes a difference where oral fluency is concerned. It is of special interest because it examined measures of fluency based on both production data and experimentally elicited data.

A key question is the relationship between the development of fluency and the proceduralization of rules. Towell's and my own research suggests that they may not be related. As, Schmidt (1992) pointed out 'there is ... little theoretical support from psychology for the common belief that the development of fluency in a second language is almost exclusively a matter of the increasingly skilful application of rules' (1992: 377). Instead, it depends on extending exemplar-based knowledge, as claimed by Skehan. The development of complexity, on the other hand, requires the extension of rule-based knowledge. Such a position, however, has been challenged, especially by researchers favouring a skill-building theory of learning. Segalowitz (2003), for example, reviewed a number of experimental studies that have investigated the development of automaticity in L2 grammar (for example, DeKeyser 1997; Robinson 1997a) and concluded that they do not provide a 'tidy picture' but do suggest that 'some kind of integration of rule-based and exemplar-based processes may ultimately be called for' (p. 400).

Communication strategies

We now turn our attention to the second aspect of procedural skill: COMMUNICATION STRATEGIES (CSs). These can be distinguished from the production phenomena considered in the previous section as follows: whereas the latter examined the general characteristics of L2 production, CSs focus on a subset of production phenomena (i.e. those that are conscious and arise as a result of a communication problem the learner is experiencing). Clearly, though, the two approaches are interrelated to a degree. For example, the extent to which a learner's production demonstrates a high level of complexity (a general phenomenon) will depend on the extent to which learners resort to reduction strategies (such as avoidance) or achievement strategies (such as paraphrase). However, these interconnections have not been investigated; the study of the general aspects of learner production and the study of CSs have proceeded separately, despite the fact that they have drawn on the same cognitive models of L2 production (for example, Levelt's model).

The term 'communication strategy' was coined by Selinker (1972) as one of the five 'processes' he identified in interlanguage development. In 1973 Varadi produced a paper (later published in 1980) that provided the first systematic analysis of CSs. Other descriptions and taxonomies of CS also appeared in the 1970s (for example, Tarone, Cohen, and Dumas 1976; Tarone 1977) but it was in the 1980s that interest in CSs really took off with, first, the publication of a collection of papers devoted specifically to CSs (Færch and Kasper 1983b), second, an influential project (the Nijmegen Project) directed at describing and theorizing CSs (Kellerman, Bongaerts, and Poulisse 1987; Poulisse 1990) and third, Bialystok's (1990) monograph linking CSs to her general theory of L2 acquisition based on the distinction between 'analysis' and 'control'. (See op. cit.: Chapter 10.) Interest in CSs has continued since with the publication of another set of collected papers (Kasper and Kellerman 1997a) and a review article by Dörnyei and Scott (1997). Since then, however, interest in CSs appears to have waned somewhat and it is pertinent to ask why.

The reason might lie in the way CS research has evolved. Early research on CSs was concerned with the mental operations that underlie the use of such strategies and focused rather narrowly on lexis. Increasingly, however, CSs have been viewed as a sociolinguistic phenomenon. This has resulted in a widening of the focus of research to include consideration of the roles of institutional setting, the socio-political context, and ethnic identity in CS use, with a corresponding diminution of interest in the role they play in acquisition. Sociolinguistic accounts of CSs have also paid greater attention to the pragmatic problems that learners experience. This change in the orientation of CS research is clearly evident if we compare the two collections of papers on CSs. Færch and Kasper's (1983b) collection included sections on defining CSs, descriptive studies of CSs, and problems in analysing CSs. Kasper and Kellerman's (1997a) collection included three parts, labelled 'psycholinguistic perspectives', 'expanding the scope', and 'sociolinguistic perspectives'. This broadening of the scope of enquiry reflects the conviction held by some SLA researchers that L2 acquisition constitutes a social, not just a cognitive, phenomenon. (See Chapter 7.) The price paid for such a development, however, is a loss of clarity and definition in the object of study. It could be argued that the term 'communicative strategies' runs the risk of becoming amorphous.

The definition of CSs and their identification and classification have, in fact, been ongoing issues and so constitute an appropriate starting point for an examination of the CS research. As my concern in this chapter is with cognitive aspects of L2 communication, I will restrict my review of the research to studies that have viewed CSs as a mental rather than a social phenomenon. I will conclude by consideration of the relationship between CSs and L2 acquisition.

Defining communication strategies

Researchers distinguish two broad theoretical approaches to CSs. They can be viewed as discourse strategies that are evident in social interactions involving learners, or they can be treated as cognitive processes involved in the use of the L2 in reception and production.

Interactional definitions

The interactional view of CSs originated in Varadi and Tarone's early work. Tarone (1981: 419) defined CSs as involving 'a mutual attempt of two interlocutors to agree on a meaning in situations where requisite meaning structures do not seem to be shared'. As such they differ from PRODUCTION STRATEGIES, which she defined as attempts to 'use one's linguistic system efficiently and clearly, with a minimum of effort'. In her 1977 study, Tarone identified and described a number of CSs by analysing transcripts of the L2 learners' attempts to refer to a number of objects and events depicted. The strategies (listed and defined in Table 10.5), therefore, were directly observable in the transcripts of the learners' productions. It is in this sense, that they are interactional—they reflect the communicative behaviours that learners employ to make themselves understood to their interlocutors. It is important to note, however, that although Tarone's strategies are clearly interactional in nature, she viewed them as a psycholinguistic phenomenon, as reflected in the definition she provided in her 1977 article: 'Conscious communication strategies are used by an individual to overcome the crisis which occurs when language structures are inadequate to convey the individual's thought' (p. 195). In other words, the interactional nature of Tarone's CSs reflects the nature of the framework she used to describe them (i.e. her methodology) rather than how she conceptualized the underlying construct.

One of the problems with the interactional approach to defining CSs is that it becomes difficult to decide exactly which interactional phenomena are 'strategic' (i.e. originate in some problem in communicating) and which reflect non-strategic production processes. For example, to what extent can the hesitation phenomena described in Table 10.5 be considered strategic. Most CS researchers have excluded these, although Dörnyei and Scott (1997) made a case for including them. They argued that learners may well hesitate not just because they are experiencing a communication problem but as a means for gaining time to find a solution.

Dörnyei and Scott (1997) distinguished three types of communication problems that can give rise to CSs: (1) own-performance problems (i.e. the learner recognizes that something he/she has said is incorrect or only partly correct), (2) other-performance problems (i.e. the learner finds something problematic in something said to him/her), and (3) processing-time pressure (i.e. the learner needs more time to plan L2 speech). Tarone's early definition covered mainly (1) although one of her strategies—'appeal for assistance' relates to (2). (2) in fact includes the strategies involved in the negotiation for meaning discussed in Chapter 6; (3) involves the production processes generally considered in accounts of fluency.

Thus, we can see that the original interactional definition of CSs has been considerably stretched, to the point where CSs overlap with other areas of study in SLA. For the sake of clarity, it might be better to restrict the definition of CSs to the strategies designed to solve 'own-performance problems' and allow the other aspects of problematic L2 production to be dealt with in terms of other, arguably more robust, theoretical frameworks.

Psycholinguistic definitions

The psycholinguistic approach is illustrated by the work of Færch and Kasper (for example, Færch and Kasper 1980, 1983b). They located CSs within a general model of speech production, in which two phases are identified: a planning phase and an execution phase. The aim of the planning phase is to develop a plan which can then be executed to allow the speaker/hearer to achieve communicative goals. In this phase 'the language user selects the rules and items which he considers most appropriate for establishing a plan, the execution of which will lead to verbal behaviour which is expected to satisfy the original goal' (1983b: 25). CSs are seen as part of the planning process. They are called upon when learners experience some problem with their initial plan which prevents them from executing it. One solution is avoidance. This occurs when learners change their original communicative goal by means of some kind of reduction strategy. The other solution is to maintain the original goal by developing an alternative plan through the use of an achievement strategy. The perspective afforded by this model is explicitly psycholinguistic.

In the Færch and Kasper model, CSs are seen as 'strategic plans', which contrast with 'production plans' in two main respects: (1) problem-orientation and (2) consciousness. Learners employ CSs because they lack the L2 resources required to express an intended meaning (a problem in the planning phase) or they cannot gain access to them (a problem in the execution phase). In either case, there is a lack of balance between means and ends (Corder 1978b). CSs are, of course, not alone in being problem-orientated, as learning strategies can also be motivated by learners' recognition of gaps in their L2 knowledge.[4]

Færch and Kasper (1980) saw consciousness as a *secondary* defining criterion of CSs. They recognized various problems in claiming that CSs are conscious and, in an attempt to deal with these, distinguished plans that are (1) always consciously employed, (2) never consciously employed, and (3) consciously employed by some but not all learners in some but not all situations. They suggested that CSs are plans belonging to (1) and (3), i.e. they 'are potentially conscious plans for solving what to an individual presents itself as a problem in reaching a particular communicative goal'.

Both the problematicity and the consciousness criteria have been criticized. Bialystok (1990) argued that it is not clear how the distinction between 'production plans' (which are non-problematic) and 'strategic plans' (which are problematic) manifests itself in actual language processing. She noted that certain non-problematic instances of language use, such as giving definitions, will result in exactly the same kind of overt linguistic behaviour associated with CSs. For example, 'an instrument for grating cheese' might be considered as a circumlocution for 'cheese-grater' in one context, but as a straightforward definition of the object in another. Bialystok also criticized Fær Kasper's claim that CSs are potentially conscious on the grounds that th no 'independent means' for deciding which plans fall into this category a that without this 'one is left to assume that *all* plans are potentially conscious (1990: 5).

Bialystok argued that the definition of CSs should be located within 'a coherent account of speech production' (1990: 82). This, of course, is exactly what Færch and Kasper tried to do but Bialystok, while approving of their attempt, considered it ultimately inadequate because the basic concepts of 'process', 'plan', and 'strategy' were ill-defined and there was insufficient evidence to support the claim that planning and execution can be distinguished in the way Færch and Kasper proposed. Bialystok's own solution to the problem of providing a psycholinguistic definition was to distinguish 'knowledge-based' and 'control-based' CSs. The former involve the speaker in making some kind of adjustment to the content of the message by exploiting knowledge of the concept, for example by providing distinctive information about it, as in a definition or circumlocution. In a control-based strategy, the speaker holds the initial intention constant and manipulates the means of expression by integrating resources from outside the L2 in order to communicate it, as in the use of many L1-based strategies and mime. Bialystok emphasized that both types of strategies need not be characterized by problematicity (gaps in knowledge or communication breakdown). Learners, like native speakers, select from their available options in order to communicate their intentions as precisely as they can within the constraints set up by particular tasks.

A psycholinguistic definition of CS similar to that of Bialystok can be found in the work of a group of Nijmegen researchers (for example, Kellerman, Bongaerts, and Poulisse 1987; Kellerman, Ammerlaan, Bongaerts, and Poulisse 1990; Poulisse 1990). The Nijmegen approach distinguished two general mental processes that underlie the surface manifestation of different CSs—'conceptual' processes and 'linguistic' (or 'code') processes. Kellerman (1991) described these as follows:

> Learners can either manipulate the concept so that it becomes expressible through their available linguistic (or mimetic) resources, or they can manipulate the language so as to come as close as possible to expressing their original intention.

Subsequently, however, Poulisse (1993) modified this definition. She argued that the distinction between conceptual and linguistic CS lacked a clear theoretical basis and proposed instead that CSs be distinguished in terms of whether they involved Levelt's (1989) conceptualizer (for example, circumlocution) or formulator (for example, approximation or morphological creativity).

The goal of psycholinguistic definitions of CSs—to locate CSs within a model of language processing—is laudable but arguments abound as to the relative virtues of the different definitions. (See for example, Kellerman and

…ique of Poulisse's redefinition.) Despite the arguments, …d from these different psycholinguistic definitions are …rprisingly perhaps, very similar to the CSs based on …n. For example, where Færch and Kasper referred …' involving 'direct' and 'indirect' appeal, Tarone …for assistance'. However, one clear advantage of …ccounts is that they provide a basis for classifying the …omies rather than simply listing them. We will now consider …xonomies.

Taxonomies of CSs

Dörnyei and Scott (1997) provided a review of nine taxonomies of CSs and, to the best of my knowledge, no new ones have emerged since. They pointed out that six of the nine taxonomies dichotomize strategies into those that involve (1) avoidance or reduction (i.e. the original message content is either abandoned or modified) and (2) achievement (i.e. the original message is maintained and modified linguistically). Five of the taxonomies organize the CSs in terms of the language devices involved (for example, the role of the L1 or the type of knowledge utilized). Tarone (1977) distinguished strategies involving paraphrase of some kind (for example, word coinage) and strategies involving conscious transfer (for example, literal translation). The other four taxonomies were based on different organizing principles. It is not possible to review all nine taxonomies here, so I will focus on three: Tarone's (1977) original taxonomy, the Nijmegen group's taxonomy, and Dörnyei and Scott's own taxonomy.

Tarone's taxonomy is shown in Table 10.5. I have chosen to present this because the CSs it identifies figure in just about all the other taxonomies and because it provides the reader with a straightforward description of the key strategies. This kind of interactional taxonomy has been criticized on the grounds that 'the criteria for assigning an utterance to a specific strategic category are sometimes vague, sometimes arbitrary and sometimes irrelevant' (Bialystok 1990: 75) with the result that the taxonomy cannot reliably be used. It has also been claimed that the CSs are not psychologically plausible. Kellerman (1991: 146) pointed out that referring to 'an art gallery' as 'a picture-place' or as 'a place where you look at pictures' clearly reflects the same underlying cognitive process. Therefore, to code them separately as 'word coinage' and 'circumlocution', as happens in Tarone's taxonomy, is misleading. Kellerman argued that it is not necessary to posit different strategies simply because they have different linguistic realizations. A third criticism is that such taxonomies are not parsimonious; categories tend to proliferate like the branches of an enormous tree.

Communication strategy		Description of strategy
1	Avoidance	
	a Topic avoidance	Avoiding reference to a salient object for which learner does not have the necessary vocabulary.
	b Message abandonment	The learner begins to refer to an object but gives up because it is too difficult.
2	Paraphrase	
	a Approximation	The learner uses an item known to be incorrect but which shares some semantic features in common with the correct item (e.g. 'worm' for 'silkworm').
	b Word coinage	The learner makes up a new word (e.g. 'person worm' to describe a picture of an animated caterpillar).
	c Circumlocution	The learner describes the characteristics of the object instead of using the appropriate TL item(s).
3	Conscious transfer	
	a Literal translation	The learner translates word for word from the native language (e.g. 'He invites him to drink' in place of 'They toast one another').
	b Language switch	The learner inserts words from another language (e.g. 'balon' for 'balloon'). NB Subsequently, Tarone (1981) refers to this as 'borrowing'.
4	Appeal for assistance	The learner consults some authority—a native speaker, a dictionary.
5	Mime	The learner uses a nonverbal device to refer to an object or event (e.g. clapping hands to indicate 'applause').

Table 10.5 Tarone's (1977) typology of communication strategies

Addressing this last criticism, the Nijmegen researchers developed a taxonomy built around two archistrategies—'conceptual' and 'linguistic' strategies. These are broken down further, as shown in Table 10.6, but are eventually traceable to many of the CSs found in interactional taxonomies such as Tarone's. However, the Nijmegen typology highlights the commonalities that underlie what are discrete strategy types in Tarone's framework. It reveals, for instance, that word coinage, circumlocution, and approximation are 'conceptual' in nature, and that they all involve an 'analytic' process. It also distinguishes between types of non-verbal behaviour instead of lumping them together in a single category, 'mime'. Thus, 'ostensive definition' (pointing at an object) is seen as the non-verbal equivalent of a linguistic strategy, whereas 'mimetic gesture' (the modelling of some feature(s) of a referent through gesture, perhaps accompanied by imitative sounds) is 'conceptual' in nature.

Archistrategies	**Communication strategies**
Conceptual	1 Analytic (circumlocution, description, and paraphrase)
	2 Holistic (the use of a superordinate, coordinate, or subordinate term)
Linguistic	1 Transfer (borrowing, foreignizing, and literal translation)
	2 Morphological creativity

Table 10.6 The typology of communication strategies used in the Nijmegen Project (based on Poulisse 1990: Chapter 7)

Dörnyei and Scott's (1997) typology aimed to be comprehensive and consequently is voluminous, consisting of 33 individual CSs. As such, it is too long to include here. Three general types of CSs are identified; direct strategies, interactional strategies, and indirect strategies. These superordinate categories reflect the manner of problem management (i.e. 'how CSs contribute to resolving conflicts and achieving mutual understanding' p. 198). The first of these involves conflict resolution and achieving mutual understanding. It includes the CSs identified in most other typologies (for example, Tarone's). The second set of strategies is concerned with preventing breakdowns and keeping the channel of communication open. It covers strategies more typically considered in accounts of the negotiation for meaning (for example, 'comprehension check' and 'asking for confirmation'). The indirect strategies also involve the management of communication but without the actual use of the L2—for example, by the use of fillers to relieve pressure on processing. Dörnyei and Scott noted that 'including indirect strategies is an equivocal and contested judgment' (p. 199).

In evaluating these taxonomies it is pertinent to ask what light they shed on the processes of L2 communication and acquisition. Is it useful, for instance to know whether students use direct, interactional, or indirect strategies? There are a number of ways of answering such a question. However, perhaps the best is to consider the empirical research based on them and the extent to which this research is illuminating. We will now turn to consider this research.

Empirical studies of CSs

Most studies have been concerned with describing and quantifying the CSs used by different learners and with identifying the factors that influence strategy choice (for example, the learners' level of L2 proficiency, the learners' PERSONALITY, the learning situation, and the nature of the task used to elicit data). A good example of the kind of study undertaken is Poulisse (1989). Poulisse investigated lexical strategies only. These were seen as referential in nature (i.e. they involve attempts by speakers to encode messages that enable hearers to identify specific referents). The participants in her study consisted of three groups of 15 Dutch learners of L2 English with varied proficiency, as indicated by the number of years they had been studying English, school grades, teacher judgements, and cloze test scores. All the participants were asked to perform four tasks in English: (1) a concrete picture description task involving everyday objects, the names of which the subjects were unlikely to know in English, (2) an abstract figure description task, (3) an oral interview, and (4) a story-retelling task, where the subjects listened to a story in Dutch and retold it in English with the help of picture prompts. (2) was also performed in the learners' L1. (3) and (4) were video-recorded and played back to the subjects for their retrospective comments, which were audio-recorded and transcribed. The study examined the effects of proficiency and task on the learners' use of CSs and also considered whether there was any evidence that learners used CSs differently from native speakers. The main findings were as follows. The less proficient learners used more CSs than the more proficient, a function of their more limited control of L2 vocabulary. There was also some evidence of proficiency-related effects on the type of strategies used. For example, the more advanced learners made greater use of holistic strategies involving superordinates. However, there were very few proficiency-related differences in the ways in which the different strategies were realized. On the other hand, the nature of the task was found to have a marked effect on strategy selection. The subjects preferred elaborate analytic strategies in task (1), while in tasks (3) and (4) they made greater use of short holistic strategies and transfer strategies. Finally, the comparison of L1 and L2 referential behaviour failed to reveal any significant differences. This indicated that CSs are not a distinctive second-language phenomenon and that L2 learners do not have to develop a special L2 strategic competence but instead can apply their L1 strategic competence.

Most studies of CSs, like Poulisse's study, have examined how learners address lexical gaps (for example, Paribakht 1985; Jourdain 2000). Kasper and Kellerman (1997b) noted that this is a direct consequence of the criteria used to define CSs (i.e. problematicity and consciousness) as learners are able to demonstrate awareness of lexical but not of grammatical problems. It is also the result of the methodology typically employed in CS studies—presenting learners with a set of pictures depicting objects they do not know the labels for and requiring them to communicate each object to the researcher. Inevitably, the main CS such a methodology elicits is circumlocution. Jourdain (2000), for example, used this methodology to examine the circumlocutions produced by native speakers and native-like speakers of French and English. Not surprisingly, given their high level of L2 proficiency, the native-like participants relied on L2 rather than L1 strategies and in general behaved very similarly in their L1 and L2. Thus, for example, they showed a strong preference for use of superordinate terms and synonymy as opposed to analogy, antonymy, metonymy, or lexical creation. Jourdain also found that these participants' attempts at circumlocution were not always successful (i.e. did not lead to the successful identification of the object they were trying to communicate). However, as she acknowledged, this was probably due to the fact that the participants were not allowed to negotiate for meaning (another feature of the standard methodology for investigating CSs). One of the problems of such studies, then, is the artificiality of the communicative context in which the CSs are elicited.

This last limitation was overcome in an interesting study by Lafford (2004), who examined the CSs used during the Oral Proficiency Interview, which arguably constitutes a more authentic context than the kinds of tasks used in the studies reported in the previous paragraph. Like Segalowitz and Freed's (2004) study this study examined the difference between stay-at-home students of L2 Spanish and study-abroad students. Lafford reported that although both groups of students possessed a wide repertoire of CSs they largely employed only two—self-repair and own accuracy checks. The most interesting finding of this study was that whereas both groups used fewer CSs in the post-test interview, the study-abroad learners reduced their reliance on them to a much greater extent. The most obvious explanation of this finding is that the increased oral proficiency of the study-abroad learners obviated their need to use CSs. However, a comparison of the language abilities of the two groups did not support such a conclusion. Instead, Lafford suggested that the study-abroad experience had made the learners less likely to be accuracy-oriented (i.e. they had become more tolerant of the mismatch between their interlanguage forms and the target-language forms).

A few studies have investigated the effects of STRATEGY TRAINING on learners' use of CSs and on acquisition.[5] This is an interesting issue given that some researchers have argued against such training. Kellerman, for example, claimed 'there is no justification for providing training in ... compensatory strategies ... Teach the learners more language and let the strategies look after themselves' (1991: 158). Other researchers have argued for training in CSs and conducted studies to investigate its effectiveness.

Dörnyei (1995) provided training to high school EFL students in Hungary in three CSs—topic-avoidance and replacement, circumlocution, and the use of fillers and hesitation to keep the communication channel open and gain time to think. Dörnyei reported a significant improvement in the instructed participants' quality and quantity of strategy use and in their overall speech performance. The participants also manifested positive attitudes towards the training. Nakatani (2005) investigated the effects of training in CSs on 62 Japanese female college students' use of these strategies and on their oral proficiency. The training consisted of explicit strategy instruction in achievement strategies (i.e. help-seeking strategies such as 'appeal for help', modified interaction strategies such as comprehension checks, modified output strategies, and time-gaining strategies such as 'providing positive comments').

These strategies were largely of the negotiation-for-meaning kind, which, as we have already seen, are excluded from some typologies of CSs. The training consisted of five phases: review of CSs use in the previous lesson, presentation of a new CS, rehearsal, performance, and evaluation. The students were also asked to keep a strategy diary to encourage self-reflection on their use of CSs. To measure the effect of the training, the students were asked to complete two oral communication tasks as a pre- and post-test which were rated by two raters. The results showed that the students increased their use of the strategies (in comparison to a control group) and significantly improved their test scores.

However, training in the use of CSs is not always effective. Lam and Wong (2000) reported a study that investigated the effects of teaching students to seek and provide clarification when communication difficulties arose in class discussions. However, although this resulted in greater use of these strategies in a post-training discussion, the strategies were often not employed effectively (for example, the students were unable to clarify something they had said) suggesting that pre-task training in the use of communication strategies may not be effective unless students also learn how to scaffold each other cooperatively when performing the task.

Reflecting perhaps the uncertainty over the value of training communication strategies, instructional materials for L2 learners are hard to find. Faucette (2001) examined a range of textbooks for ESL/EFL learners and also teachers' resource books with a review to identifying which communication strategies were introduced and what types of activities there were for practising CSs. She found that few communication strategies were to be found in the textbooks and the types of practice activities were also very limited. CSs received greater attention in the teachers' resource books but there was very little concrete guidance on how to actually teach them.

It is difficult to reach any firm conclusions on the basis of these studies. The problem lies in the fact that different researchers have operationalized CSs very differently, making a synthesis of their findings impossible.

Communication strategies and L2 acquisition

Views differ regarding whether the use of CSs assists acquisition or impedes it. Skehan (1998b) argued that CSs avoid the need for learners to develop their interlanguage resources (i.e. strategic competence compensates for lack of linguistic competence). Evidence for Skehan's position comes from Schmidt's (1983) study of Wes (see Chapter 1), who was shown to have developed his strategic competence at the apparent expense of his linguistic competence. In contrast, Kasper and Kellerman (1997b) identified a number of ways in which CSs may assist L2 acquisition. CSs

- help to keep the flow of the conversation going and thus increase learners' exposure to input

- trigger NEGOTIATION FOR MEANING which aids acquisition (See Chapter 6.)
- increase their control over their existing linguistic resources
- enable learners to obtain access to new linguistic resources when they incorporate strategic solutions into their interlanguage
- fill gaps in the learner's lexicon through positive feedback following requests for assistance
- produce PUSHED OUTPUT
- increase overall processing control.

Kasper and Kellerman concluded:

> Whether conceptualized as a cooperative venture or a purely cooperative process, the increased need to solve problems in establishing reference is both characteristic of language learners and instrumental in propelling their interlanguage forward.
> (p. 7)

These two views about the role of CSs in acquisition need not be seen as contradictory. It is possible that some learners develop their strategic competence at the expense of their linguistic competence while others exploit CSs for their learning opportunities. Littlemore (2003) found that learners' learning style (holistic versus analytic) influenced the choice of strategies and their communicative effectiveness. It is equally possible that learning style mediates the extent to which CSs benefit or impede acquisition for different learners.

There is also the question about which type of CS is most likely to facilitate acquisition. Corder (1978b) characterized reduction strategies as 'risk-avoiding' and achievement strategies as 'risk-taking', and suggested that the latter rather than the former will contribute to successful language learning. Færch and Kasper (1980) expressed the same view, arguing that achievement behaviour encourages hypothesis formation, and also that risk is essential for automatization. Tarone (1980), however, held a different view, suggesting that CSs of any kind help learners to negotiate their way to the right target-language forms. They can be seen as the means by which learners can act on Hatch's (1978b) advice to never give up.

Sadly, there have been very few studies that have actually tried to investigate whether CSs assist acquisition. Smith (2003b) investigated the effect of learners' use of 26 different strategies drawn from the various sources described above while performing two types of computer-mediated communicative tasks (jigsaw and decision-making). He found that the CS did result in learning, as measured by a post-test of lexical items that were not known prior to the learners' performance of the tasks. There was no significant difference in the effectiveness of the various CSs.

Evaluation of communication strategy research

As in many areas of research in SLA, there are competing positions, models, and frameworks for CSs. Yule and Tarone (1997) neatly summarized the main areas of divergence in terms of a distinction between the 'pros' and the 'cons'. The pros are characterized by a 'profligate, liberal expansion of categories', interactional taxonomies, an emphasis on the differences between L2 learners' and native speakers' use of CSs, an attempt to create an authentic context for the elicitation of CSs (for example, by using real-world prompts and a purpose for communicating), the study of learners with different L1s, and a commitment to teaching CSs. The cons are characterized by a 'conservative, parsimonious reduction of categories', conceptual taxonomies reflecting underlying mental processes, an emphasis on the similarities between L1 and L2 performance in the same speaker, reliance on artificial elicitation techniques (for example, the description of abstract shapes without a listening partner), the study of learners with the same L1, and the dismissal of the need to teach CSs. These stark differences might be considered to reflect confusion in the field. Alternatively, they could be taken to reflect the vibrancy of this area of study, a view I am more inclined to adopt. (See Chapter 17.)

Irrespective of whether one is a pro or a con, a number of limitations of the CS research are evident. Little has yet been discovered about the developmental nature of CSs in L2 production. Bialystok's (1983a) study suggested that there is a general switch from L1-based to L2-based strategies, but Poulisse (1990) found little evidence of proficiency-related effects on strategy choice. Jourdain (2000) found that highly proficient L2 learners used CSs in the same way as native speakers but noted that her study did not show how learners arrived at such native-like use and that little was known about this. The research to date has also made no attempt to investigate the relationship between the use of CSs and acquisition, although there has been no shortage of theorizing on this issue. This surely is one direction that future research should take.

As I noted earlier, CS research seems to have entered into limbo. This may reflect a recognition that the modelling of CSs has gone as far as it can for the time being and also the growing commitment in a number of researchers (for example, Wagner and Firth 1997) to the use of conversational analysis as a tool for investigating L2 communication, which has led to the study of CSs becoming subsumed in more general accounts of how conversations are accomplished in an L2.

Conclusion

In this chapter we have considered cognitive accounts of L2 production, focusing on just two aspects that have been of interest to SLA researchers. In the case of 'procedural skill', we considered the differences that exist between learners and native speakers, as evidenced in temporal variables and hesitation phenomena. We saw that one way of characterizing development is as progressive control of L2 resources leading to greater fluency and also that there is some evidence to suggest that this development occurs independently of the development of L2 linguistic knowledge. We also saw that learners experience difficulty in attending to all aspects of L2 production (i.e. fluency, complexity, and accuracy) simultaneously and that both pre-task planning and within-task planning impact somewhat differently depending on the aspect learners choose to prioritize. In the case of communication strategies, we observed that the research has concentrated on identifying the strategies that learners use and on developing taxonomies to account for them. Definitions and taxonomies vary according to whether they are interactional or conceptual in nature. We also considered research that has investigated learners' use of CSs, noting that this has focused on lexical compensatory strategies such as circumlocution. In addition we considered how such variables as the task learners are asked to perform affect learners' choice of strategies and the role of strategy training. We also noted the disagreement that exists regarding whether CSs facilitate or impede L2 acquisition.

This chapter points to two ways in which an account of the cognitive processes involved in L2 production can assist our understanding of L2 acquisition. First, it demonstrates the importance of recognizing that language acquisition involves more than just acquiring linguistic and pragmatic knowledge. It also entails developing control over this knowledge so that it can be accessed automatically and be used effectively in communication. Automaticity is, of course, an issue that is addressed in nearly all the cognitive theories we considered in Chapter 9 but the study of fluency enhances our understanding of L2 use and provides interesting new ways of investigating how automaticity develops over time. Second, this chapter points to the possibility of intervening in the process of L2 acquisition not directly by teaching linguistic content but indirectly by influencing the ways that L2 learners communicate. We have seen two ways in which this can be achieved. One is by manipulating the kind of planning that learners engage in when they perform a communicative task. The second is by training learners to use communication strategies. What is needed, of course, is research that shows that such intervention is effective in promoting learning. This is still largely lacking.

Notes

1 Segalowitz (2003) argued that the quantitative/qualitative distinction in discussions of fluency might be a non-issue, as 'out of quantitative changes in speed come qualitative differences in the way information is processed' (p. 387).

2 A somewhat similar model to Levelt's (Kellogg 1996) has been developed to account for the production processes involved in writing. This served as the theoretical base of Ellis and Yuan's (2004) study of the effects of planning on L2 writing.

3 Planning variability cannot account for all the variability evident in learners' use of the past tense, as demonstrated by Wolfram's (1989) review of studies that have investigated systematic variability in L2 tense marking. In particular, Wolfram drew attention to a 'lexical variable' in the early stages of acquisition. That is, learners vary in their ability to mark for past tense according to the particular verb they are using.
4 CSs also need to be distinguished from LEARNING STRATEGIES. Whereas CSs are strategies that are employed to meet a pressing communicative need—they are short-term rather than long-term solutions to a problem—learning strategies are directed at addressing a perceived gap in knowledge or skill and therefore are directed at a long-term solution. However, some typologies of learning strategies include 'compensatory strategies' (for example, Oxford 1990). Learning strategies are addressed in Chapter 12.
5 There is a good number of studies that have investigated the effects of training in the use of 'learning strategies'. These are considered in Chapter 13.

11

Sociocultural theory and second language acquisition

Introduction

The theories we examined in Chapters 9 and 10 have been informed by mainstream SLA and the COMPUTATIONAL MODEL on which this is based—i.e. the idea of the human mind as a black box, which 'contains' the knowledge that results from processing linguistic input and that is then accessed for output. Lantolf (1996) argued that this metaphor has become so pervasive 'that many people find it difficult to conceive of neural computation as a theory, it must surely be a fact' (p. 725). In this chapter we will examine an approach to explaining L2 acquisition that draws on a very different set of metaphors and affords an alternative account of both how L2 knowledge is conceptualized and the ways in which it is developed. Lantolf (2000a) labelled this paradigm SOCIOCULTURAL SLA. It is important to recognize from the outset, however, that this paradigm, despite the label 'sociocultural' does not seek to explain how learners acquire the cultural values of the L2 but rather how knowledge of an L2 is internalized through experiences of a sociocultural nature. In other words, the paradigm is essentially a cognitive one; as Lantolf (2004: 30) insisted sociocultural theory (SCT) is 'a theory of mind'.

Sociocultural SLA draws extensively on the work of Vygotsky (1987), A. N. Leont'ev (1978) and Wertsch (1985), among others. Here, however, we will consider how sociocultural theory has been appropriated by SLA researchers. Readers interested in a broader account of sociocultural theory should consult Vygotsky (1987) and the collections of Vygotsky's papers by Reiber and Carton (1987), Rieber and Wollack (1997) and Rieber (1998). Also Wertsch (1998) is a valuable source for examining how Vygotsky's ideas have been developed in the North American context. Wells (1999) considered the application of sociocultural theory to educational contexts.

It should be noted that sociocultural SLA is closely affiliated with the social approaches to SLA that were considered in Chapter 7. In particular, sociocultural researchers would endorse the general position that Watson-

Gegeo (2004) promulgated in her proposal for a language SOCIALIZATION paradigm for SLA:

> ... cognition originates in social interaction and is shaped by cultural and sociopolitical processes. That is, cultural and sociopolitical processes are central, rather than incidental, to cognitive development.
> (p. 332)

However, sociocultural SLA differs from the more general social approaches discussed in Chapter 7 in that it advances very specific claims about how social context and interaction mediate language learning and has given rise to research studies that document the intermental and intramental processes through which linguistic development takes place.

Sociocultural theory was briefly introduced in Chapter 6 where we considered the role that interaction is claimed to play in L2 acquisition from the perspective of the theory. Here we will offer an in-depth account of the theory, beginning with how 'language' is conceptualized; we will then consider the methodology used in sociocultural research and the key theoretical constructs that underpin the theory. There follows a brief account of ACTIVITY THEORY. We will then examine the SLA research based on SCT. Finally, we will consider a number of central issues in mainstream SLA (i.e. errors, the order and sequence of acquisition, L1 transfer, implicit/explicit L2 knowledge, and motivation) from an SCT perspective.

'Language' in sociocultural theory

Mitchell and Myles (1998), in the conclusion to their own survey of sociocultural SLA, offered the following criticism:

> ... sociocultural theorists of SLL (second language learning) do not offer any very thorough or detailed view of the nature of language as a formal system. What is the relative importance within the language system of words, or of grammar? Is language a creative rule-governed system, or a patchwork of prefabricated chunks and routines, available in varying degrees for recombination? Up to now, sociocultural researchers in SLL have taken little interest in such general issues.
> (p. 161)

In other words, Mitchell and Myles argued, sociocultural SLA has no theory of language. In this respect, it differs from the linguistic theories of SLA, which are considered in the following chapter, which are based on very explicit accounts of language. Mitchell and Myles are right to insist that any theory of L2 acquisition must specify the nature of the object to be acquired. To what extent are they right in claiming that sociocultural SLA is lacking in this respect?

For Vygotsky, as for sociocultural theorists in general, language is viewed as a semiotic tool; that is, language is seen as the means by which humans achieve the goals of social living. As Wells (1994a) pointed out, Vygotsky's views of language are in this respect very similar to those of Halliday:

> Halliday and Vygotsky are in agreement in seeing language as a cultural tool that has been developed and refined in the service of social action and interaction.
> (p. 49)

The differences between Vygotsky and Halliday, according to Wells, lie in the fact that as a psychologist, Vygotsky was concerned with the relationship between language and thought and saw language as the means for mediating higher levels of thinking, whereas Halliday, as a linguist, was more concerned with how language is used as a tool in communication and how its communicative uses shape language itself. For Vygotsky it is language at the level of the word that is central,[1] as it is at this level that the child discovers the symbolic function of language and at this level that the close relationship between language and thought develops. For Halliday, however, language is a semiotic system consisting of signs involving phonological, lexical, and grammatical forms that encode the intrapersonal, interpersonal, and textual functions that occur in social behaviour. The similarities, in Wells' view, however, far outweigh the differences, as according to both Vygotsky and Halliday:

> Language is a particularly powerful semiotic tool because its semantic structure:
> - encodes the culture's theory of experience, including the knowledge associated with the use of all other tools;
> - enables its users to interact with each other in order to coordinate their activity and simultaneously to reflect on and share their interpretations of experience.
>
> (p. 72)

In short, it is the semantic properties of language that are at the forefront of a sociocultural view of language rather than its formal properties. Of course, how learners acquire these semantic properties cannot be studied separately from the actual linguistic forms that encode them. Wells' exegesis of the close links between Vygotsky and Halliday suggests that sociocultural theorists might benefit from tying their enquiries more closely to a well-developed functional theory of language such as Halliday's.

The primacy of the semantic properties of language in sociocultural theory is also emphasized by Lantolf and Thorne (2006). They acknowledged the substantiveness of Mitchell and Myles' criticism and set out to address it. They presented a sociocultural perspective on language as 'communicative activity':

> ... because SCT is a theory of mediated mental development, it is most compatible with theories of language that focus on communication, cognition, and meaning rather than on formalist positions that privilege structure.
> (p. 4)

They accepted, however, that form 'matters' but argued that form cannot be considered in isolation from meaning because 'meaning and form are dialectically dependent on one another' (p. 5). They drew on a range of sources (for example, Wittgenstein, Bakhtin, Rommetveit) to dispute the Saussurian dualism between 'langue' (as a formal, abstract, and collective language system) and 'parole' (as the concrete instantiations of this system in an individual's speech) in order to argue that language needs to be studied in relation to 'social events'. They provided a revealing example of such an approach with an example from Rommetveit (1992). This shows how the same activity (Mr Smith pushing a machine across his lawn) can constitute very different social events and thus give rise to radically different meanings of the same linguistic form. Thus, in response to a friend's enquiry regarding what her lazy husband is doing, Mrs Smith might respond 'He is working, he is mowing the lawn' whereas in response to an enquiry from one of Mr Smith's friends as to whether Mr Smith is working that day she might respond 'He is not working, he is mowing the lawn'. The point that Lantolf and Thorne sought to make by this example is that a given form (such as the verb 'work') does not have a stable meaning but rather multiple personal meanings (or 'senses') that are created through interaction in accordance with the social events in which they occur.

It is possible to identify a number of linguistic paradigms that can be considered compatible with this view of meaning as 'conceptual' rather than 'referential' and language as 'communicative activity', which lies at the heart of sociocultural theory. Lantolf (2006) looked to Lakoff and Johnson's (1980, 1999) conceptual metaphor theory to provide a basis for examining how learners acquire the cultural meanings of the L2. Lantolf argued that metaphor is not at the margins of language but rather is central to both mental and linguistic activity:

> ... conceptual metaphors are culturally structured models for organizing experience that underlie, and at the same time, are made manifest in the linguistic expressions we traditionally think of as metaphors.
> (p. 85)

and gives the example of how English-speaking people construe argument as war through such linguistic metaphors as 'Your argument is indefensible'. Conceptual metaphor theory belongs to the general paradigm of COGNITIVE LINGUISTICS, which Lantolf and Thorne (2006) explicitly acknowledged as an appropriate linguistic basis for sociocultural enquiry. Another linguistic model that meets with their approval is Hopper's emergent grammar (Hopper

1998). This takes the utterance rather than the sentence as the fundamental unit of analysis and thus acknowledges that language is communicative activity. A central thesis in Hopper's grammar is that linguistic structure is derived out of communicative activity; it is 'a set of sedimented conventions that have been routinized out of the more frequently occurring ways of saying things' (Hopper 1998: 163 as cited in Lantolf and Thorne). These conventions are the formulaic sequences discussed in Chapter 2. Thus, grammar is a by-product of communication and is necessarily incomplete. Lantolf and Thorne argued that from this perspective 'learning an additional language is about enhancing one's repertoire of fragments and patterns that enables participation in a wider array of communicative activities' (p. 17).

The methodology of sociocultural research

The methodology employed by Vygotsky and adopted by SLA researchers in the Vygotskian tradition is known as the 'genetic method'. This differs from mainstream SLA research in two key respects. First, it focuses on the situational and discoursal contexts in which learner utterances are found rather than on learner language in isolation; it examines what Lave and Wenger (1991) called 'situated activity'. Second, emphasis is placed on examining the process by which new functions (for example, new utterance types) emerge rather than on the products of learning. Vygotsky (1987) specified four domains in which the genetic approach could be applied; phylogenesis (i.e. how the human species has evolved), sociocultural history (i.e. how a particular culture has developed over time), ontogenesis (i.e. how an individual develops over the course of his/her life), and MICROGENESIS (i.e. how development takes place over the course of a particular interaction in a specific sociocultural setting). Vygotsky's own research focused on ontogenesis but, as Wells (1994a) pointed out, recent research has addressed all these domains. Sociocultural SLA, however, has relied primarily on the study of acquisition in the ontogenetic and microgenetic domains.

Following Vygotsky, SLA research on ontogenesis has eschewed reaction-time and introspective research traditions as being inappropriate for studying how mental processes arise out of sociocultural activity because they focus on the product rather than the process of learning. Instead it has made use of what Vygotsky (1978) called the 'experimental-development' method. This involves exposing learners to 'double stimulation'. That is, learners are presented with tasks that are beyond their immediate capabilities and then provided with some form of assistance to enable them to solve the task. In Vygotsky's (1987) 'forbidden colour' experiments, for example, young children were required to answer questions about their homes and family but were forbidden to mention certain colours or to refer to the same colour twice. To help them in this task, Vygotsky provided the children with slips of coloured paper that they could use to remind themselves which colours they could not mention and which ones they had already mentioned. In the context of an SLA study, Ellis (1999a) asked a beginner learner to describe a 'what's wrong card' depicting a man holding an umbrella but with the rain falling inside rather than outside—a task beyond this learner's L2 abilities. The assistance in this case took the form of the teacher scaffolding the learner by prompting her and, where necessary, supplying her with the necessary vocabulary. By examining how this learner performed the task at three different times, Ellis revealed the ontogenesis of this learner's ability to perform the task more or less independently.

The bulk of socioculturally informed research in SLA, however, has employed the microgenetic method. This seeks to uncover the stages through which a learner passes en route to achieving SELF-REGULATION (i.e. the ability to control the use of a particular L2 feature by using it independently of any support provided by an interlocutor). It constitutes what Wertsch (1985: 55) called 'a very short-term longitudinal study' and reflects Vygotsky's methodological imperative that development can only be properly understood by studying its emergence. It should be noted, however, that the microgenetic method has been successfully used in studies that would be traditionally recognized as longitudinal (for example, Ohta 2001a). Lavelli *et al.* (2004) listed four key characteristics of the microgenetic method: (1) individuals are observed through a period of change, (2) observations are conducted before, during, and after the period of change, (3) observations during the period of transition are conducted regularly, and (4) observed behaviours are analysed intensively, using both qualitative and quantitative methods, in order to identify the processes that arise in the developmental change. Sociocultural research that has utilized the microgenetic method has been largely qualitative in nature; that is, it has not entailed counting instances of specific L2 phenomena but rather elucidating how a particular function/feature comes to be performed and internalized. It should be noted, however, that much of Vygotsky's research and that of other Russian researchers working in the Vygotskian tradition was often quantitative.

The choice of episodes for analysis is determined by the research question. For example, if the focus is on how corrective feedback assists the internalization of linguistic forms, then obviously episodes involving how learner errors are addressed will need to be selected. In order to determine patterns of interaction, it is necessary to obtain as full an understanding as possible of the sociocultural context in which the episodes under study occurred. This requires examining how the participants approach an activity, what roles they assume, and the level of involvement and contribution of each participant. In this respect, then, the microgenetic method avoids the limitations that Block (2003) identified in mainstream SLA research, where more often than not the participants under investigation are described in only superficial terms. (See Chapter 7.) Attention also needs to be paid to the fact that the relationships between the participants are dynamic and can change over the course of an interaction. Identifying microgenetic growth involves looking for evidence of a shift from other-regulated behaviour on the part of the learner to self-regulated behaviour. That is, the researcher inspects the interaction for examples of how assisted performance of a specific feature (for example, a word or a structure) precedes and gives way to unassisted performance either within the same interaction or in a subsequent interaction. Ellis and Barkhuizen (2005) list a number of features that the analyst will need to be on the lookout for, including the extent to which intervention by an 'expert' takes place, the quality of the intervention (i.e. the strategies used to assist the learner), the need for intervention, and the extent and nature of the learner's response to the intervention. It should be clear that such research has the capacity to demonstrate that the contextual processes are part of learning.

An important methodological issue in sociocultural SLA is the extent to which it is possible to investigate the ontogenesis and microgenesis of L2 learning in laboratory settings. As should be clear from the account of Vygotsky's and Ellis' experiments above, many SCT studies are laboratory-based. However, not all researchers accept that the laboratory constitutes a legitimate context for conducting sociocultural studies. Lantolf and Thorne (2006) discussed Newman and Holzman's (1996) 'radical position', according to which laboratory research is unacceptable in that it overlooks the fundamental fact that the laboratory constitutes a unique and unnatural setting because 'the object which the psychologist is trying to make sense of is in turn trying to make sense of the psychologist' (pp. 53–4). Lantolf and Thorne, however, found merit in laboratory research but agreed with Newman and Holzman that the focus needs to be on the behaviour of individuals rather than groups. In this respect, then, Vygotsky's 'experimental-development' method is very different from the experimental designs normally associated with the 'scientific method', which examines groups of learners in order to arrive at statistically justified generalizations concerning cause and effect. However, Vygotsky made it clear that, in his view, the approach he was proposing was compatible with the scientific method because he was using the right method for the given object of study.

Key constructs in sociocultural SLA

SCT is best seen as a holistic theory informed by a number of interlocking constructs. For this reason it is not easy to provide separate accounts of these constructs. Nevertheless, this is the approach that has been adopted in other introductions to the theory (for example, Lantolf 2000a, 2000b, 2006; Lantolf and Thorne 2006; Mitchell and Myles 1998) and so will be the approach I will follow here. As Lantolf has consistently emphasized, the key construct is that of 'mediated learning' so we will begin with this.

Mediated learning

SCT acknowledges that humans possess a biological inheritance and that this provides the basis for subsequent development. But in contrast to theories of acquisition based on Universal Grammar, SCT does not see this as determining the growth of language but rather as allowing only for relatively simple lower mental functions to be performed. For example, Vygotsky considered that our biological inheritance equips us with the same natural memory abilities found in the higher primates. Higher order mental functioning (for example, memory, attention, rational thinking) develops through the 'interweaving of our cultural and biological inheritances' (Lantolf and Thorne 2006: 59). Thus, SCT seeks to explain how mediated minds (Lantolf and Pavlenko 1995) are developed out of the social activity that is embedded in the cultural values of particular communities. It is through this social activity that genetically endowed capacities are modified and reorganized into higher order forms. In this way SCT rejects the idea of the mind and the world constituting distinct (if interrelated) entities by insisting that 'the person and the world are necessarily connected in a dialectic and inseparable relationship' (Lantolf 2005: 343). The learner is not autonomous and learning is not something that goes on exclusively inside the head of the learner but also in the world the learner inhabits. SCT brings the social and the psychological into contact through the notion of MEDIATION.

A representation of Vygotsky's model of mediated learning is shown in Figure 11.1. The model depicts a subject (in our case, an L2 learner) and the object of his/her activity (for example, to read and understand a text in the L2). If appropriate development has taken place, the subject can mediate his/her own action on the object, but if it has not, the learner will need to resort to an artefact (for example, a dictionary) to provide assistance. This results in 'tool mediated' action. Mediation, however, can involve more than just concrete artefacts. Lantolf and Thorne (2006) defined mediation as 'the process through which humans deploy culturally constructed artefacts, concepts, and activities to regulate (i.e. gain voluntary control over and transform) the material world or their own and each other's social and mental activity' (p. 79). They pointed out that artefacts can be concrete (for example, a hammer or a dictionary) or symbolic (for example, language). The specific functions that artefacts perform depend on the specific situational context; thus, although an artefact may have an established cultural function, it can serve a different mediating function in a concrete situation—what Wertsch (1998) referred to as a 'spin off' function. For example, we can use a paper clip to open up the seal on a tube of toothpaste. Artefacts are also fundamentally social in nature; that is, they reflect and forge connections between people. Artefacts are of themselves not the means of mediation but become so only as a result of repeated use—for example, a child cannot understand the function of a hammer unless it can observe someone hammering. Thus, to function as a means of mediation, an artefact must assume some conceptual value and be linked to some activity; this occurs initially through the regulatory agency of others until the individual achieves a full understanding of the artefact's conceptual value and can employ it as a mediating tool independently (= self-regulation). An artefact can also be external (i.e. employed without forethought) or internal (i.e. its use is planned in the mind before implementation).

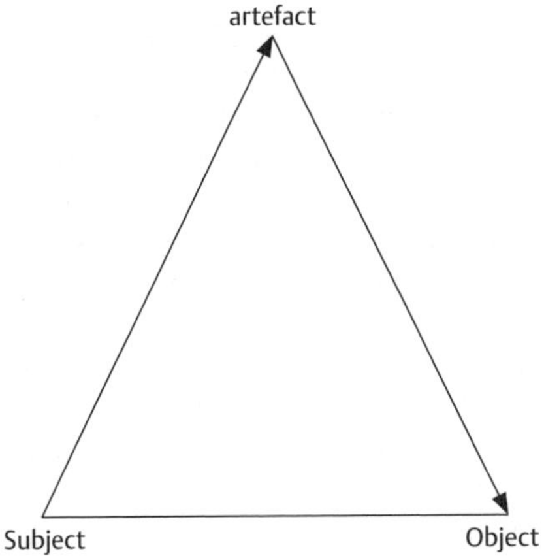

Figure 11.1 Vygotsky's model of mediated action (from Lantolf and Thorne 2006)

The most powerful artefact available for mediating thought is language. For example, alphabetic writing systems, once developed, had a profound effect on the way we view language in terms of sentences, words, and phonemes.[2] As humans acquire language they are able to use it as an autonomous tool for organizing and controlling thought. In Vygotskian theory, then, language is viewed as both a means of accomplishing social interaction and of managing mental activity, with the former serving as the basis for the latter. In the case of language learners, the L2 serves as both the object of their attention and also as the tool for mediating its acquisition. As Swain (2000) put it, L2 acquisition involves learning how to use language to mediate language learning.

Lantolf (2000a) suggested that mediation in second language learning can involve others through social interaction or the learner by him or herself through private speech. That is, mediation can occur externally, as when a novice is given assistance in the performance of some function, or internally, as when an individual uses his or her own resources to achieve control over a function. In both cases, however, these mediational resources are viewed as social in nature (i.e. they involve social interaction with others or with oneself). The essence of a sociocultural theory of mind is that external mediation serves as the means by which internal mediation is achieved. Thus, according to Lantolf (2000a) development is 'about the appropriation by individuals (and groups) of the mediational means made available by others (past or present) in their environment in order to improve control over their own mental activity'. Thus, a theory of the mediated mind claims that what originates as social speech becomes internalized as inner speech so that it can be used by the individual to regulate his/her own behaviour.

A key issue, then, is the extent to which L2 learners are able to use the L2 as inner speech to regulate their own thinking. Lantolf and Thorne (2006) outlined two positions. According to the first, advanced by Ushakova (1994), learners may succeed in learning a second language but they continue to use their L1 as inner speech. In other words, the L2 is able to serve as a tool for mediating social activity but not mental activity. According to the second position, advanced language learners are those who have acquired the ability to use the L2 for both social functions and for regulating their own thinking. In an effort to establish which of these positions is correct, Lantolf and Thorne reviewed a range of research relating to the use of gesture while speaking in an L2 and the acquisition of L2 metaphorical concepts and L2 lexical concepts. These areas were chosen in the conviction that they shed light on the extent to which learners have internalized not just the linguistic forms of the L2 and their social functions but also the deeper conceptual meanings of the L2 (what they term its 'cultural models'). Lantolf and Thorne's review is inconclusive, however. For example, they noted that there is little evidence to support the idea that conceptual metaphors are learnable but they did find evidence that some learners acquire at least some aspects of the L2 gesture system. They suggested that there may be little chance for foreign language learners who are dependent on the classroom to acquire the cultural models of the L2, but that learners who undergo intensive cultural immersion experiences may be more successful. They commented that 'what seems to be necessary is an intent and a commitment to live one's life as a member of the new community' (p. 148) and proposed that it may be that learners are able to develop a THIRD SPACE (Kramsch 1993), i.e. a world consisting of hybrid cultural models derived from both the L1 and L2.

This central notion—that learning involves mediation—underlies all the other constructs that we will now consider.

Mediation through social interaction

A primary means of mediation is verbal interaction. Thus, SCT sees learning, including language learning, as dialogically based. Artigal (1992) went so far as to suggest that the 'language acquisition device' is located in the interaction that takes place between speakers rather than inside their heads. That is acquisition occurs *in* rather than *as a result of* interaction. From this perspective, then, L2 acquisition is not a purely individual-based process but shared between the individual and other persons.

Verbal interaction is dialogic. This is self-evident in the case of interaction with another person but is also true in interactions that arise in private speech. Dialogic interaction enables an expert (such as a teacher) to create a context in which novices can participate actively in their own learning and in which the expert can fine-tune the support that the novices are given (Antón 1999). In particular, dialogic discourse is better equipped to identify what a learner can and cannot do without assistance. It serves to create the intersubjectivity that enables verbal interaction to mediate learning.

There are two ways of looking at the mediating role played by social interaction. The first is to consider the general characteristics of interaction that help learning to take place. This is the approach adopted by Wood, Bruner, and Ross (1976), who identified a number of general features of SCAFFOLDING (i.e. the dialogic process by which one speaker assists another in performing a function that he or she cannot perform alone) to explain how social interaction can assist children to acquire new linguistic forms and functions. (See Chapter 6.) This generalist approach to identifying the kinds of interactions beneficial for learning is epistemologically the same as that discussed in Chapter 6; that is, 'scaffolding' constitutes a construct of the same order as the 'negotiation of meaning'. It is, however, self-evidently much broader in scope and also differs from negotiation of meaning in that it addresses both the cognitive demands of a learning goal and the affective states of the learners attempting to achieve the goal. Foster and Ohta (2005) carried out a detailed comparison of the two constructs, concluding that in the classroom data they examined there were very few instances of the negotiation of meaning but many of learners supporting each other both affectively and cognitively in interactions where there was no evidence of any communicative problem.

Scaffolding can be seen as one feature of a more general characteristic of dialogic discourse—what Van Lier (1992) has called 'contingency'. This refers to the way in which one utterance is connected to another to produce coherence in discourse. Coherence, according to Van Lier, is achieved when the motivation for the utterance is apparent to the interlocutors and when the expectations that it sets up are subsequently met in one way or another. Drawing on Vygotskian theory, he argued that 'contingency can be seen as the essential ingredient making the transformation of social processing into cognitive processing possible' (p. 15). Contingency, then, constitutes an important condition for learning through social interaction to take place and scaffolding serves as one of the chief means of achieving it, especially with low-proficiency learners.

In more recent publications, 'scaffolding' has fallen out of favour, in part because it has been reified into an object and in part because it is difficult to apply in peer–peer interactions. Dialogic mediation needs to be viewed as an 'activity' that is jointly constructed by the participants involved and not as some kind of apparatus that one of the participants applies to conversation. Another reason is that some researchers (for example, Antón 1999) have dubiously equated scaffolding with the IRF (initiation–response–feedback) exchanges that have been shown to be so ubiquitous in classroom discourse. As Lantolf and Thorne (2006) noted, there is 'little about the IRF sequence that would structurally support creative and developmental progress in areas other than those of formal accuracy and mimicry of prescriptive norms of form and style' (p. 275). (But see Chapter 15 for a different view of IRF sequences.) The preferred terms now are COLLABORATIVE DIALOGUE and INSTRUCTIONAL CONVERSATION. Swain (2000) introduced the term collaborative dialogue, defined as 'dialogue in which speakers are engaged in problem solving and knowledge building' (p. 102). Knowledge building arises both as a result of the learners 'saying' (i.e. using the L2 to jointly address a problem) and responding to 'what is said' (i.e. consciously attending to the language forms that arise in the utterances they produce). The other frequently used term, instructional conversation (Tharp and Gallimore 1988, as cited in Donato 2000), refers to pedagogic interaction that is teacher-led and directed towards a curricular-goal (for example, enabling students to perform a structure that they have not yet internalized) but is conversational in nature (for example, it manifests equal turn-taking rights and is unpredictable).

Another essentially generalist approach to characterizing the mediating function of interaction in language learning can be found in Ohta's (2001a) description of how a learner provides assistance to a struggling peer. Ohta identified four major forms of such assistance: waiting, prompting, co-construction, and explanation. In her own study of peer interaction in a Japanese as a foreign language classroom, Ohta found that 'peer interlocutors tend to provide their partners with ample wait time' (p. 89). Prompting is a more explicit technique involving repeating a word or syllable just uttered, thereby helping the interlocutor to continue. Co-construction consists of the learner contributing some linguistic material (a word, phrase, or grammatical particle) that contributes to the completion of the partner's previous utterance. Explanations, often provided in the L1, are used to address errors the partner has made.

The second approach for examining how interaction assists learning is arguably closer to the core of SCT. According to this approach, there is no single set of general characteristics that constitute affordances for learning. Rather, affordances arise out of the successful tailoring of the interaction to the developmental level of individual learners. To be effective, mediation needs to demonstrate reciprocity and contingency. Thus, what constitutes a facilitative interaction for one learner might not be for another, either because it is pitched at a level too far in advance of the learner or because it fails to 'stretch' the learner by posing a sufficient challenge. This approach to the mediating role of interaction is well represented in Poehner and Lantolf's (2005) account of DYNAMIC ASSESSMENT. This term refers to a mode of assessment that has 'the expressed goal of modifying learner performance during the assessment itself' (p. 235) as opposed to obtaining a static measure of a learner's proficiency without feedback or intervention of any kind. Poehner and Lantolf provided a number of examples of how the procedures involved in dynamic assessment 'unfold in concrete practice' (p. 242). A number of these examples come from Aljaafreh and Lantolf's (1994) study of CORRECTIVE FEEDBACK, which is considered in detail later in this chapter. Here we will focus on the examples from Poehner's own research with advanced learners of L2 French. Poehner asked the learners to construct a past-tense oral narrative in French after watching a short video-clip. They were given no feedback or mediation in this first task. Then they repeated the task after watching a second clip. This time 'they interacted with a mediator who offered suggestions, posed questions, made corrections, and helped them think through decisions concerning selection of lexical items, verb tense, and other language difficulties' (p. 246). This interactive assistance, which was provided in English, was 'highly flexible, emerging from the interaction between the student and the mediator'. Poehner and Lantolf showed how the native-speaker interlocutor (the 'tester') varied the specific mediating strategies he used at different times with the same learner and also with different learners. For example, in the case of Sara, he initially used quite direct clues (for example, 'but in the past') and subsequently, when addressing the same linguistic problem, more indirect means (for example, 'there's something there with the verb'). Lantolf and Poehner also suggested that the nature of the mediation provided for Sara and another learner revealed them to be at different stages of development in their ability to self-regulate their use of French past tense forms. Thus, this second approach to examining the role of interaction in SCT emphasizes the need for reciprocity between the learner and mediator and draws heavily on Vygotsky's notion of the ZONE OF PROXIMAL DEVELOPMENT which was introduced in Chapter 6 and is discussed more fully later in this chapter.

Mediation by means of private speech

While interpersonal interaction holds a privileged place in SCT, it is not the only way in which language activity can mediate language learning. Self-mediation through PRIVATE SPEECH is also possible. Ohta (2001b) defines private speech as 'audible speech not adapted to an addressee' (p. 16). She suggests that it can take a number of forms including imitation, vicarious response (i.e. responses that a classroom learner produces to questions the teacher has addressed to another learner), and mental rehearsal.

Young children frequently resort to talking to themselves, even when they are in the company of others. (See Saville-Troike 1988.) This self-directed speech can take the form of questions they ask themselves, instructions regarding what to do or not to do, and evaluations of their performance. It is similar to the language used by conversationalists who are very familiar with one another—that is, it is paratactic and consists largely of comments (new information) on unstated topics (Lantolf 1999). Such talk is derived from social talk, as shown by Vygotsky and functions as a proxy for it, serving the same basic purpose of enabling the child to obtain control over the mental functioning needed to perform an activity (Vocate 1994a).

Adults as well as children employ private speech. According to the 'principle of continuous access' (Frawley and Lantolf 1985), adults continue to have access to the knowing strategies they have used previously. In difficult situations adults are able to reactivate developmentally earlier strategies as a way of achieving self-regulation. When faced with performing a new function, the adult learner is able to utilize private speech in order to achieve self-regulation. As Foley (1991) put it 'when an individual finds himself faced with a difficult task, he externalizes the inner order so that he may regulate himself' (p. 63).

Lantolf (2000a) noted that self-directed speech is well attested in the psycholinguistic literature. In Lantolf (2000b), for example, he referred to a study by Wertsch (1985) of how children learnt to carry out cognitive tasks such as using a model to reconstruct a wooden puzzle. Wertsch found that the children were initially dependent on verbal assistance from their parents but that subsequently they began to instruct themselves in what pieces of the puzzle to select and where to place them and to evaluate their actions. This occurred in the company of their parents. This study illustrates the important point that private speech can occur in social situations as well as when the individual is alone.

Because private speech is intended for the speaker, not the listener, it is not constrained by the same norms that affect social speech. In L2 learners this is evident in two ways. First, they may resort to the use of their L1 in self-directed speech. Second, if they use the L2, they may not employ target-language forms even if they have internalized these. Thus what are apparent 'errors' may simply be the private forms that learners use in their struggle to maintain control over a task. The notion of 'deviance' cannot be easily applied to private speech. Such a perspective suggests that to evaluate the accuracy of learners' productions (as described in Chapter 2), it is important to distinguish whether the talk that arises in the performance of a task is 'social' or 'private'.[3]

A key issue, however, is the extent to which learners are able to use the L2 for private speech or need to fall back on their L1. Lantolf (2000a) citing a number of L2 studies, argued that private speech by adult learners is common. Lantolf (1999) pointed out that it provides crucial evidence of the L2 forms that learners have internalized from their environment. However, more recently, Lantolf (2006) presented evidence to suggest that learners, including those of advanced proficiency, may experience difficulty in self-regulating by means of the L2. He referred to a study by Centano-Cortes and Jimenez-Jimenez (2004), which audio-recorded native speakers of both Spanish and English solving a number of cognitively challenging problems presented on a computer in Spanish. The native speakers of Spanish produced only two brief private speech utterances in the L2, while the English speakers produced much more. This led Lantolf to suggest that 'the material circumstances of a particular task (in this case, the task language) influence which language an individual is likely to access for cognitive regulation' (p. 72). The English speakers' L2 private speech was limited in a number of ways. The intermediate-level learners only used Spanish for reading aloud the problems to be solved; they switched to their L1 as they tried to reach a solution. The advanced-level learners did make fuller use of the L2 while working through a problem but interestingly were not very successful in solving it when they did so. Lantolf explained this finding by suggesting that 'producing Spanish became an intentional sub-goal of talk and, therefore, the language was unable to fully serve its function as a problem solving tool' (p. 74). This comment suggests that in considering the role of private speech in L2 acquisition it is necessary to distinguish its use for the purpose of practising/learning the L2 and for the purpose of self-regulating mental activity. As already noted, relatively few learners may fully succeed in the latter.

Our primary concern in this book, however, is whether private speech is able to mediate language learning (irrespective of whether it is able to self-regulate thought).[4] Ohta's (2001b) study of private speech in Japanese as a foreign language classrooms demonstrated that private speech may assist L2 development. She found that private speech served three broad types of overlapping language use: vicarious response, repetition, and manipulation, as shown in Table 11.1. Ohta suggested how these different types of private speech might assist learning. Thus, vicarious response served as a means of testing hypotheses about the L2. Repetition appeared to be used to achieve control over new lexical items and also phrase and sentence patterns that were the focus of explicit language practice. It functioned to assist retention. Manipulation served as a means for analysing language by building up and breaking down words and phrases and engaging in sound play. However, the test of whether private speech is effective in this way must lie in whether the forms and functions that learners have manipulated in private speech become available for subsequent use in social speech. Ohta, while making claims that this takes place, did not provide any examples. Borer (2006), however, showed that learners remembered words better when they privately vocalized deeper processing to create mnemonics.

Type	**Definition**
Vicarious response	Learner covertly answers a question addressed to another student or to the class, completes the utterance of another, or repairs another's error.
Repetition	Learner repeats words, phrases or sentences in whole or in part. Material repeated may or may not be from the immediately preceding context. The learner may repeat after him or herself. Repetition as part of choral drill is excluded from consideration here.
Manipulation	Learner manipulates sentence structure, words, or sounds.

Table 11.1 Types of L2 private speech (Ohta 2001b: 40)

The zone of proximal development

Lantolf and Thorne (2006) noted that the SCT construct that has had the greatest impact on Western scholarship and education is Vygotsky's notion of the zone of proximal development (ZPD). They gave two reasons for this. First, it is closely linked with the construct of 'assisted performance'. Second, it affords a formative view of the role of assessment; that is, assessment should focus on what learners can do with assistance at the present moment rather than what they are capable of independently. Lantolf and Thorne noted that 'there is an industry built upon educational and developmental research that has utilized, co-opted, repurposed, and expanded the ZPD concept' (p. 263). This has led to 'myriad interpretations and extensions of the concept commonly attributed to Vygotsky' (p. 263).

To understand the ZPD it is helpful to distinguish three levels of development. Vygotsky (1978) distinguished 'the actual developmental level, that is the level of development of the child's mental functions that has been established as a result of certain already completed developmental cycles' (p. 85) and a level of potential development as evidenced in problem solving undertaken with the assistance of an adult (an expert) or through collaboration with peers (novices). Another way of distinguishing these two levels is in terms of 'development' and 'learning'. The third level, not commonly mentioned by sociocultural theorists, is the level that lies beyond the learner, that is, the learner is unable to perform the task even if assistance is provided. The ZPD is the second of these levels; the level of potential development. To borrow Vygotsky's own metaphor, it is the 'bud' rather than the 'fruit' of development. Thus, the ZPD is premised on the view that development has both a social and a psychological dimension. The social dimension is where the 'buds' of learning grow and, when the functions acquired through assistance become autonomous, they develop into 'flowers'. These constitute a stable, new zone that makes possible the learning of still further skills.

The ZPD has frequently been invoked by both L2 researchers and language teaching methodologists. As Kinginger (2002) pointed out, it has been subject to a number of interpretations, not all of which are clearly justified by Vygotsky's own account of the ZPD. The 'skills interpretation' draws on the ZPD to provide a justification for the use of pair and small group work in language teaching. The 'scaffolding interpretation' of the ZPD has become synonymous with the process of expert–novice interaction even to the point where it has been used to justify the IRF sequence. Kinginger suggested a third way in which the ZPD has been appropriated by language researchers—to provide a rationale for 'collaborative dialogue'. (See Swain 2000 and Chapter 6.) Kinginger is supportive of only the third of these three interpretations on the grounds that it alone allows for 'recognition of the notion that language-in-use constitutes an object of reflection' (p. 256). Overall, she took the view that there is a danger that the construct becomes so stretched as to lose shape and meaning. In part this is because of the construct's inherent attractiveness but it is also in part due to the fact that Vygotsky himself failed to specify clearly the relationship between social interaction, the mediating function of cultural tools, and the ZPD. Thus it is not so surprising that researchers have interpreted the construct creatively in support of their own particular views about L2 acquisition. As Lantolf and Thorne (2006) concluded, there is obvious merit in interpreting the ZPD as validating the role of collaborative activity in cognitive development.

Despite the danger of over-extension, the ZPD remains a key construct in SCT. It explains a number of important phenomena about learning. First, it explains why there are some structures that learners fail to perform no matter what the external mediation; learners are unable to construct the ZPDs that make the performance of such structures possible. Second, it explains why learners are able to perform some structures with social assistance but not independently; they are able to construct ZPDs for performing these even though they have not internalized them. Third, it explains how learners come to internalize new structures; they appropriate the structures for which, with the help of external mediation, they have created the necessary ZPDs. Currently, the ZPD is conceptualized not as an attribute of the learner with 'relatively fixed dimensions' but rather as 'task-specific, reciprocal and open-ended' and, therefore, 'emergent' (Wells 1999: 345). As Newman and Holzman (1997) put it 'the ZPD is not a place at all; it is an activity ...' (p. 289).

Internalization

SCT distinguishes three forms of regulation—object-regulation, other-regulation, and self-regulation. Consider this example: a learner obtains an electronic dictionary and feels compelled to use it to check the meaning of every 'difficult' word in a reading text; this is object-regulation. The teacher then instructs learners in the strategy of 'selective dictionary use'; this is other-regulation. Finally, the learner is able to vary his/her use of the dictionary according to whether the goal is to learn new vocabulary or to comprehend a text efficiently; this is self-regulation. This process by which a person moves from object/other regulation to self-regulation constitutes INTERNALIZATION. Ohta (2001b) referred to this as 'the movement of language from environment to brain' (p. 11). More technically, Lantolf (2006) defined internalization as 'the process through which members of communities of practice appropriate the symbolic artefacts used in communicative activity and convert them into psychological artefacts that mediate their mental activity' (p. 90). Thus, internalization involves both increased control over L2 forms and functions and also, crucially, the ability to use the L2 to regulate thought.

Like children, L2 learners progress from object-regulation, where their actions are determined by the objects they encounter in the environment, to other-regulation, where they learn to exert control over an object but only with the assistance of another, usually more expert person, and finally to self-regulation, where they become capable of independent strategic functioning. As Vygotsky (1981) put it, new, elaborate psychological processes become available as a result of the initial production of these processes in social interaction. Vygotsky provided this often-cited explanation of how children develop mental skills:

> Any function in the child's cultural development appears twice, or on two planes. First it appears on the social plane, and then on the psychological plane. First it appears between people as an interpsychological category, and then within the child as an intrapsychological category ... It goes without saying that internalization transforms the process itself and changes its structure and functions. Social relations or relations among people genetically underlie all higher functions and their relationships. (p. 163)

Verbal interaction, especially dialogic, serves as the principal means by which children progress from other- to self-regulation.

SCT distinguishes 'learning' (i.e. assisted performance) from 'development' (i.e. self-regulated mental activity that results from having internalized an assisted performance). As Vygotsky (1978) put it: 'learning is not development' but 'properly organized learning results in mental development and sets in motion a variety of developmental processes that would be impossible apart from learning' (p. 90). Applied to language learning, this means that learners first manifest new linguistic forms and functions in interactions with others and subsequently internalize them so they can use them independently. Furthermore, they are likely to experience problems in using new forms when placed in communicatively demanding situations with the result that they fall back on earlier acquired and more stable skills—see, for example, Appel and Lantolf 1994—a phenomenon known as 'back-sliding' in mainstream SLA. This suggests that the extent to which specific forms and functions are internalized, and thus subject to self-regulation, is variable.

The key to understanding internalization is Vygotsky's notion of *imitation*. Lantolf (2005) emphasized that for Vygotsky imitation is not the mechanical activity it assumes in behaviourist learning theories but a creative, transformative activity. That is, it is through imitation that learners come to self-regulate. As Vygotsky (1986) put it, 'to imitate, it is necessary to possess the means of stepping from something one knows to something new' (p. 187). Nor is this something that the learner achieves in isolation; imitation arises in and out of interaction with others. As Saville-Troike's (1988) study, considered in Chapter 3, showed, imitation can arise in learners' private responses to communicative speech, as in this example between a teacher and young L2 learner:

TEACHER You guys go brush your teeth. And wipe your hands on the towel.
CHILD Wipe your hand. Wipe your teeth.

Commenting on this example, Lantolf (2005) noted that the child's utterances is not an interpersonal turn but an imitation of the teacher that results in a lexical error as the child overextends the verb 'wipe'. In this way, socially situated imitation can account for the widespread phenomenon of overgeneralization noted in Chapter 2. For Lantolf, this is an important observation because it demonstrates that such errors do not reflect purely internal, mental processes. Imitation of the kind illustrated above is both social and cognitive in nature.

Activity theory

According to Lantolf and Appel (1994b) ACTIVITY THEORY was developed by a group of Russian psychologists called the Kharkovites, of which the best known is A. N. Leont'ev. This theory was a development of Vygotskian theory. Lantolf (2000b) described it as 'a unified account of Vygotsky's original proposals on the nature and development of human behavior' (p. 8).

A. A. Leontiev (1981) proposed that people possess 'motives' that determine how they respond to a particular task. Motives can be biologically determined (for example, the need to satisfy hunger) or, more importantly from our perspective here, socially-constructed (for example, the need to learn an L2). The learners' motives determine how they construe a given situation. Thus people with different motives will perform the same learning task in different ways. For example, Wertsch, Minick, and Arns (1984) found that middle-class and rural uneducated mothers in Brazil responded differently in the kind of guidance they provided their children in a puzzle-copying task. The middle-class mothers' activity reflected their desire to teach their children the skills they needed to perform the task so they could perform other, similar tasks later (i.e. their motive was pedagogic). Thus, they consistently employed strategic statements like 'now look to see what comes next' and only when these failed did they resort to referential statements like 'try the red piece here'. In contrast, the rural mothers viewed the task as a labour activity of the kind they were familiar with in their daily work. In such activity, mistakes are costly, and, therefore, the mothers strove to prevent their children making errors by directing their actions through referential statements. Thus, the different motives that the two groups of mothers brought to the task led to different activities, reflected in different patterns of language use.

Motives, however, are not just personal; they are socially constructed, as the example from Wertsch *et al.* demonstrates. The key to understanding a learner's motive, then, lies in delineating the 'activity system' (Engestrom 1993; cited in Thorne 2004) from which a participant's motive stems. An activity system consists of the subject(s), the object of the activity, and mediational means (i.e. the symbolic or material artefacts), as in Vygotsky's model of mediated action (see Figure 11.1), but, importantly, it also involves a contextual framework made up of the community of subjects who are sharing the same object of the activity, the understood rules that govern that community, and the division of labour within the community setting (for example, the social rules subjects are expected to conform to). Together these components, which interact with each other, comprise a functional activity system. An example may help to make the model clearer. Imagine an English classroom in Japan where the teacher is conducting a lesson preparing students to sit for a university entrance examination. The students are the subjects and the teacher the mediational tool. The object of activity is a multiple choice grammar exercise of the kind commonly set in university entrance examinations. A number of material and symbolic artefacts are available to the participants. As the teacher is working through the questions one by one with the students, the interactions in which she and students participate constitute one form of mediation. Students also engage in mediation via private speech and they also have access to electronic dictionaries. The activity takes place within the classroom community, which since it is close to the end of the school year is well established, with its rules firmly understood by all the participants; and identities and roles are also well established. However, it does not follow that all the participants are part of the same functional activity system. What defines the object of the activity and therefore the specific activity system is the individual participants' motives and these can vary. For example, some students who are intent on entering a good university are likely to approach the object of activity with a view to learning specific points of grammar that may assist them when they take the examination; in contrast, other students, who for one reason or another do not aspire to enter university, may construct the object of activity as simply something to be got through with minimal effort. Subjects are constrained by the components of an activity system but they also possess agency and thus are able to reconstitute it to suit their own motives.

Thorne (2004) emphasized that a single activity system does not exist in isolation but is influenced by multiple other activity systems. Thus, to extend the example in the previous paragraph, the Japanese high school English classroom is influenced by the wider educational context in Japan and also by activity systems relating to the individuals that comprise it (for example, students' experiences of using English outside the classroom and, crucially, the goals of the individual students). Thorne summarized the main characteristics of activity theory, as he saw it, in terms of the following key points:

1 Activity theory is not a static or purely descriptive approach; rather, the use of activity theory implies transformation and innovation.
2 All activity systems are heterogeneous and multi-voiced and may include conflict and resistance as readily as cooperation and collaboration.
3 Activity is central. There is no 'student' or 'teacher' or 'technology' centred pedagogy from an activity theory perspective. Rather, agents play various roles and share an orientation to the activity.
4 Activity systems don't work alone. Multiple activity systems are always at work and will have varying influences on the local or focus activity at hand. (pp. 7–8)

One might add that activity systems are dynamic. Individuals can realign their motives in the course of carrying out an activity, thus changing the activity. For example, a student may begin by treating a communicative task as a 'game' but in the course of performing the task re-orientate to it as an 'opportunity to learn'. From the perspective of activity theory, then, it is crucially important for SLA researchers to recognize that elicitation devices (such as tasks) do not simply provide 'data' but rather constitute 'activities' that need to be examined microgenetically. (See Seedhouse 2005.)

SLA studies based on sociocultural theory

In this section we will examine a number of SLA studies that have been based on sociocultural theory. The studies have addressed a number of well-defined themes, of which we will consider the following: (1) corrective feedback, (2) collaborative dialoguing, (3) private speech, (4) metatalk, and (5) task versus activity.

Corrective feedback

In one of the most frequently cited SCT studies, Aljaafreh and Lantolf (1994) examined the one-to-one interactions arising between three L2 learners and a tutor who provided CORRECTIVE FEEDBACK on essays they had written. This study and others addressing corrective feedback from the perspective of SCT were considered in Chapter 6. Here we will focus on Samuda's (2001) classroom-based study. This was not explicitly undertaken within the framework of SCT but can usefully be interpreted within its terms. Samuda's starting point was to design a task that created a 'semantic space' for using modal verbs to express degrees of possibility/certainty (i.e. epistemic modality). The task required the learners to work in groups to speculate on the identity of a person based on the contents of their pockets. They were asked to record hypotheses about the person's name, sex, age, and marital status on a chart. During the group discussion, the learners used a number of devices for expressing possibility, deriving these both from the input of the task itself (for example, 'possible' and 'certain') and from their existing interlanguage resources (for example, 'maybe' and 'sure'). However, conspicuously missing from their speech were instances of the target feature, i.e. modal verbs such as 'may' and 'must'. During this stage the teacher did not attempt to intervene by focusing on these forms. During the next stage of the lesson, when the groups made oral presentations of their hypotheses to the whole class, the teacher did intervene—first implicitly and then explicitly. In the implicit language focus the teacher mined formulaic chunks from the input data to highlight novel form/meaning relationships in the context of assisting the learners' communicative efforts. For example, when a learner used the expression 'maybe' the teacher expanded this into 'it's possible' and introduced the modal 'might'. However, Samuda found that not one of these 'interweaves' was taken up by the learners. She suggested that this was not surprising given the learners' 'intense focus on meaning'. The teacher then switched to providing a much more explicit focus on form. This involved the teacher introducing modal verbs and offering a direct metalingual comment about their meaning or form. The learners participated actively in this explicit focus by asking questions about the forms the teacher raised to attention. In the final stage of this task in which the learners had to prepare a poster, the teacher resumed her 'communicative' role. Interestingly, the learners now spontaneously employed the modal verbs the teacher had earlier drawn explicit attention to, interweaving these into the language they mined from the input data. In terms of SCT, this study can be interpreted as demonstrating the following: (1) at the beginning of the study the students had not attained self-regulation over the use of modal verbs of possibility and thus were unable to use them, (2) implicit feedback in the form of recasts was insufficient to construct a zone of proximal development for the target features, and (3) explicit feedback was successful and resulted in the learners' internalizing the target forms and utilizing them independently.

Collaborative dialoguing

The above studies all demonstrate the value of finely tuned scaffolding on the part of an 'expert'. However, as discussed briefly in Chapter 6, scaffolding is not dependent on the presence of an expert; it can also arise in interactions between learners. DiCamilla and Antón (1997) showed how learners make use of repetition to provide scaffolded help for each other. For example, they demonstrated how it serves as a kind of platform on which the learners can rest while they struggle to find the next word and how it is used to finalize a collaborative solution. Lantolf (1997) saw repetition as a form of language play that is important for language acquisition. His learners repeated items and structures that lay within their zone of proximal development. Ohta (1995) illustrated how learners scaffold each other's contributions in a role-playing task, making the point that even a less proficient learner can assist a more proficient learner. She also noted that in learner–learner interactions the notions of novice and expert are 'fluid conceptions' (p. 109); the same learner can function as both expert and novice at different times in a conversation.

In one study, important because it provided evidence of 'development' as well as 'learning', Donato (1994) described the collective scaffolding employed by groups of university students of French performing an oral activity. In a detailed analysis of an exchange involving the negotiation of the form 'tu t'es souvenu', Donato showed how they jointly managed components of the problem, distinguished between what they had produced and what they perceived as the ideal solution, and used their collective resources to minimize frustration and risk. The scaffolding enabled the learners to construct the correct form of the verb even though no single learner knew this prior to the task. Thus this study goes further than most in demonstrating the essential claim of a sociocultural theory of mind, namely that 'higher mental functioning is situated in the dialectal processes embedded in the social context' (p. 46). Donato also provided evidence to suggest that internalization was taking place. The joint performance of new structures on one occasion was frequently followed by independent use of them by individual learners on a later occasion.

In a series of studies, Swain and her co-researchers examined the contribution of collaborative dialoguing to language learning. Kowal and Swain (1994) used a dictogloss task,[5] which required learners to first listen and take notes as their teacher read a short text containing specific grammatical features and then to work in pairs to reconstruct the text from their joint notes. In this study, the learners talked about language form and were often able to decide collectively what forms to use to reconstruct a text. However, Kowal and Swain reported that heterogeneous dyads worked less effectively together, possibly because 'neither student's needs were within the zone of proximal development of the other' (p. 86) and because they failed to respect each other's perspective. Swain (1995, 1998) also reported a study by LaPierre (1994), which used tailor-made tests to establish whether learners actually retained the forms they jointly negotiated in the 'critical language-related episodes' (LREs) that arose in the course of reconstructing a text. LaPierre found that the test results closely matched the negotiated solutions; correct and incorrect solutions led respectively to correct and incorrect test answers. Swain (1998: 79) commented that 'these results suggest rather forcibly that these LREs, during which students reflect consciously on the language they are producing, may be a source of language learning'. Further evidence of the role that collaborative dialogue can play in language learning comes from Swain and Lapkin (1998). They provided a detailed analysis of two Grade 8 French immersion students performing a jigsaw task, showing how their joint solutions to linguistic problems led to learning as measured in post-tests. Again, though, they noted that on a few occasions their solutions were incorrect. Finally, in an ingenious study involving a pre-test, treatment, post-test design, Tocalli-Beller and Swain (2007) investigated the extent to which adult ESL learners were able to collaboratively work out the meanings of jokes and puns, such as 'Waiter, I'd like a corned beef sandwich, and make it lean. Yes, sir! In which direction?' They were able to show that the learners were able to jointly interpret the jokes (even when both of them were novices in the sense that neither of them initially knew the meaning of the key lexical item in the joke) and, importantly, that, as a result of this collaborative activity, they internalized the meanings of the items as demonstrated in the subsequent post-tests. In addition to demonstrating the role that collaborative dialoguing can play in language learning, this study provided support for Vygotsky's (1987) claims regarding the importance of play (in this case involving language) for language development; play 'stretches' learners.

The importance of the *quality* of the talk between learners, emphasized by Swain, is also demonstrated in Storch (2002). This study reported an analysis of the patterns of dyadic interaction found in ESL students' performance of a range of tasks. It identified four basic patterns as shown in Figure 11.2. This is based on two intersecting dimensions involving (1) mutuality (i.e. 'the level of engagement with each other's contribution') and (2) equality (i.e. 'the degree of control or authority over a task') (p. 127). The study then went on to report the relationship between the different patterns of dyadic interaction and language development. Development was measured in accordance with SCT by examining the extent to which 'learning', as evidenced in the interactions, led to 'development', as evidenced in subsequent tasks. Storch reported that the collaborative dyad (i.e. the dyad manifesting high mutuality and high equality) manifested more instances suggesting evidence of a transfer of knowledge than both the dominant/passive and the dominant/dominant dyads, with the expert/novice group intermediate.

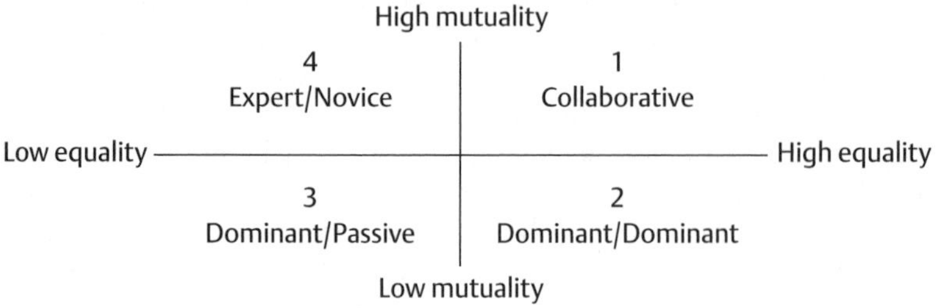

Figure 11.2 A model of dyadic interaction (Storch 2002)

In an interesting longitudinal classroom study of learners of L2 Japanese, Ohta (2001b) showed how students were able to produce utterances collaboratively that were beyond them individually and describes the various techniques that learners used to scaffold each other's L2 speech. These included the use of prompts, co-constructions, and recasts. One of the strengths of Ohta's research in comparison with work based on the Interaction Hypothesis (see Chapter 6) is that it acknowledges that interaction does not have to break down to assist the processes of internalizing new L2 forms. This view was subsequently reinforced in Foster and Ohta's (2005) study, which compared the frequency of negotiation of meaning and scaffolding sequences in the same data set.

Swain *et al.* (2003) concluded their review of peer–peer dialogue research by commenting that 'few adverse effects of working collaboratively were noted'. Ohta also reported that although the students did not always produce error-free utterances they only infrequently incorporated incorrect utterances. However, other studies have found evidence of incorrect decisions reached through dialoguing being subsequently internalized. Storch (2002), in the study referred to above, reported 10 such instances (compared to 49 instances where correct decisions were transferred). LaPierre (1994) and Swain and Lapkin (1998) also found that peer mediation did not always result in the learning of the target-language form, as the same processes were in operation for their inaccurate as for their accurate decisions. It would seem then that occasions can arise when 'expert' mediation is required. Lantolf (2000a), for example, referred to a study by Platt and Troudi (1997), which showed how a teacher's belief that peer rather than expert mediation was more effective in promoting learning had a negative effect when it came to certain content areas (for example, maths). Lantolf went on to comment 'while peer assistance is effective for learning everyday functional language, it may not be as effective for development of academic language'. There will obviously be situations in which the mediation provided by an 'expert' language user is required to negotiate a learner's ZPD.

Private speech

According to SCT, PRIVATE SPEECH occurs when learners are required to perform tasks that cause them cognitive stress, making total self-regulation impossible. In other words, private speech functions strategically to enable learners to gain control over language forms, the use of which is problematic in the context of a challenging task. Researchers working in the sociocultural tradition emphasize that when low-proficiency learners perform a task they may spend a substantial portion of the time self-regulating through the use of private speech. However, as learners become more proficient they rely less on private speech.

The bulk of the research that has investigated L2 learners' private speech has made use of oral narrative tasks. (See McCafferty (1994a) for a survey.) In an early study, Frawley and Lantolf (1985) examined the private speech of native speakers and intermediate and advanced L2 learners of English narrating a six-event picture story. Interestingly, this study reported close parallels in the use of English by a 5-year-old L1 speaker and the L2 learners. For example, both experienced problems in their choice of verb tense, opting for the use of the present progressive, which Frawley and Lantolf interpreted as evidence of object-regulation (i.e. the participants were controlled by the visual aspect of the pictures and so responded as if they were looking at photos in an album rather than at a connected narrative). Some of the L2 learners used the past tense as a means of attempting to self-regulate while the maturer native speakers opted for the atemporal present.[6] Two main points emerge from this study. The first is that private speech arises as a result of speakers' struggle to maintain and regain self-regulation. The second is that 'the function of any linguistic feature is very much task- and speaker-dependent' (Lantolf and Thorne 2006: 87). In a second study, Lantolf and Frawley (1984) used the same narrative task with intermediate and advanced learners of Spanish as a foreign language. In this study, the intermediate learners produced almost no private speech, a finding that Lantolf and Frawley explained by claiming that they were object-regulated (i.e. they treated the task as requiring them to produce grammatically well-formed sentences in accordance with the traditional language instruction they had experienced). This explanation is echoed in Tomlinson's (2001) claim that learners find it difficult to use what he called their 'inner voice' if they have only experienced formal language classrooms which require them to use a public voice from the beginning.

Other studies that have made use of oral narratives to investigate private speech are Lantolf, DiCamilla, and Ahmed (1997) and McCafferty (1994b, 1998). However, it can be argued that oral narrative tasks that learners perform by themselves are obviously biased in favour of the use of private speech. Nor is it always easy in such tasks to determine which utterances constitute private speech and which are intended to be communicative. Explicit criteria for distinguishing the two are needed. Ohta (2001) proposed a number of criteria for determining whether audible speech in an interactive instructional context constitutes private speech: (1) it is produced with a reduced volume, (2) it does not constitute a response or comment to an utterance directed at the speaker, and (3) it does not receive a response from the teacher or another classmate. However, these criteria are not clear-cut. For example, as Lantolf (2000a) noted, in some cases as when engaging in a choral exercise, it is difficult to be sure that the sotto voce repetitions are instances of private speech as they might also be 'reduced volume attempts at complying with the group nature of the exercise'.

The nature of the task is one of several factors that has been found to impact on learners' use of private speech. Narrative tasks, where the participants are shown the pictures one at a time, are more cognitively stressful than tasks where they see all the pictures together and result in greater use of private speech. In Appel and Lantolf (1994), the expository text led to more private speech than the narrative text, again because of the difficulty the participants (both native speakers and learners) experienced in achieving control in the former. Other factors that impact on the use of private speech according to McCafferty (1994a) are the proficiency of the learners, their cultural background, and how they relate to the task and to each other.

Private speech by L2 learners is also evident in interactive situations. Donato (1994), for example, suggested that the scaffolded assistance his learners provided for each other triggered the use of private talk as a means of organizing, rehearsing, and gaining control over new verbal behaviour. Probably the most extensive study of private speech in interactive contexts is Ohta's (2001b) study of adult classroom learners of L2 Japanese. One of Ohta's findings was that the instances of private speech varied greatly across students. Two students hardly produced any but one student produced an average of 54 instances per class. Ohta identified three types of private speech. (See Table 11.1.) Interestingly, the teacher-fronted setting resulted in a higher incidence of private speech than pair- or group-work, which led Ohta to suggest that the students needed a 'certain amount of privacy' (p. 66) to engage in it. Ohta considered a number of ways in which these learners' private speech may have assisted internalization: it provided a basis for further rehearsal of linguistic forms in inner speech; it enabled the learners to test out hypotheses without the pressure that accompanies speech in social interaction; it had an assimilative function; and it helped to keep the learners actively involved in classroom work.

There is, however, little clear evidence as yet that private speech contributes to language acquisition. Lantolf (1997) attempted to investigate this issue by means of a questionnaire that asked Spanish FL and ESL students to report on their use of private speech. He found that the reported frequency of private speech correlated with language proficiency and learners' goals for studying the language. Beginning level Spanish learners reported a low use of private language play but more advanced learners reported a higher level of use. The ESL learners reported less use than the Spanish FL learners, possibly because they had a much higher level of proficiency in the L2 and thus little need to use private speech for self-regulation. Learners who were learning the L2 for personal interest or for a clear instrumental purpose reported greater use of private speech than those who were taking a language class to fulfil a degree requirement. Self-report studies of this kind, however, do not demonstrate that private speech assists language learning, only that there may be a relationship between attained proficiency and reported use of private speech.

Investigating the contribution of private speech to L2 development is obviously problematic. As already noted, a major problem is deciding what constitutes private speech in a corpus of language use. At the moment the lack of a tight operational definition is an obvious threat to the reliability of studies of private speech. There is the further problem of demonstrating that private speech actually contributes to L2 development but, as noted earlier, there is now some evidence (for example, Borer 2006) that it does.

Metatalk

Two senses of METATALK can be identified. First, there is the metatalk that learners employ to establish what kind of 'activity' to make of a task and also what operations to employ in performing it. Second, there is the metatalk that arises when learners focus explicitly on language in the course of accomplishing a task.

Platt and Brooks (1994) described how university-level learners of L2 Spanish spent a considerable amount of time talking about the jigsaw task they had been asked to perform, its goals, and their own language production, using their L1 (English). Brooks and Donato (1994) described how third-year high school learners of L2 Spanish used language to mediate their goals in a two-way information-gap task that required them to describe where to draw shapes on a matrix sheet consisting of unnumbered small squares. They found that even though the teacher carefully explained the task goals, the learners often felt the need to discuss these between themselves in metatalk about the task. Typically metatalk of this kind is conducted in the L1.

Metatalk in its second sense has been investigated by Swain and her fellow researchers. They have examined the LANGUAGE RELATED EPISODES that arise in the context of collaborative dialogue between learners. In such episodes, the participants talk about linguistic form as an object. This is made possible because, as Wells (2000) puts it, an utterance can be viewed in terms of process (i.e. as 'saying') and as product (i.e. as 'what was said'). By scrutinizing and reflecting on specific forms, learners treat language products as cognitive tools and learn from them. As Swain and Lapkin (2001a) put it:

> To make their meaning as clear, coherent and precise as possible, learners will debate language form (morphosyntax through to discourse and pragmatics) and lexical choice. This talk about language (metatalk) mediates second language learning. Talk supports the process of internalization—the 'moving inwards' of joint (intermental) activity to psychological (intramental) activity.
> (p. 3)

In Chapter 9 we considered my WEAK INTERFACE HYPOTHESIS, which proposes that explicit knowledge can subsequently be used in the processes responsible for the acquisition of implicit knowledge—NOTICING and NOTICING THE GAP. In sociocultural theory, however, metatalk is seen as serving a somewhat different function. It does not just prime acquisition but rather serves to regulate thinking and through this enables learners to arrive at new knowledge.

A good example of the kind of study Swain used to investigate the role played by metatalk in language learning is Swain and Lapkin (2001b). This made use of a reformulation task (Cohen 1982) that involves asking students to write a composition, to compare their composition with a reformulated version, and finally to rewrite the composition. The full procedure that Swain and Lapkin followed is shown in Table 11.2. The discussions from stages 1, 2, and 3 were transcribed and all the language-related episodes identified. These episodes constitute occasions when metatalk occurred. Swain and Lapkin compared the changes that the students made to their initial compositions when they rewrote them in stage 4. They found that 78 per cent of both students' changes were correct. Interestingly, however, the changes did not always correspond to the reformulated version. One third of the time, the students found an alternative of their own, and out of these three quarters were correct. Swain and Lapkin suggested that the process of 'talking it through' enabled their students to find their own correct solutions by encouraging them to reflect on differences between their own compositions and the reformulated version.

More recently, Swain (2006) coined the term LANGUAGING to refer to the role that language production (oral or written) plays in making meaning when learners are faced with some problem. Languaging is a 'dynamic, never-ending process of using language to make meaning'. The particular type of languaging that Swain investigated was 'languaging about language'. She emphasized that this constitutes one of the principal ways in which advanced levels of language learning can be achieved. Languaging is not just a facilitator of learning; rather 'in languaging, we see learning taking place'. Swain illustrated how languaging works for learning by examining

Stage	Description
1 Writing	The students completed a jigsaw writing task. They were each given three pictures from a picture story, described them to each other and then wrote the story.
2 Comparing	The students were asked to compare their compositions with the reformulated version and to notice the differences. Their discussion was videotaped.
3 Simulated recall	The students were shown the videotape of their discussion and asked to comment on each difference between their own compositions and the reformulated version they had noticed in stage 2.
4 Rewriting	Each student was given a copy of her original story and asked to rewrite it independently.

Table 11.2 Reformulation writing task (from Swain and Lapkin 2001b)

in detail the responses of two learners to the reformulated version of a story they had jointly written. She showed how one of these learners developed an understanding of why *'in 19th century Japan' and *'in 19th century' were erroneous through metatalk and how, consequently, this learner was able to avoid these errors when rewriting the original story. Swain argued that such languaging about language serves two functions: (1) it articulates and transforms learners' thinking into 'an artifactual form' and (2) it provides a means for further reflection on this form.

Task versus activity

The TASK is the workplan that constitutes the stimulus for an interaction; the 'activity' consists of the actual interactions that transpire when the task is performed. The intended goal of the task may or may not be reflected in the object of the activity which the subjects construct. This claim reflects the central tenet of activity theory. (See previous section.)

The distinction between task and activity was examined in a study by Coughlan and Duff (1994). They compared the performances of five different learners (one Cambodian and four Hungarians) on a picture description task performed face-to-face with a researcher. In the case of the Cambodian learner, the task was performed as part of regular hour-long meetings at the researcher's home. In the case of the Hungarian learners, the picture description task was one of a series of tasks that were performed by the learners at their school during one-off 20-minute meetings. The activities resulting from this task varied considerably. With the Cambodian learner, the intended monologue became more like a dialogue as he constantly engaged the researcher in talk by means of comprehension checks and requests for assistance with vocabulary. Coughlan and Duff argued that it is not really possible to describe the characteristics of the discourse of the learner and the researcher independently of each other 'since both were doing the task, not just the subject' (p. 180). In contrast, the activity resulting from the Hungarian learners' performance of the task resulted in very little 'off task' talk as the researcher was concerned to complete the task in the allotted amount of time. In this context, the learners varied in the goals they established for the task. One subject treated the task as requiring her to simply name the objects in the picture. Another sought to relate the picture to her personal experience. A third listed the people in the pictures and the activities they were performing. Coughlan and Duff concluded that despite the relatively controlled nature of the task 'a range of discourse types may result from learners' multiple interpretations of that task' (p. 185). They then went on to show that the same task was interpreted very differently by the Cambodian learner when he was asked to repeat it on a later occasion.

Further support for this claim comes from a number of other studies. Platt and Brooks (1994), for example, showed how a role-play task is interpreted variably by different groups of students. One group simply carried out the instructions in a mechanical fashion. Another group reconstructed the task in accordance with their own goals. The kind of talk produced by these two groups differed greatly, with far more metatalk evident in the second. Foster (1998) reported a study which, although not conducted within the framework of SCT, testifies to the importance of the participants' motives and goals in determining the kind of activity tasks give rise to. Noting that most of the modified input/output studies have been carried out in laboratory-like settings, Foster investigated tasks that students performed as part of a timetabled lesson in their normal classroom. The tasks were (1) a grammar-based task that required students to collaborate in composing questions for given answers, (2) a spot-the-difference task, (3) a convergent opinion-gap task involving solving a problem, and (4) a map task involving split information. She found that none of the tasks led to much negotiated input or output. She suggested that the students were motivated to make the tasks fun and to this end minimized negotiation in order to keep the interaction moving. In short, the students performed the task in a way that was compatible with their own motives and goals. Wang (1996; cited in Donato 2000) also showed how different groups of learners interpreted the same task very differently and noted that this frustrated the teacher. In this case, the task required students to rank order a list of seven effects of excessive TV viewing 'from the most immediate to the most remote'. Wang reported that one group did not perform the task as instructed because they did not agree with most of the effects listed in the task materials. Another group did rank order the effects but from 'more remote to more immediate'. This caused the teacher herself to change the activity to that of simply 'finding things that go naturally together'. Roebuck (2000) showed that the way in which L2 learners of Spanish position themselves in written recall tasks has a profound effect on the actual writing they produce. Not only did the learners orient to the task in different ways but also some of them re-oriented themselves in the course of completing the task. For example, one learner began the task by trying to reproduce the text she had read only to switch half way through to just listing points she could remember. Learners who experienced difficulty in completing the task did not comply with the role they had been assigned ('subject in an experiment') but repositioned themselves in various ways (for example, by criticizing the task they had been set).

Seedhouse (2005) also pointed out that 'in practice, there is often a very significant difference between what is supposed to happen and what actually happens' (p. 537). He identified a number of reasons why this is so. Sometimes learners have a problem carrying out the communication intended by the task so the resulting activity differs from what was intended. At other times learners misunderstand the participation requirements of the task or the pedagogical focus. A task can also be transformed by the organization of the classroom interaction. Seedhouse concluded that 'task' has very poor validity as a research construct because the actual research data are not collected from it but rather from the activity that arises from it. Further, he claimed that even when researchers base their quantification of categories on the interaction arising from a task, their focus on task-as-a-workplan 'colors and even obscures the view of the task-in-process' (p. 550). He went on to argue that an 'emic methodology' that focuses on the actual interactions that arise when a task is performed is needed and illustrated how a conversational analysis perspective can provide this. In such an approach, definitions and categorizations are developed inductively and the emphasis is placed on 'socially shared cognition and learning' (p. 553).

These studies support Donato's (2000: 44) conclusion that tasks are not 'generalizable' and also that 'tasks do not manipulate learners to act in certain ways' (p. 44). Nevertheless, as we will see in Chapter 15, there is substantial evidence to show that the design features of a task do impact on the fluency, accuracy, and complexity of learner language. (See Chapter 9.) In Ellis (2003), I critiqued SCT for not taking sufficient account of this, a criticism that Lantolf (2005) acknowledged, while reaffirming the central claim of activity theory, namely that tasks cannot predetermine what learners learn because 'learning depends heavily on the significance individuals assign to the various activities they participate in' (p. 346). These apparently opposing positions can be reconciled if task features are seen as predisposing learners to behave in certain ways without predetermining their actual behaviour.

Key issues in SLA: an SCT perspective

In this section, I will briefly re-examine a number of the major issues that have emerged in the account of L2 acquisition presented in the previous chapters by taking an SCT perspective on these issues and drawing on some of the constructs and research referred to in earlier sections. I will consider critically what an SCT perspective might look like on the following: (1) errors, (2) acquisitional orders and sequences, (3) L1 transfer, (4) implicit and explicit

L2 knowledge and (as a prelude to the following chapter on individual learner differences), (5) motivation.

Errors

In mainstream SLA, ERRORS are viewed as indicators of learners' interlanguage development and also of the mental processes involved (for example, overgeneralization; L1 transfer). (See Chapter 2.) SCT affords a somewhat different account of errors. First, as Frawley and Lantolf (1985) proposed, they may reflect the forms of private speech, which are different from those of social speech. Such a proposal constitutes an account of variability in learner language from the perspective of SCT. Second, the production of errors may reflect the learner's struggle to self-regulate when performing a demanding task. In such a context, regression (or BACKSLIDING, as its is commonly called) may occur as a result of the learner falling back on a construction that was acquired earlier and has become fully internalized. Frawley and Lantolf (1985) referred to this as 'the principle of continuous access'. It arises when learners lose control and need to re-establish self-regulation. According to this perspective, then, errors may not reflect a lack of knowledge but rather the nature of the particular activity that the learners are engaging in.

One problem with such an account of errors is that it is difficult to see how it can explain overgeneralization errors. In Ellis (1997a) I wrote:

> It is not clear to me ... how Vygotskian theory can account for the prevalence of overgeneralizations errors in interlanguage (for example, 'eated'). Vysgotskian theory does acknowledge that learners have creative minds which transform knowledge obtained collaboratively but it sees the process of transformation as itself a social one. But how does interacting with others lead to the transformation that results in *eated? Such errors suggest to me that learners do indeed autonomously construct rules out of items they have gleaned through social interaction.
> (p. 244)

Responding to this, Lantolf (2005) claimed that I was guilty of the dualism inherent in mainstream SLA, namely dissociating 'embedded individuals' from 'the homogenized IDEAL learner' (p. 340). He argued that OVERGENERALIZATION can be explained in terms of internalization:

> Essentially, (over)generalization (i.e. prediction) is a process we internalize as we interact with other members of our communities ... It is normally a nonreflective process in the world of everyday activity. However, it can, and often does, become visible as it is presented to us in its 'scientific' form during schooling.
> (p. 342)

In other words, overgeneralization is something we learn to do socially or we are taught. However, such an explanation does not account for how the learner comes to extrapolate from the general process of overgeneralization, which probably is social/instructional in origin, to linguistic overgeneralization, which may be partly social/instructional in origin but surely is not entirely so, especially if linguistic overgeneralization is viewed as an unconscious process. It is difficult to see how overgeneralizations such as 'eated' can result from such social processes as imitation. The workings of 'internalization' will need to be specified more precisely if it is to satisfactorily account for the types of errors that L2 learners have been shown to make.[7]

Acquisitional orders and sequences

On the face of it the ZPD is analogous to Krashen's i + 1 (i.e. the notion that what learners can acquire is governed by their current interlanguage and what structure comes next in the natural order of acquisition). Such is the position adopted by some SCT researchers (for example, Schinke-Llano 1993). However, Dunn and Lantolf (1998) disputed such a comparison, arguing that the two constructs are incommensurable. Krashen's i + 1 is rooted in the information-processing model of cognition and the computational metaphor and relates to the acquisition of features of language by autonomous individuals. According to this view, L2 acquisition is something that goes on exclusively inside the learner's head, driven by the language acquisition device triggered by exposure to input. In contrast, the ZPD belongs to the participation metaphor; a ZPD is constructed dialogically through the mediation of social interaction or private speech. As Lantolf (2005) put it 'Krashen's is a model of language acquisition; Vygotsky's is a theory of human development' (p. 337).

SCT's insistence that learning originates in social interaction constitutes a challenge to the claimed universality of the ORDER and SEQUENCE OF ACQUISITION, as individuals' experiences will necessarily vary. Lantolf (2005) admitted this:

> SCT ... because of its fundamental theoretical assumption that development is revolutionary and therefore unpredictable, have [sic] a good deal of difficulty with the claims of universal predetermined developmental trajectories that are impervious to instructional intervention.
> (p. 339)

Similarly, Johnson (2004) argued that the adoption of Vygotskian sociocultural theory 'would require that we ... eradicate the assertion that L2 acquisition progresses along a predetermined mental path' (p. 172). In other words, while accepting that there may be developmental constraints, a key assumption of SCT is that it ought to be possible, with appropriately tailored intervention, to construct a ZPD for the performance and internalization of any linguistic feature.

To justify such a position Lantolf referred to research based on Gal'perin's pedagogical theory, the key constructs of which are materialization and internalization. For example, Carpay (1974) taught Russian speakers German adjective declensions by providing material models of the concepts and then requiring them to privately verbalize the concepts in order to internalize them. But such a study simply does not address the issue of whether there is or is not a fixed developmental route for L2 grammar. What is needed is a study that documents that learners with appropriate intervention are able to jump from one stage of development to an advanced stage without the need to pass through intermediate stages. In terms of Pienemann's Processability Theory (see Chapter 9), for example, this would involve showing that instruction enables a learner to progress from features governed by the category procedure to structures governed by the S-procedure and word-order rule without first having mastered phrasal procedures. Such a study would also need to bear in mind that as the route is evident only in spontaneous, UNPLANNED LANGUAGE USE, the measure of learning would need to tap this kind of language use. (See Chapter 16.) There is no such SCT study to date.

While it is wise to acknowledge the possibility of socially constructing alternative routes of development (as suggested by Tarone and Liu (1995)—see Chapter 7), it is also important to acknowledge the substantial body of research that has documented the existence of developmental trajectories (see Chapter 3) at least until there is an SCT study that demonstrates that intervention (social or instructional) can modify them. Nor can the research documenting the universal patterns of development be dismissed by the claim that SCT 'does not see language as a formal system with an a priori grammar but is instead an emergent system comprised of fragments that emerge and are shaped in the maelstrom of communicative interaction' (Lantolf 2005: 350). Rather, what is needed is an account of how these fragments evolve into the rule-like structures that figure in developmental orders and sequences.

L1 transfer

Whereas mainstream SLA researchers have approached LANGUAGE TRANSFER in terms of how the L1 influences interlanguage development, SCT researchers have been more concerned with whether learners are able to make use of the L2 to mediate mental activity. Lantolf (2006) presented this different approach as involving attention to the meanings of the L2 rather than the forms. He examined three areas of research: (1) the extent to which L2 learners are able to use the L2 for private speech, (2) the use of L1 gesture patterns in L2 communication (see also McCafferty 1998, 2002), and (3) the acquisition of L2 metaphorical competence. As we have already seen, Lantolf concluded that the nature of the task given to learners influenced the extent to which they were able to employ the L2 to control their mental operations, while he also emphasized the importance of distinguishing learners' ability to use the L2 for social purposes and for cognitive activity, arguing that the former is no guarantee of the latter. Lantolf investigated both L2 learners' use of gesture and their L2 metaphorical competence in the conviction that these serve as good indicators of their underlying thought processes. Drawing on Talmy's (2000) distinction between satellite-framed languages (for example, Spanish), which indicate the path of motion by means of adverbs or particles, and verb-framed languages (for example, English), which express the manner of motion within the verb itself, Lantolf concluded that 'the overall picture of the gesture–speech interface is murky' (p. 84). He found evidence to support the view that L2 speakers are able to utilize L2 gesture patterns for path of motion events but no evidence to support the view that they master L2 gestures related to the manner of motion. His review of the research that has investigated metaphorical competence similarly produced some evidence to suggest that L2 learners were capable of acquiring the metaphorical meanings of the L1 but also that this only appeared to take place in conditions of extensive cultural immersion. Thus, in SCT, language transfer is of interest because it is of major importance in what researchers see as the main goal of L2 acquisition studies—how conceptual knowledge is internalized and developed and the extent to which this knowledge is then available to regulate thinking. The position that Lantolf advanced is that learners are capable of acquiring L2 concepts but that there are strict limitations on how successful they are. In other words, the influence of L1 concepts remains pervasive.

Implicit and explicit L2 knowledge

The interface between IMPLICIT and EXPLICIT L2 KNOWLEDGE is central to cognitive accounts of L2 learning. (See Chapter 9.) It also finds a place in SCT accounts. Lantolf and Thorne (2006) reviewed the key interface positions, as described in Ellis (1994b) and DeKeyser (1998, 2001) and appeared to come out in favour of DeKeyser's claim that DECLARATIVE KNOWLEDGE can convert into PROCEDURAL KNOWLEDGE through practice, rejecting Ellis' view that, unless learners are developmentally ready, explicit knowledge cannot transform into implicit knowledge. They noted that DeKeyser's view of automaticity concurs with that of activity theory, as expressed in the work of A A Leontiev (1981), but noted that automatic behaviour can revert to consciousness whenever learners experience problems in communicating.

What is not clear in Lantolf and Thorne's account, however, is whether the *nature* of the L2 knowledge changes over time. Both DeKeyser and I (in Ellis 1994b and 2004a) acknowledged that explicit/declarative knowledge and implicit/procedural knowledge are different in kind. Lantolf and Thorne (2006) appeared to view L2 knowledge as of a single type which differs only with regard to its automaticity (i.e. how readily it can be accessed). They disputed the view that 'time is a general requirement for learners to access their explicit knowledge' (p. 298) and argued that eventually, with practice, learners can utilize this knowledge without the need for planning time. However, Luria (1970) took a different position. He argued that although intervention could enable aphasic patients to recover lost procedural ability in language it did not result in the same ability but rather entailed the reconstruction of a new structure for the damaged brain. Although Luria did not use the terms implicit/explicit knowledge, his position is certainly compatible with a clear separation of these two knowledge systems.

A number of cognitive researchers (for example, DeKeyser 1998; Krashen 1982; Bialystok 1994) argued that there are strict limitations on learners' capacity to learn explicit L2 knowledge. In part, this is due to the inadequacies of current linguistic descriptions and in part to the difficulty that many learners are likely to experience in understanding complex rules. For this reason, these researchers proposed that at least some L2 grammatical features can only be mastered through implicit learning. Lantolf and Thorne also challenged this position. In their view, cognitive linguistics affords a source of linguistic description that is mutually compatible with SCT (see earlier section in this chapter) and an adequate basis for teaching and learning explicit knowledge. Drawing on Vygotsky's notion of 'scientific concepts', they noted that 'while scientific concepts are explicit and conscious, not all explicit knowledge qualifies as scientific knowledge' (p. 301). They argued that with time explicit knowledge can become sufficiently well defined to qualify as scientific knowledge. In this respect, instruction is of special importance. Instruction needs to ensure that it avoids presenting learners with simple 'rules of thumb' as these can become impediments to learning 'coherent conceptually organized grammatical knowledge' (p. 303). Drawing on Gal'perin's model of systemic-theoretical instruction, Lantolf and Thorne described an approach to teaching explicit L2 knowledge that involves three principles: (1) orientation (i.e. presenting learners with a conceptually sound model of the knowledge to be mastered), (2) materialization (i.e. providing a concrete instantiation of the verbal explanation, involving, for example, diagrams or physical objects), and (3) verbalization (i.e. requiring learners to verbalize the rule). Lantolf and Thorne emphasized that the development of accurate and precise explicit knowledge is a gradual process that requires mediation.

It is clear, therefore, that from an SCT perspective (at least, as expressed by Lantolf and Thorne) it is explicit L2 knowledge that is viewed as central.[8] L2 learning, at least by adults, involves the gradual internalization of 'scientific' explicit grammatical concepts which subsequently become automatized. What is not clear, however, is whether young children's L2 development follows a similar pattern.

Motivation

In SCT MOTIVATION is viewed in relation to activity theory as dynamic, constructed, and reconstructed as learners respond to the context of learning. Lantolf and Genung (2002) presented a case study of a doctoral student's experiences of an intensive summer course in Chinese, which she was taking as part of her PhD programme. This learner began with the goal of developing communicative ability in Chinese but as a result of the strict, audiolingual methodology employed by the instructor, she abandoned this goal, replacing it with the lesser one of obtaining a passing grade in the course and thereby fulfilling the requirement of the PhD programme. Lantolf and Genung argued that this case study demonstrates that motivation cannot be treated as a stable force that can predict achievement. A learner's goals 'are formed and reformed under specific historic material circumstances' (p. 191). Thus, from the perspective of activity theory, motivation must be seen as constructed and dynamic, reflecting the learner's response to the learning situation and the conflict and struggle this entails. However, motivational change need not be as nugatory as in Lantolf and Genung's study. Thorne (2003) provided a counter example of a student in a fourth semester French grammar course who was teamed up with a French student in web-based chat sessions. Thorne documented how this learner shifted from approaching the chat sessions as a form of French language study to viewing them as a means of achieving a meaningful social relationship with her partner. This afforded her not only enormous personal satisfaction but also led to activity that fostered her development of French. These two case studies demonstrate that SCT can inform the study of motivation in L2 learning.

In SCT, motivation is socially constructed and serves as a tool for mediating learning. Thus it is both the product of learning and a powerful support for learning. In Chapter 13 we will consider how motivation has been addressed in SLA research in general and take a close look at some studies that have examined motivation from a SCT perspective.

Conclusion

SCT affords a radically different view of L2 acquisition from that projected in cognitive or linguistic accounts. It rejects the conduit metaphor (Reddy 1979) that underlies cognitive accounts of L2 acquisition and the modularity of mind metaphor (Fodor 1983) on which generative linguistic accounts of L2 acquisition are based. SCT views language learning as like any other type of learning—it is learning that is both social and mental, with internal mental activity originating in external dialogic activity (Swain 2000). As such, it affords important insights into the process of language learning and, in particular, the role played by instruction in this process.

For researchers schooled in the cognitive and linguistic paradigms of SLA (such as myself) it is not an easy theory to come to terms with. In part, this is because it is couched in a whole new set of concepts and technical terms for labelling them that do not relate to those employed in the other paradigms and that are not always clearly and precisely defined. Learning about SCT as it applies to L2 acquisition requires persistence and is not always effectively mediated by existing expositions of the theory![9] Nevertheless, it is clearly important that the effort is made. SCT has become a major force in SLA, as reflected in the growing number of research articles and doctoral theses that draw on it.

SCT researchers have established their own research agenda, reflecting priorities derived from the theory. As a result they have not addressed some of the established 'facts' of L2 acquisition (Long 1990c). For example, what explanation does SCT afford for the fact that most learners fail to achieve native-speaker ability in an L2? What explanation is there for the age differences apparent in the ultimate level of attainment of an L2? How would SCT account for the role played by linguistic context in explaining the patterns of variability evident in L2 production? Why is it that certain types of tasks promote fluency while others lead to greater complexity of language use? Would SCT acknowledge a role for input frequency in L2 acquisition and if so what would this role be? To be entirely convincing any theory of L2 acquisition should provide answers to such questions. It may be, however, that over time SCT researchers will turn their attention to these issues.

It is almost certainly not possible to merge a cognitive or linguistic view of L2 acquisition with a sociocultural one. Two possibilities, therefore, present themselves. One is to treat these paradigms as oppositional. This is the stance adopted by some SCT researchers, who have been at pains to demonstrate the incommensurability of SCT and other paradigms and the superiority of the SCT paradigm. Platt and Brooks (1994), for example, juxtaposed their advocacy of SCT with their opposition to input-output models, arguing that the latter afford only a mechanistic view of L2 acquisition. The other possibility is to view SCT and other theories as complementary. This is the approach adopted by Foster and Ohta (2005) in their analysis of the same data from an interactionist and a sociocultural perspective. They noted 'we believe that in this way a fuller picture emerges of the potential of interactive language learning and that our combined analysis illuminates more in the data than either approach would do on its own' (p. 423). If theories are viewed as 'artefacts' that can mediate our understanding of L2 acquisition (as I believe SCT would view them), then, arguably, we would be better off adopting Foster and Ohta's collaborative stance.

Notes

1 In her review of this chapter, Merrill Swain made the point that Vygotsky's notion of 'word' may not correspond to the general meaning of this word; rather it may refer more generally to a 'meaning unit'.

2 Such a view of the role of literacy is also reflected in Olson's work. (See Olson 1977.) Olson argued that the development of writing systems, and in particular the invention of the printing press which made mass literacy possible, radically altered the way in which people think, shifting them from analogical-type reasoning to hypothetical-deductive reasoning.

3 It can also be argued that non-standard forms should not always be considered errors even in social speech. Situations may arise where learners need

to use ungrammatical forms in order to achieve their communicative goals. See Lantolf and Ahmed (1989) for such an argument.

4 The issue of whether and to what extent L2 private speech can mediate thinking is, of course, of crucial importance in educational contexts where learners are learning subject content through the medium of the L2. The difficulty that learners experience with using the L2 to think with can be seen as one reason why the development of COGNITIVE ACADEMIC LANGUAGE PROFICIENCY (CALP) takes such a long time (7 years) to develop.

5 Dictogloss is a technique developed by Wajnryb (1990). It makes use of a short text that has been selected or devised to have a structural focus. The text is read at normal speed, sentence by sentence, while the learners note down key words and phrases (i.e. the content words). The learners then work in groups to try to reconstruct the text collaboratively. Wajnryb emphasized that the aim is not to generate an exact replica of the original text but rather to reproduce its content.

6 McCafferty (1994b) also examined L2 learners' use of present progressive and past tense in private speech in an oral narrative and produced different results from Frawley and Lantolf (1986) in that his advanced learners made extensive use of the present progressive. Lantolf and Thorne (2006) suggested that this might have been because McCafferty's learners were not so advanced as Frawley and Lantolf's. They also pointed out that 'linguistic features take on their regulatory functions in the concrete activity of people engaged in specific tasks and cannot be determined in advance of that activity' (p. 89).

7 Lantolf and Thorne (2006) did address how SCT can account for overgeneralizations like 'eated'. They drew on Tomasello's usage-based theory of acquisition (see Chapter 6) and the notion of entrenchment (the process by which forms can become habituated through frequent use). Entrenchment occurs if learners are not regularly exposed to the correct form. This, however, does not explain how learners come to use 'eated' in the first place. Lantolf and Thorne make a passing reference to 'analogy' but do not explain the status of such a self-evidently cognitive term in SCT.

8 By making explicit knowledge the key to L2 development, Lantolf and Thorne (2006) provided a basis for arguing that L2 acquisition is not subject to fixed developmental orders and sequences. As previously noted, the natural route of development is applicable only to L2 implicit knowledge. L2 explicit knowledge is not subject to the same developmental constraints.

9 Responding to this comment in her review of this chapter, Merrill Swain observed that I rely too much on Lantolf rather than reading the original works. Maybe. But I first read Vygotsky's (1962) *Thought and Language* in 1970 and have continued to read the 'original works' since. I did not find these easy in 1970 and I still don't. I have chosen to focus on how SCT has been interpreted by SLA researchers because it is their interpretation that is relevant to this book.

12

Linguistic universals and second language acquisition

Introduction

Explanations of the internal mechanisms responsible for L2 acquisition can be divided into those that emphasize the general cognitive nature of acquisition and those that emphasize its specifically linguistic nature. The former (considered in Chapter 9) discuss L2 acquisition in terms of 'processes', 'strategies', and 'operations', while the latter (to be considered in this chapter) refer to 'linguistic rules', 'linguistic principles', and, increasingly, to LINGUISTIC UNIVERSALS. Whereas cognitive theories look to psychology, linguistic theories look to linguistics.

Linguistic universals need to be distinguished from other types of universals. (See Selinker 1984.) Cognitive theories also make claims about 'universals' (for example, processing universals), while, as we have seen, evidence exists to suggest that there are also developmental 'universals' (regularities in the order and sequence of L2 development). Linguistic universals may influence and perhaps help to explain processing and developmental universals, but they are distinct from them.

There are two very different linguistic traditions in SLA; one is based on the study of TYPOLOGICAL UNIVERSALS and the other is derived from Chomsky's theory of UNIVERSAL GRAMMAR (UG) (Chomsky 1981a; 1995). Typological universals are identified 'externally' through the study of the world's languages in order to identify what features and structures they have in common. Universal Grammar is viewed 'internally'; that is, it consists of the set of general, highly abstract linguistic principles, which exist in the minds of individuals and are reflected in the rules of specific languages. These principles have traditionally been investigated by researchers examining the properties of an individual language intuitively. As Chomsky (1980: 48) wrote: 'I have not hesitated to propose a general principle of linguistic structure on the basis of observations of a single language'. However, more recent work on UG has drawn on a wide range of languages and from different historical stages of languages as well as from native-speaker intuitions about a single language.

Both the typological and UG-based approaches have recourse to the notion of 'universals', but whereas typological universals are couched in surface structure terms (for example, 'any language that has a verbal dual morpheme also has a verbal plural morpheme' (Eckman 2004a)), the universal principles of UG are highly abstract involving reference to properties like the movement of constituents, agreement between constituents, and the scope of interpretation of operators like negation and interrogation. An example of such a principle is the Overt Pronoun Constraint. This principle states 'overt pronouns cannot receive a bound variable interpretation (i.e. cannot have quantified or WH–antecedents) in situations where a null pronoun could occur' (Montalbetti 1984; cited in White 2003a). Thus, in the following sentences in Spanish (a language that permits null subjects), a null subject (indicated by Ø) can refer to 'nadie' ('nobody') while the overt pronoun 'el' must refer to someone other than 'nadie':

Nadie cree que Ø es inteligente.
Nadie cree que el es inteligente.
'Nobody believes that he is intelligent.'

A matter of some debate is the relationship between these two approaches to investigating linguistic universals. Do typological universals have any relevance to the study of UG? Generative linguistics not infrequently calls on facts uncovered through the crosslinguistic study of the world's languages to support claims about general principles. For example, Towell and Hawkins (1994) referred to the work of J. Hawkins (1980), which identified the existence of 'cross-category harmony', to support their account of the projection of phrase structure in UG. The principle involved here claims that any language will have a preferred or canonical position for the head in all phrases; for example, in English the preferred position is for the head to precede its complement whereas in Japanese the opposite is the case. Clearly, a typological approach to the study of languages can help to confirm or disconfirm such a principle.[1] In general, however, considerable doubts exist regarding the utility of typological universals in UG-based enquiry. Newmeyer (2004), for example, claimed that 'the ... crosslinguistic generalizations that form the bulk of the typology literature are not within the explanatory province of UG theory' and that UG-based approaches have been 'singularly unsuccessful ... in handling typology' (p. 527). The explanation that Newmeyer gave for such a claim is that, whereas UG is concerned with 'language structure', typological universals are indicative of 'language use'; that is, UG constitutes a theory of LINGUISTIC COMPETENCE whereas typological universals describe linguistic performance. Newmeyer did make the exception of ABSOLUTE UNIVERSALS (i.e. properties shared by all languages or evident in none). However, given that most universals are not absolute but rather either 'implicational universals' (i.e. if a language has property *x*, then it will also have property *y*) or 'frequency universals' (i.e. *x* percentage of languages manifest property *y*) and that it is implausible to claim that such universals are part of a child's genetic inheritance (as UG is claimed to be), he concluded that overall typological universals remain 'irrelevant to the construction of a theory of UG' (p. 531). Nevertheless, in the field of SLA, attempts have continued to relate observations of acquisition based on typological universals to those based on UG. (See, for example, Gass 1997b.)

I will accept Newmeyer's basic argument that the study of typological universals and UG are best treated as distinct lines of enquiry and examine the SLA based on these two types of universals separately in the sections that follow. First, though, I will briefly revisit the notion of 'interlanguage' from a linguistic (as opposed to a cognitive perspective).

I also need to make an admission. I have limited technical knowledge of the linguistic models that underlie the study of typological universals and UG. Whereas the former models are couched in descriptive terminology with which I am familiar and thus allow me to some extent at least direct access to the primary literature, the latter are more problematic because they draw on a generative linguistic framework with which I am not very familiar. Thus, I am dependent on the second-hand accounts provided by UG-inspired SLA researchers and cannot satisfy White's (1997) injunction that researchers should keep up with developments in theory *first-hand*. This limitation, however, will hopefully be offset by the fact that, limited though my understanding may be, it enables me to present the key issues in a form that I hope may turn out more readable than some of the more theoretically-savvy accounts.

Interlanguage theory: another perspective

According to Adjemian (1976), the *sine qua non* of the interlanguage hypothesis is that interlanguages are 'natural languages' and, therefore, subject to all the same constraints. A number of assumptions follow from this hypothesis: INTERLANGUAGES consist of 'a set of linguistic rules which can generate novel utterances' (1976: 299); claims about the structure of interlanguages can be derived from grammatical theory; and, like natural languages, interlanguages can be idealized to make them amenable to linguistic analysis. Adjemian argued that the goal should be to describe and explain the nature of the learner's competence at different stages of development by analysing 'intuitional data' collected experimentally; the main focus should be 'the grammatical nature of a learner's IL' rather than 'strategies' (1976: 306). In this way, Adjemian put the case for a linguistic approach to the study of interlanguage.

The position which Adjemian's early paper outlined has subsequently been reaffirmed on numerous occasions. Eckman (1991: 24), for instance, invoked Adjemian in advancing what he called the Structural Conformity Hypothesis, which states:

> The universal generalizations that hold for the primary languages also hold for interlanguages.

Eckman, like Adjemian, claimed that interlanguages are languages and, further, that proposed linguistic universals are fully universal, in the sense that they apply to non-primary as well as primary languages. Eckman provided evidence from 11 adult Asian learners of English that universal phonological generalizations (for example, 'if a language has at least one final consonant sequence consisting of stop + stop, it also has at least one final sequence consisting of fricative + stop', 1991: 24) also hold for interlanguages.

SLA researchers working with UG have adopted a similar position. White (2003a), for example, noted that UG-based SLA research has its origins in the original interlanguage hypothesis, as formulated by Adjemian (1976), Corder (1967), and Selinker (1972), among others. UG is seen as applicable to the study of interlanguage because, like natural languages, it is constrained by UG principles. However, as White pointed out, interlanguage grammars are different from natural languages in some respects and thus a key focus of research in this paradigm is to determine in what ways and to what extent interlanguage is UG-governed.

Typological universals and second language acquisition

Linguistic typology and language universals

As noted above, a typological approach to linguistic analysis involves a crosslinguistic comparison of specific features such as articles, word order, or relative clause construction. The aim is to identify commonalities across languages. Three types of commonalities have been identified:

1 ABSOLUTE UNIVERSALS (i.e. features or structures present in all the world's languages). For example, all languages have nouns and verbs and vowels and consonants. However, there are probably few such universals, universal tendencies being much more common.
2 FREQUENCY UNIVERSALS (i.e. a specific feature may be found in a large number of languages, but be missing from some). For example, Dahl (1979) found that there is 'a universal tendency for Neg to have a definite position relative to the finite element' (1979: 91). ('Neg' here refers to the negator, for example, 'not' in English.) There was also a definite preference for the negator to take a pre-verbal rather than a post-verbal position. As Comrie (1984) acknowledged, universal tendencies are problematic because they raise the question as to whether it is justifiable to talk of 'universals' when there are exceptions and also just how many exceptions can be tolerated. He argued, however, that the non-random distribution of alternative features in the world's languages is of significance.
3 IMPLICATIONAL UNIVERSALS. Frequently, crosslinguistic comparisons demonstrate that there are connections between two or more features, such

that the presence of one feature implies the presence of another or others. Implicational universals take the form of 'if/then' statements. These can be 'simple' or 'complex'. A simple implicational universal involves a connection between just two features. For example, J. Hawkins (1983) provided evidence to show that 'if a language has a noun before a demonstrative, then it has a noun before a relative clause' (1983: 84). A complex implicational universal involves a relationship between several features. Hawkins gave the following example: 'If a language is SOV, then if the adjective precedes the noun, then the genitive precedes the noun'. Implicational universals have been found to be particularly prevalent in the area of word order, as these examples show. The important point about both types of implicational universals is that they logically preclude at least one combination of features. Thus, the example from Hawkins given above allows for languages that have nouns before relative clauses not to have nouns before demonstratives. Thus, whereas combinations (1), (2), and (3) below are possible, combination (4) (where the noun follows the relative clause) is not.

1 N + Dem, N + Rel Clause
2 Dem + N, Rel Clause + N (Japanese)
3 Dem + N, N + Rel Clause (English)
4 *N + Dem, Rel Clause + N

A 'fundamental concept, underlying much grammatical work in typology' is MARKEDNESS (Croft 1990: 64). Whereas the classical view of markedness, as defined by linguists in the Prague School of Linguistic Theory (for example, Trubetzkoy 1931), viewed features as either inherently unmarked or marked (for example, in the pair of features 'a' and 'an', 'a' is unmarked and 'an' is marked), language typology sees markedness primarily as a relative phenomenon (i.e. one feature is more marked than another). Reviewing Greenberg's early work on linguistic universals, Croft identified three main types of evidence for determining markedness:[2]

1 Structure: this concerns the presence or absence of a feature. For example, plural can be considered more marked than singular because it typically involves the addition of a morpheme.
2 Behaviour: this concerns whether one element is grammatically more 'versatile' than another—the more versatile it is, the more unmarked it is. Versatility is evident in both the number of inflections a specific grammatical category possesses (for example, singular third person has three forms in English—'he', 'she', and 'it'—whereas plural third person has only one—'they') and in the number of syntactic contexts in which a specific grammatical element can occur (for example, more constructions occur with the active voice than with the passive voice).
3 Frequency: the unmarked value is likely to occur with greater frequency than the marked value, both in actual use (i.e. in actual texts) and also in the world's languages.

In general, however, markedness has been considered in terms of implicational universals. Eckman (2004a) cited the following definition of typological markedness from Gundel *et al.* (1986: 108):

> A structure X is typologically marked relative to another structure, Y (and Y is typologically unmarked relative to X), if every language that has X also had Y, but every language that has Y does not necessarily have X.

In the following section I will provide a number of examples of typological markedness. For now one will suffice—given that languages that have a verbal dual morpheme also have a plural verbal morpheme but not vice versa, the latter can be considered unmarked in relation to the former.[3]

To summarize, linguistic typology involves the crosslinguistic study of samples of the world's languages. It results in the identification of various types of universals: absolute universals, frequency universals, and implicational universals. Also, it provides a principled basis for determining the degree of relative markedness of connected features.

Typologically motivated studies of second language acquisition

SLA researchers have examined phonological features (for example, Eckman 1984, 1991) as well as grammatical features (for example, Hyltenstam 1977; Rutherford 1983; Zobl 1989; Hamilton 1994; Izumi 2003). Given the extent of the SLA research based on typological universals, I will not attempt to provide a comprehensive review of this literature. Instead, I will focus on selected areas as a way of examining two major issues:

1 whether markedness can account for learning difficulty;
2 whether typological universals can explain the order of acquisition of grammatical features.

A third issue—the extent to which the typological status of grammatical features in the native and target languages affects L1 TRANSFER—was considered in Chapter 8 and so will not be considered in detail here. I will focus on one grammatical area—relative clauses—as this has attracted the attention of a number of SLA researchers. Other grammatical areas will also be considered, but more briefly.

Relative clauses

Typological studies of relative clauses focus on a number of distinct features: (1) the position of the relative clause in relation to the head noun, (2) relativization, (3) resumptive pronouns, (4) the grammatical functions of the head noun and relative pronoun, (5) the position of the relative clause in the sentence (matrix positions), and (6) the depth of embedding. Each of these will be briefly described. A number of hypotheses based on the typological findings will then be presented. This will set the scene for a review of the research findings.

1 Position of the relative clause

Languages differ according to whether modification is prenominal or postnominal. Chinese and Japanese are examples of languages that position the relative clause before the noun they are modifying, as in this example from Japanese:

Gakussi ga katta hon
Student NOM bought book
the book that the student bought ...

while English and French are examples of languages where the relative pronoun follows the head noun, as in all the examples in the sections following.

2 Relativization

The NOUN PHRASE ACCESSIBILITY HIERARCHY (NPAH), which was briefly considered in Chapter 3 (see Table 3.7), provides a hierarchy of relativized functions that typological linguists have shown to be universal. However, Shirai and Ozeki (2007), reviewing a number of studies of L2 Asian languages that had investigated the NPAH in a special issue of *Studies in Second Language Acquisition* (29: 2), concluded that they were no longer sure about its universality.

English affords examples of all six relativized functions. The relative pronoun can function as the subject of its clause:

I bought the puppy *that* (S) made me laugh.

as direct object:

The puppy *that* (DO) I bought was a nuisance.

as indirect object:

The boy *to whom* (IO) I gave the puppy was delighted.

as the object of a preposition (referred to as 'oblique'):

The kennel *in which* (OBL) I put the puppy was very expensive.

as genitive:

The boy *whose* puppy (GEN) has just died is very unhappy.

and finally as object of the comparative (OCOMP):

The boy *that the dog is bigger than* is easily frightened.

Comrie and Keenan's (1979) crosslinguistic study showed that languages varied in the noun phrases that were 'accessible' to relativization. It proposed the following hierarchy:

S < DO < IO < OBL < GEN < OCOMP

Their study showed that this hierarchy reflected both the frequency of the different relative pronoun functions possible in the languages they investigated and also the presence and absence of specific functions in a single language. For example, any language that permitted IO would also allow relativization of all the other noun phrase functions above it in the hierarchy (i.e. DO and S), but not below it (i.e. OBL, GEN, and OCOMP). Thus, the most marked relativized position is OCOMP and the most unmarked is S.

The NPAH, as originally proposed by Comrie and Keenan, is problematic in a number of ways. Keenan (1975) pointed out that indirect object and oblique are indistinguishable in most languages (including English), as both are expressed as prepositional phrases. Jones (1991a) argued that it is a mistake to include genitive in the hierarchy, as it has a separate and complete hierarchy of its own. He suggested that there are, in fact, two hierarchies, one for – Gen and the other for + Gen, as shown in Table 12.1. As we will see, this proposal is given support by the very mixed empirical results obtained for genitive, when this is viewed as part of a single hierarchy. Finally, OCOMP is problematic in English—a language that is supposed to manifest this function—because some native speakers do not accept that sentences with this function are grammatical (Izumi 2003).

Function	**- Genitive**	**+ Genitive**
Subject (SU)	The man who came ...	The man whose wife came ...
Direct object (DO)	The man (whom) I saw ...	The man whose wife I saw ...
Indirect object (IO)	The man (whom) I gave the book to ...	The man whose wife I gave the book to ...
Object of preposition (OP)	The man (whom) I looked at ...	The man whose wife I looked at ...
Object of comparative (OC)	The man (whom) I am bigger than ...	The man whose wife I am bigger than ...

Table 12.1 The Accessibility Hierarchy for – Genitive and + Genitive (from Jones 1991a)

3 Resumptive pronouns

Languages also vary according to whether they permit resumptive pronouns (i.e. pronoun copies) in relative clauses. English does not. Thus, the following sentence is ungrammatical:

*The boy who I gave the puppy to *him* was delighted.

Typologically, languages with resumptive pronouns are more common than languages without. Thus, the presence of resumptive pronouns is considered unmarked and their absence marked. However, languages that do permit resumptive pronouns do not necessarily do so in all relative clauses. The NPAH was also found to be relevant for explaining the presence or absence of pronominal copies in a language. Thus, a pronominal copy was most likely to occur with relative pronouns lower down the hierarchy (for example, IO) than with those higher up (for example, S). That is, if a language manifested resumptive pronouns in an unmarked type of relative clause it would also allow them in more marked clauses but not vice versa.

4 *Role of the head noun and the relative pronoun*

Sheldon (1977) noted that the roles of the head noun and the relative pronoun can be matching as in:

The man who saw the rabbit caught the fox

where both the head noun ('the man') and the pronoun ('who') function as subjects of their clauses, or non-matching as in:

The man saw *the fox that* caught the rabbit.

where the head noun ('the fox') functions as direct object in the main clause while the relative pronoun ('that') functions as subject of the relative clause. The prediction here is that learners do better when the head noun and the relative pronoun are matching than when they are non-matching. As Comrie (2003) pointed out such a prediction cannot be accommodated by the NPAH as it allows for the possibility that clauses relativized on S may in some cases prove more difficult than clauses relativized on DO.

5 *Matrix positions*

Relativization is not the only problem that learners face in acquiring relative clauses. There is also the question of where the relative clause occurs in the matrix sentence. Relative clauses can function as part of the direct object of the sentence as in:

The man saw *the fox that caught the rabbit.*

or they can function as part of the subject of the sentence, as in:

The man who saw the fox caught a rabbit.

In the first of these examples the relative clause is joined onto the main clause, while in the other it is embedded in the main clause. As we saw in Chapter 3, whether the relative clause is joined onto or embedded in the main clause can affect L2 acquisition.

It should be noted that the relativized positions in the NPAH can all occur in both joined and embedded relative clauses. (See Izumi 2003.)

6 Depth of embedding

Finally, relativization can vary in terms of the structural distance between the relative pronoun and the noun phrase that it replaces and that figures as a 'gap' or a 'trace' in the relative clause. Thus in the case of sentences with a relativized subject, the distance is minimal as illustrated in this sentence (where [____] indicates the position of the gap:

I bought the puppy *that* (S) [____] made me laugh.

However, in a sentence where the relativized noun phrase is extracted from a prepositional phrase such as in the following sentence, the distance is much greater:

The kennel *in which* (OBL) I put the puppy [____]was very expensive.

J. Hawkins (1999) observed that there are crosslinguistic differences relating to extraction. Languages vary in terms of the extent of the filler gap domain permitted. They vary in terms of whether the pronoun filler appears before or after the gap. Finally, as already noted, they also vary in terms of whether the 'gap' is filled with a resumptive pronoun. Hawkins suggested that these crosslinguistic differences impact on the ease with which different relative clauses can be processed.

Hypotheses involving relative clauses

Based on these typological accounts of relative clauses, SLA researchers have advanced a number of hypotheses as a basis for investigating how L2 learners handle relative clauses and the sequence in which they are acquired. Four key hypotheses will be considered.

1 The Noun Phrase Accessibility Hierarchy (NPAH) Hypothesis

This proposes that the NPAH reflects the relative ease of relativization. That is, learners will find it easier to process relativized positions that appear higher up the hierarchy than positions that appear lower down; they will acquire the relativized positions according to the implicational order of the NPAH. A further hypothesis concerns resumptive pronouns; learners will be more likely to insert a resumptive pronoun in clauses where the relativization is marked than in clauses where it is unmarked.

2 The Perceptual Difficulty Hypothesis (PDH)

Kuno's (1974) PDH drew on differences relating to the position of the relative clause in its matrix sentence. It claims that centre-embedded relative clauses will be more difficult to process and acquire than either right- or left-conjoined clauses.

3 The Structural Distance Hypothesis (SDH)

This is based on depth of embedding. O'Grady (1999: 628), for example, predicted that the relative difficulty of subject and object relative clauses is determined by the distance between the gapped noun phrase and the head noun phrase. That is, the shorter the distance, the greater the ease of processing.

4 The SO Hierarchy Hypothesis (SOHH)

Hamilton's SOHH (1994) is based on the notion of processing discontinuity and, as Izumi (2003) pointed out, is a hybrid of the previous hypotheses in that it claims that the ease/difficulty of processing/acquiring relative clauses is dependent on *both* the matrix position of the relative clause and the depth of embedding involved. The hypothesis predicts the following order of difficulty in clauses involving subject and object functions:

OS > OO/SS > SO

where the first letter in each term refers to whether the relative clause modifies the subject or object of the matrix clause and the second letter the function of the relative pronoun in the relative clause. Thus, the easiest type of relative clause is one that modifies the object of the matrix clause and where the relative pronoun functions as subject, while the most difficult is a relative clause that modifies the subject of the matrix clause and where the relative pronoun functions as object. OO/SS relative clauses are of equal difficulty and are intermediate to OS and SO.

SLA research investigating relative clauses

Table 12.2 summarizes 15 studies that have investigated the L2 acquisition of relative clauses. These studies have investigated a variety of languages, predominantly English, but also Swedish, French, Chinese, and Japanese. The vast majority have been quasi-experimental. That is, they have not involved any 'treatment' but have been based on the analysis of data collected by means of some elicitation instrument. However, three of the studies (Eckman *et al.* 1988; Doughty 1991; Yabuki-Soh 2007) were experimental. Only one study (Matthews and Yip 2003) was longitudinal.

All the studies, except that of Matthews and Yip (2003), made use of controlled elicitation instruments to collect data. The most favoured instruments are picture description tasks (involving verbal prompts), sentence joining tasks, and grammaticality judgement tasks (GJTs). Most of these tasks elicited production from learners but in two studies (Izumi 2003; Yabuki-Soh 2007) a comprehension task was used to examine learners' ability to process relative clauses receptively. A limitation of the research to date, largely determined by the need to collect data on how learners handle different kinds of relative clauses, is that it has not examined the use of relative clauses in natural language use.[4]

Study	Participants	Design	Instruments	Main findings
Tarallo and Myhill (1983)	English-speaking adult learners of L2 right-branching languages (Chinese/Japanese) and left-branching languages (German and Portuguese)	Quasi-experimental; study designed to investigate the Linear Distance Hypothesis (LDH).	GJT	Support claimed for the LDH as learners were more likely to accept direct object than subject relatives.
Gass (1980)	17 adult ESL learners; intermediate and advanced level; mixed L1s	Quasi-experimental; data collected to investigate the universality of predictions based on NPAH (i.e. the effect of L1 transfer)	(1) GJT; (2) free composition; (3) written sentence-combining task.	(1) Markedness interacts with L1 transfer in determining frequency of avoidance and resumptive pronouns but universal principles are dominant. (2) The genitive proved easier than was predicted by the AH, possibly because the relative pronoun 'whose' is very salient.
Hyltenstam (1984)	45 adult advanced learners of L2 Swedish with Farsi, Greek, Spanish, and Finnish as L1s	Quasi-experimental; participants performed a picture identification task designed to elicit a range of relative clauses.	Task consisted of eight pictures for each relativizable function; participants responded orally to questions such as 'Who is the man in picture X?'	(1) Resumptive pronouns appeared in all learners. (2) The extent to which resumptive pronouns appeared differed according to learners' L1. (3) There was little variability within a single grammatical function. (4) Resumptive pronouns were deleted 'roughly' in the order predicted by the AH.
Pavesi (1986)	Two groups; (1) 45 Italian high-school students of English; (2) 38 Italian workers in Edinburgh	Quasi-experimental/comparative; participants completed picture identification task designed to elicit relative clauses.	Same task as in Hyltenstam (1984).	(1) Order of acquisition in accordance with the NPAH for both groups of learners. (2) However, no difference evident between IO and OO and between G and OC. (3) The formal learners manifested pronoun copies; the informal noun copies. (4) The formal learners produced more instances of marked relatives.

Eckman *et al.* (1988)	36 adult ESL learners; low-intermediate or intermediate proficiency; mixed L1s	Experimental; instruction in relativization directed at three groups; (1) SO group; (2) DO group; (3) OP. There was also a control group.	Written sentence-combining test.	(1) All groups did best on the relative structure they were trained on. (2) SO group generalized somewhat to DO but neither this group nor the DO group generalized to OP. (3) Nearly all the generalization took place in the direction of the less marked structures.
R. Hawkins (1989)	Adult English- speaking learners of L2 French	Quasi-experimental: designed to investigate the 'relational view' based on the NPAH and a 'configurational view' based on discontinuity.		Evidence points in favour of a configurational explanation as only discontinuity can explain why learners experienced greater difficulty with stylistically inverted relative clauses (e.g. L'homme que connaît Pierre ...) than with conventional relative clauses (e.g. L'homme que Pierre connaît ...).
Doughty (1991)	20 adult intermediate level ESL learners with mixed L1s	Experimental: computer-based instruction in relativization to three groups: (1) A meaning-oriented group; (2) A rule-oriented group; (3) A control group.	Several tasks used: (1) GJT; (2) sentence-combination task (with and without guidance); (3) another GJT with larger variety of errors; (4) two oral elicitation tasks.	(1) Combined scores from oral and written tests produced an implication scaling in accordance with the predictions of the NPAH for learners in all three groups. (2) Instruction on marked relativized position (Object of preposition) generalized to less marked positions.
Wolfe-Quintero (1992)	35 adult Japanese learners of English; wide range of English proficiency; 17 native speakers of English	Quasi-experimental; participants performed a task designed to investigate the learners' acquisition of extraction from prepositional phrases.	Participants listened to input sentences and looked at some pictures and were then asked to write a response in the format 'This is the ____ that/which ...'.	Learners manifest a developmental sequence consisting of (1) an early no prep stage; (2) stages involving greater embeddedness of the extracted noun; (3) stranded before non-stranded prepositional structures; and (4) greater likelihood of resumptive pronouns in the early stages.

Hamilton (1994)	98 ESL learners: intermediate to advanced; mixed L1s	Non-experimental: data collected to investigate the effects of processing discontinuity in relative clauses—the Subject-Object Hierarchy Hypothesis (SOHH).	Sentence combination task requiring formation of various relative clause types.	The SOHH was supported, i.e. OS > OO/SS > SO.
Hamilton (1995)	As above	Non-experimental: data collected to investigate relativization from different types of prepositional phrases.		(1) Learners more accurate when relativizing out of PPs functioning as arguments than out of PPs functioning as adjuncts; (2) neither the grammatical relation distinction (IO versus OP) nor the thematic distinction (beneficiary versus goal) affected performance.
Izumi (2003)	61 adult ESL learners with different L1s; low- to high-intermediate level.	Non- experimental; participants completed three tasks designed to elicit relative clauses. Izumi sought to test the predictions of three hypotheses (AH; PDH; SOHH).	Three tasks: (1) sentence combination test (production task); (2) bimodal interpretation (reception) task; (3) GJT with correction	(1) Both the NPAH and the PDH were supported; they are complementary hypotheses; (2) the effects of discontinuity as predicted by the SOHH were not clearly attested; (3) task effects were evident; tasks (1) and (3) supported the AH but task (2) did not; task (2) supported the PDH.
Matthews and Yip (2003)	Two Hong Kong bilingual children (Cantonese/English)	Longitudinal case study of the two children's English relative clauses directed at investigating transfer effects.	(1) Longitudinal recordings of natural speech; (2) diary kept by parents.	(1) English; pre-nominal object relative clauses based on the Cantonese pattern emerged first followed by postnominal relatives, initially with resumptive pronouns in object and occasionally subject position; (2) Cantonese; relative clauses were target-like throughout.

O'Grady *et al*. (2003)	Adult English-speaking learners of L2 Korean; 9 NSs of Korean	Non-experimental study designed to test the claims of the Structural Distance Hypothesis.	Picture selection tasks to assess comprehension of Korean relative clauses.	Learners preferred subject to object related clauses suggesting that the key determinant is the depth of embedding of the gap as predicted by the SDH and as found in L1 learners of Korean.
Ozeki and Shirai (2007)	90 learners of L2 Japanese with mixed L2 proficiency and L1 background	Non-experimental: study designed to test the applicability of the NPAH to learners of L2 Japanese.	Oral interview; sentence-combining task.	No evidence that subject relatives were easier than direct object or oblique in the oral data or than the direct object in the sentence-combining task. The authors concluded that the NPAH did not predict the difficulty order of relative clauses.
Yabuki-Soh (2007)	60 young learners of L2 Japanese	Experimental: the effects of three types of instruction (form-based; meaning-based; form- and meaning-based) on acquisition of relative clauses.	Comprehension test; sentence-combination test.	Acquisition of relativization was non-linear. The explicit form-based instruction was most effective; generalization from marked to unmarked relatives occurred but only in the case of production (i.e. not in the comprehension test).

Table 12.2 Typologically-based SLA studies of relative clauses

Four major questions have figured in the research based on the Noun Phrase Accessibility Hierarchy: (1) does the NPAH account for avoidance behaviour? (2) does the NPAH explain the order of acquisition of relativizable NP positions? (3) does the NPAH explain the use of resumptive pronouns? and (4) does the NPAH explain the acquisition of the forms of different relativizers? In each case, the central issue is whether markedness factors, typologically determined, can be used to explain acquisitional phenomena.

Schachter's (1974) study of relative clauses, which we considered in Chapter 8, showed that learners of English whose L1 does not contain relative clauses or contains left-branching rather than right-branching clauses (for example, Japanese and Chinese) tend to avoid using relative clauses in their English production. Schachter did not investigate whether the extent of this AVOIDANCE was related to the function of the relative pronoun. However, Gass (1980: 138) did so. She used a sentence-joining task to elicit use of all the relative pronoun functions in the NPAH. She reported that her subjects (adult learners with mixed L1 backgrounds) tended to avoid relativizing on low positions in the NPAH by changing a part of one of the sentences in a sentence-joining task so as to make relativization in a higher position possible. For example, the two sentences:

He saw the woman.
The man kissed the woman.

were intended to elicit the use of a relative pronoun functioning as direct object:

He saw the woman that the man kissed.

However, several learners contrived to use a subject relative pronoun, as in:

He saw the woman who was kissed by the man.

There is clear evidence that markedness, as defined by the AH, influences the order of acquisition but one study of L2 Japanese (Ozeki and Shirai 2007) failed to find any (i.e. the learners performed as well with direct object relatives as with subject relatives). Gass (1980) found strong support for the markedness hypothesis. Thus, fewest errors were evident in the subject position, with most errors occurring in the object of comparison position. However, Gass reported that the learners found the genitive function easier than the direct object function, contrary to predictions based on the AH, a point that will be commented on below. Pavesi (1986), in a comparative study of instructed and naturalistic Italian learners of L2 English that used implicational scaling on elicited oral data, found that, in general, both groups of learners followed the order predicted by the AH. However, the pattern for indirect object and oblique and also for genitive and object of comparative was not always as expected. Learners varied with regard to which function in each pair they favoured, some preferring the unmarked before the marked member and others vice versa. Also, the genitive and object of comparison functions were almost entirely missing in the naturalistic group.

Further evidence in support of the markedness hypothesis can be found in Eckman, Bell, and Nelson (1988) and Doughty (1991) for learners with mixed L1s and Jones (1991b) for Japanese students. In all three studies, the accuracy order for the different pronoun functions on sentence-joining tasks conformed broadly to the AH, although, again, there were some discrepancies. Jones' study is of interest because he provided separate accuracy orders for genitive and non-genitive structures. He found that the subject function was considerably easier than the direct object and oblique positions (which were roughly equal) irrespective of whether the structure involved a genitive or not. Also, although non-genitive structures proved easier overall than genitive structures, accuracy levels on the genitive subject position were equivalent to those on non-genitive direct object and oblique positions. The importance of considering genitive and non-genitive structures separately is borne out by Hansen-Strain and Strain (1989), who found that the results for genitive in their study involving five different L1 groups on seven different tasks did not match the AH. The learners performed much better than expected, possibly because they were only required to produce genitive subject structures.

Four studies have examined resumptive pronouns in terms of the AH. The studies by Gass (1979, 1980) and Hyltenstam (1984) have already been considered in Chapter 8. The conclusion was that markedness interacts with L1 transfer in the sense that although pronominal copy errors were more likely in the lower positions and less likely in the higher positions of the AH, the overall error frequency reflected whether or not pronominal copies occurred in the learners' L1. Gass felt that 'it is universal principles that play the leading role since they are dominant in assigning a relative order of difficulty' (1980: 140). A third study—Tarallo and Myhill (1983)—casts doubt on this conclusion, however. English L1 subjects were asked to judge the grammaticality of sentences containing pronominal copies in two right-branching languages (German and Portuguese) and two left-branching (Chinese and Japanese). Tarallo and Myhill reported that the learners of right-branching languages were most accurate in judgements of sentences involving the subject function, while those of left-branching languages were most accurate in judgements involving the direct object function. In other words, the learners of the right-branching languages conformed to the order predicted by the NPAH but those of left-branching languages did not. Tarallo and Myhill concluded that the crucial factor was the proximity of the relativized noun phrase (NP) site to the head of the relative clause. Thus, in English, the direct object function is more difficult than the subject function because the extraction site (shown by a [____]) is further from the head NP (in italics) than is the case for subject function, for example:

The *puppy* that I bought [____]was a nuisance.
I bought the *puppy* that [____]made me laugh.

The opposite is the case in left-branching languages. Finally, Pavesi (1986) reported that whereas learners in a formal setting (high-school Italian learners of English) produced pronoun copies, learners in an informal context (Italian waiters in English) produced noun copies, as in this example:

*No 4 is the woman who the cat is looking at the woman.

In such sentences the relative pronoun appears to be functioning as a simple coordinator.

R. Hawkins (1989) examined the acquisition of the different forms of L2 French relativizers by three groups of adult English-speaking learners, who differed in their general level of proficiency. He found that the order of acquisition of the three relativizers, 'qui', 'que', and 'dont', conformed to the order predicted by the AH, but argued that this order could also be predicted on the basis of surface configurational factors. For example, 'qui' could be expected to be acquired before 'que', which in turn would be acquired before 'dont' because this order corresponds to the distance between the head and the extraction site, as shown in the following examples:

L'homme qui___connaît Pierre ... (The man who knows Pierre.)
L'homme que Pierre connaît___... (The man who Pierre knows.)
Le visiteur dont j'avais oublié le nom___... (The visitor whose name I had forgotten.)

It is not possible, therefore, on the basis of these results, to decide between a 'relational view' (based on the AH) and 'a configurational view' (based on the surface relationships between grammatical elements). However, Hawkins went on to provide evidence to suggest that the configurational view is the right one, arguing, for example, that only this view can explain why the learners experienced greater difficulty with stylistically inverted relative clauses like:

L'homme que connaît Pierre... (The man that Pierre knows ...)

than with relative clauses displaying the more conventional order. Such a conclusion may not be justified, however, given that the difficulty with such stylistically inverted sentences may derive from L1-related factors—English does not permit subject object inversion in relative clauses—rather than from configurational factors *per se*.

Clear conclusions regarding the effect of markedness, as represented by the accessibility hierarchy, on L2 acquisition are not possible from these studies. To sum up the early studies there is some evidence to show that linguistic markedness may have an effect on the extent to which learners avoid relative clauses, the order in which they acquire relative pronoun functions, and the extent to which learners make resumptive errors. The general finding is that acquisition is easier in the unmarked, higher positions and more difficult in the marked, lower positions of the hierarchy, but the evidence for L2 Japanese is somewhat mixed. There is, however, the alternative view advanced by

Tarallo and Myhill (1983) and R. Hawkins (1989), namely that learners construct rules for relative clauses on the basis of the adjacency of categories in the surface configuration (i.e. as claimed by the Structural Difference Hypothesis). According to this view, the difficulty that learners experience in learning relative clauses is not the product of the relative markedness of the relative pronoun functions, but a function of their capacity for processing sentences. We should also note that the L2 research suggests that there are problems with the AH, as formulated by Comrie and Keenan (1979). In particular, the fact that variable results have been found for genitive suggests that Jones' (1991a) proposal that there are in fact two hierarchies, one for genitive and the other for non-genitive, is right.

Later studies have attempted to investigate the claims of the different hypotheses outlined above. The key study in this respect is Izumi (2003). Izumi set out to test the predictions of three hypotheses; the Noun Phrase Accessibility Hierarchy (NPAH) Hypothesis, the Perceptual Difficulty Hypothesis (PDH) and the Subject-Object Hierarchy Hypothesis (SOHH). A particular strength of this study is the use of a variety of instruments to measure learners' ability to produce relative clauses, process them receptively, and judge their correctness. The results supported the NPAH Hypothesis with data collected from the sentence combination test and partially with data collected from the GJT, but not from data collected by means of the interpretation test. In contrast, the data from all three instruments lent support to the PDH (as did O'Grady *et al.*'s (2003) study of relative clauses in L2 Korean) and partial support for the SOHH. Izumi concluded that the NPAH Hypothesis and the PDH are complementary rather than competing hypotheses and that the results indicated some obvious task effects. He suggested that the ability to produce relative clauses is more susceptible to processing difficulties based on predictions regarding typological markedness than the ability to comprehend them. Two other later studies (Ozeki and Shirai 2007; Yabuki-Soh 2007) produced mixed support for the NPAH Hypothesis in the case of L2 Japanese. The first of these failed to show that the NPAH Hypothesis predicted the order of difficulty of relative clauses but the other produced some evidence to show that learners of Japanese were able to generalize instruction in a marked relative to a less marked relative, as predicted by the hypothesis.

Other grammatical areas

1 Negative placement

Negative placement constitutes an example of a non-implicational universal tendency, with Dahl's (1979) survey showing a clear preference for preverbal over postverbal negative position in the world's languages. As we saw in Chapter 3, there is strong evidence that in the early stages of L2 acquisition learners opt for preverbal negation, even where the L1 manifests postverbal negation. If, on the basis of language typology, preverbal negation is considered unmarked in relation to postverbal negation, it would seem that learners acquire the unmarked form before the marked. Furthermore, as Wode (1984) noted, preverbal negation appears even when it is not present in either the target language or the learner's L1. This suggests that typological universals like negator + verb phrase may occur irrespective of the formal characteristics of the languages involved.

Jordens' (1980) re-analysis of Hyltenstam's (1977) data on the acquisition of the negative placement rule in Swedish by Turkish, Serbo-Croat, and Hamito-Semitic speakers lends support to a number of predictions based on typological markedness. Swedish is of particular interest because 'in main clauses the negation is placed after the finite verb, while in subordinate clauses it is placed immediately before the finite verb' (Hyltenstam 1977: 387). As such, it appears to contradict the 'universal tendency for Neg to have a definite position relative to the FE (finite element) of the sentence' (Dahl op. cit.: 91). Jordens argued that Hyltenstam's learners initially went for a negator + main verb ordering in both main and subordinate clauses:

*han inte kommer (he not comes)
att han inte kommer (that he not comes)

The learners, therefore, appear to be behaving like other learners by opting initially for a negator in preverbal position and also by placing the negator in a definite position. Jordens also pointed out that this position is initially determined not by the finite verb element (as this is not yet represented in the learners' interlanguage) but, more simply, by the main verb.[5]

2 *Preposition stranding and pied piping*

PREPOSITION STRANDING and pied piping have been investigated by Mazurkewich (1984) and Bardovi-Harlig (1987). Preposition stranding is typologically rare and, therefore, might be expected to be acquired late. It is considered marked in relation to PIED PIPING on the grounds that any language that has preposition stranding also has pied piping, but not the reverse. Also, the relationship is considered to be implicational (i.e. languages that have preposition stranding also have pied piping). Both structures are found in WH–questions and relative clauses in English, as shown in these examples:

With whom did Mary speak? (pied piping)
The man with whom Mary spoke ... (pied piping)
Who(m) did Mary speak with? (preposition stranding)
The man who(m) Mary spoke with ... (preposition stranding)

Mazurkewich used a written question formation test to investigate the ease of acquisition of the two structures in WH–questions by French and Inuktitut speakers. The results indicated that the French speakers produced more instances of pied piping than preposition stranding, while the opposite was true for the Inuktitut speakers. In other words, the results were ambivalent, not lending clear support to the hypothesis that the unmarked structure would prove easier than the marked. One possible explanation for this could be L1 transfer; Inuktitut does not have prepositions and so, arguably, transfer is not an issue, whereas French has pied piping but not preposition stranding. The French learners may have transferred their L1 structure, therefore. However, this is not Mazurkewich's preferred explanation. She claimed that the Inuktitut speakers were more advanced than the French speakers and, thus, more likely to have acquired the marked preposition stranding. She also argued that L1 transfer is not an adequate explanation of the French learners' results because the Quebec dialect, which they spoke, does manifest incidences of preposition stranding (for example, 'le boss que je travaille pour' = 'the boss that I work for'). Mazurkewich's arguments were dismissed by both Kellerman (1985) and White (1986), both of whom considered that the transfer explanation is stronger.

Bardovi-Harlig's (1987) study indicated that the markedness hypothesis is, in fact, not tenable for pied piping/preposition stranding. This study used a similar linguistic manipulation task to Mazurkewich, but included items involving relative clauses as well as WH–questions. The subjects were 95 learners of English, divided into six proficiency levels. They had a variety of L1s, but in every case the L1 allowed only the unmarked pied piping. The results provided clear evidence that learners acquire preposition stranding before pied piping, contrary to the markedness hypothesis. Bardovi-Harlig also found that before learners attempt either rule, they omit the preposition entirely (a 'No-Prep strategy'), as in these examples:

Who did Mary give a book?
The man Mary baked a cake was Joe.

The order of acquisition, therefore, was (1) No-Prep, (2) preposition stranding, (3) pied piping. This order was evident in both WH–questions and relative clauses, although relative clauses, as the more difficult structure, were more likely to retain the 'simpler' forms (No-Prep and preposition stranding) than WH–questions. Bardovi-Harlig argued that the results indicated that the learners were not responding to linguistic factors (i.e. markedness) but to the availability of data in the input (i.e. salience). Thus, preposition stranding is acquired before pied piping because it is more frequent in the input. She suggested the following restatement of the markedness hypothesis: 'unmarked structures are acquired before marked structures, all things being equal' (1987: 402).

The role of typological universals in second language acquisition

What conclusions can we reach regarding the role of typological universals in L2 acquisition? The evidence from the studies of negation, preposition stranding/pied piping, and relativization which we have considered, indicates that the linguistic nature of the target structures may influence both the ease and the order of their acquisition. Learners seem to find it easier to acquire typologically unmarked structures than typologically marked structures. The assumption that underlies this research, namely that linguistic universals will affect interlanguages in the same way as they affect other languages because ILs constitute natural languages, is supported.

It is clear, however, that typological markedness alone cannot account for L2 acquisition. Gass (1984) suggested that it constitutes not so much an 'absolute constraint' as an 'overall shaping factor'. Bardovi-Harlig's (1987) study of preposition stranding/pied piping showed that in some features at least, acquisition may not proceed in accordance with markedness. If a linguistically marked feature is strongly represented in the input learners are exposed to, then they will acquire this before a related unmarked feature that is only weakly represented. In other words, input frequency can override the assumed difficulty of learning a marked feature. This raises a thorny question: Is it markedness *per se* or input frequency that is the real determinant of acquisition? In general, we can assume that unmarked features are likely to be frequent. Subject relative pronouns, for instance, occur more frequently than object of comparison pronouns, and probably also more frequently than indirect object pronouns. The fact that learners acquire subject relative pronouns before object of comparison and indirect pronouns may therefore simply reflect input frequency. In order to decide whether it is markedness or input frequency that determines the order of acquisition, it is necessary to look at cases like preposition stranding/pied piping in English, where the two factors do not correlate. Bardovi-Harlig's finding that learners acquire the marked but frequent structure first is very damaging to the markedness hypothesis.

It would be premature, however, to dismiss markedness. Learners do not always respond to what is in the input, as the studies of negation show. The input shows learners of L2 English that negation in English follows the auxiliary verb and precedes the main verb, and yet learners almost invariably opt for preverbal negation in the initial stages. In this case, therefore, they appear to choose the unmarked form rather than the form supplied by the input. Again, however, the question arises as to whether the initial preference that learners show for preverbal negation reflects markedness or some other factor. For example, if learners 'simplify' the input by ignoring auxiliaries, English negation will appear to be preverbal. An explanation of early preverbal negation based on ease of processing is as tenable, if not more so, than one based on typological markedness. According to the Multidimensional Model (see Chapter 9), for instance, preverbal negation occurs because learners have not yet removed the processing 'block' that prevents them inserting an element (the negator) into the middle of a string.

UG-oriented researchers have been critical of applying typological universals to the study of L2 acquisition. Gregg's (1989) verdict on typological universals was:

> ... typological generalizations are either uninteresting (no language has labiovelar stops) or interesting only in the questions they raise, not in the answers they provide.
> (1989: 32)

Rutherford (1984b: 142) also felt that typological universals are of limited value—in his view, they offer little more than 'a collection of observations', albeit 'concerning a rather wide assortment of syntactic phenomena'. White (1987b) claimed that because typological universals were 'external' to individuals (i.e. reflected facts to do with the world's languages), it was unclear how they could be applied to individuals or whether they had any psychological reality. That is, 'L2 learners cannot be assumed to have such knowledge available to them' (p. 266). Archibald (1998) argued that a typological approach to L2 acquisition was only interesting in that it provides 'an interesting *description* of the phenomena to be explained' but failed to provide an explanation.

Eckman (2004a) set out to address these criticisms. He argued that 'description' cannot be separated as neatly from 'explanation' as these criticisms imply. Rather, it is necessary to distinguish 'levels of explanation' according to the relative generality of the laws/principles invoked. Explanations couched in terms of low generality (as Eckman acknowledged many statements about L2 acquisition based on typological universals are) should not be rejected unless a higher level generalization is available. In fact, in Eckman's view, such statements are valuable precisely because they invite higher order explanations.[6] Eckman also rejected White's argument that typological universals lack psychological validity. While accepting that L2 learners cannot have explicit or implicit knowledge of these universals (as, in fact no SLA researcher in the typological tradition has ever claimed), he argued that it is entirely feasible that whatever is responsible for implicational universals being the way they are may also be at work in determining L2 acquisition.

The study of typological universals as a basis for investigating L2 acquisition, then, can be justified on the grounds that it is of value in what Hyltenstam referred to as 'the descriptive phase of research' (1990: 33) or for what Eckman preferred to call 'lower-order explanations'. However, clearly, the case can be made stronger if higher-order explanations can be developed to explain why learning difficulty and the sequence/order of acquisition appear to be influenced by the linguistic universals identified by typological linguists. We will now examine to what extent such explanations are available.

Explaining the influence of typological universals on L2 acquisition

The underlying problem is to explain how typological universals affect acquisition. Two types of explanation are possible. One is that they affect learning *directly* because the learner has inbuilt grammatical knowledge that includes a theory of grammatical markedness. This is tantamount to suggesting that learners bring a knowledge of markedness relations, such as those represented in the NPAH, to the learning task, and thus are predisposed to expect unmarked grammatical features to be more likely than marked ones. This is the view that J. Hawkins (1999) considered and rightly rejected. The alternative view is that markedness relations are only *indirectly* related to language acquisition, and that to understand how they work it is necessary to uncover the factors that cause one linguistic feature to be more marked than another. This is the view taken by most typological and L2 researchers. For example, Hyltenstam (1984) was careful to argue that the NPAH can only serve as a basis for making *predictions* about L2 acquisition and does not, in itself, provide *explanations*. There are reasons why some features are more common in the world's languages than others and it is these reasons that will explain acquisition.

What then are the factors that determine markedness? Gass and Ard (1984) identified a number of potential sources of language universals, which are summarized in Table 12.3. They acknowledged that their list is not exhaustive, and also that any one universal may have more than one source. 'There is a great deal of controversy with regard to the assignment of an origin to a particular universal' (1984: 35). They then went on to present a model which predicted that universals based on how humans interact with and/or perceive the world around them (i.e. (1), (2), and (6)) were the ones most likely to affect acquisition. In other words, typological universals are relevant to acquisition because the processing factors that explain them are the same as those that can explain L2 acquisition.

Source		**Description**
1	Physical basis	The universal reflects 'a physical fact, perhaps dependent on the way the world is, or ... on the way the human body, especially the vocal and aural apparatus, is structured'.
2	Perceptual/ cognitive	The universal reflects 'factors in the human perceptual and cognitive apparatus and processing capabilities'. Such factors affect more than just language.
3	Language acquisition device	The universal reflects innate knowledge of language that a learner brings to the learning task.
4	Neurological basis of language acquisition	The universal reflects neurological predispositions towards the use of certain types of structure.
5	Historical change	Certain patterns may be missing from all languages because they cannot diachronically arise from the types of language extant.
6	Social interaction	Universals of interactive competence influence the universal nature of language.

Table 12.3 Sources of linguistic universals (from Gass and Ard 1984: 35–8)

It remains, however, to specify more precisely what these processing factors are. J. Hawkins (1999) went some way towards achieving this goal in a detailed discussion of the processing complexity of different types of relative clauses. He argued that there is a 'first resort strategy' in parsing relative clauses, namely that 'a gap is postulated as soon as it can be and is filled with the filler' (p. 247). Thus a sentence such as:

My brother wanted to know who Ruth will bring [1] us home to [2] at Christmas.

is difficult to process because initially the parser predicts a gap at the direct object position shown by [1] only to find this is already filled by 'us', thus requiring reanalysis of the relative clause and increased processing time. Hawkins' explanation accords with the predictions of the Structural Distance Hypothesis—see above; the human processor likes the distance between the relative pronoun and the noun phrase it replaces to be as small as possible. Hawkins then went on to address why the implicational pattern for resumptive pronouns is in the opposite direction for that for relativization; for the former it is from low to high whereas for the latter it is from high to low. The answer lies again in an account of how humans process language. Hawkins suggested that humans operate an economy strategy that leads to reduced form processing (i.e. gaps) when there is little cost (as when the distance between the head noun and the gap is minimal) and an explicit strategy that leads to a pronoun copy in contexts of greater structural complexity. Hawkins' account of processing complexity is strongly reminiscent of Slobin's OPERATING PRINCIPLES. (See Chapter 9.) It assumes that language acquisition can be accounted for in terms of a set of general cognitive operations and that there is no need to postulate a distinct language faculty. In this respect it differs from the view of linguistic universals we will consider next.

Universal Grammar and second language acquisition

As Gass (1997b) noted, there has been a change in emphasis in SLA from the early focus on typological universals to the later concern with Universal Grammar (UG).

Whereas language typology is essentially data-driven and descriptive in nature, the approach that we will consider in this section is motivated by a powerful theory of language. Cook (1988: 170) distinguished a 'general level of the theory' (i.e. the precepts of the theory of Universal Grammar) from 'the most particular' (i.e. the specific model of grammar proposed to account for Universal Grammar). Whereas the former has changed little over time, the latter has. The model that initially informed UG-based SLA research was GOVERNMENT/BINDING (Chomsky 1976, 1981a, 1981b) while more recently SLA researchers have drawn on the MINIMALIST PROGRAM (Chomsky 1995), which seeks to reduce the account of UG to a minimal set of specifications. Changes in the model of grammar that informed UG-based studies of L2 acquisition are potentially problematic, however. Van Buren and Sharwood Smith (1985) asked 'when linguistics coughs, should second language acquisition catch pneumonia?' (1985: 21). They went on to answer this question by claiming that the theoretical foundations (i.e. at that time, Chomsky's Government/Binding Theory) were sufficiently robust to warrant application in SLA research. This was not a view shared by all researchers however. Lack of consensus about the details of the theory has often been evident, as, for instance, in the debate centring on Flynn's research on the head-final/head-initial parameter. (See Flynn 1987, Bley-Vroman, and Chaudron 1990; Flynn and Lust 1990.) The switch to the Minimalist Program raises questions about the status of the earlier research conducted under the Government/Binding Model. White (1997) noted that some SLA researchers (myself included) have been dismissive of UG-based research because of the constant changes in the grammatical model that informs it. But she also argued that 'there is, on the whole, agreement about what properties of language are likely to be universal ... even though the theories that account for universality or ungrammaticality vary' (p. 65). In a similar vein, R. Hawkins (2001a) noted that the goals of both the Government/Binding Model and the Minimalist Program are the same—'to characterize the mechanisms made available by the brain for building mental grammars for specific languages' (p. 2).

In this chapter, I will focus attention on the general theory and not attempt to summarize either the Government/Binding Model or the Minimalist Program, although aspects of these will be considered by way of illustration of the general theory. I will begin by briefly introducing UG as this has been treated in SLA research. I will then consider the methodology employed by UG researchers in SLA before providing a more in-depth account of key aspects of the general theory and illustrating how these have figured in empirical studies of L2 acquisition. I will conclude with a brief evaluation of UG-based research.

Introducing Universal Grammar

Universal Grammar consists of a highly abstract set of linguistic PRINCIPLES that do not constitute the actual rules found in any single language but rather act as constraints on the form that these rules can take. An analogy might be made with a set of ethical principles that constrain what kinds of human behaviour are acceptable. The theoretical case for positing UG is that a language is so complex that it would not be possible for anyone to learn it simply through exposure to input. In this respect, then, the theory of UG offers a radical alternative to the kinds of cognitive accounts of learning where input plays a central role. (See Chapters 6 and 9.) UG makes two assumptions entirely absent from cognitive accounts: (1) human beings possess a special and highly specific capacity for language learning (as opposed to a more general cognitive apparatus responsible for all types of learning) and (2) this capacity is innate and biologically determined.

The study of UG and its role in language acquisition (both first and second) belongs to the tradition of generative linguistics, which was initiated by Chomsky's (1957) *Syntactic Structures* and his (1959) critique of Skinner's behaviourist account of L1 acquisition. It is important to recognize that this tradition seeks to explain a speaker-hearer's *unconscious* representation of the language they have learnt. That is, it constitutes a theory of implicit linguistic knowledge. Fairly obviously the abstract principles that comprise UG exist only in learners' unconscious minds (except of course in the case of the generative linguists who seek to make them explicit), but so too do the specific rules relating to the target language. UG-based SLA research, as part of the generative tradition, has nothing to say about explicit knowledge or its role in acquisition.

A speaker-hearer's implicit knowledge of a language constitutes their GRAMMATICAL COMPETENCE (i.e. the representational system that underlies actual performance). Thus a theory of UG seeks to account for how linguistic knowledge is represented rather than how it is used in *performance*. In other words, it focuses on 'knowledge' rather than 'ability', and therefore pays no attention to the variability inherent in learner language, as this is seen as a reflection of learners' capacity to use their knowledge in communication rather than competence itself. However, Klein and Martohardjono (1999a: 21) argued that it is necessary to account for 'optionality' in a learner's grammar. They distinguished between a 'variable rule' (defined as a rule that 'operates in some environments or under some conditions and not others') and 'optionality' (i.e. a rule that sometimes does and sometimes does not operate in the same environment').[7] Sorace (2000) argued that optionality characterizes all stages of L2 development, although other researchers (for example, Parodi and Tsimpli 2005) have proposed that unconstrained optionality is more evident in learners of low proficiency than in advanced learners.

Readers familiar with Chomsky's view of language learning may view UG as nothing more than a re-labelling of his earlier construct—the 'language acquisition device'. However, as White (2003a) emphasized, UG is not in itself a theory of acquisition. Generative theorists, such as White, recognize that other domains, such as perception and memory, are involved in language acquisition, and that these interact with the language module. Thus, a theory of how linguistic competence is acquired constitutes only one module in an overall theory of L2 acquisition. Furthermore, even within the language module itself, it may be necessary to identify various sub-domains, including UG and language learning procedures or principles. Finally, a language parser that analyses input is needed to account for how input triggers access to UG and the other learning mechanisms. A complete theory, therefore, will have to explain how all the modules and sub-modules shown in Figure 12.1 interact.

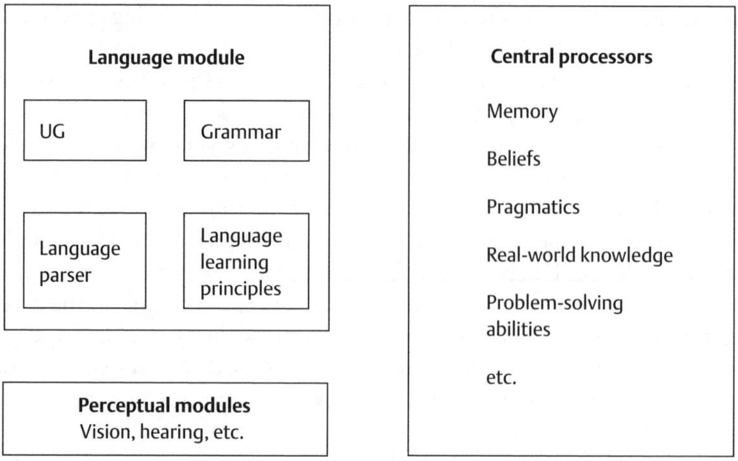

Figure 12.1 Cognitive modularity (from White 1989a: 178)

The generative approach is to focus, narrowly and perhaps sensibly (for heuristic reasons), on a specific domain (i.e. the UG box in White's model). In so doing, generative theorists are at pains to acknowledge that the explanation they provide is only a partial one. The claim is only that 'UG plays a central and vital part in L2 learning, but there are many other parts' (Cook 1988: 189). Some UG-based researchers, however, have begun to develop a more complete theory of acquisition (one that is more compatible with Chomsky's initial idea of a language acquisition device). Sharwood Smith and Truscott (2005), for example, have proposed a theory of development that seeks to account for both representation (as evidenced in discrete stages of development) and development (as evidenced in the continua that reflect gradual change) by proposing how UG interacts with general learning and processing principles. This theory is considered more fully later.

What UG seeks to explain is also limited in another important respect. While generative theorists, including Chomsky, have acknowledged that it is possible to talk of PRAGMATIC COMPETENCE in the sense that speakers also internalize a set of rules that govern how language is used to construct discourse and to perform speech acts in socially appropriate ways, they have typically excluded this from consideration. As Gregg (1989) explained:

> ... in comparison with an attempt to construct a theory of acquisition in the domain of grammar, any attempt to construct a theory of acquisition in the domain of pragmatics or communication is going to be handicapped by the lack of a well-articulated formal characterization of the domain.
> (1989: 24)

Thus, grammar is viewed as an autonomous area of language and as more amenable to scientific study than pragmatics.

In some respects, however, the scope of UG-based SLA enquiry has broadened over the years. In early versions of the theory (Chomsky 1981b), UG was considered to account for 'core' grammar only; peripheral grammatical features and vocabulary fell outside UG and thus depended on a different mechanism. However, work since the 1990s, particularly within the Minimalist Program (Chomsky 1995), has had a much broader scope, aiming to provide a principled account of the mapping of meaning to sound. As a result UG-oriented SLA researchers are now interested in almost every aspect of the linguistic knowledge of L2 speakers. If researchers have continued to concentrate on the PRINCIPLES and PARAMETERS that relate to syntax, this simply reflects the fact that this is the area in which theoretical linguists have formulated explicit proposals that can be explored in terms of L2 acquisition, not because of any *a priori* wish to delimit the scope of their enquiry. Recently, studies looking at non-syntactic areas have begun to appear, for example Slabakova's (2006) work on semantics and Lozano's (2006) work on lexical and discourse factors. The UG-program in SLA is no longer limited to the principles of 'core grammar' as outlined by Chomsky in 1981.

The methodology of UG-based studies

As noted above, UG research is directed at explaining competence, generally defined as 'grammatical competence'. However, as grammatical competence can only be viewed through some kind of performance, a key question is how researchers can be sure that what they are witnessing is reflective of learner's underlying knowledge of language. As Klein and Martohardjono (1999) pointed out, 'perhaps the biggest problem facing UG SLA research is having to evaluate competence through performance' (p. 15). A fitting starting point for our study of UG-based research, then, is an examination of the methodology researchers have employed.

There is of course no easy answer to the problem Klein and Martohardjono identified. They argued that it is essential to try to minimize what they called 'extraneous factors' (i.e. the performance factors that distort the realization of competence), noting that these factors are likely to figure more strongly in L2 learners than native speakers. They suggested a number of ways in which this can be achieved—by measuring multiple sites in the L2 grammar which a particular linguistic principle is hypothesized to govern, evaluating the extent to which the learner's grammar is internally consistent, and making use of multiple means of collecting data.

UG-based SLA research is typically quasi-experimental in nature: it involves elicited rather than naturally occurring language behaviour and control and experimental groups, but no treatment. The methodology researchers have employed is not without controversy, however, both with regard to how data are collected and also the design of studies. We will consider the key issues involved in each.

1 Methods of data collection

By and large UG-oriented researchers have preferred experimentally elicited rather than naturalistic data. This is because the hypotheses they test frequently require evidence not just of what structures learners 'allow' (i.e. actually produce) but also what they 'disallow' (i.e. do not produce because they consider them as ungrammatical). Whereas naturalistic data can shed light on what learners 'allow' it cannot show what they 'disallow'. Elicited data are also preferred because they provide researchers with the degree of control needed to minimize 'extraneous factors' and because the specific hypotheses they investigate often require evidence relating to structures that are likely to occur only very infrequently in naturalistic language use. For example, researchers would have to collect an enormous amount of naturalistic data to obtain sufficient exemplars of structures relating to the use of reflexive pronouns in such sentences such as 'Susan believed that Cynthia disliked herself'!

Researchers have employed a variety of instruments relating to what Corder (1981) called 'experimental elicitation'. In general, they have eschewed 'clinical elicitation' involving the use of communicative tasks. Klein and Martohardjono (1999a) claimed 'controlled production tasks ... serve an important purpose and are more useful for the researcher than communicative tasks' (p. 18). The experimental elicitation instruments employed can be classified into three main types: (1) grammaticality judgements, (2) production tasks, and (3) interpretation (perception) tasks. White (2003a) noted that there is no one method of collecting data that is appropriate for investigating all aspects of linguistic competence.

UG researchers have favoured the use of GRAMMATICALITY JUDGEMENT tasks (GJTs). These come in several forms (see Ellis 1991b and 2004 and Chapter 16 for an account of these), but always involve the learner in making some kind of metalingual assessment regarding the grammaticality of a mixed set of sentences, some grammatical and some ungrammatical. As White (1981) pointed out, the great advantage of this kind of task is that it forces subjects to consider sentences that are 'impossible' from a UG standpoint. There are many problems with grammaticality judgements, however. Birdsong (1989) noted that they are not appropriate for learners with poor L2 literacy, and that differences in the metalinguistic skills of literate learners are also likely to affect responses. Furthermore, when learners reject sentences it is not always clear whether this is because of their grammatical properties or because of the difficulties that they experience in trying to parse them, a point to be taken up later. Birdsong also pointed out that often learners lack confidence and, therefore, are reluctant to commit themselves to a definite judgement, a point borne out in a study reported in Ellis (1991b). I tested different groups of Chinese and Japanese learners of English on two occasions, one week apart, using sentences with dative verbs (for example, 'show' and 'explain'), and found that the learner frequently changed their judgements (up to 46 per cent of the time in one case). Variability in learners' judgements is therefore a major problem because it casts doubt on the reliability of the grammaticality judgement test.

Many of the problems that Birdsong and I raised may be overcome by better designed tests and by checking reliability. For example, Sorace (1996) has shown that 'magnitude estimation' can provide a more valid and reliable measure of learners' competence. This involves presenting learners with the first sentence in the test, asking them to assign it a numerical value in terms of its acceptability and then requiring them to assign a numerical value to each successive sentence relative to their previous judgement. Reliability can be determined by obtaining a measure of the internal consistency of responses to items in the test or by comparing two separate administrations of the same test. However, UG researchers have rarely examined the reliability of their tests. For example, as I pointed out in Ellis (2004a), of the19 studies published in *Studies in Second Language Acquisition* between 1997 and 2001 that employed some form of GJT, only two reported a measure of reliability. Nor can the need for establishing test reliability be avoided by administering the test to native speakers, as demonstrating that native speakers perform in accordance with the intuitions of the test-designer is no guarantee that the test constitutes a reliable measure for learners.

A more fundamental problem with GJTs concerns their construct validity. As Bialystok's (1979) study indicated, L2 learners make use of both IMPLICIT and EXPLICIT KNOWLEDGE in reaching judgements. Indeed, the very nature of the grammaticality judgement task encourages the use of explicit knowledge. However, as noted above, UG is a theory of *implicit* linguistic knowledge. It might be argued that learners are not likely to have explicit knowledge relating to sentences that violate UG principles, but, as several studies have shown (for example, Seliger 1979; Sorace 1988), learners' explicit knowledge is often anomalous, with the result that their judgement of any sentence, including 'impossible' ones, may be uncertain and inconsistent. Unless some way can be found to ensure that learners do not use their explicit knowledge, it is not clear how the data obtained from such a task can be used to make claims about the role of UG in L2 acquisition.[8] This problem appears to have been overlooked by UG researchers. White (2003a), for example, did not consider it in her own discussion of GJTs, preferring instead to conclude that GJTs are needed because they allow the researcher to investigate aspects of linguistic competence that would otherwise remain inaccessible.

Nevertheless, many of these problems are evident with other data collection methods.[9] All data are performance data of one kind or another and thus pose the question of how to interpret them. We are stuck with the fact that no matter what kind of information we extract from L2 speakers, we need to infer what it is that the data tell us about the learner's L2 knowledge. The key issue is not, then, whether grammaticality judgement tests constitute a non-valid and unreliable measure of what learners know about the L2, but whether the data they provide are more difficult to interpret than data obtained by other means. On this point there is disagreement. But one point is surely clear: UG-based researchers should not simply assume that grammaticality judgement tests give them the data they need to test their theories; they need to convince us that they do.

Increasingly, however, UG-oriented researchers have turned to other means of eliciting data. These include various kinds of production tasks (for example, acting-out tasks or translation tasks) and also interpretation tasks that seek to measure what kind of semantic representation learners assign to sentences. Included among the latter are multiple choice comprehension tests (i.e. learners are shown a sentence and then given two or more possible interpretations of the sentence to select from). Cairns (1999), however, pointed out that because grammars are about 'possibilities' (rather than 'preferences') it is important to ask the participants to identify which choices are disallowed as well as which one they prefer—a point that has not been observed in a number of studies considered below.

2 Design of UG-based studies

Much UG-based research in SLA has been cross-sectional in nature as it has been primarily concerned with the representation of L2 knowledge rather than L2 development. However, there have been a number of pseudo-longitudinal studies (for example, studies that compared groups of learners at different stages of development). What are still largely lacking are controlled longitudinal studies (i.e. studies that experimentally elicit data from a single learner over a period of time). Such studies are essential for examining how UG influences the developmental stages that learners have been shown to pass through.

However, UG researchers have increasingly refined the design of their cross-sectional studies, identifying a number of design features that are important for ensuring the validity of such studies. For example, there is a need to ensure that the learners have the requisite level of L2 proficiency to demonstrate whether or not a particular principle is operating in their interlanguage grammar. Many of the principles identified by UG grammarians involve complex sentences, and can therefore only be expected to manifest themselves in the later stages of development. White argued that it is essential to ensure that subjects are able to handle the necessary structures otherwise 'learners might violate a universal not because of the non-availability of UG, but because the structure in question is beyond their current capacity' (1989a: 61).

It is also essential to rule out the effects of the L1. If subjects act in accordance with UG, this might be because they have direct access to its contents or because they have indirect access through their L1. Early research inspired by the Government/Binding Model assumed that principles could be absent from languages, and investigated cases where speakers of an L1 which apparently lacked a principle were acquiring an L2 where it was apparently present. More recent research inspired by the principles-and-parameters view of Universal Grammar recognizes that principles are universal properties of the architecture of the language faculty, and do not vary from one language to another. Languages do vary, however, in how the mapping from meaning to sound is realized: the parameters of variation between languages. The options for parametric variation are themselves narrowly constrained, and determined by UG. Ruling out the effects of the L1 from this perspective involves investigating speakers of L1s where parameter values are set differently from the L2. Studies of how learners of the same L1 (for example, Chinese) learn two different languages (for example, Japanese and English) that differ with regard to whether a particular universal feature is present, and bi-directional studies (i.e. studies of how speakers of two different languages learn each other's language) are especially important for teasing out whether the learners' L1 or UG is the source of the L2 grammar.

UG researchers have typically included a control group of native speakers of the L2 in their studies. Klein and Martohardjono (1999a) argued that it is essential to compare the variability in native speakers' performance on an elicitation task with that of L2 learners. White (2003a) pointed out that a control group consisting of native speakers of the L1 is also advisable. However, she also noted that interpreting results in terms of a baseline of native speaker runs foul of the comparative fallacy (Bley-Vroman 1983) and that 'the crucial question is whether or not interlanguage grammars are UG-constrained rather than whether or not they are native like' (p. 55).

A further issue concerns the definition of 'adult'. This is of considerable importance, as a UG-based theory of L2 acquisition is, in the main, a theory of adult language acquisition. Child L2 learners are assumed to have the same access to UG as L1 learners.[10] The key issue is whether adult L2 learners are also guided by UG. To examine this issue it is necessary to investigate learners who *started* to learn an L2 in adulthood, but many of the studies do not do this. It is also necessary to determine when 'adulthood' commences. As we noted in Chapter 1, the critical age for grammar (if there is one) appears to be fairly late, around 15 years. Few of the studies to date have examined learners who began their L2 learning after this age.

Another issue—the need to go beyond examining group behaviour—has been clearly recognized by researchers. Group means can hide significant individual learner variation. Ultimately, if L2 acquisition is to be shown to be governed by UG it is necessary to demonstrate that individual learner grammars are in accord with it.

Not all the studies mentioned in the subsequent sections manifest the desirable design features considered above. Differences (and failings) in design may account for the mixed and sometimes inconclusive findings. However, in this respect, UG-based research is arguably no different from other areas of SLA research. It is comforting to note that as time passes the design of the studies has become steadily more thoughtful and rigorous.

Universal grammar and L2 acquisition: theoretical issues

The goal of UG-based SLA research is to investigate whether interlanguage grammars are constrained by the principles of UG. This involves establishing whether learners can reset parameters that differ between the L1 and the L2, and whether they can construct representations involving features not present in their L1s. It also involves considering both representation and the transition from one stage of development to another. It should be noted from the outset that these are separate issues. That is, it is possible that UG principles can be shown to constrain representation without their being involved in L2 development (this being determined by general cognitive processes).

The starting point will be a general account of the principles and parameters that comprise UG. This is followed by a description of how markedness is viewed in terms of the theory. The two central problems—the logical problem of language acquisition and the developmental problem—that inform UG-based research are then addressed. Finally, there is a brief exposition of 'learning principles', which some researchers see as a necessary adjunct to a UG theory of language acquisition.

Principles and parameters

Chomsky defined UG as 'the system of principles, conditions and rules that are elements or properties of all human languages' (1976: 29). Subsequently, Chomsky (1981a) characterized these universals as consisting of principles and parameters. The term PRINCIPLES refers to highly abstract properties of grammar which apply to language in general and which, therefore, underlie the grammatical rules of all specific languages.

The term PARAMETERS refers to the restricted ways in which different languages vary. That is, there is a finite set of options which individual languages draw on and which define the variation possible between languages. Parameters have two or more 'settings', with different languages manifesting different settings. Chomsky (1988) likened parameters to the array of switches found in a switch box; the learner's task is to use experience to determine which position each switch must be in. Principles are independent of parameters in the sense that any one principle constrains the operation of a number of different parameterized areas of the grammar.[11] The goal of generative grammar is to identify the principles and parameters that comprise UG and to specify which principles and which parameters are operative in specific languages.

Markedness

UG provides an alternative basis for determining markedness.[12] The degree of markedness depends on whether a feature is part of the 'core' or the 'periphery'. These notions have already been introduced in Chapter 8. (See Figure 8.1.) The core features of a language are those that are governed by UG, while peripheral features are those that are not. Core features are considered unmarked because they require minimal evidence for acquisition, whereas peripheral features are considered marked because they require much more substantial evidence. The degree of markedness of a feature can also vary within the core, depending on the parameter setting involved. Parameter settings can be ordered according to how marked they are. Thus, for example, Hyams (1983) considered the + null subject setting to be unmarked in relation to – null subject, with Spanish and Italian unmarked with respect to this parameter, and English marked. As White (1989a) pointed out, this view of markedness differs from that found in language typology because markedness is seen as internal to the learner, a consequence of the language faculty, rather than as something external, evident only in extant languages.

It is also possible to identify another rather different definition of markedness based on UG theory. Zobl (1983b) advanced a notion of markedness based on the learner's *projection capacity*, as shown in Figure 12.2. Here, markedness is understood in relation to the amount of primary linguistic evidence needed to acquire a given property. Zobl's PROJECTION HYPOTHESIS considers property z unmarked in relation to v, w, x, and y, on the grounds that the acquisition device does not require any actual experience of z in order to acquire it (i.e. z does not have to be attested in the input to which the learner is exposed). Instead, learners are able to infer the existence of z once they have discovered that certain other properties exist. Clusters of features—such as those associated with the Pro-Drop Parameter—provide a basis for projection; evidence of one feature in a cluster may enable learners to acquire the other features associated with it, irrespective of whether they have experienced these features in the input. Markedness based on a projection model is also a learner-internal phenomenon.

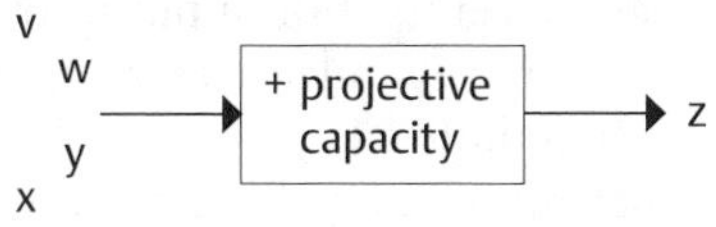

Figure 12.2 A projection model of markedness (Zobl 1983b: 294)

The logical problem of language acquisition

The logical problem of language acquisition needs to be considered separately for L1 and L2 acquisition.

1 The logical problem of L1 acquisition

Chomsky has consistently argued that UG principles are inherently impossible to learn, and that therefore, they must be innate. They make up the 'initial state', and as such provide the basis that enables a child to acquire a language. This position is based on the view that the input to which children are exposed is insufficient to enable them to acquire the grammar of their mother tongue. It is known as the POVERTY OF THE STIMULUS argument.

The LOGICAL PROBLEM OF LANGUAGE ACQUISITION concerns how all children come to acquire with ease and complete success a rich and complex body of linguistic knowledge despite both their lack of cognitive sophistication and insufficient input.

Generative theorists consider the experience which the young child has of the target language to be seriously impoverished in a number of ways. It was initially argued that input is degenerate (see Miller and Chomsky 1963; Chomsky 1965), in the sense that it contains ungrammaticalities and disfluencies which make it an inadequate source of information for language acquisition. The principal argument was that children would find it impossible to distinguish between what is grammatical and what is ungrammatical on the basis of such input. Subsequent research into caretaker talk, however, has demonstrated that simplified input of the kind most children experience in the early stages of acquisition is far less degenerate than was claimed. (See Chapter 6.)

However, the stimulus might be considered 'degenerate' in another way. Wexler and Culicover (1980) argued that the problem lies not in ungrammaticality but in the fact that the input is simplified, as this deprives children of the data they require to learn the more complex aspects of grammar. This view was subsequently endorsed by White (1989a) and Sharwood Smith (1986), among others. There are problems with this argument. First, the fact that the input is 'simplified' does not mean that children are deprived of data on all the grammatical features they have not yet learnt. Even simplified input may supply the child with some new information. Second, the caretaker research shows that input is only temporarily simplified; as the child's ability to understand grows, so the input becomes progressively more complex. (See Chapter 6.) The child, then, receives 'full' input in the course of time. The argument that children do not receive adequate input for acquisition because it is simplified does not seem to hold.

However, there are other more compelling reasons than 'degeneracy' or 'simplification' for considering the input impoverished. Input seriously underdetermines the final grammar. Two related arguments have been advanced to demonstrate this. The first is that the input does not provide the child with the data needed to determine that certain constructions in a language are *not possible*. The second is that certain facts about the grammar of a language are so subtle that it is unrealistic to expect the child to work out that they are in fact *possible*.

A child will only be exposed to a subset of the total sentences possible in the target language and has no way of determining whether a given sentence is not heard because of coincidence (i.e. it just happens that the input to date has not provided evidence of it) or because it is not possible in the language. White (1981a) gave DATIVE ALTERNATION as an example. English permits two constructions with many dative verbs, as in these examples:

Randy gave a present to Mary. (noun phrase (NP) + prepositional phrase (PP))

Randy gave Mary a present. (NP + NP)

However, other dative verbs permit only the NP + PP pattern:

Randy explained the problem to Mary.
*Randy explained Mary the problem.

Supposing the child works out that many verbs allow both patterns, how can the restriction on verbs like 'explain' be discovered? Again, positive evidence will not suffice, as the child has no way of knowing that, in time, sentences with NP + NP will not occur. One way in which this problem might be overcome is if the input provides the child with NEGATIVE EVIDENCE. Logically, there are two kinds of evidence, positive and negative. POSITIVE EVIDENCE comes from exposure to the speech of other speakers, but as we have seen, this is not adequate because it underdetermines the final grammar. It follows that if children are to learn on the basis of input alone they must receive negative evidence, i.e. be given feedback that shows them what is ungrammatical in their sentences. However, as we saw in Chapter 6, children do not typically receive direct negative feedback on the grammaticality of their utterances. If there is no negative feedback, how do children learn that sentences like the last one above are not possible sentences? The answer is that with insufficient positive evidence and no negative evidence they must rely on innate knowledge. Another possible way out of the problem is that children act in accordance with INDIRECT NEGATIVE EVIDENCE. That is, they avoid certain kinds of errors because they never hear anyone produce them. The problem with this argument is that there is ample evidence to show that children do produce errors that they could never have heard in the input. Thus, as White pointed out 'we would need a theory which would explain why children notice the non-occurrence of some sentence types but not others' (1989a: 15). Such a theory would lead, in fact, to claims that children have innate knowledge that guides them in what to avoid. Thus, arguments based on indirect negative evidence cannot replace those based on innateness. Logically, then, it must be assumed that children are prevented from making errors of the kind shown in the sentence above because they are constrained from so doing; UG constitutes the constraint.

More recent expositions of the poverty of the stimulus argument have rested on the claim that certain grammatical properties are so subtle that they cannot be induced from input. That is, UG is required to provide an 'explanation of how it is that learners come to know properties of grammar that go far beyond the input' (White 2003b: 20). A good example of this argument can be found in the Overt Pronoun Constraint. (See Table 12.5.) White (2003b) commented as follows:

> This case constitutes a clear poverty-of-the-stimulus situation. The phenomenon in question is very subtle. In many cases, overt and null pronouns will appear in the same syntactic contexts ... so it is unlikely that the absence of overt pronouns with quantified antecedents would be detected.
> (p. 22)

It would follow that the only way that learners of L2 Spanish (or Japanese which, as a + null subject language, functions like Spanish) can discover the difference in overt and null pronouns is if they are forewarned of it. UG, it is argued, provides such a forewarning.

To sum up, where L1 acquisition is concerned 'plausible theories of language acquisition must assume realistic input' (White 1990: 124). From the preceding arguments two points follow: (1) input alone cannot explain L1 acquisition, and (2) therefore the child must be equipped with knowledge that enables the deficiencies of the input to be overcome. UG assists the child in various ways. First, it ensures that relatively little evidence is needed for the child to determine that a given principle is operative in the target language or to decide which setting of a parameter is the right one. Second, it prevents children from constructing 'wild grammars' (Goodluck 1986). That is, at no point does the child construct a rule that contravenes UG. In this way, the child does not have to unlearn certain types of errors, for which negative evidence would be necessary. Of course, children do produce errors in features like third person –s (for example, 'Mommy like cake'), but these are 'benign' in the sense that they can be unlearnt on the basis of positive evidence. In essence, then, a language is learnable because the child needs to entertain only a small subset of the hypotheses that are consistent with the input data. Generative researchers argue that, without the constraints imposed by UG, L1 acquisition would be at best extremely slow and, in some respects, impossible.

2 The logical problem of L2 acquisition

A number of theorists have argued that the logical problem of language acquisition applies just as much to L2 acquisition as it does to L1 acquisition. Cook (1988), for instance, claimed that, like L1 learners, L2 learners possess knowledge of the L2 that they could not have acquired from the input and which must, therefore, have existed within their own minds. In other words, 'the poverty of the stimulus argument applies equally to L2 learning' (1988: 176). He also argued that imitation, grammatical explanation, correction and approval, social interaction, and dependence on other faculties cannot account for L2 acquisition any more than they can for L1 acquisition. For Cook, the essential difference between L1 and L2 acquisition is that L2 learners already know another language, which may serve as an alternative source to UG.

There are, however, several other significant differences between first and second language learners and it is these that theorists like Bley-Vroman (1989) and White (1989a) pointed to in arguing that the logical problem of language acquisition is somewhat different in the case of L2 acquisition. Bley-Vroman (1988) identified a number of differences (see Table 3.7) and on the basis of these argued:

> The logical problem of foreign language acquisition becomes that of explaining the quite high level of competence that is clearly possible in some cases, while permitting the wide range of variation that is possible. (1989: 49–50)

The question arises as to whether the solution to this logical problem, which is very different from that of L1 acquisition, necessitates an innate domain-specific acquisition system. Bley-Vroman's answer was a definite 'no', but, as we will see, other theorists have been more circumspect. White (1989a: 45), for instance, answered with a 'not sure', pointing out that the differences do not require the abandonment of UG-mediated L2 learning, while also noting that the arguments in favour of it are not clear-cut.

The differences discussed by Bley-Vroman are essentially quantitative in nature. But what if L2 acquisition can be shown to be qualitatively different from L1 acquisition? Schachter (1988) noted that even proficient L2 learners fail to acquire movement rules such as rules relating to topicalization and adverb placement. ('Topicalization' refers to 'the use of various grammatical devices for placing the topic of a sentence in sentence initial position (for example, "As for love, it is no substitute for money")'). Schachter argued that many learners achieve communicative fluency without complete grammatical mastery of the L2. Schachter queried whether any adult L2 learner is capable of achieving a mental state comparable to that achieved by a native speaker of the target language. In other words, she saw the L2 learner's grammatical competence as different in nature from that of the L1 learner. If this view of L2 acquisition is accepted, the logical problem becomes very different—it is that of explaining why L1 and L2 competences are qualitatively different.

White (2003b) emphasized that it is necessary to distinguish two issues: (1) the logical problem and (2) UG availability. She pointed out that it is possible for a logical problem to exist (i.e. whether learners are able to construct a mental representation of the L2 that goes beyond the input) without this necessitating appeal to UG, as learners may be able to overcome the poverty of the stimulus through reliance on their L1. She spelled out two key conditions that must be satisfied to demonstrate that a logical problem exists and that the likelihood is that this can only be overcome by means of UG:

i The phenomenon in question is underdetermined by the L2 input. That is, it must not be something that could have been acquired by simple observation of the L2 input, as an effect of input frequency, or on the basis of instruction, analogical reasoning, etc.

ii The phenomenon in question works differently in the L1 and the L2. If L2 learners show evidence of subtle and abstract knowledge, we want to exclude the possibility that such knowledge is obtained solely via the L1 grammar.
(White 2003b: 23)

To satisfy condition (ii) researchers have looked for cases where the parameter setting for the L1 and the L2 are different (as, for example, in the case of +/– NULL SUBJECT PARAMETER), as was possible when the model informing research was the Government/Binding Model. However, with the Minimalist Program serving as a model it has become increasingly difficult to identify clear differences between the L1 and the L2 except, of course, at the level of surface structure.[13]

In summary, there are different positions regarding the logical problem of L2 acquisition. One is that it is essentially the same as for L1 acquisition. Another is that it is different because L2 learners achieve variable success. A third is that it is different because L2 competence is qualitatively different from L1 competence. These positions lead to different views regarding the role of UG in L2 acquisition. To establish whether there is indeed a logical problem of L2 acquisition and whether this implicates UG, it is necessary to show not only that the L2 input underdetermines acquisition of a specific property of the L2, but also that this property is not available to the learner via the L1.

The developmental problem of L2 acquisition

As Hyams (1991) pointed out, there are in fact two problems that need to be addressed: the 'logical problem', which 'treats acquisition as an instantaneous process', and the DEVELOPMENTAL PROBLEM, which recognizes that acquisition is non-instantaneous. The developmental problem addresses whether UG plays a role in the order and sequence of acquisition. (See Chapter 3.) It poses two questions. Why do learners acquire some grammatical features before others? Why do they pass through developmental stages en route to the final state? There are three possible answers to these questions: (1) UG is subject to maturation, (2) access to UG principles and parameters is governed by markedness considerations, and (3) UG interacts with other cognitive mechanisms to determine developmental patterns.

The order of L1 acquisition might be explained by proposing that the entire contents of UG are not available to the learner immediately but become accessible at different points in time. That is, as Felix (1984) suggested, UG is subject to maturation with different principles and parameters becoming operative as acquisition proceeds. He claimed that 'the principles of Universal Grammar are themselves subject to an innately specified developmental process'—they emerge rather like teeth, in a predetermined sequence. Eubank's (1994) Valueless Features Hypothesis also claimed that access to UG changes over time. According to this hypothesis, feature strength (an abstract property of language that has consequences for word order) is initially inert, leading to optional adverb placement in sentences like:

Simon often attends football games.
*Simon attends often football games.

But such optionality disappears later on when learners access and set the parameter affecting feature strength.

Both the order and sequence of acquisition, however, could also be explained by positing that the entire contents of UG are available from the start. Such a non-maturational view of UG (as preferred by White 1981) still allows for a consideration of 'learning difficulty' if this is defined in terms of markedness. That is, learners' access to the principles and parameters is governed by whether they are marked or unmarked, with unmarked features requiring less elaborate triggering experience than marked ones. This proposal requires ordering parameters according to markedness, so that children automatically opt for an unmarked before a marked parameter and by so doing avoid building grammars that cannot subsequently be disconfirmed.

The third possibility is that there is an interaction between UG and the language parser (the mechanism responsible for processing input data), such that a certain principle is only triggered when the child is capable of perceiving the relevant input data. This is the explanation preferred by many generative theorists because it suggests that the developmental nature of L1 acquisition is the product of non-linguistic rather than linguistic factors. Researchers differ, however, regarding whether this interaction is or is not of theoretical interest.

Cook (1985) distinguished 'acquisition' and 'development'. 'Development' refers to real-time learning of a language and is influenced by non-linguistic factors such as CHANNEL CAPACITY. 'Acquisition' is language learning unaffected by maturation, and is therefore dependent entirely on the learner's language faculty (including Universal Grammar). According to this view, studies based on the analysis of performance data (for example, naturally occurring speech) only provide evidence of 'development'. In Chomsky's words, they are 'concerned with matters that may not properly belong to the language faculty' (1980: 53) and provide evidence only of the 'fluttering notions of a fledgling before the organs of flight mature' (1981a: 35). It follows from such a view that the main goal of an explanatory theory of language is to explain 'acquisition' rather than 'development'. In other words, proponents of this position argue that UG-based SLA should concern itself with 'representation' only. Cook claimed that 'acquisition' can only be examined in terms of 'an idealized "instantaneous" model in which time and experience play minimal roles' (1988: 81) and went on to argue that notions like 'order' and 'sequence', which, as we have seen, are the focus of much L2 research, have no clear place in such a model, as they only reflect the learner's developing channel capacity rather than 'acquisition' itself.

However, not all researchers working within a UG framework reject developmental data. Klein and Martohardjono (1999a), for example, argued strongly that there is a need to examine the role that UG plays in the steps involved in grammar construction rather than just focusing on representational issues. They presented a detailed specification of this role, arguing that the crucial issue is what constitutes 'triggering' for the restructuring of grammars. Their proposal is considered in a later section of this chapter.

Approaches to investigating the role of UG

This section provides an account of the different approaches that UG-based researchers have adopted. It serves as a basis for an examination of a number of UG-based empirical studies of L2 acquisition in the following section.

The poverty of the stimulus approach

Probably the predominant approach to investigating the role of UG has been to ask 'Do adult L2 learners have access to UG when learning an L2? As R. Hawkins (2001a) pointed out, this approach is motivated by the 'POVERTY OF THE STIMULUS' argument. It entails identifying whether a specific principle, realized in the L2 but not in the learners' L1 and not derivable from the input, is manifested in the grammar that L2 learners construct. If the principle can be shown to be acquired by the adult L2 learners in these circumstances, then this constitutes evidence that UG is still available to them. This approach has been subjected to recent criticism. Hawkins argued that it does little more than demonstrate whether UG is involved in L2 acquisition—'it does not go beyond offering glimpses of UG in SLA' (p. 353). He claimed that what is important is to explain within a UG framework why L2 learners behave differently in their use of the L2 from native speakers. White (2003b) also considered that the focus on access to UG, which the poverty of stimulus approach gave rise to, is limiting. She argued that terms like direct/full or indirect/partial access, which this approach gave rise to, were 'too global' and proposed that 'what is required is a greater focus on the nature of the representations that L2 learners achieve' (p. 27). As we will see later in this chapter the research based on the poverty of the stimulus approach has failed to produce a conclusive answer to the question that informed it.

Investigating the nature of L2 representations

White (2003b) noted that in the 1990s there was a shift in the approach adopted by UG-based researchers. Instead of attempting to demonstrate whether learners had broad access to UG, researchers focused narrowly on specific grammatical properties in order to investigate the nature of L2 representations. The key question they now addressed was 'Is the divergence evident between the L2 grammar and the target language grammar evidence of an impairment in UG or does it reflect UG?' In other words, it was now accepted that failure to manifest the grammatical properties of the target language need not reflect a lack of access to UG, as the L2, while clearly differing from the target language, might yet still accord with the constraints imposed by UG. In essence, then, this approach sought to establish whether or not L2 grammars belonged to the canon of natural languages or whether they constituted WILD GRAMMARS. As White noted, this new concern for representation led to studies that explored the L2 initial state.

Investigating L1–L2 differences

In contrast, the final approach focuses on the L2 final state and asks 'What L1–L2 differences are there and can these be explained by UG?' This is the approach that R. Hawkins (2001b) favoured. A difference-oriented approach attempts 'to explain why there might be observable differences between child L1 learners and adult L2 learners on the basis of how UG, the L1, primary data and perhaps other factors interact' (p. 348). The concern here is again to examine whether L2 representations fall within the 'epistemological space' defined by UG rather than whether L1 and L2 representations are the same. As with the previous approach, the emphasis is on the role that UG plays in L2 representations rather than whether L2 learners have access to UG. Hawkins considered this approach important because it provided a test of the rival claims of linguists such as Newmeyer (1998) and SLA researchers such as Bley-Vroman (1989) who considered L2 grammars as fundamentally different from L1 grammars because they are derived from general cognitive abilities rather than UG (i.e. the Fundamental Difference Hypothesis) and SLA researchers such as Robinson (1996a) who argue in favour of the Fundamental Similarity Hypothesis.

Empirical studies of second language acquisition based on Universal Grammar

Since the publication of Chomsky's *Lectures on Government and Binding* in 1981, UG-based studies of L2 acquisition have proliferated. No attempt will be made to provide a full survey of these. (See White (2003a) for a full account and the journal *Second Language Research* for recent papers.) Instead, I will focus on representative studies that have addressed a number of areas of UG—the Subjacency Principle, the Binding of Anaphors, the Null Subject Parameter, Argument Structure, and Functional Features. Each of these areas has attracted substantial interest from SLA researchers. I will first provide a brief and non-technical account of each area, followed by a review of SLA studies that have investigated it.

The Subjacency Principle

1 An account of the Subjacency Principle

SUBJACENCY defines the restrictions that govern how far one phrase can be moved from 'deep' to 'surface' structure. Thus, questions like:

What did Randy think?
What did Randy think his brother had won?

are grammatical because they involve limited movement of the WH–element (i.e. 'what') from the deep structure object position:

Randy thought _____
Randy thought his brother had won _____

whereas sentences like the following are ungrammatical:

*What did Randy wonder whether his brother would win?

because they involve movement of the WH–element from a 'remote' deep structure position:

Randy wondered whether his brother would win _____

In the Government/Binding Model, movement is discussed very precisely in terms of the restrictions imposed by 'bounding nodes', which for English consist of noun phrase, embedded sentence, and sentence. According to Berwick and Weinberg (1984) 'movement may not cross more than one bounding node' at a time. Thus, the first two sentences above are grammatical because the WH–element does not cross more than one bounding node, whereas the third sentence is ungrammatical because it crosses two embedded sentence nodes.

As R. Hawkins (2001a) noted 'if constituents do not move they cannot give rise to subjacency violations' (p. 273). Such is the case with a language such as Korean, which has no WH–phrase movement. There can also be crosslinguistic differences as to what constitutes a bounding node. However, if subjacency is a principle of UG, and L2 learners have continued access to UG, then Korean learners should have no difficulty in acquiring English WH–phrase movement.

Later accounts of subjacency took into account the fact that it was not just a question of how far a constituent moved but also both the type of constituent being moved and where it moved from. Thus, movement of a direct object results in a milder kind of ungrammaticality than movement of an adverb as illustrated by these sentences:

?What did they ask whether she could cook?
*How quickly did they ask if she could cook a curry?

This difference concerns the relative difficulty of interpreting the WH–phrase/trace relation. That is, it is much more difficult to interpret WH–questions involving adjunct extraction than direct object extraction. These facts led Chomsky (1986b) to propose the notion of 'barriers' in place of 'bounding nodes' to account for subjacency; that is, what determined whether extraction was possible was the particular structural configuration involved. The more intervening barriers there are the stronger ungrammaticality becomes. This reworking of the Subjacency Principle invites the question as to whether L2 learners can detect degrees of ungrammaticality in WH–questions depending on the number of barriers involved.

2 *SLA research investigating the Subjacency Principle*

The studies we will consider here all sought to investigate whether learners had continued access to UG. That is, they were predicated on the assumption that subjacency cannot be acquired from the input and that, therefore, if L2 learners demonstrate they have acquired knowledge of it, this must be because they can access the principle and so UG must be intact. The focus of these studies has been adult learners, although one study (Johnson and Newport 1991) also examined subjacency in younger L2 learners. The method of data collection involved grammaticality judgement tests, although some studies supplemented this with an interpretation task.

Bley-Vroman, Felix, and Ioup (1988) investigated 92 advanced Korean learners of L2 English, most of whom had been living in the United States for several years, and as a result of which they had had plenty of opportunity to learn naturalistically. Korean is not constrained by subjacency in WH–questions. The grammaticality judgement test required the subjects to indicate whether sentences were grammatical or ungrammatical, or whether they were not sure. The sentences involved WH–movement. There were also a number of sentences which did not involve the principle and which were used as controls. The results showed a response bias (the learners manifested a tendency to reject sentences irrespective of whether they were grammatical or ungrammatical) and a reluctance to make use of the 'not sure' option. However, they also showed that the learners were not guessing at random; that is, the typical response pattern resembled that of the native speakers. Bley-Vroman *et al.* concluded: 'Given these results, it is extremely difficult to maintain the hypothesis that Universal Grammar is inaccessible to adult learners' (1988: 26).

Further evidence for adult learners' continuing access to UG comes from a study by White, Travis, and Maclachlan (1992). This study looked at Malagasy learners of English, Malagasy being a language that permits extraction from complex subjects in WH–interrogatives where English does not. Thus, if the learners rejected sentences manifesting subject-extraction, this could not be explained by L1 transfer. Results from a grammaticality judgement test and a written elicited production task showed that nearly all the high-intermediate learners and half of the low-intermediate learners rejected subjacency violations. White *et al.* argued that those subjects who accepted sentences that violated this UG principle did so only because they had not reached a stage of syntactical development for the Subjacency Principle to become active (i.e. they had not yet acquired WH–movement).

Whereas Bley-Vroman *et al.*'s, and White *et al.*'s studies both supported the 'UG is alive' position, Schachter's (1989) study indicated the opposite. Schachter's participants were learners whose L1 did not reflect subjacency in

WH–questions (Korean), learners whose L1 provided only weak evidence of subjacency-based rules in WH–questions (Chinese), and learners whose L1 clearly manifested subjacency but not in WH–movement (Indonesian). In addition, there was a group of native speakers of English to act as controls. Schachter administered a grammaticality judgement test designed to assess whether the subjects had developed sufficient knowledge of the grammatical structures involved, in addition to the tests intended to show whether they violated the Subjacency Principle in different grammatical contexts. The native speakers passed both the syntax and the subjacency tests. However, many of the learners passed only the syntax test—they exhibited knowledge of the relevant syntactic construction without corresponding knowledge of the subjacency constraint. That is, the behaviour of the learners was significantly different from that of the native speakers. The Korean learners performed worse than the Chinese and Indonesian learners although this difference was not significant. Schachter concluded that even if subjacency was instantiated in the learners' L1, it did not guarantee access to it in the L2. She claimed that the results constituted 'a serious challenge' to the claim that UG is available to adult L2 learners.

Johnson and Newport (1991) also set out to examine whether the Subjacency Principle (and therefore UG) was available to L2 learners. This study is of special interest because it compared young L2 learners (L1 = Chinese) who had been living in the US for more than five years but had arrived before the age of 16 with a similar group who had had the same number of years of exposure but did not arrive until they were 18 or older. The older immersion learners varied widely in their ability to detect subjacency violations in a grammaticality judgement test. Whereas a control group of native speakers rejected on average 35 out of 36 sentences, these learners rejected on average only 22. In a detailed analysis of the subjacency violations by type, Johnson and Newport found that the learners in this group did demonstrate knowledge that some types of sentences were ungrammatical but not others. They experienced less difficulty with sentences involving extraction from noun phrases modified by relative clauses. There was also a considerable difference between the young and old arrival groups. Those learners who arrived between the ages of 4 and 7 were not significantly different from the native speakers. However, learners who arrived after the age of 7 performed differently and the difference became stronger with increasing age. Johnson and Newport concluded that whereas the very young arrivals had access to UG, the older arrivals had only partial access.

Later studies drew on the grammatical arguments which Chomsky (1986) presented in *Barriers* (a later framework than the *Government/Binding Model* used in the earlier studies). These studies continued to be concerned with whether L2 learners had access to UG but they also focused on the nature of the representations that learners formed about extraction in WH–questions. In particular, they sought to establish whether learners, like native speakers, demonstrated awareness of degrees of grammaticality depending on the site of extraction (for example, direct object or adjunct).

Uziel (1993) investigated whether L2 learners evidenced greater difficulty with extraction from complex subjects than with object-extraction. He hypothesized that subject-extraction would be rejected at a higher rate than object-extraction because it violates two principles (subjacency and another), whereas object-extraction violates only subjacency. He presented results that supported this hypothesis from a small-scale study involving grammaticality judgements by 11 adult Italian and 10 adult Hebrew ESL learners. This study, then, suggests that UG principles can help to explain why learners find some syntactic constructions more acceptable than others.

Two other studies lend support to the conclusion that L2 learners are differentially sensitive to 'strong' and 'weak' subjacency violations. Martohardjono (1993) investigated groups of advanced L2 learners of Chinese, Indonesian, and Italian by asking them to judge sentences that included strong violations (for example, extractions from relative clauses and adjunct clauses) and weak violations (for example, extractions from WH–islands). While there were differences among the L2 groups, the groups were similar in their relative ability to judge strong and weak violations. This suggests that the learners were utilizing UG in their judgements. Li (1998) investigated whether Chinese learners of L2 English, including those who had spent time in the US and those who had not, distinguished between strong and weak subjacency violations. There were differences between the US-based and China-based groups, with the former performing like native speakers, but both learner groups rejected strong violations to a greater extent than weak violations. The results obtained from the grammaticality judgement test in this study were confirmed by an interpretation test, which asked learners to specify the site of extraction in WH–questions.

There is, however, a problem with these studies. This concerns the uncertainty regarding the nature of learners' judgements when asked to judge the grammaticality of sentences like:

What did Bill think that the teacher had said?
*What did Sam believe the claim that Carol had bought?
(from Bley-Vroman *et al.* 1988: 8)

Bley-Vroman *et al.* noted that the results they obtained may have reflected ease of parsing rather than UG effects. This hypothesis has been given support by a study by Schachter and Yip (1990), which produced clear evidence of processing effects in both native speakers' and learners' judgements of sentences involving WH–movement. Both sets of learners found it more difficult to make accurate judgements in sentences with three clauses than in sentences with a single clause. Schachter and Yip suggested that this is because subjects have to keep the WH–word in short-term memory until they discover the clause in which it fits. The learners also performed much less accurately with sentences where the WH–extraction involved grammatical subjects than when it involved objects, irrespective of the number of clauses involved. In other words, both native speakers and learners treated grammatical extraction from object and subject positions differently. Schachter and Yip argued that this could not be explained by reference to UG and thus constituted further evidence of processing factors at work. However, the switch to a 'barriers' explanation of subjacency would seem to address this point, as this takes into account the extraction site. But Schachter and Yip's general point remains intact: it is still possible that the increased sensitivity that learners show to strong violations of the Subjacency Principle have nothing to do with UG and everything to do with their ability to process the sentences as input. It is, in fact, unclear how a UG explanation and a processing explanation can be distinguished. Thus, Schachter and Yips' warning that researchers should be circumspect in accepting 'pure grammatical explanations' still needs to be heeded.[14]

The Binding Principle for Anaphors

1 An account of the Binding Principle for Anaphors

The following account of the BINDING PRINCIPLE FOR ANAPHORS is a summary of the key points in R. Hawkins (2001a). The Binding Principle governs the use of anaphors such as reflexive pronouns. It states 'an anaphor must be bound in its binding domain' and accounts for the fact that a reflexive pronoun (for example, 'himself' and 'herself') must have an antecedent that it is bound to and this antecedent must be present within the 'binding domain' permitted by the target language. Thus, sentences such as the following are grammatical in English:

> Fred planned to kill *himself*. (bound by subject)
> Fred asked Cynthia some questions about *himself*. (bound by subject)
> Fred asked Cynthia some questions about *herself*. (bound by object)
> Cynthia believed that Fred was going to kill *himself*. (bound by subject of the subordinate clause)
> Cynthia wanted Mike to ask Fred some questions about *himself*. (bound by object of the non-finite clause)

whereas the following are ungrammatical:

> **Himself* asked Cynthia. (the anaphor cannot be the subject of a tensed clause)
> *Cynthia believed that Fred was going to kill *herself*. (the anaphor cannot be bound to an antecedent outside the finite clause in which it occurs)
> *Cynthia did not want Fred to kill *herself*. (the anaphor cannot be bound to an antecedent outside the non-finite clause in which it occurs)

However, whereas the Binding Principle is an invariant property of human language, languages vary in the binding domains that regulate anaphors. Wexler and Mancini's (1987) Governing Category Principle distinguished five different binding domains that can be found cross-linguistically. The different binding domains constitute the parameters of this principle. For example, whereas the binding domain for finite and non-finite clauses is the same in English (i.e. it excludes the subject of the main clause), in Russian the anaphor in a non-finite clause (but not the anaphor of a finite clause) can be bound with the subject of the main clause. In Chinese and Japanese, however, binding with the subject of the main clause can take place with anaphors in finite subordinate clauses.

Whereas the early generative accounts focused on the relationship between the anaphor and its antecedent (as in the above account), later work has addressed the nature of anaphor itself and the role that it plays in determining what antecedents are possible. Anaphors differ in terms of whether they are morphologically complex reflexives (as in English) or bare reflexives (for example, 'ziji' (= 'self') in Chinese or 'zibun' (= 'self') in Japanese). This distinction is linked to whether the anaphor permits only local binding or long-distance binding. Phrasal/complex reflexives only allow local binding (i.e. within the clause) whereas bare reflexives allow long-distance binding (i.e. the anaphor in a subordinate clause can bind with the subject of the main clause). However, interestingly, Chinese and Japanese also possess morphologically complex anaphors (for example, the Chinese 'taziji' (= 'he-self'). These languages, then, are characterized by both local and long-distance binding. There is also a link between orientation and local/distant binding. Long-distance anaphors (i.e. bare reflexives) must be subject-oriented, whereas local anaphors (i.e. complex reflexives) allow non-subject antecedents. In this reworking of the Binding Principle, then, binding domains are no longer defined independently as in Wexler's and Mancini's formulation, but are linked to the anaphor itself.

Questions of some interest, then, concern how Chinese and Japanese learners will interpret sentences such as:

Cynthia knew that Mary liked herself a lot.
Cynthia asked Mary about herself.

Do they recognize that 'herself' in the first of these sentences can refer only to Mary or do they see the sentence as ambiguous because it can refer to either Cynthia or Mary? Do they recognize that 'herself' in the second sentence can refer to both Cynthia and Mary and thus is ambiguous or do they interpret it as binding only with Mary, in accordance with how the bare reflexive in their L1 works?

2 *SLA research investigating the Binding Principle for Anaphors*

The problems in arriving at definite conclusions regarding access to UG and its role in L2 representations are also evident in the second principle we will consider—the Binding Principle for Anaphors. R. Hawkins (2001a) spelled out four problems that researchers addressing this principle have faced: (1) researchers need to be sure that the learners they are studying are able to distinguish between a pronoun and anaphor (for example, 'him' and 'himself'). If they are treating anaphors as pronouns then the Binding Principle does not apply. (2) They need to determine whether the learners are treating an anaphor as complex (polymorphemic) or bare (monomorphemic). Exposing learners to complex reflexives (for example, 'himself') in a grammaticality judgement test does not mean that the learners in fact perceive them as complex. (3) Researchers also need to determine whether learners have assigned local binding on the basis of the type of reflexive (i.e. the fact that it is complex) or on the basis of the presence of agreement inflections in the subordinate clause, as these can also signal that local binding is required. (4) Finally, researchers need to establish whether learners' interpretation of anaphors as locally bound simply reflects ease of processing (i.e. in complex sentences they find it easier to choose the closest antecedent) rather than some biologically endowed principle. Hawkins commented 'all of these factors make it difficult to draw firm conclusions currently about how performance data from L2 learners might relate to underlying knowledge of binding and to what extent UG, the L1 and the ability to reset parameters are involved' (p. 312).

There is an additional problem. Sentences require interpretation and interpretation is context-dependent. When presented with isolated sentences learners may attempt to construct a context for themselves to aid their interpretation and this may distract them, interfering with performance. Ying's (2005) study of reflexive anaphora in verb phrase ellipsis (i.e. in sentences such as 'John defended himself and Bill did too') demonstrated that L2 learners' interpretations vary depending on whether a context is provided or they have to construct a context for themselves. Ying's point is that 'L2 learners' language parsing mechanisms (or central processes) appear to be relevance-constrained' (p. 183). If this is so, the separation between linguistic and pragmatic processing that underscores UG-based research cannot be sustained.

There are three crucial aspects of reflexive binding to be considered: (1) domain (local versus non-local binding), (2) type of anaphor (complex versus bare), and (3) orientation (subject versus object binding). These aspects are interrelated (for example, complex anaphors only permit local binding; agreement inflections in a finite subordinate clause are linked to local binding) and it is their interrelationship that is in fact crucial. The studies summarized in Table 12.4 have investigated these interrelationships. They have primarily addressed whether UG is available to L2 learners, but some of the later studies have examined learners' representations of reflexives in depth. A few of the studies have also made passing reference to the L1 acquisition of reflexives—for example, Yuan (1998) noted that Chinese children opt for local binding of 'ziji' initially in much the same way as do English learners of L2 Chinese.

In general, the studies in Table 12.4 show that L2 learners do master the properties associated with the binding of anaphors (although they do not typically achieve the same degree of accuracy as native speakers). The key questions, however, are: (1) Is it possible to demonstrate that what learners acquire is underdetermined by the input and not the result of L1 transfer? (2) Is there any evidence of 'wild grammars'? All the studies in Table 12.4 simply assume that the binding properties of reflexives cannot be acquired from the input—there is no attempt to demonstrate this empirically. A number of studies failed to control for the L1 transfer. Hirakawa (1990), for example, failed to allow for the fact that Japanese has both a bare reflexive and complex reflexives and thus that acquisition of local binding in L2 English by her Japanese learners was not due to transfer. Other studies, however, did ensure that any learning could not be the result of L1 transfer. For example, Yuan's (1998) English learners of Chinese could not have acquired the distant binding rule of Chinese through L1 transfer as English has no bare equivalent of Chinese 'ziji'. A number of studies sought to answer question (1) by demonstrating a clustering effect but the results have been mixed. Christie and Lantolf (1998) failed to find any evidence of clustering, but Thomas (1998) questioned the linguistic facts on which they based their hypotheses about clustering effects. Another obvious problem with studies like Christie and Lantolf's (1998) and Akiyama's (2002) is that learners' failure to demonstrate acquisition of a cluster of reflexive features may simply reflect the fact that they have not yet reached a stage of development where this is possible. The better studies (for example, Akiyama's) did examine learners across a range of proficiency levels but there is no guarantee that even the most 'advanced' learners in these studies were 'ready' to acquire what are obviously very complex structures. Such a conclusion is supported by White's (1995) failure to find any effect for either explicit or implicit instruction on learners' acquisition of reflexive binding in English. Bennett and Progovac (1998) provided some of the best evidence to answer question (1) in the affirmative. They showed that some of the properties acquired by their Serbo-Croatian learners of L2 English could not have been derived from either the L1 or the L2, although they nevertheless still constituted an authorized parameter setting of UG.

A number of the studies have provided evidence of 'wild grammars'. Thomas (1995) reported that six low-proficiency learners and one advanced learner allowed long-distance object orientations, which is not a property of any natural language. Other studies (for example, Yuan 1998 and Christie and Lantolf 1998) also found that some of their learners behaved similarly. White (2003a) suggested that it is not unreasonable to allow a certain amount of 'noise' in the data, but this raises the thorny question (which White acknowledged) about the falsifiability of UG-based hypotheses, which, as noted earlier, apply to individuals, not just groups.

It is difficult to reach any clear conclusions from the binding studies regarding whether interlanguage is UG constrained. There is some (rather limited) evidence that learners construct grammars that could not have been derived from either their L1 or the L2, but there is also evidence of 'wild grammars'. Also, as R. Hawkins (2001a) pointed out, it is not really possible to rule out processing problems as an explanation for the findings.

Study	Participants	Research question(s)	Instruments	Main results
Finer and Broselow (1986)	6 adult Korean ESL learners in the US	Do Korean learners of English demonstrate local or distance binding in sentences with finite and non-finite clauses?	A picture identification task—learners asked to indicate whether a particular sentence matched a picture.	Learners treated reflexives in finite subordinate clauses as locally bound but reflexives in non-finite clauses as both locally and distantly bound.
Hirakawa (1990)	65 Japanese learners of L2 English in Japan	Do Japanese learners of English judge binding of reflexives in accordance with their L1 or UG?	Multiple choice grammaticality judgement test (participants given five choices for each sentence).	The learners allowed both local and distant binding in English where they allowed only distant binding in Japanese. Also, they were more likely to incorrectly accept local and distant binding in non-finite subordinate clauses than in finite clauses.
Thomas (1995)	58 high- and low-proficiency learners of L2 Japanese (including learners with L1s that permit local or long-distance binding)	Do learners of L2 Japanese accept long-distance binding with objects as well as subjects?	Grammaticality judgement test—sentences presented in the context of a story.	The high-proficiency learners generally rejected long-distance binding with objects but accepted it with subjects. The low-proficiency learners allowed long-distance binding with both objects and subjects.
White (1995)	30 adult learners of L2 English (19 francophone and 11 Japanese) in an intensive ESL summer program	Do learners of L2 English discover that long-distance binding is impossible when they are given explicit or implicit instruction showing that English allows binding to objects?	(1) A self-paced grammaticality judgement task to investigate number and gender agreement of English reflexives (2) A truth-value judgement task—students read a story and then indicated whether a statement was true or false.	No difference between francophone and Japanese learners. No evidence that lack of binding to objects and possibility of distant binding were linked. No evidence that either treatment led to improvement in the participants' knowledge of English reflexive binding.
Yuan (1998)	81 learners of L2 Chinese (58 = L1 English; 24 = L1 Japanese)	Are there any differences in the acquisition of the binding value of 'ziji' by learners with English and Japanese as their L1?	Multiple choice comprehension test—each sentence followed by three choices.	Japanese learners found it easier to acquire long-distance binding properties of 'ziji' than the English learners. English learners more likely to allow long-distance binding in non-finite clauses. Three intermediate English learners allowed long-distance binding with object.

Christie and Lantolf (1998)	92 learners and 38 NSs distributed in four groups: (1) English learners of L2 Chinese; (2) Chinese learners of L2 English; (3) English learners of L2 Spanish; and (4) Spanish learners of L2 English	To what extent do interlanguage grammars show evidence of clustering effect (e.g. involving local/distant binding with subject/object)?	Interpretation task—participants listen to or read a sentence and then choose which of two interpretations matches with a picture.	Cluster analysis provided no evidence of any clustering of the binding aspects in either learners or native speakers. There was some evidence of 'wild grammars'—3 advanced English learners of Chinese allowed binding of 'ziji' to both a subject and object antecedent.
Bennett and Progovac (1998)	73 Serbo-Croatian learners of L2 English; native-speaker controls of both Serbo-Croatian and English	Do learners transfer parameter settings for reflexives from their L1? Are the principles of UG still operative in the L2?	(1) A picture identification task (which of four pictures matched a sentence?) (2) multiple choice comprehension task.	The adolescent learners allowed long-distance binding by the matrix subject in sentences like 'Alex forced John to listen to himself', where 'Alex' is not a possible antecedent for native speakers. The learners allowed 'himself' to be bound by 'Alex', which is not attested in either English input or in Serbo-Croat.
Akiyama (2002)	411 Japanese learners of English divided into five proficiency levels; Japanese and English NS controls	Do Japanese learners of English learn that local binding of reflexives is required in embedded 'that' clauses and in infinitival clauses?	A story-based truth value judgement task as in White (1995).	(1) The locality condition is acquired better in 'that' clauses than in infinitival clauses; (2) this difference is evident at all proficiency levels; (3) 35% of the advanced learners had failed to acquire the locality condition in infinitival clauses.

Table 12.4 Selected studies investigating reflexive binding in an L2

The Null Subject Parameter

1 An account of the Null Subject Parameter

Languages vary according to whether they require an overt subject pronoun or allow it to be dropped. English, for example, is a – null subject language and so does not normally delete pronouns:

*Is the President of the United States.

Spanish, on the other hand, is a + null subject language and permits pronoun subjects to be dropped:

Es el Presidente de los Estados Unidos.

The NULL SUBJECT PARAMETER, therefore, 'determines whether the subject of a clause can be suppressed' (Chomsky 1988: 64). In this case, there are just two settings, whereas other parameters, such as the Binding Principle for Anaphors, may have multiple settings.

Parameters, like null subject are of considerable interest to linguists and, as we will see, also to SLA researchers. One reason is that the Null Subject Parameter is associated with a number of other linguistic features. That is, it is linked with a cluster of features. Chomsky (1981b) proposed that languages with null subjects, like Spanish and Italian, also have verb-subject word order as in

Viene la chica (Is coming the girl)
La chica viene (The girl is coming)

and 'that'-trace effects as in

Chi ha detto che e venuto?

In contrast, – null subject languages like English have expletives (for example, 'it' and 'there') and manifest a fixed word order with the subject placed invariably before the verb in declarative sentences:

*Is coming the girl.
The girl is coming.
*Who have you said that is come?
(Examples from Gass 1989: 509)

The Morphological Uniformity Principle (Jaeggli and Safir 1989) proposed a somewhat different cluster of features. This links subject drop with morphological uniformity (i.e. either all verbs are inflected, as in Spanish, or none, as in Japanese). In contrast, – null subject languages like English are less uniform (for example, English verbs manifest some but rather limited inflections). Huang (1984) proposed that there is also a link between the Null Subject Parameter and another parameter—the Discourse Oriented Parameter, which accounts for the topic-prominent structure of languages like Japanese. Thus, whereas Japanese is + discourse oriented and + null subject, and English is

– discourse oriented and – null subject, Spanish is – discourse oriented but + null subject. SLA researchers have examined a number of hypotheses based on these properties of the Null Subject Parameter: (1) they have hypothesized that because these various features are linked in UG they should be acquired simultaneously, and (2) they have hypothesized that there will be differences in the way in which Japanese and Spanish learners acquire L2 English.

There have also been attempts to examine the features of the Null Subject Parameter from the perspective of the Minimalist Program (MP). These will not be described here (but see Wakabayashi (2002) for an account). Suffice it to say, that an MP account emphasizes that syntactic knowledge is derived from the lexicon, which includes both substantive and functional items. This leads to the proposal that L1 transfer plays a major role and that it constitutes a gradual process as the L2 lexicon expands. Wakabayashi also showed how the MP can account for the difference between two + null subject languages like Spanish and Japanese.

Finally, more recent linguistic research has shown that pronouns in – null subject languages and + null subject languages work in subtly different ways. White (2003a), drawing on Montalbetti's (1984) Overt Pronoun Constraint, pointed out that embedded subject pronouns in – null subject languages like English can have a quantified noun phrase as an antecedent as in:

Everyone thinks he is right (where 'he' refers to 'everyone')

and can also be co-referential with a WH–question word:

Who thinks he is right? (He thinks he is right.)

Null subjects in languages like Spanish behave similarly to English overt pronouns; that is, they can take both referential and quantified antecedents. Overt pronouns in + null subject languages, however, behave differently in that they cannot have the same kind of bound interpretations with a quantified antecedent as pronouns in – null subject languages, but they can take a referential antecedent. The differences between the way pronouns work in + and – null subject languages is summarized in Table 12.5. As White demonstrated, the differences are very subtle, raising the question as to whether L2 learners are able to discover them.

	+ Null subject languages		- Null subject languages
	Null subjects	Overt subjects	Overt subjects
Referential antecedents	Yes	Yes	Yes
Quantified antecedents	Yes	No	Yes

Table 12.5 Antecedents for pronouns in null and overt subject languages (from White 2003a: 8)

2 *SLA research investigating the Null Subject Parameter*

Early studies based on the Null Subject Parameter studies investigated whether the cluster of properties associated with this parameter were acquired simultaneously. Initially, these studies focused on learners of L2 English whose L1 was Spanish, Italian, or Greek (all of which are + null subject languages). Subsequently, they considered learners of L2 English with Chinese, Korean, or Japanese as their L1 (languages that also license null subjects but which also lack person and number inflections and licence topic-orientation).

Two early studies by White (1985; 1986) indicated that initially L2 learners opt for the L1 setting of the Null Subject Parameter (referred to in these studies as the Pro-Drop Parameter), but that as their proficiency increases they switch to the L2 setting. White also investigated whether pro-drop features cluster in interlanguage grammars. The participants in the 1985 study were Spanish and French learners of L2 English, while the 1986 study also included two Italian learners. The learners were asked to judge sentences, including some with missing pronoun subjects (both expletives, 'it' and 'there', and referential pronouns, such as 'he' and 'she'), some with ungrammatical subject-verb inversion, and some with a 'that' trace. White found clear evidence of differences in the performance of the Spanish and Italian learners compared to the French. They were more inclined to accept subjectless sentences. Also, of those subjects who demonstrated the necessary syntactical development, the Spanish learners were more likely to accept 'that'-trace than the French. However, there was no difference in their judgements of sentences with ungrammatical subject-verb inversion. The accuracy level of the learners' judgements improved in accordance with their overall proficiency. The data from White's question-formation task lent support to the results obtained from the grammaticality judgement task. That is, the Spanish subjects were more likely to produce a 'that'-trace in WH–questions than the French, which White saw as further evidence of the influence of the L1 parameter setting. These results suggest the following conclusions: (1) L2 learners do not interact directly with L2 data but, instead, initially transfer the L1 setting of a parameter, (2) given time, learners succeed in resetting a parameter to the new L2 value, and (3) target-language features may cluster in interlanguage grammars, although not entirely as predicted by linguistic theory.

Another study that failed to find clear evidence in favour of the predicted clustering effect was Tsimpli and Roussou's (1991) study of intermediate and post-intermediate Greek learners of L2 English. Tsimpli and Roussou used a grammaticality judgement and translation test to investigate learners' representation of null subjects, verb-subject word order, and 'that'-trace effects. The study failed to show that these three features developed at the same time. Verb-subject word order was hardly evident. Referential pronouns were more evident than expletives. 'That'-trace effects were not recognized. There are a number of possible explanations for these findings (which we will consider at the end of this section) but Tsimpli and Roussou argued that their failure to find any clustering effect was because these learners had passed the age where they could reset the functional parameters linked to null subject when these differed between the L1 and L2. The limited success their learners manifested with some of the properties (for example, suppliance of referential pronouns) arose because they mis-analysed English pronouns as verb agreement markers, thus equating them with agreement markers in Greek. This explains why there was no connection between the acquisition of morphology and syntactic constructions. It should be noted, however, that this explanation does not constitute a denial of UG but rather of parameter resetting; that is, it claims that learners are unable to reset their L1 parameters but continue to construct grammars that are constrained by the principles of UG.

Whereas these studies were based on experimentally elicited data, other early studies utilized naturally-occurring data. Hilles's (1986, 1991) research made use of the longitudinal learner-language data collected by Cancino *et al.* (1978) in their study of the naturalistic L2 acquisition of English negatives and auxiliaries by Spanish speakers. (See Chapter 3.) In the 1986 study, Hilles looked at just one learner, Jorge, a 12-year-old Colombian. Hilles hypothesized that Jorge would begin with the L1 setting (+ pro-drop), and subsequently switch to the L2 setting (– pro-drop). She further hypothesized that this switch would co-occur with the emergence of the auxiliary, and that it would be triggered by the acquisition of the expletives 'it' and 'there'. Her analysis supported these hypotheses, although Hilles was careful to point out that more evidence was needed before firm claims could be made. The 1991 study focused on two of the features associated with the Pro-Drop Parameter—the use of pronominal subjects and verb inflection—and sought to establish the extent to which the two were correlated over time. In this study, all six of Cancino *et al.*'s subjects (two children, two adolescents, and two adults) were included, thus allowing Hilles to investigate to what extent age was a factor in the availability of UG. Three of the learners—the two children and one adolescent (Jorge)—manifested a strong correlation between the emergence of pronominal subjects and verb inflection, suggesting that their acquisition was guided by UG. Hilles argues that the developmental sequence these learners followed mirrored that found in L1 acquisition. L1 learners begin with null subjects and uniformly uninflected verbs, and subsequently switch to pronominal subjects once they realize that English is not uniform with regard to verb inflection. In contrast, the other adolescent and the two adults displayed no such correlation, indicating that they lacked access to UG. A problem of Hilles' studies is that because there are no controls (i.e. learners with non-pro-drop L1s like French), it is impossible to rule out L1 transfer as an explanation for the results.

Phinney's (1987) study also compared learners with different L1s, once again focusing on the presence and absence of subject pronouns and the verb inflectional system. In this case, however, the study was bi-directional in nature, comparing English-speaking learners of L2 Spanish and Spanish-speaking learners of L2 English. The data for this study came from written compositions. All the learners were fairly accurate in subject-verb agreement, but they differed in their use of subject pronouns. The L2 English learners omitted few referential pronouns but many expletive pronouns ('it' and 'there'), suggesting that they might have transferred the L1 value of the parameter. The L2 Spanish learners, however, provided no evidence of transfer, correctly omitting both referential and expletive pronouns. As White (1989a) pointed out, it is difficult to reach clear conclusions on the basis of this study as the two groups of subjects may not have been equivalent.

We will now consider a number of later studies, focusing on those that investigated learners of English with oriental L1s, beginning with Lakshmanan's (1991) study, which included learners with both + null subject and – null subject L1s. Lakshmanan examined longitudinal data for three learners but we will only consider two here—Marta (one of the children in Cancino *et al.*'s study) and Uguisu (the Japanese child studied by Hakuta 1974). Whereas Spanish and Japanese are both pro-drop languages, Japanese differs from Spanish in that it does not have noun and verb agreement inflections. Hilles reported that Marta began by using null pronouns, but these rapidly gave way to the inclusion of pronominal subjects. However, Marta never mastered English verb inflections in the period covered by the study. In contrast, Uguisu did not employ any null subjects, but, contrary to the claims of the Null Subject Parameter, treated English as morphologically uniform in the early stages. Clearly, then, despite the fact that both Marta's and Uguisu's L1s were + null subject, they behaved in very different ways.[15]

Other studies involving learners of oriental languages support Lakshmanan's finding for Uguisu. Yuan (1997), for example, used a grammaticality judgement test to investigate 159 Chinese learners of English, placed in seven levels of proficiency, with the top level indistinguishable from native-speaker controls. Yuan investigated these learners' acceptance of omission of both referential and expletive pronouns in both subject and object positions. Most of the learners, including those in the lower proficiency level groups, did not perform statistically differently from native speakers with regard to rejecting null subjects in subject position. But all the groups performed worse than the native speakers when it came to rejecting null subjects in object position. Yuan explained these findings as follows. First, he argued that the learners were able to recognize that English required verbal inflections for tense and agreement and thus knew that + null subject was not licensed in English. This however, does not explain why they continued to allow null pronouns in object position. To explain this, Yuan suggested, second, that the learners transfer the obligatory topic feature from their L1. This, together with their recognition that English is inflectional, leads them to recognize that English requires pronouns in subject positions. However, as the obligatory topic feature is not applicable to object position, they continue to allow sentences with null object pronouns. Yuan's explanation, then, rests on the important idea that it may be necessary to examine how principles work conjointly to explain L2 acquisition.

What these studies show is that more often than not simple hypotheses based on UG are not consistently confirmed. This has led researchers to search for ways of immunizing the central claim that UG constrains L2 acquisition. Some (for example, White 1990) have suggested that the grammatical model is wrong and have proposed revisions to the cluster of properties linked with the null subject. Others have suggested that 'developmental' factors interfere with the clustering effect; that is, the cluster of features associated with the parameter develop gradually at different rates but this does not mean that learners do not eventually reset the parameter. Still others (for example, Tsimpli and Roussou 1991) have proposed that no parameter resetting takes place but learners continue to be constrained by UG principles. Finally, researchers such as Yuan (1997) seek to link the resetting of the Null Subject Parameter with another parameter, explaining the results of their studies in terms of the interaction between two parameters. It is also possible, of course, that the data collection instruments employed in these studies failed to provide an accurate measure of learners' competence. Finally, as Hawkins (2001a), summarizing his own survey of the null subject studies noted, the problem may not be one of competence at all but of performance; 'L2 speakers have difficulty using their knowledge in real time' (p. 221).

Later studies based on the Null Subject Parameter have been less concerned to demonstrate that learners have access to UG than with trying to explain L2 representations. Wakabayashi (2002) reported a study comparing Japanese and Spanish learners of L2 English, utilizing data collected by means of a timed reading task (sentences were presented word by word on a computer screen) and a grammaticality judgement task. Wakabayashi tested the hypothesis that the acquisition of obligatory subjects in English would be more difficult for the Spanish learners than the Japanese learners. The results supported this hypothesis, showing that even low-proficiency Japanese learners rejected sentences with no subject pronoun whereas the Spanish learners initially accepted such sentences. In accordance with the Minimalist Program, Wakabayashi claimed that this difference was explicable in terms of differential L1 transfer in the two groups of learners.

Kanno (1997) investigated the Overt Pronoun Constraint by means of a judgement task consisting of 20 bi-clausal sentences administered to 28 intermediate-level English-speaking adult learners of L2 Japanese and native-speaker controls. The participants were asked to indicate whether the subject of the embedded clause could refer to the same person as the subject of the main clause or whether it referred to someone else. Both the L2 learners and the native speakers clearly differentiated between overt and null pronouns. In accordance with the Overt Pronoun Constraint, they rejected the use of an overt pronoun to refer to a quantified antecedent but accepted overt pronouns with referential antecedents. In contrast, they accepted null pronouns both with quantified and referential antecedents. Commenting on this study, White (2003b) concluded:

> It seems unlikely that there are relevant surface patterns in the L2 input that could be noticed by the learner, leading to this result ... Suggesting that L2 representations must be constrained by UG.
> (p. 25)

Thus, whereas the early studies based on the Null Subject Parameter were unable to produce clear evidence of UG access, the later studies, which examined L2 representations of null subjects from a UG perspective, have produced clearer evidence that L2 acquisition is UG controlled.

Argument Structure

1 An account of Argument Structure and dative alternation

ARGUMENT STRUCTURE refers to the information encoded in the lexical entries of verbs, regarding the thematic roles they can take. This determines the syntactic patterns that verbs figure in. For example, the dative verb 'pass' allows for an agentive role, a goal, and an object:

Mary passed John (NP) the butter (NP).
Agent V Goal Object

'Pass' allows an alternation:

Mary passed the butter (NP) to John (PP).
Agent V Object Goal

but not all dative verbs allow such an alternation:

Mary indicated the house to John.
*Mary indicated John the house.

This creates a potential learnability problem as there is a likelihood of overgeneralization (i.e. learners will treat verbs like 'indicate' as having a similar Argument Structure to 'pass' and, as a result, produce errors as in the sentence above. This has led some researchers to argue that there must be some kind of constraint to prevent errors such as this occurring.

2 SLA research investigating dative alternation

One such constraint may be markedness. Mazurkewich (1984, 1985) argued that the NP + PP pattern is unmarked and the NP + NP pattern marked. One reason she gave is that the former is more productive than the latter (i.e. almost all dative verbs take NP + PP complements while only some take NP + NP). Another reason is that case assignment is transparent in the NP + PP pattern but is problematic in the NP + NP pattern. Mazurkewich considered the NP + PP complement to be a core rule and NP + NP a peripheral rule. She hypothesized that sentences like:

John baked a cake for Mary. (__NP + PP)

would be easier to acquire than sentences like:

John baked Mary a cake. (___NP + NP)

The subjects in Mazurkewich's (1984) study were 45 French-speaking high-school and college students and 38 Inuktitut-speaking high-school students. They were divided into beginner, intermediate, and advanced levels on the basis of scores on a cloze test. There was also a group of native-speaker controls. Judgements about sentences containing dative verbs with both the NP + PP and the NP + NP patterns were elicited from all the learners and the controls. Mazurkewich found that both the French and Inuktitut speakers judged the sentences with the unmarked NP + PP pattern more accurately than the sentences with marked NP + NP. She also found that the level of accuracy in the marked pattern increased with proficiency. Taken together, these results suggest that the learners acquired the unmarked structure first.

There have been several criticisms of Mazurkewich's research, however. Kellerman (1985) pointed to a number of design flaws. White (1989a) noted that the French learners may have been influenced by their L1 (which permits only the NP + PP pattern) rather than by markedness, and she also noted that the results obtained for the Inuktitut speakers were very similar to those obtained for the native speakers. She argued, therefore, that the study fails to provide any evidence for an acquisition sequence determined by markedness.

R. Hawkins' (1987) study of DATIVE ALTERNATION investigated ten adult French speakers spending a year at a British university. They were given a grammaticality judgement task similar to Mazurkewich's and a sentence construction task that required them to add a preposition ('to' or 'for') to any sentences they thought required them. Through a highly detailed analysis of the results, Hawkins provided evidence of a series of stages in the acquisition of dative alternation, reflecting the progressive introduction of syntactic features into the interlanguage grammar. To begin with, learners distinguish dative verbs according to whether they take a pronominal or a lexical object (for example, '... give Mary it' versus '... give a present to Mary'). Later they introduce a distinction between 'to' and 'for' verbs for example, 'give' and 'cook'), while later still they distinguish native and non-native verb forms (for example, 'give' and 'donate'). These stages were evident in individual dative verbs rather than across the board, suggesting that there was 'a progressive spread through the verbs of the learner's lexicon' (1987: 24). On the basis of these findings, Hawkins argued that it is misleading to isolate a single aspect of dative alternation, as Mazurkewich did, and raise it to the status of a UG-determined feature of L2 acquisition. His own preference was for a theory of markedness based on cognitive notions of 'learning complexity'.

There have been a number of subsequent studies of dative alternation summarized in White (2003a). She considered Bley-Vroman and Yoshinaga's (1992) study in detail. This study sought to investigate whether Japanese learners of English had access to the 'narrow constraints' that Pinker (1989) proposed to explain why some English dative verbs alternate and others do not (for example, 'pass' alternates but 'push' does not). Bley-Vroman and Yoshinaga hypothesized that because learners do not have access to UG and because these 'narrow constraints' do not exist in their L1, the Japanese learners will fail to distinguish subclasses of verbs that do or do not permit dative alternation. They argued that their results supported this hypothesis, but White convincingly showed this was not the case. This study, like many that have investigated the issue of UG access, is inconclusive.

Functional Features

1 *The Failed Functional Features Hypothesis*

Hawkins and Chan (1997) advanced what they called the FAILED FUNCTIONAL FEATURES HYPOTHESIS. This claims that:

> Parameterized functional features (PFFs) cannot be acquired after childhood unless they are instantiated in the L1.

A key assumption of this hypothesis is that functional categories determine the parametric differences between languages with regard to grammatical features such as inflections on nouns, adjectives, and verbs. A second assumption is that parameterized functional features are subject to a critical period. When this is past, learners no longer have access to the 'virtual, unspecified features' that constitute UG but only to how these features are encoded in the lexical entries of their L1. These assumptions serve as the basis for claiming that (1) the main difference between L1 and L2 learners lies in the properties of the input that they can assimilate into their mental grammars, and (2) that when the critical period is past learners are unable to assimilate features from the input unless they are also instantiated in some form in their L1. In the case of a grammatical area such as gender agreement, therefore, it follows that adult learners whose L1 lacks gender agreement will experience difficulty in acquiring L2 gender agreement whereas those adult learners whose L1 contains gender agreement will have no such (or less) difficulty.

2 *The acquisition of Spanish gender*

Francheschina (2005) tested the FAILED FUNCTIONAL FEATURES HYPOTHESIS by examining the acquisition of gender in L2 Spanish by adult learners whose L1s included similar gender features (+ gen languages) and did not include them (– gen languages). She argued that as there is unambiguous positive evidence available to learners regarding gender agreement in the input, any failure to acquire it could only be explained in terms of the unavailability of UG. In a carefully designed study, Francheschina demonstrated that '+ gen L1 speakers can perform at NS levels in a range of tasks designed to test knowledge of grammatical gender, whereas – gen L1 speakers are ... consistently less targetlike than the + gen group' (p. 187). This key finding held irrespective of the modality (oral versus written) of the data or whether the data involved production, comprehension, or metalinguistic judgements.

Francheschina argued that these results are compatible with the failed Functional Features Hypothesis. She proposed that although the computational resources for human language (viewed as one component of UG) are available throughout a person's life, representational resources are not. A subset of these features is selected during L1 acquisition and only these are subsequently available to the adult language learner through the L1. However, she acknowledged that access to the parametric settings of the L2 through the L1, although a necessary condition for native-like attainment in the L2, it is not a sufficient condition, as input is also needed. It follows from this statement that non-native-like competence may reflect either lack of access to the appropriate parametric settings (because these are not present in the L1) or lack of adequate input. Francheschina did not specify what constitutes 'adequate input', except to suggest that it might involve 'many years of (preferably naturalistic) exposure to the L2' (p. 198). This observation is reminiscent of Lantolf and Thorne's recognition that native-like conceptualizations are only possible in learners who experience lengthy immersion in the L2. (See Chapter 11.)

Learning Principles

As already noted, SLA researchers have acknowledged that UG cannot by itself account for the whole of language acquisition. LEARNING PRINCIPLES constitute one proposal for supplementing UG to account for why learners are able to avoid building 'wild grammars' that cannot be later rejected solely through positive evidence. An example of such a principle is the Subset Principle (Berwick 1985). This is seen as extraneous to UG, part of a separate module of the language faculty. If learners construct a conservative grammar, Y, which generates a subset of the sentences generated by some other grammar, X, this grammar can subsequently be expanded on the basis of positive evidence. (See Figure 12.3.) However, if learners begin with a superset grammar, X, they would require negative evidence to narrow its scope in order to construct Y.

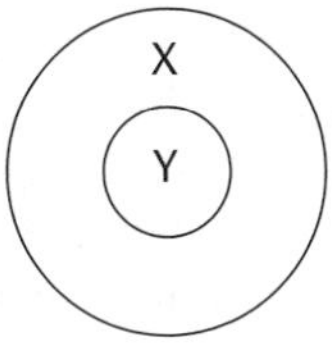

Figure 12.3 The Subset Condition of two grammars (White 1989a: 145)

For example, White (1989b) pointed out that whereas French allows adverbs to be positioned between the verb and the direct object:

Marie a mangé rapidement le dîner.

English does not:

*Mary ate rapidly her dinner.

White argued that adverb placement is related to a binary parameter of UG, the Adjacency Condition on Case Assignment, which requires that an NP with case must be next to its case assigner. She proposed that the Subset Principle should lead the learners to opt for a grammar that excluded adverb placement between verb and direct object (the conservative option), although L1 transfer would result in an L2 grammar that allowed this placement.

The Subset Principle can also be applied to anaphor binding. In this case, it would lead learners to assume that only local binding was possible (the subset condition), leaving them to recognize later on that reflexives can also be bound long-distance (the superset condition) when the input provides positive evidence that this is the case.

White (1989b) investigated the L2 acquisition of adverb placement by adult French-speaking learners of English. Three different data collection tasks were used: a paced grammaticality judgement test, an unpaced multiple choice grammaticality judgement test, and a preference task (where the subjects were asked to examine pairs of sentences and indicate which seemed 'better'). These tests were administered to the 43 learners and to a group of native-speaker controls. The results showed that the learners were much more likely to accept the ungrammatical sentences (i.e. those where the adverb was placed between verb and direct object) than the native speakers in the grammaticality judgement tests, and were much more likely to rate the grammatical and ungrammatical sentences as the same in the preference test. White concluded that these results support a transfer rather than a subset hypothesis.

This study and others (for example, Zobl 1988; Thomas 1989) suggest that the Subset Principle is non-operative in L2 acquisition. L2 learners appear to construct a superset grammar when such a grammar is suggested by their L1. This raises the question as to whether learners are subsequently able to readjust to a subset grammar. Evidence that they are able to reconstruct their grammars in this way would indicate that UG is still available to them (i.e. they have access to new, non-L1 parameter settings). Conversely, evidence that they cannot do so would suggest that they are stuck with the L1 settings of parameters because UG is not available. In essence, this takes us back to the same question we addressed when we considered parameter setting. Thomas (1989) suggested that even though learners construct superset grammars, contrary to the Subset Principle, some at least ultimately arrive at the target-language setting.

How, then, do L2 learners move from a superset to a subset grammar? Logically, this is not possible on the basis of positive evidence. Indeed, the Subset Principle was set up to account for the impossibility of eliminating problematic errors, by means of positive evidence. The French learner of L2 English can never be certain that sentences like:

*Mary ate rapidly her dinner.

are not permitted. One possible solution to this conundrum, proposed by White (1989a), is that L2 learners make use of grammatical explanations and negative evidence (in the form of corrections of their errors) to help them establish what is grammatical and what is ungrammatical. In other words, L2 learners differ from L1 learners because they do not have access to learning principles like the Subset Principle, but they are able to overcome the difficulties that this gets them into by utilizing negative evidence not available to the L1 learner. Another possibility, of course, is that the Subset Principle is incorrect and the linguistic theory is wrong.

Subsequently, adverb placement has been addressed in terms of the Verb Movement Parameter. This concerns differences in 'feature strength', an abstract property that manifests itself as 'strong' or 'weak' in different languages and has associated with it a cluster of word-order properties, including adverb placement. French is considered a language with strong features and English a language with weak features on the basis that French verbs have tense and agreement features whereas English verbs largely do not. Yuan (2001) investigated whether there were any differences between adult French and English learners of L2 Chinese, a language that like English has weak features and thus does not allow adverbs between the verb and direct object. Yuan reported no difference, suggesting that the French learners had full access to UG without transfer. However, this result contrasts with that of White (1992). In White's study French learners of L2 English accepted sentences with the adverb positioned between the verb and the direct object, in accordance with their L1.

To sum up, the available research strongly suggests that L2 learners do not have access to learning principles like the Subset Principle. Consequently, they build a superset L2 grammar, often influenced by their L1. Subsequently, however, they restructure this grammar by restricting rule application, thus creating a subset grammar. It has been suggested by White that this requires negative evidence.[16]

The role of UG in L2 acquisition: key issues

I will now reconsider the main theoretical issues in UG accounts of L2 acquisition. It should be noted that many of the studies reported in the previous two sections produced indeterminate and/or contradictory results while other studies have provided results that lend support to a UG-based account of L2 acquisition. It is, therefore, not surprising to find very different positions among UG-based SLA researchers. In 1991a, Eubank characterized the state of research on UG in SLA as one of 'point counterpoint'. The situation is not greatly different today. In fact, the number of competing positions has, if anything, grown. The key issues to be considered are: (1) access to UG, (2) the role of the L1, and (3) the role of negative evidence.

Access to UG

A number of different views relating to the availability of UG in L2 acquisition can be distinguished. These are: (1) the complete access view, (2) the no access view (sometimes referred to as 'the Fundamental Difference Hypothesis', (3) the partial access view, and (4) the dual access view. We will outline each position before attempting an evaluation of them.

The complete access view is evident in Flynn's (1984, 1987) PARAMETER SETTING MODEL. Flynn argued that 'the essential faculty for language evidenced in L1 acquisition is also critically involved in L2 acquisition' (1987: 29). However, Flynn also acknowledged a crucial role for the L1. In cases where the L1 and L2 parameter settings are the same, learning is facilitated because 'these L2 learners are able to consult the structural configuration established for the L1 in the construction of the L2 grammar' (op. cit.: 30). Where the L1 and L2 parameter settings are different, the learner has to assign new values and, although this is not problematic according to Flynn, it does add to the learning burden. Flynn (1987) hypothesized that where the L1 and L2 have identical settings, the pattern of acquisition of complex sentence structures (of the kind that UG principles typically address) will correspond to the later stages of L1 acquisition. She also hypothesized that where the L1 and L2 have different settings, the pattern of acquisition will correspond to the early stages of L1 acquisition, as the learners need to first discover the relevant structural configuration in the L2.

Flynn's Parameter Setting Model rests on the assumption that adult L2 learners have access to the same language faculty as L1 learners.[17] As such it rejects the claim advanced by other theorists that age is a significant factor in L2 learning. Flynn and Manuel (1991) explicitly addressed the age issue and concluded that 'it is impossible to argue for a monolithic critical period in L2 learning' (1991: 140). They presented three arguments in favour of this position. First, like L1 learners, L2 learners possess grammatical knowledge that could not have been learnt purely on the basis of input. Second, L2 learners possess knowledge that is structure-dependent. Third, they exhibit the same infinite productivity of new sentences as L1 learners. In essence, Flynn and Manuel are asserting that the logical problems of L1 and L2 acquisition are the same.

A number of theorists support a no access view (for example, Clahsen and Muysken 1986; Meisel 1991). This position rests on two related claims. The first is that adult L2 acquisition is very different from L1 acquisition. The second is that this difference arises because whereas L1 learners make use of their language faculty, adult L2 learners resort to general learning strategies. Not surprisingly, advocates of the no access position place considerable emphasis on identifying differences between L1 and adult L2 acquisition. Clahsen and Muysken (1986), for instance, compared the acquisitional sequences of German word order in L1 and L2 acquisition and found 'essential differences'. They argued that these reflect the existence of 'learning capacities specific to language' in the case of children and 'acquisition strategies which may be derived from principles of information processing and general problem solving strategies' (1986: 111) in the case of adults. In effect, Clahsen and Muysken were arguing that where L1 acquisition requires a linguistic theory, L2 acquisition requires a cognitive theory of the kind provided by the Multidimensional Model. (See Chapter 9.)

The partial access position draws on the distinction between principles that have parameters and those that do not. Schachter (1988) raised the interesting possibility that learners may have access to linguistic principles but not to the full range of parametric variation. This view makes two assumptions. One is that adult learners will not manifest 'wild grammars' (i.e. they will not produce 'impossible errors') because they are constrained by UG principles. The other is that they will not be able to acquire the L2 values of parameters when these differ from the L1.

Finally, Felix (1985) advanced a dual access position. According to his Competition Model (not to be confused by the model of the same name discussed in Chapter 9), adults have continued access to UG but also make use of 'a general problem solving module', which competes with the language-specific system. Felix claimed that the problem-solving system is 'a fundamentally inadequate tool to process structures beyond a certain elementary level' (1985: 51) and that this accounts for why adults fail to attain native-speaker levels of competence. Thus, when learners reach the Piagetian stage of formal operations at the onset of puberty, they develop the ability to form hypotheses about abstract phenomena. They are now able to call on two distinct and, in Felix's view, autonomous cognitive systems to deal with abstract linguistic information. Adult learners are unable to suppress the operation of the problem-solving module. This 'interferes' with UG, which alone is capable of ensuring complete grammatical competence.

How can we evaluate these different positions? As we have already seen, it is doubtful whether the empirical studies of the kind considered in the previous section provide an adequate basis for evaluation. White (1990) claimed that these studies 'at the very least ... indicate that there is accessibility via the L1' (1990: 131) and thus supported a partial access position. However, before such a conclusion can be reached, it must be shown that the L1 effects evident in L2 acquisition are explicable *only* in terms of a UG framework and not in terms of some other cognitive framework. The most convincing evidence would entail demonstrating that L2 learners access a cluster of features associated with a particular parameter, but as we have seen, such evidence is, at best, weak. In contrast to White's position, a meta-analytic study of 16 studies published between 1981 and 1999 that investigated adult L2 learners concluded that their performance on various kinds of grammar tasks was 'fundamentally different' from that of native speakers (Dinsmore 2006). Dinsmore interpreted this as showing that these learners did not have full access to UG. However, what this meta-analysis showed is simply that adult L2 learners do not typically achieve full native-speaker competence. It did not show that the reason for this failure is lack of full access to UG (there could have been many other reasons). Nor does it show that the learners in the studies investigated were not capable of further learning and ultimately achieving full native-speaker competence, as is possible. (See Chapter 1.) We must conclude that the available research does not produce a clear answer as to the availability of UG to adult L2 learners.

We are left, therefore, with indirect evidence and theoretical arguments. Table 12.6 summarizes the different positions on UG access and indicates the main assumptions of each position. The assumption that there is no critical period for the acquisition of L2 syntax is perhaps the most questionable, as the available evidence on the age issue (see Chapter 1) indicates that adults rarely if ever achieve native-speaker levels of competence. However, as we also saw in Chapter 1, there is now clear evidence that some late-starting learners achieve full grammatical (and also phonological) competence and that many learners achieve very high levels of ability in an L2. Thus, there is a basis for the 'complete access' position. The 'no access' and 'partial access' positions share two related assumptions, namely that there is a critical period beyond which full grammatical competence is unobtainable and that L2 is not the same as L1 acquisition. Both assumptions are tenable, although it does not follow that differences between L1 and L2 acquisition are the result of lost or diminished access to UG, as they may reflect other variables, such as general cognitive development and socio-affective factors. The 'no access' and 'partial access' positions are distinguished in terms of their assumptions regarding 'wild grammars'. This is clearly an aspect of acquisition that needs further study and it is probably premature to reach any firm conclusion. It is difficult, therefore, to choose between the 'no access' and 'partial access' positions. It is also difficult to evaluate the dual access position although it can be noted that the dual system that Felix proposed is supported by neurolinguistic evidence that points to distinct neurological structures for implicit and explicit knowledge. (See Chapter 14.) However, the neurolinguistic evidence is not clear as to whether child and adult learners utilize different neurological systems when learning an L2, as would be predicted by the dual system model.

It is clear from this discussion that no verdict can be reached. It is worth asking why. R. Hawkins (2001a) suggested two main reasons. First, researchers differ in how they see the modules of the language faculty interacting with each other and with other non-language faculties. Second, researchers have also differed as to what constitutes competence in the 'messiness of performance data'. There has been some movement to address the first of these issues (see the section below on the development of a comprehensive theory) but the problem of how to interpret performance data in order to investigate UG remains essentially unsolved.

Position	Description	Main assumptions
Complete access	L1 provides learners with a 'quick' setting for the L2 parameter if the value is the same, otherwise, the L2 learner proceeds in same way as the L1 learner. L2 learners have full access to UG principles.	L2 learners will be able to attain full linguistic competence; there is no critical period blocking L2 acquisition.
No access (the Fundamental Difference Hypothesis)	L2 learners no longer have access to the principles and parameters of UG; general learning strategies replace UG.	L2 ≠ L1 acquisition; adults fail to achieve full linguistic competence; 'wild grammars' can occur.
Partial access (i.e. via L1)	L2 learners have full access to UG principles but can only access those parameters operative in their L1; they may be able to reset L1 parameters by means of general learning strategies.	L2 and L1 acquisition are the same in part; adults fail to achieve full linguistic competence; no 'wild grammars' are evident.
Dual access (the Competition Model)	L2 learners have access to UG but this is partly blocked by the use of general learning strategies.	L2 = L1 acquisition in part; adults fail to achieve full linguistic competence; adults manifest similar and different linguistic behaviour from children.

Table 12.6 Alternative positions regarding access to UG in L2 acquisition

White (2003a) pointed that the 'access question' was an issue that characterized the first decade of UG-based research on L2 acquisition. She argued that since then researchers have moved on to a detailed look at the grammatical properties of interlanguage grammars. However, for UG researchers, clearly this must still entail investigating whether these properties are constrained by UG. Thus, while current research speaks of 'constraints' rather than 'access', the access issue is still the key.

The role of the L1

The question of whether learners have access to UG is, indirectly, related to the question of what role the L1 plays, as one route to UG is through the L1. It is not surprising, therefore, that UG researchers also demonstrate disagreement regarding the role that the L1 plays in activating UG principles and parameters, both in the initial L2 state and in subsequent development. Wakabayashi (2002) provided a useful summary of the main positions:

1 The Minimal Trees Model (Vainikka and Young-Scholten 1996)

According to this model, the initial state of L2 acquisition is only partly dependent on the L1; that is, the learner has access to the lexical categories of the L1 together with associated properties. However, learners do not have access to the functional properties of their L1 at this stage. Gradually learners master these categories because they can access them through UG, when they are triggered by input. L1 transfer in this model, therefore, is limited and disappears over time.

2 The Weak Transfer Model (Eubank 1994)

This model also proposes that L1 transfer is a partial phenomenon. Like the Minimal Trees Model, it claims that L1 lexical categories are available at the start, but it also claims that L1 functional categories can be accessed. However, the feature values of these functional categories are not available. Thus, the initial state has 'inert' features. Consequently, French learners of English will produce ungrammatical sentences like

*Simon plays often soccer.

while English learners of French will produce ungrammatical sentences like

*Simon souvent joue au soccer.

3 The Full Transfer/Limited Access Model (Tsimpli and Roussou 1991)

This assumes that the initial state is entirely the product of L1 transfer and that subsequent parameter setting is impossible or very difficult. However, this model does not claim that UG is not available. That is, learners do respond to the triggering effect of L2 input by constructing grammars that are compatible with UG principles.

4 Full Transfer/Full Access Model (Schwartz and Sprouse 1996)

Like the previous model, this assumes that learners have full access to the abstract properties of their L1 grammar in the initial state but (obviously) not to specific lexical items. This model differs from the previous one in claiming that learners are able to restructure their initial grammar. This takes place when the L2 input demonstrates to the learner that an L1 setting is incorrect and, as a result, the learner selects an alternative setting that is compatible with the input from those available in UG.

5 Lexical Transfer/Lexical Learning Model

This is Wakabayashi's own model. This proposes that the initial state is influenced by both L2 input and L1 transfer. Thus L1 transfer is partial and emerges gradually in the course of development. L2 functional categories are acquired from the input (i.e. they are not derived via the L1). However, the L2 lexicon is constructed by selectively transferring L1 lexical items (providing that learners believe such transfer is possible), or by learning from input. Transfer is itself triggered by input. Thus, this model allocates a bigger role for input than most UG-based models. Wakabayashi limited the influence of UG to the computational mechanism that constructs a grammar from information derived from the lexical items, in accordance with the Minimalist Program.

All these models acknowledge that interlanguage grammars are constrained by UG—that is, they constitute full- or partial-access models. All the models recognize that L1 transfer plays some kind of role in the initial state. However, they differ in terms of whether they view the learner's initial state as constituting a 'complete' grammar or as a 'defective' grammar (i.e. missing key features of UG). They also differ in how they view the extent and nature of the role of the L1 and also whether UG is seen as contributing, either via the L1 or independently, in subsequent L2 development. It is difficult to reach any clear conclusion regarding these various proposals. As White (2003a), following her own extensive review of the different models, admitted 'it is hard to find evidence to distinguish between them' (p. 95).

The role of negative evidence

A third issue of considerable theoretical importance is the role of negative evidence in L2 acquisition. We have already seen that UG theorists consider that this is typically not available to the L1 learner, while recognizing that the adult L2 learner may have access to it through both CORRECTIVE FEEDBACK and to explicit grammatical information. The key issue is whether negative evidence plays any role in UG-based L2 acquisition. There are a number of different positions.

One position is that negative evidence is beneficial to L2 learning because it enables learners to acquire grammatical properties that would otherwise be lost due to the fact they do not have continued access to learning principles. This is the view that White (1991) adopted. She provided evidence to show that adverbial placement rules in L2 English, which are typically not acquired by learners whose L1 lacks them (see the earlier section relating to Learning Principles), can be successfully learnt through formal instruction. According to this position, then, negative evidence triggers the resetting of a parameter to its L2 value.

An alternative position, associated with Schwartz (for example, Schwartz 1986 and Schwartz and Gubala-Ryzak 1992), is that UG can be activated only by means of positive evidence and that negative evidence, therefore, plays no role in UG-based acquisition. Schwartz acknowledged that negative evidence can result in the acquisition of grammatical knowledge, but argued that there is no mechanism that can 'translate' this knowledge into input of the type required by UG. In support of this position, Schwartz and

Gubala-Ryzak re-analysed the data from White (1991) in order to argue that, while the learners were clearly successful in temporarily eliminating an incorrect adverbial placement rule, they achieved this without restructuring their interlanguage grammars. This is tantamount to claiming that negative evidence aids the development of explicit L2 knowledge, but not implicit. (See Chapter 9.)

A third position is that negative evidence can play a role in certain stages of L2 development but not others. This position has been advanced by Carroll (1997, 2001). She argued that for corrective feedback to contribute to L2 acquisition it is necessary to assume that linguistic cognition is modular (i.e. is not dependent entirely on UG) but rather involves an interaction between UG and other cognitive faculties. She then went on to propose that corrective feedback must be interpretable. She sought to demonstrate that it is not interpretable at the beginning stages of L2 learning, as learners lack the metalinguistic awareness that is essential for processing corrective feedback and, also, that it is not effective at an advanced stage because correctors are less able to discern errors since these generally do not cause communication problems. Thus, she concluded that negative evidence via corrective feedback is only available and usable in the intermediate stages of development. For this reason, Carroll maintained that it is unlikely that it plays a central role in a general theory of L2 acquisition.

There is increasing evidence that negative evidence is available, usable, and actually used by L2 learners, i.e. it satisfies Pinker's (1989) three tests. (See Long (1996) and Chapter 6.) The question thus arises as to whether negative evidence has a role in a UG-based theory of L2 acquisition (i.e. whether negative evidence can activate UG) or whether its role is limited to more general cognitive operations of the kind discussed in Chapters 6 and 9. Those UG theorists who claim that negative evidence does not constitute the kind of data that UG requires are thus in a position where they must acknowledge that its role is limited to those aspects of L2 acquisition that are not UG-determined. The problem here is that there is no satisfactory means of determining which aspects are UG-based and which rely on general cognitive operations. A more convincing position would to be to accept that UG can make use of negative evidence. But, if such a position is adopted, the poverty of the stimulus argument, which, as we have seen, underlies the theoretical stance of many UG-based researchers, becomes less convincing.

Towards a comprehensive theory of L2 acquisition incorporating UG

UG researchers have long acknowledged that UG cannot provide a complete account of L2 acquisition. Increasingly, they are also acknowledging that a full explanation of the acquisition of even core grammatical features must take account of general cognitive faculties. The position that most UG-oriented

SLA researchers are now adopting is that UG constitutes *one* component in a comprehensive theory. We will briefly look at a number of proposals on how UG can be incorporated into such a theory.

Towell and Hawkins (1994) developed a model of L2 acquisition based on the view that multiple sources are involved. They list the multiple sources as:

> ... the contribution made to the L2 learning process by Universal Grammar, by the L1, by explicit instruction with negative feedback and by exposure to formulaic language in context.
> (p. 245)

They also insisted on the need for learners to be able to communicate in real time in order to develop automatized production systems. UG is seen as an essential component of this model because of the poverty of the stimulus and the need to avoid the possibility of 'wild grammars'. After the age of 7, learners access UG via their L1 but where L1 rules are incompatible with L2 input, they can 'mimic' L2 rules in a fashion constrained by UG (as suggested by Tsimpli and Roussou 1991). Initial hypotheses are modified and transformed using data obtained from explicit instruction, negative feedback, and formulaic language, which are analysed without reference to UG by means of information-processing mechanisms of the kind discussed in Chapters 9 and 10. Thus, in this model UG and the L1 serve as a basis for internally generated hypotheses (i.e. competence) whereas other sources account for how L2 performance skills are developed.

Klein and Martohardjono (1999a) also acknowledged that UG knowledge must interact with a 'learning mechanism' and thus emphasized the joint contribution of UG and other faculties (such as those involved in parsing) to L2 acquisition. They distinguished between the 'properties' of grammar that account for representation and the 'mechanism' that is responsible for L2 development. They then suggested that what makes L2 acquisition different from L1 acquisition (the logical problem of L2 acquisition) is not access to UG but rather the mechanism responsible for development. Thus, the failure of researchers to confirm the existence of clusters of grammatical features associated with a particular parameter in L2 acquisition is not because of their failure to access UG, but because the specific properties in the cluster pose different processing loads on learners and thus emerge at different stages of development. Klein and Martohardjono list seven essential premises of their model, which are shown in Table 12.7.

Sharwood Smith and Truscott (2005) also developed a model that acknowledges a role for both UG and other cognitive faculties. Their model is motivated by the need to account for the fact that L2 acquisition involves both identifiable stages of development and continua that reflect an ongoing and gradual pattern of development. They argued that L2 acquisition needs to be viewed in both ways and that both need to be accommodated in a theory of grammatical development. They sought to show how this can be achieved in their Modular On-Line Growth and Use of Language (MOGUL)

1 Principles and parameters of UG constitute the domain-specific knowledge that guides human language acquisition by constraining the representation of language-particular core grammars.
2 However, the language acquisition process cannot be determined by knowledge of UG alone. Rather, in the specification of language-particular core grammars, UG must interact with a learning mechanism to allow convergence on a particular representation of grammar (i.e. the one required by the target language).
3 Input from the ambient language is critical to allow convergence on the right (i.e. target) representation.
4 The grammar construction mechanism must encompass a language parser to process input. In addition, in order for the mechanism to operate properly, certain conditions must be met to satisfy (some specification of) learnability theory, i.e. a theory of how input interacts with UG knowledge to allow convergence.
5 Language acquisition can be characterized as a sequence of restructuring grammars, and the developmental changes observed during the course of acquisition are the result of grammar restructuring.
6 Restructuring is driven by input. Restructuring only takes place if the input is not compatible with the grammar available.
7 Completion is attainment of a steady state. At this point, no more restructuring occurs.

Table 12.7 Premises of a UG-based acquisition model (from Klein and Martohardjono 1999a: 11)

framework. This is based on a view of the language faculty as highly modular. One module is the parser, which is composed of three 'submodules'—a phonological processor, a syntactic processor, and a conceptual processor. There is competition as a result of the activation of these processors and this affects both online processing and acquisition. Options are gradually reduced as one option becomes strengthened and wins out over the others. Change is gradual because it takes time to resolve the competition between the different options. Thus optionality disappears only slowly. But stages of development are evident when the failure of one option and the success of another becomes clearly evident. All this seems to resemble a connectionist account of learning (see Chapter 9), but Sharwood Smith and Truscott argued that it is clearly different because it involves 'a very indirect, internally controlled response to the linguistic environment' (p. 234). That is, the source of the competing representations is not input, as in a connectionist theory, but UG.

These proposals differ from earlier theories which distinguished between UG-based 'acquisition' and cognitively driven 'development' in that they acknowledge that acquisition (i.e. L2 representations) cannot be satisfactorily explained entirely in terms of UG. UG and cognitive mechanisms are now seen as interacting with each other, with UG (directly or indirectly) affording the hypotheses that initiate acquisition, but acquisition also encompassing the 'triggering' processes that account for how input enables learners to select from competing hypotheses and the processes involved in the restructuring of grammars. At this point, however, these proposals are programmatic; they do not provide precise specifications of how UG and general cognitive mechanisms interact to shape learning.

An evaluation of UG-based research and theory

Some researchers are strongly committed to a UG-based theory of L2 acquisition, while others are equally strongly opposed. We will begin this evaluation by considering some of the objections that have been levelled at the theory. We will conclude with a consideration of the theory's strengths.

The domain of the theory

In the early days of UG-based research into L2 acquisition, theory and research was directed at explaining a fairly restricted phenomenon—that part of grammatical competence that is determined by an innately specified and abstract knowledge of grammatical principles. Much, therefore, was excluded. The theory did not address how learners acquire the 'skill' of using their grammatical knowledge, and it also ignored other aspects of competence—how learners develop their lexicon, how they construct form–meaning networks, and how they learn to perform speech acts appropriately, for example. Indeed, the theory did not even fully explain how 'grammar' is acquired, as it concerned itself only with those aspects of grammar that fell within the 'core'.

There has been considerable development from the 1990s onwards, as pointed out in the introduction to the section on Universal Grammar and is evident in the wide-ranging nature of many of the more recently published studies. If there is still an apparent restrictedness in recent work, it follows not from a limitation in the range of L2 linguistic phenomena of interest but from the fact that the research is in its infancy.

Another development is in the recognition of the need to develop a comprehensive theory that incorporates both a UG module and a cognitive 'processing module'. Recent accounts of the role of UG clearly acknowledge that it cannot constitute a complete theory, and present proposals for how UG interacts with other cognitive faculties such as the parser. (See previous section.)

Methodological problems

A number of methodological problems were considered earlier. The central problem, acknowledged by UG-oriented researchers such as White (2003a), is how to interpret performance data as evidence of grammatical competence. There is no obvious solution to this problem. Certainly, the continued reliance that researchers place on various kinds of grammaticality judgement tasks constitutes a major weakness, especially as UG-oriented researchers have consistently failed to provide evidence of the reliability of the tasks they have used. However, this too is changing. More studies like Francheschina (2005) are needed. She collected data using multiple tasks (i.e. a guessing game, a missing word task, a cloze/multiple choice task, a grammaticality judgement task and a gender assignment check) and examined both the commonalities and differences in gender agreement features in the different data sets. This allowed her to present her findings with conviction.

A further problem arises from the fact that learners' behaviour is not categorical, but variable, or as Hilles (1986: 234) called it, 'fuzzy'. Can this be dismissed as performance variability, or does it reflect an indeterminate competence—'a period during which the parameters may waver between two values'? We have seen that currently some UG-oriented researchers acknowledge that optionality is a feature of interlanguage grammars. This raises an important issue. How does one distinguish whether learners are entertaining optional rules from performance variability? For example, if a learner accepts the following two sentences as grammatical:

He looked at the picture.
He looked the picture.

does this demonstrate that this learner has adopted two parameter settings or does it demonstrate that the learner 'knows' the target-language setting but 'slips up' occasionally. If Bley-Vroman *et al.*'s (1988) point is accepted:

> Universal Grammar, after all, is concerned with the notion of possible grammar. The consequences of UG are not merely statistical. Violations ... are not just ungrammatical 'more often than not'. They are ungrammatical—period.
> (1988: 27)

then one would have to conclude that this learner is not demonstrating optionality but has not yet arrived at the appropriate setting. Thus, the claim made by some researchers that interlanguage grammars permit optionality is methodologically problematic.

The indeterminacy of the results obtained from empirical research

Given these methodological problems, it is perhaps not surprising to find that the empirical research has produced such indeterminate results. We examined studies directed at three issues—the availability of UG in adult L2 acquisition, the role of markedness, and learners' access to learning principles such as the Subset Principle. While some studies did suggest that learners have at least partial access to UG, more specific conclusions were not possible. Again, this need not be seen as a serious defect, for as White (1989a) pointed out 'what we are witnessing here is developing theories being applied to a particular domain' (1989a: 137). In such a case, indeterminacy can be expected. However, it is not clear that the current situation (some sixteen years later) is much different. We are still in a period of 'developing theories'. Indeed, the number of theories, models, and frameworks on offer now has grown rather than narrowed. In this respect, though, UG-based SLA is not so different from any other area of SLA. (See Chapter 17.)

The poverty of the stimulus argument

The claim that input is insufficient for learners to acquire the complex, subtle properties of grammar is the kingpin of UG-based SLA. It is also problematic. It is challengeable in two ways. First, it has been argued that principles that UG researchers argue are complex and abstract might not be so. For example, O'Grady (1999) presented linguistic arguments to demonstrate that certain types of knowledge, such as those found in the Subjacency Principle and the Pro-Drop Parameter, are not as 'abstract' as Chomsky and others have claimed, and can be accounted for in terms of input. He provided an interesting, non-UG-based explanation for pro-drop phenomena in the L1 and L2 acquisition of English. He suggested that initially learners are unable to distinguish between finite and non-finite verbs and thus are unable to distinguish between subject-taking and non-subject-taking verbs. He presented evidence to show that subjects emerge in the speech of L1 learners when they acquire tense. Second, the insufficiency of the input and the non-availability of negative evidence need to be demonstrated not taken for granted. The UG SLA literature is replete with statements such as the following:

> It seems unlikely that there are relevant surface patterns in the L2 input that could be noticed by the learner ... Nevertheless, L2 learners demonstrate knowledge of the restriction (relating to the use of overt and null pronouns ...), suggesting that L2 representations must be constrained by UG.
> (White 2003b: 25)

But something that is 'unlikely' can in fact occur and thus cannot be ruled out. If UG researchers are to convince other SLA researchers of the legitimacy of the poverty of the stimulus argument they need to provide evidence to support their claims about the indeterminacy of the input. In fact, some of the earlier claims made about the insufficiency of the input have been shown to be incorrect (or, at least, not entirely correct). For example, speakers of English do drop pronouns, as we saw in Chapter 6 when discussing the study by Gass and Lakshmanan (1991). Also, certain dialects and registers of English permit the pronoun to be dropped.[18]

The legitimacy of the poverty of the stimulus argument and the associated logical problem of language acquisition has been the subject of extensive debate. Klein (1991), for example, disputed the existence of both on the grounds that (1) L1 acquisition is not instantaneous (it is 'a difficult and cumbersome process that extends over many years'), (2) it is an 'essentially accumulative process', and (3) 'it presupposes a vast amount of input' that obviates the need for a specific language faculty. Klein challenged the assumption that a theory of language acquisition needs to posit the existence of a special language faculty.

Hyams (1991) tackled each of Klein's claims head on. She pointed out: (1) that children are able to learn certain complex structures with 'remarkably little effort' (1991: 73), (2) that 'the assumption that acquisition is cumulative in no way eliminates the logical problem inherent in the instantaneous model' (1991: 76), and (3) that even if large amounts of input are required by the child (a point she doubts), this does not justify the claim that input is more than just a trigger of the language acquisition device. Hyams' responses, however, do not demonstrate that a language faculty must exist, only that Klein is not necessarily right. Hyams missed Klein's essential point, namely that the assumption of such a faculty runs up against Occam's razor—the requirement that no theory should contain unnecessary principles:

> A theory that can do without the assumption of a specific 'language module' is much better than a theory which requires the assumption ... If everything can be explained without an extra cognitive capacity, why assume it?
> (Klein 1991)

Arguably, until UG-based researchers can demonstrate (and not merely assume) the poverty of the stimulus, Klein's objection will hold.

The case for a specific language module is probably better made by arguing the need to explain L1–L2 differences, as R. Hawkins (2001b) suggested. If it can be shown that advanced learners fail to acquire an L2 property that has no equivalent in their L1 but is clearly and plentifully substantiated in the input (as was the case with gender agreement in Franceschina's study), it would seem not unreasonable to conclude that this can only be explained by the loss of the language faculty (or some part of it) in the adult language learner. In other words, the logical case for L2 acquisition rests more clearly on the fact that L2 learners typically fail to acquire target-language competence than on the insufficiency of the input. However, it still remains to be shown that it is UG that has been lost rather than some other cognitive ability.

Conclusion

I have adopted a rather critical stance in my presentation of the theoretical claims that UG-inspired researchers have made about L2 acquisition and the empirical studies they have conducted to find support for these claims. In particular I have challenged UG researchers to examine the assumptions that underpin the theory (in particular the poverty of the stimulus assumption), as in a number of cases they may prove difficult to uphold. This said, I acknowledge that it would be unwise to dismiss the possibility that at least some aspects of linguistic competence are governed by a highly specialized language faculty. As Bialystok (1997) rightly pointed out 'learning language is never exactly like learning anything else, no matter how much general cognitive apparatus is shared' (p. 60) and as she then went on 'it is probably syntax that most significantly makes language unlike other domains, even other communicative ones'. UG affords a highly principled account of syntax and, as such, clearly cannot be ignored by SLA researchers. The real challenge is to identify which aspects of L2 acquisition are best explained in terms of 'a general cognitive apparatus' and which ones require an explanation founded on a theory of syntax such as UG.

In this respect, it should again be noted that SLA researchers have been careful to point out that UG is very strictly defined, covering only part of the total phenomena which a comprehensive theory of L2 acquisition will need to account for. While in the eyes of some this constitutes a limitation, in the eyes of many it is an enormous strength, as it provides a means for delimiting the field of enquiry to manageable proportions. Also, as a strictly defined theory of L2 acquisition, UG, in contrast to many cognitive theories, affords very precise hypotheses about the nature of learners' interlanguage grammars. These are real strengths.

Finally, the fact that there are abundant controversies in UG-based SLA can be seen as a strength rather than a weakness. As R. Hawkins (2001a) pointed out, they help to generate further empirical research in order to confirm or disconfirm hypotheses based on the different theories. UG-based research, like any other area of SLA, is still in its infancy.

Final comment

In this chapter, we have examined research that has explored how the study of linguistic universals can help us to understand L2 acquisition. In the typological approach, universals are identified externally by studying how specific linguistic features occur crosslinguistically. They are then explained with reference to general processing operations. In the UG approach, universals are viewed as innate and internal. They are viewed as comprising a specific language faculty. However, both approaches imply a nativist view of language learning, differing with regard to the precise nature of this nativism. O'Grady (1999) distinguished what he called 'special nativism' and 'general nativism'. Special nativism is 'grammatical' and is reflected in the claims about UG we have considered in this chapter. General nativism has a weak and strong form but neither involves claims about an inborn Universal Grammar. The weak form claims that the computational principles that underlie language are agrammatical in nature (i.e. draw on very general cognitive mechanisms); this is the view that is reflected in the theories we considered in Chapter 9. The strong form views the principles as grammatical in nature but 'independently attested outside language' (p. 623) and (although O'Grady did not explicitly note this) reflects the position adopted by typological linguists. It may be, however, that special nativism and strong general nativism are converging. O'Grady argued that 'work on UG (in the form of the Minimalist Program) has made significant strides in the direction of a more general nativism in the last few years' (p. 625). This being so, the two linguistic traditions that have informed the study of how linguistic universals shape L2 acquisition may prove to be less distinct in the future than they have appeared in this chapter.

Notes

1 In fact, not all languages are uniformly directional and thus, apparently, do not support this principle. German, for example, manifests mixed phrase structure, with the verb appearing head first in main clauses but head final in subordinate clauses. The position adopted by generative linguists, however, is that the order of phrase structure constituents in such languages is only 'superficially mixed' and that linguistic arguments relating to their 'deep structure' can be presented to demonstrate that there is a 'preferred' order—for example, German is viewed as a head-final language.

2 Croft identified a fourth factor involved in markedness—'neutral value' (for example, 'old' is used in both statements and in neutral questions referring to someone's age)—but argued that this is of less importance in typological study.

3 In fact, as Eckman (2004a) noted, there is an exception to this implicational universal—a language called Imonda. This exception points to the fact that implicational universals are often probabilistic rather than absolute.

4 In fact, relative clauses do not commonly occur in naturally occurring language use if this is conversational in nature. Matthews and Yip (2003), for example, in their longitudinal study of two children reported no instances of relative clauses in the longitudinal recordings in the children's homes and had to rely on data collected in the diaries of the parents.

5 Evidence for the claim that learners position the negator in relation to the 'main verb' rather than the 'finite element' can be found in the fact that initially learners produce sentences like:

han kan inte komma (he can not come)

which are grammatically correct. It is counter-intuitive, however, to argue that learners acquire correct negator position in verb phrases with an auxiliary before those consisting simply of main verbs. As Jordens points out, it is more plausible to argue that negative placement is determined initially by the learners' recognition of what constitutes the main verb. The early rule, negator + main verb, accounts for negator position in all sentences.

6 Eckman is critical of UG-based explanations because, by claiming the domain-specific nature of UG, they actually preclude questioning that leads to 'explanatory ascent' and thus block deeper understanding of the constructs involved.

7 Klein and Martohardjono's definition of 'optionality' would seem to equate it with FREE VARIATION. (See Chapter 4.)

8 Eubank (1987) also argued that failure in parsing can account for the difficulties learners experience with pronominal reference in sentences like 'When *he* entered the office, the janitor questioned the man'. Eubank

pointed out that 'any study that considers performance data must take into account multiple sources of variation' and must be prepared to consider 'multiple cognitive mechanisms' (1987: 63). In other words, Eubank queried whether the results obtained from UG-inspired studies can be interpreted solely in terms of UG.

9 Roger Hawkins, in his review of a draft of this chapter, drew this point to my attention. While I remain critical of the way grammaticality judgement tests have been used in UG-based SLA, I acknowledge that the problem of interpretation is certainly not limited to them.

10 The assumption that child L2 learners acquire grammar in the same way as L1 learners needs to be tested, of course. Some studies (such as Hilles 1991) have done so.

11 Roger Hawkins provided me with the example of the head-movement constraint to illustrate how a given principle can apply to a number of parameterized areas of the grammar. This principle is not just restricted to the particular case of verb raising but generally constrains operations involving heads.

12 This section on markedness reflects early work in UG-based SLA. The shift in thinking that occurred in the 1990s eliminated markedness on the grounds of its dubious explanatory value. That is, as it became clear that each value of a parameter needs to be triggered separately by positive evidence. For example, it is now clear that dative alternation can only be acquired if learners obtain evidence for both the double object pattern ('I gave John the book') and the prepositional object pattern ('I gave the book to John') and that any markedness relationships between the two patterns is not a factor.

13 Hawkins, in his review of this chapter, disputed the claim that the Minimalist Program makes it difficult to identify L1–L2 differences. He claimed that WH–movement in interrogatives and relative clauses, verb raising, null subjects and concord in number and gender are all areas addressed in the Minimalist Program where there can be L1–L2 differences.

14 Another problem concerning the investigation of the Subjacency Principle concerns differences among linguists as to whether languages like Japanese do or do not manifest subjacency. White (1989a), for example, cited Saito (1985) as arguing that subjacency does in fact exist in Japanese. If this is the case, the assumption of several of the studies (for example, Bley-Vroman *et al.*) that Japanese and Korean learners do not have access to subjacency in WH–questions via their L1 is not justified.

15 Lakshmanan offered a number of interesting explanations for her findings. For instance, she suggests that Uguisu used subject pronouns from the start because English, unlike Japanese, does not permit null subjects of any kind. In other words, her hypothesis might have been 'If no null subjects, then no null pronouns'. This, of course, has nothing to do with UG.

16 Hawkins has pointed out to me that later research represents a rather different view of binary parameters: that they are not seen as in a subset-superset relation, but rather each value of the parameter is determined by different kinds of positive evidence in the input. The value of this shift is that it allows one to eliminate the need for a Subset Principle.

17 In the case of L2 acquisition, parameter setting is frequently 'parameter resetting'. It should be noted that the idea of 'parameter resetting' is not restricted to proponents of complete access. Theorists like White, who adopt the view that learners can only access UG via their L1, also allow the parameter resetting with the help of negative evidence.

18 Hawkins responded to my comment that speakers of English drop pronouns by pointing out that the way English speakers drop subjects is nothing like what happens in pro-drop languages. For example, in pro-drop languages embedded subjects of tensed clauses can be null, as in:

Mr Smith said (that) ___ leaves tomorrow.

but such sentences are not possible in any variety of English. He also claimed 1st, 2nd, or 3rd person can be dropped in pro-drop languages, but not in English. This may be true (although I personally doubt it) but the point is that claims about the input need to be demonstrated not simply asserted. There are now available substantial corpora of spoken English that would make the testing of such claims relatively easy to undertake.

PART FIVE
Explaining individual differences in second language acquisition

Introduction

In Chapter 7 we examined how various social factors (in particular social class, sex, and ethnicity) influence the kinds of interaction learners participate in and learning outcomes. These factors affected learners as groups—hence the label 'social'. In this section, we focus on factors that affect learners as individuals and that are psychological in nature. A full account of how learners differ with regard to how, how much, and how fast they learn an L2 will need to take account of both social and psychological factors, and how these interact.

The chapters in the previous section of the book treated second language (L2) acquisition as a phenomenon that has universal, structural properties, and advanced various explanations for them. The underlying assumption, based on the observed regularities in learner language described in Part Two, was that all learners construct their interlanguages in much the same way, although we noted differences in how different theories explain these universal psycholinguistic processes. It is also the case that learners vary enormously in both the ways they set about learning an L2 and also in what they actually succeed in learning. The study of individual learner differences (IDs) comprises an important area of work in SLA research and contributes to theory development.

The study of IDs in SLA research seeks answers to four basic questions: (1) In what ways do language learners differ? (2) What effects do these differences have on learning outcomes? (3) How do learner differences affect the process of L2 acquisition? and (4) How do individual learner factors interact with instruction in determining learning outcomes? We will consider the first three questions in this part of the book. Answers to question (4) will be delayed until Chapter 16, when we consider the role of formal instruction in L2 acquisition.

In the first edition of this book I devoted separate chapters to what I called 'individual difference factors' and 'learning strategies'. However, in this edition, I have elected to deal with both in a single chapter. I have a number of reasons for this change. First, there is a close connection between individual difference factors and learning strategies. Secondly, I do not wish to position 'learning strategies' as such a significant area of enquiry in SLA as allocating them their own separate chapter would do. Like other researchers (for example, Dörnyei 2005), I have developed reservations about the validity of 'learning strategies' as a construct for investigating L2 learning, mainly because of the difficulties in defining them and in obtaining valid and reliable measurements of them. There is a danger that 'learning strategies' become something of a research industry in their own right, spawning endless PhD theses and journal articles of doubtful value. I do not wish to promote such an industry. Learning strategies clearly have their place in any account of individual learner differences but it should be a circumscribed one. Compared with other constructs, such as language aptitude and motivation, they are rather unconvincing.

The bulk of the chapter in this section, then, is given over to a detailed account of the theory and research relating to specific ID factors—intelligence, working memory, language aptitude, learning and cognitive style, personality, motivation, anxiety and, a latecomer on the scene, willingness to communicate. These constructs figure strongly in general psychology and, indeed, the account of them will draw considerably on the psychological literature.

13

Individual learner differences and second language learning

Introduction

The study of INDIVIDUAL LEARNER DIFFERENCES (IDs) has a long history that pre-dates the beginning of SLA as a field of enquiry. Early treatments of individual differences were largely motivated by the felt need to identify which learners should receive foreign language instruction by devising testing instruments (such as the Modern Language Aptitude Battery—Carroll and Sapon 1959) that would *predict* which learners would be successful. Learners were classified as 'good and bad, intelligent and dull, motivated and unmotivated' (Horwitz 2000a). More recent research, however, has sought to *explain* why some learners succeed more than others, and has been seen as complementary to mainstream research in SLA, which has focused on the universalistic aspects of L2 acquisition. As Horwitz pointed out, learners were now referred to by 'a myriad of new terms such as 'integratively and instrumentally motivated, anxious and comfortable, field independent and field sensitive, auditory and visual' (p. 532). Dörnyei (2005) pointed out that IDs such as these have been consistently shown to correlate strongly with L2 achievement—to a degree that no other SLA variable can match. Despite this, the study of IDs has remained somewhat marginalized in SLA, in part because of the overriding concern with universalistic aspects of acquisition but also because, as Segalowitz (1997) noted, researchers have paid scant attention to how IDs impact on the cognitive processes responsible for acquisition. There are, however, signs of a change in this direction.

What, then, are the individual differences that SLA researchers have examined? Dörnyei (2005) defines them broadly as 'enduring personal characteristics that are assumed to apply to everybody and on which people differ by degree' (p. 4). An early work (Altman 1980) presented a long list of such characteristics for consideration. Increasingly, however, researchers have honed in on a relatively small number of factors. Table 13.1 shows that Skehan (1989), Robinson (2002a), and Dörnyei (2005) all included LANGUAGE APTITUDE, MOTIVATION, PERSONALITY, and ANXIETY in their lists. These, then, can be considered 'core factors'. In addition, there are a number of factors considered less central but which figured in the lists of one or two of these authors (for example, INTELLIGENCE, LEARNING STRATEGIES, and AGE).

Skehan (1989)	**Robinson (2002)**	**Dörnyei (2005)**
1 Language aptitude 2 Motivation 3 Language learning strategies 4 Cognitive and affective factors: a extroversion/introversion b risk-taking c intelligence d field independence e anxiety	1 Intelligence 2 Motivation 3 Anxiety 4 Language aptitude 5 Working memory 6 Age	1 Personality 2 Language aptitude 3 Motivation 4 Learning and cognitive styles 5 Language learning strategies 6 Other learner characteristics a anxiety b creativity c willingness to communicate d self-esteem e learner beliefs

Table 13.1 Factors listed as influencing individual learner differences in language learning in three surveys

What has been lacking in this area of SLA, however, is a framework for examining these factors. This is, in part, because there is no unifying theory of individual differences in L2 acquisition, and in part, perhaps, because the factors overlap in vague and indeterminate ways. My own attempt to impose some order on this field of enquiry (see Ellis 2004b) is shown in Table 13.2. I distinguished factors according to whether they constitute (1) 'abilities' (i.e. cognitive capabilities for language learning that are relatively immutable), (2) 'propensities' (i.e. cognitive and affective qualities involving preparedness or orientation to language learning that can change as a result of experience), (3) 'learner cognitions about L2 learning' (i.e. conceptions and beliefs about L2 learning), and (4) 'learner actions' (i.e. learning strategies). However, as Zoltán Dörnyei pointed out in his review of this chapter, it is not always easy to decide whether a particular ID factor constitutes an 'ability' or a 'propensity' while 'actions' cannot easily be viewed as an ID factor at all. For this reason, I will not attempt to classify the various ID factors but, instead, treat them separately. One factor that is included in Robinson's list and which I also included in the chapter on individual learner differences in the first edition of this book (Ellis 1994a) is 'age'. I have omitted consideration of age here because I dealt with it in Chapter 1 and because it is of such central importance to SLA that it has figured in just about every chapter of this book.

Category	Factors
A Abilities	1 Intelligence 2 Working memory 3 Language aptitude
B Propensities	1 Learning style 2 Motivation 3 Anxiety 4 Personality 5 Willingness to communicate
C Learner cognitions about L2 learning	Learner beliefs
D Learner actions	Learning strategies

Table 13.2 Factors responsible for individual differences in L2 learning (from Ellis 2004b: 530)

This chapter begins with a discussion of the methods used in individual difference research in SLA. There follows a series of sections addressing the main factors held responsible for individual differences in L2 learning.

The methodology of individual difference research

Skehan (1989) distinguishes two general approaches to the study of IDs: (1) the HIERARCHICAL APPROACH, and (2) the CONCATENATIVE APPROACH. The hierarchical approach has as its starting point a theory that affords predictions about how particular IDs affect learning. These predictions generally take the form of specific hypotheses which can be tested empirically (i.e. they can be confirmed or disconfirmed by carrying out studies that have been specially designed to investigate them). The concatenative approach is a research-then-theory approach. Its starting point is the identification of a general research question (such as 'To what extent does motivation account for L2 achievement?'). Data are then collected with a view to identifying various IDs and the relationships among them and also between them and learning. Such research is typically correlational in nature; that is, it can demonstrate the existence of relationships but cannot easily determine what is cause and what is effect. Nevertheless, it can contribute to theory development. Much of the early research, such as Naiman, Fröhlich, Stern, and Todesco's (1978) seminal study of the GOOD LANGUAGE LEARNER, was concatenative in approach but, increasingly, researchers have turned to the hierarchical approach in order to investigate specific hypotheses drawn from a theory of a particular ID, as in, for example, Dewaele and Furnham's (2000) study of EXTRAVERSION and L2 use.

Much of the individual difference research has relied on quantitative methods of data collection and analysis. A popular method is the survey questionnaire consisting of Likert scale items that require learners to self-report on some aspect of their language learning. In some cases, such as the Group Embedded Figures Test, established tests from the field of psychology have been used. Considerable effort has gone into the development of questionnaires to ensure their validity and reliability and there now exist a number of well-established instruments. (See Table 13.3.) The data collected by means of these instruments is then subjected to statistical analysis. Correlational statistics such as Pearson Product Moment, Multiple Regression Analysis, and Factor Analysis have been widely employed to identify the strength of the relationship between variables (for example, between measures of different IDs or between a measure of an ID and a measure of L2 proficiency). As noted above, these techniques do not permit statements about cause and effect to be made, only how the variables are related to each other—but see Gardner 2000 for a different view. However, recent studies have also made use of a technique knows as Structural Equation Modeling (SEM). This allows for testing and estimating causal relationships. It caters to confirmatory rather than purely exploratory modelling and thus can be used for theory testing rather than just theory development.

Doubts about the use of questionnaires in ID research, especially about their validity, have been voiced on the grounds that asking learners to report general tendencies (as when they are required to respond to questions like 'I ask questions in English') is invalid because learners can only report their approach to learning in relation to the specific learning activities they engage in.[1] Doubts also exist about the construct validity of some of the psychological tests used in ID research. For example, there is controversy over whether the Group Embedded Figures Test (GEFT) is a measure of field independence (i.e. the perceptual ability to distinguish the details that comprise a whole), as it claims to be, or is simply a measure of general intelligence, as Griffiths and Sheen (1992) claimed. Despite these problems, researchers have continued to use the instruments in question.

The limitations of quantitative approaches have led some researchers to turn to qualitative methods of data collection. Detailed observation of learners in language-learning settings would seem a promising approach but this method has not been very successful in the study of IDs, as what learners do often does not reveal much about their psychological states or the strategies they use to learn. (See Rubin 1975 and Cohen 1984.) For this reason, researchers have favoured self-reports by means of interviews, diaries, and autobiographical narratives.

Individual difference factor	**Research instrument**	**Brief description**
Language aptitude	Modern Language Aptitude Test (Caroll and Sapon 1959)	Battery of tests measuring phonemic coding ability, grammatical sensitivity, and rote learning ability.
	Pimsleur Language Aptitude Battery (Pimsleur 1966)	Battery of tests measuring verbal intelligence, motivation, and auditory ability.
	Cognitive Ability for Novelty of Acquisition of Language (Grigorenko *et al.* 2000)	Battery of tests measuring learners' ability to handle novelty and ambiguity in language learning.
Learning style	Group Embedded Figures Test (Witkin *et al.* 1971)	Test requiring learners to identify geometrical shapes embedded in larger figures.
	Perceptual Learning Style Preference Questionnaire (Reid 1987)	Questionnaire measuring four perceptual learning styles (visual, auditory, kinaesthetic, tactile) and two social styles (group and individual).
	Learning Style Questionnaire (Ehrman and Leaver 2003)	Questionnaire measuring a number of dimensions relating to one superordinate dimension (ecstasis versus synopsis)
Motivation	Attitude Motivation Index (Gardner 1985)	Questionnaire designed to measure learner attitudes, orientations, desire to learn the L2, and motivational intensity.
Anxiety	Foreign Language Classroom Anxiety Scale (Horwitz, Horwitz, and Cope 1986)	Questionnaire measuring the degree and sources of learners' classroom language anxiety.
	Input Anxiety Scale, Processing Anxiety Scale, and Output Anxiety Scale (MacIntyre and Gardner 1994)	Three short questionnaires designed to investigate learners' anxiety at three levels of processing.
Personality	Eysenck Personality Inventory (Eysenck and Eysenck 1964)	Psychological questionnaire measuring different personality traits, including extraversion/introversion.
	Myers Briggs Type Indicator (Myers and Briggs 1976)	Questionnaire targeting four personality dichotomies: (1) extraversion-introversion, (2) sensing-intuition, (3) thinking-feeling, and (4) judging-perceiving.

Willingness to communicate	WTC Scale (MacIntyre, Baker, Clement and Conrad (2001)	The scale operationalizes willingness to communicate in terms of listening, speaking, reading, and writing both inside and outside of the classroom.
Learner beliefs	Beliefs about Language Learning Inventory (Horwitz 1987a)	Questionnaire investigating five areas of learner beliefs: language aptitude, difficulty of language learning, the nature of language learning, effective learning, and communication strategies and motivation.
Learning strategies	The Strategy Inventory for Language Learning (Oxford 1990)	Questionnaire that exists in several forms (e.g. for ESL learners and for English-speaking learners of foreign languages) measuring direct and indirect learning strategies.
	Language Strategy Survey (Cohen and Chi 2001)	Questionnaire measuring learning strategies related to listening, vocabulary, speaking, reading, writing, and translation.

Table 13.3 Frequently used instruments in researching individual difference factors in SLA (from Ellis 2004b)

Some researchers have been vocal in their rejection of quantitative methods. (See, for example, Spielman and Radnofsky's (2001) dismissal of the use of questionnaires for examining the role of anxiety in L2 learning.) However, a better approach, as Spolsky (2000) pointed out, is to use quantitative methods alongside qualitative approaches. For example, Abraham and Vann (1987) and Ellis (1989a) conducted case studies of individual learners involving a qualitative approach that included self-report, performance, and quantitative test data. Such research, which allows for triangulation (the use of diverse kinds of data as a means of achieving more accurate and reliable results), seems particularly promising in shedding light on the complex relationships that exist among ID variables. However, there are few such examples in the published literature on individual differences, doubtless because this kind of research is very time consuming.

Another method, somewhat underused in ID research, involves the collection and analysis of samples of learner language, an approach characteristic of the descriptive research in mainstream SLA research. (See Part Two of this book.) However, whereas mainstream research has focused on identifying general features of learner language in order to establish universal processes of L2 acquisition, ID research has sought to identify differences in the language produced by individual learners. The general procedure consists of obtaining data from two or more learners performing the same or similar tasks, analysing the data in order to identify differences, and then trying to identify different 'performance styles' or 'task orientations'. Hatch's (1974) distinction between 'rule formers' and 'data gatherers' (see the section on 'Learning styles' later in this chapter) was based on a series of studies of individual learners.

We turn now to a survey of the research which has investigated IDs.

Intelligence

INTELLIGENCE is the general set of cognitive abilities involved in performing a wide range of learning tasks. It constitutes 'a general sort of aptitude that is not limited to a specific performance area but is transferable to many sorts of performance' (Dörnyei 2005: 32). Intelligence, working memory, and language aptitude (the next two IDs to be considered) are clearly all closely linked. They all refer to cognitive capacities and the difference between their conceptualizations lies largely in how broad and how language-specific the terms are.

The very earliest work in individual differences in psychology focused on intelligence. In 1905 Binet produced the first intelligence test with the purpose of identifying students who would experience difficulty in handling regular instruction. This led to sustained interest in the construct through the work of such researchers as Spearman, Guilford, and Cattell, each of whom gave his name to intelligence tests. Somewhat surprisingly, however, there have been few studies that have investigated the relationship between general intelligence and language learning. Dörnyei (2005) in his survey of ID research in language learning does not mention a single one.

A reasonable hypothesis is that intelligence is a factor where COGNITIVE ACADEMIC LANGUAGE PROFICIENCY (CALP) is concerned, but less so where BASIC INTERPERSONAL COMMUNICATION SKILLS (BICS) are involved. Cummins (1983) distinguished these two types of language proficiency in terms of two intersecting continua: (1) the ability to participate in context-embedded as opposed to context-reduced communication and (2) the extent to which the communication involved is cognitively demanding or undemanding. CALP concerns the proficiency needed to engage in the kinds of context-reduced and cognitively demanding tasks characteristic of academic study whereas BICS consists of those skills required for oral fluency and the sociolinguistically appropriate use of a language in face-to-face interaction. A number of studies support this hypothesis. Genesee (1976) found that intelligence was strongly related to the development of academic L2 French language skills (reading, grammar, and vocabulary) but was largely unrelated to ratings of oral productive ability. Ekstrand (1977) also found low-level correlations between intelligence and proficiency as measured on tests of listening comprehension and free oral production, but much higher correlations when proficiency was measured by tests of reading comprehension, dictation, and free writing. Further support can be found in Skehan's (1990) study of the relationship between language aptitude and measures of L1 and L2 acquisition, which we will consider more fully later. Skehan distinguished (1) an underlying language learning capacity, which is similar in L1 and L2 learning, and (2) an ability to handle decontextualized material, such as that found in formal language tests. The former is clearly related to BICS whereas the latter reflects CALP and thus is likely to implicate general intelligence.

Intelligence can also be hypothesized to be related to EXPLICIT L2 KNOWLEDGE. (See Chapter 9.) However, the only study I am aware of that has examined the relationship between general intelligence and explicit L2 knowledge (measured by means of a GRAMMATICALITY JUDGEMENT test) failed to find such a relationship (Masny 1987). Interestingly, this study did report a relationship between a measure of language aptitude and general intelligence.

A key issue is the extent to which intelligence (however defined) is separate from language aptitude. Sasaki (1996), in a study that factor-analysed the scores of Japanese learners of English on a language aptitude test and a test of verbal intelligence, reported three first-order factors, reflecting different aspects of language aptitude, but a single second-order factor, on which measures of both language aptitude and verbal intelligence loaded. This study, along with Skehan's, suggests that language aptitude, notably the ability to analyse linguistic structure (but less so ability to discriminate sounds and memory), and intelligence are related, but also that there are other aspects of language aptitude that are distinct. Obler (1989b), however, in a study of one exceptional learner who had a record of 'picking up' languages with great rapidity and ease, concluded that 'generally superior cognitive functioning is not necessary for exceptional L2 acquisition' (1989b: 153).

Much depends on how intelligence is defined and operationalized. The studies referred to above viewed intelligence as a general ability involving the capacity to engage in analytical thinking. Sternberg (2002), however, proposed a theory of 'successful intelligence', developed through general research on native speaking students. This distinguishes three types of intelligence; analytical intelligence (i.e. the ability to analyse, compare, and evaluate), creative intelligence (i.e. the ability to produce novel solutions to problems) and practical intelligence (i.e. the capacity to adapt, to shape, and to select environments suited to one's abilities). Sternberg argued that intelligence tests have generally targeted analytic and, to a lesser extent, creative intelligence, largely because teaching methods have typically emphasized these. One possible implication of such a model is that different types of intelligence are implicated in different aspects of language proficiency.

Working memory

WORKING MEMORY (WM) is 'a memory store of very limited capacity that holds information for a few seconds' (Eysenck 2001), as when we try to remember a telephone number in order to dial it. There are a number of models of working memory but the one that has figured strongly in SLA is that of Baddeley and Hitch (1974). This identifies three key components. The 'phonological loop' holds information briefly in a phonological form which allows for articulatory rehearsal (i.e. where the phonological string is repeated in inner speech to prevent it from decaying). Rehearsal occurs within a limited time span (about 2 seconds) and is an optional process. The 'visual sketchpad' is used in the temporary storage and manipulation of spatial and visual information. The 'central executive' is the most important component. It serves a variety of functions, including selective attention to specific stimuli while ignoring others, temporary activation of material in long-term memory, and resolution of potential conflicts between schema. All three components are seen as having limited capacity. That is, they are constrained in the amount of information and processing they can handle.

Individuals' working memory capacity differs. For example, N. Ellis (2001) noted that individuals differ in their ability to repeat phonological sequences (a process he considers important for learning). He suggested that this difference can be genetic (for example, dyslexics have poorer phonological memory) and/or the result of experience (as when language learners have no representations in LONG-TERM MEMORY to aid them in chunking the input signals). He further suggested that a learner's ability to repeat novel verbal sequences such as a phone number serves as a good predictor of their ability to acquire vocabulary and grammar. He viewed phonological memory as a key component of language aptitude. Skehan (1998b) argued that the role of memory in general has been underestimated in SLA and suggested that those learners with larger working memories are better equipped to attend to and process input.

SLA researchers' interest in working memory is slowly growing. (See Juffs in press.) Harrington and Sawyer (1992) reported that learners with greater working memory capacity achieved higher scores on a measure of L2 reading skill. Miyake and Friedman (1998) found that a measure of working memory (the English Listening Span Test) predicted syntactic comprehension as measured by a task that required the Japanese subjects to draw pictures to show the thematic roles of nouns in sentences. They argued that their study demonstrated that learners with a larger working memory are better placed to take advantage of word order information because they can hold more information in their minds. Mackey, Philp, Egi, Fujii, and Tatsumi (2002) utilized tests of both Phonological Short Term Memory (STM) and Verbal Working Memory (using a test of listening span). They found that listeners who reported less noticing of question forms as they performed tasks tended to have low working memory capacities while those that reported more noticing tended to have high capacities. However, the learners' developmental stage was also a factor; less-advanced learners with high Phonological STM noticed more than more advanced learners with similar levels of phonological STM. Erlam (2005) gave school learners of L2 French a test of working memory that required learners to write down lists of five-syllable words they heard. She was interested in the relationship between these learners' working memory and their ability to learn from three different instructional approaches. The measure of working memory correlated significantly only with a measure of acquisition derived from a written production test in those learners who had been taught by means of input processing (an approach to grammar instruction that requires learners to attend to form–function mappings in input. (See Chapter 16.) In other words, learners with greater working memory were better able to process input, as claimed by Skehan. Robinson (2005b) reported that a measure of working memory using a reading span test was significantly correlated with a measure of INCIDENTAL LEARNING in an experimental study of L2 Samoan based on written input. Robinson suggested that this may be because incidental learning entails some conscious, explicit learning. (See Chapter 9.) These studies all demonstrate some kind of advantage for learners with larger working memories. Juffs (in press), however, reviewed a number of studies and concluded that it was unclear for what aspects of L2 acquisition (for example, vocabulary, morphosyntax) and for which type of learner working memory capacity was able to make reliable predictions.

A key issue is to what extent working memory is to be considered a separate individual difference factor. Miyake and Friedman and Mackey *et al.* reported that working memory scores correlated with measures of language aptitude, as did Robinson (2005b). Erlam, however, reported a non-significant correlation between her measure of working memory and of language aptitude. There are, however, good reasons to believe that working memory is a component of language aptitude. Sawyer and Ranta (2001) concluded their own review of L2 studies of working memory with the claim that 'it is likely that WM serves as an arena in which the effects of other components of aptitude are integrated'. (p. 342)

Language aptitude

LANGUAGE APTITUDE constitutes a special ability for learning an L2. It is typically held to involve a number of distinct abilities including auditory ability, linguistic ability, and memory ability (Skehan 1989). We have noted that intelligence and working memory both seem to be implicated in language aptitude. This is not surprising. Both of these general abilities are likely to be implicated in any kind of learning task, including language learning. Nevertheless, the theory and research reviewed below indicate that, in addition to these general abilities, language learning also involves more specific abilities. Language aptitude, then, is best viewed as a composite of general and specific abilities.

In an article reviewing early aptitude research, Carroll (1981) identified a number of key aspects of language aptitude. The first is that aptitude is separate from achievement. Carroll argued that they are conceptually distinct and also that they can be distinguished empirically (by demonstrating that there is no relationship between measures of aptitude and measures of proficiency at the beginning of a language programme, but that there is a relationship at the end of the programme). Second, aptitude must be shown to be separate from motivation. On this point, however, there is some disagreement, as Pimsleur (1966) treated motivation as an integral part of aptitude. Carroll argued that research by Lambert and Gardner (reviewed later in this chapter) has consistently shown that aptitude and motivation are separate factors. Third, aptitude must be seen as a stable factor, perhaps even innate. In support of this claim, Carroll referred to studies which show that learners' aptitude is difficult to alter through training. This claim, however, was challenged by Grigorenko *et al.* (2000). (See below.) Fourth, aptitude is to be viewed not as a prerequisite for L2 acquisition (all learners, irrespective of their aptitude, may achieve a reasonable level of proficiency), but as a capacity that enhances the rate and ease of learning. Aptitude tests, therefore, provide a prediction of rate of learning.

Finally, Carroll argued that aptitude should be considered distinct from general intelligence. He referred again to research by Lambert and Gardner which has shown that aptitude and intelligence measurements are not related. However, Pimsleur considered intelligence an important part of aptitude. Oller and Perkins (1978) also argued that verbal intelligence is a major factor, as it is needed to answer tests of the kind used to measure aptitude and language proficiency and thus is a common factor to both. Also, we have seen that subsequent studies have shown general intelligence (especially verbal intelligence) and language aptitude to be related. A balanced position, as presented above, is that intelligence is related to language aptitude but is not isomorphic with it.

The two main instruments used to measure aptitude were developed in the 1950s and 1960s. The Modern Language Aptitude Test (MLAT) (Carroll and Sapon 1959) was developed initially as a means of screening candidates for foreign language instruction at the Foreign Service Institute in the United States. It exists in various forms. There is a full form, a short form, and an MLAT-Elementary, which was designed for selecting, guiding, and placing children in the Foreign Language in the Elementary School (FLES) programme. Versions have also been developed for use with languages other than English—French, Italian, and Japanese. The Pimsleur Language Aptitude Battery (PLAB) (Pimsleur 1966) was developed as an alternative to the MLAT and, in particular, with a view for use in the junior high school. It measures a very similar range of abilities to MLAT. The components of these two tests are shown in Table 13.4. Other less well-known aptitude tests include the Defence Language Aptitude Battery (Petersen and Al-Haik 1976). This tested learners' ability to learn an artificial language through auditory and visual materials. It was designed for use with learners at the higher ends of the ability range. The York Language Aptitude Test (Green 1975) tested the ability of learners to use analogy to produce forms in an unknown language (Swedish). MLAT and PLAB are the most commonly used in aptitude research. Two more recent language aptitude tests (Grigorenko *et al.* 2000; Kiss and Nikolov 2005) are considered in detail below.

The Modern Language Aptitude Test (MLAT)	**The Pimsleur Language Aptitude Battery (PLAB)**
1 Number learning (after auditory practice in hearing some numbers in a new language, learners are asked to translate 15 numbers into English)	1 Grade point average
2 Phonetic script (learners hear sets of nonsense words and must choose from four printed alternatives)	2 Interest in foreign language learning
3 Spelling clues (learners read a phonetically spelled word and choose the word nearest in meaning from five choices)	3 Vocabulary (learners' knowledge of the meaning of 24 difficult adjectives is tested in a multiple choice format)
4 Words in sentences (learners read a sentence part of which is underlined and then select from five underlinings the functionally equivalent part in another sentence)	4 Language analysis (learners are asked to select the best translation for 15 English phrases into a fictitious language after being presented with a list of words and phrases in this language)
5 Paired associates (learners are given four minutes to memorize 24 Kurdish/English pairs and then select the English equivalent from five choices for each Kurdish word)	5 Sound discrimination (learners are taught three similar-sounding words in a foreign language and then indicate which of these three words they hear in 30 oral sentences)
	6 Sound–symbol association (learners hear a two- or three-syllable nonsense word and choose which word it is from four printed alternatives)

Table 13.4 Summary of the components of the MLAT and PLAB

The MLAT measures shown in Table 13.4 were selected because they were shown statistically to be representative of a number of underlying constructs comprising language aptitude. Carroll (1965) identified four key constructs:

1 Phonemic coding ability (the ability to code foreign sounds in a way that they can be remembered later). This ability is seen as related to the ability to spell and to handle sound–symbol relationships.
2 Grammatical sensitivity (the ability to recognize the grammatical functions of words in sentences).
3 Inductive language-learning ability (the ability to identify patterns of correspondence and relationships involving form and meaning).

4 Rote-learning ability (the ability to form and remember associations between stimuli). This ability is hypothesized to be involved in vocabulary learning.

Somewhat surprisingly, however, the MLAT does not include a separate measure of (3), inductive language-learning ability, perhaps because this is very close to (2), grammatical sensitivity. The PLAB covers a similar set of constructs, but has no test of rote-learning ability. Also, the PLAB included 'intelligence', measured by means of 'grade point average in academic areas'. Skehan (1998b) proposed that Carroll's original four-part model be collapsed into a three-part one by incorporating grammatical sensitivity and inductive language-learning ability into a single construct—'language analytic ability'.

Both the MLAT and the PLAB were developed in the heyday of audiolingualism and one criticism that has been levelled against them is they are based on an outmoded view of learning. Skehan (1991) suggested that there was a need to revise the basic model to take account of current theories of language and language learning in order to reflect the kind of abilities involved in BICS and informal as well as formal learning contexts. Carroll himself, however, was 'somewhat sceptical about the possibilities for greatly improving foreign language aptitude predictions beyond their present levels' (1990: 27). He reported that he had addressed the possibility of including tests of verbal fluency factors—which might be considered of importance in communicative language teaching—but had found they did not make any significant contribution to prediction.

There have, in fact, been a number of attempts to develop alternative language aptitude tests. Parry and Child (1990) developed VORD, based on an artificial language. The development consisted of incorporating a component designed to test language aptitude in a contextual framework by requiring subjects to apply general rules to particular segments of texts. However, in a small-scale study involving 36 adult subjects, many of whom were experienced language learners, Parry and Child found that MLAT was a better overall predictor of language-learning success than VORD. This study, then, bears out Carroll's scepticism. More recently, Grigorenko, Sternberg, and Ehrman (2000) offered an entirely new model of language aptitude based on an analysis of 'acquisition processes'. However, their test appears to perform very similarly to earlier tests. When factor-analysed, the scores loaded on two factors—an intelligence-related factor and a language-specific factor, with considerable overlap between the two, while correlations with measures of language learning were of a similar size to those reported for the MLAT. However, this test does afford the possibility of achieving a closer match between specific aptitudes and specific psycholinguistic processes—a development in language aptitude research that will be considered below. Kiss and Nikolov (2005) reported the development of a new test for children. This consisted of four separate tests measuring (1) sound-symbol association, (2) the identification of semantic and syntactic functions, (3) the recognition of structural patterns (involving deductive thinking ability), and (4) the memorization of lexical items. In other words, it was very similar in composition to the MLAT. The aptitude test and a test of English language proficiency were administered to 419 primary school students in Hungary. A strong correlation between the total aptitude score and the proficiency measure ($r = .63$; $p < .01$) was obtained. This exceeds that commonly reported in aptitude studies. (See below.) The aptitude measure was also shown to account for a larger portion of the variance in the proficiency scores than any of the other variables investigated (English grade, hours of English, motivation, gender, or stated preference for English). The authors also reported no relationship between the time spent learning English and the aptitude scores, suggesting that language aptitude does not improve as a product of practice and exposure. Overall, Kiss and Nikolov's language aptitude test for children looks very promising. However, these researchers did not also administer the elementary version of the MLAT, which might have proven equally effective in predicting proficiency. To date, then, the various attempts at developing new tests of language aptitude have not convincingly demonstrated that they have greater predictive power than the MLAT.

As Kiss and Nikolov's study illustrates, language aptitude research has typically adopted a concatenative approach. That is, measures of language aptitude have been correlated with measures of language proficiency and achievement, with the aim of establishing to what extent it is possible to predict learning outcomes. A general assumption of the research is that aptitude will only have an effect on learning outcomes if the learners are sufficiently motivated to learn (i.e. make the effort to use their intrinsic abilities). A fairly strong relationship has been consistently found between language aptitude and proficiency. In early research, Carroll (1981) reported that the studies he carried out using the MLAT produced correlations between .40 and .60 with a variety of criterion measures (final course grades, objective foreign language attainment tests, and instructors' estimates of learners' language learning abilities). Gardner (1980), in a review of several studies of the effects of motivation and aptitude on the learning of French in schools throughout Canada, reported a median correlation for aptitude of .41. Later research also reported similar sized correlations. Studies by Horwitz (1987b), Skehan (1986a, 1986b, 1990), Ehrman and Oxford (1995), Harley and Hart (1997), Grigorenko *et al.* (2000), and Kiss and Nikolov (2005) reported correlations in the same range as the earlier research. As Gardner and MacIntyre (1992) commented:

> Research makes it clear that in the long run language aptitude is probably the single best predictor of achievement in a second language.
> (1992: 215)

The later research, however, was less concerned with just confirming the relationship between aptitude and proficiency than with exploring a number of different issues concerning the role that language aptitude plays in language learning. These issues are considered below.

Is language aptitude relevant to informal (naturalistic) as well as formal language learning?

Krashen (1981) argued that language aptitude was only a factor in LEARNING (i.e. conscious study of the L2) and thus would only be related to measures of explicit L2 knowledge. However, Horwitz's (1987b) study showed otherwise. It investigated 61 female high school students of French in the United States. Aptitude scores on the MLAT correlated significantly with scores on a discrete-point written grammar test (r = .41) and with scores on a series of oral tasks requiring relatively spontaneous language (r = .40). Skehan (1986a, 1986b, 1990) reported significant correlations between aptitude and measures of all four language skills (including speaking) in 13-year-old children learning foreign languages in schools in the UK. Harley and Hart (1997) reported strong correlations between language aptitude and L2 measures of proficiency involving both formal and informal tasks in IMMERSION learners. In short, there is now clear evidence to show that language aptitude predicts successful learning in learners with informal as well as formal learning experiences and correlates with measures of communicative as well as controlled language use. However, it is also possible that different aspects of language aptitude are involved in informal and formal learning. For example, if, as Grigorenko, Sternberg, and Ehrman (2000) suggested, intelligence is a factor in EXPLICIT LEARNING, we might expect measures of linguistic-analytic ability to be important here, while the phonemic-coding and memory abilities may play a bigger role in informal learning.

Is language aptitude best viewed as a cumulative aggregation of abilities or as differentiated, affording more than one route to success?

Skehan's research addressed the extent to which the effect of aptitude is to be viewed 'globally', as the aggregation of aptitude strengths in the different components, or differentially, with learners finding different routes to success in language learning depending on the nature of their aptitude. Skehan (1986a) reported a study in which he used cluster analysis to identify different kinds of learners who were studying colloquial Arabic in the Army School of Languages in Britain. The results were not entirely clear, but they suggested that whereas some learners were grammatically sensitive and demonstrated finely-tuned inductive language-learning ability, others were strong on memory and 'chunk-learning'. This led Skehan (1989) to propose that there are two types of foreign language learners: analytic and memory-orientated. Both kinds can achieve a high level of success. Robinson (2005a) distinguished ten basic cognitive abilities in what he called the 'aptitude complex' and proposed that different abilities are required for such processes as noticing-the-gap and memory for contingent speech. Robinson's model, then, affords a highly differentiated view of language aptitude.

Is there any relationship between L1 language skills and language aptitude?

Two studies suggest that language aptitude is a factor in L1 language skills as well as L2 proficiency. Skehan (1986b, 1990) conducted a study in which he administered a battery of aptitude tests to the children whom Wells (1985) had investigated as young children in the Bristol Language Project. Skehan reported a number of significant correlations between language aptitude at age 13 years and measures of acquisition derived from the children's speech when they were 42 months (for example, a measure of grammatical sensitivity and a measure of mean length of utterance). Sparks, Ganschow, and Patton (1995) reported that children who demonstrated strong L1 skills at school were also strong in language aptitude and likely to achieve higher grades in foreign languages. It would seem, then, that language aptitude is a factor in L1 development as well as L2 learning.

To what extent is language aptitude immutable or responsive to training?

Here the results are somewhat conflicting. We have already seen that Kiss and Nikolov (2005) found no evidence to suggest that language aptitude improved as a result of increased learning experiences. Sawyer (1992) also failed to find any correlation between language aptitude and biographical variables such as the amount of exposure to other languages in learners of Southeast Asian languages. Harley and Hart (1997) likewise found no difference in the levels of language aptitude between immersion learners who had begun in Grade 1 and those who had started in Grade 7. In contrast, an experimental study by Sparks, Ganschow, Fluharty, and Little (1995) found that a 'multisensory, structured language approach' involving the explicit, systematic teaching of phonology/orthography resulted in significant gains in language aptitude in learning-disabled students taking a Latin course. No such gains were found in similar students taking the regular Latin course. Sawyer and Ranta (2001) concluded from these and other studies that 'aptitude is much more than a matter of skill development' (p. 334).

To what extent and in what ways is language aptitude related to the processes of L2 acquisition?

As we have seen, the majority of studies have addressed the relationship between aptitude and L2 proficiency. As such, they lie outside the mainstream of SLA, which has been primarily concerned with identifying the cognitive processes involved in L2 acquisition (Doughty and Long 2003). However, recently attempts have been made to align aptitude research with internal processing. Robinson (2001a) argued for a research programme that systematically examines the interactions between task demands, language aptitude, and language learning. He suggested that 'the information processing demands of tasks draw differentially on cognitive abilities' (p. 386) and that we need to discover how this affects learning outcomes. In line with this proposal, Nagata, Aline, and Ellis (1999) examined learners' language aptitude in relation to performance on a one-way information-gap task involving listening to and carrying out instructions that contained new L2 words. They reported moderate but statistically significant correlations between measures of sound–symbol association, grammatical–semantic sensitivity and memory for words on the one hand, and comprehension of the instructions on the other. In contrast, only memory for words was systematically related to post-test measures of the acquisition of the new words. This study suggests that different aspects of language aptitude may be implicated in different kinds of language processing.

Skehan (1998b) proposed that different aspects of language aptitude operate differently during the course of adult language learning. Language analytic ability, which is closely related to general intelligence, is involved throughout, while phonemic-coding ability plays a major role only in the early stages. Memory ability is involved in all stages but in the case of exceptional learners it is enhanced, allowing them to achieve a more or less native-like level of proficiency. In a later publication, Skehan (2002) suggested the need to relate different components of aptitude to four macro stages in language acquisition: noticing (for example, phonemic coding and working memory), patterning (for example, language analytic ability), controlling (memory retrieval processes) and lexicalizing (for example, memory abilities).

Final comment

To sum up, language aptitude research was initially motivated by the wish to identify those learners who could benefit most from language instruction. To this end, a number of language aptitude tests were developed (for example, the MLAT and the PLAB). Early research showed that these tests had predictive power, but doubts about their validity arose with the switch in language pedagogy to communicative language teaching. Interest rekindled, however, when it became clear that language aptitude was a factor in informal learning and communicative language use. This led to attempts to develop new language aptitude tests (although the old ones were found to be equally powerful) and, importantly, to relate aptitude to the kinds of internal processing responsible for acquisition. It is now clear that language aptitude is an important factor in both formal and informal language learning.

Learning styles

The idea of LEARNING STYLE comes from general psychology and much of the research in SLA has drawn on tests and questionnaires taken from general psychology (for example, The Group Embedded Figures Test (Witkin *et al.* 1971) and the Productivity Environmental Preference Survey (Dunn *et al.* 1991)). This might be considered a weakness as these instruments constitute 'global psychological measures', which may not be well suited to identifying the specific nature of the learning styles that influence language learning. For this, more 'situation-specific scales' (Ehrman 1996) may be needed. As we will see, research examining the relationship between learning styles and language learning has been plagued by problems of construct definition and of measurement and, in many respects, has proved the least satisfactory of all areas of enquiry concerning individual differences in SLA. Nevertheless, as Ehrman (1996) pointed out, the clinical experience of people who work with language learners points to the need to take account of differences in the ways in which they choose to learn.

Learning style refers to the characteristic ways in which individuals orientate to problem solving. Keefe (1979a) defines learning style as:

> ... the characteristic cognitive, affective and physiological behaviours that serve as relatively stable indicators of how learners perceive, interact with and respond to the learning environment ... Learning style is a consistent way of functioning, that reflects underlying causes of behaviour. (p. 4)

Learning styles, therefore, reflect 'the totality of psychological functioning' (Willing 1987). They can be distinguished from abilities (such as language aptitude) in that they constitute preferences that orient a learner to how they approach the learning task rather than capacities that determine how well they learn. Whereas abilities relate linearly to language achievement (for example, the greater the aptitude, the higher the achievement), learning styles are typically bi-polar, with both styles affording advantages and disadvantages for learning.[2]

Dörnyei (2005), drawing on Rayner (2000), distinguished 'learning style' and COGNITIVE STYLE. Cognitive style refers to the stable, pervasive way in which people process information. This manifests itself in activity in specific contexts and thus is intermingled with other affective, physiological, and behavioural factors. The totality is 'learning style'. It is little wonder that defining the latter has proved so problematic! In fact, learning style, so defined, cannot be clearly distinguished from other individual difference factors such as personality and motivation. The distinction between cognitive and learning styles is helpful, however, as it helps to resolve a contradiction in the literature. On the one hand cognitive styles are seen as relatively fixed (as suggested by Keefe's definition) but on the other learning styles are often seen as mutable, changing according to experience, and potentially trainable (Little and Singleton 1990; Holec 1987).

Cognitive style

Much of the earlier work on cognitive style was based on the distinction between field dependence/independence in general psychology. More recently, Ehrman and Leaver (2003) have developed a new approach, based on an instrument designed to measure cognitive style in language learning.

Field dependence/independence

The distinction between FIELD DEPENDENCE/INDEPENDENCE is taken from the work of Witkin and associates. Witkin, Oltman, Raskin, and Karp (1971) provide the following description:

> In a field-dependent mode of perceiving, perception is strongly dominated by the overall organization of the surrounding field, and parts of the field are experienced as 'fused'. In a field-independent mode of perceiving, parts of the field are experienced as discrete from organized ground ... 'field dependent' and 'field independent', like the designations 'tall' and 'short' are relative.
> (1971: 4)

To investigate subjects' perception of a 'field' as 'fused' or as composed of 'discrete parts', a variety of tests of space-orientation (for example, the body-adjustment test, which measured subjects' perception of an upright position) were developed. Later, Witkin and his associates developed various pencil-and-paper tests that required subjects to locate a simple geometrical figure within a more complex design. Witkin claimed that they measured the same construct as the space orientation tests. The version most widely used in SLA research is the Group Embedded Figures Test (GEFT).[3] This provides a measure of the extent to which individuals are field independent but, as McLaughlin (1985) pointed out there is no separate measure of field dependency.

As a result of research with the GEFT conducted by Witkin and his associates, various claims regarding the relationship between field independence (FI)/field dependence (FD) and other variables have been advanced. (See Table 13.5.) Precisely what the test measures, however, is a matter of some controversy. Griffiths and Sheen (1992) suggested that many of Witkin's claims are 'expansive'. They argued that it is not possible to extrapolate from visual-spatial abilities, which they claim the test measures, to other cognitive abilities or to personality dimensions. They suggested that the GEFT is a test of 'ability' rather than 'style', 'specifically in the visuo-spatial domain, but also related to general intelligence' (1992: 141). This is a view shared by Chapelle and Green (1992). They pointed to Witkin's later work (for example, Witkin and Goodenough 1981), which defined FI/FD as involving three major constructs: reliance on internal versus external referents, cognitive restructuring skills, and interpersonal competencies. However, they argued that the GEFT only measures 'cognitive restructuring ability'. They also suggested it constitutes a measure of one type of intelligence, 'fluid ability' (the ability that is independent of any body of content knowledge and that is involved in problem solving). The value of the L2 research based on the GEFT, then, would seem to lie more in the light it throws on aptitude, as Chapelle and Green's (1992) subsequent discussion demonstrated, than in illuminating the role of cognitive style. It is discussed in this section only because the bulk of L2 studies have treated the GEFT as a measure of style.

Another problem with the GEFT is that it may be culturally biased, favouring certain groups over others. (See Willing 1987.) Griffiths (1991b) reported marked differences in the scores obtained by nationals of different Asian countries (for example, 10 out of a maximum of 18 by Samoans as opposed to 15 plus for Japanese). Certainly, the characterization of FI and FD individuals, as shown in Table 13.5, is contentious.

Field independence	**Field dependence**
adolescents/adults	children
males	females
object-oriented jobs	people-oriented jobs
urban, technological societies	rural, agrarian societies
free social structures	rigid social structures
individualistic people	group-centred people

Table 13.5 Variables associated with field independence and field dependence

A considerable number of early studies investigated the relationship between FI/FD and L2 learning. (See Table 13.6.) One hypothesis that was investigated is that FI learners do better in formal language learning, while FD learners do better in informal language learning. However, with the exception of Abraham and Vann (1987), who studied only two learners, this hypothesis did not receive support. In general, FI learners do better on measures of formal language learning (for example, discrete point tests). But FI learners also do better on integrative tests and tests of communicative competence, designed to favour FD learners. Also, a number of studies failed to find a significant relationship between GEFT scores and measures of learning. Other studies commented on the weakness of the relationship. D'Anglejan and Renaud (1985), for instance, reported that FI explained less than 1 per cent of the variance in tests of all four language skills. Even some of the studies that reported a stronger relationship between FI and L2 achievement also commented that it loses significance once the effects of the learners' general scholastic ability have been statistically removed (for example, Hansen 1984). D'Anglejan and Renaud (1985) found a considerable overlap between FI/FD, as measured by the GEFT, and verbal intelligence, as measured by Raven's Progressive Matrices, a result that led them to question Witkin and Berry's (1975) insistence that the two cognitive traits were distinct and that reinforces the views expressed by Griffiths and Sheen (1992) and Chapelle and Green (1992) that GEFT is really an aptitude test.

Study	Participants	Setting	Proficiency level	Measures of learning	Results
Tucker, Hamayan, and Genesee 1976	School learners of L2 French in Canada	Second language	Lower intermediate	Listening comprehension; reading comprehension; oral production task; achievement test of general language skills	FI/FD failed to correlate significantly with any of the learning measures except the achievement test.
Seliger 1977	Adult learners at university in USA	Second language	Upper intermediate	Frequency of interaction in the classroom; structure test; aural comprehension test; cloze test	FI correlated significantly with all measures of learning and with the measure of classroom interaction.
Naiman *et al*. 1978	School learners of L2 French in Canada	Second language	Intermediate and above, Grades 8, 10, and 12	Listening comprehension; imitation	FI correlated at 5 per cent level with imitation and at the 1 per cent level with comprehension.
Bialystok and Fröhlich 1978	31 learners of L2 French in Canada	Second language	Intermediate, Grades 9 and 10	Reading comprehension	No significant correlation between FI/FD and learning. FI significantly related to measure of aptitude (MLAT).
Hansen and Stansfield 1981	253 learners of L2 Spanish at university in USA	Foreign language	Beginners	6 measures of linguistic competence, communicative competence, and integrative competence	Significant correlations between FI and all 6 measures of learning at 5 per cent or better; relationship weakened when scholastic ability partialled out.
Stansfield and Hansen 1983	250 learners of L2 Spanish at university in USA	Foreign language	Beginners	The students' written exam grade average; the students' oral grade; cloze test	Modest relationship between all achievement measures and FI found. Correlation between FI and cloze scores was highest ($r = .43$).
Abraham 1983	Adult ESL learners	Second language	High intermediate	Use of monitoring strategy in three language learning tasks	FI related to higher incidence of monitoring.
Hansen 1984	Adult learners of L2 English from different Pacific island cultures	Second language	Mixed levels	Cloze test	Significant relationships between FI and cloze performance found but there was considerable variation according to sub-group; also, effects of FI largely disappeared when scholastic attainment partialled out.
Day 1984	25 adult learners of L2 English in Hawaii; divided into high and low input generators	Second language	Intermediate	Oral proficiency; interview assessment of learners' grammatical, pragmatic, and socio-linguistic competence; cloze test	No relationship found between GEFT scores and measures of learning or between GEFT scores and measures of participation in classroom interaction.

Abraham 1985	61 15–19-year-old learners of L2 English; mixed language backgrounds; two treatments (deductive and examples)	Second language	High intermediate	Sentence-joining task testing participle structures	FI learners did better if they received deductive treatment and FD learners did better with examples.
Chapelle and Roberts 1986	61 adult learners of L2 English (Japanese, Spanish, and Arabic)	Second language	Intermediate	TOEFL test; MC grammar test; cloze test; dictation; oral test of communicative competence	FI significantly related to all measures of learning at beginning and end of semester; relationship strongest with TOEFL scores; FD not related to measure of communicative competence.
Abraham and Vann 1987	Two adult learners of L2 English and L1 Spanish	Second language	Both intermediate; one high and one low proficiency	Michigan English Placement test; TOEFL; test of spoken English; performance on different language learning tasks	FI related to TOEFL; FD related to oral ability; FI also related to greater variety of strategy use and to greater concern with correctness.
Bacon 1987	95 learners of L2 Spanish in supportive instructional group and 93 in non-supportive	Foreign language	Beginner	Oral interview used to measure quantity and quality of L2 production (using NS raters)	No relationship between GEFT scores and quantity/quality of L2 production—irrespective of treatment provided. FD learners attached more importance to speaking another language.
Carter 1988	72 learners of L2 Spanish taught in two courses—formal and more functional	Foreign language	Beginner/low intermediate	Regular written final examination; ACTEFL/ELTS Oral Proficiency interview; questionnaire about learners' views regarding utility of different learning strategies	FI related to both formal linguistic achievement and to functional language use; this relationship was evident in both formal and functional courses. FI students in both types of course considered focus on meaning more important than FD students.
Ellis 1990b	39 learners of L2 German; mixed L1s	Foreign language	Beginner	Measure of German acquisition; measure of spoken fluency; vocabulary test; grammar test; cloze test	Relationship between GEFT scores and all measures of learning very weak and non-significant.
Johnson, Prior, and Artuso 2000	28 native speakers; 29 adults ESL students (mainly Asian)	Second language	Intermediate	Teacher ratings of pragmatic competence; various measures based on T-units in a two-minute conversation; metaphor fluency; measure of academic language proficiency; self-ratings	For L2 group significant correlations (–.50) between GEFT and total T-units, error-free T-units and simple T-units; significant correlations also found with teacher ratings. Near zero correlations with academic language proficiency.

Table 12.6 Survey of studies which investigated the effect of cognitive style on L2 acquisition

Other hypotheses also failed to receive convincing support from the studies in Table 13.6. There is no clear evidence that FD learners interact more and seek out more contact with other users of the L2 than FI learners or that they are more concerned with meaning than FI learners. Nor is there much support for learner–instruction matching. Abraham (1985) did find that FI learners did better with a deductive method of instruction, while FD learners benefited from being given examples. However, Carter (1988) found that FI learners did better than FD learners in both a formal and a functional language course. A number of studies (for example, Bialystok and Fröhlich 1978) reported a general relationship between FI and language aptitude, questioning whether the distinction is really distinguishable from other more robust constructs. H Brown (1987) suggested that some learners may have 'flexible' cognitive styles, combining FI and FD modes of processing and adapting their approach to suit different learning tasks. However, the GEFT (which only provides a measure of FI) cannot be used to investigate the presumed advantages of a flexible learning style.

This survey of the early studies investigating the FI/FD distinction in language learning suggests that, as Skehan (1989) argued, it is 'a seam which has been mined for all the value that is going to be found' (p. 240). The dismissal of the distinction may be premature, however. The failure of the earlier research to find any relationship between GEFT scores and measures of L2 proficiency/performance may have arisen because of methodological problems in the design of the studies, in particular with how proficiency/achievement was measured. Johnson, Prior, and Artuso (2000) argued that in many of the earlier studies there was no satisfactory measure of communicative ability. They reported a study in which significant negative correlations (in the order of –.50) were found between GEFT scores and measures derived from conversations with an interviewer and some lower but still significant negative correlations (–.30) between GEFT scores and teachers' ratings of the learners' pragmatic competence. The negative correlations indicate that learners who were field dependent and thus scored poorly on the GEFT achieved higher scores in communicative language use, as predicted by the theory. Interestingly, they found near zero correlations between GEFT scores and measures of academic language proficiency. Skehan (1998b) has also shifted his view somewhat, seeing a similarity between the FI/FD distinction and his own distinction, based on measures of language aptitude, between analysis-oriented and memory-oriented learners.

Cognitive style analysis (Riding 1991)

One of the main problems of the FI/FD research is that it was based on the GEFT, which only provided a measure of FI. A very different approach to measuring cognitive style was developed by Riding (1991). This approach differed in two ways. First, it involved a more complex view of cognitive style, distinguishing two superordinate dimensions. The wholist-analytic learning dimension distinguished individuals in terms of whether they preferred to organize information as an integrated whole or as a set of parts making up the whole. This corresponds closely to the FI/FD distinction. The verbal-imagery dimension distinguishes individuals in terms of whether they are outward going and represent information verbally or are more inward looking and think visually or spatially. These dimensions were shown to be independent of each other and not correlated with measures of intelligence. Second, Riding developed an instrument (the Cognitive Style Analysis) that measured people's style preferences with reference to their response time to test items rather than the correctness of their responses. Scores on Riding's test consist of ratios (for example, the ratio of verbal response time to visual response time). Riding's approach to cognitive style is promising but, as yet, there has been only one SLA study based on it (Littlemore 2001), which is considered in a later section of this chapter.

Synopsis and ectasis (Ehrman and Leaver 2003)

Another problem of the GEFT was that it constituted a general style instrument rather than a language-dependent instrument. Ehrman and Leaver (2003) developed a new instrument for measuring the cognitive style of language learners. This instrument was based on a general distinction between ectasis and synopsis, which addresses 'the degree of conscious control of learning desired or needed' (p. 395) by learners. Thus ecstasic learners prefer to learn by exerting conscious control over the learning process whereas synoptic learners prefer an unconscious approach or, as Ehrman and Leaver put it, to 'trust their guts'. This distinction is reflected in ten further distinctions (each with its own scale), summarized in Table 13.7.[4] Ehrman and Leaver developed a questionnaire (the Learning Style Questionnaire) to measure these distinctions. This presents learners with two statements and requires them to respond on a 9-point scale which statement most reflects the way they learn. Ecstasic learners are characterized as field sensitive, field independent, random, global, inductive, synthetic, analogical, concrete, levelling, and impulsive. Synoptic learners have the characteristics of the polar opposites of these. Ehrman and Leaver claimed that their questionnaire has the advantage of providing both a general and specific picture of learners' cognitive style. They noted that 'all ten of the subscales, though correlated in a greater or lesser degree, can also operate independently of each other' (pp. 411–12). Such an approach to investigating cognitive style is promising. However, Ehrman and Leaver do not report any research based on it. Rather, they present it as a tool to be used alongside other tools for identifying learners' approaches to language learning as a basis for counselling sessions with individual adult learners in the context of the Foreign Service Institute in the USA.

Scale	Description
Field dependent and field sensitive	These are viewed as separate constructs, yielding four types of learners: (1) field independent and field sensitive learners who can learn from material in and out of context; (2) field independent and field insensitive who are comfortable with out-of-context material; (3) field dependent and field sensitive who are comfortable with in-context material; and (4) field dependent and field sensitive who have difficulties with both types of material.
Random (non-linear)–sequential (linear)	Random learners like to work out their own learning sequence and tolerate ambiguity well; sequential learners prefer to learn step-by-step, are systematic and good planners, but dislike open-ended activities.
Global–particular	Global learners focus on the 'big picture' using top-down processing; particular learners focus on details using bottom-up processing.
Inductive–deductive	Inductive learners prefer to take as their starting point language data and extract generalizations from it; deductive learners prefer to start with a rule and apply it to specific cases.
Synthetic–analytic	Synthetic learners construct hypotheses intuitively and build wholes from parts; analytic learners break down wholes into parts and build up hypotheses consciously.
Analogue–digital	Digital learners engage in logical, sequential processing and use an 'on/off mechanism'; analogical learners engage in non-linear processing and use a 'more or less mechanism'.
Concrete–abstract	Concrete learners prefer concrete activities like role-plays and grammar drills; abstract learners show more interest in the system of language than in actually using it.
Levelling–sharpening	This distinction relates to how learners perceive, store, and retrieve information. Levellers combine information from different sources ('data clumping'); sharpeners perceive and retrieve fine distinctions.
Impulsive–reflective	This distinction concerns the speed with which learners can respond to a stimulus. Impulsive learners respond rapidly but lack accuracy; reflective learners are slower and are more accurate.

Table 13.7 Ehrman and Leaver's questionnaire

Learning style

Learning style has also been investigated primarily by means of survey-style instruments. Again, some of these instruments have been taken from general psychology (for example, Dunn *et al.*'s (1991) Productivity Environmental

Preference Survey and Kolb's (1984) Learning Style Inventory) while others have been specifically designed to investigate language learners (for example, Reid's (1987) Perceptual Learning Style Questionnaire and Willing's (1987) Learning Style Questionnaire). I will focus on the language-specific research although I will consider one study (Bailey *et al.* 2000) that made use of a general questionnaire. In addition, a number of researchers have attempted to investigate learning styles by analysing samples of learner language.

Dunn *et al.*'s complex model of learning styles

Dunn *et al.*'s (1991) Productivity Environmental Preference Survey measures learning styles in four areas: (1) preferences for environmental stimuli, (2) quality of emotional stimuli, (3) orientation towards sociological stimuli, and (4) preferences related to physical stimuli. Overall, the questionnaire surveys preferences in 20 different modalities based on these areas. It is designed to reflect preferences related to both personality and learning style. Bailey, Onwuegbuzie, and Daley (2000) administered this general questionnaire to 100 students enrolled in French and Spanish first- and second-semester courses in a US university. A multiple regression analysis was used to investigate the extent to which different styles predicted foreign language achievement at the end of the learners' courses. The main finding was that higher achievers tended to like informal classroom designs and not to receive information via the kinaesthetic mode. Overall, however, learning style predicted only a very modest proportion of the variance in achievement scores (15.1 per cent), leading Bailey *et al.* to conclude that 'learning style may not be a strong predictor of foreign language proficiency' (p. 126).

Reid's perceptual learning styles

Reid (1987) distinguished four PERCEPTUAL LEARNING MODALITIES:

1 visual learning (for example, reading and studying charts)
2 auditory learning (for example, listening to lectures or to audio tapes)
3 kinaesthetic learning (involving physical responses)
4 tactile learning (hands-on learning, as in building models).

In addition, Reid distinguished two social learning styles:

1 group preference (learning with other learners)
2 individual preference (learning by oneself).

To measure these styles Reid developed the Perceptual Learning Styles Questionnaire, an instrument especially designed for use with language learners. This instrument was subsequently subjected to careful validation by Wintergerst, DeCapua, and Itzen (2001). Using factor analysis (a statistical procedure designed to discover if there were any combinations of items which afforded parallel responses), they found that Reid's questions did not show a good fit with the constructs that informed its design. They suggested that one reason for this might have been the model of learning styles itself and therefore explored an alternative learning style model, finding support for a three-factor model: (1) Group Activity Orientation, (2) Individual Activity Orientation, and (3) a Project Orientation (incorporating tactile, visual, and kinaesthetic items). Isemonger and Sheppard (2007) also used factor analysis (including in this case a confirmatory factor analysis) to question the psychometric validity of a Korean version of Reid's questionnaire.

DeCapua and Wintergerst (2005) reported a further study in which they sought to test the validity of a new instrument (the Learning Styles Indicator) based on the findings of the earlier study. They interviewed graduate students in a TESOL Master's degree programme, asking them to comment on the items in the questionnaire. Various concerns with the items were raised, including the decontextualized nature of the statements—the informants indicated that they would have made different responses depending on the context of learning. DeCapua and Wintergerst concluded by suggesting that there was a need to employ multiple methods to collect data about learning styles rather than relying on Likert-scale questionnaires. The Learning Styles Inventory has continued to undergo piloting and modification.

In her original study, Reid (1987) administered the Perceptual Learning Style Questionnaire to 1,388 students of varying language backgrounds to investigate their preferred modalities. This revealed that the learners' preferences often differed significantly from those of native speakers of American English. They showed a general preference for kinaesthetic and tactile learning styles (with the exception of the Japanese), and for individual as opposed to group learning. With regard to the latter, Reid comments: 'Every language background, including English, gave group work as a minor or negative preference'. Proficiency level was not related to learning style preference, but length of residence in the United States was—the longer the period, the more an auditory style was preferred, reflecting perhaps an adaptation to the prevailing demands of the American educational system. Wintergerst, DeCapua, and Verna (2003) reported a study based on the Learning Style Inventory (the modified version of Reid's questionnaire), which they administered to three groups of learners—Russian EFL learners, Russian ESL learners, and Asian ESL learners. All three groups expressed a preference for group activity over individual work. In addition, the Russian EFL and Asian EFL learners favoured project work. The findings of this study, therefore, contradict the findings of Reid's study. The explanation for this offered by Wintergerst *et al.* is that classroom instructional techniques had changed since Reid's study but another possibility is simply that different groups of learners will vary in their social learning style. It is not clear that any useful generalizations can be based on the research undertaken to date.

Willing's two-dimensional learning style

Willing (1987) identified two major dimensions of learning style. One was cognitive and corresponded closely to that of field independence/dependence. The other was more affective in nature; it concerned how active learners were in the way they reported approaching L2 learning tasks. Skehan (1991) suggested that the second dimension reflects a personality as much as a learning style factor. Based on these two dimensions, Willing described four general learning styles (summarized in Table 13.8). Using a questionnaire designed to measure these styles, Willing investigated the learning styles of 517 adult ESL learners in Australia. Their responses to a 30-item questionnaire were analysed by means of factor analysis. Willing's study is interesting, but it suffers from a number of methodological problems which cast doubt on the results obtained. Gieve (1991) administered the questionnaire (in a slightly adapted form) to 156 first-year female students at a junior college in Japan. His analysis of the data produced very different results from those reported by Willing. It suggested that the strength and nature of learners' motivation was the major dimension of learning style measured by the questionnaire. Gieve also made the interesting point that the students' responses reflected their environment at least as much as innate qualities, as shown by the fact that significant differences were found in learners' responses depending on whether the questionnaire was administered by a Japanese or native-speaker researcher! Gieve's study raises doubts about the validity and reliability of Willing's questionnaire.

General learning style	Main characteristics
1 Concrete learning style	Direct means of processing information; people-orientated; spontaneous; imaginative; emotional; dislikes routinized learning; prefers kinaesthetic modality.
2 Analytical learning style	Focuses on specific problems and proceeds by means of hypothetical-deductive reasoning; object-orientated; independent; dislikes failure; prefers logical, didactic presentation.
3 Communicative learning style	Fairly independent; highly adaptable and flexible; responsive to facts that do not fit; prefers social learning and a communicative approach; enjoys taking decisions.
4 Authority-orientated learning style	Reliant on other people; needs teacher's directions and learning style explanations; likes a structured learning environment; intolerant of facts that do not fit; prefers a sequential progression; dislikes discovery learning.

Table 13.8 Four learning styles used by adult ESL learners (based on Willing 1987)

Product analyses

Further evidence of differences in learning styles comes from product analyses of learner language. Researching L1 acquisition, Nelson (1973) distinguished 'referential' and 'expressive' learners. The former use language to name things while the latter prefer to use it to indicate feelings, needs, and social forms. Peters (1977) suggested that some learners are 'analytic' (i.e. are word-learners and progress incrementally through a recognizable sequence of stages of acquisition) and some are 'Gestalt' (i.e. are sentence-learners who begin with whole sentences which are used to perform functions that are important to them). In SLA research, somewhat similar types of learners have been identified. Hatch (1974), for example, talked of 'rule-formers', who pay close attention to linguistic form, sort out the rules, and develop steadily, and 'data-gatherers', who show greater concern for communication and make extensive use of FORMULAIC SEQUENCES. Krashen (1978) distinguished 'monitor-over-users' and 'monitor-under-users', allowing also for 'optimal monitor users'. Dechert (1984) compared the styles of two advanced learners in a narrative reproduction task. One was 'analytic' (manifesting long pauses at chunk boundaries, few corrections, and serial processing) while the other was 'synthetic' (manifesting shorter pauses throughout, more corrections, and episodic processing). The terms used to characterize the differences in language produced by different learners proliferate, but it is tempting to identify one general distinction that seems to underlie many of those mentioned above—the experiential, communicatively-orientated learner as opposed to the analytical, norm-orientated learner. This distinction mirrors the ecstasic/synoptic distinction of Ehrman and Leaver.

Final comment

The above survey of learning styles research in SLA is not all inclusive. There have been a number of other learning style instruments developed (for example, Oxford's (1999) Style Analysis Survey[5] and Cohen, Oxford, and Chi's (2001) Learning Style Survey). There have also been a number of studies that have investigated the relationship between learning styles and proficiency/achievement (for example, Ehrman 1994; Ehrman and Oxford 1995). These studies almost invariably reported only a weak relationship between learning styles and L2 learning.

In the earlier edition of this book, I concluded my examination of SLA research on learning styles as follows:

> At the moment there are few general conclusions that can be drawn from the research on learning style. Learners clearly differ enormously in their preferred approach to L2 learning, but it is impossible to say which learning style works best. Quite possibly it is learners who display flexibility who are most successful, but there is no real evidence yet for such a conclusion. One of the major problems is that the concept of 'learning style' is ill-defined, apparently overlapping with other individual differences of both an affective and a cognitive nature. It is unlikely that much progress will be made until researchers know what it is they want to measure.
> (Ellis 1994a: 508)

Dörnyei (2005) ended his own survey by quoting my conclusion. I see little reason to change my position. The problem of definition has not been solved and there is very little evidence to show that learning styles (as currently conceptualized) are strongly related to L2 proficiency and, a major limitation, none to show how they relate to the processes of learning. If I have dealt somewhat lengthily with learning styles this is simply a reflection of the ongoing attention it has received from researchers.

Personality

PERSONALITY can be defined as those characteristics of a person that 'account for consistent patterns of feeling, thinking and behaving' (Pervin and John 2001: 4, cited in Dörnyei 2005). It is generally conceived of as composed of a series of traits such as EXTRAVERSION/INTROVERSION and neuroticism/stability.

In the eyes of many language teachers, the personality of their students constitutes a major factor contributing to success or failure in language learning. Griffiths (1991b), for example, conducted a survey of 98 teachers of ESL/EFL in England, Japan, and Oman in order to determine how important they rated personality and two other IDs. He reported a mean rating of 4 on a 5-point scale—slightly higher than the rating for intelligence and just below that for memory. Learners also consider personality factors to be important. Of the 'good language learners' investigated by Naiman *et al.* (1978) 31 per cent believed that extroversion was helpful in acquiring oral skills. It is somewhat surprising, therefore, to find that the research that has investigated personality variables and L2 learning is quite scanty and, in many ways, unsatisfactory.

Personality is typically measured by means of some kind of self-report questionnaire. A number of language-specific questionnaires have been developed by SLA researchers (for example, Ely 1986a). These have been used to measure particular dimensions of personality such as risk-taking (i.e. willingness to use complex language and preparedness to speak in the L2) or tolerance of ambiguity (i.e. the ability to deal with ambiguous new stimuli without frustration and without appeals to authority). Also, researchers have made use of general personality questionnaires such as the Eysenck Personality Inventory (Eysenck and Eysenck 1964) and the Myers-Briggs Type Indicator (Myers and Briggs 1976). One of the problems with this multiplicity of measurement instruments is that it is very difficult to draw general conclusions, as it is difficult to identify to what extent the constructs being measured are the same or different.

One of the earliest approaches to investigating personality in L2 learning, however, did not use questionnaires, but instead adopted an experimental methodology to examine self-esteem. In a series of studies (Guiora, Lane, and Bosworth 1967; Guiora *et al.* 1972), Guiora and associates used an instrument known as the Micro-Momentary Expression Test to measure learners' empathy by having them identify when a woman in a film changed her facial expression. In the first of the studies a positive correlation between empathy (so measured) and accuracy of pronunciation by fourteen French teachers was reported. A subsequent study, however, found no such relationship, while a third study found a positive relationship for some languages and a negative one for others. In another set of studies (Guiora *et al.* 1972; Guiora, Acton, Erard, and Strickland 1980) learners were administered quantities of alcohol and Valium in order to reduce their level of inhibition. Alcohol resulted in better pronunciation but Valium did not—a result that has interesting possibilities for application in language teaching! However, as H Brown (1987) pointed out, even the positive results obtained for alcohol cannot be interpreted as showing that reduced inhibition facilitates L2 pronunciation, as it is possible that the effects of the alcohol were due to reduced muscular tension (a purely physical phenomenon).

Other early studies adopted a more conventional approach using questionnaires. However, the results obtained by different studies were inconsistent and inconclusive. Thus, for example, whereas Naiman *et al.* (1978) found a positive relationship between tolerance of ambiguity and scores on a listening comprehension test, they failed to find any relationship with scores on an imitation test. Chapelle and Roberts (1986) also reported low correlations between this personality factor and criterion measures of L2 proficiency. Similar inconsistencies can be observed in the main results for extroversion, empathy, and self-esteem. One explanation is that different instruments were used to measure the same personality variable, but this is not always the case (as can be seen in Naiman *et al.*'s results). The main problem was that there was no clear theoretical basis for predicting which personality variables would be positively or negatively related to which aspects of L2 proficiency. However, the dimension of personality that has attracted the most attention from researchers—extraversion/introversion—has proved more rewarding.

Extraversion and introversion

Extraversion/introversion represents a continuum (i.e. individuals can be more or less extraverted), but it is also possible to identify idealized types:

> Extraverts are sociable, like parties, have many friends and need excitement; they are sensation-seekers and risk-takers, like practical jokes and are lively and active. Conversely introverts are quiet, prefer reading to meeting people, have few but close friends and usually avoid excitement. (Eysenck and Chan 1982: 154)

The extent to which individuals verge towards one of these types is usually measured by analysing responses to self-report questions such as those in the Eysenck Personality Questionnaire or the Myers Briggs Type Indicator.

There are two major hypotheses regarding the relationship between extraversion/introversion and L2 learning. The first—which has been the most widely researched—is that extraverted learners will do better in acquiring basic interpersonal communication skills (BICS). The rationale for this hypothesis is that sociability (an essential feature of extraversion) will result in more opportunities to practise, more input, and more success in communicating in the L2. The second hypothesis is that introverted learners will do better at developing cognitive academic language ability (CALP). The rationale for this hypothesis comes from studies which show that introverted learners typically enjoy more academic success, perhaps because they spend more time reading and writing. (See Griffiths 1991b.)

There is some support for the first hypothesis. Strong (1983) reviewed the results of 12 studies which had investigated extraversion or similar traits (sociability, empathy, outgoingness, and popularity). He showed that in the eight studies where the criterion measure was 'natural communicative language' and which, therefore, provided an indication of BICS, 6 of them showed that extraversion was an advantage. Strong then reported his own study of 13 Spanish-speaking kindergarten children in which various dimensions of personality were investigated using both classroom observation and Coan and Cattell's (1966) Early School Personality Questionnaire. Interestingly, he found that those measures derived from observation accounted for nearly all the statistically significant correlations with language measures based on the children's natural communicative language. The important variables were talkativeness, responsiveness, and gregariousness, all of which are behaviours associated with extraversion.

However, not all studies have shown that extraversion is positively related to learners' oral language. Dörnyei and Kormos (2000), for example, failed to find any relationship between measures of social cohesiveness or of sociometric interrelationships in 46 Hungarian EFL students and measures of engagement in an oral argumentative task (i.e. number of turns or words used). They suggested that learners may adopt a 'learning mode' when performing a task in the L2 and this negates the effect of social factors such as their relationship to their interlocutor.

The crucial factor might be the task used to elicit samples of oral language and the choice of criterion measure. Dewaele and Furnham (1999) reviewed some 30 studies of personality and concluded:

> Extraverts were found to be generally more fluent than introverts in both the L1 and L2. They were not, however, necessarily more accurate in their L2, which reinforced the view that fluency and accuracy are separate dimensions in second language proficiency.
> (p. 32)

They pointed out that the strength of the relationship depends on the task—the more complex the task, the stronger the relationship. Drawing on Eysenck's theory of personality, they claimed that extraverts are less easily distracted when operating from short-term memory, are better equipped physiologically to resist stress and thus have lower levels of anxiety, which allows for greater attentional selectivity. They suggested that extraverts and introverts may make different choices in the accuracy–speed trade off, especially when they are required to perform in the L2 under pressure or stress. Dewaele and Furnham (2000) reported a study designed to test this hypothesis. They investigated 21 Flemish advanced learners of L2 French, recording their oral production in two tasks—an oral exam (considered to constitute an interpersonally stressful context) and a relaxed, informal conversation. They found a number of clear differences between the extraverts and introverts. The former had a higher speech rate in both tasks and in the informal task opted for shorter utterances. The introverts used a more explicit speech style (measured in terms of a preference for nominal as opposed to verbal constructions) and a much richer vocabulary in the formal task. Dewaele and Furnham concluded 'the formality of the situation, or rather the interpersonal stress that it provokes, has the strongest effect on the speech production processes of the introverts'.

The second hypothesis has received less support. Strong's survey of studies that investigated the effects of introversion on 'linguistic task language' reveals that less than half report a significant relationship. Busch (1982), in a study not included in Strong's survey, also failed to find a relationship. She used the Eysenck Personality Inventory to obtain measures of extraversion/introversion. Her subjects were adolescent and adult Japanese learners of English in Japan. The correlations between introversion and scores on a four-part written proficiency test were non-significant (with one exception) and generally negative in the case of the adolescents, and non-significant but positive in the case of the adults. This study, then, also fails to lend much support to the hypothesis that introversion aids the development of academic language skills. Later studies have also reported non-significant or weak relationships between measures of extraversion/introversion and formal proficiency measures. Carrell, Prince, and Astika (1996) in a study of Indonesian learners of English found few direct relationships between a measure of extraversion/introversion derived from the Myers Briggs Type Indicator and their performance on a battery of discrete-point tests. Similarly, Ehrman and Oxford (1995) found little evidence of any relationship in a study of 855 Foreign Service Institute students.

One profitable line of enquiry might be to investigate the relations between personality variables and the different kinds of behaviour that learners engage in. Ehrman (1990) examined the relationship between personality and choice of learning strategies. Robson (1992) undertook a small-scale study of Japanese college students, measuring personality by means of the Yatabe/Guilford Personality Inventory, and obtaining measures of voluntary participation from oral English classes. His general finding was that learners who are extravert and emotionally stable were more likely to engage in oral participation than introverts and neurotics. It does not follow, of course, that such learners will be more successful, as high levels of classroom participation may not enhance L2 learning. (See Chapter 15.)

The big five

The theory of personality currently dominant in psychology is the 'big five' model. This distinguishes five dimensions of personality: (1) openness to experience, (2) conscientiousness, (3) extraversion–introversion, (4) agreeableness, and (5) neuroticism–emotional stability. Somewhat surprisingly, there have been few L2 studies based on this model. A study by Verhoeven and Vermeer (2002) suggested that it may yield some interesting results. They developed a rating instrument consisting of 30 pairs of statements designed to reflect the five personality traits. They asked a teacher to assess the personality of 241 native-speaking and L2-learning children in the Netherlands based on this instrument. The dependent variables in this study were measures of different aspects of the children's COMMUNICATIVE COMPETENCE (organizational competence, PRAGMATIC COMPETENCE, and strategic competence). In the case of both the L1 and the L2 children a number of significant correlations were found. For the L2 children, openness to experience was related to all three aspects of communicative competence, extraversion was related to strategic competence, and conscientiousness was related to organizational competence. Verhoeven and Vermeer suggested that the powerful result they obtained for openness to experience might reflect the fact that 'children who display a great desire to belong and identify with the target language speaking peers tend to make the best progress in learning' (p. 373), suggesting a connection between this dimension of personality and motivation. The relationship between extraversion and strategic competence is also intuitively convincing in that extraverted learners are more likely to employ strategies to compensate for their limited language skills. This study bears out the results of other studies that suggest that personality figures in the development of communicative rather than formal linguistic competence and points to the need for further studies based on the big five model.

Final comment

To sum up, whereas early research failed to demonstrate a clear relationship between personality and language learning, a number of later studies have been more successful. There is growing evidence that traits such as extraversion and openness to experience are related to measures of communicative language use, especially fluency. Nevertheless, the research overall has been somewhat disappointing. Dörnyei (2005) offered a number of reasons for this:

1 The effects of personality may be situation-dependent, evident in some learning contexts or tasks but not in others. This may be why generalized linear associations are frequently not found.
2 The correlational approach to investigating the relationship between personality and L2 learning is somewhat naïve, as it ignores the fact that the

effects of personality may be mediated by other variables such as language-related attitudes, motivation, and situational anxiety.

3 The failure to find any clear relationship between personality dimensions such as extraversion and academic success may be because researchers have concentrated on 'supertraits' (such as introversion) rather than adopting a more fine-grained approach based on 'primary traits' (i.e. the specific characteristics that together comprise a supertrait).
4 Various methodological deficiencies (for example, the use of convenience samples, the time gap between the measurement of personality and language proficiency, the use of different measures of L2 performance/proficiency).

However, these limitations are evident in individual differences research in general. What is especially limiting in the case of the personality research is the failure to explore specific interactions between personality measures and learners' performance under different instructional conditions, as suggested by Griffiths (1991b) and as exemplified in Dewaele and Furnham's (2000) study. In particular, the role that personality plays in language learning needs to be examined in terms of how traits such as extraversion/introversion influence the way that learners process language.

Motivation

No single individual difference factor in language learning has received as much attention as MOTIVATION. Initially in the 1970s and 1980s, theorizing and research about motivation centred on Gardner and Lambert's (1972) social psychological construct of integrative motivation. Then, in the 1990s, attention switched to a more cognitive-situated view of motivation where the significance of situation-specific factors such as the classroom learning situation was examined (for example, Crookes and Schmidt 1991; Williams and Burden 1997). Recently, a more process-oriented view of motivation has emerged. This emphasizes the dynamic nature of motivation and its temporal variation (for example, Dörnyei 2001a). The 1990s in particular show an explosion of interest in the role motivation played in language learning. Dörnyei (2005) claimed that there were almost 100 studies published in this decade.

This shifting theoretical and research focus in motivation studies makes a brief survey difficult to undertake. Two possible approaches suggest themselves. One is to adopt a historical perspective tracing the developments that took place over some thirty odd years of research. This was the approach adopted by Dörnyei (2005). The second approach is to identify the key motivational constructs that have figured to date and consider these. I have elected for this latter approach, in part because it can incorporate a historical perspective, but mainly because it affords the reader a rapid view of the 'state-of-art' of language-learner motivation research. The key constructs I will address are:

1 integrative motivation
2 instrumental motivation
3 linguistic self-confidence
4 attributions
5 intrinsic motivation and self-determination
6 self-regulation
7 motivational phases
8 the ideal language self.

In the subsections that follow, I will describe each construct and examine some of the research related to each. I will conclude by considering how research on motivation can align itself more closely with mainstream SLA research by focusing on the processes of acquisition.

Integrative motivation

Dörnyei (2005) pointed out that the term INTEGRATIVE MOTIVATION has often been misunderstood and suggested that this is because the term 'integrative' figures in three separate, distinct, but related constructs—'integrative orientation', 'integrativeness', and the 'integrative motive/motivation'. In line with Dörnyei's elucidation of this terminological confusion, 'integrative motivation' can be defined as involving three subcomponents:

1 integrativeness (including integrative orientation, interest in foreign languages, and attitudes toward the L2 community)
2 attitudes towards the learning situation (i.e. attitudes towards the teacher and the L2 course)
3 motivation (i.e. the effort, desire, and attitude toward L2 learning).

As we saw in Chapter 6, Gardner's research rests on the use of self-report questionnaires. Table 13.9 shows the variables that Gardner and MacIntyre (1991) included in their composite measure of this factor. It is important to recognize, as MacIntyre (2002) put it, that 'the student who endorses integrative attitudes, or more simply an integrative orientation or goal, but who does not show effort or engagement with the language, is simply not a motivated learner' (p. 48).

Mixed results have been reported for the relationship between integrative motivation and L2 learning. Au (1988) reviewed 14 studies carried out by Gardner and his associates. Out of these, seven found a nil relationship and four found a negative relationship between at least some integrative motive measures and L2 achievement. Out of 13 studies conducted by other researchers, only a minority produced evidence of even a modest positive relationship. Au argued that 'there is little evidence that integrative motive is a unitary concept' (1988: 82) and criticized Gardner for failing to address why some components are found to relate to L2 achievement, while others are not. Gardner's (1988) response to Au's criticisms was to claim that it is 'simplistic'

Variable	Questionnaire items	Example
Attitudes towards French Canadians	Five positively-worded and five negatively-worded items.	'If Canada should lose the French culture of Quebec, it would indeed be a great loss.'
Interest in foreign languages	Five items expressing a positive interest and five a relative lack of interest.	'I enjoy meeting and listening to people who speak other languages.'
Integrative orientation	Four items expressing the importance of learning French for integrative reasons.	'Studying French can be important because it allows people to participate more freely in the activities of other cultural groups.'
Attitudes towards the learning situation	Four items referring to French teachers in general and four referring to French courses—half positive and half negative.	'French courses offer an excellent opportunity for students to broaden their cultural and linguistic horizons.'
Desire to learn French	Three positive and three negative items.	'I wish I were fluent in French.'
Attitudes towards learning French	Three positive and three negative items.	'I would really like to learn French.'

Table 13.9 An operational definition of 'integrative motivation' (based on Gardner and MacIntyre 1991)

to assume that the measures of the different components that make up an integrative motive will be equivalent to each other and he then referred to other studies not mentioned by Au (reviewed in Gardner 1980; Lalonde and Gardner 1985), which show that a composite index of motivation predicts L2 achievement.

A consistent correlation between integrative motivation and L2 achievement has been found in studies of anglophone Canadians learning French. In the earlier research (for example, Gardner and Lambert 1972), integrative orientation was seen as a more powerful predictor of achievement in formal learning situations than instrumental orientation (i.e. valuing the L2 for the practical advantages it confers on the learner). In later research, Gardner (1985) continued to assert the importance of integrative motivation but also acknowledged that learners can have both integrative and instrumental motivation, as demonstrated in studies of foreign language learners such as that of Muchnick and Wolfe (1982). This study showed that measures of the integrative and instrumental motivation of 337 students of Spanish in high schools in the United States loaded on the same factor, suggesting that for these learners, it was impossible to separate the two kinds of motivation. Similarly, Ely (1986b) investigated the types of motivation found in first-year university students of Spanish in the United States and found evidence of both strong integrative and strong instrumental motivation. In this study, the two types emerged as separate factors, but they were both present in the same students.

In order to demonstrate the overall effect of motivation on L2 achievement, Gardner (1980, 1985) chose to report the effects of a general measure of motivation (based on the Attitude Motivation Test Battery (AMTB), which includes variables relating to both integrative and instrumental motivation). A survey of seven different geographical areas in Canada revealed a median correlation of 0.37 between the AMTB scores and French grades. Thus, general motivation (comprised primarily of measures of integrative motivation) accounted for approximately 14 per cent of the variance in achievement scores. According to Gardner, this constituted a 'remarkably strong' relationship.

Integrative motivation does not affect language learning directly; rather its effect is mediated by the learning behaviours that it instigates. In a series of studies inspired by Gardner's socio-educational model (see Chapter 7 for an account of this), Gliksman (for example, in Gliksman 1976; Gliksman, Gardner, and Smythe 1982) provided evidence to show that students studying French in Canadian high schools received directed teacher questions, volunteered answers, gave correct answers, and received positive reinforcement according to the strength of their integrative motivation. The higher their integrative motivation, the more these classroom behaviours were evident.

There have also been a number of studies that have investigated the relationships between motivation, persistence, and achievement. Clement, Smythe, and Gardner (1978) investigated what factors caused Canadian students in Grades 9, 10, and 11 to drop out of a French programme. They found that motivation proved a more powerful predictor than language aptitude, classroom anxiety, or even L2 achievement. Ramage (1990) investigated the factors causing high-school students of French and Spanish to drop out in the United States. Her most significant finding was that students who chose to continue their studies beyond the second year attached very low importance to fulfilling curriculum requirements, and instead reported an interest in the target-language cultures (which suggests an integrative orientation) and the desire to attain proficiency in all language skills.

Gardner's SOCIO-EDUCATIONAL MODEL (with integrative motivation the key construct) was the dominant theory in early motivation research. It did not go unchallenged, however. Some studies failed to find a positive relationship between integrative motivation and L2 achievement. For example, Oller, Baca, and Vigil (1977) reported that Mexican women in California who rated Anglo people negatively were more successful in learning English than those who rated them positively. Oller and Perkins (1978) suggested that some learners may be motivated to excel because of negative attitudes towards the target-language community. In this case negative feelings may lead to a desire to manipulate and overcome the people of the target language—a phenomenon which they refer to as MACHIAVELLIAN MOTIVATION. In other studies (for example, Chihara and Oller 1978) the relationship between measures of integrative motivation and achievement was weak and insignificant. Kruidenier and Clement (1986) also failed to find any evidence in support for Gardner's integrative orientation in a study of language learners in Quebec. Instead they found evidence of a number of different orientations (friendship, travel, knowledge, and instrumental) with different groups of learners revealing different dominant orientations, depending on their learning situation. For example, learners of a minority language like Spanish were more influenced by a travel orientation, whereas Francophone learners of English were more influenced by a friendship orientation. One possibility raised by Dörnyei (1990), however, is that these various orientations are all part of a general integrative orientation, with different groups of learners emphasizing different constituents of this.

Gardner's construct has also been challenged on methodological and theoretical grounds. (See, for example, Au 1988.) First, the content validity of the AMTB has been criticized. Dörnyei (2005) argued that the items in the 'motivation' sub-component conflate the mental phenomenon of 'being motivated' with the behaviours this gives rise to, i.e. it 'assesses both motivation and motivated behaviour' (p. 73). As a result 'it is not easy to decide the exact nature of the underlying trait that the instrument targets'. Second, as noted above, other research in Canada has shown that Francophone learners display a number of different orientations. Noels, Pelletier, Clement, and Vallerand (2000), for example, claimed that the integrative orientation is 'not fundamental to the motivational process' (p. 60). Third, it has become clear that learners' orientations change over time, reflecting both shifting societal patterns and technological developments. Thus, in a replication of the Kruidenier and Clement study (referred to above), using a sample drawn from the same population, Belmechri and Hummel (1998) found some of the same orientations (for example, travel and friendship) but also some new ones (for example, self-understanding and instrumental). Fourth, for some time Gardner failed to acknowledge the resultative dimension of motivation. Gardner viewed motivation as causative (i.e. it led to L2 achievement) but a number of studies indicated that, in some learners, motivation resulted from success in learning. Fifth, other researchers attacked the definition of integrative orientation on the grounds that many learners have little real interest in the 'other' (i.e. target-language) community but rather seek to develop a global language identity (at least where the acquisition of a world language like English is concerned). Lamb (2004), for example, provided evidence that Indonesian learners of English oriented to English as 'an integral part of the globalization process' (p. 15). Sixth, Gardner was seen as presenting motivation in too static a way, failing to acknowledge that it was dynamic, shifting all the time as a result of learners' learning experiences and, no doubt, countless other purely personal factors. Finally, from a pedagogic perspective, the social psychological perspective was seen as too deterministic—motivation was treated as something that learners brought to the task of learning an L2 that determined their success. It did not allow for the possibility that learners could develop intrinsic interest in the process of their attempts to learn. For this reason, in particular, the theory was seen as lacking in pedagogic relevance (Crookes and Schmidt 1991).

Gardner has been vigorous in defence of integrative motivation as a primary factor accounting for L2 achievement and has somewhat stubbornly refused to entertain alternative models of motivation. In defence of the construct, Masgoret and Gardner (2003) conducted a meta-analysis of 75 independent samples totalling 10,489 individual learners drawn from a range of earlier studies. The results of this analysis demonstrated that there was a consistent relationship between the three components of integrative motivation (integrativeness, attitudes towards the learning situation, and motivation) and both objective and self-rating measures of achievement and, also, that the measure of motivation was more strongly related to achievement than the other components of integrative motivation, thus supporting Gardner's long-held view that motivation was more directly related to achievement than integrativeness or attitudes towards the learning situation. Interestingly, however, this meta-analysis did not support the claim that the learning environment had a moderating effect; the measures of integrative motivation were as strongly related to achievement in foreign as in second language environments. Masgoret and Gardner admitted that these findings may simply reflect the Canadian setting from which all the samples were drawn but consider this unlikely. Overall, the meta-analysis supports the claim that integrative motivation is an important factor in L2 achievement.

Motivation research has clearly moved on from Gardner's early formulation of integrative motivation, as to some extent has Gardner himself. (See, for example, Tremblay and Gardner 1995.) However, the developments in motivational theory in the 1990s and beyond all took Gardner's 'integrative motivation' as their starting point. Most current theories of motivation continue to include some notion of integrativeness. Csizer and Dörnyei (2005a), for example, proposed that 'integrativeness' be viewed as a projection of the learner's 'ideal self', which is discussed later in this section.

Instrumental motivation

INSTRUMENTAL MOTIVATION is also a component of Gardner's socio-educational model; it is important to recognize that it can work in conjunction with, rather than in opposition to, integrative motivation. It refers to the motivation that derives from a perception of the concrete benefits that learning the L2 might bring about. Here it is again useful to distinguish 'orientation' and 'motivation'. Gardner and MacIntyre (1991) measured the former by means of a self-report questionnaire in which learners responded to statements such as 'Studying French can be important because it is useful for one's career'. They equated 'instrumental motivation' with giving students a financial reward for performing a task successfully. Later, Gardner (2001) proposed that the 'motivation' subcomponent of integrative motivation could be combined with instrumental orientation to constitute a questionnaire-derived measure of instrumental motivation, reflecting his view that the 'motivation' component of the socio-educational model is independent of but influenced by learners' orientations.

Much of the research has investigated the effects of an instrumental orientation (as opposed to instrumental motivation) on learning. The results have been variable, reflecting the situational/cultural context of learning. Thus, whereas instrumental motivation has been found to be only a weak predictor of foreign language achievement, in several Canadian studies (see Gardner and Lambert 1972; Masgoret and Gardner 2003), it appears to be much more powerful in other contexts where learners have little or no interest in the target-language culture and few or no opportunities to interact with its members. For example, Gardner and Lambert (1972) found that a measure of instrumental orientation accounted for a significant proportion of the variance in Tagalog learners of L2 English in the Philippines. Similarly, Lukmani (1972) found that an instrumental orientation was more important than an integrative orientation in non-Westernized female learners of L2 English in Bombay. The social situation helps to determine both what kind of orientation learners have and what kind is most important for language learning.

Surprisingly, there have been few studies which have investigated the direct effect of an instrumental motivation through the provision of some kind of incentive to learn. In a very early study, Dunkel (1948) (cited in Gardner and MacIntyre 1992) offered financial rewards to students learning Farsi and found that although this did not result in a significantly better performance on a grammar test, there was a tendency in this direction. Gardner and MacIntyre (1991) reported a study in which 46 university psychology students were rewarded with $10 if they succeeded in a paired-associate (English-French) vocabulary task, while the same number were just told to do their best. The students offered the reward did significantly better. They also spent more time viewing the pairs of words, except on the sixth and last trial in the task, when the possibility of a reward no longer existed. This led Gardner and MacIntyre to claim that once any chance for receiving a reward is eliminated, learners may cease applying extra effort. They see this as a major disadvantage of instrumental motivation.

To sum up, learners with an instrumental reason for learning an L2 can be successful although overall it appears less influential than integrative motivation. In some 'second' as opposed to 'foreign' settings an instrumental orientation may be the most important one. Providing learners with incentives (such as money) may also aid learning by increasing the time learners spend studying, but the effects may cease as soon as the reward stops.

Linguistic self-confidence

Another influential group of Canadian researchers proposed a different model of motivation based on the construct of linguistic SELF-CONFIDENCE. (See Clement and Kruidenier 1983, 1985; Clement 1986; Kruidenier and Clement 1986.) Clement (1986), for example, investigated 293 francophone students at the University of Ottawa, dividing them into a majority and minority group, depending on whether francophones were in the majority or minority in their home areas. The subjects completed a questionnaire designed to produce measures of variables such as integrativeness, fear of assimilation, motivation (defined in terms of 'attitudes' and 'desire'), self-confidence, frequency of contact, and acculturation. English language ability was measured by means of an oral interview and a general proficiency test. One of the main findings of this study was that integrativeness was not related to language outcomes, nor was it influenced by the status of the learners (i.e. whether they belonged to the majority or minority group). The best predictor of language proficiency proved to be self-confidence (i.e. belief in one's ability to learn an L2 successfully), a finding that held for both groups. Clement pointed out that many of Gardner's earlier studies had investigated school students and that the rather different results he obtained might reflect the greater maturity and autonomy of his (Clement's) subjects, who typically learnt and used English on a day-to-day basis, mainly outside the classroom. Clement suggested that for such learners 'frequency of contact and the concomitant self-confidence might be more important in determining second language proficiency than socio-contextual or affective factors' (1986: 287). In a later study, Clement, Dörnyei and Noels (1994) showed that linguistic self-confidence also contributed to learning in foreign language learning situations where the learners had little contact with the L2 outside of the classroom.

Attributions

The term ATTRIBUTIONS refers to the explanations learners give for their progress in learning an L2. As Dörnyei (2005) put it 'the subjective reasons to which we attribute our past successes and failures considerably shape our motivational disposition underlying future action' (p. 79). The key attributions are ability and effort.

The recognition that such attributions can affect a learner's motivation originated in research showing that motivation can result from as well as lead to success in L2 learning. Initially, motivation researchers were reluctant to acknowledge this. Gardner (1985) claimed that motivation constituted a causative variable, although he was always prepared to accept that some modification of learners' attitudes could arise as a result of positive learning experiences, particularly in courses of a short duration. Spolsky (1989) reviewed a number of studies which suggested that 'while greater motivation and attitudes lead to better learning, the converse is not true' (1989: 153).

Other studies, however, suggested that learners' motivation was strongly affected by their achievement. Strong (1983, 1984) investigated motivation and English language attainment in Spanish-speaking kindergarten children and found that fluency in English preceded an inclination to associate with target-language groups. Hermann (1980) also suggested that it was success that contributed to motivation rather than vice versa and advanced the 'Resultative Hypothesis', which claims that learners who do well are more likely to develop motivational intensity and to be active in the classroom. Such research led Gardner (see Tremblay and Gardner 1995) to acknowledge the effect that learning could have on motivation.

However, while the role of learner attributions in shaping motivation is now fully acknowledged, there have been few studies that have investigated it. Dörnyei (2001a) suggested that this is because motivation research has typically been quantitative, based on surveys, a method that does not easily lend itself to investigating attributions. He argued that qualitative studies are needed. An example of such a study is Ushioda (2003). She carried out in-depth interviews with adult Irish learners of French to investigate what factors enabled these learners to maintain a positive self-concept and their belief in their capacity to learn French. She identified two attributional patterns that contributed to this: (1) attributing positive L2 outcomes to personal ability and/or effort and (2) attributing negative L2 outcomes to temporary shortcomings, such as lack of effort or of opportunity to learn, which could be overcome. Williams and Burden (1999) also used interviews in a study of school learners of French in English schools. They found differences in the reasons given for success according to the children's age. The younger learners (10–12-year-olds) gave listening and concentration as their reasons, while the older children (13–17-year-olds) gave a wider range of reasons such as their ability and the influence of others. Ellis, Hacker, and Loewen (2006) examined whether prior language study in a primary school context influenced New Zealand secondary school students' motivation to learn a foreign language. They reported that those who had experienced two years of foreign language study in their primary schools reported greater intrinsic interest in learning a foreign language and for learning local indigenous languages (i.e. Maori and Pacific Island languages).

Both of these studies investigated foreign language settings, where the attributions learners form may be especially potent in influencing motivation. Berwick and Ross's (1989) study of 90 first-year Japanese university students majoring in international commerce and taking obligatory English classes, although not specifically undertaken to examine the role of attributions, nevertheless points to their importance in such a group of learners. They had a strong instrumental motivation to learn English, as they needed to pass the university entrance examinations, but typically became demotivated once they were at university. Berwick and Ross found little evidence of any motivation whatsoever on a pre-test administered at the beginning of the English course, but much more on a post-test given at the end. The students' motivation appeared to broaden as a result of the course with two new motivational factors, labelled 'support' and 'interest', emerging. This study provides clear evidence of 'an experiential dimension to learner's motivation'.

It is likely that the relationship between motivation and achievement is an interactive one. A high level of motivation does stimulate learning, but perceived success in achieving L2 goals can help to maintain existing motivation and even create new types. Conversely, a vicious circle of low motivation → low achievement → lower motivation can develop especially if learners attribute their failure to factors they feel powerless to alter.

Intrinsic motivation and self-determination

The notion of INTRINSIC MOTIVATION is an old one in psychology, although until recently it has not figured strongly in L2 research. It was developed as an alternative to goal-directed theories of motivation that emphasize the role of extrinsic rewards and punishments. Keller (1984) (cited in Crookes and Schmidt 1991) identified 'interest' as one of the main elements of motivation, defining it as a positive response to stimuli based on existing cognitive structures in such a way that learners' curiosity is aroused and sustained. It is this view that underlies discussions of motivation in language pedagogy. Crookes and Schmidt (1991) observed that 'it is probably fair to say that teachers would describe a student as motivated if s/he becomes productively engaged in learning tasks, and sustains that engagement, without the need for continual encouragement or direction' (p. 480). Teachers see it as their job to motivate students by engaging their interest in classroom activities.

One possibility, supported by a strong pedagogic literature (see Holec 1980; Dickinson 1987), is that interest is engendered if learners become self-directed (i.e. are able to determine their own learning objectives, choose their own ways of achieving these, and evaluate their own progress). Dickinson referred to a study by Bachman (1964) which indicated that involving learners in decision-making tended to lead to increased motivation and, thereby, to increased productivity. Gardner, Ginsberg, and Smythe (1976) compared the effects of two sorts of instructional programmes on 25 learners of French at Dalhousie University in Canada. One was very traditional—lockstep teaching with a heavy focus on grammatical accuracy—while the other was innovative, with individualized instruction and opportunity for free communication. The students who experienced the traditional programme indicated that they were more likely to withdraw and had a more negative view of their French teacher. Those who experienced the innovatory programme reported a greater desire to excel and a more positive attitude to learning French. Diary studies also provide evidence to suggest that self-direction is important to learners. For example, J. Schumann (Schumann and Schumann 1977) reported frustration with the instructional programme he was following because of his wish to maintain a personal language learning agenda.

Noels, Pelletier, Clement, and Vallerand (2000) developed a detailed model based on the distinction between intrinsic and EXTRINSIC MOTIVATION. They defined extrinsically motivated behaviours as 'those actions carried out to achieve some instrumental end' (p. 61) and distinguished three types: (1) external regulation, which involves behaviour motivated by sources external to the learner such as tangible benefits and costs, (2) introjected regulation, which involves behaviour that results from some kind of pressure that individuals have incorporated into the self, and (3) identified regulation, consisting of behaviour that stems from personally relevant reasons. Intrinsic motivation was defined as 'motivation to engage in an activity because it is enjoyable and satisfying to do so' (p. 61). Again, three types were distinguished: (1) knowledge (i.e. the motivation derived from exploring new ideas and knowledge), (2) accomplishment (i.e. the pleasant sensations aroused by trying to achieve a task or goal), and (3) stimulation (i.e. the fun and excitement generated by actually performing a task). Noels *et al.* also considered amotivation (i.e. the absence of any motivation to learn). A factor-analytic study based on responses to a questionnaire by anglophone learners of L2 French in Canada largely confirmed this model of motivation, clearly distinguishing the extrinsic and intrinsic motivations. As expected, amotivation was negatively correlated with measures of perceived competence and intention to continue study. Interestingly, the measures of intrinsic motivation were more strongly correlated with the criterion measures than the measures of extrinsic motivation. Noel *et al.* interpreted the results in terms of self-determination theory, arguing that the more self-determined a learner's motivation is the greater the achievement. This study, then, bears out the general claim that intrinsic motivation contributes strongly to L2 learning.

Self-regulation

SELF-REGULATION refers to the ability to monitor one's learning and make changes to the strategies that one employs. Dörnyei (2005) writes:

> The basic assumption underlying the notion of motivational self-regulation is that students who are able to maintain their motivation and keep themselves on-task in the face of competing demands and attractions should learn better than students who are less skilled at regulating their motivation.
> (p. 91)

This involves both the ability to exercise control over one's attitudinal/motivational state and to engage in self-critical reflection of one's actions and underlying belief systems. As such, it will be considered in more detail in later sections of this chapter when learners' beliefs and learning strategies are examined.

Motivational phases

One of the major developments in the study of L2 learner motivation has been the recognition of its dynamic, temporal aspect. In effect, the study of learner attributions acknowledges the temporal aspect, as it recognizes that motivation can change over the course of learning an L2 as a result of how learners evaluate and explain their progress (or lack of it). However, this does not so clearly address the fluctuating nature of motivation during the course of learning events (for example, a language lesson). For this, a more process-oriented approach is needed.

Williams and Burden (1997) distinguished three motivational phases: (1) 'reasons for doing something', (2) 'deciding to do something', and (3) 'sustaining the effort or persisting'. Similarly, Dörnyei's process model of learning motivation for the L2 classroom (Dörnyei 2001a) distinguished a 'preactional stage' involving 'choice motivation', which relates closely to the idea of orientation, an 'actional stage' involving 'executive motivation', which concerns the effort the learner is prepared to invest to achieve the overall goal and which is heavily influenced by the quality of the learning experience, and a 'postactional stage' involving 'motivational retrospection', where the learner evaluates the learning experience and progress to date and determines preparedness to continue. Such a model is able to account for how motivation changes over time and, as such, is far superior to the static models of motivation that have dominated research to date. It is also capable of integrating other models of motivation. For example, the preactional stage incorporates such constructs as integrative motivation, the actional stage incorporates instrumental motivation (if this is operationalized in terms of rewards for task performance) and intrinsic motivation, and the postactional stage incorporates attribution theory.

Arguably, the stage that has been most neglected by L2 researchers is the actional stage. This is characterized by three motivational functions in Dörnyei's model—generating and carrying out sub-tasks, ongoing appraisal, and action control or self-regulation. Motivation during this stage is influenced by a number of factors—the quality of the learning experience, the learner's sense of autonomy, the influence of teachers and parents, classroom rewards, the influence of the learner group, and the learner's knowledge and use of self-regulatory strategies. Dörnyei emphasized that actional processes do not occur in isolation. Thus a new action may be initiated while a previous one is being evaluated. Also, actional processes need to be understood in terms of the broader social context in which learning takes place. For example, foreign language learning in school needs to be understood in terms of learners' overall attitude to school and academic study. Dörnyei (2005) noted, however, that to date there has been hardly any research that has examined how learners deal with multiple actions and goals.

One study that addressed motivation in the actional stage is Egbert's (2003) investigation of 'flow' in the context of fourth-semester university Spanish learners' performance of a number of learning tasks. 'Flow' is defined as 'an experiential state characterized by intense focus and involvement that leads to improved performance on a task' (p. 499). Egbert identified a number of conditions that are likely to promote flow: (1) a perceived balance of skills and challenges, (2) opportunities for intense concentration, (3) feedback showing one is succeeding, (4) a lack of self-consciousness, and (5) the perception of time passing quickly. The study investigated the extent to which the learners exhibited flow when performing seven communicative tasks over the course of a whole semester. Multiple sources of data were collected (i.e. a perceptions survey, observations of the learners performing the tasks, the task products, and post-task interviews). The extent to which the students evidenced flow on the different tasks was examined in terms of four dimensions of performance: (1) control, (2) focus, (3) interest, and (4) challenge. One of the main findings was that the nature of the task influenced flow. The task that elicited the greatest flow was one that required the students to engage in an electronic chat about artists while the one that produced the least flow was reading out loud in Spanish and asking questions. Egbert concluded that because the patterns of flow across tasks were very similar it was possible to 'talk about tasks that support flow' (p. 514). This study is interesting both methodologically in that it demonstrates how quantitative and qualitative data can mutually inform the study of motivation and theoretically in that it provides clear evidence of how instructional choices can influence learners' levels of motivation.

The ideal language self

Based on the findings from a large-scale study of 8,593 Hungarian school learners of foreign languages, Csizer and Dörnyei (2005a, 2005b), advanced a new theory of motivation centred on the notion of the 'ideal language self'. I will first briefly summarize the main findings of the research project and then outline the theory.

The instrument used to measure the students' motivation was a questionnaire consisting of items eliciting information related to the target languages (English, German, French, Italian, and Russian), the target-language communities, and a variety of non-language specific variables (i.e. attitudes toward the L2 community, contact with foreign languages, fear of assimilation, self-confidence, language learning milieu, language choice, and personal variables). As such, the questionnaire was an attempt to examine the range of variables that earlier research had indicated were important for motivation. Using structural equation modelling (a statistical technique designed to show the causal relationships between variables), Csizer and Dörnyei (2005a) located 'integrativeness' as the core variable influencing effort and language choice. Integrativeness subsumed 'attitudes towards L2 speakers', but, contrary to Gardner's claims (1985), it was also found to subsume instrumentality. Csizer and Dörnyei's (2005b) study was based on the same data set but employed a different method of analysis—cluster analysis, which is a statistical procedure that identifies homogeneous subgroups of learners within a sample. This revealed four broad motivational profiles that were independent of the language being learnt: (1) least motivated learners who had no interest in foreign languages, cultures or language learning, (2) learners who were more positively disposed towards the L2 culture and community, (3) learners who had a strong instrumental orientation, and (4) the most motivated learners who had high scores on all the motivational dimensions. Students who were studying more than one language (English and German) varied in their motivational profile and there was also evidence of 'competition' between the languages, with English (as a world language) the clear winner.

Csizer and Dörnyei (see also Dörnyei 2005) suggested that there is a need to reinterpret 'integrativeness' and proposed the construct of the 'ideal language self' to describe the attributes that a person would ideally like to possess. Thus 'motivation in this sense involves the desire to reduce the discrepancy between one's actual and ideal or ought-to selves' (Dörnyei 2005: 101). From this perspective 'integrativeness' can be reconceptualized as an L2 facet of one's ideal self. That is, if a learner's ideal self includes becoming proficient in an L2, then this indicates an integrative disposition. Dörnyei suggested that a learner's self-image as an L2 speaker is partly based on actual experiences of the L2 community and partly on imagination. Instrumentality can be related to the learner's ideal language self when extrinsic motives have become internalized. Dörnyei characterized this type of instrumentality as 'long-term instrumental motivation'. He contrasted it with the 'short-term instrumental motivation', evident when learners are simply focused on external incentives such as good grades, and suggested it is closely related to the 'ought-to L2 self'.

Final comment

There have been substantial developments in the study of L2 motivation. Whereas early social psychological research focused on a construct (integrative motivation) that had no clear links with the study of motivation in education or psychology, later research has increasingly aligned itself with constructs taken from these disciplines and is certainly the richer for it. Another development, which can be traced to the emphasis on intrinsic motivation and its dynamic, temporal aspect, is the attention being paid to how teachers can motivate their students. Drawing on this research (and perhaps even more so on his common sense), Dörnyei (2001b) proposed thirty-five strategies for the language classroom. Dörnyei emphasized that although the efficacy of many of these strategies remains to be confirmed, 'there is no doubt that student motivation can be consciously increased by using creative techniques' (p. 144).

However, the study of L2 motivation research continues to lie outside mainstream SLA. In motivation research L2 learning has typically been viewed as 'L2 achievement', operationalized in a variety of different ways (course grades, standardized achievement tests, or specific language tasks) rather than as a process of interlanguage development. An exception is Manolopoulo-Sergi (2004). She has argued convincingly that motivation of one kind or another is likely to influence the way in which learners process input, integrate intake into their interlanguage systems, and process output. She suggested, for example, that extrinsically motivated learners are likely to attend only to the surface characteristics of the input, whereas intrinsically motivated learners will process input in a more elaborated, deeper manner. However, to date, there has been no empirical study of how motivation influences learning at the micro- as opposed to macro-linguistic level by examining how it affects the key cognitive processes involved in input processing, interlanguage restructuring, and production described in Chapter 9.

Anxiety

Both naturalistic and classroom learners react to the learning situations in which they find themselves in a variety of affective ways. For example, F. Schumann (Schumann and Schumann 1977) reported being unable to settle down to studying Farsi and Arabic (in Iran and Tunisia) until she had achieved order and comfort in her physical surroundings. Bailey (1980) discussed a 'classroom crisis' that occurred when her French teacher administered a test that the class considered unfair. Language learning is an inherently emotional affair (Pavlenko 2006b).

The affective aspect that has received the most attention in SLA is ANXIETY. (See, for example, full-length books by Horwitz and Young (1991), Arnold (1999) and Young (1999).) A distinction can be made between TRAIT ANXIETY, STATE ANXIETY, and SITUATION-SPECIFIC ANXIETY. Scovel (1978), drawing on work in general psychology, defined trait anxiety as 'a more permanent predisposition to be anxious'. It is perhaps best viewed as an aspect of personality. State anxiety can be defined as apprehension that is experienced at a particular moment in time as a response to a definite situation (Spielberger 1983). It is a combination of trait and situation-specific anxiety. This latter type consists of the anxiety which is aroused by a specific type of situation or event such as public speaking, examinations, or class participation. Our concern here will be with a particular type of situation anxiety—'language anxiety' largely independent of other types of anxiety. It constitutes a 'primary emotion'. MacIntyre (2002), drawing on Buck (1984), distinguished two systems of emotion—a primary, primitive, subcortical system and a secondary, consciously evaluative system located in the cerebral cortex—and suggested that anxiety belongs to the former. It constitutes a physiological and automatic response to external events and manifests itself in particular in a reluctance to communicate in the L2.

Language anxiety has been studied in a number of ways. Some of the earliest studies (for example, Bailey 1983) used diary data to identify the sources of anxiety in language learners. More recently, studies have been correlational in nature (i.e. measures of language anxiety derived from questionnaire responses are correlated with measures of achievement). There has also been an attempt to examine experimentally how language anxiety affects language processing (MacIntyre and Gardner 1994). Ethnographic studies based on rich descriptions of learners' reactions to their learning situations have also begun to appear (for example, Spielman and Radnofsky 2001). The research has addressed three key issues: (1) the sources of language anxiety, (2) the nature of the relationship between language anxiety and language learning, and (3) how anxiety affects learning.

Sources of anxiety

The diary studies indicated that learners' competitive natures can act as a source of anxiety. Bailey (1983) analysed the diaries of 11 learners and found that they tended to become anxious when they compared themselves with other learners in the class and found themselves less proficient. She noted that as the learners perceived themselves becoming more proficient, and therefore better able to compete, their anxiety decreased. Bailey also identified other sources of anxiety, including tests and learners' perceived relationship with their teachers. Ellis and Rathbone (1987) reported that some of their diarists found teachers' questions threatening. For example, one of their subjects, Monique, commented:

> I was quite frightened when asked questions again. I don't know why; the teacher does not frighten me, but my mind is blocked when I'm asked questions. I fear lest I give the wrong answer and will discourage the teacher as well as be the laughing stock of the class maybe. Anyway, I felt really stupid and helpless in class.
> (Ellis 1989a: 257)

However, other learners experienced no worries about using German in class. When anxiety does arise relating to the use of the L2, it seems to be restricted mainly to speaking and listening, reflecting learners' apprehension at having to communicate spontaneously in the L2 (Horwitz, Horwitz, and Cope 1986). Matsumoto's (1987) learner, M, for example, displayed little anxiety but when she did it was in connection with her perceived problems in listening to and speaking English. Woodrow (2006) used interviews to investigate the sources of anxiety in speaking L2 English by 47 advanced EAP students in Australia. The three most prominent 'stressors' were 'performing English in front of classmates', 'giving an oral presentation', and 'speaking in English to native speakers' (p. 39). Woodrow found evidence of two types of anxious learner: those who experienced retrieval interference and those with a skills deficit.

Learners can also experience anxiety as a result of fear or experience of 'losing oneself' in the target culture. As Oxford (1992) pointed out, this is closely related to the idea of 'culture shock'. She listed the affective states associated with this source of anxiety: 'emotional regression, panic, anger, self-pity, indecision, sadness, alienation, "reduced personality" ...'. Gregersen and Horwitz (2002) found evidence in a qualitative study of university learners of English in Chile that anxiety was related to the personality trait of perfectionism. The anxious learners in this study reported higher standards, a greater tendency to procrastinate and to worry about the opinions of others, and more concern about making errors than the less anxious learners.

While it has been possible to identify a number of general sources of anxiety, it is important to bear in mind that learners differ in what they find anxiety-provoking. As Horwitz (2001) noted in her review of studies that have investigated the effects of instruction on anxiety 'in almost all cases, any task that was judged "comfortable" by some learners was also judged "stressful" by others' (p. 118).

The various sources of anxiety in the foreign language classroom are reflected in the questionnaires which researchers have devised to measure learner anxiety. Gardner and Smythe (1975) developed a French Class Anxiety Scale, and in subsequent studies developed scales to tap English Use Anxiety and English Test Anxiety. Horwitz, Horwitz, and Cope (1986) developed a Foreign Language Classroom Anxiety Scale, based on conversations with beginner learners who identified themselves as anxious. This questionnaire consists of thirty-three items relating to three general sources of anxiety: (1) communication apprehension, (2) tests, and (3) fear of negative evaluation. Examples of the kinds of statements learners are asked to respond to on a five-point scale are:

> I tremble when I know I am going to be called on in language class.
> I keep thinking that other students are better at language than I am.
> I get nervous when I don't understand every word the language teacher says.

MacIntyre and Gardner (1991b) have also developed an extensive set of scales (23 in all) to measure various forms of anxiety.

The sources and questionnaires referred to above all relate to the anxiety associated with speaking or listening in an L2. However, researchers have also identified sources of anxiety associated with the other language skills and developed questionnaires to measure them—for example, for writing see Cheng, Horwitz, and Schallert (1999). This raises a question regarding whether reading or writing anxiety are separate from or closely related to general language anxiety, with Horwitz (2001) arguing that they are.

Language anxiety and language learning

While there is wide agreement about the sources of language anxiety, especially in classroom settings, there is less agreement about the relationship between language anxiety and learning. Three different positions can be identified: (1) anxiety facilitates language learning, (2) anxiety has a negative impact on language learning, and (3) language anxiety is the result of difficulties with learning rather than their cause.

Eysenck (1979) noted that low levels of anxiety can lead to more effort. This suggests a connection between anxiety and motivation. Facilitative anxiety leads to increased motivation with concomitant benefits for learning.[6] Scovel (2001) pointed out that in sports psychology anxiety is not perceived as necessarily having a negative effect on performance. In accordance with the Yerkes-Dodson law, psychological arousal resulting from anxiety can facilitate performance. MacIntyre (2002) adopted a similar position. There is also empirical support for this position. In an early study, Chastain (1975) found that measures of anxiety in American university students were positively related to marks achieved by one group of audio-lingual French learners, indicating that the learners with higher levels of anxiety did best. Kleinmann (1978) provided evidence to show that Spanish- and Arabic-speaking learners of English who reported anxiety (i.e. responded positively to statements like 'Nervousness while using English helps me do better') were less likely to avoid complex grammatical structures such as infinitive complements and the passive voice than those students who reported no such anxiety.

In general, however, language anxiety has been found to have a negative effect on learning. In the Chastain study referred to above, anxiety was negatively and significantly related to marks in Spanish. Horwitz (1986) reported sizeable negative correlations (around –0.5) between foreign language classroom anxiety and final grades achieved by American university students. Young (1986) found that measures of anxiety correlated significantly and negatively with measures of oral proficiency in a group of prospective language teachers, although the relationship disappeared after controlling for ability, measured by means of other proficiency measures. Gardner, Moorcroft, and MacIntyre (1987) found a significant relationship between various measures of anxiety and scores on a word production task, but, interestingly, no relationship between the anxiety measures and free speech quality. Ely (1986a) reported that those learners with a high level of discomfort were less likely to take risks in class suggesting that high anxiety negatively affected motivation. MacIntyre and Gardner (1991b) found that language anxiety was negatively and significantly correlated with L2 performance, whereas no such correlation was found between anxiety and the learners' L1 (English). Woodrow (2006) found significant negative correlation between language anxiety both in and out of class and oral performance in 275 predominantly Asian advanced EAP students. MacIntyre and Gardner (1991a), in a comprehensive review of a number of studies, concluded:

> Covering several measures of proficiency, in several different samples, and even in somewhat different conceptual frameworks, it has been shown that anxiety negatively affects performance in the second language. In some cases, anxiety provides some of the highest simple correlations of attitudes with achievement
> (1991a: 103).

Other studies, however, have failed to show any relationship whatsoever between language anxiety and learning. Chastain (1975) reported that anxiety was positively but not significantly related to marks in German and, not related at all to marks in a 'regular' French group. This study, then, provided evidence of all three possible relationships—negative, positive, and none! Parkinson and Howell-Richardson (1990) also failed to find a relationship between measures of anxiety, based on an analysis of 51 diaries kept by adult learners of L2 English in Scotland, and rate of improvement—a result they considered 'surprising'.

As with motivation, a key issue is whether anxiety is the *cause* of poor achievement or the *result*. This issue has aroused considerable debate. Based on a series of studies of foreign language classroom learning, Sparks, Ganschow, and Javorsky (2000) promulgated the Linguistic Coding Difference Hypothesis, which claims that success in foreign language learning is primarily dependent on language aptitude and that students' anxiety about learning an L2 is a consequence of their learning difficulties. They dismissed the research carried out by Horwitz and her associates as 'misguided'. Not surprisingly, Horwitz (2000b) has reacted strongly to this dismissal of her work, arguing that while processing difficulties may cause anxiety in some learners it is not the cause in all learners, as even advanced, successful learners have reported experiencing anxiety. As Horwitz (2001) pointed out 'the challenge is to determine the extent to which anxiety is a cause rather than a result of poor language learning' (p. 118). What is needed is a dynamic model that shows how cognitive abilities and the propensity for anxiety interact in contributing to L2 achievement over time.

Language anxiety and the process of learning

The developmental model proposed by MacIntyre and Gardner (1991a) is summarized in Table 13.10. According to this model, the relationship between anxiety and learning is moderated by the learners' stage of development and by situation-specific learning experiences. The model hypothesizes that learners initially experience little anxiety so there is no effect on learning. This can explain findings such as those of Parkinson and Howell-Richardson (1990). Subsequently, language anxiety develops if learners have bad learning experiences (such as those documented in the diary studies). This then has a debilitative effect on learning. Not all studies support this model, however. Elkhafaifi (2005), for example, found higher levels of listening anxiety in beginner learners than in intermediate and advanced learners. It is possible, therefore, that in some learners, anxiety reduces as they develop. The model also recognizes that poor performance can be the cause as well as the result of anxiety, as claimed by Skehan (1989) and shown by Sparks *et al.* (2000).

Stage	Type of anxiety	Effect on learning
Beginner	Very little—restricted to state anxiety.	None.
Post-beginner	Situation anxiety develops if learner develops negative expectations based on bad learning experiences.	Learner expects to be nervous and performs poorly.
Later	Poor performance and continued bad learning experiences result in increased anxiety.	Continued poor performance.

Table 13.10 A model of the role of anxiety in the developmental process (based on MacIntyre and Gardner 1991a)

MacIntyre and Gardner (1991b) also pointed out that anxiety can be hypothesized to affect the different stages of the learning process; the input stage (i.e. when learners encounter material for the first time), the processing stage (i.e. when they make connections between the new information and existing knowledge), and the output stage (i.e. when they demonstrate the new knowledge). They set out to test this in an experimental study involving four groups of learners (MacIntyre and Gardner 1994). They used a video camera to induce anxiety at each of the three stages of cognitive processing in a computer-mediated vocabulary learning activity. They devised sets of questionnaire items to provide separate measures of Input Anxiety, Processing Anxiety and Output Anxiety.[7] They found that anxiety increased and performance decreased most immediately after the introduction of the video camera. However, as the learners grew used to the presence of the camera their anxiety declined and performance picked up. The study also showed that the learners were able to compensate for anxiety experienced at an earlier stage through increased effort at a later stage, thus demonstrating that anxiety could enhance motivation. MacIntyre and Gardner argued that this study demonstrated that anxiety is related causally to language achievement through the effect it has on learning processes.

The dynamic aspect of L2 learning, however, is not easily captured through questionnaires. It is more clearly evident in the early diary studies and also from Spielman and Radnofsky's (2001) ethnographic study of the 'tension' generated in a highly intensive residential French course for adults. This study showed that anxiety cannot be examined in purely quantitative terms (i.e. as more or less intense) but that it has a qualitative dimension as well. They proposed that anxiety can be 'euphoric/non-euphoric' (i.e. an event can be viewed as stressful but still viewed as positive or at least as not possessing negative characteristics) or dysphoric/non-dysphoric (i.e. a stressful event can be viewed negatively or as lacking in positive attributes). They documented how the students they studied experienced euphoric tension as the product of their attempts to re-invent themselves in the target language. Dysphoric tension arose largely as a result of the mismatch between the instructional programme and the students' own ideas about how best to learn and their need to be treated as adult, thinking people. The authors concluded that the causes of anxiety defy systematization but suggested that a pedagogic programme needs not just to avoid dysphoric tension but also to maximize the benefits to learning from euphoric tension.

Final comment

There is clear evidence to show that anxiety is an important factor in L2 acquisition. However, anxiety (its presence or absence) is best seen not as a necessary condition of successful L2 learning, but rather as a factor that contributes in differing degrees in different learners, depending in part on other individual difference factors such as their motivational orientation and personality. Research into language anxiety has made use of qualitative as well as quantitative methods. It has attempted to relate language anxiety to the developmental aspects of language learning and to a model of language processing. These are both positive aspects of anxiety research.

Willingness to communicate

A propensity factor that has attracted recent attention is WILLINGNESS TO COMMUNICATE (WTC), defined as 'the intention to initiate communication, given a choice' (MacIntyre, Baker, Clement, and Conrad 2001: 369).[8] As presented in MacIntyre's research, WTC is a complex construct, influenced by a number of other individual difference factors such as 'communication anxiety', 'perceived communication competence' and 'perceived behavioural control'. MacIntyre, Clement, Dörnyei, and Noels (1998) presented a schematic model of the WTC construct showing multiple layers of variables (such as those just mentioned) that feed into WTC. In other words WTC is seen as a final-order variable, determined by other factors, and the immediate antecedent of communication behaviour. Considerable research effort has gone into the attempt to validate this model.

It is very likely, however, that the precise pattern of factors influencing WTC is not fixed but situation-dependent. As Yashima (2002) noted 'a careful examination of what it means to learn a language in a particular context is necessary before applying a model developed in a different context' (p. 62). Yashima's own study investigated the WTC model in a Japanese-as-a-foreign-language context. Using structural equation modelling, Yashima showed that WTC figured in both an indirect path between other ID variables (international posture, motivation, self-confidence in communication) and language proficiency, and a direct path (i.e. international posture was directly related to WTC). The key variable influencing WTC in this context, therefore was 'international posture', defined as 'a general attitude towards the international community that influences English learning and communication among Japanese learners' (pp. 62–3).[9] Kang (2005) reported a qualitative study of the situated WTC of four adult male Korean learners of English in the United States. The learners were paired off with native speakers and invited to engage in free conversation. In this context 'international posture' did not appear to play any role. Rather 'the participants' situational WTC in their L2 appeared to emerge under psychological conditions of excitement, responsibility and security' (p. 282). Cao and Philp (2006) also provided evidence to show the situated nature of WTC. They found no statistically significant relationship between the eight adult learners of English self-reported WTC and their actual WTC as evidenced through observation of three interactional classroom contexts (whole class, pair work, and group work). Nor was there a clear relationship among manifested WTC in these three contexts.

WTC is of obvious interest to communicative language teaching (CLT), which places a premium on learning through communicating; learners with a strong willingness to communicate may be able to benefit from CLT while those who are not so willing may learn better from more traditional instructional approaches. Interestingly, MacIntyre *et al.* reported that WTC inside the classroom correlated strongly with WTC outside in anglophone learners of L2 French in Canada, demonstrating that WTC is a stable, trait-like factor. Dörnyei and Kormos (2000) found that Hungarian students' WTC in the classroom was influenced by their attitudes to the instructional task. Strong, positive correlations were found between a measure of WTC and the amount of English produced while performing a communicative task in the case of learners who expressed positive attitudes to the task but near zero correlations in the case of learners with low task attitudes. It would seem then that learners' willingness to communicate depends in part on their personality and in part on their intrinsic motivation to perform specific classroom activities.

Work on WTC is in its infancy. It is a promising construct in several respects. It constitutes an obvious link between other, more thoroughly investigated constructs (such as learner attitudes and motivation) and language proficiency. It is a construct of obvious relevance to language teaching. Dörnyei (2005) suggested that developing WTC is 'the ultimate goal of instruction' (p. 210).

Learners' beliefs

Language learners form 'mini theories' of L2 learning (Hosenfeld 1978) which shape the way they set about the learning task. These theories are made up of beliefs about language and language learning. Clearly 'beliefs' constitute an individual difference variable notably different from the other variables we have examined in that they are neither an ability nor a trait-like propensity for language learning. For this reason, Dörnyei (2005) queried whether they constitute 'a proper ID variable'. However, this would seem a little obtuse as clearly learners do vary considerably in their beliefs about language and language learning and it is reasonable to assume that their beliefs influence both the process and product of learning. Also, as we have seen, many of the other variables examined are also not really stable and trait-like but rather dynamic and situated.

Three different approaches to investigating learners' beliefs can be distinguished (Barcelos 2003). According to the normative approach, beliefs are seen as 'preconceived notions, myths or misconceptions', which can be studied by means of Likert-style questionnaires such as the Beliefs About Language Learning Inventory—BALLI (Horwitz 1987a). The metacognitive approach views learners' metacognitive knowledge about language learning as 'theories in action' (Wenden 1999); these are examined by means of the content analysis of learner self-reports in semi-structured interviews. Finally, the contextual approach views learner beliefs as varying according to context; it involves collecting a variety of data types and diverse means of data analysis. Barcelos argued that the contextual approach is superior because rather than viewing beliefs as a 'mental trait', it takes into account the 'experience-based nature of beliefs' (p. 26). A fourth approach can also be identified—metaphor analysis (Ellis 2001c; Kramsch 2003). This entails analysing the metaphors used by learners to describe their learning and constitutes an indirect means of identifying beliefs.

Much of the research has been concerned with describing and classifying the types of beliefs learners hold (based on responses to questionnaires), the sources of beliefs, and the situated and dynamic nature of learners' belief systems. Somewhat disappointingly, very few studies have examined the relationship between beliefs and language learning.

Types of learner beliefs

In an early attempt to identify the types of beliefs held by language learners, Horwitz (1987a) administered the BALLI to groups of learners. Five general areas of beliefs emerged from the analysis of the responses relating to (1) the difficulty of language learning, (2) aptitude for language learning, (3) the nature of language learning, (4) learning and communication strategies, and (5) motivation and expectations. Wenden (1986, 1987) grouped the beliefs she identified in 25 adults enrolled in a part-time advanced-level class at an American university into three general categories: (1) use of the language (for example, the importance of 'learning in a natural way'), (2) beliefs relating to learning about the language (for example, the importance of learning grammar and vocabulary), and (3) the importance of personal factors (i.e. beliefs about the feelings that facilitate or inhibit learning, self-concept, and aptitude for learning). Both of these early studies, then, identified a very similar set of learner beliefs. For example, the learners in both Horwitz's and Wenden's studies demonstrated beliefs about the need to study grammar. This dominant belief was also reported by Schulz (2001), who found that both Columbian learners of English in Columbia and American learners of foreign languages in the US placed great store on explicit grammar study and error correction.

Later research attempted to classify rather than simply list types of beliefs and to link them to metacognitive knowledge (Wenden 1999). Benson and Lor (1999), for example, distinguished higher-order 'conceptions' and lower-order 'beliefs'. They defined 'conceptions' as 'concerned with what the learner thinks the objects and processes of learning are' whereas beliefs are 'what the learner holds to be true about these objects and processes' (p. 464). A number of studies, including that of Benson and Lor, who investigated Chinese undergraduate students at the University of Hong Kong, suggest that learners hold conceptions about what language is and how to learn and that these conceptions fall into two broad categories, which can be glossed as 'quantitative/analytic' and 'qualitative/experiential'. These categories, it should be noted, bear a close resemblance to the cognitive styles discussed above (for example, the distinction between field independence and field dependence). Table 13.11 indicates the kinds of beliefs related to each. It should be noted that these two general conceptions are not mutually exclusive; learners can and often do hold a mixed set of beliefs. A number of studies (for example, Tanaka 2004) also suggest a third general conception—'self-efficacy/confidence' in language learning. This conception has more to do with how learners perceive their ability as language learners and their progress in relation to the particular context in which they are learning.

Conception	**Nature of language**	**Nature of language learning**
Quantitative/ analytic	Learning an L2 is mostly a matter of learning grammar rules.	To understand the L2 it must be translated into my L1.
	In order to speak an L2 well, it is important to learn vocabulary.	Memorization is a good way for me to learn an L2.
Qualitative/ experiential	Learning an L2 involves learning to listen and speak in the language.	It is okay to guess if you do not know a word.
	To learn a language you have to pay attention to the way it is used.	If I heard a foreigner of my age speaking the L2 I would go up to that person to practise speaking.

Table 13.11 Types of learner beliefs (based on Benson and Lor 1999)

The sources of learners' beliefs

An interesting question is what determines learners' beliefs about language learning. Little, Singleton, and Silvius (1984, reported in Little and Singleton 1990) surveyed random samples of undergraduate and postgraduate students of foreign languages at Trinity College, Dublin. They found that 'past experience, both of education in general and of language learning in particular, played a major role in shaping attitudes to language learning' (1990: 14). For example, the students stated that they preferred to learn by production activities (repeating orally and writing) rather than through receptive activities involving listening and reading. Little and Singleton claimed that this belief reflected the general nature of the instruction they had experienced (i.e. was shaped by their instructional experiences).

Another possibility is that beliefs are culturally determined. However, Horwitz (1999) in her review of the research into L2 beliefs, concluded that there was insufficient evidence to show that learners' beliefs varied systematically according to cultural background. It is possible, however, that learners' beliefs are more substantially influenced by general factors such as personality and cognitive style but this remains to be shown.

The situated and dynamic nature of learner beliefs

Learner beliefs are situation specific and dynamic. Kern (1995), for example, reported changes in the beliefs of 180 students studying first-year level French at a university in the US over the course of one semester (15 weeks). He administered Horwitz's BALLI to the students during the first and last week of the semester. Analysing the responses of 180 students, Kern reported that 35 per cent to 59 per cent of the responses changed over the 15-week period. A significant change was observed in the response to the statement 'If you are allowed to make mistakes in the beginning, it will be hard to get rid of them later on', with 37 per cent of the students reporting greater agreement and 15 per cent lesser agreement. This suggests that many students had become increasingly conscious of their mistakes and were having difficulty in avoiding them. The learners also changed their responses to the statement 'Learning a foreign language is mostly a matter of learning a lot of grammar rules', with 32 per cent showing greater agreement and 20 per cent lesser agreement. Tanaka (2004), in a longitudinal study of Japanese students learning English in New Zealand over a 12-week period, also showed that learners change their beliefs markedly over time. Many of the learners in this study began by believing that they would automatically learn English once they came to live in an English-speaking country but by the end of the 12 weeks had recognized that this was not the case. Interestingly, they began by rejecting grammar study as important (probably as a response to their negative language learning experiences in Japan) but eventually came to recognize the need for 'grammar'.

The relationship between beliefs and learning

There have to date been very few studies of the relationship between learner beliefs and learning outcomes. Abraham and Vann (1987) found some evidence that beliefs might affect learning outcomes in a case study of two learners, Gerardo and Pedro. Both learners believed that it was important to create situations for using English outside the classroom, to practise as much as possible, and to have errors corrected. Both also believed it important to participate actively in class. Gerardo, however, believed that paying conscious attention to grammar was important, while Pedro did not and expressed a strong dislike of meta-language. Also, Gerardo thought that it was important to persevere in communicating or understanding an idea, while Pedro considered topic abandonment the best strategy in some cases. Abraham and Vann characterized Gerardo's philosophy of language learning as 'broad' and Pedro's as 'narrow'. They suggested that this might have contributed to Gerardo's better TOEFL score (523 versus 473) at the end of a course of instruction. Pedro, however, did better on a test of spoken English, which might suggest that different views about language learning result in different kinds of success.

Park (1995) investigated 332 Korean university EFL students' beliefs about language learning, their language learning strategies, and the relationships among their beliefs, strategy use, and L2 proficiency. Park found three variables predicted students TOEFL scores to some extent. One was a belief variable (i.e. beliefs about self-efficacy and social interaction) and two were strategy variables (i.e. independent/interactive strategies and metacognitive strategies). Those learners who reported having confidence in learning English and the intention of speaking to others in English tended to use English actively, especially outside the classroom, and to monitor their progress in English carefully. These behaviours were also related to improvement in L2 proficiency.

Mori (1999) investigated the beliefs of 187 university students enrolled in Japanese at various proficiency levels in the US. She examined the relationship between epistemological beliefs (i.e. beliefs about learning in general) and beliefs about language learning and also the relationship between beliefs and L2 achievement. She found that strong beliefs in innate ability (i.e. the ability to learn is inherited and cannot be improved by effort) and in avoidance of ambiguity (i.e. the need for single, clear-cut answers) were associated with lower achievement. Learners who believed that L2 learning was easy manifested higher levels of achievement. In addition, this study showed that there were belief differences between novices and advanced learners. Advanced learners were less likely to believe in simple, unambiguous knowledge or the existence of absolute, single answers than novice learners. This study also revealed that epistemological beliefs and beliefs about language learning were for the most part unrelated. In other words, learner beliefs about language learning seemed to be task and domain specific.

Tanaka and Ellis (2003) reported a study of a 15-week study-abroad programme for Japanese university students, examining changes in the students' beliefs about language learning (measured by means of a questionnaire) and in their English proficiency (measured by means of the TOEFL). The results showed statistically significant changes in the students' beliefs relating to analytic language learning, experiential language learning and especially self-efficacy/confidence during the study-abroad period. Statistically significant gains in proficiency were also reported. However, Pearson's Product Moment correlations between the students' responses to the Belief Questionnaire and their TOEFL scores both before and after the study abroad period were weak and generally statistically non-significant. There was also no relationship between changes in beliefs after a three-month period of study abroad and gains in proficiency.

Overall these studies do not show a strong relationship between beliefs and learning/proficiency. However, it is perhaps not surprising that the relationship between beliefs and proficiency is weak, as the fact that learners hold a particular belief is no guarantee they will act on it; conflicts with other strongly held beliefs, situational constraints, or personal reasons may prevent them. If beliefs do impact on learning it is likely that they do so indirectly by influencing the kinds of learning strategies learners employ.

Learning strategies

LEARNER STRATEGIES define the approach learners adopt in learning an L2. They are influenced directly by learners' explicit beliefs about how best to learn. In particular, learners' strategies are governed by self-efficacy beliefs, as quite naturally they opt for an approach they feel comfortable with and able to implement and avoid actions that they consider exceed their ability to perform. A number of studies have shown a fairly strong relationship between self-efficacy beliefs and learners' actions. Yang (1999), for example, found that Taiwanese university students' self-efficacy beliefs were strongly related to their reported use of LEARNING STRATEGIES, especially functional practice strategies (i.e. the stronger their belief in their ability to learn English and the more positive their attributions of learning English, the greater their reported use of strategies). The study of learning strategies has been motivated by both the wish to contribute to SLA theory by specifying the contribution that learners can make to L2 learning and by the applied purpose of providing a research-informed basis for helping learners to learn more efficiently through identifying strategies that 'work' and training them to make use of these.

Definition of learning strategies

The actions that learners perform in order to learn a language have been variously labelled—behaviours, tactics, techniques, and strategies. The term most commonly used is 'learning strategies', defined as 'behaviors or actions which learners use to make language learning more successful, self-directed and enjoyable' (Oxford 1989).

A distinction is often made between production, communication, and learning strategies. Tarone (1980: 419) defined a PRODUCTION STRATEGY as 'an attempt to use one's linguistic system efficiently and clearly, with a minimum of effort'. Examples are simplification, rehearsal, and discourse planning. COMMUNICATION STRATEGIES consist of attempts to deal with problems of communication that have arisen in interaction. A language learning strategy is 'an attempt to develop linguistic and sociolinguistic competence in the target language' (for example, memorization, initiation of conversation with native speakers, and inferencing). However, it is not easy to distinguish these different types as there is no way of telling whether a strategy is motivated by a desire to learn or a desire to communicate. Tarone also distinguished language learning strategies and skills learning strategies. The former are concerned with the learners' attempts to master new linguistic and sociolinguistic information about the target language, while the latter are concerned with the learners' attempts to become skilled listeners, speakers, readers, or writers. Again, however, the distinction is not an easy one and the literature on learning strategies does not always distinguish clearly between these two types. Cohen (1990: 15), for instance, referred to learning strategies directed at the 'language skill' of 'vocabulary learning', although this is clearly an aspect of linguistic knowledge.

There are a number of other problems. There is uncertainty about the precise nature of the behaviours that are to count as learning strategies. Stern (1983) distinguished 'strategies' and 'techniques'. The former are defined as general and more or less deliberate 'approaches' to learning (for example, 'an active task approach'), whereas the latter constitute observable forms of language learning behaviour evident in particular areas of language learning such as grammar (for example, 'inferring grammar rules from texts') and vocabulary (for example, 'using a dictionary when necessary'). Other researchers, however, have used the term 'strategy' to refer to the kind of behaviours Stern calls techniques. Seliger (1984) distinguished 'strategies' and 'tactics'. He defined the former as 'basic abstract categories of processing by which information perceived in the outside world is organized and categorized into cognitive structures as part of a conceptual network' (1984: 4). In contrast, 'tactics' are variable and idiosyncratic learning activities, which learners use to organize a learning situation, respond to the learning environment, or cope with input and output demands. However, not all researchers make such a clear distinction between 'strategies' and 'tactics' on the basis of consciousness. Some consider that what starts out as a conscious 'tactic' may evolve into a subconscious 'strategy'. To complicate matters further, what Seliger called 'tactics' is actually what most other researchers call 'learning strategies'.

Learning strategies are perhaps best defined in terms of a set of characteristics that figure in most accounts of them:

- Strategies refer to both general approaches and specific actions or techniques used to learn an L2.
- Strategies are problem-orientated—the learner deploys a strategy to overcome some particular learning or communication problem.
- Learners are generally aware of the strategies they use and can identify what they consist of if they are asked to pay attention to what they are doing/thinking.
- Strategies involve linguistic behaviour (such as requesting the name of an object) and non-linguistic (such as pointing at an object so as to be told its name).
- Linguistic strategies can be performed in the L1 and in the L2.
- Some strategies are behavioural while others are mental. Thus some strategies are directly observable, while others are not.
- In the main, strategies contribute indirectly to learning by providing learners with data about the L2 which they can then process. However, some strategies may also contribute directly (for example, memorization strategies directed at specific lexical items or grammatical rules).
- Strategy use varies considerably as a result of both the kind of task the learner is engaged in and individual learner preferences.

However, arguments continue as to how to define learning strategies. Macaro (2006), for example, defined learning strategies as cognitive and rejected the view that they can also be considered in terms of overt behaviour.

Classifying learner strategies

Considerable effort has gone into classifying the strategies that learners use. Two of the most commonly cited taxonomies are O'Malley and Chamot (1990) and Oxford (1990). (See Table 13.12.) The former is based on a three-way distinction between COGNITIVE STRATEGIES (i.e. strategies involving analysis, transformation, or synthesis of learning materials), METACOGNITIVE STRATEGIES (i.e. strategies involving an attempt to regulate learning through planning, monitoring, and evaluating), and socio-affective learning strategies (i.e. strategies concerning ways in which learners interact with other users of the L2). Oxford's taxonomy is hierarchical, with a general distinction made between direct and indirect strategies, each of which is then broken down into a number of subcategories. Direct strategies are those that 'directly involve the target language' in the sense that 'they require mental processing of the language', whereas indirect strategies 'provide indirect support for language learning through focusing, planning, evaluating, seeking opportunities, controlling anxiety, increasing cooperation and empathy and other means' (Oxford 1990: 151). Oxford has developed versions of the Strategy Inventory for Language Learning (SILL) to measure learners' self-reported strategy use in both second and foreign language settings.

Problems exist regarding the construct validity of these taxonomies. As Hsiao and Oxford (2002) acknowledged:

> ... empirical research on the underlying constructs of L2 learning strategies has reported neither the three factor pattern theorized in O'Malley and Chamot nor the six factor solution implied in Oxford.
> (p. 372)

Doubts exist, therefore, about the psychometric properties of the SILL. Different factor analytic studies based on the SILL have produced a five-factor solution (for example, Nyikos and Oxford 1993) and a nine-factor solution. (See Oxford and Burry-Stock 1995.) Robson and Midorikawa (2001) challenged the reliability of the SILL in a study that showed a low level of test-retest reliability when the SILL was administered twice to the same group of Japanese learners of English. Tseng, Dörnyei, and Schmitt (2006) also challenged the SILL, arguing in particular that quantifying the use of different strategies runs contrary to learning strategy theory according to which it is the quality not quantity of use that matters.

In an attempt to test rival models of learning strategies, Hsiao and Oxford (2002) carried out a confirmatory factor analysis of 534 adult university-level learners of English in Taiwan, based on their responses to the SILL. The results provided support for Oxford's six-factor model as this was shown to more convincingly account for the data than O'Malley and Chamot's three-factor model, although this is perhaps not surprising, given that the SILL was designed to measure six rather than three factors. This study failed to support the higher-order categories of direct and indirect strategies in Oxford's model. Hsiao and Oxford concluded with some suggestions as to how the classification of learning strategies might be improved. They differentiated between L2 learning and L2 use strategies, recognizing that different systems may be needed for second and foreign language situations. They reclassified a number of items, ensuring that the level of specificity of particular items in the SILL is consistent and also created a task-based strategy survey. However, these suggestions do not really address Tseng, Dörnyei, and Schmitt's criticism that is the quality of strategy use that really matters.

There have been a number of other taxonomies of learning strategies. Two will be mentioned here. A particularly promising approach is that adopted by Purpura (1999). Based on a model of cognitive processing, Purpura distinguished strategies in terms of whether they related to comprehending processes, storing/memory processes, or using/retrieval processes. The advantage of such a model is that it aligns the study of learning strategies with mainstream thinking about the nature of language learning. We have already seen a number of attempts to link other ID variables (for example, motivation, anxiety, and willingness to communicate) to a general model of L2 processing. Another interesting taxonomy is Cohen and Chi's (2001) Language Strategy Survey. Unlike other taxonomies, the 89 items in this questionnaire are constructed around the traditional distinction between skills

O'Malley and Chamot (1990)	Oxford (1990)
A Metacognitive strategies, e.g. 'selective attention' (deciding in advance to attend to specific aspects of language input) B Cognitive strategies, e.g. 'inferencing' (using available information to guess meanings of new items, predict outcomes, or fill in missing information) C Social/affective strategies, e.g. 'question for clarification' (asking a teacher or another native speaker for repetition, paraphrasing, explanation and/or examples)	A Direct 1 Memory strategies, e.g. 'grouping' (classifying or reclassifying materials into meaningful units) 2 Cognitive strategies, e.g. 'practising' (repeating, formally practising, recognizing and using formulas, recombining, and practising naturalistically) 3 Compensation strategies, e.g. 'switching to mother tongue' B Indirect 1 Metacognitive strategies, e.g. 'setting goals and objectives' 2 Affective strategies, e.g. 'taking risks wisely' 3 Social strategies, e.g. 'asking for clarification or verification'

Table 13.12 Two taxonomies of learning strategies

(listening, speaking, reading, and writing) and two other aspects (vocabulary and translation). It was especially designed as a basis for strategy training in students preparing for a study-abroad period.

Finally, it should be noted that much of the strategy research (and the instruments used) has been directed at adult or adolescent learners. What research there has been that has focused on children has identified a rather different set of strategies from those mentioned above. Perhaps the best known study is Wong Fillmore's (1976, 1979) nine-month study of five Mexican children learning English in the United States. Wong Fillmore collected natural spoken data by pairing each learner with a native-speaking child in a play situation. She identified a series of social strategies, each linked to a cognitive strategy. One social strategy was 'Join a group and act as if you understand what is going on, even if you don't' while the associated cognitive strategy was 'Assume what people are saying is relevant to the situation at hand and guess'. (See Chapter 1.)

Good language learner studies

Early research on learning strategies took the form of GOOD LANGUAGE LEARNER studies. A summary of the main studies is provided in Table 13.13. One of the best-known and frequently cited of these studies is Naiman *et al.* (1978/1996). This was a double-barrelled study of highly successful adult L2 learners and adolescent classroom learners of L2 French, using intensive face-to-face interviews with the former and classroom observation with the latter. Like other studies they found that interviewing learners was more effective than observation as many of the strategies learners use are mental and so not directly observable. Also like other studies, Naiman *et al.* found that successful language learners use a mixture of analytic strategies for attending to form and experiential strategies for realizing language as a means of communication.

There are, perhaps, five major aspects of successful language learning, as evidenced by the various studies summarized in Table 13.13: (1) a concern for language form, (2) a concern for communication (functional practice), (3) an active task approach, (4) an awareness of the learning process, and (5) a capacity to use strategies flexibly in accordance with task requirements.

Looking back at these early studies, two points seem to stand out. The first is that they were considerably more illuminating and of practical value to the teaching profession than the survey-based, quantitative studies that dominate the scene today. The second is that what seems to characterize successful learners above all is the flexible use of learning strategies. Good language learners have a range of strategies at their disposal and select which strategies to use in accordance with both their long-term goals for learning the L2 and the particular task to hand. This bears out Tseng *et al.*'s (2006) point about the importance of looking at the qualitative aspects of strategy use.

There have been a few later studies of good language learners. Gan, Humphreys, and Hamp-Lyons (2004) reported a comparative study of successful and unsuccessful learners of English in Chinese universities. They distinguished the two types of learners in terms of their scores on a standard test of English proficiency used with Chinese university students and their teachers' perceptions of their proficiency. This study investigated a number of differences between the two types, including their use of learning strategies. They noted clear differences in the ways in which they went about learning vocabulary; whereas the unsuccessful students relied on rote-memorization, the successful students supplemented rote-learning with strategies for reinforcing what they had learnt (for example, doing vocabulary exercises or reading). The successful learners also reported having a systematic plan for mastering a particular set of new words. This reflected another major difference. The successful students set particular objectives for themselves and identified systematic ways of achieving these. In contrast, the unsuccessful learners did not appear to have a clear agenda and experienced difficulty in identifying their learning problems. Halbach (2000) reached a similar conclusion after analysing the learning strategies evident in the diaries of successful and weaker students of English. She found that the weaker students demonstrated a lack of critical self-awareness (i.e. they made little use of the monitoring and self-evaluation strategies). She suggested that weaker students experience a vicious circle; they are weak because they lack the strategies needed to advance, while they also lack the proficiency needed to

Study	Learners	Method	Results
Rubin 1975	Learners of mixed ages in classroom settings	Observation—Rubin emphasized the importance of using a video camera	Following strategies discussed: 1 preparedness to guess 2 attempt to communicate (i.e. get the message across) 3 willingness to appear foolish 4 attention to form 5 practising (e.g. by initiating conversation) 6 monitoring own and others' speech 7 attending to meaning (e.g. by attending to context)
Naiman et al. 1978	1 34 graduate L2 learners—many multilingual 2 students of L2 French in grades 8, 10, and 12	1 interview questionnaire—semi-directed and directed parts 2 classroom observation schedule—not successful	Following general strategies identified: 1 active task approach 2 realization of language as a system 3 realization of language as a means of communication and interaction 4 management of affective demands 5 monitoring L2 performance Each major strategy further divided into more specific sub-strategies Also various 'techniques' identified, e.g. having contact with native speakers
Rubin 1981	Young adults in classroom settings	1 classroom observation schedule—not successful 2 observation of learner performance on specific language learning tasks 3 unstructured self-reports—learners varied in ability to report but many vague 4 directed self-report—focus on specific strategies	Strategies in these areas identified: 1 clarification/verification 2 monitoring 3 memorization 4 guessing/inductive inferencing 5 deductive reasoning 6 practice (i.e. learner practises on own)
Reiss 1983	College learners of L2 French/German—18 'A' and 18 'C'/'D' students compared	Questionnaire presenting 3 hypothetical learning situations	Characteristics of successful learners: 1 they are specific in their learning task 2 they constantly look for meaning 3 they seem to know themselves and to know how to internalize information Successful learners also gave more specific answers to questionnaire

Huang and Van Naersson 1985	20 high- and 20 low-proficiency Chinese learners of English in China	1 written questionnaire on use of formal practice, functional practice, and monitoring 2 in-depth interview	The main results were: 1 No significant differences between high- and low-proficiency learners with regard to formal practice and monitoring 2 Significant differences for some functional practice strategies: speaking L2 with others, thinking in English, and participation in oral group activities
Reiss 1985	College learners at elementary and intermediate levels—some identified as good language learners	1 general questionnaire about personality variables and learning strategies 2 strategies questionnaire listing 19 strategies from which students selected the ones they used most often	Strategies identified (in rank order): 1 monitoring 2 attention to form 3 attention to meaning Reiss argued that a good language learner is 'active' in process of conscious language learning, but learner can be active by being a 'silent speaker' (i.e. practising silently while listening to others)
Gillette 1987	Two beginners of L2 Spanish/ successful learners of L2 French	1 extensive classroom observation 2 classroom notes from one of the learners 3 attitude/motivation questionnaire (Lambert and Gardner) 4 interview 5 teachers' comments	Instrumental motivation; democratic, anti-authoritarian; high self-esteem or confident; tolerant of ambiguity; one learner risk-taker but other learner rarely volunteers in class; good at getting 'big picture' without worrying about details; aware of learning process; 'active thinking'; self-regulated; individualized approach to learning; focus on meaning rather than on conscious rules; errors seen as useful tool for learning
Lennon 1989	4 Germans learning L2 English in UK—advanced	1 written answers to general questionnaire 2 personal interview	Aware of progression, performance and state of competence; switch modes of production; aware of gaps in their knowledge; stressed linguistic experimentation; concentrated on both communicating and learning (trading one off against other in different situations)

Table 13.13 Studies of the good language learner

employ effective strategies. Griffiths (2008) edited a collection that explored good language learners in relation to such individual difference factors as motivation, age, and personality.

Factors influencing choice of learning strategies

Learners have been found to vary considerably in both the overall frequency with which they employ strategies and also the particular types of strategies they use (O'Malley *et al.* 1985a; Chamot *et al.* 1987, 1988; Ehrman 1990). A range of factors have been found to affect strategy choice, some relating to the learner and others to the situational and social context of learning.

Learner factors

Age emerges as a clear factor affecting the way strategies are used. Young children have been observed to employ strategies in a task-specific manner, while older children and adults make use of generalized strategies, which they employ more flexibly. (See Brown *et al.* 1983, cited in O'Malley and Chamot 1990.) Ehrman and Oxford (1989) reported adults using more sophisticated strategies.

Another factor, which is clearly related to the use of learning strategies, is motivation. Oxford and Nyikos (1989), in a study of students of foreign languages in universities in the United States, found that 'the degree of expressed motivation was the single most powerful influence on the choice of language learning strategies' (1989: 294). Highly motivated learners used more strategies relating to formal practice, functional practice, general study, and conversation/input elicitation than poorly motivated learners. The type of motivation may also influence strategy choice. Oxford and Nyikos reported that formal practice and general study strategies were more popular than functional practice strategies, perhaps reflecting the students' strong instrumental goal of fulfilling course requirements and obtaining good grades in a programme that stressed analytical skills. However, in a different context an instrumental motivation can result in a preference for more communication-orientated strategies, as Ehrman's (1990) study of adult students at the US Foreign Service Institute learning languages for career reasons showed. Schmidt and Watanabe (2001) in a study of over 2,000 university students also found that motivation affected strategy use, with the link between strategy choice and different motives also supported.

While there is little evidence to support the intuitively appealing hypothesis that personality is related to strategy choice, there is some to suggest that learning style plays a role. Littlemore (2001) reported a study of Belgian university students learning English, demonstrating that those learners who had a holistic cognitive style, as measured by Riding's (1991) Cognitive Style Analysis (see section in this chapter on cognitive style) were more likely to utilize holistic communication strategies (for example, involving comparison) than analytic strategies (for example, involving componential analysis) and that the reverse was true for those learners with an analytic style. Also, Carson and Longhini (2002), in a diary study of Carson's naturalistic acquisition of Spanish in Argentina, showed that her choice of learning strategies were affected by her learning styles. For example, her preference for metacognitive strategies reflected her analytic learning style. Finally, a number of studies have shown that learner beliefs are related to strategy choice. Bialystok (1981b) found that Grade 10 and 12 learners of L2 French in Canada varied in the extent to which they believed that language learning involved formal as opposed to functional practice, and this influenced their choice of strategies. Wenden (1987) also found that learners who emphasized the importance of learning tended to use cognitive strategies that helped them to understand and remember specific items of language, while learners who emphasized the importance of using language relied on communication strategies.

Finally, there is considerable evidence to support a link between learners' experience with language and/or language learning and strategy use. Ehrman (1990) found that professional linguists reported using more strategies more frequently than untrained instructors and students. Also, students with at least five years of study reported using more functional practice strategies than students with four years or fewer. Nation and McLaughlin (1986) also provided evidence of the superiority of experienced language learners over inexperienced ones. They taught groups of monolingual, bilingual, and multilingual subjects an artificial language and found that the multilinguals did better on an IMPLICIT LEARNING task, a result they explained by suggesting that multilinguals were more able to utilize learning strategies automatically. Levine, Reves, and Leaver (1996) compared the learning strategies of immigrants from the former Soviet Union with those of immigrants who had been living in Israel for five years or longer. The former preferred safe, traditional strategies (for example, rote learning) while the latter preferred riskier, communicative strategies. The results indicated that 'learners studying in a highly structured and uniform educational system will develop learning strategies reflecting that system (p. 45).

Social and situational factors

The language being learnt can influence strategy choice. Chamot *et al.* (1987) found that FL students of Russian in the United States reported greater strategy use than students of Spanish. Wharton (2000) in a study of bi- and multilingual university students studying French and Japanese as foreign languages in Singapore found that students studying French had a higher overall mean for strategy use than students studying Japanese. Studies of classroom learners suggest that social strategies are rare. Chamot *et al.* (1988), for example, noted that their classroom learners mentioned social and affective strategies infrequently, the only exception being 'questioning for clarification'. Wharton reported that the strategy use of the classroom learners she investigated was lower than that in second language learning situations and that affective strategies in particular were less preferred. There may also be differences in strategy use according to whether the classroom setting is a second or foreign language one. The FL students investigated by Chamot *et al.* (1987) claimed to use some strategies not mentioned by O'Malley *et al.*'s (1985a) ESL students (for example, rehearsal, translation, note-taking, substitution, and contextualization). The FL students also reported relying on cognitive strategies (in relation to metacognitive and socio-affective strategies) to a lesser extent than the ESL students. It is likely, though, that it is not so much macro-differences (such as the FL/SL distinction) as micro-differences to do with the specific learning settings in classrooms that have the greater effect on strategy use. Chamot *et al.* (1987) and Chamot *et al.* (1988), for example, found evidence that task type had a marked influence on learners' choice of both cognitive and metacognitive strategies. For example, vocabulary tasks led to the use of the cognitive strategies of 'resourcing' and 'elaboration' and the metacognitive strategies of 'self-monitoring' and 'self-evaluation', while listening tasks led to 'note-taking', 'elaboration', 'inferencing', and 'summarizing' as cognitive strategies, and to 'selective attention', 'self-monitoring', and 'problem-identification' as metacognitive strategies. However, although specific tasks may predispose learners to use particular strategies, they cannot predetermine the actual strategies that will be used, as learners construct a task in accordance with their understanding of what is required and their own learning goals, as claimed by sociocultural theory. (See Donato and McCormick 1994.) Finally, Oxford and Nyikos (1989) found that gender had 'a profound effect on strategy choice' in their study of university students learning foreign languages. Females used more overall strategies than males. A number of other studies have corroborated Oxford and Nyikos' finding (for example, Ehrman 1990; Kaylani 1996; Peacock and Ho 2003). However, Wharton (2000) found no effect for gender. The general picture that emerges is that different populations of learners employ strategies in different ways, suggesting that we cannot expect to find a set of universal good language learning strategies.

The relationship between learning strategies and language learning

Oxford (2001) claimed that learning strategies are one of the main factors determining how and how well learners learn an L2. However, attempts to demonstrate a relationship between learning strategies and L2 proficiency have met with mixed success.

In a series of studies, Bialystok explored the relationship between four strategies and L2 proficiency. Two concerned the learning resulting from communicating in an L2 ('functional practice' and 'inferencing'), and two concerned more conscious attempts to learn the L2 ('formal practice' and 'monitoring'). In her main study, Bialystok (1981b) investigated students studying French in Grades 10 and 12 in Canada. She used a questionnaire to collect information on the students' reported use of the four strategies in both oral and written tasks. Proficiency was measured by means of oral and written tasks that required attention to meaning and to form. The results are not easy to interpret and in some respects are counter-intuitive. For example, Bialystok failed to find any relationship between inferencing and proficiency, although elsewhere a strong theoretical case for the importance of inferencing in L2 learning has been made out. (See Carton 1971; Bialystok 1983a.) Another result that seems a little odd is that only functional practice correlated significantly with proficiency in the Grade 10 students, whereas three strategies (functional practice, formal practice, and monitoring) were related to proficiency in the Grade 12 students. It is possible that this reflects a shift in strategy use as proficiency develops, but it is also possible that the data elicited by means of the questionnaire were not reliable.

If Bialystok's attempt to show a statistical relationship between strategy use and proficiency was only partly successful, Politzer and McGroarty's (1985) attempt was even less so. The study elicited information about the behaviours learners reported using in (1) study inside the classroom, (2) individual study, and (3) social interaction outside the classroom. The subjects in this study were 37 learners from two major ethnic groups (Hispanics and Asians) enrolled on an eight-week intensive ESL course at American universities. Learning gains were calculated from scores on three tests (a comprehension test, a discrete item test of linguistic competence, and a test of communicative ability), which were administered at the beginning and the end of the course. Very few statistically significant correlations were found. However, different clusters of strategies were found to be related to gains in different tests. For example, reported behaviours associated with active inquiry concerning language use (for example, 'asking teacher about an expression' and 'asking for confirmation of correctness') were correlated with gains in listening comprehension and communicative ability, while reported behaviours involving attention to form (such as 'keeping track of new vocabulary' and 'trying to use new words') were linked to gains in linguistic competence. This finding suggests that strategies need to be considered in groups rather than in isolation.

This was the approach adopted by Griffiths (2003) in a study of 348 students from 21 different countries studying in New Zealand. On the basis of their responses to the SILL, Griffiths identified 19 'plus' strategies, which she classified into eight groups. These groups included strategies relating to interaction with others, strategies related to specific areas of language learning such as reading, vocabulary, and language systems, strategies related to tolerance of ambiguity, and managing feelings.

Mangubhai (1991) studied the strategies of five adult beginner learners of L2 Hindi who received four weeks of instruction by means of TOTAL PHYSICAL RESPONSE (Asher 1977)—a method based mainly on the use of oral commands that students have to listen to and carry out. Information about the learning strategies they used came from concurrent think-aloud tasks, immediate retrospective reports, and discussions at the end of each instructional session. Three sets of strategies were identified, depending on whether the focus of the different behaviours was (1) on form, (2) on meaning, or (3) on memory (retrieval and storage). Achievement was measured by means of a test consisting of oral commands similar to those used in the instruction, a sentence repetition test, and a listening comprehension test. On the basis of these tests, the learners were divided into two groups: Group A, consisting of three 'high' achievers, and Group B of two 'low' achievers. The 'high' achievers used more memory strategies, were more likely to direct their attention to chunks than to individual words, relied less on translation, and paid more attention to the form of the commands once they had extracted the meaning. The strength of Mangubhai's study is that it elicited information relating to strategy use in a variety of ways, making it possible to compare what learners reported doing retrospectively with what they reported doing during an actual language learning task.

A number of other studies explored the relationship between vocabulary learning strategies and learning. Cohen and Aphek (1980) suggested that the use of mnemonic association aids vocabulary learning. They investigated 17 English-speaking students (nine beginners, six intermediate, and two advanced) learning Hebrew over a 100-day period. Not surprisingly perhaps, the learners' main approach was simply to try to memorize the words they did not know. Most of the learners reported using associations of various kinds and Cohen and Aphek were able to identify eleven different types, involving the target language, the learners' L1, and extralinguistic signs. The general conclusion was that any attempt to form an association involving the target word aided retention. Another interesting finding of Cohen and Aphek's study was that there was an interaction between the learners' overall level of proficiency and the kind of task that worked best for vocabulary learning. Beginners found tasks that involved listing best, while the intermediate learners found tasks that involved contextualization more effective, suggesting that contextualization strategies work better for learners who already possess a fair level of L2 knowledge.

A study by Brown and Perry (1991) investigated the success of three vocabulary-learning strategies: (1) keyword, (2) semantic, and (3) keyword–semantic. The keyword strategy involves asking learners to form a visual association between the target word and some acoustically similar word they already know (the keyword). For example, to learn the Japanese word 'ski' (= 'like'), learners might use the keyword 'skiing' and imagine themselves enjoying skiing down a mountain slope. A semantic strategy involves some kind of attempt to integrate the target word into the learner's existing semantic systems, for example by identifying how a word relates to other known words. A keyword–semantic strategy involves a combination of (1) and (2). Brown and Perry hypothesized that strategies that involved greater 'depth of processing' (see Craik and Lockhart 1972) would result in better retention. Their prediction was that processing at the 'shallow' sensory level of the kind involved in the keyword strategy aids retention less than processing at the 'deep' semantic level. Processing that involves both shallow and deep levels was hypothesized to be more effective still. An experimental study of six intact upper-level classes at the English Language Institute of the American University of Cairo lent support to Brown and Perry's hypothesis; the class taught to use the semantic–keyword strategy retained significantly more words, as measured by cued-recall and multiple choice tests, than the class taught the keyword strategy, while the results for the class taught the semantic strategy were intermediate.

A general problem with many of the correlational studies is that it is not really possible to determine what is cause and what is effect. Do learners develop high proficiency because of the strategies they use or is it learners' proficiency that determines their choice of strategies? Only longitudinal studies such as Mangubhai's and experimental studies such as Brown and Perry's are able to establish clearly if (and which) strategies are causal. Unfortunately, there is still a paucity of such studies. It is also possible that there are no absolutely 'good' or 'bad' strategies. Ehrman, Leaver and Oxford (2003) suggested that:

> a strategy is useful under these conditions: (a) the strategy relates well to the L2 task at hand, (b) the strategy fits the particular student's learning style preferences to one degree or another, (c) the strategy employs the strategy effectively and links it with other relevant strategies.
> (p. 315)

The problem, of course, is establishing if and to what extent these conditions have been met, which is no mean task given that we still know very little about the relationships between learning strategies and specific tasks and learners' learning styles or what constitutes effective use and clustering of strategies.

Thus, the following conclusions regarding the role played by learning strategies in L2 learning are necessarily tentative:

1 The strategies that learners elect to use reflect their general stage of L2 development. For example, there is some evidence to suggest that strategies that relate to the functional use of language and that involve processing chunks of language precede those that involve close attention to form and single words. Metacognitive strategies are more evident in advanced learners.
2 More proficient learners appear to use learning strategies more frequently and in qualitatively different ways than learners who are less proficient.
3 Different kinds of learning strategies may contribute to different aspects of L2 proficiency. Thus, strategies that involve formal practice may contribute to the development of linguistic competence, while strategies involving functional practice aid the development of communicative competence.
4 Learners need to employ strategies flexibly by selecting those strategies that are appropriate for performing a particular learning task.

5 Metacognitive strategies involving goal identification, planning, monitoring, and evaluation assume considerable importance, at least for adults. However, many learners appear to under-utilize these types of strategy.
6 The learning strategies used by children and adults may differ; social and interactional strategies may be more important with young learners.

Perhaps, though, the clearest conclusion is that offered by McDonough (1999) in his own review of learning strategies research:

> The relationship between strategy use and proficiency is very complicated. Issues such as frequency and quality of strategy use do not bear a simple linear relationship to achievement in a second language.
> (p. 13)

Current views of learning strategies emphasize the importance of clusters of strategies, with metacognition playing a major role in determining which clusters to employ in order to achieve particular learning goals (Macaro 2006).

Learner training

The study of learning strategies has been motivated in part by the desire to identify how to assist learners to become more effective. It is for this reason that a number of researchers have attempted to design learner training programmes, despite the uncertainty about which strategies and which combinations of strategies work best for learning. As Macaro (2006) pointed out, the lack of standardization of either the intervention packages or the manner in which learning was assessed makes it difficult to reach any firm conclusions regarding the effectiveness of strategy training.

A number of early studies investigated the effects of vocabulary strategy training. Bialystok (1983b) reported that a 15-minute lesson on how to inference led to better overall comprehension than providing the Grade 10 learners of L2 French with picture cues or letting the learners use a dictionary. However, dictionary use (but not picture cues) resulted in better scores on a vocabulary test than did the strategy training. In a second experiment the strategy training proved less effective in promoting either comprehension or vocabulary acquisition than the other two conditions. O'Malley *et al.* (1985b) studied the effects of two kinds of training on 75 intermediate-level ESL students of mixed ethnic backgrounds (Hispanic and Asian). One group received training in the use of 'imagery and grouping' (a cognitive strategy), while a second group received training in this strategy and also in 'self-evaluation' (a metacognitive strategy). There was also a control group. Although no significant differences among the treatment groups were found, a detailed analysis of the results showed that while the Hispanic training groups outperformed the Hispanic control group, the reverse was the case for the Asian groups as the latter preferred to rely on their well-tried strategy of rote memorization instead.[10]

Later studies have continued to report somewhat mixed results. (See McDonough 1999 and Chamot 2001 for reviews.) We will consider one study here. Cohen, Weaver, and Tao-Yuan Li (1998) reported a study of the impact of strategy-based instruction on speaking in a foreign language. The participants were 55 intermediate-level learners studying foreign languages at the University of Minnesota. An experimental group received strategy instruction throughout their 10-week class. This instruction was directed at a broad range of strategies relevant to speaking in an L2 and was sometimes explicit and sometimes embedded into classroom activities. The learners' speaking proficiency was measured by means of three free oral production tests, administered as a pre- and post-test. The learners also completed strategy checklists before, during, and after completing each task. These were designed to capture a three-stage process in strategy use (i.e. preparation, self-monitoring during the task, and self-reflection on completion). The experimental group outperformed the control group (which did not receive strategy training) on only one of the three oral tasks in the post-test. The relationships between reported frequency of strategy use and ratings of task performance were complex and difficult to interpret as increases in reported use of strategies were linked to improvement in both the experimental and control groups. Cohen *et al.* concluded 'it would appear beneficial to engage learners in discussions of speaking strategies, having them review checklists of possible strategies ... and practice those strategies in class' (p. 152). However, the evidence supporting this conclusion from the study itself seems rather meagre.

Swain (2000) reported an interesting study by Holunga (1995) that provides support for strategy training. This experimental study investigated the effects of metacognitive strategy training on the accurate use of verb forms by advanced learners of English. It involved three instructional conditions: (1) metacognitive strategy training plus communicative practice, (2) metacognitive strategy training plus a requirement to verbalize the strategies plus communicative practice, and (3) communicative practice only. During the instructional period the learners performed a focused task (i.e. a communicative task designed to elicit a specific linguistic feature). A detailed analysis of the three groups' performance of this task showed marked differences. Whereas groups (1) and (3) attended predominantly to message content producing interaction that was typical of a 'negotiation of meaning' task, group (2) focused on both message content and the conditional verb form that the task required. In a detailed discussion of an interaction involving a pair of learners in group (2), Swain commented 'through their collaborative effort, they produce the appropriate verb form accurately, and propose a concrete plan to monitor its accuracy in future use' (p. 108). This study is of particular interest because immediate and delayed post-tests of both a closed and open-ended nature demonstrated significantly greater gains in the ability to use complex verb forms accurately in group (2). This study was undertaken in the context of Swain's research on COLLABORATIVE DIALOGUING. (See Chapter 11.) It suggests that if strategy training involves verbalizing the strategies employed together with opportunity to use the strategies explicitly in the context of communicative activity it can be effective.

It is clear, however, that teaching learners strategies is not universally successful. Nevertheless, this has not prevented a number of researchers proposing strategy instruction schemes. Harris (2003) compared four training models—O'Malley and Chamot (1990), Oxford (1990), Chamot *et al.*(1999) and Grenfell and Harris (1999). There are also additional models, such as in Macaro (2001) and Cohen (2002). There is clearly very considerable commitment among researcher/educators to strategy training but as Dörnyei (2005) noted:

> Although the available strategy and training materials are generally creative and impressive, it is not clear whether the benefits of their explicit employment warrant the time and effort spent on them in comparison to spending the same amount of creative energy designing 'ordinary' learning activities.
> (pp. 176–7)

Final comment

Learning strategies have proved a gold mine to which many researchers have rushed and, indeed, continue to do so. (See Cohen and Macaro (2008) and Griffiths (2008).) However, the results to date are somewhat disappointing. One reason for this is the lack of a sufficiently rigorous definition of learning strategies that would enable researchers to reliably determine which learning behaviours constitute strategies and which do not. Linked to this difficulty is the problem of measurement. Learning strategy questionnaires have proliferated, with one (the SILL) proving especially popular. Other methods of investigating learning strategies (for example, through diaries, personal histories, and interviews) have increasingly figured but this has added to the confusion over what exactly constitutes a learning strategy. Finally, there is a continuing lack of any theoretical account of how learning strategies relate to the psycholinguistic processes involved in L2 acquisition.

Dörnyei (2005) noted that whereas research into learning strategies was popular in general educational research in the 1980s, it declined dramatically in the 1990s, with researchers turning their attention to a related concept, self-regulation (i.e. 'the degree to which individuals are active participants in their own learning' (p. 191)). Dörnyei claimed that researchers should do the same in SLA, as the study of SELF-REGULATION offers a broader perspective and shifts the focus from the product (strategies) to the process. Tseng, Dörnyei, and Schmitt (2006) described an instrument to measure self-regulatory capacity for vocabulary learning in a situated manner. The items in this instrument were designed to capture general trends and inclinations rather than specific behaviours (as in the SILL). They measured five facets of self-regulation: (1) commitment control (i.e. involving preserving or increasing the learner's original goal commitment), (2) metacognitive control (i.e. involving monitoring and controlling concentration), (3) satiation control (involving eliminating boredom and extending interest), (4) emotion control (i.e. involving the management of disruptive states or moods), and (5) environmental control (i.e. involving the elimination of negative environmental influences). Confirmatory and factor analyses supported this model of self-regulation. Tseng *et al.* argued that an approach based on self-regulation provides a more satisfactory way of empowering learners than traditional strategy training as the real goal should be that of assisting learners to achieve self-regulation not to use specific strategies. To date, however, there are no studies that have investigated this claim.

Conclusion

No account of L2 acquisition will be complete without due consideration of the factors that induce individual differences in learners. In Chapter 7 we examined the social factors that account for some differences. In this chapter we have focused on psychological factors. Research into these factors has advanced considerably in a number of ways, especially since the beginning of the 1990s:

1 There is now greater diversity in the methods used to investigate individual difference factors. In particular, more studies employing qualitative methods have appeared. Also, encouragingly, researchers are adopting a multi-method approach to investigating individual differences in learners.
2 Attempts have been made to improve measurement of individual difference factors. These attempts have involved borrowing instruments from general psychology (for example, Riding's Cognitive Style Analysis) and also developing language specific instruments (for example, McIntyre and Gardner's (1994) Input Anxiety Scale, Processing Anxiety Scale, and Output Anxiety Scale).
3 There has also been a growth in more theoretically driven research as opposed to fishing expeditions based on crude correlational analyses (for example, Dewaele and Furnham's (2000) study of extraversion). More sophisticated statistical techniques (such as structural equational modelling) that are capable of showing cause and effect relationships are in evidence.
4 Researchers are increasingly attempting to explore the interrelationships between individual difference factors (for example, between learning style and learning strategies). Such studies are important because they will help to identify to what extent the differently named constructs are in fact measuring differing aspects of learners and also because they will help to build a theory of individual differences.

5 The 'big two' (i.e. language aptitude and motivation) have been confirmed as the main psychological factors contributing to individual differences in learning.
6 Researchers are increasingly acknowledging that propensity factors (for example, motivation, learning style, anxiety) are situated and dynamic rather than trait-like. That is, they operate differently in different social contexts and they fluctuate as a result of learner internal and external factors.
7 A number of attempts have been made to interrelate some of the key individual difference factors (for example, language aptitude and motivation) to a processing account of L2 acquisition by identifying how they influence input processing, central processing, and output processing. This is especially encouraging as it suggests that the divide between mainstream SLA, with its emphasis on the universal, cognitive dimensions of L2 learning, and the study of individual differences is diminishing.

In 1991 Skehan pointed out that there is no comprehensive theory of IDs in SLA research (i.e. a theory that would explain the interrelationships of the different factors, how they affect the behavioural and cognitive processes involved in L2 acquisition, and their combined effect on achievement). The situation has not changed 15 years later. Perhaps, though, one should not be too critical of this lacuna, as the same could be said of mainstream SLA. A promising approach to developing a theory of individual differences is that outlined by Spolsky (1989). This was based on the observation that IDs constitute 'typical' and 'graded' rather than 'necessary' conditions and learners vary in how successful they are according to how well they satisfy the conditions relating to these IDs. This suggests that the way forward is to establish the weighted contributions of different 'conditions' and also the situational constraints that influence these contributions. Spolsky's approach, however, does not consider how ID factors influence cognitive processing. In this respect, the approach proposed by Robinson (2001a, 2002a) is better. His approach is based on the claim that 'sets of cognitive abilities, or "aptitude complexes" are differentially related to language learning under different psycholinguistic processing conditions' (2001a: 369). A theory should ideally combine the comprehensiveness of Spolsky's 'conditions' (of which 'aptitude' is just one) and the psycholinguistic dimension of Robinson's 'complexes'. However, developing such a theory constitutes a very considerable challenge.

By way of a final cautionary word, research into individual differences would do well to heed Larsen-Freeman's (1997) warning:

> Progress in understanding L2 acquisition will not be made simply by identifying more and more variables that are thought to influence language learners.
> (p. 156).

The study of individual differences might be best served by focusing on those variables (for example, language aptitude and motivation) that have been shown to have a major effect on acquisition.

Notes

1 Readers interested in the use of questionnaires in ID research are referred to Dörnyei's (2003) excellent presentation of questionnaire design and survey type research in this field of research.

2 However, Skehan (1991) argued that aptitude tests can also be used to identify learners with different orientations (for example, analytic versus memory) as well as learners with strong, combined orientations (for example, analytic and memory). In other words, language aptitude tests can also serve to indicate what kind of approach to learning individual learners are inclined to adopt.

3 There is also the Embedded Figures Test (EFT) and the Child Embedded Figures Test (CEFT). Different versions of these tests also exist. One of the problems claimed by Griffiths and Sheen (1991) is the lack of equivalence of these different versions.

4 Ehrman and Leaver (2003) viewed the distinction between ectasis and synopsis as relating to cognitive style. However, it could equally be considered a 'learning style' given the breadth of the constructs it incorporates. Dörnyei (2005) viewed it as relating to 'learning style'. However, I have included it under 'cognitive style' as most of the scales do reflect the way in which information is processed.

5 Isemonger and Watanabe (2007) reported a psychometric evaluation of an administration of a Japanese version of the perceptual component of the Style Analysis Survey. They concluded 'the perceptual component of the SAS should not be taken at face value until further studies can demonstrate valid scores' (p. 143).

6 MacIntyre (2002) suggested that language anxiety and motivation are reciprocally related—'anxiety affects motivation and motivation affects anxiety' (p. 64).

7 MacIntyre and Gardner's anxiety questionnaire was subsequently subjected to a validity check by Onwuegbuzie, Bailey and Daley (2000). After a few changes to the items had been made, the three-stage model of anxiety was confirmed.

8 Initially, willingness to communicate was conceptualized as a trait-like disposition in general psychology but in its application to L2 learning it has been reconceptualized as dynamic and situational.

9 Dörnyei (2005) suggests that Yashima's 'international posture' is a reflection of his 'ideal L2 self' construct.

10 O'Malley *et al.* also investigated the effects of strategy training on the learners' performance on a listening and a speaking task. They reported that a group taught 'functional planning' (a metacognitive strategy) outperformed both the control group and another experimental group taught 'cooperation' (a social/affective strategy) in the speaking task. There was no effect for strategy training in the listening task.

PART SIX
The brain and L2 acquisition

Introduction

This section examines L2 acquisition from the perspective of what is known about the neural mechanisms and pathways of the brain involved in processing and acquiring language. This is a new section—the first edition of the book did not consider the role of these mechanisms. Its inclusion in this second edition reflects the growth of neurolinguistic research in the 1990s. While there is a considerable history of research into aphasia, including aphasia in bilinguals, which has demonstrated a number of relationships between linguistic and neural functioning, the use of sophisticated neuroimaging devices that plot the activity of the different parts of the brain involved in language use and learning, and that became available in the 1990s, has led to a marked increase in neurolinguistic enquiry. This research has allowed researchers to examine the neurobiological plausibility of the 'black box' constructs that have been advanced to explain L2 acquisition. (See Section 4.) It has the potential to add greatly to our understanding of the processes involved. For this reason a chapter examining how the brain handles language and its acquisition is clearly necessary in any up-to-date account of SLA.

The contribution that this research can make to SLA is, however, a matter of some controversy. We can identify three positions. The first is that an understanding of the neural foundation of L2 acquisition is necessary to achieve explanatory adequacy. This is the position that Schumann (2004b) adopted. The second, a weaker version of the first, is that brain neurobiological research can help to establish the legitimacy of the constructs proposed in cognitive SLA. This position acknowledges that cognitive and neurobiological accounts are best viewed as separate and alternative ways of explaining L2 acquisition and emphasizes the advantages of a combined approach. The third position is more dismissive of neurobiological enquiry into L2 acquisition on the grounds that the 'mind' and the 'brain' are separate entities, that neurological explanations are no more 'real' or 'basic' than cognitive explanations and that, in any case, brain science is still at a very primitive stage of development (Gregg 2003). The position I have adopted in the chapter in this section accords most closely with the second of these positions. That is, I have elected to examine a number of the key issues raised in previous chapters (for example, the implicit/explicit knowledge distinction, the nature of the L2 learner's motivation, and fossilization) in the light of insights to be gleaned from neuroscientific research.

14

The neuropsychology of second language acquisition

Introduction

This chapter examines how the human brain handles the acquisition of a second language (L2). It is helpful to distinguish two somewhat different approaches in neuropsychological accounts of L2 acquisition: NEUROLINGUISTIC SLA and NEUROBIOLOGICAL SLA.

Neurolinguistic SLA (see, for example, Paradis 2004) draws on research that has examined how damage to different parts of the human brain (as a result of some traumatic experience, natural ageing, or genetic deficiency) affects a person's ability to use a previously learnt L2. This damage is of two kinds. In the case of APHASIA, the damage results in a loss of procedural ability to use the L2 (i.e. learners cannot automatically and accurately access all aspects of their IMPLICIT KNOWLEDGE of the L2 for purposes of communication). As a result there may be a failure in comprehending L2 messages or in producing spontaneous sentences that are grammatically correct. In the case of amnesia, learners' declarative memory is affected, making it difficult for them to access their explicit knowledge of the L2. In such cases, learners experience difficulty locating the specific word they want but are still able to produce utterances that are grammatical.

Neurobiological SLA (see, for example, Schumann *et al.* 2004) aims to correlate cognitive operations (such as NOTICING and NOTICING THE GAP) with neural functioning. Researchers attempt to show the locations in the brain and the neural circuits that are linked to the formation and consolidation of memories for language. That is, neurobiological SLA starts with the brain and moves on to language. Neural mechanisms are examined and theoretical arguments developed for how they might be involved in language.

These two approaches complement each other. They both involve some degree of speculation given the limits of current knowledge and the relative infancy of the techniques available both for correlating neurological damage with linguistic functioning and imaging the parts of the brain involved in language acquisition.

Brain research into L2 learning is not new. Lenneberg's (1967) *Biological Foundations of Language* sought to use studies of aphasia to support his (and Chomsky's) claims regarding the existence of a biologically-based language faculty in the brain and the non-availability of this faculty once a critical age had been passed. Luria's (1973) *The Working Brain: An Introduction to Neuropsychology* drew on a very different tradition in psychology—Vygotsky's views about the sociocultural basis of mental development. (See Chapter 11.) Like Lenneberg, Luria drew on cases of aphasia but argued against the existence of any innately determined localization of higher mental functions, such as language, in brain structures. In addition to Lenneberg and Luria's work, there is a long tradition of empirical study of aphasia in bilinguals and of methods for treating linguistic impairment. (See, for example, Obler and Alpert 1978.) This research (see Vaid 1983) has addressed such issues as the role of lateralization in language learning (i.e. the location of language functions in one of the brain's two hemispheres, usually the left hemisphere) and, in some cases, has served as a basis for making idiosyncratic proposals about language teaching (for example, Shannahoff-Khalsa's (1984) suggestion that foreign language learners should breathe through their left nostril as a way of activating the learning potential of their right hemisphere). This early research was largely neurolinguistic in orientation.

The 1990s, however, are sometimes referred to as the 'decade of the brain' (Gernsbacher and Kaschak 2003), as it was during this decade that there was a substantial growth in brain studies. This growth was motivated by the availability of techniques for imaging the functioning of the brain as learners performed specific tasks involving language. This more recent research, then, has been neurobiological in orientation.

This chapter will not attempt an in-depth account of the neurolinguistic and neurobiological research into L2 learning. Such an approach is impossible for me, as I am not trained in either of these areas. Instead, I will take as my starting point the key issues in SLA that brain research has shed light on. In other words, I will not attempt to describe the neural mechanisms involved in L2 learning but rather will endeavour to elucidate what brain research has shown about such central issues in SLA as the existence of an innate language faculty, the critical period for language learning, IMPLICIT and EXPLICIT L2 KNOWLEDGE, ATTENTION, and MOTIVATION. It is for this reason that I have entitled this chapter 'neuropsychological SLA' rather than 'neurolinguistic SLA' or 'neurobiological SLA'.

A necessary starting point is an account of the neural structures of the brain so I will begin with this—offering a simple description of the main regions and structures of the brain that will be referred to later in the chapter. I will also briefly describe the methods that have been used to examine the neural substrate of language in the brain. The main section of this chapter will then address what brain research has shown us about SLA. The chapter will conclude with a critical look at the role of brain research in SLA studies.

The anatomy of the human brain

Lamb (1999) insisted that any theory of language, language use, or language acquisition must have 'neurological plausibility'. That is:

> A successful theory has to be compatible with what is known about the brain from neurology and from cognitive science.
> (p. 294)

A starting point for understanding how the brain functions when learners are acquiring an L2, then, is an account of the basic anatomy of the human brain. The description that follows is a gross simplification of an extremely complex organ but it will hopefully suffice to provide a frame of reference for the explanation of the neural basis of different aspects of L2 acquisition, which follows later in this chapter.

It is important to recognize that different people have different brains—as Schumann (2004a) insisted, they are as different as faces. Some brain areas vary in size by a factor of ten between different people. This is reflected in the considerable differences in abilities among people, including the abilities involved in language learning. As Schumann put it, 'the implicit hypothesis ... is that the variation in abilities manifest across individuals is caused by differences in the physical and chemical structure of the brain' (p. 9). However, the basic structure and components of the brain are the same in all humans and it is these that we will concentrate on here.

Left and right hemispheres

The brain consists of two hemispheres (left and right), with language located primarily in the left hemisphere in most people (who are right-handed). The hemispheres are divided by the longitudinal fissure (i.e. a very deep groove). They are connected by means of the corpus callosum, a broad, thick band running from side to side and consisting of millions and millions of nerve fibres. Much of the inter-hemispheric communication in the brain is conducted across the corpus callosum.

The two hemispheres, although not identical, are very similar in structure. Where language is concerned (and many other functions as well), both the cerebral cortex, which spreads across the surface of each hemisphere, and a number of subcortical portions of the brain are important.

The cerebral cortex

The human cerebral cortex covers the surface of the brain and is only 2–4 mm (0.08–0.16 inches) thick. It plays a central role in such functions as memory, attention, perceptual awareness, language, and consciousness. The outermost part of the cortex is grey in colour—hence, the common term 'grey matter'. The inner layers are white. The white matter consists of bundles of fibres which connect the different parts of the cortex and also the cortex with subcortical structures.

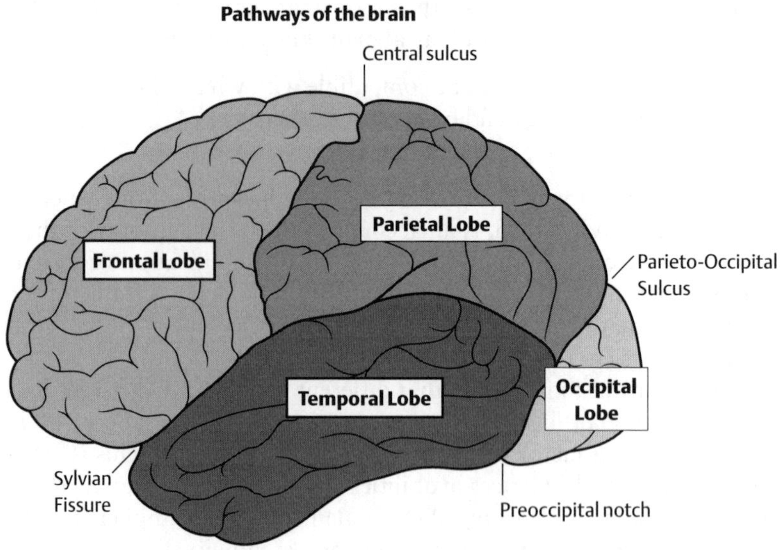

Figure 14.1 Outer surface of the left cerebral hemisphere

Despite the small size of the brain, the cortex has a very large surface. This is because it consists of grooves, referred to technically as sulci (singular sulcus) or fissures. If spread out, the cortex would cover 1400 square centimetres. The grooves divide the brain into lobes: the frontal lobe, the parietal lobe, the occipital lobe, and the temporal lobe. Figure 14.1 (from Lamb 1999: 300) shows the division of the left hemisphere into these four lobes. Each of these lobes is further divided by smaller sulci into gyri (singular gyrus). The temporal lobe is divided into three gyri: superior, middle, and inferior. The frontal lobe consists of the superior frontal gyrus, the middle frontal gyrus, and the inferior frontal gyrus, the last of which has an important role to play linguistically. The frontal pole is the most anterior portion of the frontal lobe and the temporal pole. The occipital lobe controls visual processing. It plays little role in language except, of course, in reading. The parietal lobe, which is important where language is concerned, is divided into two lobules (the superior parietal lobule and the inferior parietal lobule), each with its own gyri. In the inferior parietal lobule, there are the supramarginal gyrus and the angular gyrus.

The cortex can also be divided into layers, which can be distinguished in terms of the relative distribution of different types of neurons that compose each layer. It is traditional to recognize six layers. Layer 1 is the outer surface of the cortex and layer 6 the innermost, adjacent to the white matter.

Based on a detailed clinical examination of the neuronal make-up of the surface of the cortex, Brodmann (1909) divided the cerebral cortex into 52 areas that he judged to be anatomically distinct. Thus, Brodmann's 'map' serves as a further means for referring to the different parts of the cortex. However, the extent to which it is possible to identify the specific functions of the various areas delineated in the map is controversial. A notable limitation is that the map plots only the exposed surface of the cortex, which is only about one third of the total surface, with the other two thirds hidden in the sulci.[1]

The cerebellum

The cerebellum or 'little brain' is anatomically distinct from the cortex but is linked by means of neural pathways to the motor cortex. The cerebellum plays a role in motor coordination and has been shown to be involved in word production, especially when the task is a complex one such as, for example, one that requires the production of low-frequency words.

Subcortical areas

Subcortical portions of the brain of significance for language are the hippocampus, the amygdala, and the basal ganglia.

The hippocampus is phylogenetically one of the oldest parts of the brain. Humans, like other animals, have two hippocampi, one in each hemisphere located under the temporal lobes. They are anatomically part of the limbic system (i.e. the structures of the human brain involved in emotion) but have in fact evolved to serve a different function in the human brain. Although the precise function of the hippocampus is a matter of some dispute, there is general agreement that it is important for the formation of new memories about experienced events (i.e. episodic memories). Once formed, however, these memories are transferred to parts of the cortex, with the hippocampus ceasing to be involved. Damage to the hippocampus leads to difficulty in forming new declarative memories. For example, people suffering from Alzheimer's disease experience damage to the hippocampus and consequent memory problems.

The amygdala, which is also phylogenetically ancient, is located in the medial temporal lobe of the cerebrum. As part of the limbic system, it plays an important role in motivation and emotional behaviour. The amygdala prompts releases of hormones into the blood stream that serve to either arouse or inhibit behaviour.

The basal ganglia are a group of nuclei in the brain that interconnect with a number of other parts—the cerebral cortex, the thalamus, and the brainstem. They have been found to be related to a number of functions, including motor control, cognition, emotions, and learning. Procedural memory for language is dependent on the basal ganglia.

Neurons

The human nervous system, including the brain, is composed of cells called neurons. These transmit electric signals from one part of the nervous system to another.

A neuron consists of a cell body with a nucleus and two kinds of branching structures—an axon and dendrites. Dendrites have extensive branching that reaches out into adjacent neurons. Input is received via the cell body and the dendrites, and output is transmitted via the axon. However, dendrites and axons often act in ways contrary to their main function. Synapses are the points at which a neuron connects to other neurons. Lamb (1999) estimates that the average human cortex has about 480 trillion synapses. Thus neurons 'communicate' with each by receiving input from and transmitting output to other neurons.

There are different types of neurons in the human brain, with each type most plentiful in one of the layers of the cortex. The most common (amounting to about 70 per cent of the total number of neurons) and the most important is the pyramidal neuron. It is this type of neuron which provides the extensive connections in the central nervous system. Neurons can also be distinguished according to function. Excitatory neurons have excitatory connections with other neurons (i.e. they cause other neurons to 'fire') whereas inhibitory neurons prevent target neurons from firing. There are also modulatory neurons that have more complex effects.

Learning, including language learning, is a process of building connections between the neurons located in different parts of the brain. Connections are established by the coordinated firing of neurons. The more frequently the neurons involved in a particular connection are fired, the stronger the connection becomes, a view of learning that is clearly compatible with the connectionist model of learning we considered in Chapter 9. Frequently interconnected neurons create pathways in the brain. One pathway of particular significance for language is the arcuate fasciculus, which connects the posterior part of the temporal-parietal junction with the frontal cortex.

Methods for investigating the 'language brain'

Broadly speaking two approaches for investigating the neuronal architecture of language and language learning are possible, reflecting the distinction between an inductive approach (i.e. research-then-theory) and a deductive approach (i.e. theory-then-research). In the case of the former, an attempt is made to link the observed use of language in some kind of task with specific parts of the brain or neuronal pathways. This is the approach that has been adopted in much of the research investigating aphasia and amnesia and also in the neural imaging research of more recent years. In the case of the deductive approach, a theory of language is used to form specific hypotheses regarding the functioning of the brain which are then tested against the available evidence.

Much of the earlier research was of the research-then-theory kind, based on correlating damage to known areas of the brain with specific language functions. For example, Broca, a French professor of surgical pathology, carried out autopsies of the brains of brain-damaged patients, including one who had major difficulties in producing speech. This led him to hypothesize that it was possible to localize psychological functions in the brain and that speech production was located in the left inferior frontal lobe. In a similar vein, a German neuroscientist, Wernicke, reporting on research with patients suffering from strokes, identified an area of the brain responsible for phonological recognition and comprehension. This empirical tradition has continued, as reflected, for example, in the work of Penfield and Roberts (1959) and, more relevant to our concern for L2 language acquisition, in Paradis' (1994, 2004) account of the aphasia symptoms in two languages. It should also be noted that the research-then-theory approach is not limited to neurolinguistic studies involving aphasia or amnesia; it is also evident in much of the neurobiological research.

The case for a theoretically-informed approach has been forcefully made by Paradis (2004: 166–7):

> Without a neurolinguistically informed theory, we can only observe that a particular parameter (task, procedure, baseline, etc.) has a particular effect but we do not know why.

A good example of such a theory is Lamb's (1999) Proximity Hypothesis. Lamb argued that it is unlikely that every location in the cortex has connections to every other one. He proposed that there are three kinds of connections: (1) to neighbouring layers of the same subsystem, (2) within neighbouring subsystems, and (3) to distant subsystems. He then argued that, in general, each subsystem of language (for example, phonology, lexis, grammar, and semantics) will be served by areas of the cortex that are proximate and also that areas that are connected to two or more other areas will lie intermediate to these areas. He then mustered evidence from both aphasia studies and NEUROIMAGING to support these hypotheses. Another example of a theory-led approach to investigating the language brain is Luria's (1973) neuropsychology. For Luria the starting point was a characterization of the mental functions in psychological theory—in this case Vygotsky's sociocultural theory of the mind. (See Chapter 11.) That is, Luria saw complex functional brain systems developing as a product of the mediation of culturally-defined external aids.

We will now examine in some detail the two major methods used to collect data about the 'language brain': (1) the investigation of bilingual aphasia, and (2) neuroimaging studies of learners' use of the L2.

Investigating bilingual aphasia

Investigations of bilingual aphasia aim to identify (1) which parts of the brain have been damaged and (2) which functions in which language(s) have been affected. In this way, it is possible to relate areas of the brain to particular linguistic functions. Ahlsen (2006) listed three ways that have been used to investigate (or simulate) brain damage. As noted above, early studies, such as those by Broca and Wernicke, involved autopsies of brains to identify lesions. The intracarotid sodium amytal test involves injecting a drug into one of the arteries feeding the brain resulting in the part of the brain supplied by that artery to become anaesthetized and so making it possible to study how each hemisphere handles language. Radiography has also been used to identify malformations affecting the blood vessels in the brain. Loss of linguistic function is identified by observing language behaviour and/or testing.

BILINGUALISM is a complex phenomenon. Ahlsen (2006: 126) listed the following questions that need to be considered when examining an aphasic's ability to use both languages:

1 How comparable are investigations of the two languages?
2 Are the tests that are used comparable?
3 Have typological considerations, such as potential processing load and differences in cue validity and cue cost, been considered in constructing the tasks?
4 Have cultural, social, and individual factors that might affect the use of the two languages been considered in interpreting the results?

Paradis (2004) emphasized that the diagnosis of aphasia in bilinguals requires that both languages are tested and also that each language is tested by means of an equivalent instrument. He provided a detailed account of how test equivalence can be established. For example, he pointed out that in tests of comprehension it was important to test patients' understanding of grammatical structures of equal complexity in the two languages. Paradis also emphasized the importance of establishing the facts relating to the patient's history of bilingualism. For example, there is likely to be a difference between early and late bilinguals, with the former having developed equal implicit knowledge in both languages and the latter compensating for gaps in their implicit knowledge of the second language through explicit and pragmatic knowledge. An example of a testing instrument that sought to address these various concerns is the Bilingual Aphasia Test (Paradis and Libben 1987).

Studies of bilingual aphasia focus on which functions in which language are lost as a result of damage to the brain and also on patterns of recovery. It is possible to distinguish a number of different types of bilingual aphasia. (See Ahlsen 2006 and Paradis 2004.) These are shown in Table 14.1. 'Selective aphasia' relates to the pattern of loss in the two languages. In an overview of studies reporting aphasia, Paradis (2004) reported that 76 per cent of cases involved equal impairment in both languages, 12.3 per cent differential impairment, 6.5 per cent blended impairment, 4.3 per cent selective and 0.7 per cent antagonistic impairment. Each of these types of impairment is associated with a different recovery pattern. There are two general patterns—'parallel recovery' and 'dissociated recovery' (which can be further distinguished as shown in types 3, 4, and 5). Paradis (2004) reported that parallel recovery is the norm.

Type	**Description**
1 Selective aphasia	Brain-damaged symptoms appear in only one language.
2 Parallel recovery	Recovery takes place equally in both languages.
3 Differential recovery	One language is recovered much better than the other.
4 Selective recovery	One language is recovered and the other is not.
5 Mixed recovery	The two languages are blended in inappropriate ways.
6 Alternating antagonism	Only one language is available at one time but which language is available changes.

Table 14.1 Types of bilingual aphasia

To explain these different types of aphasia it is necessary to address three questions:

1 What brain mechanism makes these various patterns possible?
2 What determines that a given patient undergoes one type of recovery, and another patient a different type of recovery?
3 Assuming a patient exhibits a selective recovery, why is one language (say, English) preserved rather than the other (say, Japanese)?

(Paradis 2004: 69)

However, judging from Paradis' own review of the explanations provided by a number of researchers (for example, Albert and Obler 1978; Green 2002), there are no clear answers to these questions, although there is now general acceptance that the two languages are not located in different hemispheres (i.e. the L1 in the left and the L2 in the right hemisphere)—a point further considered below.

The treatment of aphasia provides a further means of investigating the language brain. Obviously, the main purpose of a treatment regime is the rehabilitation of the patient but it can also shed light on the normal activity of the brain and the organization of mental functions. For example, Luria (1970) devised a treatment that involved assisting patients to consciously enact language functions that had been damaged through external auxiliary means. He used evidence of the success of this treatment to refute the view that mental functions, such as language, are localized in specific, innately determined brain areas.

Neuroimaging

Neuroimaging involves the use of a technique for identifying which parts of the brain are activated when learners are asked to perform a language task. This technique is based on the notion that increases in the blood flow to one particular part of the brain are indicative of increases in the neural activity of that part. Gernsbacher and Kaschak (2003) described a typical neuroimaging study as one that 'relates stimulus- and task-related changes to changes in neural activity in an attempt to discern what brain regions underlie a particular type of processing and how these regions go about their work' (p. 92). Changes in neural activity can also be instigated by asking participants to perform a task involving receptive or productive language use. An example of the kind of study that has employed neuroimaging will help to elucidate the methodology employed.

Chee, Tan, and Thiel (1999) used a technique known as FUNCTIONAL MAGNETIC RESONANCE IMAGING (fMRI) to investigate whether the processing of Mandarin logographic script activated different brain areas from those activated by the processing of English alphabetic script and, also, whether there was any difference in the brain areas used by early and late bilinguals. The participants were 15 early Chinese–English bilinguals who had been exposed to English from the age of 6 years and 9 late bilinguals who had not been exposed to English before the age of 12 years. These participants were given two word tasks to perform. In the first task they were told to silently complete word stems in the case of English (for example, 'cou—' → 'couple') and to complete a compound word in Mandarin. In the second task they were given the end of an English word and asked to complete it (for example, '__ter' → 'water') and to complete Mandarin words when given a right-hand radical. The words were presented in blocks of 15 stimuli with each block separated by asking the participants to fixate on a picture of a small cross. A total of six hundred images of brain activity were collected by means of an fMRI machine. The images were interpreted by comparing those elicited from the two tasks with those elicited during the period of fixation, the latter serving as a baseline. The results indicated no difference in brain activation according to either language or age of acquisition of English.

A variety of different techniques are available for examining brain activity. Ahlsen (2006) classified these into two groups: those involving static recording and those involving dynamic recording. We will consider the main techniques used in language research here.

Magnetic resonance imaging (MRI) is a static recording technique. It was formerly referred to as magnetic resonance tomography. It is a non-invasive method used to render images of the inside of the brain. It can provide very clear images. Electroencephalography (EEG) is a dynamic recording technique that involves measuring the electrical activity generated by the brain when metal electrodes are placed on the scalp. It records brain waves generated by the different lobes in the two hemispheres. A development of this technique is the measurement of event-related potentials (ERPs). Measurements are again obtained from placing electrodes on the scalp but these are averaged over many events from the same stimulus in order to eliminate disturbances due to unwanted activity such as blinking and head movements. The advantage of ERPs is that they provide clear evidence of temporal events in the brain but they provide only poor evidence of which regions of the brain are involved. Positron emission tomography (PET) registers physiological changes in brain cells. It involves injecting water molecules tagged with radioactive isotopes into the body. It produces a map of the functional processes in the brain and has shown that when the brain is damaged in one area as a result of aphasia, changes in other more distant areas also occur. Functional magnetic resonance imaging (fMRI)—the method used in the Chee *et al.* study—is another dynamic imaging technique which identifies changes in regional blood oxygen levels in cortical areas. These latter two methods provide good spatial resolution.

On the face of it these techniques afford an excellent method for identifying both the parts of the brain and the neural pathways involved in performing different language tasks. However, there are a number of problems. Paradis (2004), in particular, is critical of neuroimaging studies arguing that they 'suffer from a lack of linguistic sophistication'. The problems he identified included the following:

1 The tasks used are often not linguistic tasks (i.e. are not part of natural language use) and hence to do not involve the normal linguistic processes involved in understanding and producing messages. Chee *et al.*'s study, for example, involved the highly artificial task of completing words from cues provided.
2 The language tasks used often result in activation in several cortical regions making it difficult to determine which of the activated areas serves which component of the task.
3 The activation patterns revealed by the imaging technique used need to be interpreted and interpretation depends on the baseline and the statistical procedures used.
4 Different neuroimaging techniques can reveal very different results.
5 There is likely to be substantial 'noise' in the images obtained as a result of 'multiple unintended secondary processes' (p. 158).
6 The evidence that neuroimaging provides often conflicts with that from other sources (for example, aphasia studies).
7 The results obtained are averaged with the result that inter-individual variation is lost.

Paradis' review of neuroimaging studies with bilingual participants revealed substantial contradictions in the results obtained. He concluded that 'cognitive neuroimaging is still by and large at the "poking" stage' (p. 186).

Concluding comment

From this brief review of the methods of studying the language brain, it should be clear that there is no one 'best' method. Brain research suffers from similar problems to those faced in psychological SLA. Whereas mainstream SLA faces the problem of deciding which observable behaviours constitute evidence of which mental processes, research into the language brain faces the problem of correlating evidence of neuronal impairment/activity with identifiable mental processes. The solution to this problem, as in mainstream SLA, is to look for converging evidence. Theoretically-derived hypotheses about the mental functioning involved in L2 acquisition are best tested by collating evidence obtained from a variety of sources including studies of aphasia and amnesia and studies using neuroimaging techniques.

Neuropsychological aspects of L2 acquisition

I will now examine research that has studied the neural mechanisms involved in L2 acquisition. This research is quite extensive and often very technical, so my approach will be to identify the main findings and illustrate these with reference to selected studies. I will work top-down rather than bottom-up; that is, my starting point will not be the brain itself but rather the key issues in SLA that the neurolinguistic and neurobiological research has addressed. The questions I will consider are:

1 Does learning an L2 involve a specialized language faculty or rely on general cognitive mechanisms?
2 Are the mental processes involved in learning an L2 different from those involved in learning an L1?
3 To what extent are the processes involved in comprehending and producing an L2 distinct?
4 How valid is the distinction between implicit (procedural) knowledge and explicit (declarative) knowledge of an L2?
5 What is the role of 'attention' in L2 acquisition?
6 What is 'motivation' and how does it affect the acquisition of an L2?
7 How do speakers control access to the L2 and L1?
8 Is there evidence of a critical period?
9 Is defossilization possible?

These are all questions that have figured in the preceding chapters; they all address highly controversial issues in SLA.

A specialized language faculty

In Chapter 11 we examined the claim made by researchers working within the tradition of generative linguistics regarding the existence of a specialized language faculty. Chomsky (1980) postulated that there is a language organ, which is part of a human's biological endowment and which houses the universal principles and parameters without which a child would be unable to develop full LINGUISTIC COMPETENCE. We also saw that this has led to researchers questioning whether this Universal Grammar is available to the older learner. In contrast, psychologists in the Piagetian mould and, more recently, emergentists, such as N Ellis (1998), have argued that language acquisition, whether first or second, is driven by general cognitive mechanisms responsible for learning of all types. What light does what is known about the language brain throw on this dispute?

The claim that language constitutes an 'organ' in the brain is based on the assumption that it is possible to identify a specific area of the brain that handles language. Thus, a preliminary issue that needs to be addressed is whether language is localized or distributed in the human brain—that is, whether it is possible to identify a specific area of the brain that controls language and language learning or whether a number of different areas and neural pathways account for language. Ahlsen (2006) identified a number of different views relating to this issue. Localists seek specific centres in the brain to account for different functions, an approach that is compatible with a specialized language faculty. Associationists view language functions as arising from the coordinated activity of different areas of the brain, a view that might still be compatible with a Chomskyan account of language if one of these areas or circuits can be shown to relate to 'core grammar'. Supporters of the dynamic localization of function propose a set of localized subfunctions. In their view language systems are dynamic in the sense that they can be reorganized during language development or after loss of language due to neurological damage. Such a view is less obviously compatible with the idea of specialized language faculty.

There are few pure localists today. There is much more support for the associationist position. Paradis (2004), for example, argued that the brain is composed of neurofunctional modules that are isolable, autonomous, domain-specific, and purposeful. These modules can interact but the interactions do not alter their computational procedures. Each module has access only to the output of another module. Paradis claimed that the neurofunctional systems that underlie implicit competence (which, as we have seen in earlier chapters, is what both generative and connectionist accounts of language acquisition seek to explain) contain distinct modules for phonology, syntax, and semantics, each of which has its own internal organization. In general, then, Paradis' account of neurofunctional modularity is compatible with the idea of a specific language organ for grammar. However, the demonstration of modularity does not in and of itself justify the claim that linguistic competence depends on a specific and innate language faculty. Paradis was careful to point out that innateness is not a necessary attribute of the language module. Also, he noted that 'dedicated weighted connections for a particular task constitute the connectionist equivalent of a module, a different metaphor for a modular system' (p. 122). In other words, the acceptance of neuronal modularity does not necessitate acceptance of a dedicated module for grammar.

The crucial evidence for determining whether a Chomskyan or a connectionist account of language learning is to be preferred comes from studies that have investigated whether language learning draws on the same neural mechanisms as other types of learning. Here we will focus on what has been discovered about the neural structures involved in the acquisition of implicit knowledge. Lee (2004) reported research that demonstrated the role played by the basal ganglia in the development of procedural memory. The basal ganglia are massively connected to cortical and other subcortical brain structures, all of which contribute to performance of a diverse set of functions, only one of which is language. Learning is initiated in the area of the cortex responsible for motor activity and in the anterior basal ganglia. There is a direct and indirect pathway running from the basal ganglia to the motor cortex. As a result of repetitive inputs, the synapses in the basal ganglia and cortex grow stronger until the learner can execute rules through the direct pathway, with the indirect pathway serving to inhibit incorrect patterns. Once automatized through the direct pathway, procedural memories (corresponding to chunks) are stored in pathways between the cortex and the posterior part of the basal ganglia. Clearly, such an account of the mechanisms responsible for the development of implicit linguistic knowledge does not support the idea of a specialized language faculty. As Lee commented 'automatization is not a function of an innate grammar, but a process that occurs through a domain-general learning mechanism in the brain that is used not only for language but also for motor and other cognitive skill learning' (p. 43). This view of learning, however, is clearly commensurate with a connectionist model.

An account of language acquisition based on Universal Grammar (UG) was forcibly rejected by Jacobs and Schumann (1992). They challenged it on two grounds. First, they argued that the neurobiological evidence gave no support for a specifically language-related mental module as the 'dynamic plasticity' of the brain allows for a far greater environmental effect on the development of language than is recognized by UG theorists. Second, they claimed that language learning is like any other type of learning in that it 'involves alteration of the microanatomical and molecular neural structure to the point where information can be retained and retrieved so as to be able to effect behavior' (p. 287). Eubank and Gregg (1995) addressed both of these arguments. They argued that dynamic plasticity is not a feature of all neural processes and that there is evidence of a 'bounded period of sensitivity and response specificity' in some sets of neurons, such as those found in the hippocampus. They also argued that it is necessary to posit the existence of innate mechanisms for some domains (for example, to explain phenomena such as the highly-complex tail-wagging dance performed by European honeybees to communicate information about food sources) and also a CRITICAL PERIOD for language learning. These arguments are problematic, however. For a start, the hippocampus is associated with the learning of DECLARATIVE

KNOWLEDGE rather than the kind of PROCEDURAL KNOWLEDGE that UG addresses. Second, as we saw in Chapter 1, the existence of a critical period for language acquisition is highly questionable. While it is very likely that there is biological propensity for certain motor skills (such as the bees' tail-wagging dance), it does not follow that there is a unique neural apparatus for language. Indeed, if there is one clear message from brain research it is that neural systems are not discrete but highly inter-connected and multi-functional.

The neurobiological basis of L1 and L2 acquisition

If it is assumed that the brain (like the mind) is modular, then the question arises as to whether there are separate modules for the L1 and the L2. This is related to whether there is a specific faculty for language (i.e. Universal Grammar). If there is, then the further question arises as to whether it remains available to L2 learners. If it does, then the neurobiological basis must be the same for L2 acquisition as L1 acquisition. If it does not, then it must be assumed that the neurobiological basis is different. As we have already seen, the available evidence does not support the evidence of a brain area dedicated to language (i.e. there is no apparent neurobiological foundation for Universal Grammar). Neurological modularity is of a more distributed nature.

The question can now be reformulated as whether the neural mechanisms responsible for the acquisition of the L1 are the same as those for the acquisition of the L2 (irrespective of the fact that they are distributed) and, also, whether L1 representations are stored together with or separate from L2 representations.

The early work on HEMISPHERIC DIFFERENTIATION in bilinguals (Albert and Obler 1978) suggested that L1 and L2 learning drew on different mechanisms. Studies of aphasia indicated that bilinguals were less hemisphere dominant than monolinguals. Albert and Obler claimed:

> Language is organized in the brain of the bilingual in a manner different from that which might have been predicted by studies of cerebral organization for language monolinguals. Studies of monolinguals have indicated that the left hemisphere is dominant for language in most individuals. Studies on bilinguals demonstrate not only the left hemispheric role in language but also a major right hemispheric contribution.

Galloway (1980) also noted differences in the aphasias of monolinguals and bilinguals. She found that 98 per cent of aphasias in monolinguals were due to left-hemisphere lesions and only 2 per cent to right-hemisphere lesions, while for bilinguals the ratio was 85 per cent and 15 per cent. However, the research cited in support of the Hemispheric Differentiation Hypothesis has come in for considerable criticism. Genesee (1980), in a review of Albert and Obler (1978), noted that 'there is a disturbing number of inaccuracies throughout the neuropsychological sections of the book'. Solin (1989) pointed out that

Galloway's sample was biased and noted that more recent brain research points to greater right-hemisphere involvement in L1 acquisition than Albert and Obler were aware of.

The belief that L2 learning involved greater right-hemisphere involvement than L1 acquisition was, in part, based on the claim that lateral specialization is progressive (i.e. that it increases gradually until it reaches completion in adolescence). However, it is now widely accepted that lateralization is completed much earlier (possibly even before birth). We can safely conclude, therefore, that lateralization is not the explanation for any neurobiological differences between L1 and L2 learners.

There is much greater support for DIFFERENTIAL LOCALIZATION (i.e. the existence of neurobiological differences within the same hemisphere). Paradis (2004) suggests two ways in which differential localization might occur:

1 L1 and L2 acquisition draw on partly overlapping and partly different anatomical areas in the dominant hemisphere.
2 Both the L1 and the L2 are served by the same language areas but involve different circuits within these areas.

Paradis rejected (1) on the grounds that there is no evidence that the L1 and L2 are represented in different anatomical areas—a position apparently supported by the results of Chee *et al.*'s study considered earlier in this chapter. This study, it will be recalled, failed to find any difference in the areas of the brain activated by a word completion task in early and late English–Mandarin bilinguals. Similarly, Hernandez *et al.* (2000) used fMRI to study six Spanish–English bilinguals, all of whom had learnt both languages before the age of six. They found no significant differences in localization. On the basis of such studies, Paradis concluded in favour of (2):

> Both language systems seem to be represented as distinct microanatomical subsystems located in the same gross anatomical areas.
> (p. 116)

Paradis' position is largely confirmed by Indefrey's (2006) review of neuroimaging studies that examined the activation patterns during L1 and L2 processing. Indefrey concluded that 'there are no L2-specific regions of activation' (p. 299).

Some studies, however, have shown anatomical differences between the L1 and L2. Studies of aphasia that point to a clear dissociation of the two languages suggest that, in some learners at least, the two languages are stored in different parts of the brain. For example, Gomez-Tortosa *et al.* (1995) reported on a balanced Spanish–English bilingual who underwent surgery to her left temporal lobe and subsequently reported finding trouble with accessing words in Spanish but not in English. Neuroimaging studies also provide evidence of anatomical differentiation of languages. Price *et al.* (1999) observed that comprehension of words in the L1 yielded greater activation of the left temporal lobe than did words in the L2. As Dehaene

(1999) noted, this replicates several earlier studies which all showed that the 'language organ' in the left temporal lobe is more activated when listening to the mother tongue than to any other lesser-known language. Mueller (2005) reviewed a range of ERP studies and concluded that while they pointed to similarities in the lexical–semantic domain between L1 and L2 speakers, differences were evident in both syntactic processing and speech segmentation. Mueller suggested that highly automatic syntactic processes and native-like speech segmentation mechanisms may not be fully available to even advanced late L2 learners. Finally, as Indefrey (2006) noted, even if the same regions of the brain are implicated in L1 and L2 processing in the population at large, this does not preclude the possibility that L2-specific sites might be found at the single-learner level.

There is substantial evidence in support of differences reflecting smaller-scale specialized circuits. Dehaene (1999) cited a study by Kim *et al.* (1997) which showed that whereas sentence production tasks in the L1 and L2 activated the same areas in learners who had acquired the L2 early and were balanced bilinguals, they activated two non-overlapping sub-regions of Broca's area in the case of learners who had acquired the L2 late and were clearly dominant in their L1. Dehaene *et al.* (1997) reported similar results for sentence comprehension.

One possibility is that the crucial factor determining whether L1 and L2 acquisition are neurobiologically the same is the degree of fluency rather than the age L2 acquisition started. Thus whereas major anatomical differences may be evident when the comparison involves non-fluent L2 learners, only micro-anatomical differences will be observed when the learner is fluent in the L2. Dehaene (1999) concluded:

> ... a weak consensus seems to be emerging to suggest that the level of fluency is a critical determinant of brain activation patterns in language tasks. In fluent individuals, processing differences between L1 and L2 may be supported by differences in cerebral microcircuitry that are hardly visible with the present resolution of brain-imaging methods.
> (p. 2208)

Again, though, not all studies are compatible with such a conclusion. Chee *et al.*'s study, for example, failed to find anatomical differences even though there was undoubtedly a difference between the degree of fluency of the late bilinguals (who came from China) and the L1 speakers and early bilinguals. Also, as Mueller's (2005) survey of ERP studies showed, it may depend on the particular aspect of language under examination (for example, lexical–semantic versus syntactic).

The study of aphasias and the neuroimaging and event-related potential (ERP) research serve as means for testing the L2 = L1 acquisition hypothesis. (See Chapter 3.) This hypothesis is predicated on the assumption that L2 acquisition is either like (wholly or in part) or unlike L1 acquisition. But this is perhaps the wrong way to look at this issue. Grosjean (1989) proposed that the bilingual is a unique language user; that is, the bilingual's competence is distinct from that of monolinguals' competence in the two languages. In other words, bilinguals possess a unified, integrated system—a view clearly compatible with the claim that bilinguals' two languages share the same anatomical areas but with different micro-circuitry. Jerkiewicz (2000) reviewed the evidence for Grosjean's hypothesis. He cited a study by Ardal *et al.* (1990). This examined monolinguals' and bilinguals' L1 and L2 responses to sentences that were semantically congruous (for example, 'For breakfast I ate cereal with milk') and incongruous (for example, 'For breakfast I ate cereal with socks') using EEG to measure ERPs. The bilingual participants had significantly better recognition scores in their L1 compared to the monolinguals, suggesting that L2 learning has an impact on L1 processing. Also the monolinguals' ERPs peaked earlier than the bilinguals. This study then supports Grosjean's hypothesis. However, Indefrey (2006) felt that there was insufficient evidence to support the claim that the bilingual processing resulted in structural brain changes of the kind implied by Grosjean's hypothesis.

What conclusions can we reach regarding the neurobiological basis of L1 and L2 acquisition? If there are differences, these are not because of the non-availability of the 'language organ' to L2 learners because there is no convincing evidence to support the existence of a language organ. We can also confidently dismiss the early view that the difference is hemispheric as a result of lateralization. However, if there are differences (and there is conflicting evidence on this point), it is not yet clear whether the differences are anatomical or in the micro-circuitry of the same anatomical areas or, indeed, in both. Green, Crinion, and Price (2006) concluded their review of the current research by stating that it indicates 'that the neural representation of an L2 converges with that of an L1' but then went on to say that this 'does not deny that there might be language-specific neuronal sites within these regions' (p. 111). Rodriguez-Fornells, Balaguer, and Munte (2006) concluded that the brain regions involved in L1 and L2 learning are 'partially overlapping and partially segregated' (p. 137).

One final comment is in order. It is entirely possible that the neural commonalities of the L1 and L2 will depend to a considerable extent on the languages involved. It is not unreasonable to suppose that where the language distance is small (for example, English–Dutch) the neural commonalities will be more extensive than when the language distance is great (for example, English–Japanese). Such a hypothesis is compatible with the role that language distance has been shown to play in LANGUAGE TRANSFER. (See Chapter 8.)

The neurobiological bases of comprehension and production in an L2

The claim that there are distinct parts of the brain responsible for comprehending and producing language originated in the early work of Paul Broca and Carl Wernicke, who demonstrated a dissociation between comprehension and production and the parts of the brain responsible for these in brain-damaged people. Broca identified a section of the brain in the inferior gyrus of the frontal lobe that was involved in language production. People who suffer from Broca's aphasia have difficulty in creating grammatically complex sentences. Their speech is telegraphic, lacking function words and morphological markers. In contrast, their comprehension is relatively normal, although studies have demonstrated that Broca's aphasics can also have trouble understanding certain kinds of syntactically complex sentences. Wernicke identified a different section of the brain—the posterior part of the first or superior temporal gyrus and adjacent areas—responsible for comprehension. Patients suffering from Wernicke's aphasia lose the ability to understand language. However, although they can speak clearly, their sentences are sometimes jumbled and make no sense, a phenomenon that has been explained by the loss of the connection between Broca's and Wernicke's areas which makes patients unable to monitor their own speech for comprehension.

More recent neuroimaging research, however, suggests a much more complicated picture of the neural mechanisms involved in comprehension and production, indicating that multiple areas in the left and right hemispheres are involved. The general picture is of a many-to-many mapping of regions of the brain to language processing. Table 14.2, based on Gernsbacher and Kaschak's (2003) summary of the neuroimaging studies of language production and comprehension, demonstrates this many-to-many mapping of structure and function. However, Gernsbacher and Kaschak acknowledged that this mapping is somewhat crude both because the functional labels are very broad and therefore vague and because of the methodological difficulty of ascertaining which specific regions are activated by a particular task. They acknowledged that 'the rules of the game are still being developed' (p. 109).

We will now consider which regions of the brain are involved in L2 comprehension and production. Abutalebi, Cappa, and Perani (2001) provided a helpful review of the neuroimaging studies that have investigated comprehension and production. They concluded that L2 proficiency is the crucial factor. For comprehension, they noted studies (for example, Perani *et al.* 1996, 1998) that reported differing cortical responses in low- and high-proficiency L2 learners. In the case of advanced L2 learners the neural machinery involved when listening to a story was the same as that found in L1 subjects (i.e. it comprised all the classical language areas in the temporal lobe and also the temporal pole, a structure that is involved in sentence and discourse processing). In the case of less proficient learners, fewer areas are active (i.e. only the right superior and middle temporal areas). Differences according to proficiency are also evident for L2 production. That is, there is a common neural network involving the left prefrontal cortex for production in the L1 and the L2 when the L2 learner is advanced. Interestingly, cerebral activation (i.e. in brain structures such as Broca's area and the basal ganglia) increases in learners of low proficiency—the opposite of what was observed for comprehension. Abutalebi *et al.* commented: 'When a language is not used regularly, a larger network may be necessary for its processing' (p. 183).

Region of the brain	**Main functions**
A Frontal regions	
Left hemisphere	
1 Middle and superior frontal regions	Semantic decision tasks.
2 Supplementary motor area and Broca's area	Production of verbal and non-verbal motor responses to tasks; maintenance of phonological representations; production of subvocalizations; syntactic processing.
Right hemisphere	
1 Inferior frontal region	Processing of abstract words; sentence processing; discourse processing; detection of emotional content in speech.
2 Middle and superior frontal regions	Semantic decision tasks; integrative aspects of discourse processing.
B Temporal and posterior regions	
Left hemisphere	
1 Superior temporal regions	Auditory processing of sounds; semantic processing; syntactic processing.
2 Middle temporal region	Phonological and semantic processing.
3 Temporal pole	Discourse processing.
4 Wernicke's area	Semantic processing; certain aspects of phonological processing, e.g. translating written words into their phonological representations.
5 Posterior inferior-temporal regions	Early visual processing of words.
6 Superior parietal regions	Discourse processing.
7 Cerebellum	Complex cognitive tasks (e.g. difficult word completion tasks).
Right hemisphere	
1 Superior parietal regions	Discourse processing.
2 Superior temporal regions	Early speech processing; processing difficult sentences; discourse processing.
3 Right temporal regions	Processing of prosody.

Table 14.2 Neural activation in language production and comprehension (based on Gernsbacher and Kaschak 2003: 107–8)

Another difference between more and less proficient learners' L2 production that was noted by Golestani *et al.* (2006) concerns the components responsible for procedural memory. This will be considered in the following section.

Two conclusions are possible. The first is that, to a degree at least, different brain structures are involved in comprehension and production, although in both cases these structures are multiple and partly overlapping. The second is that for both comprehension and production the same structures figure in native speakers and advanced L2 learners but that some differences in brain regions are evident between these and low-proficiency learners.

Implicit versus explicit L2 knowledge

As I noted in Chapter 9, the distinctions between implicit and explicit memory and between procedural and declarative knowledge are now generally acknowledged to refer to the same mental phenomena. I will therefore use these terms interchangeably in the discussion that follows.

So far we have found very limited evidence to support the macro-localization of language functions. However, the evidence we will now consider suggests a relatively clear-cut differentiation in the areas of the brain responsible for implicit/procedural and explicit/declarative memory. I will begin by describing the key neural regions associated with each type of memory and the specific language functions associated with each, and then move on to consider the evidence that supports this differentiation. I will conclude this section by revisiting the INTERFACE positions considered in Chapter 9 in the light of the neuroscientific findings.

Procedural memory relies on circuits in the basal ganglia. According to the account provided by Lee (2004), the pre-supplementary motor cortex and the anterior part of the basal ganglia are recruited to initiate learning. Once a sequence is automatized, the cerebellar dentate nucleus and the posterior part of the basal ganglia serve as the sites for storing and retrieving procedural memory. Cortical inputs through the basal ganglia go on to the thalamus and return to the cortical areas, forming a loop. There are two pathways for this loop: a direct pathway, which facilitates the flow of information through the thalamus and the consequent excitation of the cerebral cortex, and an indirect pathway, which inhibits the flow of information and consequently decreases the activity of the cerebral cortex. Automatization occurs when numerous and repetitive inputs build up stronger synapses in neurons in the cortex and basal ganglia enabling the learner to execute rules through the direct pathway, while the indirect pathway serves to inhibit incorrect patterns. Procedural memory is not dedicated to language; it also underlies the learning and performance of motor skills in general. However, whereas the neural structures involved are domain general, the circuits within this domain that serve non-linguistic and linguistic processes may be specific.

The storage of declarative memories involves various regions of the brain but some regions are more important than others. The hippocampus plays a major role, especially in the initial formation of declarative knowledge (Crowell 2004). Thus, the surgical removal of the hippocampus makes the formation of new declarative memories difficult if not impossible. More permanent storage of episodic and semantic knowledge involves those areas of the cerebral cortex (i.e. the temporal and parietal neocortical regions) that were originally involved in processing. Crowell noted, however, that recent research also indicates that episodic memory traces may remain in the hippocampus and that whether the storage of declarative knowledge in the hippocampus is just temporary or more permanent is a matter of debate. Two processes are involved in the development of long-term declarative memory; long-term potentiation and long-term depression. The former involves an increase in synaptic transmission and is responsible for forming and storing memories. A synapse is strengthened when stimulated—a response that 'potentiates' the synapse and simultaneously activates the neurons connected to the synapse. The potentiation can last for minutes, hours, days, months, or even years, depending on the extent of the stimulation. Late-phase potentiation constitutes 'a stage where temporary short-term memories first begin the process of changing into more stable long-term memories' (Crowell 2004; 87). Long-term depression brings about a decrease in learning. Hippocampal long-term depression is believed to be important for clearing old memory traces. The declarative memory system is also not specific to language. It is involved in both the learning of facts (semantic knowledge) and events (episodic knowledge).

These two systems have been linked to quite separate aspects of language. Ullman (2001) argued that procedural memory is 'largely informationally encapsulated' (p. 47) and develops as a result of implicit, non-conscious processes of learning. It is specialized for sequences (i.e. linguistic chunks) and houses a rule system consisting of representations of linguistic patterns extracted from input that has repeatedly stimulated the relevant neural circuits. It is associated with grammatical processing (both syntax and morphology) as this occurs in real time. Ullman (2001) characterized the declarative memory system as 'an associative memory of distributed representations' (p. 41) housing the mental lexicon, that is, the sounds and meanings of morphologically simple and complex words. He suggested that, unlike procedural memory it might not be informationally encapsulated. Thus, according to Ullman, the brain is so organized as to support a mental model consisting of two largely separate systems—the lexicon and the grammar, each with distinct neural bases. He illustrated this model with reference to the processing of morphological forms such as regular and irregular past-tense verbs forms. He proposed that procedural memory permits the computation of regular morphological features (for example, V–ed) by concatenating the phonological forms of the base and an affix (for example, walk +ed → walked). In contrast, declarative memory handles irregular forms. However, an irregular form such as 'ate' is not stored as a whole in declarative memory but rather in a distributed fashion 'as a structured assembly of its parts'. Ullman suggested that 'for a given morphosyntactic configuration, both systems attempt to compute an appropriately complex form' but that 'if a form is found in memory (*sang*), the rule-based computation is inhibited' (p. 39).

However, as Ullman himself admitted, language cannot be so neatly divided into 'regular' and 'irregular' forms; there are also subregular forms (i.e. forms that manifest some degree of regularity without being entirely regular). A good example can be found in the plural forms of German nouns. The default, regular form is –s, but other forms are partially regular (for example, the –(e)n plural form which occurs predominantly with feminine nouns). An event-related potential study by Bartke, Rösler, Streb, and Wiese (2005) found differences in brain responses depending on whether the stimulus was a complete irregular or a subregular and suggested that, like regular forms, subregular forms may be represented as rules. They suggested that the dual-mechanism account proposed by Ullman and others (see Chapter 9) may need to be modified to incorporate a third processing component to explain how the brain processes subregular forms.

Such a proposal appears speculative, however. In general, neurolinguists prefer a dual-mechanism model. Paradis (2004), for example, made a clear-cut distinction between the functions of two systems. He claimed that 'the neural structures that mediate controlled processing and those that subserve automatic processing each have their own evolutionary history and place in ontogeny' (p. 42). Implicit memory is primary where language is concerned as it allows automatic and entirely involuntary processing. In contrast, explicit memory operates through controlled processes which are under voluntary execution. Whereas implicit memory serves grammar, explicit memory is necessary for learning phonological forms and the referential meaning of words.

Evidence for this functional differentiation of the two memory systems comes from studies of neurological impairment and neuroimaging studies. For example, the nature of the language loss suffered by people experiencing neurodegeneracy or neurodevelopmental disorders can be explained in terms of the existence of two separate systems, each with their own distinct functions. These differences are summarized in Table 14.3 below, based on the account provided by Ullman (2001). For example, the implicit memory system is damaged in the case of Parkinson's Disease, resulting in problems in grammatical processing. The explicit memory system is impaired in Alzheimer's Disease and Williams Syndrome, leading to difficulty in accessing items stored lexically. What is particularly compelling evidence of the separateness of the two memory systems is the fact that damage to one system does not lead to loss of functions associated with the other system.

This separateness has also been noted in studies of bilingual aphasia. Paradis, for example, provided evidence demonstrating that 'some bilingual aphasic patients who have lost access to parts of their linguistic competence (i.e. their implicit memory) will still have access to their metalinguistic knowledge' (p. 53). He distinguished between aphasia and amnesia, the former arising as a result of damage to the neural sites responsible for implicit memory and the latter occurring when there is neurological damage to the sites involved in

Implicit linguistic memory	Explicit linguistic memory
Parkinson's disease: degeneration in dopaminergic neurons in the basal ganglia causing inhibition in motor activity; difficulty experienced in both comprehension and production of grammar (e.g. regular past tense forms) but not with lexis (e.g. irregular past tense forms).	Alzheimer's disease: degeneration of temporal and temporoparietal areas of the neocortex; difficulty experienced in retrieving and recognizing words (e.g. errors in irregular past tense forms) while syntactic processing (e.g. regular past tense forms) remains unimpaired.
Huntington's disease—degeneration in dopaminergic neurons projecting to the basal ganglia leading to difficulty in suppressing movements; patients unable to control application of rules in production resulting in errors such as 'walkeded' and 'dugged' but without similar errors in purely lexical forms.	Williams Syndrome—children have more difficulty producing irregular than regular past tenses and plurals and frequently over-regularize (e.g. 'digged', 'mouses').
Specific Language Impairment—difficulty experienced in producing novel regular forms and over-generalizations indicating inability to learn grammatical rules; reliance on memorization of discrete lexical forms.	

Table 14.3 Linguistic difficulties associated with neurological impairments (based on Ullman 2001)

explicit memory. Paradis cited a study by Obler and Mahecha (1991), which showed that aphasic bilinguals with less than high school education tend not to recover their native language as well as their second because they have minimal metalinguistic knowledge of their L1. He also noted aphasic cases where learners perform better in their L2 than their L1, which he claimed is explicable in terms of their greater L2 metalinguistic knowledge. He suggested that educated aphasics may give the impression of having recovered their L1 but in fact are relying on their explicit knowledge of this language, a point which will be taken up later when we consider Luria's proposals regarding the treatment of aphasia. Damage to the basal ganglia has been linked to impairments in grammar often in conjunction with the other functions associated with this region such as the expression of motor skills. In contrast, damage to the cortical areas that house explicit memory is linked to loss of vocabulary.

Neuroimaging studies also support a two-system account of language functioning. Different patterns of neural activity for irregular and regular verbs have been observed. Ullman, Bergida, and O'Craven (1997), for example, asked adults to silently produce the past tense forms of irregular (for example, 'sleep') and regular (for example, 'slip') verbs. Using fMRI, they found that the irregular verbs resulted in greater activation in the left frontal cortex and the regular verbs in the left and right temporal lobe regions.

Electroencephalography has been used to investigate to what extent there is evidence of implicit processing in the very early stages of L2 acquisition. This constitutes a controversial issue, with some researchers (for example, DeKeyser 1998) arguing that the starting point is declarative knowledge and others (for example, N Ellis 2002) claiming that implicit processing operates in L2 acquisition, as it does in L1 acquisition (i.e. from the start). Tokowicz and MacWhinney (2005) examined the ERPs recorded for beginner learners when responding to three kinds of grammatical violations in L2 Spanish: (1) a tense feature that was similar in the L2 (Spanish) and the learners' L1 (English), (2) a feature that was formed differently in the L1 and L2 (i.e. number agreement), and (3) a feature unique to the L2 (i.e. gender agreement). The learners were asked to judge sentences containing these errors. The ERPs provided evidence of implicit processing, while the untimed judgements served as indicators of their explicit knowledge of these features.[2] The beginner learners did not demonstrate any ability to judge whether the sentences were grammatical or ungrammatical, suggesting that they lacked any explicit knowledge of them. However, the ERPs data indicated they were responsive to two of the three types of grammatical violations (i.e. types (1) and (3) but not type (2)). Tokowicz and McWhinney concluded that 'learners are able to implicitly process some aspects of L2 syntax even in early stage of learning but that this knowledge depends on the similarity between the L1 and L2'. (p. 174)

We will turn now to a reconsideration of the interface positions discussed in Chapter 9. Here we will find some support for the NON-INTERFACE POSITION, the STRONG INTERFACE POSITION, and the WEAK INTERFACE POSITION.

Luria's (1970) proposals regarding the treatment of aphasia are compatible with a non-interface position. Luria developed a programme of rehabilitation directed at constructing a new structure to take over the function of the damaged part of the brain. He used external means as auxiliary aids to assist the patients to transfer the performance of the disturbed function to a higher, conscious level. Initially the transference was achieved only with much effort with the result that the restored function could be performed only slowly. However, when the patients had successfully internalized the auxiliary means, the disordered function reorganized and became more automatic, although the signs of the reorganization never entirely disappeared. Luria illustrated his proposal by reference to patients whose speech had become agrammatical as a result of a lesion (presumably to the part of the brain responsible for procedural memory). By directing such patients to a conscious reorganization of the damaged function (presumably, by activating the function through explicit memory) improvement was possible. Luria's proposal suggests two separate components that do not interact. But, unlike Krashen, who claimed only a minimal role for explicit knowledge ('learning'), he saw explicit memory as a substitute, albeit not a perfect one, for implicit memory.

Lee (2004) suggested that neuroanatomy allows for an interface between declarative and procedural memory. As shown in Figure 14.2, he proposed that the interface is achieved in two ways. First, the basal ganglia, which serve procedural memory, are directly connected to the hippocampus, which serves declarative memory, allowing one to influence the other. Second, to an extent, procedural and declarative memories share the same cortical areas. Lee hypothesized that the learner is able to use declarative information to repair incorrect procedures. He explained this process as follows:

> When (the learner) utters a sentence that violates the rule, his or her declarative memory may send a signal indicating that the utterance is wrong. This signal may prevent the formation of connections among neurons that could have represented the incorrect rule. On the other hand, when the speaker executes a correct sentence, this information aligns with that of declarative memory, and the connection that represents the sentence or the rule involved in the sentence may become stronger. (p. 67)

Lee's account appears to lend support to both a strong interface position (i.e. declarative memory can convert into procedural memory) and a weak interface position (i.e. declarative memory can help adjust the neural circuits in which procedural memory is housed).

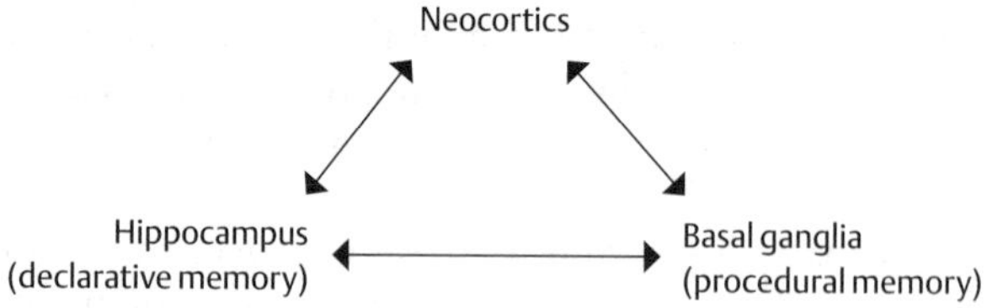

Figure 14.2 Schematic representation of the interrelationship between declarative and procedural memory (Lee 2004: 68)

Other neuroscientific researchers, however, have rejected the possibility of a strong interface and emphasized the weak interface position. Paradis (2004) is adamant that explicit knowledge does not convert into implicit knowledge; acquisition may commence with an explicit rule (controlled processing), but subsequently the learner acquires implicit computational procedures involving automatic processing. Thus 'acquisition is not a process of automatizing rules' (p. 41). Paradis argued that L2 development involves a gradual shift from using explicit knowledge to using implicit competence, but in an acquisition-rich context implicit competence develops first. Paradis also proposed that metalinguistic knowledge can assist the development of implicit competence, but only indirectly through focusing attention on the items that need to be practised and through MONITORING. Crowell (2004) argued that my own predictions regarding the role of declarative memory in language learning (see Chapter 9 and Ellis 1994c) are supported by what is known about the underlying biology of the two memory systems. That is, declarative knowledge is not converted into procedural knowledge but rather the two types of knowledge are learnt and stored involving different neural loops. She commented 'what would appear on the behavioural level to be a "conversion" is, in actuality, probably a strengthening of connections in the non-declarative loop that is sometimes accompanied by weakening of connections in the declarative loop' (p. 101). Crowell considered that my proposals concerning the role of declarative knowledge in noticing and noticing the gap were supported by the underlying biology of the brain.

To sum up, the neuroscientific research that has investigated procedural/implicit memory and declarative/explicit memory indicates a substantial degree of anatomical localization within the brain. It has demonstrated that procedural memory is responsible for grammar (both morphology and syntax) and that declarative memory is responsible for lexis (including those aspects of grammar that are lexical). It would follow that proficiency in an L2 is dependent on the development of both implicit and explicit memories. In this case, then, there is a relatively clear correlation between anatomical and functional localization. However, the neuroscientific research does not provide a conclusive answer to the debate surrounding the interface position. That is, it is not able to show whether or not there is an interface between the two types of memory and, if there is, what the nature of this interface is.

The role of attention in L2 acquisition

Cognitive accounts of L2 acquisition (see Chapter 9) have emphasized the important role played by attention. Attention is viewed as a mainly conscious process involving WORKING MEMORY. What, then, is the neuroscientific basis of attention and working memory?

Suchert (2004) argued that attention, as defined in psychology and in language learning research, is 'a creation of culture and does not map isomorphically onto the brain' (p. 144). She took the position that attention is not served by a dedicated substrate but involves diverse anatomy and functions. She defined attention as follows:

> a process in which biological mechanisms interact when goal-directed behaviours and stimulus-driven responses converge in action.
> (p. 144)

and saw it as consisting of a series of moments in a continuous process of evaluation, action, and reaction. She claimed that the psychological distinctions between attention, perception, cognition, and action have no biological correlates. Attention is 'an ongoing, interactive process that defies singular definition' (p. 173).

Suchert identified the cortical regions involved in working memory and attention, showing that there is no one-to-one relationship between the brain's anatomy and cognitive functions. For example, the dorsolateral prefrontal cortex is implicated in SHORT-TERM MEMORY, working memory, attentional control, and attentional demands, suggesting that aspects of memory and attention are part of the same process. She also argued that visual-spatial processing and motor planning are integrative parts of the attention process, citing research which shows that participants perform attentional tasks more rapidly if, while waiting for a stimulus, they covertly attend to the motor action they will make during a response rather than thinking about the expected visual response.

The basic neurobiological model of attention that Suchert proposed is one where there is constant competition for neural resources:

> ... there is a constant cycle of stimulus detection, refinement and redefinition according to the goals and plans for action. The anterior cingulate cortex weighs the influence of goals and stimuli to determine priorities and so ensure that the strongest influences are represented in the organism's response.
> (p. 146)

Inattentional blindness can occur when participants fail to attend to a visual stimulus because they are guided by their internal goal. But conscious attention can take place if the neurons that are innately receptive to stimulus properties are activated by some change to the stimulus environment. Also, some external stimuli possess properties that elicit automatic neural responses which can override the behavioural goal. In other cases, internal stimuli derived from previous experience and memory can evoke an automatic neural response. Covert attention involving activation of neurons in the dorsolateral prefrontal cortex can also occur when an object in the visual field is noticed without physically orienting to it. This suggests that attention may not always be conscious. Both inattentional blindness and covert attention reflect the ongoing competition among external and internal stimuli for processing resources as the brain balances the demands of behavioural goals (intentions), external stimuli, and internal stimuli.

The anterior cingulate plays a special role in managing this competition. Its anatomical form ensures contact with diverse neuroanatomical areas, including the premotor areas, the amygdala, and the hippocampus. Suchert cited Carter *et al.*'s (1998) proposal that the anterior cingulate performs a comparator function by monitoring competition between conflicting aspects of the attention process. It does this through inhibiting possible response or action plans that have an inferior influence or weight (i.e. it provides negative FEEDBACK).

As Suchert pointed out, this account of the neural mechanisms involved in attention has some obvious implications for L2 learning. Linguistic input that is salient can elicit attention (what is called the 'pop-out effect') but also a learner may fail to attend to novel features simply because they are not familiar. Recently activated neurons may remain primed and become active again when exposed to subsequent stimuli that are the same or related. This can explain why recent learning of a grammatical rule that is held in declarative memory can exert influence over the initial processing of an external stimulus. The neurobiological correlates of attention may also be important for overcoming FOSSILIZATION, a point discussed in a later section of this chapter.

Motivation and L2 acquisition

The neurobiological basis of the motivation for L2 learning has been extensively examined by Schumann. (See Schumann 1997; Schumann and Wood 2004.) Schumann's theory is rooted in the notions of 'value':

1 Homeostatic value: 'the biological tendency for an organism to maintain its physiological system within a certain range' (Schumann and Wood 2004: 24).
2 Sociostatic value: the instinct to interact by, for example, paying attention to faces or voices.
3 Somatic value: 'preferences and aversions acquired in the life-time of the individual through experience, socialization, enculturation, and education' (Schumann and Wood 2004: 24–5).

Organisms develop memory for value based on stimulus-appraisal. This involves assessing the emotional relevance of stimuli on the basis of their novelty, pleasantness, and relevance to the individual's goals or needs, the ability to cope, and compatibility with the individual's self and social image. As a result of these appraisals the learner either opts to engage in the sustained learning needed for successful L2 acquisition or to curtail learning. 'This STIMULUS-APPRAISAL SYSTEM ... is a major factor in the wide range of proficiencies seen in second language acquisition' (Schumann 1997: 36).

The neural mechanisms involved in stimulus appraisal consist of the amygdala, the orbitofrontal cortex (above the orbits of the eyes), and the body proper. The amygdala is important in assessing positive or negative value of stimuli. It is a phylogenetically old part of the brain and probably assesses value based on inherited homeostats and sociostats. The orbitofrontal cortex, which is highly connected to the amygdala, is involved in reasoning about social and personal issues, that is, somatic value. Because the neural mechanisms extend beyond the brain to the peripheral nervous system, the body proper also contributes to stimulus appraisal. Messages sent from the orbitofrontal cortex either directly or through the amygdala either stimulate or inhibit reactions in different parts of the body, fostering positive or negative values.

Schumann (1997) drew on Damasio (1995) to outline how the stimulus appraisal mechanism works. A stimulus generates mental images in the early sensory cortices where they are organized as thoughts guided by 'dispositional representations' consisting of potential or dormant neuronal patterns located in the higher order association cortices in the brain. These house the somatic values acquired over a lifetime and thus contain memories of past stimulus appraisals. Dispositional representations relating to innate homeostatic and sociostatic values that govern survival and interaction behaviours are mediated by the amygdala. Dispositional representations in the orbitofrontal cortex and the amygdala are activated in response to a stimulus situation creating a bodily state which Damasio refers to as a 'somatic marker', interpreted by the brain as a feeling. Once this stimulus appraisal has been made, chemical messengers such as dopamine are released into various parts of the brain to regulate how the person attends to characteristics of the stimulus. In this way the link between affective response and cognitive activity is made. Positive appraisals enable learning to take place. Negative appraisals lead to avoidance behaviour. Finally, Schumann (1997) suggested that stimulus appraisals may be consolidated during rapid-eye-movement (REM) sleep.

Schumann and Wood (2004) further developed Schumann's (1997) theory by characterizing learning as 'a form of mental or intellectual foraging involving motor activity to acquire knowledge or skill' (p. 29) and hypothesized a neural system for mental foraging. A successful forager/learner takes actions that result in an increase in dopamine activity in the basal ganglia and that avoid actions that involve decreased dopamine activity. Learners remember actions that increase dopamine in order that they can repeat those actions to increase learning. Positive appraisal results in conscious or unconscious attention to the components of the language involved.

The role of the amygdala, the orbitofrontal cortex, and the peripheral nervous system in making stimulus appraisals is supported by the findings of studies of brain-damaged patients. These indicate that appraisals involving goal/need significance, coping potential and norm/self compatibility involve the orbitofrontal cortex, while appraisals involving pleasantness and perhaps novelty/familiarity entail the amygdala, possibly in conjunction with the orbitofrontal cortex. However, there is no neurobiological research that shows that activity or changes in the amygdala, orbitofrontal cortex, body proper, or basal ganglia are related to L2 acquisition. Thus indirect evidence for this comes from other sources: (1) language learner autobiographies and (2) drugs of abuse. Schumann (1997) discussed a number of language learner diaries and autobiographies. He claimed that these 'provide a particularly clear demonstration of how stimulus appraisals enhance or inhibit the cognitive effort necessary to become bilingual' (p. 170). They show the 'unique affective trajectory' that characterizes individual learners' preparedness to persist or withdraw, as would be predicted by a stimulus appraisal perspective. He also claimed that the diaries and autobiographies show that LANGUAGE APTITUDE and motivation are not independent factors, as learners' abilities affect their appraisals. Schumann and Wood discussed the effect of various drugs such as nicotine, cocaine, and opiates on dopamine, the neurotransmitter responsible for effecting stimulus appraisals. These drugs produce the same affective state as positive stimulus appraisals. Just as positive appraisals motivate the learner to do the hard work needed to acquire an L2, so drugs motivate the addict to continue to use them.

The theory of motivation that Schumann promulgated is predicated on the assumption that motivation for language learning can ultimately be reduced to the neurobiological mechanisms that govern persistence or withdrawal. It follows, as Schumann and Wood pointed out, 'that there may not be a best motivation. What seems to be necessary is sufficient positive appraisals along one or more dimensions suggested to sustain the effort for the 5 to 8 years necessary to learn the second language well' (p. 42). In other words, it makes little sense to argue the merits of integrative or instrumental motivation and a lot more sense to suggest that motivation to learn a language is more a matter of the place that language holds in the 'ideal self' (Dörnyei 2005) that a learner constructs as a result of the values accrued over a lifetime of appraising stimuli.

Controlling access to the L2 and L1

Earlier we noted that the neuroscientific evidence points to no distinct brain regions devoted to the L1 and L2 but rather to differences in the micro-circuitry within these regions. This raises the question of how access to the different languages is controlled and what neurobiological mechanisms are involved in this control.

In accordance with the general claim that language functions are not localized in specific regions of the brain but rather share regions associated with non-linguistic behaviour (see the section on a 'specialized language faculty'), it seems reasonable to assume that the processes associated with language control (as evidenced, for example, in lexical selection and language switching in bilinguals) are the same as those involved in the control of action in general. This is the position advanced by Abutalebi and Green (2007) in their survey of the neurolinguistic and neurobiological research that has addressed this issue. They argued that cognitive control is achieved through the interaction of a number of separate systems and identified four of these. The main device is the prefrontal cortex, which is involved in top-down decision-making through its influence on the neural functioning of other sites. The prefrontal cortex has been linked to a number of cognitive functions, including decision-making, response selection, response inhibition, and working memory. In the case of the bilingual, the executive function of the prefrontal cortex is evident when there is a need to block 'stronger responses' (i.e. in the L1) in order to produce 'weaker responses' (i.e. in the L2). A second device implicated in cognitive control is the left parietal cortex. Whereas the prefrontal cortex is involved in selecting between competing responses, the left parietal cortex is activated when there is a need to maintain a representation among possible responses. The anterior cingulate cortex contributes in another way; it detects conflict between competing resources and sends a signal to the prefrontal cortex that greater control is needed. Thus, it contributes to control by activating attention, monitoring conflict, and detecting errors. The fourth device involves the basal ganglia. As we have already seen this is associated with motor control. In the case of cognitive activity it assists sequence planning and the suppression of competing alternatives. It is implicated in language switching, as evidenced in cases of aphasia where lesions to the basal ganglia can result in inappropriate blending of languages or selective recovery.

These control mechanisms serve both the L1 and L2 and also regulate switching from one language to another. Abutalebi and Green cited studies that showed that bilinguals use identical brain areas when performing the same task in their two languages and, furthermore, that this is evident irrespective of their age of L2 acquisition. However, the extent to which the mechanisms are activated will depend on the degree of proficiency in the languages involved. That is, there are more extensive activations of the prefrontal cortex in the case of tasks performed in the L2 when the learners are of low proficiency or have experienced only limited exposure to the L2. Interestingly, the region of the prefrontal cortex involved lies outside the areas generally associated with language representation but in areas linked to cognitive control. The explanation for the difference in neural activity lies in whether the language operations involve automatic or controlled processing. That is 'the non-automatic language (generally L2 when not mastered to a high degree of proficiency) engages more extended portions of the prefrontal cortex whereas the more automatic language does not' (p. 262).

However, even highly proficient bilinguals need inhibition mechanisms. This is demonstrated in Rodriguez-Fornells *et al.*'s (2002) study of Catalan–Spanish bilinguals who possessed a high level of proficiency in both languages. Compared to monolingual Spanish speakers, the bilinguals manifested greater activation in an area of the prefrontal cortex. It is possible, therefore, that the superior cognitive functioning of bilinguals in comparison to monolinguals reported by Bialystok *et al.* (2004) is the result of their enhanced capacity to select responses in the face of competing cues. In other words neural capacity is increased as a result of the demands placed on the bilingual brain. Such a conclusion is also supported by Mechelli *et al.*'s (2004) finding that, in comparison to monolinguals, bilinguals display increased grey matter in the left parietal cortex and that the density of this grey matter correlated with L2 proficiency.

The study of the control mechanisms involved in language and lexical selection is of potential importance to the understanding of L1 transfer in L2 acquisition. (See Chapter 8.) Perani *et al.* (1998) proposed that low-proficiency students recruit multiple and variable brain regions to handle dimensions of the L2 that differ from the L1 whereas highly proficient bilinguals use the same machinery for both languages. Rodriguez-Fornells *et al.* (2006) surveyed a number of studies that showed that neural activity linked to cognitive control is reduced when the L1 and L2 are similar lexically, morphologically, and phonologically and increased when they differ. One interpretation of such studies is that negative transfer arises when the executive brain areas struggle but fail to deactivate or suppress the stronger response evoked by the L1. However, as proficiency increases, learners succeed in separating the neural microcircuits for the L1 and L2 with the result that there is no longer the need to exert strenuous control over L1 responses as normal control mechanisms suffice to regulate the choice of linguistic form. L1 transfer may also be influenced by dopamine as damage to the supply of dopamine has been shown to affect the executive systems. Birdsong (2006) speculated that dopamine may play a role in suppressing and supplanting L1 routines in syntax and phonology. However, as our understanding of control mechanisms is still limited (Indefrey and Gullberg 2006), neuroscientific studies are not yet able to shed light on the complex set of conditions that govern why L1 transfer takes place on some occasions and not others.

The Critical Period Hypothesis

In Chapter 1 we examined whether there is a critical period for learning an L2—that is, whether after a given age, it becomes impossible to acquire full native-speaker competence in an L2. The review of the literature suggested no agreement on this issue. While there is substantial evidence to show that many L2 learners who begin learning an L2 at puberty or beyond fail to acquire native-speaker competence, there is also evidence to show that at least some learners appear to be able to do so and also that the ability to acquire an L2 declines gradually with age rather than abruptly when a specific age is reached. Birdsong (1999a) admitted that after many years of supporting the Critical Period Hypothesis, he had become a doubter. What then does the neuroscientific evidence suggest about this issue?

A number of neuroscientific researchers have accepted the existence of a critical period and have sought to explain this in terms of maturational changes in the brain. Lenneberg (1967) saw a correlation between the process of lateralization, which is not completed until puberty, and a critical period for language learning. MacWhinney (2006) reviewed the evidence for lateralization as an explanation for the critical period and concluded that there was little to show that lateralization can account for age-related effects in language learning after the first three years of life. Pinker (1994) suggested that the decline in metabolic rate and the number of neurons during the early school years explains the loss of language-learning ability, but MacWhinney argued that Pinker 'placed the neurological cart before the neurological horse' as there was no evidence of an overall loss of metabolic rate when learners are confronted with new tasks. Pulvermuller and Schumann (1994) argued that full knowledge of a language can only be achieved if two conditions are met—the learner is motivated to learn the language and the learner possesses the ability to acquire grammatical knowledge. They then went on to argue that the second condition is not met in the case of older learners due to the maturation of the brain brought about by the processes of myelination and loss of plasticity.

A somewhat different argument is advanced by Paradis (2004). He argued that the critical period needs to be understood as relating only to procedural memory for language. He proposed that the acquisition of implicit competence declines with the gradual loss of plasticity that begins at 5 years of age and with the increased reliance on declarative memory which begins at 7 years. Thus, the critical period applied only to those aspects of language that depend on procedural memory (i.e. prosody, phonology, morphology, and syntax). As there is no maturational effect evident in declarative memory, there is no critical period for vocabulary. According to this view, then, learners switch from a reliance on the neural mechanisms that feed incidental, IMPLICIT LEARNING to those that govern intentional, explicit learning once the critical period is ended. This view is endorsed by Jones (2004) in her account of the neural bases of lexis. She emphasized that the elements necessary for learning vocabulary exist in non-language-specific neural systems and that words group together according to their sensory features, or object features, or by contextual factors involved in their acquisition. These systems operate similarly in L1 and L2 acquisition irrespective of age.

Some support for the existence of a critical period can be found in an interesting ERP-based study of the acquisition of a miniature version of Japanese. Mueller (2006) conducted two studies in which he compared native speakers of Japanese with both non-advanced and advanced German-speaking learners of Mini-Nihongo. The assumption was that native Japanese speakers would process the miniature version of their language in a similar way to natural Japanese. Mueller reported that even when the learners achieved native-like accuracy in grammaticality judgements, differences in their ERPs were evident, a result that she interpreted as supporting a strong version of the Critical Period Hypothesis. However, as Mueller admitted, the learning environment was a very special one and the learners had received only limited exposure. For these reasons the validity of the comparison between the native and non-native speakers of the miniature language is open to question.

There is, however, neuroscientific evidence that disputes the existence of a critical period of any kind for language. Studies that have examined whether acquisition prior to and after a critical age is related to differences in neural processes need to control for differences in proficiency. This is essential, for, as has already been demonstrated, proficiency has been shown to influence neural functioning. The key question is whether learners of similar proficiency who started learning before or after the critical period manifest different or similar types of neural activity. Birdsong (2006), in a review of neuroimaging studies that have investigated brain areas activated in relation to age and proficiency, concluded 'in studies of production, it is L2 proficiency level not AoA (age of arrival) that emerges as the strongest predictor of degree of similarity between late learners and monolingual natives' (p. 24). He also reached a similar conclusion for comprehension. These findings indicate that brain functioning does not differ as a product of age and therefore do not lend support to a critical period. It should be noted, however, that while the starting age does not affect the brain areas employed by L2 learners, differences in the degree of activation have been observed. Learners who start late appear to need to process the L2 with more effort than those who start early, who function like native speakers (Wartenburger *et al.* 2003), a finding that accords with the discussion above of the effects of proficiency on the neurobiological mechanisms involved in bilingual control. It should also be noted that many of the neuroimaging studies that have investigated L2 processing in comparison to L1 processing have made use of vocabulary retrieval tasks and therefore may be tapping the neural mechanisms of declarative rather than procedural memory, which, as Paradis (2004) pointed out, are not susceptible to maturation in the same way as those involving procedural memory.

Another approach to investigating whether there is a neurobiological basis for a critical period in language learning is to examine what is known about the ageing brain. If there is clear evidence of a maturational effect for ageing, this would allow for the possibility of a critical period. If, on the other hand, the effect is biological in nature, this would constitute evidence against a critical period. Birdsong (2006) considered two age-related aspects of changes in the structure of the brain—brain volume and dopamine systems. Drawing on a survey by Raz (2005), he concluded that the volumes of the key areas of the brain associated with language decrease in a linear and continuous fashion. Nor does the onset of this decrease coincide with the age typically associated with the end of the critical period (i.e. puberty). In many cases the decline does not begin until much later (i.e. the twenties or middle age). Birdsong also concluded that the relationship between the decline in brain volume and cognitive functioning was also linear in many cases. Similarly, the decline in dopamine receptors does not begin until the early twenties and then continues across the life span. Birdsong concluded 'none of the evidence from the cognitive, brain volume, or dopamine literature is consistent with a maturational account because the observed declines commence after the end of maturation' (p. 35) while also, the declines are linear in nature. In other words studies of the ageing brain provide no obvious support for the existence of a critical period.

From this review of the neuroscientific research that has addressed the issue of a critical period for language learning it should be clear that contradictory findings and views exist. As Hyltenstam and Abrahamsson (2001) noted, 'this research is indeed still at the stage of hypothesis formation' (p. 160). What is clear is that there is a general decline in the neural capacity for language learning with age. What is less clear is whether this decline is due (partially or fully) to the loss of access to those neural mechanisms that ensure that L1 acquisition is normally complete and relatively effortless and, if there is such a loss, what changes in the brain are responsible for it.

The neurobiological basis of fossilization

Irrespective of whether or not there is a critical period (or periods) for the acquisition of language, it is clear that the typical end state of L2 acquisition is not the same as L1 acquisition. This has led some researchers to propose that L2 acquisition is characterized by fossilization, by backsliding, low proficiency and persistent errors. As we saw in Chapter 1, it is difficult to establish behaviourally whether fossilization has in fact set in, leading some commentators (for example, Birdsong 2004) to suggest the concept is not helpful in advancing our understanding of L2 acquisition, but, for the purposes of the following discussion, it will be accepted that such a condition can and does arise. What, then, are the neurobiological correlates of fossilization?

According to MacWhinney (2006), fossilization is best explained in terms of two processes—parasitic reliance on the L1 and ENTRENCHMENT. That is, the learner borrows linguistic forms from the L1, which become entrenched through constant use. However, there can be other sources of entrenchment. Wu (2000, cited in Lee 2004) argued that fossilization is due to automatized routines consisting of 'holistic units that are mapped onto neural representations of the context in which they typically occur' (p. vii). Such routines are formed from years of repetition and are resistant to executive control. Lee (2004) suggested that they correspond to the processes of automatization associated with basal ganglia. (See earlier section on implicit versus explicit knowledge.) He noted that fossilized learners are often communicatively fluent reflecting their ability to produce utterances without cognitive planning or conscious effort. Such an explanation, then, views fossilization as the result of neural circuits involved in the development of procedural knowledge. Because procedural memory develops more slowly than declarative memory, it is also more resistant to change.

The question arises as to whether entrenched procedural routines can be changed—in other words whether defossilization is possible. Lee argued that although fossilized rules are difficult to alter or suppress, change is not impossible. He gave two reasons: (1) the brain retains some degree of plasticity, even in older learners, and (2) connections between the hippocampus and the basal ganglia make it possible to use declarative memory to induce change in procedural memory providing that there is sufficient motivational input from the amygdala and the orbitofrontal cortex. In other words, defossilization involves the combined operation of those parts of the brain responsible for stimulus appraisal, declarative memory, and procedural memory. Control mechanisms are also likely to be involved. Suchert (2004: 170) considered the role of attention in overcoming fossilization, arguing that to break the habit of an over-used linguistic behaviour, five elements of attention need to be in alignment:

1 The overall behavioural goal (for example, to improve speaking)
2 The task-related goal or attentional template/working memory (for example, to execute an utterance with correct grammar)

3 Motor planning (for example, planning to change motor schemata in order to overcome a proceduralized motor response plan)
4 Stimulus qualities (a salient stimulus—such as a declarative rule—that evokes a neural response strong enough to override a proceduralized response)
5 The anterior cingulate (assessing the competing influences of the four previous elements).

Only when these five elements are aligned, which is difficult to achieve, will a learner notice and change fossilized habits. A possible explanation for why some learners avoid fossilization or successfully defossilize is their superior ability for increased alignment of these attentional mechanisms.

Fossilization may also involve declarative memory. Birdsong (2006) suggested that with age learners may have greater difficulty in learning irregular forms than regular. As we have seen, irregular forms involve declarative memory. Thus, older learners are more likely to experience difficulty in ridding themselves of overgeneralized –ed verb forms. Birdsong saw neuroanatomical changes in the regions of the brain serving declarative memory as responsible for this. If Ullman (2001) is correct and older learners also rely more on their declarative memories than younger learners then this would explain the increased difficulty in learning an L2 and the greater likelihood of fossilization that has been observed to correlate with age.

These accounts of fossilization are speculative, however. They involve an attempt to relate a behavioural and cognitive phenomenon to neural mechanisms on the basis of what is known about the workings of these mechanisms but with very little empirical evidence to support the relationships that have been posited.

Summary

It should be clear that few firm conclusions regarding key SLA issues are yet possible on the basis of the neuroscientific evidence currently available. The following summary of the main findings related to these issues, therefore, are to be viewed as tentative.

1 Controversy continues as to the existence of a specialized language faculty. Overall, however, the evidence points to the language function being non-localized in the brain. It relies on the same neural mechanisms as other types of learning (for example, the basal ganglia are implicated in the development of procedural memory for language as they are in other forms of procedural memory). These findings weigh against the existence of a 'language organ' as proposed by Chomsky and SLA researchers in the generative tradition.
2 There is a growing consensus that the neurobiological mechanisms that serve the L1 and L2 are the same. Whereas early views (for example, Albert and Obler 1978) claimed that there were hemispheric differences in L1 and

L2 representation due to lateralization, more recent evidence has shown that both languages involve the same regions of the brain although there may be differences in the neural circuitry within these regions. It is also possible that the question of similarity or difference may depend on the area of language involved (for example, similarity in the case of lexico-semantics but differences in the case of grammar and phonology). The crucial factor may be fluency; similar areas are activated when the L2 is fluent. In the view of some theorists the evidence supports the claim that bilinguals possess a unified, integrated system but this is disputed by other researchers.

3 There is some evidence that different parts of the brain are involved in language production (for example, Broca's area) and comprehension (for example, WERNICKE'S AREA) but recent neuroimaging studies have shown that a more accurate picture is of a many-to-many mapping of structure to function. The same production and comprehension structures figure in native speakers and advanced learners but some differences are evident in the case of low-proficiency learners.

4 There is clear evidence of the mediation of procedural/implicit memory in the basal ganglia and of declarative/explicit memory in the hippocampus and areas of the cerebral cortex. This lends support to a dual-mechanism account of L2 learning, with procedural memory housing grammar and declarative memory lexis. However, neurolinguists do not agree on the nature of the interface between these two mechanisms, with some arguing for a non-interface and others for a strong or weak interface. In this respect, then, the neuroscientific evidence is unable to resolve the debates surrounding the interface positions discussed in Chapter 9.

5 Attention has a neurobiological basis, although not a clearly localized one. There is competition between internal goals and stimulus arousal. Attention occurs when neurons innately receptive to a stimulus are activated, overriding the inattentional blindness induced by an internal goal.

6 Schumann has developed a theory of motivation for language learning based on the notion of a biologically based system of stimulus-appraisal. This system involves the amygdala, responsible for assessing the positive or negative value of stimuli; the orbitofrontal cortex, responsible for reasoning about social and personal issues; and the body proper. Thus, there is a clear link between the learner's affective response, cognitive evaluation, and action. Positive appraisals are stored in memory, leading learners to continue to seek out the stimuli that produced them and thus ensuring persistence in learning. Negative appraisals lead to withdrawal.

7 Bilinguals need to be able to control the use of their languages. Research indicates that the parts of the brain used to achieve this are not specific to language and involve an interaction of a number of different systems (i.e. the prefrontal cortex, the left parietal cortex, the anterior cingulate, and the basal ganglia). These areas become more active in the case of low L2 proficiency and also when the L1 and L2 are linguistically different. There is some evidence to suggest that the effort spent in linguistic control leads to an increase in the neural capacity of bilinguals.

8 Various neurobiological explanations of a critical period in language learning have been provided—lateralization (Lenneberg), the decline in metabolic rate and the number of neurons (Pinker), myelination and loss of plasticity (Pulvermuller and Schumann). One possibility advanced by Paradis is that the critical period only applies to those aspects of language governed by implicit memory. Neuroimaging studies, however, have failed to show any differences in brain functioning as a product of age, once proficiency is controlled for. Likewise there is no clear support for a critical period from studies of the ageing brain as decline in neural capacity is linear and continuous.

9 Fossilization arises when neural circuits involved in the development of procedural knowledge become resistant to change. Neuroscientists have suggested that it may be possible to bring about change in these circuits but this will involve the integrative functioning of those parts of the brain responsible for stimulus appraisal, declarative memory, procedural memory, and control and, thus, is an exacting process. It has been suggested that fossilization can also occur in declarative memory, especially in older learners.

Conclusion

Mainstream SLA has sought to explain the behaviours that occur when learners endeavour to learn an L2 in terms of psycholinguistic mechanisms and processes. (See Chapters 8, 9, and 10.) Neuroscientific SLA aims to identify the neural mechanisms and circuits responsible for the same observable behaviours. As Figure 14.3 below suggests, this raises the possibility of matching the psycholinguistic and neurobiological dimensions of SLA. This has been the approach I have adopted in this chapter. I have revisited a number of key issues in SLA in order to examine whether the mental constructs postulated to explain L2 acquisition are supported by the findings of neuroscientific research.

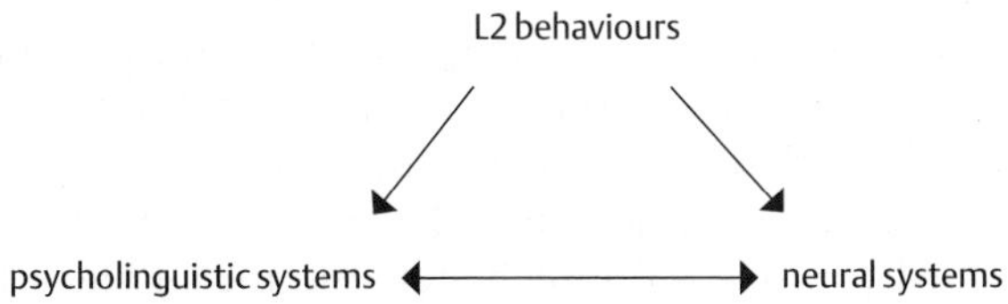

Figure 14.3 Neuropsychological SLA

Such an approach is not unproblematic, however. First, just as it is not always easy to make reliable inferences about the mental systems that underlie L2 behaviours, so too it has not proved easy to determine which regions of the brain and which neural pathways are activated by specific L2 behaviours. For example, in considering the neurolinguistic bases of L1 and L2 behavioural responses, Mueller (2005) pointed out:

> ... the absence of differences in behavioural measures taken from L1 and L2 speakers does not necessarily mean that the underlying neural processing mechanisms are the same. Similarly, differences in behavioural measures, such as reaction times, are not necessarily the result of the involvement of different neuronal structures, even if they show qualitatively different patterns.
> (p. 153)

If it is not easy to match behavioural and neuroscientific evidence, the question must be asked whether much is to be gained from a neuropsychological account of L2 acquisition. There are differing answers to this question.

Not surprisingly, perhaps, opposition to neuropsychological SLA has come from the proponents of Universal Grammar. Earlier we noted that there is no neuroscientific evidence to support the existence of an independent language faculty. Instead, we saw that linguistic functioning is distributed over a number of regions of the brain which also contribute to non-linguistic functioning. This constitutes a challenge to the claim that there is a specific language mental module—a claim that lies at the centre of most generative linguistic accounts of L2 acquisition. (See Chapter 11.) Eubank and Gregg (1995) responded to this challenge in two ways. First, as previously discussed, they disputed the neuroscientific evidence cited in support of the non-localization of language function (see p. 746). Second, they critiqued neuroscientific SLA on epistemological grounds. Reiterating the central position of UG-based SLA, namely, that the goal of a theory of L2 acquisition must be an explanation of linguistic competence, they argued that the attempt to achieve this goal by means of 'lower level, neurobiological theory is reductionist and fundamentally flawed given the impossibility of identifying neuronal counterparts of linguistic constructs such as "subject" or "empty category" '. They maintained that it was impossible to escape from some 'higher order' account of language—'you cannot have an explanation if you do not have an explanandum' (p. 53). Eubank and Gregg's critique, then, points to two legitimate problems with neuroscientific SLA in its current state.

First, as the previous sections of this chapter have shown, in many cases the neuroscientific evidence is mixed, making it difficult to reach clear conclusions on such issues as the L2 = L1 acquisition hypothesis, the interface positions, the existence of a critical period for L2 acquisition, or, indeed, the validity of UG.[3] There is, however, clearer evidence to support the distinction between implicit and explicit L2 knowledge.

Second, matching psycholinguistic (or linguistic) constructs with neurobiological structures remains clearly problematic. For a neuroscientific account of L2 acquisition to have any meaning we must first know what the constructs are that need to be explained; there must be a theory of language/acquisition that serves as the basis for neurological or neurobiological enquiry. The problem with Eubank and Gregg's argument, of course, is their insistence that this theory must necessarily be UG. As Schumann (1995) noted, and as we have seen in earlier chapters in this book, this constitutes a narrow view of language, and one that is not shared by many SLA researchers. Thus, if neurobiological SLA is to progress it will need to keep an open mind about the nature of the description of the phenomenon that needs to be explained (the explanandum) and test out the claims of different theories. This, however, is more easily said than done, as it is not yet clear what constitutes confirming or disconfirming evidence at the neurobiological level of constructs at the mental level.

Other researchers, however, have been more optimistic. Schumann (2004b) argued that the value of a neurobiological approach to SLA lies in the constraints it imposes on the metaphors we use to explain L2 acquisition. He noted:

> Historically, the language acquisition mirror, as it were, has reflected behaviour back into the 'black box' of theoretical mechanisms with little concern for the neurobiological plausibility of those mechanisms' (p. ix)

For Schumann, it is necessary to investigate whether metaphors (such as UG)[4] have an underlying neural foundation. He saw neurobiological studies (and I would add neurolinguistic studies too) as providing a way of validating such mental constructs as operating principles, noticing, monitoring, or learning strategies. Schumann insisted that the approach should not be a bottom-up one, driven by the available technology for investigating the activity of the brain, but rather a top-down one, informed by hypotheses drawn from mainstream SLA, which can be systematically tested by searching for their neurobiological correlates. It is likely that there will be an increasing number of studies attempting this in the years ahead and that, over time, researchers will increasingly succeed in mapping the cognitive functions involved in L2 acquisition onto distinct brain mechanisms and pathways.

Notes

1 More recent attempts to develop an 'atlas' of the human brain include those by Talairach and Tournoux (1988) and Zilles *et al.* (2002).

2 It is, of course, arguable whether grammaticality judgements elicit explicit or implicit knowledge or a mixture of the two. (See Chapter 17 for a discussion of this point.)

3 The available evidence, however, would seem to weigh against the existence of a specific language organ. Schumann (2004c) reached the following conclusion after reviewing the available evidence: 'The neural equipment for every aspect of the L2 acquisition process is available in general learning systems distributed throughout the brain' (p. 177).

4 Eubank and Gregg (1995), of course, dispute that UG constitutes a 'metaphor', preferring to claim its literal status.

PART SEVEN
Classroom second language acquisition

Introduction

The previous sections of this book have been concerned with questions of general import to the study of second language acquisition. They have endeavoured to provide descriptions of how an L2 is acquired, and to explain the structural processes that account for its universal properties and the social and individual factors that account for variation in the rate and success of individual learners. Although some attention has been given to the impact that the acquisitional setting can have on outcomes (see Chapter 7) the primary concern has been to account for the regularities in acquisition evident across settings. Thus, no clear distinction has been drawn between the acquisition that takes place in untutored and tutored settings.

Much of the research that has been reported in the earlier sections, however, has involved classroom learners. This is particularly true of experimental or correlational studies (for example, studies based on the competition or skill-building models or research on motivation in Canada). One reason is that the large numbers of learners needed for such research are more accessible in *educational* than in *naturalistic* settings. However, this research has not been concerned with classroom L2 acquisition *per se*; rather it has used classroom learners to investigate questions of general significance to SLA research.

In this section, we focus our attention specifically on classroom L2 acquisition. While there may be many similarities in the ways that learners learn an L2 inside and outside a classroom, there are also differences with regard to the nature of the input they are exposed to, the kinds of interactions they participate in, and, crucially, the extent to which they attend to form as opposed to meaning. In naturalistic settings, learners will primarily treat the L2 as a tool for communicating (and, if they develop sufficient competence, perhaps also for thinking). In classroom settings, it is also possible that the L2 will be viewed as a tool for communicating (as is the case in task-based teaching) but it is also likely that learners will approach the L2 as an object to be studied and intentionally learnt. These differences point to the need to treat classroom L2 acquisition ('instructed SLA') as worthy of separate attention.

Instructed SLA is an area of enquiry of interest to both researchers and language teachers. Researchers have investigated form-focused instruction in order to develop and test theories of second language (L2 acquisition). For example, studies have sought to examine the relative effectiveness of implicit versus explicit instruction and of production-based and input-based grammar instruction, issues of key significance to the cognitive theories we considered in Chapter 9. Other studies have focused on issues that are widely discussed in handbooks for language teachers, such as error correction. Here the goal has been to try to identify what constitutes effective pedagogic practice. Instructed SLA constitutes an area of enquiry, then, where the concerns of researchers and teachers can be brought together. It is perhaps for this reason that this area has attracted considerable attention over the last 30 years with a number of full-length books (for example, Ellis 1984a, 1990a; Doughty and Williams 1998; Long and Doughty, forthcoming) devoted to it.

The study of how acquisition takes place in a classroom context will entail revisiting many of the general issues raised earlier in the book—for example, the role of interaction in shaping learning, the difference between implicit and explicit knowledge, the role of corrective feedback, the significance of acquisition orders and sequences, and the role of individual learner differences. In fact, the classroom constitutes an ideal setting for examining the key theoretical issues because it is possible to observe closely how input is made available to the learner and what kinds of output learners produce in specific classroom contexts. It is also possible to engineer what input learners are exposed to and what output they produce in order to investigate specific hypotheses about how learning takes place.

The reason for focusing on the classroom, however, is not merely to shed further light on how L2 acquisition takes place. It is also motivated by a desire to discover what classroom conditions are most likely to facilitate acquisition. In other words, it has a pedagogic purpose. However, this pedagogic purpose is not quite the same as that addressed in methodological handbooks for teachers, where the aim is to suggest specific techniques or activities that teachers can use. The research we will consider in this section invites us to consider pedagogy not in terms of 'techniques' or 'activities', but in terms of what kinds of classroom behaviours teachers need to engage in to promote learning—what questions to ask, when and how to correct learners' errors, how to instigate negotiation for meaning, how to induce learners to attend to form during a communicative task, etc.

It is possible to identify two major strands in classroom L2 acquisition research, corresponding to two ways of viewing the classroom. According to one view, what happens in the classroom provides opportunities for learning, which can be explored by examining the relationship between the interactions that take place in the classroom—the means by which the opportunities are provided—and L2 learning. An alternative is to view the classroom as a place where attempts are made to intervene directly in the process of L2 learning—to ask, in other words, 'Do learners learn what they have been taught?' Chapter 15 examines research belonging to the first strand, while Chapter 16 looks at the effects on learning of direct intervention.

15

Classroom interaction and second language acquisition

Introduction

This chapter draws on the theoretical perspectives and research relating to the role of input and interaction in L2 acquisition that we considered in Chapters 6 and 11. The underlying assumption is, as Allwright (1984: 156) proposed, that interaction is 'the fundamental fact of classroom pedagogy' because 'everything that happens in the classroom happens through a process of live person-to-person interaction'. This perspective has led researchers to observe and describe the interactional events that take place in a classroom in order to understand how learning opportunities are created and, also, to examine how different kinds of classroom interaction lead to learning.

First of all, this chapter will consider some of the principal research methods that have been used to investigate the role of classroom interaction in language learning. There follows a brief historical overview of L2 classroom research. The chapter then surveys research that has examined the general characteristics of classroom discourse followed by an account of specific aspects of the teacher's and the learner's contributions to this discourse. Next there is a review of research that has examined tasks and the interaction they give rise to. The chapter concludes with an account of studies that have attempted to demonstrate a relationship between classroom interaction and L2 learning, in particular those that have drawn on the important construct of 'focus-on-form'.

Methods of researching the second language classroom

A distinction can be drawn between 'classroom research' and 'classroom-orientated research' (Nunan 1991: 249). The former consists of studies that have investigated learners inside actual classrooms, while the latter consists of studies conducted outside the classroom in a 'laboratory' setting but which have been motivated by issues of clear relevance to classroom L2 acquisition. A key methodological issue concerns whether laboratory interactions and classroom interactions are sufficiently similar to allow for extrapolation from the former to the latter. Here opinions differ. Nunan argued that findings from laboratory experiments may not generalize to classrooms because variables cannot be so easily controlled in the latter. Foster (1998), in the study reported in Chapter 11, found that NEGOTIATION OF MEANING, which has been found to occur frequently in laboratory studies, arose only rarely in task-based interactions in a classroom setting. However, Gass, Mackey, and Ross-Feldman (2005) reported a study that specifically set out to compare three aspects of interaction (negotiation of meaning, language-related episodes, and recasts) in a laboratory setting (with a researcher present) and in their normal classroom setting and found no statistically significant differences in any of the aspects. They argued that the results of their study demonstrated that laboratory-based research findings could be cautiously generalized to classroom settings. However, one problem with such a claim (which Gass *et al.* acknowledged) is that both laboratory and classroom settings are not monolithic. There is, in fact, plenty of evidence to show that interactional behaviours vary according to the particular classroom setting. (See, for example, Sheen's (2004) study of corrective feedback strategies in immersion, ESL, and EFL classroom contexts.) It is also clear that laboratory settings can vary in a number of ways—for example, the background of the learners, the types of tasks used to elicit data, and the composition of the groups/dyads. Thus, care needs to be taken both in making generalizations on the basis of single studies conducted in a laboratory or a classroom and in extrapolating from laboratory-based studies to the classroom.

In fact, it is no longer easy to define what is meant by a 'language classroom'. Stereotypically, this consists of a teacher and a number of students who meet face to face in a confined space. But this definition raises questions. Is a 'content' or 'immersion' classroom also a language classroom? In such classrooms, there may be not any planned, direct attempt to teach language, but they nevertheless constitute sites in which many L2 learners find themselves and they afford opportunities for language learning as well as content learning. SLA researchers have generally viewed such classrooms as 'language classrooms'. Another issue is whether academic advising sessions between an instructor/tutor and a language learner constitute a 'language classroom'. A number of often-cited studies (for example, Aljaafreh and Lantolf 1994; Bardovi-Harlig and Hartford 1993; Mondada and Doehler 2004) have examined this kind of setting. Finally, there is an increasing SLA literature (for example, Smith 2005) examining computer-mediated interaction, which itself can take a number of different forms (for example, learners working together on a computer-delivered activity, online lessons), which, it can be argued, take place in cyber classrooms. Where appropriate I will draw on research that has investigated all these types of language classrooms but, in general, reflecting the bulk of the research to date, I will focus on the stereotypical language classroom.

Types of classroom research

A broad distinction can be drawn between 'formal research' and 'practitioner research'. The former is research that is conducted by an external researcher drawing on one or more of the established research traditions considered below. Practitioner research is research conducted by teachers in their own classrooms drawing on the principles of action research (for example, Carr and Kemmis 1986) or exploratory practice (Allwright 2003). The extent to which such teacher-based research can contribute to our theoretical understanding of instructed L2 acquisition is debated, especially as it is not designed to test or develop theory but to solve practical problems in the case of action research, or to develop the participants' understanding of 'the quality of life' in the classroom in the case of exploratory practice (Allwright 2003) and, in the eyes of some (for example, Crookes 1993), it need not conform to the normal requirements of reliability, validity, and trustworthiness. Most of the research addressed in this chapter will be of the formal type but, where appropriate, I will also draw on practitioner research, reflecting Van Lier's (1994b) argument that practice can inform theory as well as theory informing practice.

The research traditions evident in SLA input/interaction research—descriptive, experimental, self-report, and introspective (see Chapter 6)—can also be found in L2 classroom research. Broadly speaking, L2 classroom researchers have followed two general approaches, sometimes combining both: (1) descriptive and (2) confirmatory.

Descriptive research

Descriptive research focuses on 'the form and functions of classroom interactions, how these interactions are shaped and become meaningful, and what the implications may be for students' learning' (Zuengler and Mori 2002: 283). By and large such research does not examine how input/interaction leads to language learning although it has considered how it affords opportunities for learning. Descriptive studies of L2 classrooms can be qualitative or quantitative (i.e. the frequency of specific descriptive categories such as 'confirmation checks' or 'display questions' can be calculated). Descriptive research has drawn on a number of tools.

1 *Interaction analysis*

This involves the use of a schedule consisting of a set of categories for coding specific classroom behaviours. Long (1980b) referred to three different types of INTERACTION ANALYSIS: in a category system each event is coded each time it occurs, in a sign system each event is recorded only once within a fixed time span, while in a rating scale an estimate of how frequently a specific type of event occurred is made after the period of observation. Initially, schedules were developed for content classrooms (see Flanders 1970 for an account of this early work), but these were rapidly adapted to the language classroom (for example, Moskowitz 1967). Frequently, the categories listed in a schedule reflected the researcher's assumptions about what behaviours were important and were not theoretically motivated. The Marburg schedule (Freudenstein 1977) included categories such as 'phases of instruction', assuming that the basic pattern of a lesson would follow the pattern 'warming up', 'presentation', 'learning', and 'using'. However, subsequent schedules (for example, Fanselow 1977; Allwright 1980) attempted to produce more comprehensive and method-neutral sets of categories, while some (for example, Spada and Fröhlich 1995) have been based on a theoretical understanding of the nature of L2 acquisition.[1]

Long (1980b) listed twenty-two interaction analysis systems, to which several more must now be added. This proliferation reflects differences in research foci. It makes comparison across studies extremely difficult. Also, because the behaviour of the teacher and the learners is often treated separately, information is lost about 'the sequential flow of classroom activities' (McLaughlin 1985: 149). Often interaction analysis runs the risk of producing disconnected tallies of behaviours that obscure the general picture, as there is no basis for deciding which *combinations* of features might be important. Interaction analysis depends on a number of assumptions—for example, that it is possible for an observer to 'read' the intentions of the teacher and students. Such assumptions can be questioned, thus casting doubt on the reliability and validity of the measurements. However, this is more of a problem with 'high inference' categories (for example, 'degree of teacher control exercised over materials') than with 'low inference' categories (for example, 'type of materials—text, audio or visual'), as Long (1980b) pointed out.

2 *Discourse analysis*

Discourse analysis serves as a device for systematically describing the kinds of interactions that occur in language classrooms. Drawing on initial work on content classrooms by Bellack *et al.* (1966) and by the Birmingham school of linguists (Sinclair and Coulthard 1975), discourse analysts give attention not only to the function of individual utterances but also to how these utterances combine to form larger discoursal units. They aim to account for the joint contributions of teacher and student and to describe all the data, avoiding the kind of 'rag bag' category found in many interaction analysis schedules.

McTear (1975) showed how the Birmingham framework could be adapted to account for the discourse structure found in language lessons. Researchers at the Centre de Recherche et d'Applications Pédagogiques en Langues (CRAPEL) in the University of Nancy (for example, Gremmo, Holec, and Riley 1978; Riley 1985) also made use of discourse analysis to show how 'natural' discourse is distorted in the language classroom as a result of the teacher's dominance. Other researchers (for example, Ellis 1984a; Van Lier 1988) developed frameworks based on discourse analysis to characterize the different types of interaction that can occur in the L2 classroom. More commonly, researchers have used the techniques of discourse analysis to develop comprehensive accounts of specific areas of discourse. Chaudron (1977), for example, provided an analysis of teacher feedback, Long and Sato (1984) offered a discourse-based analysis of teachers' questions, and Sheen (2006a) developed a taxonomy of recasts.

3 Conversational analysis (CA)

Like discourse analysis, CONVERSATIONAL ANALYSIS provides a tool for conducting micro-analyses of classroom discourse and, in particular, for examining the sequential development of classroom talk. (See, for example, Mori 2002.) CA derives from a branch of sociology—ethnomethodology. Seedhouse (2004) identified five key principles of this method of enquiry: (1) indexicality (i.e. the use that interactants make of shared background knowledge and context), (2) the documentary method of interpretation (i.e. each real-world action is treated as an exemplar of a previously known pattern), (3) the reciprocity of perspectives (i.e. the interactants' willingness to follow the same norms in order to achieve intersubjectivity), (4) normative accountability (i.e. there are norms that are constitutive of action and enable speakers to produce and interpret actions), and (5) reflexivity (i.e. the same methods and procedures apply to the production and interpretation of actions). In accordance with these principles, conversational analysis seeks to explain how 'talk in interaction' takes place. It aims to 'characterize the organization of interaction by abstracting from exemplars of specimens of interaction and to uncover the emic logic underlying the organization' (Seedhouse 2004: 13). This emic perspective, which contrasts with the etic perspective of mainstream SLA accounts of interaction (for example, Gass 1997a), is achieved by recording naturally occurring interactions, transcribing them narrowly and deriving bottom-up interpretations of the underlying order.

CA has been used to contrast the interactions that occur in naturalistic settings with those that occur in classrooms (Lörscher 1986), the organization of TURN-TAKING (Van Lier 1988; Seedhouse 2004), the structure of repair sequences (Kasper 1986; Seedhouse 1999), the basic structure of classroom discourse, and how context is jointly constructed by the participants (Seedhouse 2004).

'CA for SLA', the term coined by Markee and Kasper (2004), affords rich and illuminative accounts of classroom interaction. It serves as a tool 'for researchers to be able to assess what environments may be more or less conducive to learning ... because such settings would recommend themselves as scenes on which to focus research efforts' (Kasper 2004: 552). However, according to Rampton, Roberts, Leung, and Harris (2002), there are limits to its adequacy. One concerns the principle of 'reciprocity of perspectives' as it cannot be assumed that students (as L2 learners) do act in accordance with the same norms as the teacher (native or non-native speaker). Rampton *et al.* noted that it is not so easy to interpret the participants' orientation to such phenomena as silences, stretched syllables, and non-verbal behaviour in the L2 classroom as in interaction involving co-members. They also asked whether CA is capable of accounting for 'learning' as opposed to language use and concluded that 'CA alone can't cope'. Other disadvantages include the difficulty of generalizing results and the danger of ignoring superordinate variables relating to the learners' social context.

4 *Ethnography of communication*

Ethnographic approaches involve the kind of detailed descriptive work advocated by Johnson (1995). They emphasize the importance of obtaining multiple perspectives through triangulation. Watson-Gegeo (1997) distinguished four approaches to classroom ethnography: (1) ETHNOGRAPHY OF COMMUNICATION, (2) micro-ethnography, (3) discourse analysis, and (4) critical ethnography. However, as Duff (2002) pointed out, classroom researchers have often utilized a mixture of these approaches. She suggested that research in this tradition may best be described simply as 'ethnographic'.

The ethnography of communication has its origins in anthropology and, in particular, in the work of Hymes (1974). It aims to identify the workings of specific 'speech communities' by obtaining multiple perspectives on what participants in a particular social setting understand their interactive behaviours to mean. It requires both etic and emic analyses of 'ways of speaking', including non-verbal signals such as silences and gaze. It adopts both macro- and micro-methods of analysing discourse. The ethnography of communication differs from conversational or discourse analysis in that it 'looks for strategies and conventions governing larger units of communication and involves more holistic interpretation' (Saville-Troike 1996: 354).

The ethnographic tradition has been particularly evident in research into bilingual classrooms or mainstream classrooms containing L2 learners (for example, Phillips 1972; Heath 1983; Ernst 1994; Duff 2002). Gaies (1983) gave three advantages of such research: (1) it can account for learners who do not participate actively in class, (2) it can provide insights into the conscious thought processes of participants, and (3) it helps to identify variables which have not previously been acknowledged. Many of the disadvantages noted for conversational analysis also apply to the ethnography of communication. In particular, studies in this tradition have not typically shown how the interactional opportunities afforded a learner in a classroom contribute to learning.

Confirmatory research

Confirmatory L2 classroom research differs from the descriptive research considered above in that it is typically theory-driven, seeking to compare different instructional approaches, to test specific hypotheses, or to identify relationships between pre-determined variables. It involves either an experimental or a correlational design.

COMPARATIVE METHOD STUDIES, programme–product comparisons of the kind used to evaluate different types of immersion programmes and studies of different types of FORM-FOCUSED INSTRUCTION, all of which we will examine in the next chapter, are examples of experimental research. In this chapter we will examine experimental studies that have investigated the effect of learners focusing on form while performing meaning-focused tasks.

Well-designed experimental studies have the following features: participants randomly assigned to the experimental and control groups, a pre-test, both an immediate and a delayed post-test to establish if any learning has taken place and is durable, and, ideally, a process element to provide information about the actual events that take place inside the classroom. Whereas many of the early studies lacked one or more of these features, later studies are increasingly well designed.

Confirmatory research is also evident in correlational studies that have examined the relationship between specific classroom behaviours, such as teachers' requests, and learning outcomes (for example, Politzer, Ramirez, and Lewis 1981). Chaudron (1988: 30) noted that these studies often suffer from a failure to validate the categories used to measure instructional features, as well as from a failure to establish theoretical links between the processes observed and learning outcomes. However, more recent research, such as the studies that have investigated the relationship between different kinds of CORRECTIVE FEEDBACK and learner UPTAKE (for example, Lyster 1998b; Ellis, Basturkmen, and Loewen 2001; Loewen and Philp 2006), has been more theoretically driven.

Final comment

It is probably true to say that there has been a bias towards confirmatory research in the journals that publish L2 classroom research (i.e. *Language Learning*, *Modern Language Journal*, *Studies in Second Language Acquisition* and *TESOL Quarterly*). Lazaraton (2000) reported the results of a study of data-based articles in these journals over a seven-year period. She found that 88 per cent of the articles were quantitative, 10 per cent were qualitative and 2 per cent were 'partially qualitative'. However, qualitative articles are on the increase, stimulated in part by Firth and Wagner's (1997) call for a reappraisal of research in SLA. (See Chapter 7.) Also, L2 classroom research is becoming increasingly hybrid. A hybrid approach, whether evidenced through the eclectic use of different descriptive approaches or through a mixture of descriptive and experimental approaches has much to recommend it. Finally, there is a growing recognition amongst teacher educators that practitioner research has an important role to play in knowledge-making about teaching and learning (Allwright 2006).

A historical overview of L2 classroom research

There is no up-to-date historical review of L2 classroom research, but see Chaudron's account of the research up to the date of the publication of his book in 1988. It is clear however, that L2 classroom research pre-dated the establishment of SLA in the 1960s. Chaudron (2001) undertook a review of articles reporting L2 classroom research published in *The Modern Language Journal* (*MLJ*) from 1916 to 2000 and this provides us with the best snapshot of how research developed during this period. Table 15.1 summarizes the trends that Chaudron identified. A number of points stand out. The first is that method comparisons of one kind or another have been pervasive. The second is that the main focus of research has shifted somewhat from one period to another (for example, individualized instruction was the focus of the 70s, individual learner factors figured in the 1980s, and classroom process features in the 1990s). It should be noted, however, that there is considerably more to L2 classroom research than that reported in *MLJ*. Chaudron's review, therefore, is only an incomplete reflection of trends in this domain. A final point, emphasized by Chaudron, is that the research has improved notably in methodological sophistication and rigour over the years.

Period	**Main research topics**	**Main characteristics**	**Main findings**	**Sample study**
Early period (1916–1935)	Methods comparisons	Increasing sophistication in experimental design, procedures and statistical analysis.	More effective programmes employed more oral work and more meaningful reading rather than grammar-translation.	Peters (1934). Method comparison (direct method versus grammar); different tests favoured different methods.
The war years and 1950s	Very little classroom research published; methods comparisons	This period was characterized by the rise of audiolingualism; published articles dealt with its methodology and presumed successes.	No clear findings	Beck (1951). Method comparison of audiolingual approach versus grammar translation.
1960s	Methods comparisons; documentation of actual classroom processes; students' attitudes to instruction	Greater variety of research; experimental and observational studies. Research employed more complex statistics and demonstrated more detailed accounting of materials and procedures used in instructional treatments.	More mixed results for methods comparison studies—students shown to learn what they are taught. Evidence provided of aptitude-treatment interaction effects.	Jarvis (1968). Classroom observation scheme for quantifying teacher and learner classroom behaviours.

1970s	Methods comparisons; individualization of instruction	Methods comparisons focused on comprehension-based approaches; various approaches to individualized teaching investigated.	In general, individualized approaches found to be more effective than traditional instruction but variables difficult to control for in these studies.	Nieman and Smith (1978). Comparison of a self-paced with a traditional group; self-paced students did better overall but high-aptitude students did better with traditional instruction.
1980s	Focus on the learner: individual learner variables; focus on the teacher: method comparisons studies still evident but less prominent	Attempts were made to relate learner variables to achievement; attempts made to verify actual class practice. Methods studies investigated implicit (Nieman and Smith 1978) versus explicit and inductive versus deductive approaches.	The research evidenced a general dissatisfaction with 'method' as a construct; teaching characterized in terms of 'activities', 'strategies', and 'time' on task.	Swaffar, Arens, and Morgan (1982). Questionnaire study of teachers' classroom practices; supposed different methods not distinguishable in terms of specific activities.
1990s and beyond	Focus on 'tasks'; analyses of teacher talk; social perspectives on language classrooms	Experimental studies were now more clearly theory-driven (e.g. input-processing studies); descriptive studies used discourse and conversational analysis to examine interaction in classroom settings; a social perspective evident in studies based on sociocultural/sociocognitive theory but these lacked formal assessment of learning.	Input-processing instruction and negotiation of meaning shown to promote L2 acquisition. Other studies provided a detailed and quantified analysis of actual classroom uses of language (e.g. L1 versus L2) and how the design features of tasks influenced interaction.	Cadierno (1995). Input-processing instruction found to be more effective than traditional production-based instruction.

Table 15.1 Historical review of L2 classroom research (based on Chaudron's (2001) survey of language classroom studies published in The Modern Language Journal)

The nature of second language classroom discourse

In this section we will examine a number of general characteristics of the interaction typically found in L2 classrooms. Classroom discourse mediates between pedagogic decision-making and the outcomes of language instruction, as Figure 15.1 from Allwright and Bailey (1991) shows. Teachers plan their lessons by making selections with regard to what to teach (syllabus), how to teach (method), and perhaps also the nature of the social relationships they want to encourage (atmosphere). When acted on, their plans result in 'classroom interaction'. This is not planned in advance, but rather is 'co-produced' with the learners. In part, it will reflect the pedagogic decisions that have been taken, but it will also evolve as part of the process of accomplishing the lesson. The interaction provides learners with opportunities to encounter input or to practise the L2. It also creates in the learners a 'state of receptivity', defined as 'an active openness, a willingness to encounter the language and the culture' (op cit.: 23). Although classroom interactions are not usually designed in advance of a lesson, they have been found to manifest distinct and fairly predictable characteristics. These will be considered in terms of (1) the structure and general characteristics of classroom discourse, (2) types of language use, (3) turn-taking, and (4) differences between classroom and naturalistic discourse.

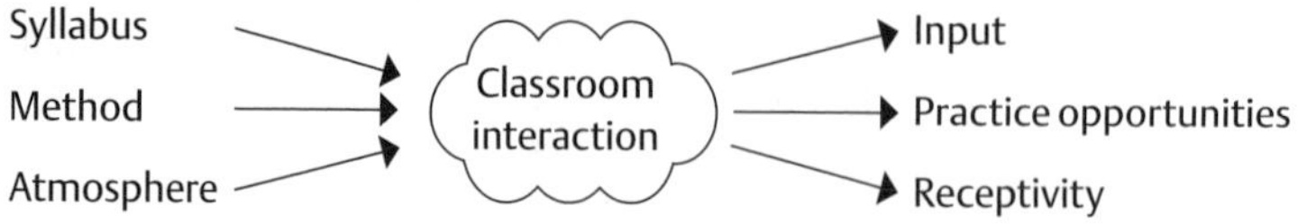

Figure 15.1 The relationship between plans and outcomes (from Allwright and Bailey 1991: 25)

Structure and general characteristics of teacher-centred discourse

Early work on teacher-centred classrooms made use of interaction analysis systems. The aim of these was to identify significant aspects of L2 classroom discourse and to develop specific categories that would allow for quantification. By so doing they provided a basis for investigating which interactional features are important for language acquisition. However, as we noted earlier in this chapter, they have a number of drawbacks. Some of the most frequently cited systems are Fanselow (1977), Allwright (1980) and Allen, Fröhlich, and Spada (1984). We will focus on the last of these here.

The COMMUNICATIVE ORIENTATION IN LANGUAGE TEACHING (COLT) (Allen, Fröhlich, and Spada 1984) differs from the systems that preceded it in that it was not only informed by current theories of COMMUNICATIVE COMPETENCE and communicative language teaching but also by research into L1 and L2 acquisition.[2] The authors commented:

> The observational categories are designed (a) to capture significant features of verbal interaction in L2 classrooms and (b) to provide a means of comparing some aspects of classroom discourse with *natural* language as it is used outside the classroom.
> (1984: 232)

The system is in two parts. The first part, 'A description of classroom activities', is designed for use in real-time coding. It consists of a set of general categories broken down into narrower sub-categories, in line with earlier systems. The main unit of analysis is 'activity type'; examples of the kinds of activities that might be identified are drill, translation, discussion, game, and dialogue. Each activity is then described in terms of participant organization (whether whole class, group work, or individual work), content (the subject matter of the activities), student modality (the various skills involved in the activity), and materials (type, length, and source/purpose). This part, therefore, relies on pedagogic rather than interactional constructs. However, the second part, 'Communicative Features', reflects a more discoursal perspective on the classroom. Coding is based on an audio recording of the classes observed. Seven communicative features are identified relating to use of the target language, whether and to what extent there is an information gap, sustained speech, whether the focus is on code or message, the way in which incorporation of preceding utterances takes place, discourse initiation, and the degree to which linguistic form is restricted. Table 15.2 illustrates Part 2 of the system by comparing extracts from two lessons, one reflecting a 'stereotyped routine', and the other communication that is closer to natural language behaviour. Unlike other interaction analysis systems, COLT has been used quite extensively in classroom research to distinguish the types of interaction that occur in different L2 classrooms (Spada 1987; Harley, Allen, Cummins, and Swain 1990).

A Analytical instruction

	Utterance	Communicative features
T	What's the date today?	L2/pseudo-request/minimal speech
S1	April 15th.	L2/predictable information/ultra-minimal speech/ limited form
T	Good.	L2/comment/minimal speech
T	What's the date today?	L2/pseudo-request/minimal speech
S2	April 15th.	L2/predictable information/ultra-minimal speech/ limited form
T	Good.	L2/comment/minimal speech

B Experiential instruction

	Utterance	Communicative features
T	What did you do on the weekend?	L2/genuine request/minimal speech
S	I went to see a movie.	L2/giving unpredictable information/minimal speech/unrestricted form
T	That's interesting. What did you see?	L2/comment/elaboration (genuine request for information)/sustained speech
S	ET. I really liked it. He's so cute.	L2/giving unpredictable information/sustained speech/unrestricted form
T	Yes. I saw it too and really liked it. Did anyone else see it?	L2/comment/expansion/elaboration (genuine request for information)/sustained speech

Table 15.2 Interaction in analytical and experiential type lessons (from Allen, Fröhlich, and Spada 1984)

A rather different approach to describing teacher-centred classroom discourse involved the use of discourse and conversational analysis to identify key features. In one of the best known accounts of classroom discourse, Sinclair and Coulthard (1975) developed a hierarchical model by identifying the following 'ranks' in the structure of a lesson: (1) lesson, (2) transaction, (3) exchange, (4) move, and (5) act. Overall, a 'lesson' has only a weakly defined structure, consisting of 'an unordered series of transactions'. A 'transaction' consists of a 'preliminary', one or more 'medial', and a 'terminal' exchange. It is most easily identifiable by means of 'boundary exchanges', signalled by framing and focusing moves. The element of structure that is most clearly defined, however, is that of 'teaching exchange', which typically has three phases, involving an 'initiating' move, a 'responding' move, and a 'follow-up' move, as in this example:

T Ask Anan what his name is. (initiating)
S What's your name? (responding)
T Good. (follow-up)

This exchange became known as IRF. Each move is realized by means of various kinds of 'acts'—the smallest unit in the discourse system. For example, the follow-up move can be performed by means of an 'accept' (for example, 'yes'), an 'evaluate' (for example, 'good') or a 'comment' (for example, 'that's interesting').

This system was not developed to account for language lessons, but, as McTear (1975) has shown, it fits remarkably well. Only small changes are necessary. For example, students in the L2 classroom often produce an additional response after the follow-up move in IRF exchanges, which has become known as 'uptake' (Lyster and Ranta 1997):

T What do you do every morning?
S I clean my teeth.
T You clean your teeth every morning.
S I clean my teeth every morning.

The exchange structure is, therefore, IRF(R). It should be noted, however, that this structure is only likely to arise in classroom discourse that is teacher-controlled.

IRF exchanges, constituting what Lemke (1990) called 'triadic dialogue', have often been viewed as limiting opportunities for learning. They are associated with the pedagogy of transmission (Barnes 1976), affording learners few opportunities for extended utterances, limiting the range of language functions to be performed and providing few occasions for negotiating meaning as communication breakdown is infrequent. As Van Lier (1996) put it 'in the IRF exchange, the student's response is hemmed in, squeezed between a demand to display knowledge and a judgment on its competence' (p. 151). However, an alternative view is possible. Van Lier went on to acknowledge that IRF exchanges can also facilitate students' contribution by SCAFFOLDING their attempts to use the L2. Much depends on how the exchange is enacted. Thus, if the initiation move involves teacher questions that 'introduce issues as for negotiation' (Nassaji and Wells 2000: 400) richer contributions from students can arise. Also, where the follow-up move serves to extend the student's response and to make connections with what has gone before and what will follow, rather than evaluate the student's response, the discourse can become less pedagogic and more conversational. Ohta (2001b), for example, reported that the Japanese learners she investigated appropriated the language they were exposed to in IRF exchanges for use in subsequent group work. Gourlay (2005) showed how teachers in business English lessons with L2 learners exploited the IRF exchange by means of 'embedded extensions', which introduced new input and allowed students to engage in covert activities where they enacted their own agendas. From these studies it is clear that IRF is not a monolithic structure but, in fact, highly varied. Van Lier (1996) identified the following dimensions in which it can vary: (1) conduct of initiation (i.e. a general, unspecific elicitation directed at the whole class or a specific, personal elicitation directed at a single student), (2) response function (i.e. whether the teacher's follow-up move requires students to repeat something, to recall material from their memory, or to express themselves more precisely), and (3) pedagogical purpose (i.e. display or assessment orientation). Clearly, the IRF exchange is capable of affording a greater range of learning opportunities than was once thought.

Although IRF exchanges tend to dominate, other kinds of exchange can also be found. Van Lier (1988) pointed out that it is easy to overstate the lack of flexibility evident in L2 classroom discourse. He found that although the discourse is often strictly controlled by the teacher, learners do sometimes initiate exchanges, and 'schismic talk' (talk that deviates from some predetermined plan) also occurs, at least in some classrooms. Other studies (for example, Ernst 1994; Johnson 1995; Walsh 2002) have also pointed to the variety of discourse that is possible in teacher-led exchanges.

Types of language use

Other researchers have sought to describe classroom interaction by identifying the different types of language use or interaction found in L2 classrooms. We will now examine a number of such frameworks.

Allwright (1980: 166) provided what he called 'a macro-analysis of language teaching and learning' by identifying three basic elements:

1 samples: instances of the target language, in isolation or in use;
2 guidance: instances of communication concerning the nature of the target language;
3 management activities: aimed at ensuring the profitable occurrence of (1) and (2).

These elements are not mutually exclusive, as instances of guidance and management activities automatically provide samples. Classrooms vary according to the relative proportion of the different elements, their distribution between teacher and learner, sequencing, and the language used (target or other).

Other accounts of types of classroom use distinguish between interaction where the focus is the code itself (a key feature of the language classroom) and interactions which centre on genuine meaning exchange. McTear (1975), for instance, identified four types of language use based on this general distinction:

1 mechanical: no exchange of meaning is involved
2 meaningful: meaning is contextualized but there is still no information conveyed
3 pseudo-communicative: i.e. new information is conveyed but in a manner that is unlikely in naturalistic discourse
4 real communication: i.e. spontaneous speech resulting from the exchange of opinions, jokes, classroom management, etc.

Mechanical and meaningful language use involve a focus on the code, while real communication by definition entails genuine information exchange with pseudo-communicative language use lying somewhere in between.

The frameworks developed by myself and Van Lier are a little more complicated, as they involve two dimensions rather than one. In Ellis 1984a, I distinguished 'goal' (the overall purpose of an interaction) and 'address' (who talks to whom). Three goals were specified: (1) core goals, where the focus is on the language itself (medium), on some other content (message), or embedded in some ongoing activity such as model-making (activity); (2) framework goals associated with the organization and management of classroom events; and (3) social goals. I discussed interactional sequences taken from an ESL classroom in Britain to illustrate how the type of goal influences the discourse, and then speculated about the learning opportunities each type affords. I pointed out that interactional events with core goals are likely to restrict learners to a responding role, whereas framework and social goals provide opportunities for them to initiate discourse and to perform a wider range of language functions. Kaneko (1991) used this framework to examine the effect of language choice (target or the learners' L1) on learning. She found that the items that Japanese high-school students reported learning in English lessons occurred most commonly in interactional events with core goals where there was an element of spontaneous language use.

In Van Lier's (1988) framework, there are four basic types of classroom interaction, according to whether the teacher controls the topic (i.e. what is talked about) and the activity (i.e. the way the topic is talked about). Type 1 occurs when the teacher controls neither topic nor activity, as in the small talk sometimes found at the beginning of a lesson or in private talk between students. In Type 2 the teacher controls the topic but not the activity; it occurs when the teacher makes an announcement, gives instructions, or delivers a lecture. Type 3 involves teacher control of both topic and activity, as when the teacher elicits responses in a language drill. In Type 4 the teacher controls the activity but not the topic, as in small-group work where the procedural rules are specified but the students are free to choose what to talk about. In a further development of this framework, Van Lier (1991) added a third dimension—the function that the language serves. He followed Halliday (1973) in distinguishing three types of function: (1) ideational (telling people facts or experiences), (2) interpersonal (working on relationships with people), and (3) textual (signalling connections and boundaries, clarifying, summarizing, etc.).

Johnson (1995) adopted a similar holistic approach based on a distinction between 'academic task structures' (i.e. how the subject matter is sequenced in a lesson and the sequential steps involved) and 'social participation structures' (i.e. how the allocation of interactional rights and obligations shapes the discourse). These two structures are interrelated. Where the academic task structure is rigid, the social participation structures are also tightly controlled. In such cases, classroom communication becomes ritualized. In contrast, when the academic task structure and social participation structure are more fluid, classroom communication can become highly spontaneous and adaptive. Johnson considered that topic control plays a crucial role in determining how fluid the communication is. Drawing on Ellis (1990a) and Van Lier (1988), she suggested the 'optimal conditions' for L2 acquisition. These include creating opportunities for students to have a reason for attending to language, providing ample opportunity for students to use language, helping students to participate in language-related activities that are beyond their current level of proficiency, and offering a full range of contexts that cater for a 'full performance' of the language. Johnson argued that these optimal conditions are more likely to occur in discourse where the academic task structure and social participation structure are more relaxed.

These broad frameworks have been developed through descriptive and ethnographic studies of language classrooms, utilizing detailed analysis of transcripts of actual classroom interactions. While they were not intended to serve as schemes for coding specific classroom behaviours, they have provided a tool for understanding classroom interaction and how it might affect learning. Their disadvantage is that they do not permit precise quantification, and thus cannot easily be used in experimental or correlational research that seeks to establish relationships between classroom processes and L2 learning statistically.

Turn-taking

Research which has specifically examined turn-taking in the L2 classroom has drawn extensively on ethnomethodological studies of naturally occurring conversations (for example, Sacks, Schegloff, and Jefferson 1974). These identified a number of rules that underlie speaker selection and change: only one speaker speaks at a time; a speaker can select the next speaker by nominating or by performing the first part of an adjacency pair (for example, asking a question that requires an answer); a speaker can alternatively allow the next speaker to self-select; and there is usually competition to take the next turn. Classroom researchers frequently highlight the differences between turn-taking in natural and classroom settings. McHoul (1978), for instance, showed that in the latter there is a strict allocation of turns in order to cope with potential transition and distribution problems and that who speaks to whom at what time is firmly controlled. As a result there is less turn-by-turn negotiation and competition, and individual student initiatives are discouraged.

Turn-taking in language classrooms is much the same as that in general subject classrooms. Lörscher (1986) examined turn-taking in English lessons in different types of German secondary schools and found that turns were almost invariably allocated by the teacher, the right to speak returned to the teacher when a student turn was completed, and the teacher had the right to interrupt or stop a student turn. Lörscher argued that these rules are determined by the nature of the school as a public institution and by the teaching–learning process.

There are a number of extensive discussions of turn-taking in the L2 classroom. Van Lier (1988) set out to identify how turn-taking in the L2 classroom differs from that found in ordinary conversation. He identified the following 'basic rule' governing classroom turn-taking:

1 In L2 classrooms, whenever centralized attention is required:
   a one speaker speaks at any one time;

b many can speak at once if they say (roughly) the same thing, or at least if (a proportion of) the simultaneous talk remains intelligible.

2 If not (a) or (b), repair work will be undertaken. (p. 139)

Van Lier suggested that this rule is, in fact, not so different from that observed in other forms of verbal interaction, with the real difference lying in the fact that classroom turn-taking is typically regulated by means of 'some form of centralized control' to ensure 'intelligibility'.

Interest in the turn-taking mechanisms found in classroom discourse has continued over the years. Markee (2000) identified the following general characteristics of turn-taking in classroom talk:

- the pre-allocation of different kinds of turns to teachers and learners
- the frequent production by learners of turns in chorus
- the frequent production of long turns by the teacher and short turns by the student
- the requirement that learners produce elaborated sentence-length turns in order to display knowledge
- a pre-determined topic.

Markee saw turn-taking of this kind as a reflection of 'unequal power speech exchange systems'.

In contrast to Markee's generalized account, Seedhouse (2004) offered a more differentiated description of classroom turn-taking mechanisms according to whether the context was 'form and accuracy' or 'meaning and fluency'. He argued that there is no single speech exchange system in L2 classrooms. Thus, Seedhouse emphasized 'the reflexive relationship between the pedagogical focus of the interaction and the organization of turn-taking and sequence' (p. 138). However, Seedhouse (2004) admitted that despite its flexibility the classroom speech exchange systems he examined 'remain identifiably L2 classroom interaction' (p. 139) and that conversational exchanges are difficult if not impossible in the L2 classroom. In an earlier publication he wrote:

> As soon as the teacher instructs the learners to 'have a conversation in English', the institutional purpose will be invoked, and the interaction could not be a conversation ... To replicate conversation, the lesson would have to cease to be a lesson in any understood sense of the term and become a conversation which did not have any underlying pedagogical purpose ...
> (Seedhouse 1996: 18)

In other words, conversational exchanges are only possible in 'off-the-record' business. Richards (2006), however, took a different position, based on a series of illuminative analyses of how identity is constructed through talk in the classroom. The 'default identities' of the participants (i.e. teacher and student) result in the standard speech exchange system described above. But other identities are possible when the participants draw on some 'transportable identity' (i.e. an identity relating to some aspect of a person's life not directly connected to the situation in which the talk occurs—for example, 'movie goer'). When this happens, a change in 'discourse identity' occurs and more conversational-like exchanges can arise. In short, conversational exchanges are possible when 'transportable identity' is privileged over 'situational identity'.

We can see two related issues running through these accounts of classroom turn-taking. The first is the tension between the felt need to identify a set of general characteristics of classroom speech exchange systems and the recognition that there is considerable variety as well. This variety derives in part from the fact that the participants are able to transgress from the routinized 'basic rule' that guides turn-taking and in part from the fact that turn-taking mechanisms differ according to the pedagogic purpose. The second issue concerns the differences between L2 classroom turn-taking mechanisms and those found in ordinary conversation. All the studies of classroom turn-taking referred to above take as their point of comparison the speech exchange system documented by analysts of ordinary conversation. It is now time to consider this comparison in greater depth.

The difference between classroom and naturalistic discourse

The discourse that results when the focus is on trying to learn a language is different from that which results when the focus is on trying to communicate. Edmondson (1985) drew on Labov's idea of the Observer's Paradox (see Chapter 4) to suggest that there is also 'the teacher's paradox', which states:

> We seek in the classroom to teach people how to talk when they are not being taught.
> (1985: 162)

Thus, there is a tension between discourse that is appropriate to pedagogic goals and discourse that is appropriate to pedagogic settings. Studies have shown that natural discourse occurs rarely in the classrooms. Pica and Long (1986), for example, found that there was very little negotiation of meaning in elementary ESL classrooms in Philadelphia in comparison to NS–NNS conversations outside the classroom, as evident in significantly fewer conversational adjustments by the teachers. Politzer, Ramirez, and Lewis (1981) reported that 90 per cent of all student moves were responses, testifying to the limited nature of opportunities to participate that learners are afforded in classrooms—a point we will take up later. These and other studies (for example, Kasper 1986) testify to the restricted nature of pedagogic discourse.

The teacher's control over the discourse is the main reason given for the prevalence of pedagogic discourse. Researchers at CRAPEL (for example, Gremmo, Holec, and Riley 1978) argued that in the classroom setting discourse rights are invested in the teacher. It is the teacher who has the right to participate in all exchanges, to initiate exchanges, to decide on the length of exchanges, to close exchanges, to include and exclude other participants, etc. When teachers act as 'informants' or 'knowers' (Corder 1977b), they are likely to make full use of their rights, and as a consequence the learners are placed in a dependent position. As a result there is a preponderance of teacher acts over student acts (typically in a 2:1 ratio), because teachers open and close each exchange. In the opinion of some, pedagogic discourse constitutes a 'falsification of behaviour' and a 'distortion' (Riley 1977), but other researchers see it as inevitable and even desirable (for example, Edmondson 1985 and Cullen 1998).

However, classroom discourse is not invariably pedagogic—a point that Seedhouse (2004) made in his discussion of how the participants' purpose determines the turn-taking mechanisms. Kramsch (1985) argued that the classroom is characterized by 'co-existing discourse worlds'. She suggested that the nature of classroom discourse will depend on the roles the participants adopt, the nature of the learning tasks, and the kind of knowledge that is targeted. Instructional discourse arises when the teacher and the students act out institutional roles, the tasks are concerned with the transmission and reception of information and are controlled by the teacher, and there is a focus on knowledge as a product and accuracy. Natural discourse is characterized by more fluid roles established through interaction, tasks that encourage equal participation in the negotiation of meaning, and a focus on the interactional process itself and on fluency. One way in which the two worlds can be brought together is through communicating about learning itself, as suggested by Breen (1985).

In Ellis (1999a), I argued that, when teachers relinquish control of the topic and of how it is developed, a different type of discourse arises—one that is potentially acquisition-rich. A good example of this can be found in Ernst's (1994) study of one particular classroom event which occurred regularly in the elementary ESL classroom she was studying. The event was the 'talking circle', where the students were asked to gather round the teacher in a semicircle in order to share and discuss experiences and to introduce the weekly theme of the class. Ernst noted that this repetitive event had a clear five-part structure consisting of (1) getting ready, (2) entry into the circle, (3) a core phase, when students had the chance to talk about topics of interest to them, (4) the teacher's exposition of her agenda for the week, and (5) moving on. Ernst provided a detailed analysis of one 16-minute talking circle in order to demonstrate how the five phases differed with regard to topic development, the social demands placed on the children, and the particular communicative functions performed by the teacher's and students' speech. This demonstrated clearly that when the students are in control of the topic, the quality of the discourse is markedly richer than when the teacher is in control. We will revisit the question of learner control later in this chapter.

Final comment

The research we have considered in this section has been entirely descriptive. It has drawn on a range of methodologies, all informed by the felt need to develop a rich understanding of the learning process through examining classroom discourse. Thus, the underlying theoretical perspective has been the same—(1) learning arises out of the interactions that take place and (2) different types of classroom interaction afford variable opportunities for learning. The relationship between 'interaction' and 'learning', however, has not been directly investigated in this research. Rather, the research has provided descriptions of the discourse to be found in classrooms (often in very illuminating ways) and, then, on the basis of a theoretical view of how interaction shapes learning, hypothesized which types of interaction are 'acquisition rich'. As we will see in the conclusion to this chapter, the value of this descriptive research is a matter of controversy.

The research has also been challenged in another way. The underlying theoretical premise is that classroom interaction is more likely to foster learning when the classroom talk mirrors that found in naturalistic discourse. However, Widdowson (1990) argued that '... the very concept of pedagogy (whether defined as art or science) presupposes invention and intervention which will direct learners in ways they would not, left to their own devices, have an opportunity or inclination to pursue' (p. 48). In a similar vein, Cullen (1998) reasoned that classrooms did not need to replicate the kind of communicative behaviour found outside the classroom. He argued that discourse can be pedagogically effective when the teacher successfully combines the role of 'instructor' and 'interlocutor'. This claim mirrors that made in the revisionist accounts of the value of IRF exchanges, which we considered earlier.

The teacher's contribution to classroom discourse

Whereas the previous section looked in a relatively holistic fashion at the nature of L2 classroom discourse, this section will consider research that has investigated a number of specific aspects of the teacher's contribution to the discourse.

Teacher talk

L2 TEACHER TALK can be viewed as a special register, analogous to foreigner talk. (See Chapter 6.) Studies of teacher talk, like those of foreigner talk, have sought to describe its phonological, lexical, grammatical, and discoursal properties. They have been motivated by the felt need to document the nature of the 'input' that learners are exposed to in classroom environments. Wong Fillmore (1985) identified a number of features of teacher talk that she claimed were facilitative of acquisition in kindergarten classrooms with both L1 and L2 speaking children: avoidance of translation, an emphasis on communication and comprehension by ensuring message redundancy, the avoidance of ungrammatical teacher talk, the frequent use of patterns and routines, repetitiveness, tailoring questions to suit the learners' level of proficiency, and general richness of language. Chaudron (1988: Chapter 3) provided a comprehensive survey of the teacher-talk studies. His main conclusions are summarized in Table 15.3. The research indicates that teachers modify their speech when addressing L2 learners in the classroom in a number of ways and also that they are sensitive to their learners' general proficiency level. Many of these modifications are the same as those found in foreigner talk but some seem to reflect the special characteristics of classroom settings—in particular the need to maintain orderly communication. However, in general, little is known about what constitutes optimal teacher talk. Nor is it clear on what basis teachers make their modifications. Hakansson (1986) speculated that they may aim at some hypothetical average learner, in which case the input is not likely to be tuned very accurately to the level of many of the learners in some classrooms.

Feature	**Main conclusions**	**Main studies**
Amount of talk	In general, the research confirms the finding for L1 classrooms—namely, that the teacher takes up about two-thirds of the total talking time.	Legaretta 1977; Bialystok *et al.* 1978; Ramirez *et al.* 1986
Functional distribution	There is considerable evidence of variability among teachers and programs, but the general picture is again one of teacher dominance in that teachers are likely to explain, question, and command and learners to respond.	Shapiro 1979; Bialystok *et al.* 1978; Ramirez *et al.* 1986
Rate of speech	Teachers, like native speakers in general, slow down their rate of speech when talking to learners as opposed to other native speakers and also do so to a greater extent with less proficient learners. However, there is considerable variability among teachers.	Henzl 1973; Dahl 1981; Wesche and Ready 1985; Griffiths 1990
Pauses	Teachers are likely to make use of longer pauses when talking to learners than to other native speakers.	Downes 1981; Hakansson 1986; Wesche and Ready 1985
Phonology, intonation, articulation, stress	There have been few studies which have attempted to quantify these aspects of teacher talk, but teachers appear to speak more loudly and to make their speech more distinct when addressing L2 learners.	Henzl 1973, 1979; Downes 1981; Mannon 1986

Modifications in vocabulary	Several studies provide evidence of a lower type–token ratio and teachers also vary in accordance with the learners' proficiency level, but Wesche and Ready (1985) found no significant vocabulary modifications in university lectures to L2 learners.	Henzl 1979; Mizon 1981
Modifications in syntax	There is a trend towards shorter utterances with less proficient learners, but some studies which use words per utterance as a measure report no modifications. The degree of subordination tends to be lower, but again results have been mixed. Teachers use fewer marked structures such as past tense. More declaratives and statements than questions are used in comparison to natural discourse. Ungrammatical teacher talk is rare.	Pica and Long 1986; Gales 1977; Kleifgen 1985; Early 1985; Wesche and Ready 1985
Modifications in discourse	There is some evidence that teachers use more self-repetitions with L2 learners, in particular when they are of low-level proficiency.	Hamayan and Tucker 1980; Ellis 1985d

Table 15.3 Main features of teacher talk (summarized from Chaudron 1988: Chapter 3)

There have been few studies of teacher talk since Chaudron's review. In one study, Consolo (2000) compared functional aspects of the teacher talk of native and non-native speaking teachers in Brazilian private language schools, reporting no differences, due to the fact that both sets of teachers were constrained to enact the same roles resulting in standardized patterns of interaction. One reason for the demise of teacher-talk studies is that register-like descriptions such as those summarized in Table 15.3 are viewed as being of limited value because they fail to take account of the individual, contextual, and sociocultural factors that shape teachers' choice of language on a moment-by-moment basis. More recent accounts, therefore, have moved beyond viewing teacher talk as a source of input in order to examine how it shapes learners' contributions to the discourse. Walsh (2002), for example, identified a number of characteristics of teacher talk that, in his view, either inhibited or increased learner participation. Learning potential was increased if the corrective feedback was direct (as opposed to indirect), if teachers provided 'content feedback' (i.e. personal reactions made to learners), frequently 'pushed' learners by requesting confirmation or clarification, allowed extended wait-time, and scaffolded learners' production. Learning opportunities were inhibited if the teacher attempts to ensure the smooth progression of the discourse by means of 'latching' (i.e. completing student turns for them), echoing students' contributions, and interrupting students' in mid-flow. Some of the characteristics identified by Walsh are considered in detail later in this chapter.

Teachers' questions

Teachers, whether in content classrooms or in language classrooms, typically ask a lot of questions. For example, Long and Sato (1984) observed a total of 938 questions in six elementary level ESL lessons. One reason for the prevalence of questioning is undoubtedly the control it gives the teacher over the discourse. Thus, a question is likely to occupy the first part of the ubiquitous three-phase IRF exchange.

Much of the work on questions has centred on developing taxonomies to describe the different types. In one of the earliest taxonomies, Barnes (1969, 1976) distinguished four types of questions he observed in secondary school classrooms in Britain: (1) factual questions ('what?'), (2) reasoning questions ('how?' and 'why?'), (3) OPEN QUESTIONS that do not require any reasoning, and (4) social questions (questions that influence student behaviour by means of control or appeal). Barnes made much of the distinction between CLOSED QUESTIONS (i.e. questions that are framed with only one acceptable answer in mind) and open questions (i.e. questions that permit a number of different acceptable answers). Barnes also pointed out that many questions have the appearance of being open, but, in fact, when the teacher's response to a student's answer is examined, turn out to be closed; he called these PSEUDO-QUESTIONS.

Long and Sato (1984) modified Kearsley's (1976) taxonomy of questions to account for the different types of teachers' questions they observed in ESL lessons in the USA. The key distinction was between echoic questions, which ask for the repetition of an utterance or confirmation that it has been properly understood, and epistemic questions, which serve the purpose of acquiring information. The latter type include REFERENTIAL and DISPLAY QUESTIONS, which Long and Sato discussed in some detail. This distinction is similar but not identical to the open/closed distinction of Barnes. Referential questions are genuinely information-seeking, while display questions 'test' the learner by eliciting already known information, as in this example:

T What's the capital of Peru?
S Lima.
T Good.

Referential questions are likely to be open, while display questions are likely to be closed, but it is possible to conceive of closed referential questions and of open display questions.

Other taxonomies have focused on different aspects of teachers' questions. Koivukari (1987), for example, was concerned with depth of cognitive processing. Rote questions (those calling for the reproduction of content) are considered to operate at the surface level, while two kinds of 'comprehension' questions (those calling for the reproduction of content and those calling for the generation of new content) operate at progressively deeper levels. Hakansson and Lindberg (1988) distinguished questions in terms of their form (i.e. 'yes/no' questions, alternative questions, or WH–questions), cognitive level (i.e. questions that require reproduction of information or convergent thinking), communicative value (i.e. whether they were referential or display), and orientation (i.e. whether the question is focused on language or real-life content). Hakansson and Lindberg's taxonomy is one of the most comprehensive available.

Whereas there are few problems in assigning teachers' questions to formal categories, difficulties arise with functional, communicative, or cognitive categories. These are 'high inference' and often call for substantial interpretative work on the part of the analyst. For example, the teacher's questions in the following example from White (1992) might be considered display in that they were clearly designed to elicit a specific grammatical structure but also referential in that they concerned an area of the student's private life that the teacher had no knowledge of.

T How long have you worn glasses? How long have you had your glasses?
S I have worn glasses for about six years.
T Very good. Same glasses?

Such 'pseudo-communication' (McTear 1975) makes the coding of questions problematic.

Studies of teachers' questions in the L2 classroom have focused on the frequency of the different types of questions, wait-time (the length of time the teacher is prepared to wait for an answer), the nature of the learners' output when answering questions, the effect of the learners' level of proficiency on questioning, the possibility of training teachers to ask more 'communicative' questions, and the variation evident in teachers' questioning strategies. Much of the research has been informed by the assumption that L2 learning will be enhanced if the questions result in active learner participation and meaning negotiation.

In general, language teachers prefer closed, display questions. Long and Sato (1984) found that the ESL teachers in their study asked far more display than referential questions (476 as opposed to 128). This contrasted with native-speaker behaviour outside the classroom where referential questions predominate (999 as opposed to 2 display questions in the sample they studied). They concluded that 'ESL teachers continue to emphasize form over meaning, accuracy over communication' (1983: 283–4). Other studies (for example, White and Lightbown 1984; Early 1985; Ramirez *et al.* 1986; White 1992) also showed that display/closed questions are more common than referential/open questions in the L2 classroom.[3]

Teachers also seem to prefer instant responses from their students. White and Lightbown (1984) found that the teachers in their study rarely gave enough time for students to formulate answers before repeating, rephrasing, or redirecting the question at another student. The shorter the wait-time is, however, the fewer and the shorter the student responses are.

One way in which teachers' questions might affect L2 acquisition is in terms of the opportunities they provide for learner output. A key issue, therefore, is whether teachers' questions encourage PUSHED OUTPUT. (See Chapter 6.) Brock (1986) found that responses to referential questions (mean length = 10 words) were significantly longer than responses to display questions (mean length = 4.23 words) in four advanced ESL classes at the University of Hawaii. Similar results have been obtained by Long and Crookes (1987), Nunan (1990a), and White (1992), suggesting that the findings are fairly robust. However, as White illustrated, it does not follow that all display questions produce short responses. It is obvious that 'there is no meaning left to negotiate' in exchanges such as the following:

T What's this?
S It's a cup.
T Good.
(Long and Crookes 1987)

However, this is not the case in the following exchange based on a reading comprehension lesson, even though it also begins with a display question:

T Did anyone manage to find some reasons for this?
S With the decline of religion there is no pressure on woman to get married.
(White 1992: 26)

White argued that there is a need for a more delicate categorization of display questions to allow for the different types of student response evident in these two exchanges. Banbrook (1987) also showed that referential questions can elicit responses of varying lengths and complexity. It should be noted, however, that the length of the student's response to a question is only one of several possible measures of learner output. Of equal interest, perhaps, is the length of the sequence initiated by a question. In this respect, Long and Crookes (1987) report that display questions elicited more student turns than referential questions. Clearly, more work is needed to tease out the relationship between question type and learner output.

Very few studies have examined the relationship between teachers' choice of questions and the learners' proficiency level. In Ellis (1985d), I found no difference in the use a teacher made of open and closed questions with two learners over a nine-month period, but I did find evidence to suggest that the cognitive complexity of the questions changed, with more questions requiring some form of comment as opposed to object identification evident at the end of the period. White (1992) found that one of his teachers used more referential questions with a high-level class and more display questions with a low-level class, but the other teacher in this study followed the opposite pattern.

Given the indeterminate nature of the findings of many of the studies, it might seem premature to prescribe questioning strategies in teacher education. A number of studies, however, have investigated the effect of training teachers to ask specific types of questions. Brock (1986) and Long and Crookes (1987) found that instructors given training in the use of referential questions did respond by increasing the frequency of this type of question in their teaching. Koivukari (1987) found that training led teachers to use more 'deep' comprehension questions and fewer superficial rote questions, and was also able to demonstrate that an experimental group showed improved comprehension scores from this treatment.

Finally, several studies have pointed to the necessity of acknowledging individual variation in teachers' questioning strategies. Studies by Long and Sato (1984), Long and Crookes (1987), and Koivukari (1987) reported extensive differences, although not all these researchers bothered to draw the reader's attention to them explicitly. Banbrook and Skehan (1990) provided illustrative evidence to argue that there is both intra- and inter-teacher variation. They identified three sources of intra-teacher variation: '(a) general teacher variation, (b) variation that takes place over the phases of the lesson and (c) variation in question asking ... that is the consequence of the teaching tasks or activities engaged in' (1990: 150). They argued that although variation in teachers' questions is well attested, its parameters are not yet well understood.

These studies of teachers' questions in the L2 classroom have been 'etic' in orientation. That is, they have attempted to code questions in terms of a pre-determined classification system and then quantify the different types. In Van Lier's (1988) view, however, a more 'emic' approach might be more rewarding. Van Lier commented:

> the practice of questioning in L2 classrooms, pervasive though it is, has so far received only superficial treatment ... An analysis must go beyond simple distinctions such as display and referential to carefully examine the purposes and the effects of questions, not only in terms of linguistic production, but also in terms of cognitive demands and interactive purpose.
> (1988: 224)

Recent qualitative, socially-oriented accounts of teachers' questions have sought to challenge the received view that certain types of questions (for example, display questions) impact negatively on acquisition because they fail to engage learners in the kinds of language use believed to be facilitative.

The sociocultural context may influence teachers' choice of questioning strategies. Poole (1992), suggested that the use of display or closed questions in most of the classrooms that have been studied may reflect the caretaker practices evident in white, middle-class Western society. Teachers from such a background ask questions because they provide a means by which an expert (the teacher) and a novice (the learner) can jointly construct a proposition across utterances and speakers. Poole suggested that this may be why such questions are so ubiquitous and why they are difficult to get rid of—teachers are being asked to reject a strategy that they feel to be culturally warranted.

Other researchers, such as Seedhouse (1996), argued that display questions can be viewed as well suited to promoting learning from an institutional discourse perspective. McCormick and Donato's (2000) semester-long study of ESL teachers' questions was premised on a view of instruction as goal-directed actions. From this perspective, the role of teachers' questions can only be understood in relation to the goals they are trying to achieve. McCormick and Donato sought to show that simply assigning questions to some pre-determined functional category is misleading. They argued that questions need to be viewed as 'dynamic discursive tools' that serve 'to build collaboration and to scaffold comprehension and comprehensibility'. They sought to demonstrate this by examining questions in relation to Wood, Bruner, and Ross's (1976) scaffolding framework. (See Chapter 6.) Finally, Ho (2005) examined the questions asked by three non-native speaking ESL teachers in Brunei to demonstrate the dangers of assigning teachers' questions to fixed categories and to argue, like Seedhouse and McCormick and Donato, that display-type questions can be purposeful and effective in terms of institutional goals.

The work on teachers' questions summarized in this section reflects the general shift in approach evident in some other areas of L2 classroom research—from a predominantly etic perspective to a more mixed one where etic and emic accounts vie for a place in the sun. What is missing from both approaches, however, is any demonstration of how teachers' questioning practices result in learning.

Use of the L1

The teacher's use of the L1 in the L2 classroom remains a complex and controversial issue. It is complex because clearly the utility of using the L1 will depend on the instructional context. Auerbach (1993), for example, made a compelling case for the use of the learners' L1 in ESL classrooms in majority-language contexts (such as the USA), but the situation is clearly very different in foreign language contexts where learners' only source of exposure to the L2 may be the classroom. It is controversial because different theories of L2 acquisition afford very different hypotheses about the value of L1 use in the classroom. From an interactionist perspective, for example, emphasis needs to be given to ensuring learners receive maximum exposure to L2 input, whereas from a sociocultural perspective the L1 can serve as a tool for scaffolding learner production in the L2 (for example, Anton and DiCamilla 1998; Swain and Lapkin 2000). Not surprisingly, commentators differ widely in their recommendations regarding L1 use. Cook (2001), for example, recommended that teachers use the L1 to explain grammar, organize tasks, discipline students, and implement tests. In Ellis (1984), however, I argued that the L1 should be used as little as possible.

Turnball and Arnett (2002) surveyed the research on the teacher's use of the L1. They noted that a number of studies have found a direct correlation between achievement and teacher use of the target language and concluded 'since teachers are often the primary source of linguistic input in the TL, it is therefore reasonable to argue that maximizing the TL in the classroom is a favourable practice' (p. 205). Studies of L1 use, however, have focused on how much and in which contexts teachers use the L1 in classrooms. Not surprisingly, the results of these studies reveal enormous variation. Duff and Polio (1991) investigated the use of the L1 (English) and L2 in foreign language classrooms at the University of Southern California. They observed considerable variation among teachers (from 10 to 100 percent use of the L2) and identified a number of variables that might explain this variation (for example, the specific language being taught, departmental guidelines, the actual lesson content, the nature of the teaching materials, and the extent to which the instructors had had formal teacher training). Polio and Duff (1994) provided a more detailed analysis of the specific uses of the L2 in these classrooms but noted that it was difficult to make firm predictions regarding the specific purposes a given teacher would choose to use the L2 or English. Kim and Elder (2005) also reported considerable variation in the use of the L2 and the L1 by four secondary school foreign language teachers in New Zealand. They also found no systematic relationship between the teachers' choice of language and particular pedagogic functions. As Turnball and Arnett noted, there is a real need for process–product studies to determine the relationship between teachers' use of the L2 and L1 and learner achievement and, apart from a number of small-scale studies (for example, Kaneko's (1991) study referred to earlier), these are currently lacking.

Use of metalanguage

Clearly, when teachers elect to use metalanguage they are treating language as an 'object' rather than using it as a 'tool' for communication. Thus, implicit in the use of metalanguage is an explicit (rather than implicit) approach to teaching the L2. However, teachers make use of metalanguage in communicative-type lessons as well as more traditional, form-focused lessons. Samuda (2001), for example, described a study based on a communicative task where the teacher interrupted the task to provide a metalinguistic account of modal verbs of possibility in order to elicit the use of these verbs when students went back into performing the task. (See Chapter 11 for a fuller account of this study.)

Relatively few studies have examined teachers' use of metalanguage. Borg (1999) examined four teachers' use of grammatical terminology in relation to their expressed beliefs about teaching. The teachers varied considerably in the extent to which they used metalanguage, depending on whether or not they believed that learning grammar explicitly was important for language learning and on their assessment of their students' ability to handle technical terms. Basturkmen, Loewen, and Ellis (2002) investigated the extent to which teachers used metalanguage in lessons based on communicative tasks.

Interestingly, metalanguage occurred more frequently in teacher-initiated form-focused episodes (i.e. where the teacher elected to draw attention to language even though no problem had arisen) than in reactive episodes. Altogether metalanguage occurred in 32 per cent of the total form-focused episodes but most of the terms used were of a semi-technical nature (for example, 'mean', 'question' and 'verb'), reflecting the teachers' assessment of their students' knowledge of metalanguage.

To date, no study has investigated the relationship between teachers' use of metalanguage and L2 acquisition. Basturkmen *et al.*, however, examined whether metalanguage was related to student uptake and repair. (See Chapter 6 for a discussion of these terms.) They found no evidence of any relationship, although this may simply have reflected the low incidence of metalanguage in the communicatively-oriented discourse they investigated. As we will see later, there is clear evidence that corrective feedback containing metalinguistic explanations assists acquisition.

Corrective feedback

Corrective feedback (CF) was considered in some detail in Chapter 6. (See, in particular, the section dealing with discourse repair). It was also examined in Chapter 11, where a sociocultural theoretical perspective on CF was considered. Readers may like to revisit these chapters as a preliminary to the classroom-based and classroom-oriented research we will discuss in this section. In this section, we will consider the descriptive research that has examined corrective feedback. Later in this chapter we will revisit corrective feedback in the context of the discussion of 'focus-on-form'. Examination of the confirmatory research is reserved until Chapter 16.

In general, most classroom learners like to be corrected. Cathcart and Olsen (1976) found that the ESL learners they investigated liked to be corrected by their teachers and wanted more correction than they are usually provided with. Chenoweth *et al.* (1983) found that learners liked to be corrected not only during form-focused activities, but also when they were conversing with native speakers. This liking for correction contrasts with the warnings of Krashen (1982) that correction is both useless for ACQUISITION and dangerous in that it may lead to a negative affective response. Krashen may be partly right, though, as Cathcart and Olsen also reported that when a teacher attempted to provide the kind of correction the learners in their study said they liked, it led to communication which the class found undesirable. Other studies have investigated which type of corrective feedback students prefer. Kim and Mathes (2001) and Nagata (1993) reported a clear preference for more EXPLICIT FEEDBACK. Learners, however, are likely to differ in how much, when, and in what way they want to be corrected in specific instructional activities; to date, the studies investigating learners' viewpoints about error correction have failed to explore this variation in any depth.

Not all errors get corrected. The main conclusions Chaudron (1988) reached in his review of a number of studies which have investigated this issue were that (1) many errors are not treated at all, (2) discourse, content, and lexical errors receive more attention than phonological or grammatical errors, (3) the more often a particular type of error is made, the less likely the teacher is to treat it, and (4) there is considerable variation among teachers regarding how frequently ERROR TREATMENT takes place. Edmondson (1985) pointed out teachers sometimes correct 'errors' that have not in fact been made!

In general, it is teachers (rather than the students) who correct errors. Studies of repair in naturally-occurring conversations have shown a preference for self-initiated and self-completed repair. (See Chapter 6.) However, in classroom contexts, where, as we have seen, discourse rights are unevenly invested in the teacher, other-initiated and other-completed repair are predominant (Van Lier 1988). Other patterns of repair can also occur, however. Kasper (1985) found that in the language-centred phase of an English lesson in a Grade 10 Danish gymnasium, the trouble sources were identified by the teacher but they were repaired either by the learners responsible for them or by other learners. In the content phase of the same lesson, self-initiated and self-completed repair was evident, although the learners were inclined to appeal for assistance from the teacher.

Much of the research has focused on the types of corrective strategies teachers employ. (See Table 6.3 in Chapter 6 for a description of the most common strategies.) The choice of strategy varies according to the instructional context. Van Lier (1988: 211) pointed out that the type of repair work will reflect the nature of the context which the teacher and learners have jointly created. Seedhouse (2004) also emphasized that there is 'no single, monolithic organization of repair in the L2 classroom' (p. 179), with the type of organization varying with the pedagogic focus. Sheen (2004) reported significant differences in the types of CF observed in four teaching contexts (Canada immersion, Canada ESL, New Zealand ESL, and Korea EFL). The frequency of recasts, for example, varied significantly from one context to the next. So too did other types—for example, EXPLICIT CORRECTION was rare in Canada ESL classes but quite common in New Zealand ESL ones. Irrespective of these general contextual differences, a teacher's personal teaching style may also influence the type of corrective work that occurs, as Nystrom's (1983) study of the correction styles of four teachers in bilingual classrooms demonstrated.

However, some generalization is possible. Seedhouse (1997, 2004), reviewing data from a number of descriptive studies, reported that in general teachers were reluctant to utilize unmitigated, direct repair strategies, preferring instead indirect ones such as recasts. He suggested that this reflected the pedagogical advice that teachers had received as part of their teacher education (i.e. use indirect strategies to avoid embarrassing students). He argued that, in fact, given the interactional organization of the L2 classroom and the expectancies that result from this, it would be more natural for the teacher to use direct, unmitigated repair, as in the context of the classroom this marks errors as unimportant and unembarrassing.

Probably the main finding of studies of error treatment is that it is an enormously complex process. This is evident in the elaborative decision-making systems that have been developed (Long 1977; Day *et al.* 1984; Chaudron 1977) and also in the extensive taxonomies of the various types of teachers' corrective reactions (Allwright 1975a; Chaudron 1977; Van Lier 1988; Seedhouse 1997). Chaudron's system, for example, consists of a total of 31 'features' (corrective acts that are dependent on context) and 'types' (acts capable of standing independently). These descriptive frameworks provide a basis for examining teachers' preferences regarding types of error treatment. Studies have shown, for instance, that repetitions of various kinds are a common type of corrective feedback (Nystrom 1983).

Further evidence of the complexity of the decision-making process during error treatment is the inconsistency and lack of precision that teachers manifest. Long (1977) noted that teachers often give more than one type of feedback simultaneously and that often their feedback moves go unnoticed by the students. Teachers are likely to use the same overt behaviour for more than one purpose. A teacher repetition can occur after a learner error and serve as a model for imitation, or it can function as a reinforcement of a correct response. Teachers often fail to indicate where or how an utterance is deviant. They respond positively even when the learners continue to make the error. They correct an error in one part of the lesson but ignore it in another. They may give up on the task of correction if learners do not seem able to cope. Nystrom (1983) summed it all up with this comment:

> teachers typically are unable to sort through the feedback options available to them and arrive at the most appropriate response.

However, some researchers (for example, Allwright 1975a) consider inconsistency inevitable and even desirable, as it reflects the teacher's attempts to cater for individual differences among the learners.

Whereas the early research focused on addressing key theoretical issues and describing the corrective practices of teachers, later research has attempted to investigate whether CF is uptaken by learners and whether it actually assists acquisition. In a series of articles, Lyster and co-researchers (for example, Lyster and Ranta 1997; Lyster 1998a, 1998b) examined the nature of French immersion students' uptake of corrective feedback. Lyster distinguished two broad types of uptake: 'repair' (i.e. the student's utterance successfully repairs the initial problem) and 'needs repair' (i.e. the student's response fails to successfully repair the initial utterance). In Lyster and Ranta (1997) a number of ways students perform these two types of uptake are distinguished. (See Table 15.4.) Lyster (1998a) examined the relationship between different types of corrective feedback and uptake. He found that learner repair of lexical and grammatical errors was more likely after elicitations, requests for clarification, and metalinguistic clues (which he called 'negotiation of form') than other types. For example, 61 per cent of the repairs of grammatical errors occurred after negotiation of form and only 39 per cent after explicit correction or recasts.

However, as with corrective feedback strategies, variation in the rate and nature of uptake has been found. Sheen (2004), in the study referred to above, found marked differences in both the level of uptake and repair in the four contexts she investigated. In particular, there was variation in the effectiveness of recasts in eliciting uptake and repair, which she suggested reflected differences in the pedagogical focus of these contexts, the age of the students, their L2 proficiency, and educational background. Lyster and Mori (2006) also reported differences in uptake and repair according to instructional context, in this case two different immersion contexts—French immersion in Canada and Japanese immersion in Japan. The negotiation of form (now relabelled 'prompts') induced higher levels of uptake and repair in Canada but recasts did so in Japan. On the basis of these findings they advanced the 'counterbalance hypothesis', which predicts that the extent to which different CF strategies lead to uptake/repair is influenced by whether the overall instruction orients learners to attend to form, as it did in Japan but not in Canada. Finally, Oliver and Mackey (2003) found differences in both the frequency of feedback, uptake, and modified output in the specific contexts found within child ESL classrooms. Feedback occurred most frequently in explicit language contexts. Uptake and modified output were also more likely to occur in explicit language contexts. Feedback, uptake, and modified output were least frequent in management-related exchanges.

A Repair

1. Repetition (i.e. the student repeats the teacher's feedback).
2. Incorporation (i.e. the student incorporates repetition of the correct form in a longer utterance).
3. Self-repair (i.e. the student corrects the error in response to teacher feedback that did not supply the correct form).
4. Peer-repair (i.e. a student other than the student who produced the error corrects it in response to teacher feedback).

B Needs repair

1. Acknowledgement (e.g. a student says 'yes' or 'no').
2. Same error (i.e. the student produces the same error again).
3. Different error (i.e. the student fails to correct the original error and in addition produces a different error).
4. Off target (i.e. the student responds by circumventing the teacher's linguistic focus).
5. Hesitation (i.e. the student hesitates in response to the teacher feedback).
6. Partial repair (i.e. the student partly corrects the initial error).

Table 15.4 Types of uptake following corrective feedback (from Lyster and Ranta 1997)

The learner's contribution to classroom discourse

There has been substantially less work done on the learner's contribution to classroom discourse, probably for the obvious reason—learners typically contribute a lot less than teachers to the discourse and also do so in quite limited ways. In classrooms dominated by IRF exchanges, for example, the learner is frequently limited to the 'response' move. However, a number of studies have explored different aspects of the learner's contribution especially in the context of small group work. Much of the more recent research has been informed by the theory and methodology of SOCIOCULTURAL SLA; that is, it has attempted to identify ways in which classroom learners construct learning opportunities in interactions either with the teacher or among themselves. We will consider first aspects of the learner's participation in classrooms and then focus on research that has examined small group work.

Learner participation

What evidence is there that learners who participate actively in language lessons learn more rapidly than those who remain more passive? In other words, does frequent practice in using the L2 in the classroom promote learning? Or is it not so much a question of the frequency as the quality of learner participation that counts? These are the questions that classroom researchers have attempted to answer.

Quantity of participation

There is no clear evidence that the extent to which learners participate productively in the classroom affects their rate of development. Table 15.5 summarizes a number of correlational studies that have examined the relationship between amount of learner classroom participation and L2 achievement/proficiency. The results are mixed. Whereas studies by Seliger (1977),[4] Naiman *et al.* (1978), and Strong (1983, 1984) reported positive correlations between various measures of learner participation and proficiency, Day (1984) (in a careful replication of Seliger's study) and to a large extent Ely (1986a) found no such relationships. Allwright (1980) also found that the learner who participated the most in the lesson he analysed was not among those who showed the greatest advances. As Chaudron (1988) and I (Ellis 1988b) have pointed out, correlational studies of learner participation are not easy to interpret, as there is no way of telling whether a 'participation-causes-learning' or 'proficiency-causes-participation' explanation is correct when a significant relationship is discovered. For this reason perhaps, such studies have been discontinued.

An alternative approach is to examine experimentally whether language practice leads to actual gains in L2 knowledge. In Ellis (1984b), I investigated whether there was any relationship between the number of times a group of ESL learners practised producing 'when' questions in a teacher-led activity and their development of this structure. Somewhat surprisingly, the 'low interactors' manifested greater development than the 'high interactors'. Sciarone and Meijer (1995) investigated the effects of students' engaging in computer-based controlled practice exercises on acquisition. They found no difference in the test results of students who completed the exercises and those who did not. They noted that even the 'good' students in their sample did not appear to benefit from the practice. In Ellis (1992), I found that differences in the accuracy with which adult beginners of L2 German performed the difficult 'verb-end' word order rule in communicative speech could not be accounted for by differences in the amount of practice in this structure they had received over a six-month period. However, I did note that many of the classroom learners appeared to have achieved greater accuracy in the use of verb-end than the purely naturalistic learners studied in the ZISA project. (See Meisel 1983.) It is possible, then, that the instruction did have some effect but that this effect was not readily explicable in terms of amount of practice. Overall, these studies do not demonstrate that sheer quantity of practice is what matters for acquisition.

However, the term 'language practice' can mean very different things. DeKeyser (2007b) offered the following definition:

> ... specific activities in the second language, engaged in systematically, deliberatively, with the goal of developing knowledge of and skills in the second language
> (p. 1)

The types of practice in the studies referred to above were largely of the mechanical and, to a lesser extent, the meaningful types described by Paulston and Bruder (1976). As DeKeyser noted, mechanical drills are of little value for L2 acquisition as they do not require the learner to establish form–meaning connections. Lightbown (2000), reconsidering her earlier claim that 'practice does not make perfect' (Lightbown 1985a), also noted that she was thinking of audiolingual-type drills and went on to suggest that 'when "practice" is defined as opportunities for meaningful language use (both receptive and productive) and for thoughtful, effortful practice of difficult language features, then the role of practice is clearly beneficial and even essential' (p. 443). This, then, might explain why the studies described above failed to find any clear effect for practice, although, as Lightbown (2006) pointed out, even meaningful practice does not necessarily ensure high levels of FLUENCY and ACCURACY.

Another key concept in understanding the limitations of practice is 'transfer-appropriate processing'. Drawing on Segalowitz and Lightbown (1999), Lightbown (2006) proposed the transfer appropriate-processing principle:

> ... according to the principle of *transfer appropriate processing*, the learning environment that best promotes rapid, accurate retrieval of what

> has been learnt is that in which the psychological demands placed on the learner resemble those that will be encountered later in natural settings.

DeKeyser (2007b) noted that the notion of 'transfer' applies to both the receptive/productive distinction and the declarative/procedural distinction as well as to whether knowledge acquired in a formal context is available for use in an informal one. In accordance with skill-learning theory (see Chapter 9) he also suggested that transfer to procedural knowledge requires that an adequate declarative base has been established first.

There is danger in overextending the meaning of the term 'practice'. For example, I do not think it helpful to use this term to refer to the kinds of interaction derived from communicative tasks, as do several of the articles in DeKeyser's (2007a) collection of papers on 'practice'. My own definition of language practice is as follows:

> Intentional and persistent activity conducted with awareness with the aim of mastering the use of a specific language feature or skill.

Quality of learner participation

Lightbown's comments are indicative of the importance of examining the nature of learners' participation in classroom discourse more closely. Here I will consider a number of characteristics of learner participation that have been hypothesized to facilitate acquisition.

Learner initiative

Opportunities for learner initiative do arise in the L2 classroom. Van Lier (1988) identified a number of turn-taking behaviours that he considered indicative of learner initiative (for example, the student turn is off-stream, introducing something new or disputing a proposition in a previous turn). He went on to challenge McHoul's claim that 'only teachers can direct speakership in any creative way' (1978: 188). He noted that in the L2 classroom data he collected the learners frequently did self-select. Van Lier argued that learners need such opportunities because they cater for experimentation with language that is at the cutting edge of their linguistic development.

One of the factors that seems to determine the quality of learner participation in classroom settings is the degree of control the learners exercise over the discourse—a point we briefly touched on when discussing turn-taking. Cathcart (1986) studied the different kinds of communicative acts performed by eight Spanish-speaking children in a variety of school settings (recess, seatwork, free play, ESL instruction, playhouse, interview, and storytelling). She found that situations where the learner had control of the talk were characterized by a wide variety of communicative acts and syntactic structures, whereas the situations where the teacher had control seemed to produce single-word utterances, short phrases, and FORMULAIC SEQUENCES. Other researchers have also found marked differences in the quality of learners' participation depending on the kind of activity they are involved in. House (1986), for

Study	Subjects	Measures of participation	Measures of learning	Results
Seliger 1977	6 adults learning English	Amount of verbal interaction; any student speech act counted as interaction; initiations and responses scored separately	Cloze test; structure test; aural comprehension test	Total interaction scores correlated significantly with structure and aural comprehension tests; proportion of initiations correlated significantly with aural comprehension test.
Naiman *et al*. 1978	Learners of L2 French in Grades 8, 10, and 12 in schools in Canada	Various measures of classroom behaviour (e.g. student hand-raising, student complete/partial responses; student correct/incorrect responses	Comprehension test; imitation test	Hand-raising, complete responses, correct responses, and number of responses over 10 significantly related to both criterion measures. Negative correlations for incorrect/partially correct responses found.
Strong 1983, 1984	13 kindergarten pupils in bilingual classrooms	Responses to utterances produced by others	Various measures of linguistic correctness, vocabulary and pronunciation based on classroom speech	Children's responsiveness correlated significantly with proficiency measures.
Day 1984	26 adult learners of L2	Responses to teacher general solicits; English self-initiated turns	Oral proficiency assessment of grammatical, pragmatic, and sociolinguistic competence; cloze test	No significant relationships between measures of participation and criterion measures reported.
Ely 1986b	72 first-year adult learners of L2 Spanish; half in first and half in second quarter	Number of self-initiated utterances in Spanish, i.e. volunteering a question or a response	Oral fluency in a story-reproduction task; oral correctness (based on error count); written correctness	Weak relationship between participation and oral correctness found for first quarter students; no other significant relationships found.

Table 15.5 Classroom-based studies of learner participation

instance, compared the performance of advanced German learners of L2 English in a role-play situation, where they had considerable freedom, and a teacher-led discussion. She found that the learners confined themselves to an 'interactional core' in the discussion, failing to use 'discourse lubricants' such as topic introducers (for example, 'You know ...') and various kinds of supportive and amplifying moves. In contrast, the role-play conversations sounded much more natural.

Further evidence of learner-initiated discourse in L2 classrooms can be found in Ellis, Basturkmen, and Loewen's (2001) study of 'pre-emptive focus-on-form'. This refers to episodes that arose in the context of task-based lessons where either the students or the teacher initiated attention to form in the absence of any attested learner error. The study found that the majority of the pre-emptive FOCUS-ON-FORM episodes (FFEs), dealt with vocabulary, were direct (i.e. they dealt with form explicitly rather than implicitly) and were initiated by students rather than the teacher. Students were more likely to 'uptake' a form (i.e. incorporate it into an utterance of their own) if the FFE was student-initiated than if it was teacher-initiated. This may have been because student-initiated focus-on-form addressed *actual* gaps in the students' knowledge whereas teacher-initiated focus-on-form only dealt with forms the teacher *hypothesized* might be problematic.

The key question, however, is whether learner initiation results in acquisition. Few studies have addressed this. Slimani (1989) investigated a series of lessons taught to a group of adult Algerian students. At the end of each lesson she asked the students to record on an 'uptake chart' what they thought they had learnt. In the main, they listed vocabulary items. She then examined transcripts of the lessons to try to identify what it was in the classroom interactions that might have caused them to remember the items. In general, the lessons were activity oriented and the teacher controlled the discourse. However, there were occasions when individual students nominated their own topics, i.e. learner topicalization occurred. Slimani found that 'whatever is topicalized by the learners rather than the teacher has a better chance of being claimed to have been learnt'.

In Ellis (1999a) I proposed a number of theoretical reasons why learner initiation assists acquisition—from the perspective of the INTERACTION HYPOTHESIS it creates the conditions that lead to the negotiation of meaning while from the perspective of sociocultural theory it ensures the learner's interest in the activity, helps the teacher to identify what speech forms may lie within the learner's zone of proximal development, and provides a basis for determining the kind of scaffolding needed to assist the learner to use and subsequently internalize more complex language.

Learner questions

One way in which learners can seize the initiative is by asking questions. Unfortunately, learners do not typically ask questions in teacher-fronted lessons. Also, when learners ask the teacher questions as a result of some problem they encountered during group work, the teacher tends to subvert learner control of the discourse. Markee (2000) showed that rather than give direct answers to students in such situations, teachers are likely to respond with a counter-question of the display type, as in this example:

L I don't understand 'stake'. What does it mean 'stake'?
T Who can define 'stake'?

Markee argued that teachers adopt this strategy because it enables them to regain control over the discourse. He also pointed out that it is ineffective because the fact that the students had asked for help indicates that they had been able unable to fill the gap in their knowledge by themselves.

However, Ohta and Nakone's (2004) study of student questions in Japanese language classes showed that not all teachers behave like Markee's ESL teachers. As in other studies, the students asked few questions in teacher-fronted lessons (only 20 in 40 hours of instruction) although they directed slightly more questions (23 in total) at the teacher while working in groups. Ohta and Nakone reported that the teacher provided direct answers to 21 of these. They suggested that direct answers were potentially facilitative of L2 acquisition in that they enabled the students to act as equal partners in the discourse and provided them with solutions to their real problems. They concluded that how teachers respond to learner questions varies depending on their cultural background or the training they have received.

Learner repetition

Repetition is traditionally associated with audio-lingual drill practice and, as such, has been largely discredited as a tool for facilitating acquisition. However, the contribution that repetition can make to acquisition has recently been reassessed. From a cognitivist perspective repetition can serve several functions, as Skehan (1998b) noted:

> Repetition in the language we produce provides more time to engage in micro and macro conversational planning. In acquisitional terms, repetition in conversation can serve to consolidate what is being learnt, since conversation may act as an unobtrusive but effective scaffold for what is causing learning difficulty.
> (p. 33)

Clearly, though, the kind of repetition that Skehan has in mind is not the kind of rote-parroting associated with audiolingualism but rather the repetition that arises naturally in the course of attempts to communicate, reflecting the need for 'context appropriate practice' referred to above.[5] From a sociocultural perspective, too, repetition is seen as a valuable tool for achieving self-regulation. (See Lantolf's (2006) arguments in support of what he refers to as 'imitation' in Chapter 11.)

Duff (2000) reviewed previous classroom research on repetition and then went on to document numerous instances of repetition in learners' speech involving both young learners, adolescents, and young adults in high-school language immersion classes in Hungary and university foreign language classrooms. She showed how repetition serves a variety of social, cognitive, linguistic, and affective purposes. She also illustrated through the analysis of two extended sequences how repetition can become burdensome when insisted on by the teacher. In these sequences, repetition was pervasive as the learners struggled to master the production of specific linguistic expressions. Duff suggested that the repetition made the learners weary of the focus-on-forms, causing them to diverge from the teacher's topic by introducing their own, less taxing but more meaningful topic. In this respect, then, the repetition might be considered to have resulted in a favourable shift in the discourse.

Other studies have focused on learners' use of repetition in group work interactions. DiCamilla and Anton (1997), for example, showed how learners' repetition served the important function of achieving intersubjectivity. They examined five dyads discussing how to write a common composition. They repeated phrases, words, and sometimes syllables as a means of accepting and extending each other's contributions. Repetition, DiCamilla and Anton suggested, serves to give the members of a dyad a single voice by ensuring that they work with a shared perspective. They emphasized that repetition does far more than increase the frequency of input, or make the input comprehensible; it serves as a socio-cognitive tool for accomplishing the task.

Roebuck and Wagner (2004) showed that classroom learners can be taught to use repetition as an effective tool. Like DiCamilla and Anton, they based their research on sociocultural theory, arguing that repetition served both communicative and cognitive functions and that 'by first using repetition as a communicative tool, students should begin to master the mediational means of conversation' (p. 74). They sought to train students in a fourth-semester university Spanish course to use repetition (for example, by requiring them to repeat part of the teacher's question before answering it). They found that the students did subsequently use unscripted repetition in peer interviews and also in more demanding dramatizations. They noted this was especially beneficial for the weaker students.

Small-group work and interaction

In this section I will briefly review the extensive research on group work in L2 classrooms. I will then consider its advantages and disadvantages.

Both educators (for example, Gibbons 2002) and SLA researchers (for example, Long and Porter 1985) have espoused the advantages of small group work for language learning. A summary of the main advantages can be found in Table 15.6.

Advantage	Comment
1 The quantity of learner speech can increase.	In teacher-fronted classrooms, the teacher typically speaks 80% of the time; in group work more students talk for more of the time.
2 The variety of speech acts can increase.	In teacher-fronted classrooms, students are cast in a responsive role, but in group work they can perform a wide range of roles, including those involved in the negotiation of meaning.
3 There can be more individualization of instruction.	In teacher-fronted lessons teachers shape their instruction to the needs of the average student but in group work the needs of individual students can be attended to.
4 Anxiety can be reduced.	Students feel less nervous speaking in an L2 in front of their peers than in front of the whole class.
5 Motivation can increase.	Students will be less competitive when working in groups and are more likely to encourage each other.
6 Enjoyment can increase.	Students are 'social animals' and thus enjoy interacting with others in groups; in teacher-fronted classrooms student–student interaction is often proscribed.
7 Independence can increase.	Group activities help students to become independent learners.
8 Social integration can increase.	Group activities enable students to get to know each other.
9 Students can learn how to work together with others.	In typical teacher-fronted classrooms students are discouraged from helping each other; group work helps students to learn collaborative skills.
10 Learning can increase.	Learning is enhanced by group work because students are willing to take risks and can scaffold each other's efforts.

Table 15.6 The potential advantages of group activities in language instruction (based on Jacobs 1998)

A number of studies compared the interaction in teacher-centred lessons with that found in group work. Long, Adams, McLean, and Castaños (1976) reported that students working in small groups produced a greater quantity of language and also better quality language than students in a teacher-fronted, lockstep classroom setting. Small-group work provided more opportunities for language production and greater variety of language use in initiating discussion, asking for clarification, interrupting, competing for the floor, and joking. Pica and Doughty (1985a), however, found no difference in the overall quantity of INTERACTIONAL ADJUSTMENTS in a one-way task performed in a lockstep setting and in small-group work, but when they replicated this study using a two-way task (Pica and Doughty 1985b), they did find significant differences. Thus, these two studies showed that group-work results in more negotiation of meaning but only if the task is of the required-information exchange type. Rulon and McCreary (1986) investigated the effect of participation pattern on the negotiation of content, defined as 'the process of spoken interaction whereby the content of a previously encountered passage (aural or written) is clarified to the satisfaction of both parties' (1986: 183). They found little difference between small-group and teacher-led discussions with regard to length of utterance, syntactic complexity, or interactional features, but they did find that significantly more negotiation of content occurred in the small-group discussions. From these studies it seems reasonable to conclude that group work can provide the interactional conditions which have been hypothesized to facilitate acquisition more readily than can interaction involving teachers. A meta-analysis of 12 studies that have investigated the effect of group-based interaction on L2 acquisition (Keck, Iberri-Shea, Ventura, and Wa-Mbaleka (2006) afforded convincing evidence that such interaction is facilitative of acquisition.

The studies referred to in the previous paragraph were guided by Long's Interaction Hypothesis. Bygate (1988), however, emphasized the role of learner output in collaborative discourse construction. He suggested that group work facilitates acquisition by affording learners opportunities to build up utterances through the use of satellite units. These are words, phrases, or clauses that constitute either moodless utterances that lack a finite verb or some kind of syntactically dependent unit, as in the following example:

S1 at the door
S2 yes in the same door I think
S3 besides the man who is leaving
S2 behind him.

Bygate found numerous examples of such units in the speech produced by learners working in small groups. He argued that the use of satellite units allows for flexibility in communication, gives the learner time to prepare messages, and enables messages to be built up collaboratively, thus helping to extend learners' capabilities.

Other studies of learner interaction have focused on the learner variables that affect the quality of the talk in group work. One variable, already mentioned is the choice of task. This will be considered in greater detail later in this chapter. Other variables that have been found to be important are gender (see Chapter 7) and the proficiency level of the learners. Porter (1986) found that intermediate learners got more input and better quality input from advanced than from other intermediate learners while advanced learners get more opportunity to practise when they are communicating with intermediate learners. Porter felt that mixed pairings offer something to both sets of learners. In a very careful study involving a task that required the resolution of a number of 'referential conflicts' (the subjects were given maps that differed in a number of ways), Yule and McDonald (1990) examined the effects of proficiency in mixed-level dyads, where in some interactions the sender of the information was of low proficiency and the receiver high proficiency (L>H) and in others the opposite (H>L). They found that the L>H interactions were at least twice as long as the H>L interactions. Furthermore, negotiated solutions to the referential problems were much more likely to take place in the L>H condition than in the H>L (a 67.5 per cent success rate as opposed to 17.5 per cent). Where mixed-ability pairings are involved, therefore, success (and perhaps also acquisition) is more likely if the lower-level learner is in charge of the key information that has to be communicated. Flanigan's (1991) study of pairs of non-native-speaker elementary school children lends further support to this hypothesis. In this study, the more linguistically competent children were asked to assist the less competent in how to use a computer in a graded reading and listening 'station'. Flannigan found that little negotiation of meaning took place, as the less proficient learners lacked the ability to respond. Also, although the more proficient children made use of the same discourse strategies as those observed in adult caretakers and teachers (i.e. repetitions, expansions, explanations, rephrased questions, and comprehension checks), they made no attempt to simplify their talk grammatically or lexically.

A growing number of studies have made use of the theoretical constructs and methodology of sociocultural theory to explore the acquisitional benefits of group interaction. (See, in particular, Storch 2002.) These were reviewed in the section on 'collaborative scaffolding' in Chapter 11 and so will not be considered in detail here. The key findings were that learners are capable of scaffolding one another, that structures produced collaboratively during group work are internalized so that they can be produced independently at a later time, and that adolescent and adult learners are able to engage in METATALK that facilitates task performance and attention to form.

Researchers and educators have noted a number of potential limitations of small group work. One concerns the ephemeral nature of spoken discourse. Wells (1999) pointed out that 'memory for the exact words spoken is extremely short and, without recourse to a definitive text of what is said, it is difficult to work systematically to improve it and the understanding that it embodies' (p. 115). In other words, in the case of language learning, learners may have difficulty engaging in the psycholinguistic processing necessary to turn input into INTAKE. Jessica Williams (1999) suggested, for example, that group work may not be conducive to students paying attention to form. She found that beginner and intermediate proficiency learners rarely focused on form while performing communicative tasks and when they did so it was only when the teacher was in attendance. Advanced level learners addressed form more frequently. However, the actual forms attended to by learners, irrespective of their proficiency, were lexical; there were very few occasions when they addressed grammatical problems. One way of enabling closer attention to grammatical form is when the group talk is centred on a written text as the outcome, as in many of Swain's studies (for example, Swain and Lapkin 2001b). (See Chapter 11.)

A second problem concerns the INTERLANGUAGE TALK that inevitably occurs in group work. Both Pica and Doughty (1985a) and Porter (1986) found that interlanguage talk is less grammatical than teacher talk. Thus, it is possible that exposure to incorrect peer input may lead to FOSSILIZATION. However, two of Porter's findings give reason to believe that this may not be the case. She reported that when learners corrected each other's errors, they did so wrongly only 0.3 per cent of the time and also that only 3 per cent of the errors the learners produced could be attributed to repetition of a fellow-learner's error. In general, therefore, learners do not appear to be unduly disadvantaged by exposure to deviant input from other learners.

A third problem concerns the lack of any sociolinguistic need to adjust one's speech to take account of social context in group work. Porter found that L2 speakers did not provide sociolinguistically appropriate input and suggests that learners may not be able to develop sociolinguistic competence from each other. This, however, may be a limitation not just of small group but of classroom interaction in general, as suggested by Ellis' (1992) study of two learners' requesting strategies. (See Chapter 5.) One solution to this problem may lie in electronically enabled interaction between L2 learners and native-speaking peers. Belz and Kinginger (2003) showed that American classroom learners of L2 German showed progression towards native-speaking norms in the use of 'du' and 'Sie' as a result of participating in such interaction with expert-speaking German peers. Such interaction has the advantage of being available to the learners in written form.

As Pica (1994a) noted, the effectiveness of group work depends very much on the specific context, with factors such as whether the group is monolingual or heterogeneous, the cultural background of the learners, and the nature of the classroom task influencing outcomes. Pica concluded that while group work definitely has a role in the classroom, it does not guarantee success in L2 learning.

One way of reconciling the potential advantages of group work with the possible problems lies in ensuring that learners engage cooperatively with each other in order to support each other's language learning. Naughton (2006) described a study in which the effects of training university learners of L2 English in cooperative strategies (the use of follow-up questions, requesting and giving clarification, repair by means of recasts, and requesting and giving help) were examined. Naughton reported that the cooperative strategy training had a positive effect on both overall participation (measured by the number of turns taken) and the students' use of interaction strategies (in particular the use of follow-up questions and repair) in subsequent group work.

Summary

Despite the commonly held belief among teachers that learner participation is important for language learning, SLA researchers have not been able to demonstrate a clear relationship between frequency of participation and L2 acquisition in either correlational or experimental studies. What may be more important than the sheer quantity of practice is the quality, in particular whether it ensures task-appropriate transfer. Researchers have examined a number of qualitative aspects of learners' contribution to classroom discourse—opportunities for learners to initiate discourse, questions, and repetition—and hypothesized that these will facilitate learning. There has also been extensive study of group work interactions from both an interactionist and sociocultural perspective. This has lent support to many of the claims regarding the advantages that group work holds. However, researchers have also noted a number of disadvantages. A crucial factor is likely to be the extent to which there is learner cooperation during group work, which has been shown to be trainable. There is now considerable evidence that the interactions that take place during group work facilitate language acquisition.

Tasks and interaction

The study of TASKS has proved to be one of the most productive seams of L2 classroom research. It has been motivated in part by proposals for 'task-based syllabuses' (see Long 1985b; Prabhu 1987; Long and Crookes 1992; Ellis 2003; Nunan 2004; Van den Branden 2006), which specify the content to be taught in terms of a series of tasks to be performed by the students, either with the teacher or in small group work. 'Task' has also figured as an important construct in SLA research, serving both as a device for delivering instructional treatment in experimental studies and for measuring the outcomes of this treatment. Thus, 'task' serves as a bridge between pedagogy and research (Pica 1997).

Various definitions of 'task' exist. (See Ellis 2003: 4; Van den Branden 2006: 3–8). However, the essential characteristics are as follows:

1 There is a primary focus on meaning (as opposed to form).
2 There is some kind of gap (information, opinion, or reasoning), which needs to be filled through performance of the task.
3 Learners need to use their own linguistic resources to perform the task.

4 There is a clearly defined communicative outcome other then the display of 'correct' language.

In these crucial respects, tasks differ from 'exercises'.[6] Tasks can involve any of the four language skills either in isolation or in various combinations. However, SLA researchers have been predominantly concerned with speaking tasks and these will be our focus here.

In Ellis (2003), I distinguished two kinds of tasks: unfocused and focused. Unfocused tasks may predispose learners to choose from a range of forms but they are not designed with the use of a specific form in mind. In contrast, focused tasks aim to induce learners to process, receptively or productively, some particular linguistic feature(s), such as a grammatical structure. A common type of focused task is what Loschky and Bley-Vroman (1983) called a 'structure based production task'.

Tasks, or rather the performance of them, create opportunities for learning, which can be assessed in relation to some theory of L2 acquisition. Thus, one of the goals of SLA research has been to identify the design features and methods of implementation that influence how tasks are performed and thereby, hypothetically, afford opportunities for learning. It is probably true that the bulk of the research to date has been undertaken with this general goal. Swan (2005) criticized SLA researchers and proponents of task-based language teaching for this 'legislation by hypothesis', arguing that what was needed were studies that demonstrated that learners actually learn the L2 when they perform tasks. In fact, there have been a number of such studies. In this section, we will consider the descriptive research that has examined the relationship between task features and language use. These divide fairly clearly into three groups: (1) tasks and the negotiation of meaning, (2) tasks and learner production, and (3) the co-construction of tasks through interaction. In the section that follows we will review studies that demonstrate that tasks can serve as a device for facilitating learning.

Tasks and the negotiation of meaning

As in much of the research considered in this chapter, researchers have drawn on both mainstream interactionist and cognitive theories of the kind reviewed in Chapters 6 and 9 and also sociocultural theory (see Chapter 11) to investigate and interpret the interactions that derive from tasks.

Long's Interaction Hypothesis (Long 1983b, 1996) has proved especially fruitful in motivating studies of tasks. The underlying assumption of research on tasks from this perspective is that 'it ought to be possible to build up a multidimensional classification, organizing tasks in terms of their potential for second language learning on the basis of psycholinguistically motivated dimensions' (Long and Crookes 1987). A number of task variables have been examined but we will focus on three main ones here; (1) required versus optional information exchange, (2) one-way versus two-way information exchange, (3) open versus closed tasks. (See Ellis (2003) and Ondarra (1997) for full reviews of the literature.)

As noted in the section on small-group work, Pica and Doughty (1985a, 1985b) found that small-group work in language classrooms only resulted in more negotiation work than teacher-fronted lessons when the task was of the required information type. Newton (1995) found almost double the quantity of negotiation in tasks where the information provided was split among the learners when compared to tasks where the information was shared. Foster (1998) reported that required information exchange tasks consistently elicited more negotiation and more MODIFIED OUTPUT than the optional information exchange tasks, especially when the students worked in pairs, although, in this study, neither type of task elicited much negotiation. The superiority of required information exchange tasks has been challenged. Nakahama, Tyler, and Van Lier (2001) found that although a required information exchange task resulted in more negotiation exchanges, these exchanges were rather mechanical, centring on lexical items. In contrast, the interactions derived from a conversation task, where there was no required information exchange, resulted in greater negotiation of global problems (for example, problems relating to anaphoric reference and interpretation of an entire utterance), significantly longer and more complex turns and wider use of discourse strategies (for example, paraphrase). The authors concluded that the conversational activity offered 'a larger range of opportunities for language use' (p. 401) than the information gap task.

A number of studies (Long 1980a; Doughty and Pica 1986; Newton 1991) examined the effects on interaction of tasks that involve a one-way exchange of information as opposed to those that require a two-way exchange. Examples of the former include giving instructions and telling a personal story, while an example of the latter is a jigsaw activity in which the participants each hold part of the information needed to complete the task. Long (1989) considered the results of these studies sufficiently robust to claim that 'two-way tasks produce more negotiation work and more useful negotiation work than one-way tasks' (1989: 13). However, other studies have failed to show that two-way tasks promote more negotiation than one-way tasks. Gass and Varonis (1985) compared the NNS–NNS interactions resulting from a 'describe and draw' task and a jigsaw listening task, which required participants to share information in order to work out who had committed a robbery. They found that more indicators of non-understanding occurred in the one-way task, although the difference was not significant. Jauregi (1990, reported in Ondarra 1997) also found that a one-way task (describe and draw) produced more negotiation work than a two-way task that involved talking about future plans.

Open tasks are those where the participants know there is no predetermined solution. Closed tasks are those that require students to reach a single, correct solution or one of a small finite set of solutions. Long (1989) argued that closed tasks are more likely to promote negotiation work than open tasks because they make it less likely that learners will give up when faced with a challenge. A number of other studies lend support to Long's claim (for example, Crookes and Rulon 1985; Berwick 1990; Newton 1991). Manheimer (1995) compared Spanish L2 learners' performance on an open task where students had to decide whose life should be saved from a crashing plane and a closed task involving the solution to a mystery murder, reporting that learners modified their output more in the closed task, which also produced greater sentence COMPLEXITY.

In Ellis (2003) I pointed out that one of the problems with the research reported above is that we have no idea how the task variables interact to influence negotiation of meaning. One study that has attempted to investigate the combined effect of design features is Hardy and Moore (2004). They examined two binary variables. In the case of 'structural task support', high support was defined as a high amount of linguistic information, a clear ordering of parts of the task, and a requirement to select a response, while low task support entailed little linguistic information, left open the sequence needed to achieve a solution, and imposed no need for learners to construct their own response. The other variable 'content familiarity' was operationalized in terms of the students' familiarity with the plot, characters, and cultural setting of the video material that comprised the input for the tasks. The results showed that low support resulted in more negotiation (broadly defined to include content as well as meaning) than high support. The ordering of the tasks was also a factor. When a task with low structural support was preceded by a task with high structural support, it led to more negotiation than in the reverse order. However, content familiarity had no effect on negotiation and there was also no evidence of any interaction between the two design variables. One of the points Hardy and Moore emphasized in discussing their results was that 'task affordances should not be conceptualized as fixed parameters with precalculated properties' but rather 'individuals' perception of affordances is itself a constructive process of meaning-making within a larger context' (p. 365), a view that we will explore more fully below.

Other studies of tasks in the interactionist tradition have focused on implementational variables, such as planning and participant role. Planning was considered in some depth in Chapter 10 and so we will concentrate on participant role here. In a laboratory study, Polio and Gass (1998) found that native speakers comprehended learners better when the learners were adept at providing the right information and the learners were allowed to 'lead' the interaction. Thus, the effectiveness of the one-way task used in this study depended on the extent to which the learners were able to take control of the discourse, bearing out the earlier conclusion regarding the importance of learner initiative. (See also the earlier account of Yule and McDonald 1990.) Other implementational variables that have been studied include task repetition (Yule, Powers and McDonald 1992), interlocutor familiarity (Plough and Gass 1993), and type of feedback, i.e. clarification requests as opposed to confirmation checks, (Pica, Holliday, Lewis, and Morganthaler 1989). These have been found to impact on both the frequency of negotiation sequences and modified output.

Tasks and L2 production

Researchers who have explored the relationship between task design and implementation variables have also drawn on cognitive theories of the kind described in Chapter 9. In particular, Skehan's (1998b) theory based on the distinction between exemplar-based and rule-based knowledge has informed a large number of studies. These have sought to show how tasks and the way they are performed influence the fluency, complexity, and accuracy of learners' L2 production. Table 15.7 summarizes the results of studies conducted by Skehan and Foster (for example, Foster and Skehan 1996; Skehan and Foster 1997, 1999) that investigated a number of different design features. These studies investigated such design variables as 'familiarity of information', the 'degree of structure' and the 'complexity of outcome'. They also considered implementational variables such as pre- and within-task planning and task rehearsal (i.e. repetition of a task) which were discussed in Chapter 10 (see in particular Table 10.3) and so will not be examined further here.

Task characteristic	**Accuracy**	**Complexity**	**Fluency**
Familiarity of information	No effect	No effect	Slightly greater
Dialogic versus monologic	Greater	Slightly greater	Lower
Degree of structure	No effect	No effect	Greater
Complexity of outcome	No effect	Greater	No effect
Transformations (i.e. whether the task requires learners to reproduce or transform information)	No effect	Planned condition leads to greater	No effect

Table 15.7 Effects of different task characteristics on L2 production (based on Skehan 2001)

The co-construction of tasks through interaction

Whereas interactionist and cognitive theories view tasks as devices that predispose learners to engage in interactions which are, therefore, to some extent predictable on the basis of the design features of the tasks and the methodological procedures for implementing them, sociocultural theory emphasizes that the activity that derives from a task is unstable, varying in accordance with the specific goals and motives of the participants. In other words, from the perspective of sociocultural theory there is no straightforward relationship between task-as-workplan and task-in-process. (See the discussion of the distinction between 'task' and 'activity' in Chapter 11.) This led Seedhouse (2005) to argue that researchers have erred in investigating the task-as-workplan and that the conceptual and methodological focus needs to switch to task-in-process. Such an approach acknowledges that the interaction that results from a task is 'dynamic, fluid, and locally managed on a turn-by-turn basis to a considerable extent' (p. 556). This being so, the appropriate methodology for investigating tasks is not the quantification of a priori constructs (as in the research based on Long's Interaction Hypothesis or Skehan's cognitive theory) but rather the emic perspective afforded by conversational analysis as this provides a tool for demonstrating how 'socially distributed cognition' arises from a task. The view of 'learning' that underlies this perspective is that of a competence that is co-constructed and embedded in interaction. A number of studies have explored tasks from this perspective. (See, in particular, the collection of papers in Hall and Verplaeste 2000.)

Using the techniques of conversational analysis, Mori (2002) examined how a 'zadankai' task (i.e. a task involving a discussion between small groups of learners of Japanese and native-speaker visitors to the classroom) panned out. She reported that what unfolded as the learners engaged in the discussions was not exactly what was intended by the task. The task-as-workplan required the learners to ask the native speaker questions and to comment on the replies and allow the native speaker to ask them questions. In actuality, in one group the task-in-process took the form of a structured interview, with the students functioning as the interviewer and only minimally acknowledging the native speaker's responses before moving on to the next question. Mori suggested that one reason for this might have been the pre-task planning that the students engaged in, which oriented them to the information transfer aspect of the task and inhibited attention to the moment-by-moment development of the talk. In other words, pre-task planning had a nugatory rather than beneficial effect on the way the task was performed, as it denied the students the opportunity to engage in authentic conversation.

Ko, Schallert, and Walters (2003) used sociocultural theory to investigate how a story-telling task created opportunities for 'scaffolding' that enabled adult ESL learners to elicit feedback that helped them to improve the quality of the stories when they retold them. In this task, each student told a story to two classmates and the teacher, engaged in negotiation-of-meaning exchanges with them about the story, and then retold the story to a group of other students. Out of the 21 students, 11 scored higher for the retold story than the original one, while 10 scored the same or lower. In other words, not all the students told better stories at the second attempt. Through detailed analyses of a number of these exchanges, Ko *et al.* showed that the teacher was a critical factor in explaining this finding; for example, whereas some teachers drew the storyteller's attention to places where the story lacked essential information, others did not. However, they found that the storytellers themselves played an even more important role in influencing the quality of the negotiation-of-meaning exchanges by their active response to the negotiation that transpired. Ko, Schallert, and Walters concluded that 'scaffolding' is very much a co-construction, with learners playing as important a role as the 'experts'.

Platt and Brooks (2002) investigated 'task engagement' (i.e. the attainment of intersubjectivity and control over a task) from a sociocultural perspective. Using microgenetic analysis, they traced a task activity from its origin to its end. They asked groups of students of L2 Spanish and Swahili to complete a jigsaw task. They showed how initial difficulty in understanding what was required of the task was resolved in a number of different ways—through the intervention of the researcher, the use of the L1, or through assistance from a task participant. Engagement was manifested in the participants arriving at procedural strategies that enabled them to accomplish the task by focusing on the content-relevant information. Platt and Brooks identified 'the moment of engagement' (p. 392) that motivated the learners to move through the complex task. They concluded that performing a task is a 'struggle' that can only be successfully managed when learners achieve control over the task and suggested that it is during the engagement period that 'transformation' (i.e. the movement from interpsychological to intrapsychological functioning) becomes evident.

These studies show how the emic perspective afforded by studies based on sociocultural theory and utilizing conversational analysis can enrich and help revise our understanding of constructs such as pre-task planning, negotiation of meaning, and task engagement. However, as I pointed out in Ellis (2000), although it is clearly necessary to recognize that task performances are always constructed rather than determined by task design features and methodological procedures, it is also the case that the task-as-workplan *will* predispose learners to behave in certain ways. The study of the relationship between tasks and interaction can benefit from both an etic and an emic approach, which therefore should be seen as complementary rather than oppositional.

Interaction and L2 learning

In this final section we will consider research that has sought to demonstrate how classroom communication results in learning. We will begin by considering to what extent successful L2 learning is possible in communicative classrooms (i.e. classrooms where the instruction is content- or task-based). We will then examine research that has drawn on the central theoretical construct of 'focus-on-form'. Our focus will still be on classroom input and interaction. Consideration of experimental studies that have examined the effect that particular kinds of instruction had on learning will be taken up in the next chapter.

Second language learning in communicative classrooms

A number of scholars have proposed that the most effective way of developing successful L2 competence in a classroom is to ensure that the learners have sufficient opportunities to participate in discourse directed at the exchange of information. (See Krashen 1982; Swain 1985; Prabhu 1987.) According to this view, the failure of many classroom learners derives from the lack of COMPREHENSIBLE INPUT and/or COMPREHENSIBLE OUTPUT. One way of investigating this claim is by studying the extent to which a communicative classroom, presumably rich in such acquisition-rich features, results in successful L2 learning.

There is now convincing evidence that learners can learn 'naturally' in a communicative classroom setting. Terrell, Gomez, and Mariscal (1980) showed that elementary learners of L2 Spanish can successfully acquire various question forms simply as a result of being exposed to questions in the input. Prabhu (1987) developed a programme known as the COMMUNICATIONAL TEACHING PROJECT (CTP), which had as its aim the development of linguistic competence through a task-based approach to language teaching. This project, which was conducted in a number of secondary schools in Bangalore and Madras with beginner learners of L2 English, was evaluated by Beretta and Davies (1985). Although not all the results showed an advantage for the project schools over the control schools, which were taught by means of the structural-oral-situational method, Davies and Beretta interpreted the results as 'being, on the whole, positive' and concluded that 'they provide tentative support for the CTP'. Finally, Lightbown (1992b) reported on a project in New Brunswick, in which Canadian French children in Grades 3–6 were taught English by listening to tapes and following the written text. Results at the end of the third year of the project showed that 'students in this program have succeeded in learning at least as much English as those whose learning had been guided by the teacher in a more traditional program' (1992: 362). They were as good even at speaking English. These studies, therefore, demonstrate that classrooms where the focus is placed on meaning rather than on form are effective in promoting L2 acquisition. However, it should be noted that in all these studies the learners were at an elementary level. Other studies suggest that such classrooms may not be so successful in promoting high levels of linguistic competence. Krashen (1982) claimed that immersion classrooms have succeeded in developing very high levels of L2 proficiency, but there is growing evidence that they are not quite as successful as Krashen claims. Researchers have for some time recognized that immersion learners generally fail to acquire certain grammatical distinctions. (See Chapter 7.) Other studies also suggest there may be limitations to what can be achieved in communicative classrooms. Spada and Lightbown (1989) found that an intensive ESL course (5 hours a day for 5 months), which was taught by means of communicative methods emphasizing tasks leading to natural interaction, produced little evidence of syntactic development. For example, the students were only 50 per cent accurate in their use of plural –s and only 20 per cent in the case of V + –ing. My study of the requests produced by two classroom learners (Ellis 1992; see Chapter 5) also suggested that the communicative classroom may not be well suited to the achievement of sociolinguistic competence. This is because 'the classroom constitutes an environment where the interactants achieve great familiarity with each other, removing the need for the careful face-work that results in the use of indirect request-types and extensive modification' (1992a: 20). Lightbown, Halter, White, and Horst (2002) reported a follow-up study to the New Brunswick comprehension-based programme first reported in Lightbown (1992; see above), looking at the same students when they had reached Grade 8 after six years of the programme. These students performed as well as the comparison groups on measures of comprehension and some measures of oral production measures but were inferior on measures of written production. The students in the regular ESL programme, for example, were more likely to mark verbs for past and were less likely to make errors like substituting 'his' for 'is'.

A somewhat different approach to investigating communicative classrooms involves the attempt to compare the L2 learning that takes place in classrooms that differ in a number of major ways. The advantage of this approach is that it serves to identify those characteristics of the classroom environment that are important for learning. Wong Fillmore (1982) distinguished two basic types of classroom organization in a longitudinal study of classroom ESL learners in a kindergarten setting: (1) teacher-directed classrooms, where interaction involved the teacher and the class, and (2) learner-centred organization, where interactions between teacher and individual students and between the learners themselves took place. The classrooms she investigated also differed with regard to the proportion of L2 learners and native-English-speaking children in them. Wong Fillmore found that these two factors interacted to influence L2 learning. Successful language learning occurred in classes that had a high proportion of L2 learners and were teacher-directed, and also in classes that were more mixed in composition (i.e. had more native-English-speaking children) and an open organization. Conversely, much less learning took place in mixed, teacher-directed classes and open classes with large numbers of L2 learners.

One interpretation of the research on communicative classrooms is as follows:

1 Giving beginner learners opportunities for meaningful communication in the classroom helps to develop communicative abilities and also results in initial linguistic abilities no worse than those developed through more traditional, form-focused approaches.
2 The extent to which meaning-focused classrooms are successful in promoting L2 acquisition depends on a number of micro factors such as the choice of participatory structure.

3 Overall, however, meaning-focused classroom settings may not be sufficient to ensure the development of high levels of linguistic and sociolinguistic competence, although they may be very successful in developing fluency and effective discourse skills.

The fact that communicating in a language does not guarantee full target-language competence accords with the arguments of Higgs and Clifford (1982) regarding the limitations of 'natural' learning.

Focus-on-form and acquisition

One reason why learners fail to achieve high levels of competence in communicative classrooms may be their failure to attend to form. That is, because the activities they engage in are meaning-focused, they do not notice features such as past tense markings or unusual word order, or have many opportunities for 'pushed output'. Such an interpretation is compatible with the NOTICING and OUTPUT HYPOTHESES, which we discussed in Chapter 6. This has led researchers to investigate 'focus-on-form' instruction. Long (1991: 45–6) provided the following definition:

> ... focus-on-form ... overtly draws students' attention to linguistic elements as they arise incidentally in lessons whose overriding focus is on meaning or communication.

However, there are problems with this definition. In fact, two main types of focus-on-form instruction can be distinguished—incidental and planned (Ellis 2001a). Incidental focus-on-form occurs when learners' attention is drawn to form while they are performing an unfocused task (i.e. the linguistic focus is not pre-determined). In this case, the focus-on-form is typically extensive (i.e. addresses a wide range of linguistic features). Planned focus-on-form requires a focused task and is intensive (i.e. it is concentrated on the linguistic feature(s) that is the target of the task). Focus-on-form has attracted considerable attention from researchers and teachers alike. (See, for example, the collections of papers in Doughty and Varela 1998 and in Fotos and Nassaji 2006.)

The theoretical rationale for focus-on-form is as follows:

1 To acquire the ability to use new linguistic forms communicatively, learners need the opportunity to engage in meaning-focused language use.
2 However, such opportunity will only guarantee full acquisition of the new linguistic forms if learners also have the opportunity to attend to form *while* engaged in meaning-focused language use. Long (1991) argued that only in this way can attention to form be made compatible with the immutable processes that characterize L2 acquisition and thereby overcome persistent developmental errors.
3 Given that learners have a limited capacity to process the second language (L2) and have difficulty in simultaneously attending to meaning and form they will prioritize meaning over form when performing a communicative activity (VanPatten 1990).

4 For this reason, it is necessary to find ways of drawing learners' attention to form *during* a communicative activity. As Doughty (2001) noted 'the factor that distinguishes focus-on-form from other pedagogical approaches is the requirement that focus-on-form involves learners briefly and perhaps simultaneously attending to form, meaning and use during one cognitive event' (p. 211).

Ellis, Basturkmen, and Loewen (2002) summarized the various options for inducing attention to form in the context of meaning-focused language use. (See Table 15.8.) Doughty and Williams (1998) offered a taxonomy of focus-on-form tasks and techniques based on whether they were unobtrusive (for example, RECASTS) or obtrusive (for example, CONSCIOUSNESS-RAISING TASKS).

Options	**Description**
A Reactive focus-on-form	The teacher or another student responds to an error that a student makes in the context of a communicative activity.
1 Negotiation	
a Conversational	The response to the error is triggered by a failure to understand what the student meant. It involves 'negotiation of meaning'.
b Didactic	The response occurs even though no breakdown in communication has taken place; it constitutes a 'time-out' from communicating. It involves 'negotiation of form'.
2 Feedback	
a Implicit feedback	The teacher or another student responds to a student's error without directly indicating an error has been made, e.g. by means of a recast.
b Explicit feedback	The teacher or another student responds to a student's error by directly indicating that an error has been made, e.g. by formally correcting the error or by using metalanguage to draw attention to it.
B Pre-emptive focus-on-form	The teacher or a student makes a linguistic form the topic of the discourse even though no error has been committed.
1 Student initiated	A student asks a question about a linguistic form.
2 Teacher-initiated	The teacher gives advice about a linguistic form he/she thinks might be problematic or asks the students a question about the form.

Table 15.8 Options for focus-on-form (Ellis, Basturkmen, and Loewen 2002: 429–30)

Incidental focus-on-form

Establishing whether the performance of unfocused tasks contributes to acquisition is problematic from a methodological standpoint. This is because it is not possible to pre-determine the linguistic features that learners might learn and thus no pre-testing is possible. Thus, experimental designs are precluded. Two approaches have resulted. One seeks to examine to what extent focus-on-form arises in the course of meaning-focused instruction and the extent to which it draws attention to problematic forms. The other approach is correlational; that is, it seeks to establish a relationship between the forms attended to in class and measures of learning.

Lightbown and Spada (1990) examined the effects of corrective feedback in the context of communicative language teaching. This study investigated a number of classrooms which were part of an intensive communicative ESL programme in Quebec. Lightbown and Spada found that, although the teaching was mainly communicative in focus, some of the teachers paid more attention to the students' formal errors than others. They found that the learners who received error correction achieved greater accuracy in the production of some structures (for example, the use of the correct 'There is ...' in place of the L1-induced error 'It has ...') but not of others (for example, adjectival placement). Lightbown (1992a) interpreted this result as follows:

> In the 'successful' intensive programme class, the situations in which the teacher drew students' attention to their be/have error were precisely those situations in which the students knew what they wanted to say and the teacher's interventions made clear to them that there was a particular way to say it.
> (p. 209)

Pica (2002) examined the extent to which learners and their teachers modified the interaction that arose in content-based instruction in order to attend to developmentally difficult form-meaning relationships (for example, English articles). Data were collected over a seven-week period from teacher-led discussions about the cultural, thematic, or story content of a literary text or film. These discussions took place in a university-based English language institute. The analysis of the data focused on negotiation of meaning sequences and instances of form-focused intervention (corresponding broadly to the pre-emptive and reactive focus-on-form options described in Table 15.8). Pica reported very little attention to form. She commented 'one of the most striking findings of the study was that the majority of student non-target utterances went unaddressed in any way' (p. 9). One reason for this was that the students' utterances, although often ungrammatical, did not require any adjustment in order to be understood. In other words, the interesting and meaningful content that comprised these lessons drew learners' attention from the need to attend to form. This study, then, provides an explanation for why learners do not appear to achieve advanced levels of linguistic competence in communicative classrooms. Pica (2005) suggested that one way of addressing this is to develop focused tasks (especially information-gap tasks) that direct learners' attention to form and described a number of such tasks and procedures for implementing them in the classroom.

Pica's research focused on an instructional context that encouraged learners to focus on meaning rather than form. Ellis, Basturkmen, and Loewen's (2001) study examined incidental focus-on-form in classrooms in private language schools involving learners of lower proficiency than Pica's participants. This study found that attention to form in teacher-directed, task-based lessons was surprisingly frequent, with a form-focused episode of one kind or another occurring every 1.6 minutes. It also showed a very high level of student uptake in these episodes (73.9 per cent) with the large majority of these being successful (for example, demonstrating repair of an initial error). Clearly, there are contextual factors at work that influence the extent to which focus-on-form occurs.

The other studies we will consider have attempted to demonstrate a relationship between attention to form and learning. One approach has been to ask classroom learners to complete an 'uptake chart' by recording the items that they think they noticed and think they learnt during a particular lesson. (It should be noted that this is a different use of the term 'uptake' from the earlier use of this term in the chapter, where 'uptake' referred to the student move following corrective feedback). After the lesson has been recorded and transcribed, the researcher identifies where the uptaken items occurred during the lesson. This provides a means for exploring the interactional conditions that might have caused learners to uptake items. Studies that have adopted this approach are Slimani (1989) and Ellis (1995b). We considered Slimani's study earlier in this chapter. Its key finding was that items 'topicalized' by other students—rather than by the teacher—were most likely to figure as 'uptake'. Ellis examined the 'uptake' reported by groups of Japanese learners of L2 English who performed a listen-and-do task that exposed them to three kinds of input: baseline, premodified, and interactionally modified. The learners reported learning a mean of 2.71, 3.88, and 5.89 words respectively in these input conditions. Thus, this study lends apparent support to the claims regarding the value of interactionally modified input. However, as Ellis pointed out, learners were exposed to considerably more input in the interactionally modified condition than in the other conditions simply as a result of the increased time it took to complete the task in this condition.

Another approach has been to identify LANGUAGE-RELATED EPISODES that arise when learners engage with linguistic problems while performing a task. Language-related episodes are defined as 'any part of a dialogue where students talk about language they are producing, question their language use, or other- or self-correct their language production' (Swain and Lapkin 2001b: 104). Researchers have investigated the factors that result in such episodes when learners are performing tasks. Leeser (2004), for example, found that learner proficiency was a factor; the higher the proficiency of the dyads completing a dictogloss task, the more they attended to form, the more likely they were to attend to grammar rather than vocabulary, and the more likely they were to solve their linguistic problems correctly. Such studies, however, do not demonstrate that attending to form during task-based interaction actually results in acquisition—only that they engage in behaviours likely to do so. However, other studies have attempted to demonstrate that when learners solve language-related episodes successfully, acquisition occurs. These studies administered tailor-made tests directed at the problems the learners experienced. The strength of this approach is that it focuses on identifiable gaps in learners' L2 competence and provides measures of acquisition that are separate from the interactional work that the learners have done to try to fill these gaps. Swain and her co-researchers (for example, Swain 1998; Swain and Lapkin 1998) carried out a number of studies using this methodology. We will consider one here. Swain and Lapkin (2001b) asked Grade 8 mixed-ability French immersion students to complete two tasks in pairs—a jigsaw task and a dictogloss task—both of which involved producing narratives. Language-related episodes were identified in the dyadic interactions. Swain and Lapkin then documented a number of episodes where the learners successfully addressed a grammatical problem and then produced the problematic form correctly in the tailor-made test administered two weeks later.

Loewen (2005) adopted a similar approach. He recorded teacher-led task-based lessons involving adult ESL learners and then identified what Ellis, Basturkmen, and Loewen (2001) called 'form-focused episodes' in the transcripts of the lessons. Form-focused episodes (FFEs) are very similar to 'language related episodes' except that they include occasions when the teacher directed attention to form either pre-emptively or reactively. The FFEs were then coded for a number of characteristics—for example, uptake, successful uptake (i.e. repair), complexity (i.e. length of episode), and source (i.e. whether the episode was triggered by a communication breakdown or by the desire to attend to form for its own sake). Tailor-made tests were administered one or two days after the lessons or two weeks later. These were of three kinds—'suppliance' (i.e. testing knowledge of lexical items), 'correction' (i.e. correcting grammatical errors in sentences) and 'pronunciation' (i.e. pronouncing words written on cards). The learners' responses were scored as correct, partially correct, or incorrect. Out of the 473 FFEs tested, 62.4 per cent were either correct or partially correct in the immediate tests and 49.1 per cent in the delayed tests. A logistic regression analysis showed that both uptake and successful uptake (i.e. uptake that repaired the original error) predicted the scores for the correction and suppliance tests, lending credence to the claim that uptake has a role to play in language acquisition. In the case of the pronunciation tests the predictor variables were complexity (short, simple FFEs), source (i.e. the FFE centred around a communication breakdown), and successful uptake. Loewen noted that these results suggest that different types of focus-on-form may be needed to treat different aspects of language. In a subsequent article, Loewen (2006) extended the analysis of his data to investigate the extent to which the learners used the items targeted in the FFEs in subsequent classroom discourse, which might be considered another measure of acquisition. He reported that 20 per cent of the total forms targeted occurred subsequently in spontaneous communication. He also found that the accuracy of these forms in classroom use was greater after the FFE than before, suggesting the focus-on-form had had some effect.

Planned focus-on-form

Planned focus-on-form is much easier to research because it is possible to adopt a standard experimental design. The procedure adopted has been to identify a target linguistic feature that is known to be problematic to a group of learners, administer a pre-test measuring learners' knowledge of this feature, have the learners perform a focused task during which attention is drawn to the target feature (the instructional treatment), and then administer an immediate and delayed post-test. The learners' performance on the post-tests is then compared to that of learners in a control group. Much of the research has focused on the effects of reactive focus-on-form (i.e. corrective feedback). As it constitutes a clear example of form-focused instruction, it will be considered in detail in the following chapter.

A number of studies have examined whether focused tasks do result in learners producing the language feature that has been targeted. In a key article, Loschky and Bley-Vroman (1993) distinguished three ways in which a 'structure-based production task' can be designed to incorporate a specific target language feature. The first is 'task-naturalness'. In this case, the target structure may not be necessary for completion of the task but nevertheless can be expected to arise naturally and frequently in performing the task. The second way is in terms of 'task-utility'. By this Loschky and Bley-Vroman mean that even though a targeted feature is not essential for completing the task it is very 'useful'. The third way of designing a focused task is to try to ensure the 'task-essentialness' of the targeted feature. This requires that learners *must* use the feature in order to complete the task successfully—if they fail to use it they will not be able to achieve a satisfactory outcome. However, the examples Loschky and Bley-Vroman gave are all of comprehension rather than production tasks. They acknowledged that it may be impossible to design tasks that make the production of the target feature essential and that, in fact, task-essentialness can only be achieved by receptive tasks.

In Ellis (2003), I reviewed a number of studies that utilized focused tasks and reached the following conclusions. First, it is possible to design tasks that successfully target the use of specific grammatical structures. Second, it seems to be easier to elicit some features than others. Eliciting the use of modals or the use of question forms, for example, is easier than eliciting noun phrases with multiple attributive adjectives (for example, 'a small, red house'). Third, there is likely to be individual learner variation. Whereas some learners use the structure that has been targeted other learners do not. This lends support to Loschky and Bley-Vroman's claim that whether a task is successful in eliciting use of the target structure will depend on the learner's stage of development.

Fourth, there is evidence that when performing focused tasks, learners treat them as opportunities for communicating rather than for learning. Thus, any learning that does occur as a result of performing a structure-based task is likely to be incidental.

Final comment

In this section we have examined studies which suggest that, in some cases at least, communicative classrooms may not lead to high levels of linguistic competence (although they certainly do produce learners capable of fluent and confident communication). We have seen that one reason for this is that learners in these classrooms may have only limited opportunities to focus-on-form. We then considered a number of studies that have examined whether attention to form results in language learning. We have seen that there is now substantial evidence that when learners' attention is directed at linguistic forms and the meanings they encode—in the context of meaning-focused activities—learning takes place. Sheen (2003) criticized SLA researchers for advocating focus-on-form as a pedagogic strategy on the grounds that there is a lack of empirical evidence to demonstrate its effectiveness for learning. He is clearly wrong. (See also the section on corrective feedback in the following chapter.)

Conclusion

The research that we have reviewed in this chapter attests to the intense interest that exists in the interactional 'life' of L2 classrooms. Its achievements are clear. They include (1) a demonstration of the importance of balancing 'external' accounts of language pedagogy of the kind found in methodology handbooks with 'internal' accounts of what actually happens inside the classroom; (2) the availability of a substantial body of descriptive information about specific interactional behaviours (for example, regarding teacher questions, error treatment, learner initiative, and focus-on-form); (3) a developing understanding of how specific variables (for example, the learners' proficiency and the participatory pattern) affect interaction; (4) useful information about how tasks can be designed and implemented to construct sites for language learning; (5) insights into how attention to form in the context of meaning-focused interaction takes place and how it can assist learning; and (6) the availability of a broad set of tools for examining classroom interaction that can be used not only for formal research purposes but also in teacher education and by teachers who wish to join in what Allwright (1988) called 'the research enterprise'.

However, many of the weaknesses that Long (1990b) identified and gave as reasons why the findings are not yet ready to be passed on to teachers are still apparent: (1) the studies have generally been small scale, (2) they have tended to be short term with the result that little is known about the long-term effects of specific classroom behaviours, (3) the findings have tended to be partial or fragmented in that they have focused on isolated aspects of classroom life, and (4) many of the studies are methodologically flawed (i.e. the analyses have not been tested for reliability or for statistical significance).

The bulk of the work has been descriptive. It has documented how teachers and learners interact in a language classroom. How useful this is in accounting for acquisition remains a matter of some controversy. As Gass (2004) pointed out in her response to a series of articles examining classroom talk from a CA perspective published in *The Modern Language Journal* Volume 88/4, the key issue is whether such research documents learning or merely provides a detailed description of classroom talk. This is precisely the issue we considered in Chapter 7 when we examined the claims and counter-claims emanating from social accounts of language learning (cf. Firth and Wagner 1997 and Long 1998). Here, following Markee and Kasper (2004), we can distinguish two different positions. The weak position is that interaction constitutes a site for learning—for example, through learner participation and initiation. The strong position, reflecting sociocultural theory, is that learning is actually evident in the interactions that take place. In addressing the weak position, Gass noted that there is the problem of deciding what interactional environments are conducive to learning if there is no documentation of the learning that takes place in them. She then queried the strong position by asking whether simply documenting the 'process of acquisition' in terms of learners' participation in interaction is theoretically compelling if no link is made with the psycholinguistic and linguistic processes involved in learning. However, researchers in this tradition emphasize the importance of rich, emic accounts of classroom interaction as a means of documenting 'learning in process' and point to the limitations of research that views learning simply as a 'product'. There is no easy resolution to this controversy and it is likely to continue for the foreseeable future. In this chapter, I have tried to represent both positions.

Notes

1 What distinguishes these interaction analysis schedules from the earlier ones is the attempt to provide a comprehensive rather than selective account of classroom discourse. Not surprisingly, therefore, they require the analyst to work with recorded lessons rather than through observation of classroom events in real time.

2 Mitchell, Parkinson, and Johnstone (1981) described another very comprehensive observational schedule which they used in a series of studies of foreign language classrooms in Scotland. Four basic dimensions were identified: (1) topic of discourse, (2) language activity, (3) pupil mode of involvement, and (4) class organization.

3 Chaudron (1988) cited one study (by Bialystok, Fröhlich, and Howard 1978) which showed teachers preferring general information questions,

which Chaudron considered 'potentially referential'. However, general information questions can also be of the display/closed types. It is a mistake, therefore, to associate referential/open questions with information exchange and display/closed questions with a focus on language form.

4 As Chaudron (1988) pointed out, there are methodological problems with Seliger's study which make the results he obtained very questionable. For example, it is based on only six learners selected from a group of twelve learners, and misuses correlational statistics.

5 McDonough's (2006) study is a good example of the kind of repetition Skehan had in mind. In a laboratory study she used a technique called 'confederate priming', which involved the learner repeating a confederate's picture description before describing their own picture. McDonough showed that this had a beneficial effect on the acquisition of dative constructions with 'to' (for example, 'The man takes the doll to his friend'). However, comprehension primes where the learners just listened to the confederate's description without repeating worked just as well.

6 It should be noted that definitions of 'tasks' differ considerably. Breen's (1989) definition incorporates both 'a brief practice exercise' and 'a more complex workplan that requires spontaneous communication of meaning'. Many studies of tasks have adopted Breen's wider definition.

16

Form-focused instruction and second language acquisition

Introduction

Two kinds of instructional intervention in language learning can be distinguished: indirect and direct. In R. Ellis (2005c), I defined indirect intervention as instruction that aimed at creating the conditions for learners to learn experientially through learning how to communicate in the L2, and noted that this can be achieved by means of a task-based curriculum. In direct intervention, the instruction specifies what it is that the learners will learn and when they will learn it. That is, it is based on a prior specification of the language forms and/or functions and their linguistic realizations to be taught. Direct intervention, then, is based on what R. White (1988) referred to as a Type A Curriculum—that is, a curriculum that is synthetic rather than analytic and is accuracy rather then fluency oriented. It is aimed at 'skill-getting' and constitutes 'an investment for future use' (Widdowson 1989). The content of a Type A Curriculum can be specified either in linguistic terms (i.e. as a list of phonological, lexical, or grammatical items to be taught) or in notional/functional terms and their linguistic realizations (as in the Common European Framework of Reference for Languages, Council of Europe (2001)). Our concern in this chapter is with instruction as direct intervention—FORM-FOCUSED INSTRUCTION (FFI). There is now a substantial literature in SLA addressing the effects of FFI in all these aspects of language. However, for reasons of space we will only consider studies that have investigated grammar and L2 pragmatics.

The review of the FFI literature presented in this chapter is of the traditional kind (as, indeed, the reviews of SLA research presented in other chapters have been). That is, my goal is an integrative and narrative review of the empirical and theoretical research that has investigated FFI. It should be noted, however, that other approaches to reviewing the FFI literature are becoming common, in particular the kind of research synthesis conducted by means of meta-analysis of quantitative studies. I will draw on the results of a number of meta-analytic studies in my own review.

I will first consider the methodology of form-focused instruction studies. I will then briefly describe a number of different theoretical positions relating to the role of FFI in L2 acquisition. The review of FFI studies will begin with an examination of the COMPARATIVE METHOD STUDIES. This is followed by an account of early FFI research that sought to investigate the effects of form-focused instruction by comparing learners in naturalistic and instructed situations, by examining whether instruction could change the natural ORDER/SEQUENCE OF ACQUISITION, and by determining whether the effects of form-focused instruction are durable. In the following two sections I will examine research that has investigated the relative effect of different types of form-focused instruction and (a key issue) whether FFI leads to the development of implicit knowledge. In all of these sections I will be primarily concerned with the effects of FFI on the acquisition of L2 grammar. The last two sections will consider research that has investigated the effects of FFI on learners' L2 PRAGMATIC COMPETENCE and the role of mediating factors such as LANGUAGE-LEARNING APTITUDE and MOTIVATION on the effects of FFI.

Methodology of FFI studies

Whereas most of the studies we considered in Chapter 15 were descriptive and ethnographic in nature, the studies to be examined in this chapter are largely experimental in design. A true experiment requires: (1) random sampling from a well-defined population, (2) random distribution of participants into groups, and (3) a control group. In fact, in FFI research (1) and (2) have rarely been achieved as researchers have usually had to use intact classes. For this reason, the studies we will consider are best described as quasi-experimental. Key features of such studies are that they include a pre-test (essential if intact classes are used in order to ensure that the groups are equivalent at the beginning of the study) and both an immediate and delayed post-test in order to establish whether any immediate effects of the instruction are durable and also whether the effects only become evident after a period of time. Also, FFI studies should include a control group and, while some have, others have just included a comparison group.

Two methodological issues are of special importance in the design of FFI studies: (1) the choice of linguistic target and (2) the design of the instruments for measuring learning.

Choice of linguistic target

The key criterion in selecting the linguistic target is problematicity (i.e. the feature chosen should constitute a learning problem). Problematicity can be determined in different ways. These are summarized in Table 16.1 and discussed below.

Method	Comment
1 Remedial	Choice of target feature is based on previous empirical research which demonstrates that learners have difficulty in acquiring the feature.
2 Grammatical complexity	Choice is based on either some a priori notion of grammatical complexity or on expert's assessment of what constitutes an easy/hard feature to learn.
3 Acquisition sequences	Choice is based on an attested acquisition sequence, which allows researchers to define acquisition in terms of movement through the sequence.
4 Linguistic theory (e.g. the parameter-setting model of UG)	Choice is based on some linguistic theory that predicts that a given grammatical feature will be difficult to learn.
5 Psycholinguistic theory (e.g. VanPatten's input processing principles)	Choice is based on a theory of input (or output) processing that predicts that a given grammatical feature will be difficult to learn.

Table 16.1 Determining problematicity in the choice of target feature (from Ellis 2006a)

In some studies, the choice of the target feature is based on previous empirical findings that have demonstrated the feature is problematic to learners. In Harley's (1989) study, for example, the French *passé composé* and *imparfait* were selected because earlier studies of immersion learners had shown that even after several years of content-based instruction, anglophone learners of L2 French were consistently failing to use these tenses accurately.

Problematicity has also been defined in terms of grammatical complexity. The assumption here is that a feature that is grammatically complex can be predicted to be difficult to learn. There are, however, considerable problems with this approach, given that there is no convincing linguistic theory of grammatical complexity. DeKeyser's (1995) approach was to define complexity in terms of whether a specific grammatical rule was categorical or prototypical (i.e. whether a rule applied invariably or whether it applied probabilistically due to allomorphic variation). Robinson's (1996b) approach was to elicit the judgements of experts (experienced L2 teachers) as to whether listed grammatical features were 'simple' or 'complex'. Ultimately, however, whether a particular linguistic feature is easy or difficult is relative to the learner's level of proficiency (and the learner's L1), so it is necessary to consider what is easy/hard for the particular learners participating in the study. Answering this question requires knowledge of the learners' stage of development and also some means of determining what is easy/hard at different stages.

It is for this reason that a number of researchers have sought to base their selection on what is currently known about acquisition sequences. Mackey

(1999) based her choice of English question forms on the well-established sequence of development of this feature. (See Chapter 3 and Pienemann, Johnston, and Brindley 1988.) She identified five developmental stages for questions, giving examples of specific interrogative forms for each stage. She then undertook to identify which stage each learner was at prior to the instructional treatment and thus was able to determine the effects of the treatment in terms of whether individual learners made any movement through the sequence. A similar approach was adopted by Spada and Lightbown (1999). In these studies, then, the choice of target feature was largely dictated by the availability of robust information about developmental sequences. Unfortunately, however, similar information is not available for many other features.

Other researchers have selected their target features in accordance with a theoretical account of L2 acquisition. Trahey and White's (1993) study was designed to investigate whether pre-emption operates in L2 acquisition, as it is claimed to do in L1 acquisition. That is, they wanted to examine whether positive L2 input was sufficient to force parameter setting. Thus, they needed a target feature that would enable them to test this. The parameter they choose was Agreement (Agr), where there are differences between English and French. (See Chapter 12.) VanPatten (1996) drew on a psycholinguistic account of input-processing (see Chapter 9) to identify target features for study.

The measurement of learning in FFI studies

In order to measure a construct it is necessary to define it carefully. Bialystok and Sharwood Smith (1985) distinguished two senses of acquisition: (1) the internalization of completely new forms and (2) increased control over forms that have already been partially acquired. There is also a third sense: (3) progress along a sequence of acquisition (i.e. movement from an early to later stage of development in an attested sequence). This third sense of conceptualizing acquisition is important because it avoids the comparative fallacy (Bley-Vroman 1983); that is, it avoids the need to base measurement on target language norms. Table 16.2 summarizes the methods of measurement associated with these definitions.

Researchers have differed in how they have defined and therefore measured the acquisition of 'new' forms. Meisel *et al.* (1981) proposed 'emergence'—the first appearance of the form in a learner's spontaneous language production. The problem here is that a form may first appear in a FORMULAIC SEQUENCE and thus not be representative of true emergence. This problem could be overcome if reliable procedures for distinguishing formulaic and creative language use were available. However, as we noted in Chapter 3, they are not. Mackey (1999) imposed a more stringent criterion—the presence of at least two examples of a structure in two different post-tests. In effect, she redefined 'emergence' as 'sustained development'.

Most studies have measured acquisition in terms of increased control over the target form. As Norris and Ortega (2003) noted, how such 'control' is operationalized depends on the theoretical framework of the study. They commented:

> Generative linguistic studies of SLA are likely to rely almost exclusively on the outcomes of GRAMMATICALITY JUDGEMENT tasks of various kinds, where *acquired* means native like levels of rejection of illegal exemplars of the target grammar ... Interactionist SLA researchers maintain that acquisition of L2 forms cannot be demonstrated until such forms are productively used in a variety of contexts in spontaneous performance; a multiplicity of performance data is therefore required to produce a complete picture of language development ... *Acquired* for emergentists, means fast, accurate, and effortless performance attained along attested learning curves that reflect non-linear, exemplar-driven learning.
> (pp. 727–8)

However, what is common to studies in all three paradigms is a concern for accuracy. That is, instruction is said to have had an effect if learners demonstrate a statistically significant gain in accuracy over time (for example, from pre-test to post-test). A variety of instruments have been used to measure accuracy. Norris and Ortega (2000) distinguished four types: (1) metalinguistic judgements (i.e. learners evaluate the appropriateness or grammaticality of L2 target structures presented in a series of isolated sentences), (2) selected response (i.e. learners choose the correct response from a range of alternatives, as in multiple choice tests), (3) constrained constructed response (i.e. learners produce the target form within a highly controlled linguistic context, as in fill-in-the-gap tests), and (4) free constructed response (i.e. learners produce the target form in a task that involves meaningful communication). Doughty (2004) provided a useful list of specific measures for each of Norris and Ortega's four types.

What is lacking in many studies that use these measures is any consideration of the construct validity of the instruments used (Douglas 2001). That is, the studies do not specify what their measuring instruments are actually measuring. A key issue is whether the instruments measure IMPLICIT or EXPLICIT KNOWLEDGE. (See Ellis 2005b.) If acquisition is to be characterized in terms of gains in implicit knowledge—the position adopted by all three of Norris and Ortega's theoretical paradigms—then clearly, researchers need to be confident that they are indeed measuring this type of knowledge. As Doughty (2003a) rightly pointed out there has been a notable bias in favour of testing explicit knowledge.

Studies that have measured progress along an acquisition sequence have typically been conducted within the interactionist paradigm and have involved the collection of samples of learner language by means of tasks that elicit communicative language use (i.e. free constructed responses). These samples are then submitted to what Ellis and Barkhuizen (2005) called FREQUENCY ANALYSIS and Doughty and Varela (1998) called INTERLANGUAGE ANALYSIS. These involve identifying the different devices that a learner uses to perform the target feature and then calculating the frequency with which each device is used at different points in time (i.e. in the pre-test and post-tests). Stages of acquisition are determined by identifying which device is dominant at different points in time. Acquisition is said to have taken place if there is clear evidence that learners have shifted from the use of one device to another as a result of the instruction. For example, Doughty and Varela distinguished between (1) verbs with no past tense marking in obligatory contexts (for example, 'take'), (2) verbs that were marked for past tense but in non-target-like ways (for example, 'toke') and (3) verbs that were marked for past tense in accordance with target language norms (for example, 'took'). They considered progress from (1) to (2) as evidence of acquisition as well as progress from (1) or (2) to (3). Relatively few studies have measured acquisition in this way.

Definition of acquisition	**Method of measurement**	**Instruments**
Internalization of a new linguistic feature	The presence of at least two exemplars of a structure that was not evident in the pre-test in two consecutive post-tests. This method requires production data.	The data for analysis can be collected by a variety of means but commonly a communicative task is chosen.
Increased control over use of a linguistic feature	Increased control is measured by means of a gain in accuracy from pre-test to post-test. This method employs both comprehension and production data.	A variety of instruments involving: 1 metalinguistic judgement, 2 selected response, 3 constrained selected, response, 4 free constructed response.
Progress along an acquisition sequence	Progress is measured in terms of changes in the frequency with which learners produce different constructions for performing the target variable. This method requires production data.	A communicative task that elicits a free constructed response.

Table 16.2 Methods of defining and measuring acquisition

Another important issue concerning the measurement of learning in FFI studies is the timing of the measurement. Early FFI studies typically measured learning only once, immediately following the completion of the instruction. Later studies, however, included a delayed post-test administered up to a whole year after the period of instruction. Delayed post-tests are now considered essential for two reasons. First, they enable the research to establish whether the effects of the instruction are durable or short-lived. Second, they show whether the effects of the instruction do not emerge immediately but only after a further period of time has elapsed. The ideal, however, is 'process testing' (i.e. a whole series of tests) as only this is capable of showing the accumulated effect of instruction on developmental transitions over time.

Theoretical positions

One of the main issues in language pedagogy is what Stern (1983) called the 'code-communication dilemma'. There are advocates of what Widdowson (1984) referred to as 'pure education ... and its associated permissive pedagogy of non-intervention' (for example, Krashen 1981). There are also those who argue that while instruction may not be necessary for L2 acquisition, it does help learners to acquire more quickly (Ellis 1993). Finally, there are a number of scholars who maintain that for some aspects of language at least, formal instruction is necessary (for example, L. White 1989a). We will briefly consider each of these theoretical positions.

The 'zero option'

The zero option advocates the abandonment of formal instruction. As a result of early work in L2 acquisition which provided evidence of a 'natural' route of development (see Chapter 3), a number of researchers (for example, Dulay and Burt 1973; Krashen 1982) and also educationalists (for example, Newmark 1966; Corder 1976; Terrell 1977; Prabhu 1987) proposed that classroom language learning will proceed more effectively if language learners are allowed to construct their interlanguages 'naturally', in the same way as they would if they were learning grammar through the process of learning how to communicate. Prabhu, for instance, argued:

> ... the development of competence in a second language requires not systematization of language inputs or maximization of planned practice, but rather the creation of conditions in which learners engage in an effort to cope with communication.
> (1987: 1)

The COMMUNICATIONAL TEACHING PROJECT in southern India, under Prabhu's leadership, sought to demonstrate that 'form can best be learnt when the learner's attention is focused on meaning' (Beretta 1989: 233). It should be noted, however, that Prabhu did not actually claim that grammar cannot be learnt through formal instruction, only that learning it through communication is more effective.

In contrast, Krashen (1982) argued that grammatical competence cannot be taught. His position, which might be referred to as a NON-INTERFACE HYPOTHESIS,[1] is that LEARNING does not become ACQUISITION. (See Chapter 9.) Formal instruction, therefore, is rejected because it does not contribute to the development of the kind of implicit knowledge needed for normal communication. No matter how much the learner practises, explicit knowledge cannot be converted into implicit knowledge, a view also espoused by Paradis (2004). Krashen did accept, however, that formal instruction can contribute to the learning of explicit knowledge,[2] although he saw this as of limited use because only rules that are formally simple and deal with meanings that are easy to explain can be 'learnt'. Most rules have to be 'acquired'. Krashen also claimed that explicit knowledge is of limited value because it can only be used in MONITORING when the learner is focused on form and has sufficient time.

The zero position, as advocated by Krashen and Prabhu, entails not only a rejection of planned intervention by means of the presentation and practice of different items and rules but also of unplanned intervention in the form of error correction. Krashen (1982: 74) referred to error correction as a 'serious mistake' and argued that it should be limited to rules that can be 'learnt'. He claimed that it puts students on the defensive and encourages them to avoid using difficult constructions. Also, it is likely to disrupt the all-important focus on communication. However, negative feedback in the form of communicative responses to learners' efforts to convey messages—of the kind found in caretaker and foreigner talk (see Chapter 6)—is permitted. Thus, although systematic correction is prohibited, incidental feedback is allowed. Beretta (1989), in research based on classrooms in the Communicational Teaching Project, demonstrated that such a distinction is pedagogically operational.

Instruction as facilitation

The essential claim of the facilitative position is that although formal instruction is not necessary to acquire an L2, it helps learning, in particular by speeding up the process of 'natural' acquisition. There are, in fact, several different versions of the facilitative position. One is the INTERFACE HYPOTHESIS—the claim that by practising specific structures learners can 'control' them i.e. that explicit knowledge gradually becomes implicit (DeKeyser 1998). The second is the VARIABILITY HYPOTHESIS, according to which instruction can directly affect the learners' ability to perform structures in some kinds of use but not in others. The third, associated in particular with Pienemann (1985), is the TEACHABILITY HYPOTHESIS. The fourth is that formal instruction helps to make the internalization of rules easier in the long term by helping learners to notice them. We can refer to this as the WEAK INTERFACE HYPOTHESIS.

The Interface Hypothesis

According to the Interface Hypothesis, instruction facilitates acquisition by (1) supplying learners with conscious rules, and (2) providing practice to enable them to convert this conscious, 'controlled' knowledge into 'automatic' knowledge. Sharwood Smith (1981) built on the work of Bialystok and McLaughlin (see Chapter 9) in order to develop a full interface model. He claimed that 'it is quite clear and uncontroversial to say that most spontaneous performance is attained by dint of practice' (1981: 166). DeKeyser (1998) made a similar claim, drawing on skill-building theory; DECLARATIVE KNOWLEDGE is converted into PROCEDURAL KNOWLEDGE by means of practice that involves the learner in communicative behaviour.

The Variability Hypothesis

The Variability Hypothesis differs from the interface hypothesis in one major respect: it claims that teaching learners new structures will affect their *careful style* but not their *vernacular style*. (See Chapter 4 for an account of the STYLISTIC CONTINUUM and Chapter 9 for an account of the VARIABLE COMPETENCE MODEL.) Thus, its effects will be evident when learners are performing in planned language use but not in unplanned language use. In my earlier publications (for example, Ellis 1987c), I claimed that the explanation for this lies in the relationship between different types of classroom interaction and the learner's variable interlanguage system:

> Participation in the kind of planned discourse that results from teacher-directed language drills leads to the acquisition of target language norms in the learner's careful style ... Participation in the more freely-structured discourse that results from unfocused activities requires the performance of a greater range of speech acts and induces the NEGOTIATION OF MEANING required for the development of the vernacular style. (1987c: 191–2)

In addition to the direct effect that FFI has on learners' careful styles, it can have an indirect effect on their vernacular styles. Tarone (1983) suggested that there is movement along the stylistic continuum over time, while Dickerson (1974, cited in Tarone 1982) claimed that the continued advancement in the careful style may have a 'pull effect' on the vernacular style. In other words, forms that enter a learner's interlanguage in the careful style will gradually become available for use in unplanned discourse.

The Teachability Hypothesis

The third version of the facilitative position—the Teachability Hypothesis—has a considerable history (see Nickel 1973; Bailey, Madden, and Krashen 1974; Valdman 1978) but by far the most detailed proposal came from Pienemann (1985). His teachability hypothesis, based on his views about processability (see Chapter 9), 'predicts that instruction can only promote language acquisition if the interlanguage is close to the point when the structure to be taught is acquired in the natural setting (so that sufficient processing prerequisites are developed)' (p. 37). The corollaries of this hypothesis are:

1 Do not demand a learning process which is impossible at a given stage (i.e. order of teaching objectives to be in line with stages of acquisition).
2 But do *not* introduce deviant (i.e. interlanguage) forms.[3]
3 The general input may contain structures which were not introduced for production.

(p. 63)

Pienemann considered that 'teachability' only applied to developmental features, not to variational features (i.e. features that could be acquired at any stage).

Lightbown (1985b) rightly pointed out that our knowledge of natural acquisition sequences is too limited to make specific recommendations about how they should be related to teaching sequences. Pienemann and his fellow researchers subsequently attempted to overcome this problem by developing a broad theoretical framework with predictive power for when specific structures will be acquired. (See the account of Processability Theory in Chapter 9.)

The Weak Interface Hypothesis

The fourth version of the facilitative position claims that formal instruction acts as an aid to acquisition, not by actually bringing about the internalization of new linguistic features, but rather by providing the learner with 'hooks, points of access'. In other words, instruction does not enable learners to fully acquire what is taught when it is taught, but prepares the way for its subsequent acquisition. As Gass put it, instruction 'triggers the initial stages in what eventually results in grammar restructuring' (1991: 137). Instruction works by helping learners to pay SELECTIVE ATTENTION to form and form–meaning connections in the input. It provides learners with tools that help them to recognize those features in their interlanguages which are in need of modification. According to my Weak Interface model (see Chapter 9), instruction directed at explicit knowledge can indirectly facilitate the acquisition of implicit knowledge by priming the processes involved in its development (i.e. NOTICING and NOTICING THE GAP).

The necessity of FFI

While there is general recognition that much of the L2 can be learnt naturally (i.e. without any form-focused instruction), it is also clear that most L2 learners (especially adults) do not achieve full target-language competence as a result of exposure (see the account of FOSSILIZATION in Chapter 1) and thus need assistance. That is, there may be certain linguistic properties that cannot be acquired by L2 learners unless they receive instruction in them.

One occasion on which instruction may be necessary is when the learner is in danger of constructing an over-inclusive grammar. We saw in Chapter 12 that principles such as the subset principle may not operate effectively in L2 acquisition, with the result that certain types of 'problematic overgeneralization' occur as when francophone learners of L2 English attempt to insert an adverb between the verb and the direct object (for example, *'John drank yesterday some coffee'). White (1989b) argued that this type of error cannot be eliminated purely on the basis of the positive evidence supplied by communicative input, because the learner could never be sure that such sentences were not possible. In such cases, NEGATIVE EVIDENCE in the form of a grammar lesson or CORRECTIVE FEEDBACK is required.[4]

It has also been suggested that even 'benign OVERGENERALIZATIONS' (i.e. errors that can be eliminated on the basis of positive evidence) may require instruction. Rutherford (1989) argued that learners may fail to expunge such errors on the basis of positive evidence because they have come to understand that language tolerates synonymy. Thus, noticing 'went' in the input may not be sufficient to eliminate 'goed', if the learner operates with the hypothesis that both forms are possible. This might explain why learners like Patty (Lardiere 2007; see Chapter 1) fail to learn many of the morphological properties of a language even after years of intensive exposure. Such learners may need to have the fact that 'goed' and 'went' are not acceptable synonyms brought to their conscious attention. Adult learners may also fail to eliminate errors naturally because they can only access those parts of Universal Grammar that are instantiated in the L1. (See the account of the FAILED FUNCTIONAL FEATURES HYPOTHESIS in Chapter 12.)

In effect, these arguments bear upon the results of the research we considered in Chapter 15, which indicated that even under favourable conditions, classroom learners fail to develop full L2 linguistic competence simply by communicating. It should be noted, however, that it does not follow that formal instruction is the answer. It is possible that many adult learners will fail to develop high levels of grammatical competence no matter what the instructional conditions. D'Anglejan, Painchaud, and Renaud (1986) concluded their study of the effects of intensive mixed instruction (teaching that combined form-focused work with more communicative activities) on adult immigrant learners of L2 French in Canada as follows:

> It is both disappointing yet challenging to discover that after 900 hours of formal instruction, the vast majority of the subjects have attained proficiency levels which at best can be described as minimal.
> (1986: 199)

In other words, there may be limits to what is achievable through classroom learning for the simple reason that there are limits regarding what many learners are capable of achieving under any conditions, although, as we noted in Chapter 1, there will always be exceptional learners (for example, Moyer

1999) for whom instruction may provide the assistance they need to achieve an advanced level of competence.

I will now turn to an examination of the FFI research.

Effects of FFI on L2 acquisition

Comparative method studies

The earliest research investigating the effects of FFI was 'method' oriented; that is, it consisted of global comparisons of language teaching methods that differed in their conceptualizations of how to teach language. At the time when a number of key studies took place (in the 1960s and 1970s), language pedagogy assumed that the teaching of language necessarily and essentially involved focusing on form (primarily grammatical form) and the principal debate concerned how form should best be taught. Thus, methods were distinguished in terms of whether form was to be taught deductively (as in the grammar-translation method) or inductively (as in the audiolingual method). The aim of comparative method studies is to establish which of two or more methods or general approaches to language teaching is the most effective in terms of the actual learning (the 'product') that is achieved after a given period of time. Many of the earlier studies were 'global' in nature, conducted over weeks, months, and even years. Later ones have tended to examine differences resulting from shorter periods of exposure to different methods.

The 1960s were characterized by what Diller (1978) called 'the language teaching controversy'. This pitted the claims of rationalist approaches to language teaching against those of empiricists. Methods such as the traditional grammar-translation method and the cognitive-code method emphasized the provision of explicit knowledge through rule explanation and learning through all four skills simultaneously, while so-called 'functional' methods such as audiolingualism and the oral approach emphasized inductive rule learning through listening and extensive oral practice. At the time, it seemed logical to investigate which method produced the better results.

In an early study, Scherer and Wertheimer (1964) compared the grammar-translation method and the audiolingual approach by following the progress of different groups of college-level students of L2 German taught by each method and tested at the end of the their first and second years of study. The results showed that students in the grammar-translation group did better in reading and writing while the students in the audiolingual group did better at listening and speaking. In other words, each method resulted in learning 'products' that reflected the instructional emphasis.

A subsequent large-scale study known as the Pennsylvania Project (Smith 1970) compared the effects of three methods on beginning and intermediate French and German classes at the high-school level. The three methods were (1) 'traditional' (i.e. grammar-translation), (2) 'functional skills' (essentially the audiolingual approach), and (3) 'functional skills plus grammar'. Student achievement in the four skills of listening comprehension, speaking, reading, and writing was evaluated at mid-year and at the end of the year using a battery of standardized tests. The results in general showed no significant differences between the three methods, except that the 'traditional' group was superior to the other two groups on two of the reading tests. After two years, the 'traditional' group again surpassed the 'functional skills' group in reading ability but did significantly worse on a test of oral mimicry. No differences were found in the students' performance on the other tests.

In general, therefore, these studies failed to provide convincing evidence that one method was superior to another. One possible explanation, as suggested by Clark (1969) in his detailed discussion of the Pennsylvania Project, was that the distinctions between the different methods were not in fact clear. Clark commented:

> If ostensibly different teaching methods tend in the course of the experiment to resemble one another in terms of what actually goes on in the classroom, the likelihood of finding significant differences in student performance is accordingly reduced.

As Allwright (1988) documented, this led to the development of instruments for observing what actually takes place during the course of instruction (for example, Jarvis 1968) and a focus on describing language lessons at the level of technique rather than method (for example, Politzer 1970).

Comparative method studies were not abandoned, however. Asher and associates (see Asher 1977 for a review) conducted a number of studies designed to compare the effects on learning of TOTAL PHYSICAL RESPONSE (TPR), a method devised and promoted by Asher, and other methods, in particular the audiolingual approach. Asher claimed that the results of these studies show that TPR produces greater short-term and long-term retention of new linguistic material and better understanding of novel utterances. He also suggested they indicate that learners are able to transfer the training they received in listening to other skills—speaking, reading, and writing. Furthermore, Asher reported that students taught by TPR were more likely to continue studying the foreign language and displayed more positive attitudes. Krashen (1982: 156) concluded his survey of Asher's studies by claiming that 'the TPR results are clear and consistent, and the magnitude of superiority of TPR is quite striking'. A number of caveats are in order, however. First, as an advocate of his own method, Asher had a vested interest in finding in favour of it; second, the period of instruction was relatively short—only 20 hours in some studies; third, only beginners were investigated. We do not know, therefore, whether the method is equally effective in the long term or with advanced learners. Nevertheless, the TPR studies stand out in comparative method studies as providing evidence that support the superiority of a particular method.

More recent discussions of language teaching methodology have emphasized the importance of providing opportunities for learners to communicate.

The few studies that have investigated the effectiveness of communicative language teaching, however, have led to the same kind of indeterminate results found in the early global method studies. Palmer (1979) compared the effects of 'traditional' instruction and 'communicative' instruction involving extensive peer-communication based on language games. The subjects were Thai learners of English. No significant differences between the groups were found. One possible explanation for this unexpected finding, according to Krashen (1981), was that while teacher talk was in the target language in the traditional group, it was in the learners' L1 in the communicative class. Hammond (1988) compared groups of students in a Spanish programme at two universities. Eight experimental groups were taught by means of the Natural Approach (Krashen and Terrell 1983) and 52 comparison groups were taught by means of the grammar-translation method, which emphasized the deductive learning of grammar. Although in general the experimental groups outperformed the comparison groups in both a mid-term and a final examination, many of the differences were not significant. This study did show, however, that students in a communicative classroom did no worse in learning grammar than those in a traditional programme—a finding replicated in Beretta and Davies' (1985) evaluation of Prabhu's Communicational Teaching Project.

The difficulties of conducting effective comparisons between 'communicative' and 'non-communicative' classrooms are also evident in a carefully planned study by Allen, Swain, Harley, and Cummins (1990). This was based on Stern's (1990) distinction between 'experiential' and 'analytic' teaching strategies. (See Table 16.3.) Allen *et al.* used an interaction analysis schedule (the COMMUNICATIVE ORIENTATION TO LANGUAGE TEACHING, or COLT—see Chapter 15) to describe the teaching strategies used in eight Grade 11 French classes in Toronto. The information provided by this was used to rank the classes according to how experiential/analytic they were. This study differs from the earlier ones, then, in that the comparison involved examining classrooms that varied in terms of the actual processes observed to take place (in other words, it had a process element). It was hypothesized that the analytic classes would perform better on the written and grammatical accuracy measures and that the experiential classes would do better on measures of sociolinguistic and discourse competence, but when pre- and post-test measures were compared, this was not found to be the case. There were a few statistically significant differences between the two most experiential and the two most analytic classes. Allen *et al.* admitted that the results were 'somewhat disappointing'.

Experiential features	Analytic features
1 Substantive or motivated topic or theme (topics are not arbitrary or trivial).	1 Focus on aspects of L2, including phonology, grammar functions, discourse, and sociolinguistics.
2 Students engage in purposeful activity (tasks or projects), not exercises.	2 Cognitive study of language items (rules and regularities are noted; items are made salient, and related to other items and systems).
3 Language use has characteristics of real talk (conversation) or uses any of the four skills as part of purposeful action.	3 Practice or rehearsal of language items or skill aspects.
4 Priority of meaning transfer and fluency over linguistic error avoidance and accuracy.	4 Attention to accuracy and error avoidance.
5 Diversity of social interaction.	5 Diversity of social interaction desirable.

Table 16.3 Experiential and analytic features in language pedagogy (from Stern 1990)

With the exception of the TPR studies, then, comparative method studies have failed to produce evidence that one method results in more successful learning than another. There are many reasons for this. As Lightbown (1990) noted in her discussion of Allen *et al.*'s study, one is that foreign language lessons of any type often result in relatively little progress. Another is that individual learners benefit from different types of instruction (a point taken up later in this chapter). A third reason is that language classes tend to offer very similar opportunities for learning irrespective of their methodological orientation. It is probably true to say that comparative method studies, even when conducted with due regard for classroom 'processes', have afforded little insight into how instructional events contribute to learning. 'Method' may not be the most appropriate unit for investigating the effect that language teaching has on L2 learning, although this has not prevented some researchers from continuing to advocate method comparisons.[5]

Comparisons of naturalistic and instructed L2 learners

At around the same time as the comparative method studies, SLA researchers, drawing on the findings and methods of first language acquisition research, began to investigate how learners acquired an L2 in naturalistic settings (i.e. when exposed to the use of the L2 in non-pedagogic contexts). This research, which was reviewed in Chapter 3, indicated that learners tended to follow a natural ORDER OF ACQUISITION and also manifested fairly well-defined sequences in the acquisition of specific target structures. These findings led to a questioning of whether FFI was necessary for acquisition (i.e. they were used to support the zero position). The research that ensued compared the ultimate level of achievement and rate of learning of groups of learners who had received instruction (which was assumed to consist of FFI) with groups who had not.

In one of the first reviews of the literature on FFI, Long (1983c) considered a total of eleven studies that had investigated whether learners who receive formal instruction achieve higher levels of proficiency than those who do not. He concluded that most of the studies (Carroll 1967; Chihara and Oller 1978; Briere 1978; Krashen, Seliger, and Hartnett 1974; Krashen, Jones, Zelinski, and Usprich 1978) lent support to formal instruction. Three studies (Upshur 1968; Mason 1971; Fathman 1975) indicated that instruction did not help, while one study (Martin 1980) showed that exposure without formal instruction was beneficial. Long considered two other studies to be 'ambiguous cases' because, although they produced negative results for instruction, this was because they had been wrongly interpreted. For example, Long pointed out that variables to do with instruction, socio-economic background, amount of exposure, and parental attitudes were conflated in Hale and Budar's (1970) study, with the result that it was impossible to determine which factors were responsible for the observed differences in proficiency level.

Long's general conclusion was that 'there is considerable evidence to indicate that SL instruction does make a difference' (1983c: 374). He claimed that the studies suggested that instruction was advantageous (1) for children as well as adults, (2) for both intermediate and advanced learners, (3) irrespective of whether acquisition was measured by means of integrative or discrete-point tests, and (4) in acquisition-rich as well as acquisition-poor environments.

A study published since Long's review lends support to these general conclusions. Weslander and Stephany (1983) examined the effects of instruction on 577 children with limited English proficiency in Grades 2 to 10 in public schools in Iowa. Students who received more instruction did better on the Bilingual Syntax Measure. (See Chapter 3.) The effects were strongest at the lowest levels of proficiency in the first year of schooling and diminished in later years. Weslander and Stephany's results contrast with those obtained by Hale and Budar (1970).

In general, then, these early studies show an advantage for FFI over exposure. Long, in his original review, claimed that this conclusion was damaging to Krashen's position on FFI (i.e. the zero position). Krashen (1985: 28–31) responded by arguing that the studies did not in fact show an advantage for formal instruction *per se*, but only that learning in a classroom was helpful for 'beginners', who found it difficult to obtain the COMPREHENSIBLE INPUT they needed in normal communication outside the classroom. In this respect, it should be noted that Weslander and Stephany (1983) reported that it was the beginners who benefited most from formal instruction in their study. To protect himself against Long's conclusion that the studies also showed FFI was advantageous for advanced learners, Krashen argued that the subjects in some of the studies had been wrongly classified as 'intermediate' and 'advanced'. In a response to this, Long (1988) pointed out that his other main conclusions (i.e. (1), (3), and (4) above) were also problematic for the INPUT HYPOTHESIS and that the conclusion that Krashen himself had reached in an earlier paper was, in fact, the right one—'formal instruction is a more efficient way of learning English for adults than trying to learn it in the streets' (Krashen, Jones, Zelinski, and Usprich 1978: 260).

These studies—and Long's and Krashen's subsequent debate—are based on comparisons of the relative effects of formal instruction and exposure. However, many learners—including many of those in the studies Long reviewed—experienced both together. It is conceivable, therefore, that what works best is some form of combination of the two. This possibility was examined directly in three other studies.

Savignon (1972), in a frequently cited study of communicative language teaching, compared the grammatical and communicative skills of three classes of learners of French as a foreign language who had received four hours of instruction per week. The experimental group, which was given an extra hour of communicative tasks, outperformed the other two groups on a number of 'communicative' measures, but not on 'linguistic' measures. This study, then, suggests that a combination of direct and indirect intervention aids the development of communicative language skills in foreign language learners.

Spada (1986) sought to establish whether there was any interaction between type of contact and type of instruction. She investigated the effects of instruction and exposure on 48 intermediate-level adult learners enrolled in an intensive six-week ESL course at a Canadian university. Spada found that although type and amount of contact appeared to account for variation in some aspects of the learners' proficiency before the effects of instruction were considered, it did not account for differences in the learners' improvement during the course. Overall, instruction was more important than contact in accounting for differences in the learners' L2 proficiency. She also found evidence of an interaction between the type of instruction that different groups of learners received and commented:

> ... contact positively accounted for differences in learners' improvement on the grammar and writing tests when the instruction was more form-focused, and negatively accounted for differences on those measures when the instruction was less form-focused
> (1986: 97).

In other words, those learners who had access both to formal instruction and to exposure to English showed the greatest gains in proficiency. As Spada (1987: 133) commented, 'attention to both form and meaning works best' for L2 learners.

This conclusion is also given support by another study (Montgomery and Eisenstein 1985). This compared the gains in proficiency observed in a group of working-class Hispanic students who, in addition to regular ESL classes aimed primarily at improving grammatical accuracy, also enrolled in a special oral communication course, involving field trips to sites where they routinely needed to communicate in English, and a group of similar learners who experienced only the regular ESL classes. The two groups were compared for accent, grammar, vocabulary, fluency, and comprehension. Both groups improved their rating from pre- to post-test, but the group who had experienced the oral communication programme showed greater gains in grammar and accent and were also more successful in passing the ESL course (86 per cent pass rate as opposed to 57 per cent). Montgomery and Eisenstein proposed that 'a combination of form-oriented and meaning-oriented language teaching was more beneficial than form-oriented teaching alone' (1985: 329). It should be noted, however, that the group in the joint programme received more overall instruction and that it might have been the total amount of instruction, rather than the type that accounted for their advantage.

In general, then, there is support for the claim that FFI helps language learners (both foreign and second) to develop greater L2 proficiency, particularly if it is linked with opportunities for natural exposure. Foreign language learners appear to benefit by developing greater communicative skills, while second language learners benefit by developing greater linguistic accuracy. As I pointed out in Ellis 1990a, however, there are several reasons for exercising caution in interpreting the studies considered in this section.

First, many of the studies, like that of Montgomery and Eisenstein, failed to control for overall amount of combined contact and instruction. Studies which show that learners who receive instruction and exposure do better than learners with just exposure are, by themselves, not very convincing, as this may simply reflect their greater overall contact. To counter this objection, Long (1983c) pointed out that whereas some studies showed that differences in amounts of instruction were related to differences in proficiency in learners with the same overall exposure, the reverse was not the case—differences in the amount of exposure had no effect on the proficiency of learners matched for amount of instruction. Long argued that these contrasting results enable us to be more confident in finding a positive effect for instruction in studies which failed to control for overall opportunities for learning. However, if such studies are removed on the grounds of this design flaw, the number of studies in Long's original review that unambiguously show that instruction helps is reduced to two.

Another problem is that the studies do not take account of individual differences in learners. Fathman (1978) found that the informal learners in her study varied in English oral proficiency much more than the formal learners, leading her to suggest that some were skilful at learning informally while others had difficulty. Similar points have been made about differences in the ability of formal learners. (See the section on language aptitude in Chapter

13 and the section dealing with the mediating effect of individual difference factors later in this chapter.) It is also possible that motivation functions as an important intervening variable. As Krashen, Jones, Zelinski, and Usprich (1978) recognized, students who are more highly motivated to learn are more likely to enrol in classes. The positive effect found for instruction may simply reflect stronger motivation rather than the instruction itself.

Perhaps the most serious problem, however, is that many of the studies made no attempt to ascertain what took place in the name of 'instruction'. They simply equated FFI with the number of years spent in the classroom. As a result, we do not know for certain, whether the instruction was form-focused, communication-orientated, or a mixture of the two. We cannot be sure whether the classroom learners did better than the naturalistic learners because of FFI or because of access to comprehensible input.

More convincing is the evidence provided by the three later studies, which suggest that learners progress most rapidly when they experience both FFI and communicative exposure. It should be noted that this accords with the findings of the 'good language learner' studies (see Chapter 13), which have indicated that successful learners pay attention to language form and also seek out opportunities for communicating in the L2. As we will see in a later section, it is possible that the long-term effectiveness of FFI is contingent on the availability of opportunities to communicate in the L2.

The effects of FFI on production accuracy

Like the earlier research, this research was motivated by both theoretical and pedagogic considerations. On a theoretical level, the studies sought to test the claims advanced by Krashen (1981) and later Schwartz (1993) that teaching grammar or correcting learner errors has no effect on the learner's 'acquired' system. On the pedagogical level, the studies explored whether FFI could help learners to acquire those grammatical structures they had failed to acquire even after years of exposure to comprehensible input or those structures that were known to be difficult to acquire from studies of naturalistic learners. Harley (1989), for example, investigated French *imparfait* and *prétérit*, which immersion learners typically fail to acquire.

The studies that have investigated the effects of FFI on production accuracy have produced mixed results. (See Table 16.4.) In Chapter 15 we considered research (for example, Ellis 1984c and 1992) that suggested that learner participation in classroom FFI activities is not related to gains in accuracy. However, as Long (1988) pointed out, an explanation for these findings might be that the instruction was directed at a structure too far in advance of the learners' stage of development.

Other studies have produced results more supportive of FFI, although typically only when acquisition was measured by means of constrained constructed responses or metalinguistic judgements. Lightbown, Spada, and Wallace (1980), for example, reported that 175 French-speaking school learners of English improved by 11 per cent on a grammaticality judgement test when instructed on a range of grammatical features whereas a control group improved by only 3 per cent. Lightbown *et al.* (1980) emphasized, however, that the learners may not have acquired the functions of the various forms or, in other words, that acquisition was only partial. Pica (1983, 1985) also produced evidence to suggest that some grammatical features are performed more accurately if learners have access to formal instruction. She compared the accuracy with which three groups of learners (a natural group, a mixed group, and an instructed group) performed a number of grammatical morphemes in unplanned speech. The instructed learners performed plural –s more accurately than the naturalistic learners. However, they performed progressive –ing less accurately, while no difference between the groups was found for another feature (articles). Pica explained these interesting results by suggesting that instruction only aids the acquisition of features which are formally easy to acquire and which manifest transparent form–function relationships.

Some studies have compared the effect of FFI on accuracy in planned and unplanned production. Kadia (1988), for example, studied the effects of 40 minutes of one-to-one instruction on a Chinese learner's acquisition of di-transitive (for example, 'I showed him the book') and phrasal verb constructions such as 'I called him up'. She concluded:

> ... formal instruction seemed to have very little effect on spontaneous production, but it was beneficial for controlled performance.
> (1988: 513)

It should be noted, however, that the structures that Kadia investigated are complex and typically acquired late. In the Pica study, instructional effects were evident in unplanned language use when the target structure was easy to acquire.

Another intriguing possibility is that FFI may have a delayed effect, as claimed by the Weak Interface Hypothesis. Ellis, Loewen, and Erlam (2006), for example, reported that corrective feedback in the form of metalinguistic comments did not result in statistically significant gains in the accuracy with which English past tense –ed was used by adult L2 learners in an immediate post-test but did in a delayed test administered two weeks later.

However, there is also some evidence to suggest that formal instruction can have a deleterious effect. Lightbown (1983) showed that francophone learners over-learnt progressive –ing as a result of teaching. They overgeneralized it, using it in contexts that required the simple form of the verb, which they had used correctly prior to the instruction. Pica (1983) also found evidence that instruction can trigger the oversuppliance of a number of regular morphological features such as past tense –ed and progressive –ing. Weinert (1987) and VanPatten (1990b) also provided evidence to suggest that instruction can impede acquisition of negatives in L2 German and clitic pronouns in L2 Spanish. In all these studies the reason given for the failure of the formal instruction was that it distorted the input made available to the learner and thus prevented the normal processes of acquisition from operating smoothly.

The general picture which emerges from the studies we have examined so far is that FFI often does not work, particularly when acquisition is measured in relation to spontaneous speech. However, a number of other studies carried out in Canada suggest that grammar teaching can have positive effects on learning. These studies examined the role of FFI in the context of communicative language teaching (i.e. when opportunities for communicating in the L2 are supplemented with grammar lessons). A feature of all the studies was the provision of instruction that had been carefully planned in accordance with current pedagogic views about what constitutes 'good' grammar teaching. A second feature was that the instruction has been extensive.

Harley (1989) devised a set of functional-grammar materials to teach French immersion students the distinction between *passé composé* and *imparfait* which, as we have seen, is one of the features that is typically not acquired by immersion learners. She found that eight weeks of instruction resulted in significant improvement in the accuracy with which the two verb tenses were used in a written composition, in a rational cloze test, and in an oral interview. The instructional effects were therefore evident in both planned and unplanned language use. However, a control group subsequently caught up with the experimental group. Harley suggested that this might have been because the control group also subsequently received formal instruction directed at this feature. The Harley study is encouraging for supporters of FFI.

Two other Canadian studies also support this view. White (1991) investigated the effects of instruction on adverb placement, examining whether it was successful in eliminating this error made by French learners of L2 English:

*John kissed often Mary. (SVAO)

and in teaching these learners to use adverbs between subject and verb, a position not allowed in French:

*Jean souvent embrasse Marie. (SAVO)

White argued that the latter structure is learnable through positive input (i.e. through input obtained from communicative exposure), but that avoidance of the adverb placement error requires negative evidence such as that provided by formal instruction. The learners were children in Grades 5 and 6 in an intensive ESL program. Two weeks of instruction in the use of frequency and manner adverbs was provided three months into the program. The instructed learners showed significantly greater gains in accuracy in a number of manipulative tasks (a grammaticality judgement task, a preference task, and a sentence construction task) in comparison to control groups. These results held true for both use of SAVO and for avoidance of SVAO word order.

White was also interested in whether the learners recognized that sentences of the kind:

John ran quickly to the end of the street. (i.e. SVAPP)

were permitted in English even though they had not been taught this. However, the subjects did not learn that SVAPP was possible where SVAO was not, and White suggested that they made 'a conscious overgeneralization' to the effect that 'adverbs must not appear between the verb and something else'. This study indicates that the learners responded to instruction, but that they were unable to make fine distinctions (i.e. between SVAO and SVAPP) that they had not been taught.

The second study (White *et al.* 1991) studied the effects of instruction on question formation (WH– and 'yes/no') on the same groups of learners as those used in the adverb study. Five hours of instruction over a two-week period were provided. Acquisition was measured by means of a cartoon task, a preference grammaticality judgement task, and an oral communication task. In comparison to a control group, the experimental group showed substantial gains in accuracy in all three tasks. The instructed learners in this case showed that they had learnt how to use inversion in questions.

The clearest evidence for the positive effect that FFI can have on learners' accuracy of production comes from Norris and Ortega's (2000) meta-analysis of 49 studies. The mean effect size[6] for all the treatments in these studies (a total of 98) was $d = 0.96$, considered to be 'large'. The point of comparison here was with groups of learners who received no instruction in the target feature or with learners who experienced only naturalistic exposure to the target language. However, Norris and Ortega pointed out that the high overall standard deviation (0.87) indicated a high level of heterogeneity among studies. In other words, as noted in the discussion of the specific studies above, FFI was variably effective and sometimes not effective at all. A number of other analyses carried out by Norris and Ortega are indicative of the factors that might account for this variability. One analysis (to be reported in a later section of this chapter) analysed the effect of different types of instruction, finding that this varied considerably. Another important analysis examined the magnitude of effect according to the types of outcome measure. Interestingly, the effect size for free constructed response ($d = 0.55$) was much smaller than those for selected response ($d = 1.46$) and constrained constructed response ($d = 1.20$). In other words, FFI was found to be more effective if learning outcomes were measured in ways that tapped into learners' explicit knowledge. The effect on implicit knowledge (as evidenced by free constructed response measures) was still substantial, however. Another factor that was found to influence the overall effectiveness of FFI was the length of the duration of the treatment. Surprisingly, 'brief treatments' (i.e. less than one hour) and 'short treatments' (i.e. between 1 and 2 hours) resulted in larger mean effect sizes ($d = 1.06$ and $d = 1.08$ respectively) than medium treatments (between 3 and 6 hours) or 'long treatments' (i.e. more than 7 hours), where the effect size for both was

Study	Type of classroom	Participants	Proficiency	Data	Results
Lightbown *et al.* 1980	ESL in Canadian schools	Children and adolescents in Grades 6, 8, and 10; N sizes varied for the analyses carried out but were between 75 and 25 for the different grade levels.	Mixed ability levels	Grammaticality judgement test.	Instruction resulted in increased accuracy in grammaticality judgements in the short term. However, accuracy fell away in follow-up test 5 months later.
Lightbown 1983	ESL in schools in Canada	The same children were followed through Grades 6, 7, and 8 (they numbered 75 at the start).	Mainly lower intermediate	Spontaneous speech on a picture task.	V + –ing over-used by grade 6 children; replaced by simple verb form in grade 7. Progressive aux followed similar pattern of development. Forms 'overlearnt' but natural processing takes over later. Effect of instruction delayed.
Pica 1983, 1985	EFL in Mexico/ESL in the United States	6 adult EFL learners, 6 adult ESL learners, and 6 natural learners	Mixed levels of ability	Audiotaped conversations with researcher.	Instructed learners more accurate in some forms (e.g. plural –s), less accurate in others (e.g. V + –ing) and the same in others (e.g. articles).
Kadia 1988	ESL in Canadian university	One adult learner	Fossilized, i.e. no development taking place	Spontaneous speech substitution and grammaticality judgement tests.	Instruction had no effect on spontaneous production. Performance on grammaticality judgement test declined but that on substitution test improved.
Harley 1989	French as a FL in Canada	319 Grade 6 learners in immersion programmes	Intermediate and upper intermediate	Ratings based on written compositions; cloze test scores; error scores based on oral interview.	The instructed students better than control students on cloze and oral interview scores on immediate post-test. Gains maintained in follow-up test 3 months later.
L. White 1991	ESL in Canada	82 Grade 5 and 6 students	Post-beginner/ low intermediate	Grammaticality judgement task, preference task, and card-sorting task.	Instructed learners made fewer judgement errors and scored higher scores on card-sorting task than did control. However, gains largely disappeared in follow-up test administered 5 months later.
L. White *et al.* 1991	ESL in Canada	56 Grade 5 and 6 students	Post-beginner/ low intermediate	Grammaticality judgement task, preference task, and oral production task.	Instructed learners performed better on all three tasks than controls. Gains maintained in follow-up test 6 months later.

Table 16.4 Selected studies investigating the effects of instruction on accuracy

d = 0.79. Norris and Ortega noted, however, that this difference probably reflected a number of moderator variables such as the intensity and type of instruction, which they were unable to investigate.

What general conclusions can we come to on the basis of the research which has investigated the effects of FFI on accuracy? There is clear evidence to show that FFI can result in definite gains in accuracy. However, additional research is needed to determine the factors that influence whether and to what extent FFI is effective. Of particular importance is whether FFI leads to improved accuracy in unplanned language use (i.e. Norris and Ortega's 'free constructed response') and under what conditions it does so. This issue is addressed further in a later section of this chapter.

The effects of FFI on the order and sequence of acquisition

Irrespective of whether FFI results in increased accuracy, it is also important to ask whether classroom learners (who are presumed to have received FFI) manifest a different accuracy/acquisition *order* from naturalistic learners. Table 16.5 summarizes a number of studies that addressed this question. (For the distinction between 'order' and 'sequence', see the Introduction to Chapter 3.)

Early studies

Studies by Fathman (1978) of EFL and ESL learners, by Makino (1980) of Japanese learners of English, and by Pica (1983) of Spanish-speaking learners of English failed to find any significant differences between naturalistic and instructed learners. Turner (1979) found that the accuracy/acquisition orders manifested by three 18-year-old Spanish learners of English enrolled in an intensive English language program correlated highly with each other but not with the order of instruction. Perkins and Larsen-Freeman (1975) found that the order obtained for twelve Venezuelan students at the beginning of a course of instruction did not differ significantly from that obtained at the end. These studies were used to claim the inviolability of the morpheme order. Sajavaara (1981b), in a study of adolescent EFL learners in Finland, and also Lightbown (1983), in the study referred to earlier, however, found differences between the instructed and natural morpheme orders and those produced by the learners who had received formal instruction. It should also be noted that there was evidence in some studies that specific morphemes were performed more accurately as a result of instruction. (See, for example, Perkins and Larsen-Freeman (1975) and Pica (1983), and the discussion in the previous section.)

A number of other studies that have focused on the order of acquisition in specific grammatical sub-systems also suggested that instruction is powerless to alter the general pattern of development. In Chapter 3 we saw that the functions of relative pronouns are acquired in a predictable order that reflects their typological status. Pavesi (1984, 1986) found this 'universal' order of acquisition in both a group of instructed EFL learners in an Italian high school and a group of waiters learning English naturalistically in Edinburgh, Scotland. Once again, however, this study found that the instructed group showed higher levels of acquisition, both in the sense that they had progressed further along the universal order and in the sense that the errors they manifested were less 'primitive' (for example, they used pronoun copies rather than noun copies).

Given the doubts that have been expressed about the construct of *order* of acquisition (see Chapter 3), the research that has examined the effects of formal instruction on the *sequence* of acquisition is arguably of greater theoretical interest. Research on German word order rules has indicated that FFI is unable to affect acquisition sequences. This work is based on studies of naturalistic learners, which showed there is a definite sequence of acquisition of word order rules. (See Chapter 3.) Pienemann (1984), in a frequently cited experimental study, showed that instruction in inversion was successful in the case of a learner who had reached the immediately preceding stage, but not in the case of another learner who was at a much earlier stage. Drawing on the claims of Processability Theory (see Chapter 9), Pienemann advanced what he called the Teachability Hypothesis. (See the section in this chapter on 'Theoretical positions'.) Subsequent longitudinal studies of the classroom acquisition of German by university students in Australia (Pienemann 1986, 1989) further demonstrated the immutability of the word order sequence and the failure of instruction to alter it. My study of 39 adult learners of L2 German in higher education in Britain (Ellis 1989b) also suggested that instruction is powerless to alter the sequence of acquisition of these word order rules. Two cross-sectional studies (Daniel 1983 and Westmoreland 1983) also show that the sequence of acquisition for German word order rules is the same in instructed and naturalistic acquisition.

Later studies

A number of later studies investigated the effects of instruction on the acquisition of English question forms and produced somewhat less convincing support for the claim that instruction is powerless to affect the sequence of development. We will consider two here. Mackey's (1999) research involved planned FOCUS-ON-FORM through PREMODIFIED INPUT or INTERACTIONALLY MODIFIED INPUT (see Chapter 6) in the context of performing a number of communicative tasks. Mackey distinguished 'interactors' who were 'ready' to progress to a more developmentally advanced stage and learners who were 'unready'. However, the difference in the progress of the 'ready' and 'unready' learners was minimal, with both demonstrating more advanced types of questions although only in the second post-test (i.e. the effect of the treatment was delayed). The 'unreadies' actually produced more instances of advanced type questions, although Mackey reported that their overall development was 'less systematic'. It should be noted, however, that the treatment in Mackey's study exposed learners to a variety of question types, not just those questions one stage beyond that which they had already reached. Spada and Lightbown (1999), however, did just this. They determined the precise developmental stage of 150 francophone children, establishing that most of them were at stage 2 (i.e. produced SVO questions with rising intonation). The children were then exposed to hundreds of questions mainly at stage 4 (for example, 'yes/no' questions with auxiliary inversion) and stage 5 (i.e. WH– questions with auxiliary second) in communicative activities over a two-week period. By and large, the learners moved up only one stage (i.e. those at stage 2 moved up to stage 3, while those at stage 3 moved up to stage 4). However, there were two learners at stage 2 who made the leap to stage 4[7] and also many of the students who were at the more advanced stages initially failed to progress at all. Spada and Lightbown concluded that these results failed to support the Teachability Hypothesis.

Taken together, these studies suggest that there are developmental constraints on whether FFI is effective, but they do not provide clear support for the idea that, to be effective, instruction needs to be directed at just one stage above the one the learner has already reached. However, there is another possible explanation for why instruction can sometimes enable learners to 'beat' the natural sequence. Lightbown (1998) suggested that those utterances that seemingly show a learner has beaten the natural sequence may in fact be formulaic sequences rather than creative speech. Lightbown went on to suggest that even if this were the case, the learners clearly knew the meanings of these memorized chunks and that, as such, they could serve as 'auto-input' for subsequent development.

Projection studies

Another possibility, compatible with the results obtained by Spada and Lightbown (1999), is that teaching a 'marked' structure will help learners to acquire both that structure and associated unmarked structures. Following Zobl (1983b), I refer to this as the PROJECTION HYPOTHESIS. It has been investigated primarily with reference to relative pronoun functions, as described in the Accessibility Hierarchy. (See Chapter 12.) Gass (1982) and Eckman, Bell, and Nelson (1988) found that instruction directed at the object of preposition function (for example, 'This is the man who we spoke about') triggered acquisition of the less marked features (direct object and subject functions), as demonstrated in a written production task. The reverse, however, did not occur to the same extent: for example, students taught the subject function did not show much gain on the object and object of preposition functions. Subsequent studies by A. Jones (1991b, 1992) replicated these results for Japanese college-level learners of English, and also showed that the predicted order was evident in oral as well as written production.[8] Yabuki-Soh (2007) also found some support for the Projection Hypothesis in a sentence-combining test but not in a comprehension test. However, Hamilton (1994) reported that although the instructed learners in his study advanced along the sequence predicted by the Accessibility Hierarchy, they did not necessarily acquire the unmarked functions as a result of being taught a marked function. Finally, a study by Zobl (1985) also lent support to the triggering effect achieved by teaching marked structures. It showed that French learners of English who received instruction directed at the marked use of possessive pronouns (possessive + human entity, for example, 'his mother') improved in both this feature and in the unmarked use of possessive pronouns (possessive + inanimate entity, for example, 'her car'). These studies have not produced consistent results but they do suggest that, in some cases at least, learners can generalize from instruction they receive in a marked feature to an unmarked feature, at least when learning is measured in terms of controlled production. Also, it needs to be pointed out that not all grammatical structures are subject to MARKEDNESS relations in the same way as relative clauses and possessive pronouns.

Summary and commentary

On the face of it the results of the 'natural sequence' and 'projection' studies are incompatible. However, this need not be the case. Projection theories do not claim that input rich in marked features enables learners to learn 'out of sequence', but only that it will enable them to acquire a cluster of features simultaneously. Second, projection may only be applicable to the reactivation of items that have been learnt earlier but which have become dormant. It is noticeable that none of the projection studies have examined the effects of instruction on completely new grammatical structures.

The following tentative conclusions attempt to reconcile the various findings:

1 Instructed learners manifest the same order of morpheme acquisition as naturalistic learners (for example, Fathman 1978).
2 Instructed learners also manifest the same order of acquisition of features comprising grammatical sub-systems such as relative pronoun functions as naturalistic learners (for example, Pavesi 1986).
3 Grammar instruction may prove powerless to alter the natural sequence of acquisition of developmental structures, as these are manifest in learner production (for example, Pienemann 1989). However, grammar instruction does not need to be directed at just one stage above the learner's developmental level to be effective. Also, there may not be the same developmental constraints on learners' ability to comprehend the function of grammatical structures.
4 Grammar instruction can be effective in enabling learners to progress along the natural order more rapidly. One way in which this might be achieved is by teaching marked features within the sequence (for example, Eckman *et al.* 1988).

It should be noted, however, that the existence of acquisition orders and sequences has not gone unchallenged. They are widely acknowledged in cognitive theories of L2 acquisition but are disputed in sociocultural accounts

Study	Type of classroom	Participants	Proficiency	Data	Results
Morpheme order studies					
Fathman 1978	EFL in Germany versus ESL in United States	48 EFL learners in Hauptschule in Germany and 67 ESL learners in public schools in the US	Mixed ability	Oral production task.	Morpheme order for EFL and ESL learners were significantly correlated, but differences in types of errors found (for example, EFL learners made more overgeneralization errors).
Makino 1980	EFL in Japan	777 students in Grades 9 and 10 of high school	Lower intermediate	Written data based on picture stimuli.	Order of morpheme acquisition same as natural order and different from order in textbooks.
Sajavaara 1981b	EFL in Finland	Adolescents in high school		Elicited speech.	Morpheme order differed from natural order—articles ranked lower.
Pica 1983	EFL in Mexico/ESL in USA	6 adult EFL learners/6 adult ESL learners and 6 natural learners	Mixed ability	Audio-taped conversations with the researcher.	Morpheme order the same as natural order.
Order of acquisition in grammatical sub-system					
Pavesi 1984, 1986	EFL in Italy; ESL in Scotland	48 adolescents in high school; 38 Italian workers	Mixed ability	Oral data on relative clauses elicited by picture cues.	Instructed and untutored learners displayed same acquisition order, but the instructed learners showed greater quantitative development.
Sequence of acquisition					
Pienemann 1984	German as a SL in Germany	10 children aged 7–9 years	Mixed ability	Oral interviews and hidden recordings.	Inversion rule acquired by one learner who was developmentally ready, but not acquired by another who was not ready; accuracy in copula increased initially but decreased some 9 months later; instruction in inversion caused learner who was not developmentally ready to abandon already acquired rule.
Pienemann 1986, 1989	German as a FL in Australia	3 adult learners at university	Complete beginners	Oral interviews.	Learners acquired 'easy' word order rules when taught, but difficult rules (e.g. general order of acquisition) corresponded to natural order.

Ellis 1989b	German as a FL in Britain	39 adult learners in higher education	Beginners and false beginners	Spontaneous speech in information-gap tasks.	Order of development of word order rules same as in naturalistic learners and different from instructional order, but instructed learners displayed greater development in the late-acquired verb-end rule.
Mackey (1999)	English as a SL in Australia	34 adult learners in private language schools	Beginners and low intermediate	Spontaneous speech in information-gap tasks.	Conversational interaction facilitated acquisition for learners who were developmentally 'ready' and also those who were 'unready'.
Spada and Lightbown (1999)	Intensive ESL in Canada	144 Grade 6 (age 11–12) French-speaking learners	Most learners at early stage of question-form development	Oral production; elicited written production; metalinguistic judgements.	Learners at stage 3 in the 5-stage sequence for the acquisition of questions did not progress more than those at stage 2.
'Projection' studies					
Gass 1982	ESL in the United States	Adults at university	Intermediate	Grammaticality and sentence-joining tasks.	Group that received instruction on marked relative pronoun function showed improvement on this function and on unmarked functions; group that received instruction on unmarked relative function showed improvement primarily on this function only.
Zobl 1985	ESL French speakers in Canada	162 French-speaking adults	Low level	Oral questions based on pictures, designed to elicit noun phrases with possessive adjectives.	One group that received instruction in human-possessed entities (= marked) generalized to non-human possessed entities (= unmarked) but reverse did not occur. Types of error also differed.
Eckman *et al.* 1988	ESL in the United States	36 adults in an intensive university course	Low intermediate and intermediate	Sentence-joining task.	Generalization of learning occurred from marked to unmarked structures, but little took place in opposite direction.

Table 16.5 Selected studies investigating the effect of FFI on the course of L2 acquisition

of L2 learning (see Chapter 11), which see learning as socially constructed through scaffolded interaction and thus potentially variable. Also, the claims about order and sequence relate to implicit knowledge. There is no evidence that explicit knowledge of grammatical rules is acquired in a fixed order or sequence. In Ellis (2006c), I demonstrated that the learning difficulty of 17 grammatical structures differs according to whether this is measured in terms of explicit or implicit knowledge and that the order of difficulty predicted by studies of naturalistic learning is only evident in measures of implicit knowledge. It is likely, then, that formal instruction directed at explicit knowledge may not be subject to the same processing constraints as those governing implicit knowledge.

It is also not at all clear what practical use teachers can make of the research which has examined the effects of instruction on the order/sequence of acquisition. While it may not be necessary to ensure that grammar instruction is timed to match individual learners' exact stage of development, it is clearly desirable to check if learners are generally ready to acquire the target structure. Pienemann, Johnston, and Brindley (1988) outlined a procedure which teachers can use to establish this, but the procedure is a complicated one, calling for the accurate completion of an observation form in order to identify individual learners' developmental gaps. It is doubtful if most teachers would be able to use this with sufficient precision. To overcome this problem, and also to facilitate the analysis of L2 data for research purposes, Pienemann and his co-workers (see Pienemann 1992) developed a software computer package called COALA. However, this package requires the data to be prepared manually before it can be analysed, and so may not be readily usable by teachers. COALA does not appear to have been widely used by either teachers or SLA researchers.

Problems also exist in applying the Projection Hypothesis. So far, the evidence for this hypothesis is restricted to a few structures. Attempts to extend it to other areas such as adverb position (L. White 1991) have not proved successful. It would seem that projection which is predicted to occur on the basis of markedness relations identified by linguistic theory does not always occur. In such cases, researchers tend to query the linguistic theory. It is possible, however, that it is the Projection Hypothesis itself that is faulty.

The durability of FFI effects

It is possible that, even in cases where FFI appears to have worked, the beneficial effects may be only temporary. The increased levels of accuracy that result from instruction may prove to be impermanent or the acquisition of a new grammatical feature illusory. As time passes the effects may gradually atrophy and the learners return to similar levels of performance to those observed before the instruction. If this were to be the case, the utility of formal instruction would be severely limited.

A number of studies already referred to (see Tables 16.4 and 16.5) indicate that the effects of grammar instruction may not last. Lightbown *et al.* (1980) found that the overall scores of the learners they investigated dropped to a level approximately halfway between that of the pre-test and the immediate post-test in a follow-up test administered six months after the instruction. Pienemann (1984) found that the gains which one learner made in the accurate use of the copula as a result of instruction began to disappear after as little as one week. L. White (1991) found that gains in the correct positioning of adverbs were largely lost five months after the instruction.

However, other studies have found that the effects of instruction are durable. Harley (1989), for example, retested her subjects three months after the instruction and found that the learners' improved ability to use French *imparfait* and *passé composé*, as evident in an immediate post-test, had not only been maintained but extended even further. L. White *et al.* (1991) found that increased accuracy in the formation of questions, evident in the same learners that White had investigated, did not slip back to pre-instruction levels. In fact, the learners were still improving some six months later.

Norris and Ortega (2000) meta-analysed twelve FFI studies that reported results for both immediate and delayed post-tests. The mean effect size for the immediate post-tests was $d = 1.32$ while that for the delayed post-tests was $d = 1.17$ (delayed post-test 1) and $d = 1.06$ (delayed post-test 2). They noted that although there was a decrease from the immediate post-test to the second delayed post-test, this was relatively small (i.e. on average less than three-tenths of a standard deviation point). They also noted that the decrease was less in studies with longer-term treatments (i.e. 3 hours or more in duration) than in studies where the instruction lasted less than two hours. Overall, then, this analysis indicated that the effects of instruction are durable. Keck *et al.*'s (2006) meta-analysis supported Norris and Ortega's findings. They found an effect for interaction treatments in post-tests administered 8–29 days (considered a short delay; $d = 1.12$) and 30–60 days (considered a long delay; $d = 1.18$) after the treatment.

There is, however, sufficient evidence to suggest that instruction does not *always* have a long-term effect. Why might this be? One very plausible possibility is that advanced by Lightbown (1992a). She suggested:

> ... when form-focused instruction is introduced in a way which is divorced from the communicative needs and activities of the students, only short-term effects are obtained.

In other words, learners benefit most from FFI that is embedded in communicative activities; they may also need subsequent and possibly continuous access to communication that utilizes the target features after the instruction has ceased.

Although this is an attractive explanation, it does not appear to account fully for the results of all the studies mentioned above. It is reasonable to assume, for instance, that the structures investigated by Lightbown *et al.*

(1980)—various –s morphemes, copula 'be', and locative prepositions—and that investigated by Pienemann (1984)—copula 'be'—are frequent in classroom input and that opportunities for producing them were available to the learners. Yet the effects of instruction directed at these features tended to disappear. It would seem, then, that other factors are involved. One possibility is the saliency of the target feature. Features such as copula 'be' and –s morphemes are not very salient. Thus, although they occur frequently, they may not easily be perceived in continuous speech. These features may also not be seen as very important for message conveyance. If learners are motivated primarily by communicative need, then they will probably retain only those features that they perceive to be important for communication, as suggested by Meisel, Clahsen, and Pienemann (1981) and by proponents of some functional theories of L2 acquisition. (See Chapter 9.) It should be noted that these explanations are subtly different from the one Lightbown has advanced. Whereas Lightbown emphasized opportunity for hearing and using a structure, these explanations suggest that such opportunity constitutes a necessary but not sufficient condition to ensure retention of learnt grammar—the learner needs to be able to perceive structures in the input and requires a motive for remembering them.

Another possible explanation for the absence of durable effects can be found in Tode (2007). Tode examined the effects of IMPLICIT and EXPLICIT INSTRUCTION on Japanese high-school students' acquisition of copula 'be'. She found that the explicit instruction had a positive effect that declined somewhat but was still evident in a delayed post-test, but subsequently disappeared after the same learners had been provided with instruction in progressive 'be'. This study suggested that the effects of FFI might be lost if learners receive instruction in a related structure and are unable to sort out the two structures in their interlanguage systems.

It should be noted that a number of studies (for example, Mackey 1999; Ellis, Loewen, and Erlam 2006) reported that statistically significant effects for instruction were not immediately evident but only emerged in the delayed post-tests. Thus, it is also necessary to explain why this might occur. The likely explanation again lies in the nature of the target structure. In Ellis (2007), for example, I reported that whereas explicit corrective feedback had an immediate effect on the acquisition of comparative adjectives, it only had a delayed effect on the acquisition of past tense –ed. This might be because the learners possessed solid explicit knowledge of past tense –ed but not of comparative –er prior to the instruction. The instruction served to develop the learners' explicit knowledge of comparative –er, which accounted for its immediate effect. In the case of past tense –ed, however, the instruction activated learners' existing explicit knowledge, which primed them to attend to this feature in subsequent input with the result that gains became apparent in the delayed test.

It is clearly essential to establish whether the learning that results from instruction persists (or only emerges later); a positive feature of most recent

FFI studies is that they include one or more delayed post-tests. In general, the effects of FFI appear to be durable but there are exceptions and these are important for both language pedagogy and SLA theory building.

The effects of different types of formal instruction

The research that we have considered so far has attempted to answer the question 'Does formal instruction result in the acquisition of the features that have been taught?' This research has viewed formal instruction generically as involving attention to form and the provision of corrective feedback. (See Krashen and Seliger 1975.) In taking this view, researchers have been able to gain insight into the nature of the complex relationship between instruction and L2 learning, and also to shed light on the processes of acquisition. From the teacher's perspective, however, another question is of equal if not of greater importance: 'What kind of formal instruction works best?' Later research has focused on this question by distinguishing a number of methodological options available to teachers.[9]

Methodological options for FFI

There are now a number of frameworks specifying the various methodological options involved in FFI (for example, Ellis 1997, 1998, 2001; Doughty and Williams 1998; Norris and Ortega 2000). Such frameworks are valuable for a number of reasons. First, they provide a basis for describing the types of FFI available to teachers. Second, they enable SLA researchers to systematically investigate the effects of specific options on L2 acquisition. This is important for SLA theory development; carefully designed FFI studies provide a means of testing fine-grained hypotheses concerning the relationship between features of input/interaction/output and learning.

My own framework of options (see Ellis 1998) distinguished four macro-options:

1 Input-based options (i.e. instruction that involves the manipulation of the input that learners are exposed to or are required to process). They include input flooding (i.e. input that contains many examples of the target structure), enhanced input (i.e. input with the target feature made salient to the learners, for example, by means of emphatic stress or bolding), and structured input (i.e. input that has been contrived to induce processing of the target feature). These options are all comprehension-based.
2 Explicit options (i.e. instruction directed at helping learners develop explicit knowledge of the target structure). They include both direct explicit instruction (i.e. learners are provided with metalinguistic descriptions of the target feature) and indirect explicit instruction (i.e. learners are provided with data illustrating the target feature and are required to 'discover' the rule for themselves).

3 Production options (i.e. instruction directed at enabling/inducing learners to produce utterances containing the target structure). Production options can be distinguished in terms of whether they involve text-manipulation (for example, fill-in-the-blank exercises) or text-creation (for example, focused tasks). (See Chapter 15.) They can also be distinguished in terms of whether they are error-avoiding or error-inducing.
4 CORRECTIVE FEEDBACK options. As discussed in Chapters 6 and 15, corrective feedback can be implicit (for example, by means of RECASTS or REQUESTS FOR CLARIFICATION) or explicit (for example, metalinguistic explanation or elicitation). It can also be input-providing (for example, recasts or metalinguistic explanation) or output-prompting (for example, requests for clarification or elicitation).

The research that we will consider below has sought to compare the relative effectiveness of different pairs of options. One comparison, for example, involves implicit (input-based) instruction versus explicit instruction. Another involves input-based versus production instruction. However, these macro-distinctions have been variously operationalized by researchers, as each involves a number of possible micro-options, making it difficult to synthesize the results obtained by different studies. As Norris and Ortega (2000) pointed out, FFI research has not been designed and reported 'in a manner accessible for further cumulative analysis'. It should also be noted that what is often considered best practice in FFI, as attested in popular handbooks for teachers (for example, Ur 1996), is a combination of options (for example, explicit instruction + production options).

Another macro-distinction that has figured strongly in recent FFI research is FOCUS-ON-FORMS versus FOCUS-ON-FORM (Long 1991; Doughty and Williams 1998). Focus-on-forms refers to instruction that seeks to isolate linguistic forms in order to teach them one at a time as when language teaching is based on a structural syllabus. Focus-on-form was defined and considered in some detail in Chapter 15. It involves 'alternating in some principled way between a focus on meaning and a focus-on-form' (Long 1991) and involves the use of tasks as opposed to exercises. This distinction involves all the macro-options listed above, as shown in Table 16.6.

The definition of focus-on-form and focus-on-forms types of instruction is debated, however. In Ellis (2001b), I chose to define these in terms of whether learners attend to form while they are primarily oriented towards message-comprehension/production in order to achieve the outcome of some 'task' as opposed to whether they attend to form in activities whose principal goal is accurate language use (i.e. in 'exercises' of one kind of another). This corresponds closely to Long's original definition (Long 1991; Long and Robinson 1998) and is reflected in Table 16.6. An alternative definition, favoured by some, is to view focus-on-form as instruction that is directed at establishing form–meaning mappings, and focus-on-forms as instruction directed solely

Macro-option	Focus-on-forms	Focus-on-form
Input-based	Any input-based option can be used; learners are directed to pay attention to the target form.	Any input-based option that centres on form–meaning mapping; learners are not told what the target form is so any attention to it is incidental.
Explicit instruction	Typically direct explicit instruction but also indirect instruction by means of consciousness-raising tasks.	No explicit instruction of any kind is provided.
Output-based	A variety of text-manipulation and text creation options. Also, both error-avoiding and error-inducing options are possible.	Only text creation options with no attempt made to either avoid or induce errors.
Corrective feedback	Typically explicit types of feedback.	Typically implicit types of feedback.

Table 16.6 Focus-on-forms and focus-on-form types of instruction

at formal accuracy by means of traditional, controlled exercises. For example, Doughty and Williams (1998) distinguished the two types as follows:

> ... a focus-on-form entails a focus on the formal elements of language, whereas focus-on-forms is not limited to such a focus ... the fundamental assumption of focus-on-form instruction is that meaning and use must be evident to the learner at the time that attention is drawn to the linguistic apparatus needed to get the meaning across.
> (p. 4)

Further, Doughty and Williams argued that both types can include explicit instruction and that the distinction between the two types constitutes a continuum rather than a dichotomy.

We will begin our examination of the different types of instruction by examining research that has investigated the focus-on-forms versus focus-on-form distinction. We will then consider input-based options, implicit versus explicit FFI and inductive versus deductive FFI. Finally, we will look at research that has investigated error-inducing production practice and corrective feedback.

Focus-on-forms versus focus-on-form

While there have been a number of studies that have investigated whether focus-on-form is effective in enabling learners to acquire the target feature (see Chapter 15), there have been relatively few studies that have explicitly attempted to compare the two types of FFI. Indeed, this lacuna lies at the core of R. Sheen's (2003) critique of advocates of focus-on-form in task-based language teaching. In order to conduct a comparison, therefore, it is necessary to code studies that were designed to investigate some other aspect of FFI as either focus-on-forms or focus-on-form.

In the 49 studies that Norris and Ortega (2000) included in their meta-analysis, 56 per cent of the instructional treatments were categorized as focus-on-forms, with 80 per cent of these involving some form of explicit instruction. Of the 44 per cent of treatments coded as focus-on-form, 58 per cent involved explicit techniques. They distinguished the two types of instruction in terms of whether there was evidence of an integration of form or meaning via the use of focused tasks that required primary attention to meaning, or evidence of an attempt to ensure that the instruction was unobtrusive, or evidence of the documentation of the learners' mental processes (for example, 'noticing'). If any of these strategies were found, the treatment was coded as focus-on-form. If none was found, it was coded as focus-on-forms. These operationalizations of the two types of instruction differ somewhat from Table 16.6, in particular because they include as focus-on-form treatments where learners are explicitly required to attend to the target structure.

Norris and Ortega's meta-analysis provided evidence that both focus-on-forms and focus-on-form instruction are effective. The mean effect size for focus-on-form was $d = 1.92$ while that for focus-on-forms was slightly smaller: $d = 1.47$. Both effect sizes are considered to be 'large'. However, Norris and Ortega noted that the standard deviations for both types were also large and that, therefore, the analyses could not be considered trustworthy. They concluded that there was no real difference between the two types of instruction.

There are a number of problems with Norris and Ortega's comparison of focus-on-forms and focus-on-form. The first is their operationalizations of the two types of instruction. To my mind, Norris and Ortega have failed to recognize that an essential feature of focus-on-form instruction is that it involves incidental rather than intentional learning. (See Chapter 9 for definitions of these.) That is, learners must *not* approach the treatment activities with the goal of learning some pre-determined and explicitly presented target structure. I believe this is unlikely if learners receive explicit instruction in the target structure, which was the case in more than half of the studies they coded as focus-on-form. The second is that because the bulk of both the studies classified as focus-on-form and focus-on-forms involved some kind of explicit instruction, there was a bias towards instruction likely to lead to METALINGUAL KNOWLEDGE about language (Doughty 2003). The third problem, related to the second, is that the methods of measuring learning outcomes in the studies investigated again favoured treatments that included explicit instruction.

Thus, it is not clear to me that we are in a position to decide which type of instruction (focus-on-forms or focus-on-form) is the more effective. Nor is it likely that the situation will become clearer until there are explicit, operationalizable, and widely accepted definitions of these instructional types. It may be that, theoretically interesting as this distinction is, the range of micro-options entailed in each precludes a convincing comparison. Indeed, it could be argued that any attempt to compare the two approaches will run into the same problems as the global method studies considered in an earlier section of this chapter.

Input-based instruction

Input-based instruction is directed at enabling learners to (1) notice the presence of a specific feature in the input, (2) comprehend the meaning of the feature, and (3) rehearse the feature in short-term memory. One of the assumptions of input-based FFI is that it is psycholinguistically easier to manipulate the processes involved in intake than it is to induce learners to restructure their interlanguage systems. Pienemann (1985) noted that 'the input to the comprehension system does not need to be adjusted to the level of complexity of the production learning task since there are different types of processing procedures in the two systems' (1985: 53). Input-based FFI can be distinguished in terms of whether it involves ENRICHED INPUT or processing instruction. I will consider each separately as they have different theoretical bases.

Enriched input

Studies that have investigated enriched input options have drawn on Schmidt's Noticing Hypothesis and the Frequency Hypothesis. (See Chapter 6.) Enriched input can take the form of oral or written texts that learners simply listen to or read (i.e. input-flooding) or texts where the target structure has been highlighted in some way (for example, through the use of underlining or bold print). Three groups of enriched input studies can be identified: (1) studies designed to investigate whether the forms targeted in the enriched input are noticed by learners, (2) studies designed to investigate whether enriched input promotes acquisition, and (3) studies comparing the effects of enriched input with some other instructional option. (See Ellis 1999b.) We will consider (1) and (2) in this section and (3) below.

In accordance with the Noticing Hypothesis, enriched input can only work for acquisition if learners actually pay attention to the target structure. It is, therefore, important to demonstrate that noticing does in fact occur. Jourdenais, Ota, Stauffer, Boyson and Doughty (1995) found that English speaking learners of L2 Spanish were more likely to make explicit reference to preterite and imperfect verb forms when thinking aloud during a narrative writing task if they had previously read texts where the forms were typologically highlighted. They also found that the learners exposed to the enhanced text were more likely to use past tense forms than the learners who read the non-enhanced text even though both texts had been enriched. Yoshimura (2006) asked groups of Japanese learners of English to read a text under three conditions—to memorize it, to retell it, and to draw a picture based on it. In this study, then, it was not the input *per se* that was manipulated but rather the learners' orientation to the input—a different way of viewing 'enrichment'. Yoshimura hypothesized that more noticing would occur in conditions one and two than condition three. This was largely supported in a fill-in-the-blanks production post-test of verbs in the text.

Studies that have investigated the effects of enriched input on L2 acquisition have produced mixed results. Trahey and White (1993) examined whether enriched input (viewed as 'positive input') was sufficient to enable francophone learners of L2 English to learn that English permits adverb placement between the subject and the verb (French does not) but does not permit placement between the verb and object (French does). Exposure occurred 1 hour a day for 10 days. The learners succeeded in learning the SAV position but failed to 'unlearn' the ungrammatical SVAO position. Trahey (1996) found the same pattern of results in a follow-up test administered one year after the treatment. Leeman, Arteagoitia, Fridman, and Doughty (1995) examined the effects of INPUT ENHANCEMENT on the acquisition of preterite and imperfect verbs forms that were highlighted in written input. The learners were told to pay special attention to how temporal relations were expressed in Spanish and received corrective feedback from the teacher. Post-tests showed that the learners outperformed a comparison group that did not receive the enhanced input. However, because they received instruction involving several options, it is not possible to claim that the benefits were solely due to the enriched input. J. White (1998) compared the effects of three types of enriched input: (1) typographically enhanced input flood plus extensive listening and reading, (2) typographically enhanced input by itself, and (3) typically unenhanced input flood. This study found that the three types of enriched input worked equally effectively in assisting francophone learners to acquire the possessive pronouns 'his' and 'her', leading White to conclude that the target structure was equally salient in all three.

What conclusions are possible about the efficacy of enriched input as an FFI option? There is some evidence that enriched input involving either highlighting or orienting learners to attend to form induces noticing of target features. However, little is yet known about which approach to enrichment works best. There is fairly convincing evidence that enriched input can help L2 learners acquire some new grammatical features and use partially learnt features more consistently, although it may not enable learners to eradicate erroneous rules from their interlanguage. Also, clear positive effects may only be evident when the treatment provides learners with extensive exposure to the target features and is relatively prolonged.

Input processing instruction

PROCESSING INSTRUCTION makes use of STRUCTURED INPUT but cannot be equated with it. I will begin by considering structured input and then move on to examine processing instruction.

Structured input differs from enriched input in that it presents learners with input in a context that requires them to demonstrate that they have correctly processed the target structure for meaning. The demonstration takes the form of a learner response to an input stimulus, with the response being either non-verbal (for example, choosing the picture that matches the stimulus) or minimally verbal (for example, indicating whether they agree/disagree with some statement). This is achieved by means of 'interpretation tasks' (Ellis 1995a). In Ellis (1995a), I provided a set of guidelines for designing interpretation tasks:

1 An interpretation task consists of a stimulus to which learners must make some kind of response.
2 The stimulus can take the form of spoken or written input.
3 The response can take various forms (for example, indicate true/false, check a box, select the correct picture, draw a diagram, perform an action) but in each case the response will be completely nonverbal or minimally verbal.
4 The activities in the task can be sequenced to require first attention to meaning, then noticing the form and function of the grammatical structure, and finally error identification.
5 Learners should have the opportunity to make some kind of personal response (i.e. relate the input to their own lives).

Interpretation tasks are the essential feature of input-processing instruction. However, as we will see, not all studies that have investigated FFI by means of such tasks have involved input-processing instruction.

VanPatten (1996) defined processing instruction as 'a type of grammar instruction whose purpose is to affect the ways in which learners attend to input data. It is input-based rather than output-based ...' (p. 2). What is distinctive about it is the theoretical basis for identifying instructional targets. This consists of a set of principles that is hypothesized to govern how learners process input. (See Chapter 9.) Only grammatical features that are governed by these principles are deemed suitable targets for investigating input-processing instruction.

VanPatten argued that instruction that draws attention to form–meaning mappings will prove more effective than traditional production practice. This claim has been tested in a series of studies that compared the relative effects of practice involving structured input activities and controlled production activities on learners' acquisition of target structures governed by one of the processing principles. Acquisition in these studies was measured by both comprehension (interpretation) and production tests. Two points need to be noted about these studies. The first is that the instructional treatments generally included metalinguistic explanations. The second is that, with a few exceptions, the tests measuring acquisition did not measure learners' ability to process the target structures in unplanned language use. Summaries of a representative selection of these studies are provided in Table 16.7.

In the initial study, VanPatten and Cadierno (1993) compared the effects of two instructional treatments, one directed at manipulating learners' output to effect change in their developing interlanguage systems (i.e. production practice), and the other aimed at changing the way the learners perceived and processed input (i.e. interpretation). Learners of Spanish at university level who received interpretation training relating to Spanish word order rules and the use of clitic pronouns performed better in comprehension tests than a group of similar learners who received production training. This result is not perhaps surprising, as it can be argued that the comprehension test favoured the interpretation group. However, this group also performed at the same level as the traditional practice group in a production task that favoured the latter. This study, then, provided evidence that processing instruction was superior to traditional production practice.

One of the problems with this study was that both the experimental groups received explicit instruction. Thus, what the study really showed was that explicit instruction + input processing practice was more effective than explicit instruction + production practice. However, VanPatten argued that explicit instruction is not an essential element of processing instruction. In a subsequent study he set out to investigate whether this was in fact the case. VanPatten and Oikennon (1996) compared three groups: (1) received explicit information about the target structure followed by structured input activities, (2) received only explicit information, and (3) just completed the structured input activities. Acquisition was measured by means of both interpretation and production tests. In the comprehension test, significant gains were evident in groups (1) and (3), but not in (2). In the production test, group (1) did better than group (2). VanPatten and Oikennon interpreted these results as showing that it was the structured input rather than the explicit information that was important for acquisition. Other studies (for example, Sanz and Morgan-Short 2004; Benati 2004) have since replicated these results. Benati concluded that explicit information does not play a major role in input-processing instruction.

Thus, by and large the studies support VanPatten's theoretical claims. That is, they show that input-based instruction results in superior performance to controlled output-based instruction when acquisition is measured by means of interpretation tests, and in equal performance in discrete item production tests. They also show that explicit instruction is not required for input processing to be effective. Nevertheless, there are a number of remaining doubts. First, most of the studies have not examined whether input-processing

Study	Participants	Target structure	Treatments	Measures of acquisition	Results
VanPatten and Cadierno (1993)	129 second-year university-level learners of L2 Spanish	Position of object clitic pronouns in Spanish	Two instructional conditions: (1) traditional instruction (TI) (explanation + mechanical form-oriented practice; (2) input-processing instruction (IP) (explanation + structured-input activities).	(1) interpretation test: sentence-matching; (2) production test: picture-cued sentence-completion test; immediate and delayed post-tests.	IP group outperformed TI group on the interpretation test and performed as well on the production test. Differences maintained in delayed test.
VanPatten and Sanz (1995)	44 third- semester university learners of L2 Spanish	As in VanPatten and Cadierno (1993)	Processing instruction (explicit instruction + structured input; control group.	(1) interpretation test; (2) discrete point production test; (3) structured interview; (4) oral and written video narration.	The PI group outperformed the control on tests (1), (2), and (4) written production. No effect evident on (4) oral production. (3) provided insufficient obligatory occasions for analysis.
VanPatten and Oikennon (1996)	59 fourth semester learners of L2 Spanish in a high school	As in VanPatten and Cadierno (1993)	Three instructional conditions: (1) explicit instruction + structured input; (2) explicit information only; (3) structured input only.	As in VanPatten and Cadierno (1993)	(1) and (3) resulted in significant gains in the interpretation tests but not (2). All three led to gains on the production test with the gains for (1) greatest.
Allen (2000)[10]	140 fourth semester high-school learners of L2 French	French causative (e.g. use of 'faire' in sentences like 'faire du ski nautique')	Three groups: (1) processing instruction (explicit instruction + structured input); (2) production activities involving both controlled and communicative activities but with no explicit instruction; (3) no instruction.	(1) interpretation test; (2) distractor test (on a different grammatical structure); (3) open-ended written production test.	No difference between (1) and (2) on the interpretation test (both were superior to control group); (2) outperformed (1) on the production test.
Wong (2004)	72 first quarter university learners of L2 French	Article use in negative and affirmative statements (i.e. 'un'/ 'une' versus 'de')	Three instructional conditions: (1) full processing instruction (explanation instruction (EI) + structured input (SI); (2) EI only; (3) SI only. Control group.	(1) interpretation test; (2) sentence completion production task.	PI and SI group were significantly better than EI and control group on the interpretation test. PI and SI groups were better than the control group on the production test but only the PI group was better than the EI group.
Sanz and Morgan-Short (2004)	69 first- and second-year university learners of L2 Spanish	As in VanPatten and Cadierno (1993)	Computer-delivered structured-input activities in four conditions: (1) + explicit instruction (EI)/ + feedback (F); (2) – EI/ – F; (3) + EI/ – F; (4) – EI/ + F.	(1) Interpretation test; (2) sentence completion production test; (3) written video-retelling task.	All groups improved significantly and similarly on all three measures.

Table 16.7 Selected input processing studies

instruction results in the ability to use the target structure in unplanned language use. VanPatten and Sanz (1995) did attempt to address this issue by including measures of free constructed responses. The input-processing group significantly improved their accuracy in producing the target structure (preverbal object pronouns in L2 Spanish) on all the written tests, outperforming the control group, which showed no improvement. However, no statistically significant difference was found between the two groups on an oral video narration test. Marsden (2006), however, found that processing instruction did result in statistically significant gains in measures obtained from oral narratives and guided conversation tasks in the first of the two studies she reported but not in the other. Also, even in the first study the gains were marginal and much weaker than those evident in discrete point tests. Overall, then, there is still no convincing evidence that input-processing instruction is effective (or more effective than other instructional techniques) in developing the implicit knowledge needed to use the target structure in oral communication.

A second doubt arises because some studies failed to find an advantage for input-processing over production practice (for example, DeKeyser and Sokalski 1996). In fact, in some studies (for example, Allen 2000) production-based practice was shown to result in higher scores in the production tests. Two explanations for these non-predicted findings have been offered. VanPatten (2002) argued that input-processing instruction is only effective for those target structures that involve learners overcoming default-processing strategies (i.e. structures governed by his input-processing principles) and that studies where no advantage was found for input-based practice had selected inappropriate target structures. The second explanation is that some studies (for example, Erlam 2003) compared input-based practice with *meaning-based* production practice rather than with traditional production and that such instruction, like input-processing instruction, enables learners to map meaning onto form. However, this latter explanation does not explain why the meaning-based production practice was shown to be superior in both Allen's and Erlam's studies.

Input-processing instruction continues to attract the attention of researchers (for example, the collection of studies in VanPatten 2004b) and also debate (for example, DeKeyser, Salaberry, Robinson, and Harrington's (2002) commentary on VanPatten's (2002) defence of input-processing instruction).

Implicit versus explicit instruction

DeKeyser (2003) drew a distinction between explicit/implicit instruction and deductive/inductive instruction.[11] I will consider implicit versus explicit instruction in this section and inductive versus deductive explicit instruction in the section following.

Explicit FFI involves 'some sort of rule being thought about during the learning process' (DeKeyser 1995). In other words, learners are encouraged to develop metalinguistic awareness of the rule. This can be achieved deductively or inductively. (See next section.) Implicit instruction is directed at enabling learners to infer rules without awareness. Thus it contrasts with explicit instruction in that there is an absence of externally-prompted awareness of what is being learnt. Housen and Pierrard (2006a) differentiated implicit and explicit FFI in terms of a number of characteristics, as shown in Table 16.8.

It should be noted that the terms explicit and implicit instruction can only be defined from a perspective external to the learner—i.e. the teacher's, material writer's, or course designer's perspective. In contrast, the terms implicit/explicit learning and INTENTIONAL/INCIDENTAL L2 LEARNING (see Chapter 9) refer to the learner's perspective. These distinctions should not be treated as isomorphic. That is, it does not follow that implicit instruction results in implicit/incidental learning nor that explicit instruction necessarily leads to explicit/intentional learning.

Implicit FFI	**Explicit FFI**
• *attracts* attention to target form	• directs attention to target form
• is delivered *spontaneously* (e.g. in an otherwise communication-oriented activity)	• is *predetermined* and *planned* (e.g. as the main focus and goal of a teaching activity)
• is unobtrusive (minimal interruption of communication of meaning)	• is obtrusive (interruption of communicative meaning)
• presents target forms in context	• presents target forms in isolation
• makes no use of metalanguage	• uses metalinguistic terminology (e.g. rule explanation)
• encourages free use of the target form	• involves controlled practice of target form

Table 16.8 Implicit and explicit FFI (Housen and Pierrard 2006a: 10)

Norris and Ortega's (2000) meta-analysis reported an overall effect size for 29 implicit treatments of $d = 0.54$ and $d = 1.13$ for the 69 explicit treatments. In other words, there was a clear advantage for explicit treatments. In fact, this was the single trustworthy finding for the overall effect of FFI that they were able to report. It should be noted, however, that the studies they included in their analysis operationalized both implicit and explicit instruction in very different ways. For example, implicit instruction could be either enriched input which learners were asked to process for comprehension or a set of sentences containing the target feature which learners were asked to memorize.[12] In the case of studies classified as explicit instruction, some of the treatments consisted solely of metalinguistic explanation while others also included production practice.

Studies where implicit instruction involved enriched input include Doughty (1991), Alanen (1995), and Williams and Evans (1998). Doughty compared the effects of 'meaning-oriented instruction' and 'rule-oriented instruction' on the acquisition of relative clauses by 20 intermediate-level ESL students from different language backgrounds. The materials consisted of computer-presented reading passages, specially written to contain examples of clauses where the direct object had been relativized. All the subjects skimmed the texts first. The meaning-oriented group received support in the form of lexical and semantic rephrasings and sentence clarification strategies (i.e. input enhancement). The rule-oriented group received instruction in the form of explicit rule statements and on-screen sentence manipulation. A control group simply read the text again. The results showed that the meaning-oriented group and the rule-oriented group both outperformed the control group in their ability to relativize. There was no difference between the two experimental groups. The group that received input-enhancement, however, demonstrated an advantage with regard to comprehension of the content of the text.

In Alanen's study there were four groups: (1) a control group, (2) an 'enhancement group' which received just enriched input in two fifteen-minute instructional periods, (3) a 'rule group' that received just explicit instruction, and (4) a 'rule + enhanced group' that received both enriched input and explicit instruction. The enriched input took the form of two short texts in which the target features had been italicized. Learning was measured by means of a sentence completion task, a grammaticality judgement task, and a rule statement task. The learners were also asked to think aloud during the treatment. The main finding was that groups (3) and (4) outperformed groups (1) and (2). Also, there was no difference between groups (1) and (2) or between groups (3) and (4). One possible reason why the enriched input had no clear effect on acquisition in this study was that the period of instruction may have been too short.

Williams and Evans (1998) compared the effects of enriched input (consisting of an artificially increased incidence of the highlighted target forms) and the same input plus explicit instruction and corrective feedback on the acquisition of English participial adjectives (for example, 'boring/bored') and present passive. For participial adjectives, the explicit instruction group did better than both the enriched input group and the control group on a grammaticality judgement test and a sentence completion test while the difference between the enriched group and the control did not reach statistical significance. For the passive, both the implicit and explicit groups outperformed the control group on a sentence completion test, but no group differences were evident on a narrative test.

I will now consider representative studies that have operationalized implicit instruction by requiring learners to memorize a set of sentences containing the target feature but without any requirement that they comprehend the sentences. N. Ellis (1993) compared the effects of three kinds of instruction on adult university students' ability to learn the rules of soft mutation in Welsh. These rules require that initial consonants in Welsh nouns mutate (for example, /t/→/d/) in accordance with a complex set of contextual factors.

Learners taught implicitly (i.e. given randomly ordered examples of mutating and non-mutating nouns in different contexts they were asked to memorize) showed very uncertain knowledge of the rules of soft mutation. Learners taught explicitly (i.e. given an account of the rules for soft mutation) developed a solid knowledge of the rules but could not always make accurate use of them when asked to judge correct and incorrect noun forms. Learners given a 'structured' treatment (i.e. rules and examples of how to apply them) did best. They learnt the rules and they were also successful in using them in judging the grammaticality of sentences. Ellis noted that 'this group alone knows when novel phrases are ungrammatical'.

Robinson (1996b) investigated adult Japanese learners' acquisition of two English structures—one easy (subject–verb inversion following adverbial fronting) and one difficult (pseudo-clefts of location). There were four instructional conditions: (1) an implicit condition (remembering sentences), (2) an incidental condition (exposure in meaning-centred task), (3) a rule-search condition (identifying rules), and (4) an instructed condition (written explanations of rules). Acquisition was measured by means of grammaticality judgement tests with response times also recorded. There was also a debriefing questionnaire to measure awareness of the rules. The instructed condition proved more effective than the implicit condition in accuracy of judgements for both the easy and difficult structures but the difference only reached statistical significance for the easy structure. The instructed learners were also better than the implicit learners at verbalizing the easy rule but, interestingly, the implicit learners were better at verbalizing the hard rule.

Rosa and O'Neill (1999) compared the effects of instruction directed at the Spanish contrary-to-fact conditional (a complex structure) by university-level learners of L2 Spanish. Four types of instruction were included in this study: (1) rule explanation + rule search, (2) rule explanation + no rule search; (3) no rule explanation + rule search; and (4) no rule explanation + no rule search. Acquisition was measured by means of a time-pressured multiple-choice recognition task while think-aloud protocols were used to measure awareness of the rule. The instructed condition (i.e. (1)) proved superior to the implicit condition (i.e. (4)). Groups (1) and (2) performed equally. However, all the groups (including the implicit group) improved from pre- to post-test.

By and large, these studies bear out Norris and Ortega's finding that explicit instruction is more effective than implicit instruction. Five of the studies (Alanen; Williams and Evans; N. Ellis; Robinson; Rosa and O'Neill) found that learners receiving explicit instruction outperformed learners receiving implicit instruction. This general conclusion applies irrespective of how the implicit instruction was operationalized (i.e. whether in terms of enriched input or through an instruction to memorize a set of sentences). However, a number of caveats are in order. The studies suggest that explicit instruction is more effective when it is directed at easy rather than difficult structures. Both Williams and Robinson found no statistically significant differences between the implicit and explicit learners for the complex structures in their studies.

Also, one study (Doughty) found no difference between the implicit and explicit instruction. A key feature of this study is that the implicit condition did not just expose learners to input but provided them with an opportunity to view reformulations and clarifications of it. There is plenty of other evidence to suggest that premodified input facilitates learning. (See Chapter 6.)

The final caveat concerns how acquisition was measured in these studies—the same problem that we noted in the discussion of the input-processing studies. In the Williams and Evans (1998) study, for example, the beneficial effects of explicit instruction were evident in the sentence-completion test but not in the narrative test. The key question, then, is whether explicit instruction is effective when learning is measured in terms of 'free constructed responses'. In Ellis (2008), I reviewed a number of studies that suggest it is effective but in all of these studies explicit instruction was combined with some other instructional option (typically production practice). Evidence showing that explicit instruction by itself results in improved accuracy in free production is still lacking.

Inductive versus deductive explicit instruction

Explicit instruction can take the form of an inductive treatment, where learners are required to induce rules from examples given to them, or an explicit treatment, where learners are given a rule which they then practise using. This distinction underlies the 'language teaching controversy' (Diller 1978) of the 1960s and early 1970s, in which the claims of an empiricist approach (such as the audiolingual method) were pitted against those of a rationalist approach (such as the cognitive code method).[13]

Several studies have compared deductive and inductive explicit instruction when these are combined with practice activities. Unfortunately, these two types of instruction have been operationalized very differently, making comparison of their results difficult. Seliger (1975), for example, investigated the effects of presenting metalinguistic information *before* and *after* practice activities, whereas Robinson (1996b) and Rosa and O'Neill (1999) investigated the effects of giving students a rule as opposed to asking them to search for a rule. In a review of such studies, Erlam (2005), not surprisingly, found conflicting results, with some studies favouring DEDUCTIVE INSTRUCTION, others INDUCTIVE INSTRUCTION and some finding no difference. Erlam's own study investigated the effects of these two types of instruction on the acquisition of direct object pronouns in French as a foreign language. She reported a distinct advantage for the deductive instruction in both comprehension and production tests but she also noted that there was much greater individual variation in the deductive group. A tentative general conclusion might be that deductive FFI is more effective than inductive FFI (when both involve practice activities) but it is possible that this may in part depend on the learner's preferred learning style (Eisenstein 1980).

Other studies have examined the relative effects of metalinguistic explanations provided by the teacher (i.e. deductive FFI) and consciousness-raising (CR) tasks[14] where learners discover rules for themselves (i.e. inductive FFI). Fotos and Ellis (1991) found that both teacher-provided metalinguistic explanation and a CR task resulted in significant gains in understanding of the target structure (dative alternation), although the former seemed to produce the more durable gains. However, Fotos (1994) found no statistically significant difference between these two types in a follow-up study that investigated three different grammatical structures (adverb placement, dative alternation, and relative clauses). Mohamed (2001) found that a CR task was more effective than metalinguistic explanation with groups of high-intermediate ESL learners from mixed L1 backgrounds but not with a group of low-intermediate learners. This study suggests that the effectiveness of CR tasks may depend on the proficiency of learners. Leow (1997b) asked learners to think aloud while they completed a crossword puzzle designed to develop awareness of Spanish irregular third person singular and plural preterite forms of stem-changing –ir verbs such as 'repetir'. He found that increased levels of meta-awareness correlated with greater 'conceptually-driven processing' such as hypothesis-testing and morphological rule formation. Furthermore, discrete-item post-tests showed that those learners who demonstrated high levels of meta-awareness were better able to both recognize and produce the correct target forms.

However, none of these studies produced convincing evidence that deductive explicit FFI results in L2 implicit knowledge, as the tests they used to measure learning were of the kind that were likely to tap explicit knowledge. Fotos (1993) was able to show that the explicit knowledge the learners gained from her CR tasks may have aided the processes believed to be involved in the acquisition of implicit knowledge. She showed that completing the CR tasks aided subsequent noticing of the targeted features. Several weeks after the completion of the CR tasks, the learners in her study completed a number of dictations that included exemplars of the target structures. They were then asked to underline any particular bit of language they had paid special attention to as they did the dictation. Fotos found that they frequently underlined the structures that had been targeted in the CR tasks.

Production practice—error-inducing

Most production practice is directed at enabling learners to produce the correct target language forms (i.e. by avoiding errors). However, Tomasello and Herron (1988, 1989) compared the effects of two kinds of instruction directed at problematic constructions that led to overgeneralization and transfer errors in beginner learners of L2 French. In one treatment, the problems were explained and illustrated to the students (i.e. explicit instruction). In the other, which Tomasello and Herron referred to as the 'down the garden path' treatment, the typical errors were induced and then immediately corrected.

The results of this study show that leading students down the garden path was more effective. Two explanations for the results were offered. First, Tomasello and Herron suggested that the 'garden path' technique encourages learners to carry out a 'cognitive comparison' between their own deviant utterances and the correct target-language utterances. Second, they suggested this technique may increase motivation to learn by arousing curiosity regarding rules and their exceptions. This study indicates that L2 learners can benefit from the negative evidence provided by corrective feedback.

Corrective feedback

A frequently cited study of corrective feedback is Doughty and Varela (1998). This provided corrective feedback directed at past tense verbs in the context of students' production of oral and written science reports. The feedback consisted of 'corrective recasting', where the teacher first repeated a learner utterance with a past tense error, highlighting the error through emphasis, and then, if this did not result in a learner self-correction, the teacher recast the utterance using the correct verb form (see p. 229 for an example). The students showed significant post-test gains in oral science report tasks, which were largely maintained over time. These gains reflected both increased use of the correct target language forms and also progression to more advanced interlanguage stages. However, only small gains in the written post-test were found and these were not durable.

A number of other studies have compared the effect of different types of corrective feedback on acquisition. These are summarized in Table 16.9. Not all the studies showed such a clear effect for corrective feedback as the Doughty and Varela one and it is not easy to come to clear conclusions due to a number of factors. Implicit feedback in these studies typically took the form of recasts but this constitutes a general cover term for a variety of error-reformulating practices (Ellis and Sheen 2006) so the studies were not necessarily all investigating the same phenomenon. Explicit feedback was also operationalized in very different ways—for example, simply by indicating that an error has been committed (for example, Carroll and Swain's (1993) 'explicit rejection' or Leeman's (2003) 'negative evidence') or by means of more extensive treatment involving the provision of metalinguistic knowledge. Overall, the results point to an advantage for explicit over implicit corrective feedback. There is also some evidence (Nagata 1993; Rosa and Leow 2004) that more detailed METALINGUISTIC FEEDBACK works better. However, not all the studies point to an advantage for explicit feedback. DeKeyser (1993) found no difference between the group receiving extensive explicit feedback and the group receiving limited explicit feedback, although individual difference factors played a role in this study, as discussed in a later section in this chapter. Kim and Mathes (2001), in a study that replicated Carroll and Swain (1993), also failed to find any statistically significant differences in the scores of the explicit and implicit groups. Explicit feedback that consists of simply indicating that a problem exists does not appear to be helpful (Leeman 2003). In the one study (Sanz 2003) which examined feedback as part of input-processing instruction, explicit metalinguistic feedback did not confer any advantage. It is also important to recognize that these studies also provided evidence that implicit methods of feedback can assist learning. The implicit groups in Carroll and Swain (1993), Carroll (2001), Muranoi (2000), Leeman (2003), and Lyster (2004) all scored more highly than the control groups in the post-tests. However, some studies (for example, Ellis, Loewen, and Erlam 2006; Sheen 2006a) found that implicit feedback in the form of recasts was ineffective, possibly because the period of instruction was insufficient for this type of feedback to impact on acquisition.

A number of studies have also investigated another key difference in corrective feedback—whether it is input-providing (as in the case of recasts) or output-prompting (as in the case of elicitations, requests for clarification and metalinguistic clues). In line with his general position that output-prompting feedback is more likely to promote L2 acquisition (at least in the sense of assisting learners to achieve greater control over their existing knowledge), Lyster (2004) compared the relative effects of recasts and prompts on the acquisition of French gender, reporting that both resulted in learning gains, but prompts more so. Ammar and Spada (2006) reported similar results, with low-proficiency learners in particular benefiting from prompts.

The study of corrective feedback constitutes one of the richest veins of enquiry in classroom SLA research. There is clear evidence that corrective feedback contributes to learning. Russell and Spada's (2006) meta-analysis of 15 studies (9 of which investigated classroom learning) reported a mean effect size of 1.16—'a very large effect' (p. 152). Thus, the CF research does not support Truscott's (1999) claim that 'oral correction does not improve learners' ability to speak grammatically' (p. 437). Although Russell and Spada were unable to comment on the relative effectiveness of different CF strategies, due to the small number of studies that met the conditions for meta-analysis, the studies reviewed in Table 16.9 indicate that while implicit types do promote acquisition, explicit and output-prompting types may be more effective. However, this is still a matter of controversy, with some SLA researchers (for example, Doughty 2003) continuing to argue in favour of more implicit, input-providing types of focus-on-form. Overall, the studies reviewed in this section indicate that negative evidence plays an important role in L2 acquisition, contrary to the claims of the zero option.

However, it may not be possible to arrive at a clear-cut conclusion regarding which type of corrective feedback is most effective for L2 learning. It is likely that there are contextual and individual difference factors that mediate any effect that corrective feedback has. The individual learner factors are considered in a later section of this chapter. In Chapter 15, we observed that there are differences regarding the type of feedback that occur in different instructional contexts. (See for example, Lyster and Mori's (2006) comparison of corrective feedback in French and Japanese immersion classrooms.)

Study	Participants	Target structure	Design	Tests	Results
Carroll and Swain (1993)	100 Spanish adult ESL learners (low intermediate)	Dative verbs	Five groups: (A) direct metalinguistic feedback, (B) explicit rejection, (C) recast, (D) indirect metalinguistic feedback, (E) control. Treatment consisted of two feedback sessions, each followed by recall (i.e. production without feedback).	Recall production tasks following each feedback session.	All the treatment groups performed better than the control group on both recall tasks. Group A (direct metalinguistic feedback) outperformed the other groups.
Nagata (1993)	32 second-year university learners of L2 Japanese	Japanese passive structures; verbal predicates and particles	Learners performed computer-based exercises requiring them to respond to sentences produced by an imaginary partner. Sentences were computer-parsed and feedback on errors provided in two forms: (A) traditional group received feedback indicating what was missing or not expected, (B) intelligent group received same feedback + metalinguistic explanations.	Written test using same format as treatment task.	Group (B) significantly outperformed Group (A) on particles but not verbal predicates. Learners expressed preference for metalinguistic explanation.
DeKeyser (1993)	25 Dutch high-school seniors learning L2 French	Variety of features, predominantly morphosyntact-ical	Two groups: (A) extensive explicit corrective feedback during normal class activities, (B) limited explicit corrective feedback. 10 class periods.	Three oral communication tasks (interview, picture description and storytelling); a fill-in-the-blank test. Tests administered twice.	No statistically significant differences evident between groups (A) and (B).
Muranoi (2000)	114 first-year Japanese college students	Indefinite article to denote new information	Three groups: (A) interaction enhancement (IE) by means of requests for repetition and recasts in communicative task + formal debriefing (explicit grammar explanation), (B) IE + meaning-focused debriefing, (C) control (no IE with meaning-focused debriefing).	Grammaticality judgement test; oral production task; written production task; two post-tests 5 weeks apart.	Both experimental groups outperformed the control group on both post-tests; Group A outperformed Group B on post-test 1 but not on post-test 2.

Kim and Mathes (2001)	20 Korean adult ESL learners (high beginners and intermediate)	Dative verbs	One group received explicit metalinguistic feedback; the other recasts; feedback was presented in two sessions one week apart each followed by production with no feedback.	Controlled production tasks (as in the treatment) without feedback.	Differences between performance on first and second production tasks not significant; differences between groups for gains in production not significant. Learners expressed preference for explicit feedback.
Carroll (2001)	100 adult low-intermediate ESL learners	Forming nouns from verbs (e.g. 'help' (V) > 'help'/ 'helping' (N)) and distinguishing THING and EVENT nouns	Five groups as in Carroll and Swain (1993).	Elicited verb–noun conversions in a sentence format.	All types of feedback helped learners to learn the items targeted by the feedback but only explicit metalinguistic information (Group A) and indirect prompting (Group D) enabled learners to form a generalization. Modelling/correction (i.e. recasts) did not facilitate generalization.
Havranek and Cesnik (2003)	207 university students specializing in English	Variety of English phonological, lexical and grammatical features	Data on 1700 corrective feedback episodes from normal English lessons.	Class-specific tests (written, spoken completion tasks; translation; correction and reading-aloud) directed at corrected items.	Effectiveness of corrective feedback techniques was, in order: (1) elicited self-correction, (2) explicit rejection + recast, (3) recast alone.
Leeman (2003)	74 first-year university learners of Spanish	Spanish noun–adjective agreement	Four groups performing communicative task one-on-one with researcher: (A) recast group, (B) negative evidence group (source or problem indicated but not corrected), (C) enhanced salience with no feedback, (D) control group.	Post and delayed post picture descriptions tasks.	Only Groups A and C outperformed the control group on any post-test measure. No difference between A and C.
Sanz (2003)	28 first-year university learners of Spanish	Position of clitic pronouns between object and verb	Computer-delivered input processing instruction without prior explicit instruction. Three groups: (A) explicit metalinguistic feedback, (B) implicit feedback (e.g. 'Sorry, try again.').	(1) Interpretation tests; (2) production tests: (a) sentence completion and (b) written video retelling.	Both groups significantly increased ability to interpret and accurately produce the target structure with no difference between the groups on any measure.
Lyster (2004)	148 (Grade 5) 10–11-year-olds in a French immersion programme	French grammatical gender (articles + nouns)	Group 1 received form-focused instruction (FFI) + recasts; Group 2 FFI + prompts (including explicit feedback); Group 3 FFI only. Control group.	Four tests: (1) binary choice test, (2) text completion test, (oral production tasks), (3) object identification test, (4) picture description test. Two post-tests (PT) with PT2 administered 8 weeks after PT1.	FFI-prompt group was only group to outperform control group on all 8 measures (PT1 and PT2). FFI-recast group outperformed control group on 5 out of 8 measures. FFI-only group outperformed control group on 4 out 8 measures. Statistically significant differences between FFI-prompt and FFI-only groups but not between FFI-recast and FFI-prompt.

Rosa and Leow (2004)	100 adult university learners of L2 Spanish enrolled in advanced courses	Contrary-to-the-fact conditional sentences in the past	Computer-based exposure to input-based jigsaw task characterized by 'task essentialness'. Two groups: (A) explicit feedback to both correct and incorrect responses involving metalinguistic explanation + opportunity to try again if incorrect, (B) implicit feedback indicating whether the answer was right or wrong. Control group.	Three multiple choice recognition tests and three written controlled production tests; immediate and delayed post-tests.	Results presented in terms of 'old' and 'new' items. For the recognition tests a statistically significant difference was evident between (A) and (B) for new but not old items. For the production tests a statistically significant difference was evident for the old but not the new items. Both groups outperformed the control group.
Ellis, Loewen, and Erlam (2006)	34 intermediate-level adult ESL students in private language schools	Regular past tense –ed	Classroom-based exposure to either recasts or metalinguistic feedback (without correction of the error).	(1) Oral imitation tests—OIT (designed to measure implicit knowledge); (2) untimed grammaticality judgement test—UGJT (to measure explicit knowledge; (3) metalinguistic knowledge test (to measure explicit knowledge).	No effect evident for CF on the immediate post-test but the group receiving metalinguistic feedback outperformed both the recast and control groups on both the delayed OIT and UGJT.
Sheen (2006b)	Low-intermediate ESL learners in a community college in the USA	Indefinite and definite articles	Classroom-based exposure to recasts and correction—metalinguistic explanation in the context of performing an oral narrative task.	(1) Dictation test; (2) written narrative test; (3) error corrections test.	Whereas the metalinguistic correction resulted in significant gains in learning in both immediate and post-tests, the recasts did not.
Ammar and Spada (2006)	64 mixed-proficiency learners in three Grade 6 intensive ESL classes	Third-person possessive determiners ('his' and 'her')	Classroom-based corrective feedback consisting of recasts and prompts.	(1) Written passage correction task; (2) Oral picture description task.	High-proficiency learners benefited equally from recasts and prompts; low-proficiency learners benefited more from prompts.

Table 16.9 Empirical studies investigating the effects of different kinds of corrective feedback on L2 acquisition

From a sociocultural perspective, the effectiveness or otherwise of CF does not depend on whether the feedback is implicit or explicit, or input-providing or output-prompting. Rather it depends on the choice of corrective strategy being suited to the construction of a zone of proximal development for the individual learner. (See Chapter 11.)

FFI and implicit knowledge

In the preceding sections we have repeatedly noted that a problem with FFI research is the failure to demonstrate that instruction has any effect on learners' implicit knowledge by including measures based on free and spontaneous production—especially oral production. In this section, I will examine a number of studies that have included such a measure. These studies enable us to address the question 'Does FFI in general have any effect on learners L2 implicit knowledge?'. However, they do not enable us to consider whether different types of FFI are differentially effective in this respect.

Whether FFI is able to affect implicit knowledge is a controversial issue. Krashen (1981, 1982, 1994) has argued consistently that the effect of FFI is only peripheral; it can affect only the 'learning' of 'simple' structures as explicit knowledge, not the 'acquisition' of implicit knowledge. There are a number of arguments to support such a claim. First, FFI is invariably based on explicitly formulated rules derived from a reference grammar of some kind or another. Thus what it seeks to teach, whether through implicit or explicit methods, may bear no resemblance whatsoever to how this feature is represented in the learner's store of implicit knowledge. Second, FFI entails artificially adjusting the frequency and distribution of a property through instruction and so may artificially distort the input and actually mislead the learner, as Lightbown (1983) found when Grade 5 classroom learners were taught V–ing. (See Table 16.4.) Third, it is not clear that even highly intensive FFI is capable of providing the sheer number of exemplars needed for implicit knowledge to develop. However, other researchers have claimed that FFI can lead to changes in learners' implicit knowledge. DeKeyser (1998) saw FFI as providing the means for converting DECLARATIVE into PROCEDURAL KNOWLEDGE. In Ellis (1993), I suggested that FFI (in the form of consciousness-raising activities) can have an indirect effect on learners' implicit knowledge by facilitating the processes of noticing and noticing-the-gap. (See section on deductive and inductive FFI.)

These different positions can only be resolved empirically. In Ellis (2002b), I reviewed eight FFI studies that included a measure of free written or oral production. To these several more can now be added. Table 16.10 provides a summary of a representative sample of these studies. These studies suggest that FFI can contribute to the acquisition of implicit knowledge and points to two variables that appear to influence its success—the choice of the target structure and the extent of the instruction. FFI involving extensive instruction directed at 'simple' structures was more likely to succeed in developing implicit

Study	Subjects	Target structure	Treatment	Measure of acquisition	Results
Day and Shapson (1991)	315 Grade 7 early French immersion students	French hypothetical conditions	5–7 weeks of analytic-functional grammar materials.	(1) Oral interviews with prompts to rephrase more politely; (2) written composition with prompts. Both scored for accuracy in obligatory contexts.	(1) On immediate post-test (PT) the difference between experimental and control was non-significant in the oral interview but significant in the written composition; (2) Results were the same for the delayed PT.
Salaberry (1997)	65 third-semester university students of L2 Spanish	Pre-verbal object pronouns; word order	1.5 hours of input-processing instruction/production based instruction consisting of explicit explanation and structured input activities/production practice.	Oral narrative based on one-minute silent video clips. Both immediate and delayed PT.	No significant differences between experimental group and control group. Number of tokens of target structure very low.
Mackey and Philp (1998)	35 adult ESL learners	English question forms	Subjects performed three information gap tasks under two conditions: interaction (1) with and (2) without intensive recasts.	Performance on similar information gap tasks to those used for treatment; analysis in terms of developmental stages.	Group that was developmentally 'ready' and received intensive recasts showed significantly greater stage increase.
Spada, Lightbown, and White (2006)	90 French-speaking 11–12-year-old learners of L2 English	(1) the possessive pronouns 'his' and 'her' (2) inversion in questions	4 weeks of instruction (4 hours per day) involving opportunities to hear and produce the target structures in a variety of activities + explicit instruction (rule of thumb).	Possessive pronouns; oral production task based on describing a cartoon; written production task requiring students to write questions based on an imaginary situation and oral communicative task.	Possessive pronouns: both experimental and control group showed development over time but with much stronger gains for the experimental group. Questions: no difference on written test between experimental and control groups on progress through acquisition stages but clearer differences in oral production task in favour of experimental group.
Housen, Pierrard, and Van Daele (2006)	69 14–15-year-old Dutch-speaking learners of L2 French	(1) French sentence negation (simple structure) (2) French passive constructions (complex structure)	4 weeks of instruction consisting of: (1) metalinguistic pedagogical rule; (2) reading text; (3) identification of exemplars in the text; (4) description of these examples; (5) controlled practice exercises (sentence-transformation and answering semi-open questions).	An unplanned written production task consisting of an oral interview with open questions about pictures and objects, which they had to answer instantly.	No difference between experimental and control groups on absolute number of tokens of target structure produced on the immediate post-test, but experimental group significantly outperformed the control group in accuracy of production. Same pattern for delayed post-test. The complexity of the target structure did not affect the results.

knowledge. However, limited instruction directed at complex structures also proved effective provided that the target structures are readily available in non-instructional input.

Effects of instruction on L2 pragmatic development

Whereas the majority of FFI studies have addressed L2 grammatical development, there has been a growing interest in the effects of instruction on L2 pragmatic development. These studies have focused mainly on speech acts such as requests (for example, Takimoto 2006) or compliments (Rose and Kwai-fun 2001) but have also addressed other areas of pragmatics such as socio-pragmatic aspects of politeness (for example, Lyster 1994) and implicature (for example, Kubota 1995). In a meta-analysis of 13 experimental studies, Jeon and Kaya (2006) identified a number of issues that these studies have addressed: (1) whether the teaching of L2 pragmatics is necessary, (2) the differential effectiveness of different instructional options, (3) whether the method of measurement of learning affects the results obtained, and (4) the effect of different lengths of instruction on learning. These issues are essentially the same issues as those investigated by FFI research in general, as reflected in Norris and Ortega's (2000) meta-analysis. Table 16.11 summarizes a representative sample of studies that have investigated the effects of instruction on L2 pragmatic development. I will draw on these studies in addressing the four issues raised by Jeon and Kaya.

The studies summarized in Table 16.11 investigated the effects of FFI on pragmalinguistic features. That is, the studies have been primarily concerned with learners' use of linguistic realization devices rather than with sociopragmatic aspects of L2 use. The pragmalinguistic features investigated include both formulaic devices associated with early L2 development (for example, Tateyama 2001) and more complex devices likely to be found in more advanced learners (for example, Takimoto 2006). The studies were conducted mainly in foreign language classroom contexts, a notable exception being Lyster's (1994) study of address forms in an immersion context. A possible reason for the absence of studies in second language contexts is that instruction is seen as less important when learners have exposure to communicative language use outside the classroom. However, Schmidt's (1993) assertion that simple exposure to the target language does not suffice, as pragmatic features are often not salient to learners, suggests that instruction is needed in second as well as foreign language contexts.

As with FFI studies in general, there has been a general shift from early studies (for example, Lyster 1994) which were informed by pedagogical theory and which sought to address whether L2 pragmatic features are teachable, to later studies (for example, Takimoto 2006) that have drawn on SLA theory (for example, Schmidt's Noticing Hypothesis). Later studies have also followed general FFI research in investigating the mediating effect of individual difference factors on the effects of instruction (for example,

Study	Participants	Instruction	Design	Assessment	Results
Lyster (1994)	108 Grade 8 early immersion students in Canada	Focus: sociopragmatic French address forms ('tu' and 'vous'). Type: functional-analytic involving input and output materials (text manipulation and text creation) and explicit instruction. Length: 12 hours over 5-week period.	Pre-test, post-test, delayed post-test comparison.	Written production test, oral production test, multiple choice test.	Immediate and delayed post-tests showed clear gains in oral and written production and also in awareness of socio-stylistic differences.
Liddicoat and Crozet (2001)	10 second-year university-level students of L2 French in an ab initio programme in Australia	Focus: interactional norms in responding to question 'Did you have a good weekend?'. Type: awareness-raising of cross-cultural comparison of Australian and French norms followed by experimentation phase, free production practice, and feedback. Length: not specified. Part of a 13-week instructional module.	Descriptive comparison of role-plays preceding and following instruction.	Analysis focused on performance features relating to content (e.g. question leads directly to talk on topic) and form (e.g. use of repetition).	Prior to instruction learners' talk displayed few of the content or form characteristics of NS talk. Following instruction learners' talk displayed NS-like content features but less so NS form features. Gains still evident one year later.
Rose and Kwai-fun (2001)	103 Cantonese speaking undergraduates in a university in Hong Kong	Focus: English compliments. Type: (1) inductive: consciousness-raising activities based on a film input; (2) deductive: explicit instruction + practice activities based on a film. Length: 3 hours spread over 6 weeks.	Pre-test, post-test (administered 4 weeks after treatment); control group.	Self-assessment, written discourse completion tests, meta-pragmatic assessment questionnaire.	No overall effect for the instruction; the deductive group outperformed the control group on the discourse completion test.
Tateyama (2001)	102 English-speaking university beginner learners of L2 Japanese	Focus: Formulaic expressions for getting attention, apologizing, and expressing gratitude. Type: (1) explicit instruction video input, awareness-raising activities; (2) implicit instruction: Length: 4 x 20-minute lessons over an 8-week period.	Pre-test (administered after first treatment) and post-test (administered after last treatment).	Multiple choice test (MCT), role-plays (RP) and self-reports.	Both multiple choice test and role-plays indicated no difference between the two groups. The explicit group's scores increased on the MCT while the implicit group's decreased; the reverse occurred for the RP.
Takimoto (2006)	45 Japanese adult intermediate students	Focus: lexical/phrasal/syntactic downgraders of English requests. Type: (1) structured input (SI) and (2) structured input with explicit feedback. Length: 4 x 40-minute lessons over 2- week period.	Pre-test, immediate post-test, and delayed post-test; control group.	(1) open-ended discourse completion test, (2) role-play test, (3) listening test and (4) acceptability judgement test.	Structured input (SI) resulted in significant and sustained gains. No difference between the SI and SI + explicit feedback groups.

Table 16.11 Representative studies investigating the effects of instruction of L2 pragmatic development

Takahashi 2005). (See following section.) Many of the studies have been experimental or, rather, quasi-experimental (for example, Lyster 1994; Rose and Kwai-fun 2001) but there have also been some descriptive studies (for example, Liddicoat and Crozet 2001).

The teachability of L2 pragmatic features was investigated in a number of the studies listed in Table 16.11, with mixed results. The studies by Rose and Kwai-fun and by Takahashi found that instruction had no overall effect on the acquisition of the pragmalinguistic devices for performing compliments in the case of the former and on awareness of bi-clausal complex request forms in the case of the latter. However, Lyster (1994) reported clear gains in both an oral and written production test and in awareness of the appropriate use of 'tu' and 'vous', while Liddicoat and Crozet found that instruction resulted in a more native-like performance of a specific communicative task. Clearly, then, FFI directed at pragmatic features is effective at least some of the time. Jeon and Kaya's meta-analysis of 13 FFI studies reported a considerable range of effect sizes—from a high of $d = 5.93$ in the case of Lyster, to a low of $d = -0.43$ in the case of Fukaya and Clark's (2001) study of English mitigators. The mean effect size for six studies which involved experimental versus control groups was $d = 0.59$ (considered a medium effect size) while that for pre- to post-test comparisons was $d = 1.57$ (considered a large effect size). They concluded that, overall, these effect sizes showed that L2 pragmatic features are teachable. Future research will need to investigate to what extent the choice of target features affects the success of the instruction. It is possible that instruction is successful when it is directed at relatively simple features (for example, formulaic expressions) but is less successful when it is directed at syntactically complex realization devices (for example, bi-clausal requests). Such an interpretation would accord with the research considered in earlier sections of this chapter.

Studies that have addressed the relative effectiveness of different teaching approaches have focused primarily on the implicit versus explicit instructional options. Examples of such studies in Table 16.11 are Tateyama and Takimoto. Tateyama found no difference between the implicit and explicit groups in her study, although on a multiple choice test, the explicit group's scores improved from pre- to post-test whereas the implicit group's scores declined. Takimoto also found no difference between a group that received only structured input (the implicit group) and a group that received structured input plus explicit feedback. Takimoto suggested that this was because both treatments were optimal in enabling the learners to develop clear explicit knowledge of the target features. Rose and Kwai-fun investigated the difference between direct and indirect explicit instruction, reporting that the direct explicit group outperformed the control group on a discourse completion test. All three studies, it should be noted, reported a clear overall effect for instruction. Jeon and Kaya's meta-analysis also found that both implicit and explicit instruction were effective, with the mean effect sizes for explicit instruction notably larger than those for implicit instruction. However, they warned against concluding that explicit FFI is superior given the small number of studies included in their analysis and the fact that the two types of instruction had been operationalized in different ways. They noted that the inconclusiveness of their analysis contrasted with the clear advantage that Norris and Ortega (2000) reported for explicit instruction in their meta-analysis of studies that had targeted mainly L2 grammar.

As we have already noted, how learning outcomes are measured is important for evaluating the effects of FFI. Of particular importance is whether the instruction can be shown to have an effect on natural language data as well as elicited data. As with FFI studies in general, the studies in Table 16.11 show a bias towards elicited data, but a number (Lyster; Liddicoat and Crozet; Tateyama) employed instruments that elicited unplanned, natural language data. Two of these studies (Lyster; Liddicoat and Crozet) reported that the instruction led to improvements in oral language use suggesting that FFI can result in implicit knowledge of pragmatic features. Jeon and Kaya compared studies that collected just elicited language data with those that collected both elicited and natural language data. They reported that there was a large difference in the mean effect sizes in favour of the elicited plus natural data. However, they acknowledged that this finding was not reliable, given the low number of observations they were able to include in their analysis. Also, their analysis merely showed that FFI has a stronger effect on pragmatic ability when multiple as opposed to single measures of learning are obtained; that is, it did not address the crucial question of the effects of FFI on implicit and explicit pragmatic knowledge. As Rose and Kasper (2002) pointed out in their own survey of the effects of FFI on learning second language pragmatics, 'far more attention needs to be paid to the development of outcome measures' (p. 271).

A fourth issue concerns the differential effect of length of instruction. A general feature of the studies summarized in Table 16.11 is that the length of the instruction in L2 pragmatic studies is typically greater than that in L2 grammar studies, many of which have involved only very short periods of instruction. Lyster, for example, provided a total of 12 hours of instruction, while no study in Table 16.11 offered less than one hour. Also notable is the fact that instruction was generally spread over a number of weeks. It would appear, then, that L2 pragmatic researchers recognize the importance of ensuring that the instruction learners receive is substantial. Jeon and Kaya compared studies that provided less than five hours of instruction with those that provided more than five hours. The mean effect sizes for the latter were notably larger than those for the former, suggesting that extended instruction is more beneficial. However, they again cautioned about reaching a firm conclusion, pointing out that their finding contradicted Norris and Ortega (2000), who found that a shorter period of instruction was more effective.

The research investigating the effects of FFI on L2 pragmatics is limited in a number of respects. First, there are still relatively few studies. Second, the research suffers from a failure to operationalize FFI in precise and systematic ways, reflecting perhaps the pedagogical as opposed to theoretical orientation of many of the studies. Third, there are a number of other design problems—for example, insufficient attention to ensuring the reliability and validity of measurements of learning outcomes and a general failure to include delayed post-tests. Thus, the only clear finding to date is that FFI can lead to improvements in pragmatic ability at least in the short term. It is not yet possible to conclude with confidence which type of instruction is more effective or whether the instruction results in gains in implicit or explicit knowledge or both.

The mediating effects of individual difference factors

The research we have considered in the previous sections examined the effects of FFI on learners in general. The underlying assumption was that it is possible to identify whether instruction or what types of instruction work best for all learners. However, it would seem likely that learners differ in the kind of instruction they are best equipped to benefit from. In other words, individual difference factors of the kind we investigated in Chapter 13 may mediate the effects of the instruction. In this section we examine a number of studies that have investigated this. Table 16.12 describes a selection of these studies.

The studies are of two principal kinds; (1) APTITUDE–TREATMENT–INTERACTION (ATI) studies (Cronbach and Snow 1977) and (2) correlational studies. In ATI studies, learners who differ in terms of some individual difference factor (for example, field dependence/independence) are taught by means of two instructional approaches (for example, traditional versus functional) so that there are both matching and complementary conditions. The prediction is that learners in the matching conditions will outperform learners in the complementary conditions. Thus, ideally, an ATI study needs to be factorial in order to account for two or more independent variables. (See Hatch and Lazaraton 1991: 369 ff.) However, relatively few L2 studies have been truly factorial. In many cases, only two groups were used and the interaction between treatment and individual differences was computed statistically after the event. This constitutes a weakness in the research. Willing (1987) pointed out a number of other problems with ATI research. It is not clear, for instance, what dimension of individual difference is pivotal where instruction is concerned. Also, given that learners can differ on a number of factors (language aptitude, learning style, personality, etc.) matching based on a single factor may be ineffective. ATI research in general has focused on cognitive factors (in particular learning style) and has tended to ignore affective factors. Another problem is that many of the studies have failed to ascertain whether the intended 'treatment' was actually manifest in the instructional practices that occurred, as there was no 'classroom process' element.

Many of the earlier studies were of the ATI kind. Several of these investigated learning style—in particular, field dependence/independence, which, as we saw in Chapter 11, has exerted considerable fascination for SLA researchers.

In general, the results have not been very impressive. Only Abraham's (1985) produced a significant interaction effect: field-dependent learners performed better with an inductive treatment, while the field-independent ones did better with a deductive treatment. Other studies (for example, Carter 1988) failed to find a significant interaction between FI/FD and treatment.

A much more impressive study is Wesche (1981). This examined the relationship between language aptitude and instruction. Wesche started with the assumption that 'learning conditions which are optimal for one individual may be inappropriate for another' (1981: 125), and that aptitude tests could be used to identify the special abilities and weaknesses of individual learners. Two types of student were identified. Those in type A had a high overall score on the MLAT and PLAB tests. (See Chapter 12.) Those in type B manifested a high level of analytical ability but demonstrated problems with phonetic coding and listening. The two treatments consisted of (1) an audiovisual, inductive approach organized around the presentation of linguistic structures sequenced according to order of difficulty and (2) a more deductive, analytical approach, which taught oral and literacy skills together and provided explanations of grammatical points and of how to produce specific sounds. In an initial study, type A students were taught by approach (1), and type B students by approach (2). The results were encouraging. There were no significant differences in achievement between A and B students, suggesting that the matched condition led to equal achievement. Wesche then used a standard ATI design, assigning students of both types to matched and complementary conditions. The results of an achievement test showed that students in the matched conditions gained higher scores. Also, when interviewed, these students reported greater interest in foreign language study, more initiative in practising French outside the classroom, and less ANXIETY in class.

The second kind of study is correlational. Here no attempt is made to match instruction to the individual learner. Instead, the mediating effects of IDs are investigated *post hoc* by examining the extent to which achievement is affected by individual factors. In some of these studies (for example, Robinson 1997b), two or more types of instruction were examined while in others the influence of individual factors on the effects of a single type of instruction (for example, White and Ranta 2002) was investigated. A strength of this approach is that it avoids the need to dichotomize IDs (as in ATI research), as it allows for gradations in the traits investigated.[15] A weakness is that correlational statistics do not easily permit statements about cause and effect.

Many of the later studies are correlational in design, reflecting the difficulty of conducting ATI studies and the problems with these. A number of these studies investigated the effects of language aptitude (especially language analytical ability). DeKeyser (1993) found no interaction between language analytical ability and instruction (possibly because this study did not investigate specific grammatical targets) but three other studies (which targeted specific structures) did find a relationship. Robinson (1997b) reported that learners with high analytical ability benefited in three of the conditions he investigated—implicit, rule-search, and instructed—but not in the incidental condition. Erlam (2005) found that language analytic ability was a factor when learners were taught by means of an inductive or structured input instruction. Sheen (2006b) found that learners with high language analytical ability achieved higher scores on tests of English articles as a result of a treatment that included metalinguistic explanations but not as a result of the same treatment with recasts. Thus, in the case of Robinson and Sheen it would appear that language analytical ability is of benefit when the instruction encourages direct attention to form but not when learners' attention is primarily focused on meaning. On the surface, Erlam's study suggests the opposite, but a careful scrutiny of her instructional treatments reveals that both the inductive and deductive treatments involved conscious attention to linguistic form. The deductive treatment in this study may have enabled learners with weaker analytical abilities to benefit from the instruction. This interpretation is borne out by J. White and Ranta's (2002) study, which produced results to show that metalinguistic instruction can compensate for limitations in aptitude.

Another cognitive factor that has attracted attention is memory. Robinson (1997b) found that memory, as measured by means of a paired-associate task, was related to learning in his more explicit conditions but not in the more implicit ones. Mackey *et al.* (2002) reported that short-term memory correlated with learners' ability to notice grammatical forms during communicative interaction and also with their long-term development. Erlam also found that working memory was associated with the learning that resulted from an input-based type of instruction. It is possible, then, that long-term and short-term memory interact with instruction in different ways.

A few studies have investigated affective factors. It is tempting to hypothesize that these may be more important when attention to form occurs in instruction that is primarily meaning-oriented. Two studies support this hypothesis. Takahashi (2005) found that intrinsic motivation led to higher achievement in input-based instruction, while Sheen (2006b) reported that learners with low language classroom anxiety were able to benefit from corrective feedback in the form of recasts to a greater extent than those with high anxiety.

In an early review of research examining the role of IDs in instructed language learning, Skehan (1989) reached three conclusions:

> ... first, that the completed condition-seeking research has been some of the most fascinating in applied linguistics; second, that there are many studies whose interpretation is not clear for research/design reasons; and third, that abysmally little research of this sort has actually been done.

To what extent are these conclusions still valid some 20 years after Skehan wrote his review? I am not sure about the first of them—this is a matter of opinion. The second still holds—much of the research seems to me methodologically flawed. However, the third is no longer the case. An increasing

Study	Subjects	Individual differences	Treatment	Results
Wesche (1981)	Adult learners of L2 French	High aptitude overall versus high-analytical ability but low phonetic coding ability.	Audio-visual inductive approach versus deductive, analytical approach.	Students in matched condition achieved higher scores and reported greater interest in learning French.
Abraham (1985)	Adult ESL learners	Field dependent (FD) versus field independent (FI).	Inductive versus deductive approach to teaching participle phrases.	No main effect for method evident, but interactional effect found: FI learners did better with deductive lesson and FD learners with inductive.
Carter (1988)	72 beginner/low-intermediate learners of L2 Spanish	Field dependent versus field independent.	Learners taught using formal and more functional approaches.	Main effect found for cognitive style (i.e. FI learners did better) but no interactional effect evident.
DeKeyser (1993)	35 Dutch-speaking high-school learners of L2 French	Language analytical ability; extrinsic motivation; French class anxiety.	Systematic error correction versus infrequent error correction.	Systematic error correction benefited those learners with low extrinsic motivation and low anxiety; infrequent error correction benefited learners with high extrinsic motivation. No effect for language analytical ability.
Robinson (1997b)	94 intermediate Asian (mainly Japanese) learners of L2 English in Hawaii	Language aptitude: language analytical ability and verbal memory.	4 conditions: (1) implicit, (2) incidental, (3) rule-search and (4) instructed.	Language analytical ability correlated with measures of easy and hard rules for implicit, rule-search, and instructed conditions but not for incidental. Memory correlated with measures of both rules for instructed condition and for measure of easy rule for rule-search condition.
White and Ranta (2002)	59 francophone Grade 6 learners of English in an intensive ESL program in Quebec, Canada	Language aptitude: L1 metalinguistic task (error identification and correction).	2 conditions: (1) communicative instruction + metalinguistic instruction in use of French possessive pronouns (his and her); (2) communicative language instruction with no metalinguistic instruction.	Performance on a metalinguistic and an oral production task correlated significantly for learners in both (1) and (2) prior to instruction but not after. (1) outperformed (2) on both tasks following instruction.

Mackey, Philp, Egi, Fujii, and Tatsumi (2002)	30 low-intermediate adult Japanese ESL learners in the USA	Working memory.	Learners performed communicative tasks with NSs; stimulated recall used to elicit learners' comments about their performance.	Learners with high working memory reported more noticing and showed greater development over time (but learners with low working memory showed more development initially).
Takahashi (2005)	80 Japanese university learners of English (non majors)	Motivation.	Input-based instruction directed at bi-clausal complex English request forms.	Intrinsic motivation strongly related to awareness of a number of bi-clausal request features.
Erlam (2005)	60 high-school learners of L2 French in New Zealand	Phonemic coding ability; language analytic ability; working memory.	Deductive instruction; inductive instruction; structured input instruction.	Phonemic coding ability related to gains in listening test for the deductive group; language analytical ability related to gains in listening and written production test for the inductive and SI groups; working memory related to gains in written production for the SI group.
Sheen (2006b)	143 low-intermediate ESL students in a community college in the USA	Language analytical ability; language classroom anxiety; attitudes towards error correction and grammatical accuracy.	2 types of oral corrective feedback (CF) : (1) implicit: recasts and (2) explicit: metalinguistic explanation.	High language analytical ability and positive attitudes towards correctness led to higher achievement in the metalinguistic group but not in the recast group; learners with low anxiety benefited from both types of CF.

Table 16:12 Studies investigating the interaction between individual differences and FFI

number of studies have examined the inter-relationships between ID variables, instruction, and learning outcomes. There is now evidence that cognitive and affective IDs do mediate the effects of FFI. Bialystok (1985) noted commonsensically that there needs to be a 'minimal congruity' between the learner's preferred way of learning and the type of instruction for L2 acquisition to proceed efficiently. The research reported in this section may not permit a clear statement about what this 'minimal congruity' consists of but it has certainly pointed the way.

Conclusion

There are now a large number of studies that have investigated the effects of FFI on L2 acquisition but clear conclusions are difficult to arrive at. Norris and Ortega (2000, 2003) noted problems with the research methods employed, relating to both the overall design of the studies (for example, no control group or no pre-test) and to the instruments used to measure learning outcomes (for example, the failure to demonstrate validity and reliability). Another major problem is the lack of an agreed framework for describing and thereby operationalizing instructional options. For example, the definitions of 'focus-on-form' and 'focus-on-forms'—a key distinction in current thinking about FFI—are in dispute. Researchers are often torn between the desire to test theoretical claims about L2 acquisition, which requires the investigation of precise and discrete instructional options, and the desire to ensure that FFI is ecologically valid, which leads to combining options into treatments that are pedagogically defensible. As a result of these problems, care must be taken in reaching conclusions about the role of FFI. Thus the following conclusions must be viewed as programmatic.

1 FFI is effective in helping learners acquire an L2

The case for form-focused instruction is strengthening and the case for the zero option is weakening. FFI results in increased accuracy and accelerates progress through developmental sequences. It is effective in promoting both the learning of grammar and L2 pragmatics. Two important caveats, however, are that FFI may not be necessary for learning many of the features of an L2 (i.e. many features can be learnt naturally) and FFI may not ensure that learners achieve full target-language competence. In general, however, learners who receive FFI will learn faster and progress further than those who do not. Also, certain 'marked' L2 features may only be acquirable with FFI.

2 The effects of FFI are not always positive

A number of studies have shown that FFI can sometimes have negative effects. FFI directed at features that are formally simple but functionally complex may result in their overuse. FFI directed at a feature similar to one previously taught and learnt may lead to confusion and loss of learning.

3 FFI facilitates natural language acquisition

This is a more contentious claim. Krashen (1981, 1993a) maintained that FFI assists 'learning' but plays no role in 'acquisition', a position also adopted by some UG-based researchers (for example, Schwartz 1993). However, there is now clear evidence that although FFI may be powerless to alter a developmental sequence it facilitates progress through it. Initially, this finding led to the claim that learners had to be at the stage immediately preceding the stage targeted by the instruction, but this may no longer be the case. Instruction directed more than one stage ahead can enable learners to progress, although they will still follow the sequence. The available evidence suggests that FFI can work by facilitating the processes involved in natural L2 acquisition.

4 FFI also offers an alternative mode of learning

In addition to facilitating natural language acquisition, FFI can teach learners metalinguistic facts about the L2 and thereby contribute to their explicit knowledge. Explicit knowledge is of value in itself as it is available for formulating and monitoring utterances, especially in planned language use. There is also growing evidence that explicit knowledge developed through instruction can assist learners' acquisition of implicit knowledge. That is, teaching 'rules' (or assisting learners to discover rules for themselves) leads ultimately to improved accuracy in unplanned as well as planned language use. There is growing theoretical and empirical support for the Weak Interface Hypothesis.

5 FFI can result in implicit as well as explicit L2 knowledge

This claim is a corollary of the preceding two claims. In this chapter I analysed a number of studies that investigated whether FFI had any effect on learners' ability to produce the targeted forms in 'free constructed responses'. I demonstrated that this was indeed the case providing that the target feature was not too complex for the learners and the instruction was of sufficient quantity. This claim is a key one. It addresses the criticism levelled at much FFI research by Doughty (2003)—namely, that the choice of measurement in many studies is biased towards explicit knowledge. It remains uncertain, however, how FFI results in implicit knowledge. One possibility is that it enables learners to convert explicit knowledge into implicit knowledge through practice in accordance with skill-building theory and the Strong Interface Hypothesis. Another possibility is that it serves to facilitate the processes involved in natural language acquisition in accordance with the claims that have been advanced in favour of focus-on-form instruction or input-processing instruction.

6 There are constraints on the teachability of specific features

There are constraints on whether FFI works. Factors such as the degree of markedness, form–function transparency, and the nature of the processing operations involved determine how difficult different structures are to teach. Thus, it does not follow that FFI will always be effective. However, little is currently known about whether these constraints apply to explicit knowledge as well as implicit knowledge or whether there are different constraints that apply to the two types of knowledge.

7 The effects of FFI may or may not be evident immediately and may or may not be durable

A number of studies have found that the effects of the FFI do not appear in the immediate post-test but do emerge some time later in a delayed post-test. These studies support the Weak Interface Hypothesis. Instruction raises learners' consciousness about a feature which is then attended to selectively in subsequent input, resulting in acquisition. Other studies have found that instruction can have an immediate effect but that this may not last (i.e. it disappears in a delayed post-test). An explanation of this phenomenon is that the instruction resulted only in explicit (declarative) knowledge which then atrophies because the learner was not developmentally 'ready' to acquire it or because of no subsequent communicative exposure to it.

8 Both focus-on-forms and focus-on-form instruction are effective

This claim is also contentious. Doughty (2003), for example, argued that 'the completely decontextualized nature of explicit focus-on-forms ... promotes a mode of learning that is arguably unrelated to L2 acquisition ... in that the outcome is merely the accumulation of metalinguistic knowledge about language' (p. 271). In other words, Doughty claimed that focus-on-forms only results in explicit knowledge. The preceding review of FFI studies in this chapter, however, suggests that focus-on-forms can contribute to implicit knowledge (i.e. several of the studies listed in Table 16.11 are of the focus-on-forms type). There is also growing evidence that focus-on-form instruction facilitates acquisition. However, it is not possible to claim that one type of instruction is superior to the other. I have argued that given the disagreements in the definitions of these two constructs and the fact that they are composites involving a number of distinct options it may not be possible to conduct a convincing comparison.

9 The type of instruction influences learning outcomes

A major section of this chapter investigated the relative effects of a number of different instructional options (input-based, explicit as opposed to implicit, inductive versus deductive, error-inducing production practice, and corrective feedback). It is not easy to reach clear conclusions, due to the fact that most of the studies did not investigate discrete options but rather combinations of options, making it difficult to determine what aspect of the instruction was effective. There is clear evidence that input-based instruction can assist acquisition although it may be premature to claim that this is more effective than production-based instruction. There is clearer evidence that explicit instruction (especially when combined with practice activities) is more effective than implicit instruction (i.e. practice activities alone). Both inductive and deductive explicit instruction appear to work with no clear evidence in favour of either. Inducing errors in order to correct also appears effective. Arguably, some of the best research has examined corrective feedback, providing an accumulation of evidence to suggest that explicit types of feedback (for example, metalinguistic explanation) are more effective than implicit types (for example, recasts) and that output-prompting types (for example, elicitation) are more effective than input-providing (for example, recasts) at least for features that learners have already partially acquired. Ultimately, however, trying to establish which type of instruction is most effective may be a mistaken enterprise as it may depend on contextual and individual learner factors.

10 Individual difference factors mediate the effects of FFI

Researchers are increasingly examining whether, to what extent, and in what ways individual difference factors such as learning style, language aptitude, memory, anxiety, and learner attitudes interact with different types of FFI. There is clear evidence that they do, although, again, it may be premature to offer any conclusions. Learners' language analytical abilities influence their capacity to process instruction, especially when this is of the more formal, explicit kind. Working memory and affective factors such as motivation and anxiety have been shown to have an impact when the instruction is of the more implicit kind.

FFI is a complex phenomenon. So is L2 acquisition. It is therefore not surprising to find that controversy abounds in discussions about the relationship between them (see Ellis 2006b). I will end by mentioning one key issue of contention—the role of explicit instruction. Doughty (2003) concluded her own review of the instructed L2 acquisition research by arguing that the 'guiding principle' should be for instruction 'to engage perceptual processes during implicit learning rather than to promote metalinguistic awareness' (p. 298). In contrast, N. Ellis (2005) argued the case for teaching explicit knowledge to help learners fine-tune the processes of implicit learning. To resolve this controversy will require more careful definition, operationalization, and measurement of the constructs involved than has been the case with much of the research reported in this chapter.

Notes

1 Krashen suggested that his Input Hypothesis constitutes a 'weaker-interface position' on the grounds that learner output produced with the help of 'learnt' knowledge can serve as comprehensible input for the purposes of 'acquisition'. However, in so far as Krashen claimed that 'learnt' knowledge does not convert directly into 'acquired' knowledge, his position is tantamount to a strong non-interface position.

2 Krashen (1982) also recognized a second use of FFI—it can serve as subject matter for 'language appreciation lessons'.

3 Acquisition sequences include deviant forms (for example, the pre-verbal stage in negation). Pienemann's point is that in attempting to teach in accordance with a developmental sequence, teachers should not teach the deviant stages in this sequence.

4 It should be noted that White did not argue that formal instruction should be limited to 'problematic overgeneralizations'. She also argued that it can have a valuable facilitative effect when 'benign errors' occur.

5 Sheen (2003), for example, argued for a comparative study of 'focus-on-forms' and 'focus-on-form' in order to determine which of these FFI 'methods' is the more effective. In doing so, Sheen showed a lack of understanding of the problems involved in conducting method comparisons.

6 In inferential statistics, an effect size is the size of a statistically significant difference. In meta-analytical studies, effect sizes are used as a common measure which can be calculated for different studies and then combined into an overall mean effect size. Cohen (1992) claimed that $d = 0.2$ is indicative of a small effect, $d = 0.5$ a medium, and $d = 0.8$ a large effect size.

7 As the reviewer of this chapter (Lourdes Ortega) pointed out, it is always possible that the failure of just two learners to conform with the predictions of the Teachability Hypothesis was simply due to a measurement problem (for example, the pre-test failed to elicit the tokens needed to determine their exact stage of development).

8 Jones (1992) queried whether the order found in the oral production task can be adequately explained by the Accessibility Hierarchy (AH). He suggested that, although the distinction between DO and OP is clear to grammarians, his learners did not see it the same way. Their performance on the oral task indicated that they treated verbs with prepositional phrases (for example, 'working on the floor') as if they were VP + NP constructions, where the verb consisted of a two-word chunk 'working on'. This bears out the conclusion reached in Chapter 12, namely that the acquisition of relative pronoun functions may be best explained in terms of processing difficulty rather than the AH.

9 It is not intended to suggest that these 'options' constitute 'approaches'. Any particular lesson may be made up by selecting from the range of options available.

10 Allen attempted to demonstrate how the target structure in her study related to one of VanPatten's input-processing principles, but VanPatten (2002) disputed her rationale.

11 The terms 'explicit' and 'implicit' are not to be equated with the terms 'analytic' and 'experiential'. (See Table 16.3.) The term 'formal instruction' can be equated with 'analytic' instruction; such instruction can be either 'explicit' or 'implicit'. It should be noted, however, that, rather confusing-

ly, the term 'implicit' is sometimes used in connection with communicative language teaching (i.e. 'experiential' instruction) by other authors.

12 This way of operationalizing implicit instruction (i.e. as an instruction to memorize a set of sentences) reflects how this type of instruction has been investigated in cognitive psychology (for example, Reber 1976).

13 Inductive instruction is sometimes viewed as a form of implicit instruction. However, if the goal of the inductive instruction is to enable learners to develop some explicit representation of the target structure, then it is better treated as a type of explicit instruction.

14 The term CONSCIOUSNESS-RAISING has been widely used in SLA research by researchers interested in the role of formal instruction. It is frequently used to refer to any attempt to focus the learner's attention on a specific target structure, i.e. as a synonym for form-focused instruction—see Sharwood Smith's (1981) use of the term. In this sense, language practice activities also involve consciousness-raising. In a later article, Sharwood Smith (1991) suggested a better term might be 'input enhancement'. He argued that we can only know what we do with input, not what effect our attempts have on the learner (i.e. whether the input actually raises consciousness). However, the term 'consciousness-raising' is preferred in this chapter in acknowledgement of its wide currency. It is used with the narrow definition given in Ellis (1991e), which distinguishes 'consciousness-raising' from 'practice'.

15 Lourdes Ortega correctly pointed out to me that some researchers do dichotomize continuous data. Mackey *et al.* (2002), for example, elected to divide their learners *post hoc* into 'low' and 'high working memory' groups.

PART EIGHT
Conclusion

Introduction

Long (1990c) wrote an article in which he referred to the 'well-established findings about learners, environments, and interlanguages' (p. 656) and went on to describe these. In the first edition of this book, I queried the extent to which it was in fact possible to identify findings that were well established. It would be pleasing to report that some fifteen years later the situation has changed and that it is now possible to identify consensual findings. However, I do not believe this is the case. Indeed, if anything, there is now more disagreement about the facts of L2 acquisition. For example, there are researchers who challenge the existence of acquisition orders and sequences (which I have been inclined to treat as a 'well-established finding') and there are others who dispute whether there are any such things as a critical period for learning an L2 or fossilization. There are also more theories of L2 acquisition on the scene than in 1994, including those that are being actively pursued by different groups of researchers (for example, interactionist theories, emergentist theories, skill-building theories, UG-based theories).There is an ongoing controversy as to whether SLA should be viewed as a field of cognitive psychology or, more broadly, as encompassing sociolinguistic lines of enquiry. In short, the picture of SLA that I have painted in the preceding chapters resembles a collage of contrasting and sometimes competing images rather than a sharp, well-defined photograph.

Not surprisingly, then, I will not attempt a neat summary of what is currently known about L2 acquisition in the final chapter of this book. Given the complex and multi-faceted nature of SLA as reflected in the preceding chapters, it would be unwise and probably impossible to produce such a summary.

Instead, I will consider the continuing tendency in SLA research to turn in on itself—to examine its own navel, so to speak—by addressing a number of epistemological issues of considerable importance to the whole enterprise. These issues concern the kind of data used in SLA research, theory construction, and the application of the findings of SLA research to other fields.

17

Epistemological issues in second language acquisition

Introduction

In this chapter, we will address three questions:

1 What kinds of data are required to investigate L2 acquisition?
2 How should theory-building proceed in SLA research?
3 Can the results of SLA research be applied to other fields, in particular language pedagogy, and, if so, how?

These questions are, of course, interrelated. For example, the kind of data we collect to investigate L2 acquisition is likely to reflect our theoretical views. The applicability of SLA research to language pedagogy will depend on both the perceived relevance of the research (which, in turn, is likely to depend on the kind of data used), and the nature of the theory advanced to explain the results obtained. The nature of these interrelationships will become more apparent in the following sections.

The issues discussed in this chapter relate to issues of wide epistemological concern. However, it is not my intention to embark on a full examination of them, although there is undoubtedly a need for such as examination. (See Jordan 2003 for an attempt at this.) I have set myself a narrower goal, one that accords with the general aim of this book (i.e. to provide a balanced and, as far as possible, objective account of work undertaken in SLA). I shall seek only to identify the issues relating to data, theory, and pedagogical applications as these have been reflected in the SLA literature to date.

The choice of data in second language acquisition research

We have come up against the difficulties that SLA researchers face with regard to data at various points in this book: in Chapter 2, where we considered the data needed to examine learners' errors; in Chapter 4, where we noted that the descriptive 'facts' of learner language vary according to the 'task' used to collect data; in Chapter 5, where we considered the merits of discourse completion questionnaires for investigating pragmatic features of learner language; in Chapter 12, where we examined some of the problems attendant on using data from GRAMMATICALITY JUDGEMENT tests; and in Chapter 13, where we saw the importance attached to the use of self-report data in the study of learner differences but also noted the doubts that exist regarding the validity and reliability of such data. In Chapter 16 we noted the problems that have arisen in investigating the effects of form-focused instruction, due to the different ways in which researchers have measured acquisition. As in other social sciences, there is no agreement about what constitutes the 'right stuff' in SLA research.

Ellis and Barkhuizen (2005) identified three broad types of data commonly used in SLA: (1) performance data that do not involve production, (2) samples of learner production, and (3) reports from learners about their own learning. Performance data that do not involve production consist of measurements of learners' non-verbal responses to linguistic stimuli. They include measures of learners' reaction times to linguistic stimuli as in sentence-matching tests, non-verbal measures of learners' comprehension of linguistic input as in picture-matching tests, and measures of learners' intuitions about the grammaticality or acceptability of sentences. Learner production data can consist of oral or written samples of naturally occurring language use (i.e. the samples are produced in a real-life situation in order to satisfy some communicative or aesthetic need) or elicited data. Following Corder (1976, reproduced in 1981), two kinds of elicitation can be distinguished: clinical and experimental elicitation. Corder defined clinical elicitation as 'getting the informant to produce data of any sort' and suggests that it is used 'where the investigator has not yet formed any well-formed hypothesis about the nature of the language he [*sic*] is investigating' (p. 69). In contrast, experimental elicitation involves getting the informant 'to produce data incorporating particular features which the linguist is interested in at that moment' and constitutes, therefore, 'a carefully controlled procedure'. Following Cohen (1987), verbal-report data can be divided into SELF-REPORT, 'self-observation', and 'self-revelation'. There is also a fourth type—self-assessment. Figure 17.1 displays these main data types.

Different kinds of SLA research have tended to favour different data types. Thus, the early descriptive work that led to claims about the 'order' and 'sequence' of acquisition showed a clear preference for language-use data—natural language use in the early case studies, and clinical and experimental elicitation in the cross-sectional studies (for example, the MORPHEME STUDIES). The study of interlanguage pragmatics, however, has relied extensively on experimentally elicited data, using, for example, Discourse Completion Questionnaires, although some work has also been based on natural language use. In contrast, research based on 'strong' theories, such as Universal Grammar and the Competition Model, has relied heavily on non-linguistic performance data. Research into INDIVIDUAL LEARNER DIFFERENCES has found language-use data of limited value, and has turned to

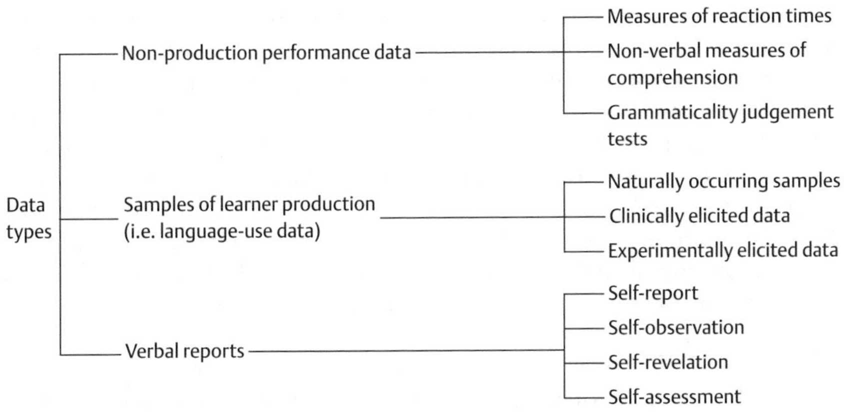

Figure 17.1 The main data types used in second language acquisition research

various kinds of verbal reports. In other words, the type of data used closely reflects the research goals. We will now discuss each of the main data types in more detail and then conclude this section with some general comments about the validity of L2 data.

Non-production data

Measures of performance that do not involve production enable inferences to be made about learners' linguistic knowledge based on their ability to process language receptively.

Measuring learners' reaction time

A good example of the use of this measure can be found in sentence-matching tests. These present learners with two sentences, which are either both grammatical or both ungrammatical, and ask them to determine whether the two sentences are identical or not. The time it takes learners to make an online judgement is then measured. Gass (2001) describes the standard procedure as follows:

> Participants are seated in front of a computer and are presented with one sentence that is either grammatical or ungrammatical. After a short delay, a second sentence appears on a screen, with the first sentence remaining in place. Participants are asked to decide as quickly as possible if the sentences match or do not match, entering their decision by pressing specific keys. The time from the appearance of the second sentence to the participant's pressing the key is recorded and forms the data base for the analysis. (p. 423)

It is this reaction-time that is used to determine the status of learners' L2 knowledge. Following research conducted by native speakers (for example, Freedman and Forster 1985), it is argued that participants take longer to judge the equivalence of ungrammatical sentences than grammatical ones. Thus, by examining the reaction times, it becomes possible to determine to what extent specific structures are deemed to be grammatical or ungrammatical by a particular learner.[1] The validity of this method of examining learners' intuitive L2 knowledge remains uncertain, however. Gass (2001), for example, found no difference in the response time of L2 learners of French between pairs of grammatical and ungrammatical sentences.

Measuring comprehension

Non-verbal measures of comprehension have been used to establish whether learners are able to process specific linguistic features in the input—for example, the interpretation tests used in Processing Instruction research. (See Chapter 16.) In a picture-matching test, for example, learners are presented with a sentence and then asked to select which picture from an array of two or more the sentence matches. For example, they might be shown the following sentence:

The dog was bitten by Thomas.

and then asked to match the sentence with the correct picture from a pair of pictures, which show a dog biting a man and a man biting a dog. There are variations in this procedure. In some studies (for example, Montrul 2001), participants are asked to judge the extent to which a particular sentence matches a picture on a Likert scale ('very natural'–'very unnatural'). In other studies (for example, Bley-Vroman and Joo 2001), participants are given pairs of sentences and pictures and asked to say which sentence matches which picture, with the option of choosing 'neither'. Such data are not only used to measure comprehension, but are also used to make claims about the grammatical/linguistic system that underlies a particular performance.

Obviously, comprehension tests such as picture-matching only work with grammatical structures that have clear, identifiable functions—such as the passive voice in English. They cannot be used for structures that are semantically redundant (for example, third person -s in English or noun-adjectival agreement in French).

Grammaticality judgement tests

Grammaticality judgement tests (GJTs) vary on two dimensions—the design of the GJT and the procedures for implementing the test. Variables in design relate to the way in which learners are asked to make their judgements and in whether they are asked to perform some additional operation. In the 'standard' GJT, learners are simply asked to judge whether the sentences are grammatical or ungrammatical, with (sometimes) the additional option of choosing a 'not sure' option. They can also be offered a wider selection of choices in a multiple choice format (for example, 'clearly grammatical', 'probably grammatical', 'probably ungrammatical' and 'clearly ungrammatical') or given a scale of grammaticality to respond to. Sorace (1996) made a strong case for the use of 'magnitude estimation'. (See Chapter 12.) Learners can also be given a set of sentences and asked to rank them in terms of grammaticality or they can be given a pair of sentences and asked to choose which sentence in the pair is grammatical. In addition to judging the grammaticality of the sentences in these ways, learners can also be asked to carry out further operations on the sentences they consider ungrammatical: (1) indicate the parts they consider ungrammatical (for example, by underlining) and (2) write out the sentences correctly.

Procedures for administering a GJT also vary considerably. Perhaps the most crucial variable is whether the test is administered in a speeded or unspeeded format. In a speeded test learners are given a specified amount of time to judge each sentence. The idea is to elicit judgements based on IMPLICIT KNOWLEDGE by preventing them from consulting their metalinguistic knowledge. In an unspeeded test learners have as much time as they want to judge each sentence. In such a test, learners are more able to utilize their EXPLICIT KNOWLEDGE of learnt rules.

GJTs provide three kinds of data. First and foremost they provide information about learners' intuitions as to what is grammatical or ungrammatical. Second, if the time it takes learners to judge each sentence is recorded, GJTs provide information about reaction times which can be used to evaluate what kind of knowledge (implicit or explicit) the learners used to make their judgements. Third, if learners are asked to correct the ungrammatical sentences, the GJT serves as a device for eliciting samples of learner language. In this respect, a GJT constitutes an example of 'experimental elicitation'. These different types of data are then used to draw conclusions about the nature of the learners' L2 grammatical representations. For example, information about reaction times can be used to determine whether learners are able to access implicit knowledge of grammatical features (Ellis 2005d).

The pros and cons of GJTs were considered in some detail in Chapter 12. The central problem concerns the type of knowledge that they measure. As Sorace (1996) commented:

> It can be a complex task to decide about the kind of norm consulted by learners in the process of producing a judgment, particularly in a learning environment that fosters the development of metalinguistic knowledge. It is difficult to tell whether subjects reveal what they think or what they think they should think.
> (p. 385)

This problem is exacerbated by the fact that learners' knowledge systems are typically indeterminate. When learners are not sure they may resort to a variety of strategies in order to produce a judgement. (See Ellis 1991c and

Davies and Kaplan 1998.) There have been two responses to these problems of validity. Some researchers have argued that GJTs are inherently flawed and should not be used in SLA (for example, Goss, Ying-Hua, and Lantolf 1994). Other researchers, such as Sorace, claim that the problems can be overcome through the careful design of GJTs (for example, by using magnitude estimation in tests administered in a speeded format). In Ellis (2004a), I suggested that by manipulating the design features of a GJT it may be possible to obtain relatively separate measures of learners' implicit and explicit knowledge. For example, learners are more likely to draw on their implicit knowledge in judging grammatical sentences in a speeded test and their explicit knowledge in judging ungrammatical sentences in an unspeeded test.

The reliability of GJTs has been examined by asking learners to take the same test a second time after only a short intervening period and then comparing their judgements on the two tests (i.e. test/re-test reliability). Mixed results have been forthcoming. Ellis (1991c) found that learners changed up to 45 per cent of their unspeeded judgements, lending support to the point made above about the indeterminacy of L2 knowledge. Han (1996) also reported low levels of test/re-test reliability in a study that examined learners' judgements in a speeded GJT. However, Gass (1994) reported a much higher level of reliability. Interestingly, though, Gass reported that learners were much more likely to keep to the same judgement in the case of sentences where the grammatical structure was relatively simple than where it was more complex. An interpretation of Gass' study is that the reliability of judgements is higher when learners' L2 knowledge is more determinate, as is likely with simple structures that are acquired early, and lower when their knowledge is more indeterminate. This suggests that GJTs may lack reliability when learners are asked to judge sentences containing features they have no or very limited knowledge of.

Given the doubts that exist regarding non-production data, SLA researchers need to give careful consideration to the validity and reliability of their chosen instrument. Unfortunately, they have often neglected to do so. (See Douglas 2001.) Researchers have been happy to report results based on non-production data without bothering to demonstrate that the instruments they have used are reliable and valid. Nevertheless, such instruments are valuable providing that their reliability and validity can be established, as they enable researchers to test hypotheses by investigating specific grammatical structures that often prove difficult, or even impossible, to elicit in learner production.

Learner production data

The three major types of production data (naturally occurring samples, clinically elicited samples, and experimentally elicited samples) constitute a data continuum as shown in Figure 17.2 below. At one end of the continuum are naturally occurring samples, where the researcher exercises no control whatsoever. At the other end is language use involving very close control of the language produced, as in experimentally elicited samples. Between these two poles lie clinically elicited samples, where some control is exercised through the choice of task but learners are expected to be primarily engaged in message conveyance for a pragmatic purpose, as in naturally occurring language use. In the eyes of many SLA researchers the ideal data are naturally occurring samples, as they reflect what learners can 'do' with the L2 when engaged in the kind of language use for which language is designed. However, because it is often not possible to obtain naturally occurring samples in sufficient quantity or that contain the specific linguistic features a researcher wishes to investigate, it is often necessary to fall back on clinically or experimentally elicited data.

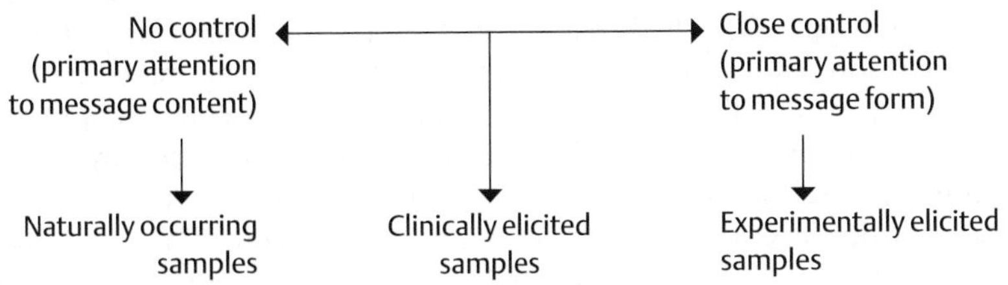

Figure 17.2 Three types of samples of learner language

Naturally occurring samples of learner language

In Labovian terms, natural language use shows us the learner's vernacular style, which some researchers consider to be 'basic' in the sense that it reflects the most normal way knowledge of language is utilized. However, the very fact that learners know they are being researched is likely to result in a shift towards a more 'careful style'. This led Labov to formulate the Observer's Paradox. This states that the only way to obtain good data is through systematic observation but that such observation is likely to contaminate the data collected, making it difficult to sample the vernacular style. Whereas sociolinguistically oriented research of the kind considered in Chapter 4 has paid close attention to the Observer's Paradox, psycholinguistically-oriented SLA research generally has not.

Oral samples of naturally occurring learner language can be collected by means of (1) pencil-and-paper, (2) audio recording, and (3) video recording. Generally, (2) and (3) are preferred to (1), as it is difficult to obtain reliable data relating to the interactional context in which specific learner utterances occur. Audio recording is now widely used in sampling naturally occurring language use. The main disadvantage is that the presence of a cassette recorder may induce learners to attend to their speech, thus making it less likely that the resulting samples will reflect their vernacular style. However, the use of modern clip-on radio microphones has minimized this problem and has even allowed researchers to obtain clear samples of learners' 'private speech'.

(See, for example, studies by Saville-Troike (1988) and Ohta (2001b).) Another possibility is to use mini-disc recorders, which learners carry in their pockets. These provide digital recordings that can be directly entered into a computer program as a sound file for analysis. Video recording has the obvious advantage of providing detailed visual information relating to the context of an utterance, including important paralinguistic information such as gesture and facial expression. Researchers are increasingly making use of such information. In fact, video data are essential for conducting the kind of detailed analyses of gesture that are becoming a feature of SLA research. (See, for example, the special issue of *International Review of Applied Linguistics* Volume 44/2.)

Methods for transcribing oral data can be 'broad' or 'narrow', reflecting the research purpose. The broadest of transcriptions will simply provide a written record in standard orthography, perhaps noting major pauses. A narrower system will indicate such phenomena as pause length, and simultaneous/overlapping speech. Very narrow systems will employ phonetic notation and/or provide means for indicating a variety of characteristics of speech delivery (for example, intonation, extension of a sound, abrupt halts, emphasis, volume, audible aspirations, and inhalations). Conversation analysts such as Seedhouse (2004) make use of such systems. Dubois (1991) discussed a number of design principles for transcription systems. Two of these are 'Make the system accessible' by, for example, ensuring that all the notations are 'motivated' in terms of the purpose of the research, and 'Make representations robust' by, for example, avoiding 'fragile contrasts'.

Written samples are relatively permanent and, for this reason, easier to collect. In recent years there have been large-scale projects of learner language based on written samples and motivated by the availability of computer-based concordancing tools for analysing the samples.[2] One of the best known of these projects is the International Corpus of Learner English (ICLE) (Granger 1998a). The ICLE is a computerized corpus of argumentative essays on different topics written by advanced learners of English (i.e. university students of English in their second or third years). It is made up of a set of sub-corpora from learners with different L1 backgrounds, including Asian languages (Chinese and Japanese) and European languages (for example, French and Russian). Another project based on an extensive sample of university-level academic essays can be found in Hinkel (2002). A key decision in collecting written samples concerns the genre to be sampled. In the case of the ICLE only argumentative essays were collected. Another key decision concerns the conditions under which the written samples are produced. Two conditions are especially important: (1) whether the written sample is timed or untimed and (2) whether the learners have access to reference tools such as dictionaries and grammars while they write. The Swedish component of the ICLE (www.englund.lu.se/research/corpus/corpus/swicle.html) consists of both untimed and timed essays.

Clinically elicited samples

Clinically elicited samples of learner language differ from naturally occurring samples in that they are collected specifically for the purpose of research. It is important to distinguish two broad types of clinically elicited data depending on whether the researcher's goal is to collect a *general* sample of learner language or a *focused* sample. In the case of a general sample, the elicitation instrument is designed to provide a context for learners to speak or write in the L2 in a purposeful manner. In the case of a focused sample, the elicitation instrument is designed to induce learners to use some specific linguistic feature when speaking or writing. In the case of a general sample, then, there is no attempt to pre-determine what linguistic forms the learners will use whereas in a focused sample there is. However, a clinically elicited focused sample remains distinct from an experimentally elicited sample. While both types of sample reflect an attempt to elicit specific linguistic features for study, a clinically elicited focused sample requires learners to be oriented primarily to message-conveyance (i.e. fluency) while an experimentally elicited sample involves a primary orientation to form (i.e. accuracy). This is an important distinction, as the learner's orientation to the elicitation task can have a profound effect on the language used. (See, for example, Larsen-Freeman 1976b; Tarone 1988.)

General samples of learner language are elicited by means of some kind of *task*. (See Chapter 15.) A task can be 'authentic' (i.e. correspond to some real-world activity) or 'pedagogic' (i.e. only be found in an instructional setting).[3] Both kinds of tasks, however, can lay claim to 'some sort of relationship with the real world' in that they involve the kinds of communicative processes involved in the real-world (for example, repairing non-understanding or misunderstanding). Tasks can be used to elicit both oral and written samples. There is no recognized typology of tasks. Below is an account of some of the tasks commonly used in SLA research. These include both tasks that involve social interaction and result in dialogic discourse (for example, role-plays) and tasks that are performed by individual learners, thus providing samples of monologic discourse (for example, text-reconstruction).

Common types of tasks used in SLA research are (1) tasks that involve some kind of gap, (2) open role-plays, (3) text reconstruction, (4) picture narratives, and (5) oral interviews. Information- and opinion-gap tasks have figured strongly in SLA as a data collection method for some time, especially in research directed at investigating the role of interaction and input in L2 acquisition. (See, for example, Pica, Kanagy, and Falodun 1993 and Chapter 6.) More recently they have become objects of enquiry in their own right. (See Skehan 1998b and Chapter 15.) As we saw in Chapter 10, researchers have become interested in how task variables influence learner production. Role-plays have been commonly used by researchers who wish to investigate pragmatic aspects of learner language (for example, how learners perform speech acts such as requests or apologies when speaking to different addressees). The advantage, as Kasper and Dahl (1991) pointed out, is that they enable learner-language to be studied in its full discourse context. In a text reconstruction task learners listen to or read a text. This is then removed and the learners are asked to reconstruct the text in their own words. The assumption underlying this task is that in processing a text for meaning learners store the propositional content but not the linguistic forms used to encode the content. Thus, when asked to reconstruct the text, they are forced to draw on their own linguistic resources. A popular means of eliciting learner production is to use a picture composition or a short video film. The basic procedure is to show the learners the picture composition/video and then ask them to retell the story in their own words, either in writing or orally. However, there are a number of options available to the researcher. Skehan and Foster (1999), for example, compared learner production in a watch-and-tell condition (i.e. the subjects had to simultaneously watch a Mr. Bean video and speak) and a 'watch-then-tell' condition (i.e. they told the story after they had finished watching the video), finding that the watch-then-tell condition led to more complex language use. Interviewing learners provides an obvious means of obtaining samples of learner language but doubts exist regarding the 'interactional authenticity' of the data so collected (Van Lier 1989). However, this problem of authenticity is arguably implicit in the very idea of trying to 'elicit' samples of learner language and thus applies to all the methods.

Focused tasks can be used to elicit production of specific linguistic features. These were discussed in Chapter 15. One common type of focused task is 'dictogloss' (Wajnryb 1990). This involves the use of a short text that contains several exemplars of the target structure. The text is read aloud twice while the learners take notes. The learners then work collaboratively in small groups to reconstruct the text using the notes they have taken. A problem with both dictogloss and other types of focused tasks is that learners are adept at avoiding the use of linguistic features they find difficult. For example, Kowal and Swain (1997) reported that in completing a dictogloss task learners 'go beyond the assigned grammatical feature' and 'follow their own agenda'.

Experimentally elicited samples

Experimental elicitation results in 'constrained constructed responses' (Norris and Ortega 2000), i.e. the production of short L2 segments (ranging from a single word up to a full sentence) within highly controlled linguistic contexts. In the case of many linguistic features, experimental elicitation may serve as the only way of obtaining sufficient data. However, as we noted previously, experimental elicitation may only tell us what learners can produce under conditions of experimental elicitation and may or may not reflect what they can do under more natural conditions of language use, as the samples of spontaneous and elicited speech from Schumann (1978b) shown in Table 17.1 illustrate.

Spontaneous utterances	Elicited data
I no understand this question. You after no talk nothing English I no can You no like Coca-Cola?	SHE WANTS SOME DINNER She don't want some dinner. SHE SAW HIM She don't saw him. THE BABY IS CRYING The baby is don't crying. THE DOG CAN BARK The dog don't can bark.

Table 17.1 Comparison of spontaneous and elicited language use (based on Schumann 1978b)

It is helpful to distinguish two broad types of experimental elicitation that differ in the degree to which the learner's response is constrained. The first type consists of 'discrete point tests' where learners are not expected to provide any language of their own or, at most, a single word (for example, traditional language exercise formats such as fill-in-the-blanks, cloze passages, elicited imitation, and elicited translation). The second type consists of 'prompts' where learners are provided with some stimulus, such as the beginning of a sentence, and use it to produce a complete sentence. Prompts can be distinguished from focused tasks involved in clinical elicitation, however, in that the learners' responses are still highly constrained (i.e. are no longer than a sentence). Examples include sentence completion, discourse completion, question-and-answer, as in the Bilingual Syntax Measure (Burt, Dulay, and Hernandez-Chavez 1973) and Rose's (2000) questions based on a cartoon to elicit requests, apologies, and compliment responses.

In the case of both discrete point tests and prompts a key procedural issue is whether the learners' responses to the stimulus provided are oral or written and whether they are speeded or unspeeded. When given plenty of time to produce a response, learners are able to plan carefully and also pre-monitor their output. This enables them to search their linguistic resources thoroughly and access declarative knowledge of L2 forms. In contrast, when required to respond more immediately learners are forced to rely on their implicit knowledge. Given that natural language relies primarily on implicit knowledge, it can be argued that samples obtained from speeded experimental elicitation are more likely to match those obtained naturally.

Verbal reports

Verbal reports can serve the double purpose of providing samples of learner language (as long as the learners' responses are in the L2 and not their L1) and important information about what Grotjahn (1991) called 'learners' subjective theories',[4] which can assist in providing explanations of L2 acquisition.

It should be noted, however, that there is some disagreement over the validity of verbal reports, with some researchers such as Seliger (1984) arguing that much of language learning is unconscious and thus not reportable by learners.

Self-report

Cohen (1987) defined self-report as 'learner's descriptions of what they do characterized by generalized statements about learning behaviour ... or labels they apply to themselves' (p. 84). He noted that such statements 'are based on beliefs or concepts that learners have about the way they learn language, and are often not based on the observation of any specific event'. Three of the most common methods used to obtain self-reports from learners are questionnaires (see Dörnyei (2003) for an account of the use of these in L2 research), interviews (both structured and unstructured), and personal learning histories (i.e. a learner's narrative account of learning an L2 over time). An interesting example of the last of these can be found in Schumann (1997). As part of a course in SLA, Schumann asked his students to write five-page autobiographical accounts of their language learning. Later in the course, as a final project, he asked them to write a second time about their personal learning experiences, but this time to analyse them from a particular theoretical perspective.

Self-observation

Cohen described self-observation as involving 'the inspection of specific behaviour, either while the information is still in short-term memory, i.e. introspectively, or after the event, i.e. retrospectively' (p. 84). The retrospection can be relatively immediate (i.e. within a day) or delayed. What distinguishes self-observation from self-report is the recency and specificity of the events under consideration. The two main methods of collecting self-observation data are diary studies and stimulated recall. Like questionnaires and interviews, diaries can be more or less structured. That is, learners can be given a very general instruction (for example, 'Please write something every day about your experiences in learning English') or much more specific instructions. Diaries have been widely used in SLA, proving especially useful in investigating affective variables such as anxiety. (See Bailey 1991 and Schumann 1997.) Stimulated recall is an introspective method used to prompt learners to comment on the thoughts and feelings they had while participating in a specific learning event. A common method is to replay a video or audio recording of learners as they engaged in a teaching–learning event, stopping it at particular points to ask the learners to comment. For example, Mackey, Gass, and McDonough (2000) used video playbacks to obtain comments from learners on what they noticed about the feedback they had received on utterances produced while performing a communicative task.

Self-revelation

Self-revelation entails a verbal report made while the learner is still engaged in a teaching–learning event. The report, therefore, is concurrent with the event. The theoretical basis of this method is provided by information-processing models, which claim that information recently attended to is kept in short-term memory (STM) and thus is available for reporting. As Ericsson and Simon (1987) pointed out, a crucial assumption is that 'the information contained in attention and STM remains the same with the verbal report procedure as it would be without the reporting procedure' (p. 32). This assumption has been challenged by some researchers, however. Smagorinsky (1998), for example, argued that verbal reports can change the very process they seek to uncover given that speech activity itself is a powerful way of organizing cognition. Swain (2005) reported evidence that supports Smagorinsky's claim. She demonstrated that from the perspective of sociocultural theory verbal reports contribute to learning. In SLA research, think-aloud has been primarily used in writing tasks as writing allows for 'dual-tasking' (for example, Cumming 1989).

Self-assessment

Self-assessment involves asking learners to report on their own knowledge of the L2. A good example is to be found in Paribakht and Wesche's (1999) instrument for eliciting learners' self-assessments of their lexical knowledge. The crucial issue regarding self-assessment is its validity. A number of studies have investigated this. Oscarson (1997), in a review of such studies, concluded that 'although no consensus has been reached on the merits of the self-assessment approach, a clear majority of the studies surveyed report generally favourable results' (p. 182).

Two final points about the use of self-reports in SLA need to be emphasized. First, it is vital that the instruments and procedures used to collect self-report data are chosen/developed with due regard to both their theoretical underpinnings and also the accumulated wisdom of researchers who have utilized this approach to data collection. In this respect handbooks such as Brown (2001), Brown and Rodgers (2002), and Mackey and Gass (2005) should be referred to because they provide concrete guidelines about how to proceed. Second, because of the doubts that exist about the validity and reliability of self-report methods, it is advisable to combine two or more self-report methods (for example, questionnaires and in depth interviews or think-aloud and stimulus recall).

The question of validity

Underlying this discussion of the pros and cons of the different types of data is the central problem of validity. What constitutes valid L2 data? One answer is that valid data are those that enable a researcher to infer underlying phenomena. The distinction between 'data' and 'phenomena' is made much of by Gregg (1993). Gregg emphasized that theory construction is concerned with phenomena (i.e. some generalized aspect or event such as the melting point of lead) and not with data (i.e. particular observations such as the actual measurements of the temperature at which samples of lead melt). The questions that arise, of course, are what constitute the 'phenomena' to be investigated and how the 'phenomena' can be derived from the 'data'. Gregg has much to say about the nature of the phenomena that he believes should constitute the object of enquiry (see following section) but nothing to say about how data can be related to phenomena.

The answer customarily given is that data provide evidence of phenomena when the results they provide are consistent. To demonstrate consistency, it is necessary to show that the data are not just a reflection of the instrument used to collect them. This can be achieved by comparing the results obtained from one set of data with those obtained from another–ideally, some 'baseline' such as natural language use. There is, however, a logical objection to such a procedure:

> One must be aware that not all tasks, linguistic or metalinguistic, tap the same source of linguistic knowledge. Thus the results of one type of test may not be useful in proving the concurrent validity of another source. (Birdsong 1989: 118)

In effect, Birdsong is acknowledging the position adopted by variabilists. Learners vary in the way they use their linguistic knowledge in accordance with a variety of linguistic, situational, and psycholinguistic factors. (See Chapter 4.) It is to be expected, therefore, that data collected from one source will not completely match those collected from another.

Ultimately, as Gregg recognized, the validity of data must be decided in relation to some clearly articulated theoretical position. This means that validity is essentially a relative issue. What are viewed as valid data from one theoretical perspective may not be from another, different perspective. Nevertheless, two general observations can be made. First, in any study it is necessary to *demonstrate* the validity of the data that have been collected. As Douglas (2001) pointed out, too many studies simply assume that the data are valid. Where the data consist entirely of experimentally elicited samples this is dangerous and, perhaps, theoretically untenable. For example, does the fact that learners can join two sentences together using relative clauses provide convincing evidence that they have acquired relative clauses? Second, there is an obvious need to employ multiple data collection methods on the grounds that no one method will provide an entirely valid picture of what a learner knows. In particular, there is a need to supplement experimentally elicited data with clinically elicited and/or naturally occurring data or both. It is encouraging to note that many researchers now acknowledge the need for multiple types of data.

Good data, then, are data that are relevant to the particular descriptive or theoretical goals of the research. It is theory that decides what counts as valid data. Good research, then, is based on data that can convincingly address the theoretical concerns that inform the research. This is more likely to be achieved if multiple sources of data are collected. Finally, good research gives recognition to the limitations of the data sources used. In Birdsong's words, researchers should recognize that 'each method carries with it impediments to the translation of data to theory' (1989: 613).

The construction and evaluation of SLA theories

While much of the earlier work in SLA was primarily concerned with describing the object of enquiry (the language produced by L2 learners), subsequent research has increasingly been directed at developing theories to explain the wide range of phenomena that have been discovered and to predict new phenomena. Since the 1980s, theories have appeared at a startling rate, leading to debates regarding the merits of one theory as opposed to another. Gregg, in particular, has been at the forefront of these debates staunchly defending his own preferred theory—a Chomskian account of how learners acquire LINGUISTIC COMPETENCE. Starting with his attack on Krashen's Monitor Theory (Gregg 1984), he then moved on to a dismissal of my and Tarone's variabilist theories (Gregg 1990). More recently, he has taken on postmodernist accounts of L2 acquisition (Gregg 2000, 2002), EMERGENTISM (Gregg 2003) and the language socialization paradigm (Gregg 2006). However, Gregg is not the only combatant in these theory wars. As we saw in Chapter 7, there is ongoing controversy between those SLA researchers who favour a cognitive, universalistic theory of L2 learning (for example, Long 1997) and those who support a social, constructivist theory (Firth and Wagner 1997).

Thomas (2005) reviewed three books (Block 2003; Johnson 2004; Jordan 2003), all of which developed arguments in favour of one particular theoretical position in opposition to some other. Block argued for a socially oriented theory in opposition to the dominant Input–Interaction–Output Model; Johnson advocated SOCIOCULTURAL THEORY of L2 acquisition as a replacement for the 'cognitive-computational tradition' (p. 11); Jordan staked out the case for a rationalist approach to theory development and evaluation, and rejected relativist positions. The prevailing approach is to present theories as oppositional and incommensurable rather than as mutually-informing and complementary. It should be noted, too, that the disagreements centre not just on the nature of the phenomena that a theory of L2 acquisition needs to explain (i.e. whether universalistic and cognitive phenomena or social and individualistic phenomena) but also on how theory development should proceed (i.e. whether deductively by testing hypotheses or inductively by collecting observations in order to formulate generalizations).

There has also been disagreement regarding what to do about the plethora of theories that have emerged over the years and which show little sign of thinning out. According to one view (for example, Long 1993), 'culling' is needed to enable SLA to advance from what Kuhn (1962) called the 'pre-paradigm stage' to the 'normal science stage', where researchers agree on a particular theoretical approach, enabling them to get on with the business of solving more and more problems and expanding knowledge without expending their energies in fruitless controversies. The alternative view is that multiple theories are inevitable given the complexity of the phenomena under investigation and the subjective nature of all knowledge and so we should 'let all the flowers bloom' (Lantolf 1996). Such a view is also compatible with COMPLEXITY THEORY as advanced by Larsen-Freeman (See Chapter 9.) As Larsen-Freeman and Cameron (2008) pointed out 'multiple blended methods' constitute 'a pragmatic solution to the demands of a theoretical perspective that seeks to understand the dynamics of change in complex systems'.

The purpose of this section is not to adjudicate on these disagreements by arguing my own position but, in line with the tenor of the entire book, to identify the key issues and present the different positions that have been advanced. The questions that have motivated the various debates are these:

1 What approach to theory-building should SLA research adopt?
2 What should the scope of a theory of L2 acquisition be?
3 What form should a theory take?
4 How can different theories be evaluated?

Approaches to theory-building in SLA research

Long (1985a) drew on the work of Reynolds (1971) to identify two broad approaches to theory building: the 'research-then-theory' approach and the 'theory-then-research' approach. This broadly corresponds to the difference between an inductive (empiricist) approach to theory-building and a deductive (rationalist) approach.

Long suggested that a research-then-theory approach involves the following four activities:

1 Select a phenomenon and list all its characteristics.
2 Measure all the characteristics in as many and as varied situations as possible.
3 Analyse the resulting data by looking for systematic patterns.
4 Formalize significant patterns as theoretical statements (the laws of nature).

This accurately describes much of the early SLA research. The phenomenon under study was 'learner language', its characteristics (errors, developmental features, variability, etc.) were examined, and 'systematic patterns' were identified. This led to the formulation of a number of 'laws' in the form of generalizations about L2 acquisition (for example, 'in the early stages of development learners tend to simplify by omitting both grammatical functors and content words'). Examples of sets-of-laws theories are CREATIVE

CONSTRUCTION theory (Dulay and Burt 1973) and my own VARIABLE COMPETENCE MODEL. Beretta (1991: 505) referred to this approach to theory-building as a 'bottom-up strategy' and argued that researchers should seek plentiful data before proceeding to formulate a theory. He argued that the tendency of researchers to formulate theoretical statements prematurely constitutes a weakness of this approach.

However, others would disagree. Strong theories (such as Chomsky's theory of linguistic competence) have arisen without plentiful data. Not surprisingly, Gregg (1993), with his strong commitment to Chomsky's theory, is dismissive of the research-then-theory approach, arguing that it results in 'shallow theories' (i.e. theories that stick as closely as possible to what is observable and, therefore, do not address 'phenomena'). Another weakness of this approach is that it leads to theories that are particularistic rather than general (i.e. theories that seek to explain only a limited set of data). However, the best known sets-of-laws theory, Spolsky's (1989) 'general theory of second language learning', is very comprehensive (perhaps too much so), consisting of 74 'conditions' for second language learning, which Spolsky extracted from a wide range of SLA findings.

The theory-then-research approach is characterized by Reynolds (as in Long 1985a: 390) in terms of the following activities:

1 Develop an explicit theory in axiomatic or causal process form.
2 Derive a testable prediction from the theory.
3 Conduct research to test the prediction.
4 If the prediction is disconfirmed, modify the theory and test a new prediction (or abandon the theory altogether).
5 If the research findings confirm the prediction, test a new one.

In Gregg's view, this approach lends itself to the construction of 'deep theories' (i.e. theories that go beyond what has been observed by acknowledging the importance of those aspects of nature that cannot be observed). Importantly, such theories allow for predictions to be formulated, tested, and modified. One possibility afforded by this approach is the adoption of a theory for step (1) from outside the realm of SLA research. This has increasingly happened: for example, the emergentist and skill-building models adopted from cognitive psychology (see Chapter 9), the constructionist models derived from sociocultural theory (see Chapter 11) or the linguistic models taken from theoretical linguistics (see Chapter 12).

It is unnecessary and, indeed, unwise, to try to argue that one approach to theory-building is superior to the other. Long (1985a) rightly recognized that both approaches have their strengths and weaknesses. He argued that researchers in the research-then-theory approach are less likely to be 'wrong' because their theoretical claims are based firmly on empirical evidence—always providing, of course, that their observations are valid and reliable—but the end result of their efforts may be 'limited' and perhaps ultimately 'irrelevant'. Researchers in the theory-then-research tradition are more likely to bring about a paradigm shift, as it is this approach that is associated with 'scientific revolutions'. Long recognized, however, that researchers tend to resist abandoning their theories, preferring, if necessary, to modify or add parts to them in order to immunize them against disconfirming evidence. A good example of this is Krashen's continuing attempts to maintain his theory (the INPUT HYPOTHESIS). Arguing the merits of one approach over the other is also unwise for another reason: the two approaches can interlock in a cyclical endeavour. That is, there is no reason why a 'shallow theory' should not develop into a 'deep theory' over time, as in fact often happens when theorists in the research-then-theory tradition go beyond the empirical evidence. Arguably, this is exactly what has happened with Long's own theory (the INTERACTION HYPOTHESIS—see Chapter 6). This originated in Long's observations about the differences between unmodified, premodified, and interactionally modified input (Long 1983) and thus was clearly an example of the research-then-theory approach; it subsequently evolved into a 'deep theory' by incorporating other theoretical perspectives (for example, the OUTPUT and NOTICING HYPOTHESES). As described in Long (1996), the Interaction Hypothesis has clearly become an explicit theory of the causal-process type.

Other commentators, however, have come out more forcibly in favour of the theory-then-research approach. Gregg (1989) argued for a theory-first approach and against a data-led one on the grounds that SLA is to be seen as a sub-field of cognitive science and needs, therefore, to adopt a similar approach to theory development. Beretta (1993) noted that there are advantages to advocacy of a 'tribal model' (a theory that is aggressively promoted so that it stimulates others to explore and elaborate). Examples of 'tribal models' that have attracted allegiance in SLA are the INTERACTIONIST HYPOTHESIS, UNIVERSAL GRAMMAR and, more recently, SOCIOCULTURAL THEORY. However, there is still no single causal-process theory in SLA that commands total (or even near total) allegiance.

Jordan (2003) presented a powerful argument for a rationalist approach to research in SLA. Like Gregg, he sought to brand SLA as a 'science', claiming that 'what distinguishes science from other types of enquiry is that its theories are couched in such a way that they make powerful predictions which are open to falsification through empirical observations and experiments' (p. 86). He identified a number of assumptions that inform the construction of a rational theory of L2 acquisition. (See Table 17.2.) It should be noted, however, that although he argued strongly for a theory-then-research approach, he rejected the minimalist stance of the likes of Gregg and Long by recognizing the advantages of a pluralist approach to theory development. Jordan's commitment to a rationalist approach to theory development, however, is unlikely to be accepted by either those SLA researchers, such as Schumann (1983), who view all knowledge as subjective and reality as multiple, or those, such as Markee (1994), who see 'thick description' as the basis for developing an understanding of the complex factors involved in L2 learning.

Assumptions	Commentary
1 An external world exists independently of our perceptions.	This amounts to a 'minimally realist epistemology'.
2 Research is inseparable from theory.	Theory-free observation of the world is impossible. Thus this assumption contradicts the behaviourist and logical positivist positions.
3 Theories attempt to explain phenomena.	Like Gregg, Jordan distinguished 'phenomena' and 'data'. The former occur in a wide variety of situations and in most cases are not directly observable—a good example being 'linguistic competence' for those researchers working on UG-based SLA.
4 Research is fundamentally concerned with problem-solving.	Problem-solving requires an explanatory theory. Hypotheses can serve as an initial attempt to solve a problem but need to lead to theories. The overall goal should be to unify low-level descriptive theories into a general causal theory.
5 We cannot formalize 'the scientific method'.	There is no one method for arriving at a theory; SLA will benefit from a multi-method approach.
6 There is no need for paradigmatic theories.	Multiple theories are desirable providing they can be supported by evidence. Young theories should be tolerated. All theories should be subject to criticism.

Table 17.2 Assumptions underlying the construction of theories in SLA (Jordan 2003: 115–16)

The scope of a theory of second language acquisition

Second language acquisition is an enormously complex phenomenon—so complex, perhaps, that it is not yet clear exactly what a theory of L2 acquisition needs to account for. One way of specifying the scope of such a theory might be to start by listing the 'well-established findings' of SLA (Long 1990c). These constitute generalizations or 'laws' and are, in Long's view, 'the least that a second language acquisition theory needs to explain' (p. 656). Such an approach makes obvious sense and, incidentally, provides a justification for a book such as this one, which has as one of its major goals a review of what has been discovered about L2 acquisition. Nevertheless, it also has its problems. The first is that there is often no agreement about what constitutes the 'well-established findings', nor whether these findings represent 'phenomena' or 'data'. While it is often possible to agree on broad generalizations (for example, 'age differences systematically affect how fast learners learn'), it is less easy to reach agreement on more specific statements (such as 'the "critical period" for the acquisition of a native-like phonology ends at the age of six'). Even apparently well-established facts come to be challenged (for example, Lantolf's (2005) rejection of acquisition orders and sequences). Second, there is the question of deciding how many of the well-established findings a theory needs to account for. Long, for instance, stated that 'a theory must account for at least *some* of the *major* accepted findings' (1990c: 660, my emphasis added), inviting questions as to what 'some' and 'major' mean, questions for which, not surprisingly, no answers are provided. It is probably true to say that, to date, there is no agreement in SLA research about what facts or how many facts need to be accounted for. This, above all, is why the field is characterized by a multiplicity of theories.

Three views regarding the scope of an L2 acquisition theory can be identified. One is that the field should strive towards a single, comprehensive theory. Jordan (2003) posed three questions that such a theory should address:

> What is L2 competence?
> How is L2 competence acquired?
> How is L2 competence put to use? (p. 260)[5]

The second view is that a modular approach will work best, informed, perhaps, by an over-reaching framework that enables researchers to identify fairly specific domains in which to theorize. The third view, which in fact follows on from the second, is that the scope of the theory should be informed by a particular epistemological stance regarding what is significant in L2 acquisition.

General theories of L2 acquisition

As noted above, the most substantial attempt to construct a comprehensive theory is Spolsky's (1989) 'general theory'. The statements that describe the 'conditions' under which L2 learning can take place are of various kinds—'necessary', 'typical', and 'graded'—depending on the nature of the relationship between a particular condition and a particular outcome. Because many of the conditions are of the 'typical' and 'graded' kind, Spolsky referred to his theory as a 'preference model'. The model contains a total of 74 statements of conditions, which Spolsky claims are 'the natural and logical conclusion of current research in second language learning' and 'a description of the state of the art' (1988: 384). In addition, Spolsky (1989: 28) provided a schematic outline of the different components of the model. This is important because it provides a basis for grouping the various conditions (for example, under such headings as 'social context', 'attitudes', and 'learning opportunities') and also because it indicates the nature of the relationship among the various components.

A comprehensive theory such as Spolsky's general theory is attractive to SLA research because it affords a basis for systematic enquiry. It provides a framework in which individual researchers can locate their specific lines of enquiry; it allows for specific predictions based on the conditions to be tested; and it provides a blueprint for investigating the whole of L2 acquisition (i.e. for determining which factors contribute to the universal and variant properties of L2 acquisition and to what extent they do so). In other words, it helps to shape the whole field and caters for research with both micro and macro goals. Such a comprehensive theory has a number of drawbacks, however. First—and perhaps most serious—it could be argued that Spolsky's theory is not really a theory but merely a long list of conditions and that the interrelationships among these conditions are underspecified, since to specify them fully would run the risk of producing a model of unwieldy complexity.

Second, there is the danger—acknowledged by Spolsky—that the statements will be pitched at such a high level of generality as to be of doubtful value. One wonders, for example, about the explanatory value of conditions such as the 'Attitude Condition', which blandly states that 'a learner's attitudes affect the development of motivation' (Spolsky 1989: 23). Finally, it is not clear how the whole theory can be falsified (although, as we will shortly see, the notion of 'falsification' is itself problematic). It may be possible to falsify the specific conditions, but how many conditions have to be shown to be false before the whole theory becomes untenable? Spolsky's general theory results in a 'messy, fuzzy, overlapping picture' (Hatch, Shirai, and Fantuzzi 1990: 711). However, some researchers find this tolerable because of the importance they attach to forming a whole picture.

These criticisms of Spolsky's theory make assumptions regarding what constitutes a 'good' theory—for example, that a theory should provide a parsimonious, integrated, and cohesive set of statements. Such assumptions are challengeable, however. For example, it could also be argued that a theory needs to be comprehensive. The thorny question of the criteria to be used to evaluate theories is considered below.

Modular theories

Theories of SLA can be unitary or modular. Unitary theories see acquisition as governed by a single general learning mechanism. Modular theories view acquisition as involving a number of distinct mental faculties each functioning differently and responsible for some different aspect of language. Emergentism and UG are respectively examples of a unitary and modular theory. As Gregg (2003) noted, two sorts of modules can be distinguished—specialized data-based modules (Chomsky modularity) and input-processing modules (Fodor modularity). UG is premised on a data-based module (i.e. it is a theory of representation—linguistic competence. In emergentism, however, the distinction between representation and processing is blurred.

A modular approach to theory-building is premised on the idea that a complete explanation of L2 acquisition needs to be accounted for in terms of a number of distinct mental modules, which can best be achieved by constructing theories for each of these modules. Thus, a modular theory must specify (1) the domain covered by the theory, as narrowly as possible, and (2) the domains that are not covered by the theory.

The nearest to a full modular theory is Towell and Hawkin's (1994) Model of Second Language Acquisition. This is based on the view that acquisition needs to be conceptualized in terms of 'the way the L2 learner learns the language system, learns to use the L2 system, and possibly creates interaction between these two processes' (p. 245). Towell and Hawkins proposed that learners draw on a number of separate 'sources' to achieve this; UG, the L1, authentic input data, and (potentially) explicit instruction. Thus, a full account of L2 acquisition requires an explanation for how L2 knowledge is represented, the role of the L1, and how control over L2 knowledge is developed. Towell and Hawkins' model is modular both in terms of what needs to be learnt and in terms of the sources of learning.

The advantage of a theory based on a single module is that it simplifies the task of what needs to be explained, resulting (at best) in a highly articulated theory that affords precise and testable hypotheses, as arguably is the case with UG. The case for such modularity can be made on theoretical or procedural grounds or, of course, both. In the case of UG, the case for modularity is clearly theoretical; the identification of the 'language module' is theoretically motivated in that language is seen as distinct from other aspects of cognition (such as perception) and conforms to principles not observed in other modules. In other cases, authors have elected to address some specific aspect of L2 learning and the mental operations involved on the grounds that this is what interests them or because it makes the job of testing the theory easier. Arguably, Long's Interaction Hypothesis was procedurally motivated; that is, it focused on one specific aspect of interaction (the NEGOTIATION OF MEANING), which Long's (1980a) descriptive research had indicated was significant. (See Chapter 6.) Similarly, my own THEORY OF INSTRUCTED LANGUAGE ACQUISITION was motivated by my desire to explain the interface between implicit and explicit L2 knowledge in such a way as to inform language pedagogy. (See Chapter 9.)

One of the dangers of modularity is unwarranted reductionism (i.e. the domain of investigation is delimited over-narrowly and without theoretical justification). Jordan (2003), for example, criticized UG because its domain is too limited, i.e. many aspects of acquisition lie outside it (a point we noted in Chapter 12). Another serious problem is atomism (i.e. the investigation of one domain takes place in total isolation from the study of other domains). An explanation may satisfactorily account for a delimited set of phenomena and yet be found wanting when these same phenomena are viewed as part of the complete picture. As Hatch, Shirai, and Fantuzzi put it, 'to make our research feasible, we try to limit our investigations to one area, but in so doing, we may advance explanations that are faulty' (1990: 702).[6] This led them to argue that 'partial theories are misleading'. Ultimately, therefore, a modular theory has to be tested in relation to the whole picture. It is valid only in the extent to which its explanation of a single domain holds true when this domain is considered in relation to other domains.

Epistemologically driven theories

Most theories of L2 acquisition are neither comprehensive nor truly modular. Rather they tackle a particular area or adopt a particular perspective (often derived from a parent discipline—cognitive psychology, social psychology, sociolinguistics, linguistics, neurolinguistics, education) without reference to other areas or perspectives. A multiplicity of theories is the result, as is amply demonstrated in this book (see Part Four in particular) and in other survey books. In Ellis 1985a I reviewed seven theories, McLaughlin (1987) considered five, Larsen-Freeman and Long (1991) also examined five (although not the same five as McLaughlin), Mitchell and Myles (1998) discussed six general theoretical 'perspectives', and VanPatten and Williams (2006) examined ten. Furthermore, this theoretical pluralism shows no signs of abating, for, as Spolsky has observed, 'new theories do not generally succeed in replacing their predecessors, but continue to coexist with them uncomfortably' (1990: 609).

It is possible, however, to classify theories into 'schools' by examining their underlying epistemology. Norris and Ortega (2003) identified four broad theoretical schools in this way:

1 linguistically-oriented theories based on some version of Universal Grammar (for example, White 2003a)
2 interactionist theories (such as Long's (1996) Interaction Hypothesis), which are informed by the view that acquisition is the product of a relationship between learner-internal and external processes
3 sociocultural theory (Lantolf 2005) based on Vygotsky's claims that all higher forms of learning are mediated through culturally-determined social interaction
4 emergentist theories (N. Ellis 1998), which see language learning as like any other type of learning, driven by exposure to input that fine-tunes the networked connections that comprise implicit linguistic knowledge.

Norris and Ortega considered the differences in these theories 'fundamental'. That is, the theories differ in their underlying epistemologies, which shape their central constructs (i.e. the phenomena to be investigated), determine what are considered to be the relevant data for investigating L2 acquisition, and inform the methods used to measure acquisition.

The existence of these epistemologically driven theories has inevitably given rise to sharp divisions regarding their relative merits. The arguments that have ensued—referred to in the opening paragraph of this section on theory construction—have been tendentious and ongoing. This is not the place to enter into an extended account of these arguments, but, by way of example, I will consider one: Gregg's (2003) attack on emergentism (as articulated by N. Ellis) and his defence of what he calls 'mad dog nativism'.

Gregg is a staunch advocate of UG. In Eubank and Gregg (1995), for example, he claimed that UG 'is the only theory that there is' (p. 51). As Gregg (2003) made clear, UG is based on two key premises: (1) linguistic competence constitutes a separate module of the mind ('concepts like SUBJECT or C-COMMAND ... have no analogues in other domains', p. 123) and (2) learners must possess innate knowledge of linguistic facts (for example, 'subject') because these facts are not discoverable from the input (i.e. the poverty of stimulus argument). Emergentism is an obvious challenge to Gregg as it disputes both these premises. That is, it views language learning as like any other learning (i.e. it involves associative learning) and views the environment as 'massive and complex' (N. Ellis 1998: 27), fully capable of enabling learners to induce facts such as 'subject'. Gregg's approach is first to reject the arguments that emergentists have used to attack UG accounts of acquisition—the argument that evoking innateness solves nothing; that a simple theory is preferable to a complex theory; that UG is neurologically implausible; and that it is highly unlikely that UG could have evolved as a result of natural selection. Gregg then embarks on a detailed analysis of Ellis and Schmidt's (1997, 1998) connectionist modelling of the acquisition of a plural morpheme (see Chapter 9) in order to demonstrate that assigning some form of innate knowledge is unavoidable and that there are some obvious differences between input as operationalized in their study and natural input. Gregg makes a number of telling points but also conveniently ignores evidence and scholarship that might be used to refute his arguments (for example, he does not acknowledge the work of variabilists who have shown that learners do indeed 'tend to generalize' in a manner very similar to Ellis and Schmidt's computer, rather than categorically apply a morphological feature, as Gregg seems to think they do). However, the key point I wish to make here concerns the *tone* of Gregg's critique. In a series of footnotes in which Gregg addresses points raised by N. Ellis (who was a pre-publication reviewer of his article) he makes free with terms like 'nonsense', 'asinine claim', and 'wretched excuse'—strong language! SLA's epistemological debates arouse emotion as well as reason—even among the so-called rationalists! This is unfortunate as, far from encouraging the 'challenge', which Gregg is apparently keen to see, it discourages it.

The existence of epistemologically incompatible theories as exemplified by UG and emergentism raises the question as to whether such incommensurability should be accepted as inevitable in a complex field of enquiry such as SLA or whether, through a process of evaluation, one theory can emerge victorious. This is an issue considered below.[7] First, though, we will briefly consider the form that theories can take.

The form of a theory of second language acquisition

There has been far less discussion about the form that a theory of L2 acquisition should take. Crookes (1992) and Gregg (1993) distinguished 'property theories' and 'transition theories'. The former are concerned with providing accounts of static systems; they are 'ways of representing dispositions, competencies, or bodies of knowledge' (Crookes 1992: 433). Such theories are useful in that they help to identify the states of L2 knowledge and the components of such states to be found in learners at different stages of their development. Much of the modelling of L2 knowledge found in UG-based theories of L2 acquisition is of this nature. But there is general recognition that property theories in themselves cannot satisfactorily explain L2 acquisition. A transition theory that seeks to account for how changes in the state of a system take place is also needed. Crookes argued that an adequate theory must specify the 'mechanisms' that are responsible for such changes. Long (1990c: 654) defined 'mechanisms' as 'devices that specify how cognitive functions operate on input to move a grammar at Time 1 to its new representation at Time 2', although this probably needs to be broadened to include mechanisms of a more affective nature, such as motivation. A satisfactory theory, then, must identify the mechanisms—cognitive and affective—responsible for acquisition.

We find opposing views about whether SLA theorists should focus on developing a PROPERTY THEORY or a TRANSITION THEORY. Gregg (2001) argued that the first task is to develop a property theory. He argued that UG provides the basis for this but has not yet achieved it. According to Gregg, only when a satisfactory property theory has been formulated should attention be paid to developing a transition theory to explain the mechanisms that operate on linguistic input in order to account for the different states learners pass through en route to linguistic competence. Jordan (2003), however, argued that there is no need to wait until the property theory has been fully worked out before venturing solutions to the 'developmental problem' of L2 acquisition. Jordan noted that the main interest in SLA lies not in the development of a property theory (especially as it is not clear if there is such a thing as a 'steady state' in L2 acquisition) but in explaining interlanguage (i.e. the route learners follow to whatever final state they arrive at).

There is also the question of how theories should be articulated. Crookes pointed out that traditionally theories have taken the form of a series of deductively related sentences, often utilizing a highly formalist language such as that provided by mathematics or logic. However, this kind of theory has never figured strongly in SLA research, which instead has preferred what Crookes calls 'a statement-picture complex' form. According to this, a theory consists of some kind of pictorial element (the 'model') and a supporting set of statements containing generalizations based on and supporting the model. The 'model' provides an iconic element and is likely to employ an analogy of some kind, which may or may not be explicitly acknowledged. For example,

Crookes suggested that Krashen's MONITOR THEORY incorporates a ladder analogy (in the Natural Order Hypothesis) and a learner-as-sponge analogy (in his account of how ACQUISITION takes place). Schumann (1983), with tongue only partly in cheek, discussed a number of pictorial models of L2 acquisition from the perspective of a 'curator of an exhibition of SLA art' (1983: 67) to make his point that theories need to be considered from an aesthetic point of view. The supporting statements, Crookes suggested, need to be clear and explicit, which can be achieved through the appropriate use of formalisms, although few L2 acquisition theories have attempted this. However, it is noteworthy that the two dominant theories in developmental psychology over the past century, Piagetian and Vygotskian, used very few formalisms.

Thus, there is no consensus on the form a theory should take—neither on whether it should contain both property and transition components (and specify how these are related) nor on whether it should be articulated formalistically or iconically and metaphorically.

Evaluating second language acquisition theories

Gregg (2003) wrote 'it is not really clear that we have anything worth calling a theory of SLA, in which case it may seem premature to discuss evaluating them' (p. 849). Such a statement is contradictory, however, as presumably Gregg must have engaged in some form of evaluation in order to conclude that there was no worthwhile theory currently available! Evaluation is about deciding what is and what isn't a theory and what is a good or bad theory.

We have seen that there is a multiplicity of theories of L2 acquisition. The first question that arises is to what extent this multiplicity is to be viewed positively or negatively. Beretta (1991) noted that opinions differ considerably on this point. On the one hand there are the 'relativists' who view SLA research as an 'art' rather than a 'science', and argue that 'in art perspectives are neither right or wrong; they are simply more or less appealing to various audiences' (Schumann 1983: 66). On the other hand, there are those like Long (1993), and, to a certain extent, Beretta himself, who see multiple theories as problematic for SLA research and consider the elimination of some theories in favour of others a necessary goal if the field is to advance. Long pointed out that, whereas some theories can be seen as complementary, others are clearly oppositional. He gives examples of rival claims in choice of domain (for example, UG-based theories versus variationist theories), within a single domain (for example, the conflicting theories relating to the availability of UG in adult learners), and with regard to the specific variables considered important by MENTALIST, environmentalist and INTERACTIONIST THEORIES. He argued that where opposition exists, 'culling' needs to take place, pointing out that the history of science shows that successful sciences are those that are guided by a 'dominant theory'.

Three approaches to theory evaluation can be identified. One consists of identifying a set of criteria that can be applied to all theories as a way of eliminating those that are unsatisfactory. This, according to Beretta (1991) and Long (1993), should be the goal of SLA research. The second approach is to abandon any attempt to evaluate theories on rational grounds, and to turn instead to aesthetic criteria. The third approach is to accept that theoretical pluralism is not just a temporary feature of an immature discipline, but is here to stay and to try to avoid the attendant problems of absolute relativism by evaluating theories in relation to their particular contexts and purposes. We will briefly consider these three approaches.

Table 17.3 shows the criteria for evaluating theories that have been proposed by a number of SLA researchers. Synthesizing these assessment frameworks, the following five general criteria can be identified:

1 Scope of the theory. There is general agreement that a theory with a broad scope is preferable to a theory with a narrow scope. McLaughlin proposed that a theory should fit the body of established knowledge about L2 acquisition. Both Mitchell and Myles and Jordan explicitly mentioned the need for a theory to be broad in scope. Towell and Hawkins were more specific, identifying five 'core areas' that a theory should account for.
2 Empirical support. McLaughlin, Long, Mitchell and Myles, and Jordan all recognized the importance of this criterion. A good theory must be compatible with what is known about L2 acquisition.
3 Internal consistency. Long and Jordan both considered that the extent to which the theory is internally consistent (i.e. coherent and cohesive) is important. Long saw internal consistency as a criterion that should be applied prior to empirical testing.
4 External consistency. A theory that is consistent with other recognized theories is better than one that is not. However, this does raise the question as to what theories the theory being evaluated should be compared with. McLaughlin referred to 'related theories' and Long to 'accepted theories in other fields'. However, the question then arises as how to establish 'relatedness' and 'acceptability' in other fields.
5 Fruitfulness. McLaughlin, Long, and Jordan all considered that an indicator of a strong theory is whether it motivates substantial research and is likely to continue to do so in the future. The theory should help to establish new knowledge and to challenge established knowledge.

In addition to these five general criteria, a number of other criteria are mentioned by individual researchers. Two of these—simplicity and falsifiability—warrant closer consideration.

In accordance with Occam's razor, Jordan stated baldly that 'theories should be simple'. He claimed that a theory 'with the simplest formula, and the fewest number of basic types of entity postulated, is to be preferred for reasons of economy' (p. 97). However, Gregg (2003) considered 'simplicity' a 'red herring', noting that while rationalists (such as Jordan) are happy to

McLaughlin (1987, 1990c)	Long (1993)	Towell and Hawkins (1994)	Mitchell and Myles (1998)	Jordan (2003)
The following criteria are identified: 1 Norms of correspondence: the extent to which the theory fits the facts that it seeks to explain. 2 Norms of coherence: the extent to which the theory fits the body of knowledge that has already been established, and is consistent with other related theories. 3 Practicality: the extent to which a theory is 'heuristically rich' in stimulating and guiding research (McLaughlin 1990c: 619). 4 Falsifiability: the extent to which the theory affords hypotheses that can be disconfirmed.	Five sets of 'assessment strategies' are identified: 1 Criteria applicable before the empirical testing of a theory (for example, internal consistency). 2 Criteria for assessing the empirical adequacy of a theory (for example, explanatory adequacy, and generality). 3 Criteria for assessing a theory's future potential (for example, fruitfulness). 4 Consistency with accepted theories in other fields. 5 Metaphysical and methodological constraints (for example, experimental testability).	Theories are to be evaluated in terms of whether they account for 'five core areas of observed L2 behaviour' (p. 5): • language transfer • staged development • systematicity across L2 learners • variability • incompleteness.	Theories are to be evaluated with reference to: • the claims and scope of the theory • the view of language • the view of the language-learning process • the view of the learner • the nature and extent of empirical support.	Jordan lists five criteria for assessing SLA theories: 1 Research hypotheses should be coherent, cohesive, and expressed in the clearest possible terms. 2 Theories should have empirical content. 3 Theories should be fruitful. 4 Theories should be broad in scope. 5 Theories should be simple.

Table 17.3 Criteria for evaluating SLA theories

appeal to simplicity, empiricists are not. While acknowledging that he himself applied the simplicity criterion in dismissing Krashen's Monitor Model (see Gregg 1984), he considered 'such easy targets' rare. Nor is it always easy to determine what constitutes relative simplicity, given the difficulty of comparing theories that are formulated in different ways (for example, in terms of general axioms or in terms of statements based on formal logic). Also, an ambitious theory that is broad in scope is likely to be more complex than a theory that is limited to explaining a highly restricted domain of SLA. In short, the validity of 'simplicity' as an evaluative criterion is questionable, and it is certainly difficult to apply.

Falsifiability (i.e. the extent to which the theory affords hypotheses that can be disconfirmed) is also controversial. Beretta (1991) argued that it is problematic because of the impossibility of obtaining neutral, objective data with which to test theoretical claims and, also, because L2 acquisition theories tend to be formulated in such a way that they allow for *ad hoc* or auxiliary hypotheses as a way of immunizing initial hypotheses against disconfirming evidence. Schumann (1993) made the same point when he pointed out that it is very difficult to test a hypothesis in isolation because every hypothesis is embedded in 'a network of auxiliary assumptions'. Thus, when the results fail to support the hypothesis, we cannot tell whether this is because the hypothesis is wrong or because one or more of the auxiliary hypotheses is wrong. He argued that 'falsification is ... extremely difficult, if not impossible to achieve' (1993: 296). However, other researchers have argued for falsifiability as a criterion. Long (1993), while acknowledging problems, saw merit in this criterion. Jordan (2003) mounted a robust defence of it, aligning himself with the Popperian view that falsifiability is 'the hallmark on a scientific theory, and allows us to make a demarcation line between science and non-science' (p. 31). The essence of Popper's position is that we can never confirm a theory as, at some time or another, evidence may be forthcoming to demonstrate that the theory is wrong. Therefore, all we can do is show that the theory is not compatible with the empirical facts although this raises the thorny question of how we determine what constitutes disconfirming evidence.[8] Like Long, Jordan argued that falsification and empirical adequacy are criteria that should be applied once the internal consistency of a theory has been established. In this sense, then, falsification can be considered an important second-order criterion.

Finally, it is worth noting another approach to theory evaluation—one that rests not on the relationship between theory and evidence but on the social value of the theory. This is the approach adopted by Vygotsky, who, in accordance with Marx's philosophy, saw the role of theory as contributing to beneficial changes in the material circumstances of people's lives.

The second approach to theory evaluation acknowledges the inherent subjectivity involved. Schumann (1983) made much of the fact that scientists working in the physical sciences now acknowledge that there is no 'objective reality'. The recognition that 'we create the reality we study' leads to an acceptance of 'philosophical flexibility' (1983: 51) and to treating science as 'art'. Clearly, a very different set of criteria are called for if this perspective is adopted. Schumann suggested that 'innovation', 'tone of voice', and 'metaphor' can be used to evaluate theories, and goes on to apply these criteria to a number of L2 acquisition theories. This approach to theory evaluation is attractive, not least because it may reflect what many of us covertly do when we consider theories, but ultimately it is unsatisfactory because it does not take into account empirical evidence. Ultimately a theory is not 'good' because it is 'beautiful' (although it is obviously desirable that it should be), but because it 'fits the available evidence'.

In a later article, Schumann (1993) suggested that theory development should be seen as a process of 'exploration'. This refers to 'efforts to expand, revise, alter, and ultimately to understand and assess the validity of the construct' (1993: 301). Schumann proposed that one way in which exploration can take place is by trying to understand a phenomenon at a different level of organization or in relation to another field. For example, socio-affective theories, which are the main focus of his own research (see Chapter 7), can be explored in terms of social/psychological factors and through neurological enquiry. (See Chapter 14.) Schumann sees a 'reductionist' approach that accommodates explanation at different levels as preferable to a 'closurist' approach of the kind favoured by Long.

It is clear, then, that that there is no universally accepted set of criteria. Acknowledgement of this is a recurring refrain in the commentaries on SLA theory evaluation. Beretta (1991) concluded his discussion of the various evaluative criteria with the assertion that there are no foolproof, indispensable criteria available. Jordan (2003), some twelve years later, commented 'there are no golden rules for theory assessment, no hard and fast rules, except the obvious requirement that a theory has empirical content' (p. 97). It is unlikely that any consensus will be reached in the years ahead given the philosophical disagreements about such fundamental issues as 'objective evidence'.

The third approach is to accept that multiple theories are inevitable and to abandon any attempt to evaluate and cull theories. Relativists argue that it is not possible to determine which theories are 'good' and which 'bad' on purely objective grounds and therefore the existence of multiple theories should be accepted and welcomed. Such a view stands in clear opposition to the views of rationalists, who view evaluation as essential if SLA is to achieve maturity. The debate between the rationalists and the relativists in SLA is fierce and ongoing.

Lined up on the rationalist team are (among others) Long, Gregg, and Jordan. Long (1993) argued that even if there is no set of universally valid assessment criteria, researchers need to act as if there is. He suggested that different criteria may be important at different stages of theory development, and that the failure to identify a universal set of criteria may reflect a 'problem in the timing of their application, not conflicts in principle' (1993: 242). He went on to suggest that criteria, like theories, should be subjected to empirical testing and adjusted when they are found to be 'false'. Gregg (2000) staked out the standard rationalist position:

> Scientists test claims. They test them by making predictions about the world, which they try to confirm or disconfirm by experiment and observation.

He dismissed the postmodernist and constructivist arguments that underlie relativism, concluding in his customary robust style that relativists need to 'get real'. According to Gregg, most SLA researchers are advocates of 'scientism'. That is, they recognize that the 'goals of scientific enquiry include the discovery of objective empirical truths' (Fodor 1998: 189). If such truths are discoverable (and that is a matter of philosophical debate), then, theories can be evaluated in terms of whether they match up to them. Theories that fail to do so (or do so less well than others) should be eliminated. Jordan (2003) pleaded for SLA researchers to unite into 'a broad rationalist community' and to accept a rationalist approach to assessing theories. However, unlike Gregg, he acknowledged the need to question the 'objectivity' of science and the role played by individual and social factors in theory construction. He is also in favour of 'unlikely' theories being developed—SLA researchers should be encouraged to 'fly any kite' they like. But like Long and Gregg he argued that theories need to be evaluated. He saw contradictions among theories as problematic, to be resolved through 'rational discussion' and the use of criteria such as those shown in Table 17.3.

Lined up on the relativist team are Schumann, Block, and Lantolf[9] (among others). Schumann's views on theory evaluation were outlined above. They are relativistic in the sense that he disputed the possibility of identifying which theories were 'good' or 'bad' except on aesthetic grounds. Block (1996), responding to the series of articles published in *Applied Linguistics* 14/3 by Long *et al.*, took objection to what he saw as a ruling clique in SLA. He challenged the assumptions he viewed as strangling SLA enquiry—namely that there is such a thing as 'normal science', that there is an 'ample body' of 'accepted findings', and that replication studies are useful. He argued that the multiplicity of theories in SLA is not problematic. In his 2003 book, Block again confronted the 'self-proclaimed authorities/gatekeepers of SLA' (i.e. Long, Gass *et al.*) and sought to 'circumvent exclusionary stances' (p. 7). He argued for a broadening of SLA with regard to what is understood by the terms 'second', 'language', and 'acquisition' and thus (implicitly) for a multiplicity of approaches. Lantolf (1996) most clearly set out the case for relativism in his aptly named article 'SLA theory building: letting all the flowers bloom!' Lantolf viewed theories as 'discourses', rejecting a 'readerly' stance towards texts in favour of a 'writerly' one on the grounds that texts do not have objective content. Theories are inherently metaphorical—'theories are metaphors that have achieved the status of acceptance by a group of people we refer to as scientists' (p. 721). It is thus a small step to the claim that 'the greater the acceptance of an acquiescence to standard scientific language within a discipline, the greater the chances that the productivity of the scientific endeavour will diminish' (p. 723). To avoid this, SLA researchers need to create new metaphors to represent multiple realities. Lantolf explicitly favoured a plurality of theories, seeing relativism as a defence against the hegemony of a dominant theory (such as Chomsky's).

The rationalists have not been slow to respond to the attacks of the relativists. Gregg, Long, Jordan, and Beretta (1997) responded to Block (1996). Gregg (2000) responded to Lantolf (1996). And the debate goes on. Lantolf (2002) offered 'a commentary from the flower garden' in response to Gregg (2000), while Gregg (2002) was kindly given the last word—'a garden ripe for weeding'. Long (2006c) reviewed this exchange of views, concluding that 'it is not true that a multiplicity of theories in a field is unproblematic' and arguing that to adopt such a position is 'tantamount to a declaration of irresponsibility or else a belief that progress is unattainable' (p. 156). Long also weighed in against the editors of the journals who publish the 'shoddily argued material' of the relativists, thereby evidencing the hegemonic tendency that relativists have frequently complained about.

Is there a way out of this increasingly acrimonious debate? One possibility might lie in the distinction that Lantolf (1996) made between 'judgmental relativism' and 'epistemic relativism'. Whereas the former views all knowledge as equally valid, the latter claims that theories can be distinguished 'in terms of their relevance and adequacy for attaining particular goals' (p. 734). Epistemic relativism is the position I adopted (and still favour) in the first edition of this book. I argued that theories should be evaluated in relation to the context in which they were developed and the purpose(s) they were intended to serve. A UG-based theory, for example, is to be understood in terms of the field of Chomskian linguistics from which it was developed, and needs to be evaluated with regard to the contributions that it makes to this field. It would be entirely inappropriate to try to understand and evaluate such a theory from the point of view of a foreign language teacher. In contrast, sociocultural SLA has been developed by researchers interested in language pedagogy; constructs such as mediation and the zone of proximal development (see Chapter 12) have obvious relevance to teachers. An approach to evaluation that acknowledges that theories are contextually determined allows for an acceptance of complementarity without a commitment to absolute relativism, for it can still be argued that among theories constructed for the same purpose and context, one does a better job than another because it is more complete, fits the facts (if these can be agreed upon) better, affords more interesting predictions, is more consistent with other theories, etc. Bialystok's Theory of L2 Learning (see Chapter 9), for example, might be considered a better theory than Krashen's Monitor Theory because it allows for an interface between explicit and implicit knowledge, for which there is growing empirical support. The important point here is the one I raised in Ellis (1995c)—that ultimately it is not the SLA theorist who will decide whether a particular theory is relevant to a particular purpose but the consumers of the theory. SLA is in essence an applied discipline and any attempt to evaluate its products without reference to their applications is doomed to failure.

It follows that theories designed to meet different purposes in different contexts should be allowed to co-exist. This is one reason why theories of L2 acquisition are great survivors. SLA theories are not usually dismissed as a result of empirical study or powerful argumentation but instead tend to slip slowly and gently into oblivion because they are no longer seen as useful. Thus, over the years, it is possible to detect a gradual waning of influence of some theories (such as the Monitor Theory or my own Variable Competence Theory), although many of their ideas live on and are incorporated into other models (for example, my views on variability have been incorporated into emergentist accounts of L2 acquisition).

To sum up, we have seen that there is considerable disagreement among SLA scholars about theories. This is evident in the role of theory in SLA research, the scope of a theory, the form it should take, and how it should be evaluated. We can detect two poles, with many shades of opinion in between. At one pole there is 'a healthy and unusually polite acceptance of the possibility of pluralism in the answers proposed, a willingness to concede that different models might be needed for different aspects of the problem, an acceptance that different points of view might lead to different theories' (Spolsky 1990: 613). At the other there is the belief that research should follow the assumed methods of the hard sciences, with little or no room allowed for complementarity or personal preference. At the moment the pluralists are winning out over the closurists. This is perhaps as it should be; those theories that are found useful by researchers and practitioners (such as teachers) for their varying purposes will continue to flourish.

The application of second language acquisition research to other fields of enquiry

On a number of occasions in the preceding chapters, we noted that the study of L2 acquisition may be of value to other disciplines. One of the most obvious ways in which it can be of service is by providing a rich body of data that can be used to address theoretical issues of importance in the 'parent' disciplines. For example, the study of how L2 learners grammaticalize their interlanguages (see Chapter 9) can inform functional theories of grammar. Similarly, experimental studies designed to test UG-based hypotheses can be used to refine the model of grammar on which they are based. SLA research and linguistics enjoy a symbiotic relationship, for as Gass (1989) put it:

> ... facts of second-language learners force us to look deeper into questions of language. Facts of language force us to consider them in the light of second-language learners. Whether it is the chicken first or the egg first comes largely from one's major interest and not in anything inherent in the chicken or the egg. (p. 526)

We might note, though, that this symbiosis is not without its problems. It is not an easy matter to determine what the relevant 'facts' are. Nor is it clear what should give way—the 'facts of second-language learners' or the 'facts of language'—when the results of empirical studies of L2 learners are not in conformity with the predictions of linguistic theory.[10]

The main area of application, however, is probably L2 pedagogy. As Spolsky notes, 'we have a traditional concern to consider not just the explanatory power of a theory but also its relevance to second language pedagogy' (1990: 610). Similarly, Long (2006c) viewed SLA as 'a field with considerable social consequences for millions of people all over the world' (p. 156); he had teachers and teacher educators specifically in mind.

This concern with language teaching is reflected in a series of articles by SLA researchers over the years that have addressed the relationship between SLA research and second/foreign language teaching and language teacher education (for example, Tarone, Cohen, and Dumas 1976; Hatch 1978e; Lightbown 1985a, 2000; Widdowson 1990; Long 1990b, 2006a; Nunan 1990b, 1991; Ellis 1994b, 1997b, 1999c; Schachter 1993; Van Lier 1994a; Gass 1995; Crookes 1997; Markee 1997; the articles in the special issue of *The Modern Language Journal* 89/3 on methodology, epistemology, and ethics in instructed SLA research). In these articles we can identify a number of different positions:

1 The results of SLA research cannot be safely applied to language pedagogy because they are too uncertain.[11]
2 SLA research provides a basis for teacher 'education' but not for teacher 'training'. That is, it can help teachers develop reasonable expectations about what they can achieve in their teaching, but cannot be used to tell them how to teach.
3 The results of SLA research (and in particular of classroom-oriented research) provide 'hard evidence' which should be used to advise teachers about what techniques and procedures work best.
4 SLA research provides information and actual data that can be used in the construction of tasks designed to raise teachers' awareness of and stimulate reflection about the likely relationship between teaching/learning behaviours and L2 acquisition.
5 The results of SLA research constitute a source of 'provisional specifications' (Stenhouse 1975) that teachers need to test through teacher research in their own classrooms.
6 SLA researchers need to collaborate with teachers in identifying how SLA can best inform language pedagogy and, also, in conducting classroom-based research into L2 learning.
7 The relationship between SLA and language pedagogy should be two-way; that is, language pedagogy should inform SLA and SLA should inform language pedagogy.

As we can see, these positions range from a super-cautious 'don't apply' to a confident 'go ahead and apply' while also claiming that SLA and language pedagogy should relate symbiotically.

Early commentaries (for example, Tarone *et al.* 1976; Hatch 1978e) tended to evince an either 'don't apply' or 'apply with caution' position. Tarone *et al.* gave seven reasons why SLA research failed to provide the teacher with satisfactory guidelines. These included: it was restricted in scope; it had only just begun to investigate the cognitive processes and learning strategies involved in L2 acquisition; the contribution of individual variables such as personality and motivation had not been evaluated; the methodology for both the collection and analysis of data was still uncertain; and few studies had been replicated. Tarone and her colleagues also noted that the practices of teaching and research were very different, for, whereas teachers had immediate needs they must meet, researchers could afford to follow a slow, bit-by-bit approach. Hatch (1978e) thought that researchers had been over-ready to make applications for pedagogy, commenting: '... our field must be known for the incredible leaps in logic we make in applying our research findings to classroom teaching'.

There have clearly been considerable advances in SLA since but doubts still exist about whether its findings are sufficiently robust to warrant a direct application to language teaching. Lightbown (1985a), for example, concluded that 'second-language acquisition research does not tell teachers *what* to teach, and what it says about *how* to teach they have already figured out' (p. 182). However, Lightbown did find one role for SLA research: she suggested that knowledge of the findings of SLA research will help teachers to have 'much more realistic expectations about what can be accomplished'. Fifteen years later, Lightbown (2000) is somewhat more optimistic, recognizing that although it is still not possible to 'apply' the findings of individual studies, it is feasible to apply 'the general principles that they reflect' (p. 454). Lightbown was careful to acknowledge, however, that SLA constitutes only one and possibly not even the main source of information for guiding teachers.

Some researchers, however, have argued for the direct application of SLA to language pedagogy. Corder (1980) sensibly pointed out that teachers cannot wait until researchers have got it right and that it is natural to expect them to go ahead and make use of the best information available. In this respect, information obtained from research conducted inside real classrooms as opposed to laboratories may prove more valuable for, as Spada (2005) noted, teachers are more willing to heed it. Long (1990b) argued that teaching and teacher training should be grounded in 'hard evidence about what works'. He claimed that the teaching profession, like the medical profession, needs to be informed by specialized knowledge unknown to the lay person, and to be guided by research information. He was critical of the ungrounded 'assertions and prescriptions' found in teaching manuals. Thus, although, like others, he acknowledged the limitations of the research, he believed that there are sufficient studies affording reliable results to make it possible to transmit them to teachers in the form of information about what and how to teach. Long (2006c) saw SLA as a defence against 'drastic pendulum swings of fashion' and 'Wonder Methods' (p. 157). It caters to evidence-based practice although, as Long (echoing Lightbown) was careful to acknowledge, it is not the only source of evidence. Long pointed to a number of insights that language teaching has quietly absorbed from SLA theory and research but also lamented the 'disappointing unwillingness' to recognize these.

A number of other commentators have noted that the procedures involved in conducting research and in language teaching are not the same and have claimed that for this reason the direct application of theory and research to language pedagogy is impossible. Widdowson (1990), for example, argued that theory and research involve 'an abstraction', whereas teaching takes place in concrete and varied contexts. It follows that 'application cannot simply model itself on the procedures of empirical research' (1990: 60). One conclusion from this line of argument might be that theory and research are of no use to the teacher. This was the view adopted by Clarke (1994), who saw the discourses of researchers and teachers as fundamentally different and the relationship between researchers and teachers as inherently dysfunctional. However, this is not the position Widdowson adopted. Instead, he argued that what is needed is an attempt to mediate between 'outsider research' and 'insider research' (i.e. actual teaching). This mediation requires 'teacher education' (rather than 'teacher training') and should take the form of discussion of 'issues of current pedagogic concern' (1990: 66), informed by 'generalities' and 'principles' supported by theory and research. By engaging in a 'process of pragmatic mediation', teachers can examine how their particular pedagogic problems can be addressed. In Ellis (1997c), I identified two basic ways in which 'mediation' between researchers and teachers can be accomplished: (1) by making SLA relevant and accessible to teachers, as in books on SLA written specifically for teachers (for example, Lightbown and Spada 1999) and (2) evaluating language pedagogy through SLA, for example by addressing questions that have originated from teachers (as in Pica 1994a). This view of the relationship between theory/research and teaching, then, emphasizes the inevitability of variable solutions, as teachers seek to utilize the information available to them in terms of their own teaching context.

One way in which SLA can be made relevant to teacher education is by viewing it as a rich source of information and data which can be used to foster the processes that lie at the centre of teacher development (i.e. the formation of a language teaching ideology, the acquisition of techniques and procedures for action, and the evaluation of these through reflection). In Ellis (1994b), I suggested that one way of making practical use of SLA research is by developing activities to raise teachers' awareness about such issues as the relationship between the kinds of questions they ask and L2 learning. The research, then, serves as a basis for the development of teacher education tasks designed to promote reflection on different aspects of language pedagogy.

All of the above approaches involve making use of SLA to inform language pedagogy. The assumption, therefore, is that researchers do the research which is then packaged in various ways to address pedagogic issues. A more radical alternative, however, is for teachers themselves to become SLA researchers in their own classrooms. There are compelling educational arguments for involving teachers in researching in their own classrooms. (See, for example, the arguments presented in support of action research by Crookes (1993) and for practitioner research by Allwright (2003).) Teacher research ensures that the research is relevant to the specific context in which a teacher is working and it engages teachers in reflective practice. Teacher research can originate in the pedagogical problems a teacher has identified (i.e. from within teaching) or from SLA (i.e. from without). In this latter case, proposals emanating from SLA need to be treated, as Stenhouse (1975) recommended, as 'provisional specifications', the validity of which need to be tested by teachers themselves in their own classrooms. SLA can assist teacher researchers in another way—it can provide them with information about the instruments and procedures they will need to collect and analyse data.

There are, however, problems with trying to turn teachers into SLA researchers, desirable as this might be. Teachers do not always make good researchers[12] and may find the burden of researching their classrooms time-consuming and onerous. An alternative approach, therefore, might be for teachers to collaborate with SLA researchers in researching their classrooms. This is the approach favoured by Gass (1995). It becomes most feasible when the interests of teachers and researchers coincide, as, for example, in investigating whether specific types of tasks result in the kinds of interaction likely to foster acquisition, or the relative effectiveness of different types of corrective feedback. A good example of researcher-teacher collaboration can be found in Doughty and Varela's (1998) study of corrective recasts. In the opinion of some (for example, Louden 1992), collaborative research of this kind will work best when there is mutual trust between researcher and teacher engendered by the researcher's acceptance of the teacher's autonomy.

Finally, as Van Lier (1994b) pointed out, consideration also needs to be given to how language pedagogy can serve as a source of theoretical and empirical knowledge about L2 acquisition. Van Lier advocated a critical scientific method that uses 'participation in the practical affairs of the field to fuel theory, which is then put back into the service of progress in practical affairs' (p. 338). However, given the power imbalance between 'research' and 'teaching' and the differences in the discourses that underlie and construct this imbalance, it is doubtful whether such a fruitful symbiosis will come about. One way might be for SLA researchers to become teachers.

There is a consensus among SLA researchers that SLA is indeed of value to teachers even if precisely how remains a matter of controversy. Some teacher educators, however, are not so convinced that SLA has much to offer the teaching profession, especially if SLA is seen as a 'content' that dictates how teachers should teach. The focus of much language teacher education has shifted from the learner to the teacher. Johnson (2006), for example, disputed Yates and Muchisky's (2003) claim that the central role of teacher educators is to ensure that teachers are equipped with 'core disciplinary knowledge about the nature of language and language acquisition' (p. 136) and argued that instead they should focus on how teachers learn to teach and how they carry out their work. In line with such a view, teacher cognition research has taken off, but sadly, as Johnston herself admitted, the relationship between 'teacher learning' and 'student learning' has gone unexplored. What is missing from teacher cognition research is the recognition that the cognitions that really matter are those that are associated with *effective* teaching (i.e. teaching that contributes to student learning). Certainly, teachers need to probe their own mental worlds, but they also need to be able to evaluate their beliefs and their teaching in terms of whether they foster learning. Investigating teacher learning cannot be a substitute for examining how teaching facilitates learning. SLA must constitute an essential component of any teacher education programme—especially if it is used as a resource to help teachers question their own theories about L2 acquisition.

Conclusion

In this chapter we have examined a number of issues that are of epistemological and philosophical importance to SLA research. I have restricted the discussion to those positions reflected in the SLA literature to date. In accordance with the main aim of this book, I have not attempted to argue strongly in favour of particular positions, although my own views have necessarily intruded.

I would like to conclude with two proposals for improving SLA research. The first is that SLA researchers should pay more attention to the replication of published studies in SLA. The second is that SLA researchers should commit more to longitudinal studies of L2 learners.

Replication is one way in which some of the disputes concerning what constitute the 'facts of L2 acquisition' might be resolved. It offers a way of achieving objectivity. To date, there have been relatively few replication studies, which, as Polio and Gass (1997) pointed out, constitutes a serious lacuna, given that so many published studies are methodologically limited in one way or another (for example, in terms of the sample size or the lack of randomized groups in experimental designs). Polio and Gass distinguished 'virtual replications' and 'conceptual replications'. The former involve a more or less complete copy of the original study, while the latter involve alterations to the original study with a view to confirming the generalizability or external validity of the research. Polio and Gass suggested that virtual replications are difficult to achieve in SLA given the problems in ensuring identical learning conditions. Conceptual replications are more feasible. Such replications, however, need to be conducted by researchers who do not have a vested interest in confirming the results of the original study. The journal

Studies in Second Language Acquisition has set an example by encouraging submissions of replication studies. Unfortunately, however, to date few have been published.

The early years of SLA were characterized by a number of longitudinal studies of L2 learners that did much to define the research agenda of SLA. (See Chapter 1 for a summary of a number of these studies.) With some notable exceptions (for example, Lardiere's (1997) study of Patty) longitudinal studies have given way to experimental studies of short duration (even when a delayed post-test is included) or micro analyses of highly localized interactions involving L2 learners. The need for longitudinal research has recently been forcibly made by Ortega and Byrnes (2008). They argued that learners' interlanguage development is inherently emergent, variable, and non-linear and so can only be properly understood through longitudinal study. However, they do not equate longitudinal study simply with length. Rather they argued that it needs to be characterized by multi-wave data collection that focuses, in particular on transition points (for example, when learners shift from the classroom to a study-abroad context), a focus on documenting change in learners' systems, and prolonged tracking of specific phenomena in context. They also argued that it needs to examine non-linguistic as well as linguistic development. The case they make for longitudinal research is a convincing one.

SLA research, some forty years after its inception as an identifiable field of enquiry, is still characterized by facts, opinions, explanations, positions, and perspectives that frequently exist in an uneasy state of complementarity and opposition. SLA is a diverse and divided field of enquiry. Differences are evident in the kind of data researchers collect to investigate acquisition, in the attitudes they hold towards theory development and evaluation, and in how researchers and educators think SLA should inform language pedagogy. In this chapter, we have seen that there are opposing views about what to do about this state of affairs. One is that SLA needs to cull 'bad' theories and eschew mindless relativism and ill-informed challenges. The other is that whether or not progress is being made is not the issue (for after all progress is difficult, perhaps impossible, to measure) and that what matters most is that SLA has established itself as a vibrant field of enquiry with a willingness to explore a wide range of issues by means of alternative paradigms and methods. I have indicated my sympathy with the latter view. However, I hope that in the years ahead SLA researchers can settle on a set of 'well-established findings' as a basis for both theory-evaluation and pedagogical applications and, to this end, more replication of published studies and more longitudinal research will surely be helpful.

Notes

1 Whether learners are correct in their judgements in a sentence-matching test is immaterial. The time taken to make a judgement serves as the meas-

ure of whether a particular structure is deemed grammatical (and thus part of the learner's interlanguage) or ungrammatical (and thus not part).

2 Spoken corpora have also been collected (for example, The Louvain International Database of Spoken English Interlanguage (LINDSEI) Project—http://www.fltr.ucl.ac.). The Vienna-Oxford International Corpus of English (VOICE), a corpus of English as a lingua franca, currently in preparation, is another relevant example (http://www.univie.ac.at/voice/).

3 It can be argued, of course, that so-called 'pedagogic tasks' are authentic in the context of a classroom. Indeed, it might be argued that they are more authentic than so called 'authentic tasks' in such a setting.

4 Grotjahn (1991: 188) defines 'subjective theories' as follows:

> ... complex cognitive structures that are highly individual, relatively stable, and relatively enduring, and that fulfil the task of explaining and predicting such human phenomena as action, reaction, thinking, emotion and perception.

5 As Jim Lantolf pointed out to me in his review of this chapter, precisely what a general theory of L2 acquisition should account for is itself a matter of controversy. Jordan formulated the scope of such a theory in terms of competence but competence itself is a construct from a particular theory—generative grammar. Other theories reject the idea of underlying competence. It is doubtful whether it is possible to delineate the scope of a theory of L2 acquisition in theoretically neutral terms.

6 This is really a restatement of the data problem. One source of data may afford results that are not supported by other data sources. In particular, there may be differences between what data elicited experimentally show and what natural data show.

7 I should come out and make clear my own position here. I doubt that SLA researchers will ever agree to settle on a single theory (or even a single theoretical perspective) but if this does happen it will probably not be through the process of evaluation but through tribal power and affiliation.

8 A good example of the problem of determining what constitutes disconfirming evidence can be found in the debate concerning the Piraha language from Brazil. The language is claimed to have no relative clauses or grammatical recursion and thus serves as a counter-example to the theory proposed by Hauser, Chomsky, and Fitch (2002), which views recursion as a crucial and uniquely human language property. I thank Jim Lantolf for bringing this example to my attention.

9 In his review of this chapter, Lantolf indicated that as a researcher he was not a relativist but a realist and that he did believe in an objective world. He commented that he made the relativist argument to 'open up room for other theories'. He accepted, however, that he is happy to be included among the relativists based on his 1996 article and the 2002 exchange with Gregg.

10 This is an obvious problem in UG-based SLA research. If L2 learners fail to provide evidence of access to a particular principle of UG, this might suggest (1) that they do not have access to UG or (2) the principle has been incorrectly formulated in linguistic theory.

11 In his review of this chapter, Lantolf argued that the field of SLA is characterized by a dualism, where 'research' and 'practice' are viewed as distinct activities. He noted that from the point of view of sociocultural theory there can be no separation—'research is praxis'. While I have no argument with the view that good research will inevitably be of some value to practice, I find it difficult to accept that there is not a distinction to be made between what SLA researchers do and what teachers do and also in the 'discourses' they typically engage in.

12 In the opinion of some, the fact that teachers may not be good researchers does not matter. Wells (1994b) argued that because the goal was 'the personal and professional growth of the practitioner', teacher research 'should be judged less in terms of the quality of the product or the rigor of its methodology, and more in terms of the learning that results from the person carrying it out' (p. 28).

Glossary

absolute universals See *typological universals*.

Accessibility Hierarchy (AH) The Accessibility Hierarchy is a statement of the markedness of various relative pronoun functions (for example, subject, direct object). It lists these functions in an implicational ordering, such that a given function implies the existence of all other functions above it. The hierarchy is an example of a *typological universal* and has been widely used as a basis for SLA research.

Accommodation Theory Accommodation Theory is a social-psychological model of language use proposed by Giles to account for the dynamic nature of variation within the course of a conversation. Speakers can converge (i.e. make their speech similar to the style of their addressee) or diverge (i.e. make their speech different from the style of their addressee). In some situations speech maintenance occurs (i.e. speakers make no changes).

Acculturation Model This is a theory of L2 acquisition developed by Schumann (1978a). It treats L2 acquisition as one aspect of acculturation (the process by which the learner becomes adapted to a new culture). Various factors influence the social and psychological 'distance' of the learner from the target-language culture and thereby the rate and ultimate success of L2 acquisition. See also *social distance* and *psychological distance*.

accuracy Accuracy 'concerns the extent to which the language produced conforms to target language norms' (Skehan 1996; 22). A typical measure of accuracy is percentage of error-free clauses.

acquisition Krashen (1981) uses the term *acquisition* to refer to the spontaneous and incidental process of rule internalization that results from natural language use, where the learner's attention is focused on meaning rather than form. It contrasts with *learning*.

action research Action research is research conducted by teachers to investigate solutions to their own pedagogic problems. It constitutes a type of practitioner research.

Activity Theory Activity theory was a development of Vygotsky's views about learning. The theory emphasizes the social nature of learning, how individuals' motives affect the nature of the activity they engage in, and the mediating role of artefacts in learning.

Adaptive Control of Thought (ACT) Model This is Anderson's (1980, 1983) model of skill-learning. The model accounts for how learners' ability to perform a skill develops from a declarative stage, where information is stored as facts, to an autonomous stage, where information is stored as easily accessed procedures.

additional language The term 'additional language' is preferred to 'second language' in some settings (for example, South Africa and in the UK, where students from ethnic minority backgrounds are incorporated into mainstream education). This is because it suggests that the L2 will exist alongside the L1 and be of equal but not necessarily greater importance to the learner.

additive bilingualism See *bilingualism*.

affective state The learner's affective state is influenced by a number of factors, for example, anxiety, a desire to compete, and whether learners feel they are progressing or not. It is hypothesized that it can influence the rate of L2 acquisition and the ultimate level of achievement.

analytical strategy Peters (1977) found that some children seemed to analyse the input into parts. They manifested systematic development involving first a one-word and then a two-word stage, etc. Hatch (1974) refers to L2 learners who learn in this way as 'rule-formers'. See also *gestalt strategy*.

anomie Anomie is experienced by L2 learners (usually in natural settings) who feel disconnected from the target social group and from their own speech group. Such learners feel insecure because they believe they do not belong to any social group.

anxiety Anxiety is one of the affective factors that have been found to affect L2 acquisition. Different types of anxiety have been identified: (1) trait anxiety (a characteristic of a learner's personality), (2) state anxiety (apprehension that is experienced at a particular moment in response to a definite situation), and (3) situation-specific anxiety (the anxiety aroused by a particular type of situation). Anxiety may be both facilitating (i.e. it has a positive effect on L2 acquisition), or debilitating (i.e. it has a negative effect).

aphasia Aphasia is a loss of the ability to produce and/or comprehend language, due to injury to the brain. Bilingual aphasia occurs when there is loss in some aspect of one language without any in the other.

aptitude-treatment interaction (ATI) See *learner-instruction matching*.

Argument Structure Argument Structure refers to the information encoded in the lexical entries of verbs regarding the thematic roles they can take. This determines the syntactic patterns that verbs figure in.

Aspect Hypothesis The Aspect Hypothesis claims that the distribution of interlanguage verbal morphology is determined by the lexical aspectual class. It draws on Vendler's (1967) classification of verb phrases into those that refer to states (for example, 'seem' and 'know'), achievements (for example, 'arrive' and 'fall asleep'), activities (for example, 'sleep' and 'study'), and accomplishments (for example, 'build a house' or 'paint a picture').

attention In SLA, attention is the cognitive process by which learners perceive linguistic features in input or their own output. Attention can be 'focused' or 'divided'. The extent to which attention is an entirely conscious process or is subconscious remains a matter of some controversy. See also *Noticing Hypothesis*.

attributional motivation The term 'attributions' refers to the subjective reasons by which we explain our past successes and failures. These have an effect on a learner's motivational disposition. Key attributions are ability and effort.

avoidance Avoidance is said to take place when specific target-language features are under-represented in the learner's production in comparison to native-speaker production. Learners are likely to avoid structures they find difficult as a result of differences between their native language and the target language.

backsliding L2 learners are likely to manifest correct target-language forms on some occasions but deviant forms on other occasions. When this happens they are said to 'backslide'. Backsliding involves the use of a rule belonging to an earlier stage of development. It can occur when learners are under some pressure, as, for instance, when they have to express difficult subject matter or are feeling anxious (Selinker 1972).

balanced bilingualism See *bilingualism*.

Basic Interpersonal Communication Skills (BICS) Cummins (1981) used the term 'Basic Interpersonal Communication Skills' (BICS) to refer to the kind of L2 proficiency that learners require in order to engage effectively in face-to-face interaction. BICS involve the mastery of context-embedded uses of language in communicative tasks that are relatively undemanding.

basic variety This constitutes an early stage of L2 acquisition identified by researchers in the *European Science Foundation Project*. It is characterized by the absence of grammatical functors. Learners rely instead on pragmatic means to convey semantic concepts such as pastness. Learner utterances at this stage consist of noun + verb + noun (e.g. *Mädchen nehme Brot* (girl take bread)) or verb + noun. Verbs are non-finite. The 'basic variety' is preceded by the 'pre-basic variety' (characterized by nominal organization) and followed by the 'post-basic variety' (where finite verb forms appear).

behaviourist learning theory Behaviourist learning theory is a general theory of learning (i.e. it applies to all kinds of learning). It views learning as the formation of habits. These are formed when the learner is confronted with specific stimuli which lead to responses, which are, in turn, reinforced by rewards, or are corrected. Behaviourist learning theory emphasizes environmental factors as opposed to internal, mental factors.

bi-directional transfer This is transfer of linguistic forms both from L1 to L2 and from L2 to L1. It is most evident in vocabulary.

bilingualism Bilingualism refers to the use of two languages by an individual or a speech community. There are various types of bilingualism. In the case of *additive bilingualism*, a speaker adds a second language without any loss of competence to the first language. This can lead to *balanced bilingualism*. In the case of *subtractive bilingualism*, the addition of a second language leads to gradual erosion of competence in the first language.

Bilingual Syntax Measure (BSM) Burt, Dulay and Hernandez-Chavez (1975) developed the Bilingual Syntax Measure to elicit sentences containing specific grammatical structures, using pictures. This instrument was used in a number of morpheme studies.

Binding Principle for Anaphors This principle of Universal Grammar (UG) governs the use of anaphors such as reflexive pronouns. It accounts for the fact that a reflexive pronoun (for example, 'himself' and 'herself') must have an antecedent that it is bound to and this antecedent must be present within the 'binding domain' permitted by the target language.

blocking See *overshadowing*.

borrowing transfer See *language transfer.*

breadth of knowledge This is a term used in vocabulary acquisition research to refer to the number of words a learner has either receptive or productive knowledge of as determined by their performance on vocabulary tests such as Laufer and Nation's (1995) Productive Vocabulary Level Test.

Broca's area A section of the brain in the inferior gyrus of the frontal lobe that is involved in language production. This section was named after Paul Broca who first identified it.

capability This is the term used by Tarone (1983) to refer to the learner's actual ability to use particular rules in language use. Tarone intended it to contrast with *competence*. As such, it seems very similar in meaning to L2 *proficiency*.

careful style This is a term used by Labov (1970) to refer to the language forms evident in speech that has been consciously attended to and monitored. Such forms are used more frequently with higher-status interlocutors. A careful style is used in formal language tasks such as reading pairs of words or doing a grammar test. See also *vernacular style* and *stylistic continuum*.

caretaker talk When adults (or older children) address young children, they typically modify their speech. These modifications are both formal (for example, the use of higher pitch or simple noun phrases) and interactional (for example, the use of expansions).

casual style See *vernacular style*.

change from above This refers to changes to the dialect spoken by a social group as a result of social pressures. Speakers are aware of the change. The linguistic feature involved in the change can be stigmatized or prestigious. Preston (1989) sees 'change from above' as analogous to *monitoring* in L2 acquisition.

channel capacity This refers to the language learner's ability to process utterances in comprehension or production. It involves the ability to recover rules and items from memory and to use them easily and spontaneously. In the early stages of L2 acquisition, learners have limited channel capacity and slowly develop this at the same time as they acquire L2 knowledge.

Chaos Theory This is a theory developed in the physical sciences and is based on the idea that complex systems are random, non-linear, unpredictable, self-organizing, and tend to hone in on a particular pattern. Larsen-Freeman (1997) applied her interpretation of Chaos Theory to L2 acquisition.

classroom process research The aim of classroom process research is to subject the teaching–learning behaviours that occur in a classroom to careful observation with a view to describing as fully as possible what takes place. It views language lessons as 'socially constructed events' and seeks to understand how they take place.

closed question A closed question is one that is framed with only one acceptable answer in mind (for example, 'What is the name of the day after Tuesday?')

code-switching Code-switching is one kind of intra-speaker variation. It occurs when a speaker changes from one variety or language to another variety or language in accordance with situational or purely personal factors.

Cognitive Academic Language Proficiency (CALP) Cummins (1981) used the term 'Cognitive Academic Language Proficiency' (CALP) to refer to the kind of L2 proficiency required to engage effectively in academic study. In particular, CALP involves the ability to communicate messages that are precise and explicit in tasks that are context-reduced and cognitively demanding.

Cognitive Linguistics Cognitive Linguistics is a school of linguistics that seeks to examine language in terms of general cognitive principles and mechanisms that are not specific to language. As such it contrasts with the generative school of linguistics which views syntax as a separate component of the mind.

cognitive strategies O'Malley and Chamot defined cognitive strategies as learning strategies that 'operate directly on incoming information, manipulating it in ways that enhance learning' (1990: 44). They involve such operations as rehearsal, organizing information, and inferencing.

cognitive style Some psychologists consider that individuals have characteristic ways of perceiving phenomena, conceptualizing, and recalling information. Various dimensions of cognitive style have been identified, including *field dependence* and *field independence*. See also *learning style*.

collaborative dialogue Swain (2000) defined collaborative dialogue as 'dialogue in which speakers are engaged in problem solving and knowledge building' (p. 102).

communication strategy Communication strategies are employed when learners are faced with the task of communicating meanings for which they lack the requisite linguistic knowledge (for example, when they have to refer to some object without knowing the L2 word). Various typologies of learning strategies have been proposed.

Communicational Teaching Project This was a project carried out in Southern India designed to investigate the feasibility of task-based language teaching. (See Prabhu 1987.)

communicative competence Communicative competence consists of the knowledge that users of a language have internalized to enable them to understand and produce messages in the language. Various models of communicative competence have been proposed, but most of them recognize that it entails both linguistic competence (for example, knowledge of grammatical rules) and pragmatic competence (for example, knowledge of what constitutes appropriate linguistic behaviour in a particular situation).

Communicative Orientation in Language Teaching (COLT) This is an interaction analysis system designed by Allen, Fröhlich, and Spada (1984). The observational categories were designed to capture significant features of verbal interaction in L2 classrooms and to provide a means of comparing some aspects of classroom discourse with *natural* language as it is used outside the classroom.

comparative fallacy Bley-Vroman (1983) referred to methods that seek to account for learner language solely in terms of target-language norms as inadequate because they fail to acknowledge that learners develop their own unique systems. He called this the comparative fallacy.

comparative method studies These are studies carried out to measure the different learning outcomes achieved by two different teaching methods. An example of such a study is the Pennsylvania Project (Smith 1970), which compared the cognitive-code and audiolingual methods.

competence This term refers to a language user's underlying knowledge of language, which is drawn on in actual performance. Theories of language vary in how they define competence. See also *linguistic competence*, *pragmatic competence*, and *proficiency*.

Competition Model This is a functional model of language use and language acquisition, proposed initially by Bates and MacWhinney (1982). It views the task of language learning as that of discovering the particular form–function mappings that characterize the target language. These mappings are viewed as having varying 'strengths' in different languages. For example, in English, case is a relatively weak signal of agency, whereas in Russian, it is a strong signal. See also *emergentism*.

complexity Complexity 'concerns the elaboration of the language that is produced' and reflects learners' preparedness to take risks (Skehan 1996: 22). One common measure is the number of clauses per T-unit.

Complexity Theory See *Chaos Theory*.

comprehensible input 'Input' refers to language that learners are exposed to. Input that can be understood by a learner has been referred to as 'comprehensible input'. (See Krashen 1981.) Input can be made comprehensible in various ways: through simplification, with the help of context, or by negotiating non-understanding and misunderstanding. Some researchers (such as Krashen) consider comprehensible input a necessary condition for L2 acquisition.

Comprehensible Output Hypothesis 'Output' is language produced by the learner. It can be comprehensible or incomprehensible to an interlocutor. Swain (1985) has proposed that when learners have to make efforts to ensure that their output is comprehensible (i.e. produce 'pushed output'), acquisition may be fostered.

computational model A computational model of L2 acquisition adopts the information processing approach common in cognitive psychology. It views acquisition as the result of processing mechanisms that operate on input to construct interlanguage systems that evolve gradually over time.

concatenative research In a concatenative approach to the study of individual learner differences, a general research question serves as a basis for collecting data, which then are used to investigate the relationships among learner factors and between these factors and L2 acquisition. Such research is typically correlational in nature.

conceptual transfer This addresses how an L1-specific world view affects the acquisition of another language. That is, transfer effects are seen as not just linguistic but as reflecting the underlying ways in which learners perceive and conceptualize the world.

confirmation check An utterance immediately following the previous speaker's utterance intended to confirm that the utterance was understood.

connectionism Connectionist accounts of L2 learning view language as an elaborative neural network rather than as a set of rules. The network changes over time as a response to input frequencies and corrective feedback. The underlying assumption is that L2 learning is a complex phenomenon but can be accounted for by a relatively simple associationist mental mechanism that is not specific to language learning.

consciousness-raising The term 'consciousness-raising' is used by some researchers with much the same meaning as 'formal instruction' (i.e. an attempt to focus the learner's attention on the formal properties of the language). In Ellis (1991d), I used this term with a narrower meaning. I contrasted 'consciousness-raising' with 'practice', the former term referring to attempts to help learners understand a grammatical structure and learn it as explicit knowledge. An alternative term for consciousness-raising is *intake enhancement* (Sharwood Smith 1993).

constructions Constructions are 'recurrent patterns of linguistic elements that serve some well-defined linguistic function' (N. Ellis 2003: 66). They can be at sentence level or below. Emergentist accounts of L2 acquisition view acquisition as a process of internalizing and subsequently analysing constructions. See also *formulaic sequences*.

context The 'context' of an utterance can mean two different things: (1) the situation in which an utterance is produced—this is the situational context; (2) the linguistic environment—the surrounding language—this is the linguistic context. Both types of context influence the choice of language forms, and therefore have an effect on output. See also *psycholinguistic context*.

contextualization cues These consist of signals that trigger how speakers view the context they are attempting to build through interaction in order to channel the listeners' interpretations of what is being said.

contrastive analysis Contrastive analysis is a set of procedures for comparing and contrasting the linguistic systems of two languages in order to identify their structural similarities and differences.

Contrastive Analysis Hypothesis According to the Contrastive Analysis Hypothesis, L2 errors are the result of differences between the learner's L1 and the L2. The strong form of the hypothesis claims that these differences can be used to predict all errors that will occur. The weak form of the hypothesis claims that these differences can be used only to identify some out of the total errors that actually occur.

contrastive interlanguage analysis This is the term used by Granger (1998a) to refer to the contrastive study of the interlanguages of learners with different L1s. It has been made possible by the advent of concordancing tools for analysing learner corpora.

conversational analysis (CA) CA is a method for analysing social interactions in order to uncover their orderliness, structure, and sequential patterns. CA is used to investigate both institutional interactions (i.e. in the school, doctor's surgery, or law court) and casual conversation. Key aspects of interaction studied in CA are turn-taking and repair.

corrective feedback In language acquisition, the term 'feedback' refers to information given to learners which they can use to revise their interlanguage. A distinction is often made between 'positive' and 'negative' feedback (sometimes referred to as 'negative evidence'); negative feedback refers to information that indicates a hypothesis is incorrect. The term 'corrective feedback' is increasingly used in preference to negative feedback. Corrective feedback can be implicit or explicit; it can also be input-providing or output-prompting.

covert error See *error*.

creative construction Dulay, Burt, and Krashen defined 'creative construction' as 'the subconscious process by which language learners gradually organize the language they hear, according to the rules they construct to understand and generate sentences' (1982: 276).

creole A creole is a pidgin language that has become the native language of a group of speakers. A creole is generally more linguistically complex than a pidgin language as a result of a process known as 'creolization'. This results in a 'creole continuum', made up of 'lects' (i.e. varieties) that vary in complexity depending on whether they are closest to a pidgin or the standard language. An example of an English-based creole is Jamaican Creole.

Critical Period Hypothesis This states that there is a period (i.e. up to a certain age) during which learners can acquire an L2 easily and achieve native-speaker competence, but that after this period L2 acquisition becomes more difficult and is rarely entirely successful. Researchers differ over when this critical period comes to an end.

Cross-cultural Speech Act Realization Project This was a project carried out in the 1980s with the goal of investigating cross-cultural variation in verbal behaviour. The project focused on two speech acts: requests and apologies. An account of the main findings of the project can be found in Blum-Kulka, House, and Kasper (1989).

crosslinguistic influence This is a term proposed by Sharwood Smith and Kellerman (1986: 1) to refer to 'such phenomena as "transfer", "interference", "avoidance", "borrowing" and L2-related aspects of language loss'. Whereas the term 'transfer' is closely associated with *behaviourist* learning theory, 'crosslinguistic influence' is theory-neutral.

dative alternation English permits two constructions (NP + PP and NP + NP) with many dative verbs such as 'give', but only one of these constructions (NP + PP) with other dative verbs such as 'explain'.

debilitating anxiety See *anxiety.*

declarative L2 knowledge Declarative knowledge is characterized by Anderson (1983) as 'knowledge that'. In the case of language, it consists of factual information about the L2 such as explicit knowledge of L2 grammatical rules.

deductive instruction Deductive instruction involves providing learners with an explicit rule which they then practise in one way or another. It contrasts with *inductive instruction.*

depth of knowledge This is a term used in vocabulary acquisition research to refer to the extent to which learners have acquired various properties of words such as their syntactical functions and their collocations.

descriptive adequacy An account of a language (i.e. a 'grammar') is considered to have 'descriptive adequacy' if it constitutes a complete and explicit description of the rules and items that comprise native-speaker competence. See also *explanatory adequacy.*

developmental error Developmental errors occur when the learner attempts to build up hypotheses about the target language on the basis of limited experience.

developmental feature See *Multidimensional Model.*

developmental pattern See *pattern of development.*

developmental problem of L2 acquisition This recognizes that acquisition is non-instantaneous and seeks to address whether *Universal Grammar* plays a role in the order and sequence of acquisition.

developmental sequence One of the main findings of L2 research is that learners pass through a series of identifiable stages in acquiring specific grammatical structures such as negatives, interrogatives, and relative clauses. To a large extent, these sequences are not affected by the learner's L1. See also *sequence of development.*

differential localization This term refers to the existence of neurobiological differences within the same hemisphere of the brain in bilinguals. It contrasts with *hemispheric differentiation.*

discourse completion questionnaire A discourse completion questionnaire provides learners with a description of a situation designed to elicit a specific *illocutionary act* (for example, an apology) and then asks learners to write down what they would say in such a situation or asks them to select what they would say from choices provided. It is used to investigate learners' L2 *pragmatic competence*.

Discourse Hypothesis The discourse hypothesis states that speakers will systematically distinguish between foregrounded and backgrounded information when performing narratives.

discourse management When native speakers (or other L2 learners) are addressing L2 learners, they may seek to modify their speech interactionally in order to avoid communication problems. For example, they may restrict the kind of information they try to convey or use comprehension checks.

discourse repair When native speakers (or other L2 learners) experience a communication problem with an L2 learner, they may seek to repair the breakdown (for example, by *negotiation of meaning*) or to repair a learner error through correction.

display question A display question is one designed to test whether the addressee has knowledge of a particular fact or can use a particular linguistic item correctly (for example, 'What's the opposite of "up" in English?'). See also *closed question*.

Dual-Mechanism Model According to this model computation of regular morphological features such as past tense –ed in English involves rule-based or symbolic processing, whereas irregular features such as irregular past tense forms like 'swam' are stored as items.

dual-mode system Skehan (1998b) proposed that a person's knowledge of language (first or second) is comprised of two distinct systems—a rule-based system and a memory-based system, where 'exemplars' are stored. This view corresponds closely to that of the dual-mechanism model.

dynamic assessment This term refers to a mode of assessment that has 'the expressed goal of modifying learner performance during the assessment itself' (Poehner and Lantolf 2005: 235) as opposed to obtaining a static measure of a learner's proficiency without feedback or intervention of any kind.

educational settings Whereas many researchers are happy to talk of 'foreign' (as opposed to 'second') language acquisition, others, including the author of this book, prefer to distinguish different types of language acquisition in terms of context or setting. A key distinction is between acquisition that takes place in 'educational settings' (such as schools) and that which takes place in 'natural settings' (such as the street or the workplace).

elaborative simplification This is a term used by the ZISA researchers (for example, Meisel 1980) to refer to the simplification that occurs when learners are trying to complexify their *interlanguage* systems (for example, through the use of *overgeneralization*). It contrasts with *restrictive simplification*.

emergentism In the context of SLA, emergentism refers to theories that assume that language use and acquisition emerge from basic processes that are not specific to language. Examples of emergentist theories are MacWhinney's *Competition Model* and O'Grady's (2005) account of syntax in terms of a 'general efficiency-driven processor'. (p. xi)

English as a Lingua Franca (ELF) This term is used to refer to the communication in English that takes place between speakers with different first languages.

English as an International Language (EIL) This term is used to refer to the use of English across a wide range of contexts throughout the world.

enriched input Enriched input is one type of form-focused instruction. It can take the form of oral or written texts that learners simply listen to or read (i.e. input-flooding) or texts where the target structure has been highlighted in some way (e.g. through the use of underlining or bold print).

entrenchment Linguistic forms, including interlanguage forms, that are in constant use become entrenched in the learners' interlanguage system. One source of entrenchment is the learner's L1. Entrenchment is a feature of *fossilization.*

epenthesis This is insertion of one or more sounds in a word. L2 learners frequently insert a vowel in a consonant cluster.

error According to Corder (1967), an 'error' is a deviation in learner language which results from lack of knowledge of the correct rule. It contrasts with a *mistake*. An error can be overt (the deviation is apparent in the surface form of the utterance) or covert (the deviation is only evident when the learner's meaning intention is taken into account). Various frameworks for describing errors have been developed, including descriptive taxonomies, which focus on the observable surface features of errors, and surface strategy taxonomies, which reflect the way in which target language surface structure is altered by learners.

Error Analysis Error Analysis involves a set of procedures for identifying, describing, and explaining errors in learner language. (See Corder 1974.) Error Analysis for pedagogical purposes has a long history but its use as a tool for investigating how learners learn a language is more recent (it began in the 1960s).

error evaluation Error evaluation involves a set of criteria and procedures for evaluating the effect that different errors in learner language have on addressees, both native speakers and non-native speakers. Error evaluation results in an assessment of *error gravity*.

error gravity Error gravity concerns the seriousness of an *error*. This can be determined with reference to such criteria as intelligibility, acceptability, and irritation (Khalil 1985).

error treatment Error treatment concerns the way in which teachers (and other learners) respond to learners' errors. Error treatment is discussed in terms of whether errors should be corrected, when, how, and by whom. An alternative term is *corrective feedback*.

ethnography Ethnography makes use of procedures such as detailed observation, interviews, and questionnaires to collect data that are 'rich' and that afford multiple perspectives. It has been extensively used in the study of bilingual classrooms.

ethnography of communication Ethnography of communication has its origins in anthropology and, in particular, in the work of Hymes (1974). It aims to identify the workings of specific 'speech communities' by obtaining multiple perspectives on what participants in a particular social setting understand their interactive behaviours to mean.

ethnolinguistic identity theory This theory addresses how people from different ethnic groups communicate with each other. Giles and Johnson (1981) propose that the members of an in-group may or may not adopt positive linguistic distinctiveness strategies when communicating with members of an out-group.

European Science Foundation Project on Adult Second Language Acquisition This was a longitudinal project that investigated the acquisition of a number of European languages as second languages by adult migrants. (See, for example, Perdue 1993.) The project was informed by a functionalist theory of L2 acquisition.

explanatory adequacy An account of a language (i.e. a 'grammar') is considered to have 'explanatory adequacy' if it not only provides a complete and explicit description of native-speaker competence but also provides an explanation for how this competence is achieved. That is, it must explain how children learn their mother tongue. The theory of *Universal Grammar* seeks to achieve explanatory adequacy.

explicit correction This is a type of feedback that provides the learner with the correct form while at the same time indicating an error was committed.

explicit instruction Explicit instruction involves 'some sort of rule being thought about during the learning process' (DeKeyser 1995). That is, learners are encouraged to develop metalinguistic awareness of the rule. This can be achieved by means of *deductive instruction* or *inductive instruction.*

explicit L2 knowledge Explicit L2 knowledge is the knowledge of rules and items that exists in an analysed form so that learners are able to report what they know. Explicit L2 knowledge is closely linked to *metalingual knowledge.* It contrasts with *implicit knowledge.*

explicit L2 learning Explicit learning is a conscious process and is also likely to be intentional. It can be investigated by giving learners an explicit rule and asking them to apply it to data or by inviting them to try to discover an explicit rule from an array of data provided.

explicit memory This is memory that is based on conscious recollections of events and phenomena. Explicit memory houses explicit L2 knowledge.

external variation This is variation in language use that results from factors related to the social context. See also *style-shifting.*

externalized (E) approach Chomsky (1986a) distinguished an 'E-approach' and an 'I-approach' to language study. The former involves the collection of samples of a particular language or languages which are then used to develop a 'descriptive grammar'. See also *internalized (I) approach.*

extraversion/introversion These terms describe the dimension of personality which has been most thoroughly investigated in SLA research. They reflect a continuum: at one end are learners who are sociable and risk-takers, while at the other end are learners who are quiet and avoid excitement.

facilitating anxiety See *anxiety.*

Failed Functional Features Hypothesis Hawkins and Chan (1997) advanced what they called the Failed Functional Features Hypothesis. This claims that parameterized functional features (e.g. gender agreement) cannot be acquired after childhood unless they are instantiated in the L1.

field dependence/independence Field dependence/independence constitutes one kind of *cognitive style.* Field-dependent learners are believed to operate holistically (i.e. they see the field as a whole), whereas field-independent learners operate analytically (i.e. they perceive the field in terms of its component parts). Although a number of L2 researchers have made use of this distinction to account for differences in learners, others dispute its usefulness.

fluency Various definitions exist. Skehan (1996: 22) defines it as concerning 'the learner's capacity to produce language in real time without undue pausing or hesitation'. Segalowitz (2003, 2007) operationalized it in terms of 'access fluidity' and 'attention control'. A common measure of fluency is the number of syllables per minute.

focus-on-form 'Focus-on-form' is a type of form-focused instruction; it 'overtly draws students' attention to linguistic elements as they arise incidentally in lessons whose overriding focus is on meaning or communication' (Long 1991: pp. 45–6). It is distinct from both *focus-on-forms* and *focus-on-meaning instruction.*

focus-on-forms 'Focus-on-forms' is evident in the traditional approach to grammar teaching based on a structural syllabus. The underlying assumption is that language learning is a process of accumulating distinct entities.

foreign language acquisition A number of researchers distinguish 'foreign language acquisition' (for example, the learning of French in schools in the United States) and 'second language acquisition' (for example, the learning of English by speakers of other languages in the United States). Other researchers find this distinction problematic. See *educational settings.*

foreigner talk When native speakers address learners, they adjust their normal speech in order to facilitate understanding. These adjustments, which involve both language form and language function, constitute 'foreigner talk'. Foreigner talk has been hypothesized to aid L2 acquisition in a number of ways (for example, by making certain features more salient to the learner).

form-focused instruction Form-focused instruction involves some attempt to focus learners' attention on specific properties of the L2 so that they will learn them. Different types of form-focused instruction can be distinguished, including *explicit instruction* and *implicit instruction.*

form–function analysis In a form–function analysis, all instances of a specific linguistic form are identified in the data and the different meanings realized by this form are identified.

formulaic sequences Wray (2000: 465) gives the following definition:

> A sequence, continuous or discontinuous, of words or other meaning elements, which is, or appears to be, prefabricated; that is stored and retrieved whole from memory at the time of use, rather than being subject to generation or analysis by the language grammar.

See also *routines* and *patterns.*

fossilization Selinker (1972) noted that most L2 learners fail to reach target-language competence. That is, they stop learning while their internalized rule system contains rules different from those of the target system. This is referred to as 'fossilization'. It can also be viewed as a cognitive process, whereby new learning is blocked by existing learning. It remains a controversial construct with some researchers arguing that there is never a complete cessation of learning.

fragile features Fragile features of language are those that are acquired late, often with effort, and only when there is access to adequate input. Examples of fragile features are plural and tense markings. Fragile features contrast with *resilient features.*

free variation When a speaker uses two or more variants of a variable structure randomly (e.g. selects variants without reference to the linguistic or situational context), free variation occurs. In Ellis (1985c), I argued that free variation arises in learner language when learners acquire a new form side by side with a previously acquired form and use it to realize the same meaning.

frequency analysis This is the method of analysing learner language that involves identifying the *variants* of a given structure and examining the frequency of occurrence of each variant. For example, a learner may make negative utterances using (1) 'no' + verb, (2) 'don't' + verb and (3) auxiliary + verb. A frequency analysis of the negative utterances produced by this learner would involve counting each occurrence of the three variants. It is also known as *interlanguage analysis.*

Frequency Hypothesis The Frequency Hypothesis states that the order of development in L2 acquisition is determined by the frequency with which different linguistic items occur in the input.

frequency universals These are determined by showing that a specific linguistic feature may be found in a large number of languages even if it is missing from some. However, it can be argued that it is not justifiable to talk of 'universals' when there are exceptions.

functionalist model Functionalist models of L2 acquisition view the task of learning a language as involving the construction of form–function networks. That is, learners have to discover which forms perform which meanings in the L2. These models recognize that learners are likely to construct idiosyncratic form–function networks (i.e. use forms to perform functions not performed by these forms in the target language). Functionalist models emphasize the role that communication plays in the acquisition process.

gestalt strategy Peters (1977) found that some children in L1 acquisition remain silent for a long time and then suddenly begin producing full sentences. Hatch (1974) refers to this kind of L2 learner as a 'data-gatherer'. See also *analytical strategy* and *silent period.*

gestural accent L2 learners have been observed to transfer the gestural systems of the L1 into their use of the L2. This results in what has been called 'gestural accent'.

global error Global errors are errors that affect overall sentence organization (for example, wrong word order). They are likely to have a marked effect on comprehension. See also *local error.*

good language learner Researchers have investigated the individual learner factors that contribute to L2 learning by investigating what expert, successful L2 learners do in order to learn an L2. These studies are known as the 'good language learner studies'. One of the best known is Naiman *et al.* 1978.

Government/Binding Model The Government/Binding (GB) Model is a competence theory of grammar. It proposes a system of innate principles and constraints which govern all languages and a set of parameter values that define the syntax of particular languages (Chomsky, 1981). 'Government' addresses the nature of abstract syntactic relations whereas 'binding' deals with the referents of features such as pronouns. The Government/Binding Model was superseded by the *Minimalist Program.*

Gradual Diffusion Model Gatbonton's (1978) Gradual Diffusion Model identifies two broad phases in L2 acquisition: an 'acquisition phase', characterized by free variation, and a 'development phase' where free variation gives way to systematic variation and categorical language use. See also *Variability Hypothesis.*

grammatical competence See *linguistic competence.*

grammaticality judgements One way of obtaining data on what learners know about the L2 is by asking them to judge whether sentences are grammatically correct or incorrect. This method is favoured by some researchers because they believe it provides information about learners' intuitions and thus caters for an *internalized (I) approach.*

grammaticalization Some *functionalist models* of L2 acquisition consider that early L2 acquisition is characterized by the use of pragmatic strategies for conveying meanings that are conveyed grammatically by native speakers. Gradually, learners move from this pragmatic mode to a grammatical mode as they learn the grammatical properties of the L2.

head act This is a term used in the study of pragmatics. Speech acts such as requests typically involve a head act (e.g. the act that performs the request) and various other supporting acts that either prepare for the head act (e.g. by attempting to get a pre-commitment to perform the act) or follow the head act (e.g. by offering a reason for performing the act).

hemispheric differentiation Early studies of bilingualism suggested that a second language is stored differently from the first language. Whereas the latter is (usually) housed in the left hemisphere of the brain, the former was believed to involve both hemispheres. However, later research has shown that there is no clear hemispheric differentiation of the two languages.

hierarchical research In the hierarchical approach to the study of *individual learner differences* (IDs), predictions based on a theory of IDs are made and then tested empirically. In fact, this approach has been little used, as there is no generally accepted theory of IDs.

horizontal variation This refers to the variation evident in learner language at a particular moment or stage in a learner's development. It contrasts with *vertical variation.*

hypercorrection Some native speakers overuse a linguistic form which is associated with social prestige. For example, some speakers of British English may overextend a feature like /h/ to words such as 'hour', even though this word does not have this sound in the standard dialect.

Preston (1989) has suggested that this process is analogous to *overgeneralization* in L2 acquisition.

hypocorrection This consists of the retention of an old norm in the speech of the working class because it has covert prestige. Preston (1989) suggests this is analogous to *negative transfer* in L2 acquisition.

hypothesis testing According to one view of interlanguage development, learners form hypotheses about the structures of the target language and then 'test' these out on the evidence available from input, with the result that they either accept them or abandon them and form new hypotheses. This process may or may not involve consciousness.

Ignorance Hypothesis Newmark and Reibel (1968) argue that what is commonly referred to as 'interference' is in fact merely an attempt by the learner to fill gaps of knowledge by using previous knowledge.

illocutionary act This term is taken from *speech act* theory. (See Austin 1962.) An utterance is seen as having not only propositional meaning (i.e. saying something about the world) but also functional meaning (i.e. doing something). An illocutionary act is the functional meaning performed by an utterance. Examples are 'requesting' and 'apologizing'. Searle (1969) has identified various 'conditions' that have to be met in order for a specific illocutionary act to be performed successfully. For example, for the act of 'giving an order' to be successfully performed, both speaker and hearer must recognize that the speaker is in a position of authority over the hearer.

immediate recall This method of eliciting data from learners requires them to recall what they just heard (or said) immediately after hearing (saying) it. Philp (2003), for example, cued L2 learners to repeat the last utterance they had heard by interrupting the interaction by means of two loud knocks on a table.

immersion education programme In immersion education programmes the L2 is not taught as a separate subject. Rather, it is taught by using it as the medium of instruction for teaching the content of other school subjects. Immersion education has been widely used in Canada and has now spread to other countries.

implicational scaling Implicational scaling is a technique used by sociolinguists and some SLA researchers to represent variation in L2 performance. It rests on the notion that the presence of one linguistic form in learner language occurs only if one or more forms are also present. Thus, one form 'implicates' other forms.

implicational universals An implicational universal is evident when it can be shown that the presence of one property in a language necessarily means that another different property will also be present. A good example can be found in the *Accessibility Hierarchy* for noun phrases.

implicit instruction Implicit instruction is directed at enabling learners to infer rules without awareness. It contrasts with *explicit instruction*, in that there is an absence of externally-prompted awareness of what is being learned.

implicit L2 knowledge Implicit knowledge of a language is knowledge that is intuitive and tacit. It cannot be directly reported. The knowledge that most speakers have of their L1 is implicit. The study of *linguistic competence* is the study of a speaker-hearer's implicit knowledge. See also *explicit L2 knowledge*.

implicit L2 learning Implicit learning is typically defined as learning that takes place without either intentionality or awareness. It can be investigated by exposing learners to input data, which they are asked to process for meaning, and then investigating (without warning) whether they have acquired any L2 linguistic properties as a result of the exposure.

implicit memory This is memory that does not depend on conscious recollections of events and phenomena. It houses implicit L2 knowledge.

impression management Impression management concerns the way speakers make use of their linguistic resources in interaction to create social meanings favourable to themselves. For example, L2 learners may make deliberate use of primitive interlanguage forms to mitigate the force of threatening speech acts.

incidental L2 learning This refers to learning of some specific feature that takes place without any conscious intention to learn it. It is investigated by giving learners a task that focuses their attention on one aspect of the L2 and, without pre-warning, testing on some other feature.

incorporation strategy One way in which learners can construct an utterance is by borrowing a chunk from the previous utterance and extending it by adding an element at the beginning or end. See also *vertical constructions*.

indicator An indicator is a variable form that is responsive to social factors such as social class, age, and gender. See also *marker*.

indirect negative evidence See *corrective feedback*.

individual learner differences (IDs) The term 'individual learner differences' refers to the differences in how learners learn an L2, in how fast they learn, and in how successful they are. These differences include both general factors such as language learning aptitude and motivation, and specific learner strategies. The differences can be cognitive, affective, or social in nature.

induced error Induced errors arise in learner language when learners are led to make errors that otherwise they would not make by the nature of the formal instruction they receive.

inductive instruction Inductive instruction is a form of explicit instruction that involves requiring learners to induce rules from examples given to them or simply from the opportunity to practise the rules. It contrasts with *deductive instruction*.

initiate-respond-follow up (IRF) exchange The IRF exchange was identified by Sinclair and Coulthard (1975) as a familiar pattern in classroom talk. It consists of the teacher initiating the exchange, places the student in a responding role, and allows the teacher the right to follow up on the student's response.

inner-directed learners According to Saville-Troike (1988: 568), inner-directed learners 'approach language as an intrapersonal task, with a predominant focus on the language code'.

input enhancement Sharwood Smith (1993) used this term to refer to the deliberate manipulation of the input learners are exposed to in order to induce learning. He argued that this term is preferable to *consciousness-raising* because this latter term refers to an internal state of the learner whereas instruction can only affect the external conditions of learning.

Input Hypothesis The Input Hypothesis was advanced by Krashen (1982) to explain how 'acquisition' takes place. It states that 'we acquire ... only when we understand language that contains a structure that is 'a little beyond where we are now' (1982: 21). Elsewhere Krashen has referred to the idea of input that is 'a little bit beyond' as 'i + 1'.

Input Processing Theory VanPatten (1996) proposed that because learners have a limited working memory capacity they process input in accordance with a set of principles that allocate attention selectively to input. An example of such a principle is 'Learners process input for meaning before they process it for form'. These principles account for interlanguage development.

instructed language acquisition This term refers to language acquisition that takes place as a result of attempts to teach the L2—either directly through formal instruction or indirectly by setting up the conditions that promote natural acquisition in the classroom.

instructional conversation Tharp and Gallimore (1988) used this term to refer to pedagogic interaction that is teacher-led and directed towards a curricular goal (for example, enabling students to perform a structure that they have not yet internalized), but is conversational in nature (for example, it manifests equal turn-taking rights and is unpredictable).

instrumental motivation See *motivation*.

intake Intake is that portion of the input that learners notice and therefore take into temporary memory. Intake may subsequently be accommodated in the learner's interlanguage system (i.e. become part of long-term memory). However, not all intake is so accommodated.

integration Integration is a general term that refers to the processes involved in storing items noticed and processed into long-term memory. That is, it involves modification of learners' interlanguage systems. See also *restructuring*.

integrative motivation See *motivation*.

intelligence Intelligence is the general set of cognitive abilities involved in performing a wide range of learning tasks. It constitutes 'a general sort of aptitude that is not limited to a specific performance area but is transferable to many sorts of performance'. (Dörnyei 2005: p. 32)

intentional L2 learning This is learning of a specific L2 feature that occurs when the learner consciously sets out to learn it. It is investigated by making learners aware of what they are supposed to learn and then testing whether they have learned it.

interaction analysis Interaction analysis is a research procedure used to carry out classroom observation. It involves the use of a system of categories to record and analyse the different ways in which teachers and students use language. Various types of system exist, for example: a category system for coding specific events every time they occur, a sign system for coding the events that occur within a predetermined period, and a rating system for estimating the frequency of specific events.

Interaction Hypothesis Long (1983) claimed that the interactional modifications that arise during the negotiation of meaning provide learners with comprehensible input and thereby assist acquisition. In a later version of this hypothesis Long broadened the scope of the hypothesis by claiming that 'negotiation for meaning, and especially negotiation work that triggers interactional adjustments by the NS or more competent interlocutor, facilitates acquisition because it connects input, internal learner capacities, particularly selective attention, and output in productive ways' (pp. 451–2).

interactional act An interactional act is an utterance considered in terms of its structural function in discourse, for example, whether it opens, closes, or continues a conversation.

interactionally modified input Input that is modified through the course of the learner interacting with another speaker. It contrasts with *premodified input*.

interactional modification Interactional modifications occur when some kind of communication problem arises and the participants engage in interactional work to overcome it. They take the form of discourse functions such as comprehension checks, requests for clarification, and requests for confirmation. See also *negotiation of meaning*.

interactional sociolinguistics This is a branch of sociolinguistics that examines how speakers achieve communicative effects by manipulating their linguistic and non-linguistic resources.

interactionist theories of language learning Interactionist learning theory emphasizes the joint contributions of the linguistic environment and the learner's internal mechanisms in explaining language acquisition. Learning results from an interaction between the learner's mental abilities and the linguistic input. The term 'interactionist' can also be applied to theories that explain L2 acquisition in terms of social interaction—how communication between the learner and other speakers leads to L2 acquisition.

Interdependency Principle Cummins (1981) formulated the Interdependency Principle to refer to the idea that *cognitive academic language proficiency* (CALP) is common across languages, and can therefore easily be transferred from LI use to L2 use by the learner. It explains why people who are literate in their L1 find fewer problems in developing CALP in an L2 than those who are not.

interface position/hypothesis Theories of L2 acquisition that emphasize the distinctiveness of implicit and explicit knowledge can either maintain that these are completely separate, or that each knowledge type 'leaks', so that explicit knowledge can become implicit and vice versa. This latter position is known as the 'interface position'. See also *non-interface position* and *skill-building hypothesis*.

interference According to *behaviourist learning theory*, old habits get in the way of learning new habits. Thus, in L2 acquisition the patterns of the learner's mother tongue that are different from those of the L2 get in the way of learning the L2. This is referred to as 'interference'. See also *language transfer*.

Inter-group Theory This is a theory of L2 acquisition proposed by Giles and Byrne (1982). It characterizes L2 acquisition as 'long-term convergence' and explains it in terms of attitudes relating to relationship between the learner and the target-language community. See *Accommodation Theory*.

interlanguage Selinker (1972) coined the term 'interlanguage' to refer to the systematic knowledge of an L2 which is independent of both these learner's L1 and the target language. The term has come to be used with different but related meanings: (1) to refer to the series of interlocking systems which characterize acquisition, (2) to refer to the system that is observed at a single stage of development ('an interlanguage'), and (3) to refer to particular L1/L2 combinations (for example, L1 French/L2 English versus L1 Japanese/L2 English). Other terms that refer to the same basic idea are 'approximative system' (Nemser 1971) and 'transitional competence' (Corder 1967).

interlanguage analysis See *frequency analysis*.

interlanguage talk L2 learners often obtain input from other L2 learners. For many learners interlanguage talk may the primary source of input. In classroom contexts, interlanguage talk has been referred to as 'tutor talk' (Flanigan 1991). See also *English as a Lingua Franca*.

internalization A term used in sociocultural theory to refer to the process by which a person moves from object/other-regulation to self-regulation. Ohta (2001b) referred to this as 'the movement of language from environment to brain' (p. 11).

internalized (I) approach Chomsky distinguishes an externalized (E) approach and an internalized (I) approach to the study of language. The latter makes use of native-speaker intuitions about what is grammatical and ungrammatical in order to investigate the abstract principles that underlie particular grammars. Chomsky favours the I-approach. See also *externalized (E) approach*.

internal variation This is variation in language use that results from the influence of purely linguistic factors such as the linguistic context, linguistic markedness, and the learners' L1.

International Corpus of Learner English (ICLE) (Granger 1998b) The ICLE is a computerized corpus of argumentative essays on different topics written by advanced learners of English (i.e. university students of English in their second or third years). It is made up of a set of sub-corpora from learners with different L1 backgrounds, including Asian languages (Chinese and Japanese) and European languages (French and Russian).

inter-speaker variation In some communities, no speaker has access to all the varieties used by the community. Instead, one speaker may have access to one variety, another speaker to a second variety, and so on. Inter-speaker variation contrasts with *intra-speaker variation*.

intralingual error Intralingual errors are errors in learner language that reflect learners' transitional competence and that are the result of such learning processes as *overgeneralization*. An example might be *'They explained her what to do'.

intra-speaker variation This refers to the variation in the use of specific linguistic features evident in the speech and writing produced by individual learners on any one occasion. This variation reflects linguistic, social, and psychological factors. See also *inter-speaker variation*.

intrinsic motivation This refers to the motivation that derives from a learner's internal curiosity about the target language or the interest generated by participating in a language-learning activity. It is closely linked to the idea of self-determination in language learning.

L2 = L1 hypothesis (or identity hypothesis) According to the L2 = L1 hypothesis, L2 acquisition is either identical or very similar to L1 acquisition. The similarity may be evident at the level of product (i.e. in the kind of language produced by the two kinds of learner) or process (i.e. the mechanisms responsible for acquisition). Views differ considerably on the validity of this hypothesis.

language acquisition device (LAD) Mentalist theories of language acquisition emphasize the importance of the innate capacity of the language learner at the expense of environmental factors. Each learner is credited with a 'language acquisition device' (LAD), which directs the process of acquisition. This device contains information about the possible form that the grammar of any language can take. See *Universal Grammar*.

language-learning aptitude It has been hypothesized that people possess a special ability for learning an L2. This ability, known as 'language-learning aptitude', is considered to be separate from the general ability to master academic skills, often referred to as *intelligence*. Language-learning aptitude is one of the general factors that characterize individual learner differences. Various tests have been designed to measure language-learning aptitude, for example, the Modern Language Aptitude Test.

language socialization Shieffelin and Ochs (1986) defined language socialization as the practice by which novices in a community are socialized both to the language forms and, through language, to the values, behaviours, and practices of the community in which they live. Thus, it entails 'socialization through the use of language and socialization to use language' (p. 163).

language transfer Odlin (1989) gives this 'working definition' of 'transfer':

> Transfer is the influence resulting from similarities and differences between the target language and any other language that has been previously (and perhaps imperfectly) acquired (1989: 27).

'L1 transfer' occurs when the 'influence' results from the learner's mother tongue. Two types of transfer are commonly identified: borrowing transfer (where the L2 influences the L1) and substratum transfer (where the L1 influences the L2).

languaging Swain (2006) coined the term 'languaging' to refer to the role that language production (oral or written) plays in making meaning when learners are faced with some problem.

learner corpora These are sets of oral and/or written data collected from a large number of learners and converted into electronic form to facilitate computer-based analyses by means of concordancing programmes. One of the best known learner corpora is the *International Corpus of Learner English (ICLE)* (Granger 1998).

learner-instruction matching Learner-instruction matching involves an attempt to ensure that the teaching style is suited to the learner. It is based on the assumption that learners have different learning styles and that they will learn most effectively if the instruction matches their particular learning style. Educational research based on learner-instruction matching is sometimes referred to as *aptitude-treatment interaction*.

learner strategy Learner strategies are the behaviours or actions that learners engage in, in order to learn or use the L2. They are generally considered to be conscious—or, at least, potentially conscious—and, therefore, open to inspection. See also *cognitive* and *metacognitive strategies*.

'learning' Krashen (1981) used the term 'learning' to refer to the development of conscious knowledge of an L2 through formal study. It means the same as *explicit knowledge*.

Learning Principles Learning Principles supplement a UG account of L2 acquisition. They seek to account for why learners are able to avoid building *wild grammars* (i.e. grammars that do not accord with UG principles and that cannot be rejected solely through positive evidence).

learning strategy A learning strategy is a device or procedure used by learners to develop their *interlanguages*. Learning strategies account for how learners acquire and automatize L2 knowledge. They are also used to refer to how they develop specific skills. It is possible, therefore, to talk of both 'language-learning strategies' and 'skill-learning strategies'. Learning strategies contrast with *communication* and *production strategies*, both of which account for how learners use rather than acquire L2 competence. See also *cognitive*, *metacognitive*, and *social/affective strategies*.

learning style Learning style refers to the characteristic ways in which individuals orientate to problem-solving. It reflects 'the totality of psychological functioning' (Willing 1987) involving affective as well as cognitive activity. In this respect it can be distinguished from *cognitive style*, which is narrower in scope.

Levelt's Model of Speech Production Levelt (1989) proposed that speech production could be accounted for in terms of four overlapping operations; (1) conceptualization, (2) formulation, (3) articulation, and (4) monitoring. His model has been used in studies that have investigated the effects of planning on L2 performance.

Lexicalization Hypothesis This addresses the role that the L1 plays in learners' ability to infer the meanings of L2 words. It states that learners will find it easier to infer the meanings of unknown L2 words that have equivalent L1 forms.

linguistic competence Researchers who work within the theoretical framework developed by Chomsky consider it necessary to distinguish *competence* and *performance*. 'Competence' refers to what speaker-hearers know, and 'performance' to the use of this knowledge in communication. Linguistic competence refers to the knowledge of the items and rules that comprise the formal systems of a language. It can also be distinguished from *pragmatic competence*. See also *pragmatic competence* and *communicative competence*.

linguistic context See *context*.

linguistic universals See *typological universals* and *Universal Grammar*.

local errors Local errors are errors that affect single elements in a sentence (for example, errors in the use of inflections or grammatical functors). They contrast with *global errors*.

logical problem of foreign language acquisition Bley-Vroman (1989) argued that this involves explaining the quite high level of competence that is clearly possible in some cases, while permitting the wide range of variation that is possible.

logical problem of language acquisition This is a term used by researchers in the Chomskyan tradition. It refers to the gap between what can logically be learnt from the available input and what actually is learnt. Input is considered to 'underdetermine' language acquisition. It is therefore necessary to posit the existence of innate knowledge of language to account for children's ability to achieve full linguistic competence.

Machiavellian motivation See *motivation*.

magnetic resonance imaging Magnetic resonance imaging (MRI) uses a radiology technique to produce images of body structures. It has been used in language research to investigate what parts of the brain are active in performing different language tasks and also in whether there are differences in brain functioning in L1 and L2 language use.

markedness Various definitions of linguistic markedness exist. The term refers to the idea that some linguistic structures are 'special' or 'less natural' or 'less basic' than others. For example, the use of 'break' in 'she broke my heart' can be considered marked in relation to the use of 'break' in 'she broke a cup'. SLA researchers are interested in markedness because it can help to account for patterns of attested L2 acquisition.

Markedness Differential Hypothesis This is a hypothesis advanced by Eckman (1977). It makes use of 'markedness' to explain why some L1 forms are transferred while others are not. It claims that learners transfer target-language features that are less marked than equivalent features in their L1 but do not transfer those that are more marked.

marker Some variable forms are both 'social' and 'stylistic'. That is, as well as manifesting variation according to social factors such as social class, they also manifest variation according to situational factors (for example, the addressee). See also *indicators*.

mediation This is a term used in *sociocultural SLA*. Lantolf (2000a) suggested that mediation in second language learning involves (1) mediation by others in social interaction, (2) mediation by self through private speech, and (3) mediation by artefacts (for example, tasks and technology).

mentalist theories of language learning Mentalist theories of language learning emphasize the learner's innate mental capacities for acquiring a language. Researchers in the Chomskyan tradition consider children (and possibly adults) to possess knowledge of abstract principles of language which serve as a basis for acquiring particular languages. Input is seen as a 'trigger' that activates these principles. See also *Universal Grammar* and *LAD*.

metacognitive strategy Many L2 learners are able to think consciously about how they learn and how successfully they are learning. Metacognitive strategies involve planning learning, monitoring the process of learning, and evaluating how successful a particular strategy is.

metalingual knowledge Metalingual knowledge is knowledge of the technical terminology needed to describe language. Metalingual knowledge helps to make L2 knowledge fully explicit.

metalinguistic feedback This consists of utterances that provide comments, information, or questions related to the well-formedness of the learner's utterance.

metatalk Metatalk refers to (1) the talk that learners employ to establish what kind of 'activity' to make of a task and also what operations to employ in performing it and (2) the talk that arises when learners focus explicitly on language in the course of accomplishing a task. See also *languaging*.

microgenesis Microgenesis refers to how development takes place over the course of a particular interaction in a specific sociocultural setting. In sociocultural theory, the microgenetic method has been used by researchers to investigate how learning takes place within the course of an interaction.

Minimalist Program The Minimalist Program constituted a development of the Government/Binding Model. It attempted to develop a more economical account of the principles that underlie the syntax of all languages by formulating a number of 'guidelines' that provide for a more 'minimal' representation of innate knowledge of syntax. (See Chomsky 1995.)

mistake According to Corder (1967), a 'mistake' is a deviation in learner language that occurs when learners fail to perform their competence. It is a lapse that reflects processing problems. A mistake contrasts with an *error*.

modality reduction When L2 learners are under communicative pressure, they may omit grammatical features such as modal verbs and adverbials that are associated with the expression of modal meanings like possibility and tentativeness. This is known as 'modality reduction'.

modified output Modified output occurs when learners modify a previous utterance. This may occur following feedback or as a result of self-monitoring. The modification may occur immediately following the original utterance or feedback or some turns later. It may involve repair of an initial error or some other change.

monitoring Both native speakers and learners typically try to correct any 'mistakes' they make. This is referred to as 'monitoring'. The learner can monitor vocabulary, grammar, phonology, or discourse. Krashen (1981) uses the term 'Monitoring' (with a capital 'M') to refer to the way learners use 'learned' knowledge to edit utterances generated by means of 'acquired' knowledge.

Monitor Theory This is the theory advanced by Krashen (1977) based on the distinction between 'acquisition' and 'learning'. Krashen argued that learned (i.e. explicit) knowledge was only available for use through Monitoring and that utterances need to be initiated by means of acquired (i.e. implicit) knowledge.

monolingualism This refers to speakers or speech communities who know and use only one language—their L1. It can also be characterized as a failure to learn an L2 and may be associated with a strong ethnic identity and negative attitudes towards the target language.

morpheme studies In the 1970s a number of researchers (for example, Dulay and Burt) conducted studies of a group of English morphemes (for example, V + ing, –ed, 3rd person –s) with a view to determining their order of acquisition. These studies, which were both cross-sectional and longitudinal, were known as 'morpheme studies'.

motivation In general terms, motivation refers to the effort that learners put into learning an L2 as a result of their need or desire to learn it. In one theory of motivation, Gardner and Lambert (1972) distinguished 'instrumental motivation', which occurs when a learner has a functional goal (such as to get a job or pass an examination), and 'integrative motivation', which occurs when a learner wishes to identify with the culture of the L2 group. Other types of motivation have also been identified, including (1) 'task motivation' or 'intrinsic motivation'—the interest that learners experience in performing different learning tasks, (2) 'Machiavellian motivation'—the desire to learn a language that stems from a wish to manipulate and overcome the people of the target language, and (3) attributional/ resultative motivation—the motivation that results from learners' responses to their own successes or failures in learning the L2.

multicompetence Cook (2002) has proposed the idea of multicompetence to refer to knowledge of two or more languages in the same mind. One implication of this is that the L1 of bi- or multilinguals differs from that of monolinguals and another is that multilinguals have greater cognitive flexibility than monolinguals.

Multidimensional Model Meisel, Clahsen, and Pienemann (1981) proposed a model of L2 acquisition in which a distinction is drawn between *developmental* and *variational features*. The former are acquired sequentially as certain processing strategies are mastered. The latter are acquired at any time (or not at all), depending on the learner's social and affective attitudes. The model has been elaborated by Johnston and Pienemann (1986). See also *Processability Theory*.

multilingualism This is the use of three or more languages by an individual or within a speech community. Frequently, multilingual people do not have equal control over all the languages they know and also use the languages for different purposes.

Nativization Model The Nativization Model (Andersen 1980) proposes that L2 acquisition consists of two general processes, nativization and denativization. In the former, learners make the input conform to their own internalized view of what constitutes the L2 system while in the latter they accommodate to an external norm.

naturalistic language acquisition This refers to language acquisition which takes place in *natural settings*. It contrasts with *instructed language acquisition*.

natural order See *order of development/ acquisition*.

natural settings A natural setting for L2 acquisition is one where the L2 is used normally for everyday communicative purposes (for example, in the street or the workplace). See also *educational settings*.

negative evidence Long (1996: 413) defined negative evidence as input that provides 'direct or indirect evidence of what is ungrammatical'.

negative transfer See *interference*.

negotiation of form This refers to repair that occurs when there is no communication difficulty (i.e. when the problem is entirely linguistic). Such repairs are uncommon in conversational interaction (although sometimes learners do request them), but have been shown to be very common in some classroom contexts.

negotiation of meaning Communication involving L2 learners often leads to problems in understanding and communication breakdown. Frequently, one or more of the participants—the learner or the interlocutor—attempts to remedy this by engaging in interactional work to secure mutual understanding. This work is often called 'negotiation of meaning'. It is characterized by *interactional modifications* such as comprehension checks and requests for clarification. Interactionally modified discourse also occurs when there is 'negotiation of content', defined by Rulon and McCreary (1986) as the process by which previously encountered content is clarified.

Neurobiological SLA This aims to correlate cognitive operations with neural functioning. Researchers attempt to show the locations in the brain and the neural circuits that are linked to the formation and consolidation of memories for language.

neuroimaging Neuroimaging involves the use of techniques for identifying which parts of the brain are activated when learners are asked to perform a language task. One method for achieving this is by functional *magnetic resonance imaging* (MRI), which indicates increased blood flow to different parts of the brain. Another method is electroencephalography (EEG) which measures the electrical activity generated by the brain when metal electrodes are placed on the scalp.

neurolinguistic SLA This draws on research that has examined how damage to different parts of the human brain (as a result of some traumatic experience, natural ageing, or genetic deficiency) affects a person's ability to use a previously learned L2.

non-interface position/hypothesis Theories of L2 acquisition which emphasize the distinctiveness of explicit and implicit knowledge and which claim that one type of knowledge cannot be converted directly into the other type adopt a 'non-interface position'. See also *interface position*.

Noun Phrase Accessibility Hierarchy See *Accessibility Hierarchy*.

Noticing Hypothesis The strong version of the hypothesis claims that learners will only learn what they consciously attend to in the input. The weak version allows for representation and storage of unattended stimuli in memory but claims that 'people learn about the things they attend to and do not learn much about the things they do not attend to' (Schmidt 2001).

Null Subject Parameter Languages vary according to whether they require an overt subject pronoun or allow it to be dropped. The Null Subject Parameter 'determines whether the subject of a clause can be suppressed' (Chomsky 1988: 64).

obligatory occasion analysis This involves identifying contexts that require the obligatory use of a specific grammatical feature in samples of learner language and calculating the accuracy with which the feature is actually supplied in these contexts. (See Brown 1973.) See also *target-like use analysis*.

Observer's Paradox According to Labov (1970), good data require systematic observation but the act of trying to observe contaminates the data collected. He refers to this as the Observer's Paradox.

online planning Online planning is a term used in task-based research to refer to the planning that learners do while they are performing a task.

open question An open question is one that has been framed with no particular answer in mind—a number of different answers are possible. Some questions have the appearance of being open, but are in fact closed; Barnes (1969) called these 'pseudo-questions'.

Operating Principles Slobin (1973) coined the term 'operating principles' to describe the various learning strategies employed by children during L1 acquisition. Examples include 'Pay attention to the ends of words' and 'Avoid exceptions'. Andersen (1984a, 1990) has shown how similar principles can be seen at work in L2 acquisition.

order of development/acquisition A number of studies of L2 acquisition (for example, the morpheme studies) have produced evidence to suggest that learners achieve mastery of grammatical features in a particular order irrespective of their L1 or their age. For example, verb + –ing has been found to be mastered before verb + –ed.

other-directed learner According to Saville-Troike (1988: 568), other-directed learners 'approach language as an interpersonal, social task, with a predominant focus on the message they wish to convey'. See also *inner-directed learners*.

Output Hypothesis See *comprehensible output hypothesis*.

overgeneralization Language learners in both L1 and L2 acquisition produce errors like 'comed'. These can be explained as extensions of some general rule to items not covered by this rule in the target language. Overgeneralization is one type of *over-use*.

overshadowing Overshadowing refers to a situation where two cues are associated with an outcome. Research has shown that in such cases the more subjectively salient of the two cues overshadows the weaker. As overshadowing continues over time, *blocking* results (i.e. learners learn to selectively attend to only the more salient of the two cues).

over-use Over-use involves the use of an L2 feature more frequently than the same feature is used by native speakers. It constitutes an 'over-indulgence' (Levenston 1971), which may be brought about by differences between the native and target languages. It may be reflected in errors (*overgeneralization*) or just a preference for one target-language form to the exclusion of other possible target forms.

Parallel Distributed Processing This is a theory of language use and acquisition developed by Rumelhart and McClelland. Whereas most theories view language as consisting of a set of rules and items, Parallel Distributed Processing models view it as complex networks of interconnections between 'units' that do not correspond to any linguistic construct. Learners gradually learn networks with interconnections of the same 'strengths' as those in the networks of users of the target language. See also *emergentism*.

Parameter This is a term used in Chomsky's theory of *Universal Grammar*. Some universal principles are 'parameterized': that is, they permit a finite set of options, which individual languages draw on and which thus define how languages differ. A language learner needs to discover which parameter settings apply in the target language. See also *principle* and *Parameter-setting Model*.

Parameter-setting Model This is a theory of L2 acquisition proposed by Flynn (1984). It is based on the theory of *Universal Grammar* and assumes that adult L2 learners have continued access to this. Their task is to discover how each principle is realized in the L2 (i.e. what parameter settings are needed).

pattern of development This term is used in this book to refer to the overall shape of L2 acquisition, from the initial stages to the final stages. It serves as a cover term, therefore, for both *order of development* and *sequence of development*.

patterns Patterns are one type of *formulaic sequence*. They are unanalysed units with one or more open slots, for example, 'Can I have a —?'.

Perceptual Learning Styles Reid (1987) distinguished four perceptual learning modalities: (1) visual learning, (2) auditory learning, (3) kinaesthetic learning, and (4) tactile learning. Learners vary in their preferred modality.

performance This term refers to the actual use of language in either comprehension or production. It contrasts with *competence*. See also *linguistic competence*.

personality Personality is generally conceived of as composed of a series of traits such as extraversion/introversion and neuroticism/stability. It constitutes a factor believed to account for individual differences in L2 learning.

pied piping This is a term used in grammar. It refers to the proximity of two tied grammatical elements. For example, the preposition 'for' and the pronoun 'whom' are placed next to each other in the sentence: 'For whom did you get the present?'. Pied piping contrasts with *preposition stranding*.

planned discourse Ochs (1979: 55) distinguished 'discourse that lacks forethought and organizational preparation' (i.e. unplanned discourse) and 'discourse that has been thought out and organized prior to its expression' (i.e. planned discourse). See also *speech planning*.

positive evidence 'Models of what is grammatical and acceptable' (Long 1996: 413).

positive transfer According to *behaviourist* accounts of L2 acquisition, learners will have no difficulty in learning L2 patterns when these are the same as L1 patterns. Support for positive transfer occurs when it can be shown that learners acquire L2 features which are the same as or similar to L1 features with little difficulty.

poverty of the stimulus Researchers in the Chomskyan tradition view the input available to learners as an inadequate source of information for building a grammar. The stimulus can be considered impoverished on several grounds: (1) input is degenerate (for example, it contains ungrammatical sentences), (2) input underdetermines the grammar that needs to be constructed, and (3) the input to children does not typically contain *negative evidence*.

Power Law of Practice This states that the logarithm of the reaction time and/or the error rate for a particular task decrease linearly with the logarithm of the number of practice trials taken, i.e. practice improves performance but with a gradually diminishing effect.

pragmalinguistic failure This is a term used by Thomas (1983). It arises when a learner tries to perform the right speech act but uses the wrong linguistic means.

pragmatic competence Pragmatic competence consists of the knowledge that speaker-hearers use in order to engage in communication, including how speech acts are successfully performed. Pragmatic competence is normally distinguished from linguistic competence. Both are seen as relating to 'knowledge', and are therefore distinct from actual performance.

pragmatics Pragmatics is the study of how language is used in communication. Among other aspects of language use, it includes the study of *illocutionary acts*.

pre-emption In UG-based SLA studies, the term pre-emption is used to refer to the prevention of the development of an interlanguage form that cannot be disconfirmed purely on the basis of positive evidence.

premodified input Input that is modified to make it more comprehensible prior to the learner being required to process it. Graded readers provide learners with premodified input.

preparatory act Studies of speech acts have shown that speakers frequently prepare for a *head act* (i.e. the utterance that actually performs the speech act). For example, in the case of requests, a speaker might check on the ability of the hearer to respond to the request by saying 'Are you busy?'.

preposition stranding In some languages, like English, a preposition does not always have to be proximate to the noun or pronoun to which it grammatically belongs, as in this sentence: 'Who did you get the present for?' Preposition stranding contrasts with *pied piping*.

pre-task planning Pre-task planning is a term used in task-based research to refer to the planning that learners do before they start the task. An alternative term is *strategic planning*.

Principles This is a term used in Chomsky's theory of *Universal Grammar*. It refers to highly abstract properties of grammar which govern all languages. Principles are thought to constrain the form that a specific grammar can take. They constitute part of a child's innate knowledge of language. See also *parameter*.

private speech Some L2 learners who go through a *silent period* engage in private conversations with themselves, thus, perhaps, preparing themselves for social speech later.

proactive inhibition Proactive inhibition is the way in which previous learning prevents or inhibits the learning of new habits. L2 learners are hypothesized to experience difficulty in learning target-language forms that are different from first-language forms. See *interference* and *transfer*.

procedural knowledge Two related but different uses of the term procedural knowledge can be found in SLA research. On the one hand, it is used in contrast to *declarative knowledge* to refer to knowledge that has become proceduralized so that it is available for automatic and unconscious use. On the other hand, it refers to knowledge of the various strategies that learners employ to make effective use of their L2 knowledge in communication (for example, *communication strategies*).

Processability Theory Pienemann's Processability Theory seeks to explain what is known about acquisitional orders/sequences in terms of a set of processing procedures. As Pienemann (2005a: 2) put it 'once we can spell out the sequence in which language processing routines develop we can delineate those grammars that are processable at different points of development'. It constitutes a development of the earlier *Multidimensional Model*.

Processing Instruction VanPatten (1996) defined Processing Instruction as 'a type of grammar instruction whose purpose is to affect the ways in which learners attend to input data. It is input-based rather than output-based ...' (p. 2). It is designed to assist learners to construct form–function mappings in line with the target language.

production strategy Production strategies refer to the utilization of linguistic knowledge in communication. They differ from *communication strategies* in that they do not imply any communication problem and in that they are generally used without conscious awareness.

proficiency L2 proficiency refers to a learner's skill in using the L2. It can be contrasted with the term 'competence'. Whereas, competence refers to the knowledge of the L2 a learner has internalized, proficiency refers to the learner's ability to use this knowledge in different tasks.

Projection Hypothesis Zobl (1983b) suggests that L2 learners (like L1 learners) have the ability to 'project' knowledge of one rule to enable them to acquire another, implicated rule, for which they have received no direct evidence in the input. Thus, acquiring rule x automatically enables learners to acquire rule *y*, if *x* implicates *y*.

property theory A property theory is concerned with providing an account of a static linguistic system; it is a 'way of representing dispositions, competencies, or bodies of knowledge' (Crookes, 1992: 433). UG-based theories are property theories of L2 acquisition in the main. A property theory contrasts with a *transition theory*.

prototypicality This term is used by Kellerman (1977) to refer to perceptions that learners have regarding the structure of their own language. These perceptions lead them to treat some structures as transferable and others as non-transferable.

pseudo-question See *open question*.

psycholinguistic context This is a term used in this book to refer to the extent to which a particular context of use affords time for planning linguistic production and also whether it encourages or discourages monitoring of output.

psychological distance A term used by Schumann (1978a) in his *Acculturation Model*. It refers to the distance between a learner and the target-language community resulting from various psychological factors such as language shock and rigidity of ego boundaries.

psychotypology Kellerman (1978) has suggested that learners have perceptions regarding the distance between their L1 and the L2 they are trying to learn. These perceptions constitute their psychotypology.

pushed output This is a term used by Swain (1985) to refer to learner output that is produced with effort and reflects the outer limits of their linguistic competence. See also *comprehensible output hypothesis* and *modified output*.

recast An utterance that 'rephrases the learner's utterance by changing one or more components (subject, verb, object) while still referring to its central meaning' (Long 1996).

re-creation continuum Corder (1978a) suggested that one way of viewing the interlanguage continuum is as a re-creation continuum. One possible starting point is 'some basic simple grammar', which is recalled from an early stage of L1 acquisition. Learners gradually comlexify this system.

reference group L2 learners—particularly those in natural settings—often have a choice of language variety as the target model. Their choice is influenced by the particular social group or groups they wish to identify with.

referential question A referential question is a question that is genuinely information-seeking (for example, 'Why didn't you do your homework?'). See also *open question* and *closed question*.

rehearsal In information processing theories of L2 acquisition, 'rehearsal' refers to the recycling of material attended to in working memory. In the context of studies of the effects of planning on performance, it refers to task-repetition (i.e. asking learners to perform the same task a second time).

replication A replication is the repetition of an original study. Polio and Gass (1997) distinguished 'virtual replications' and 'conceptual replications'. The former involve a more or less complete copy of the original study, while the latter involve alterations to the original study with a view to confirming the generalizability or external validity of the research.

request for clarification An utterance that elicits clarification of the preceding utterance. See also *interactional modification*.

resilient features Resilient linguistic features are those that are acquired relatively easily even when the only input available to the learner is deficient. Examples are word order rules. Resilient features contrast with *fragile features*.

restrictive simplification Researchers in the ZISA project (for example, Meisel 1980) used the term 'restrictive simplification' to refer to learners' continued use of simplified structures such as the deletion of function words, even though they have developed knowledge of corresponding non-simplified structures. It contrasts with *elaborative simplification*.

restructuring This is a term used in information-processing theories of L2 acquisition to refer to the qualitative changes that take place in learners' interlanguage at certain stages of development. (See McLaughlin 1990a.) For example, learners may begin by representing past-tense forms as separate items and then shift to representing them by means of a general rule for past-tense formation.

restructuring continuum Corder (1978a) suggested that one way of viewing the interlanguage continuum is as a restructuring continuum. The starting point is the learner's L1. The learner gradually replaces Ll-based rules with L2-based rules.

routines Routines are one type of formulaic sequence. They are units that are totally unanalysed and which are learnt as wholes. A common routine is 'I don't know'. See also *formulaic speech* and *patterns*.

scaffolding Scaffolding refers to the process by which one speaker (an expert or a novice) assists another speaker (a novice) to perform a skill that they are unable to perform independently. It is a term used in *sociocultural SLA*.

Selective Attention Hypothesis According to this hypothesis, formal instruction aids L2 acquisition not by actually causing new linguistic features to become part of the learner's interlanguage, but by providing the learner with 'hooks, points of access' (Lightbown 1985b). In particular, it has been suggested that formal instruction initiates the process of acquiring a feature by helping learners to notice a new feature in the input.

self-confidence This is a motivational factor consisting of belief in one's ability to learn an L2 successfully.

self-regulation This is the ability to monitor one's learning and make changes to the strategies that one employs. It involves both the ability to exercise control over one's attitudinal/motivational state and to engage in self-critical reflection of one's actions and underlying belief systems.

self-report One way of investigating learners' cognitive and affective states during L2 learning is by asking them to report on these. Self-report includes retrospective reports elicited by means of interviews, diaries, personal learning histories, and *stimulated recall* and also concurrent reports elicited by means of *immediate recall* and *think-aloud tasks*.

semilingualism In some contexts, when learners of an L2 develop negative attitudes towards both their own culture and that of the target language, semilingualism can result, i.e. the learners fail to develop full proficiency in either language. This idea is controversial, however.

sentence-matching tests These present learners with two sentences, which are either both grammatical or both ungrammatical, and ask them to determine whether the two sentences are identical or not. The time it takes learners to make an online judgement is then measured.

sequence of development This book distinguishes order and sequence of development. 'Sequence of development' refers to the stages of acquisition through which a learner passes in acquiring specific grammatical structures such as interrogatives, negatives, and relative clauses. See also *order of development*.

silent period Some L2 learners, especially children, undergo an often lengthy period during which they do not try to speak in the L2. However, they may be learning the L2 through listening to others speak it and may also be engaging in *private speech*.

situational context See *context*.

situation-specific anxiety See *anxiety*.

skill-acquisition theories Skill-acquisition theories are based on the view that language learning, like any other skill, is characterized by a progression from an initial declarative knowledge stage involving controlled processing, to a final procedural stage where knowledge is automatic. Skills are learnt as a result of 'practice'.

social/affective strategies These are one type of *learning strategy*. They concern the ways in which learners elect to interact with other learners and native speakers (for example, 'asking a teacher for repetition' (Chamot 1987).

social context According to a structural view of social context, social factors such as power and prestige are seen as determining social context. In an interactional view the social context is seen as created in each situation through an interplay of social factors.

social distance This is a term used by Schumann (1978a) to account for why some L2 learners learn very slowly or achieve low levels of proficiency. Various factors such as the size of the learner's L2 group and the learner's desire to acculturate influence the 'distance' between the learner and the target-language community.

social identity Norton defined 'social identity' as 'the relationship between the individual and the larger social world, as mediated through institutions such as families, schools, workplaces, social services, and law courts (Norton 1997: 420). Social identity is multiple and dynamic.

Social Identity Theory This theory claims that learners' social identities affect how successful they will be in learning an L2. Norton (2000) demonstrated through a series of case studies of immigrant women in Canada how the social identity they accepted or insisted on influenced their opportunities for learning English.

socialization See *language socialization.*

social network Milroy (1980) developed an approach to investigating linguistic variability that involved examining the social networks that individuals were members of. She distinguished social networks in terms of whether they were 'dense' (i.e. where all the individual members know each other), 'diffuse' (i.e. where the individuals are not known to each other), 'multiplex' (i.e. where the relationships among individuals are complex, involving a number of different social institutions such as family and workplace) or 'simplex' (i.e. where relationships are governed by a single role).

sociocultural SLA This is a branch of SLA that draws on the work of Vygotsky in viewing learning as the product of mediated activity. Higher order language functions are seen as developing both in and out of social interaction. Learners progress from object- and other-regulation to self-regulation through interacting with others. See also *zone of proximal development* and *scaffolding.*

Sociocultural Theory See *sociocultural SLA.*

Socio-educational Model of L2 Learning This is a model of L2 learning developed by Gardner (1985). It posits that the social and cultural milieu in which learners grow up determines the attitudes and motivational orientation they hold towards the target language, its speakers, and its culture. These in turn influence learning outcomes.

sociolinguistic variables A sociolinguistic variable is a linguistic feature that varies in accordance with factors such as age, sex, social class, and ethnic membership. For example, Labov (1970) illustrates how variation in /r/ in the speech of New Yorkers reflects the social class of a speaker.

sociopragmatic failure This is a term used by Thomas (1983). It occurs when a learner performs the wrong *illocutionary act* for the situation and constitutes a deviation with regard to appropriateness of meaning. An example is a learner who apologizes where a native speaker would thank someone.

Speech Accommodation Theory See *Accommodation Theory.*

speech act A speech act is an utterance that performs a locutionary and an illocutionary meaning in communication. For example, 'I like your dress' is a locutionary speech act concerning a proposition about a person's dress with the illocutionary force of a compliment.

speech planning In some contexts of language use, speakers have the opportunity to plan their speech, while in others they have to use the language more spontaneously. Speech planning influences the choice of linguistic form. For example,

L2 learners may use a target-language form in planned language use but an interlanguage form in unplanned language use. Speech planning is sometimes investigated by studying 'temporal variables' (for example, speech rate and pause length).

stabilization Stabilization' refers to a state of L2 development where fluctuation has temporarily ceased—and therefore contrasts with *fossilization*, which refers to a permanent cessation of development. Many L2 learners are familiar with a situation where they appear to plateau, failing to develop despite their continuing efforts to do so, but then make a 'breakthrough' some time later.

state anxiety See *anxiety*.

stereotype A stereotype is a linguistic feature with a specific social meaning that is *stigmatized* and therefore often actively avoided. A stereotype typically does not show regular stratification because everyone is so aware of it.

stimulated recall This is a technique for eliciting a retrospective report. It seeks to explore learners' thought processes at the time they performed an activity by asking them to report their thoughts after they have completed a task. (See Gass and Mackey 2000.)

stimulus-appraisal system Schumann (1997) proposed a theory of motivation involving learners assessing the emotional relevance of stimuli on the basis of their novelty, pleasantness, and relevance to their individual goals or needs, their ability to cope, and compatibility with their self and social image. He saw the stimulus-appraisal system as having a neurobiological basis.

strategic planning See *pre-task planning*.

strategy training This involves attempts to train learners to make use of specific *communication strategies* or *learning strategies*. Strategy training studies aim to measure the effect that such training has on learning.

structural and semantic simplification Learner language produced by beginners is characteristically simpler than the target language, and in many respects resembles a pidgin language. Structural simplification is evident in the omission of grammatical functors. Semantic simplification is evident in the omission of propositional elements (for example, *'Hitting' instead of 'Kurt is hitting his sister').

structured input This is input that has been specially designed to expose learners to exemplars of a specific linguistic feature. It constitutes a technique in form-focused instruction.

style shifting Both native speakers and L2 learners use different *variants* of a *variable form* depending on the degree of attention they pay to their speech (i.e. whether they are accessing their *vernacular* or *careful style*). Labov refers to these changes in speech as 'style shifting'.

stylistic continuum Tarone (1983), drawing on the work of Labov, suggested that learners internalize different 'styles' of language, ranging from a *careful* to a *vernacular style*. The stylistic continuum accounts for *variability* in learner language.

Subjacency Principle This is a principle of *Universal Grammar*. It defines the restrictions that govern how far one phrase can be moved from 'deep' to 'surface' structure.

submersion The term submersion is used to refer to educational settings where L2 learners are required to learn in classrooms where most of the students are native speakers so that few input adjustments take place.

substratum transfer See *language transfer*.

subtractive bilingualism See *bilingualism*.

syllable structure Syllables can be open or closed. An open syllable consists of an onset (one or more consonants) and a rhyme (a vowel). Closed syllables contain a coda (i.e. one or more final consonants). Closed syllables are generally considered to be more difficult to acquire than open syllables.

syntactization See *grammaticalization*.

target-like use analysis This is an extension of *obligatory occasion analysis*. It is designed to take into account the incorrect use of specific grammatical features in contexts that do not require them in the target language (for example, *'Mary and Peter likes travelling.'), as well as non-suppliance in contexts that require the feature (for example, *'Simon eat an apple every day.').

task A task is a language-teaching activity where meaning is primary, there is some kind of gap, students are required to use their own linguistic resources, and there is an outcome other than the display of language for its own sake.

task-based teaching Task-based teaching is an approach to the teaching of second/foreign languages based on a syllabus consisting of communicative tasks and utilizing a methodology that makes meaningful communication rather than linguistic accuracy primary.

task-induced variation This is a blanket term used to refer to the *variability* in language use evident when learners are asked to perform different tasks. Ultimately, it is traceable to other sources (such as *linguistic* and *situational contexts*).

Teachability Hypothesis Pienemann's (1985) Teachability Hypothesis 'predicts that instruction can only promote language acquisition if the interlanguage is close to the point when the structure to be taught is acquired in the natural setting (so that sufficient processing prerequisites are developed)' (p. 37). This hypothesis is derived from the *Multidimensional Model*.

teacher talk Teachers address classroom language learners differently from the way they address other kinds of classroom learners. They make adjustments to both language form and language function in order to facilitate communication. These adjustments are referred to as 'teacher talk'. See also *foreigner talk*.

Theory of Instructed Language Acquisition This is the theory advanced by Ellis (1993, 1994c), based on the distinction between implicit and explicit L2 knowledge. The theory seeks to explain the role played by both types of knowledge in L2 acquisition in terms of how they interface.

think-aloud tasks These are tasks designed to collect introspective data on the strategies learners use. Learners are asked to perform a task (for example, completing a cloze test) and to concurrently report the thought processes they are using to accomplish the task.

Total Physical Response (TPR) A teaching method developed by James Asher that consisted of teaching grammar by asking students to carry out a set of commands designed to provide them with comprehensible input.

trait anxiety See *anxiety*.

transfer-appropriate processing The principle of transfer-appropriate processing states that 'the learning environment that best promotes rapid, accurate retrieval of what has been learned is that in which the psychological demands placed on the learner resemble those that will be encountered later in natural settings' (Lightbown 2006).

transfer errors These are errors in learner language that can be accounted for in terms of differences between the structures of the L1 and the L2. See *language transfer* and *proactive inhibition*.

transitional constructions Dulay, Burt, and Krashen (1982) define transitional constructions as 'the interim language forms that learners use while they are still learning the grammar of a language'. For example, before learners master the rule for English negatives, they operate with interim rules (such as 'no' + verb).

transition theory A transition theory seeks to account for how changes in the state of a linguistic system take place. Crookes (1992) argued that an adequate theory must specify the 'mechanisms' that are responsible for such changes. Pienemann's *Processability Theory* is a transition theory.

turn-taking Ethnomethodological studies of naturally occurring conversations (for example, Sacks, Schegloff, and Jefferson 1974) have identified a number of rules that underlie speaker selection and change in conversations—for example, only one speaker speaks at a time.

typological universals Typological universals are identified by examining a representative sample of natural languages in order to identify features that are common to all or most of these languages. Typological universals can be absolute (i.e. occur in all languages), tendencies (i.e. occur in a large number of, but not all, languages), or implicational (i.e. the presence of one feature implies the presence of another).

Universal Grammar This is a term used by Chomsky to refer to the abstract knowledge of language which children bring to the task of learning their native language, and which constrains the shape of the particular grammar they are trying to learn. Universal Grammar consists of various *principles* which govern the form grammatical rules can take. Some of these principles are 'parameterized' (i.e. are specified as consisting of two or more options). See also *principles* and *parameters*.

unplanned discourse See *speech planning* and *planned discourse*.

uptake This is a move undertaken by the learner in response to the feedback the learner receives from another speaker on his/her previous utterance that contained an error. Uptake can involve 'repair' or 'no repair' depending on whether the learner successfully corrects his/her original error.

U-shaped behaviour L2 learners have been observed to manifest a target-language form in their output at an early stage of development only to manifest an interlanguage form in its place at a later stage. Eventually the correct target-language form reappears (for example, 'came' becomes 'comed' and, later still, 'came' again). This pattern of development is known as 'U-shaped behaviour'.

Variability Hypothesis This is a term used in this book to refer to the possibility that formal instruction may have an effect on the learner's *careful style* but that is less likely to have an effect on the learner's *vernacular* style. See also *stylistic continuum*.

Variable Competence Model The Variable Competence Model seeks to account for the variability evident in learner language by positing that this reflects a competence that is itself variable (i.e. it contains variable rules or different styles). Tarone (1983) proposed that the learner's competence comprises a *stylistic continuum*.

variable form A variable form is a phonological, lexical, or grammatical feature that is realized linguistically in more than one way. The linguistic devices that realize a variable form are known as *variants*.

variants A *variable form* has two or more variants, i.e. it can be realized by two or more linguistic structures. For example, English copula has two variants—contracted and full copula.

variational features See *Multidimensional Model*.

vernacular style This is a term used by Labov (1970) to refer to the language forms evident when speakers are communicating spontaneously and easily with interlocutors familiar to them. It contrasts with *careful style*, and for this reason is also sometimes referred to as 'casual style'. See also *stylistic continuum*.

vertical constructions Vertical constructions are learner utterances which are formed by borrowing chunks from the preceding discourse and then adding to these from the learner's own resources. For example, a learner utterance like 'No come here' could be constructed by taking 'come here' from a previous utterance and adding 'no'. According to one view of L2 acquisition, vertical constructions are the precursors of horizontal constructions.

vertical variation This refers to the differences in learner language evident from one time to another. It reflects the development that is taking place in the learner's interlanguage.

Wave Theory This is a sociolinguistic theory developed by Bailey (1973) to account for linguistic change. It explains how old rules spread from one speech community to another and how new rules arise. It also accounts for how rules spread from one linguistic environment to another.

Wernicke's area This refers to the posterior part of the first or superior temporal gyrus and adjacent areas of the brain that are responsible for comprehension. Named after the person who first identified it.

wild grammar Goodluck (1986) has used the term 'wild grammar' to refer to a grammar that contains rules that contravene *Universal Grammar*. It is argued that children do not in fact construct wild grammars.

willingness to communicate This is the extent to which learners are prepared to initiate communication when they have a choice. It constitutes a factor believed to lead to individual differences in language learning.

within-task planning This refers to the planning that speakers (or writers) undertake while they are engaged in the act of communicating. It can be pressured or unpressured. It contrasts with *pre-task planning*.

working memory Working memory is a mental construct that accounts for how the key processes of perception, attention and rehearsal take place. It is believed to play a central role in L2 acquisition. There are different models of working memory including a capacity-limited model and a multiple-resources model.

zone of proximal development This refers to 'the distance between the actual developmental level as determined by independent problem solving and the level of potential development as determined through adult guidance or in collaboration with more capable peers' (Vygotsky 1978: 86). It is a term used in *sociocultural SLA*.

Bibliography

Abbott, G. 1980. 'Toward a more rigorous analysis of foreign language errors'. *International Review of Applied Linguistics* 18: 121–34.

Abdullah, K. and **H. Jackson.** 1998. 'Idioms and the language learner: contrasting English and Syrian Arabic'. *Languages in Contrast* 1: 83–107.

Aboud, F. and **R. Meade** (eds.). 1974. *Cultural Factors in Learning and Education.* Bellingham, Washington: Fifth Western Washington Symposium on Learning.

Abraham, R. 1983. 'Relationships between use of the strategy of monitoring and cognitive style'. *Studies in Second Language Acquisition* 6: 17–32.

Abraham, R. 1985. 'Field independence-dependence and the teaching of grammar'. *TESOL Quarterly* 20: 689–702.

Abraham, R. and **R. Vann.** 1987. 'Strategies of two language learners: a case study' in A. Wenden and J. Rubin (eds.): *Learner Strategies in Language Learning.* Englewood Cliffs, N.J.: Prentice Hall.

Abrahamsson, N. 2003. 'Development and recoverability of L2 codas: a longitudinal study of Chinese/Swedish interphonology'. *Studies in Second Language Acquisition* 25: 313–49.

Abutalebi, J., S. Cappa, and **D. Pernai.** 2001. 'The bilingual brain as revealed by functional neuroimaging'. *Bilingualism, Language and Cognition* 4: 179–90.

Abutalebi, J. and **D. Green.** 2007. 'Bilingual language production: the neurocognition of language representation and control'. *Journal of Neurolinguistics* 20: 242–75.

Achiba, M. 2003. *Learning to Request in a Second Language.* Clevedon: Multilingual Matters.

Adams, K. and **D. Brinks** (eds.). 1990. *Perspectives on Official English: the Campaign for English as the Official Language of the USA.* Berlin: Mouton de Gruyter.

Adams, M. 1978. 'Methodology for examining second language acquisition' in E. Hatch (ed.): *Second Language Acquisition.* Rowley, Mass.: Newbury House.

Adamson, H. and **V. Regan.** 1991. 'The acquisition of community norms by Asian immigrants learning English as a second language: a preliminary study'. *Studies in Second Language Acquisition* 1: 1–22.

Adger, C. 1987. 'Accommodating cultural differences in conversational style: a case study' in J. Lantolf and A. Labarca (eds.): *Research in Second Language Learning: Focus on the Classroom.* Norwood, N.J.: Ablex.

Adjemian, C. 1976. 'On the nature of interlanguage systems'. *Language Learning* 26: 297–320.

Ahlsen, E. 2006. *Introduction to Neurolinguistics.* Amsterdam: John Benjamins.

Akamatsu, N. 2003. 'The effects of first language orthographic features on second language reading in text'. *Language Learning* 53: 207–31.

Akiyama, Y. 2002. 'Japanese adult learners' development of the locality condition of English reflexives'. *Studies in Second Language Acquisition* 24: 27–54.

Alanen, R. 1995. 'Input enhancement and rule presentation in second language acquisition' in R. Schmidt (ed.): *Attention and Awareness in Foreign Language Learning.* Honolulu: University of Hawai'i Second Language Teaching and Curriculum Center.

Alatis, J. (ed.). 1968. *Report of the Nineteenth Annual Round Table Meeting on Linguistics and Language Studies.* Georgetown University, Washington D.C.: Georgetown University Press.

Albert, M. and **L. Obler.** 1978. *The Bilingual Brain: Neuropsychological and Neurolinguistic Aspects of Bilingualism.* New York: Academic Press.

Albrechtsen, D., B. Henriksen, and **C. Færch.** 1980. 'Native speaker reactions to learners' spoken interlanguage'. *Language Learning* 30: 365–96.
Aljaafreh, A. and **J. Lantolf.** 1994. 'Negative feedback as regulation and second language learning in the Zone of Proximal Development'. *The Modern Language Journal* 78: 465–83.
Allen, J. P. and **S. P. Corder** (eds.). 1974. *The Edinburgh Course in Applied Linguistics Volume 3*. London: Oxford University Press.
Allen, J. P., M. Fröhlich, and **N. Spada.** 1984. 'The communicative orientation of language teaching: an observation scheme' in J. Handscombe, R. Orem, and B. Taylor (eds.): *On TESOL '83: The Question of Control*. Washington D.C.: TESOL.
Allen, J. P., M. Swain, B. Harley, and **J. Cummins.** 1990. 'Aspects of classroom treatment: toward a more comprehensive view of second language education' in B. Harley, J. P. Allen, J. Cummins, and M. Swain (eds.): *The Development of Second Language Proficiency*. Cambridge: Cambridge University Press.
Allen, L. 2000. 'Form-meaning connections and the French causative: an experiment in input processing'. *Studies in Second Language Acquisition* 22: 69–84.
Allwright, D. 1988. *Observation in the Language Classroom*. London: Longman.
Allwright, D. 2003. 'Exploratory practice: rethinking practitioner research in language teaching'. *Language Teaching Research* 7: 113–42.
Allwright, D. 2006. 'Six promising directions in applied linguistics' in S. Gieve and I. Miller (eds.). *Understanding the Language Classroom*. Basingstoke: Palgrave Macmillan.
Allwright, D. and **K. Bailey.** 1991. *Focus on the Language Classroom: An Introduction to Classroom Research for Language Teachers*. Cambridge: Cambridge University Press.
Allwright, R. 1975a. 'Problems in the study of the language teacher's treatment of learner error' in M. Burt and H. Dulay (eds.): *On TESOL '75: New Directions in Second Language Learning, Teaching and Bilingual Education*. Washington D.C.: TESOL.
Allwright, R. (ed.). 1975b. *Working Papers: Language Teaching Classroom Research*. University of Essex, Department of Language and Linguistics.
Allwright, R. 1980. 'Turns, topics and tasks: patterns of participation in language teaching and learning' in D. Larsen-Freeman (ed.): *Discourse Analysis in Second Language Research*. Rowley, Mass.: Newbury House.
Allwright, R. 1984. 'The importance of interaction in classroom language learning'. *Applied Linguistics* 5: 156–71.
Altman, H. 1980. 'Foreign language teaching: focus on the learner' in H. Altman and C. Vaughan James (eds.): *Foreign Language Teaching: Meeting Individual Needs*. Oxford: Pergamon.
Altman, H. and **C. Vaughan James** (eds.). 1980. *Foreign Language Teaching: Meeting Individual Needs*. Oxford: Pergamon.
Ammar, A. and **N. Spada.** 2006. 'One size fits all? Recasts, prompts, and L2 learning'. *Studies in Second Language Acquisition* 28: 543–74.
Ammon, U. 1997. 'Language spread policy'. *Language Problems and Language Planning* 21: 51–7.
Andersen, R. 1979a. 'Expanding Schumann's Pidginization Hypothesis'. *Language Learning* 29: 105–19.
Andersen, R. (ed.). 1979b. *The Acquisition and Use of Spanish and English as First and Second Languages*. Washington, D.C.: TESOL.
Andersen, R. 1980. 'The role of creolization in Schumann's Pidginization Hypothesis for second language acquisition' in R. Scarcella and S. Krashen (eds.): *Research in Second Language Acquisition*. Rowley, Mass.: Newbury House.
Andersen, R. (ed.). 1981. *New Dimensions in Second Language Acquisition Research*. Rowley, Mass.: Newbury House.
Andersen, R. 1983a. 'Transfer to somewhere' in S. Gass and L. Selinker (eds.). *Language Transfer in Language Learning*. Rowley, Mass.: Newbury House.

Andersen, R. 1983b. *Pidginization and Creolization as Language Acquisition*. Rowley, Mass.: Newbury House.

Andersen, R. (ed.). 1984a. *Second Language: a Crosslinguistic Perspective*. Rowley, Mass.: Newbury House.

Andersen, R. 1984b. 'The One-to-One Principle of interlanguage construction'. *Language Learning* 34: 77–95.

Andersen, R. 1990. 'Models, processes, principles and strategies: second language acquisition inside and outside of the classroom' in B. VanPatten and J. Lee (eds.): *Second Language Acquisition—Foreign Language Learning*. Clevedon: Multilingual Matters.

Andersen, R. 1991. 'Developmental sequences: the emergence of aspect marking in second language acquisition' in C. Ferguson and T. Huebner (eds.): *Second Language Acquisition and Linguistic Theories*. Amsterdam: Benjamins.

Andersen, R. and **Y. Shirai.** 1994. 'Discourse motivations for some cognitive acquisition principles'. *Studies in Second Language Acquisition* 16/2: 133–56.

Andersen, R. and **Y. Shirai.** 1996. 'Primacy of aspect in first and second language acquisition: The pidgin/creole connection' in W. Ritchie and T. Bhatia (eds.): *Handbook on Language Acquisition*. New York: Academic Press.

Anderson, J. 1976. *Language, Memory, and Thought*. Hillsdale, N.J.: Lawrence Erlbaum.

Anderson, J. 1980. *Cognitive Psychology and its Implications*. San Francisco: Freeman. (Second edition 1985).

Anderson, J. 1983. *The Architecture of Cognition*. Cambridge, Mass.: Harvard University Press.

Anderson, J. 1993. *Rules of the Mind*. Hillsdale, N.J.: Lawrence Erlbaum.

Anton, M. 1999. 'A learner-centered classroom: sociocultural perspectives on teacher–learner interaction in the second language classroom'. *The Modern Language Journal* 83: 303–18.

Anton, M. and **F. J. DiCamilla.** 1998. 'Socio-cognitive functions of Ll collaborative interaction in the L2 classroom'. *The Canadian Modern Language Review* 54: 314–42.

Appel, G. and **J. Lantolf.** 1994. 'Speaking as mediation: a study of L I and L2 text recall tasks'. *The Modern Language Journal* 78: 437–52.

Archibald, J. 1998. *Second Language Phonology*. Amsterdam: John Benjamins.

Archibald, J. (ed.). 2000. *Second Language Acquisition and Linguistic Theory*. Oxford: Blackwell.

Ardal, S., M. W. Donald, R. Meuter, S. Muldrew, and **M. Luce.** 1990. 'Brain responses to semantic incongruity in bilinguals'. *Brain and Language* 39: 187–205.

Arnaud, P. and **H. Bejoint** (eds.). 1992. *Vocabulary and Applied Linguistics*. London: Macmillan.

Arnold, J. (ed.). 1999. *Affective Language Learning*. Cambridge: Cambridge University Press.

Arthur, B., M. Weiner, J. Culver, L. Young, and **D. Thomas.** 1980. 'The register of impersonal discourse to foreigners: verbal adjustments to foreign accent' in D. Larsen-Freeman (ed.). *Discourse Analysis in Second Language Research*. Rowley, Mass.: Newbury House.

Artigal, J. 1992. 'Some considerations on why a new language is acquired by being used'. *International Journal of Applied Linguistics* 2: 221–40.

Artigal, J. 1997. 'The Catalan immersion program' in R. Johnson and M. Swain (eds.). *Immersion Education: International Perspectives*. Cambridge: Cambridge University Press.

Asher, J. 1977. *Learning Another Language Through Actions: The Complete Teachers' Guidebook*. Los Gatos, Calif.: Sky Oaks Publications.

Aston, G. 1986. 'Trouble-shooting in interaction with learners: the more the merrier?' *Applied Linguistics* 7: 128–43.

Atkinson, D. 2002. 'Toward a sociocognitive approach to second language acquisition'. *The Modern Language Journal* 86: 525–45.

Atkinson, M. 1986. 'Learnability' in P. Fletcher and M. Garman (eds.). *Language Acquisition* (Second edition). Cambridge: Cambridge University Press.

Au, S. 1988. 'A critical appraisal of Gardner's social-psychological theory of second language (L2) learning'. *Language Learning* 38: 75–100.

Auerbach, E. 1993. 'Reexaming English only in the ESL classroom'. *TESOL Quarterly* 27: 9–32.

Austin, J. 1962. *How to Do Things with Words.* Oxford: Clarendon Press.

Ayoun, D. 2004. 'The effectiveness of written recasts in the second language acquisition of aspectual distinctions in French; a follow-up study'. *The Modern Language Journal* 88: 31–55.

Bach, E. and **R. Harms** (eds.). 1968. *Universals of Linguistic Theory.* New York: Holt, Rinehart and Winston.

Bachman, J. 1964. 'Motivation in a task situation as a function of ability and control over task'. *Journal of Abnormal and Social Psychology* 69: 272–81.

Bacon, S. 1987. 'Differentiated cognitive style and oral performance' in B. VanPatten, T. Dvorak, and J. Lee (eds.): *Foreign Language Learning: A Research Perspective.* Cambridge: Newbury House.

Bacon, S. 1992. 'The relationship between gender, comprehension, processing strategies, and cognitive and affective response in second-language listening'. *The Modern Language Journal* 76: 160–78.

Bacon, S. and **M. Finnemann.** 1992. 'Sex differences in self-reported beliefs about foreign-language learning and authentic oral and written input'. *Language Learning* 42: 471–95.

Baddeley, A. 1986. *Working Memory.* Oxford: Oxford University Press.

Baddeley, A. and **G. Hitch.** 1974. 'Working memory' in G. Bower (ed.): *The Psychology of Learning and Motivation Volume 8.* New York: Academic Press.

Bahns, J. and **H. Wode.** 1980. 'Form and function in L2 acquisition' in S. Felix (ed.). *Second Language Development: Trends and Issues.* Tübingen: Gunter Narr.

Bailey, C. 1973. *Variation and Linguistic Theory.* Washington D.C.: Center for Applied Linguistics.

Bailey, K. 1980. 'An introspective analysis of an individual's language learning experience' in R. Scarcella and S. Krashen (eds.): *Research in Second Language Acquisition.* Rowley, Mass.: Newbury House.

Bailey, K. 1983. 'Competitiveness and anxiety in adult second language learning: looking at and through the diary studies' in H. Seliger and M. Long (eds.): *Classroom-oriented Research in Second Language Acquisition.* Rowley, Mass.: Newbury House.

Bailey, K. 1991. 'Diary studies of classroom language learning: the doubting game and the believing game' in E. Sadtano (ed.). *Language Acquisition and the Second/Foreign Language Classroom.* Singapore: SEAMEO Regional Language Centre.

Bailey, K., M. Long, and **S. Peck** (eds.). 1983. *Second Language Acquisition Studies.* Rowley, Mass.: Newbury House

Bailey, N. 1989. 'Theoretical implications of the acquisition of the English simple past and past progressive: putting together the pieces of the puzzle' in S. Gass, C. Madden, D. Preston, and L. Selinker (eds.). *Variation in Second Language Acquisition Volume II: Psycholinguistic Issues.* Clevedon: Multilingual Matters.

Bailey, N., C. Madden, and **S. Krashen.** 1974. 'Is there a "natural sequence" in adult second language learning?' *Language Learning* 21: 235–43.

Bailey, P., A. Onwuegbuzie, and **C. Daley.** 2000. 'Using learning style to predict foreign language achievement at college level'. *System* 28: 115–34.

Baker, C. 2006. *Foundations of Bilingual Education and Bilingualism* (Fourth edition). Clevedon: Multilingual Matters.

Ball, P., H. Giles, and **M. Hewstone.** 1984. 'The intergroup theory of second language acquisition with catastrophic dimensions' in H. Tajfel (ed.): *The Social Dimension Volume 2.* Cambridge: Cambridge University Press.

Bamgbose, A. 1998. 'Torn between the norms: innovations in world Englishes'. *World Englishes* 17: 1–14.

Banbrook, L. 1987. 'Questions about questions: an inquiry into the study of teachers' questioning behaviour in ESL classrooms'. *TESOL Quarterly* 20: 47–59.

Banbrook, L. and **P. Skehan.** 1990. 'Classroom and display questions' in C. Brumfit and R. Mitchell (eds.): *Research in the Language Classroom. ELT Documents 133*. London: Modern English Publications.

Barcelos, A. 2003. 'Researching beliefs about SLA: a critical review' in P. Kalaja and A. Barcelos (eds.): *Beliefs about SLA: New Research Approaches*. Dordrecht: Kluwer.

Bardovi-Harlig, K. 1987. 'Markedness and salience in second language acquisition'. *Language Learning* 37: 385–407.

Bardovi-Harlig, K. 1992. 'The relationship of form and meaning: a cross-sectional study of tense and aspect in the interlanguage of learners of English as a second language'. *Applied Psycholinguistics* 13: 253–78.

Bardovi-Harlig, K. 1998. 'Narrative structure and lexical aspect: conspiring factors in second language acquisition of tense-aspect morphology'. *Studies in Second Language Acquisition* 20: 471–508.

Bardovi-Harlig, K. 1999a. 'From morpheme studies to temporal semantics: tense-aspect research in SLA'. *Studies in Second Language Acquisition* 21: 341–82.

Bardovi-Harlig, K. 1999b. 'Exploring the interlanguage of interlanguage pragmatics: a research agenda for acquisitional pragmatics'. *Language Learning* 49: 677–713.

Bardovi-Harlig, K. 2000. 'Tense and aspect in second language acquisition: form, meaning and use'. *Language Learning Monograph Series*. Malden, Mass.: Blackwell.

Bardovi-Harlig, K. and **T. Bofman.** 1989. 'Attainment of syntactic and morphological accuracy by advanced language learners'. *Studies in Second Language Acquisition* 11: 17–34.

Bardovi-Harlig, K. and **Z. Dörnyei.** 1998. 'Do language learners recognize pragmatic violations? Pragmatic vs. grammatical awareness in instructed L2 learning'. *TESOL Quarterly* 32: 233–59.

Bardovi-Harlig, K. and **Z. Dörnyei** (eds.). 2006. *Themes in SLA Research AILA 19*. Amsterdam: John Benjamins.

Bardovi-Harlig, K. and **B. Hartford.** 1990. 'Congruence in native and nonnative conversations: status balance in the academic advising session'. *Language Learning* 40: 467–501.

Bardovi-Harlig, K. and **B. Hartford.** 1991. 'Saying "no" in English: native and nonnative rejections' in L. Bouton and Y. Kachru (eds.): *Pragmatics and Language Learning Monograph Series Volume* 2. Urbana-Champaign, Ill.: Division of English as an International Language, University of Illinois.

Bardovi-Harlig, K. and **B. Hartford.** 1993. 'Learning the rules of academic talk: a longitudinal study of pragmatic development'. *Studies in Second Language Acquisition* 15: 279–304.

Bardovi-Harlig, K. and **B. Hartford.** 1996. 'Input in institutional settings'. *Studies in Second Language Acquisition* 18: 171–88.

Bardovi-Harlig, K. and **B. Hartford.** (eds.). 2005a. *Interlanguage Pragmatics: Exploring Institutional Talk*. Mahwah, N.J.: Lawrence Erlbaum.

Bardovi-Harlig, K. and **B. Hartford.** 2005b. 'Institutional discourse and interlanguage pragmatics research' in K. Bardovi-Harlig and B. Hartford (eds.): *Interlanguage Pragmatics: Exploring Institutional Talk*. Mahwah, N.J.: Lawrence Erlbaum.

Bardovi-Harlig, K. and **T. Salsbury.** 2004. 'The organization of turns in the disagreements of L2 learners: a longitudinal perspective' in D. Boxer and A. D. Cohen (eds.): *Studying Speaking to Inform Second Language Learning*. Clevedon: Multilingual Matters.

Barkhuizen, G. 2004. 'Social influences on language learning' in A. Davies and C. Elder (eds.). *The Handbook of Applied Linguistics*. Oxford: Blackwell.

Barlow, M. 2005. 'Computer-based analyses of learner language' in R. Ellis and G. Barkhuizen (eds.): *Analysing Learner Language*. Oxford: Oxford University Press.

Barnes, D. 1969. 'Language in the secondary classroom' in D. Barnes, J. Britton, and M. Torbe (eds.): *Language, the Learner and the School*. Harmondsworth: Penguin.

Barnes, D. 1976. *From Communication to Curriculum*. Harmondsworth: Penguin.

Barnes, D., J. Britton, and **M. Torbe** (eds.). 1969. *Language, the Learner and the School*. Harmondsworth: Penguin.

Barnes, S., M. Gutfreund, D. Satterly, and **G. Wells.** 1983. 'Characteristics of adult speech which predict children's language development'. *Journal of Child Language* 10: 65–84.

Bartelt, G. (ed.). 1994. *The Dynamics of Language Processes: Essays in Honor of Hans W. Dechert.* Tübingen: Gunter Narr.

Bartke, S., F. Rosler, J. Streb, and **R. Wiese.** 2005. 'An ERP-study of German "regular" and "irregular" morphology'. *Journal of Neurolinguistics* 18: 29–55.

Basturkmen, H., S. Loewen, and **R. Ellis.** 2002. 'Metalanguage in focus on form in the communicative classroom'. *Language Awareness* 11: 1–13.

Bates, E. and **B. MacWhinney.** 1982. 'Functionalist approaches to grammar' in E. Wanner and L. Gleitman (eds.). *Language Acquisition: the State of the Art.* New York: Cambridge University Press.

Batstone, R. 2002. 'Contexts of engagement: a discourse perspective on "intake" and "pushed output"'. *System* 30: 1–14.

Batstone, R. 2005. 'Planning as discourse activity' in R. Ellis (ed.): *Planning and Task Performance in a Second Language.* Amsterdam: John Benjamins.

Bayley , R. 1996. 'Competing constraints on variation in the speech of adult Chinese learners of English' in R. Bayley and D. Preston (eds.): *Second Language Acquisition and Linguistic Variation.* Amsterdam: John Benjamins.

Bayley, R. and **D. Preston.** (eds.). 1996. *Second Language Acquisition and Linguistic Variation.* Amsterdam: John Benjamins.

Bayley, R. and **S. Schechter.** (eds.). 2003. *Language Socialization in Bilingual and Multilingual Societies.* Clevedon: Multilingual Matters.

Beck, M. 1997. 'Regular verbs, past tense and frequency: tracking down a potential source of NS/NNS competence differences'. *Second Language Research* 13: 93–115.

Beck, T. 1951. 'An experiment in teaching French by the Oral-Cultural Approach Method'. *The Modern Language Journal* 35: 595–601.

Beebe, L. 1974. 'Socially conditioned variation in Bangkok Thai'. PhD dissertation, University of Michigan, Ann Arbor.

Beebe, L. 1977. 'The influence of the listener on code-switching'. *Language Learning* 27: 331–9.

Beebe, L. 1980. 'Sociolinguistic variation and style-shifting in second language acquisition'. *Language Learning* 30: 433–47.

Beebe, L. 1981. 'Social and situational factors affecting the communicative strategy of dialect code-switching'. *International Journal of Sociology of Language* 32: 139–49.

Beebe, L. 1982. 'Reservations about the Labovian paradigm of style shifting and its extension to the study of interlanguage'. Plenary paper presented at Los Angeles Second Language Research Forum, Los Angeles.

Beebe, L. 1985. 'Input: choosing the right stuff' in S. Gass and C. Madden (eds.): *Input in Second Language Acquisition.* Rowley, Mass.: Newbury House.

Beebe, L. (ed.). 1988. *Issues in Second Language Acquisition: Multiple Perspectives.* New York: Newbury House.

Beebe, L. and **M. Cummings.** 1985. 'Speech act performance: a function of the data collection procedure'. Paper presented at TESOL Convention, New York.

Beebe, L. and **H. Giles.** 1984. 'Speech accommodation theories: a discussion in terms of second language acquisition'. *International Journal of the Sociology of Language* 46: 5–32.

Beebe, L. and **T. Takahashi.** 1989a. 'Do you have a bag? Social status and patterned variation in second language acquisition' in S. Gass, C. Madden, D. Preston, and L. Selinker (eds.): *Variation in Second Language Acquisition Volume I: Sociolinguistic Issues.* Clevedon: Multilingual Matters.

Beebe, L. and **T. Takahashi.** 1989b. 'Sociolinguistic variation in face-threatening speech acts' in M. Eisenstein (ed.): *The Dynamic Interlanguage: Empirical Studies in Second Language Variation.* New York: Plenum Press.

Beebe, L., T. Takahashi, and **R. Uliss-Weltz.** 1990. 'Pragmatic transfer in ESL refusals' in R. Scarcella, E. Andersen, and S. Krashen (eds.): *Developing Communicative Competence.* New York: Newbury House.

Beebe, L. and **J. Zuengler.** 1983. 'Accommodation theory: an explanation for style shifting in second language dialects' in N. Wolfson and E. Judd (eds.): *Sociolinguistics and Second Language Acquisition.* Rowley, Mass.: Newbury House.

Bell, A. 1984. 'Language style as audience design'. *Language in Society* 13: 145–204.

Bell, R. 1974. 'Error analysis: a recent pseudoprocedure in applied linguistics'. *ITL Review of Applied Linguistics* 25–6; 35–9.

Bellack, A., A. Herbert, M. Kliebard, R. Hyman, and **F. Smith.** 1966. *The Language of the Classroom.* New York: Teachers College Press.

Belmechri, F. and **K. Hummel.** 1998. 'Orientations and motivation in the acquisition of English as a second language among high school students in Quebec City'. *Language Learning* 48: 219–44.

Belz, J. and **C. Kinginger.** 2003. 'Discourse options and the development of pragmatic competence by classroom learners of German: the case of address forms'. *Language Learning* 53: 591–657.

Benati, A. 2004. 'The effects of structured input activities and explicit information on the acquisition of Italian future tense' in B. VanPatten (ed.): *Processing Instruction: Theory, Research, and Commentary.* Mahwah, N.J.: Lawrence Erlbaum.

Bennett, S. and **L. Progovac.** 1998. 'Morphological status of reflexives in second language acquisition' in S. Flynn, G. Martohardjono and W. O'Neil (eds.): *The Generative Study of Second Language Acquisition.* Mahwah, N.J.: Lawrence Erlbaum.

Benson, P. and **W. Lor.** 1999. 'Conceptions of language and language learning'. *System* 27: 459–72.

Berdan, R. 1996. 'Disentangling acquisition from language variation' in R. Bayley and D. Preston (eds.): *Second Language Acquisition and Linguistic Variation.* Amsterdam: John Benjamins.

Beretta, A. 1989. 'Attention to form or meaning? Error treatment in the Bangalore Project'. *TESOL Quarterly* 23: 283–303.

Beretta, A. 1991. 'Theory construction in SLA: complementarity and opposition'. *Studies in Second Language Acquisition* 13: 493–511.

Beretta, A. 1993. '"As God said, and I think, rightly ...". Perspectives on theory construction in SLA: an introduction'. *Applied Linguistics* 14: 221–4.

Beretta, A. and **A. Davies.** 1985. 'Evaluation of the Bangalore Project'. *ELT Journal* 39: 121–7.

Berko, J. 1958. 'The child's learning of English morphology'. *Word* 14: 150–77.

Berman, S., J. Choe, and **J. McDonough** (eds.). 1986. *Proceedings of NELS 16.* University of Massachusetts at Amherst: Graduate Linguistics Students Association.

Bernini, G. 2000. 'Negative items and negation strategies in nonnative Italian'. Studies in Second Language Acquisition 22: 399–440.

Berry, D. 1994. 'Implicit and explicit learning of complex tasks' in N. Ellis (ed.): *Implicit and Explicit Learning of Languages.* London: Academic Press.

Berwick, R. 1985. *The Acquisition of Syntactic Knowledge.* Cambridge, Mass.: MIT Press.

Berwick, R. 1990. *Task Variation and Repair in English as a Foreign Language.* Kobe University of Commerce: Institute of Economic Research.

Berwick, R. and **S. Ross.** 1989. 'Motivation after matriculation: are Japanese learners of English still alive after examination hell?'. *JALT* 11: 193–210.

Berwick, R. and **A. Weinberg.** 1984. *The Grammatical Basis of Linguistic Performance: Language Use and Acquisition.* Cambridge, Mass.: MIT Press.

Bever, T. 1981. 'Normal acquisition processes explain the critical period for language learning' in K. Diller (ed.): *Individual Differences and Universals in Language Learning Aptitude.* Rowley, Mass.: Newbury House.

Bhardwaj, M., R. Dietrich, and **C. Noyan.** 1988. *Second Language Acquisition by Adult Immigrants: Temporality. Final Report Volume 5*. Strasbourg: European Science Foundation.

Bialystok, E. 1978. 'A theoretical model of second language learning'. *Language Learning* 28: 69–84.

Bialystok, E. 1979. 'Explicit and implicit judgments of L2 grammaticality'. *Language Learning* 29: 81–104.

Bialystok, E. 1981a. 'The role of linguistic knowledge in second language use'. *Studies in Second Language Acquisition* 4: 31–45.

Bialystok, E. 1981b. 'The role of conscious strategies in second language proficiency'. *The Modern Language Journal* 65: 24–35.

Bialystok, E. 1982. 'On the relationship between knowing and using forms'. *Applied Linguistics* 3: 181–206.

Bialystok, E. 1983a. 'Some factors in the selection and implementation of communication strategies' in C. Færch and G. Kasper (eds.): *Strategies in Interlanguage Communication*. London: Longman.

Bialystok, E. 1983b. 'Inferencing: testing the "hypothesis-testing" hypothesis' in H. Seliger and M. Long (eds.). *Classroom-oriented Research in Second Language Acquisition*. Rowley, Mass.: Newbury House.

Bialystok, E. 1985. 'The compatibility of teaching and learning strategies'. *Applied Linguistics* 6: 155–262.

Bialystok, E. 1990. *Communication Strategies: A Psychological Analysis of Second-Language Use*. Oxford: Basil Blackwell.

Bialystok, E. 1991. 'Achieving proficiency in a second language: a processing description' in R. Phillipson *et al.* (eds.): *Foreign/Second Language Pedagogy Research*. Clevedon: Multilingual Matters.

Bialystok, E. 1994. 'Representation and ways of knowing: three issues in second language acquisition' in N. Ellis (ed.): *Implicit and Explicit Learning of Languages*. London: Academic Press.

Bialystok, E. 1997. 'Why we need grammar: confessions of a cognitive generalist' in L. Eubank, L. Selinker, and M. Sharwood Smith (eds.): *The Current State of Interlanguage*. Amsterdam: John Benjamins.

Bialystok, E., F. Craik, R. Klein, and **M. Viswanathan.** 2004. 'Bilingualism, aging, and cognitive control: evidence from the Simon task'. *Psychology and Aging* 19: 290–303.

Bialystok, E. and **M. Fröhlich.** 1978. 'Variables of classroom achievement in second language learning'. *The Modern Language Journal* 62: 327–36.

Bialystok, E., M. Fröhlich, and **J. Howard.** 1978. *The Teaching and Learning of French as a Second Language in Two Distinct Learning Settings. Project Report*. Toronto: Modern Language Centre, Ontario Institute for Studies in Education.

Bialystok, E. and **K. Hakuta.** 1994. *In Other Words: The Science and Psychology of Second-language Acquisition*. New York: Basic Books.

Bialystok, E. and **K. Hakuta.** 1999. 'Confounded age: linguistic and cognitive factors in age differences for second language acquisition' in D. Birdsong (ed.): *Second Language Acquisition and the Critical Period Hypothesis*. Mahwah, N.J.: Lawrence Erlbaum.

Bialystok, E. and **E. Ryan.** 1985. 'A metacognitive framework for the development of first and second language skills' in D. Forrest-Pressley, G. MacKinnon, and T. Waller (eds.): *Metacognition, Cognition, and Human Performance Volume 1*. New York: Academic Press.

Bialystok, E. and **M. Sharwood Smith.** 1985. 'Interlanguage is not a state of mind: an evaluation of the construct for second language acquisition'. *Applied Linguistics* 6: 101–17.

Biase, B. and **Kawaguchi, S.** 2002. 'Exploring the typological plausibility of processability theory: language development in Italian second language and Japanese second language'. *Second Language Research* 17: 274–302.

Biber, D. 1988. *Variation across Speech and Writing*. Cambridge: Cambridge University Press.

Bickerton, D. 1975. *Dynamics of a Creole System*. Cambridge: Cambridge University Press.

Bickerton, D. 1981. 'Discussion of "Two perspectives on pidginization as second language acquisition"' in R. Andersen (ed.): *New Dimensions in Second Language Acquisition Research*. Rowley, Mass.: Newbury House.

Bickerton, D. and **T. Givón.** 1976. 'Pidginization and syntactic change: from SXV and VSX to SVX' in S. Stever, C. Walker, and S. Mufwene (eds.): *Papers from the Parasession on Diachronic Syntax*. Chicago: Chicago Linguistic Society.

Bigelow, M., R. Delmas, K. Hansen, and **E. Tarone.** 2005. 'Literacy and the processing of oral recasts in SLA'. Paper given at AILA, Madison, Wisconsin, USA.

Billmyer, K. 1990. '"I really like your lifestyle": ESL learners learning how to compliment'. *Penn Working Papers in Educational Linguistics* 6: 31–48.

Bingaman, J. 1990. 'On the English Proficiency Act' in K. Adams and D. Brinks (eds.): *Perspectives on Official English: the Campaign for English as the Official Language of the USA*. Berlin: Mouton de Gruyter.

Birdsong, D. 1989. *Metalinguistic Performance and Interlinguistic Competence*. Berlin: Springer-Verlag.

Birdsong, D. 1992. 'Ultimate attainment in second language acquisition'. *Language* 68: 706–55.

Birdsong, D. 1999a. 'Introduction: Whys and why nots of the Critical Period Hypothesis for second language acquisition' in D. Birdsong (ed.): *Second Language Acquisition and the Critical Period Hypothesis*. Mahwah, N.J.: Lawrence Erlbaum.

Birdsong, D. (ed.). 1999b. *Second Language Acquisition and the Critical Period Hypothesis*. Mahwah, N.J.: Lawrence Erlbaum.

Birdsong, D. 2004. 'Second language acquisition and ultimate attainment' in A. Davies and C. Elder (eds.): *Handbook of Applied Linguistics*. New Malden, Mass.: Blackwell.

Birdsong, D. 2005. 'Interpreting age effects in second language acquisition' in J. Kroll and A. Groot (eds.): *Handbook of Bilingualism: Psycholinguistic Approaches*. New York: Oxford University Press.

Birdsong, D. 2006. 'Age and second language acquisition and processing: a selective overview' in M. Gullberg and P. Indefrey (eds.): *The Cognitive Neuroscience of Second Language Acquisition*. Malden, Mass.: Blackwell.

Birdsong, D. and **J. Flege.** 2001. 'Regular-irregular dissociations in L2 acquisition of English morphology' in *BLCD 25: Proceedings of the 25th Annual Boston University Conference on Language Development*. Boston, Mass.: Cascadilla Press.

Bjorklund, S. 1997. 'Immersion in Finland in the 1990s: a state of development and expansion' in R. Johnson and M. Swain (eds.): *Immersion Education: International Perspectives*. Cambridge: Cambridge University Press.

Blatchford, C. and **J. Schachter** (eds.). 1978. *On TESOL '78: EFL Policies, Programs, Practices*. Washington D.C.: TESOL.

Blau, E. 1982. 'The effect of syntax on readability for ESL students in Puerto Rico'. *TESOL Quarterly* 16: 517–28.

Bley-Vroman, R. 1983. 'The comparative fallacy in interlanguage studies: the case of systematicity'. *Language Learning* 33: 1–17.

Bley-Vroman, R. 1988. 'The fundamental character of foreign language learning' in W. Rutherford and M. Sharwood Smith (eds.): *Grammar and Second Language Teaching: A Book of Readings*. Rowley, Mass.: Newbury House.

Bley-Vroman, R. 1989. 'The logical problem of second language learning' in S. Gass and J. Schachter (eds.): *Linguistic Perspectives on Second Language Acquisition*. Cambridge: Cambridge University Press.

Bley-Vroman, R. and **C. Chaudron.** 1990. 'Second language processing of subordinate clauses and anaphora—first language and universal influences: a review of Flynn's research'. *Language Learning* 40: 245–85.

Bley-Vroman, R., S. Felix, and **G. Ioup.** 1988. 'The accessibility of Universal Grammar in adult language learning'. *Second Language Research* 4: 1–32.

Bley-Vroman, R. and **H. Joo.** 2001. 'Agentive verbs of manner of motion in Spanish and English as second languages'. *Studies in Second Language Acquisition* 23: 207–19.
Bley-Vroman, R. and **Yoshinaga, N.** 1992. 'Broad and narrow constraints on the English dative alternation: some fundamental differences between native speakers and foreign language learners'. *University of Hawai'i Working Papers in ESL* 11: 157–99.
Block, D. 1996. 'Not so fast! Some thoughts on theory culling, relativism, accepted findings and the heart and soul of SLA'. *Applied Linguistics* 17: 65–83.
Block, D. 2003. *The Social Turn in Second Language Acquisition*. Edinburgh: Edinburgh University Press.
Block, D. 2006. *Multilingual Identities in a Global City*. Basingstoke: Palgrave Macmillan.
Block, D. and **D. Cameron** (eds.). 2001. *Language Learning and Teaching in the Age of Globalisation*. London: Routledge.
Blomaert, J. and **J. Verschurren** (eds.). 1991. The *Pragmatics of Intercultural and International Communication*. Amsterdam: John Benjamins.
Bloom, L. 1970. *Language Development: Form and Function in Emerging Grammars*. Cambridge, Mass.: MIT Press.
Bloomfield, L. 1933. *Language*. New York: Holt.
Blum-Kulka, S. 1991. 'Interlanguage pragmatics: the case of requests' in R. Phillipson, E. Kellerman, L. Selinker, M. Sharwood Smith, and M. Swain (eds.): *Foreign/Second Language Pedagogy Research*. Clevedon: Multilingual Matters.
Blum-Kulka, S., J. House, and **G. Kasper.** 1989a. *Cross-cultural Pragmatics: Requests and Apologies*. Norwood, N.J.: Ablex.
Blum-Kulka, S., J. House, and **G. Kasper.** 1989b. 'Investigating cross-cultural pragmatics: An introductory overview' in S. Blum-Kulka, J. House and G. Kasper (eds.): *Cross-cultural Pragmatics: Requests and Apologies*. Norwood, N.J.: Ablex.
Blum-Kulka, S. and **E. Olshtain.** 1984. 'Requests and apologies: a cross-cultural study of speech act realization patterns (CCSARP)' . *Applied Linguistics* 5: 196–213.
Blum-Kulka, S. and **E. Olshtain.** 1986. 'Too many words: length of utterances and pragmatic failure'. *Journal of Pragmatics* 8: 47–61.
Bodman, J. and **M. Eisenstein.** 1988. 'May God increase your bounty: the expression of gratitude in English by native and non-native speakers'. *Cross Currents* 15: 1–21.
Bogaards, P. and **B. Laufer.** 2004a. 'Introduction' in P. Bogaards and B. Laufer (eds.): *Vocabulary in a Second Language*. Amsterdam: John Benjamins.
Bogaards, P. and **B. Laufer.** (eds.). 2004b. *Vocabulary in a Second Language*. Amsterdam: John Benjamins.
Bohn, O. 1986. 'Formulas, frame structures, and stereotypes in early syntactic development: some new evidence from L2 acquisition'. *Linguistics* 24: 185–202.
Bohn, O. and **J. Flege.** 1992. 'The production of new and similar vowels by adult German learners of English'. *Studies in Second Language Acquisition* 14: 131–58.
Bolinger, D. 1975. 'Meaning and memory'. *Forum Linguisticum* 1: 2–14.
Bolton, K. 2004. 'World Englishes' in A. Davies and C. Elder (eds.). *The Handbook of Applied Linguistics*. Oxford: Blackwell.
Bondevik, S. 1996. 'Foreigner talk revisited: when does it really occur and why?' Unpublished MA thesis, University of Tromso, Tromso, Norway.
Bongaerts, T. 1999. 'Ultimate attainment in L2 pronunciation: the case of the very advanced late L2 learners' in D. Birdsong (ed.): *Second Language Acquisition and the Critical Period Hypothesis*. Mahwah, N.J.: Lawrence Erlbaum.
Bongartz, C. and **M. Schneider.** 2003. 'Linguistic development in social context: A study of two brothers learning German'. *The Modern Language Journal* 87: 13–37.
Bonikowska, M. 1988. 'The choice of opting out'. *Applied Linguistics* 9: 169–81.
Borer, L. 2006. 'Depth of processing in private and social speech: Its role in the retention of vocabulary by adult EAP learners'. Paper given at the Joint AAL and ACLA/CAAL Conference, Montreal, Canada.

Borg, S. 1999. 'The use of grammatical terminology in the second language classroom'. *Applied Linguistics* 20: 95–126.

Bourdieu, P. 1977. 'The economics of linguistic exchanges'. *Social Science Information* 16: 645–68.

Bourhis, R. and **H. Giles.** 1977. 'The language of intergroup distinctiveness' in H. Giles (ed.): *Language, Ethnicity and Intergroup Relations*. New York: Academic Press.

Bouton, F. (ed.). 2001. *Pragmatics and Language Learning* (Monograph Series Volume 10). Urbana-Champaign, Ill.: Division of English as an International Language, University of Illinois.

Bouton, L. and **Y. Kachru** (eds.). 1991. *Pragmatics and Language Learning Monograph Series Volume* 2. Urbana-Champaign, Ill.: Division of English as an International Language, University of Illinois.

Bower, G. (ed.). 1974. *The Psychology of Learning and Motivation Volume 8*. New York: Academic Press.

Bowerman, M. 1985. 'What shapes children's grammar?' in D. Slobin (ed.): *The Crosslinguistic Study of Language Acquisition Volume 2, Theoretical Issues.* Hillsdale, N.J.: Lawrence Erlbaum.

Boxer, D. and **A. D. Cohen** (eds.). 2004. *Studying Speaking to Inform Second Language Learning.* Clevedon: Multilingual Matters.

Boyle, J. 1987. 'Sex differences in listening vocabulary'. *Language Learning* 37: 273–84.

Braidi, S. M. 2002. 'Reexamining the role of recasts in native-speaker/nonnative-speaker interactions'. *Language Learning* 52/1: 1–42.

Breen, M. 1985. 'The social context for language learning—a neglected situation?' *Studies in Second Language Acquisition* 7: 135–58.

Breen, M. 1989. 'The evaluation cycle for language learning tasks' in R. K. Johnson (ed.): *The Second Language Curriculum.* Cambridge: Cambridge University Press.

Breen, M. 2001a. 'Postscript: New directions for research on learner contributions' in M. Breen (ed.). *Learner Contributions to Language Learning.* Harlow: Pearson Education.

Breen, M. (ed.). 2001b. *Learner Contributions to Language Learning: New Directions in Research.* Harlow: Pearson Education.

Bremer, K., C. Roberst, M. Vasseur, M. Simonot, and **P. Broeder.** 1996. *Achieving Understanding: Discourse in Intercultural Encounters.* Harlow: Longman.

Briere, E. 1978. 'Variables affecting native Mexican children's learning Spanish as a second language' *Language Learning* 28: 159–74.

Brock, C. 1986. 'The effects of referential questions on ESL classroom discourse'. *TESOL Quarterly* 20: 47–8.

Brodmann, K. 1909. *Vergleichende Lokalisationslehre der Grosshirnrinde in ihren Prinzipien dargestellt auf Grund des Zellenbaues.* Leipzig: J. A. Barth.

Broeders, A. 1982. 'Engels in nederlandse oren: Uitspraakvookeur bij nederlandse studenten engels' in *Toegepaste Taalkunde in Artikeln Volume 9.* Amsterdam: Vu Boekhandel.

Broen, P. 1972. 'The verbal environment of the language learning child'. *American Speech and Hearing Monographs* No. 17.

Broner, M. and **E. Tarone.** 2001. 'Is it fun? Language play in a fifth grade Spanish immersion classroom'. *The Modern Language Journal* 85: 363–79.

Brooks, F. and **R. Donato.** 1994. 'Vygotskyan approaches to understanding foreign language learner discourse during communicative tasks'. *Hispania* 77: 262–74.

Brooks, N. 1960. *Language and Language Learning.* New York: Harcourt Brace and World.

Brown A., J. Bransford, R. Ferrara, and **J. Campione.** 1983. 'Learning, remembering and understanding' in J. Flavell and M. Markman (eds.): *Carmichael's Manual of Child Psychology Volume 3.* New York: Wiley.

Brown, C. 1985. 'Requests for specific language input: differences between older and younger adult language learners' in S. Gass and C. Madden (eds.): *Input in Second Language Acquisition.* Rowley, Mass.: Newbury House.

Brown, H. 1980. 'The optimal distance model of second language acquisition'. *TESOL Quarterly* 14: 157–64.
Brown, H. 1987. *Principles of Language Learning and Teaching* (Second edition). Englewood Cliffs, N.J.: Prentice Hall.
Brown, H., C. Yorio, and **R. Crymes** (eds.). 1977. *On TESOL '77*. Washington D.C.: TESOL.
Brown, J. D. 2001. *Using Surveys in Language Programs.* Cambridge: Cambridge University Press.
Brown, J. D. and **T. Rodgers.** 2002. *Doing Second Language Research.* Oxford: Oxford University Press.
Brown, K. 2000. 'World Englishes and the classroom: research and practice agendas for the year 2000' in E. Thumboo (ed.): *The Three Circles of English.* Singapore: UniPress.
Brown, P. and **S. Levinson.** 1978. 'Universals of language usage: politeness phenomena' in E. Goody (ed.). *Questions and Politeness.* Cambridge: Cambridge University Press.
Brown, R. 1973. *A First Language: the Early Stages.* Cambridge, Mass.: Harvard University Press.
Brown, R. 1977. 'Introduction' in C. Snow and C. Ferguson (eds.): *Talking to Children: Language Input and Acquisition.* Cambridge: Cambridge University Press.
Brown, R. 1987. 'A comparison of the comprehensibility of modified and unmodified reading materials for ESL'. *University of Hawai'i Working Papers in ESL* 6: 49–79.
Brown, R. and **C. Hanlon.** 1970. 'Derivational complexity and order of acquisition in child speech' in J. Hayes (ed.): *Cognition and the Development of Language.* New York: Wiley and Sons.
Brown, T. and **F. Perry.** 1991. 'A comparison of three learning strategies for ESL vocabulary acquisition'. *TESOL Quarterly* 25: 655–70
Brumfit, C. and **R. Mitchell** (eds.). 1990. *Research in the Language Classroom. ELT Documents 133.* Modern English Publications.
Brumfit, C., R. Mitchell, and **J. Hooper.** 1996. 'Grammar', 'language' and 'practice' in M. Hughes (ed.): *Teaching and Learning in Changing Times.* Oxford: Blackwell.
Buck, R. 1984. *The Communication of Emotion.* New York: Guildford Press.
Burmeister, H. and **P. Rounds** (eds.). 1990. *Variability in Second Language Acquisition: Proceedings of the Tenth meeting of the Second Language Acquisition Forum. Volume 1.* Eugene, Oreg.: Department of Linguistics, University of Oregon.
Burmeister, P., T. Piske, and **A. Rohde** (eds.). 2002. *An Integrated View of Language Development: Papers in Honor of Henning Wode.* Trier: Wissenschaftlicher Verlag.
Burstall, C. 1975. 'Factors affecting foreign-language learning: a consideration of some relevant research findings'. *Language Teaching and Linguistics Abstracts* 8: 105–25.
Burt, M. 1975. 'Error analysis in the adult EFL classroom'. *TESOL Quarterly* 9: 53–63.
Burt, M. and **H. Dulay** (eds.). 1975. *On TESOL '75: New Directions in Second Language Learning, Teaching and Bilingual Education.* Washington D.C.: TESOL.
Burt, M., H. Dulay, and **M. Finocchiaro** (eds.). 1977. *Viewpoints on English as a Second Language.* New York: Regents.
Burt, M., H. Dulay, and **E. Hernandez.** 1973. *Bilingual Syntax Measure.* New York: Harcourt Brace Jovanovich.
Burton, P., K. Dyson, and **S. Ardener** (eds.). 1994. *Bilingual Women: Anthropological Approaches to Second Language Use.* Oxford: Berg.
Busch, D. 1982. 'Introversion-extraversion and the EFL proficiency of Japanese students'. *Language Learning* 32: 109–32.
Bush, R., E. Galanter, and **R. Luce** (eds.). 1963. *Handbook of Mathematical Psychology Volume II.* New York: Wiley.
Butterworth, G. and **E. Hatch.** 1978. 'A Spanish-speaking adolescent's acquisition of English syntax' in E. Hatch (ed.): *Second Language Acquisition.* Rowley, Mass.: Newbury House.
Bygate, M. 1988. 'Units of oral expression and language learning in small group interaction'. *Applied Linguistics* 9: 59–82.

Bygate, M. 1996. 'Effects of task repetition: appraising the developing language of learners' in D. Willis and J. Willis (eds.): *Challenge and Change in Language Teaching*. Oxford: Heinemann.

Bygate, M. 1999. 'Task as the context for the framing, re-framing and unframing of language'. *System* 27: 33–48.

Bygate, M. 2001. 'Effects of task repetition on the structure and control of oral language' in M. Bygate, P. Skehan, and M. Swain (eds.): *Researching Pedagogic Tasks, Second Language Learning, Teaching and Testing*. Harlow: Longman.

Bygate, M. and **V. Samuda.** 2005. 'Integrative planning through the use of task-repetition' in R. Ellis (ed.): *Planning and Task Performance in a Second Language*. Amsterdam: John Benjamins.

Bygate, M., P. Skehan, and **M. Swain** (eds.). 2001. *Researching Pedagogic Tasks, Second Language Learning, Teaching and Testing*. Harlow: Longman.

Byrnes, H. (ed.). 2006. *Advanced Language Learning: The Contributions of Halliday and Vygotsky*. London, UK: Continuum.

Cadierno, T. 1995. 'Formal instruction from a processing perspective: an investigation into Spanish past tense'. *The Modern Language Journal* 79: 179–93.

Cairns, H. 1999. 'Common methodological issues in L1 and L2 research' in C. Klein and G. Martohardjono (eds.): *The Development of Second Language Grammars: A Generative Approach*. Amsterdam: John Benjamins.

Caldas, S. and **S. Caron-Caldas.** 2002. 'A sociolinguistic analysis of the language preferences of adolescent bilinguals: shifting allegiances and developing identities'. *Applied Linguistics* 23: 490–514.

Canale, M. 1983. 'From communicative competence to language pedagogy' in J. Richards and R. Schmidt (eds.): *Language and Communication*. London: Longman.

Cancino, H., E. Rosansky, and **J. Schumann.** 1978. 'The acquisition of English negatives and interrogatives by native Spanish speakers' in E. Hatch (ed.): *Second Language Acquisition*. Rowley, Mass.: Newbury House.

Candlin, C. and **N. Mercer** (eds.). 2001. *English Language Teaching in its Social Context*. London: Routledge.

Cao, Y. and **J. Philp.** 2006. 'Interactional context and willingness to communicate: a comparison of behaviour in whole class, group and dyadic interaction'. *System* 34: 480–93.

Carlisle, R. 1991. 'The influence of environment on vowel epenthesis in Spanish/English interphonology'. *Applied Linguistics* 12: 76–95.

Carlisle, R. 1998. 'The acquisition of onsets in a markedness relationship: a longitudinal study'. *Studies in Second Language Acquisition* 20: 245–60.

Carpay, J. 1974. 'Foreign-language teaching and meaningful learning: a Soviet point of view'. *ITL* 25–26: 161–87.

Carr, T. and **T. Curran.** 1994. 'Cognitive factors in learning about structured sequences: applications to syntax'. *Studies in Second Language Acquisition* 16: 205–30.

Carr, W. and **S. Kemmis.** 1986. *Becoming Critical: Education, Knowledge and Action Research*. London: The Falmer Press.

Carrell, P. 1981. 'Relative difficulty of request forms in L1/L2 comprehension' in M. Hines and W. Rutherford (eds.): *On TESOL '81*. Washington D.C.: TESOL.

Carrell, P. and **B. Konnecker.** 1981. 'Politeness: comparing native and nonnative judgments'. *Language Learning* 31: 17–31.

Carrell, P., M. Prince, and **G. Astika.** 1996. 'Personality types and language learning in an EFL context'. *Language Learning* 46: 75–99.

Carroll, J. 1965. 'The prediction of success in foreign language training' in R. Glaser (ed.): *Training, Research, and Education*. New York: Wiley.

Carroll, J. 1967. 'Foreign language proficiency levels attained by language majors near graduation from college'. *Foreign Language Annals* 1: 131–51.

Carroll, J. 1981. 'Twenty-five years in foreign language aptitude' in K. Diller (ed.): *Individual Differences and Universals in Language Learning Aptitude*. Rowley, Mass.: Newbury House.

Carroll, J. 1990. 'Cognitive abilities in foreign language aptitude: then and now' in T. Parry and C. Stansfield (eds.): *Language Aptitude Reconsidered*. Englewood Cliffs, N.J.: Prentice Hall.

Carroll, J. and **S. Sapon.** 1959. *Modern Language Aptitude Test—Form A*. New York: The Psychological Corporation.

Carroll, S. 1997. 'The irrelevance of verbal feedback to language learning' in L. Eubank, L. Selinker and M. Sharwood Smith (eds.): *The Current State of Interlanguage*. Amsterdam: John Benjamins.

Carroll, S. 1999. 'Input and SLA: adults' sensitivity to different sorts of cues to French gender'. *Language Learning* 49: 37–92.

Carroll, S. 2001. *Input and Evidence: The Raw Material of Second Language Acquisition*. Amsterdam: John Benjamins.

Carroll, S. and **M. Swain.** 1993. 'Explicit and implicit negative feedback: an empirical study of the learning of linguistic generalizations'. *Studies in Second Language Acquisition* 15: 357–86.

Carson, J. and **A. Longhini.** 2002. 'Focusing on learning styles and strategies: a diary study in an immersion setting'. *Language Learning* 52: 401–38.

Carter, C., T. Braver, D. Barch, M. Botvinick, D. Noll, and **J. Cohen.** 1998. 'Anterior cingulate cortex, error detection, and the online monitoring of performance'. *Science* 280: 747–9.

Carter, E. 1988. 'The relationship of field dependent/independent cognitive style to Spanish language achievement and proficiency: a preliminary report'. *The Modern Language Journal* 72: 21–30.

Carter, R. and **M. McCarthy.** 1995. 'Grammar and the spoken language'. *Applied Linguistics* 16/2: 141–58.

Carton, A. 1971. 'Inferencing: a process in using and learning language' in P. Pimsleur and T. Quinn (eds.): *The Psychology of Second Language Learning*. Cambridge: Cambridge University Press.

Cathcart, R. 1986. 'Situational differences and the sampling of young children's school language' in R. Day (ed.): *Talking to Learn: Conversation in Second Language Acquisition*. Rowley, Mass.: Newbury House.

Cathcart, R. and **J. Olsen.** 1976. 'Teachers' and students' preferences for correction of classroom errors' in J. Fanselow and R. Crymes (eds.): *On TESOL '76*. Washington D.C.: TESOL.

Cazden, C. 1972. *Child Language and Education*. New York: Holt, Rinehart, and Winston.

Cazden, C., E. Cancino, E. Rosansky, and **J. Schumann.** 1975. *Second Language Acquisition in Children, Adolescents and Adults. Final Report*. Washington D.C.: National Institute of Education.

Cazden, C., V. John, and **D. Hymes** (eds.). 1972. *Functions of Language in the Classroom*. New York: Teachers' College Press.

Cenoz, J. 2001. 'The effect of linguistic distance, L2 status and age on crosslinguistic influence in third language acquisition' in J. Cenoz, B. Hufheisen, and U. Jessner (eds.). *Cross-linguistic Influence in Third Language Acquisition: Psycholinguistic Perspectives*. Clevedon: Multilingual Matters.

Cenoz, J., B. Hufheisen, and **U. Jessner** (eds.). 2001. *Cross-linguistic Influence in Third Language Acquisition: Psycholinguistic Perspectives*. Clevedon: Multilingual Matters.

Centano-Cortes, B. and **A. Jimenez-Jimenez.** 2004. 'Problem-solving tasks in a foreign language: the importance of the L1 in private verbal thinking'. *International Journal of Applied Linguistics* 14: 7–35.

Chalhoub-Deville, M., C. Chapelle, and **P. Duff** (eds.). 2005. *Inference and Generalizability in Applied Linguistics: Multiple Perspective*. Amsterdam: John Benjamins.

Chambers, J. and **P. Trudgill.** 1980. *Dialectology*. Cambridge: Cambridge University Press.

Chamot, A. 1978. 'Grammatical problems in learning English as a third language' in E. Hatch (ed.): *Second Language Acquisition*. Rowley, Mass.: Newbury House.

Chamot, A. 1979. 'Strategies in the acquisition of English structures by a child bilingual in Spanish and French' in R. Andersen (ed.): *The Acquisition and Use of Spanish and English as First and Second Languages*. Washington D.C.: TESOL.

Chamot, A. 1987. 'The learning strategies of ESL students' in A. Wenden and J. Rubin (eds.). *Learner Strategies in Language Learning*. Englewood Cliffs, N.J.: Prentice Hall.

Chamot, A. 2001. 'The role of learning strategies in second language acquisition' in M. Breen (ed.): *Learner Contributions to Language Learning: New Directions in Research*. Harlow: Longman.

Chamot, A., S. Barnhardt, P. El-Dinary, and **J. Robbins.** 1999. *The Learning Strategies Handbook*. White Plains, N.Y.: Addison Wesley Longman.

Chamot, A., L. Kupper, and **M. Impink-Hernandez.** 1988. *A Study of Learning Strategies in Foreign Language Instruction: Findings of the Longitudinal Study.* McLean, Va.: Interstate Research Associates.

Chamot, A., J. O'Malley, L. Kupper, and **M. Impink-Hernandez.** 1987. *A Study of Learning Strategies in Foreign Language Instruction: First Year Report*. Rosslyn, Va.: Interstate Research Associates.

Chapelle, C. and **P. Green.** 1992. 'Field independence/dependence in second language acquisition research'. *Language Learning* 42: 47–83.

Chapelle, C. and **C. Roberts.** 1986. 'Ambiguity tolerance and field independence as predictors of proficiency in English as a second language'. *Language Learning* 36: 27–45.

Chastain, K. 1975. 'Affective and ability factors in second language acquisition'. *Language Learning* 25: 153–61.

Chastain, K. 1981. 'Native-speaker evaluation of student composition errors'. *The Modern Language Journal* 65: 288–94.

Chaudron, C. 1977. 'A descriptive model of discourse in the corrective treatment of learners' errors'. *Language Learning* 27: 29–46.

Chaudron, C. 1983. 'Foreigner talk in the classroom—an aid to learning?' in H. Seliger and M. Long (eds.): *Classroom-oriented Research in Second Language Acquisition*. Rowley, Mass.: Newbury House.

Chaudron, C. 1988. *Second Language Classrooms: Research on Teaching and Learning*. Cambridge: Cambridge University Press.

Chaudron, C. 2001. 'Progress in language classroom research: evidence from *The Modern Language Journal*, 1916–2000'. *The Modern Language Journal* 85: 57–76.

Chaudron, C. and **J. Richards.** 1986. 'The effect of discourse markers on the comprehension of lectures'. *Applied Linguistics* 7: 113–27.

Chee, M., E. Tan, and **T. Thiel.** 1999. 'Mandarin and English single word processing studies with functional magnetic resonance imaging'. *The Journal of Neuroscience* 19: 3050–6.

Cheng, Y., E. Horwitz, and **D. Schallert.** 1999. 'Language anxiety: Differentiating writing and speaking components'. *Language Learning* 49: 417–46.

Chenoweth, N., R. Day, A. Chun, and **S. Luppescu.** 1983. 'Attitudes and preferences of nonnative speakers to corrective feedback'. *Studies in Second Language Acquisition* 6: 79–87.

Chiang, D. 1980. 'Predictors of relative clause production' in R. Scarcella and S. Krashen (eds.): *Research in Second Language Acquisition*. Rowley, Mass.: Newbury House.

Chick, K. 1985. 'The interactional accomplishment of discrimination in South Africa'. *Language in Society* 14: 299–326.

Chihara, T. and **J. Oller.** 1978. 'Attitudes and attained proficiency in EFL: a sociolinguistic study of adult Japanese speakers'. *Language Learning* 28: 55–68.

Chomsky, C. 1969. *The Acquisition of Syntax in Children from 5 to 10*. Cambridge, Mass.: MIT Press.

Chomsky, N. 1957. *Syntactic Structures*. The Hague: Mouton.

Chomsky, N. 1959. 'Review of *Verbal Behavior* by B. F. Skinner'. *Language* 35: 26–58.
Chomsky, N. 1965. *Aspects of the Theory of Syntax*. Cambridge, Mass.: MIT Press.
Chomsky, N. 1976. *Reflections on Language*. London: Temple Smith.
Chomsky, N. 1980. *Rules and Representations*. New York: Columbia University Press.
Chomsky, N. 1981a. 'Principles and parameters in syntactic theory' in N. Hornstein and D. Lightfoot (eds.): *Explanation in Linguistics: the Logical Problem of Language Acquisition*. London: Longman.
Chomsky, N. 1981b. *Lectures on Government and Binding*. Dordrecht: Foris.
Chomsky, N. 1986. *Barriers*. Cambridge, Mass.: MIT Press.
Chomsky, N. 1988. *Language and Problems of Knowledge: the Nicaraguan Lectures*. Cambridge, Mass.: MIT Press.
Chomsky, N. 1995. *The Minimalist Program*. Cambridge, Mass.: MIT Press.
Christie, K. and **J. Lantolf.** 1998. 'Bind me up and bind me down: reflexives in L2' in S. Flynn, G. Martohardjono and W. O'Neil (eds.): *The Generative Study of Second Language Acquisition*. Mahwah, N.J.: Lawrence Erlbaum.
Chun, A., R. Day, A. Chenoweth, and **S. Luppescu.** 1982. 'Errors, interaction, and correction: a study of non-native conversations'. *TESOL Quarterly* 16: 537–47.
Clahsen, H. 1980. 'Psycholinguistic aspects of L2 acquisition' in S. Felix (ed.): *Second Language Development: Trends and Issues*. Tübingen: Gunter Narr.
Clahsen, H. 1982. *Spracherwerb in der Kindheit: eine Untersuchung zur Entwicklung der Syntax bei Kleinkindern*. Tübingen: Gunter Narr.
Clahsen, H. 1984. 'The acquisition of German word order: a test case for cognitive approaches to L2 development' in R. Andersen (ed.): *Second Language: a Crosslinguistic Perspective*. Rowley, Mass.: Newbury House.
Clahsen, H. 1988. 'Critical phases of grammar development: a study of the acquisition of negation in children and adults' in P. Jordens and J. Lalleman (eds.): *Language Development*. Dordrecht: Foris.
Clahsen, H. 1990. 'The comparative study of first and second language development'. *Studies in Second Language Acquisition* 12: 135–54.
Clahsen, H., J. Meisel, and **M. Pienemann.** 1983. *Deutsch als Zweitsprache: der Spracherwerb auslandischer Arbeiter*. Gunter Narr: Tübingen.
Clahsen, H. and **P. Muysken.** 1986. 'The availability of universal grammar to adult and child learners—the study of the acquisition of German word order'. *Second Language Research* 2: 93–119.
Clapham, C. and **D. Corson** (eds.). 1997. *Encyclopedia of Language and Education, Volume 7: Language Testing and Assessment*. Dordrecht: Kluwer Academic.
Clark, H. and **E. Clark.** 1977. *Psychology and Language: an Introduction to Psycholinguistics*. New York: Harcourt Brace Jovanovich.
Clark J. 1969. 'The Pennsylvania Project and the "Audio-Lingual vs. Traditional" question'. *The Modern Language Journal* 53: 388–96.
Clark, R. 1974. 'Performing without competence'. *Journal of Child Language* 1: 1–10.
Clarke, M. 1994. 'The dysfunctions of theory/practice discourse'. *TESOL Quarterly* 28: 9–26.
Clarke, M. and **J. Handscombe** (eds.). 1983. *On TESOL '82*. Washington D.C.: TESOL.
Claude, S. and **W. Weaver.** 1949. *The Mathematical Theory of Communication*. Urbana, Ill.: University of Illinois Press.
Clement, R. 1980. 'Ethnicity, contact and communicative competence in a second language' in H. Giles, W. Robinson, and P. Smith (eds.): *Language: Social Psychological Perspectives*. Oxford: Pergamon Press.
Clement, R. 1986. 'Second language proficiency and acculturation: an investigation of the effects of language status and individual characteristics'. *Journal of Language and Social Psychology* 5: 271–90.
Clement, R., Z. Dörnyei, and **K. Noels.** 1994. 'Motivation, self-confidence and group cohesion in the foreign language classroom' *Language Learning* 44: 417–48.

Clement, R. and **B. Kruidenier.** 1983. 'Orientations in second language acquisition: 1. The effects of ethnicity, milieu and target language on their emergence'. *Language Learning* 33: 273–91.

Clement, R. and **B. Kruidenier.** 1985. 'Aptitude, attitude and motivation in second language proficiency: a test of Clement's model'. *Journal of Language and Social Psychology* 4: 21–38.

Clement, R., P. Smythe, and **R. Gardner.** 1978. 'Persistence in second language study: motivational considerations'. *Canadian Modern Language Review* 34: 688–94.

Clyne, M. 1978. 'Some remarks on foreigner talk' in N. Dittmar, H. Haberland, T. Skuttnab-Kangas, and U. Telman (eds.): *Papers from the First Scandinavian-German Symposium on the Language of Immigrant Workers and their Children.* Linguistgruppen, Roskilde Universiteits Center.

Coan, R. and **R. Catell.** 1966. *Early School Personality Questionnaire.* Champaign, Ill.: Institute for Personality and Ability Testing.

Cochrane, R. 1980. 'The acquisition of /r/and /l/ by Japanese children and adults learning English as a second language'. *Journal of Multilingual and Multicultural Development* 1: 331–60.

Cohen, A. 1982. 'Writing like a native: the process of reformulation'. *ERIC ED* 224–338.

Cohen, A. 1984. 'Studying second-language learning strategies: how do we get the information?' *Applied Linguistics* 5: 101–12. Also in A. Wenden and J. Rubin (eds.). 1987. *Learner Strategies in Language Learning.* Englewood Cliffs, N.J.: Prentice Hall.

Cohen, A. 1987. 'Using verbal reports in research on language learning' in C. Færch and G. Kasper (eds.). *Introspection in Second Language Research.* Clevedon: Multilingual Matters.

Cohen, A. 1990. *Language Learning: Insights for Learners, Teachers, and Researchers.* New York: Newbury House/Harper Row.

Cohen, A. 1997. 'Developing pragmatic ability' in H. Cook, K. Hijirada, and M. Tahara (eds.): *New Trends and Issues in Teaching Japanese Language and Culture Technical Report No. 15.* Honolulu: University of Hawai'i, Second Language Teaching and Curriculum Center.

Cohen, A. (ed.). 1998. *Strategies in Learning and Using a Second Language.* London: Longman.

Cohen, A. 2002. 'Preparing teachers for styles and strategies-based instruction' in V. Crew, C. Davison, and B. Mak (eds.): *Reflecting on Language in Education.* Hong Kong: Hong Kong Institute of Education.

Cohen, A. and **E. Aphek.** 1980. 'Retention of second language vocabulary over time: investigating the role of mnemonic associations'. *System* 8: 221–35.

Cohen, A. D. and **J. C. Chi.** 2001. 'Language strategy use survey'. Minneapolis, Minn.: Center for Advanced Research on Language Acquisition, University of Minnesota. Downloadable from the CARLA website: http://www.carla.umn.edu/about/profiles/Cohen.

Cohen, A. D. and **E. Macaro** (eds.). 2008. *Language Learner Strategies: Thirty Years of Research and Practice.* Oxford: Oxford University Press.

Cohen, A. and **E. Olshtain.** 1981. 'Developing a measure of sociocultural competence; the case of apology'. *Language Learning* 31: 113–34.

Cohen, A., R. Oxford, and **C. Chi.** 2001. 'Learning style survey'. Online: http://carla.acad.umn.edu/profiles/Cohen-profiloe.html.

Cohen, A. and **M. Swain.** 1979. 'Bilingual education: the "immersion" model in the North American context' in J. Pride (ed.): *Sociolinguistic Aspects of Language Learning and Teaching.* Oxford: Oxford University Press.

Cohen, A., S. Weaver, and **T. Li.** 1998. 'The impact of strategies-based instruction on speaking a foreign language' in A. Cohen (ed.): *Strategies in Learning and Using a Second Language.* London: Longman.

Cohen, J. 1992. 'A power primer'. *Psychological Bulletin* 112/1: 155–59.

Cole, P. and **J. Morgan** (eds.). 1975. *Syntax and Semantics 3: Speech Acts.* New York: Academic Press.

Collentine, J. and **B. Freed.** 2004. 'Learner context and its effects on second language acquisition'. *Studies in Second Language Acquisition* 26: 153–72.

Collier, V. 1992. 'The Canadian bilingual immersion debate: a synthesis of research findings'. *Studies in Second Language Acquisition* 14: 87–97.

Collins, L. 2002. 'The roles of L1 influence and lexical aspect in the acquisition of temporal morphology'. *Language Learning* 52: 43–94.

Comrie, B. 1984. *Language Universals and Linguistic Typology.* Oxford: Basil Blackwell.

Comrie, B. 2003. 'Typology and language acquisition: the case of relative clauses' in A. Ramat (ed.): *Typology and Second Language Acquisition.* Berlin: Mouton de Gruyter.

Comrie, B. and **E. Keenan.** 1979. 'Noun phrase accessibility revisited'. *Language* 55: 649–64.

Conrad, L. 1989. 'The effects of time-compressed speech on native and EFL listening comprehension'. *Studies in Second Language Acquisition* 11: 1–16.

Consolo, A. 2000. 'Teachers' action and student oral participation in classroom interaction' in J. Hall and L. Verplaetse (eds.): *Second and Foreign Language Learning Through Classroom Interaction.* Mahwah, N.J.: Lawrence Erlbaum.

Cook, G. 2000. *Language Play, Language Learning.* Oxford: Oxford University Press.

Cook, G. and **B. Seidlhofer** (eds.). 1995. *Principle and Practice in Applied Linguistics: Studies in Honour of H. G. Widdowson.* Oxford: Oxford University Press.

Cook, H., K. Hijirada, and **M. Tahara** (eds.). 1997. *New Trends and Issues in Teaching Japanese Language and Culture Technical Report No. 15.* Honolulu: University of Hawai'i, Second Language Teaching and Curriculum Center.

Cook, V. 1971. 'The analogy between first and second language learning' in R. Lugton (ed.): *Toward a Cognitive Approach to Second Language Acquisition.* Philadelphia, Penn.: Center for Curriculum Development.

Cook, V. 1973. 'The comparison of language development in native children and foreign adults'. *International Review of Applied Linguistics* 11: 13–28.

Cook, V. 1977. 'Cognitive processes in second language learning'. *International Review of Applied Linguistics* 15: 1–20.

Cook, V. 1985. 'Chomsky's universal grammar and second language learning'. *Applied Linguistics* 6: 2–18.

Cook, V. (ed.). 1986. *Experimental Approaches to Second Language Acquisition.* Oxford: Pergamon.

Cook, V. 1988. *Chomsky's Universal Grammar: An Introduction.* Oxford: Basil Blackwell.

Cook, V. 1989. 'Universal grammar theory and the classroom'. *System* 17: 169–82.

Cook, V. 1999. 'Going beyond the native speaker in language teaching'. *TESOL Quarterly* 33/2: 185–209

Cook, V. 2001. 'Using the first language in the classroom'. *Canadian Modern Language Review* 57: 402–23.

Cook, V. (ed.). 2002. *Portraits of the L2 User.* Clevedon: Multilingual Matters.

Cook, V. (ed.). 2003. *Effects of the Second Language on the First.* Clevedon: Multilingual Matters.

Coppetiers, R. 1987. 'Competence differences between native and near-native speakers'. *Language* 63: 544–73.

Corder, S. P. 1967. 'The significance of learners' errors'. *International Review of Applied Linguistics* 5: 161–9.

Corder, S. P. 1971a. 'Idiosyncractic dialects and error analysis'. *International Review of Applied Linguistics* 9: 149–59.

Corder, S. P. 1971b. 'Describing the language learner's language'. *CILT Reports and Papers* No. 6. CILT.

Corder, S. P. 1973. 'The elicitation of interlanguage' in J. Svartvik (ed.): *Errata: Papers in Error Analysis.* Lund, Sweden: CWK Gleerup.

Corder, S. P. 1974. 'Error analysis' in J. P. Allen and S. P. Corder (eds.). *The Edinburgh Course in Applied Linguistics Volume 3*. London: Oxford University Press.
Corder, S. P. 1976. 'The study of interlanguage' in *Proceedings of the Fourth International Conference of Applied Linguistics*. Munich, Hochschulverlag. Also in Corder 1981.
Corder, S. P. 1977a. 'Language teaching and learning: a social encounter' in H. Brown, C. Yorio, and R. Crymes (eds.): *On TESOL '77*. Washington D.C.: TESOL.
Corder, S. P. 1977b. '"Simple codes" and the source of the learner's initial heuristic hypothesis'. *Studies in Second Language Acquisition* 1: 1–10.
Corder, S. P. 1978a. 'Language distance and the magnitude of the learning task'. *Studies in Second Language Acquisition* 2: 27–36.
Corder, S. P. 1978b. 'Strategies of communication'. *AFinLa* 23. Also in Corder 1981. *Error Analysis and Interlanguage*. Oxford: Oxford University Press.
Corder, S. P. 1980. 'Second language acquisition research and the teaching of grammar'. *BAAL Newsletter* 10.
Corder, S. P. 1981. *Error Analysis and Interlanguage*. Oxford: Oxford University Press.
Corder, S. P. 1983. 'A role for the mother tongue' in S. Gass and L. Selinker (eds.): *Language Transfer in Language Learning*. Rowley, Mass.: Newbury House.
Corsaro, W. and **P. Miller** (eds.). 1992. *New Directions for Child Development Volume 58*. San Francisco: Jossey Bass.
Coughlan, P. and **P. A. Duff.** 1994. 'Same task, different activities: analysis of a SLA task from an activity theory perspective' in J. Lantolf and G. Appel. (eds.): *Vygotskian Approaches to Second Language Research*. Norwood, N.J.: Ablex.
Coulmas, F. 1981. *Conversational Routines: Explorations in Standardized Communication Situations and Prepatterned Speech*. The Hague: Mouton.
Coulmas, F. (ed.). 1997. *The Handbook of Sociolinguistics*. Oxford: Blackwell.
Council of Europe. 2001. *The Common European Framework of Reference for Languages*. Cambridge: Cambridge University Press.
Coupland, N. 2001. 'Introduction: Sociolinguistic theory and social theory' in N. Coupland, S. Sarangi, and C. Candlin (eds.): *Sociolinguistic and Social Theory*. Harlow: Pearson Education.
Coupland, N., H. Giles, and **J. Wiemann** (eds.). 1991. *Miscommunication and Problematic Talk*. Newbury Park: Sage Publications.
Coupland, N., S. Sarangi, and **C. Candlin** (eds.). 2001. *Sociolinguistic and Social Theory*. Harlow: Pearson Education.
Courchene, R., J. Glidden, J. St. John, and **C. Therien** (eds.). 1992. *Comprehension-based Second Language Teaching*. Ottowa: University of Ottawa Press.
Craik, F. and **R. Lockhart.** 1972. 'Levels of processing: a framework for memory research'. *Journal of Verbal Learning and Verbal Behavior* 11: 671–84.
Craik, F. and **T. Salthouse** (eds.). 2005. *The Handbook of Aging and Cognition* (Second edition). Mahwah, N.J.: Lawrence Erlbaum.
Crew, V., C. Davison and **B. Mak** (eds.). 2002. *Reflecting on Language in Education*. Hong Kong: Hong Kong Institute of Education.
Croft, W. 1990. *Typology and Universals*. Cambridge: Cambridge University Press.
Cronbach, L. and **R. Snow.** 1977. *Aptitudes and Instructional Methods*. New York: Irvington.
Crookes, G. 1989. 'Planning and interlanguage variability'. *Studies in Second Language Acquisition* 11: 367–83.
Crookes, G. 1991. 'Second language speech production research: a methodologically oriented review'. *Studies in Second Language Acquisition* 13: 113–32.
Crookes, G. 1992. 'Theory format and SLA theory'. *Studies in Second Language Acquisition* 14: 425–49.
Crookes, G. 1993. 'Action research for SL teachers—going beyond teacher research'. *Applied Linguistics* 14: 130–44.

Crookes, G. 1997. 'SLA and language pedagogy: a socioeducational perspective'. *Studies in Second Language Acquisition* 19: 93–116.

Crookes, G. and **S. Gass** (eds.). 1993. *Tasks and Language Learning: Integrating Theory and Practice.* Clevedon: Multilingual Matters.

Crookes, G. and **K. Rulon.** 1985. *Incorporation of Corrective Feedback in Native Speaker/Non-native Speaker Conversation. Technical Report No. 3.* Honolulu: Center for Second Language Classroom Research, Social Science Research Institute, University of Hawai'i.

Crookes, G. and **R. Schmidt.** 1991. 'Language learning motivation: reopening the research agenda'. *Language Learning* 41: 469–512.

Cross, T. 1977. 'Mothers' speech adjustments: the contribution of selected child listener variables' in C. Snow and C. Ferguson (eds.): *Talking to Children: Language Input and Acquisition.* Cambridge: Cambridge University Press.

Cross, T. 1978. 'Mothers' speech and its association with rate of linguistic development in young children' in N. Waterson and C. Snow (eds.): *The Development of Communication.* Wiley: New York.

Crowell, S. 2004. 'The neurobiology of declarative memory' in J. Schumann *et al.* (eds.): *The Neurobiology of Learning: Perspectives from Second Language Acquisition.* Mahwah, N.J.: Lawrence Erlbaum.

Crystal, D. 1976. *Child Language Learning and Linguistics: An Overview for the Teaching and Therapeutic Professions.* London: Edward Arnold.

Crystal, D. 1997. *English as a Global Language* . Cambridge: Cambridge University Press.

Csizer, K. and **Z. Dörnyei.** 2005a. 'The internal structure of language learning motivation and its relationship with language choice and learning effort'. *The Modern Language Journal* 89: 19–36.

Csizer, K. and **Z. Dörnyei.** 2005b. 'Language learners' motivational profiles and their motivated learning behaviour'. *Language Learning* 55: 613–59.

Cullen, R. 1998. 'Teacher-talk and the classroom context'. *ELT Journal* 52: 179–87.

Cumming, A. 1989. 'Writing expertise and second-language proficiency'. *Language Learning* 39: 81–141.

Cummins, J. 1981. *Bilingualism and Minority Children.* Ontario: Ontario Institute for Studies in Education.

Cummins, J. 1983. 'Language proficiency and academic achievement' in J. Oller (ed.): *Issues in Language Testing Research.* Rowley, Mass.: Newbury House.

Cummins, J. 1988. 'Second language acquisition within bilingual education programs' in L. Beebe (ed.): *Issues in Second Language Acquisition: Multiple Perspectives.* New York: Newbury House.

Cummins, J. 1992. 'Heritage language teaching in Canadian schools'. *Journal of Curriculum Studies* 24: 281–6.

Cummins, J., B. Harley, M. Swain, and **J. P. Allen.** 1990. 'Social and individual factors in the development of bilingual proficiency' in Harley *et al.* (eds.): *The Development of Second Language Proficiency.* Cambridge: Cambridge University Press.

Cummins, J. and **K. Nakajima.** 1987. 'Age of arrival, length of residence, and interdependence of literacy skills among Japanese immigrant students' in B. Harley, J. P. Allen, J. Cummins and M. Swain (eds.): *The Development of Bilingual Proficiency: Final Report. Volume III: Social Context and Age.* Toronto: Modern Language Centre, Ontario Institute for Studies in Education.

Curtiss, S. (ed.). 1977. *Genie: Psycholinguistic Study of a Modern-day 'Wild Child'.* London: Academic Press.

Dagut, M. and **B. Laufer.** 1985. 'Avoidance of phrasal verbs—a case for contrastive analysis'. *Studies in Second Language Acquisition* 7: 73–9.

Dahl, D. 1981. 'The role of experience in speech modifications for second language learners'. *Minnesota Papers in Linguistics and Philosophy of Language* 7: 78–93.

Dahl, O. 1979. 'Typology of sentence negation'. *Linguistics* 17: 79–106.

Damasio, A. 1995. 'Toward a neurobiology of emotion and feeling: operational concepts and hypotheses'. *Neuroscientist* 1: 19–25.

d'Anglejan, A. 1978. 'Language learning in and out of classrooms' in J. Richards (ed.): *Understanding Second and Foreign Language Learning: Issues and Approaches*. Rowley, Mass.: Newbury House.

d'Anglejan, A., G. Painchaud, and **C. Renaud.** 1986. 'Beyond the classroom: a study of communicative abilities in adult immigrants following intensive instruction'. *TESOL Quarterly* 20: 185–205.

d'Anglejan, A. and **C. Renaud.** 1985. 'Learner characteristics and second language acquisition: a multivariate study of adult immigrants and some thoughts on methodology'. *Language Learning* 35: 1–19.

Daniel, I. 1983. 'On first-year German foreign language learning: a comparison of language behavior in response to two instructional methods'. Unpublished PhD dissertation, University of Southern California.

Danoff, M., G. Coles, D. McLaughlin, and **D. Reynolds.** 1978. *Evaluation of the Impact of ESEA Title VII Spanish/English Bilingual Education Program: Overview of Study and Findings*. Palo Alto, Calif.: American Institutes for Research.

Das, B. (ed.). 1987. *Patterns of Classroom Interaction*. Singapore: SEAMEO Regional Language Centre.

Davies, A. 1989. 'Is international English an interlanguage?' *TESOL Quarterly* 23: 447–67.

Davies, A., C. Criper, and **A. Howatt** (eds.). 1984. *Interlanguage*. Edinburgh: Edinburgh University Press.

Davies, A. and **C. Elder.** (eds.). 2004. *The Handbook of Applied Linguistics*. Oxford: Blackwell.

Davies, E. 1983. 'Error evaluation: the importance of viewpoint'. *ELT Journal* 37: 304–11.

Davies, W. and **T. Kaplan.** 1998. 'Native speaker vs. L2 learner grammaticality judgments'. *Applied Linguistics* 19: 183–203.

Day, E. and **S. Shapson.** 1991. 'Integrating formal and functional approaches to language teaching in French immersion: an experimental study'. *Language Learning* 41: 25–58.

Day, R. 1984. 'Student participation in the ESL classroom, or some imperfections of practice'. *Language Learning* 34: 69–102.

Day, R. 1985. 'The use of the target language in context and second language proficiency' in S. Gass and C. Madden (eds.): *Input in Second Language Acquisition*. Rowley, Mass.: Newbury House.

Day, R. (ed.). 1986. *Talking to Learn: Conversation in Second Language Acquisition*. Rowley, Mass.: Newbury House.

Day, R., N. Chenoweth, A. Chun, and **S. Leppescu.** 1984. 'Corrective feedback in native-nonnative discourse'. *Language Learning* 34: 19–45.

De Angelis, J. 2005. 'Interlanguage transfer of function words'. *Language Learning* 55: 379–414.

De Beaugrande, R. and **W. Dressler.** 1981. *Introduction to Text Linguistics*. London: Longman.

De Bot, K. 1992. 'A bilingual production model: Levelt's "Speaking" model adapted'. *Applied Linguistics* 13: 1–24.

De Bot, K., R. Ginsberg, and **C. Kramsch** (eds.). 1991. *Foreign Language Research in Cross-cultural Perspective*. Amsterdam: John Benjamin.

De Jong, J. and **D. Stevenson** (eds.). 1990. *Individualizing the Assessment of Language Abilities*. Clevedon: Multilingual Matters.

De la Fuente, M. 2002. 'Negotiation and oral acquisition of L2 vocabulary: the roles of input and output in the receptive and productive acquisition of words'. *Studies in Second Language Acquisition* 24: 81–112.

De Villiers, J. and **P. de Villiers.** 1973. 'A cross-sectional study of the development of grammatical morphemes in child speech'. *Journal of Psycholinguistic Research* 1: 299–310.

Decamp, D. 1971. 'Implicational scales and sociolinguistic theory'. *Linguistics* 17: 79–106.

DeCapua, A. and **A. Wintergerst.** 2005. 'Assessing and validating a learning styles instrument'. *System* 33: 1–16.

Dechert, H. 1983. 'How a story is done in a second language' in C. Færch and G. Kasper (eds.). *Strategies in Interlanguage Communication*. London: Longman.

Dechert, H. 1984. 'Individual variation in language' in H. Dechert, D. Möhle and M. Raupach (eds.): *Second Language Productions*. Tübingen: Gunter Narr.

Dechert, H. (ed.). 1990. *Current Trends in European Second Language Acquisition Research*. Clevedon: Multilingual Matters.

Dechert, H., D. Möhle, and **M. Raupach** (eds.). 1984. *Second Language Productions*. Tübingen: Gunter Narr.

Dechert, H. and **M. Raupach** (eds.). 1989. *Interlingual Processes*. Tübingen: Gunter Narr.

Dehaene, S. 1999. 'Fitting two languages into one brain'. *Brain* 122: 2207–08.

Dehaene, S., E. Dupoux, J. Mehler, L. Cohen, E. Oaulesu, D. Pernai, P. van de Moortele, S. Lehericy, and **D. Le Bihan.** 1997. 'Anatomical variability in the cortical representation of first and second language'. *NeuroReport* 8: 3809–15.

DeKeyser, R. 1993. 'The effect of error correction on L2 grammar knowledge and oral proficiency'. *The Modern Language Journal* 77: 501–14.

DeKeyser, R. 1995. 'Learning second language grammar rules: an experiment with a miniature linguistic system'. *Studies in Second Language Acquisition* 17: 379–410.

DeKeyser, R. 1997. 'Beyond explicit rule learning: Automatizing second language morphosyntax'. *Studies in Second Language Acquisition* 19: 195–221.

DeKeyser, R. 1998. 'Beyond focus on form: cognitive perspectives on learning and practicing second language grammar' in C. Doughty and J. Williams (eds.): *Focus on Form in Classroom Second Language Acquisition*. Cambridge: Cambridge University Press.

DeKeyser, R. 2000. 'The robustness of critical period effects in second language acquisition'. *Studies in Second Language Acquisition* 22: 499–533.

DeKeyser, R. 2001. 'Automaticity and automatization' in P. Robinson (ed.): *Cognition and Second Language Instruction*. Cambridge: Cambridge University Press.

DeKeyser, R. 2003. 'Implicit and explicit learning' in C. Doughty and M. Long (eds.): *Handbook of Second Language Acquisition*. Malden, Mass.: Blackwell.

DeKeyser, R. (ed.). 2007a. *Practice in a Second Language*. Cambridge: Cambridge University Press.

DeKeyser, R. 2007b. 'Introduction: situating the concept of practice' in R. DeKeyser (ed.): *Practice in a Second Language*. Cambridge: Cambridge University Press.

DeKeyser, R., R. Salaberry, P. Robinson, and **M. Harrington.** 2002. 'What gets processed in processing instruction? A commentary on Bill VanPatten's "Processing instruction: an update"'. *Language Learning* 52: 805–24.

DeKeyser, R. and **K. Sokalski.** 1996. 'The differential role of comprehension and production practice'. *Language Learning* 46: 613–42.

Derwing, T. 1989. 'Information type and its relation to nonnative speaker comprehension'. *Language Learning* 39: 157–72.

Derwing, T. 1996. 'Elaborative detail: help or hindrance to the NNS listener?' *Studies in Second Language Acquisition* 18: 283–98.

Dewaele, J. 1998. 'Lexical inventions: French interlanguage as L2 versus L3'. *Applied Linguistics* 19: 471–90.

Dewaele, J. and **A. Furnham.** 1999. 'Extraversion: the unloved variable in applied linguistic research'. *Language Learning* 49: 509–44.

Dewaele, J. and **A. Furnham.** 2000. 'Personality and speech production: A pilot study of second language learners'. *Personality and Individual Differences* 28: 355–65.

DiCamilla, F. and **M. Anton.** 1997. 'The function of repetition in the collaborative discourse of L2 learners'. *The Canadian Modern Language Review* 53: 609–33.

Dickerson, L. 1974. 'Internal and external patterning of phonological variability in the speech of Japanese learners of English'. Unpublished PhD dissertation, University of Illinois, Urbana.

Dickerson. L. 1975. 'The learner's interlanguage as a system of variable rules'. *TESOL Quarterly* 9: 401–7.

Dickinson, L. 1987. *Self-instruction in Language Learning.* Cambridge: Cambridge University Press.

Dienes, Z. and **J. Perner.** 1999. 'A theory of implicit and explicit knowledge'. *Behavioral and Brain Sciences* 22: 735–808.

Dietrich. R., W. Klein, and **C. Noyau** (eds.). 1995. *The Acquisition of Temporality in a Second Language.* Amsterdam: John Benjamins.

Diller, K. 1978. *The Language Teaching Controversy.* Rowley, Mass.: Newbury House.

Diller, K. (ed.). 1981. *Individual Differences and Universals in Language Learning Aptitude.* Rowley, Mass.: Newbury House.

Dinsmore, T. 2006. 'Principles, parameters, and SLA: a retrospective meta-analytical study investigation into adult L2 learners' access to Universal Grammar' in J. Norris and L. Ortega (eds.): *Synthesizing Research on Language Teaching and Learning.* Amsterdam: John Benjamins.

Dittmar, N. and **H. Terborg.** 1991. 'Modality and second language learning' in C. Ferguson and T. Huebner (eds.): *Crosscurrents in Second Language Acquisition and Linguistic Theories.* Amsterdam: John Benjamins.

Dittmar, N., H. Haberland, T. Skuttnab-Kangas, and **U. Telman** (eds.). 1978. *Papers from the First Scandinavian-German Symposium on the Language of Immigrant Workers and their Children.* Linguistgruppen, Roskilde Universiteits Center.

Doi, T. and **K. Yoshioka.** 1990. 'Speech processing constraints on the acquisition of Japanese particles: applying the Pienemann-Johnston model to Japanese as a second language' in T. Hayes and K. Yoshioka (eds.): *Proceedings of the First Conference on Second Language Acquisition and Teaching Volume 1.* Language Programs of the International University of Japan.

Donato, R. 1994. 'Collective scaffolding in second language learning' in J. Lantolf and G. Appel (eds.): *Vygotskian Approaches to Second Language Research.* Norwood, N.J.: Ablex.

Donato, R. 2000. 'Sociocultural contributions to understanding the foreign and second language classroom' in Lantolf, J. (ed.): *Sociocultural Theory and Second Language Learning.* Oxford: Oxford University Press.

Donato, R. and **D. McCormack.** 1994. 'A sociocultural perspective on language learning strategies: the role of mediation'. *The Modern Language Journal* 78: 453–64.

Dörnyei, Z. 1990. 'Conceptualizing motivation in foreign language learning'. *Language Learning* 40: 46–78.

Dörnyei, Z. 1995. 'On the teachability of communication strategies'. *TESOL Quarterly* 29: 55–85.

Dörnyei, Z. 2001a. *Motivational Strategies in the Language Classroom.* Cambridge: Cambridge University Press.

Dörnyei, Z. 2001b. *Teaching and Research Motivation.* Harlow: Longman.

Dörnyei, Z. 2003. *Questionnaires in Second Language Research: Construction, Administration, and Processing.* Mahwah, N.J.: Lawrence Erlbaum.

Dörnyei, Z. 2005. *The Psychology of the Language Learner: Individual Differences in Second Language Acquisition.* Mahwah, N.J.: Lawrence Erlbaum.

Dörnyei, Z. and **J. Kormos.** 2000. 'The role of individual and social variables in oral task performance'. *Language Teaching Research* 4: 275–300.

Dörnyei, Z. and **R. Schmidt** (eds.). 2001. *Motivation and Second Language Acquisition.* Honolulu: University of Hawai'i Press.

Dörnyei, Z. and **M. Scott.** 1997. 'Communication strategies in a second language: definitions and taxonomies'. *Language Learning* 47: 173–210.

Doughty, C. 1991. 'Second language instruction does make a difference: evidence from an empirical study on SL relativization'. *Studies in Second Language Acquisition* 13: 431–69.

Doughty, C. 2001. 'Cognitive underpinnings of focus on form' in P. Robinson (ed.): *Cognition and Second Language Instruction.* Cambridge: Cambridge University Press.

Doughty, C. 2003. 'Instructed SLA: constraints, compensation and enhancement' in C. Doughty and M. Long (eds.): *The Handbook of Second Language Acquisition.* Malden, Mass.: Blackwell.

Doughty, C. 2004. 'Effects of instruction on learning a second language: A critique of instructed SLA research' in B. VanPatten, J. Williams and S. Rott (eds.): *Form–Meaning Connections in Second Language Acquisition.* Mahwah, N.J.: Lawrence Erlbaum.

Doughty, C. and **M. Long** (eds.) 2003: *The Handbook of Second Language Acquisition.* Malden, Mass.: Blackwell.

Doughty, C. and **T. Pica.** 1986. '"Information gap" tasks: do they facilitate second language acquisition'. *TESOL Quarterly* 20: 305–25.

Doughty, C. and **Varela, E.** 1998. 'Communicative focus-on-form' in C. Doughty and J. Williams (eds.): *Focus-on-form in Classroom Second Language Acquisition.* Cambridge: Cambridge University Press.

Doughty, C. and **J. Williams** (eds.). 1998. *Focus-on-form in Classroom Second Language Acquisition.* Cambridge: Cambridge University Press.

Douglas, D. 2001. 'Performance consistency in second language acquisition and language testing research: a conceptual gap'. *Second Language Research* 17: 442–56.

Dowd, J., J. Zuengler, and **D. Berkowitz.** 1990. 'L2 social marking: research issues'. *Applied Linguistics* 11: 16–29.

Downes, N. 1981. 'Foreigner talk inside and outside the classroom'. Unpublished paper, Department of Linguistics, University of Pittsburgh (cited in Chaudron 1988).

Dubois, J. 1991. 'Transcription design principles for spoken discourse research'. *Pragmatics* 1: 71–106.

Dubois, S. and **B. Horvath.** 1999. 'When the music changes, you change too: gender and language change in Cajun English'. *Language Variation and Change* 11: 287–314.

Duda, R. and **P. Riley** (eds.). 1990. *Learning Styles.* Nancy, France: University of Nancy.

Duff, P. 1997. 'Immersion in Hungary: an EFL experiment' in R. Johnson and M. Swain (eds.): *Immersion Education: International Perspectives.* Cambridge: Cambridge University Press.

Duff, P. 2000. 'Repetition in foreign language classroom interaction' in J. Hall and L. Verplaetse (eds.): *Second and Foreign Language Learning Through Classroom Interaction.* Mahwah, N.J.: Lawrence Erlbaum.

Duff, P. 2002. 'The discursive co-construction of knowledge, identity, and difference; An ethnography of communication in the high school mainstream'. *Applied Linguistics* 22: 289–322.

Duff, P. and **C. Polio.** 1991. 'How much foreign language is there in the foreign language classroom?' *The Modern Language Journal* 74: 154–66.

Duff, P., P. Wong, and **M. Early.** 2002. 'Learning language for work and life: The linguistic socialization of immigrant Canadians seeking careers in healthcare'. *The Modern Language Journal* 86: 297–422.

DuFon, M. 2000. 'The acquisition of negative responses to experience questions in Indonesian as a second language by sojourners in naturalistic interactions' in B. Swierzbin, F. Morris, M. Anderson, C. Klee, and E. Tarone (eds.): *Social and Cognitive Factors in Second Language Acquisition.* Somerville, Mass.: Cascadilla Press.

Dulay, H. and **M. Burt.** 1972. 'Goofing, an indicator of children's second language strategies'. *Language Learning* 22: 234–52.

Dulay, H. and **M. Burt.** 1973. 'Should we teach children syntax?' *Language Learning* 23: 245–58.

Dulay, H. and **M. Burt.** 1974a. 'You can't learn without goofing' in J. Richards (ed.): *Error Analysis*. London: Longman.
Dulay, H. and **M. Burt.** 1974b. 'Errors and strategies in child second language acquisition'. *TESOL Quarterly* 8: 129–36.
Dulay, H. and **M. Burt.** 1974c. 'Natural sequences in child second language acquisition'. *Language Learning* 24: 37–53.
Dulay, H. and **M. Burt.** 1974d. 'A new perspective on the creative construction processes in child second language acquisition'. *Language Learning* 24: 253–78.
Dulay, H. and **M. Burt.** 1975. 'Creative construction in second language learning and teaching' in M. Burt and H. Dulay (eds.). *On TESOL '75: New Directions in Second Language Learning, Teaching and Bilingual Education*. Washington D.C.: TESOL.
Dulay, H. and **M. Burt.** 1980. 'On acquisition orders' in S. Felix (ed.): *Second Language Development: Trends and Issues*. Tübingen: Gunter Narr.
Dulay, H., M. Burt, and **S. Krashen.** 1982. *Language Two*. New York: Oxford University Press.
Dunkel, H. 1948. *Second Language Learning*. Boston: Ginn.
Dunn, R., K. Dunn, and **G. Price.** 1991. *Productivity Environmental Preference Survey*. Lawrence, Kans.: Price Systems, Inc.
Dunn, W. and **J. P. Lantolf.** 1998. 'i + 1 and the ZPD: incommensurable constructs; incommensurable discourses'. *Language Learning* 48: 411–42.
Dupuy, B. and **S. Krashen.** 1993. 'Incidental vocabulary acquisition in French as a foreign language'. *Applied Language Learning* 4: 55–63.
Duskova, L. 1969. 'On sources of errors in foreign language learning'. *International Review of Applied Linguistics* 7: 11–36.
Early, M. 1985. 'Input and interaction in content classrooms: foreigner talk and teacher talk in classroom discourse'. Unpublished PhD dissertation, University of California at Los Angeles. (Cited in Chaudron 1988.)
Eckert, P. 1997. 'Age as a sociolinguistic variable' in F. Coulmas (ed.): *The Handbook of Sociolinguistics*. Oxford: Blackwell.
Eckert, P. and **S. McConnel-Ginet.** 1999. 'New generalizations and explanations in language and gender research'. *Language and Society* 28: 185–201.
Eckman, F. 1977. 'Markedness and the contrastive analysis hypothesis'. *Language Learning* 27: 315–30.
Eckman, F. 1981. 'On the naturalness of interlanguage phonological rules'. *Language Learning* 31: 195–216.
Eckman, F. 1984. 'Universals, typologies and interlanguage' in W. Rutherford (ed.): *Typological Universals and Second Language Acquisition*. Amsterdam: John Benjamins.
Eckman, F. 1985. 'Some theoretical and pedagogical implications of the markedness differential hypothesis'. *Studies in Second Language Acquisition* 7: 289–307.
Eckman, F. 1991. 'The structural conformity hypothesis and the acquisition of consonant clusters in the interlanguage of ESL learners'. *Studies in Second Language Acquisition* 13: 23–41.
Eckman, F. 2004a. 'Universals, innateness and explanation in second language acquisition'. *Studies in Language* 28: 682–703.
Eckman, F. 2004b. 'From phonemic differences to constraint rankings: research on second language phonology'. *Studies in Second Language Acquisition* 26: 513–49.
Eckman, F., L. Bell, and **D. Nelson** (eds.). 1984. *Universals of Second Language Acquisition*. Rowley, Mass.: Newbury House.
Eckman, F., L. Bell, and **D. Nelson.** 1988. 'On the generalization of relative clause instruction in the acquisition of English as a second language'. *Applied Linguistics* 9: 1–20.
Eckman, F., A. Elreyes, and **G. Iverson.** 2003. 'Some principles of second language phonology'. *Second Language Research* 19: 169–208.
Eckman, F., D. Highland, P. Lee, J. Mileham, and **R. Weber** (eds.). 1995. *Second Language Acquisition Theory and Pedagogy*. Mahwah, N.J.: Lawrence Erlbaum.

Eckman, F., E. Moravcsik, and **J. Wirth** (eds.). 1986. *Markedness*. New York: Plenum Press.

Eckman, F., E. Moravcsik, and **J. Wirth.** 1989. 'Implicational universals and interrogative structures in the interlanguage of ESL learners'. *Language Learning* 39: 173–205.

Edmondson, W. 1985. 'Discourse worlds in the classroom and in foreign language'. *Studies in Second Language Acquisition* 7: 159–68.

Edmondson, W. and **J. House.** 1991. 'Do learners talk too much? The waffle phenomenon in interlanguage pragmatics' in R. Phillipson, E. Kellerman, L. Selinker, M. Sharwood Smith and M. Swain (eds.): *Foreign/Second Language Pedagogy Research*. Clevedon: Multilingual Matters.

Edwards, G. 1977. *Second Language Retention in the Canadian Public Service*. Ottowa: Public Service Commission of Canada.

Egbert, J. 2003. 'A study of flow theory in the foreign language classroom'. *The Modern Language Journal* 87: 499–518.

Egi, T. 2007. 'Interpreting recasts as linguistic evidence: the roles of linguistic target, length, and degree of change'. *Studies in Second Language Acquisition* 29/4: 511–37.

Ehrlich, S. 1997. 'Gender as social practice: implications for second language acquisition'. *Studies in Second Language Acquisition* 129: 421–46.

Ehrlich, S. 2004. 'Language and gender' in A. Davies and C. Elder (eds.): *The Handbook of Applied Linguistics*. Malden, Mass.: Blackwell.

Ehrlich, S., P. Avery, and **C. Yorio.** 1989. 'Discourse structure and the negotiation of comprehensible input'. *Studies in Second Language Acquisition* 11: 397–414.

Ehrman, M. 1990. 'The role of personality type in adult language learning: an ongoing investigation' in T. Parry and C. Stansfield (eds.): *Language Aptitude Reconsidered*. Englewood Cliffs, N.J.: Prentice Hall.

Ehrman, M. 1994. 'The type differentiation indicator and adult foreign language learning success'. *Journal of Psychological Type* 30: 10–29.

Ehrman, M. 1996. *Understanding Second Language Difficulties*. Thousand Oaks, Calif.: Sage.

Ehrman, M. and **B. Leaver.** 2003. 'Cognitive styles in the service of language learning'. *System* 31: 391–415.

Ehrman, M., B. Leaver, and **R. Oxford.** 2003. 'A brief overview of individual differences in language learning'. *System* 31: 313–30.

Ehrman, M. and **R. Oxford.** 1989. 'Effects of sex differences, career choice, and psychological type on adult language learning strategies'. *The Modern Language Journal* 73: 1–13.

Ehrman, M. and **R. Oxford.** 1995. 'Cognition plus: correlates of language learning success'. *The Modern Language Journal* 79: 67–89.

Eisenstein, M. 1980. 'Grammatical explanations in ESL: teach the student, not the method'. *TESL Talk* 11: 3–13.

Eisenstein, M. 1982. 'A study of social variation in adult second language acquisition'. *Language Learning* 32: 367–92.

Eisenstein, M. (ed.). 1989. *The Dynamic Interlanguage: Empirical Studies in Second Language Variation*. New York: Plenum Press.

Eisenstein, M., N. Bailey, and **C. Madden.** 1982. 'It takes two: contrasting tasks and contrasting structures'. *TESOL Quarterly* 16: 381–93.

Eisenstein, M. and **J. Bodman.** 1986. '"I very appreciate": expressions of gratitude by native and non-native speakers of American English'. *Applied Linguistics* 7: 167–85.

Ekstrand, L. 1977. 'Social and individual frame factors in L2 learning: comparative aspects' in T. Skuttnab-Kangas (ed.): *Papers from the First Nordic Conference on Bilingualism*. Helsingfors: Universitet.

Elder, C. and **N. Iwashita.** 2005. 'Planning for test performance: Does it make a difference?' in R. Ellis (ed.): *Planning and Task Performance in a Second Language*. Amsterdam: John Benjamins.

Eliasson, S. and **E. Jahr** (eds.). 1997. *Language and its Ecology*. Berlin: Mouton.

Elkhafaifi, H. 2005. 'Listening comprehension and anxiety in the Arabic language classroom'. *The Modern Language Journal* 89: 206–20.

Elley, W. 1989. 'Vocabulary acquisition from listening to stories'. *Reading Research Quarterly* 24: 174–87.

Ellinger, B. 2000. 'The relationship between ethnolinguistic identity and English language achievement for native Russian speakers and native Hebrew speakers in Israel'. *Journal of Multilingual and Multicultural Development* 21: 292–307.

Ellis, N. 1993. 'Rules and instances in foreign language learning: interactions of explicit and implicit knowledge'. *European Journal of Cognitive Psychology* 5: 289–319.

Ellis, N. 1994a. 'Introduction: Implicit and explicit language learning—an overview' in N. Ellis (ed.): *Implicit and Explicit Learning of Languages*. San Diego: Academic Press.

Ellis, N. (ed.). 1994b. *Implicit and Explicit Learning of Languages*. San Diego: Academic Press.

Ellis, N. 1996. 'Sequencing in SLA: phonological memory, chunking, and points of order'. *Studies in Second Language Acquisition* 18: 91–126.

Ellis, N. 1997. 'Vocabulary acquisition: word structure, collocation, word-class, and meaning' in N. Schmitt and M. McCarthy (eds.): *Vocabulary: Description, Acquisition and Pedagogy*. Cambridge: Cambridge University Press.

Ellis, N. 1998. 'Emergentism, connectionism, and language learning'. *Language Learning* 48: 631–64.

Ellis, N. 1999. 'Cognitive approaches to SLA'. *Annual Review of Applied Linguistics* 19: 22–42.

Ellis, N. 2001. 'Memory for language' in P. Robinson (ed.): *Cognition and Second Language Instruction*. Cambridge: Cambridge University Press.

Ellis, N. 2002. 'Frequency effects in language processing: a review with implications for theories of implicit and explicit language acquisition'. *Studies in Second Language Acquisition* 24: 143–88.

Ellis, N. 2003. 'Constructions, chunking, and connectionism: the emergence of second language structure' in C. Doughty and M. Long (eds.): *Handbook of Second Language Acquisition*. Malden, Mass.: Blackwell.

Ellis, N. 2005. 'At the interface: dynamic interactions of explicit and implicit knowledge'. *Studies in Second Language Acquisition* 27: 305–52.

Ellis, N. 2006a. 'Language acquisition as rational contingency learning'. *Applied Linguistics* 27: 1–24.

Ellis, N. 2006b. 'Cognitive perspectives in SLA: the Associative-Cognitive CREED'. *AILA Review* 19: 100–21.

Ellis, N. 2006c. 'Selective attention and transfer phenomena in SLA: contingency, cue competition, salience, interference, overshadowing, blocking and perceptual learning'. *Applied Linguistics* 27: 164–94.

Ellis, N. 2007. 'The weak interface, consciousness, and form-focused instruction: mind the door' in S. Fotos and H. Nassaji (eds.): *Form-focused Instruction and Teacher Education: Studies in Honour of Rod Ellis*. Oxford: Oxford University Press.

Ellis, N. and **D. Larsen-Freeman.** 2007. 'Language emergence: implications for applied linguistics—introduction to the special issue'. *Applied Linguistics* 27: 558–99.

Ellis, N. and **P. Robinson** (eds.). 2007. *Handbook of Cognitive Linguistics and Second Language Acquisition*. Mahwah, N.J.: Lawrence Erlbaum.

Ellis, N. and **R. Schmidt.** 1997. 'Morphology and longer distance dependencies: laboratory research illuminating the A in SLA'. *Studies in Second Language Acquisition* 19: 145–72.

Ellis, N. and **R. Schmidt.** 1998. 'Rules or associations in the acquisition of morphology? The frequency by regularity interaction in human and PDP learning or morphosyntax'. *Language and Cognitive Processes* 13: 307–36.

Ellis, R. 1982. 'The origins of interlanguage'. *Applied Linguistics* 3: 207–23.

Ellis, R. 1984a. *Classroom Second Language Development*. Oxford: Pergamon.

Ellis, R. 1984b. 'Formulaic speech in early classroom second language development' in J. Handscombe, R. Orem, and B. Taylor (eds.): *On TESOL '83: The Question of Control.* Washington D.C.: TESOL.

Ellis, R. 1984c. 'Can syntax be taught? A study of the effects of formal instruction on the acquisition of WH questions by children'. *Applied Linguistics* 5: 138–55.

Ellis, R. 1985a. *Understanding Second Language Acquisition.* Oxford: Oxford University Press.

Ellis, R. 1985b. 'The L1 = L2 Hypothesis: a reconsideration'. *System* 13: 9–24.

Ellis, R. 1985c. 'Sources of variability in interlanguage'. *Applied Linguistics* 6: 118–31.

Ellis, R. 1985d. 'Teacher–pupil interaction in second language development' in S. Gass and C. Madden (eds.): *Input in Second Language Acquisition.* Rowley, Mass.: Newbury House.

Ellis, R. (ed.). 1987a. *Second Language Acquisition in Context.* London: Prentice Hall International.

Ellis, R. 1987b. 'Interlanguage variability in narrative discourse: style-shifting in the use of the past tense'. *Studies in Second Language Acquisition* 9: 1–20.

Ellis, R. 1987c. 'Contextual variability in second language acquisition and the relevancy of language teaching' in R. Ellis (ed.): *Second Language Acquisition in Context.* London: Prentice Hall International.

Ellis, R. 1988a. 'The effects of linguistic environment on the second language acquisition of grammatical rules'. *Applied Linguistics* 9: 257–74.

Ellis, R. 1988b. 'The role of practice in classroom language learning'. *AILA Review* 5: 20–39.

Ellis, R. 1989a. 'Classroom learning styles and their effect on second language acquisition: a study of two learners'. *System* 17: 249–62.

Ellis, R. 1989b. 'Are classroom and naturalistic acquisition the same? A study of the classroom acquisition of German word order rules'. *Studies in Second Language Acquisition* 11: 305–28.

Ellis, R. 1989c. 'Sources of intra-learner variability in language use and their relationship to second language acquisition' in S. Gass, C. Madden, D. Preston and L. Selinker (eds.). *Variation in Second Language Acquisition Volume II: Psycholinguistic Issues.* Clevedon: Multilingual Matters.

Ellis, R. 1990a. *Instructed Second Language Acquisition.* Oxford: Blackwell.

Ellis, R. 1990b. 'Individual learning styles in classroom second language development' in J. de Jong and D. Stevenson (eds.): *Individualizing the Assessment of Language Abilities.* Clevedon: Multilingual Matters.

Ellis, R. 1990c. 'A response to Gregg'. *Applied Linguistics* 11: 384–91.

Ellis, R. 1991a. 'The interaction hypothesis: a critical evaluation' in E. Sadtono (ed.): *Language Acquisition and the Second/Foreign Language Classroom.* Singapore: RELC.

Ellis, R. 1991b. 'Grammaticality judgments and second language acquisition'. *Studies in Second Language Acquisition* 13: 161–86.

Ellis, R. 1991c. 'Grammaticality judgements and learner variability' in R. Burmeister and P. Rounds (eds.): *Variability in Second Language Acquisition: Proceedings of the Tenth Meeting of the Second Language Research Forum Volume 1.* Eugene, Oreg.: University of Oregon: Department of Linguistics.

Ellis, R. (ed.). 1991d. *Second Language Acquisition and Second Language Pedagogy.* Clevedon: Multilingual Matters.

Ellis, R. 1991e. 'Grammar teaching—practice or consciousness-raising' in R. Ellis (ed.): *Second Language Acquisition and Second Language Pedagogy.* Clevedon: Multilingual Matters.

Ellis, R. 1992. 'Learning to communicate in the classroom'. *Studies in Second Language Acquisition* 14: 1–23.

Ellis, R. 1993. 'Second language acquisition and the structural syllabus'. *TESOL Quarterly* 27: 91–113.

Ellis, R. 1994a. *The Study of Second Language Acquisition.* Oxford: Oxford University Press.

Ellis, R. 1994b. 'Second language acquisition research and teacher development: the case of teachers' questions' in D. Li, D. Mahoney, and J. Richards (eds.): *Exploring Second Language Teacher Development*. Hong Kong: City Polytechnic.

Ellis, R. 1994c. 'A theory of instructed second language acquisition' in N. Ellis (ed.): *Implicit and Explicit Learning of Languages*. San Diego: Academic Press.

Ellis, R. 1995a. 'Interpretation tasks for grammar teaching'. *TESOL Quarterly* 29: 87–106.

Ellis, R. 1995b. 'Uptake as language awareness'. *Language Awareness* 4: 147–60.

Ellis, R. 1995c. 'Appraising second language acquisition theory in relation to language pedagogy' in G. Cook and B. Seidlhofer (eds.): *Principle and Practice in Applied Linguistics: Studies in Honour of H. G. Widdowson*. Oxford: Oxford University Press.

Ellis, R. 1995d. 'Modified input and the acquisition of word meanings'. *Applied Linguistics* 16: 409–41.

Ellis, R. 1997a. *Second Language Acquisition*. Oxford: Oxford University Press.

Ellis, R. 1997b. *SLA Research and Language Teaching*. Oxford: Oxford University Press.

Ellis, R. 1997c. 'SLA and language pedagogy: an educational perspective'. *Studies in Second Language Acquisition* 19: 69–92.

Ellis, R. 1998. 'Teaching and research: options in grammar teaching'. *TESOL Quarterly* 32: 39–60.

Ellis, R. 1999a. 'From communicative language teaching to developmental pedagogy'. *English in Aotearoa* 38: 14–22.

Ellis, R. 1999b. 'Input-based approaches to teaching grammar: a review of classroom-oriented research'. *Annual Review of Applied Linguistics* 19: 64–80.

Ellis, R. 1999c. 'Item versus system learning: explaining free variation'. *Applied Linguistics* 20: 460–80.

Ellis, R. 1999d. *Learning a Second Language Through Interaction*. Amsterdam: John Benjamin.

Ellis, R. 2000. 'Task-based research and language pedagogy'. *Language Teaching Research* 4: 193–220.

Ellis, R. (ed.) 2001a. *Form-focused Instruction and Second Language Learning*. Malden, Mass.: Blackwell.

Ellis, R. 2001b. 'Investigating form-focused instruction' in R. Ellis (ed.): *Form-Focused Instruction and Second Language Learning*. Malden, Mass.: Blackwell.

Ellis, R. 2001c. 'The metaphorical construction of second language learners' in M. Breen (ed.): *Learner Contributions to Language Learning: New Directions in Research*. Harlow: Longman.

Ellis, R. 2002. 'Does form-focused instruction affect the acquisition of implicit knowledge? A review of the research'. *Studies in Second Language Acquisition* 24: 223–36.

Ellis, R. 2003. *Task-based Language Learning and Teaching*. Oxford: Oxford University Press.

Ellis, R. 2004a. 'The definition and measurement of L2 explicit knowledge'. *Language Learning* 54: 227–75.

Ellis, R. 2004b. 'Individual differences in language learning' in C. Elder and A. Davies (eds.): *Handbook of Applied Linguistics*. Oxford: Blackwell.

Ellis, R. 2005a. *Planning and Task-Performance in a Second Language*. Amsterdam: John Benjamins.

Ellis, R. 2005b. 'Planning and task-based research: theory and research' in R. Ellis (ed.): *Planning and Task-Performance in a Second Language*. Amsterdam: John Benjamins.

Ellis, R. 2005c. 'Instructed language learning and task-based teaching' in E. Hinkel (ed.): *Handbook of Research in Second Language Teaching and Learning*. Mahwah, N.J.: Lawrence Erlbaum.

Ellis, R. 2005d. 'Measuring implicit and explicit knowledge of a second language: a psychometric study'. *Studies in Second Language Acquisition* 27: 141–72.

Ellis, R. 2006a. 'Researching the effects of form-focused instruction on L2 acquisition' in K. Bardovi-Harlig and Z. Dörnyei (eds.): *Themes in SLA Research AILA 19*. Amsterdam: John Benjamins.

Ellis, R. 2006b. 'Current issues in the teaching of grammar: an SLA perspective'. *TESOL Quarterly* 40: 83–108.

Ellis, R. 2006c. 'Modelling learning difficulty and second language proficiency: the differential contributions of implicit and explicit knowledge'. *Applied Linguistics* 27: 431–63

Ellis, R. 2007. 'The differential effects of corrective feedback on two grammatical structures' in A. Mackey (ed.): *Conversational interaction and Second Language Acquisition: A Series of Empirical Studies*. Oxford: Oxford University Press.

Ellis, R. 2008. 'Explicit form-focused instruction and second language acquisition' in B. Spolsky and F. Hult (eds.): *The Handbook of Educational Linguistics*. Oxford: Blackwell.

Ellis, R. and **G. Barkhuizen.** 2005. *Analysing Learner Language*. Oxford: Oxford University Press.

Ellis, R., H. Basturkmen, and **S. Loewen.** 2001. 'Learner uptake in communicative ESL lessons'. *Language Learning* 51: 281–318.

Ellis, R., H. Basturkmen, and **S. Loewen.** 2002. 'Doing focus on form'. *System* 30: 419–32.

Ellis, R., P. Hacker, and **S. Loewen.** 2006. 'The relationship between an early start in language learning in New Zealand schools and students' motivation'. *New Zealand Studies in Applied Linguistics* 12: 16–34.

Ellis, R. and **X. He.** 1999. 'The roles of modified input and output in the incidental acquisition of word meanings'. *Studies in Second Language Acquisition* 21: 319–33.

Ellis, R. and **R. Heimbach.** 1997. 'Bugs and birds: children's acquisition of second language vocabulary through interaction'. *System* 25: 247–59.

Ellis, R., S. Loewen, and **R. Erlam.** 2006. 'Implicit and explicit corrective feedback and the acquisition of L2 grammar'. *Studies in Second Language Acquisition* 28: 339–68.

Ellis, R. and **M. Rathbone,** 1987. *The Acquisition of German in a Classroom Context.* Mimeograph, London: Ealing College of Higher Education.

Ellis, R. and **Y. Sheen.** 2006. 'Re-examining the role of recasts in SLA'. *Studies in Second Language Acquisition* 28: 575–600.

Ellis, R., Y. Tanaka, and **A. Yamazaki.** 1994. 'Classroom interaction, comprehension and the acquisition of word meanings'. *Language Learning* 44: 449–91.

Ellis, R. and **G. Wells.** 1980. 'Enabling factors in adult-child discourse'. *First Language* 1: 46–82.

Ellis, R. and **F. Yuan.** 2004. 'The effects of planning on fluency, complexity and accuracy in second language narrative writing'. *Studies in Second Language Acquisition* 26: 59–84.

Ely, C. 1986a. 'An analysis of discomfort, risktaking, sociability, and motivation in the L2 classroom'. *Language Learning* 36: 1–25.

Ely, C. 1986b. 'Language learning motivation: a descriptive and causal analysis'. *The Modern Language Journal* 70: 28–35.

Engestrom, Y. 1993. 'Developmental studies of work as a test bench of activity theory: the case of primary care in medical practice' in J. Lave and S. Chalkin (eds.): *Understanding Practice: Perspectives on Activity and Context.* Cambridge: Cambridge University Press.

Epstein, N. 1977. *Language, Ethnicity and the Schools.* Washington D.C.: Institute for Educational Leadership.

Erickson, F. and **J. Schultz.** 1982. *The Counselor as Gatekeeper: Social Interaction in Interviews.* New York: Academic Press.

Ericsson, K. and **H. Simon.** 1987. 'Verbal reports on thinking' in C. Færch and G. Kasper (eds.): *Introspection in Second Language Research.* Clevedon: Multilingual Matters.

Erlam, R. 2003. 'Evaluating the relative effectiveness of structured-input and output-based instruction in foreign language learning: Results from an experimental study'. *Studies in Second Language Acquisition* 25: 559–82.

Erlam, R. 2005. 'Language aptitude and its relationship to instructional effectiveness in second language acquisition'. *Language Teaching Research* 9: 147–72.

Erman, B. and **B. Warren.** 2000. 'The idiom principle and the open-choice principle'. *Text* 20: 29–62.

Ernst, S. 1994. '"Talking Circle": Conversation, negotiation in the ESL classroom'. *TESOL Quarterly* 28: 293–322.

Ervin-Tripp, S. 1974. 'Is second language learning like the first?' *TESOL Quarterly* 8: 111–27.

Ervin-Tripp, S., A. Strage, M. Lampert, and **N. Bell.** 1987. 'Understanding requests'. *Linguistics* 25: 107–43.

Eubank, L. 1987. 'Parameters in L2 learning: Flynn revisited'. *Second Language Research* 5: 43–73.

Eubank, L. 1990. 'Linguistic theory and the acquisition of German negation' in B. VanPatten and J. Lee (eds.). *Second Language Acquisition—Foreign Language Learning.* Clevedon: Multilingual Matters.

Eubank, L. 1991a. 'Introduction' in L. Eubank (ed.). *Point Counterpoint: Universal Grammar in the Second Language.* Amsterdam: John Benjamins.

Eubank, L. (ed.). 1991b. *Point Counterpoint: Universal Grammar in the Second Language.* Amsterdam: John Benjamins.

Eubank, L. 1994. 'Optionality and the initial state in L2 development' in T. Hoekstra and B. Schwartz (eds.). *Language Acquisition Studies in Generative Grammar.* Amsterdam: John Benjamins.

Eubank, L. and **K. Gregg.** 1995. '"Et in amygdale ego?": UG, (S)LA, and neurobiology'. *Studies in Second Language Acquisition* 17: 35–58.

Eubank, L., L. Selinker, and **M. Sharwood Smith** (eds.). 1997. *The Current State of Interlanguage.* Amsterdam: John Benjamins.

Eysenck, M. 1979. 'Anxiety, learning and memory: a reconceptualisation'. *Journal of Research in Personality* 13: 363–85.

Eysenck, M. 2001. *Principles of Cognitive Psychology* (Second edition). Hove: Psychology Press.

Eysenck, S. and **J. Chan.** 1982. 'A comparative study of personality in adults and children: Hong Kong vs. England'. *Personality and Individual Differences* 3: 153–60.

Eysenck, H. and **S. Eysenck.** 1964. *Manual of the Eysenck Personality Inventory.* London: Hodder and Stoughton.

Fabbro, F. (ed.). 2002. *Advances in the Neurolinguistics of Bilingualism.* Udine: Forum-Udine University Press.

Færch, C. and **G. Kasper.** 1980. 'Processes and strategies in foreign language learning and communication'. *Interlanguage Studies Bulletin* 5: 47–118.

Færch, C. and **G. Kasper** (eds.). 1983a. *Strategies in Interlanguage Communication.* London: Longman.

Færch, C. and **G. Kasper.** 1983b. 'Plans and strategies in foreign language communication' in C. Færch and G. Kasper (eds.): *Strategies in Interlanguage Communication.* London: Longman.

Færch, C. and **G. Kasper.** 1986. 'The role of comprehension in second language learning'. *Applied Linguistics* 7: 257–74.

Færch, C. and **G. Kasper** (eds.). 1987. *Introspection in Second Language Research.* Clevedon: Multilingual Matters.

Færch, C. and **G. Kasper.** 1989. 'Internal and external modification in interlanguage request realization' in S. Blum-Kulka, J. House and G. Kasper (eds.): *Cross-cultural Pragmatics: Requests and Apologies.* Norwood: N.J.: Ablex.

Fanselow, J. 1977. 'Beyond "Rashomon"—conceptualizing and describing the teaching act'. *TESOL Quarterly* 10: 17–39.

Fanselow, J. and **R. Crymes** (eds.). 1976. *On TESOL '76.* Washington D.C.: TESOL.

Farrar, M. 1990. 'Discourse and the acquisition of grammatical morphemes'. *Journal of Child Language* 17: 607–24.

Farrar, M. 1992. 'Negative evidence and grammatical morpheme acquisition'. *Developmental Psychology* 28: 9–98.

Fasold, R. and **R. Shuy** (eds.). 1975. *Analyzing Variation in Language*. Washington D.C.: Georgetown University Press.

Fathman, A. 1975. 'Language background, age, and the order of acquisition of English structures' in M. Burt and H. Dulay (eds.): *On TESOL '75: New Directions in Second Language Learning, Teaching and Bilingual Education*. Washington D.C.: TESOL.

Fathman, A. 1978. 'ESL and EFL learning: similar or dissimilar?' in C. Blatchford and J. Schachter (eds.): *On TESOL '78: EFL Policies, Programs, Practices*. Washington D.C.: TESOL.

Faucette, P. 2001. 'A pedagogical perspective on communication strategies: benefits of training and an analysis of English language teaching materials'. *Second Language Studies* 19: 1–40.

Felix, S. 1978. 'Some differences between first and second language acquisition' in N. Waterson and C. Snow (eds.): *The Development of Communication*. John Wiley: New York.

Felix, S. (ed.). 1980a. *Second Language Development: Trends and Issues*. Tübingen: Gunter Narr.

Felix, S. 1980b. 'Interference, interlanguage and related issues' in S. Felix (ed.): *Second Language Development: Trends and Issues*. Tübingen: Gunter Narr.

Felix, S. 1981. 'The effect of formal instruction on second language acquisition'. *Language Learning* 31: 87–112.

Felix, S. 1984. 'Maturational aspects of Universal Grammar' in A. Davies, C. Criper and A. Howatt (eds.): *Interlanguage*. Edinburgh: Edinburgh University Press.

Felix, S. 1985. 'More evidence on competing cognitive systems'. *Second Language Research* 1: 47–72.

Felix-Brasdefer, J. 2004. 'Interlanguage refusals: linguistic politeness and length of residence in the target community'. *Language Learning* 54: 587–653.

Ferguson, C. 1971. 'Absence of copula and the notion of simplicity: a study of normal speech, baby talk, foreigner talk and pidgins' in D. Hymes (ed.): *Pidginization and Creolization of Languages*. Cambridge: Cambridge University Press.

Ferguson, C. 1975. 'Towards a characterization of English foreigner talk'. *Anthropological Linguistics* 17: 1–14.

Ferguson, C. 1977. 'Baby talk as a simplified register' in C. Snow and C. Ferguson (eds.): *Talking to Children: Language Input and Acquisition*. Cambridge: Cambridge University Press.

Ferguson, C. and **C. DeBose.** 1977. 'Simplified registers, broken languages and pidginization' in A. Valdman (ed.): *Pidgin and Creole*. Indiana University Press.

Ferguson, C. and **T. Huebner** (eds.). 1991. *Crosscurrents in Second Language Acquisition and Linguistic Theories*. Amsterdam: John Benjamins.

Ferrier, L. 1978. 'Some observations of error in context' in N. Waterson and C. Snow (eds.): *The Development of Communication*. Wiley: New York.

Ferris, D. 2002. *Treatment of Error in Second Language Writing*. Ann Arbor: University of Michigan Press.

Fidler, A. 2006. 'Reconceptualizing fossilization in second language acquisition: a review'. *Second Language Research* 22: 398–411.

Field, J. 2003. *Psycholinguistics: A Resource Book for Students*. London: Routledge.

Fiksdal, S. 1989. 'Framing uncomfortable moments in crosscultural gatekeeping interviews' in S. Gass, C. Madden, D. Preston and L. Selinker (eds.): *Variation in Second Language Acquisition Volume I: Sociolinguistic Issues*. Clevedon: Multilingual Matters.

Fillmore, C. 1968. 'The case for case' in E. Bach and R. Harms (eds.): *Universals of Linguistic Theory*. New York: Holt, Rinehart, and Winston.

Fillmore, C., D. Kempler, and **W. Wang** (ed.). 1979. *Individual Differences in Language Ability and Language Behavior*. New York: Academic Press.

Finer, D. and **E. Broselow.** 1986. 'Second language acquisition of reflexive binding' in S. Berman, J. Choe, and J. McDonough (eds.): *Proceedings of NELS 16*. University of Massachusetts at Amherst: Graduate Linguistics Students Association.

Firth A. and **J. Wagner.** 1997. 'On discourse, communication, and (some) fundamental concepts in SLA'. *The Modern Language Journal* 81: 285–300.

Fischer, J. 1958. 'Social influences in the choice of a linguistic variant'. *Word* 14: 47–56.

Fisher, J., M. Clarke, and **J. Schachter** (eds.). 1980. *On TESOL '80*. Washington D.C.: TESOL.

Fishman, J., C. Ferguson, and **J. Das Gupta** (eds.). 1998. *Language Problems of Developing Nations*. New York: Wiley.

Fisiak, J. (ed.). 1981a. *Contrastive Linguistics and the Language Teacher*. Oxford: Pergamon.

Fisiak, J. 1981b 'Some introductory notes concerning contrastive linguistics' in J. Fisiak (ed.): *Contrastive Linguistics and the Language Teacher*. Oxford: Pergamon.

Fitikides, T. 1936. *Common Mistakes in English*. London: Longman.

Fitzpatrick, F. 1987. *The Open Door: The Bradford Bilingual Project*. Clevedon: Multilingual Matters.

Flanders, N. 1970. *Analyzing Teaching Behavior*. Reading, Mass.: Addison Wesley.

Flanigan, B. 1991. 'Peer tutoring and second language acquisition in the elementary school'. *Applied Linguistics* 12: 141–58.

Flavell, J. and **M. Markman** (eds.). 1983. *Carmichael's Manual of Child Psychology Volume 3*. New York: Wiley.

Flege, J. 1995. 'Second language speech learning: theory, findings and problems' in W. Strange (ed.): *Speech Perception and Linguistic Experience: Issues in Cross-language Research*. Timonoium, Md.: York Press.

Flege, J. 1999. 'Age of learning and second language speech' in D. Birdsong (ed.): *Second Language Acquisition and the Critical Period Hypothesis*. Mahwah, N.J.: Lawrence Erlbaum.

Fletcher, P. and **M. Garman** (eds.). 1986. *Language Acquisition* (Second edition). Cambridge: Cambridge University Press.

Flick, W. 1979. 'A multiple component approach to research in second language acquisition' in R. Andersen (ed.): *The Acquisition and Use of Spanish and English as First and Second Languages*. Washington, D.C.: TESOL.

Flick, W. 1980. 'Error types in adult English as a second language' in B. Ketterman and R. St. Clair (eds.): *New Approaches to Language Acquisition*. Heidelberg: Julius Groos.

Flores d'Arcais, G. and **W. Levelt** (eds.). 1970. *Advances in Psycholinguistics*. Amsterdam: North-Holland Publishing.

Flowerdew, J. 1992. 'Definitions in science lectures'. *Applied Linguistics* 13: 202–21.

Flynn, S. 1984. 'A universal in L2 acquisition based on a PBD typology' in F. Eckman, L. Bell and D. Nelson (eds.): *Universals of Second Language Acquisition*. Rowley, Mass.: Newbury House.

Flynn, S. 1987. *A Parameter-setting Model of L2 Acquisition*. Dordrecht: Reidel.

Flynn, S. and **B. Lust.** 1990. 'In defense of parameter-setting in L2 acquisition: a reply to Bley-Vroman and Chaudron '90'. *Language Learning* 40: 419–49.

Flynn, S. and **S. Manuel.** 1991. 'Age-dependent effects in language acquisition: an evaluation of the "critical period" hypothesis' in L. Eubank (ed.): *Point Counterpoint: Universal Grammar in the Second Language*. Amsterdam: John Benjamins

Flynn, S., G. Martohardjono and **W. O'Neil** (eds.). 1998. *The Generative Study of Second Language Acquisition*. Mahwah, N.J.: Lawrence Erlbaum.

Fodor, J. 1983. *Modularity of Mind: An Essay on Faculty Psychology*. Cambridge, Mass.: MIT Press.

Fodor, J. 1998. *In Critical Condition: Polemical Essays on Cognitive Science and the Philosophy of the Mind.* Cambridge, Mass.: MIT Press.

Foley, J. 1991. 'A psycholinguistic framework for task-based approaches to language teaching'. *Applied Linguistics* 12: 62–75.

Forrest-Pressley, D., G. MacKinnon, and **T. Waller** (eds.). 1985. *Metacognition, Cognition, and Human Performance Volume 1.* New York: Academic Press.

Foster, P. 1996. 'Doing the task better: how planning time influences students' performance' in J. Willis and D. Willis (eds.): *Challenge and Change in Language Teaching.* London: Heinemann.

Foster, P. 1998. 'A classroom perspective on the negotiation of meaning'. *Applied Linguistics* 19: 1–23.

Foster, P. 2001. 'Rules and routines: a consideration of their role in the task-based language production of native and non-native speakers' in M. Bygate *et al.* (eds.): *Researching Pedagogic Tasks, Second Language Learning, Teaching and Testing.* Harlow: Longman.

Foster, P. and **A. Ohta.** 2005. 'Negotiation for meaning and peer assistance in second language classrooms'. *Applied Linguistics* 26: 402–30.

Foster P. and **P. Skehan.** 1996. 'The influence of planning on performance in task-based learning'. *Studies in Second Language Acquisition* 18/3: 299–324.

Foster, P. and **P. Skehan.** 1999. 'The influence of source of planning and focus of planning on task-based performance'. *Language Teaching Research* 3: 215–47.

Foster-Cohen, S. 2001. 'First language acquisition ... second language acquisition: "What's Hecurba to him or he to Hecuba?"' *Second Language Research* 17: 329–44

Foster-Cohen, S. and **A. Nizegorodzew** (eds.). 2003. *EUROSLA Yearbook 1.* Amsterdam: John Benjamins.

Fotos, S. 1993. 'Consciousness-raising and noticing through focus-on-form: grammar task performance vs. formal instruction'. *Applied Linguistics* 14: 385–407.

Fotos, S. 1994. 'Integrating grammar instruction and communicative language use through grammar consciousness-raising tasks'. *TESOL Quarterly* 28: 323–51.

Fotos, S. and **R. Ellis.** 1991. 'Communicating about grammar: a task-based approach'. *TESOL Quarterly* 25: 605–28.

Fotos, S. and **H. Nassaji.** 2006. *Form-focused Instruction and Teacher Education: Studies in Honour of Rod Ellis.* Oxford: Oxford University Press.

Fowler, H. 1906. *The King's English.* Oxford: Clarendon Press.

Franceshina, F. 2005. *Fossilized Second Language Grammars: The Acquisition of Grammatical Gender.* Amsterdam: Benjamins.

Francis, W. and **H. Kucera.** 1982. 'Frequency analysis of English usage: lexicon and grammar' in T. Huckin, M. Haynes, and J. Coady (eds.): *Second Language Reading and Vocabulary Learning.* Norwood, N.J.: Ablex.

Fraser, B. 1981. 'On apologizing' in F. Coulmas (ed.): *Conversational Routines: Explorations in Standardized Communication Situations and Prepatterned Speech.* The Hague: Mouton.

Fraser, B. 1983. 'The domain of pragmatics' in J. Richards and J. Schmidt (eds.): *Language and Communication.* London: Longman.

Fraser, B., E. Rintell, and **J. Walters.** 1980. 'An approach to conducting research on the acquisition of pragmatic competence in a second language' in D. Larsen-Freeman (ed.): *Discourse Analysis in Second Language Research.* Rowley, Mass.: Newbury House.

Frawley, W. and **J. Lantolf.** 1985. 'Second language discourse: a Vygotskyan perspective'. *Applied Linguistics* 6: 19–44.

Frawley, W. and **J. Lantolf.** 1986. 'Private speech and self-regulation: a commentary of Frauenglass and Diaz'. *Developmental Psychology* 22: 706–8.

Freed, B. 1980. 'Talking to foreigners vs. talking to children: similarities and differences' in R. Scarcella and S. Krashen (eds.): *Research in Second Language Acquisition.* Rowley, Mass.: Newbury House.

Freed, B. 1981. 'Foreigner talk, baby talk, native talk'. *International Journal of the Sociology of Language* 28: 19–39.
Freed, B. (ed.). 1995. *Second Language Acquisition in a Study Abroad Context*. Amsterdam: John Benjamins.
Freedman, S. and **K. Forster.** 1975. 'The psychological status of overgenerated sentences'. *Cognition* 19: 101–31.
Freudenstein, R. 1977. 'Interaction in the foreign language classroom' in M. Burt, H. Dulay, and M. Finocchiaro (eds.): *Viewpoints on English as a Second Language*. New York: Regents.
Fromkin, V. 1971. 'The non-anomalous nature of anomalous utterances'. *Language* 47: 27–52.
Fukaya, Y. and **M. Clark.** 2001. 'A comparison of input enhancement and explicit language instruction of mitigators' in F. Bouton (ed.): *Pragmatics and Language Learning* (Monograph series Volume 10). Urbana-Champaign, Ill.: Division of English as an International Language, University of Illinois.
Fuller, J. 1999. 'Between three languages: composite structure in interlanguage'. *Applied Linguistics* 20: 534–61.
Furrow, D., K. Nelson, and **H. Benedict.** 1979. 'Mothers' speech to children and syntactic development: some simple relationships'. *Journal of Child Language* 6: 423–42.
Gaies, S. 1977. 'The nature of linguistic input in formal second language learning: linguistic and communicative strategies' in H. Brown, C. Yorio, and R. Crymes (eds.): *On TESOL '77*. Washington D.C.: TESOL.
Gaies, S. 1982. 'Native speaker–nonnative speaker interaction among academic peers'. *Studies in Second Language Acquisition* 5: 74–82.
Gaies, S. 1983. 'The investigation of language classroom processes'. *TESOL Quarterly* 17: 205–18.
Gal, S. 1978. 'Peasant men can't get wives: language change and sex roles in a bilingual community'. *Language in Society* 7: 1–16.
Gallaway, C. and **B. Richards** (eds.). 1994. *Input and Interaction in Language Acquisition*. Cambridge: Cambridge University Press.
Galloway, L. 1980. 'Towards a neuropsychological model of bilingualism and second language performance: a theoretical article with a critical review of current research and some new hypotheses' in M. Long, S. Peck, and K. Bailey (eds.): *Research in Second Language Acquisition*. Rowley, Mass.: Newbury House.
Gan, Z., G. Humphreys, and **L. Hamp-Lyons.** 2004. 'Understanding successful and unsuccessful EFL students in Chinese universities'. *The Modern Language Journal* 88: 229–44.
Garcia, O. 2002. 'Language spread and its study: narrowing its spread as a scholarly field' in R. Kaplan (ed.): *The Oxford Handbook of Applied Linguistics*. New York: Oxford.
Gardner, R. 1979. 'Social psychological aspects of second language acquisition' in H. Giles and R. St. Clair (eds.): *Language and Social Psychology*. Oxford: Blackwell.
Gardner, R. 1980. 'On the validity of affective variables in second language acquisition: conceptual, contextual, and statistical considerations'. *Language Learning* 30: 255–70.
Gardner, R. 1983. 'Learning another language: a true social psychological experiment'. *Journal of Language and Social Psychology* 2: 219–40.
Gardner, R. 1985. *Social Psychology and Second Language Learning: The Role of Attitude and Motivation*. London: Edward Arnold.
Gardner, R. 1988. 'The socio-educational model of second language learning: assumptions, findings and issues'. *Language Learning* 38: 101–26.
Gardner, R. 2000. 'Correlation, causation, motivation, and second language acquisition'. *Canadian Psychology* 41: 1–24.
Gardner, R. 2001. 'Integrative motivation and second language acquisition' in Z. Dörnyei and R. Schmidt (eds.): *Motivation and Second Language Learning*. Honolulu: University of Hawai'i Press.

Gardner, R. and **R. Clement.** 1990. 'Social psychological perspectives on second language acquisition' in H. Giles and W. Robinson (eds.): *Handbook of Language and Social Psychology*. Chichester: John Wiley and Sons.

Gardner, R., R. Ginsberg, and **P. Smythe.** 1976. 'Attitudes and motivation in second language learning: course related changes'. *The Canadian Modern Language Review* 32: 243–66.

Gardner, R., R. Lalonde, and **J. MacPherson.** 1985. 'Social factors in second language attrition'. *Language Learning* 35: 519–40.

Gardner, R., R. Lalonde, and **R. Pierson.** 1983. 'The socio-educational model of second language acquisition: an investigation using LISREL causal modeling'. *Journal of Language and Social Psychology* 2: 1–15.

Gardner, R. and **W. Lambert.** 1959. 'Motivational variables in second language acquisition'. *Canadian Journal of Psychology* 13: 266–72.

Gardner, R. and **W. Lambert.** 1972. *Attitudes and Motivation in Second Language Learning.* Rowley, Mass.: Newbury House.

Gardner, R. and **P. MacIntyre.** 1991. 'An instrumental motivation in language study: who says it isn't effective?' *Studies in Second Language Acquisition* 13: 57–72.

Gardner, R. and **P. MacIntyre.** 1992. 'A student's contributions to second language learning. Part 1: Cognitive variables'. *Language Teaching* 25: 211–20.

Gardner, R., R. Moorcroft, and **P. MacIntyre.** 1987. *The Role of Anxiety in Second Language Performance of Language Dropouts. Research Bulletin* 657. London, Ontario: University of Western Ontario.

Gardner, R. and **P. Smythe.** 1975. 'Second language acquisition: a social psychological approach'. *Research Bulletin* 332. Department of Psychology, University of Western Ontario. Canada. (Cited in Gardner 1985.)

Garnica, O. 1977. 'Some prosodic and paralinguistic features of speech to young children' in C. Snow and C. Ferguson (eds.): *Talking to Children: Language Input and Acquisition.* Cambridge: Cambridge University Press.

Gaskill, W. 1980. 'Correction in native speaker–nonnative speaker conversation' in D. Larsen-Freeman (ed.): *Discourse Analysis in Second Language Research*. Rowley, Mass.: Newbury House.

Gass, S. 1979. 'Language transfer and universal grammatical relations'. *Language Learning* 29: 327–44.

Gass, S. 1980. 'An investigation of syntactic transfer in adult second language learners' in R. Scarcella and S. Krashen (eds.): *Research in Second Language Acquisition*. Rowley, Mass.: Newbury House.

Gass, S. 1981. 'From theory to practice' in M. Hines and W. Rutherford (eds.): *On TESOL '81*. Washington, D.C.: TESOL.

Gass, S. 1983. 'Language transfer and universal grammatical relations' in S. Gass and L. Selinker (eds.): *Language Transfer in Language Learning*. Rowley, Mass.: Newbury House.

Gass, S. 1984. 'A review of interlanguage syntax: language transfer and language universals'. *Language Learning* 34: 115–32.

Gass, S. 1987. 'The resolution of conflicts among competing systems: a bidirectional perspective'. *Applied Psycholinguistics* 8: 329–50.

Gass, S. 1988. 'Integrating research areas: a framework for second language studies'. *Applied Linguistics* 9: 198–217.

Gass, S. 1989. 'Language universals and second language acquisition'. *Language Learning* 39: 497–534.

Gass, S. 1990. 'Second and foreign language learning: same, different or none of the above?' in B. VanPatten and J. Lee (eds.): *Second Language Acquisition—Foreign Language Learning*. Clevedon: Multilingual Matters.

Gass, S. 1991. 'Grammar instruction, selective attention, and learning' in R. Phillipson, E. Kellerman, L. Selinker, M. Sharwood Smith, and M. Swain (eds.): *Foreign/Second Language Pedagogy Research*. Clevedon: Multilingual Matters.

Gass, S. 1994. 'The reliability of second language grammaticality judgments' in E. Tarone, S. Gass, and A. Cohen (eds.): *Research Methodology in Second Language Research*. Hillsdale, N.J.: Lawrence Erlbaum.

Gass, S. 1995. 'Learning and teaching: the necessary intersection' in F. Eckman, D. Highland, P. Lee, J. Mileham, and R. Weber (eds.): *Second Language Acquisition Theory and Pedagogy*. Mahwah, N.J.: Lawrence Erlbaum.

Gass, S. 1997a. *Input, Interaction and the Second Language Learner*. Mahwah, N.J.: Lawrence Erlbaum.

Gass, S. 1997b. 'Universals, SLA, and language pedagogy: 1984 revisited' in L. Eubank, L. Selinker, and M. Sharwood Smith (eds.): *The Current State of Interlanguage*. Amsterdam: John Benjamins.

Gass, S. 2001. 'Sentence matching: a re-examination'. *Second Language Research* 17: 421–41.

Gass, S. 2003. 'Input and Interaction' in C. Doughty and M. Long (eds.): *The Handbook of Second Language Acquisition*. Malden, Mass.: Blackwell.

Gass, S. 2004. 'Conversation analysis and input-interaction'. *The Modern Language Journal* 88: 597–616.

Gass, S. and **J. Ard.** 1980. 'L2 data: their relevance for language universals'. *TESOL Quarterly* 16: 443–52.

Gass, S. and **J. Ard.** 1984. 'Second language acquisition and the ontology of language universals' in W. Rutherford (ed.): *Typological Universals and Second Language Acquisition*. Amsterdam: John Benjamins.

Gass, S. and **N. Houck.** 1999. *Interlanguage Refusals*. Berlin: Mouton de Gruyter.

Gass, S. and **U. Lakshmanan.** 1991. 'Accounting for interlanguage subject pronouns'. *Second Language Research* 7: 181–203.

Gass, S. and **A. Mackey.** 2000. *Stimulated Recall Methodology in Second Language Research*. Mahwah, N.J.: Lawrence Erlbaum.

Gass, S. and **A. Mackey.** 2002. 'Frequency effects and second language acquisition: a complex picture?' *Studies in Second Language Acquisition* 24: 223–36.

Gass, S., A. Mackey, M. Fernandez, and **M. Alvarez-Torres.** 1999. 'The effects of task repetition on linguistic output'. *Language Learning* 49: 549–80.

Gass, S., A. Mackey, and **T. Pica.** 1998. 'The role of input and interaction in second language acquisition: Introduction to the special issue'. *The Modern Language Journal* 82: 299–305.

Gass, S., A. Mackey, and **L. Ross-Feldman.** 2005. 'Task-based interactions in classroom and laboratory settings'. *Language Learning* 55: 575–611.

Gass, S. and **C. Madden** (eds.). 1985. *Input in Second Language Acquisition*. Rowley, Mass.: Newbury House.

Gass, S., C. Madden, D. Preston, and **L. Selinker** (eds.). 1989a. *Variation in Second Language Acquisition Volume I: Sociolinguistic Issues*. Clevedon: Multilingual Matters.

Gass, S., C. Madden, D. Preston, and **L. Selinker** (eds.). 1989b. *Variation in Second Language Acquisition Volume II: Psycholinguistic Issues*. Clevedon: Multilingual Matters.

Gass, S. and **J. Neu** (eds.). 1996. *Speech Acts Across Cultures: Challenges in Communication in a Second Language*. Berlin: de Gruyter.

Gass, S. and **J. Schachter** (eds.). 1989. *Linguistic Perspectives on Second Language Acquisition*. Cambridge: Cambridge University Press.

Gass, S. and **L. Selinker** (eds.). 1983. *Language Transfer in Language Learning*. Rowley, Mass.: Newbury House.

Gass, S. and **L. Selinker** (eds.). 1992. *Language Transfer in Language Learning* (Revised edition). Amsterdam: John Benjamins.

Gass, S., I. Svetics, and **S. Lemelin.** 2003. 'Differential effects of attention'. *Language Learning* 53: 497–545.

Gass, S. and **M. Varonis.** 1985. 'Task variation and nonnative/nonnative negotiation of meaning' in S. Gass and C. Madden (eds.): *Input in Second Language Acquisition*. Rowley, Mass.: Newbury House.

Gass, S. and **E. Varonis.** 1986. 'Sex differences in NNS/NNS interactions' in R. Day (ed.): *Talking to Learn: Conversation in Second Language Acquisition*. Rowley, Mass.: Newbury House.

Gass, S. and **E. Varonis.** 1991. 'Miscommunication in nonnative speaker discourse' in N. Coupland, H. Giles, and J. Wiemann (eds.): *Miscommunication and Problematic Talk*. Newbury Park: Sage Publications.

Gass, S. and **E. Varonis.** 1994. 'Input, interaction and second language production'. *Studies in Second Language Acquisition* 16: 283–302.

Gasser, M. 1990. 'Connectionism and universals of second language acquisition'. *Studies in Second Language Acquisition* 12: 179–99.

Gatbonton, E. 1978. 'Patterned phonetic variability in second language speech: a gradual diffusion model'. *Canadian Modern Language Review* 34: 335–47.

Gatbonton, E., P. Trofimovich, and **M. Magid.** 2005. 'Learners' ethnic group affiliation and L2 pronunciation accuracy: a sociolinguistic investigation'. *TESOL Quarterly* 39: 489–511.

Genesee, F. 1976. 'The role of intelligence in second language learning'. *Language Learning* 26: 267–80.

Genesee, F. 1980. 'Review of *The Bilingual Brain: Neuropsychological and Neurolinguistic Aspects of Bilingualism*'. *American Anthropologist* 82: 625–6.

Genesee, F. 1984. 'French immersion programs' in S. Shapson and V. D'Oyley (eds.): *Bilingual and Multicultural Education: Canadian Perspectives*. Clevedon: Multilingual Matters.

Genesee, F. 1987. *Learning Through Two Languages: Studies of Immersion and Bilingual Education*. Cambridge, Mass.: Newbury House.

George, H. 1972. *Common Errors in Language Learning: Insights from English*. Rowley, Mass.: Newbury House.

Gernsbacher M. and **M. Kaschak.** 2003. 'Neuroimaging studies of language production and comprehension'. *Annual Review of Psychology* 54: 91–114.

Giacalone Ramat, A. 1997. 'Progressive periphrases, markedness, and second language data' in S. Eliasson and E. Jahr (eds.): *Language and its Ecology*. Berlin: Mouton.

Gibbons, J. 1985. 'The silent period: an examination'. *Language Learning* 35: 255–67.

Gibbons, P. 2002. *Scaffolding Language, Scaffolding Learning: Teaching Second Language Learners in the Mainstream*. Portsmouth, N.H.: Heinemann.

Gieve, S. 1991. 'Goals and preferred language styles of Japanese English majors' in *Proceedings of the Conference on Second Language Research in Japan*. International University of Japan.

Gieve, S. and **I. Miller.** (eds.). 2006. *Understanding the Language Classroom*. Basingstoke: Palgrave Macmillan.

Giles, H. 1971. 'Our reactions to accent'. *New Society*, 14 October.

Giles, H. (ed.). 1977. *Language, Ethnicity and Intergroup Relations*. New York: Academic Press.

Giles, H. and **J. Byrne.** 1982. 'An intergroup approach to second language acquisition'. *Journal of Multicultural and Multilingual Development* 3: 17–40.

Giles, H. and **P. Johnson.** 1981. 'The role of language in ethnic group relations' in J. Turner and H. Giles (eds.): *Intergroup Behavior*. Chicago, Ill.: University of Chicago Press.

Giles, H., W. Robinson, and **P. Smith** (eds.). 1980. *Language: Social Psychological Perspectives*. Oxford: Pergamon Press.

Giles, H. and **W. Robinson** (eds.). 1990. *Handbook of Language and Social Psychology*. Chichester: John Wiley and Sons.

Giles, H. and **E. Ryan.** 1982. 'Prolegomena for developing a social psychological theory of language attitudes' in E. Ryan and H. Giles (eds.): *Attitudes Towards Language Variation*. London: Edward Arnold.

Giles, H. and **R. St. Clair** (eds.). 1979. *Language and Social Psychology*. Oxford: Blackwell.

Gingras, R. (ed.). *Second Language Acquisition and Foreign Language Teaching.* Arlington, Va.: Center for Applied Linguistics.

Givón, T. 1979. *On Understanding Grammar.* New York: Academic Press.

Givón, T. 1984. 'Universals of discourse structure and second language acquisition' in W. Rutherford (ed.): *Typological Universals and Second Language Acquisition.* Amsterdam: John Benjamins.

Givón, T. 1995. *Functionalism and Grammar.* Amsterdam: John Benjamins.

Glaser, R. (ed.). 1965. *Training, Research, and Education.* New York: Wiley.

Glass, W. and **A. Perez-Leroux** (eds.). 1997. *Contemporary Perspectives on the Acquisition of Spanish.* Somerville, Mass.: Cascadilla Press.

Gleitman, L., E. Newport, and **H. Gleitman.** 1984. 'The current status of the motherese hypothesis'. *Journal of Child Language* 11: 43–79.

Gliksman, L. 1976. 'Second language acquisition: the effects of student attitudes on classroom behavior'. Unpublished MA thesis, University of Western Ontario.

Gliksman, L., R. Gardner, and **P. Smythe.** 1982. 'The role of integrative motivation on students' participation in the French classroom'. *Canadian Modern Language Review* 38: 625–47.

Godfrey, D. 1980. 'A discourse analysis of tense' in D. Larsen-Freeman (ed.): *Discourse Analysis in Second Language Research.* Rowley, Mass.: Newbury House.

Golato, A. 2003. 'Studying compliment responses: a comparison of DCTs and recordings of naturally occurring talk'. *Applied Linguistics* 24: 90–121.

Goldberg, A. 2006. *Constructions at Work: The Nature of Generalization in Language.* Oxford: Oxford University Press.

Goldin-Meadow, S. 1982. 'The resilience of recursion: a study of a communication system developed without a conventional language model' in E. Wanner and L. Gleitman (eds.): *Language Acquisition: The State of the Art.* Cambridge: Cambridge University Press.

Goldschneider, J. and **R. DeKeyser.** 2001. 'Explaining the "Natural Order of L2 Morpheme Acquisition" in English: a meta-analysis of multiple determinants'. *Language Learning* 51: 1–50.

Goldstein, L. 1987. 'Standard English: the only target for nonnative speakers of English?' *TESOL Quarterly* 21: 417–36.

Goldstein, L. 1995. '"Nobody is talking bad": creating community and claiming power on the production line' in K. Hall and M. Bucholtz (eds.): *Gender Articulated: Language and the Socially Constructed Self.* New York: Routledge.

Golestani, N., F. Alaria, S. Meriaux, D. le Bihan, S. Dehaane, and **C. Pallaier.** 2006. 'Syntax production in bilinguals'. *Neuropsychologia* 44: 1029–40.

Gomez-Tortosa, E., E. M. Martin, M. Gaviria, F. Charbel, and **J. I. Ausman.** 1995. 'Selective deficit of one language in a bilingual patient following surgery in the left perisylvian area'. *Brain and Language* 48: 320–5.

Goodluck, H. 1986. 'Language acquisition and linguistic theory' in P. Fletcher and M. Garman (eds.): *Language Acquisition* (Second edition). Cambridge: Cambridge University Press.

Goody, E. (ed.). 1978. *Questions and Politeness.* Cambridge: Cambridge University Press.

Goss, N, Z. Ying-Hua, and **J. Lantolf.** 1994. 'Two heads may be better than one: mental activity in second language grammaticality judgements' in E. Tarone, S. Gass and A. Cohen (eds.): *Research Methodology in Second Language Research.* Hillsdale, N.J.: Lawrence Erlbaum.

Goulden, R., P. Nation, and **J. Read.** 1990. 'How large can a receptive vocabulary be?' *Applied Linguistics* 11: 341–73.

Gourlay, L. 2005. 'OK, who's got number one? Permeable triadic dialogue, covert participation and the co-construction of checking episodes'. *Language Teaching Research* 9: 403–22.

Graddol, D. 1997. *The Future of English?* London: The British Council.

Graham, C. and **C. Brown.** 1996. 'The effects of acculturation on second language proficiency in a community with a two-way bilingual program'. *The Bilingual Research Journal* 20: 235–60.

Granger, S. 1998a. 'The computerized learner corpus: a versatile new source of data for SLA research' in S. Granger (ed.): *Learner English on Computer.* London: Addison Wesley Longman.
Granger, S. 1998b. *Learner English on Computer.* London: Addison Wesley Longman.
Granger, S. 1999. 'Uses of tenses by advanced EFL learners: evidence from an error-tagged computer corpus' in H. Hasselgrad and S. Oksefjell (eds.): *Out of Corpora—Studies in Honour of Stig Johansson.* Amserdam and Atlanta: Rodopi.
Granger, S. and **S. Tyson.** 1996. 'Connector usage in the English essay writing of native and non-native EFL speakers of English'. *World Englishes* 15: 19–29.
Grauberg, W. 1971. 'An error analysis in the German of first-year university students' in G. Perren and J. Trim (eds.): *Applications of Linguistics.* Cambridge: Cambridge University Press.
Green, D. 2002. 'Representation and control: exploring recovery patterns in bilingual aphasics' in F. Fabbro (ed.): *Advances in the Neurolinguistics of Bilingualism.* Udine: Forum-Udine University Press.
Green, D. 2005. The neurocognition of recovery patterns in bilingual aphasia. In J. Kroll and A. de Groot (eds.): *Handbook of Bilingualism: Psycholinguistic Approaches.* New York: Oxford University Press.
Green, D., J. Crinion, and **C. Price.** 2006. 'Convergence, degeneracy and control' in M. Gullberg and P. Indefrey (eds.): *The Cognitive Neuroscience of Second Language Acquisition.* Malden, Mass.: Blackwell.
Green, P. 1975. 'Aptitude testing: an ongoing experiment'. *Audio-Visual Language Journal* 12: 205–10.
Green, P. and **K. Hecht.** 1992. 'Implicit and explicit grammar: an empirical study'. *Applied Linguistics* 13: 168–84.
Greenfield, P. and **C. Dent.** 1980. 'A developmental study of the communication of meaning: the role of uncertainty of information' in K. Nelson (ed.): *Children's Language Volume 2.* Gardner's Press.
Gregersen, T. and **E. Horwitz.** 2002. 'Language learning and perfectionism: anxious and non-anxious language learners' reactions to their own oral performance'. *The Modern Language Journal* 86: 562–70.
Gregg, K. 1984. 'Krashen's Monitor and Occam's Razor'. *Applied Linguistics* 5: 79–100.
Gregg, K. 1989. 'Second language acquisition theory: the case for a generative perspective' in S. Gass and J. Schachter (eds.): *Linguistic Perspectives on Second Language Acquisition.* Cambridge: Cambridge University Press.
Gregg, K. 1990. 'The variable competence model of second language acquisition and why it isn't'. *Applied Linguistics* 11: 364–83.
Gregg, K. 1993. 'Taking explanation seriously: or, let a couple of flowers bloom'. *Applied Linguistics* 14: 276–94.
Gregg, K. 2000. 'A theory for every occasion: postmodernism and SLA'. *Second Language Research* 16: 383–99.
Gregg, K. 2001. 'Learnability and SLA theory' in P. Robinson (ed.): *Cognition and Second Language Instruction.* Cambridge: Cambridge University Press.
Gregg, K. 2002. 'A garden ripe for weeding: a reply to Lantolf'. *Second Language Research* 18: 79–81.
Gregg, K. 2003. 'The state of emergentism in second language acquisition'. *Second Language Research* 19: 95–128.
Gregg, K. 2006. 'Taking a social turn for the worse: the language socialization paradigm for second language acquisition'. *Second Language Research* 22: 413–42.
Gregg, K., M. Long, G. Jordan, and **A. Beretta.** 1997. 'Rationality and its discontents in SLA'. *Applied Linguistics* 18/4: 538–58.

Gremmo, M., H. Holec, and P. Riley. 1978. *Taking the Initiative: Some Pedagogical Applications of Discourse Analysis.* Melanges Pedagogiques, University of Nancy: CRAPEL.

Grenfell, M. and **V. Harris.** 1999. *Modern Languages and Learning Strategies.* London: Routledge.

Griffiths, C. 2003. 'Patterns of language learning strategy use'. *System* 31: 367–83.

Griffiths, C. (ed.). 2008. *Lessons from Good Language Learners.* Cambridge: Cambridge University Press.

Griffiths, R. 1990. 'Speech rate and NNS comprehension: a preliminary study in time-benefit analysis'. *Language Learning* 40: 311–36.

Griffiths, R. 1991a. 'Pausological research in an L2 context: a rationale and review of selected studies'. *Applied Linguistics* 12: 345–64.

Griffiths, R. 1991b. 'Personality and second-language learning: theory, research and practice' in E. Sadtano (ed.): *Language Acquisition and the Second/Foreign Language Classroom.* Singapore: SEAMEO Regional Language Centre.

Griffiths, R. and **R. Sheen.** 1992. 'Disembedded figures in the landscape: a reappraisal of L2 research on field dependence/independence'. *Applied Linguistics* 13: 133–48.

Grigorenko, E., R. Sternberg, and **M. Ehrman.** 2000. 'A theory-based approach to the measurement of foreign language learning ability: the Canal-F theory and test'. *The Modern Language Journal* 84: 390–405.

Grosjean, F. 1989. 'Neurolinguists, beware! The bilingual is not two monolinguals'. *Brain and Language* 36: 3–15.

Grotjahn R. 1991. 'The research programme subjective theories: a new approach in second language research'. *Studies in Second Language Acquisition* 13: 187–214.

Guiora, A., W. Acton, R. Erard, and **F. Strickland.** 1980. 'The effects of benzodiazepine (valium) on permeability of language ego boundaries'. *Language Learning* 30: 351–63.

Guiora, A., B. Beit-Hallahmi, R. Brannon, C. Dull, and **T. Scovel.** 1972. 'The effects of experimentally induced changes in ego states on pronunciation ability in a second language: an exploratory study'. *Comprehensive Psychiatry* 13: 421–8.

Guiora, A., H. Lane, and **L. Bosworth.** 1967. 'An explanation of some personality variables in authentic pronunciation in a second language' in H. Lane and E. Zale (eds.): *Studies in Language and Language Behavior* 4. New York: Appleton-Century.

Gullberg, M. and **P. Indefrey.** (eds.). 2006. *The Cognitive Neuroscience of Second Language Acquisition.* Malden, Mass.: Blackwell.

Gumperz, J. 1982. *Discourse Strategies.* Cambridge: Cambridge University Press.

Gundel, J., K. Houlihan, and **G. Sanders.** 1986. 'Markedness distribution in phonology and syntax' in F. Eckman, E. Moravcsik and J. Wirth (eds.): *Markedness.* New York: Plenum Press.

Gupta, A. 1994. *The Step-Tongue: Children's English in Singapore.* Clevedon: Multilingual Matters.

Haastrup, K. and **B. Henriksen.** 1998. 'Vocabulary acquisition: from partial to precise understanding' in K. Haastrup and A. Viberg (eds.): *Perspectives on Lexical Acquisition in a Second Language.* Lund: Lund University Press.

Haastrup, K. and **A. Viberg** (eds.). 1998. *Perspectives on Lexical Acquisition in a Second Language.* Lund University: Lund University Press.

Hakansson, G. 1986. 'Quantitative studies of teacher talk' in G. Kasper (ed.): *Learning, Teaching and Communication in the Foreign Language Classroom.* Aarhus: Aarhus University Press.

Hakansson, G. 2001. 'Against full transfer—evidence from Swedish learners of German'. *Lund University Department of Linguistics Working Papers* 48: 67–86.

Hakansson, G. and **I. Lindberg.** 1988. 'What's the question? Investigating second language classrooms' in G. Kasper (ed.). Classroom Research. *AILA Review* 5: 73–88.

Hakuta, K. 1974. 'A preliminary report on the development of grammatical morphemes in a Japanese girl learning English as a second language'. *Working Papers on Bilingualism* 3: 18–43.

Hakuta, K. 1976. 'A case study of a Japanese child learning English as a second language'. *Language Learning* 26: 321–51.

Hakuta, K. and **E. Cancino.** 1977. 'Trends in second language acquisition research'. *Harvard Educational Review* 47: 294–316.

Halbach, A. 2000. 'Finding out about students' learning strategies by looking at their diaries: a case study'. *System* 28: 85–96.

Hale, T. and **E. Budar.** 1970. 'Are TESOL classes the only answer?' *The Modern Language Journal* 54: 487–92.

Hall, B. and **W. Gudykunst.** 1986. 'The intergroup theory of second language ability'. *Journal of Language and Social Psychology* 5: 291–302.

Hall, J. and **L. Verplaetse.** 2000. *Second and Foreign Language Learning Through Classroom Interaction*. Mahwah, N.J.: Lawrence Erlbaum.

Hall, K. and **M. Bucholtz** (eds.). 1995. *Gender Articulated: Language and the Socially Constructed Self*. New York: Routledge.

Hall, S. 1992. 'The question of cultural identity' in S. Hall, D. Held, and T. McGrew (eds.): *Modernity and its Futures*. Cambridge: Polity Press/Open University.

Hall, S., D. Held, and **T. McGrew** (eds.). 1992. *Modernity and its Futures*. Cambridge: Polity Press/Open University.

Halliday, M. 1973. *Explorations in the Functions of Language*. London: Edward Arnold.

Hamayan, E. and **R. Tucker.** 1980. 'Language input in the bilingual classroom and its relations to second language achievement'. *TESOL Quarterly* 14: 453–68.

Hamilton, R. 1994. 'Is implicational generalization unidirectional and maximal? Evidence from relativization instruction in a second language'. *Language Learning* 44: 123–57.

Hamilton, R. 1995. 'The Noun Phrase Accessibility Hierarchy in SLA: determining the basis for developmental effects' in F. Eckman, D. Highland, P. Lee, J. Milcham, and R. Weber (eds.): *Second Language Acquisition Theory and Pedagogy*. Mahwah, N.J.: Lawrence Erlbaum.

Hammarberg, B. 1973. 'The insufficiency of error analysis' in J. Svartvik (ed.): *Errata: Papers in Error Analysis*. Lund, Sweden: CWK Gleerup.

Hammarberg, B. 1979. 'On intralingual, interlingual and developmental solutions in interlanguage' in K. Hyltenstam and M. Linnarud (eds.): *Interlanguage Workshop at the Fifth Scandinavian Conference of Linguistics* 27–29: 7–24.

Hammarberg, B. 1988. 'Acquisition of phonology'. *Annual Review of Applied Linguistics* 9: 23–41.

Hammerley, H. 1987. 'The immersion approach: litmus test of second language acquisition through classroom communication'. *The Modern Language Journal* 71: 395–401.

Hammerley, H. 1989. *French Immersion: Myths and Reality*. Calgary, Alberta: Detselig Enterprises.

Hammond, R. 1988. 'Accuracy versus communicative competency: the acquisition of grammar in the second language classroom'. *Hispania* 71: 408–17.

Han, Y. 1996. 'L2 learners' explicit knowledge of verb complement structures and its relationship to implicit knowledge'. Unpublished doctoral dissertation, Philadelphia, Temple University.

Han, Y. and **R. Ellis.** 1998. 'Implicit knowledge, explicit knowledge and general language proficiency'. *Language Teaching Research* 2: 1–23.

Han, Z. 1998. 'Fossilization: an investigation into advanced L2 learning of a typologically distant language'. Unpublished PhD Thesis, University of London.

Han, Z. 2000. 'Persistence of the implicit influence of NL: the case of the pseudo-passive'. *Applied Linguistics* 21: 78–105.

Han, Z. 2002. 'A study of the impact of recasts on tense consistency in L2 output'. *TESOL Quarterly* 36: 543–72.

Han, Z. 2004. *Fossilization in Adult Second Language Acquisition*. Clevedon: Multilingual Matters.

Han, Z. and **T. Odlin** (eds.). 2006. *Studies of Fossilization in Second Language Acquisition*. Clevedon: Multilingual Matters.

Hanania, E. and **H. Gradman.** 1977. 'Acquisition of English structures: a case study of an adult native speaker of Arabic in an English-speaking environment'. *Language Learning* 27: 75–91.

Handscombe, J., R. Orem, and **B. Taylor** (eds.). 1984. *On TESOL '83: The Question of Control.* Washington D.C.: TESOL.

Hansen, D. 1995. 'A study of the effect of the acculturation model on second language acquisition' in F. Eckman, D. Highland, P. Lee, J. Milcham, and R. Weber (eds.): *Second Language Acquisition Theory and Pedagogy*. Mahwah, N.J.: Lawrence Erlbaum.

Hansen, J. 2001. 'Linguistic constraints on the acquisition of English syllabic codas by native speakers of Mandarin Chinese'. *Applied Linguistics* 22: 338–65.

Hansen, J. and **C. Stansfield.** 1981. 'The relationship of field dependent-independent cognitive styles to foreign language achievement'. *Language Learning* 31: 349–67.

Hansen, L. 1984. 'Field dependence-independence and language testing: evidence from six Pacific island cultures'. *TESOL Quarterly* 18: 311–24.

Hansen-Strain, L. and **J. Strain.** 1989. 'Variation in the relative clause of Japanese learners'. *JALT Journal* 11: 211–37.

Harder, P. 1980. 'Discourse as self-expression—on the reduced personality of the second language learner'. *Applied Linguistics* 1: 262–70.

Hardy, I. and **J. Moore.** 2004. 'Foreign language students' conversational negotiations in different task environments'. *Applied Linguistics* 25: 340–70.

Hargreaves, A. and **M. Fullan** (eds.). 1992. *Understanding Teacher Development*. London and New York: Cassell and Teachers College Press.

Harkness, S. 1977. 'Aspects of social environment and first language acquisition in rural Africa' in C. Snow and C. Ferguson (eds.): *Talking to Children: Language Input and Acquisition*. Cambridge: Cambridge University Press.

Harley, B. 1986. *Age in Second Language Acquisition*. Clevedon: Multilingual Matters.

Harley, B. 1989. 'Functional grammar in French immersion: A classroom experiment'. *Applied Linguistics* 19: 331–59.

Harley, B., J. P. Allen, J. Cummins, and **M. Swain** (eds.). 1987. *The Development of Bilingual Proficiency: Final Report. Volume III: Social Context and Age*. Toronto: Modern Language Centre, Ontario Institute for Studies in Education.

Harley, B., J. P. Allen, J. Cummins, and **M. Swain.** 1990. *The Development of Second Language Proficiency*. Cambridge: Cambridge University Press.

Harley, B. and **D. Hart.** 1997. 'Language aptitude and second language proficiency in classroom learners of different starting ages'. *Studies in Second Language Acquisition* 19: 379–400.

Harley, B. and **M. Swain.** 1978. 'An analysis of the verb system by young learners of French'. *Interlanguage Studies Bulletin* 3: 35–79.

Harrington, M. 1987. 'Processing transfer: language-specific processing strategies as a source of interlanguage variation'. *Applied Psycholinguistics* 8: 351–77.

Harrington, M. and **M. Sawyer.** 1992. 'L2 working memory capacity and L2 reading skill'. *Studies in Second Language Acquisition* 14: 25–38.

Harris, R. 1995. 'Disappearing language' in J. Mace (ed.): *Literacy, Language and Community Publishing*. Clevedon: Multilingual matters.

Harris, R., C. Leung, and **B. Rampton.** 2001. 'Globalisation, diaspora and language education in the UK' in D. Block and D. Cameron (eds.): *Language Learning and Teaching in the Age of Globalisation*. London: Routledge.

Harris, V. 2003. 'Adapting classroom-based strategy instruction to a distance learning context'. *TESL-EJ* 7: 1–19.

Harvey, P. 1994. 'The presence and absence of speech in the communication of gender' in P. Burton, K. Dyson, and S. Ardener (eds.): *Bilingual Women: Anthropological Approaches to Second Language Use*. Oxford: Berg.

Hasselgrad, H. and **S. Oksefjell** (eds.). 1999. *Out of Corpora—Studies in Honour of Stig Johansson*. Amsterdam and Atlanta: Rodopi.

Hatch, E. 1974. 'Second language learning—universals?' *Working Papers on Bilingualism* 3: 1–17.

Hatch, E. (ed.). 1978a. *Second Language Acquisition*. Rowley, Mass.: Newbury House.

Hatch, E. 1978b. 'Discourse analysis and second language acquisition' in E. Hatch (ed.): *Second Language Acquisition*. Rowley, Mass.: Newbury House.

Hatch, E. 1978c. 'Acquisition of syntax in a second language' in J. Richards (ed.): *Understanding Second and Foreign Language Learning: Issues and Approaches*. Rowley, Mass.: Newbury House.

Hatch, E. 1978d. 'Apply with caution'. *Studies in Second Language Acquisition* 2: 123–43.

Hatch, E. 1983a. 'Simplified input and second language acquisition' in R. Andersen (ed.): *Pidginization and Creolization as Language Acquisition*. Rowley, Mass.: Newbury House.

Hatch, E. 1983b. *Psycholinguistics: a Second Language Perspective*. Rowley, Mass.: Newbury House.

Hatch, E. and **H. Farhady.** 1982. *Research Design and Statistics for Applied Linguistics*. Rowley, Mass.: Newbury House.

Hatch, E. and **A. Lazaraton.** 1991. *The Research Manual: Design and Statistics for Applied Linguistics*. New York: Newbury House/Harper Collins.

Hatch, E. and **M. Long.** 1980. 'Discourse analysis, what's that?' in D. Larsen-Freeman (ed.): *Discourse Analysis in Second Language Research*. Rowley, Mass.: Newbury House.

Hatch, E., S. Peck, and **J. Wagner-Gough.** 1979. 'A look at process in child second language acquisition' in E. Ochs and B. Schieffelin (eds.): *Developmental Pragmatics*. New York: Academic Press.

Hatch, E., R. Shapira, and **J. Wagner-Gough.** 1978. 'Foreigner talk discourse'. *ITL Review of Applied Linguistics* 39/40: 39–60.

Hatch, E., Y. Shirai, and **C. Fantuzzi.** 1990. 'The need for an integrated theory: connecting modules'. *TESOL Quarterly* 24: 697–716.

Hatch, E. and **J. Wagner-Gough.** 1976. 'Explaining sequence and variation in second language acquisition'. *Language Learning* (Special issue) 4: 39–47.

Hauser, E. 2005. 'Coding "corrective recasts": the maintenance of meaning and more fundamental problems'. *Applied Linguistics* 26: 293–316.

Hauser, M., N. Chomsky, and **T. Fitch.** 2002. 'The faculty of language: what is it, who has it, and how did it evolve? *Science* 298: 1569–79.

Havranek, G. and **H. Cesnik.** 2003. 'Factors affecting the success of corrective feedback' in S. Foster-Cohen and A. Nizegorodzew (eds.): *EUROSLA Yearbook 1*. Amsterdam: John Benjamins.

Hawkins, B. 1985. 'Is the appropriate response always so appropriate' in S. Gass and C. Madden (eds.): *Input in Second Language Acquisition*. Rowley, Mass.: Newbury House.

Hawkins, J. 1980. 'On implicational and distributional universals of word order'. *Journal of Linguistics* 16: 193–235.

Hawkins, J. 1983. *Word Order Universals*. New York: Academic Press.

Hawkins, J. 1999. 'Processing complexity and filler-gap dependencies across grammars'. *Language* 75: 244–85.

Hawkins, R. 1987. 'Markedness and the acquisition of the English dative alternation by L2 learners'. *Second Language Research* 3: 20–55.

Hawkins, R. 1989. 'Do second language learners acquire restrictive relative clauses on the basis of relational or configurational information? The acquisition of French subject, direct object and genitive restrictive relative clauses by second language learners'. *Second Language Research* 5: 158–88.

Hawkins, R. 2001a. *Second Language Syntax: A Generative Introduction*. Oxford: Blackwell.

Hawkins, R. 2001b. 'The theoretical significance of Universal Grammar in second language acquisition'. *Second Language Research* 17: 345–367.

Hawkins, R. and **C. Chan.** 1997. 'The partial availability of UG in second language acquisition. The "failed functional features hypothesis"'. *Second Language Research* 13: 187–226.

Hayes, J. (ed.). 1970. *Cognition and the Development of Language*. New York: Wiley and Sons.

Hayes, T. and **K. Yoshioka** (eds.). 1990. *Proceedings of the First Conference on Second Language Acquisition and Teaching Volume 1*. Language Programs of the International University of Japan.

Healy, A. and **L. Bourne** (eds.). 1998. *Foreign Language Learning: Psycholinguistic Studies on Training and Retention*. Hillsdale, N.J.: Lawrence Erlbaum.

Heath, S. 1983. *Ways with Words: Language, Life and Work in Communities and Classrooms*. Cambridge: Cambridge University Press.

Hedgcock, J. 1993. 'Well-formed vs. ill-formed strings in L2 metalingual tasks: specifying features of grammaticality judgements'. *Second Language Research* 9: 1–21.

Heidelberger Forschungsprojekt. 1978. 'The acquisition of German syntax by foreign migrant workers' in D. Sankoff (ed.): *Linguistic Variation: Model and Methods*. New York: Academic Press.

Heller, M. 1999. *Linguistic Minorities and Modernity*. Harlow: Longman.

Heller, M. 2001. 'Gender and public space in a bilingual school' in A. Pavlenko, A. Backledge, I. Piller, and M. Teutsch-Dwyer (eds.): *Multilingualism, Second Language Learning, and Gender*. Berlin: Mouton de Gruyter.

Hendrickson, J. 1978. 'Error correction in foreign language teaching: recent theory, research and practice'. *The Modern Language Journal* 62: 387–98.

Henning, C. (ed.). 1977. *Proceedings of the Los Angeles Second Language Research Forum*. University of California at Los Angeles.

Henzl, V. 1973. 'Linguistic register of foreign language instruction'. *Language Learning* 23: 207–27.

Henzl, V. 1979. 'Foreigner talk in the classroom'. *International Review of Applied Linguistics* 17: 159–65.

Herbert, R. 1989. 'The ethnography of compliments' in W. Oleksy (ed.): *Contrastive Pragmatics*. Amsterdam: John Benjamins.

Hermann, G. 1980. 'Attitudes and success in children's learning of English as a second language: the motivational vs. the resultative hypothesis'. *ELT Journal* 34: 247–54.

Hernandez, A. E., A. Martinez, and **K. Kohnert.** 2000. 'In search of the language switch: an fMRI study of picture naming in Spanish–English bilinguals'. *Brain and Language* 73: 421–31.

Higgs, T. (ed.). 1982. *Curriculum, Competence and the Foreign Language Teacher*. Skokie, Ill.: National Textbook Company.

Higgs, T. and **R. Clifford.** 1982. 'The push toward communication' in T. Higgs (ed.): *Curriculum, Competence and the Foreign Language Teacher*. Skokie, Ill.: National Textbook Company.

Hill, J. 1987. 'Women's speech in modern Mexicano' in S. Philips, S. Steele, and C. Tanz (eds.): *Language, Gender and Sex in Comparative Perspective*. Cambridge: Cambridge University Press.

Hill, T. 1997. 'The development of pragmatic competence in an EFL context'. Unpublished PhD dissertation, Japan, Temple University.

Hilles, S. 1986. 'Interlanguage and the pro-drop parameter'. *Second Language Research* 2: 33–52.

Hilles, S. 1991. 'Access to Universal Grammar in second language acquisition' in L. Eubank (ed.): *Point Counterpoint: Universal Grammar in the Second Language*. Amsterdam: John Benjamins.

Hines, M. and **W. Rutherford** (eds.). 1981. *On TESOL '81*. Washington D.C.: TESOL.

Hinkel, E. 2002. Second *Language Writers' Text: Linguistic and Rhetorical Features (ESL and Applied Linguistics Professional Series)*. Mahwah, N.J.: Lawrence Erlbaum.

Hinkel, E. (ed.). 2005. *Handbook of Research in Second Language Teaching and Learning*. Mahwah, N.J.: Lawrence Erlbaum.

Hirakawa, M. 1990. 'A study of the L2 acquisition of English reflexives'. *Second Language Research* 6: 60–85.

Ho, D. 2005. 'Why do teachers ask the questions they ask?' *RELC Journal* 36: 297–310.

Hoekstra, T. and **B. Schwartz** (eds.). 1994. *Language Acquisition Studies in Generative Grammar*. Amsterdam: John Benjamins.

Holec, H. 1980. 'Learner training: meeting needs in self-directed learning' in H. Altman and C. Vaughan James (eds.): *Foreign Language Teaching: Meeting Individual Needs*. Oxford: Pergamon.

Holec, H. 1987. 'The learner as manager: managing learning or managing to learn?' in A. Wenden and J. Rubin (eds.): *Learner Strategies in Language Learning*. Englewood Cliffs, N.J.: Prentice Hall.

Holmes, J. 1988. 'Paying compliments: a sex-preferential positive politeness strategy'. *Journal of Pragmatics* 12: 445–65.

Holobrow, N., F. Genesee, and **W. Lambert.** 1991. 'The effectiveness of a foreign language immersion program for children from different ethnic and social class backgrounds: Report 2'. *Applied Psycholinguistics* 12: 179–98.

Holunga, S. 1995. 'The effect of metacognitive strategy training with verbalization on the oral accuracy of adult second language learners'. Unpublished doctoral dissertation, University of Toronto (Ontario Institute for Studies in Education).

Hopper, P. 1979. 'Aspect and foregrounding in discourse' in T. Givón (ed.): *Syntax and Semantics: Discourse and Syntax*. New York: Academic Press.

Hopper, P. 1998. 'Emergent grammar' in M. Tomasello (ed.). *The New Psychology of Language: Cognitive and Functional Approaches to Language Structure*. Mahwah, N.J.: Lawrence Erlbaum.

Hornberger, N. and **D. Corson** (eds.). 1997. *Encyclopedia of Language and Education Volume 8: Research Methods in Language and Education*. The Netherlands: Kluwer.

Hornstein, N. and **D. Lightfoot** (eds.). 1981. *Explanation in Linguistics: The Logical Problem of Language Acquisition*. London: Longman.

Horst, M., T. Cobb, and **P. Meara.** 1998. 'Beyond a Clockwork Orange: acquiring a second language vocabulary through reading'. *Reading in a Foreign Language* 11: 207–23.

Horwitz, E. 1986. 'Preliminary evidence for the reliability and validity of a foreign language anxiety scale'. *TESOL Quarterly* 20: 559–62.

Horwitz, E. 1987a. 'Surveying student beliefs about language learning' in A. Wenden and J. Rubin (eds.). *Learner Strategies in Language Learning*. New York: Prentice Hall.

Horwitz, E. 1987b. 'Linguistic and communicative competence: reassessing foreign language aptitude' in B. VanPatten, T. Dvorak, and J. Lee (eds.): *Foreign Language Learning: A Research Perspective*. New York: Newbury House.

Horwitz, E. 1999. 'Cultural and situation influences on foreign language learners' beliefs about language learning: a review of BALLI studies'. *System* 27: 557–76.

Horwitz, E. 2000a. 'Teachers and students, students and teachers: an ever-evolving partnership'. *The Modern Language Journal* 84: 523–35.

Horwitz, E. 2000b. 'It ain't over till it's over: on foreign language anxiety, first language deficits, and the confounding of variables'. *The Modern Language Journal* 84: 256–9.

Horwitz, E. 2001. 'Language anxiety and achievement'. *Annual Review of Applied Linguistics* 21: 112–26.

Horwitz, E., M. Horwitz, and **J. Cope.** 1986. 'Foreign language classroom anxiety'. *The Modern Language Journal* 70: 125–32.

Horwitz, E. and **D. Young.** 1991. *Language Learning Anxiety: from Theory and Research to Classroom Implications*. Englewood Cliffs, N.J.: Prentice Hall.

Hosenfeld, C. 1978. 'Students' mini-theories of second language learning'. *Association Bulletin* 29: 2.

House, J. 1986. 'Learning to talk: talking to learn. An investigation of learner performance in two types of discourse' in G. Kasper (ed.): *Learning, Teaching and Communication in the Foreign Language Classroom*. Aarhus: Aarhus University Press.

House, J. 1989. 'Excuse me please: Apologizing in a foreign language' in B. Ketterman *et al.* (eds.): *Englisch als Zweitsprache*. Tübingen: Gunter Narr.

House, J. and **G. Kasper.** 1987. 'Interlanguage pragmatics: requesting in a foreign language' in W. Lörscher and R. Schultze (eds.): *Perspectives on Language in Performance*. Tübingen: Gunter Narr.

Housen, A. and **M. Pierrard.** 2006a. 'Investigating instructed second language acquisition' in A. Housen and M. Pierrard (eds.): *Investigations in Instructed Second Language Acquisition*. Berlin: Mouton de Gruyter.

Housen, A. and **M. Pierrard** (eds.). 2006b. *Investigations in Instructed Second Language Acquisition*. Berlin: Mouton de Gruyter.

Housen, A., M. Pierrard, and **S. Vandaele.** 2006. 'Structure complexity and the efficacy of explicit grammar instruction' in A. Housen and M. Pierrard (eds.): *Investigations in Instructed Second Language Acquisition*. Berlin: Mouton de Gruyter.

Howard, G. 1994. *The Good English Guide*. London, Macmillan

Hsiao, T. and **R. Oxford.** 2002. 'Comparing theories of language learning strategies: a confirmatory factor analysis'. *The Modern Language Journal* 86: 368–83.

Hu, G. 2002. 'Psychological constraints on the utility of metalinguistic knowledge in second language production'. *Studies in Second Language Acquisition* 24: 347–86.

Huang, C. 1984. 'On the distribution and reference of empty pronouns'. *Linguistic Inquiry* 15: 531–74.

Huang, J. 1970. 'A Chinese child's acquisition of syntax'. Unpublished MA TESL thesis, University of California at Los Angeles.

Huang, J. and **E. Hatch.** 1978. 'A Chinese child's acquisition of English'. in E. Hatch (ed.): *Second Language Acquisition*. Rowley, Mass.: Newbury House.

Huckin, T. and **J. Coady.** 1999. 'Incidental vocabulary acquisition in a second language: a review'. *Studies in Second Language Acquisition* 21: 181–94.

Huckin, T., M. Haynes, and **J. Coady** (eds.). 1982. *Second Language Reading and Vocabulary Learning*. Norwood, N.J.: Ablex.

Hudson, T. 1993. 'Nothing does not equal zero: problems with applying developmental sequence findings to assessment and pedagogy'. *Studies in Second Language Acquisition* 15: 461–93.

Huebner, T. 1979. 'Order-of-acquisition vs. dynamic paradigm: a comparison of method in interlanguage research'. *TESOL Quarterly* 13: 21–8.

Huebner, T. 1980. 'Creative construction and the case of the misguided pattern' in J. Fisher, M. Clarke, and J. Schachter (eds.). *On TESOL '80*. Washington D.C.: TESOL.

Huebner, T. 1983. *A Longitudinal Analysis of the Acquisition of English*. Ann Arbor: Karoma Publishers.

Huebner, T. 1985. 'System and variability in interlanguage syntax'. *Language Learning* 35: 141–63.

Hughes, A. and **C. Lascaratou.** 1982. 'Competing criteria for error gravity'. *ELT Journal* 36: 175–82.

Hughes, M. (ed.). 1996. *Teaching and Learning in Changing Times*. Oxford: Blackwell.

Hulstijn, J. 1987. 'Onset and development of grammatical features: two approaches to acquisition orders'. Paper given at Interlanguage Conference, La Trobe University, Melbourne.

Hulstijn, J. 1989. 'Implicit and incidental second language learning: experiments in the processing of natural and partly artificial input' in H. Dechert and M. Raupach (eds.): *Interlingual Processes*. Tübingen: Gunter Narr.

Hulstijn, J. 1990. 'A comparison between the information-processing and the analysis/control approaches to language learning'. *Applied Linguistics* 11: 30–45.

Hulstijn, J. 1992. 'Retention of inferred and given word meanings: experiments in incidental vocabulary learning' in P. Arnaud and H. Bejoint (eds.): *Vocabulary and Applied Linguistics*. London: Macmillan.

Hulstijn, J. 2002. 'Towards a unified account of the representation, processing and acquisition of second language knowledge'. *Second Language Research* 18: 193–223.

Hulstijn, J. 2003. 'Incidental and intentional learning' in C. Doughty and M. Long (eds.): *The Handbook of Second Language Acquisition*. Malden, Mass.: Blackwell.

Hulstijn, J. and **R. De Graaf.** 1994. 'Under what conditions does explicit knowledge of a second language facilitate the acquisition of implicit knowledge? A research proposal' in J. Hulstijn and R. Schmidt (eds.): *Consciousness in Second Language Learning. AILA Review* 11.

Hulstijn, J. and **W. Hulstijn.** 1984. 'Grammatical errors as a function of processing constraints and explicit knowledge'. *Language Learning* 34: 23–43.

Hulstijn, J. and **E. Marchena.** 1989. 'Avoidance: grammatical or semantic causes'. *Studies in Second Language Acquisition* 11: 242–55.

Hulstijn, J. and **R. Schmidt** (eds.). 1994. *Consciousness in Second Language Learning. AILA Review* 11.

Hyams, N. 1983. 'The acquisition of parameterized grammars'. Unpublished PhD dissertation, City University of New York.

Hyams, N. 1991. 'Seven not-so-trivial trivia of language acquisition: comments on Wolfgang Klein' in L. Eubank (ed.): *Point Counterpoint: Universal Grammar in the Second Language*. Amsterdam: John Benjamins.

Hyltenstam, K. 1977. 'Implicational patterns in interlanguage syntax variation'. *Language Learning* 27: 383–411.

Hyltenstam, K. 1984. 'The use of typological markedness conditions as predictors in second language acquisition: the case of pronominal copies in relative clauses' in R. Andersen (ed.): *Second Language: a Crosslinguistic Perspective*. Rowley, Mass.: Newbury House.

Hyltenstam, K. 1990. 'Typological markedness as a research tool in the study of second language acquisition' in H. Dechert (ed.): *Current Trends in European Second Language Acquisition Research*. Clevedon: Multilingual Matters.

Hyltenstam, K. and **N. Abrahamsson.** 2001. 'Age and L2 learning: the hazards of matching practical "implications" with theoretical "facts"'. *TESOL Quarterly* 35: 151–69.

Hyltenstam, K. and **N. Abrahamsson.** 2003. 'Maturational constraints in SLA' in C. Doughty and M. Long (eds.): *The Handbook of Second Language Acquisition*. Malden, Mass.: Blackwell.

Hyltenstam, K. and **M. Pienemann** (eds.). 1985. *Modelling and Assessing Second Language Acquisition*. Clevedon: Multilingual Matters.

Hymes, D. (ed.). 1971. *Pidginization and Creolization of Languages*. Cambridge: Cambridge University Press.

Hymes, D. 1974. *Foundations in Sociolinguistics: An Ethnographic Approach*. Philadelphia: University of Pennsylvania Press.

Indefrey, P. 2006. 'A meta-analysis of hemodynamic studies of first and second language processing: which suggested differences can we trust and what do they mean?' in M. Gullberg and P. Indefrey (eds.): *The Cognitive Neuroscience of Second Language Acquisition*. Malden, Mass.: Blackwell.

Indefrey, P. and **M. Gullberg.** 2006. 'Introduction' in M. Gullberg and P. Indefrey (eds.): *The Cognitive Neuroscience of Second Language Acquisition.* Malden, Mass.: Blackwell.

Ioup, G. 1977. 'Interference versus structural complexity as a predictor of second language relative clause acquisition' in C. Henning (ed.): *Proceedings of the Los Angeles Second Language Research Forum.* University of California at Los Angeles.

Ioup, G. 1996. 'Grammatical knowledge and memorized chunks: a response to Ellis'. *Studies in Second Language Acquisition* 18: 355–60.

Ioup, G., E. Boustagui, M. El Tigi, and **M. Moselle.** 1994. 'Reexamining the critical period hypothesis: the influence of maturational state on the acquisition of English as a second language'. *Studies in Second Language Acquisition* 16: 73–98.

Ioup, G. and **S. Weinberger** (eds.). 1987. *Interlanguage Phonology: The Acquisition of a Second Language Sound System.* Rowley, Mass.: Newbury House.

Isemonger, I. and **C. Sheppard.** 2007. 'A construct-related validity study on a Korean version of the Perceptual Learning Styles Preference questionnaire'. *Educational and Psychological Measurement* 67: 1–12.

Isemonger, I. and **K. Watanabe.** 2007. 'The construct validity of scores on a Japanese version of the perceptual component of the Style Analysis Survey'. *System* 35: 134–47.

Ishida, M. 2004. 'Effects of recasts on the acquisition of the aspectual form of –te i (ru) by learners of Japanese as a foreign language'. *Language Learning* 54: 311–94.

Issidorides, D. and **J. Hulstijn.** 1992. 'Comprehension of grammatically modified and nonmodified sentences by second language learners'. *Applied Psycholinguistics* 13: 147–71.

Itoh, H. and **E. Hatch.** 1978. 'Second language acquisition: a case study' in E. Hatch (ed.): *Second Language Acquisition.* Rowley, Mass.: Newbury House.

Iwashita, N. 2003. 'Negative feedback and positive evidence in task-based interaction: differential effects of L2 development'. *Studies in Second Language Acquisition* 25: 1–36.

Iwashita N., C. Elder, and **T. McNamara.** 2001. 'Can we predict task difficulty in an oral proficiency test? Exploring the potential of an information-processing approach to task design'. *Language Learning* 51/3: 401–36.

Izumi, E., K. Uchimoto, and **H. Isahara.** 2004. 'SST speech corpus of Japanese learners' English and automatic detection of learners' errors'. *ICAME Journal* 28: 31–48.

Izumi, S. 2003. 'Processing difficulty in comprehension and production of relative clauses by learners of English as a second language'. *Language Learning* 53: 285–323.

Izumi, S. and **M. Bigelow.** 1999. 'Does output promote noticing and second language acquisition?' *TESOL Quarterly* 34: 239–78.

Izumi, S., M. Bigelow, M. Fujiwara, and **S. Fearnow.** 1999. 'Testing the output hypothesis: effects of output on noticing and second language acquisition'. *Studies in Second Language Acquisition* 21: 421–52.

Jackson, H. 1981. 'Contrastive analysis as a predictor of errors, with reference to Punjabi learners of English' in J. Fisiak (ed.): *Contrastive Linguistics and the Language Teacher.* Oxford: Pergamon.

Jackson, K. and **R. Whitnam.** 1971. *Evaluation of the Predictive Power of Contrastive Analyses of Japanese and English. Final report.* Contract No. CEC-0-70-5046 (-823), US Office of Health, Education and Welfare.

Jacobs, B. and **J. Schumann.** 1992. 'Language acquisition and the neurosciences: towards a more integrative perspective'. *Applied Linguistics* 13: 282–301.

Jacobs, G. 1998. 'Cooperative learning or just grouping students: the difference makes a difference' in W. Renandya and G. Jacobs (eds.): *Learners and Language Learning.* Singapore: SEAMEO Regional Language Centre.

Jaeggli, O. and **K. Safir.** 1989. 'The null subject parameter and parametric theory' in O. Jaeggli and K. Safir (eds.): *The Null Subject Parameter.* Dordrecht: Kluwer.

Jain, M. 1974. 'Error analysis: Source, cause and significance' in J. Richards (ed.): *Error Analysis.* London: Longman.

Jakobovits, L. 1970. *Foreign Language Learning: a Psycholinguistic Analysis of the Issue.* Rowley, Mass.: Newbury House.

James, C. 1971. 'The exculpation of contrastive linguistics' in G. Nickel (ed.): *Papers in Contrastive Analysis.* Cambridge: Cambridge University Press.

James, C. 1977. 'Judgments of error gravity'. *ELT Journal* 31: 116–24.

James, C. 1980. *Contrastive Analysis.* London: Longman.

James, C. 1990. 'Learner language'. *Language Teaching* 23: 205–13.

James, C. 1998. *Errors in Language Learning and Use.* London: Longman

Janicki, K. 1985. *The Foreigner's Language: a Sociolinguistic Perspective.* Oxford: Pergamon Press.

Jarvis G. 1968. 'A behavioral observation system for classroom foreign language learning'. *The Modern Language Journal* 52: 335–41.

Jarvis, S. 2000. 'Methodological rigor in the study of transfer: identifying L1 influence in the interlanguage lexicon'. *Language Learning* 50: 245–309.

Jauregi, K. 1990. 'Task-variation in non-native/non-native conversation'. Unpublished master's thesis, University of Reading.

Jenkins, J. 2000. *The Phonology of English as an International Language.* Oxford: Oxford University Press.

Jeon, E. and **T. Kaya.** 2006. 'Effects of L2 instruction on interlanguage pragmatic development: a meta-analysis' in J. Norris and L. Ortega (eds.): *Synthesizing Research on Language Teaching and Learning.* Amsterdam: John Benjamins.

Jerzkiewicz, L. 2000. (Untitled paper). http://webhost.bridgew.edu/ljerzykiewicz/Papers/SLA%20Neuroscience.pdf.

Jiang, N. 2000. 'Lexical representation and development in a second language'. *Applied Linguistics* 21: 47–77.

Jiang, N. 2002. 'Form-meaning mapping in vocabulary acquisition in a second language'. *Studies in Second Language Acquisition* 24: 617–36.

Johansson, S. 1973. 'The identification and evaluation of errors in foreign languages: a functional approach' in J. Svartvik (ed.): *Errata: Papers in Error Analysis.* Lund, Sweden: CWK Gleerup.

Johnson, D. 1992. *Approaches to Research in Second Language Learning.* New York: Longman.

Johnson, J. and **E. Newport.** 1989. 'Critical period effects in second language learning: the influence of maturational state on the acquisition of English as a second language'. *Cognitive Psychology* 21: 60–99.

Johnson, J. and **E. Newport.** 1991. 'Critical period effects on universal properties'. *Cognition* 39: 215.

Johnson, J., S. Prior, and **M. Artuso.** 2000. 'Field dependence as a factor in second language communicative production'. *Language Learning* 50: 529–67.

Johnson, K. 1988. 'Mistake correction'. *ELT Journal* 42: 89–101.

Johnson, K. (ed.). 1989. *The Second Language Curriculum.* Cambridge: Cambridge University Press.

Johnson, K. 1995. *Understanding Communication in Second Language Classrooms.* Cambridge: Cambridge University Press.

Johnson, K. 1996. *Language Teaching and Skill Learning.* Oxford: Blackwell.

Johnson, K. 2006. 'The sociocultural turn and its challenges for second language teacher education'. *TESOL Quarterly* 40: 235–57.

Johnson, M. 2004. *A Philosophy of Second Language Acquisition.* New Haven, Conn.: Yale University Press.

Johnson, P. 1981. 'Effects on reading comprehension of language complexity and cultural background of a text'. *TESOL Quarterly* 15: 169–81.

Johnson, R. and **M. Swain.** (eds.). 1997. *Immersion Education: International Perspectives.* Cambridge: Cambridge University Press.

Johnston, M. and **M. Pienemann.** 1986. *Second Language Acquisition: a Classroom Perspective*. New South Wales Migrant Education Service.

Jones, A. 1991a. 'Review of studies on the acquisition of relative clauses in English'. Unpublished paper, Temple University, Japan.

Jones, A. 1991b. 'Learning to walk before you can run'. Unpublished paper, Temple University, Japan.

Jones, A. 1992. 'Relatively speaking'. Unpublished paper, Temple University, Tokyo.

Jones, B. 2004. 'The neurobiology of memory consolidation' in J. Schumann *et al.* (eds.): *The Neurobiology of Learning: Perspectives from Second Language Acquisition*. Mahwah, N.J.: Lawrence Erlbaum.

Jordain, S. 2000. 'A native-like ability to circumlocute'. *The Modern Language Journal* 84: 185–95.

Jordan, G. 2003. *Theory Construction in Second Language Acquisition*. Amsterdam: John Benjamins.

Jordens, P. 1980. 'Interlanguage research: interpretation and explanation'. *Language Learning* 30: 195–207.

Jordens, P. 1988. 'The acquisition of word order in L2 Dutch and German' in P. Jordens and L. Lalleman (eds.): *Language Development*. Dordrecht: Foris.

Jordens, P. and **L. Lalleman** (eds.). 1988. *Language Development*. Dordrecht: Foris.

Jourdenais, R. 2001. 'Cognition, instruction and protocol analysis' in P. Robinson (ed.): *Cognition and Second Language Instruction*. Cambridge: Cambridge University Press.

Jourdenais, R., M. Ota, S. Stauffer, B. Boyson, and **C. Doughty.** 1995. 'Does textual enhancement promote noticing? A think-aloud protocol analysis' in R. Schmidt (ed.): *Attention and Awareness in Foreign Language Learning*. Honolulu: University of Hawai'i Press.

Judd, E. 1978. 'Language policy and TESOL: socio-political factors and their influences on the profession' in C. Blatchford and J. Schachter (eds.). *On TESOL '78: Policies, Programs and Practices*. Washington D.C.: TESOL.

Juffs, A. (in press). 'Working Memory, second language acquisition, and low-educated second language and literacy learners'. *LOT Occasional Papers*: Netherlands Graduate School of Linguistics.

Kachru, B. 1982. *The Other Tongue: English Across Cultures*. Urbana Ill.: University of Illinois Press

Kachru, B. 1986. *The Alchemy of English*. Oxford: Pergamon Press.

Kachru, B. 1999. 'Asian Englishes: contexts, constructs and creativity'. Keynote address, the 12th World Congress of the International Association of Applied Linguistics, Tokyo.

Kachru, B. and **C. Nelson.** 1996. 'World Englishes' in S. McKay and N. Hornberger (eds.): *Sociolinguistics and Language Teaching*. Cambridge: Cambridge University Press.

Kadia, K. 1988. 'The effect of formal instruction on monitored and spontaneous naturalistic interlanguage performance'. *TESOL Quarterly* 22: 509–15.

Kalaja, P. and **A. Barcelos** (eds.). 2003. *Beliefs about SLA: New Research Approaches*. Dordrecht: Kluwer.

Kamimoto, T., A. Shimura, and **E. Kellerman.** 1992. 'A second language classic reconsidered—the case of Schachter's avoidance'. *Second Language Research* 8: 231–77.

Kanagy, R. 1999. 'Interactional routines as a mechanism for L2 acquisition and socialization in an immersion context'. *Journal of Pragmatics* 31: 1467–92.

Kaneko, T. 1991. 'The role of the L1 in second language classrooms'. Unpublished EdD dissertation, Temple University, Japan.

Kang, S. 2005. 'Dynamic emergence of situational willingness to communicate in a second language'. *System* 33: 277–92.

Kanno, K. 1997. 'The acquisition of null and overt pronominals in Japanese by English speakers'. *Second Language Research* 13: 265–87.

Kaplan, R. (ed.). 2002. *The Oxford Handbook of Applied Linguistics*. New York: Oxford.

Karmiloff-Smith, A. 1986. 'From metaprocess to conscious access: evidence from children's metalinguistic and repair data'. *Cognition* 28: 95–147.

Karmiloff-Smith, A. 1992. *Beyond Modularity: A Developmental Perspective on Cognitive Science.* Cambridge, Mass.: MIT Press.

Kasper, G. 1981. *Pragmatische Aspeckte in der Interimsprache.* Tübingen: Gunter Narr.

Kasper, G. 1984a. 'Pragmatic comprehension in learner–native speaker discourse'. *Language Learning* 34: 1–20.

Kasper, G. 1984b. 'Perspectives on language transfer'. *BAAL Newsletter* 24.

Kasper, G. 1985. 'Repair in foreign language teaching'. *Studies in Second Language Acquisition* 7: 200–15.

Kasper, G. (ed.). 1986. *Learning, Teaching and Communication in the Foreign Language Classroom.* Aarhus: Aarhus University Press.

Kasper, G. 1990. 'Linguistic politeness: current research issues'. *Journal of Pragmatics* 14: 193–218.

Kasper, G. 1992. 'Pragmatic transfer'. *Second Language Research* 8: 203–31.

Kasper, G. 2001. 'Four perspectives on L2 pragmatic development'. *Applied Linguistics* 22: 502–30.

Kasper, G. 2004. 'Participant orientations in German conversation-for-learning'. *The Modern Language Journal* 88: 551–67.

Kasper, G. and **S. Blum-Kulka** (eds.). 1993. *Interlanguage Pragmatics.* Oxford: Oxford University Press.

Kasper, G. and **M. Dahl.** 1991. 'Research methods in interlanguage pragmatics'. *Studies in Second Language Acquisition* 12: 215–47.

Kasper, G. and **E. Kellerman** (eds.). 1997a. *Communication Strategies: Psycholinguistic and Sociolinguistic Perspectives.* London: Longman.

Kasper, G. and **E. Kellerman.** 1997b. 'Introduction: Approaches to communication strategies' in G. Kasper and E. Kellerman (ed.): *Communication Strategies: Psycholinguistic and Sociolinguistic Perspectives.* London: Longman.

Kasper, G. and **K. Rose.** 2002. *Pragmatic Development in a Second Language.* Language Learning Monograph Series. Oxford: Blackwell.

Kasper, G. and **R. Schmidt.** 1996. 'Developmental issues in interlanguage pragamatics'. *Studies in Second Language Acquisition.* 18: 149–69.

Kawaguchi, S. 2005. 'Argument structure and syntactic development in Japanese as a second language' in M. Pienemann (ed.): *Cross-linguistic Aspects of Processability Theory.* Amsterdam: John Benjamins.

Kaylani, C. 1996. 'The influence of gender and motivation on EFL learning strategy use in Jordan' in R. Oxford (ed.): *Language Learning Strategies Around the World: Cross-cultural Perspectives.* Honolulu: University of Hawai'i Press.

Kearsley, G. 1976. 'Questions and question-asking in verbal discourse: a cross-disciplinary review'. *Journal of Psycholinguistic Research* 5: 355–75.

Keck, C. M., G. Iberri-Shea, N. Tracy-Ventura, and **S. Wa-Mbaleka.** 2006. 'Investigating the empirical link between task-based interaction and acquisition: a meta-analysis' in J. M. Norris and L. Ortega (eds.): *Synthesizing Research on Language Learning and Teaching.* Philadelphia, Penn.: John Benjamins.

Keefe. J. 1979a. 'Learning style: an overview' in J. Keefe (ed.): *Student Learning Styles: Diagnosing and Describing Programs.* Reston Va.: National Secondary School Principals.

Keefe, J. (ed.). 1979b. *Student Learning Styles: Diagnosing and Describing Programs.* Reston Va.: National Secondary School Principals.

Keenan, E. 1975. 'Variation in universal grammar' in R. Fasold and R. Shuy (eds.): *Analyzing Variation in Language.* Washington D.C.: Georgetown University Press.

Kelch, K. 1985. 'Modified input as an aid to comprehension'. *Studies in Second Language Acquisition* 7: 81–90.

Keller, J. 1984. 'Motivational design of instruction' in C. Reigeluth (ed.): *Instructional Design Theories and Models*. Hillsdale, N.J.: Lawrence Erlbaum.

Kellerman, E. 1977. 'Towards a characterization of the strategies of transfer in second language learning'. *Interlanguage Studies Bulletin* 2: 58–145.

Kellerman, E. 1978. 'Giving learners a break: native language intuitions as a source of predictions about transferability'. *Working Papers on Bilingualism* 15: 59–92.

Kellerman, E. 1979. 'Transfer and non-transfer: where are we now?' *Studies in Second Language Acquisition* 2: 37–57.

Kellerman, E. 1983. 'Now you see it, now you don't' in S. Gass and L. Selinker (eds.): *Language Transfer in Language Learning*. Rowley, Mass.: Newbury House.

Kellerman, E. 1985. 'Dative alternation and the analysis of data: a reply to Mazurkewich'. *Language Learning* 35: 91–106.

Kellerman, E. 1986. 'An eye for an eye: crosslinguistic constraints on the development of the L2 lexicon' in E. Kellerman and M. Sharwood Smith (eds.): *Cross-linguistic Influence in Second Language Acquisition*. Oxford: Pergamon.

Kellerman, E. 1987. 'Aspects of transferability in second language acquisition. Chapter 1: Crosslinguistic influence: a review'. Unpublished manuscript, University of Nijmegen.

Kellerman, E. 1989. 'The imperfect conditional' in K. Hyltenstam and L. Obler (eds.): *Bilingualism Across the Lifespan: Aspects of Acquisition, Maturity and Loss*. Cambridge: Cambridge University Press.

Kellerman, E. 1991. 'Compensatory strategies in second language research: a critique, a revision, and some (non-) implications for the classroom' in R. Phillipson *et al.* (eds.): *Foreign/Second Language Pedagogy Research*. Clevedon: Multilingual Matters.

Kellerman, E. 1992. 'Another look at an old classic; Schachter's avoidance'. Lecture notes, Temple University Japan.

Kellerman, E. 1995. 'Crosslinguistic influence: transfer to nowhere?' *Annual Review of Applied Linguistics* 15: 125–50.

Kellerman, E. 2001. 'New uses for old language: cross-linguistic and cross-gestural influence in the narratives of non-native speakers' in J. Cenoz, B. Hufheisen, and U. Jessner (eds.): *Cross-linguistic Influence in Third Language Acquisition: Psycholinguistic Perspectives*. Clevedon: Multilingual Matters.

Kellerman, E., A. Amerlaan, T. Bongaerts, and **N. Poulisse.** 1990. 'System and hierarchy in L2 compensatory strategies' in R. Scarcella, E. Andersen, and S. Krashen (eds.). *Developing Communicative Competence*. New York: Newbury House.

Kellerman, E. and **E. Bialystok.** 1997. 'On the psychological plausibility in the study of communication strategies' in G. Kasper and E. Kellerman (ed.): *Communication Strategies: Psycholinguistic and Sociolinguistic Perspectives*. London: Longman.

Kellerman, E., T. Bongaerts, and **N. Poulisse.** 1987. 'Strategy and system in L2 referential communication' in R. Ellis (ed.): *Second Language Acquisition in Context*. London: Prentice Hall International.

Kellerman, E. and **M. Sharwood Smith** (eds.). 1986. *Cross-linguistic Influence in Second Language Acquisition*. Oxford: Pergamon.

Kellog, R. 1996. 'A model of working memory in writing' in C. Levy and S. Ransdell (eds.): *The Science of Writing*. Mahwah N.J.: Lawrence Erlbaum.

Kelly, P. 1982. 'Interlanguage, variation and social/psychological influences within a developmental stage'. Unpublished MA in TESL thesis, University of California at Los Angeles.

Kelsky, K. 2001. *Women on the Verge*. Durham, N.C.: Duke University Press.

Kempe, V. and **B. MacWhinney.** 1998. 'The acquisition of case marking by adult learners of Russian and German'. *Studies in Second Language Acquisition* 20: 543–87.

Kerekes, J. 2005. 'Before, during and after the event: getting the job (or not) in an employment interview' in K. Bardovi-Harlig and B. Hartford (eds.): *Interlanguage Pragmatics: Exploring Institutional Talk*. Mahwah, N.J.: Lawrence Erlbaum.

Kern, R. 1995. 'Students' and teachers' beliefs about language learning'. *Foreign Language Annals* 28: 71–91.

Ketterman, B. *et al.* (eds.). 1989. *Englisch als Zweitsprache*. Tübingen: Gunter Narr.

Ketterman, B. and **R. St. Clair** (eds.). 1980. *New Approaches to Language Acquisition*. Heidelberg: Julius Groos.

Khalil, A. 1985. 'Communicative error evaluations: native speakers' evaluation and interpretation of written errors of Arab EFL learners'. *TESOL Quarterly* 19: 225–351.

Kilborn, K. 1987. 'Sentence processing in a second language: seeking a performance definition of fluency'. Unpublished PhD dissertation, University of California, San Diego.

Kilborn, K. and **A. Cooremann.** 1987. 'Sentence interpretation strategies in adult Dutch-English bilinguals'. *Applied Psycholinguistics* 8: 415–31.

Kilborn, K. and **T. Ito.** 1989. 'Sentence processing strategies in adult bilinguals' in B. MacWhinney and E. Bates (eds.): *The Crosslinguistic Study of Sentence Processing*. Cambridge: Cambridge University Press.

Kim, H. and **G. Mathes.** 2001. 'Explicit vs. implicit corrective feedback'. *The Korea TESOL Journal* 4: 1–15.

Kim, K., N. Relkin, K. Lee, and **J. Hirsch.** 1997. 'Distinct cortical areas associated with native and second languages'. *Nature* 388: 171–4.

Kim, S. and **C. Elder.** 2005. 'Language choices and pedagogic functions in the foreign language classroom: a cross-linguistic functional analysis of teacher talk'. *Language Teaching Research* 9: 335–80.

Kinginger, C. 2002. 'Defining the zone of proximal development in US foreign language education'. *Applied Linguistics* 23: 240–61.

Kiss, C. and **M. Nikolov.** 2005. 'Developing, piloting, and validating an instrument to measure young learners' aptitude'. *Language Learning* 55: 99–150.

Kleifgen, J. 1985. 'Skilled variation in a kindergarten teacher's use of foreigner talk' in S. Gass and C. Madden (eds.): *Input in Second Language Acquisition*. Rowley, Mass.: Newbury House.

Klein, E. and **G. Martohardjono.** 1999a. 'Investigating second language grammars' in E. Klein and G. Martohardjono (eds.): *The Development of Second Language Grammars: A Generative Approach*. Amsterdam: John Benjamins.

Klein, E. and **G. Martohardjono.** (eds.). 1999b. *The Development of Second Language Grammars: A Generative Approach*. Amsterdam: John Benjamins.

Klein, W. 1986. *Second Language Acquisition*. Cambridge: Cambridge University Press.

Klein, W. 1991. 'Seven trivia of language acquisition' in L. Eubank (ed.): *Point Counterpoint: Universal Grammar in the Second Language*. Amsterdam: John Benjamins.

Klein, W. 1995. 'The acquisition of English' in R. Dietrich, W. Klein and C. Noyau (eds.): *The Acquisition of Temporality in a Second Language*. Amsterdam: John Benjamins.

Klein, W. and **N. Dittmar.** 1979. *Developing Grammars: the Acquisition of German Syntax by Foreign Workers*. Berlin: Springer.

Klein, W. and **C. Perdue.** 1992. *Utterance Structure: Developing Grammars Again*. Amsterdam: John Benjamins.

Klein, W. and **C. Perdue.** 1997. 'The basic variety (or: Couldn't natural languages be much simpler?)'. *Second Language Research* 13: 301–48

Kleinmann, H. 1978. 'The strategy of avoidance in adult second language acquisition' in W. Ritchie (ed.): *Second Language Acquisition Research*. New York: Academic Press.

Klima, E. and **V. Bellugi.** 1966. 'Syntactic regularities in the speech of children' in J. Lyons and R. Wales (eds.): *Psycholinguistic Papers*. Edinburgh: Edinburgh University Press.

Klingner, J. and **S. Vaughn.** 2000. 'The helping behaviors of fifth graders while using collaborative strategic reading during ESL content classes'. *TESOL Quarterly* 99: 3–22.

Knowlton, B. and **L. Squire.** 1996. 'Artificial grammar learning depends on implicit acquisition of both abstract and exemplar-based information'. *Journal of Experimental Psychology: Learning, Memory and Cognition* 22: 169–81.

Ko, J., D. Schallert, and K. Walters. 2003. 'Rethinking scaffolding: examining negotiation of meaning in an ESL storytelling task'. *TESOL Quarterly* 37: 303–24.

Koda, K. 1999. 'Developing L2 intraword orthographic sensitivity and decoding skills'. *The Modern Language Journal* 83: 51–64.

Koivukari, A. 1987. 'Question level and cognitive processing: psycholinguistic dimensions of questions and answers'. *Applied Psycholinguistics* 8: 101–20.

Kolb, D. 1984. *Experiential Learning: Experience as the Source of Learning and Development.* Englewood Cliffs, N.J.: Prentice Hall.

Kondo, S. 1997. 'The development of pragmatic competence by Japanese learners of English: Longitudinal study on interlanguage apologies'. *Sophia Linguistica* 41: 265–84.

Kormos, J. 1999. 'Monitoring and self-repair'. *Language Learning* 49: 303–42.

Kormos, J. 2000. 'The role of attention in monitoring second language speech production'. *Language Learning* 50: 343–84.

Kormos, J. 2006. *Speech Production and Second Language Acquisition.* Mahwah, N.J.: Lawrence Erlbaum.

Kowal, M. and **M. Swain.** 1994. 'Using collaborative language production tasks to promote students' language awareness'. *Language Awareness* 3: 73–93.

Kowal, M. and **M. Swain.** 1997. 'From semantic to syntactic processing: how can we promote metalinguistic awareness in the French immersion classroom?' in R. Johnson and M. Swain (eds.): *Immersion Education: International Perspectives.* Cambridge: Cambridge University Press.

Kramarae, C. 1990. 'Changing the complexion of gender in language research' in H. Giles and W. Robinson (eds.). *Handbook of Language and Social Psychology.* Chichester: John Wiley and Sons.

Kramsch, C. 1985. 'Classroom interaction and discourse options'. *Studies in Second Language Acquisition* 7: 169–83.

Kramsch, C. 1993. *Context and Culture in Language Teaching.* Oxford: Oxford University Press.

Kramsch, C. 2002. *Language Acquisition and Language Socialization*: Ecological Perspectives. London: Continuum.

Kramsch, C. 2003. 'Metaphor and the subjective construction of beliefs' in P. Kalaja and A. Barcelos (eds.): *Beliefs about SLA: New Research Approaches.* Dordrecht: Kluwer.

Kramsch, C. and **S. McConnell-Ginet** (eds.). 1992. *Text and Context: Cross-disciplinary Perspectives on Language Study.* Lexington, Mass.: D.C. Heath and Company.

Krashen, S. 1976. 'Formal and informal linguistic environments in language acquisition and language learning'. *TESOL Quarterly* 10: 157–68.

Krashen, S. 1977. 'Some issues relating to the Monitor Model' in H. Brown, C. Yorio, and R. Crymes (eds.): *On TESOL '77.* Washington D.C.: TESOL.

Krashen, S. 1978. 'Individual variation in the use of the monitor' in W. Ritchie (ed.): *Second Language Acquisition Research.* New York: Academic Press.

Krashen, S. 1981. *Second Language Acquisition and Second Language Learning.* Oxford: Pergamon.

Krashen, S. 1982. *Principles and Practice in Second Language Acquisition.* Oxford: Pergamon.

Krashen, S. 1983. 'Newmark's ignorance hypothesis and current second language acquisition theory' in S. Gass and L. Selinker (eds.): *Language Transfer in Language Learning.* Rowley, Mass.: Newbury House.

Krashen, S. 1985. *The Input Hypothesis: Issues and Implications.* London: Longman.

Krashen, S. 1989. 'We acquire vocabulary and spelling by reading: additional evidence for the Input Hypothesis'. *The Modern Language Journal* 73: 440–64.

Krashen, S. 1993a. 'The effect of grammar teaching: still peripheral'. *TESOL Quarterly* 27: 717–25.

Krashen, S. 1993b. *The Power of Reading.* Englewood, Colo.: Libraries Unlimited.

Krashen, S. 1994. 'The input hypothesis and its rivals' in N. Ellis (ed.). *Implicit and Explicit Learning of Languages*. London: Academic Press.

Krashen, S. 1998. 'Comprehensible output?' *System* 26: 175–82.

Krashen, S. 2003. *Explorations in Language Acquisition and Use: The Taipei lectures*. Portsmouth, N.H.: Heinemann.

Krashen, S., J. Butler, R. Birnbaum, and **J. Robertson.** 1978. 'Two studies in language acquisition and language learning'. *ITL: Review of Applied Linguistics* 39/40: 73–92.

Krashen, S., C. Jones, S. Zelinksi, and **C. Ursprich.** 1978. 'How important is instruction?' *ELT Journal* 32: 257–61.

Krashen, S., M. Long, and **R. Scarcella.** 1979. 'Age, rate and eventual attainment in second language acquisition'. *TESOL Quarterly* 13: 573–82. Also in S. Krashen, R. Scarcella, and M. Long (eds.): 1982. *Child-adult Differences in Second Language Acquisition*. Rowley, Mass.: Newbury House.

Krashen, S. and **R. Scarcella.** 1978. 'On routines and patterns in second language acquisition and performance'. *Language Learning* 28: 283–300.

Krashen, S. and **H. Seliger.** 1975. 'The essential characteristics of formal instruction'. *TESOL Quarterly* 9: 173–83.

Krashen, S., H. Seliger, and **D. Hartnett.** 1974. 'Two studies in second language learning'. *Kritikon Litterarum* 3: 220–8.

Krashen, S. and **T. Terrell.** 1983. *The Natural Approach: Language Acquisition in the Classroom*. Oxford: Pergamon.

Kroll, J. and **A. De Groot** (eds.). 1997. *Tutorials in Bilingualism: Psycholinguistic Perspectives*. Mahwah, N.J.: Lawrence Erlbaum.

Kroll, J. and **A. De Groot** (eds.). 2005. *Handbook of Bilingualism: Psycholinguistic Approaches*. New York: Oxford University Press.

Kruidenier, B. and **R. Clement.** 1986. *The Effect of Context on the Composition and Role of Orientations in Second Language Acquisition*. Quebec: International Centre for Research on Bilingualism.

Kubota, M. 1995. 'Teachability of conversational implicature to Japanese EFL learners'. *IRLT Bulletin* 9: 35–67.

Kuczaj, S. 1977. 'Old and new forms, old and new meanings: the form-function hypothesis revisited'. Paper presented at the Society for Research in Child Development, New Orleans.

Kuhl, P. 2000. 'A new view of language acquisition'. *Proceedings of the National Academy of the Sciences* 92: 11850–7.

Kuhn, T. 1962. *The Structure of Scientific Revolutions*. Chicago, Ill.: University of Chicago Press.

Kumagai, T. 1993. 'Remedial interactions as face-management: the case of Japanese and Americans' in S. Y. T. Matsuda, M. Sakurai, and A. Baba (eds.): *In honor of Tokuichiro Matsuda: Papers Contributed on the Occasion of his Sixtieth Birthday*. Tokyo: Iwasaki Linguistic Circle.

Kumpf, L. 1984. 'Temporal systems and universality in interlanguage: a case study' in F. Eckman, L. Bell and D. Nelson (eds.): *Universals of Second Language Acquisition*. Rowley, Mass.: Newbury House.

Kuno, S. 1974. 'The position of relative clauses and conjunctions'. *Linguistic Inquiry* 5: 117–36.

Labov, W. 1969. 'Contraction, deletion, and inherent variability of the English copula'. *Language* 45: 715–52.

Labov, W. 1970. 'The study of language in its social context'. *Studium Generale* 23: 30–87.

Labov, W. 1971. 'The notion of "system" in Creole languages' in D. Hymes (ed.). *Pidginization and Creolization of Languages*. Cambridge: Cambridge University Press.

Labov, W. 1991. 'The intersection of sex and social class in the course of linguistic change'. *Language Variation and Linguistic Change* 2: 205–51.

Lado, R. 1957. *Linguistics Across Cultures: Applied Linguistics for Language Teachers.* Ann Arbor, Michigan: University of Michigan.

Lafford, B. 2004. 'The effect of the context of learning on the use of communication strategies by learners of Spanish as a second language'. *Studies in Second Language Acquisition* 26: 201–25.

Lakoff, G. and **M. Johnson.** 1980. *Metaphors We Live By.* Chicago: Chicago University Press.

Lakoff, G. and **M. Johnson.** 1999. *Philosophy in the Flesh.* New York: Basic Books.

Lakshmanan, U. 1991. 'Morphological uniformity and null subjects in child second language acquisition' in L. Eubank (ed.): *Point Counterpoint: Universal Grammar in the Second Language.* Amsterdam: John Benjamins.

Lalonde, R. and **R. Gardner.** 1985. 'On the predictive validity of the Attitude/Motivation Test Battery'. *Journal of Multilingual and Multicultural Development* 6: 403–12.

Lam, W. and **J. Wong.** 2000. 'The effects of strategy training on developing discussion skills in an ESL classroom'. *ELT Journal* 54: 245–55.

Lamb, M. 2004. 'Integrative motivation in a globalizing world'. *System* 32: 3–19.

Lamb, S. 1999. *Pathways of the Brain: The Neurocognitive Basis of Language.* Amsterdam: John Benjamins.

Lambert, W. 1974. 'Culture and language as factors in learning and education' in F. Aboud and R. Meade (eds.): *Cultural Factors in Learning and Education.* Bellingham, Washington: Fifth Western Washington Symposium on Learning.

Lambert, W. and **G. Tucker.** 1972. *The Bilingual Education of Children: the St. Lambert Experiment.* Rowley, Mass.: Newbury House.

Lane, H. and **E. Zale** (eds.). 1967. *Studies in Language and Language Behavior* 4.

Langacker, R. 1987. *Foundations of Cognitive Grammar.* Stanford, California: Stanford University Press.

Lange, D. 1979. 'Negation in naturlichen Englisch-Deutschen Zweitsprachenerwerb: eine Fallstudie'. *International Review of Applied Linguistics* 17: 331–48.

Lanoue, G. 1991. 'Language loss, language gain: cultural camouflage and social change among the Sekani of Northern British Columbia'. *Language in Society* 20: 87–115.

Lantolf, J. 1996. 'Second language theory building: letting all the flowers bloom!' *Language Learning* 46: 713–49.

Lantolf, J. 1997. 'The function of language play in the acquisition of Spanish as a second language' in W. Glass and A. Perez-Leroux (eds.): *Contemporary Perspectives on the Acquisition of Spanish.* Somerville, Mass.: Cascadilla Press.

Lantolf, J. 1999. 'The role of inner speech in SLA: a theoretical perspective'. Plenary address, September, Annual Conference of the Applied Linguistics Association of New Zealand, Auckland, New Zealand.

Lantolf, J. (ed.). 2000a. *Sociocultural Theory and Second Language Learning.* Oxford: Oxford University Press.

Lantolf, J. 2000b. 'Second language learning as a mediated process'. *Language Teaching* 33: 79–96.

Lantolf, J. 2000c. 'Introducing sociocultural theory' in J. Lantolf (ed.): *Sociocultural Theory and Second Language Learning.* Oxford: Oxford University Press.

Lantolf, J. 2002. 'Commentary from the flower garden: responding to Gregg 2000'. *Second Language Research* 18: 72–8.

Lantolf, J. 2004. 'Sociocultural theory and second foreign language learning. An overview of sociocultural theory' in K. Van Esch, and O. St. John (eds.): *Vygotsky's Theory of Education in Cultural Context.* Frankfurt am Main: Peter Lang.

Lantolf, J. 2005. 'Sociocultural and second language learning research: an exegesis' in E. Hinkel (ed.): *Handbook of Research on Second Language Teaching and Learning.* Mahway, N.J.: Lawrence Erlbaum.

Lantolf, J. 2006. 'Sociocultural theory and L2'. *Studies in Second Language Acquisition* 28: 67–109.

Lantolf, J. and **M. Ahmed.** 1989. 'Psycholinguistic perspectives on interlanguage variation' in S. Gass, C. Madden, D. Preston, and L. Selinker (eds.): *Variation in Second Language Acquisition: Psycholinguistic Issues.* Clevedon: Multilingual Matters.

Lantolf, J. and **A. Aljaafreh.** 1995. 'Second language learning in the zone of proximal development: A revolutionary experience'. *International Journal of Educational Research* 23: 619–32.

Lantolf, J. and **G. Appel.** 1994a. 'Theoretical framework: an introduction to Vygotskian perspectives on second language research' in J. Lantolf and G. Appel (eds.). *Vygotskian Approaches to Second Language Research.* Norwood, N.J.: Ablex.

Lantolf, J. and **G. Appel.** (eds.). 1994b. *Vygotskian Approaches to Second Language Research.* Norwood, N.J.: Ablex.

Lantolf, J., F. DiCamilla, and **M. Ahmed.** 1997. 'The cognitive function of linguistic performance: tense/aspect use by L1 and L2 speakers' *Language Sciences* 19: 153–65.

Lantolf, J. and **W. Frawley.** 1984. 'Second language performance and Vygotskyan psycholinguistics: implications for L2 instruction' in A. Manning, P. Martin, and K. McCalla (eds.): *The Tenth LACUS Forum 1983.* Columbia, S.C.: Hornbeam Press.

Lantolf, J. and **P. Genung.** 2002. '"I'd rather switch than fight": an activity-theoretic study of power, success and failure in a foreign language' in C. Kramsch (ed.): *Language Acquisition and Language Socialization: Ecological Perspectives.* London: Continuum.

Lantolf, J. and **A. Labarca.** (eds.). 1987. *Research in Second Language Learning: Focus on the Classroom.* Norwood, N.J.: Ablex.

Lantolf, J. and **A. Pavlenko.** 1995. 'Sociocultural theory and second language acquisition'. *Annual Review of Applied Linguistics* 15: 108–124.

Lantolf, J. and **S. Thorne.** 2006. *Sociocultural Theory and the Genesis of Second Language Development.* Oxford: Oxford University Press.

LaPierre, D. 1994. 'Language output in a cooperative learning setting: determining its effects on second language learning'. Unpublished MA thesis, University of Toronto (Ontario Institute for Studies in Education).

Lardiere, D. 2007. *Ultimate Attainment in Second Language Acquisition: A Case Study.* Mahwah, N.J.: Lawrence Erlbaum.

Larsen-Freeman, D. 1975. 'The acquisition of grammatical morphemes by adult ESL students'. *TESOL Quarterly* 9: 409–30.

Larsen-Freeman, D. 1976a. 'Teacher speech as input to the ESL learner'. *University of California Working Papers in TESL* 10: 45–9.

Larsen-Freeman, D. 1976b. 'An explanation for the morpheme acquisition order of second language learners'. *Language Learning* 26: 125–34.

Larsen-Freeman, D. (ed.). 1980. *Discourse Analysis in Second Language Research.* Rowley, Mass.: Newbury House.

Larsen-Freeman, D. 1983. 'The importance of input in second language acquisition' in R. Andersen (ed.): *Pidginization and Creolization as Language Acquisition.* Rowley, Mass.: Newbury House.

Larsen-Freeman, D. 1997. 'Chaos/complexity science and second language acquisition'. *Applied Linguistics* 18: 141–65.

Larsen-Freeman, D. 2005. 'Second language acquisition and fossilization: there is no end, and there is no state' in Z-H. Han and T. Olden (eds.): *Studies of Fossilization in Second Language Acquisition.* Clevedon: Multilingual Matters.

Larsen-Freeman, D. and **M. Long.** 1991. *An Introduction to Second Language Acquisition Research.* London: Longman.

Laufer, B. 1998. 'The development of passive and active vocabulary in a second language: same or different?' *Applied Linguistics* 19: 255–71.

Laufer, R. and **S. Eliasson.** 1993. 'What causes avoidance in L2 learning: L1–L2 difference, L1–L2 similarity, or L2 complexity?' *Studies in Second Language Acquisition* 15: 35–48.

Laufer, B. and **P. Nation.** 1995. 'Vocabulary size and use: lexical richness in L2 written production'. *Applied Linguistics* 16: 307–22.

Laufer, B. and **P. Nation.** 1999. 'A vocabulary-size test of controlled productive ability'. *Language Testing* 16: 33–51.

Lave, J. and **S. Chalkin** (eds.). 1993. *Understanding Practice: Perspectives on Activity and Context.* Cambridge: Cambridge University Press.

Lave, J. and **E. Wenger.** 1991. *Situated Learning: Legitimate Peripheral Participation.* Cambridge: Cambridge University Press.

Lavelli, M., A. P. F. Pantoja, H. Hsu, D. Messinger, and **A. Fogel.** 2004. 'Using microgenetic designs to study change processes' in D. M. Teti (ed.): *Handbook of Research Methods in Developmental Psychology.* Baltimore, Md.: Blackwell Publishers.

Lazaraton, A. 2000. 'Current trends in research methodology and statistics in applied linguistics'. *TESOL Quarterly* 34: 175–81.

Leather, J. 1999a. 'Second language research: an introduction' in J. Leather (ed.): *Language Learning* 49: Supplement 1.

Leather, J. (ed.). 1999b. 'Phonological issues in language learning'. *Language Learning* 49: Supplement 1.

Leather, J. and **A. James.** 1991. 'The acquisition of second language speech'. *Studies in Second Language Acquisition* 13: 305–41.

Lee, C. and **P. Smagorinsky** (eds.). 2000. *Vygotskian Perspectives on Literacy Research.* New York: Cambridge University Press.

Lee, N. 2004. 'The neurobiology of procedural memory' in J. Schumann *et al.* (eds.): *The Neurobiology of Learning: Perspectives from Second Language Acquisition.* Mahwah, N.J.: Lawrence Erlbaum.

Lee, W. 1968. 'Thoughts on contrastive linguistics in the context of language teaching' in J. Alatis (ed.): *Report of the Nineteenth Annual Round Table Meeting on Linguistics and Language Studies.* Georgetown University, Washington D.C.: Georgetown University Press.

Leech, G. 1983. *Principles of Pragmatics.* London: Longman.

Leeman, J. 2003. 'Recasts and L2 development: beyond negative evidence'. *Studies in Second Language Acquisition* 25: 37–63.

Leeman, J., I. Arteagoitia, D. Fridman, and **C. Doughty.** 1995. 'Integrating attention to form in content-based Spanish instruction' in R. Schmidt (ed.): *Attention and Awareness in Foreign Language Learning.* Honolulu: University of Hawai'i Press.

Leeser, M. 2004. 'Learner proficiency and focus on form during collaborative dialogue'. *Language Teaching Research* 8: 55–81.

Legaretta, D. 1977. 'Language choice in bilingual classrooms'. *TESOL Quarterly* 11: 9–16.

Lemke, J. 1990. *Talking Science: Language. Learning and Values* (Language and Classroom Processes Volume 1). Norwood, N.J.: Ablex Publishing.

Lenneberg, E. 1967. *Biological Foundations of Language.* New York: Wiley and Son.

Lennon, P. 1989. 'Introspection and intentionality in advanced second-language acquisition'. *Language Learning* 39: 375–95.

Lennon, P. 1991. 'Error: some problems of definition, identification and distinction'. *Applied Linguistics* 12: 180–95.

Lennon, P. 1994. 'Self-correction and error in advanced learner spoken narrative' in G. Bartelt (ed.): *The Dynamics of Language Processes: Essays in Honor of Hans W. Dechert.* Tübingen: Gunter Narr.

Leontiev, A. A. 1981. *Psychology and the Language Learning Process.* London: Pergamon.

Leont'ev, A. N. 1978. *Activity, Consciousness, and Personality.* Englewood Cliffs, N.J.: Prentice Hall.

Leow, R. 1993. 'To simplify or not to simplify: a look at intake'. *Studies in Second Language Acquisition* 15: 333–55.

Leow, R. 1997a. 'The effects of input enhancement and text length on adult L2 readers comprehension and intake in second language acquisition'. *Applied Language Learning* 8: 151–82.

Leow, R. 1997b. 'Attention, awareness, and foreign language behavior'. *Language Learning* 47: 467–505.

Leow, R. 1998. 'Toward operationalizing the process of attention in SLA: evidence for Tomlin and Villa's (1994) fine-grained analysis of attention'. *Applied Psycholinguistics* 19: 133–59.

Leow, R. 2000. 'A study of the role of awareness in foreign language behavior: Aware vs. unaware learners'. *Studies in Second Language Acquisition* 22: 557–84.

Leow, R. and **K. Morgan-Short.** 2004. 'To think aloud or not to think aloud: the issue of reactivity in SLA research methodology'. *Studies in Second Language Acquisition* 26: 35–58.

Le Page, R. and **A. Tabouret-Keller.** 1985. *Acts of Identity: Creole-based Approaches to Language and Ethnicity*. Cambridge: Cambridge University Press.

Leung, C., R. Harris, and **B. Rampton.** 1997. 'The idealized native speaker, reified ethnicities, and classroom realities'. *TESOL Quarterly* 31: 543–60.

Levelt, W. 1983. 'Monitoring and self-repair in speech'. *Cognition* 14: 41–104.

Levelt, W. 1989. *Speaking: From Intention to Articulation*. Cambridge: Cambridge University Press.

Levenston, E. 1971. 'Over-indulgence and under-representation: aspects of mother tongue interference' in G. Nickel (ed.): *Papers in Contrastive Linguistics*. Cambridge, Cambridge University Press.

Levenston, E. 1979. 'Second language lexical acquisition: issues and problems'. *Interlanguage Studies Bulletin* 4: 147–60.

Levine, A., T. Reves, and **B. Leaver.** 1996. 'Relationship between language learning strategies and Israeli versus Russian cultural-educational factors' in R. Oxford (ed.): *Learning Strategies Around the World: Cross-cultural Perspectives*. Honolulu: University of Hawai'i Press.

Levinson, S. 1983. *Principles of Pragmatics*. Cambridge: Cambridge University Press.

Li, D. 2000. 'The pragmatics of making requests in the L2 workplace: A case study of language socialization'. *Canadian Modern Language Review* 8757: 58–87.

Li, D., D. Mahoney, and **J. Richards** (eds.). 1994. *Exploring Second Language Teacher Development*. Hong Kong: City Polytechnic.

Li, X. 1998. 'Adult L2 accessibility to UG: an issue revisited' in S. Flynn, G. Martohardjono, and W. O'Neil (eds.). *The Generative Study of Second Language Acquisition*. Mahwah, N.J.: Lawrence Erlbaum.

Liao, Y. and **Y. Fukuya.** 2004. 'Avoidance of phrasal verbs: the case of Chinese learners of English'. *Language Learning* 54: 193–226.

Liceras, J. 1985. 'The role of intake in the determination of learners' competence' in S. Gass and C. Madden (eds.): *Input in Second Language Acquisition*. Rowley, Mass.: Newbury House.

Liddicoat, A. and **C. Crozet.** 2001. 'Acquiring French interactional norms through instruction' in K. Rose and G. Kasper (eds.): *Pragmatics in Language Teaching*. Cambridge: Cambridge University Press.

Lieven, E. 1994. 'Crosslinguistic and crosscultural aspects of language addressed to children' in C. Gallaway and B. Richards (eds.): *Input and Interaction in Language Acquisition*. Cambridge: Cambridge University Press.

Lightbown, P. 1983. 'Exploring relationships between developmental and instructional sequences in L2 acquisition' in H. Seliger and M. Long (eds.): *Classroom-oriented Research in Second Language Acquisition*. Rowley, Mass.: Newbury House.

Lightbown, P. 1984. 'The relationship between theory and method in second language acquisition research' in A. Davies, C. Criper and A. Howatt (eds.): *Interlanguage*. Edinburgh: Edinburgh University Press.

Lightbown, P. 1985a. 'Great expectations: second language acquisition research and classroom teaching'. *Applied Linguistics* 6: 173–89.

Lightbown, P. 1985b. 'Can language acquisition be altered by instruction?' in K. Hyltenstam and M. Pienemann (eds.): *Modelling and Assessing Second Language Acquisition*. Clevedon: Multilingual Matters.

Lightbown, P. 1990. 'Process-product research on second language learning in classrooms' in Harley *et al.* (eds.): *The Development of Second Language Proficiency*. Cambridge: Cambridge University Press.

Lightbown, P. 1992a. 'Getting quality input in the second/foreign language classroom' in C. Kramsch and S. McConnell-Ginet (eds.): *Text and Context: Cross-disciplinary Perspectives on Language Study.* Lexington, Mass.: D.C. Heath and Company.

Lightbown, P. 1992b. 'Can they do it themselves? A comprehension-based ESL course for young children' in R. Courchene *et al.* (eds.): *Comprehension-based Second Language Teaching*. Ottowa: University of Ottawa Press.

Lightbown, P. 1998. 'The importance of timing in focus-on-form' in C. Doughty and J. Williams (eds.): *Focus-on-form in Classroom Second Language Acquisition*. Cambridge: Cambridge University Press.

Lightbown, P. 2000. 'Anniversary article: classroom SLA research and language teaching'. *Applied Linguistics* 21: 431–62.

Lightbown, P. 2006. 'Perfecting practice'. Plenary talk given at the IRAAL/BAAL Conference, Cork, Ireland.

Lightbown, P. and **A. d'Anglejan.** 1985. 'Some input considerations for word order in French L1 and L2 acquisition' in S. Gass and C. Madden (eds.): *Input in Second Language Acquisition*. Rowley, Mass.: Newbury House.

Lightbown, P., R. Halter, J. White, and **M. Horst.** 2002. 'Comprehension-based learning: the limits of "Do it yourself"'. *Canadian Modern Language Journal* 58: 427–64.

Lightbown, P. and **N. Spada.** 1990. 'Focus-on-form and corrective feedback in communicative language teaching: effects on second language learning'. *Studies in Second Language Acquisition* 12: 429–48.

Lightbown, P. and **N. Spada.** 1999. *How Languages Are Learned.* (Second edition). Oxford: Oxford University Press.

Lightbown, P., N. Spada, and **R. Wallace.** 1980. 'Some effects of instruction on child and adolescent ESL learners' in R. Scarcella and S. Krashen (eds.): *Research in Second Language Acquisition*. Rowley, Mass.: Newbury House.

Lin, Y. 2003. 'Interphonology variability: Sociolinguistic factors affecting L2 simplification'. *Applied Linguistics* 24: 439–64.

Linnell, J., F. L. Porter, H. Stone, and **W. Chen** 1992. 'Can you apologize me? An investigation of speech act performance among non-native speakers of English'. *Working Papers in Educational Linguistics* 8/2: 33–53.

Little, D. and **D. Singleton.** 1990. 'Cognitive style and learning approach' in R. Duda and P. Riley (eds.): *Learning Styles*. Nancy, France: University of Nancy.

Little, D., D. Singleton, and **W. Silvius.** 1984. *Learning Second Languages in Ireland: Experience, Attitudes and Needs*. Dublin: Trinity College, Centre for Language and Communication Studies.

Littlemore, J. 2001. 'An empirical study of the relationship between cognitive style and the use of communication strategy'. *Applied Linguistics* 22: 241–65.

Littlemore, J. 2003. 'The communicative effectiveness of different types of communication strategy'. *System* 31: 331–48.

LoCoco, V. 1976. 'A comparison of three methods for the collection of L2 data: free composition, translation and picture description'. *Working Papers on Bilingualism* 8:59–86.

Loewen, S. 2005. 'Incidental focus on form and second language learning'. *Studies in Second Language Acquisition* 27: 361–86.

Loewen, S. 2006. 'The prior and subsequent use of forms targeted in incidental focus on form' in S. Fotos and H. Nassaji (eds.): *Form-focused Instruction and Teacher Education: Studies in Honour of Rod Ellis*. Oxford: Oxford University Press.

Loewen, S. and **J. Philp.** 2006. 'Recasts in the adult English L2 classroom; characteristics, explicitness, and effectiveness'. *The Modern Language Journal* 90: 536–56.

Logan, G. 1988. 'Towards an instance theory of automatisation'. *Psychological Review* 95: 492–527.

Long, M. 1977. 'Teacher feedback on learner error: mapping cognitions' in H. D. Brown, C. Yorio, and R. Crymes (eds.): *On TESOL '77*. Washington D.C.: TESOL.

Long, M. 1980a. 'Input, interaction and second language acquisition'. Unpublished PhD dissertation, University of California at Los Angeles.

Long, M. 1980b. 'Inside the "black box": methodological issues in classroom research on language learning'. *Language Learning* 30: 1–42.

Long, M. 1981. 'Input, interaction and second language acquisition' in H. Winitz (ed.): *Native Language and Foreign Language Acquisition*. Annals of the New York Academy of Sciences 379.

Long, M. 1983a. 'Native speaker/non-native speaker conversation and the negotiation of comprehensible input'. *Applied Linguistics* 4: 126–41.

Long, M. 1983b. 'Native speaker/non-native speaker conversation in the second language classroom' in M. Clarke and J. Handscombe (eds.): *On TESOL '82*. Washington D.C.: TESOL.

Long, M. 1983c. 'Does second language instruction make a difference? A review of the research'. *TESOL Quarterly* 17: 359–82.

Long, M. 1985a. 'Input and second language acquisition theory' in S. Gass and C. Madden (eds.): *Input in Second Language Acquisition*. Rowley, Mass.: Newbury House.

Long, M. 1985b. 'A role for instruction in second language acquisition: task-based language teaching' in K. Hyltenstam and M. Pienemann (eds.): *Modelling and Assessing Second Language Acquisition*. Clevedon: Multilingual Matters.

Long, M. 1988. 'Instructed interlanguage development' in L. Beebe (ed.): *Issues in Second Language Acquisition: Multiple Perspectives*. New York: Newbury House.

Long, M. 1989. 'Task, group, and task-group interactions'. *University of Hawai'i Working Papers in ESL* 8: 1–26.

Long, M. 1990a. 'Maturational constraints on language development'. *Studies in Second Language Acquisition* 12: 251–86.

Long, M. 1990b. 'Second language classroom research and teacher education' in C. Brumfit and R. Mitchell (eds.): *Research in the Language Classroom. ELT Documents 133*. Modern English Publications.

Long, M. 1990c. 'The least a second language acquisition theory needs to explain'. *TESOL Quarterly* 24: 649–66.

Long, M. 1991. 'Focus on form: a design feature in language teaching methodology' in K. de Bot, R. Ginsberg, and C. Kramsch (eds.): *Foreign Language Research in Cross-cultural Perspective*. Amsterdam: John Benjamin.

Long, M. 1993. 'Assessment strategies for SLA theories'. *Applied Linguistics* 14: 225–49.

Long, M. 1996. 'The role of the linguistic environment in second language acquisition' in W. Ritchie and T. Bhatia (eds.): *Handbook of Second Language Acquisition*. San Diego: Academic Press.

Long, M. 1997. 'Construct validity in SLA research: a response to Firth and Wagner'. *The Modern Language Journal* 81: 318–23.

Long, M. 1998. 'SLA breaking the siege'. *University of Hawai'i Working Papers in ESL* 17: 79–129.

Long, M. 2003. 'Stabilization and fossilization in interlanguage development' in C. Doughty and M. Long (eds.): *Handbook of Second Language Acquisition*. Malden, Mass.: Blackwell.

Long, M. (ed.). 2006a. *Problems in SLA*. Mahwah, N.J.: Lawrence Erlbaum.

Long, M. 2006b. 'Recasts in SLA: the story so far' in M. Long (ed.): *Problems in SLA*. Mahwah, N.J.: Lawrence Erlbaum.

Long, M. 2006c. 'SLA: breaking the siege' in M. Long (ed.): *Problems in SLA*. Mahwah, N.J.: Lawrence Erlbaum.

Long, M., L. Adams, M. McLean, and **F. Castanos.** 1976. 'Doing things with words: verbal interaction in lockstep and small group classroom situations' in J. F. Fanselow and R. Crymes (eds.): *On TESOL '76*. Washington D.C.: TESOL.

Long, M. and **G. Crookes.** 1987. 'Intervention points in second language classroom processes' in B. Das (ed.): *Patterns of Classroom Interaction*. Singapore: SEAMEO Regional Language Centre.

Long, M. and **G. Crookes.** 1992. 'Three approaches to task-based syllabus design'. *TESOL Quarterly* 26: 27–56.

Long, M. and **C. Doughty.** 2003. 'SLA and cognitive science' in C. Doughty and M. Long (eds.): *Handbook of Second Language Acquisition Research*. Malden, Mass.: Blackwell.

Long, M. and **C. Doughty** (eds.). Forthcoming. *Handbook of Second and Foreign Language Teaching*. Oxford: Blackwell.

Long, M., S. Gambhir, V. Gambhir, and **M. Nishimura.** 1982. 'Regularization in foreigner talk and interlanguage'. Paper presented at the 17th Annual TESOL Convention, Toronto, Canada.

Long, M., S. Inagaki, and **L. Ortega.** 1998. 'The role of implicit negative feedback in SLA: models and recasts in Japanese and Spanish'. *The Modern Language Journal* 82/3: 357–71.

Long, M., S. Peck, and **K. Bailey** (eds.). 1980. *Research in Second Language Acquisition*. Rowley, Mass., Newbury House.

Long, M. and **P. Porter.** 1985. 'Group work, interlanguage talk, and second language acquisition'. *TESOL Quarterly* 19: 207–28.

Long, M. and **P. Robinson.** 1998. 'Focus-on-form: theory, research and practice' in C. Doughty and J. Williams (eds.): *Focus-on-form in Classroom Second Language Acquisition*. Cambridge: Cambridge University Press.

Long, M. and **S. Ross.** 1993. 'Modifications that preserve language and content' in M. Tickoo (ed.): *Simplification: Theory and Application*. Singapore: SEAMEO Regional Language Centre.

Long, M. and **C. Sato.** 1984. 'Methodological issues in interlanguage studies: an interactionist perspective' in A. Davies, C. Criper, and A. Howatt (eds.): *Interlanguage*. Edinburgh: Edinburgh University Press.

Lörscher, W. 1986. 'Conversational structures in the foreign language classroom' in G. Kasper (ed.): *Learning, Teaching and Communication in the Foreign Language Classroom*. Aarhus: Aarhus University Press.

Lörscher, W. and **R. Schultze** (eds.). 1987. *Perspectives on Language in Performance*. Tübingen: Gunter Narr.

Loschky, L. 1994. 'Comprehensible input and second language acquisition: what is the relationship'. *Studies in Second Language Acquisition* 16: 303–23.

Loschky, L. and **R. Bley-Vroman.** 1993. 'Grammar and task-based methodology' in G. Crookes and S. Gass (eds.): *Tasks and Language Learning: Integrating Theory and Practice*. Clevedon: Multilingual Matters.

Lott, D. 1983. 'Analysing and counteracting interference errors'. *ELT Journal* 37: 256–61.

Louden, W. 1992. 'Understanding reflection through collaborative research' in A. Hargreaves and M. Fullan (eds.): *Understanding Teacher Development*. London and New York: Cassell and Teachers College Press.

Lowenberg, P. 1986. 'Non-native varieties of English: nativization, norms, and implications'. *Studies in Second Language Acquisition* 8: 1–18.

Lozano, C. 2006. 'Focus and split-transivity: the acquisition of word order alternations in non-native Spanish'. *Second Language Research* 22: 145–87.

Ludwig, J. 1982. 'Native-speaker judgements of second-language learners' efforts at communication: a review'. *The Modern Language Journal* 66: 274–83.

Ludwig, J. 1983. 'Attitudes and expectations: a profile of female and male students of college French, German and Spanish'. *The Modern Language Journal* 67: 216–27.

Lugton, R. (ed.). 1971. *Toward a Cognitive Approach to Second Language Acquisition.* Philadelphia, Penn.: Center for Curriculum Development.

Lujan, M., L. Minaya, and **D. Sankoff.** 1984. 'The universal consistency hypothesis and the prediction of word order acquisition stages in the speech of bilingual children'. *Language* 60: 343–71.

Lukmani, Y. 1972. 'Motivation to learn and language proficiency'. *Language Learning* 22: 261–73.

Luria, A. 1970. *Traumatic Aphasia.* The Hague: Mouton.

Luria, A. 1973. *The Working Brain.* Harmondsworth: Penguin.

Lynch, A. 1988. 'Speaking up or talking down: foreign learners' reactions to teacher talk'. *ELT Journal* 42: 109–16.

Lynch, T. and **J. Maclean.** 2000. 'Exploring the benefits of task repetition and recycling for classroom language learning'. *Language Teaching Research* 4: 221–50.

Lynch, T. and **J. Maclean.** 2001. 'Effects of immediate task repetition on learners' performance' in M. Bygate, P. Skehan, and M. Swain (eds.): *Researching Pedagogic Tasks, Second Language Learning, Teaching and Testing.* Harlow: Longman.

Lyons, J. 1968. *Introduction to Theoretical Linguistics.* Cambridge: Cambridge University Press.

Lyons, J. and **R. Wales** (eds.). 1966. *Psycholinguistic Papers.* Edinburgh. Edinburgh University Press.

Lyster, R. 1994. 'The effect of functional-analytic teaching on aspects of French immersion students' sociolinguistic competence'. *Applied Linguistics* 15: 263–87.

Lyster, R. 1998a. 'Recasts, repetition and ambiguity in L2 classroom discourse'. *Studies in Second Language Acquisition* 20/1: 51–81.

Lyster, R. 1998b. 'Negotiation of form, recasts, and explicit correction in relation to error types and learner repair in immersion classrooms'. *Language Learning* 48: 183–218.

Lyster, R. 2002. 'The importance of differentiating negotiation of form and meaning in classroom interaction' in P. Burmeister, T. Piske, and A Rohde (eds.): *An Integrated View of Language Development: Papers in Honor of Henning Wode.* Trier: Wissenschaftlicher Verlag.

Lyster, R. 2004. 'Differential effects of prompts and recasts in form-focused instruction'. *Studies in Second Language Acquisition* 26/3: 399–432.

Lyster, R. and **H. Mori.** 2006. 'Interactional feedback and instructional counterbalance'. *Studies in Second Language Acquisition* 28: 269–300.

Lyster, R. and **L. Ranta.** 1997. 'Corrective feedback and learner uptake: negotiation of form in communicative classrooms'. *Studies in Second Language Acquisition* 19: 37–66.

Macaro, E. 2001. *Learning Strategies in Foreign and Second Language Classrooms.* London: Continuum.

Macaro, E. 2006. 'Strategies for language learning and for language use: revising the theoretical framework'. *The Modern Language Journal* 90: 320–37.

Mace, J. (ed.). 1995. *Literacy, Language and Community Publishing.* Clevedon: Multilingual matters.

MacIntyre, P. 2002. 'Motivation, anxiety and emotion in second language acquisition' in P. Robinson (ed.): *Individual Differences in Second Language Acquisition.* Amsterdam: John Benjamins.

MacIntyre, P. and **R. Gardner.** 1991a. 'Methods and results in the study of foreign language anxiety: a review of the literature'. *Language Learning* 41: 25–57.

MacIntyre, P. and **R. Gardner.** 1991b. 'Language anxiety: its relationship to other anxieties and to processing in native and second languages'. *Language Learning* 41: 513–34.

MacIntyre, P. and **R. Gardner.** 1994. 'The subtle effects of induced anxiety on cognitive processing in the second language'. *Language Learning* 44: 283–305.

MacIntyre, P., S. Baker, R. Clement, and **S. Conrad.** 2001. 'Willingness to communicate, social support, and language learning orientations of immersion students'. *Studies in Second Language Acquisition* 23: 369–88.

MacIntyre, P., R. Clement, Z. Dörnyei, and **K. Noels.** 1998. 'Conceptualizing willingness to communicate in a L2: a situated model of confidence and affiliation'. *The Modern Language Journal* 82: 545–62.

Mackey, A. 1999. 'Input, interaction and second language development: an empirical study of question formation in ESL'. *Studies in Second Language Acquisition* 21: 557–87.

Mackey. A. 2007a. 'Introduction' in A. Mackey (ed.): *Conversational Interaction in Second Language Acquisition: A Collection of Empirical Studies.* Oxford: Oxford University Press.

Mackey, A. (ed.). 2007b. *Conversational Interaction in Second Language Acquisition: A Collection of Empirical Studies.* Oxford: Oxford University Press.

Mackey, A. and **S. Gass.** 2005. *Second Language Research.* Mahwah, N.J.: Lawrence Erlbaum.

Mackey, A. and **S. Gass.** 2006. 'Introduction'. *Studies in Second Language Acquisition* 28: 169–78.

Mackey, A., S. Gass. and **K. McDonough.** 2000. 'How do learners perceive interactional feedback?' *Studies in Second Language Acquisition* 22: 471–97.

Mackey, A. and **J. Goo.** 2007. 'Interaction research in SLA: a meta-analysis and research synthesis' in A. Mackey (ed.): *Conversational Interaction in Second Language Acquisition: A Collection of Empirical Studies.* Oxford: Oxford University Press.

Mackey, A., R. Oliver, and **J. Leeman.** 2003. 'Interactional input and the incorporation of feedback: an exploration of NS–NNS and NNS–NNS adult and child dyads'. *Language Learning* 53: 35–66.

Mackey, A. and **J. Philp.** 1998. 'Conversational interaction and second language development: recasts, responses, and red herrings?' *The Modern Language Journal* 82/3: 338–56.

Mackey, A., J. Philp, T. Egi, A. Fujii, and **T. Tatsumi.** 2002. 'Individual differences in working memory, noticing of interactional feedback and L2 development' in P. Robinson (ed.): *Individual Differences in L2 Learning.* Amsterdam: John Benjamins.

Macrory, G. and **V. Stone.** 2000. 'Pupil progress in the acquisition of the perfect tense in French: the relationship between knowledge and use'. *Language Teaching Research* 4: 55–82.

MacWhinney, B. 1989. 'Competition and connectionism' in B. MacWhinney and E. Bates (eds.): *The Crosslinguistic Study of Sentence Processing.* Cambridge: Cambridge University Press.

MacWhinney, B. 2001. 'The competition model: the input, the context' in P. Robinson (ed.): *Cognition and Second Language Instruction.* Cambridge: Cambridge University Press.

MacWhinney, B. 2006. 'Emergent fossilization' in Z. Han and T. Odlin (eds.): *Studies of Fossilization in Second Language Acquisition.* Clevedon: Multilingual Matters.

MacWhinney, B. 2007a. 'Emergentism—use often and with care'. *Applied Linguistics* 27: 729–40.

MacWhinney, B. 2007b. 'A unified model' in N. Ellis and P. Robinson (eds.): *Handbook of Cognitive Linguistics and Second Language Acquisition.* Mahwah, N.J.: Lawrence Erlbaum.

MacWhinney, B. and **E. Bates** (eds.). 1989. *The Crosslinguistic Study of Sentence Processing.* Cambridge: Cambridge University Press.

MacWhinney. B., E. Bates, and **R. Kligell.** 1984. 'Cue validity and sentence interpretation in English, German and Italian'. *Journal of Verbal Learning and Verbal Behavior* 23: 127–50.

MacWhinney, B., C. Pleh, and **E. Bates.** 1985. 'The development of sentence interpretation in Hungarian'. *Cognitive Psychology* 17: 178–209.

Maeshiba, N., N. Yoshinaga, G. Kasper, and **S. Ross.** 1996. 'Transfer and proficiency in interlanguage apologizing' in S. Gass and J. Neu (eds.): *Speech Acts Across Cultures: Challenges in Communication in a Second Language.* Berlin: de Gruyter.

Magnet, J. 1990. 'Canadian perspectives on official English' in K. Adams and D. Brink (eds.): *Perspectives on Official English: the Campaign for English as the Official Language of the USA.* Berlin: Mouton de Gruyter.

Major, R. 1987. 'A model for interlanguage pronunciation' in G. Ioup and S. Weinberger (eds.): *Interlanguage Phonology: the Acquisition of a Second Language Sound System*. Rowley, Mass.: Newbury House.
Major, R. 1996a. 'Chunking and phonological memory: a response to Ellis'. *Studies in Second Language Acquisition* 18: 351–4.
Major, R. 1996b. 'Markedness in second language acquisition consonant clusters' in R. Bayley and D. Preston (eds.): *Second Language Acquisition and Linguistic Variation*. Amsterdam: John Benjamins.
Major, R. 2001. *Foreign Accent*. Amsterdam: John Benjamin.
Major, R. and **E. Kim.** 1996. 'The similarity differential rate hypothesis'. *Language Learning* 46: 465–96.
Makino, T. 1980. 'Acquisition order of English morphemes by Japanese secondary school students'. *Journal of Hokkaido University Education* 30: 101–48.
Malouf, R. and **C. Dodd.** 1972. 'Role of exposure, imitation and expansion in the acquisition of an artificial grammatical rule'. *Developmental Psychology* 7: 195–203.
Mangubhai, F. 1991. 'The processing behaviours of adult second language learners and their relationship to second language proficiency'. *Applied Linguistics* 12: 268–98.
Manheimer, R. 1995. 'Close the task: improve the discourse'. Paper given at Annual Conference of American Association of Applied Linguists, Long Beach, California.
Manning, A., P. Martin, and **K. McCalla** (eds.). 1984. *The Tenth LACUS Forum 1983*. Columbia, S.C.: Hornbeam Press.
Mannon, T. 1986. 'Teacher talk: a comparison of a teacher's speech to native and non-native speakers'. Unpublished MA TESL thesis, University of California at Los Angeles.
Manolopoulo-Sergi, E. 2004. 'Motivation within the information processing model of foreign language learning'. *System* 32: 427–42.
Maple, R. 1982. 'Social distance and the acquisition of English as a second language: a study of Spanish-speaking adult learners'. Unpublished PhD dissertation, University of Texas at Austin.
Marcel, J. 1983. 'Conscious and unconscious perception: experiments on visual masking and word recognition'. *Cognitive Psychology* 15: 197–237.
Markee, N. 1994. 'Towards and ethnomethodological respecification of second language acquisition studies' in E. Tarone, S. Gass, and A. Cohen (eds.): *Research Methodology in Second Language Acquisition*. Mahwah, N.J.: Lawrence Erlbaum.
Markee, N. 1997. 'SLA research: a resource for changing teachers' professional cultures?' *The Modern Language Journal* 81: 80–93.
Markee, N. 2000. *Conversation Analysis*. Mahwah, N.J.: Lawrence Erlbaum.
Markee, N. and **G. Kasper.** 2004. 'Classroom talks: an introduction'. *The Modern Language Journal* 88: 491–500.
Marsden, E. 2006. 'Exploring input processing in the classroom: an experimental comparison of processing instruction and enriched input'. *Language Learning* 56: 507–66.
Martin, G. 1980. 'English language acquisition: the effects of living with an American family'. *TESOL Quarterly* 14: 388–90.
Martohardjono, G. 1993. 'Wh-movement in the acquisition of a second language: a crosslinguistic study of three languages with and without movement'. Unpublished PhD dissertation, Cornell University.
Masgoret, A. and **R. Gardner.** 2003. 'Attitudes, motivation, and second language learning: a meta-analysis of studies conducted by Gardner and associates'. *Language Learning* 53: 123–63.
Masny, D. 1987. 'The role of language and cognition in second language metalinguistic awareness' in J. Lantolf and A. Labarca (eds.): *Research in second Language learning: Focus on the classroom*. Norwood, N.J.: Ablex.
Mason, B. and **S. Krashen.** 1997. 'Extensive reading in English as a foreign language'. *System* 25: 91–102.

Mason, C. 1971. 'The relevance of intensive training in English as a foreign language for university students'. *Language Learning* 21: 197–204.

Matsuda, S. Y. T., M. Sakurai, and **A. Baba** (eds.). 1993. *In honor of Tokuichiro Matsuda: Papers contributed on the occasion of his sixtieth birthday*. Tokyo: Iwasaki Linguistic Circle.

Matsumura, S. 2001. 'Learning the rules for offering advice: A quantitative approach to second language socialization'. *Language Learning* 51: 635–79.

Matsumara, S. 2003. 'Modelling the relationships among interlanguage, pragmatic development, L2 proficiency, and exposure to L2'. *Applied Linguistics* 24: 465–91.

Matsumoto, K. 1987. 'Factors involved in the L2 learning process'. *JALT Journal* 11: 167–92.

Matsuura, H. 1998. 'Japanese EFL learners' perception of politeness in low imposition requests'. *JALT Journal* 20/1: 33–48.

Matthews, P. 1997. *The Concise Oxford Dictionary of Linguistics*. Oxford: Oxford University Press.

Matthews, S. and **V. Yip.** 2003. 'Relative clauses in early bilingual development; transfer and universals' in A. Ramat (ed.): *Typology and Second Language Acquisition*. Berlin: Mouton de Gruyter.

May, S. 2001. *Language and Minority Rights*. London: Longman.

Mazurkewich, I. 1984. 'The acquisition of the dative alternation by second language learners and linguistic theory'. *Language Learning* 34: 91–109.

Mazurkewich, I. 1985. 'Syntactic markedness and language acquisition'. *Studies in Second Language Acquisition* 7: 15–35.

McCafferty, S. 1994a. 'Adult second language learners' use of private speech: a review of studies'. *The Modern Language Journal* 78: 421–36.

McCafferty, S. 1994b. 'The use of private speech by adult ESL learners at different levels of proficiency' in J. Lantolf and G. Appel (eds.): *Vygotskian Approaches to Second Language Research*. Norwood, N.J.: Ablex.

McCafferty, S. 1998. 'Nonverbal expression and L2 private speech'. *Applied Linguistics* 19: 73–96.

McCafferty, S. 2002. 'Gesture and creating zones of proximal development in second language learning'. *The Modern Language Journal* 86: 192–203.

McClelland, J., D. Rumelhart, and **G. Hinton.** 1986. 'The appeal of parallel distributed processing' in D. Rumelhart *et al.* (eds.). *Parallel Distributed Processing: Explorations in the Microstructure of Cognition Volume 1: Foundations*. Cambridge, Mass.: MIT Press.

McClelland, J., D. Rumelhart, and the **PDP Research Group** (eds.). 1986. *Parallel Distributed Processing: Explorations in the Microstructure of Cognition Volume 2: Psychological and Biological Models*. Cambridge, Mass.: MIT Press.

McCormick, D. and **R. Donato.** 2000. 'Teacher question as scaffolding assistance in an ESL classroom' in J. Hall and L. Verplaetse (eds.): *Second and Foreign Language Learning Through Classroom Interaction*. Mahwah, N.J.: Lawrence Erlbaum.

McDonald, J. 1986. 'The development of sentence comprehension strategies in English and Dutch'. *Journal of Experimental Child Psychology* 41: 317–35.

McDonald, J. and **K. Heilenman.** 1991. 'Determinants of cue strength in adult first and second language speakers of French'. *Applied Psycholinguistics* 12: 313–48.

McDonough, K. 2006. 'Interaction and syntactic priming: English L2 speakers' production of dative constructions'. *Studies in Second Language Acquisition* 28: 179–208.

McDonough, K. and **A. Mackey.** 2006. 'Responses to recasts: Repetitions, primed production, and linguistic development'. *Language Learning* 56: 693–720.

McDonough, S. 1999. 'Learner strategies'. *Language Teaching* 32: 1–18.

McHoul, A. 1978. 'The organization of turns at formal talk in the classroom'. *Language and Society* 7: 183–213.

McKay, S. 2005. 'Sociolinguistics and second language learning' in E. Hinkel (ed.): *Handbook of Research in Second Teaching and Learning*. Mahwah, N.J.: Lawrence Erlbaum.

McKay, S. and **S. Wong.** 1996. 'Multiple discourses, multiple identities: Investment and agency in second language learning among Chinese adolescent immigrant students'. *Harvard Educational Review* 3: 577–608.
McLaughlin, B. 1978a. *Second Language Acquisition in Childhood.* Hillsdale, N.J.: Lawrence Erlbaum.
McLaughlin, B. 1978b. 'The Monitor Model: some methodological considerations'. *Language Learning* 28: 309–32.
McLaughlin, B. 1980. 'Theory and research in second-language learning: an emerging paradigm'. *Language Learning* 30: 331–50.
McLaughlin, B. 1985. *Second Language Acquisition in Childhood. Volume 2: School-age Children.* Hillsdale, N.J.: Lawrence Erlbaum.
McLaughlin, B. 1987. *Theories of Second Language Learning.* London: Edward Arnold.
McLaughlin, B. 1990. 'Restructuring'. *Applied Linguistics* 11: 113–28.
McLaughlin, B. and **M. Harrington.** 1989. 'Second-language acquisition'. *Annual Review of Applied Linguistics* 10: 122–34.
McLaughlin, B. and **R. Heredia.** 1996. 'Information processing approaches to research on second language acquisition and use' in R. Ritchie and T. Bhatia (eds.). *A Handbook of Second Language Acquisition.* San Diego: Academic Press.
McLaughlin, B., T. Rossman, and **B. McLeod.** 1983. 'Second language learning: an information-processing perspective'. *Language Learning* 33: 135–58.
McNamara, J. 1973. 'Nurseries, streets and classrooms: some comparisons and deductions'. *The Modern Language Journal* 57: 250–55.
McNamara, T. 1997. 'What do we mean by social identity? Competing frameworks, competing discourses'. *TESOL Quarterly* 31: 561–6.
McNeill, D. 1970. *The Acquisition of Language.* New York: Harper Row.
McTear, M. 1975. 'Structure and categories of foreign language teaching sequences' in R. Allwright (ed.): *Working Papers: Language Teaching Classroom Research.* University of Essex, Department of Language and Linguistics.
Meara, P. 1984. 'The study of lexis in interlanguage' in A. Davies *et al.* (eds.): *Interlanguage.* Edinburgh: Edinburgh University Press.
Meara, P. (ed.). 1986. *Spoken Language.* London: Centre for Information on Language Teaching.
Meara, P. 1997. 'Towards a new approach to modeling vocabulary acquisition' in N. Schmitt and M. McCarthy (eds.): *Vocabulary: Description, Acquisition and Pedagogy.* Cambridge: Cambridge University Press.
Mechelli, A., J. Crinion, U. Noppeney, J. O'Doherty, J. Ashburner, and **R. Frackowiack.** 2004. 'Neurolinguistics: structural plasticity in the bilingual brain'. *Nature* 431: 757.
Mehnert U. 1998. 'The effects of different lengths of time for planning on second language performance'. *Studies in Second Language Acquisition* 20: 52–83.
Meisel, J. 1980. 'Linguistic simplification' in S. Felix (ed.): *Second Language Development: Trends and Issues.* Tübingen: Gunter Narr.
Meisel, J. 1983. 'Strategies of second language acquisition: more than one kind of simplification' in R. Andersen (ed.): *Pidginization and Creolization as Language Acquisition.* Rowley, Mass.: Newbury House.
Meisel, J. 1991. 'Principles of Universal Grammar and strategies of language learning: some similarities and differences between first and second language acquisition' in L. Eubank (ed.): *Point Counterpoint: Universal Grammar in the Second Language.* Amsterdam: John Benjamins.
Meisel, J., H. Clahsen, and **M. Pienemann.** 1981. 'On determining developmental stages in natural second language acquisition'. *Studies in Second Language Acquisition* 3: 109–35.
Mesthrie, R. and **T. Dunne.** 1990. 'Syntactic variation in language shift: the relative clause in South African English'. *Language Variation and Change* 2: 31–56.
Michieka, M. 2005. 'English in Kenya: a sociolinguistic profile'. *World Englishes* 24: 173–86.

Miller, G. and **N. Chomsky.** 1963. 'Finitary models of language users' in R. Bush, E. Galanter, and R. Luce (eds.): *Handbook of Mathematical Psychology Volume II*. New York: Wiley.
Miller, J. 2004. 'Identity and language use: the politics of speaking ESL in schools' in A. Pavlenko and A. Blackledge (eds.): *Negotiation of Identities in Multilingual Contexts*. Clevedon: Multilingual Matters.
Milon, J. 1974. 'The development of negation in English by a second language learner'. *TESOL Quarterly* 8: 137–43.
Milroy, J. and **L. Milroy.** 1997. 'Varieties and variation' in F. Coulmas (ed.): *The Handbook of Sociolinguistics*. Malden, Mass.: Blackwell.
Milroy, L. 1980. *Language and Social Networks*. Oxford: Basil Blackwell.
Mitchell, R. and **F. Myles.** 1998. *Second Language Learning Theories*. London: Hodder Arnold.
Mitchell, R. and **F. Myles.** 2004. *Second Language Learning Theories* (Second edition). London: Hodder Arnold.
Mitchell, R., B. Parkinson, and **R. Johnstone.** 1981. 'The foreign language classroom: an observational study'. *Stirling Educational Monographs No. 9*. Stirling: Department of Education, University of Stirling.
Miyake, A. and **N. Friedman.** 1998. 'Individual differences in second language proficiency: working memory as language aptitude' in A. Healy and L. Bourne (eds.): *Foreign Language Learning: Psycholinguistic Studies on Training and Retention*. Hillsdale, N.J.: Lawrence Erlbaum.
Mizon, S. 1981. 'Teacher talk: a case study from the Bangalore/Madras communicational ELT project'. Unpublished MA thesis, University of Lancaster.
Mohamed, N. 2001. 'Teaching grammar through consciousness-raising tasks'. Unpublished MA thesis, University of Auckland, Auckland.
Möhle, D. and **M. Raupach.** 1989. 'Language transfer and procedural knowledge' in H. Dechert and M. Raupach (eds.): *Interlingual Processes*. Tübingen: Gunter Narr.
Mondada, L. and **S. Doehler.** 2004. 'Second language acquisition as situated practice: Task accomplishment in the French second language classroom'. *The Modern Language Journal* 88: 501–18.
Montalbetti, M. 1984. 'After binding: on the interpretation of pronouns'. Unpublished PhD thesis, MIT.
Montgomery, C. and **M. Eisenstein.** 1985. 'Real reality revisited: an experimental communicative course in ESL'. *TESOL Quarterly* 19: 317–33.
Montrul, S. 2001. 'Agentive verbs of manner of motion in Spanish and English as second languages'. *Studies in Second Language Acquisition* 22: 229–73.
Mori, J. 2002. 'Task design, plan, and development of talk-in-interaction: an analysis of a small group activity in a Japanese language classroom'. *Applied Linguistics* 23: 323–47.
Mori, Y. 1999. 'Epistemological beliefs and language learning beliefs: what do language learners believe about their learning'. *Language Learning* 49: 377–415.
Morris, C. 1938. *Foundations of the Theory of Signs*. Chicago: University of Chicago Press.
Morris, R. (ed.). 1989. *Parallel Distributed Processing: Implications for Psychology and Neurobiology*. Oxford: Clarendon Press.
Morrison, D. and **G. Low.** 1983. 'Monitoring and the second language learner' in J. Richards and R. Schmidt (eds.): *Language and Communication*. London: Longman.
Moskowitz, G. 1967. 'The FLint system: an observational tool for the foreign language classroom' in. A. Simon and E. Boyer (eds.): *Mirrors for Behavior: an Anthology of Classroom Observation Instruments*. Philadelphia: Center for the Study of Teaching at Temple University.
Moyer, A. 1999. 'Ultimate attainment in L2 phonology: the critical factors of age, motivation, and instruction'. *Studies in Second Language Acquisition* 21: 81–108.
Moyer, A. 2004. *Age, Accent and Experience in Second Language Acquisition: An Integrated Approach to Critical Period Inquiry*. Clevedon: Multilingual Matters.

Muchnick, A. and **D. Wolfe.** 1982. 'Attitudes and motivations of American students of Spanish'. *Canadian Modern Language Review* 38: 262–81.

Mueller, J. 2005. 'Electrophysiological correlates of second language processing'. *Second Language Research* 21: 152–74.

Mueller, J. 2006. 'L2 in a nutshell: the investigation of second language processing in the miniature language model' in M. Gullberg and P. Indefrey (eds.): *The Cognitive Neuroscience of Second Language Acquisition*. Malden, Mass.: Blackwell.

Mukkatesh, L. 1977. *Problematic Areas in English Syntax for Jordanian Students*. University of Amman, Jordan.

Muñoz, C. 2006. 'The effects of age on foreign language learning: The BAF project' in C. Muñoz (ed.): *Age and the Rate of Foreign Language Learning*. Clevedon: Multilingual Matters.

Muranoi, H. 2000. 'Focus-on-form through interaction enhancement: integrating formal instruction into a communicative task in EFL classrooms'. *Language Learning* 50: 617–73.

Murphy, B. and **J. Neu.** 1996. 'My grade's too low: the speech act set of complaining' in S. Gass and J. Neu (eds.): *Speech Acts Across Cultures: Challenge to Communication in a Second Language*. Berlin: de Gruyter.

Murphy, V. 2004. 'Dissociable systems in second language inflectional morphology'. *Studies in Second Language Acquisition* 26: 433–59.

Muysken, P. 1984. 'The Spanish that Quechua speakers learn' in R. Andersen (ed.): *Second Language: a Crosslinguistic Perspective*. Rowley, Mass.: Newbury House.

Myers, I. and **K. Briggs.** 1976. *The Myers-Briggs Type Indicator, Form G*. Paolo Alto, Calif.: Consulting Psychologists Press.

Myles, F. 2004. 'From data to theory: the over-representation of linguistic knowledge in SLA'. *Transactions of the Philological Society* 102: 139–68.

Myles, F., J. Hooper, and **R. Mitchell.** 1998. 'Rote or rule? Exploring the role of formulaic language in classroom foreign language learning'. *Language Learning* 48: 323–63.

Myles, F., R. Mitchell, and **J. Hooper.** 1999. 'Interrogative chunks in French L2: a basis for creative construction?' *Studies in Second Language Acquisition* 21: 49–80.

Nabei, I. and **M. Swain.** 2002. 'Learner awareness of recasts in classroom interaction: a case study of an adult EFL student's second language learning'. *Language Awareness* 11: 43–63.

Nagara, S. 1972. *Japanese Pidgin English in Hawai'i: a Bilingual Description*. Honolulu: University Press of Hawai'i.

Nagata, H., D. Aline, and **R. Ellis.** 1999. 'Modified input, language aptitude and the acquisition of word meanings' in R. Ellis (ed.): *Learning a Second Language Through Interaction*. Amsterdam: John Benjamins.

Nagata, N. 1993. 'Intelligent computer feedback for second language instruction'. *The Modern Language Journal* 77: 330–39.

Naiman, N., M. Fröhlich, H. Stern, and **A. Todesco.** 1978. 'The Good Language Learner'. *Research in Education Series No 7*. Toronto: The Ontario Institute for Studies in Education. Reprinted in 1996 by Multilingual Matters.

Nakahama, Y., A. Tyler, and **L. Van Lier.** 2001. 'Negotiation of meaning in conversational and information gap activities: a comparative discourse analysis'. *TESOL Quarterly* 35: 377–405.

Nakatani, Y. 2005. 'The effects of awareness-raising training on oral communication strategy use'. *The Modern Language Journal* 89: 76–91.

Naro, A. 1983. 'Comments on "Simplified Input and Second Language Acquisition"' in R. Andersen (ed.): *Pidginization and Creolization as Language Acquisition*. Rowley, Mass.: Newbury House.

Nassaji, H. and **M. Swain.** 2000. 'A Vygotskian perspective on corrective feedback in L2: the effect of random versus negotiated help in the learning of English articles'. *Language Awareness* 9: 34–51.

Nassaji, H. and **G. Wells.** 2000. 'What's the use of "triadic dialogue"? An investigation of teacher–student interaction'. *Applied Linguistics* 21: 376–406.

Nation, P. 2001. *Learning Vocabulary in Another Language*. Cambridge: Cambridge University Press.

Nation, R. and **B. McLaughlin.** 1986. 'Experts and novices: an information-processing approach to the "good language learner" problem'. *Applied Psycholinguistics* 7: 41–56.

Nattinger, J. and **J. DeCarrico.** 1992. *Lexical Phrases and Language Teaching*. Oxford: Oxford University Press.

Naughton, D. 2006. 'Cooperative strategy training and oral interaction: enhancing small group communication in the language classroom'. *The Modern Language Journal* 90: 169–84.

Nayar, P. 1997. 'ESL/EFL dichotomy today: language policies and pragmatics'. *TESOL Quarterly* 31: 9–37.

Negueruela, E. 2003. 'A sociocultural approach to teaching and researching second language: Systemic-theoretical instruction and second language development'. PhD dissertation, Penn State University, University Park, Penn.

Nelson, K. 1973. 'Structure and strategy in learning to talk'. *Monographs of the Society for Research in Child Development* 38.

Nelson, K. 1977. 'Facilitating children's syntax acquisition'. *Developmental Psychology* 13: 101–7.

Nelson, K. (ed.). 1980. *Children's Language Volume* 2. Gardner's Press.

Nemser, W. 1971. 'Approximative systems of foreign language learners'. *International review of Applied Linguistics* 9: 115–23. Also in J. Richards (ed.). 1978. *Understanding Second and Foreign Language Learning: Issues and Approaches*. Rowley, Mass.: Newbury House.

Newman, F. and **L. Holzman.** 1996. *Unscientific Psychology. A Cultural-Performatory Approach to Understanding Human Life*. New York: Praeger.

Newman, F. and **L. Holzman.** 1997. *The End of Knowing: A New Developmental Way of Learning*. London: Routledge.

Newman, J. and **L. White.** 1999. 'A pilot study of language awareness at the New Zealand tertiary level'. *New Zealand Language Teacher* 25: 41–53.

Newmark, L. 1966. 'How not to interfere in language learning'. *International Journal of American Linguistics* 32: 77–87.

Newmark, L. and **D. Reibel.** 1968. 'Necessity and sufficiency in language learning'. *International Review of Applied Linguistics in Language Teaching* 6: 145–64.

Newmeyer, F. 1998. *Language Form and Language Function*. Cambridge: MIT Press.

Newmeyer, F. 2004. 'Typological evidence and universal grammar'. *Studies in Language* 28: 527–48.

Newport, E. 1976. 'Motherese: the speech of mothers to young children'. Unpublished PhD thesis, University of Pennsylvania, Penn.

Newport, E., H. Gleitman, and **L. Gleitman.** 1977. '"Mother, I'd rather do it myself": some effects and non-effects of maternal speech styles' in C. Snow and C. Ferguson (eds.): *Talking to Children: Language Input and Acquisition*. Cambridge: Cambridge University Press.

Newton, J. 1991. 'Negotiation: negotiating what?' Paper given at SEAMEO Conference on Language Acquisition and the Second/Foreign Language Classroom, RELC, Singapore.

Newton, J. 1995. 'Task-based interaction and incidental vocabulary learning: a case study'. *Second Language Research* 11/2: 159–77.

Nicholas, H. 1986. 'The acquisition of language as the acquisition of variation'. *Australian Working Papers on Language Development* 1: 1–30.

Nicholas, H., P. Lightbown, and **N. Spada.** 2001. 'Recasts as feedback to language learners'. *Language Learning* 51/4: 719–58.

Nickel, G. (ed.). 1971. *Papers in Contrastive Analysis*. Cambridge: Cambridge University Press.

Nickel, G. 1973. 'Aspects of error analysis and grading' in J. Svartvik (ed.): *Errata: Papers in Error Analysis*. Lund, Sweden: CWK Gleerup.

Nieman, L. and **W. Smith.** 1978. 'Individualized instruction: its effects upon achievement and interest in beginning college Spanish'. *The Modern Language Journal* 62: 157–67.

Niezgoda, K. and **C. Rover.** 2001. 'Pragmatic and grammatical awareness: A function of learning environment?' in K. Rose and G. Kasper (eds.): *Pragmatics in Language Teaching.* New York: Cambridge University Press.

Nobuyoshi, J. and **R. Ellis.** 1993. 'Focused communication tasks'. *ELT Journal* 47: 203–10.

Noels, K., L. Pelletier, R. Clement, and **R. Vallerand.** 2000. 'Why are you learning a second language? Motivational orientations and self-determination theory'. *Language Learning* 50: 57–85.

Nonaka, K. 2000. 'Apology is not necessary: an in-depth analysis of my own intercultural and intracultural miscommunication'. *Journal of Hokkaido University of Education at Kushiro* 32: 155–86.

Norris, J. and **L. Ortega.** 2000. 'Effectiveness of L2 instruction: a research synthesis and quantitative meta-analysis'. *Language Learning* 50: 417–528.

Norris, J. and **L. Ortega.** 2003. 'Defining and measuring SLA' in C. Doughty and M. Long (eds.): *Handbook of Second Language Acquisition.* Oxford: Blackwell.

Norris, J. and **L. Ortega.** 2006a. 'The value and practice of research synthesis for language learning and teaching' in J. Norris and L. Ortega (eds.): *Synthesizing Research on Language Learning and Teaching.* Amsterdam: John Benjamins.

Norris, J. and **L. Ortega** (eds.). 2006b. *Synthesizing Research on Language Teaching and Learning.* Amsterdam: John Benjamins.

Norton, B. 1997. 'Language, identity, and the ownership of English'. *TESOL Quarterly* 31: 409–29.

Norton, B. 2000. *Identity and Language Learning: Gender, Ethnicity and Educational Change.* Harlow: Longman.

Norton, B. and **A. Pavlenko.** 2004a. 'Gender and English language learners' challenges and possibilities' in B. Norton and A. Pavlenko (eds.): *Gender and English Language Learners.* Washington D.C.: Teachers of English to Speakers of Other languages.

Norton, B. and **A. Pavlenko** (eds.). 2004b. *Gender and English Language Learners.* Washington D.C.: Teachers of English to Speakers of Other languages.

Noyau, C., B. Dorriots, S. Sjostrom, and **K. Voionmaa.** 1995. 'The acquisition of Swedish' in R. Dietrich, W. Klein, and C. Noyau (eds.): *The Acquisition of Temporality in a Second Language.* Amsterdam: John Benjamins.

Nunan, D. 1990a. 'The questions teachers ask'. *JALT Journal* 12: 187–202.

Nunan, D. 1990b. 'The teacher as researcher' in C. Brumfit and R. Mitchell (eds.): *Research in the Language Classroom. ELT Documents 133.* Modern English Publications.

Nunan, D. 1991. 'Methods in second language classroom-oriented research: a critical review'. *Studies in Second Language Acquisition* 13: 249–74.

Nunan, D. 2004. *Task-based Language Teaching.* Cambridge: Cambridge University Press.

Nyikos, M. 1990. 'Sex related differences in adult language learning: socialization and memory factors'. *The Modern Language Journal* 3: 273–87.

Nyikos, M. and **R. Oxford.** 1993. 'A factor-analytic study of language-learning strategy use: interpretations from information-processing theory and social psychology'. *The Modern Language Journal* 77: 11–22.

Nystrom, N. 1983. 'Teacher–student interaction in bilingual classrooms: four approaches to error feedback' in H. Seliger and M. Long (eds.). *Classroom-oriented Research in Second Language Acquisition.* Rowley, Mass.: Newbury House.

Obler, L. 1989. 'Exceptional second language learners' in S. Gass, C. Madden, D. Preston, and L. Selinker (eds.): *Variation in Second Language Acquisition Volume I: Sociolinguistic Issues.* Clevedon: Multilingual Matters.

Obler, L. and **M. Alpert.** 1978. 'A monitor system for bilingual language processing' in M. Paradis (ed.): *Aspects of Bilingualism.* Columbia, S. C.: Hornbeam Press.

Obler, L. and **N. Mahecha.** 1991. 'First language loss in bilingual and polyglot aphasics' in H. Seliger and R. Vago (eds.): *First Language Attrition*. Cambridge: Cambridge University Press.

Ochs, E. 1979. 'Planned and unplanned discourse' in T. Givón (ed.): *Syntax and Semantics Volume 12: Discourse and Semantics*. New York: Academic Press.

Ochs, E. 1982. 'Talking to children in Western Samoa'. *Language in Society* 11: 77–104.

Ochs, E. and **B. Schieffelin** (eds.). 1979. *Developmental Pragmatics*. New York: Academic Press.

Ochs, E. and **B. Schieffelin.** 1984. 'Language acquisition and socialization: three developmental stories and their implications' in R. Shweder and R. LeVine (eds.): *Culture and its Acquisition*. New York: Cambridge University Press.

Odlin, T. 1989. *Language Transfer*. Cambridge: Cambridge University Press.

Odlin, T. 1990. 'Word-order transfer, metalinguistic awareness and constraints on foreign language learning' in B. VanPatten and J. Lee (eds.): *Second Language Acquisition—Foreign Language Learning*. Clevedon: Multilingual Matters.

Odlin, T. 2003. 'Cross-linguistic influence' in C. Doughty and M. Long (eds.): *The Handbook of Second Language Acquisition*. Malden, Mass.: Blackwell.

Odlin, T. 2005. 'Crosslinguistic influence and conceptual transfer: what are the concepts'. *Annual Review of Applied Linguistics* 25: 3–25.

O'Grady, W. 1999. 'Toward a new nativism'. *Studies in Second Language Acquisition* 21: 621–35.

O'Grady, W. 2005. *Syntactic Carpentry: An Emergentist Approach to Syntax*. Mahwah, N.J.: Erlbaum.

O'Grady, W., M. Lee, and **M. Choo.** 2003. 'A subject-object asymmetry in the acquisition of relative clauses in Korean as a second language'. *Studies in Second Language Acquisition* 25: 433–47.

Oh, S-Y. 2001. 'Two types of input modification and EFL reading comprehension: simplification versus elaboration'. *TESOL Quarterly* 35: 69–96.

Ohta, A. 1995. 'Applying sociocultural theory to an analysis of learner discourse: learner–learner collaborative interaction in the zone of proximal development'. *Issues in Applied Linguistics* 612: 93–122.

Ohta, A. 2000. 'Rethinking recasts: a learner-centered examination of corrective feedback in the Japanese language classroom' in J. K. Hall and L. S. Verplaeste. (eds.): *The Construction of Second and Foreign Language Learning through Classroom Instruction*. Mahwah, N.J.: Lawrence Erlbaum.

Ohta, A. 2001a. 'A longitudinal study of the development of expression of alignment in Japanese as a foreign language' in K. Rose and G. Kasper (eds.): *Pragmatics in Language Teaching*. New York: Cambridge University Press.

Ohta, A. 2001b. *Second Language Acquisition Processes in the Classroom: Learning Japanese*. Mahwah, N.J.: Lawrence Erlbaum.

Ohta, A. and **T. Nakone.** 2004. 'When students ask questions: teacher and peer answers in the foreign language classroom'. *International Review of Applied Linguistics* 42: 217–37.

Okamura-Bichard, F. 1985. 'Mother tongue maintenance and second language learning: a case of Japanese children'. *Language Learning* 35: 63–89.

Oleksy, W. (ed.). 1989. *Contrastive Pragmatics*. Amsterdam: John Benjamins.

Oliver, R. 1997. 'Negotiation of meaning in child interactions'. *The Modern Language Journal* 82: 372–86.

Oliver, R. 2000. 'Age differences in negotiation and feedback in classroom and pairwork'. *Language Learning* 50: 119–51.

Oliver, R. 2002. 'The patterns of negotiation for meaning in child interactions'. *The Modern Language Journal* 86: 97–111.

Oliver, R. and **A. Mackey.** 2003. 'Interactional context and feedback in child ESL classrooms'. *The Modern Language Journal* 87: 519–33.

Oller, J. 1977. 'Attitude variables in second language acquisition' in M. Burt, H. Dulay, and M. Finocchiaro (eds.): *Viewpoints on English as a Second Language*. New York: Regents.

Oller, J. (ed.). 1983. *Issues in Language Testing Research*. Rowley, Mass.: Newbury House.

Oller, J., L. Baca, and **A. Vigil.** 1977. 'Attitudes and attained proficiency in ESL: a sociolinguistic study of Mexican Americans in the Southwest'. *TESOL Quarterly* 11: 173–83.

Oller, J. and **K. Perkins.** 1978. 'Intelligence and language proficiency as sources of variance in self-reported affective variables'. *Language Learning* 28: 85–97.

Olsen, L. and **S. Samuels.** 1973. 'The relationship between age and accuracy of foreign language pronunciation'. *Journal of Educational Research* 66: 263–67. Reprinted in S. Krashen, R. Scarcella, and M. Long (eds.).

Olshtain, E. 1983. 'Sociocultural competence and language transfer: the case of apologies' in S. Gass and L. Selinker (eds.): *Language Transfer in Language Learning*. Rowley, Mass.: Newbury House.

Olshtain, E. 1989. 'Apologies across languages' in S. Blum-Kulka, J. House, and G. Kasper (eds.): *Cross-cultural Pragmatics: Requests and Apologies*. Norwood: N.J.: Ablex.

Olshtain, E. and **A. Cohen.** 1983. 'Apology: a speech act set' in N. Wolfson and E. Judd (eds.): *Sociolinguistics and Second Language Acquisition*. Rowley, Mass.: Newbury House.

Olshtain, E. and **S. Blum-Kulka.** 1985. 'Degree of approximation: non-native reactions to native speech act behavior' in S. Gass and C. Madden (eds.): *Input in Second Language Acquisition*. Rowley, Mass.: Newbury House.

Olshtain, E. and **A. Cohen.** 1989. 'Speech act behavior across languages' in H. Dechert and M. Raupach (eds.): *Interlingual Processes*. Tübingen: Gunter Narr.

Olshtain, E., E. Shohamy, J. Kemp, and **R. Chatow.** 1990. 'Factors predicting success in EFL among culturally different learners'. *Language Learning* 40: 23–44.

Olshtain, E. and **L. Weinbach.** 1985. 'Complaints: a study of speech act behavior among native and non-native speakers of Hebrew' in J. Verschuren and M. Bertucelli-Papi (eds.): *The Pragmatic Perspective*. Amsterdam: Benjamins.

Olson, D. R. 1977. 'From utterance to text: the bias of language in speech and writing'. *Harvard Educational Review* 47: 257–81.

O'Malley, J. 1987. 'The effects of training in the use of learning strategies on acquiring English as a second language' in A. Wenden and J. Rubin (eds.): *Learner Strategies in Language Learning*. Englewood Cliffs, N.J.: Prentice Hall.

O'Malley, J. and **A. Chamot.** 1990. *Learning Strategies in Second Language Acquisition*. Cambridge: Cambridge University Press.

O'Malley, J., A. Chamot, G. Stewner-Manzanaraes, L. Kupper, and **R. Russo.** 1985a. 'Learning strategies used by beginning and intermediate ESL students'. *Language Learning* 35: 21–46.

O'Malley, J., A. Chamot, G. Stewner-Manzanaraes, R. Russo, and **L. Kupper.** 1985b. 'Learning strategy applications with students of English as a second language'. *TESOL Quarterly* 19: 285–96.

Ondarra, K. 1997. *Collaborative Negotiation of Meaning*. Amsterdam: Rodopi.

Onwuegbuzie, A., P. Bailey, and **C. Daley.** 2000. 'The validation of three scales measuring anxiety at different stages of the foreign language learning process: the input anxiety scale, the processing anxiety scale, and the output anxiety scale'. *Language Learning* 50: 87–117.

Ortega L. 1999. 'Planning and focus on form in L2 oral performance'. *Studies in Second Language Acquisition* 21: 109–48.

Ortega, L. 2001. 'Current options in graduate-level introductory SLA textbooks'. *Second Language Research* 17: 71–89.

Ortega, L. 2005. 'What do learners plan? Learner-driven attention to form during pre-task planning' in R. Ellis (ed.): *Planning and Task Performance in a Second Language*. Amsterdam: John Benjamins.

Ortega, L. and **H. Byrnes.** 2008. 'Theorizing advancedness, setting up the longitudinal research agenda' in L. Ortega and H. Byrnes (eds.): *The Longitudinal Study of Advanced L2 Capacities.* Mahwah, N.J.: Lawrence Erlbaum/Taylor and Francis.

Ortony, A. (ed.). 1979. *Metaphor and Thought.* Cambridge: Cambridge University Press.

Osburne, A. 1996. 'Final cluster reduction in L2 speech: a case study of a Vietnamese speaker'. *Applied Linguistics* 17: 164–81.

Oscarson, M. 1997. 'Self-assessment of foreign and second language proficiency' in C. Clapham and D. Corson (eds.): *Encyclopedia of Language and Education, Volume 7: Language Testing and Assessment.* Dordrecht: Kluwer Academic.

Oxford, R. 1989. 'Use of language learning strategies: a synthesis of studies with implications for teacher training'. *System* 17: 235–47.

Oxford, R. 1990. *Language Learning Strategies: What Every Teacher Should Know.* Rowley, Mass.: Newbury House.

Oxford, R. 1992. 'Who are our students? A synthesis of foreign and second language research on individual differences with implications for instructional practice'. *TESL Canada Journal* 9: 30–49.

Oxford, R. (ed.). 1996. *Language Learning Strategies Around the World: Cross-cultural Perspectives.* Honolulu: University of Hawai'i Press.

Oxford, R. 1999. '"Style wars" as a source of anxiety in language classrooms' in D. Young (ed.): *Affect in Foreign Language and Second Language Learning.* Boston: McGraw Hill.

Oxford, R. 2001. 'Language learning styles and strategies' in M. Celce-Murcia (ed.): *Teaching English as a Second or Foreign Language* . Boston: Heinle and Heinle.

Oxford, R. and **J. Burry-Stock.** 1995. 'Assessing the use of language learning strategies worldwide with the ESL/EFL version of the Strategy Inventory for Language Learning (SILL)' . *System* 23: 1–35.

Oxford, R. and **M. Nyikos.** 1989. 'Variables affecting choice of language learning strategies by university students'. *The Modern Language Journal* 73: 291–300.

Oyama, S. 1976. 'A sensitive period in the acquisition of a non-native phonological system'. *Journal of Psycholinguistic Research* 5: 261–85.

Ozeki, H. and **Y. Shirai.** 2007. 'Does the Noun Phrase Accessibility Hierarchy predict the difficulty order in the acquisition of Japanese relative clauses?' *Studies in Second Language Acquisition* 29: 169–96.

Palmberg, R. (ed.). 1979. *Perception and Production of English: Papers on Interlanguage. AFTIL Volume* 6. Publications of the Department of English, Åbo Akademi.

Palmberg, R. 1987. 'Patterns of vocabulary development in foreign-language learners'. *Studies in Second Language Acquisition* 9: 201–20.

Palmer, A. 1979. 'Compartmentalized and integrated control: an assessment of some evidence for two kinds of competence and implications for the classroom'. *Language Learning* 29: 169–80.

Pankhurst, J., M. Sharwood Smith, and **P. Van Buren** (eds.). 1988. *Learnability and Second Languages: a Book of Readings.* Dordrecht: Foris.

Panova, I. and **R. Lyster.** 2002. 'Patterns of corrective feedback and uptake in an adult ESL classroom'. *TESOL Quarterly* 36: 573–95.

Paradis, M. 1994. 'Neurolinguistic aspects of implicit and explicit memory: implications for bilingualism and second language acquisition' in N. Ellis (ed.): *Implicit and Explicit Language Learning.* London: Academic Press.

Paradis M. 2004. *A Neurolinguistic Theory of Bilingualism.* Amsterdam: John Benjamins.

Paradis M. and **G. Libben.** 1987. *The Assessment of Bilingual Aphasia.* Hillsdale, N.J.: Lawrence Erlbaum.

Paribakht, T. 1985. 'Strategic competence and language proficiency'. *Applied Linguistics* 6: 132–46.

Paribakht, T. 2005. 'The influence of first language lexicalization on second language lexical inferencing: a study of Farsi-speaking learners of English as a foreign language'. *Language Learning* 55: 701–48.

Paribakht, T. and **M. Wesche.** 1993. 'Reading comprehension and second language development in a comprehension-based ESL programme'. *TESL Canada Journal* 11: 9–27.

Paribakht, T. and **M. Wesche.** 1999. 'Reading and incidental L2 vocabulary acquisition: an introspective study of lexical inferencing'. *Studies in Second Language Acquisition* 21: 195–224.

Park, G. 1995. 'Language learning strategies and beliefs about language learning of university students learning English in Korea'. Unpublished PhD dissertation, University of Texas at Austin.

Parker, K. and **C. Chaudron.** 1987. 'The effects of linguistic simplifications and elaborative modifications on L2 comprehension'. *University of Hawai'i Working Papers in ESL* 6: 107–33.

Parkinson, B. and **C. Howell-Richardson.** 1990. 'Learner diaries' in C. Brumfit and R. Mitchell (eds.): *Research in the Language Classroom. ELT Documents 133*. Modern English Publications.

Parry, T. and **J. Child.** 1990. 'Preliminary investigation of the relationship between VORD, MLAT and language proficiency' in T. Parry and C. Stansfield (eds.): *Language Aptitude Reconsidered*. Englewood Cliffs, N.J.: Prentice Hall.

Parry, T. and **C. Stansfield.** (ed.). 1990. *Language Aptitude Reconsidered*. Englewood Cliffs, N.J.: Prentice Hall.

Parodi, T. and **I. Tsimpli.** 2005. '"Real" and "apparent" optionality in second language grammars: finiteness and pronouns in null operator structures'. *Second Language Research* 21: 250–85.

Patkowski, M. 1980. 'The sensitive period for the acquisition of syntax in a second language'. *Language Learning* 30: 449–72.

Paulston, C. and **M. Bruder.** 1976. *Teaching English as a Second Language: Techniques and Procedures*. Englewood Cliffs, N.J.: Prentice Hall.

Pavesi, M. 1984. 'The acquisition of relative clauses in a formal and informal context' in D. Singleton and D. Little (eds.). *Language Learning in Formal and Informal Contexts*. Dublin: IRAAL.

Pavesi, M. 1986. 'Markedness, discoursal modes and relative clause formation in a formal and informal context'. *Studies in Second Language Acquisition* 8: 38–55.

Pavlenko, A. 2002. 'Poststructuralist approaches to the study of social factors in second language learning and use' in V. Cook (ed.): *Portraits of the L2 User*. Clevedon, England: Multilingual Matters.

Pavlenko, A. 2004. 'Gender and sexuality in foreign and second language education: Critical and feminist approaches' in B. Norton and K. Toohey (eds.): *Critical Pedagogies and Language Learning*. Cambridge: Cambridge University Press.

Pavlenko, A. 2006a. *Bilingual Minds: Emotional Experience, Expression and Representation*. Clevedon: Multilingual Matters.

Pavlenko, A. 2006b. *Emotions and Multilingualism*. Cambridge: Cambridge University Press.

Pavlenko, A. and **A. Blackledge** (eds.). 2004. *Negotiation of Identities in Multilingual Contexts*. Clevedon: Multilingual Matters.

Pavlenko, A., A. Blackledge, I. Piller, and **M. Teutsch-Dwyer** (eds.). 2001. *Multilingualism, Second Language Learning, and Gender*. Berlin: Mouton de Gruyter.

Pavlenko, A. and **S. Jarvis.** 2002. 'Bidirectional transfer'. *Applied Linguistics* 23: 190–214.

Pawley, A. and **F. Syder.** 1983. 'Two puzzles for linguistic theory: nativelike selection and nativelike fluency' in J. Richards and R. Schmidt (eds.): *Language and Communication*. London: Longman.

Peacock, M. and **M. Ho.** 2003. 'Student learning strategies across eight disciplines'. *International Journal of Applied Linguistics* 11: 1–20.

Peck, S. 1978. 'Child-child discourse in second language acquisition' in E. Hatch (ed.): *Second Language Acquisition*. Rowley, Mass.: Newbury House.

Peirce, B. 1995. 'Social identity, investment and language learning'. *TESOL Quarterly* 29: 9–31.

Penfield, W. and **L. Roberts.** 1959. *Speech and Brain Mechanisms*. New York: Atheneum Press.

Pennycook, A. 1990. 'Towards a critical applied linguistics for the 1990s'. *Issues in Applied Linguistics* 1: 8–28.

Pennycook, A. 2001. *Critical Applied Linguistics*. Hillsdale, N.J.: Lawrence Erlbaum.

Perani, D., S. Dehaene, F. Grassi, L. Cohen, S. Cappa, E. Dupoux, F. Fazio, and **J. Mehler.** 1996. 'Brain processing of native and foreign languages'. *NeuroReport* 7: 2439–44.

Perani, D., E. Paulesu, D. Sebastian-Galles, E. Duoux, S. Dehaene, V. Bettibardi, S. Cappa, F. Fazio, and **J. Mehler.** 1998. 'The bilingual brain: proficiency and age of acquisition in a second language'. *Brain* 121: 1841–52.

Perdue, C. 1991. 'Cross-linguistic comparisons: organizational principles in learner languages' in C. Ferguson and T. Huebner (eds.): *Crosscurrents in Second Language Acquisition and Linguistic Theories*. Amsterdam: John Benjamins.

Perdue, C. (ed.). 1993. *Adult Language Acquisition: Cross-linguistic Perspectives. Volume 2: The Results*. Cambridge: Cambridge University Press.

Perdue, C. 2000. 'Introduction to special issue on the structure of learner varieties'. *Studies in Second Language Acquisition* 22: 299–305.

Perdue, C. and **W. Klein.** 1992. 'Why does the production of some learners not grammaticalize?' *Studies in Second Language Acquisition* 14: 259–72.

Perkins, K. and **D. Larsen-Freeman.** 1975. 'The effects of formal language instruction on the order of morpheme acquisition'. *Language Learning* 25: 237–43.

Perren, G. and **J. Trim** (eds.). 1971. *Applications of Linguistics*. Cambridge: Cambridge University Press.

Pervin, L. and **O. John.** 2001. *Personality: Theory and Research* (Eighth edition). New York: John Wiley and Sons.

Peters, A. 1977. 'Language learning strategies: does the whole equal the sum of the parts?' Language 53: 560–73. Also in K. Diller (ed.): 1981. *Individual Differences and Universals in Language Learning Aptitude*. Rowley, Mass.: Newbury House.

Peters, M. 1934. 'An experimental comparison of grammar translation method and direct method in the learning of French'. *The Modern Language Journal* 18: 528–42.

Petersen, C. and **A. Al-Haik.** 1976. 'The development of the Defense Language Aptitude Battery (DLAB)' . *Educational and Psychological Measurement* 36: 369–80.

Pfaff, C. (ed.). 1987. *First and Second Language Acquisition Processes*. Cambridge, Mass.: Newbury House.

Pfaff, C. 1992. 'The issue of grammaticalization in early German second language'. *Studies in Second Language Acquisition* 14: 273–96.

Philips, S., S. Steele, and **C. Tanz** (eds.). *Language, Gender and Sex in Comparative Perspective*. Cambridge: Cambridge University Press.

Phillips, S. 1972. 'Participation structures and communicative competence: Warm Springs children in community and classroom' in C. Cazden, V. John, and D. Hymes (eds.): *Functions of Language in the Classroom*. New York: Teachers' College Press.

Phillipson, R. 1992. *Linguistic Imperialism*. Oxford: Oxford University Press.

Phillipson, R. 1994. 'English language spread policy'. *International Journal of the Sociology of Language* 107: 7–24.

Phillipson, R., E. Kellerman, L. Selinker, M. Sharwood Smith, and **M. Swain** (eds.). 1991. *Foreign/Second Language Pedagogy Research*. Clevedon: Multilingual Matters.

Philp, J. 2003. 'Constraints on "noticing the gap": non-native speakers' noticing of recasts in NS–NNS interaction'. *Studies in Second Language Acquisition* 25: 99–126.

Phinney, M. 1987. 'The pro-drop parameter in second language acquisition' in T. Roeper and E. Williams (eds.): *Parameter Setting*. Dordrecht: Reidel.

Pica, T. 1983. 'Adult acquisition of English as a second language under different conditions of exposure'. *Language Learning* 33: 465–97.

Pica, T. 1984. 'Methods of morpheme quantification: their effect on the interpretation of second language data'. *Studies in Second Language Acquisition* 6: 69–78.

Pica, T. 1985. 'The selective impact of instruction on second language acquisition'. *Applied Linguistics* 6: 214–22.

Pica, T. 1987. 'Second language acquisition, social interaction in the classroom'. *Applied Linguistics* 7: 1–25.

Pica, T. 1988. 'Interlanguage adjustments as an outcome of NS–NNS negotiated interaction'. *Language Learning* 38: 45–73.

Pica, T. 1991. 'Classroom interaction, participation and comprehension: redefining relationships'. *System* 19: 437–52.

Pica, T. 1992. 'The textual outcomes of native speaker–non-native speaker negotiation: what do they reveal about second language learning' in C. Kramsch and S. McConnell-Ginet (eds.): *Text and Context: Cross-disciplinary Perspectives on Language Study.* Lexington, Mass.: D.C. Heath and Company.

Pica, T. 1994a. 'Questions from the language classroom: research perspectives'. *TESOL Quarterly* 28: 49–79.

Pica, T. 1994b. 'Research on negotiation: what does it reveal about second-language learning conditions, processes, and outcomes?' *Language Learning* 44: 493–527.

Pica, T. 1996. 'The essential role of negotiation in the communicative classroom'. *JALT Journal* 78: 241–68.

Pica, T. 1997. 'Second language teaching and research relationships: a North American view'. *Language Teaching Research* 1: 48–72.

Pica, T. 2002. 'Subject-matter content: how does it assist the interactional and linguistic needs of classroom language learners?' *The Modern Language Journal* 86: 1–19.

Pica, T. 2005. 'Classroom learning, teaching and research: a task-based perspective'. *The Modern Language Journal* 89: 339–52.

Pica, T. and **C. Doughty.** 1985a. 'Input and interaction in the communicative language classroom: a comparison of teacher-fronted and group activities' in S. Gass and C. Madden (eds.): *Input in Second Language Acquisition.* Rowley, Mass.: Newbury House.

Pica, T. and **C. Doughty.** 1985b. 'The role of group work in classroom second language acquisition'. *Studies in Second Language Acquisition* 7: 233–48.

Pica, T., L. Holliday, N. Lewis, D. Berducci, and **J. Newman.** 1991. 'Language learning through interaction: what role does gender play?' *Studies in Second Language Acquisition* 13: 343–76.

Pica, T., L. Holliday, N. Lewis, and **L. Morgenthaler.** 1989. 'Comprehensible output as an outcome of linguistic demands on the learner'. *Studies in Second Language Acquisition* 11: 63–90.

Pica, T., R. Kanagy, and **J. Falodun.** 1993. 'Choosing and using communication tasks for second language research and instruction' in. G. Crookes and S. Gass (eds.): *Task-based Learning in a Second Language.* Clevedon: Multilingual Matters.

Pica, T. and **M. Long.** 1986. 'The linguistic and conversational performance of experienced and inexperienced teachers' in R. Day (ed.): *Talking to Learn: Conversation in Second Language Acquisition.* Rowley, Mass.: Newbury House.

Pica, T., R. Young, and **C. Doughty.** 1987. 'The impact of interaction on comprehension'. *TESOL Quarterly* 21: 737–58.

Pienemann, M. 1980. 'The second language acquisition of immigrant children' in S. Felix (ed.): *Second Language Development: Trends and Issues.* Tübingen: Gunter Narr.

Pienemann, M. 1981. *Der Zweitsprachenerwerb Auslandischer Arbeitskinder.* Bonn: Bouvier.

Pienemann, M. 1984. 'Psychological constraints on the teachability of languages'. *Studies in Second Language Acquisition* 6: 186–214.

Pienemann, M. 1985. 'Learnability and syllabus construction' in K. Hyltenstam and M. Pienemann (eds.): *Modelling and Assessing Second Language Acquisition*. Clevedon: Multilingual Matters.

Pienemann, M. 1986. 'Is language teachable? Psycholinguistic experiments and hypotheses'. *Australian Working Papers in Language Development* 1: 3.

Pienemann, M. 1989. 'Is language teachable? Psycholinguistic experiments and hypotheses'. *Applied Linguistics* 10: 52–79.

Pienemann, M. 1992. 'COALA - A computational system for interlanguage analysis'. *Second Language Research* 8: 59–92.

Pienemann, M. 1998. *Language Processing and Second Language Development: Processability Theory*. Amsterdam: John Benjamins.

Pienemann, M. 2005a. 'An introduction to processability theory' in M. Pienemann (ed.). *Cross-linguistic Aspects of Processability Theory*. Amsterdam: John Benjamins.

Pienemann, M. (ed.). 2005b. *Cross-linguistic Aspects of Processability Theory*. Amsterdam: John Benjamins.

Pienemann, M., B. Di Biase, S. Fawaguchi, and **G. Hakansson.** 2005. 'Processability, typological distance and language transfer' in M. Pienemann (ed.): *Cross-linguistic Aspects of Processability Theory*. Amsterdam: John Benjamins.

Pienemann, M. and **G. Hakansson.** 1999. 'A unified approach toward the development of Swedish as L2: a processability account'. *Studies in Second Language Acquisition* 21: 383–420.

Pienemann, M., M. Johnston, and **G. Brindley.** 1988. 'An acquisition-based procedure for second language assessment'. *Studies in Second Language Acquisition* 10: 217–43.

Piller, I. 2002. 'Passing for a native speaker: identity and success in second language learning'. *Journal of Sociolinguistics* 6: 179–206.

Piller, I. and **K. Takahashi.** 2006. 'A passion for English: desire and the language market' in A. Pavlenko (ed.): *Bilingual Minds: Emotional Experience, Expression and Representation*. Clevedon: Multilingual matters.

Pimsleur, P. 1966. *Pimsleur Language Aptitude Battery (PLAB)*. New York: Harcourt Brace Jovanovich.

Pimsleur, P. and **T. Quinn** (eds.). 1971. *The Psychology of Second Language Learning*. Cambridge: Cambridge University Press.

Pine, J. 1994. 'The language or primary caregivers' in C. Gallaway and B. Richards (eds.): *Input and Interaction in Language Acquisition*. Cambridge: Cambridge University Press.

Pinker, S. 1989. *Learnability and Cognition: The Acquisition of Argument Structure*. Cambridge, Mass.: MIT Press.

Pinker, S. 1994. *The Language Instinct: How the Mind Creates Language*. New York: William Morrow and Co.

Pinker, S. 1999. *Words and Rules*. New York: Basic Books.

Pinker, S. and **A. Prince.** 1989. 'Rules and connections in human language' in R. Morris (ed.): *Parallel Distributed Processing: Implications for Psychology and Neurobiology*. Oxford: Clarendon Press.

Platt, E. and **F. Brooks.** 1994. 'The "acquisition-rich environment" revisited'. *The Modern Language Journal* 78: 497–511.

Platt, E. and **R. Brooks.** 2002. 'Task engagement: a turning point in foreign language development'. *Language Learning* 52: 365–400.

Platt, E. and **S. Troudi.** 1997. 'Mary and her teachers: a brego-speaking child's place in the mainstream classroom'. *The Modern Language Journal* 81: 28–59.

Pleh, C. 1990. 'The search for universal operating principles in language acquisition'. *Studies in Second Language Acquisition* 12: 233–41.

Plough, I. and **S. Gass.** 1993. 'Interlocutor and task familiarity effects on interaction structure' in G. Crookes and S. Gass (eds.): *Tasks in a Pedagogical Context: Integrating Theory and Practice*. Clevedon: Multilingual Matters.

Plunkett, K. 1988. 'Parallel distributed processing'. *Psyke and Logos* 9/2: 307–36.
Poehner, M. and **J. Lantolf.** 2005. 'Dynamic assessment in the language classroom'. *Language Teaching Research* 9: 233–65.
Polio, C. and **P. Duff.** 1994. 'Teachers' language use in university foreign language classrooms: a qualitative analysis of English and target language alternation'. *The Modern Language Journal* 78: 313–26.
Polio, C. and **S. Gass.** 1997. 'Replication and reporting: a commentary'. *Studies in Second Language Acquisition* 19: 499–508.
Polio, C. and **S. Gass.** 1998. 'The role of interaction in native speaker comprehension of nonnative speaker speech'. *The Modern Language Journal* 82: 308–19.
Politzer, R. 1970. 'Some reflections on "good" and "bad" language teaching behaviors'. *Language Learning* 20: 31–43.
Politzer, R. and **M. McGroarty.** 1985. 'An exploratory study of learning behaviors and their relationship to gains in linguistic and communicative competence'. *TESOL Quarterly* 19:103–23.
Politzer, R. and **A. Ramirez.** 1973. 'An error analysis of the spoken English of Mexican-American pupils in a bilingual school and a monolingual school'. *Language Learning* 18: 35–53.
Politzer, R., A. Ramirez, and **S. Lewis.** 1981. 'Teaching standard English in the third grade: classroom functions of language'. *Language Learning* 31: 171–93.
Polyani, L. 1995. 'Language learning and living abroad: stories from the field' in B. Freed (ed.): *Second Language Acquisition in a Study Abroad Context* . Amsterdam: John Benjamins.
Poole, D. 1992. 'Language socialization in the second language classroom'. *Language Learning* 42: 593–616.
Porter, J. 1977. 'A cross-sectional study of morpheme acquisition in first language learners'. *Language Learning* 27: 47–62.
Porter, P. 1986. 'How learners talk to each other: input and interaction in task-centred discussions' in R. Day (ed.): *Talking to Learn: Conversation in Second Language Acquisition*. Rowley, Mass.: Newbury House.
Posner, M. and **S. Petersen.** 1990. 'The attention system of the human brain'. *Annual Review of Neural Science* 13: 25–42.
Poulisse, N. 1989. 'Variation in learners' use of communication strategies' in R. Duda and P. Riley (eds.). *Learning Styles.* Nancy, France: University of Nancy.
Poulisse, N. 1990. *The Use of Compensatory Strategies by Dutch Learners of English.* Enschede: Sneldruk.
Poulisse, N. 1993. 'A theoretical account of lexical communication strategies' in R. Schreuder and B. Weltens (eds.): *The Bilingual Lexicon.* Amsterdam: John Benjamins.
Poulisse, N. and **T. Bongaerts.** 1994. 'First language use in second language production'. *Applied Linguistics* 15: 35–57.
Prabhu, N. S. 1987. *Second Language Pedagogy*. Oxford: Oxford University Press.
Prasada, S. and **S. Pinker.** 1993. 'Generalizations of regular and irregular morphological patterns'. *Language and Cognitive Processes* 8: 1–56.
Prator, C. 1968. 'The British heresy in TESL' in J. Fishman, C. Ferguson, and J. Das Gupta (eds.): *Language Problems of Developing Nations*. New York: Wiley.
Preston, D. 1981. 'The ethnography of TESOL'. *TESOL Quarterly* 15: 105–16.
Preston, D. 1989. *Sociolinguistics and Second Language Acquisition.* Oxford: Blackwell.
Preston, D. 1996. 'Variationist perspectives on second language acquisition' in R. Bayley and D. Preston (eds.): *Second Language Acquisition and Linguistic Variation* . Amsterdam: John Benjamins.
Preston, D. 2002. 'A variationist perspective on second language acquisition' in R. Kaplan (ed.): *The Oxford Handbook of Applied Linguistics.* New York: Oxford University Press.
Price, C, D. Green, and **R. Von Studnitz.** 1999. 'Functional imaging study of translation and language switching'. *Brain* 122: 2221–36.

Pride, J. (ed.). 1979. *Sociolinguistic Aspects of Language Learning and Teaching.* Oxford: Oxford University Press.

Pulvermuller, F. and **J. Schumann.** 1994. 'Neurobiological mechanisms of language acquisition'. *Language Learning* 44: 681–734.

Purcell, E. and **R. Suter.** 1980. 'Predictors of pronunciation accuracy: a reexamination'. *Language Learning* 30: 271–87.

Purpura, J. 1999. *Learner Strategy use and Performance on Language Tests: A Structural Equation Modelling Approach.* Cambridge: Cambridge University Press.

Quirk, R. 1982a. 'International communication and the concept of nuclear English' in R. Quirk (ed.): *Style and Communication in the English Language.* London: Edward Arnold.

Quirk, R. (ed.). 1982b. *Style and Communication in the English Language.* London: Edward Arnold.

Quirk, R. 1985. 'The English language in a global context' in R. Quirk and H. Widdowson (eds.): *English in the World: Teaching and Learning the Language and Literatures.* Cambridge: Cambridge University Press.

Quirk, R. and **H. Widdowson** (eds.). 1985. *English in the World: Teaching and Learning the Language and Literatures.* Cambridge: Cambridge University Press.

Ramage, K. 1990. 'Motivational factors and persistence in foreign language study'. *Language Learning* 40: 189–219.

Ramat, A. 1992. 'Grammaticalization processes in the area of temporal and modal relations'. *Studies in Second Language Acquisition* 14: 297–322.

Ramat, A. (ed.). 2003. *Typology and Second Language Acquisition.* Berlin: Mouton de Gruyter.

Ramirez, J., S. Yuen, D. Ramey, and **B. Merino.** 1986. *First Year Report: Longitudinal Study of Immersion Programs for Language Minority Children.* Arlington, Va.: SRA Technologies.

Rampton, B. 1987. 'Stylistic variability and no speaking 'normal' English: some post-Labovian approaches and their implications for the study of interlanguage' in R. Ellis (ed.): *Second Language Acquisition in Context.* London: Prentice Hall International.

Rampton, B. 1995. *Crossing: Language and Ethnicity among Adolescents.* London: Longman.

Rampton, B. 1997. 'Retuning in applied linguistics'. *International Journal of Applied Linguistics* 7: 3–25.

Rampton, B. 1999. 'Crossing'. Special issue entitled 'A Lexicon for the Millenium'. *Journal of Linguistic Anthropology* 9/1–2: 54–6.

Rampton, B. 2006. *Language in Later Modernity: Interaction in an Urban School.* Cambridge: Cambridge University Press.

Rampton, B., C. Roberts, C. Leung, and **R. Harris.** 2002. 'Methodology in the analysis of classroom discourse'. *Applied Linguistics* 2002: 373–92.

Raschka, C., L. Wei, and **S. Lee.** 2002. 'Bilingual development and social networks of British-born Chinese children'. *International Journal of Sociology* 153: 9–25.

Raupach, M. 1983. 'Analysis and evaluation of communication strategies' in C. Færch and G. Kasper (eds.). *Strategies in Interlanguage Communication.* London: Longman.

Ravem, R. 1968. 'Language acquisition in a second language environment'. *International Review of Applied Linguistics* 6: 165–85.

Rayner, S. 2000. 'Reconstructing style differences in thinking and learning: profiling learner performance' in R. Riding and S. Rayner (eds.): *Interpersonal Perspectives on Individual Differences. Volume 1: Cognitive Styles.* Stamford, Conn.: Ablex.

Raz, N. 2005. 'The aging brain observed in vivo: differential changes and their modifiers' in F. Craik and T. Salthouse (eds.): *The Handbook of Aging and Cognition* (Second edition). Mahwah, N.J.: Lawrence Erlbaum.

Read, J. 1997. 'Vocabulary and testing' in N. Schmitt and M. McCarthy (eds.): *Vocabulary: Description, Acquisition and Pedagogy.* Cambridge: Cambridge University Press.

Read, J. and **P. Nation.** 2004. 'Measurement of formulaic sequences'. in N. Schmitt (ed.): *Formulaic Sequences.* Amsterdam: John Benjamins.

Reber, A. 1976. 'Implicit learning of synthetic learners: the role of instructional set'. *Journal of Experimental Psychology, Human Learning and Memory* 2: 88–94.
Reber, A. 1989. 'Implicit learning and tacit knowledge'. *Journal of Experimental Psychology: General* 118: 219–35.
Reber, A. 1993. *Implicit Learning and Tacit Knowledge: An Essay on the Cognitive Unconscious*. Oxford: Oxford University Press.
Reber, A., R. Allen, and **P. Reber.** 1999. 'Implicit vs. explicit learning' in R. Sternberg (ed.): *The Nature of Cognition*. Cambridge, Mass.: MIT Press.
Reber, A., F. Walkenfeld, and **R. Hernstadt.** 1991. 'Implicit and explicit learning: individual differences and IQ'. *Journal of Experimental Psychology: Learning Memory and Cognition* 11: 888–96.
Reddy, M. 1979. 'The conduit metaphor' in A. Ortony (ed.). *Metaphor and Thought*. Cambridge: Cambridge University Press.
Regan, V. 1996. 'Variation in French interlanguage: a longitudinal study of sociolinguistic competence' in R. Bayley and D. Preston (eds.): *Second Language Acquisition and Linguistic Variation*. Amsterdam: John Benjamins.
Rehner, K., R. Mougeon, and **T. Nadsasdi.** 2003. 'The learning of sociolinguistic variation by advanced ESL learners'. *Studies in Second Language Acquisition* 25: 127–56.
Reiber, R. and **A. Carton.** (eds.). 1987. *The Collected Works of L.S. Vygotsky*. New York: Plenum Press.
Reid, J. 1987. 'The learning style preferences of ESL students'. *TESOL Quarterly*, 21: 87–111.
Reigeluth, C. (ed.). 1984. *Instructional Design Theories and Models*. Hillsdale, N.J.: Lawrence Erlbaum.
Renandya, W. and **G. Jacobs** (eds.). 1998. *Learners and Language Learning*. Singapore: SEAMEO Regional Language Centre.
Rescorla, L. and **S. Okuda.** 1987. 'Modular patterns in second language acquisition'. *Applied Psycholinguistics* 8: 281–308.
Reynolds, P. 1971. *A Primer in Theory Construction*. Indianapolis, Bobbs Merrill.
Ricento, T. 2005. 'Considerations of identity in L2 learning' in E. Hinkel (ed.): *Handbook of Research in Second Language Teaching and Learning*. Mahwah, N.J.: Lawrence Erlbaum.
Richards, J. 1971. 'A non-contrastive approach to error analysis'. *ELT Journal* 25: 204–19.
Richards, J. 1972. 'Social factors, interlanguage and language learning'. *Language Learning* 22: 159–88.
Richards, J. (ed.). 1974. *Error Analysis*. London: Longman.
Richards, J. 1976. 'The role of vocabulary teaching'. *TESOL Quarterly* 10: 77–89.
Richards, J. (ed.). 1978. *Understanding Second and Foreign Language Learning: Issues and Approaches*. Rowley, Mass.: Newbury House.
Richards, J., J. Platt, and **H. Platt** (eds.). 1992. *Longman Dictionary of Language Teaching and Applied Linguistics*. London: Longman.
Richards, J. and **T. Rodgers.** 2001. *Approaches and Methods in Language Teaching* (Second edition). Cambridge: Cambridge University Press.
Richards, J. and **R. Schmidt** (eds.). 1983. *Language and Communication*. London: Longman.
Richards, K. 2006. '"Being the teacher": Identity and classroom conversation'. *Applied Linguistics* 27: 51–77.
Riding, R. 1991. *Cognitive Styles Analysis*. Birmingham: Learning and Training Technology.
Riding, R. and **S. Rayner** (eds.). 2001. *Interpersonal Perspectives on Individual Differences. Volume 1: Cognitive Styles*. Stamford, Conn.: Ablex.
Rieber, R. (ed.). 1998. *The Collected Works of L. S. Vygotsky. Volume 5: Child Psychology*. New York: Plenum Press.
Rieber, R. and **J. Wollack** (eds.). 1997. *The Collected Works of L. S. Vygotsky. Volume 4: The History of the Development of Higher Mental Functions*. New York: Plenum Press.
Riley, P. 1977. *Discourse Networks in Classroom Interaction: Some Problems in Communicative Language Teaching*. Melanges Pedagogiques, University of Nancy: Crapel.

Riley, P. 1985. *Discourse and Learning.* London: Longman.

Riley, P. 1989. 'Well don't blame me! On the interpretation of pragmatic errors' in W. Oleksy (ed.): *Contrastive Pragmatics.* Amsterdam: John Benjamins.

Riney, T. 1990. 'Age and open syllable preference in interlanguage phonology' in H. Burmeister and P. Rounds (eds.): *Variability in Second Language Acquisition: Proceedings of the Tenth meeting of the Second Language Acquisition Forum. Volume 1.* Eugene: Department of Linguistics, University of Oregon.

Ringbom, H. 1976. 'Crosslinguistic influence and the foreign language learning process' in E. Kellerman and M. Sharwood Smith (eds.): *Cross-linguistic Influence in Second Language Acquisition.* Oxford: Pergamon.

Ringbom, H. 1978. 'The influence of the mother tongue on the translation of lexical items'. *Interlanguage Studies Bulletin* 3: 80–101.

Ringbom, H. 1987. *The Role of the First Language in Foreign Language Learning.* Clevedon: Multilingual Matters.

Ringbom, H. 1992. 'On L1 transfer in L2 comprehension and L2 production'. *Language Learning* 42: 85–112.

Ringbom, H. 2002. 'Levels of transfer from L1 and L2 in L3 acquisition' in J. Ytsma and M. Hooghiemestra (eds.): *Proceedings of the Second International Conference on Trilingualism.* Leeuwarden, Holland: Fryske Academie [CD-ROM].

Ringbom, H. 2007. *The Importance of Cross-linguistic Similarity in Foreign Language Learning: Comprehension, Learning and Production.* Clevedon: Multilingual Matters.

Ringbom, H. and **R. Palmberg** (eds.): 1976. *Errors Made by Finns and Swedish-speaking Finns in the Learning of English.* Åbo, Finland: Department of English, Åbo Akademi. ERIC Report ED 122628.

Rintell, E. 1981. 'Sociolinguistic variation and pragmatic ability: a look at learners'. *International Journal of the Sociology of Language* 27: 11–34.

Rintell, E. and **C. Mitchell.** 1989. 'Studying requests and apologies' in S. Blum-Kulka, J. House, and G. Kasper (eds.): *Cross-cultural Pragmatics: Requests and Apologies.* Norwood: N.J.: Ablex.

Ritchie, W. (ed.). 1978. *Second Language Acquisition Research.* New York: Academic Press.

Ritchie, W. and **T. Bhatia** (eds.). 1996. *Handbook on Language Acquisition.* New York: Academic Press.

Roberts, C. 2001. 'Language acquisition or language socialisation in and through discourse? Towards a redefinition of the domain of SLA' in C. Candlin and N. Mercer (eds.): *English Language Teaching in its Social Context.* London: Routledge.

Roberts, C. and **M. Simonot.** 1987. '"This is my life": how language acquisition is interactionally accomplished' in R. Ellis (ed.): *Second Language Acquisition in Context.* London: Prentice Hall International.

Robinson, P. 1995a. 'Attention, memory, and the "noticing" hypothesis'. *Language Learning* 45: 283–331.

Robinson, P. 1995b. 'Task complexity and second language narrative discourse'. *Language Learning* 45: 99–140.

Robinson, P. 1996a. *Consciousness, Rules, and Instructed Second Language Acquisition.* New York/Frankfurt: Peter Lang.

Robinson, P. 1996b. 'Learning simple and complex rules under implicit, incidental rule-search conditions, and instructed conditions'. *Studies in Second Language Acquisition* 18: 27–67.

Robinson, P. 1997a. 'Generalizability and automaticity of second language learning under implicit, incidental, enhanced and instructed conditions'. *Studies in Second Language Acquisition* 19: 223–47.

Robinson, P. 1997b. 'Individual differences and the fundamental similarity of implicit and explicit adult language learning'. *Language Learning* 47: 45–99.

Robinson, P. 2001a. 'Individual differences, cognitive abilities, aptitude complexes and learning conditions in second language acquisition'. *Second Language Research* 17: 368–92.

Robinson P. 2001b. 'Task complexity, cognitive resources, and syllabus design: a triadic framework for examining task influences on SLA' in P. Robinson (ed.): *Cognition and Second Language Instruction.* Cambridge: Cambridge University Press.

Robinson, P. (ed.). 2001c. *Cognition and Second Language Instruction.* Cambridge: Cambridge University Press.

Robinson, P. 2002a. 'Learning conditions, aptitude complexes and SLA: A framework for research and pedagogy' in P. Robinson (ed.): *Individual Differences and Instructed Language Learning.* Amsterdam, John Benjamins.

Robinson, P. (ed.). 2002b. *Individual Differences and Instructed Language Learning.* Amsterdam, John Benjamins.

Robinson, P. 2003. 'Attention and memory during SLA' in C. Doughty and M. Long (eds.): *Handbook of Second Language Acquisition.* Malden, Mass.: Blackwell.

Robinson, P. 2005a. 'Aptitude and second language acquisition'. *Annual Review of Applied Linguistics* 25: 46–73.

Robinson, P. 2005b. 'Cognitive abilities, chunk strength, and frequency effects in implicit artificial grammar and incidental L2 learning: replications of Reber, Wakenfeld, and Hernstadt (1991) and Knowlton and Squire (1996) and their relevance to SLA'. *Studies in Second Language Studies* 27: 235–68.

Robson, G. 1992. 'Individual learner differences and classroom participation: a pilot study'. Unpublished paper, Temple University, Japan.

Robson, G. and **H. Midorikawa.** 2001. 'How reliable and valid is the Japanese version of the Strategy Inventory for Language Learning (SILL)?' *JALT Journal* 23: 202–26.

Rodrigo, V., S. Krashen, and **B. Gribbons.** 2004. 'The effectiveness of two comprehensible-input approaches to foreign language instruction at the intermediate level'. *System* 32: 53–60.

Rodriguez, R. 1982. *Hunger of Memory: the Education of Richard Rodriguez.* Boston: David R. Godine.

Rodriquez-Fornells, A., R. Balaguer, and **T. Muente.** 2006. 'Executive control in bilingual language processing' in M. Gullberg and P. Indefrey (eds.): *The Cognitive Neuroscience of Second Language Acquisition.* Malden, Mass.: Blackwell.

Rodriquez-Fornells, A., M. Rotte, H. Heinze, T. Noesselt, and **T. Muente.** 2002. 'Brain potential and functional MRI evidence for how to handle two languages with one brain'. *Nature* 415: 1026–9.

Roebuck, R. 2000. 'Subjects speak out: how learners position themselves in a psycholinguistic task' in J. Lantolf (ed.): *Sociocultural Theory and Second Language Learning.* Oxford: Oxford University Press.

Roebuck, R. and **L. Wagner.** 2004. 'Teaching repetition as a communicative and cognitive tool: evidence from a Spanish conversation class'. *International Journal of Applied Linguistics* 14: 70–89.

Roeper, T. and **E. Williams** (eds.). 1987. *Parameter Setting.* Dordrecht: Reidel.

Rogers, S. (ed.). 1976. *They Don't Speak Our Language.* London: Edward Arnold.

Rogoff, B. and **J. Lave** (eds.). 1984. *Everyday Cognition: Its Development in Social Contexts.* Cambridge, Mass.: Harvard University Press.

Romaine, S. 1984. *The Language of Children and Adolescents*: Oxford: Blackwell.

Romaine, S. 2003. 'Variation' in C. Doughty and M. Long (eds.): *The Handbook of Second Language Acquisition.* Malden, Mass.: Blackwell.

Rommetveit, R. 1992. 'Outlines of a dialogically based social-cognitive approach to human cognition and communication in' A. Wold (ed.): *The Dialogical Alternative. Towards a theory of Language and Mind.* Oslo: Scandinavian University Press.

Rosa, E. M. and **R. P. Leow.** 2004. 'Awareness, different learning conditions, and second language development'. *Applied Psycholinguistics* 25: 269–92.

Rosa, E. and **D. O'Neill.** 1999. 'Explicitness, intake, and the issue of awareness: another piece to the puzzle'. *Studies in Second Language Acquisition* 21: 511–53.

Rosansky, E. 1976. 'Methods and morphemes in second language acquisition'. *Language Learning* 26: 409–25.

Rose, K. 1994. 'On the validity of discourse completion tests in non Western contexts'. *Applied Linguistics* 15: 1–14.

Rose, K. 2000. 'An exploratory cross-sectional study of interlanguage pragmatic development'. *Studies in Second Language Acquisition* 22: 27–67.

Rose, K. and **G. Kasper** (eds.). 2001. *Pragmatics in Language Teaching*. Cambridge: Cambridge University Press.

Rose, K. and **C. Kawai-fun.** 2001. 'Inductive and deductive teaching of compliments and compliment responses' in K. Rose and G. Kasper (eds.): *Pragmatics in Language Teaching*. Cambridge: Cambridge University Press.

Rose, K. and **R. Ono.** 1995. 'Eliciting speech act data in Japanese: the effect of questionnaire type'. *Language Learning* 45: 191–223.

Rost, M. 1990. *Listening in Language Learning*. London: Longman.

Rubin, J. 1975. 'What the "good language learner" can teach us'. *TESOL Quarterly* 9: 41–51.

Rulon, K. and **J. McCreary.** 1986. 'Negotiation of content: teacher-fronted and small group interaction' in R. Day (ed.): *Talking to Learn: Conversation in Second Language Acquisition*. Rowley, Mass.: Newbury House.

Rumelhart, D. and **J. McClelland.** 1986a. 'On learning the past tenses of English verbs' in J. McClelland *et al.* (eds.): *Parallel Distributed Processing: Explorations in the Microstructure of Cognition. Volume 2: Psychological and Biological Models*. Cambridge, Mass.: MIT Press.

Rumelhart, D., J. McClelland, and the **PDP Research Group** (eds.). 1986b. *Parallel Distributed Processing: Explorations in the Microstructure of Cognition Volume 1: Foundations*. Cambridge, Mass.: MIT Press.

Russell, J. and **N. Spada.** 2006. 'The effectiveness of corrective feedback for the acquisition of L2 grammar: a meta-analysis of the research' in J. Norris and L. Ortega (eds.): *Synthesizing Research on Language Learning and Teaching*. Amsterdam: John Benjamins.

Rutherford, W. 1983. 'Language typology and language transfer' in S. Gass and L. Selinker (eds.): *Language Transfer in Language Learning*. Rowley, Mass.: Newbury House.

Rutherford, W. (ed.). 1984a. *Typological Universals and Second Language Acquisition*. Amsterdam: John Benjamins.

Rutherford, W. 1984b. 'Description and explanation in interlanguage syntax: state of the art'. *Language Learning* 34: 127–55.

Rutherford, W. 1988. *Second Language Grammar: Learning and Teaching*. London: Longman.

Rutherford, W. 1989. 'Preemption and the learning of L2 grammars'. *Studies in Second Language Acquisition* 11: 441–57.

Rutherford, W. and **M. Sharwood Smith** (eds.). 1988. *Grammar and Second Language Teaching: A Book of Readings*. Rowley, Mass.: Newbury House.

Ryan, E. and **H. Giles** (eds.). 1982. *Attitudes Towards Language Variation*. London: Edward Arnold.

Sachs, J. 1977. 'The adaptive significance of linguistic input to prelinguistic infants' in C. Snow and C. Ferguson (eds.): *Talking to Children: Language Input and Acquisition*. Cambridge: Cambridge University Press.

Sacks, H., E. Schegloff, and **G. Jefferson.** 1974. 'A simplest systematics for the organization of turn taking in conversation'. *Language* 50: 696–735.

Sadtano, E. (ed.). 1991. *Language Acquisition and the Second/Foreign Language Classroom*. Singapore: SEAMEO Regional Language Centre.

Saito, M. 1985. 'Some asymmetries in Japanese and their theoretical implications'. Unpublished PhD dissertation, Cambridge, Mass.: MIT.

Sajavaara, K. 1981a. 'Contrastive linguistics past and present and a communicative approach' in J. Fisiak (ed.): *Contrastive Linguistics and the Language Teacher*. Oxford: Pergamon.

Sajavaara, K. 1981b. 'The nature of first language transfer: English as L2 in a foreign language setting'. Paper presented at the first European-North American Workshop in Second Language Acquisition Research. Lake Arrowhead, California.

Salaberry, R. 1997. 'The role of input and output practice in second language acquisition'. *The Canadian Modern Language Review* 53: 422–51.

Samuda, V. 2001. 'Guiding relationships between form and meaning during task performance: the role of the teacher' in M. Bygate, P. Skehan, and M. Swain (eds.): *Researching Pedagogic Tasks, Second Language Learning, Teaching and Testing*. Harlow: Longman.

Sangarun, J. 2005. 'The effects of focusing on meaning and form in strategic planning' in R. Ellis (ed.): *Planning and Task Performance in a Second Language*. Amsterdam: John Benjamins.

Sankoff, D. (ed.). 1978. *Linguistic Variation: Model and Methods*. New York: Academic Press.

Santos, T. 1987. 'Markedness theory and error evaluation: an experimental study'. *Applied Linguistics* 8: 207–18.

Sanz, C. 2003. 'Computer delivered implicit vs. explicit feedback in processing instruction' in B. VanPatten (ed.): *Processing Instruction: Theory, Research, and Commentary* (Second Language Acquisition Research). Mahwah, N.J.: Lawrence Erlbaum.

Sanz, C. and **K. Morgan-Short.** 2004. 'Positive evidence versus explicit rule presentation and negative feedback: a computer-assisted study'. *Language Learning* 54: 35–78.

Saravanan, V. 1995. 'Linguistic and cultural maintenance through education for minority groups in Singapore' in M. Tickoo (ed.): *Language and Culture in Multilingual Societies*. Singapore: SEAMEO Regional Language Centre.

Sasaki, M. 1996. *Second Language Proficiency, Foreign Language Aptitude, and Intelligence*. New York: Lang.

Sasaki, Y. 1991. 'English and Japanese interlanguage comprehension strategies: an analysis based on the competition model'. *Applied Psycholinguistics* 12: 47–73.

Sasaki, Y. 1997. 'Individual variation in a Japanese sentence comprehension task: Form, functions and strategies'. *Applied Linguistics* 18: 508–37.

Sato, C. 1984. 'Phonological processes in second language acquisition: another look at interlanguage syllable structure'. *Language Learning* 34: 43–57. Also in G. Ioup and S. Weinberger (eds.). 1987. *Interlanguage Phonology: the Acquisition of a Second Language Sound System*. Rowley, Mass.: Newbury House.

Sato, C. 1985. 'Task variation in interlanguage phonology' in S. Gass and C. Madden (eds.): *Input in Second Language Acquisition*. Rowley, Mass.: Newbury House.

Sato, C. 1986. 'Conversation and interlanguage development: rethinking the connection' in R. Day (ed.): *Talking to Learn: Conversation in Second Language Acquisition*. Rowley, Mass.: Newbury House.

Sato, C. 1987. 'Phonological processes in second language acquisition: another look at interlanguage syllable structure' in G. Ioup and S. Weinberger (eds.): *Interlanguage Phonology: the Acquisition of a Second Language Sound System*. Rowley, Mass.: Newbury House.

Sato, C. 1988. 'Origins of complex syntax in interlanguage development'. *Studies in Second Language Acquisition* 10: 371–95.

Saunders, N. 1987. 'Morphophonemic variations in clusters in Japanese English'. *Language Learning* 37: 247–72.

Savignon, S. 1972. *Communicative Competence: an Experiment in Foreign Language Teaching*. Philadelphia: Center for Curriculum Development.

Saville-Troike, M. 1988. '"Private speech": evidence for second language learning strategies during the "silent period"'. *Journal of Child Language* 15: 567–90.

Saville-Troike, M. 1996. 'The ethnography of communication' in S. McKay and N. Hornberger (eds.): *Sociolinguistics and Language Teaching*. Cambridge: Cambridge University Press.

Savord, J. G. and **L. Laforge** (eds.). 1981. *Proceedings of the Fifth Conference of AILA*. Laval: University of Laval Press.

Sawyer, M. 1992. 'Language aptitude and language experience: are they related'. *The Language Programs of the International University of Japan Working Papers* 3: 27–45.

Sawyer, M. and **L. Ranta**: 2001. 'Aptitude, individual differences, and instructional design' in P. Robinson (ed.): *Cognition and Second Language Instruction*. Cambridge: Cambridge University Press.

Saxton, M. 1997. 'The contrast theory of negative input'. *Journal of Child Language* 24: 139–61.

Scarcella, R. 1979. 'On speaking politely in a second language' in C. Yorio, K. Perkins and J. Schachter. (eds.): *On TESOL '79*. Washington D.C.: TESOL.

Scarcella, R., E. Andersen, and **S. Krashen** (eds.). 1990. *Developing Communicative Competence*. New York: Newbury House.

Scarcella, R. and **C. Higa.** 1981. 'Input, negotiation and age differences in second language acquisition'. *Language Learning* 31: 409–37.

Scarcella, R. and **S. Krashen** (eds.). 1980. *Research in Second Language Acquisition*. Rowley, Mass.: Newbury House.

Schachter, J. 1974. 'An error in error analysis'. *Language Learning* 27: 205–14.

Schachter, J. 1983. 'A new account of language transfer' in S. Gass and L. Selinker. *Language Transfer in Language Learning*. Rowley, Mass.: Newbury House.

Schachter, J. 1986. 'In search of systematicity in interlanguage production'. *Studies in Second Language Acquisition* 8: 119–34.

Schachter, J. 1988. 'Second language acquisition and its relationship to Universal Grammar'. *Applied Linguistics* 9: 219–35.

Schachter, J. 1989. 'Testing a proposed universal' in S. Gass and J. Schachter (ed.): *Linguistic Perspectives on Second Language Acquisition*. Cambridge: Cambridge University Press.

Schachter, J. 1993. 'Second language acquisition: perceptions and possibilities'. *Second Language Research* 9: 173–87.

Schachter, J. and **M. Celce-Murcia.** 1977. 'Some reservations concerning error analysis'. *TESOL Quarterly* 11: 141–51.

Schachter, J. and **W. Rutherford.** 1979. 'Discourse function and language transfer'. *Working Papers on Bilingualism* 19: 3–12.

Schachter, J. and **V. Yip.** 1990. 'Grammaticality judgments: why does everyone object to subject extraction?' *Studies in Second Language Acquisition* 12: 379–392.

Schecter, S. and **R. Bayley.** 1997. 'Language socialization practices and cultural identity: case studies of Mexican-descent families in California and Texas'. *TESOL Quarterly* 31: 513–41.

Scherer, A. and **M. Wertheimer.** 1964. *A Psycholinguistic Experiment in Foreign Language Teaching*. New York: McGraw Hill.

Schieffelin, B. and **E. Ochs.** 1986. 'Language socialization'. *Annual Review of Anthropology* 15: 163–91.

Schinke-Llano, L. 1990. 'Can foreign language learning be like second language acquisition? The curious case of immersion' in B. VanPatten and J. Lee (eds.): *Second Language Acquisition—Foreign Language Learning*. Clevedon: Multilingual Matters.

Schinke-Llano, L. 1993. 'On the value of a Vygotskian framework for SLA theory'. *Language Learning* 43: 121–9.

Schlyter, S. 1990. 'The acquisition of French temporal morphemes in adults and in bilingual children' in G. Bernini and A. Giacalone Ramat (eds.): *La Temporalita nell'Acquisaizione di Lingue Seconde*. Milan: Franco Angeli.

Schmidt, M. 1980. 'Coordinate structures and language universals in interlanguage'. *Language Learning* 30: 397–416.

Schmidt, R. 1977. 'Sociolinguistic variation and language transfer in phonology'. *Working Papers on Bilingualism* 12: 79–95.

Schmidt, R. 1983. 'Interaction, acculturation and the acquisition of communication competence' in M. Wolfson and E. Judd (eds.). *Sociolinguistics and Second Language Acquisition.* Rowley, Mass.: Newbury House.

Schmidt, R. 1988. 'The potential of parallel distributed processing for S.L.A. theory and research'. *University of Hawai'i Working Papers in ESL* 7: 55–6.

Schmidt, R. 1990. 'The role of consciousness in second language learning'. *Applied Linguistics* 11: 129–58.

Schmidt, R. 1992. 'Psychological mechanisms underlying second language fluency'. *Studies in Second Language Acquisition* 14: 357–85.

Schmidt, R. 1993. 'Consciousness, learning and interlanguage pragmatics' in G. Kasper and S. Blum-Kulka (eds.): *Interlanguage Pragmatics.* Oxford: Oxford University Press.

Schmidt, R. 1994. 'Deconstructing consciousness in search of useful definitions for applied linguistics'. *AILA Review* 11: 11–26.

Schmidt, R. 1995a. 'Consciousness and foreign language learning: a tutorial in the role of attention and awareness in learning' in R. Schmidt (ed.): *Attention and Awareness in Foreign Language Learning.* Honolulu: University of Hawai'i Press.

Schmidt, R. (ed.). 1995b. *Attention and Awareness in Foreign Language Learning.* Honolulu: University of Hawai'i Press.

Schmidt, R. 2001. 'Attention' in P. Robinson (ed.): *Cognition and Second Language Instruction.* Cambridge: Cambridge University Press.

Schmidt, R. and **S. Frota.** 1986. 'Developing basic conversational ability in a second language: a case-study of an adult learner' in R. Day (ed.). *Talking to Learn: Conversation in Second Language Acquisition.* Rowley, Mass.: Newbury House.

Schmidt, R. and **Y. Watanabe.** 2001. 'Motivation, strategy use, and pedagogical preferences in foreign language learning' in Z. Dörnyei and R. Schmidt (eds.): *Motivation and Second Language Acquisition.* Honolulu: University of Hawai'i Press.

Schmitt, N. 1998. 'Tracking the incremental acquisition of second language vocabulary: a longitudinal study'. *Language Learning* 48: 281–317.

Schmitt, N. (ed.). 2004. *Formulaic Sequences.* Amsterdam: John Benjamins.

Schmitt, N. and **M. McCarthy.** (eds.). 1997. *Vocabulary: Description, Acquisition and Pedagogy.* Cambridge: Cambridge University Press.

Schmitt, N. and **P. Meara.** 1997. 'Researching vocabulary through a word knowledge framework: Word associations and verbal suffixes'. *Studies in Second Language Acquisition* 19: 17–36.

Schreuder, R. and **B. Weltens** (eds.). 1993. *The Bilingual Lexicon.* Amsterdam: John Benjamins.

Schulz, R. 2001. 'Cultural differences in student and teacher perceptions concerning the role of grammar instruction'. *The Modern Language Journal* 85: 244–58.

Schumann, F. and **J. Schumann.** 1977. 'Diary of a language learner: an introspective study of second language learning' in H. Brown, C. Yorio, and R. Crymes (eds.): *On TESOL '77.* Washington D.C.: TESOL.

Schumann, J. 1978a. 'The acculturation model for second language acquisition' in R. Gingras (ed.): *Second Language Acquisition and Foreign Language Teaching.* Arlington, Va.: Center for Applied Linguistics.

Schumann, J. 1978b. *The Pidginization Process: a Model for Second Language Acquisition.* Rowley, Mass.: Newbury House.

Schumann, J. 1978c. 'Social and psychological factors in second language acquisition' in J. Richards (ed.): *Understanding Second and Foreign Language Learning: Issues and Approaches.* Rowley, Mass.: Newbury House.

Schumann, J. 1979. 'The acquisition of English negation by speakers of Spanish: a review of the literature' in R. Andersen (ed.): *The Acquisition and Use of Spanish and English as First and Second Languages.* Washington, D.C.: TESOL.

Schumann, J. 1980. 'The acquisition of English relative clauses by second language learners' in R. Scarcella and S. Krashen (eds.): *Research in Second Language Acquisition*. Rowley, Mass.: Newbury House.

Schumann, J. 1983. 'Art and science in second language acquisition research'. *Language Learning Special Issue* 33: 49–75.

Schumann, J. 1986. 'Research on the acculturation model for second language acquisition'. *Journal of Multilingual and Multicultural Development* 7: 379–92.

Schumann, J. 1987. 'The expression of temporality in basilang speech'. *Studies in Second Language Acquisition* 9: 21–41.

Schumann. J. 1993. 'Some problems with falsification: an illustration from SLA research'. *Applied Linguistics* 14: 295–306.

Schumann, J. 1995. 'Ad minorem theoriae gloriam; a response to Eubank and Gregg'. *Studies in Second Language Acquisition* 17: 59–63.

Schumann, J. 1997. *The Neurobiology of Affect in Language. Language Learning Monograph Series*. Malden, Mass.: Blackwell.

Schumann, J. 2004a. 'Introduction' in Schumann *et al.* (eds.): *The Neurobiology of Learning: Perspectives from Second Language Acquisition*. Mahwah, N.J.: Lawrence Erlbaum.

Schumann, J. 2004b. 'Preface' in J. Schumann *et al.* (eds.): *The Neurobiology of Learning: Perspectives from Second Language Acquisition*. Mahwah, N.J.: Lawrence Erlbaum.

Schumann, J. 2004c. 'Conclusion' in J. Schumann *et al.* (eds.): *The Neurobiology of Learning: Perspectives from Second Language Acquisition*. Mahwah, N.J.: Lawrence Erlbaum.

Schumann, J., S. Crowell, N. Jones, N. Lee, A. Suchert, and **L. Wood** (eds.). 2004. *The Neurobiology of Learning: Perspectives from Second Language Acquisition*. Mahwah, N.J.: Lawrence Erlbaum.

Schumann, J. and **N. Stenson** (eds.). 1974. *New Frontiers in Second Language Learning*. Rowley, Mass.: Newbury House.

Schumann, J. and **L. Wood.** 2004. 'The neurobiology of motivation' in J. Schumann *et al.* (eds.): *The Neurobiology of Learning: Perspectives from Second Language Acquisition*. Mahwah, N.J.: Lawrence Erlbaum.

Schwartz, B. 1986. 'The epistemological status of second language acquisition'. *Second Language Research* 2: 120–59.

Schwartz, B. 1993. 'On explicit and negative data effecting and affecting competence and linguistic behaviour'. *Studies in Second Language Acquisition* 15: 147–63.

Schwartz, B. and **B. Gubala-Ryzak.** 1992. 'Learnability and grammar reorganization in L2A: against negative evidence causing the unlearning of verb movement'. *Second Language Research* 8: 1–38.

Schwartz, B. and **R. Sprouse.** 1996. 'L2 cognitive states and the full transfer/full access model'. *Second Language Research* 12: 40–7.

Schwartz, J. 1980. 'The negotiation for meaning: repair in conversations between second language learners of English' in D. Larsen-Freeman (ed.): *Discourse Analysis in Second Language Research*. Rowley, Mass.: Newbury House.

Sciarone, A. and **P. Meijer.** 1995. 'Does practice make perfect? On the effect of exercises on second/foreign language acquisition'. *ITL Review of Applied Linguistics* 107–108: 35–7.

Scollon, R. 1976. *Conversations with a One-year Old*. Honolulu: The University of Hawai'i Press.

Scollon, R. and **S. Scollon.** 1983. 'Face in interethnic communication' in J. Richards and R. Schmidt (eds.): *Language and Communication*. London: Longman.

Scollon, R. and **S. Scollon.** 2001. *Intercultural Communication: A Discourse Approach* (Second edition). (First edition 1995). Oxford: Blackwell.

Scovel, T. 1978. 'The effect of affect on foreign language learning: a review of the anxiety research'. *Language Learning* 28: 129–42.

Scovel, T. 1981. 'The recognition of foreign accents in English and its implications for psycholinguistic theories of language acquisition' in J. G. Savord and L. Laforge (eds.): *Proceedings of the Fifth Conference of AILA*. Laval: University of Laval Press.

Scovel, T. 2001. *Learning New Languages: A Guide to Second Language Acquisition*. Boston: Heinle and Heinle.

Scribner, S. and **M. Cole.** 1973. 'Cognitive consequences of formal and informal learning'. *Science* 182: 553–9.

Searle, J. 1969. *Speech Acts*. Cambridge: Cambridge University Press.

Searle, J. 1975. 'Indirect speech acts' in P. Cole and J. Morgan (eds.): *Syntax and Semantics 3: Speech Acts*. New York: Academic Press.

Searle, J. 1976. 'The classification of illocutionary acts'. *Language in Society* 5: 1–24.

Seedhouse, P. 1996. 'Classroom interaction: possibilities and impossibilities'. *ELT Journal* 50: 17–24.

Seedhouse, P. 1997. 'The case of the missing "no"; the relationship between pedagogy and interaction'. *Language Learning* 47: 547–83.

Seedhouse, P. 1999. 'Task-based interaction'. *ELT Journal* 53: 149–56.

Seedhouse, P. 2004. *The Interactional Architecture of the Language Classroom: A Conversation Analysis Perspective*. Malden, Mass.: Blackwell.

Seedhouse, P. 2005. '"Task" as research construct'. *Language Learning* 55/3: 533–70.

Segalowitz, N. 1997. 'Individual differences in second language acquisition' in A. de Groot, M. Kroll, and J. Kroll (eds.): *Tutorials in Bilingualism: Psycholinguistic Perspectives*. Mahwah, N.J.: Lawrence Erlbaum.

Segalowitz, N. 2003. 'Automaticity and second languages' in C. Doughty and M. Long (eds.): *Handbook of Second Language Acquisition*. Malden, Mass.: Blackwell.

Segalowitz, N. 2007. 'Access fluidity, attention control, and the acquisition of fluency in a second language'. *TESOL Quarterly* 41: 181–6.

Segalowitz, N. and **B. Freed.** 2004. 'Context, contact, and cognition in oral fluency: learning Spanish in at home and study abroad context'. *Studies in Second Language Acquisition* 26: 173–99.

Segalowitz, N. and **P. Lightbown.** 1999. 'Psycholinguistic approaches to SLA'. *Annual Review of Applied Linguistics* 19: 43–63.

Segalowitz, N. and **S. Segalowitz.** 1993. 'Skilled performance, practice, and the differentiation of speed-up from automatization effects: evidence from second language word recognition effects'. *Applied Psycholinguistics* 14: 369–85.

Segalowitiz, S. (ed.). 1983. *Language Functions and Brain Organization*. New York: Academic Press.

Seidlhofer, B. 2002. 'The shape of things to come? Some basic questions about English as a lingua franca' in K. Knapp and C. Meierkord (eds.): *Lingus Franca Communication*. Frankfurt/Main: Peter Lang.

Seidlhofer, B. 2005. 'English as a lingua franca'. *ELT Journal* 59: 339–41.

Seliger, H. 1975. 'Inductive method and deductive method in language teaching: a re-examination'. *International Review of Applied Linguistics* 13: 1–18.

Seliger, H. 1977. 'Does practice make perfect? A study of the interaction patterns and L2 competence'. *Language Learning* 27: 263–78.

Seliger, H. 1978. 'Implications of a multiple critical periods hypothesis for second language learning' in W. Ritchie (ed.): *Second Language Acquisition Research*. New York: Academic Press.

Seliger, H. 1979. 'On the nature and function of language rules in language teaching'. *TESOL Quarterly* 13: 359–69.

Seliger, H. 1984. 'Processing universals in second language acquisition' in F. Eckman, L. Bell, and D. Nelson (eds.). *Universals of Second Language Acquisition*. Rowley, Mass.: Newbury House.

Seliger, H. 1989. 'Semantic transfer constraints in foreign language speakers' reactions to acceptability' in H. Dechert and M. Raupach (eds.): *Interlingual Processes*. Tübingen: Gunter Narr.

Seliger, H. and **M. Long** (eds.). 1983. *Classroom-oriented Research in Second Language Acquisition*. Rowley, Mass.: Newbury House.

Seliger, H. and **R. Vago** (eds.). 1991. *First Language Attrition*. Cambridge: Cambridge University Press.

Selinker, L. 1969. 'Language transfer'. *General Linguistics* 9: 67–92.

Selinker, L. 1972. 'Interlanguage'. *International Review of Applied Linguistics* 10: 209–31.

Selinker, L. 1984. 'The current state of interlanguage studies: an attempted critical summary' in A. Davies, C. Criper, and A. Howatt (eds.): *Interlanguage*. Edinburgh: Edinburgh University Press.

Selinker, L. and **D. Douglas.** 1985. 'Wrestling with context in interlanguage theory'. *Applied Linguistics* 6: 190–204.

Selinker, L. and **U. Lakshmanan.** 1992. 'Language transfer and fossilization: the multiple effects principle' in S. Gass and L. Selinker (eds.): *Language Transfer in Language Learning* (Revised edition). Amsterdam: John Benjamins.

Selinker, L. and **J. Lamendella.** 1978. 'Two perspectives on fossilization in interlanguage learning'. *Interlanguage Studies Bulletin* 3: 143–91.

Selinker, L., M. Swain, and **G. Dumas.** 1975. 'The interlanguage hypothesis extended to children'. *Language Learning* 25: 139–91.

Sfard, A. 1998. 'On two metaphors for learning and the dangers of choosing just one'. *Educational Researchers* 27: 4–13.

Shannahoff-Khalsa, D. 1984. 'Rhythms and reality: the dynamics of the mind'. *Psychology Today* Sept.: 72–3.

Shapiro, F. 1979. 'What do teachers actually *do* in language classrooms?' Paper presented at the 13th Annual TESOL Convention, Boston.

Shapson, S. and **V. D'Oyley** (eds.). 1984. *Bilingual and Multicultural Education: Canadian Perspectives*. Clevedon: Multilingual Matters.

Sharwood Smith, M. 1981. 'Consciousness-raising and the second language learner'. *Applied Linguistics* 2: 159–69.

Sharwood Smith, M. 1986. 'Comprehension vs. acquisition: two ways of processing input'. *Applied Linguistics* 7: 239–56.

Sharwood Smith, M. 1991. 'Speaking to many minds: on the relevance of different types of language information for the L2 learner'. *Second Language Research* 7: 118–32.

Sharwood Smith, M. 1993. 'Input enhancement in instructed SLA: theoretical bases'. *Studies in Second Language Acquisition* 15: 165–79.

Sharwood Smith, M. and **E. Kellerman.** 1986. 'Crosslinguistic influence in second language acquisition: an introduction' in E. Kellerman and M. Sharwood Smith (eds.): *Cross-linguistic Influence in Second Language Acquisition*. Oxford: Pergamon.

Sharwood Smith, M. and **J. Truscott.** 2005. 'Stages or continua in second language acquisition: a MOGUL solution'. *Applied Linguistics* 26: 219–40.

Shatz, M. 1978. 'On the development of communicative understanding: an early strategy for interpreting and responding to message'. *Journal of Cognitive Psychology* 10: 271–301.

Sheen, R. 2003. 'Focus-on-form—a myth in the making'. *ELT Journal* 57: 225–33.

Sheen, Y. 2004. 'Corrective feedback and learner uptake in communicative classrooms across instructional settings'. *Language Teaching Research* 8: 263–300.

Sheen, Y. 2006a. 'Exploring the relationship between characteristics of recasts and learner uptake'. *Language Teaching Research* 10/4: 361–92.

Sheen, Y. 2006b. 'Corrective feedback, individual differences and the acquisition of articles by second language learners'. Unpublished PhD thesis, University of Nottingham.

Shehadeh, A. 1999. 'Non-native speakers' production of modified comprehensible output and second language learning'. *Language Learning* 49: 627–75.

Shehadeh, A. 2002. 'Comprehensible output, from occurrence to acquisition: an agenda for acquisitional research'. *Language Learning* 52: 597–647.

Sheldon, A. 1977. 'On strategies for processing relative clauses: a comparison of children and adults'. *Journal of Verbal Learning and Verbal Behavior* 4: 305–18.

Sheorey, R. 1986. 'Error perceptions of native-speaking and non-native speaking teachers of ESL'. *ELT Journal* 40: 306–12.

Shepherd, C. 2006. 'The effect of instruction directed at gaps second language learners noticed in their oral production'. Unpublished doctoral thesis, University of Auckland. New Zealand.

Shriffrin, D. 1994. *Approaches to Discourse*. Oxford: Blackwell.

Shiffrin, R. and **W. Schneider.** 1977. 'Controlled and automatic human information processing: II. Perceptual learning, automatic attending and a general theory'. *Psychological Review* 84: 127–90.

Shin, S. and **L. Milroy.** 1999. 'Bilingual acquisition by Korean schoolchildren in New York City'. *Bilingualism: Language and Cognition* 2: 147–67.

Shirai, Y. and **H. Ozeki.** 2007. 'Introduction'. *Studies in Second Language Acquisition* 29: 155–67.

Shook, D. 1994. 'FL/L2 reading, grammatical information, and the input-to-intake phenomenon'. *Applied Language Learning* 5: 57–93.

Shore, R. 1997. *Rethinking the Brain: New Insights into Early Development*. New York: Families and Work Institute.

Siegel, J. 2003. 'Social context' in C. Doughty and M. Long (eds.): *The Handbook of Second Language Acquisition*. Malden, Mass.: Blackwell.

Simard, D. and **W. Wong.** 2001. 'Alertness, orientation and detection: the conceptualization of attentional functions in SLA'. *Studies in Second Language Acquisition* 23: 103–24.

Simon, A. and **E. Boyer** (eds.). 1967. *Mirrors for behavior: an anthology of classroom observation instruments*. Philadelphia: Center for the Study of Teaching at Temple University.

Sinclair, J. 1991. *Corpus, Concordance, Collocation*. Oxford: Oxford University Press.

Sinclair, J. and **M. Coulthard.** 1975. *Towards an Analysis of Discourse*. Oxford: Oxford University Press.

Singleton, D. 1987. 'Mother and other tongue influence on learner French: a case study'. *Studies in Second Language Acquisition* 9: 327–45.

Singleton, D. 1989. *Language Acquisition: the Age Factor.* Clevedon: Multilingual Matters.

Singleton, D. 1999. *Exploring the Second Language Lexicon*. Cambridge: Cambridge University Press.

Singleton, D. 2005. 'The critical period hypothesis: a coat of many colours'. *International Review of Applied Linguistics* 10: 209–31.

Singleton, D. and **D. Little** (eds.). *Language Learning in Formal and Informal Contexts*. Dublin: IRAAL.

Sjöholm, K. 1976. 'A comparison of the test results in grammar and vocabulary between Finnish- and Swedish-speaking applicants for English' in H. Ringbom and R. Palmberg (eds.): *Errors Made by Finns and Swedish-speaking Finns in the Learning of English*. Åbo, Finland: Department of English, Åbo Akademi. ERIC Report ED 122628.

Sjöholm, K. 1979. 'Do Finns and Swedish-speaking Finns use different strategies in the learning of English as a foreign language?' in R. Palmberg (ed.): *Perception and Production of English: Papers on Interlanguage. AFTIL Volume 6*. Publications of the Department of English, Åbo Akademi.

Sjöholm, K. 1995. *The Influence of Crosslinguistic, Semantic, and Input Factors on the Acquisition of English Phrasal Verbs: A Comparison between Finnish and Swedish Learners at an Intermediate and Advanced Level.* Åbo, Finland: Åbo Akademi University Press.

Skehan, P. 1986a. 'Cluster analysis and the identification of learner types'. in V. Cook (ed.): *Experimental Approaches to Second Language Acquisition*. Oxford: Pergamon.

Skehan, P. 1986b. 'Where does language aptitude come from?' in P. Meara (ed.): *Spoken Language*. London: Centre for Information on Language Teaching.
Skehan, P. 1989. *Individual Differences in Second-language Learning*. London: Edward Arnold.
Skehan, P. 1990. 'The relationship between native and foreign language learning ability: educational and linguistic factors' in H. Dechert (ed.): *Current Trends in European Second Language Acquisition Research*. Clevedon: Multilingual Matters.
Skehan, P. 1991. 'Individual differences in second language learning'. *Studies in Second Language Acquisition* 13: 275–98.
Skehan, P. 1996. 'Second language acquisition research and task-based instruction'. in D. Willis and J. Willis (eds.): *Challenge and Change in Language Teaching*. London: Heinemann.
Skehan, P. 1998a. 'Task-based instruction'. *Annual Review of Applied Linguistics* 18: 268–86.
Skehan, P. 1998b. *A Cognitive Approach to Language Learning*. Oxford: Oxford University Press.
Skehan, P. 2001. 'Tasks and language performance assessment' in M. Bygate *et al.* (eds.): *Researching Pedagogic Tasks, Second Language Learning, Teaching and Testing*. Harlow: Longman.
Skehan, P. 2002. 'Theorising and updating aptitude' in P. Robinson (ed.): *Individual Differences and Instructed Language Learning*. Amsterdam, John Benjamins.
Skehan, P. 2003. 'Task-based instruction'. *Language Teaching* 36: 1–14.
Skehan, P. and **P. Foster.** 1997. 'Task type and task processing conditions as influences on foreign language performance'. *Language Teaching Research* 1: 185–211.
Skehan, P. and **P. Foster.** 1999. 'The influence of task structure and processing conditions on narrative retellings'. *Language Learning* 49: 93–120.
Skehan, P. and **P. Foster.** 2005. 'Strategic and on-line planning: the influence of surprise information and task time on second language performance' in R. Ellis (ed.): *Planning and Task-Performance in a Second Language*. Amsterdam: John Benjamins.
Skuttnab-Kangas, T. (ed.). 1977. *Papers from the First Nordic Conference on Bilingualism*. Helsingfors: Universitetet.
Skuttnab-Kangas, T. 1988. 'Multilingualism and the education of minority children' in T. Skuttnab-Kangas and J. Cummins (eds.): *Minority Education*. Clevedon: Multilingual Matters.
Skuttnab-Kangas, T. 2000. *Linguistic Genocide in Education—or Worldwide Diversity in Human Rights?* Mahwah, N.J.: Lawrence Erlbaum.
Skuttnab-Kangas, T. and **J. Cummins** (eds.). 1988. *Minority Education*. Clevedon: Multilingual Matters.
Slabakova, R. 2006. 'Learnability in the second language acquisition of semantics: a bidirectional study of a semantic parameter'. *Second Language Research* 22: 498–523.
Slimani, A. 1989. 'The role of topicalization in classroom language learning'. *System* 17: 223–34.
Slobin, D. 1970. 'Universals of grammatical development in children' in G. Flores d'Arcais and W. Levelt (eds.): *Advances in Psycholinguistics*. Amsterdam: North-Holland Publishing.
Slobin, D. 1973. 'Cognitive prerequisites for the development of grammar' in C. Ferguson and D. Slobin (eds.): *Studies of Child Language Development*. New York: Appleton-Century-Crofts.
Slobin, D. (ed.). 1985a. *The Crosslinguistic Study of Language Acquisition. Volume 2, Theoretical Issues*. Hillsdale, N.J.: Lawrence Erlbaum.
Slobin, D. 1985b. 'Cross-linguistic evidence for the language-making capacity' in D. Slobin (ed.): *The Crosslinguistic Study of Language Acquisition. Volume 2, Theoretical Issues*. Hillsdale, N.J.: Lawrence Erlbaum.
Smagorinsky, P. 1998. 'Thinking and speech and protocol analysis'. *Mind, Culture, and Activity: An International Journal* 5: 157–77.

Smith, B. 2003a. 'Computer-mediated negotiated interaction: an expanded model'. *The Modern Language Journal* 87: 38–57.

Smith, B. 2003b. 'The use of communication strategies in computer-mediated communication'. *System* 31: 29–53.

Smith, B. 2005. 'The relationship between negotiated interaction, learner uptake and lexical acquisition in task-based computer-mediated communication'. *TESOL Quarterly* 39: 33–58.

Smith, L. 1983. *Readings in English as an International Language.* London: Pergamon.

Smith, P. 1970. *A Comparison of the Audiolingual and Cognitive Approaches to Foreign Language Instruction: the Pennsylvania Foreign Language Project.* Philadelphia: Center for Curriculum Development.

Smith, S., N. Scholnick, A. Crutcher, M. Simeone, and **W. Smith.** 1991. 'Foreigner talk revisited: limits on accommodation to nonfluent speakers' in J. Blomaert and J. Verschurren (eds.). *The Pragmatics of Intercultural and International Communication.* Amsterdam: John Benjamins.

Snow, C. 1972. 'Mother's speech to children learning'. *Child Development* 43: 549–65.

Snow, C. 1976. 'The language of the mother-child relationship' in S. Rogers (ed.): *They Don't Speak Our Language.* London: Edward Arnold.

Snow, C. 1986. 'Conversations with children' in P. Fletcher and M. Garman (eds.): *Language Acquisition* (Second edition). Cambridge: Cambridge University Press.

Snow, C. 1987. 'Beyond conversation: second language learners' acquisition of description and explanation' in J. Lantolf and A. Labarca (eds.): *Research in Second Language Learning: Focus on the Classroom.* Norwood, N.J.: Ablex.

Snow, C. and **C. Ferguson** (eds.). 1977. *Talking to Children: Language Input and Acquisition.* Cambridge: Cambridge University Press.

Snow, C. and **M. Hoefnagel-Höhle.** 1978. 'The critical age for language acquisition: evidence from second language learning'. *Child Development* 49: 1114–28.

Snow, C. and **M. Hoefnagel-Höhle.** 1982. 'School age second language learners' access to simplified linguistic input'. *Language Learning* 32: 411–30.

Solin, D. 1989. 'The systematic misrepresentation of bilingual crossed aphasia and its consequences'. *Brain and Language* 36: 92–116.

Sorace, A. 1985. 'Metalinguistic knowledge and language use in acquisition-poor environments'. *Applied Linguistics* 6: 239–54.

Sorace, A. 1988. 'Linguistic intuitions in interlanguage development: the problem of indeterminacy' in J. Pankhurst, M. Sharwood Smith, and P. Van Buren (eds.): *Learnability and Second Languages: a Book of Readings.* Dordrecht: Foris.

Sorace, A. 1996. 'The use of acceptability judgments in second language acquisition research' in W. Ritchie and T. Bhatia (eds.): *Handbook of Second Language Acquisition.* San Diego, Calif.: Academic Press.

Sorace, A. 2000. 'Syntactic optionality in non-native grammars'. *Second Language Research* 16: 93–102.

Spada, N. 1986. 'The interaction between types of content and type of instruction: some effects on the L2 proficiency of adult learners'. *Studies in Second Language Acquisition* 8: 181–99.

Spada, M. 1987. 'Relationships between instructional differences and learning outcomes: a process-product study of communicative language teaching'. *Applied Linguistics* 8/2: 137–55.

Spada, N. 2005. 'Conditions and challenges in developing school-based SLA research programs'. *The Modern Language Journal* 89: 328–38.

Spada, N. and **M. Fröhlich.** 1995. *COLT—Communicative Orientation of Language Teaching Observation Scheme: Coding Conventions and Applications.* Sydney: National Centre for English Language Teaching and Research.

Spada, N. and **P. Lightbown.** 1989. 'Intensive ESL programmes in Quebec primary schools'. *TESL Canada* 7: 11–32.

Spada, N. and **P. Lightbown.** 1999. 'First language influence and developmental readiness in second language acquisition'. *The Modern Language Journal* 83: 1–21.
Spada, N., P. Lightbown, and **J. White.** 2006. 'The importance of form/meaning mappings in explicit form-focused instruction' in A. Housen and M. Pierrard (eds.): *Investigations in Instructed Second Language Acquisition.* Berlin: Mouton de Gruyter.
Sparks, R., L. Ganschow, K. Fluharty, and **S. Little.** 1995. 'An exploratory study on the effects of Latin on the native language skills and foreign language aptitude of students with and without disabilities'. *The Classical Journal* 91: 165–84.
Sparks, R., L. Ganschow, and **J. Javorsky.** 2000. 'Déjà vu all over again: a response to Saito, Horwitz, and Garza'. *The Modern Language Journal* 84: 251–9.
Sparks, R., L. Ganschow, and **J. Patton.** 1995. 'Prediction of performance in first-year foreign language courses: connections between native and foreign language learning'. *Journal of Educational Psychology* 87: 638–55.
Spielberger, C. 1983. *Manual for the State-Trait Anxiety Inventory (Form Y).* Palo Alto, Calif.: Consulting Psychologists Press.
Spielman, G. and **M. Radnofsky.** 2001. 'Learning language under tension: new directions from a qualitative study'. *The Modern Language Journal* 85: 259–78.
Spolsky, B. 1986a. 'Overcoming language barriers to education in a multilingual world' in B. Spolsky (ed.): *Language and Education in Multilingual Settings.* Clevedon: Multilingual Matters.
Spolsky, B. (ed.). 1986b. *Language and Education in Multilingual Settings.* Clevedon: Multilingual Matters.
Spolsky. B. 1988. 'Bridging the gap: a general theory of second language learning'. *TESOL Quarterly* 22: 377–96.
Spolsky, B. 1989. *Conditions for Second Language Learning.* Oxford: Oxford University Press.
Spolsky, B. 1990. 'Introduction to a colloquium: the scope and form of a theory of second language learning'. *TESOL Quarterly* 24: 609–16.
Spolsky, B. 2000. 'Anniversary article: Language motivation revisited'. *Applied Linguistics* 21: 157–69.
Spolsky, B. and **F. Hult** (eds.). 2008. *The Handbook of Educational Linguistics.* Oxford: Blackwell.
Sridhar, S. and **K. Sridhar.** 1986. 'Bridging the paradigm gap: second language acquisition theory and indigenized varieties of English'. *World Englishes* 5: 3–14.
St. John, O., K. van Esch, and **E. Schalkwijk** (eds.). 2004. *New Insights into Foreign Language Learning and Teaching.* Peter Lang Verlag, Frankfurt (Germany).
Stam, G. 2006. 'Changes in patterns of thinking with second language acquisition'. Unpublished PhD thesis, University of Chicago.
Stansfield, C. and **L. Hansen.** 1983. 'Field-dependence-independence as a variable in second language cloze test performance'. *TESOL Quarterly* 17: 29–38.
Stauble, A. 1984. 'A comparison of a Spanish–English and a Japanese–English second language continuum: negation and verb morphology' in R. Andersen (ed.): *Second Languages: A Cross-linguistic Perspective.* Rowley, Mass.: Newbury House.
Stenhouse, L. 1975. *An Introduction to Curriculum Research and Development.* London: Heinemann.
Stenson, B. 1974. 'Induced errors'. in J. Schumann and N. Stenson (eds.): *New Frontiers in Second Language Learning.* Rowley, Mass.: Newbury House.
Stern, H. 1983. *Fundamental Concepts of Language Teaching.* Oxford: Oxford University Press.
Stern, H. 1990. 'Analysis and experience as variables in second language pedagogy' in B. Harley, J. P. Allen, J. Cummins, and M. Swain (eds.): *The Development of Second Language Proficiency.* Cambridge: Cambridge University Press.
Sternberg, R. (ed.). 1999. *The Nature of Cognition.* Cambridge, Mass.: MIT Press.

Sternberg, R. 2002. 'The theory of successful intelligence and its implication for language aptitude-testing' in P. Robinson (ed.): *Individual Differences and Instructed Language Learning*. Amsterdam, John Benjamins.
Stever, S., C. Walker, and **S. Mufwene** (eds.). 1976. *Papers from the Parasession on Diachronic Syntax*. Chicago: Chicago Linguistic Society.
Stockwell, R. and **J. Bowen.** 1965. *The Sounds of English and Spanish*. Chicago: Chicago University Press.
Stockwell, R., J. Bowen, and **J. Martin.** 1965. *The Grammatical Structures of English and Spanish*. Chicago: Chicago University Press.
Storch, N. 2001. 'How collaborative is pair work? ESL tertiary students composing in pairs'. *Language Teaching Research* 5: 29–53.
Storch, N. 2002. 'Patterns of interaction in ESL pair work'. *Language Learning* 52: 119–58.
Strange, W. (ed.). 1995. *Speech Perception and Linguistic Experience: Issues in Cross-language Research*. Timonoium, Md.: York Press.
Strevens, P. 1980. *Teaching English as an International Language*. Oxford: Pergamon.
Strong, M. 1983. 'Social styles and second language acquisition of Spanish-speaking kindergarteners'. *TESOL Quarterly* 17: 241–58.
Strong, M. 1984. 'Integrative motivation: cause or result of successful second language acquisition?' *Language Learning* 34: 1–14.
Suchert, A. 2004. 'The neurobiology of attention' in J. Schumann, S. Crowell, N. Jones, N. Lee, S. Shuchert, and L. Wood (eds.): *The Neurobiology of Learning: Perspectives from Second Language Acquisition*. Mahwah, N.J.: Lawrence Erlbaum.
Sure, K. 1991. 'Language functions and language attitudes in Kenya'. *English World-Wide* 12: 245–60.
Svanes, B. 1988. 'Attitudes and "cultural distance" in second language acquisition'. *Applied Linguistics* 9: 357–71.
Svartvik, J. (ed.) 1973a. *Errata: Papers in Error Analysis*. Lund, Sweden: CWK Gleerup.
Svartvik, J. 1973b. 'Introduction' in Svartvik, J. (ed.): *Errata: Papers in Error Analysis*. Lund, Sweden: CWK Gleerup.
Swaffar, J., K. Arens, and **M. Morgan.** 1982. 'Teacher classroom practices: redefining method as task hierarchy'. *The Modern Language Journal* 66: 24–32.
Swain, M. 1985. 'Communicative competence: some roles of comprehensible input and comprehensible output in its development' in S. Gass and C. Madden (eds.): *Input in Second Language Acquisition*. Rowley, Mass.: Newbury House.
Swain, M. 1995. 'Three functions of output in second language learning' in G. Cook and B. Seidlhofer (eds.). *Principles and Practice in the Study of Language: Studies in Honour of H. G. Widdowson*. Oxford: Oxford University Press.
Swain, M. 1998. 'Focus on form through conscious reflection' in C. Doughty and J. Williams (eds.): *Focus-on-form in Classroom Second Language Acquisition*. Cambridge: Cambridge University Press.
Swain, M. 2000. 'The output hypothesis and beyond: mediating acquisition through collaborative dialogue' in J. Lantolf (ed.): *Sociocultural Theory and Second Language Learning*. Oxford: Oxford University Press.
Swain, M. 2005. 'Verbal protocols: what does it mean for research to use speaking as a data collection tool?' in M. Chalhoub-Deville, C. Chapelle, and P. Duff (eds.): *Inference and Generalizability in Applied Linguistics: Multiple Perspectives*. Amsterdam: John Benjamins.
Swain, M. 2006. 'Languaging, agency and collaboration in advanced second language learning' in H. Byrnes (ed.): *Advanced Language Learning: The contributions of Halliday and Vygotsky*. London: Continuum.
Swain, M., L. Brooks, and **A. Tocalli-Beller.** 2003. 'Peer–peer dialogue as a means of second language learning'. *Annual Review of Applied Linguistics* 23: 171–85.

Swain, M. and **J. Cummins.** 1979. 'Bilingualism, cognitive functioning and education' reprinted in V. Kinsella (ed.). 1982. *Surveys 1: Eight State-of-the-art Articles on Key Areas in Language Teaching.* Cambridge: Cambridge University Press.

Swain, M. and **S. Lapkin.** 1982. *Evaluating Bilingual Education: a Canadian Case Study.* Clevedon: Multilingual Matters.

Swain, M. and **S. Lapkin.** 1991. 'Heritage language children in an English-French bilingual program'. *Canadian Modern Language Review* 47: 635–41.

Swain, M. and **S. Lapkin.** 1995. 'Problems in output and the cognitive processes they generate: a step towards second language learning'. *Applied Linguistics* 16: 371–91.

Swain, M. and **S. Lapkin.** 1998. 'Interaction and second language learning: two adolescent French immersion students working together'. *The Modern Language Journal* 82: 320–37.

Swain, M. and **S. Lapkin.** 2000. 'Task-based second language learning: the use of the first language'. *Language Teaching Research* 4: 251–74.

Swain, M. and **S. Lapkin.** 2001a. 'Talking it through: two French immersion learners' response to reformulation'. Unpublished paper, Ontario Institute for Studies in Education, University of Toronto, Canada.

Swain, M. and **S. Lapkin.** 2001b. 'Focus on form through collaborative dialogue: exploring task effects' in M. Bygate, P. Skehan, and M. Swain (eds.): *Researching Pedagogic Tasks, Second Language Learning, Teaching and Testing.* Harlow: Longman.

Swain, M. and **S. Lapkin.** 2005. 'The evolving socio-political context of immersion education in Canada: some implications for program development'. *International Journal of Applied Linguistics* 15: 169–86.

Swan, M. 2005. 'Legislating by hypothesis: the case of task-based instruction'. *Applied Linguistics* 26: 376–401.

Swan, M. and **B. Smith.** 2001. *Learner English: A Teacher's Guide to Interference and Other Problems* (Second edition). Cambridge: Cambridge University Press.

Swanborn, M. and **K. de Glopper.** 2002. 'Impact of reading purpose on incidental word learning from context'. *The Modern Language Journal* 52: 95–117.

Swierzbin, B., F. Morris, M. Anderson, C. Klee, and **E. Tarone** (eds.). 2000. *Social and Cognitive Factors in Second Language Acquisition.* Somerville, Mass.: Cascadilla Press.

Tabouret-Keller, A. 1997. 'Language and identity'. in F. Coulmas (ed.): *The Handbook of Sociolinguistics.* Oxford: Blackwell.

Tajfel, H. 1974. 'Social identity and intergroup behaviour'. *Social Science Information* 13: 65–93.

Tajfel, H. (ed.). 1984. *The Social Dimension Volume 2.* Cambridge: Cambridge University Press.

Takahashi, S. 1996. 'Pragmatic transferability'. *Studies in Second Language Acquisition* 18: 189–223.

Takahashi, S. 2005. 'Pragmalinguistic awareness: is it related to motivation and proficiency?' *Applied Linguistics* 26: 90–120.

Takahashi, S. and **L. Beebe.** 1987. 'The development of pragmatic competence by Japanese learners of English'. *JALT Journal* 8: 131–55.

Takahashi, T. 1989. 'The influence of the listener on L2 speech' in S. Gass, C. Madden, D. Preston, and L. Selinker (eds.): *Variation in Second Language Acquisition Volume I: Sociolinguistic Issues.* Clevedon: Multilingual Matters.

Takimoto, M. 2006. 'The effects of explicit feedback on the development of pragmatic proficiency'. *Language Teaching Research* 10: 393–417.

Talairach, J. and **P. Tournoux.** 1988. *Co-planar Stereotaxic Atlas of the Human Brain.* Thieme Medical, New York.

Talmy, L. 2000. *Toward a Cognitive Semantics. Volume II: Typology and Process in Concept Structuring.* Cambridge, Mass.: MIT Press.

Tanaka, K. 2004. 'Changes in Japanese students' beliefs about language learning and English language proficiency in a study-abroad context'. Unpublished PhD thesis, University of Auckland.

Tanaka, K. and **R. Ellis.** 2003. 'Study abroad, language proficiency, and learner beliefs about language learning'. *JALT Journal* 25: 63–85.

Tanaka, N. 1988. 'Politeness: some problems for Japanese speakers of English'. *JALT Journal* 9: 81–102.

Tanaka, S. and **S. Kawade.** 1982. 'Politeness strategies and second language acquisition'. *Studies in Second Language Acquisition* 5: 18–33.

Tarallo, F. and **J. Myhill.** 1983. 'Interference and natural language in second language acquisition'. *Language Learning* 33: 55–76.

Tarone, E. 1977. 'Conscious communication strategies in interlanguage: a progress report' in H. Brown, C. Yorio, and R. Crymes (eds.). *On TESOL '77*. Washington D.C.: TESOL.

Tarone, E. 1978. 'The phonology of interlanguage' in J. Richards (ed.): *Understanding Second and Foreign Language Learning: Issues and Approaches*. Rowley, Mass.: Newbury House.

Tarone, E. 1980. 'Communication strategies, foreigner talk, and repair in interlanguage'. *Language Learning* 30: 417–31.

Tarone, E. 1981. 'Some thoughts on the notion of communication strategy'. *TESOL Quarterly* 15: 285–95.

Tarone, E. 1982. 'Systematicity and attention in interlanguage'. *Language Learning* 32: 69–82.

Tarone, E. 1983. 'On the variability of interlanguage systems'. *Applied Linguistics* 4: 143–63.

Tarone, E. 1985. 'Variability in interlanguage use: a study of style-shifting in morphology and syntax'. *Language Learning* 35: 373–403.

Tarone, E. 1988. *Variation in Interlanguage*. London: Edward Arnold.

Tarone, E. 1990. 'On variation in interlanguage: a response to Gregg'. *Applied Linguistics* 11: 392–400.

Tarone, E. 2000. 'Still wrestling with context'. *Annual Review of Applied Linguistics* 20: 181–98.

Tarone, E., A. Cohen, and **G. Dumas.** 1976. 'A closer look at some interlanguage terminology: a framework for communication strategies'. *Working Papers on Bilingualism* 9: 76–90.

Tarone, E., S. Gass, and **A. Cohen** (eds.). 1994. *Research Methodology in Second Language Research*. Hillsdale, N.J.: Lawrence Erlbaum.

Tarone, E. and **G. Liu.** 1995. 'Situational context, variation, and second language acquisition theory' in G. Cook and B. Seidlhofer (eds.): *Principle and Practice in Applied Linguistics: Studies in Honour of H. G. Widdowson*. Oxford: Oxford University Press.

Tarone, E. and **B. Parrish.** 1988. 'Task-related variation in interlanguage: the case of articles'. *Language Learning* 38: 21–44.

Tarone, E. and **M. Swain.** 1995. 'A sociolinguistic perspective on second-language use in immersion classrooms'. *The Modern Language Journal* 79: 166–78.

Tarone, E. and **B. Swierzbin.** 2005. 'Features of interlanguage in oral narratives: the impact of literacy level'. Paper given at AILA, Madison, Wisconsin, USA.

Tateyama, Y. 2001. 'Explicit and implicit teaching of pragmatic routines: Japanese sumimasen' in K. Rose and G. Kasper (eds.): *Pragmatics in Language Teaching*. Cambridge: Cambridge University Press.

Tavakoli, P. and **S. Skehan.** 2005. 'Strategic planning, task structure, and performance testing' in R. Ellis (ed.): *Planning and Task-Performance in a Second Language*. Amsterdam: John Benjamins.

Taylor, B. 1975. 'The use of overgeneralization and transfer learning strategies by elementary and intermediate students of ESL'. *Language Learning* 25: 73–107.

Taylor, D. 1980. 'Ethnicity and language: a social psychological perspective' in H. Giles, W. Robinson, and P. Smith. (eds.): *Language: Social Psychological Perspectives*. Oxford: Pergamon.

Taylor, D. 1988. 'The meaning and use of the term "competence" in linguistics and applied linguistics'. *Applied Linguistics* 9: 148–68.

Taylor, G. 1986. 'Errors and explanations'. *Applied Linguistics* 7: 144–66.

Terrell, T. 1977. 'A natural approach to second language acquisition and learning'. *The Modern Language Journal* 61: 325–36.

Terrell, T., E. Gomez, and **J. Mariscal.** 1980. 'Can acquisition take place in the classroom' in R. Scarcella and S. Krashen (eds.): *Research in Second Language Acquisition.* Rowley, Mass.: Newbury House.

Tharp, R. and **R. Gallimore.** 1988. *Rousing Minds to Life: Teaching, Learning and Schooling in a Social Context.* New York: Cambridge University Press.

Thomas, J. 1983. 'Cross-cultural pragmatic failure'. *Applied Linguistics* 4: 91–112.

Thomas, M. 1989. 'The interpretation of English reflexive pronouns by non-native speakers'. *Studies in Second Language Acquisition* 11: 281–303.

Thomas, M. 1995. 'Acquisition of the Japanese reflexive zibun and movement of anaphors in logical form'. *Second Language Research* 11: 206–34.

Thomas, M. 1998. 'Programmatic ahistoricity in second language acquisition theory'. *Studies in Second Language Acquisition* 20: 387–405.

Thomas, M. 2005. 'Theories of second language acquisition: three sides, three angles, three points'. *Second Language Research* 21: 393–414.

Thorne, S. 2003. 'Artifacts and cultures-of-use in intercultural communication'. *Language Learning and Technology* 7: 38–67.

Thorne, S. 2004. 'Cultural historical activity theory and the object of innovation' in O. St. John, K. van Esch, and E. Schalkwijk (eds.): *New Insights into Foreign Language Learning and Teaching.* Frankfurt: Peter Lang Verlag.

Tocalli-Beller, A. and **M. Swain.** 2007. 'Riddles and puns in the ESL classroom: adults talk to learn' in A. Mackey (ed.): *Conversational Interaction and Second Language Acquisition: A Series of Empirical Studies.* Oxford: Oxford University Press.

Tode, T. 2007. 'Durability problems with explicit instruction in an EFL context: the learning of copula be before and after the introduction of auxiliary be'. *Language Teaching Research* 11: 11–30.

Tokowicz, N. and **B. MacWhinney.** 2005. 'Implicit and explicit measures of sensitivity to violations in second language grammar: an even-related potential investigation'. *Studies in Second Language Acquisition* 27: 173–204.

Tollefson, J. 1991. *Planning Language, Planning Inequality.* London: Longman.

Tomasello, M. 2000a. 'Do young children have adult syntactic competence?' *Cognition* 74: 209–53.

Tomasello, M. 2000b. 'The item-based nature of children's early syntactic development'. *Trends in Cognitive Science* 4: 156–63.

Tomasello, M., N. Akhtar, K. Dodson, and **L. Rekau.** 1997. 'Differential productivity in young children's use of nouns and verbs'. *Journal of Child Language* 24: 373–87.

Tomasello, M. and **C. Herron.** 1988. 'Down the garden path: inducing and correcting overgeneralization errors in the foreign language classroom'. *Applied Psycholinguistics* 9: 237–46.

Tomasello, M. and **C. Herron.** 1989. 'Feedback for language transfer errors: the garden path technique'. *Studies in Second Language Acquisition* 11: 385–95.

Tomiyana, M. 1980. 'Grammatical errors and communication breakdown'. *TESOL Quarterly* 14: 71–9.

Tomlin, R. and **V. Villa.** 1994. 'Attention in cognitive science and second language acquisition'. *Studies in Second Language Acquisition* 16: 183–203.

Tomlinson, B. 2001. 'The inner voice: a critical factor in L2 learning'. *The Journal of Imagination in Language Learning and Teaching* VI: 26–33.

Tono, Y., T. Kaneko, H. Isahara, T. Saiga, E. Izumi, M. Narita, and **E. Kaneko.** 2001. 'The Standard Speaking Test (SST) Corpus: a 1 million-word spoken corpus of Japanese learners of English and its implications for L2 lexicography' in S. Lee (ed.): *ASIALEX 2001 Proceedings: Asian Bilingualism and the Dictionary*. The Second Asialex International Congress, 8–10 August 2001, Yonsei University, Korea.

Tosi, A. 1984. *Immigration and Bilingual Education*. Oxford: Pergamon.

Towell, R. 1987. 'Variability and progress in the language development of advanced learners of a foreign language' in R. Ellis (ed.): *Second Language Acquisition in Context*. London: Prentice Hall International.

Towell, R. 2002. 'Relative degrees of fluency: A comparative case study of advanced learners of French'. *International Review of Applied Linguistics* 40: 117–50.

Towell, R. and **R. Hawkins.** 1994. *Approaches to Second Language Acquisition*. Clevedon: Multilingual Matters.

Towell, R., R. Hawkins, and **N. Bazergui.** 1993. 'Systematic and non-systematic variability in advanced language learning'. *Studies in Second Language Acquisition* 15: 439–60.

Towell, R., R. Hawkins, and **N. Bazergui.** 1996. 'The development of fluency in advanced learners of French'. *Applied Linguistics* 17/1: 84–115.

Trahey, M. 1996. 'Positive evidence in second language acquisition: some long term effects'. *Second Language Research* 12: 111–39.

Trahey, M. and **L. White.** 1993. 'Positive evidence and preemption in the second language classroom'. *Studies in Second Language Acquisition* 15: 181–204.

Tran-Chi-Chau 1975. 'Error analysis, contrastive analysis and students' perceptions: a study of difficulty in second language learning'. *International Review of Applied Linguistics* 13: 119–43.

Tremblay, P. and **R. Gardner.** 1995. 'Expanding the motivation construct in language learning'. *The Modern Language Journal* 79: 505–20.

Trosberg, A. 1995. *Interlanguage Pragmatics*. Berlin de Gruyter.

Trubetzkoy, N. 1931. 'Die phonologischen Systeme'. *Travaux du Cercle Linguistique de Prague* 4: 96–116.

Trudgill, P. 1983. *Sociolinguistics: An Introduction to Language and Society*. Harmondsworth: Penguin.

Truscott, J. 1999. 'What's wrong with oral grammar correction'. *The Canadian Modern Language Review* 55: 437–55.

Tseng, W., Z. Dörnyei, and **N. Schmitt.** 2006. 'A new approach to assessing strategic learning: the case for self-regulation in vocabulary acquisition'. *Applied Linguistics* 27: 78–102.

Tsimpli, I. and **A. Roussou.** 1991. 'Parameter resetting in L2'. *UCL Working Papers in Linguistics* 3: 149–69.

Tucker, G., E. Hamayan, and **F. Genesee.** 1976. 'Affective cognitive and social factors in second language acquisition'. *Canadian Modern Language Review* 32: 214–16.

Tulving, E. and **D. Schachter.** 1990. 'Priming and human memory'. *Science* 247: 301–6.

Turnball, M. and **K. Arnett.** 'Teachers' uses of the target and first languages in second and foreign language classrooms'. *Annual Review of Applied Linguistics* 22: 204–18.

Turner, D. 1979. 'The effect of instruction on second language learning and second language acquisition' in R. Andersen (ed.): *The Acquisition and Use of Spanish and English as First and Second Languages*. Washington, D.C.: TESOL.

Turner, J. and **H. Giles** (eds.). 1981. *Intergroup Behavior*. Chicago, Ill.: University of Chicago Press.

Turton, J. and **N. Heaton.** (eds.). 1996. *Longman Dictionary of Common Errors*. London: Longman.

Ullman, M. 2001. 'The declarative/procedural model of lexicon and grammar'. *Journal of Psycholinguistic Research* 30: 37–69.

Ullman, M., R. Bergida, and **K. O'Craven.** 1997. 'Distinct fMRI activation patterns for regular and irregular past tense'. *NeuroImage* 5: S549.

Upshur, J. 1968. 'Four experiments on the relation between foreign language teaching and learning'. *Language Learning* 18: 111–24.

Ur, P. 1996. *A Course in Language Teaching*. Cambridge: Cambridge University Press.

Ushakova, T. 1994. 'Inner speech and second language acquisition: an experimental-theoretical approach' in J. Lantolf and G. Appel (eds.): *Vygotskian Approaches to Second Language Research*. Hillsdale, N.J.: Ablex.

Ushioda, E. 2003. 'Motivation as a socially mediated process' in D. Little, J. Ridley, and E. Ushioda (eds.): *Learner Autonomy in the Foreign Language Classroom: Teacher, Learner, Curriculum, Assessment*. Dublin: Authentik.

Uziel, S. 1993. 'Resetting universal grammar parameters: evidence from second language acquisition of Subjacency and the Empty Category Principle'. *Second Language Research* 9: 49–83.

Vaid, J. 1983. 'Bilingualism and brain lateralization' in S. Segalowitz (ed.): *Language Functions and Brain Organization*. New York: Academic Press.

Vainikka, A. and **M. Young-Scholten.** 1996. 'Gradual development of L2 phrase structure'. *Second Language Research* 12: 7–39.

Vainikka, A. and **M. Young-Scholten.** 1998. 'The initial state in the L2 acquisition of phrase structure' in S. Flynn, G. Martohardjono and W O'Neil (eds.): *The Generative Study of Second Language Acquisition*. Mahwah, N.J.: Lawrence Erlbaum.

Valdman, A. (ed.). 1977. *Pidgin and Creole*. Indiana University Press.

Valdman, A. 1978. 'On the relevance of the pidginization-creolization model for second language learning'. *Studies in Second Language Acquisition* 1: 55–77.

Valdman, A. 1992. 'Authenticity, variation and communication in the foreign language classroom' in C. Kramsch and S. McConnell-Ginet (eds.): *Text and Context: Cross-disciplinary Perspectives on Language Study*. Lexington, Mass.: D.C. Heath and Company.

Van Buren, P. and **M. Sharwood Smith.** 1985. 'The acquisition of preposition stranding by second language learners and parametric variation'. *Second Language Research* 1: 18–26.

Van den Branden, K. 1997. 'Effects of negotiation on language learners' output'. *Language Learning* 47: 589–636.

Van den Branden, K. (ed.). 2006. *Task-based Language Education*. Cambridge: Cambridge University Press.

Van Els, T., T. Bongaerts, G. Extra, C. Van Os, and **A. Janssen-Van Dieten.** 1984. *Applied Linguistics and the Learning and Teaching of Foreign Languages*. London: Edward Arnold.

Van Esch, K. and **O. St. John** (eds.). 2004. *Vygotsky's Theory of Education in Cultural Context*. Frankfurt am Main: Peter Lang.

Van Lier, L. 1988. *The Classroom and the Language Learner*. London: Longman.

Van Lier, L. 1989. 'Reeling, writing, drawling, stretching and fainting in coils: oral proficiency interviews as conversation'. *TESOL Quarterly* 23: 489–508.

Van Lier, L. 1991. 'Inside the classroom: learning processes and teaching procedures'. *Applied Language Learning* 2: 29–69.

Van Lier, L. 1992. 'Not the nine o'clock linguistics class: investigating contingency grammar'. *Language Awareness* 1: 91–108.

Van Lier, L. 1994a. 'Forks and hopes: pursuing understanding in different ways'. *Applied Linguistics* 15: 328–46.

Van Lier, L. 1994b. 'Some features of a theory of practice'. *TESOL Journal* 4: 6–10.

Van Lier, L. 1996. *Interaction in the Language Curriculum: Awareness, Autonomy and Authenticity*. London: Longman.

Van Lier, L. 2000. 'From input to affordance: social-interactive learning from an ecological perspective' in J. Lantolf (ed.): *Sociocultural Theory and Second Language Learning*. Oxford: Oxford University Press.

Van Naerssen, M. 1980. 'How similar are Spanish as a first and foreign language?' in R. Scarcella and S. Krashen (eds.): *Research in Second Language Acquisition*. Rowley, Mass.: Newbury House.

Vann, R., D. Meyer, and **F. Lorenz.** 1984. 'Error gravity: a study of faculty opinion of ESL errors'. *TESOL Quarterly* 18: 427–40.

VanPatten, B. 1990a. 'Attending to form and content in the input'. *Studies in Second Language Acquisition* 12: 287–301.

VanPatten, B. 1990b. 'The acquisition of clitic pronouns in Spanish: two case studies' in B. VanPatten and J. Lee (eds.): *Second Language Acquisition—Foreign Language Learning.* Clevedon: Multilingual Matters.

VanPatten, B. 1996. *Input Processing and Grammar Instruction in Second Language Acquisition.* Norwood, N.J.: Ablex.

VanPatten, B. 2002. 'Processing instruction: an update'. *Language Learning* 52: 755–804.

VanPatten, B. (ed.). 2003. *Processing Instruction: Theory, Research, and Commentary (Second Language Acquisition Research).* Mahwah, N.J.: Lawrence Erlbaum.

VanPatten, B. 2004a. 'Input-processing in Second Language Acquisition' in B. VanPatten (ed.): *Processing Instruction: Theory, Research, and Commentary.* Mahwah, N.J.: Lawrence Erlbaum.

VanPatten, B. 2004b. *Processing Instruction: Theory, Research, and Commentary.* Mahwah, N.J.: Lawrence Erlbaum.

VanPatten, B. and **T. Cadierno.** 1993. 'SLA as input processing: a role for instruction'. *Studies in Second Language Acquisition* 15: 225–43.

VanPatten, B., T. Dvorak, and **J. Lee** (eds.). 1987. *Foreign Language Learning: a Research Perspective.* New York: Newbury House.

VanPatten, B. and **J. Lee.** (eds.). 1990. *Second Language Acquisition—Foreign Language Learning.* Clevedon: Multilingual Matters.

VanPatten, B. and **S. Oikennon.** 1996. 'Explanation vs. structured input in processing instruction'. *Studies in Second Language Acquisition* 18: 495–510.

VanPatten, B. and **C. Sanz.** 1995. 'From input to output: Processing instruction and communicative tasks' in F. Eckman *et al.* (eds.): *Second Language Acquisition Theory and Pedagogy.* Mahwah. N.J.: Lawrence Erlbaum.

VanPatten, B. and **J. Williams.** (eds.). 2006. 'Introduction' in *Theories in Second Language Acquisition.* Mahwah, N.J.: Lawrence Erlbaum.

Varadi, T. 1980. 'Strategies of target language learner communication: message adjustment'. *International Review of Applied Linguistics* 6: 71–90.

Varonis, E. and **S. Gass.** 1985. 'Non-native/non-native conversations: a model for negotiation of meaning'. *Applied Linguistics* 6: 71–90.

Vendler, Z. 1967. *Linguistics in Philosophy.* Ithaca, N.Y.: Cornell University Press.

Verhoeven, L. 1991. 'Predicting minority children's bilingual proficiency: child, family and institutional factors'. *Language Learning* 41: 205–33.

Verhoeven, L. and **A. Vermeer.** 2002. 'Communicative competence and personality dimensions in first and second language learners'. *Applied Psycholinguistics* 23: 361–74.

Veronique, D. 1987. 'Reference to past events and actions in narratives in a second language: insights from North African workers' French' in C. Pfaff (ed.): *First and Second Language Acquisition Processes.* Cambridge, Mass.: Newbury House.

Verschuren, J. and **M. Bertucelli-Papi** (eds.). 1985. *The Pragmatic Perspective.* Amsterdam: Benjamins.

Vocate, D. 1994a. 'Self-talk and inner speech: Understanding the uniquely human aspects of intrapersonal communication' in D. Vocate (ed.): *Intrapersonal Communication, Different Voices, Different Minds.* Hillsdale, N.J.: Lawrence Erlbaum.

Vocate, D. (ed.). 1994b. *Intrapersonal Communication, Different Voices, Different Minds.* Hillsdale, N.J.: Lawrence Erlbaum.

Vogel, T. and **J. Bahns.** 1989. 'Introducing the English progressive in the classroom: insights from second language acquisition research'. *System* 17: 183–94.

Von Stutterheim, C. 2003. 'Linguistic structures and information organization: the case of advanced learners'. *EUROSLA Yearbook* 3: 183–206.

Von Stutterheim, C. 2005. 'Advanced learner languages: the impact of grammatical categories on principles of information organisation as a learning problem'. Paper given at the University of Bern Summer School on Understanding Second Language Acquisition. Bern, Switzerland.

Vygotsky, L. 1962. *Thought and Language*. Cambridge, Mass.: MIT Press

Vygotsky, L. 1978. *Mind in Society*. Cambridge: Mass.: MIT Press.

Vygotsky, L. 1981. 'The genesis of higher mental functions' in J. Wertsch (ed.): *The Concept of Activity in Soviet Psychology*. Armonk, N.Y.: M. E. Sharpe.

Vygotsky, L. 1986. *Thought and Language* (Newly revised and edited by A. Kozulin). Cambridge, Mass.: MIT Press.

Vygotsky, L. 1987. *The Collected Works of L. S. Vygotsky Volume 1: Thinking and Speaking*. New York: Plenum Press.

Wagner, J. and **A. Firth.** 1997. 'Communication strategies at work' in G. Kasper and E. Kellerman (ed.): *Communication Strategies: Psycholinguistic and Sociolinguistic Perspectives*. London: Longman.

Wagner-Gough, J. 1975. *Comparative Studies in Second Language Learning*. CAL-ERIC/CLL Series on Language and Linguistics 26.

Wajnryb, R. 1990. *Grammar Dictation*. Oxford: Oxford University Press.

Wakabayashi, S. 2002. 'The acquisition of non-null subjects in English: a minimalist account'. *Second Language Research* 18: 28–71.

Walsh, S. 2002. 'Construction or obstruction: teacher talk and learner involvement in the EFL classroom'. *Language Teaching Research* 6: 3–24.

Walters, J. 1979. 'The perception of deference in English and Spanish' in C. Yorio, K. Perkins, and J. Schachter (eds.): *On TESOL '79*. Washington D.C.: TESOL.

Walters, J. 1980. 'Grammar, meaning and sociocultural appropriateness in second language acquisition'. *Canadian Journal of Psychology* 34: 337–45.

Wang. M. and **K. Koda.** 2005. 'Commonalities and differences in word identification skills among learners of English as a second language'. *Language Learning* 55: 71–98.

Wang, M., K. Koda, and **C. Perfetti.** 2003. 'Alphabetic and non-alphabetic L1 effects in English word identification: a comparison of Korean and Chinese English L2 learners'. *Cognition* 87: 129–49.

Wang, X. (ed.). 1996. *A View from Within: A Case Study of Chinese Heritage Community Language Schools in the United States*. Washington, D.C.: National Foreign Language Center.

Wanner, E. and **L. Gleitman** (eds.). 1982. *Language Acquisition: The State of the Art*. Cambridge: Cambridge University Press.

Wardhaugh, R. 1970. 'The Contrastive Analysis Hypothesis'. *TESOL Quarterly* 4: 123–30.

Wartenburger, I., H. Heekeren, J. Abutalebi, S. Cappa, A. Villringer, and **D. Perani.** 2003. 'Early setting of grammatical processing in the bilingual brain'. *Neuron* 37: 159–70.

Waterson, N. and **C. Snow.** 1978. *The Development of Communication*. Wiley: New York.

Watson-Gegeo, K. 1992. 'Thick explanation in the ethnographic study of child socialization and development: a longitudinal study of the problem of schooling for Kwara'ae (Solomon Islands) children' in W. Corsaro and P. Miller (eds.): *New Directions for Child Development Volume 58*. San Francisco: Jossey Bass.

Watson-Gegeo, K. 1997. 'Classroom ethnography' in N. Hornberger and D. Corson (eds.): *Encyclopedia of Language and Education Volume 8: Research Methods in Language and Education*. The Netherlands: Kluwer.

Watson-Gegeo, K. 2004. 'Mind, language, and epistemology: toward a language socialization paradigm for SLA'. *The Modern Language Journal* 88: 331–50.

Weedon, C. 1997. *Feminist Practice and Poststructuralist Theory*. London: Blackwell.

Weinberger, S. 1987. 'The influence of linguistic context on syllable structure simplification' in G. Ioup and S. Weinberger (eds.): *Interlanguage Phonology: The Acquisition of a Second Language Sound System*. Rowley, Mass.: Newbury House.

Weinert, R. 1987. 'Processes in classroom second language development: the acquisition of negation in German'. in R. Ellis (ed.): *Second Language Acquisition in Context.* London: Prentice Hall International.

Weinreich, U. 1953. *Languages in Contact.* The Hague: Mouton.

Wells, G. 1980. 'Apprenticeship in meaning' in K. Nelson (ed.): *Children's Language Volume 2.* New York: Gardner Press.

Wells, G. 1985. *Language Development in the Pre-school Years.* Cambridge: Cambridge University Press.

Wells, G. 1986a. *The Meaning Makers: Children Learning Language and Using Language to Learn.* London: Hodder and Stoughton.

Wells, G. 1986b. 'Variation in child language' in P. Fletcher and M. Garman (eds.): *Language Acquisition* (Second edition). Cambridge: Cambridge University Press.

Wells, G. 1994a. 'The complementary contributions of Halliday and Vygotsky to a "language-based theory of learning"'. *Linguistics and Education* 6: 41–90.

Wells, G. 1994b. 'Introduction: Teacher research and educational change' in G. Wells *et al.* (eds.): *Changing Schools from Within: Creating Communities of Enquiry.* Toronto, Canada: Ontario Institute for Studies in Education.

Wells, G. 1999. *Dialogical Enquiry: Toward a Sociocultural Practice and Theory of Education.* Cambridge: Cambridge University Press.

Wells, G. 2000. 'Dialogic enquiry in education: Building on the legacy of Vygotsky' in C. Lee and P. Smagorinsky (eds.): *Vygotskian Perspectives on Literacy Research.* New York: Cambridge University Press.

Wells, G. *et al.*, (eds.). 1994 *Changing Schools from Within: Creating Communities of Enquiry.* Toronto, Canada: Ontario Institute for Studies in Education.

Wells, G. and **M. Montgomery.** 1981. 'Adult-child interaction at home and at school' in P. French and M. McLure (eds.): *Adult-child Conversation.* New York: St Martin's Press.

Wendel, J. 1997. 'Planning and second language narrative production'. Unpublished doctoral dissertation, Temple University, Japan.

Wenden, A. 1986. 'What do second language learners know about their language learning? A second look at retrospective accounts'. *Applied Linguistics* 7: 186–201.

Wenden, A. 1987. 'How to be a successful learner: insights and prescriptions from L2 learners' in A. Wenden and J. Rubin (eds.): *Learner Strategies in Language Learning.* Englewood Cliffs, N.J.: Prentice Hall.

Wenden, A. 1999. 'An Introduction'. *System* 27: 435–41.

Wenden, A. and **J. Rubin.** (eds.). 1987. *Learner Strategies in Language Learning.* Englewood Cliffs, N.J.: Prentice Hall.

Wenk, B. 1986. 'Crosslinguistic influence in second language phonology: speech rhythms' in E. Kellerman and M. Sharwood Smith (eds.): *Cross-linguistic Influence in Second Language Acquisition.* Oxford: Pergamon.

Wertsch, J. (ed.). 1981. *The Concept of Activity in Soviet Psychology.* Armonk, N.Y.: M. E. Sharpe.

Wertsch, J. 1985. *Vygotsky and the Social Formation of Mind.* Cambridge, Mass.: Harvard University Press.

Wertsch, J. 1998. *Mind as Action.* Oxford: Oxford University Press.

Wertsch, J., N. Minick, and **F. Arns.** 1984. 'The creation of context in joint problem solving' in B. Rogoff and J. Lave (eds.): *Everyday Cognition: Its Development in Social Contexts.* Cambridge, Mass.: Harvard University Press.

Wesche, M. 1981. 'Language aptitude measures in streaming, matching students with methods, and diagnosis of learning problems' in K. Diller (ed.): *Individual Differences and Universals in Language Learning Aptitude.* Rowley, Mass.: Newbury House.

Wesche, M. and **T. Paribakht.** (eds.). 1999. 'Incidental L2 vocabulary acquisition: theory, current research, and instructional implications'. *Studies in Second Language Acquisition* 21: 175–80.

Wesche, M. and **D. Ready.** 1985. 'Foreigner talk in the university classroom' in S. Gass and C. Madden (eds.): *Input in Second Language Acquisition*. Rowley, Mass.: Newbury House.

Weslander, D. and **G. Stephany.** 1983. 'Evaluation of an English as a second language program for Southeast Asian students'. *TESOL Quarterly* 17: 473–80.

West, C. 1992. 'A matter of life and death'. *October* 61: 20–3.

Westmoreland, R. 1983. 'German acquisition by instructed adults'. Unpublished paper. Hawai'i: University of Hawai'i.

Wexler, K. and **P. Culicover.** 1980. *Formal Principle of Language Acquisition*. Cambridge Mass.: MIT Press.

Wexler, K. and **R. Mancini.** 1987. 'Parameters and learnability in binding theory' in T. Roeper and E. Williams (eds.): *Parameter Setting*. Dordrecht: Reidel.

Wharton, G. 2000. 'Language learning strategy use of bilingual foreign language learners in Singapore'. *Language Learning* 50: 203–43.

White, J. 1998. 'Getting learners' attention: a typographical input enhancement study' in C. Doughty and J. Williams (eds.): *Focus-on-form in Classroom Second Language Acquisition*. Cambridge: Cambridge University Press.

White, J. and **P. Lightbown.** 1984. 'Asking and answering in ESL classes'. *Canadian Modern Language Review* 40: 228–44.

White, J. and **L. Ranta.** 2002. 'Examining the interface between metalinguistic task performance and oral production in a second language'. *Language Awareness* 11: 259–90.

White, L. 1977. 'Error-analysis and error-correction in adult learners of English as a second language'. *Working Papers on Bilingualism* 13: 42–58.

White, L. 1981. 'The responsibility of grammatical theory to acquisitional data' in N. Hornstein and D. Lightfoot (eds.): *Explanation in Linguistics: the Logical Problem of Language Acquisition*. London: Longman.

White, L. 1985. 'The pro-drop parameter in adult second language acquisition'. *Language Learning* 35: 47–62.

White, L. 1986. 'Implications of parametric variation for adult second language acquisition: an investigation of the "pro-drop" parameter' in V. Cook (ed.): *Experimental Approaches to Second Language Acquisition*. Oxford: Pergamon.

White, L. 1987a. 'Against comprehensible input: the input hypothesis and the development of second language competence'. *Applied Linguistics* 8: 95–110.

White, L. 1987b. 'Markedness and second language acquisition: the question of transfer'. *Studies in Second Language Acquisition* 9: 261–86.

White, L. 1989a. *Universal Grammar and Second Language Acquisition*. Amsterdam: John Benjamins.

White, L. 1989b. 'The adjacency condition on case assignment: do learners observe the Subset Principle?' in S. Gass and J. Schachter (eds.): *Linguistic Perspectives on Second Language Acquisition*. Cambridge: Cambridge University Press.

White, L. 1990. 'Second language acquisition and universal grammar'. *Studies in Second Language Acquisition* 12: 121–33.

White, L. 1991. 'Adverb placement in second language acquisition: some effects of positive and negative evidence in the classroom'. *Second Language Research* 7: 133–61.

White, L. 1992. 'Long and short verb movement in second language acquisition'. *Canadian Journal of Linguistics* 37: 273–86.

White, L. 1995. 'Input, triggers, and second language acquisition: can binding be taught?' in F. Eckman *et al.* (eds.): *Second Language Acquisition Theory and Pedagogy*. Mahwah, N.J.: Lawrence Erlbaum.

White, L. 1997. 'Chasing after linguistic theory: how minimal should we be?' In L. Eubank, L. Selinker, and M. Sharwood Smith (eds.): *The Current State of Interlanguage*. Amsterdam: John Benjamins.

White, L. 2000. 'Second language acquisition: from initial to final state' in J. Archibald (ed.): *Second Language Acquisition and Linguistic Theory*. Oxford: Blackwell.

White, L. 2003a. *Second Language Acquisition and Universal Grammar*. Cambridge: Cambridge University Press.

White, L. 2003b. 'On the nature of interlanguage representation; Universal Grammar in the second language' in C. Doughty and M. Long (eds.): *The Handbook of Second Language Acquisition*. Malden, Mass.: Blackwell.

White, L., N. Spada, P. Lightbown, and **L. Ranta.** 1991. 'Input enhancement and question formation'. *Applied Linguistics* 12: 416–32.

White, L., L. Travis, and **A. Maclachlan.** 1992. 'The acquisition of wh-question formation by Malagasy learners of English: evidence for Universal Grammar'. *Canadian Journal of Linguistics* 37: 341–68.

White, M. 1992. 'Teachers' questions—form, function, and interaction: a study of two teachers'. Unpublished paper, Temple University, Japan.

White, R. 1988. *The ELT Curriculum*. Oxford: Blackwell.

Widdowson, H. 1979a. *Explorations in Applied Linguistics*. Oxford: Oxford University Press.

Widdowson, H. 1979b. 'The significance of simplification' in H. Widdowson (ed.): *Explorations in Applied Linguistics*. Oxford: Oxford University Press. Previously published in *Studies in Second Language Acquisition 1*.

Widdowson, H. 1979c. 'Rules and procedures in discourse analysis' in T. Myers (ed.): *The Development of Conversation and Discourse*. Edinburgh: Edinburgh University Press.

Widdowson, H. 1983. *Learning Purpose and Language Use*. Oxford: Oxford University Press.

Widdowson, H. 1989. 'Knowledge of language and ability for use'. *Applied Linguistics* 10: 128–37.

Widdowson, H. 1990. *Aspects of Language Teaching*. Oxford: Oxford University Press.

Wiese, R. 1984. 'Language production in foreign and native languages: same or different?' in H. Dechert, D. Möhle and M. Raupach (eds.): *Second Language Productions*. Tübingen: Gunter Narr.

Wigglesworth, G. 1997. 'An investigation of planning time and proficiency level on oral test discourse'. *Language Testing* 14/1: 21–44.

Wigglesworth, G. 2001. 'Influences on performance in task based oral assessments' in M. Bygate, P. Skehan, and M. Swain (eds.): *Researching Pedagogic Tasks, Second Language Learning, Teaching and Testing*. Harlow: Longman.

Wigglesworth, G. 2005. 'Current approaches to researching second language learner processes'. *Annual Review of Applied Linguistics* 25: 98–111.

Wilkinson, L. (ed.). 1982. *Communicating in the Classroom*. New York: Academic Press.

Willett, J. 1995. 'Becoming first graders in an L2: an ethnographic study of L2 socialization'. *TESOL Quarterly* 29: 473–503.

Williams, Jessica. 1999. 'Learner-generated attention to form'. *Language Learning* 49: 583–625.

Williams, Jessica. 2005. 'Writing center interaction: institutional discourse and the role of peer tutors' in K. Bardovi-Harlig and B. Hartford (eds.): *Interlanguage Pragmatics: Exploring Institutional Talk*. Mahwah, N.J.: Lawrence Erlbaum.

Williams, Jessica and **J. Evans.** 1998. 'What kind of focus and on which forms?' in C. Doughty and J. Williams (eds.): *Focus-on-form in Classroom Second Language Acquisition*. Cambridge: Cambridge University Press.

Williams, John. 1999. 'Memory, attention and inductive learning'. *Studies in Second Language Acquisition* 21: 1–48.

Williams, John. 2005. 'Learning with awareness'. *Studies in Second Language Acquisition* 27: 269–304.

Williams, John and **P. Lovatt.** 2003. 'Phonological memory and rule learning'. *Language Learning* 53: 67–121.

Williams, M. and **R. Burden.** 1997. *Psychology for Language Teachers*. Cambridge: Cambridge University Press.

Williams, M. and **R. Burden.** 1999. 'Students developing conceptions of themselves as language learners'. *System* 83: 193–201.

Williams, S. and **B. Hammarberg.** 1998. 'Language switches in L3 production: implications for a polyglot speaking model'. *Applied Linguistics* 19: 295–333.

Willing, K. 1987. *Learning Styles and Adult Migrant Education.* Adelaide: National Curriculum Resource Centre.

Willis, J. and **D. Willis** (eds.). 1996. *Challenge and Change in Language Teaching.* London: Heinemann.

Winitz, H. (ed.). 1981. *Native Language and Foreign Language Acquisition.* Annals of the New York Academy of Sciences 379.

Wintergerst, A., A. DeCapua, and **R. Itzen.** 2001. 'The construct validity of one learning style instrument'. *System* 29: 385–403.

Wintergerst, A., A. DeCapua, and **M. Verna.** 2003. 'Conceptualizing learning style modalities for EFL/ESL students'. *System* 31: 85–106.

Witkin, H. and **J. Berry.** 1975. 'Psychological differentiation in cross-cultural perspective'. *Journal of Cross-cultural Psychology* 6: 4–87.

Witkin, H. and **D. Goodenough.** 1981. *Cognitive Styles: Essence and Origins—Field Dependence and Independence.* Psychological Issues Monograph 51.

Witkin, H., O. Oltman, E. Raskin, and **S. Karp.** 1971. *A Manual for the Embedded Figures Test.* Palo Alto, Calif.: Consulting Psychology Press.

Wode, H. 1976. 'Developmental sequences in naturalistic L2 acquisition'. *Working Papers on Bilingualism* 11:1–13.

Wode, H. 1977. 'The L2 acquisition of /r/'. *Phonetica* 34: 200–17.

Wode, H. 1978. 'The L1 vs. L2 acquisition of English negation'. *Working Papers on Bilingualism* 15: 37–57.

Wode, H. 1980. 'Phonology in L2 acquisition' in S. Felix (ed.): *Second Language Development: Trends and Issues.* Tübingen: Gunter Narr.

Wode, H. 1981. *Learning a Second Language 1: an Integrated View of Language Acquisition.* Tübingen: Gunter Narr.

Wode, H. 1983. *Papers on Language Acquisition, Language Learning and Language Teaching.* Heidelberg: Julius Groos.

Wode, H. 1984. 'Some theoretical implications of L2 acquisition research' in A. Davies, C. Criper and A. Howatt (eds.): *Interlanguage.* Edinburgh: Edinburgh University Press.

Wode, H., A. Rohde, F. Gassen, B. Weiss, M. Jekat, and **P. Jung.** 1992. 'L1, L2, L3: continuity vs. discontinuity in lexical acquisition' in P. Arnaud and H. Bejoint (eds.): *Vocabulary and Applied Linguistics.* Basingstoke: Macmillan.

Wold, A. (ed.). 1992. *The Dialogical Alternative. Towards a theory of Language and Mind.* Oslo: Scandinavian University Press.

Wolfe-Quintero, K. 1992. 'Learnability and the acquisition of extraction in relative clauses and wh-questions'. *Studies in Second Language Acquisition* 14: 39–70.

Wolfram, W. 1985. 'Variability in tense marking: a case for the obvious'. *Language Learning* 35: 229–53.

Wolfram. W. 1989. 'Systematic variability in second-language tense marking' in M. Eisenstein (ed.): *The Dynamic Interlanguage: Empirical Studies in Second Language Variation.* New York: Plenum Press.

Wolfram, W. 1991. 'Interlanguage variation: a review article'. *Applied Linguistics* 12: 102–6.

Wolfson, N. 1976. 'Speech events and natural speech: some implications for sociolinguistic methodology'. *Language in Society* 5: 182–209.

Wolfson, N. 1983. 'Rules of speaking' in J. Richards and R. Schmidt (eds.): *Language and Communication.* London: Longman.

Wolfson, N. 1989a. *Perspectives: Sociolinguistics and TESOL.* Rowley, Mass.: Newbury House.

Wolfson, N. 1989b. 'The social dynamics of native and nonnative variation in complimenting behavior' in M. Eisenstein (ed.): *The Dynamic Interlanguage: Empirical Studies in Second Language Variation*. New York: Plenum Press.

Wolfson, N. and **E. Judd** (eds.). 1983. *Sociolinguistics and Second Language Acquisition*. Rowley, Mass.: Newbury House.

Wolfson, N., T. Marmor, and **S. Jones.** 1989. 'Problems in the comparison of speech acts across cultures' in S. Blum-Kulka, J. House, and G. Kasper (eds.): *Cross-cultural Pragmatics: Requests and Apologies*. Norwood: N.J.: Ablex.

Wong, H. 1934. 'The best English: a claim for the superiority of received standard English'. *Society for Pure English* 39: 603–21.

Wong, W. 2001. 'Modality and attention to meaning and form in the input'. *Studies in Second Language Acquisition* 23: 345–68.

Wong, W. 2004. 'Processing instruction in French: the roles of explicit information and structured input' in B. VanPatten (ed.): *Processing Instruction: Theory, Research, and Commentary*. Mahwah: N.J.: Lawrence Erlbaum.

Wong Fillmore, L. 1976. 'The second time around: cognitive and social strategies in second language acquisition. Unpublished PhD dissertation, Stanford University.

Wong Fillmore, L. 1979. 'Individual differences in second language acquisition' in C. Fillmore, D. Kempler, and W. Wang (ed.): *Individual Differences in Language Ability and Language Behavior*. New York: Academic Press.

Wong Fillmore, L. 1982. 'Instructional language as linguistic input: second language learning in classrooms' in L. Wilkinson (ed.): *Communicating in the Classroom*. New York: Academic Press.

Wong Fillmore, L. 1985. 'When does teacher talk work as input?' in S. Gass and C. Madden (eds.): *Input in Second Language Acquisition*. Rowley, Mass.: Newbury House.

Wood, D., J. Bruner, and **G. Ross.** 1976. 'The role of tutoring in problem-solving'. *Journal of Child Psychology and Psychiatry* 17: 89–100.

Woodrow, L. 2006. 'Anxiety and speaking English as a second language'. *RELC Journal* 37: 308–28.

Wray, A. 2000. 'Formulaic sequences in second language teaching: principle and practice'. *Applied Linguistics* 21: 463–89.

Wray, A. 2002. *Formulaic Language and the Lexicon*. Cambridge: Cambridge University Press.

Wu, Y. 2000. 'The neurobiology of language acquisition'. Unpublished MA thesis, UCLA.

Wu, Z. 1981. *Speech act—apology*. Los Angeles: ESL Section, Department of English, UCLA.

Yabuki-Soh, N. 2007. 'Teaching relative clauses in Japanese: exploring different types of instruction and the projection effect'. *Studies in Second Language Acquisition* 29: 219–52.

Yang, N. 1999. 'The relationship between EFL learners' beliefs and learning strategy use'. *System* 27: 515–35.

Yano, Y. 2001. 'World Englishes on 2000 and beyond'. *World Englishes* 20: 119–31.

Yashima, T. 2002. 'Willingness to communicate in a second language: the Japanese EFL context'. *The Modern Language Journal* 86: 54–66.

Yates, R. and **D. Muchisky.** 2003. 'On reconceptualising teacher education'. *TESOL Quarterly* 37: 135–47.

Ying, H. 2005. 'Relevance and L2 learners' interpretation of reflexive anaphora in VP-ellipsis: an exploration of the relationship between relevance theory and typological universals'. *Journal of Universal Language* 6: 159–94.

Yorio, C. 1980. 'Conventionalized language forms and the development of communicative competence'. *TESOL Quarterly* 24: 433–42.

Yorio, C., K. Perkins, and **J. Schachter.** (eds.). 1979. *On TESOL '79*. Washington D.C.: TESOL.

Yoshida, M. 1978. 'The acquisition of English vocabulary by a Japanese-speaking child' in E. Hatch (ed.): *Second Language Acquisition*. Rowley, Mass.: Newbury House.

Yoshimi, D. 1999. 'L1 language socialization as a variable in the use of ne by L2 learners of Japanese'. *Journal of Pragmatics* 31: 1513–25.

Yoshimura, F. 2006. 'Does manipulating foreknowledge of output tasks lead to differences in reading behaviour, text comprehension and noticing of language form?' *Language Teaching Research* 10: 419–34.

Yoshioka, K. 2005. 'Linguistic and gestural introduction and tracking of referents in L1 and L2 discourse'. Unpublished PhD thesis, University of Groningen, Netherlands.

Yoshioka, K. and **T. Doi.** 1988. 'Testing the Pienemann-Johnston model with Japanese: a speech-processing view of the acquisition of particles and word order'. Paper presented at the 8th Second Language Research Forum, Hawai'i, University of Hawai'i.

Young, D. 1986. 'The relationship between anxiety and foreign language oral proficiency ratings'. *Foreign Language Annals* 19: 439–45.

Young, D. 1999. *Affect in Foreign Language and Second Language Learning.* Boston: McGraw Hill.

Young, R. 1988a. 'Variation and the interlanguage hypothesis'. *Studies in Second Language Acquisition* 10: 281–302.

Young, R. 1988b. 'Input and interaction'. *Annual Review of Applied Linguistics* 9: 122–34.

Young, R. 1991. *Variation in Interlanguage Morphology.* New York: Peter Lang.

Young, R. 1996. 'Form-function relations in articles in English interlanguage' in R. Bayley and D. Preston (eds.): *Second Language Acquisition and Linguistic Variation.* Amsterdam: John Benjamins.

Young, R. and **R. Bayley.** 1996. 'VARBUL analysis for second language acquisition research' in R. Bayley and D. Preston (eds.): *Second Language Acquisition and Linguistic Variation.* Amsterdam: John Benjamins.

Young, R. and **C. Doughty.** 1987. 'Negotiation in context: a review of research' in J. Lantolf and A Labarca (eds.): *Research in Second Language Learning: Focus on the Classroom.* Norwood, New Jersey: Ablex.

Ytsma, J. and **M. Hooghiemestra** (eds.). 2002. *Proceedings of the Second International Conference on Trilingualism.* Leeuwarden, Holland: Fryske Academie [CD-ROM].

Yuan, B. 1997. 'Asymmetry of null subjects and null objects in Chinese speakers' L2 English'. *Studies in Second Language Acquisition* 19: 467–97.

Yuan, B. 1998. 'Interpretation of binding and orientation of the Chinese reflexive ziji by English and Japanese speakers'. *Second Language Research* 14: 324–40.

Yuan, B. 2001. 'The status of thematic verbs in the second language acquisition of Chinese'. *Second Language Research* 17: 248–72.

Yuan, F. and **R. Ellis.** 2003. 'The effects of pre-task and on-line planning on fluency, complexity and accuracy in L2 monologic oral production'. *Applied Linguistics* 24/1: 1–27.

Yuan, K. 2001. 'An inquiry into empirical pragmatics data-gathering methods: Written DCTs, oral DCTs, field notes, and natural conversations'. *Journal of Pragmatics* 33: 271–92.

Yule, G. and **D. McDonald.** 1990. 'Resolving referential conflicts in L2 interaction: the effect of proficiency and interactive role'. *Language Learning* 40: 539–56.

Yule, G., M. Powers, and **D. McDonald.** 1992. 'The variable effects of some task-based learning procedures on L2 communicative effectiveness'. *Language Learning* 42: 249–77.

Yule, G. and E. Tarone. 1997. 'Investigating communication strategies in L2 reference: pros and cons' in G. Kasper and E. Kellerman (ed.): *Communication Strategies: Psycholinguistic and Sociolinguistic Perspectives.* London: Longman.

Zielonka, B. 2005. *The Role of Linguistic Context in the Acquisition of the Pluperfect.* Gdansk: Wydawnictwo Uniwersytetu Gdanksiego.

Zilles K., N. Palomero-Gallagher, C. Grefkes, F. Scheperjans, C. Boy, K. Amunts, and **A. Schleicher.** 2002. 'Architectonics of the human cerebral cortex and transmitter receptor fingerprints: reconciling functional neuroanatomy and neurochemistry'. *European Neuropsychopharmacology* 12: 587–99.

Zobl, H. 1980a. 'The formal and developmental selectivity of L1 influence on L2 acquisition'. *Language Learning* 30: 43–57.

Zobl, H. 1980b. 'Developmental and transfer errors: their common bases and (possibly) differential effects on subsequent learning'. *TESOL Quarterly* 14: 469–79.

Zobl, H. 1982. 'A direction for contrastive analysis: the comparative study of developmental sequences'. *TESOL Quarterly* 16: 169–83.

Zobl, H. 1983a. 'Contact-induced language change, learner-language, and the potentials of a modified contrastive analysis' in K. Bailey, M. Long, and S. Peck. (eds.): *Second Language Acquisition Studies*. Rowley, Mass.: Newbury House.

Zobl, H. 1983b. 'Markedness and the projection problem'. *Language Learning* 33: 293–313.

Zobl, H. 1984. 'Cross-language generalizations and the contrastive dimension of the interlanguage hypothesis' in A. Davies, C. Criper, and A. Howatt (eds.): *Interlanguage*. Edinburgh: Edinburgh University Press.

Zobl, H. 1985. 'Grammars in search of input and intake' in S. Gass and C. Madden (eds.): *Input in Second Language Acquisition*. Rowley, Mass.: Newbury House.

Zobl, H. 1986. 'Word order typology, lexical government, and the prediction of multiple, graded effects in L2 word order'. *Language Learning* 36: 159–83.

Zobl, H. 1988. 'Configurationality and the subset principle: the acquisition of V' by Japanese learners of English' in J. Pankhurst, M. Sharwood Smith, and P. Van Buren (eds.): *Learnability and Second Languages: a Book of Readings*. Dordrecht: Foris.

Zobl, H. 1989. 'Canonical typological structures and ergativity in English L2 acquisition' in S. Gass and J. Schachter (eds.): *Linguistic Perspectives on Second Language Acquisition*. Cambridge: Cambridge University Press

Zobl, H. and **J. Liceras.** 1994. 'Functional categories and acquisition orders'. *Language Learning* 44: 159–80.

Zuengler, J. 1989. 'Assessing an interactive paradigm: how accommodative should we be?' in M. Eisenstein (ed.): *The Dynamic Interlanguage: Empirical Studies in Second Language Variation*. New York: Plenum Press.

Zuengler, J. and **K. Cole.** 2005. 'Language socialization and second language learning' in E. Hinkel (ed.): *Handbook of Second Language Teaching and Learning*. Mahwah, N.J.: Lawrence Erlbaum.

Zuengler, J. and **J. Mori.** 2002. 'Microanalyses of classroom discourse: a critical consideration of method'. *Applied Linguistics* 23: 283–8.

Author index

See the subject index for names of informants, research projects and organizations.

References to chapter notes are indicated by page and note number, e.g. 66n7. References to tables and entries in the glossary are indicated as, e.g., 98t and 955g. Tables are indexed separately only if they contain references to authors not mentioned elsewhere on the page.

Subject index

The Index covers the Introduction, Parts One to Eight, and the Glossary. Entries are arranged in letter-by-letter alphabetical order, in which spaces between words are ignored: 'bilingualism' is therefore listed after 'bilingual classrooms' and before 'bilingual settings'.

References to chapter notes are indicated by page and note number, e.g. 37n3. Glossary references and references to tables and figures are indicated by 'g', 't' and 'f' respectively, e.g. 970g, 183t, 330f. Tables and figures are indexed separately only if they contain information that is found nowhere else on that page.

Headings referring to specific groups of L2 learners are constructed in the following manner: [L1]-[L2] speakers, for example Spanish-English speakers.